SEC Staff Accounting
Bulletin
Revenue Recognition

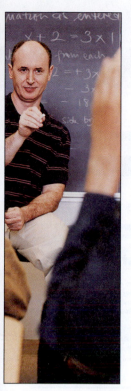

Prepare & Present

Create outstanding class presentations using a wealth of resources, such as PowerPoint™ slides, interactive simulations, and more. Plus you can easily upload any materials you have created into your course, and combine them with the resources Wiley provides you with.

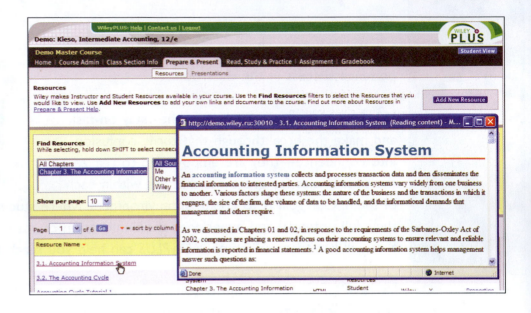

Create Assignments

Automate the assigning and grading of homework or quizzes by using the provided question banks, or by writing your own. Student results will be automatically graded and recorded in your gradebook. *WileyPLUS* also links homework problems to relevant sections of the online text, hints, or solutions—context-sensitive help where students need it most!

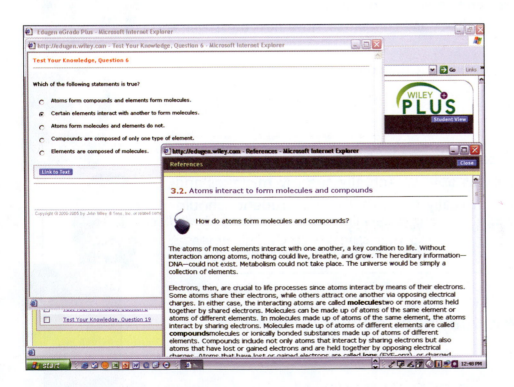

Track Student Progress

Keep track of your students' progress via an instructor's gradebook, which allows you to analyze individual and overall class results. This gives you an accurate and realistic assessment of your students' progress and level of understanding.

Now Available with WebCT and Blackboard!

Now you can seamlessly integrate all of the rich content and resources available with *WileyPLUS* with the power and convenience of your WebCT or BlackBoard course. You and your students get the best of both worlds with single sign-on, an integrated gradebook, list of assignments and roster, and more. If your campus is using another course management system, contact your local Wiley Representative.

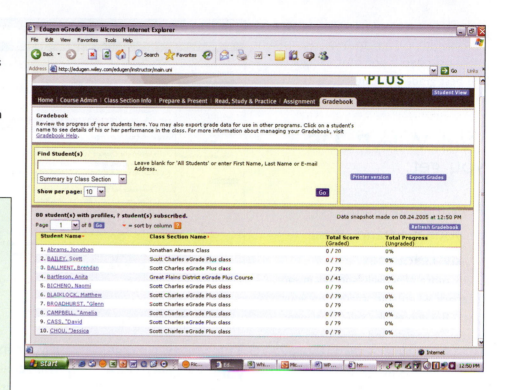

"I studied more for this class than I would have without *WileyPLUS*."

Melissa Lawler, *Western Washington Univ.*

For more information on what *WileyPLUS* can do to help your students reach their potential, please visit

www.wiley.com/college/wileyplus

76% of students surveyed said it made them better prepared for tests.*

*Based on a spring 2005 survey of 972 student users of *WileyPLUS*

You have the potential to make a difference!

WileyPLUS is a powerful online system packed with features to help you make the most of your potential, and get the best grade you can!

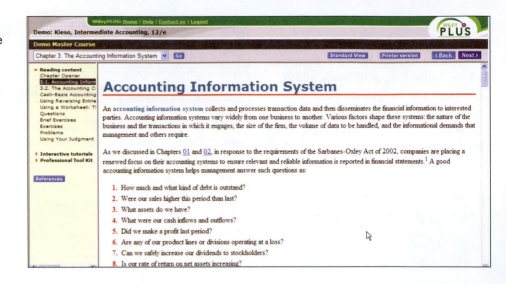

With Wiley**PLUS** you get:

A complete online version of your text and other study resources

Study more effectively and get instant feedback when you practice on your own. Resources like self-assessment quizzes, tutorials, and animations bring the subject matter to life, and help you master the material.

Problem-solving help, instant grading, and feedback on your homework and quizzes

You can keep all of your assigned work in one location, making it easy for you to stay on task. Plus, many homework problems contain direct links to the relevant portion of your text to help you deal with problem-solving obstacles at the moment they come up.

The ability to track your progress and grades throughout the term.

A personal gradebook allows you to monitor your results from past assignments at any time. You'll always know exactly where you stand.

If your instructor uses *WileyPLUS*, you will receive a URL for your class. If not, your instructor can get more information about *WileyPLUS* by visiting www.wiley.com/college/wileyplus

---

"It has been a great help, and I believe it has helped me to achieve a better grade."

Michael Morris, *Columbia Basin College*

69% of students surveyed said it helped them get a better grade.*

*Based on a spring 2005 survey of 972 student users of *WileyPLUS*

TWELFTH EDITION

INTERMEDIATE ACCOUNTING

Volume 2

TWELFTH EDITION

INTERMEDIATE ACCOUNTING

Volume 2

DONALD E. KIESO PH.D., C.P.A.
KPMG Peat Marwick Emeritus Professor of Accounting
Northern Illinois University
DeKalb, Illinois

JERRY J. WEYGANDT PH.D., C.P.A.
Arthur Andersen Alumni Professor of Accounting
University of Wisconsin
Madison, Wisconsin

TERRY D. WARFIELD PH.D.
Associate Professor
University of Wisconsin
Madison, Wisconsin

WILEY

John Wiley & Sons

*Dedicated to our wives, Donna, Enid, and Mary, for their love,
support, and encouragement*

PUBLISHER	Susan Elbe
EXECUTIVE EDITOR	Christopher DeJohn
SENIOR ACQUISITIONS EDITOR	Mark Bonadeo
ASSISTANT EDITOR	Brian Kamins
DEVELOPMENT EDITOR	Ann Torbert
PRODUCTION SERVICES MANAGER	Jeanine Furino
SENIOR MARKETING MANAGER	Amy Scholz
CREATIVE DIRECTOR	Harry Nolan
TEXT DESIGNER	Nancy Fields
PRODUCTION SERVICES MANAGEMENT	Ingrao Associates
SENIOR ILLUSTRATION EDITOR	Anna Melhorn
SENIOR MEDIA EDITOR	Allie Morris
PROJECT EDITOR	Ed Brislin
EDITORIAL ASSISTANT	Alison Stanley
MARKETING ASSISTANT	Vanessa Ahrens
PRODUCTION ASSISTANT	Andrea Juda
COVER PHOTO	© Jan Stromme/Lonely Planet Images/Getty Images, Inc.
COVER DESIGN	Howard Grossman

This book was set in Palatino by Techbooks and printed and bound by Von Hoffmann. The cover was printed by Lehigh Press.

This book is printed on acid free paper. ∞

To order books or for customer service, please call 1-800-CALL WILEY (225-5945).

Material from the Uniform CPA Examinations and Unofficial Answers, copyright © 1965, 1966, 1967, 1968, 1969, 1970, 1971, 1972, 1973, 1974, 1975, 1976, 1977, 1978, 1979, 1980, 1981, 1982, 1983, 1984, 1985, 1986, 1987, 1988, 1990, 1991, 1992, and 1993 by the American Institute of Certified Public Accountants, Inc., is adapted with permission.

This book contains quotations from *Accounting Research Bulletins, Accounting Principles Board Opinions, Accounting Principles Board Statements, Accounting Interpretations,* and *Accounting Terminology Bulletins,* copyright © 1953, 1956, 1966, 1968, 1969, 1970, 1971, 1972, 1973, 1974, 1975, 1976, 1977, 1978, 1979, 1980, 1981, 1982 by the American Institute of Certified Public Accountants, Inc., 1211 Avenue of the Americas, New York, NY 10036.

This book contains citations from various FASB pronouncements. Copyright © by Financial Accounting Standards Board, 401 Merritt 7, P.O. Box 5116, Norwalk, CT 06856 U.S.A. Reprinted with permission. Copies of complete documents are available from Financial Accounting Standards Board.

Material from the Certificate in Management Accounting Examinations, copyright © 1975, 1976, 1977, 1978, 1979, 1980, 1981, 1982, 1983, 1984, 1985, 1986, 1987, 1988, 1989, 1990, 1991, 1992, and 1993 by the Institute of Certified Management Accountants, 10 Paragon Drive, Montvale, NJ 07645, is adapted with permission.

Material from the Certified Internal Auditor Examinations, copyright © May 1984, November 1984, May 1986 by The Institute of Internal Auditors, 249 Maitland Ave., Altemonte Springs, FL 32701, is adapted with permission.

The financial statements and accompanying notes reprinted from the 2004 Annual Report of Procter & Gamble Company are courtesy of P&G, copyright © 2004, all rights reserved.

ISBN-13 978-0-471-77193-7
ISBN-10 0-471-77193-7

Printed in the United States of America

10 9 8 7 6 5 4 3 2 1

ABOUT THE AUTHORS

Donald E. Kieso, Ph.D., C.P.A., received his bachelor's degree from Aurora University and his doctorate in accounting from the University of Illinois. He has served as chairman of the Department of Accountancy and is currently the KPMG Peat Marwick Emeritus Professor of Accounting at Northern Illinois University. He has public accounting experience with Price Waterhouse & Co. (San Francisco and Chicago) and Arthur Andersen & Co. (Chicago) and research experience with the Research Division of the American Institute of Certified Public Accountants (New York). He has done postdoctorate work as a Visiting Scholar at the University of California at Berkeley and is a recipient of NIU's Teaching Excellence Award and four Golden Apple Teaching Awards. Professor Kieso is the author of other accounting and business books and is a member of the American Accounting Association, the American Institute of Certified Public Accountants, and the Illinois CPA Society. He has served as a member of the Board of Directors of the Illinois CPA Society, the AACSB's Accounting Accreditation Committees, the State of Illinois Comptroller's Commission, as Secretary-Treasurer of the Federation of Schools of Accountancy, and as Secretary-Treasurer of the American Accounting Association. Professor Kieso served as a charter member of the national Accounting Education Change Commission. He is the recipient of the Outstanding Accounting Educator Award from the Illinois CPA Society, the FSA's Joseph A. Silvoso Award of Merit, and the NIU Foundation's Humanitarian Award for Service to Higher Education.

Jerry J. Weygandt, Ph.D., C.P.A., is Arthur Andersen Alumni Professor of Accounting at the University of Wisconsin—Madison. He Holds a Ph.D. in accounting from the University of Illinois. Articles by Professor Weygandt have appeared in the *Accounting Review, Journal of Accounting Research, Accounting Horizons, Journal of Accountancy,* and other academic and professional journals. These articles have examined such financial reporting issues as accounting for price-level adjustments, pensions, convertible securities, stock option contracts, and interim reports. Professor Weygandt is author of other accounting and financial reporting books and is a member of the American Accounting Association, the American Institute of Certified Public Accountants, and the Wisconsin Society of Certified Public Accountants. He has served on numerous committees of the American Accounting Association and as a member of the editorial board of the *Accounting Review;* he also has served as President and Secretary-Treasurer of the American Accounting Association. In addition, he has been actively involved with the American Institute of Certified Public Accountants and has been a member of the Accounting Standards Executive Committee (AcSEC) of that organization. He has served on the FASB task force that examined the reporting issues related to accounting for income taxes and as a trustee of the Financial Accounting Foundation. Professor Weygandt has received the Chancellor's Award for Excellence in Teaching and the Beta Gamma Sigma Dean's Teaching Award. He is on the board of directors of M & I Bank of Southern Wisconsin. He is the recipient of the Wisconsin Institute of CPA's Outstanding Educator's Award and the Lifetime Achievement Award. In 2001 he received the American Accounting Association's Outstanding Accounting Educator Award.

Terry D. Warfield, Ph.D., is associate professor of accounting at the University of Wisconsin—Madison. He received a B.S. and M.B.A. from Indiana University and a Ph.D. in accounting from the University of Iowa. Professor Warfield's area of expertise is financial reporting, and prior to his academic career, he worked for five years in the banking industry. He served as the Academic Accounting Fellow in the Office of the Chief Accountant at the U.S. Securities and Exchange Commission in Washington, D.C. from 1995–1996. Professor Warfield's primary research interests concern financial accounting standards and disclosure policies. He has published scholarly articles in *The*

Accounting Review, Journal of Accounting and Economics, Research in Accounting Regulation, and *Accounting Horizons,* and he has served on the editorial boards of *The Accounting Review, Accounting Horizons,* and *Issues in Accounting Education.* He has served as president of the Financial Accounting and Reporting Section, the Financial Accounting Standards Committee of the American Accounting Association (Chair 1995–1996), and on the AAA-FASB Research Conference Committee. Professor Warfield has received teaching awards at both the University of Iowa and the University of Wisconsin, and he was named to the Teaching Academy at the University of Wisconsin in 1995. Professor Warfield has developed and published several case studies based on his research for use in accounting classes. These cases have been selected for the AICPA Professor-Practitioner Case Development Program and have been published in *Issues in Accounting Education.*

THE ACCOUNTING ENVIRONMENT

Since the 11th Edition of *Intermediate Accounting*, much has happened in the financial reporting arena. Given the series of accounting scandals and eroding public confidence in auditing and financial reporting, Congress passed the most important legislation since the Securities Act of 1934, the Sarbanes-Oxley Act of 2002. That legislation and the resulting Public Accounting Oversight Board established as a result of it now compel the profession to reexamine its most fundamental concepts and principles.

With this reexamination come many questions related to financial reporting: How, for example, should we value assets and liabilities? What should be the proper reporting for off-balance-sheet financing transactions? How should we account for the complex hybrid and derivative securities that are increasing in use? What should be the proper reporting for the many restatements that are taking place in corporate America? How quickly should we converge international and U.S. GAAP? What is the proper reporting for defined-benefit pension plans? These are difficult questions, but ones that need serious study and action.

Some judge these questions mundane compared to larger questions faced by society, such as what we should do with Social Security, health-care reform, or international relationships. Yet, the accounting scandals have focused attention on the importance of proper accounting to all of us. Consider, for example, the over 90 million Americans who have investments in stocks either directly, through mutual funds, or through employer-sponsored retirement funds. Consider the numerous retirees who are now suffering hardship because the companies they worked for reported incorrect information in attempts to hype stock prices or compensation. Or think of the many Americans who trusted corporate financial reports and invested in companies like **WorldCom**, **Enron**, and **Fannie Mae**, only to find that the numbers were wrong. What these events tell us is that accounting is essential for our economy to function effectively. Without high-quality accounting standards, capital markets cannot efficiently allocate capital to its best use in building and maintaining our economy and way of life. Thus, we must get the accounting right!

We believe that recent legislation will be helpful, because it puts increased emphasis on proper and high-quality reporting. Companies, and the individuals who run these companies, must adhere to sound reporting practices or face severe sanctions. It is an exciting time for those involved in financial reporting. Interest has never been higher in developing and reporting information that will be useful to interested parties. We therefore believe it imperative that *every student of business understands the fundamentals of accounting and financial reporting to ensure that the system will be continually developed and improved.*

LINKING THE ACCOUNTING ENVIRONMENT WITH ACCOUNTING EDUCATION

In this edition of *Intermediate Accounting*, we continue a tradition, begun over 30 years ago, of helping students understand, prepare, and use financial information by linking accounting education with the "real-world" accounting environment. As indicated above, the importance of students understanding the role of financial information in capital markets has never been more important.

An important feature of *Intermediate Accounting,* therefore, is an enhanced effort to provide more perspective on the information provided by financial reporting. As a result, special boxed insights titled "What Do the Numbers Mean?" illustrate how reporting methods affect the decisions of financial statement users. By means of these boxes, originally introduced in the 11th Edition, we hope to convey the excitement and ever-changing nature of accounting, illuminating its significance and highlighting its importance.

In addition, for the 12th Edition, we have added at the *Gateway to the Profession* portal (the book's companion website) a "B set" of additional exercises online, as well as information about access to additional versions of the Professional Simulations and a new "Accounting in Action" continuing problem. The continuing problem provides students a real-world context in which to apply the concepts they are learning in the textbook. The *Gateway to the Profession* also provides students and instructors access to all the material previously delivered on the *Take Action! CD.*

The 12th Edition of *Intermediate Accounting* introduces a revised element to the "Using Your Judgment" section of the end-of-chapter material. A "Professional Simulation" in each chapter provides students with a new and integrative context for applying the concepts introduced in the chapter. To complement the Professional Simulation, in the 12th Edition we have introduced in each chapter a "Professional Research" case. These cases give students an opportunity to conduct authoritative research using the Financial Accounting Research System (FARS). These new and enhanced elements are patterned after the computerized CPA exam. They expand the focus of many of the elements of the *Gateway to the Professional* portal (writing, working in teams, using the analyst's toolkit) to help students learn how to use accounting facts and procedures in various business contexts.

Another key feature of this edition is the introduction of **WileyPLUS**, an online suite of resources, including access to an online version of the complete text. Within WileyPLUS, the online version of the text will be integrated with the Accounting Research database (FARS). Students will be able to conduct authoritative research in a seamless environment. In addition, WileyPLUS contains all of the elements of the *Gateway to the Profession* portal, plus a homework management system and resources for creating class presentations. (See page xviii for a complete description of this content-rich resource.)

Throughout the book, we continue to strive for a balanced discussion of conceptual and procedural presentations so that these elements are mutually reinforcing. In addition, text discussions explain the rationale behind business transactions before addressing the accounting and reporting for those transactions. As in prior editions, we have thoroughly revised and updated the text to include all the latest developments in the accounting profession and practice. For example, we have completely revised the chapter on accounting changes and error corrections to reflect new accounting standards for accounting changes. Benefiting from the comments and recommendations of adopters of the 11th Edition, we have made significant revisions: We have expanded explanations where necessary; simplified complicated discussions and illustrations; integrated realism to heighten interest and relevancy; and added new topics and coverage to maintain currency. Finally, to provide the instructor with flexibility of use and no loss in topic coverage, we have moved discussions of less commonly used methods and more complex or specialized topics to the *Gateway to the Profession* portal.

NEW FEATURES

Based on extensive reviews, focus groups, and interactions with other intermediate accounting instructors and students, we have developed a number of new pedagogical features and content changes, designed both to help students learn more effectively and to answer the changing needs of the course.

Editorial Review

The 12th Edition of *Intermediate Accounting* has undergone an editorial review and line-by-line editing process to improve the readability of the text. The goals of this process were to retain the book's numerous examples and analogies that set the standard in the intermediate accounting course, but to simplify words and reduce sentence and paragraph length wherever possible without sacrificing precision. This review placed emphasis on introducing an active voice and conversational style in the presentation.

Major Chapter Revisions

In response to new FASB standards, we have significantly revised several chapters:

- Chapters 4 and 22 have been revised in response to the new standard on *accounting changes*. They now include comprehensive illustrations with a focus on the presentation of comparative statements when reporting accounting changes and errors.
- Chapter 10 presents a revised section on exchanges of nonmonetary assets and introduces the concept of commercial substance in accounting for exchanges.
- Chapter 16 has been revised in light of the new standard on stock-based compensation, which requires recognition of compensation expense using the fair-value model. A revised chapter-end appendix covers the accounting for restricted stock and stock appreciation rights.

New Appendixes

In addition to the revised appendix for Chapter 16 (see above), we also developed two new appendixes: on the accounting for variable-interest entities (Chapter 17), and on international accounting (Chapter 24). We added Appendix 24B in order to provide additional insight into the issue of convergence of U.S. and international accounting standards. We believe that convergence will continue to gain momentum and that students should be aware of this issue as their careers develop.

FARS Cases

In response to increased demand for accounting research skills and the requirements of the computerized CPA exam, each chapter now has a Professional Research case. These new cases give students an opportunity to conduct authoritative research, using either the Financial Accounting Research System (FARS) CD-ROM or FARS Online. Both of these products are available through John Wiley & Sons Higher Education Division.

Updated Supplements

All supplements are updated. In particular, the Solutions Manual questions are newly classified by textbook learning objective, the PowerPoint presentations are newly designed, and there are more review questions and over 400 new Test bank questions.

Gateway to the Profession Portal

The book companion *website at www.wiley.com/college/kieso* (with separate areas for instructors and for students) has been completely revamped. At this website, now titled *Gateway to the Profession*, students can access the following resources:

- A "B set" of additional exercises, providing additional practice opportunities for students (solutions available to instructors).
- For each chapter, a new "Accounting in Action" continuing problem, which follows the evolution of CM^2 Corporation from a start-up to an initial public offering (IPO). The continuing problem provides students with a real-world context in which to apply the concepts they are learning in the textbook. Instructors can use the continuing problem in its entirety or in parts, as desired.

- Information about access to online and additional versions of the Professional Simulations, which are found in each chapter of the text.
- Financial statements for **The Procter & Gamble Company**, **The Coca-Cola Company**, and **PepsiCo.**
- Access to the Student, Analyst, and Professional Toolkits previously delivered on the *Take Action! CD*. We describe the content of these three toolkits later in the preface (see pages xix–xxii).

ENHANCED FEATURES OF THE 12TH EDITION

We have continued and enhanced many of the features of the 11th Edition of *Intermediate Accounting*, including the following.

Real-World Emphasis

One of the goals of the intermediate accounting course is to orient students to the application of accounting principles and techniques in practice. Accordingly, we have continued our practice of using numerous examples from real companies throughout the text. The names of these real companies are highlighted in red. Illustration and exhibits marked by the icon shown here in the margin, or by company logos, are excerpts from actual financial statements of real firms.

Johnson & Johnson

WHAT DO THE NUMBERS MEAN?

P&G

The Coca-Cola Company

PEPSICO

At the start of each chapter, we have updated and introduced new chapter-opening vignettes to provide an even better real-world context that helps motivate student interest in the chapter topic. Also, throughout the chapters, the "What Do the Numbers Mean?" boxed inserts also provide real-world extensions of the material presented in the text.

In addition, Appendix 5B contains the 2004 annual report of **The Procter & Gamble Company (P&G)**. The book's website contains the 2004 annual reports of **The Coca-Cola Company** and of **PepsiCo, Inc.** Problems in the *Using Your Judgment* section (see description below) involve study of the P&G annual report or comparison of the annual reports of The Coca-Cola Company and PepsiCo. Also, links to many real-company financial reports appear in the company database at the *Gateway to the Profession* portal.

Currency and Accuracy

Accounting continually changes as its environment changes; an up-to-date book is therefore a necessity. As in past editions, we have strived to make this edition the most up-to-date and accurate textbook available.

International Coverage

INTERNATIONAL INSIGHT

Having a basic understanding of international accounting is becoming ever more important as the profession moves toward convergence of GAAP and international standards. Thus, we continue to include marginal *International Insights*, marked with the icon shown here, which we updated throughout to reflect changes in international accounting. These paragraphs describe or compare IASB standards and accounting practices in other countries with U.S. GAAP. This feature helps students understand that other countries sometimes use different recognition and measurement principles to report financial information. In addition, a *new* appendix on international accounting follows Chapter 24.

Streamlined Presentation

We also have continued our efforts to keep the topic coverage of *Intermediate Accounting* in line with the way instructors are *currently* teaching the course. Accordingly, we have moved some optional topics into chapter-end appendixes, and we have omitted altogether some topics that formerly were covered in appendixes. Often, these omitted topics have been moved to the *Gateway to the Profession* portal. Details are noted in the list of specific content changes below and in the list of portal content later in the preface.

Additional Exercises

Our study of the intermediate accounting course indicates the importance of the end-of-chapter Exercises for teaching and practicing important accounting concepts. In the 12th Edition, therefore, we have prepared an additional set of exercises. These new exercises are available at the *Gateway to the Profession* portal. (Solutions are available at the instructor's portion of the website.)

Using Your Judgment Section

We have revised and updated the *Using Your Judgment* section at the end of each chapter. Elements included in this section include the following:

- A Financial Reporting Problem, featuring **The Procter & Gamble Company**.
- A Financial Statement Analysis Case that asks students to use the information in published accounting reports to conduct financial analysis.
- A Comparative Analysis Case, featuring **The Coca-Cola Company** and **PepsiCo, Inc.**, that asks students to compare and contrast the financial reporting for these two companies.
- A Research Case, that asks students to read articles from the popular financial press and apply them to the chapter topic.
- An International Reporting Case that explores differences in reporting by international companies.
- A Professional Research: Financial Accounting and Reporting case that gives students practice conducting authoritative research using the Financial Accounting Research System (FARS).
- A Professional Simulation, newly revised for this edition, which models the computerized CPA exam.

The *Using Your Judgment* assignments are designed to help develop students' critical thinking, analytical, and research skills.

CONTENT CHANGES

The following list outlines the content revisions and improvements made in chapters of the 12th Edition.

Chapter 1
- Enhanced discussion of the hierarchy of generally accepted accounting principles.
- Reduced emphasis on AICPA.
- Updated international discussion.
- Enhanced discussion of the Sarbanes-Oxley Act of 2002.

Chapter 2
- Enhanced discussion of fair values and their use in financial accounting.

Chapter 3
- Enhanced coverage of the accounting cycle, with complete discussion and comprehensive example of Pioneer Advertising from inception to preparation of the financial statements.

- Improved discussion of financial statements in the chapter with illustration of the use of a worksheet in an appendix.

Chapter 4
- Updated illustration in the chapter-opening vignette.
- New chart on irregular items.
- New discussion of income statement reporting of a change in accounting principle.

Chapter 5
- Updated chapter-opening vignette on balance sheet and cash flow quality.
- New "What Do the Numbers Mean?" box on contractual commitments.
- Incorporated "significant non-cash financing and investing activities" into the statement of cash flows.

Chapter 7
- New chapter-opening vignette on abuse of allowance accounts.
- New illustration of the role of credit card operations and bad debts at major retailers.

Chapter 8
- Updated chapter-opening vignette on the importance of inventory information.

Chapter 9
- New "What Do the Numbers Mean?" box on the deficient reporting of lower-of-cost-or-market recoveries.

Chapter 10
- Updated chapter-opening vignette on variation in fixed assets across companies.
- Major rewrite of the discussion of nonmonetary exchanges in response to the recent FASB standard.

Chapter 11
- Updated chapter-opening vignette on recent changes in international accounting for impairments.

Chapter 12
- New "What Do the Numbers Mean?" box on impairment issues at **Krispy Kreme**.
- Rewrite of negative goodwill discussion.

Chapter 13
- New chapter-opening vignette related to international differences in the definition of a liability.
- Enhanced introduction to the discussion of contingencies.

Chapter 14
- New "What Do the Numbers Mean?" box on the economics of bonds.
- Enhanced "What Do the Numbers Mean?" box on bond ratings and default risk.
- Expanded discussion of required disclosures of long-term liabilities, including the recent SEC rule on contractual obligations.

Chapter 15
- New chapter-opening vignette on the importance of dividends in stock yields.
- New illustration on the prevalence of stock buy-backs.
- Updated discussion on responses to the new standard on redeemable preferred stock.

Chapter 16

- New chapter-opening vignette on stock options.
- Enhanced discussion of the distinctions between debt and equity and its relationship to hybrid or dilutive securities.
- Major rewrite of the discussion of stock-based compensation in response to the recent standard, including new illustrations and exhibits.
- New "What Do the Numbers Mean?" box on contingently convertible bonds (CoCos).
- New appendix on restricted stock and stock appreciation rights, based on the accounting guidance in the recent standard.

Chapter 17

- Updated chapter-opening vignette on international accounting for equity investments.
- New "What Do the Numbers Mean?" box on fair value accounting at **Morgan Stanley**.
- New "What Do the Numbers Mean?" box on off-balance-sheet transactions.
- New "What Do the Numbers Mean?" box on impairments.
- Reorganized discussion of fair value hedges in Appendix 17A.
- New appendix (Appendix 17B) on variable-interest entities.

Chapter 18

- New chapter-opening vignette on revenue recognition.
- New "What Do the Numbers Mean?" box on the revenue recognition challenges of gift cards.

Chapter 19

- New chapter-opening vignette on uncertain tax provisions.
- Enhanced discussion of net operating losses (NOLs) and when they can be used.
- New "What Do the Numbers Mean?" box on NOLs.

Chapter 20

- New chapter-opening vignette on changes in pension plan use.
- New "What Do the Numbers Mean?" box on mix of defined-benefit and defined-contribution plans.
- New "What Do the Numbers Mean?" box on pension underfunding.
- New illustration of pension worksheet in Excel format.
- Updated discussion on the **Pension Benefit Guarantee Corporation**.
- Eliminated discussion in appendix of OPEB transition adjustment, given its limited applicability.

Chapter 21

- New discussion of the leasing market, with special emphasis on lessors.
- New chart on equipment leasing growth.
- New "What Do the Numbers Mean?" box on recognition problems related to operating leases.

Chapter 22

- Complete rewrite of first section concerning accounting changes and errors, incorporating the guidance in the recent FASB standard.
- New emphasis on preparation of comparative statements.

Chapter 23

- Updated the treatment of stock options in response to the recent standard.

- Updated "What Do the Numbers Mean?" box on manipulation of operating cash flow.

Chapter 24

- New discussion of expanded disclosure requirements in the wake of the Sarbanes-Oxley Act of 2002.
- New "What Do the Numbers Mean?" box on the importance of disclosure for efficient securities markets.
- New discussion of managements' reporting on and auditor attestation on the effectiveness of internal controls.
- Enhanced discussion of Internet reporting with emphasis on "XBRL."
- New appendix (Appendix 24B) on international accounting.

END-OF-CHAPTER ASSIGNMENT MATERIAL

At the end of each chapter, we have provided a comprehensive set of review and homework material. This section consists of Questions, Brief Exercises, Exercises, Problems, and short Concepts for Analysis exercises. These materials are followed by the Using Your Judgment section, described earlier (see page xv). For this edition, we have updated many of these end-of-chapter materials. All of the assignment materials have been class-tested and/or double-checked for accuracy and clarity.

The Questions are designed primarily for review, self-testing, and classroom discussion purposes, as well as for homework assignments. Typically a Brief Exercise covers one topic, and an Exercise covers one or two topics. The Problems are designed to develop a professional level of achievement and are more challenging and time-consuming to solve than the Exercises. In the 12th Edition, the Brief Exercises, Exercises, and Problems now are classified by learning objective number. All Brief Exercises and Exercises and selected Problems are available in WileyPLUS with automatic grading capability.

The Concepts for Analysis (formerly called Conceptual Cases) generally require discussion, as opposed to quantitative solutions. They are intended to confront the student with situations calling for conceptual analysis and the exercise of judgment in identifying issues and problems and in evaluating alternatives.

Separate icons next to Exercises, Problems, and Concepts for Analysis indicate homework materials that offer more than just a quantitative challenge. Homework materials that are especially suited for group assignments, for example, are identified by the red icon shown here in the margin. Homework materials suitable as writing assignments are marked with the pencil icon shown here in the margin. Items that address ethics issues are identified by the scale (balance) icon. Homework materials that can be solved using the Excel Problems supplement are identified by the spreadsheet icon shown at left.

Probably no more than one-fourth of the total exercise, problem, and concepts for analysis material must be used to cover the subject matter adequately. Consequently, problem assignments may be varied from year to year without repetition. As noted earlier, a *new* additional set of Exercises is available at the book's website, to provide an even wider assortment of exercises from which to choose.

WileyPLUS

As described earlier, **WileyPLUS** is a suite of resources that contains online homework, with access to an online version of the text, plus all of the elements of the *Gateway to the Profession* portal. WileyPLUS gives you the technology to create an environment where students reach their full potential and experience academic success. Instructor resources include a wealth of presentation and preparation tools, easy-to-navigate assignment and assessment tools, and a complete system to administer and manage your course exactly as you wish. In addition, a premium version of WileyPLUS is available that will include access to FARS (Financial Accounting Research System) Online, a series of active learning modules titled *Mastering FARS Online: An Active Leaning Approach*, the *Rockford Practice Set* powered by new general ledger software, and Excel Working Papers.

WileyPLUS is built around the activities you regularly perform:

- **Prepare and present class presentations** using relevant Wiley resources such as PowerPoint™ slides, image galleries, animations, and other WileyPLUS materials. You can also upload your own resources or web pages to use in conjunction with Wiley materials.

- **Create assignments** by choosing from end-of-chapter exercises, selected problems, and test bank questions organized by chapter, study objective, level of difficulty, and source—or add your own questions. WileyPLUS automatically grades students' homework and quizzes and records the results in your gradebook.

- **Offer context-sensitive help to students, 24/7.** When you assign homework or quizzes, you decide if and when students get access to hints, solutions, or answers where appropriate. Or they can be linked to relevant sections of their complete, online text for additional help whenever and wherever they need it most.

- **Track student progress.** You can analyze students' results and assess their level of understanding on an individual and class level using the WileyPLUS gradebook, and you can export data to your own personal gradebook.

- Seamlessly integrate all of the rich WileyPLUS content and resources with the power and convenience of your **WebCT** or **Blackboard** course—with a single sign-on.

In addition to the classroom presentation tools, the homework management system, and the online version of the text, **WileyPLUS** offers rich content in the *Gateway to the Profession* portal.

Content of the *Gateway to the Profession* Portal

As noted earlier, the *Gateway to the Profession* portal includes the Analyst's Toolkit, the Professional Toolkit, and the Student Toolkit, whose content is described below.

Analyst's Toolkit

Tools in the Analyst's Toolkit consist of the following items.

Database of Real Companies. Links to more than 20 annual reports of well-known companies, including three international companies, are provided at the *Gateway to the Profession* portal. Classes can use these annual reports in a variety of ways. For example, they can use them to illustrate different presentations of financial information or to compare note disclosures across companies. In addition, classes can use these reports to analyze a company's financial condition and compare its prospects with those of other companies in the same industry. Assignment material provides some examples of different types of analysis that students can perform. Each of the companies in the database of real companies is identified by a Web address to facilitate the gathering of additional information, if desired.

Additional Enrichment Material. An online chapter on Financial Statement Analysis is provided at the portal, along with related assignment material. This chapter can also be used in conjunction with the database of annual reports of real companies.

Spreadsheet Tools. Present value templates are provided. These templates can be used to solve time value of money problems.

Additional Internet Links. A number of useful links related to financial analysis are provided to expand expertise in analyzing real-world reporting.

Professional Toolkit

Consistent with expanding beyond technical accounting knowledge, the *Gateway to the Profession* materials emphasize certain skills necessary to become a successful accountant or financial manager. The following materials will help students develop needed professional skills.

Writing Materials. A primer on professional communications gives students a framework for writing professional materials. This primer discusses issues such as the top-ten writing problems, strategies for rewriting, how to do revisions, and tips on clarity. This primer has been class-tested and is effective in helping students enhance their writing skills.

Group-Work Materials. Recent evaluations of accounting education have identified the need to develop more skills in group problem solving. The *Gateway to the Profession* portal provides a second primer dealing with the role that work-groups play in organizations. Information is included on what makes a successful group, how you can participate effectively in the group, and do's and don'ts of group formation.

Ethics. The Professional Toolkit contains expanded materials on the role of ethics in the profession, including references to speeches and articles on ethics in accounting; codes of ethics for major professional bodies; and examples and additional case studies on ethics.

Career Professional Spotlights. Every student should have a good understanding of the profession he or she is entering. Career vignettes on the *Gateway to the Profession* portal indicate the types of work that accountants do. Other aspects of the spotlights on careers are included at the *Gateway to the Profession* to help students make successful career choices. These include important links to websites that can provide useful career information to facilitate the student's efforts in this area.

Student Toolkit

Also included at the *Gateway to the Profession* are features that help students process and understand the course materials. They are:

Interactive Tutorials. To help students better understand some of the more difficult topics in intermediate accounting, we have developed a number of interactive tutorials that provide expanded discussion and explanation in a visual and narrative context. Topics addressed are:

- the accounting cycle
- accounting for bad debts (recording uncollectible accounts)
- disposition (transfer) of receivables
- inventory methods
- dollar-value LIFO
- interest capitalization
- depreciation methods

These tutorials are for the benefit of the student and should require no use of class time on the part of instructors.

Expanded Discussion and Illustrations. The Expanded Discussion section provides additional topics not covered in depth in the textbook. *The Gateway to the Profession* gives the flexibility to enrich or expand the course by discussion of additional topics such as those listed below. Topics included, with appropriate chapter linkage, are as follows.

Gateway to the Profession Topics

Chapter 1

- Expanded discussion of ethical issues in financial accounting.

Chapter 2

- Discussion of accounting for changing prices.

Chapter 3
- Presentation of worksheet using the periodic inventory method.
- Specialized journals and methods of processing accounting data.
- Tutorial on the accounting cycle.

Chapter 6
- Present-value–based measurements, including an expanded discussion of spreadsheet tools for solving present-value problems.

Chapter 7
- Discussion of how a four-column bank reconciliation (the proof of cash) can be used for control purposes.
- Expanded example, with accounting entries, of transfers of receivables without recourse.
- Tutorial on the accounting for bad debts.
- Tutorial on transfer of receivables.

Chapter 8
- Tutorial on inventory methods (cost flow assumptions).
- Tutorial on LIFO issues, including dollar-value LIFO.

Chapter 10
- Tutorial on interest capitalization.

Chapter 11
- Discussion of lesser-used depreciation methods, such as the retirement and replacement methods.
- Tutorial on depreciation methods.

Chapter 12
- Expanded discussion on valuing goodwill.

Chapter 13
- Expanded discussion on property taxes.

Chapter 15
- Expanded discussion on the par value method for treasury stock.
- Expanded discussion on quasi-reorganizations.

Chapter 16
- Comprehensive earnings per share illustration.

Chapter 17
- Illustration of accounting entries for transfers of investment securities.
- Expanded discussion of special issues related to investments.

Chapter 19
- Discussion of the conceptual aspects of interperiod tax allocation, including the deferred and net of tax methods.
- Discussion, with examples, of accounting for intraperiod tax allocations.

Chapter 21
- Discussion of real estate leases and leveraged leases.

Chapter 23
- Discussion, with a detailed example, of the T-account method for preparing a statement of cash flows.

Chapter 24

- Discussion of accounting for changing prices, both for general and specific price-level changes.
- Financial analysis primer.

In addition to these materials, illustrative disclosures of financial reporting practices are provided.

Self-Study Tests and Additional Self-Tests. Each chapter on the *Gateway to the Profession* portal includes two sets of self-tests, to allow students to check their understanding of key concepts from the chapter. The software automatically grades the tests and points students to material they need to study further.

Glossary. A complete glossary of all the key terms used in the text is provided, in alphabetical order as well as via Wiley's Flash card technology for drill and practice. Page numbers show where these key terms appear in the text.

Learning-Style Survey. Research on left brain/right brain differences and also on learning and personality differences suggests that each person has preferred ways to receive and communicate information. After taking this learning-style quiz, students will be able to identify their particular learning styles and pinpoint the study aids in the textbook that will help them learn the material.

In summary, the *Gateway to the Profession* portal is a comprehensive complement to the 12th Edition of *Intermediate Accounting,* providing new materials as well as a new way to communicate those materials.

SUPPLEMENTARY MATERIALS

Accompanying this textbook is an improved and expanded package of student learning aids and instructor teaching aids. The *Intermediate Accounting,* 12th Edition, *Gateway to the Profession* portal at *www.wiley.com/college/kieso* provides various tools for students and instructors. This portal offers expanded materials in the three toolkits previously described. In addition, as described earlier, WileyPLUS offers resources to help you prepare class presentations, create assignments, offer help to students, and track student progress.

Other teaching and learning aids to supplement the textbook are described below.

Instructor Teaching Aids

The following teaching aids are available to support instructors using the 12th Edition.

Instructor's Resource CD. The *Instructor's Resource CD* contains electronic versions of the Instructor's Manual, Solutions Manual, Test Bank, computerized Test Bank, PowerPoint™ presentations, and other instructor resources.

Solutions Manual, Vols. 1 and 2. The *Solutions Manual* provides answers to all end-of-chapter questions, brief exercises, exercises, problems, and case materials. Classification tables categorize solutions by topic, and the new solutions manual also categorizes solutions by textbook learning objective. The estimated time to complete exercises, problems, and cases is provided.

Test Bank: Vols. 1 and 2. The 12th Edition Test Bank contains *over 400 new testing questions.* Exercises, problems, true/false, multiple choice, and conceptual short-answer questions help instructors test students' knowledge and communication skills.

Computerized Test Bank. This easy-to-use program allows instructors to create multiple versions of the same test. This computerized test bank also has authoring capabilities and randomizing functions.

Instructor's Manual, Vols. 1 and 2. The *Instructor's Manual* contains lecture outlines, chapter reviews, sample syllabi, printed teaching transparency masters, and much more.

Solutions Transparencies, Vols. 1 and 2. These acetate transparencies contain solutions to textbook end-of-chapter material. The transparencies contain large, bold type for classroom presentation.

PowerPoint™ Presentations. The PowerPoint™ presentations are designed to enhance classroom presentation of chapter topics and examples. The 12th Edition templates now have a new design with review questions and many examples illustrating textbook content.

Teaching Transparencies. These four-color acetates provide illustrations of key concepts for classroom viewing.

Solutions to Rockford Practice Set. This supplement provides solutions to the *Rockford Practice Set*, which is available in print form or electronically through the premium version of WileyPLUS.

Solutions to Excel Workbook Templates. Available for download from the KWW website, these are solutions to the *Solving Problems Using Excel Workbook* templates.

Course Management Resources. Course content cartridges are available from both WebCT and Blackboard.

Periodic Newsletters. The textbook is supplemented by the publication of periodic newsletters. These faculty-oriented supplements include the following sections:

- "Update"—Provides the latest information about new accounting standards promulgated since the text was published.
- "Financial Reporting Challenges"—Addresses a contemporary issue being debated by accounting professionals and standard setters, which may result in a new accounting standard.
- "By the Way. . ."—Provides a "heads up" to instructors on topics addressed in the text (usually the subject of a recent change in accounting standards), to increase instructors' awareness of its implications for their courses.
- "CPA Exam Update"—Offers the latest information about the CPA exam. This item is prepared by Debra R. Hopkins (CPA, CIA), CPA Review Director, Northern Illinois University, DeKalb, Illinois.

Student Learning Aids

Student Study Guide, Vols. 1 and 2. Each chapter of the Study Guide contains a chapter review, chapter outline, and a glossary of key terms. Demonstration problems, multiple-choice, true/false, matching, and other exercises are included.

Problem-Solving Survival Guide, Vols. 1 and 2. This study guide contains exercises and problems that help students develop their intermediate accounting problem-solving skills. Explanations assist in the approach, set-up, and completion of accounting problems. Tips alert students to common pitfalls and misconceptions.

Working Papers, Vols. 1 and 2. The working papers are printed templates that can help students correctly format their textbook accounting solutions. Working paper templates are available for all end-of-chapter brief exercises, exercises, problems, and cases.

Excel Working Papers, Vols. 1 and 2. The *Excel Working Papers* are Excel templates that students can use to correctly format their textbook accounting solutions. Working paper templates are available for all end-of-chapter brief exercises, exercises, problems, and cases.

Solving Problems Using Excel Workbook. A useful introduction to Excel, this workbook helps students work with preprogrammed spreadsheets, and it explains how students can design their own spreadsheet. This workbook is packaged with a CD containing Excel templates that allow students to complete the selected end-of-chapter exercises and problems identified by a spreadsheet icon in the margin of the main textbook.

Rockford Corporation: An Accounting Practice Set. This practice set helps students review the accounting cycle and the preparation of financial statements.

Rockford Corporation: A Computerized Accounting Practice Set. The computerized Rockford practice set is a general ledger software version of the printed practice set. Available within WileyPLUS Premium Version.

ACKNOWLEDGMENTS

We thank the many users of our 11th Edition who contributed to the revision through their comments and instructive criticism. Special thanks are extended to the focus group participants and the primary reviewers of and contributors to our 12th Edition manuscript.

Lisa Bostick
University of Tampa

Greg Brookins
Santa Monica College

Laura Delaune
Louisiana State University

Lynda Dennis
University of Central Florida

Claire Eckstein
CUNY—Baruch

Dave Farber
Michigan State University

Clyde Galbraith
West Chester University

Ellen Goldberg
Northern Virginia Community College

Marty Gosman
Quinnipiac College

Julia Higgs
Florida Atlantic University

Geoffrey Horlick
St. Francis College

Marilyn Hunt
University of Central Florida

Cynthia Jeffrey
Iowa State University

Mary Jo Jones
Eastern University

Art Joy
University of South Florida

Celina Jozci
University of South Florida

Lisa Koonce
University of Texas at Austin

Timothy Lindquist
University of Northern Iowa

Barbara Lippincott
University of Tampa

Gary Luoma
University of Southern California

Daphne Main
University of New Orleans

Ed Nathan
University of Houston

Hugo Nurnberg
CUNY – Baruch

Ann O'Brien
University of Wisconsin—Madison

Anne Oppegard
Augustana College, SD

Alee Phillips
University of Kansas

Marlene Plumlee
University of Utah

Wing Poon
Montclair State University

Jay Price
Utah State University

Paul (Jep) Robertson
Henderson State University

Larry Roman
Cuyahoga Community College

Bob Rouse
College of Charleston

Tim Shea
University of Wisconsin – Madison

Jerry Siebel
University of South Florida

Karen Squires
University of Tampa

Douglas Smith
Samford University

Gary Taylor
University of Alabama

Lynn Thomas
Kansas State University

Tom Tierney
University of Wisconsin—Madison

Steve Zeff
Rice University

David Weiner
University of San Francisco

   We also thank other colleagues who provided helpful criticism and made valuable suggestions as members of focus groups, survey participants, or as adopters and reviewers of previous editions.

Diana Adcox
University of North Florida

Noel Addy
Mississippi State University

Roberta Allen
Texas Tech University

James Bannister
University of Hartford

Charles Baril
James Madison University

Kathleen Buaer
Midwestern State University

Janice Bell
California State University at Northridge

Larry Bergin
Winona State University

Lynn Bible
University of Nevada, Reno

John C. Borke
University of Wisconsin—Platteville

Tiffany Bortz
University of Texas, Dallas

Phillip Buchanan
George Mason University

Tom Buchman
University of Colorado, Boulder

Suzanne M. Busch
California State University—Hayward

Eric Carlsen
Kean College of New Jersey

Tom Carment
Northeastern State University

Tommy Carnes
Western Carolina University

Robert Cluskey
Tennessee State University

Edwin Cohen
DePaul University

W. Terry Dancer
Arkansas State University

Lee Dexter
Moorhead State University

Judith Doing
University of Arizona

Joanne Duke
San Francisco State University

Richard Dumont
Teikyo Post University

William Dwyer
DeSales University

Dean S. Eiteman
Indiana University—Pennsylvania

Larry R. Falcetto
Emporia State University

Richard Fern
Eastern Kentucky University

Richard Fleischman
John Carroll University

Stephen L. Fogg
Temple University

William Foster
New Mexico State University

Clyde Galbraith
West Chester University

Marshall Geiger
University of Richmond

Susan Gill
Washington State University

Harold Goedde
State University of New York at Oneonta

Lynford E. Graham
Rutgers University

Donald J. Griffin
Cayuga Community College

Marcia I. Halvorsen
University of Cincinnati

Garry Heesacker
Central Washington University

Kenneth Henry
Florida International University

Wayne M. Higley
Buena Vista University

Judy Hora
University of San Diego

Geoffrey R. Horlick
St. Francis College

Kathy Hsu
University of Louisiana, Layfayette

M. Zarar Iqbal
California Polytechnic State University—San Luis Obispo

Daniel Ivancevich
University of North Carolina at Wilmington

Susan Ivancevich
University of North Carolina at Wilmington

Cynthia Jeffrey
Iowa State University

Scott Jeris
San Francisco State University

James Johnston
Louisiana Tech University

Jeff Jones
University of Texas—San Antonio

Celina Jozsi
University of South Florida

Douglas W. Kieso
Aurora University

Paul D. Kimmel
University of Wisconsin—Milwaukee

Martha King
Emporia State University

Florence Kirk
State University of New York at Oswego

Mark Kohlbeck
Florida Atlantic University

Lisa Koonce
University of Texas—Austin

Steve Lafave
Augsburg College

Ellen Landgraf
Loyola University, Chicago

Tom Largay
Thomas College

David B. Law
Youngstown State University

Henry LeClerc
Suffolk Community College—Selden Campus

Patsy Lee
University of Texas—Arlington

Lydia Leporte
Tidewater Community College

Timothy Lindquist
University of Northern Iowa

Tom Linsmeier
Michigan State University

Ellen Lippman
University of Portland

Daphne Main
University of New Orleans

Mostafa Maksy
Northeastern Illinois University

Danny Matthews
Midwestern State University

Noel McKeon
Florida Community College

Robert J. Matthews
New Jersey City University

Robert Milbrath
University of Houston

James Miller
Gannon University

John Mills
University of Nevada—Reno

Joan Monnin-Callahan
University of Cincinnati

Mohamed E. Moustafa
California State University—Long Beach

Siva Nathan
Georgia State University

Kermit Natho
Georgia State University

Joseph Nicassio
Westmoreland County Community College

Patricia Parker
Columbus State Community College

Richard Parker
Olivet College

Obeau S. Persons
Rider University

Ray Pfeiffer
University of Massachusetts—Amherst

Robert Rambo
University of New Orleans

Debbie Rankin
Lincoln University

MaryAnn Reynolds
Western Washington University

Vernon Richardson
University of Arkansas

Richard Riley
West Virginia University

Jeffrey D. Ritter
St. Norbert College

Paul (Jep) Robertson
Henderson State University

Steven Rock
University of Colorado

Ron Stunda
Birmingham Southern College

John Rossi
Moravian College

Eric Sussman
University of California. Los Angeles

Tim Ryan
Southern Illinois University

Diane L. Tanner
University of North Florida

Victoria Rymer
University of Maryland

Gary Testa
Brooklyn College

James Sander
Butler University

Paula B. Thomas
Middle Tennessee State University

John Sander
University of Southern Maine

Elizabeth Venuti
Hofstra University

George Sanders
Western Washington University

James D. Waddington, Jr.,
Hawaii Pacific University

Howard Shapiro
Eastern Washington University

Dick Wasson
Southwestern College

Douglas Sharp
Wichita State University

Frank F. Weinberg
Golden Gate University

Phil Siegel
Florida Atlantic University

Jeannie Welsh
LaSalle University

John R. Simon
Northern Illinois University

Shari H. Wescott
Houston Baptist University

Keith Smith
George Washington University

Michael Willenborg
University of Connecticut

Pam Smith
Northern Illinois University

William H. Wilson
Oregon Health University

Billy S. Soo
Boston College

Kenneth Wooling
Hampton University

Carlton D. Stolle
Texas A&M University

Joni Young
University of New Mexico

William Stout
University of Louisville

Paul Zarowin
New York University

Pamela Stuerke
Case Western Reserve University

Stephen A. Zeff
Rice University

In addition, we thank the following colleagues who contributed to several of the unique features of this edition.

Gateway to the Profession Portal and FARS Cases

Jack Cathey
University of North Carolina—Charlotte

Andrew Prewitt
KPMG, Chicago

Michelle Ephraim
Worcester Polytechnic Institute

Jeff Seymour
KPMG, Minneapolis

Erik Frederickson
Madison, Wisconsin

Matt Sullivan
Deloitte & Touche, Milwaukee

Jason Hart
Deloitte & Touche, Milwaukee

Jen Vaughn
PricewaterhouseCoopers, Chicago

Kelly Krieg
E & Y, Milwaukee

Erin Viel
PricewaterhouseCoopers, Milwaukee

Jeremy Kunicki
Walgreens

Edward Wertheim
Northeastern University

Ancillary Authors, Contributors, Proofers, and Accuracy Checkers

Mary Ann Benson

John C. Borke
University of Wisconsin—Platteville

Jack Cathey
University of North Carolina—Charlotte

Betty Connor
University of Colorado at Denver

Robert Derstine
Villanova University

Gregory Dold
Southwestern College

Jan Duffy
Iowa State University

Jim Emig
Villanova University

Larry Falcetto
Emporia State University

Tom Forehand
State University of New York—New Paltz

Rosemary Fullerton
Utah State University

Clyde Galbraith
West Chester University

Alicia Gmeiner
Elm Street Publishing Services

Edwin Hackleman
Delta Software

Coby Harmon
University of California, Santa Barbara

Wayne Higley
Buena Vista University

Debra R. Hopkins
Northern Illinois University

Judi Hora
University of San Diego

Marilyn F. Hunt

Douglas W. Kieso
Aurora University

Mark Kohlbeck
Florida Atlantic University

Jennifer Laudermilch
PricewaterhouseCoopers

Ann Martin
University of Colorado at Denver

Barbara Muller
Arizona State University

Don Newell
Delta Software

Tom Noland
University of Houston

Paul (Jep) Robertson
Henderson State University

Rex A. Schildhouse
University of Phoenix—San Diego

Alice Sineath
Forsyth Technical Community College

Dick D. Wasson
Southwestern College, San Diego University

WileyPLUS Developers and Reviewers

James Mraz

Jan Mardon

Melanie Yon

Perspectives and "From Classroom to Career" Interviews

Stuart Weiss, *Stuart Weiss Business Writing, Inc., Portland, Oregon*

Practicing Accountants and Business Executives

From the fields of corporate and public accounting, we owe thanks to the following practitioners for their technical advance and for consenting to interviews.

Ron Bernard
NFL Enterprises

Mike Crooch
FASB

Tracy Golden
Deloitte & Touche

John Gribble
PricewaterhouseCoopers

Darien Griffin
S.C. Johnson & Son Wax

Michael Lehman
Sun Microsystems, Inc.

Michele Lippert
Evoke.com

Sue McGrath
Vision Capital Management

David Miniken
Sweeney Conrad

Robert Sack
University of Virginia

Clare Schulte
Deloitte & Touche

Willie Sutton
Mutual Community Savings Bank, Durham, NC

Lynn Turner
Glass, Lewis, LLP

Gary Valenzuela
Yahoo!

Rachel Woods
PricewaterhouseCoopers

Arthur Wyatt
*Arthur Anderson & Co., and the University
of Illinois—Urbana*

In addition, we appreciate the exemplary support and professional commitment given us by the development, marketing, production, and editorial staffs of John Wiley & Sons, including the following: Susan Elbe, Chris DeJohn, Mark Bonadeo, Amy Scholz, Alison Stanley, Ed Brislin, Allie Morris, Vanessa Ahrens, Jeanine Furino, Harry Nolan, Anna Melhorn, and Lenore Belton. Thanks to Terry Ann Kremer for her careful line edit of the book and to Ann Torbert for her editorial assistance in pulling together the various pieces of the manuscript. Thanks, too, to Suzanne Ingrao for her production work, to the management and staff at TechBooks for their work on the textbook, and to Alicia Gmeiner and the management and staff at Elm Street Publishing Services for their work on the solutions manual.

We also appreciate the cooperation of the American Institute of Certified Public Accountants and the Financial Accounting Standards Board in permitting us to quote from their pronouncements. We thank The Procter & Gamble Company for permitting us to use its 2004 annual report for our specimen financial statements. We also acknowledge permission from the American Institute of Certified Public Accountants, the Institute of Management Accountants, and the Institute of Internal Auditors to adapt and use material from the Uniform CPA Examinations, the CMA Examinations, and the CIA Examination, respectively.

If this book helps teachers instill in their students an appreciation for the challenges, worth, and limitations of accounting, if it encourages students to evaluate critically and understand financial accounting theory and practice, and if it prepares students for advanced study, professional examinations, and the successful and ethical pursuit of their careers in accounting or business, then we will have attained our objectives.

Suggestions and comments from users of this book will be appreciated.

Donald E. Kieso
Somonauk, Illinois

Jerry J. Weygandt
Madison, Wisconsin

Terry D. Warfield
Madison, Wisconsin

BRIEF CONTENTS

CONTENTS

CHAPTER FIFTEEN

STOCKHOLDERS' EQUITY

Everything Else Equal?

Not all dividend payers are created equal. Some stocks provide a good dividend yield but also promise strong earnings growth. These stocks could provide a healthy one-two punch for investors. A good example is Seattle's **Plum Creek Timber**. It pays a dividend of close to 4.2 percent, and it also expects earnings to expand about 6 percent in the next year.

General Motors has a seemingly healthy dividend of 5.8 percent. But the big automaker had a loss of $1.1 billion in a recent quarter, and it is having trouble reducing its onerous health-care benefits. There is concern that GM may be forced to trim its dividend at some point to conserve cash. The following chart shows that dividends are an important part of total stock returns.

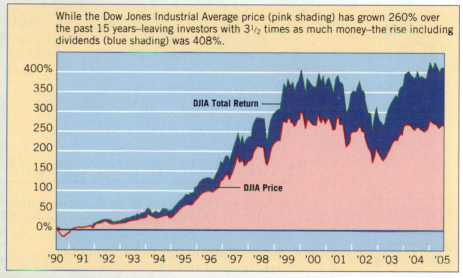

While the Dow Jones Industrial Average price (pink shading) has grown 260% over the past 15 years–leaving investors with 3½ times as much money–the rise including dividends (blue shading) was 408%.

Source: WSJ Marketing Data Group

As one analyst noted, "Investors have consistently underappreciated the value of compounding dividends in a portfolio. And dividends usually provide a strong degree of downside protection for a portfolio." But be wary when focusing on high-dividend stocks. Those with problems may find it difficult to keep their dividend payments going in the future.

Source: Adapted from Gary Zuckerman, "When Dividends Are Sweet, Be Choosy," *Wall Street Journal Online* (July 3, 2005).

Learning Objectives

After studying this chapter, you should be able to:

1 Discuss the characteristics of the corporate form of organization.

2 Identify the key components of stockholders' equity.

3 Explain the accounting procedures for issuing shares of stock.

4 Describe the accounting for treasury stock.

5 Explain the accounting for and reporting of preferred stock.

6 Describe the policies used in distributing dividends.

7 Identify the various forms of dividend distributions.

8 Explain the accounting for small and large stock dividends, and for stock splits.

9 Indicate how to present and analyze stockholders' equity.

As our opening story indicates, dividends combined with other information about a company can provide useful information to investors. In this chapter we explain the accounting issues for dividend transactions, as well as other transactions related to the stockholders' equity of a corporation. The content and organization of the chapter are as follows.

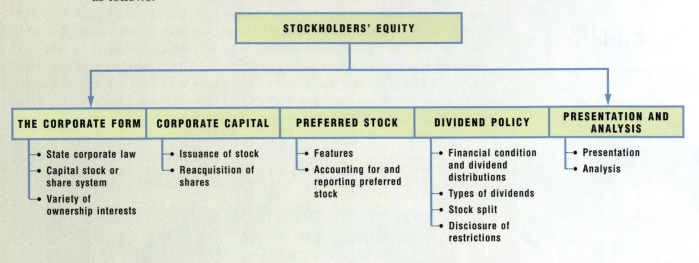

THE CORPORATE FORM OF ORGANIZATION

Of the three **primary forms of business organization**—the proprietorship, the partnership, and the corporation—the corporate form dominates. The corporation is by far the leader in terms of the aggregate amount of resources controlled, goods and services produced, and people employed. All of the "Fortune 500" largest industrial firms are corporations. Although the corporate form has a number of advantages (as well as disadvantages) over the other two forms, its principal advantage is its facility for attracting and accumulating large amounts of capital.

The special characteristics of the corporate form that affect accounting include:

1 Influence of state corporate law.
2 Use of the capital stock or share system.
3 Development of a variety of ownership interests.

State Corporate Law

Anyone who wishes to establish a corporation must submit **articles of incorporation** to the state in which incorporation is desired. After fulfilling requirements, the state issues a corporation charter, thereby recognizing the company as a legal entity subject to state law. Regardless of the number of states in which a corporation has operating divisions, it is incorporated in only one state.

It is to the company's advantage to incorporate in a state whose laws favor the corporate form of business organization. **General Motors**, for example, is incorporated in Delaware; **U.S. Steel** is a New Jersey corporation. Some corporations have increasingly been incorporating in states with laws favorable to existing management. For example, to thwart possible unfriendly takeovers, at one time, **Gulf Oil** changed its state of incorporation to Delaware. There, the board of directors alone, without a vote of the shareholders, may approve certain tactics against takeovers.

Each state has its own business incorporation act. The accounting for stockholders' equity follows the provisions of these acts. In many cases states have adopted the principles contained in the Model Business Corporate Act prepared by the American Bar Association. State laws are complex and vary both in their provisions and in their definitions of certain terms. Some laws fail to define technical terms. As a result, terms often mean one thing in one state and another thing in a different state. These problems may be further compounded because legal authorities often interpret the effects and restrictions of the laws differently.

Capital Stock or Share System

Stockholders' equity in a corporation generally consists of a large number of units or shares. Within a given class of stock each share exactly equals every other share. The number of shares possessed determines each owner's interest. If a company has one class of stock divided into 1,000 shares, a person who owns 500 shares controls one-half of the ownership interest. One holding 10 shares has a one-hundredth interest.

Each share of stock has certain rights and privileges. Only by special contract can a company restrict these rights and privileges at the time it issues the shares. Owners must examine the articles of incorporation, stock certificates, and the provisions of the state law to ascertain such restrictions on or variations from the standard rights and privileges. In the absence of restrictive provisions, each share carries the following rights:

1 To share proportionately in profits and losses.
2 To share proportionately in management (the right to vote for directors).
3 To share proportionately in corporate assets upon liquidation.
4 To share proportionately in any new issues of stock of the same class—called the **preemptive right**.[1]

INTERNATIONAL INSIGHT

In the United States, stockholders are treated equally as far as access to financial information. That is not always the case in other countries. For example, in Mexico, foreign investors as well as minority investors often have difficulty obtaining financial data. These restrictions are rooted in the habits of companies that, for many years, were tightly controlled by a few stockholders and managers.

The first three rights are self-explanatory. The last right is used to protect each stockholder's proportional interest in the company. **The preemptive right protects an existing stockholder from involuntary dilution of ownership interest.** Without this right, stockholders might find their interest reduced by the issuance of additional stock without their knowledge, and at prices unfavorable to them. However, many corporations have eliminated the preemptive right. Why? Because this right makes it inconvenient for corporations to issue large amounts of additional stock, as they frequently do in acquiring other companies.

The share system easily allows one individual to transfer an interest in a company to another investor. For example, individuals owning shares in **Circuit City** may sell **them to others at any time and at any price without obtaining the consent of the company or other stockholders**. Each share is personal property of the owner, who may dispose of it at will. Circuit City simply maintains a list or subsidiary ledger of stockholders as a guide to dividend payments, issuance of stock rights, voting proxies, and the like. Because owners freely and frequently transfer shares, Circuit City must revise the subsidiary ledger of stockholders periodically, generally in advance of every dividend payment or stockholders' meeting.

In addition, the major stock exchanges require ownership controls that the typical corporation finds uneconomic to provide. Thus, corporations often use **registrars and transfer agents** who specialize in providing services for recording and transferring stock. The Uniform Stock Transfer Act and the Uniform Commercial Code govern the negotiability of stock certificates.

Variety of Ownership Interests

In every corporation one class of stock must represent the basic ownership interest. That class is called common stock. **Common stock** is the residual corporate interest that bears the ultimate risks of loss and receives the benefits of success. It is guaranteed

---

[1]This privilege is referred to as a **stock right** or **warrant**. The warrants issued in these situations are of short duration, unlike the warrants issued with other securities.

neither dividends nor assets upon dissolution. But common stockholders generally control the management of the corporation and tend to profit most if the company is successful. In the event that a corporation has only one authorized issue of capital stock, that issue is by definition common stock, whether so designated in the charter or not.

In an effort to broaden investor appeal, corporations may offer two or more classes of stock, each with different rights or privileges. In the preceding section we pointed out that each share of stock of a given issue has the same four inherent rights as other shares of the same issue. By special stock contracts between the corporation and its stockholders, however, the stockholder may sacrifice certain of these rights in return for other special rights or privileges. Thus special classes of stock, usually called **preferred stock**, are created. In return for any special preference, the preferred stockholder always sacrifices some of the inherent rights of common stock ownership.

A common type of preference is to give the preferred stockholders a prior claim on earnings. The corporation thus assures them a dividend, usually at a stated rate, before it distributes any amount to the common stockholders. In return for this preference the preferred stockholders may sacrifice their right to a voice in management or their right to share in profits beyond the stated rate.

CLASSY STOCK

WHAT DO THE NUMBERS MEAN?

Some companies grant preferences to different shareholders by issuing different classes of common stock. Blue-chip newspaper companies, such as **The New York Times**, **Dow Jones**, and **The Washington Post**, have two classes of stock. Also, **Ford** and **Comcast** are two-class companies.

Sometimes these different classes of shares trade at dramatically different prices. For example, **Molex** has issued both common shares and Class A common stock, with the common shares trading at up to a 15 percent premium over the Class A shares. Why the difference in price? The most common explanation is voting rights. In the Molex case, the common shareholders get one vote per share; Class A shares don't get to vote.

For most retail investors, voting rights are not that important. But for family-controlled companies, issuing newer classes of lower or non-voting stock effectively creates currency for acquisitions, increases liquidity, or puts a public value on the company without diluting the family's voting control. Thus, investors must carefully compare the apparent bargain prices for some classes of stock—they may end up as second-class citizens with no voting rights.

Source: Adapted from Lauren Rublin, "Separate but Equal," *Barons Online* (August 16, 1999); and Andy Serwer, "Dual-Listed Companies Aren't Fair or Balanced," *Fortune* (September 20, 2004), p. 83.

CORPORATE CAPITAL

OBJECTIVE 2
Identify the key components of stockholders' equity.

Owner's equity in a corporation is defined as stockholders' equity, shareholders' equity, or corporate capital. The following three categories normally appear as part of stockholders' equity:

1 Capital stock.

2 Additional paid-in capital.

3 Retained earnings.

The first two categories, capital stock and additional paid-in capital, constitute contributed (paid-in) capital. **Retained earnings** represents the earned capital of the company. **Contributed capital (paid-in capital)** is the total amount paid in on capital stock—the amount provided by stockholders to the corporation for use in the business. Contributed capital includes items such as the par value of all outstanding stock and premiums less discounts on issuance. **Earned capital** is the capital that develops from profitable operations. It consists of all undistributed income that remains invested in the company.

Stockholders' equity is the difference between the assets and the liabilities of the company. That is, the owners' or stockholders' interest in a company like **Walt Disney Co.** is a **residual interest.**[2] **Stockholders' (owners') equity** represents the cumulative net contributions by stockholders plus retained earnings. As a residual interest, stockholders' equity has no existence apart from the assets and liabilities of Disney—stockholders' equity equals net assets. Stockholders' equity is not a claim to specific assets but a claim against a portion of the total assets. Its amount is not specified or fixed; it depends on Disney's profitability. Stockholders' equity grows if it is profitable. It shrinks, or may disappear entirely, if Disney loses money.

Issuance of Stock

In issuing stock, companies follow these procedures: First, the state must authorize the stock, generally in a certificate of incorporation or charter. Next, the corporation offers shares for sale, entering into contracts to sell stock. Then, after receiving amounts for the stock, the corporation issues shares. The corporation generally makes no entry in the general ledger accounts when it receives its stock authorization from the state of incorporation.

OBJECTIVE 3
Explain the accounting procedures for issuing shares of stock.

We discuss the accounting problems involved in the issuance of stock under the following topics.

1 Accounting for par value stock.
2 Accounting for no-par stock.
3 Accounting for stock issued in combination with other securities (lump-sum sales).
4 Accounting for stock issued in noncash transactions.
5 Accounting for costs of issuing stock.

Par Value Stock

The par value of a stock has no relationship to its fair market value. At present, the par value associated with most capital stock issuances is very low. For example, **PepsiCo**'s par value is $0.01, **Kellogg**'s is $0.25, and **Hershey**'s is $1. Such values contrast dramatically with the situation in the early 1900s, when practically all stock issued had a par value of $100. Low par values help companies avoid the contingent liability associated with stock sold below par.[3]

To show the required information for issuance of par value stock, corporations maintain accounts for each class of stock as follows.

1 *Preferred Stock or Common Stock.* Together, these two stock accounts reflect the par value of the corporation's issued shares. The company credits these accounts

---

[2]"Elements of Financial Statements," *Statement of Financial Accounting Concepts No. 6* (Stamford, Conn.: FASB, 1985), par. 60.

[3]Companies rarely, if ever, issue stock at a value below par value. If issuing stock below par, the company records the discount as a debit to Additional Paid-in Capital. In addition, the corporation may call on the original purchaser or the current holder of the shares issued below par to pay in the amount of the discount to prevent creditors from sustaining a loss upon liquidation of the corporation.

when it originally issues the shares. It makes no additional entries in these accounts unless it issues additional shares or retires them.

2   *Additional Paid-in Capital (also called Paid-in Capital in Excess of Par).* The **Additional Paid-in Capital** account indicates any excess over par value paid in by stockholders in return for the shares issued to them. Once paid in, the excess over par becomes a part of the corporation's additional paid-in capital. The individual stockholder has no greater claim on the excess paid in than all other holders of the same class of shares.

No-Par Stock

Many states permit the issuance of capital stock without par value, called **no-par stock**. The reasons for issuance of no-par stock are twofold: First, issuance of no-par stock **avoids the contingent liability** (see footnote 3) that might occur if the corporation issued par value stock at a discount. Second, some confusion exists over the relationship (or rather the absence of a relationship) between the par value and fair market value. If shares have no par value, **the questionable treatment of using par value as a basis for fair value never arises**. This is particularly advantageous whenever issuing stock for property items such as tangible or intangible fixed assets.

A major disadvantage of no-par stock is that some states levy a high tax on these issues. In addition, in some states the total issue price for no-par stock may be considered legal capital, which could reduce the flexibility in paying dividends.

Corporations sell no-par shares, like par value shares, for whatever price they will bring. However, unlike par value shares, corporations issue them without a premium or a discount. The exact amount received represents the credit to common or preferred stock. For example, Video Electronics Corporation is organized with authorized common stock of 10,000 shares without par value. Video Electronics makes only a memorandum entry for the authorization, inasmuch as no amount is involved. If Video Electronics then issues 500 shares for cash at $10 per share, it makes the following entry:

Cash	5,000	
Common Stock—No-Par Value		5,000

If it issues another 500 shares for $11 per share, Video Electronics makes this entry:

Cash	5,500	
Common Stock—No-Par Value		5,500

True no-par stock should be carried in the accounts at issue price without any additional paid-in capital or discount reported. But some states require that no-par stock have a **stated value**. The stated value is a minimum value below which a company cannot issue it. Thus, instead of being no-par stock, such stated-value stock becomes, in effect, stock with a very low par value. It thus is open to all the criticism and abuses that first encouraged the development of no-par stock.[4]

If no-par stock has a stated value of $5 per share but sells for $11, all such amounts in excess of $5 are recorded as additional paid-in capital, which in many states is fully or partially available for dividends. Thus, no-par value stock, with a low stated value, permits a new corporation to commence its operations with additional paid-in capital that may exceed its stated capital. For example, if a company issued 1,000 of the shares with a $5 stated value at $15 per share for cash, it makes the following entry.

Cash	15,000	
Common Stock		5,000
Paid-in Capital in Excess of Stated Value		10,000

---

[4]*Accounting Trends and Techniques—2004* indicates that its 600 surveyed companies reported 655 issues of outstanding common stock, 570 par value issues, and 54 no-par issues; 6 of the no-par issues were shown at their stated (assigned) values.

Most corporations account for no-par stock with a stated value as if it were par value stock with par equal to the stated value.

Stock Issued with Other Securities (Lump-Sum Sales)

Generally, corporations sell classes of stock separately from one another. The reason to do so is to track the proceeds relative to each class, as well as relative to each lot. Occasionally, a corporation issues two or more classes of securities for a single payment or lump sum, in the acquisition of another company. The accounting problem in such **lump-sum sales** is how to allocate the proceeds among the several classes of securities. Companies use one of two methods of allocation: (1) the proportional method and (2) the incremental method.

Proportional Method. If the fair market value or other sound basis for determining relative value is available for each class of security, **the company allocates the lump sum received among the classes of securities on a proportional basis**. For instance, assume a company issues 1,000 shares of $10 stated value common stock having a market value of $20 a share, and 1,000 shares of $10 par value preferred stock having a market value of $12 a share, for a lump sum of $30,000. Illustration 15-1 shows how the company allocates the $30,000 to the two classes of stock.

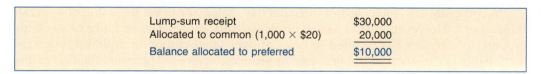

ILLUSTRATION 15-1
Allocation in Lump-Sum Securities Issuance—Proportional Method

Fair market value of common (1,000 × $20) = $20,000
Fair market value of preferred (1,000 × $12) = 12,000

Aggregate fair market value $32,000

Allocated to common: $\dfrac{\$20,000}{\$32,000} \times \$30,000 = \$18,750$

Allocated to preferred: $\dfrac{\$12,000}{\$32,000} \times \$30,000 = 11,250$

Total allocation $30,000

Incremental Method. In instances where a company cannot determine the fair market value of all classes of securities, it may use the incremental method. It uses the market value of the securities as a basis for those classes that it knows, and allocates the remainder of the lump sum to the class for which it does not know the market value. For instance, if a company issues 1,000 shares of $10 stated value common stock having a market value of $20, and 1,000 shares of $10 par value preferred stock having no established market value, for a lump sum of $30,000, it allocates the $30,000 to the two classes as shown in Illustration 15-2.

ILLUSTRATION 15-2
Allocation in Lump-Sum Securities Issuance—Incremental Method

Lump-sum receipt	$30,000
Allocated to common (1,000 × $20)	20,000
Balance allocated to preferred	$10,000

If a company cannot determine fair value for any of the classes of stock involved in a lump-sum exchange, it may need to use other approaches. It may rely on an expert's appraisal. Or, if the company knows that one or more of the classes of securities issued will have a determinable market value in the near future, it may use a best estimate basis with the intent to adjust later, upon establishment of the future market value.

Stock Issued in Noncash Transactions

Accounting for the issuance of shares of stock for property or services involves an issue of valuation. **The general rule is: Companies should record stock issued for services or property other than cash at either the fair value of the stock issued or the fair value of the noncash consideration received, whichever is more clearly determinable.**

If a company can readily determine both, and the transaction results from an arm's-length exchange, there will probably be little difference in their fair values. In such cases the basis for valuing the exchange should not matter.

If a company cannot readily determine either the fair value of the stock it issues or the property or services it receives, it should employ an appropriate valuation technique. Depending on available data, the valuation may be based on market transactions involving comparable assets or the use of discounted expected future cash flows. Companies should avoid the use of the book, par, or stated values as a basis of valuation for these transactions.

A company may exchange unissued stock or treasury stock (issued shares that it has reacquired but not retired) for property or services. If it uses treasury shares, the cost of the treasury shares should not be considered the decisive factor in establishing the fair value of the property or services. Instead, it should use the fair value of the treasury stock, if known, to value the property or services. Otherwise, if it does not know the fair value of the treasury stock, it should use the fair value of the property or services received, if determinable.

The following series of transactions illustrates the procedure for recording the issuance of 10,000 shares of $10 par value common stock for a patent for Marlowe Company, in various circumstances.

1 Marlowe cannot readily determine the fair value of the patent, but it knows the fair value of the stock is $140,000.

Patent	140,000	
Common Stock (10,000 shares × $10 per share)		100,000
Paid-in Capital in Excess of Par		40,000

2 Marlowe cannot readily determine the fair value of the stock, but it determines the fair value of the patent is $150,000.

Patent	150,000	
Common Stock (10,000 shares × $10 per share)		100,000
Paid-in Capital in Excess of Par		50,000

3 Marlowe cannot readily determine the fair value of the stock nor the fair value of the patent. An independent consultant values the patent at $125,000 based on discounted expected cash flows.

Patent	125,000	
Common Stock (10,000 shares × $10 share)		100,000
Paid-in Capital in Excess of Par		25,000

In corporate law, the board of directors has the power to set the value of noncash transactions. However, boards sometimes abuse this power. The issuance of stock for property or services has resulted in cases of overstated corporate capital through intentional overvaluation of the property or services received. The overvaluation of the stockholders' equity resulting from inflated asset values creates **watered stock**. The corporation should eliminate the "water" by simply writing down the overvalued assets.

If, as a result of the issuance of stock for property or services, a corporation undervalues the recorded assets, it creates **secret reserves**. An understated corporate structure (secret reserve) may also result from other methods: excessive depreciation or amortization charges, expensing capital expenditures, excessive write-downs of inventories or receivables, or any other understatement of assets or overstatement of liabilities. An example of a liability overstatement is an excessive provision for estimated product warranties that ultimately results in an understatement of owners' equity, thereby creating a secret reserve.

Costs of Issuing Stock

When a company like **Walgreens** issues stock, it should report direct costs incurred to sell stock, such as underwriting costs, accounting and legal fees, printing costs, and taxes, as a reduction of the amounts paid in. Walgreens therefore debits issue costs to Additional Paid-in Capital because they are unrelated to corporate operations. In effect, **issue costs are a cost of financing**. As such, issue costs should reduce the proceeds received from the sale of the stock.

Walgreens should expense management salaries and other indirect costs related to the stock issue because it is difficult to establish a relationship between these costs and the sale proceeds. In addition, Walgreens expenses recurring costs, primarily registrar and transfer agents' fees, as incurred.

THE CASE OF THE DISAPPEARING RECEIVABLE

Sometimes companies issue stock but may not receive cash in return. As a result, a company records a receivable.

Controversy existed regarding the presentation of this receivable on the balance sheet. Some argued that the company should report the receivable as an asset similar to other receivables. Others argued that the company should report the receivable as a deduction from stockholders' equity (similar to the treatment of treasury stock). The SEC settled this issue: It requires companies to use the contra-equity approach because the risk of collection in this type of transaction is often very high.

This accounting issue surfaced in **Enron**'s accounting. Starting in early 2000, Enron issued shares of its common stock to four "special-purpose entities," in exchange for which it received a note receivable. Enron then increased its assets (by recording a receivable) and stockholders' equity, a move the company now calls an accounting error. As a result of this accounting treatment, Enron overstated assets and stockholders' equity by $172 million in its 2000 audited financial statements and by $828 million in its unaudited 2001 statements. This $1 billion overstatement was 8.5 percent of Enron's previously reported stockholders' equity at that time.

As Lynn Turner, former chief accountant of the SEC, noted, "It is a basic accounting principle that you don't record equity until you get cash, and a note doesn't count as cash." Situations like this led investors, creditors, and suppliers to lose faith in the credibility of Enron, which eventually caused its bankruptcy.

Source: Adapted from Jonathan Weil, "Basic Accounting Tripped Up Enron—Financial Statements Didn't Add Up—Auditors Overlook a Simple Rule," *Wall Street Journal* (November 11, 2001), p. C1.

WHAT DO THE NUMBERS MEAN?

Reacquisition of Shares

Companies often buy back their own shares. In fact, share buybacks now exceed dividends as a form of distribution to stockholders.[5] For example, **Dell**, **Yahoo**, and **The Home Depot** had buybacks recently of $10 billion, $3 billion, and $2 billion, respectively. Illustration 15-3 (on page 734) indicates that buybacks are increasing dramatically.

> **OBJECTIVE 4**
> Describe the accounting for treasury stock.

---

[5]At the beginning of the 1990s the situation was just the opposite. That is, share buybacks were less than half the level of dividends. Companies are extremely reluctant to reduce or eliminate their dividends, because they believe that the market negatively views this action.

ILLUSTRATION 15-3
Stock Buybacks on the
Rise

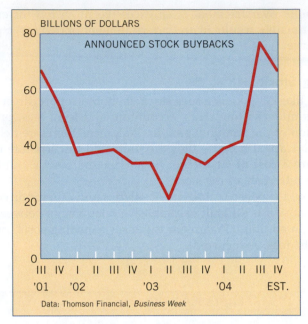

Source: *Business Week* (November 29, 2004), p.116.

Corporations purchase their outstanding stock for several reasons:

1 *To provide tax-efficient distributions of excess cash to shareholders.* Capital gain rates on sales of stock to the company by the stockholders have been approximately half the ordinary tax rate for many investors. This advantage has been somewhat diminished by recent changes in the tax law related to dividends.

2 *To increase earnings per share and return on equity.* Reducing both shares outstanding and stockholders' equity often enhances certain performance ratios. However, strategies to hype performance measures might increase performance in the short-run, but these tactics add no real long-term value.

3 *To provide stock for employee stock compensation contracts or to meet potential merger needs.* **Honeywell Inc.** reported that it would use part of its purchase of one million common shares for employee stock option contracts. Other companies acquire shares to have them available for business acquisitions.

4 *To thwart takeover attempts or to reduce the number of stockholders.* By reducing the number of shares held by the public, existing owners and managements bar "outsiders" from gaining control or significant influence. When Ted Turner attempted to acquire **CBS**, CBS started a substantial buyback of its stock. Companies may also use stock purchases to eliminate dissident stockholders.

5 *To make a market in the stock.* As one company executive noted, "Our company is trying to establish a floor for the stock." Purchasing stock in the marketplace creates a demand. This may stabilize the stock price or, in fact, increase it.

Some publicly held corporations have chosen to "go private," that is, to eliminate public (outside) ownership entirely by purchasing all of their outstanding stock. Companies often accomplish such a procedure through a **leveraged buyout (LBO)**, in which the company borrows money to finance the stock repurchases.

After reacquiring shares, a company may either retire them or hold them in the treasury for reissue. If not retired, such shares are referred to as **treasury stock** (**treasury shares**). Technically, treasury stock is a corporation's own stock, reacquired after having been issued and fully paid.

Treasury stock is not an asset. When a company purchases treasury stock, a reduction occurs in both assets and stockholders' equity. It is inappropriate to imply that a

UNDERLYING CONCEPTS

As we indicated in Chapter 2, an asset should have probable future economic benefits. Treasury stock simply reduces common stock outstanding.

corporation can own a part of itself. A corporation may sell treasury stock to obtain funds, but that does not make treasury stock a balance sheet asset. When a corporation buys back some of its own outstanding stock, it has not acquired an asset; it reduces net assets.

The possession of treasury stock does not give the corporation the right to vote, to exercise preemptive rights as a stockholder, to receive cash dividends, or to receive assets upon corporate liquidation. **Treasury stock is essentially the same as unissued capital stock.** No one advocates classifying unissued capital stock as an asset in the balance sheet.[6]

SIGNALS TO BUY?

Market analysts sometimes look to stock buybacks as a buy signal for a stock. That strategy is not that surprising if you look at the performance of companies that did buybacks. For example, in one study, buyback companies outperformed similar companies without buybacks by an average of 23 percent. In a recent three-year period, companies followed by **Buybackletter.com** were up 16.4 percent, while the S&P 500 Stock Index was up just 7.1 percent in that period. Why the premium? Well, the conventional wisdom is that companies who buy back shares believe their shares are undervalued. Thus, analysts view the buyback announcement as an important piece of inside information about future company prospects.

On the other hand, buy-backs can actually hurt businesses and their shareholders over the long-run. Whether the buy-back is a good thing appears to depend a lot on why the company did the buy-back and what the repurchased shares were used for. One study found that companies often increased their buybacks when earnings growth slowed. This allowed the companies to prop up earnings per share (based on fewer shares outstanding). Furthermore, many buybacks do not actually result in a net reduction in shares outstanding. For example, companies, such as **Microsoft**, bought back shares to meet share demands for stock option exercises, resulting in higher net shares outstanding when it re-issued the repurchased shares to the option holders upon exercise. In this case the buyback actually indicated a further dilution in the share ownership in the buyback company.

This does not mean you should never trust a buy-back signal. But if the buy-back is intended to manage the company's earnings or if the buy-back results in dilution, take a closer look.

Source: Adapted from Ann Tergesen, "When Buybacks Are Signals to Buy," *Business Week Online* (October 1, 2001); and Rachel Beck, "Stock BuyBacks Not Always Good for the Company, Shareholders," *Naples [FL] Daily News* (March 7, 2004). p. I1.

WHAT DO THE NUMBERS MEAN?

Purchase of Treasury Stock

Companies use two general methods of handling treasury stock in the accounts: the cost method and the par value method. Both methods are generally acceptable. The cost method enjoys more widespread use.[7]

- The **cost method** results in debiting the Treasury Stock account for the reacquisition cost and in reporting this account as a deduction from the total paid-in capital **and** retained earnings on the balance sheet.
- The **par** or **stated value method** records all transactions in treasury shares at their par value and reports the treasury stock as a deduction from capital stock only.

Discussion of Using Par or Stated Value for Treasury Stock Transactions

---

[6]The possible justification for classifying these shares as assets is that the company will use them to liquidate a specific liability that appears on the balance sheet. *Accounting Trends and Techniques—2004* reported that out of 600 companies surveyed, 398 disclosed treasury stock, but none classified it as an asset.

[7]*Accounting Trends and Techniques—2004* indicates that of its selected list of 600 companies, 384 carried common stock in treasury at cost and only 2 at par or stated value; 2 companies carried preferred stock in treasury at cost and none at par or stated value.

No matter which method a company uses, most states consider the cost of the treasury shares acquired as a restriction on retained earnings.

Companies generally use the cost method to account for treasury stock. This method derives its name from the fact that a company maintains the Treasury Stock account at the cost of the shares purchased.[8] Under the cost method, the company debits the Treasury Stock account for the cost of the shares acquired. Upon reissuance of the shares, it credits the account for this same cost. The original price received for the stock does not affect the entries to record the acquisition and reissuance of the treasury stock.

To illustrate, assume that Pacific Company issued 100,000 shares of $1 par value common stock at a price of $10 per share. In addition, it has retained earnings of $300,000. Illustration 15-4 shows the stockholders' equity section on December 31, 2006, before purchase of treasury stock.

ILLUSTRATION 15-4
Stockholders' Equity with
No Treasury Stock

Stockholders' equity	
Paid-in capital	
Common stock, $1 par value, 100,000 shares	
issued and outstanding	$ 100,000
Additional paid-in capital	900,000
Total paid-in capital	1,000,000
Retained earnings	300,000
Total stockholders' equity	$1,300,000

On January 20, 2007, Pacific acquires 10,000 shares of its stock at $11 per share. Pacific records the reacquisition as follows:

January 20, 2007

Treasury Stock	110,000	
Cash		110,000

Note that Pacific debited Treasury Stock for the cost of the shares purchased. The original paid-in capital account, Common Stock, is not affected because the number of issued shares does not change. The same is true for the Additional Paid-in Capital account. Pacific deducts treasury stock from total paid-in capital and retained earnings in the stockholders' equity section.

Illustration 15-5 shows the stockholders' equity section for Pacific after purchase of the treasury stock.

ILLUSTRATION 15-5
Stockholders' Equity with
Treasury Stock

Stockholders' equity	
Paid-in capital	
Common stock, $1 par value, 100,000 shares	
issued and 90,000 outstanding	$ 100,000
Additional paid-in capital	900,000
Total paid-in capital	1,000,000
Retained earnings	300,000
Total paid-in capital and retained earnings	1,300,000
Less: Cost of treasury stock (10,000 shares)	110,000
Total stockholders' equity	$1,190,000

---

[8]If making numerous acquisitions of blocks of treasury shares at different prices, a company may use inventory costing methods—such as specific identification, average, or FIFO—to identify the cost at date of reissuance.

Pacific subtracts the cost of the treasury stock from the total of common stock, additional paid-in capital, and retained earnings. It therefore reduces stockholders' equity. Many states require a corporation to restrict retained earnings for the cost of treasury stock purchased. The restriction keeps intact the corporation's legal capital that it temporarily holds as treasury stock. When the corporation sells the treasury stock, it lifts the restriction.

Pacific discloses both the number of shares issued (100,000) and the number in the treasury (10,000). The difference is the number of shares of stock outstanding (90,000). The term **outstanding stock** means the number of shares of issued stock that stockholders own.

Sale of Treasury Stock

Companies usually reissue or retire treasury stock. When selling treasury shares, the accounting for the sale depends on the price. If the selling price of the treasury stock equals its cost, the company records the sale of the shares by debiting Cash and crediting Treasury Stock. In cases where the selling price of the treasury stock is not equal to cost, then accounting for treasury stock sold **above cost** differs from the accounting for treasury stock sold **below cost**. However, the sale of treasury stock either above or below cost increases both total assets and stockholders' equity.

Sale of Treasury Stock above Cost. When the selling price of shares of treasury stock exceeds its cost, a company credits the difference to Paid-in Capital from Treasury Stock. To illustrate, assume that Pacific acquired 10,000 shares of its treasury stock at $11 per share. It now sells 1,000 shares at $15 per share on March 10. Pacific records the entry as follows.

March 10, 2007

Cash	15,000	
Treasury Stock		11,000
Paid-in Capital from Treasury Stock		4,000

There are two reasons why Pacific does not credit $4,000 to Gain on Sale of Treasury Stock: (1) Gains on sales occur when selling **assets**; treasury stock is not an asset. (2) A gain or loss should not be recognized from stock transactions with its own stockholders. Thus, Pacific should not include paid-in capital arising from the sale of treasury stock in the measurement of net income. Instead, it lists paid-in capital from treasury stock separately on the balance sheet, as a part of paid-in capital.

Sale of Treasury Stock below Cost. When a corporation sells treasury stock below its cost, it usually debits the excess of the cost over selling price to Paid-in Capital from Treasury Stock. Thus, if Pacific sells an additional 1,000 shares of treasury stock on March 21 at $8 per share, it records the sale as follows.

March 21, 2007

Cash	8,000	
Paid-in Capital from Treasury Stock	3,000	
Treasury Stock		11,000

We can make several observations based on the two sale entries (sale above cost and sale below cost): (1) Pacific credits Treasury Stock at cost in each entry. (2) Pacific uses Paid-in Capital from Treasury Stock for the difference between the cost and the resale price of the shares. (3) Neither entry affects the original paid-in capital account, Common Stock.

After eliminating the credit balance in Paid-in Capital from Treasury Stock, the corporation debits any additional excess of cost over selling price to Retained Earnings. To illustrate, assume that Pacific sells an additional 1,000 shares at $8 per share on April 10. Illustration 15-6 shows the balance in the Paid-in Capital from Treasury Stock account (before the April 10 purchase).

ILLUSTRATION 15-6
Treasury Stock Transactions in Paid-in Capital Account

Paid-in Capital from Treasury Stock			
Mar. 21	3,000	Mar. 10	4,000
		Balance	1,000

In this case, Pacific debits $1,000 of the excess to Paid-in Capital from Treasury Stock. It debits the remainder to Retained Earnings. The entry is:

April 10, 2007

Cash	8,000	
Paid-in Capital from Treasury Stock	1,000	
Retained Earnings	2,000	
Treasury Stock		11,000

Retiring Treasury Stock

The board of directors may approve the retirement of treasury shares. This decision results in cancellation of the treasury stock and a reduction in the number of shares of issued stock. Retired treasury shares have the status of authorized and unissued shares. The accounting effects are similar to the sale of treasury stock except that corporations debit the **paid-in capital accounts applicable to the retired shares** instead of cash. For example, if a corporation originally sells the shares at par, it debits Common Stock for the par value per share. If it originally sells the shares at $3 above par value, it also debits Paid-in Capital in Excess of Par Value for $3 per share at retirement.

PREFERRED STOCK

OBJECTIVE 5
Explain the accounting for and reporting of preferred stock.

As noted earlier, **preferred stock** is a special class of shares that possesses certain preferences or features not possessed by the common stock.[9] The following features are those most often associated with preferred stock issues.

1 Preference as to dividends.
2 Preference as to assets in the event of liquidation.
3 Convertible into common stock.
4 Callable at the option of the corporation.
5 Nonvoting.

The features that distinguish preferred from common stock may be of a more restrictive and negative nature than preferences. For example, the preferred stock may be nonvoting, noncumulative, and nonparticipating.

Companies usually issue preferred stock with a par value, expressing the dividend preference as a **percentage of the par value**. Thus, holders of 8 percent preferred stock with a $100 par value are entitled to an annual dividend of $8 per share. This stock is commonly referred to as 8 percent preferred stock. In the case of no-par preferred stock, a corporation expresses a dividend preference as a **specific dollar amount** per share, for example, $7 per share. This stock is commonly referred to as $7 preferred stock.

A preference as to dividends does not assure the payment of dividends. It merely assures that the corporation must pay the stated dividend rate or amount applicable to the preferred stock before paying any dividends on the common stock.

[9]*Accounting Trends and Techniques—2004* reports that of its 600 surveyed companies, 84 had preferred stock outstanding; 73 had one class of preferred, and 9 had two classes.

A company often issues preferred stock (instead of debt) because of a high debt-to-equity ratio. In other instances, it issues preferred stock through private placements with other corporations at a lower-than-market dividend rate because the acquiring corporation receives largely tax-free dividends (owing to the IRS's 70 percent or 80 percent dividends received deduction).

Features of Preferred Stock

A corporation may attach whatever preferences or restrictions, in whatever combination it desires, to a preferred stock issue, as long as it does not specifically violate its state incorporation law. Also, it may issue more than one class of preferred stock. We discuss the most common features attributed to preferred stock below.

Cumulative Preferred Stock

Cumulative preferred stock requires that if a corporation fails to pay a dividend in any year, it must make it up in a later year before paying any dividends to common stockholders. If the directors fail to declare a dividend at the normal date for dividend action, the dividend is said to have been "passed." Any passed dividend on cumulative preferred stock constitutes a dividend in arrears. Because no liability exists until the board of directors declares a dividend, a corporation does not record a dividend in arrears as a liability but discloses it in a note to the financial statements. A corporation seldom issues noncumulative preferred stock because a passed dividend is lost forever to the preferred stockholder. As a result, this stock issue would be less marketable.

Participating Preferred Stock

Holders of participating preferred stock share ratably with the common stockholders in any profit distributions beyond the prescribed rate. That is, 5 percent preferred stock, if fully participating, will receive not only its 5 percent return, but also dividends at the same rates as those paid to common stockholders if paying amounts in excess of 5 percent of par or stated value to common stockholders. Note that participating preferred stock may be only partially participating. Although seldom used, examples of companies that have issued participating preferreds are **LTV Corporation**, **Southern California Edison**, and **Allied Products Corporation**.

Convertible Preferred Stock

Convertible preferred stock allows stockholders, at their option, to exchange preferred shares for common stock at a predetermined ratio. The convertible preferred stockholder not only enjoys a preferred claim on dividends but also has the option of converting into a common stockholder with unlimited participation in earnings.

Callable Preferred Stock

Callable preferred stock permits the corporation at its option to call or redeem the outstanding preferred shares at specified future dates and at stipulated prices. Many preferred issues are callable. The corporation usually sets the call or redemption price slightly above the original issuance price and commonly states it in terms related to the par value. The callable feature permits the corporation to use the capital obtained through the issuance of such stock until the need has passed or it is no longer advantageous.

The existence of a call price or prices tends to set a ceiling on the market value of the preferred shares unless they are convertible into common stock. When a corporation redeems preferred stock, it must pay any dividends in arrears.

Redeemable Preferred Stock

Recently, more and more issuances of preferred stock have features that make the security more like debt (legal obligation to pay) than an equity instrument. For example, redeemable preferred stock has a mandatory redemption period or a redemption feature that the issuer cannot control.

Previously, public companies were not permitted to report these debt-like preferreds in equity, but they were not required to report them as a liability either. There were concerns about classification of these debt-like securities, which may have been reported as equity or in the "mezzanine" section of balance sheets between debt and equity. There also was diversity in practice as to how dividends on these securities were reported. The FASB recently issued a standard that affects the accounting for certain hybrid instruments and requires debt-like securities, like redeemable preferred stock to be classified as liabilities and be measured and accounted for similar to liabilities.[10]

Accounting for and Reporting Preferred Stock

The accounting for preferred stock at issuance is similar to that for common stock. A corporation allocates proceeds between the par value of the preferred stock and additional paid-in capital. To illustrate, assume that Bishop Co. issues 10,000 shares of $10 par value preferred stock for $12 cash per share. Bishop records the issuance as follows:

Cash	120,000	
Preferred Stock		100,000
Paid-in Capital in Excess of Par		20,000

Thus, Bishop maintains separate accounts for these different classes of shares.

In contrast to convertible bonds (recorded as a liability on the date of issue) corporations consider convertible preferred stock as a part of stockholders' equity. In addition, when exercising convertible preferred stocks, there is no theoretical justification for recognition of a gain or loss. A company recognizes no gain or loss when dealing with stockholders in their capacity as business owners. Instead, the company **employs the book value method**: debit Preferred Stock, along with any related Additional Paid-in Capital; credit Common Stock and Additional Paid-in Capital (if an excess exists).

Preferred stock generally has no maturity date. Therefore, no legal obligation exists to pay the preferred stockholder. As a result, companies classify preferred stock as part of stockholders' equity. Companies generally report preferred stock at par value as the first item in the stockholders' equity section. They report any excess over par value as part of additional paid-in capital. They also consider dividends on preferred stock as a distribution of income and not an expense. Companies must disclose the pertinent rights of the preferred stock outstanding.[11]

DIVIDEND POLICY

As indicated in the opening story, dividend payouts can be important signals to the market. The practice of paying dividends declined sharply in the 1980s and 1990s as companies focused on growth and plowed profits back into the business. A resurgence in dividend payouts is due in large part to the dividend tax cut of 2003, which reduced the rate of tax on dividends to 15 percent (quite a bit lower than the ordinary income rate charged in the past). In addition, investors who were burned by accounting scandals in recent years began demanding higher payouts in the form of dividends. Why?

---

[10]"Accounting for Certain Financial Instruments with Characteristics of Both Liabilities and Equity," *Statement of Financial Accounting Standards No. 150* (Norwalk Conn.: FASB, 2003). *SFAS No. 150* represents completion of the first phase in a broader project on liabilities and equity. In phase two, the FASB will deal with the accounting for compound financial instruments (e.g., convertible debt, covered in Chapter 16) that have characteristics of liabilities and equity, the definition of an ownership relationship, and the definition of liabilities (an amendment to *FASB Concepts Statement No. 6*, "Elements of Financial Statements.")

[11]"Disclosure of Information about Capital Structure," *Statement of Financial Accounting Standards No. 129* (Norwalk, Conn.: FASB, 1997).

A dividend check provides proof that at least some portion of a company's profits is genuine.[12]

Determining the proper amount of dividends to pay is a difficult financial management decision. Companies that are paying dividends are extremely reluctant to reduce or eliminate their dividend. They fear that the securities market might negatively view this action. As a consequence, companies that have been paying cash dividends will make every effort to continue to do so. In addition, the type of shareholder the company has (taxable or nontaxable, retail investor or institutional investor) plays a large role in determining dividend policy.

Very few companies pay dividends in amounts equal to their legally available retained earnings. The major reasons are as follows.

1 To maintain agreements (bond covenants) with specific creditors, to retain all or a portion of the earnings, in the form of assets, to build up additional protection against possible loss.

2 To meet state corporation requirements, that earnings equivalent to the cost of treasury shares purchased be restricted against dividend declarations.

3 To retain assets that would otherwise be paid out as dividends, to finance growth or expansion. This is sometimes called internal financing, reinvesting earnings, or "plowing" the profits back into the business.

4 To smooth out dividend payments from year to year by accumulating earnings in good years and using such accumulated earnings as a basis for dividends in bad years.

5 To build up a cushion or buffer against possible losses or errors in the calculation of profits.

The reasons above are self-explanatory except for the second. The laws of some states require that the corporation restrict its legal capital from distribution to stockholders, to protect against loss for creditors.[13] The applicable state law determines the legality of a dividend.

Financial Condition and Dividend Distributions

Effective management of a company requires attention to more than the legality of dividend distributions. Management must also consider economic conditions, most importantly, liquidity. Assume an extreme situation as shown in Illustration 15-7.

ILLUSTRATION 15-7
Balance Sheet, Showing a Lack of Liquidity

BALANCE SHEET			
Plant assets	$500,000	Capital stock	$400,000
	$500,000	Retained earnings	100,000
			$500,000

The depicted company has a retained earnings credit balance. Unless restricted, it can declare a dividend of $100,000. But because all its assets are plant assets used in operations, payment of a cash dividend of $100,000 would require the sale of plant assets or borrowing.

[12]Jeff Opdyke, "Tax Cut, Shareholder Pressure Stoke Surge in Dividends," *Wall Street Journal Online* (January 18, 2005).

[13]If the corporation buys its own outstanding stock, it reduces its legal capital and distributes assets to stockholders. If permitted, the corporation could, by purchasing treasury stock at any price desired, return to the stockholders their investments and leave creditors with little or no protection against loss.

Even if a balance sheet shows current assets, as in Illustration 15-8, the question remains as to whether the company needs those cash assets for other purposes.

ILLUSTRATION 15-8
Balance Sheet, Showing Cash but Minimal Working Capital

BALANCE SHEET					
Cash	$100,000	Current liabilities		$ 60,000	
Plant assets	460,000	Capital stock	$400,000		
	$560,000	Retained earnings	100,000	500,000	
				$560,000	

The existence of current liabilities strongly implies that the company needs some of the cash to meet current debts as they mature. In addition, day-by-day cash requirements for payrolls and other expenditures not included in current liabilities also require cash.

Thus, before declaring a dividend, management must consider **availability of funds to pay the dividend**. A company should not pay a dividend unless both the present and future financial position warrant the distribution.

The SEC encourages companies to disclose their dividend policy in their annual report, especially those that (1) have earnings but fail to pay dividends, or (2) do not expect to pay dividends in the foreseeable future. In addition, the SEC encourages companies that consistently pay dividends to indicate whether they intend to continue this practice in the future.

Types of Dividends

OBJECTIVE 7
Identify the various forms of dividend distributions.

Companies generally base dividend distributions either on accumulated profits (that is, retained earnings) or on some other capital item such as additional paid-in capital. Dividends are of the following types.

1 Cash dividends.
2 Property dividends.
3 Liquidating dividends.
4 Stock dividends.

Although commonly paid in cash, companies occasionally pay dividends in stock or some other asset.[14] **All dividends, except for stock dividends, reduce the total stockholders' equity in the corporation.** When declaring a stock dividend, the corporation does not pay out assets or incur a liability. It issues additional shares of stock to each stockholder and nothing more.

The natural expectation of any stockholder who receives a dividend is that the corporation has operated successfully. As a result, he or she is receiving a share of its profits. A company should disclose a liquidating dividend—that is, a dividend not based on retained earnings—to the stockholders so that they will not misunderstand its source.

Cash Dividends

The board of directors votes on the declaration of cash dividends. Upon approval of the resolution, the board declares a dividend. Before paying it, however, the company must prepare a current list of stockholders. For this reason there is usually a time lag between declaration and payment. For example, the board of directors might approve

---

[14]*Accounting Trends and Techniques—2004* reported that of its 600 surveyed companies, 370 paid a cash dividend on common stock, 54 paid a cash dividend on preferred stock, 4 issued stock dividends, and 7 issued or paid dividends in kind. Some companies declare more than one type of dividend in a given year.

a resolution at the January 10 (**date of declaration**) meeting, and declare it payable February 5 (**date of payment**) to all stockholders of record January 25 (**date of record**).[15] In this example, the period from January 10 to January 25 gives time for the company to complete and register any transfers in process. The time from January 25 to February 5 provides an opportunity for the transfer agent or accounting department, depending on who does this work, to prepare a list of stockholders as of January 25 and to prepare and mail dividend checks.

A declared cash dividend is a liability. Because payment is generally required very soon, it is usually a current liability. Companies use the following entries to record the declaration and payment of an ordinary dividend payable in cash. For example, Roadway Freight Corp. on June 10 declared a cash dividend of 50 cents a share on 1.8 million shares payable July 16 to all stockholders of record June 24.

At date of declaration (June 10)

Retained Earnings (Cash Dividends Declared)	900,000	
Dividends Payable		900,000

At date of record (June 24)

No entry

At date of payment (July 16)

Dividends Payable	900,000	
Cash		900,000

To set up a ledger account that shows the amount of dividends declared during the year, Roadway Freight might debit Cash Dividends Declared instead of Retained Earnings at the time of declaration. It then closes this account to Retained Earnings at year-end.

A company may declare dividends either as a certain percent of par, such as a 6 percent dividend on preferred stock, or as an amount per share, such as 60 cents per share on no-par common stock. In the first case, the rate multiplied by the par value of outstanding shares equals the total dividend. In the second, the dividend equals the amount per share multiplied by the number of shares outstanding. **Companies do not declare or pay cash dividends on treasury stock.**

Dividend policies vary among corporations. Some companies, such as **Bank of America**, **Clorox Co.**, and **Tootsie Roll Industries**, take pride in a long, unbroken string of quarterly dividend payments. They would lower or pass the dividend only if forced to do so by a sustained decline in earnings or a critical shortage of cash.

"Growth" companies, on the other hand, pay little or no cash dividends because their policy is to expand as rapidly as internal and external financing permit. For example, **Questcor Pharmaceuticals Inc.** has never paid cash dividends to its common stockholders. These investors hope that the price of their shares will appreciate in value. The investors will then realize a profit when they sell their shares. Many companies focus more on increasing share price, stock repurchase programs, and corporate earnings than on dividend payout.

INTERNATIONAL INSIGHT

As a less preferred but still allowable treatment, international accounting standards permit companies to reduce equity by the amount of proposed dividends prior to their legal declaration.

Property Dividends

Dividends payable in assets of the corporation other than cash are called **property dividends** or **dividends in kind**. Property dividends may be merchandise, real estate, or investments, or whatever form the board of directors designates. **Ranchers Exploration and Development Corp.** reported one year that it would pay a fourth-quarter dividend in gold bars instead of cash. Because of the obvious difficulties of divisibility of

---

[15]Theoretically, the ex-dividend date is the day after the date of record. However, to allow time for transfer of the shares, the stock exchanges generally advance the ex-dividend date two to four days. Therefore, the party who owns the stock on the day prior to the expressed ex-dividend date receives the dividends. The party who buys the stock on and after the ex-dividend date does not receive the dividend. Between the declaration date and the ex-dividend date, the market price of the stock includes the dividend.

units and delivery to stockholders, the usual property dividend is in the form of securities of other companies that the distributing corporation holds as an investment.

For example, after ruling that **DuPont**'s 23 percent stock interest in **General Motors** violated antitrust laws, the Supreme Court ordered DuPont to divest itself of the GM stock within 10 years. The stock represented 63 million shares of GM's 281 million shares then outstanding. DuPont could not sell the shares in one block of 63 million. Further, it could not sell 6 million shares annually for the next 10 years without severely depressing the value of the GM stock. DuPont solved its problem by declaring a property dividend and distributing the GM shares as a dividend to its own stockholders.

When declaring a property dividend, the corporation should **restate at fair value the property it will distribute, recognizing any gain or loss** as the difference between the property's fair value and carrying value at date of declaration. The corporation may then record the declared dividend as a debit to Retained Earnings (or Property Dividends Declared) and a credit to Property Dividends Payable, at an amount equal to the fair value of the distributed property. Upon distribution of the dividend, the corporation debits Property Dividends Payable and credits the account containing the distributed asset (restated at fair value).

For example, Trendler, Inc. transferred to stockholders some of its investments in marketable securities costing $1,250,000 by declaring a property dividend on December 28, 2006, to be distributed on January 30, 2007, to stockholders of record on January 15, 2007. At the date of declaration the securities have a market value of $2,000,000. Trendler makes the following entries.

At date of declaration (December 28, 2006)

Investments in Securities	750,000	
Gain on Appreciation of Securities		750,000
Retained Earnings (Property Dividends Declared)	2,000,000	
Property Dividends Payable		2,000,000

At date of distribution (January 30, 2007)

Property Dividends Payable	2,000,000	
Investments in Securities		2,000,000

Liquidating Dividends

Some corporations use paid-in capital as a basis for dividends. Without proper disclosure of this fact, stockholders may erroneously believe the corporation has been operating at a profit. To avoid this type of deception, intentional or unintentional, a clear statement of the source of every dividend should accompany the dividend check.

Dividends based on other than retained earnings are sometimes described as **liquidating dividends**. This term implies that such dividends are a return of the stockholder's investment rather than of profits. In other words, **any dividend not based on earnings reduces corporate paid-in capital and to that extent, it is a liquidating dividend**. Companies in the extractive industries may pay dividends equal to the total of accumulated income and depletion. The portion of these dividends in excess of accumulated income represents a return of part of the stockholder's investment.

For example, McChesney Mines Inc. issued a "dividend" to its common stockholders of $1,200,000. The cash dividend announcement noted that stockholders should consider $900,000 as income and the remainder a return of capital. McChesney Mines records the dividend as follows:

At date of declaration

Retained Earnings	900,000	
Additional Paid-in Capital	300,000	
Dividends Payable		1,200,000

At date of payment

Dividends Payable	1,200,000	
Cash		1,200,000

In some cases, management simply decides to cease business and declares a liquidating dividend. In these cases, liquidation may take place over a number of years to ensure an orderly and fair sale of assets. For example, when **Overseas National Airways** dissolved, it agreed to pay a liquidating dividend to its stockholders over a period of years equivalent to $8.60 per share. Each liquidating dividend payment in such cases reduces paid-in capital.

Stock Dividends

If management wishes to "capitalize" part of the earnings (i.e., reclassify amounts from earned to contributed capital), and thus retain earnings in the business on a permanent basis, it may issue a stock dividend. In this case, **the company distributes no assets**. Each stockholder maintains exactly the same proportionate interest in the corporation and the same total book value after the company issues the stock dividend. Of course, the book value per share is lower because each stockholder holds more shares.

A stock dividend therefore is the issuance by a corporation of its own stock to its stockholders on a pro rata basis, without receiving any consideration. In recording a stock dividend, some believe that the company should transfer the **par value of the stock issued** as a dividend from retained earnings to capital stock. Others believe that it should transfer the **fair value of the stock issued**—its market value at the declaration date—from retained earnings to capital stock and additional paid-in capital.

The fair value position was adopted, at least in part, in order to influence the stock dividend policies of corporations. Evidently in 1941 both the New York Stock Exchange and many in the accounting profession regarded periodic stock dividends as objectionable. They believed that the term dividend when used with a distribution of additional stock was misleading because investors' net assets did not increase as a result of this "dividend." As a result, these groups decided to make it more difficult for corporations to sustain a series of such stock dividends out of their accumulated earnings, by requiring the use of fair market value when it substantially exceeded book value.[16]

When the stock dividend is less than 20–25 percent of the common shares outstanding at the time of the dividend declaration, the company is therefore required to transfer the **fair market value** of the stock issued from retained earnings. Stock dividends of less than 20–25 percent are often referred to as small (ordinary) stock dividends. This method of handling stock dividends is justified on the grounds that "many recipients of stock dividends look upon them as distributions of corporate earnings and usually in an amount equivalent to the fair value of the additional shares received."[17] We consider this argument unconvincing. It is generally agreed that stock dividends are not income to the recipients. Therefore, sound accounting should not recommend procedures simply because some recipients think they are income.

To illustrate a small stock dividend, assume that Vine Corporation has outstanding 1,000 shares of $100 par value capital stock and retained earnings of $50,000. If Vine declares a 10 percent stock dividend, it issues 100 additional shares to current stockholders. If the fair value of the stock at the time of the stock dividend is $130 per share, the entry is:

At date of declaration

Retained Earnings (Stock Dividend Declared)	13,000	
Common Stock Dividend Distributable		10,000
Paid-in Capital in Excess of Par		3,000

UNDERLYING CONCEPTS

By requiring fair value, the intent was to punish companies that used stock dividends. This approach violates the neutrality concept (that is, that standards-setting should be even-handed).

OBJECTIVE 8
Explain the accounting for small and large stock dividends, and for stock splits.

---

[16]This was perhaps the earliest instance of "economic consequences" affecting an accounting pronouncement. The Committee on Accounting Procedure described its action as required by "proper accounting and corporate policy." See Stephen A. Zeff, "The Rise of 'Economic Consequences,'" *The Journal of Accountancy* (December 1978), pp. 53–66.

[17]American Institute of Certified Public Accountants, *Accounting Research and Terminology Bulletins*, No. 43 (New York: AICPA, 1961), Ch. 7, par. 10. One study concluded that *small* stock dividends do not always produce significant amounts of extra value on the date after issuance (ex date) and that *large* stock dividends almost always fail to generate extra value on the ex-dividend date. Taylor W. Foster III and Don Vickrey, "The Information Content of Stock Dividend Announcements," *The Accounting Review*, Vol. LIII, No. 2 (April 1978), pp. 360–370.

Note that the stock dividend does not affect any asset or liability. The entry merely reflects a reclassification of stockholders' equity. If Vine prepares a balance sheet between the dates of declaration and distribution, it should show the common stock dividend distributable in the stockholders' equity section as an addition to capital stock (whereas it shows cash or property dividends payable as current liabilities).

When issuing the stock, the entry is:

At date of distribution

Common Stock Dividend Distributable	10,000	
Common Stock		10,000

No matter what the fair value is at the time of the stock dividend, each stockholder retains the same proportionate interest in the corporation.

Some state statutes specifically prohibit the issuance of stock dividends on treasury stock. In those states that permit treasury shares to participate in the distribution accompanying a stock dividend or stock split, the planned use of the treasury shares influences corporate practice. For example, if a corporation issues treasury shares in connection with employee stock options, the treasury shares may participate in the distribution because the corporation usually adjusts the number of shares under option for any stock dividends or splits. But no useful purpose is served by issuing additional shares to the treasury stock without a specific purpose, since they are essentially equivalent to authorized but unissued shares.

To continue with our example of the effect of the small stock dividend, note in Illustration 15-9 that the stock dividend does not change the total stockholders' equity. Also note that it does not change the proportion of the total shares outstanding held by each stockholder.

ILLUSTRATION 15-9
Effects of a Small (10%) Stock Dividend

Before dividend	
Capital stock, 1,000 shares of $100 par	$100,000
Retained earnings	50,000
Total stockholders' equity	$150,000
Stockholders' interests:	
A. 400 shares, 40% interest, book value	$ 60,000
B. 500 shares, 50% interest, book value	75,000
C. 100 shares, 10% interest, book value	15,000
	$150,000
After declaration but before distribution of 10% stock dividend	
If fair value ($130) is used as basis for entry:	
Capital stock, 1,000 shares at $100 par	$100,000
Common stock distributable, 100 shares at $100 par	10,000
Paid-in capital in excess of par	3,000
Retained earnings ($50,000 − $13,000)	37,000
Total stockholders' equity	$150,000
After declaration and distribution of 10% stock dividend	
If fair value ($130) is used as basis for entry:	
Capital stock, 1,100 shares at $100 par	$110,000
Paid-in capital in excess of par	3,000
Retained earnings ($50,000 − $13,000)	37,000
Total stockholders' equity	$150,000
Stockholders' interest:	
A. 440 shares, 40% interest, book value	$ 60,000
B. 550 shares, 50% interest, book value	75,000
C. 110 shares, 10% interest, book value	15,000
	$150,000

Stock Split

If a company has undistributed earnings over several years, and accumulates a sizable balance in retained earnings, the market value of its outstanding shares likely increases. Stock issued at prices less than $50 a share can easily attain a market value in excess of $200 a share. The higher the market price of a stock, however, the less readily some investors can purchase it.

The managements of many corporations believe that better public relations depend on wider ownership of the corporation stock. They therefore target a market price sufficiently low to be within range of the majority of potential investors. To reduce the market value of shares, they use the common device of a stock split. For example, after its stock price increased by 25-fold, **Qualcomm Inc.** split its stock 4-for-1. Qualcomm's stock had risen above $500 per share, raising concerns that Qualcomm could not meet an analyst target of $1,000 per share. The split reduced the analysts' target to $250, which it could better meet with wider distribution of shares at lower trading prices.

From an accounting standpoint, Qualcomm **records no entry for a stock split**. However, it enters a memorandum note to indicate the changed par value of the shares and the increased number of shares. Illustration 15-10 shows the lack of change in stockholders' equity for a 2-for-1 stock split on 1,000 shares of $100 par value stock with the par being halved upon issuance of the additional shares.

Stockholders' Equity before 2-for-1 Split		Stockholders' Equity after 2-for-1 Split	
Common stock, 1,000 shares		Common stock, 2,000 shares	
at $100 par	$100,000	at $50 par	$100,000
Retained earnings	50,000	Retained earnings	50,000
	$150,000		$150,000

ILLUSTRATION 15-10
Effects of a Stock Split

SPLITSVILLE

Stock splits were all the rage in the booming stock market of the 1990s. Of major companies on the **New York Stock Exchange**, fewer than 80 companies split shares in 1990. By 1998, with stock prices soaring, over 200 companies split shares. Although the split does not increase a stockholder's proportionate ownership of the company, studies show that split shares usually outperform those that don't split, as well as the market as a whole, for several years after the split. In addition, the splits help the company keep the shares in more attractive price ranges.

What about when the market "turns south"? A number of companies who split their shares in the boom markets of the 1990s have since seen their share prices decline to a point considered too low. For example, since **Ameritrade**'s 12-for-1 split in 1999, its stock price declined over 74 percent, so that it was trading around $6 per share in March 2002. And **Lucent** traded at less than $5 a share following a 4-for-1 split. For some investors, these low-priced stocks are unattractive because some brokerage commissions rely on the number of shares traded, not the dollar amount. Others are concerned that low-priced shares are easier for would-be scamsters to manipulate.

Some companies are considering reverse stock splits in which, say, 5 shares are consolidated into one. Thus, a stock previously trading at $5 per share would be part of an unsplit share trading at $25. Unsplitting might thus avoid some of the negative consequences of a low trading price. The downside to this strategy is that analysts might view reverse splits as additional bad news about the direction of the stock price. For example, **Webvan**, a failed Internet grocer, did a 1-for-25 reverse split just before it entered bankruptcy.

Source: Adapted from David Henry, "Stocks: The Case for Unsplitting," *BusinessWeek Online* (April 1, 2002).

WHAT DO THE NUMBERS MEAN?

Stock Split and Stock Dividend Differentiated

From a legal standpoint, a stock split differs from a stock dividend. How? A stock split increases the number of shares outstanding and decreases the par or stated value per share. **A stock dividend, although it increases the number of shares outstanding, does not decrease the par value; thus it increases the total par value of outstanding shares.**

The reasons for issuing a stock dividend are numerous and varied. Stock dividends can be primarily a publicity gesture, **because many consider stock dividends as dividends**. Another reason is that the corporation may simply wish to retain profits in the business by capitalizing a part of retained earnings. In such a situation, it makes a transfer on declaration of a stock dividend from earned capital to contributed capital.

A corporation may also use a stock dividend, like a stock split, to increase the marketability of the stock, although marketability is often a secondary consideration. If the stock dividend is large, it has the same effect on market price as a stock split. **Whenever corporations issue additional shares for the purpose of reducing the unit market price, then the distribution more closely resembles a stock split than a stock dividend. This effect usually results only if the number of shares issued is more than 20–25 percent of the number of shares previously outstanding.**[18] A stock dividend of more than 20–25 percent of the number of shares previously outstanding is called a large stock dividend.[19] Such a distribution should not be called a stock dividend but instead "a split-up effected in the form of a dividend" or "stock split."

Also, since a split-up effected in the form of a dividend does not alter the par value per share, companies generally are required to transfer the par value amount from retained earnings. In other words, companies transfer from retained earnings to capital stock **the par value of the stock issued**, as opposed to a transfer of the market value of the shares issued as in the case of a small stock dividend.[20] For example, **Brown Group, Inc.** at one time authorized a 2-for-1 split, effected in the form of a stock dividend. As a result of this authorization, it distributed approximately 10.5 million shares, and transferred more than $39 million representing the par value of the shares issued from Retained Earnings to the Common Stock account.

To illustrate a large stock dividend (stock split-up effected in the form of a dividend), Rockland Steel, Inc. declared a 30 percent stock dividend on November 20, payable December 29 to stockholders of record December 12. At the date of declaration, 1,000,000 shares, par value $10, are outstanding and with a fair market value of $200 per share. The entries are:

At date of declaration (November 20)

Retained Earnings	3,000,000	
Common Stock Dividend Distributable		3,000,000

Computation: 1,000,000 shares	300,000 Additional shares
× 30%	× $10 Par value
300,000	$3,000,000

At date of distribution (December 29)

Common Stock Dividend Distributable	3,000,000	
Common Stock		3,000,000

---

[18]*Accounting Research and Terminology Bulletin No. 43*, par. 13.

[19]The SEC has added more precision to the 20–25 percent rule. Specifically, the SEC indicates that companies should consider distributions of 25 percent or more as a "split-up effected in the form of a dividend." Companies should account for distributions of less than 25 percent as a stock dividend. The SEC more precisely defined GAAP here. As a result, public companies follow the SEC rule.

[20]Often, a company records a split-up effected in the form of a dividend as a debit to Paid-in Capital instead of Retained Earnings to indicate that this transaction should affect only paid-in capital accounts. No reduction of retained earnings is required except as indicated by legal requirements. For homework purposes, assume that the debit is to Retained Earnings. See, for example, Taylor W. Foster III and Edmund Scribner, "Accounting for Stock Dividends and Stock Splits: Corrections to Textbook Coverage," *Issues in Accounting Education* (February 1998).

Illustration 15-11 summarizes and compares the effects in the balance sheet and related items of various types of dividends and stock splits.

Effect on:	Declaration of Cash Dividend	Payment of Cash Dividend	Declaration and Distribution of		Stock Split
			Small Stock Dividend	Large Stock Dividend	
Retained earnings	Decrease	–0–	Decrease[a]	Decrease[b]	–0–
Capital stock	–0–	–0–	Increase[b]	Increase[b]	–0–
Additional paid-in capital	–0–	–0–	Increase[c]	–0–	–0–
Total stockholders' equity	Decrease	–0–	–0–	–0–	–0–
Working capital	Decrease	–0–	–0–	–0–	–0–
Total assets	–0–	Decrease	–0–	–0–	–0–
Number of shares outstanding	–0–	–0–	Increase	Increase	Increase

[a]Market value of shares.   [b]Par or stated value of shares.   [c]Excess of market value over par.

ILLUSTRATION 15-11
Effects of Dividends and Stock Splits on Financial Statement Elements

INTERNATIONAL INSIGHT

Switzerland allows companies to create income reserves. That is, companies reduce income in years with good profits by allocating it to reserves on the balance sheet. In less profitable years, companies then reallocate from the reserves to improve income. This "smoothes" income across years.

Disclosure of Restrictions on Retained Earnings

Many corporations restrict retained earnings or dividends, without any formal journal entries. Such restrictions are **best disclosed by note**. Parenthetical notations are sometimes used, but restrictions imposed by bond indentures and loan agreements commonly require an extended explanation. Notes provide a medium for more complete explanations and free the financial statements from abbreviated notations. The note disclosure should reveal the source of the restriction, pertinent provisions, and the amount of retained earnings subject to restriction, or the amount not restricted.

Restrictions may be based on the retention of a certain retained earnings balance, the ability to maintain certain working capital requirements, additional borrowing, and other considerations. The example from the annual report of **Alberto-Culver Company** in Illustration 15-12 shows a note disclosing potential restrictions on retained earnings and dividends.

Alberto-Culver Company

Note 3 (in part): The $200 million revolving credit facility, the term note due September 2000, and the receivables agreement impose restrictions on such items as total debt, working capital, dividend payments, treasury stock purchases, and interest expense. At year-end, the company was in compliance with these arrangements, and $220 million of consolidated retained earnings was not restricted as to the payment of dividends.

ILLUSTRATION 15-12
Disclosure of Restrictions on Retained Earnings and Dividends

PRESENTATION AND ANALYSIS OF STOCKHOLDERS' EQUITY

Presentation

Balance Sheet

Illustration 15-13 (on page 750) shows a comprehensive stockholders' equity section from the balance sheet of Frost Company that includes most of the equity items we discussed in this chapter.

OBJECTIVE 9
Indicate how to present and analyze stockholders' equity.

ILLUSTRATION 15-13
Comprehensive
Stockholders' Equity
Presentation

FROST CORPORATION
STOCKHOLDERS' EQUITY
DECEMBER 31, 2007

Capital stock

Preferred stock, $100 par value, 7% cumulative, 100,000 shares authorized, 30,000 shares issued and outstanding		$ 3,000,000
Common stock, no par, stated value $10 per share, 500,000 shares authorized, 400,000 shares issued		4,000,000
Common stock dividend distributable, 20,000 shares		200,000
Total capital stock		7,200,000
Additional paid-in capital[21]		
Excess over par—preferred	$150,000	
Excess over stated value—common	840,000	990,000
Total paid-in capital		8,190,000
Retained earnings		4,360,000
Total paid-in capital and retained earnings		12,550,000
Less: Cost of treasury stock (2,000 shares, common)		(190,000)
Accumulated other comprehensive loss[22]		(360,000)
Total stockholders' equity		$12,000,000

Frost should disclose the pertinent rights and privileges of the various securities outstanding. For example, companies must disclose all of the following dividend and liquidation preferences, participation rights, call prices and dates, conversion or exercise prices and pertinent dates, sinking fund requirements, unusual voting rights, and significant terms of contracts to issue additional shares. Liquidation preferences should be disclosed in the equity section of the balance sheet, rather than in the notes to the financial statements, to emphasize the possible effect of this restriction on future cash flows.[23]

Statement of Stockholders' Equity

The **statement of stockholders' equity** is frequently presented in the following basic format.

1 Balance at the beginning of the period.
2 Additions.
3 Deductions.
4 Balance at the end of the period.

*Reporting of Stockholders'
Equity in Eastman-Kodak's
Annual Report*

---

[21]*Accounting Trends and Techniques—2004* reports that of its 600 surveyed companies, 535 had additional paid-in capital; 313 used the caption "Additional paid-in capital"; 111 used "Capital in excess of par or stated value" as the caption; 82 used "Paid-in capital" or "Additional capital"; and 29 used other captions.

[22]Companies may include a number of items in the "Accumulated other comprehensive loss." Among these items are "Foreign currency translation adjustments" (covered in advanced accounting), "Unrealized holding gains and losses for available-for-sale securities" (covered in Chapter 17), "Excess of additional pension liability over unrecognized prior service cost" (covered in Chapter 20), "Guarantees of employee stock option plan (ESOP) debt," "Unearned or deferred compensation related to employee stock award plans," and others.

Accounting Trends and Techniques—2004 reports that of its 600 surveyed companies reporting other items in the equity section, 477 reported cumulative translation adjustments, 389 reported minimum pension liability adjustments, 268 reported unrealized losses/gains on certain investments, and 311 reported changes in the fair value of derivatives. A number of companies had more than one item.

[23]"Disclosure of Information about Capital Structure," *Statement of Financial Accounting Standards No. 129* (Norwalk, Conn.: FASB, February 1997), par. 4.

Companies must disclose changes in the separate accounts comprising stockholders' equity, to make the financial statements sufficiently informative.[24] Such changes may be disclosed in separate statements or in the basic financial statements or notes thereto.[25]

A **columnar format** for the presentation of changes in stockholders' equity items in published annual reports is gaining in popularity. An example is **Hewlett-Packard Company**'s statement of stockholders' equity, shown in Illustration 15-14.

ILLUSTRATION 15-14
Columnar Format for Statement of Stockholders' Equity

Hewlett-Packard Company and Subsidiaries
Consolidated Statement of Stockholders' Equity

(in millions, except number of shares in thousands)	Common Stock Number of Shares	Par Value	Additional Paid-in Capital	Retained Earnings	Accumulated Other Comprehensive Income (Loss)	Total
Balance October 31, 2003	3,042,761	$30	$24,587	$13,332	$ (203)	$37,746
Net earnings				3,497		3,497
Net unrealized loss on available-for-sale securities					(20)	(20)
Net unrealized loss on cash flow hedges					(28)	(28)
Minimum pension liability, net of taxes					(13)	(13)
Cumulative translation adjustment					21	21
Comprehensive income						3,457
Assumption of stock options in connection with business acquisitions			15			15
Issuance of common stock in connection with employee stock plans and other	40,467		592			592
Repurchases of common stock	(172,468)	(1)	(3,100)	(208)		(3,309)
Tax benefit from employee stock plans			35			35
Dividends				(972)		(972)
Balance October 31, 2004	2,910,760	$29	$22,129	$15,649	$(243)	$37,564

Analysis

Analysts use stockholders' equity ratios to evaluate a company's profitability and long-term solvency. We discuss and illustrate the following three ratios below.

1 Rate of return on common stock equity.
2 Payout ratio.
3 Book value per share.

---

[24]If a company has other comprehensive income, and computes total comprehensive income only in the statement of stockholders' equity, it must display the statement of stockholders' equity with the same prominence as other financial statements. "Reporting Comprehensive Income," *Statement of Financial Accounting Standards No. 130* (Norwalk, Conn.: FASB, June 1997).

[25]*Accounting Trends and Techniques—2004* reports that of the 600 companies surveyed, 586 presented statements of stockholders' equity, 7 presented separate statements of retained earnings only, 2 presented combined statements of income and retained earnings, and 5 presented changes in equity items in the notes only.

Financial Analysis Primer

Rate of Return on Common Stock Equity

The **rate of return on common stock equity** measures profitability from the common stockholders' viewpoint. This ratio shows how many dollars of net income the company earned for each dollar invested by the owners. Return on equity (ROE) also helps investors judge the worthiness of a stock when the overall market is not doing well. For example, **Best Buy** shares dropped nearly 40 percent, along with the broader market in 2001–2002. But a review of its return on equity during this period and since shows a steady return of 20 to 22 percent while the overall market ROE declined from 16 percent to 8 percent. More importantly, Best Buy and other stocks, such as **3M** and **Procter & Gamble**, recovered their lost market value, while other stocks with less robust ROEs stayed in the doldrums.

Return on equity equals net income less preferred dividends, divided by average common stockholders' equity. For example, assume that Gerber's Inc. had net income of $360,000, declared and paid preferred dividends of $54,000, and average common stockholders' equity of $2,550,000. Illustration 15-15 shows how to compute Gerber's ratio.

ILLUSTRATION 15-15
Computation of Rate of Return on Common Stock Equity

$$\text{Rate of Return on Common Stock Equity} = \frac{\text{Net income} - \text{Preferred dividends}}{\text{Average common stockholders' equity}}$$

$$= \frac{\$360{,}000 - \$54{,}000}{\$2{,}550{,}000}$$

$$= 12\%$$

As shown in Illustration 15-15, when preferred stock is present, income available to common stockholders equals net income less preferred dividends. Similarly, the amount of common stock equity used in this ratio equals total stockholders' equity less the par value of preferred stock.

A company can improve its return on common stock equity through the prudent use of debt or preferred stock financing. **Trading on the equity** describes the practice of using borrowed money or issuing preferred stock in hopes of obtaining a higher rate of return on the money used. Shareholders win if return on the assets is higher than the cost of financing these assets. When this happens, the rate of return on common stock equity will exceed the rate of return on total assets. In short, the company is "trading on the equity at a gain." In this situation, the money obtained from bondholders or preferred stockholders earns enough to pay the interest or preferred dividends and leaves a profit for the common stockholders. On the other hand, if the cost of the financing is higher that the rate earned on the assets, the company is trading on equity at a loss and stockholders lose.

Payout Ratio

Another ratio of interest to investors, the **payout ratio**, is the ratio of cash dividends to net income. If preferred stock is outstanding, this ratio equals cash dividends paid to common stockholders, divided by net income available to common stockholders. For example, assume that Troy Co. has cash dividends of $100,000 and net income of $500,000, and no preferred stock outstanding. Illustration 15-16 shows the payout ratio computation.

ILLUSTRATION 15-16
Computation of Payout Ratio

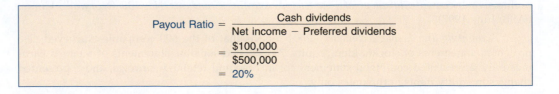

$$\text{Payout Ratio} = \frac{\text{Cash dividends}}{\text{Net income} - \text{Preferred dividends}}$$

$$= \frac{\$100{,}000}{\$500{,}000}$$

$$= 20\%$$

As discussed in the opening story, it is important to some investors that the payout be sufficiently high to provide a good yield on the stock.[26]

Book Value per Share

A much-used basis for evaluating net worth is found in the book value or equity value per share of stock. **Book value per share** of stock is the amount each share would receive if the company were liquidated **on the basis of amounts reported on the balance sheet**. However, the figure loses much of its relevance if the valuations on the balance sheet fail to approximate fair market value of the assets. Book value per share equals common stockholders' equity divided by outstanding common shares. Assume that Chen Corporation's common stockholders' equity is $1,000,000 and it has 100,000 shares of common stock outstanding. Illustration 15-17 shows its book value per share computation.

$$\frac{\text{Book Value}}{\text{Per Share}} = \frac{\text{Common stockholders' equity}}{\text{Outstanding shares}}$$
$$= \frac{\$1,000,000}{100,000}$$
$$= \$10 \text{ per share}$$

ILLUSTRATION 15-17
Computation of Book Value Per Share

SUMMARY OF LEARNING OBJECTIVES

1. Discuss the characteristics of the corporate form of organization. Among the specific characteristics of the corporate form that affect accounting are the: (1) influence of state corporate law, (2) use of the capital stock or share system, and (3) development of a variety of ownership interests. In the absence of restrictive provisions, each share of stock carries the right to share proportionately in: (1) profits and losses; (2) management (the right to vote for directors); (3) corporate assets upon liquidation; (4) any new issues of stock of the same class (called the preemptive right).

2. Identify the key components of stockholders' equity. Stockholders' or owners' equity is classified into two categories: contributed capital and earned capital. Contributed capital (paid-in capital) describes the total amount paid in on capital stock. Put another way, it is the amount that stockholders advance to the corporation for use in the business. Contributed capital includes items such as the par value of all outstanding capital stock and premiums less any discounts on issuance. Earned capital is the capital that develops if the business operates profitably; it consists of all undistributed income that remains invested in the company.

3. Explain the accounting procedures for issuing shares of stock. Accounts are kept for the following different types of stock: *Par value stock:* (a) preferred stock or common stock; (b) paid-in capital in excess of par or additional paid-in capital; and (c) discount on stock. *No-par stock:* common stock or common stock and additional paid-in capital, if stated value used. Stock issued in combination with other securities (lump-sum sales): The two methods of allocation available are (a) the proportional method; and (b) the incremental method. Stock issued in noncash transactions: When issuing stock for services or property other than cash, the company should record the property or services at either the fair market value of the stock issued, or the fair market value of the noncash consideration received, whichever is more clearly determinable.

KEY TERMS

additional paid-in capital, *730*

book value per share, *753*

callable preferred stock, *739*

cash dividends, *742*

common stock, *727*

contributed (paid-in) capital, *729*

convertible preferred stock, *739*

cost method, *735*

cumulative preferred stock, *739*

dividend in arrears, *739*

earned capital, *729*

large stock dividend, *748*

leveraged buyout (LBO), *734*

liquidating dividends, *742, 744*

lump-sum sales, *731*

no-par stock, *730*

par (stated) value method, *735*

participating preferred stock, *739*

payout ratio, *752*

preemptive right, *727*

---

[26]Analysts also closely watch the **dividend yield**—the cash dividend per share divided by the market price of the stock. This ratio indicates the rate of return that investors will receive in cash dividends from their investment.

Expanded Discussion of Quasi-Reorganization

4. Describe the accounting for treasury stock. The cost method is generally used in accounting for treasury stock. This method derives its name from the fact that a company maintains the Treasury Stock account at the cost of the shares purchased. Under the cost method, a company debits the Treasury Stock account for the cost of the shares acquired and credits it for this same cost upon reissuance. The price received for the stock when originally issued does not affect the entries to record the acquisition and reissuance of the treasury stock.

5. Explain the accounting for and reporting of preferred stock. Preferred stock is a special class of shares that possesses certain preferences or features not possessed by the common stock. The features that are most often associated with preferred stock issues are: (1) preference as to dividends; (2) preference as to assets in the event of liquidation; (3) convertible into common stock; (4) callable at the option of the corporation; (5) nonvoting. At issuance, the accounting for preferred stock is similar to that for common stock. When convertible preferred stock is converted, a company uses the book value method: It debits Preferred Stock, along with any related Additional Paid-in Capital, and credits Common Stock and Additional Paid-in Capital (if an excess exists).

6. Describe the policies used in distributing dividends. The state incorporation laws normally provide information concerning the legal restrictions related to the payment of dividends. Corporations rarely pay dividends in an amount equal to the legal limit. This is due, in part, to the fact that companies use assets represented by undistributed earnings to finance future operations of the business. If a company is considering declaring a dividend, it must ask two preliminary questions: (1) Is the condition of the corporation such that the dividend is **legally permissible**? (2) Is the condition of the corporation such that a dividend is **economically sound**?

7. Identify the various forms of dividend distributions. Dividends are of the following types: (1) cash dividends, (2) property dividends, (3) liquidating dividends (dividends based on other than retained earnings), (4) stock dividends (the issuance by a corporation of its own stock to its stockholders on a pro rata basis, but without receiving consideration).

8. Explain the accounting for small and large stock dividends, and for stock splits. Generally accepted accounting principles require that the accounting for small stock dividends (less than 20 or 25 percent) rely on the fair market value of the stock issued. When declaring a stock dividend, a company debits Retained Earnings at the fair market value of the stock it distributes. The entry includes a credit to Common Stock Dividend Distributable at par value times the number of shares, with any excess credited to Paid-in Capital in Excess of Par. If the number of shares issued exceeds 20 or 25 percent of the shares outstanding (large stock dividend), it debits Retained Earnings at par value and credits Common Stock Distributable—there is no additional paid-in capital.

A stock dividend is a capitalization of retained earnings that reduces retained earnings and increases certain contributed capital accounts. The par value per share and total stockholders' equity remain unchanged with a stock dividend, and all stockholders retain their same proportionate share of ownership. A stock split results in an increase or decrease in the number of shares outstanding, with a corresponding decrease or increase in the par or stated value per share. No accounting entry is required for a stock split.

9. Indicate how to present and analyze stockholders' equity. The stockholders' equity section of a balance sheet includes capital stock, additional paid-in capital, and retained earnings. A company might also present additional items such as treasury stock and accumulated other comprehensive income. Companies often provide a statement of stockholders' equity. Common ratios that use stockholders' equity amounts are: rate of return on common stock equity, payout ratio, and book value per share.

Dividend Preferences and Book Value Per Share

DIVIDEND PREFERENCES

Illustrations 15A-1 to 15A-4 indicate the **effects of** various **dividend preferences** on dividend distributions to common and preferred stockholders. Assume that in 2007, Mason Company is to distribute $50,000 as cash dividends, its outstanding common stock has a par value of $400,000, and its 6 percent preferred stock has a par value of $100,000. Mason would distribute dividends to each class, employing the assumptions given, as follows:

> **OBJECTIVE 10**
> Explain the different types of preferred stock dividends and their effect on book value per share.

1   If the preferred stock is noncumulative and nonparticipating:

	Preferred	Common	Total
6% of $100,000	$6,000		$ 6,000
The remainder to common		$44,000	44,000
Totals	$6,000	$44,000	$50,000

ILLUSTRATION 15A-1
Dividend Distribution, Noncumulative and Nonparticipating Preferred

2   If the preferred stock is cumulative and nonparticipating, and Mason Company did not pay dividends on the preferred stock in the preceding two years:

	Preferred	Common	Total
Dividends in arrears, 6% of $100,000 for 2 years	$12,000		$12,000
Current year's dividend, 6% of $100,000	6,000		6,000
The remainder to common		$32,000	32,000
Totals	$18,000	$32,000	$50,000

ILLUSTRATION 15A-2
Dividend Distribution, Cumulative and Nonparticipating Preferred, with Dividends in Arrears

3   If the preferred stock is noncumulative and is fully participating:[1]

---

[1] When preferred stock is participating, there may be different agreements as to how the participation feature is to be executed. However, in the absence of any specific agreement the following procedure is recommended:

    a. After the preferred stock is assigned its current year's dividend, the common stock will receive a "like" percentage of par value outstanding. In example (3), this amounts to 6 percent of $400,000.

    b. In example (3), shown in Illustration 15A-3 (on page 756), the remainder of the declared dividend is $20,000. We divide this amount by total par value ($500,000) to find the rate of participation to be applied to each class of stock. In this case, the rate of participation is 4% ($20,000 ÷ $500,000), which we then multiply by the par value of each class of stock to determine the amount of participation.

ILLUSTRATION 15A-3
Dividend Distribution, Noncumulative and Fully Participating Preferred

	Preferred	Common	Total
Current year's dividend, 6%	$ 6,000	$24,000	$30,000
Participating dividend of 4%	4,000	16,000	20,000
Totals	$10,000	$40,000	$50,000

The participating dividend was determined as follows:

Current year's dividend:	
Preferred, 6% of $100,000 = $ 6,000	
Common, 6% of $400,000 = 24,000	$ 30,000
Amount available for participation ($50,000 − $30,000)	$ 20,000
Par value of stock that is to participate ($100,000 + $400,000)	$500,000
Rate of participation ($20,000 ÷ $500,000)	4%
Participating dividend:	
Preferred, 4% of $100,000	$ 4,000
Common, 4% of $400,000	16,000
	$ 20,000

4 If the preferred stock is cumulative and is fully participating, and Mason Company did not pay dividends on the preferred stock in the preceding two years:

ILLUSTRATION 15A-4
Dividend Distribution, Cumulative and Fully Participating Preferred, with Dividends in Arrears

	Preferred	Common	Total
Dividends in arrears, 6% of $100,000 for 2 years	$12,000		$12,000
Current year's dividend, 6%	6,000	$24,000	30,000
Participating dividend, 1.6% ($8,000 ÷ $500,000)	1,600	6,400	8,000
Totals	$19,600	$30,400	$50,000

BOOK VALUE PER SHARE

Book value per share in its simplest form is computed as net assets divided by outstanding shares at the end of the year. The computation of book value per share becomes more complicated if a company has preferred stock in its capital structure. For example, if preferred dividends are in arrears, if the preferred stock is participating, or if preferred stock has a redemption or liquidating value higher than its carrying amount, the company must allocate retained earnings between the preferred and common stockholders in computing book value.

To illustrate, assume that the following situation exists.

ILLUSTRATION 15A-5
Computation of Book Value Per Share—No Dividends in Arrears

Stockholders' equity	Preferred	Common
Preferred stock, 5%	$300,000	
Common stock		$400,000
Excess of issue price over par of common stock		37,500
Retained earnings		162,582
Totals	$300,000	$600,082
Shares outstanding		4,000
Book value per share		$150.02

The situation in Illustration 15A-5 assumes that no preferred dividends are in arrears and that the preferred is not participating. Now assume that the same facts exist except that the 5 percent preferred is cumulative, participating up to 8 percent, and that dividends for three years before the current year are in arrears. Illustration 15A-6 shows how to compute the book value of the common stock, assuming that no action has yet been taken concerning dividends for the current year.

Stockholders' equity	Preferred	Common
Preferred stock, 5%	$300,000	
Common stock		$400,000
Excess of issue price over par of common stock		37,500
Retained earnings:		
Dividends in arrears (3 years at 5% a year)	45,000	
Current year requirement at 5%	15,000	20,000
Participating—additional 3%	9,000	12,000
Remainder to common		61,582
Totals	$369,000	$531,082
Shares outstanding		4,000
Book value per share		$132.77

ILLUSTRATION 15A-6
Computation of Book Value Per Share—With Dividends in Arrears

In connection with the book value computation, the analyst must know how to handle the following items: the number of authorized and unissued shares; the number of treasury shares on hand; any commitments with respect to the issuance of unissued shares or the reissuance of treasury shares; and the relative rights and privileges of the various types of stock authorized. As an example, if the liquidating value of the preferred stock is higher than its carrying amount, the liquidating amount should be used in the book value computation.

SUMMARY OF LEARNING OBJECTIVE FOR APPENDIX 15A

10. Explain the different types of preferred stock dividends and their effect on book value per share. The dividend preferences of preferred stock affect the dividends paid to stockholders. Preferred stock can be (1) cumulative or noncumulative, and (2) fully participating, partially participating, or nonparticipating. If preferred dividends are in arrears, if the preferred stock is participating, or if preferred stock has a redemption or liquidation value higher than its carrying amount, allocate retained earnings between preferred and common stockholders in computing book value per share.

Note: All **asterisked** Questions, Brief Exercises, and Exercises relate to material contained in the appendixes to the chapter.

QUESTIONS

1. In the absence of restrictive provisions, what are the basic rights of stockholders of a corporation?

2. Why is a preemptive right important?

3. Distinguish between common and preferred stock.

4. Why is the distinction between paid-in capital and retained earnings important?

5. Explain each of the following terms: authorized capital stock, unissued capital stock, issued capital stock, outstanding capital stock, and treasury stock.

6. What is meant by par value, and what is its significance to stockholders?

7. Describe the accounting for the issuance for cash of no-par value common stock at a price in excess of the stated value of the common stock.

8. Explain the difference between the proportional method and the incremental method of allocating the proceeds of lump sum sales of capital stock.

9. What are the different bases for stock valuation when assets other than cash are received for issued shares of stock?

10. Explain how underwriting costs and accounting and legal fees associated with the issuance of stock should be recorded.

11. For what reasons might a corporation purchase its own stock?

12. Discuss the propriety of showing:

(a) Treasury stock as an asset.

(b) "Gain" or "loss" on sale of treasury stock as additions to or deductions from income.

(c) Dividends received on treasury stock as income.

13. What features or rights may alter the character of preferred stock?

14. Little Texas Inc. recently noted that its 4% preferred stock and 4% participating second preferred stock, which are both cumulative, have priority as to dividends up to 4% of their par value. Its participating preferred stock participates equally with the common stock in any dividends in excess of 4%. What is meant by the term participating? Cumulative?

15. Where in the financial statements is preferred stock normally reported?

16. List possible sources of additional paid-in capital.

17. Pleasant Dolls Inc. purchases 10,000 shares of its own previously issued $10 par common stock for $290,000. Assuming the shares are held in the treasury with intent to reissue, what effect does this transaction have on (a) net income, (b) total assets, (c) total paid-in capital, and (d) total stockholders' equity?

18. Indicate how each of the following accounts should be classified in the stockholders' equity section.

(a) Common Stock

(b) Retained Earnings

(c) Paid-in Capital in Excess of Par Value

(d) Treasury Stock

(e) Paid-in Capital from Treasury Stock

(f) Paid-in Capital in Excess of Stated Value

(g) Preferred Stock

19. What factors influence the dividend policy of a company?

20. What are the principal considerations of a board of directors in making decisions involving dividend declarations? Discuss briefly.

21. Dividends are sometimes said to have been paid "out of retained earnings." What is the error, if any, in that statement?

22. Distinguish among: cash dividends, property dividends, liquidating dividends, and stock dividends.

23. Describe the accounting entry for a stock dividend, if any. Describe the accounting entry for a stock split, if any.

24. Stock splits and stock dividends may be used by a corporation to change the number of shares of its stock outstanding.

(a) What is meant by a stock split effected in the form of a dividend?

(b) From an accounting viewpoint, explain how the stock split effected in the form of a dividend differs from an ordinary stock dividend.

(c) How should a stock dividend that has been declared but not yet issued be classified in a statement of financial position? Why?

25. The following comment appeared in the notes of Alvarado Corporation's annual report: "Such distributions, representing proceeds from the sale of James Buchanan, Inc. were paid in the form of partial liquidating dividends and were in lieu of a portion of the Company's ordinary cash dividends." How would a partial liquidating dividend be accounted for in the financial records?

26. This comment appeared in the annual report of Rodriguez Lopez Inc.: "The Company could pay cash or property dividends on the Class A common stock without paying cash or property dividends on the Class B common stock. But if the Company pays any cash or property dividends on the Class B common stock, it would be required to pay at least the same dividend on the Class A common stock." How is a property dividend accounted for in the financial records?

27. For what reasons might a company restrict a portion of its retained earnings?

28. How are restrictions of retained earnings reported?

*29. Aaron Burr Corp. had $100,000 of 10%, $20 par value preferred stock and 12,000 shares of $25 par value common stock outstanding throughout 2007.

(a) Assuming that total dividends declared in 2007 were $88,000, and that the preferred stock is not cumulative but is fully participating, common stockholders should receive 2007 dividends of what amount?

(b) Assuming that total dividends declared in 2007 were $88,000, and that the preferred stock is fully participating and cumulative with preferred dividends in arrears for 2006, preferred stockholders should receive 2007 dividends totaling what amount?

(c) Assuming that total dividends declared in 2007 were $30,000, that cumulative nonparticipating preferred stock was issued on January 1, 2006, and that $5,000 of preferred dividends were declared and paid in 2006, the common stockholders should receive 2007 dividends totaling what amount?

BRIEF EXERCISES

(LO 3)   **BE15-1**   Lost Vikings Corporation issued 300 shares of $10 par value common stock for $4,100. Prepare Lost Vikings' journal entry.

(LO 3)   **BE15-2**   Shinobi Corporation issued 600 shares of no-par common stock for $10,200. Prepare Shinobi's journal entry if (a) the stock has no stated value, and (b) the stock has a stated value of $2 per share.

(LO 4, 9)   **BE15-3**   Lufia Corporation has the following account balances at December 31, 2007.

Common stock, $5 par value	$ 210,000
Treasury stock	90,000
Retained earnings	2,340,000
Paid-in capital in excess of par	1,320,000

Prepare Lufia's December 31, 2007, stockholders' equity section.

(LO 3)   **BE15-4**   Primal Rage Corporation issued 300 shares of $10 par value common stock and 100 shares of $50 par value preferred stock for a lump sum of $14,200. The common stock has a market value of $20 per share, and the preferred stock has a market value of $90 per share. Prepare the journal entry to record the issuance.

(LO 3)   **BE15-5**   On February 1, 2007, Mario Andretti Corporation issued 2,000 shares of its $5 par value common stock for land worth $31,000. Prepare the February 1, 2007, journal entry.

(LO 3)   **BE15-6**   Powerdrive Corporation issued 2,000 shares of its $10 par value common stock for $70,000. Powerdrive also incurred $1,500 of costs associated with issuing the stock. Prepare Powerdrive's journal entry to record the issuance of the company's stock.

(LO 4)   **BE15-7**   Maverick Inc. has outstanding 10,000 shares of $10 par value common stock. On July 1, 2007, Maverick reacquired 100 shares at $85 per share. On September 1, Maverick reissued 60 shares at $90 per share. On November 1, Maverick reissued 40 shares at $83 per share. Prepare Maverick's journal entries to record these transactions using the cost method.

(LO 4)   **BE15-8**   Power Rangers Corporation has outstanding 20,000 shares of $5 par value common stock. On August 1, 2007, Power Rangers reacquired 200 shares at $75 per share. On November 1, Power Rangers reissued the 200 shares at $70 per share. Power Rangers had no previous treasury stock transactions. Prepare Power Rangers' journal entries to record these transactions using the cost method.

(LO 5)   **BE15-9**   Popeye Corporation issued 450 shares of $100 par value preferred stock for $61,500. Prepare Popeye's journal entry.

(LO 6)   **BE15-10**   Micro Machines Inc. declared a cash dividend of $1.50 per share on its 2 million outstanding shares. The dividend was declared on August 1, payable on September 9 to all stockholders of record on August 15. Prepare all journal entries necessary on those three dates.

(LO 6, 7)   **BE15-11**   Ren Inc. owns shares of Stimpy Corporation stock classified as available-for-sale securities. At December 31, 2006, the available-for-sale securities were carried in Ren's accounting records at their cost of $875,000, which equals their market value. On September 21, 2007, when the market value of the securities was $1,400,000, Ren declared a property dividend whereby the Stimpy securities are to be distributed on October 23, 2007, to stockholders of record on October 8, 2007. Prepare all journal entries necessary on those three dates.

(LO 6, 7)   **BE15-12**   Radical Rex Mining Company declared, on April 20, a dividend of $700,000 payable on June 1. Of this amount, $125,000 is a return of capital. Prepare the April 20 and June 1 entries for Radical Rex.

(LO 8)   **BE15-13**   Mike Holmgren Football Corporation has outstanding 200,000 shares of $10 par value common stock. The corporation declares a 5% stock dividend when the fair value of the stock is $65 per share. Prepare the journal entries for Mike Holmgren Football Corporation for both the date of declaration and the date of distribution.

(LO 8)   **BE15-14**   Use the information from BE15-13, but assume Mike Holmgren Football Corporation declared a 100% stock dividend rather than a 5% stock dividend. Prepare the journal entries for both the date of declaration and the date of distribution.

(LO 10) **BE15-15*   Minnesota Fats Corporation has outstanding 10,000 shares of $100 par value, 8% preferred stock and 60,000 shares of $10 par value common stock. The preferred stock was issued in January 2006, and no dividends were declared in 2006 or 2007. In 2008, Minnesota Fats declares a cash dividend of $300,000. How will the dividend be shared by common and preferred stockholders if the preferred is (a) noncumulative and (b) cumulative?

EXERCISES

(LO 3)   **E15-1   (Recording the Issuances of Common Stock)**   During its first year of operations, Collin Raye Corporation had the following transactions pertaining to its common stock.

Jan. 10	Issued 80,000 shares for cash at $6 per share.
Mar. 1	Issued 5,000 shares to attorneys in payment of a bill for $35,000 for services rendered in helping the company to incorporate.
July 1	Issued 30,000 shares for cash at $8 per share.
Sept. 1	Issued 60,000 shares for cash at $10 per share.

Instructions
(a) Prepare the journal entries for these transactions, assuming that the common stock has a par value of $5 per share.
(b) Prepare the journal entries for these transactions, assuming that the common stock is no par with a stated value of $3 per share.

(LO 3)   **E15-2   (Recording the Issuance of Common and Preferred Stock)**   Kathleen Battle Corporation was organized on January 1, 2007. It is authorized to issue 10,000 shares of 8%, $100 par value preferred stock, and 500,000 shares of no par common stock with a stated value of $1 per share. The following stock transactions were completed during the first year.

Jan. 10	Issued 80,000 shares of common stock for cash at $5 per share.
Mar. 1	Issued 5,000 shares of preferred stock for cash at $108 per share.
Apr. 1	Issued 24,000 shares of common stock for land. The asking price of the land was $90,000; the fair market value of the land was $80,000.
May 1	Issued 80,000 shares of common stock for cash at $7 per share.
Aug. 1	Issued 10,000 shares of common stock to attorneys in payment of their bill of $50,000 for services rendered in helping the company organize.
Sept. 1	Issued 10,000 shares of common stock for cash at $9 per share.
Nov. 1	Issued 1,000 shares of preferred stock for cash at $112 per share.

Instructions
Prepare the journal entries to record the above transactions.

(LO 3)   **E15-3   (Stock Issued for Land)**   Twenty-five thousand shares reacquired by Elixir Corporation for $53 per share were exchanged for undeveloped land that has an appraised value of $1,700,000. At the time of the exchange the common stock was trading at $62 per share on an organized exchange.

Instructions
(a) Prepare the journal entry to record the acquisition of land assuming that the purchase of the stock was originally recorded using the cost method.
(b) Briefly identify the possible alternatives (including those that are totally unacceptable) for quantifying the cost of the land and briefly support your choice.

(LO 3)   **E15-4   (Lump-Sum Sale of Stock with Bonds)**   Faith Evans Corporation is a regional company which is an SEC registrant. The corporation's securities are thinly traded on NASDAQ (National Association of Securities Dealers Quotes). Faith Evans Corp. has issued 10,000 units. Each unit consists of a $500 par, 12% subordinated debenture and 10 shares of $5 par common stock. The investment banker has retained 400 units as the underwriting fee. The other 9,600 units were sold to outside investors for cash at $880 per unit. Prior to this sale the 2-week ask price of common stock was $40 per share. Twelve percent is a reasonable market yield for the debentures, and therefore the par value of the bonds is equal to the fair value.

Instructions
(a) Prepare the journal entry to record Evans' transaction, under the following conditions.
    (1) Employing the incremental method.
    (2) Employing the proportional method, assuming the recent price quote on the common stock reflects fair value.
(b) Briefly explain which method is, in your opinion, the better method.

(LO 3, 5) **E15-5** **(Lump-Sum Sales of Stock with Preferred Stock)** Dave Matthew Inc. issues 500 shares of $10 par value common stock and 100 shares of $100 par value preferred stock for a lump sum of $100,000.

Instructions
(a) Prepare the journal entry for the issuance when the market value of the common shares is $165 each and market value of the preferred is $230 each. (Round to nearest dollar.)
(b) Prepare the journal entry for the issuance when only the market value of the common stock is known and it is $170 per share.

(LO 3, 4) **E15-6** **(Stock Issuances and Repurchase)** Lindsey Hunter Corporation is authorized to issue 50,000 shares of $5 par value common stock. During 2007, Lindsey Hunter took part in the following selected transactions.

1. Issued 5,000 shares of stock at $45 per share, less costs related to the issuance of the stock totaling $7,000.
2. Issued 1,000 shares of stock for land appraised at $50,000. The stock was actively traded on a national stock exchange at approximately $46 per share on the date of issuance.
3. Purchased 500 shares of treasury stock at $43 per share. The treasury shares purchased were issued in 2003 at $40 per share.

Instructions
(a) Prepare the journal entry to record item 1.
(b) Prepare the journal entry to record item 2.
(c) Prepare the journal entry to record item 3 using the cost method.

(LO 4) **E15-7** **(Effect of Treasury Stock Transactions on Financials)** Joe Dumars Company has outstanding 40,000 shares of $5 par common stock which had been issued at $30 per share. Joe Dumars then entered into the following transactions.

1. Purchased 5,000 treasury shares at $45 per share.
2. Resold 2,000 of the treasury shares at $49 per share.
3. Resold 500 of the treasury shares at $40 per share.

Instructions
Use the following code to indicate the effect each of the three transactions has on the financial statement categories listed in the table below, assuming Joe Dumars Company uses the cost method: (I = Increase; D = Decrease; NE = No effect).

#	Assets	Liabilities	Stockholders' Equity	Paid-in Capital	Retained Earnings	Net Income
1						
2						
3						

(LO 3, 10) **E15-8** **(Preferred Stock Entries and Dividends)** Otis Thorpe Corporation has 10,000 shares of $100 par value, 8%, preferred stock and 50,000 shares of $10 par value common stock outstanding at December 31, 2007.

Instructions
Answer the questions in each of the following independent situations.
(a) If the preferred stock is cumulative and dividends were last paid on the preferred stock on December 31, 2004, what are the dividends in arrears that should be reported on the December 31, 2007, balance sheet? How should these dividends be reported?
(b) If the preferred stock is convertible into seven shares of $10 par value common stock and 4,000 shares are converted, what entry is required for the conversion assuming the preferred stock was issued at par value?
(c) If the preferred stock was issued at $107 per share, how should the preferred stock be reported in the stockholders' equity section?

(LO 3, 4) **E15-9 (Correcting Entries for Equity Transactions)** Pistons Inc. recently hired a new accountant with extensive experience in accounting for partnerships. Because of the pressure of the new job, the accountant was unable to review what he had learned earlier about corporation accounting. During the first month, he made the following entries for the corporation's capital stock.

May 2	Cash		192,000	
	Capital Stock			192,000
	(Issued 12,000 shares of $5 par value common stock at $16 per share)			
10	Cash		600,000	
	Capital Stock			600,000
	(Issued 10,000 shares of $30 par value preferred stock at $60 per share)			
15	Capital Stock		15,000	
	Cash			15,000
	(Purchased 1,000 shares of common stock for the treasury at $15 per share)			
31	Cash		8,500	
	Capital Stock			5,000
	Gain on Sale of Stock			3,500
	(Sold 500 shares of treasury stock at $17 per share)			

Instructions

On the basis of the explanation for each entry, prepare the entries that should have been made for the capital stock transactions.

(LO 3, 4) **E15-10 (Analysis of Equity Data and Equity Section Preparation)** For a recent 2-year period, the balance sheet of Santana Dotson Company showed the following stockholders' equity data at December 31 in millions.

	2007	2006
Additional paid-in capital	$ 931	$ 817
Common stock—par	545	540
Retained earnings	7,167	5,226
Treasury stock	1,564	918
Total stockholders' equity	$7,079	$5,665
Common stock shares issued	218	216
Common stock shares authorized	500	500
Treasury stock shares	34	27

Instructions

(a) Answer the following questions.
  (1) What is the par value of the common stock?
  (2) What is the cost per share of treasury stock at December 31, 2007, and at December 31, 2006?
(b) Prepare the stockholders' equity section at December 31, 2007.

(LO 7, 8) **E15-11 (Equity Items on the Balance Sheet)** The following are selected transactions that may affect stockholders' equity.

1. Recorded accrued interest earned on a note receivable.
2. Declared a cash dividend.
3. Declared and distributed a stock split.
4. Recorded a retained earnings restriction.
5. Recorded the expiration of insurance coverage that was previously recorded as prepaid insurance.
6. Paid the cash dividend declared in item 2 above.
7. Recorded accrued interest expense on a note payable.
8. Declared a stock dividend.
9. Distributed the stock dividend declared in item 8.

Instructions

In the table on the next page, indicate the effect each of the nine transactions has on the financial statement elements listed. Use the following code:

			Stockholders'	Paid-in	Retained	Net
Item	Assets	Liabilities	Equity	Capital	Earnings	Income

I = Increase   D = Decrease   NE = No effect

(LO 7, 8) **E15-12** **(Cash Dividend and Liquidating Dividend)** Lotoya Davis Corporation has ten million shares of common stock issued and outstanding. On June 1 the board of directors voted an 80 cents per share cash dividend to stockholders of record as of June 14, payable June 30.

Instructions
(a) Prepare the journal entry for each of the dates above assuming the dividend represents a distribution of earnings.
(b) How would the entry differ if the dividend were a liquidating dividend?

(LO 8) **E15-13** **(Stock Split and Stock Dividend)** The common stock of Alexander Hamilton Inc. is currently selling at $120 per share. The directors wish to reduce the share price and increase share volume prior to a new issue. The per share par value is $10; book value is $70 per share. Nine million shares are issued and outstanding.

Instructions
Prepare the necessary journal entries assuming the following.
(a) The board votes a 2-for-1 stock split.
(b) The board votes a 100% stock dividend.
(c) Briefly discuss the accounting and securities market differences between these two methods of increasing the number of shares outstanding.

(LO 8) **E15-14** **(Entries for Stock Dividends and Stock Splits)** The stockholders' equity accounts of G.K. Chesterton Company have the following balances on December 31, 2007.

Common stock, $10 par, 300,000 shares issued and outstanding	$3,000,000
Paid-in capital in excess of par	1,200,000
Retained earnings	5,600,000

Shares of G.K. Chesterton Company stock are currently selling on the Midwest Stock Exchange at $37.

Instructions
Prepare the appropriate journal entries for each of the following cases.
(a) A stock dividend of 5% is declared and issued.
(b) A stock dividend of 100% is declared and issued.
(c) A 2-for-1 stock split is declared and issued.

(LO 7, 8) **E15-15** **(Dividend Entries)** The following data were taken from the balance sheet accounts of Masefield Corporation on December 31, 2006.

Current assets	$540,000
Investments	624,000
Common stock (par value $10)	500,000
Paid-in capital in excess of par	150,000
Retained earnings	840,000

Instructions
Prepare the required journal entries for the following unrelated items.
(a) A 5% stock dividend is declared and distributed at a time when the market value of the shares is $39 per share.

(b) The par value of the capital stock is reduced to $2 with a 5-for-1 stock split.

(c) A dividend is declared January 5, 2007, and paid January 25, 2007, in bonds held as an investment. The bonds have a book value of $100,000 and a fair market value of $135,000.

(L0 6, 7, 8) **E15-16** **(Computation of Retained Earnings)** The following information has been taken from the ledger accounts of Isaac Stern Corporation.

Total income since incorporation	$317,000
Total cash dividends paid	60,000
Total value of stock dividends distributed	30,000
Gains on treasury stock transactions	18,000
Unamortized discount on bonds payable	32,000

Instructions

Determine the current balance of retained earnings.

(L0 9) **E15-17** **(Stockholders' Equity Section)** Bruno Corporation's post-closing trial balance at December 31, 2007, was as follows.

BRUNO CORPORATION
POST-CLOSING TRIAL BALANCE
DECEMBER 31, 2007

	Dr.	Cr.
Accounts payable		$ 310,000
Accounts receivable	$ 480,000	
Accumulated depreciation—building and equipment		185,000
Additional paid-in capital—common		
In excess of par value		1,300,000
From sale of treasury stock		160,000
Allowance for doubtful accounts		30,000
Bonds payable		300,000
Building and equipment	1,450,000	
Cash	190,000	
Common stock ($1 par value)		200,000
Dividends payable on preferred stock—cash		4,000
Inventories	560,000	
Land	400,000	
Preferred stock ($50 par value)		500,000
Prepaid expenses	40,000	
Retained earnings		301,000
Treasury stock—common at cost	170,000	
Totals	$3,290,000	$3,290,000

At December 31, 2007, Bruno had the following number of common and preferred shares.

	Common	Preferred
Authorized	600,000	60,000
Issued	200,000	10,000
Outstanding	190,000	10,000

The dividends on preferred stock are $4 cumulative. In addition, the preferred stock has a preference in liquidation of $50 per share.

Instructions

Prepare the stockholders' equity section of Bruno's balance sheet at December 31, 2007.

(AICPA adapted)

(L0 4, 7, 8) **E15-18** **(Dividends and Stockholders' Equity Section)** Anne Cleves Company reported the following amounts in the stockholders' equity section of its December 31, 2006, balance sheet.

Preferred stock, 10%, $100 par (10,000 shares authorized, 2,000 shares issued)	$200,000
Common stock, $5 par (100,000 shares authorized, 20,000 shares issued)	100,000
Additional paid-in capital	125,000
Retained earnings	450,000
Total	$875,000

During 2007, Cleves took part in the following transactions concerning stockholders' equity.

1. Paid the annual 2006 $10 per share dividend on preferred stock and a $2 per share dividend on common stock. These dividends had been declared on December 31, 2006.
2. Purchased 1,700 shares of its own outstanding common stock for $40 per share. Cleves uses the cost method.
3. Reissued 700 treasury shares for land valued at $30,000.
4. Issued 500 shares of preferred stock at $105 per share.
5. Declared a 10% stock dividend on the outstanding common stock when the stock is selling for $45 per share.
6. Issued the stock dividend.
7. Declared the annual 2007 $10 per share dividend on preferred stock and the $2 per share dividend on common stock. These dividends are payable in 2008.

Instructions

(a) Prepare journal entries to record the transactions described above.
(b) Prepare the December 31, 2007, stockholders' equity section. Assume 2007 net income was $330,000.

(LO 9) **E15-19** **(Comparison of Alternative Forms of Financing)** Shown below is the liabilities and stockholders' equity section of the balance sheet for Jana Kingston Company and Mary Ann Benson Company. Each has assets totaling $4,200,000.

Jana Kingston Co.		Mary Ann Benson Co.	
Current liabilities	$ 300,000	Current liabilities	$ 600,000
Long-term debt, 10%	1,200,000	Common stock ($20 par)	2,900,000
Common stock ($20 par)	2,000,000	Retained earnings (Cash	
Retained earnings (Cash		dividends, $328,000)	700,000
dividends, $220,000)	700,000		
	$4,200,000		$4,200,000

For the year each company has earned the same income before interest and taxes.

	Jana Kingston Co.	Mary Ann Benson Co.
Income before interest and taxes	$1,200,000	$1,200,000
Interest expense	120,000	–0–
	1,080,000	1,200,000
Income taxes (45%)	486,000	540,000
Net income	$ 594,000	$ 660,000

At year end, the market price of Kingston's stock was $101 per share, and Benson's was $63.50.

Instructions

(a) Which company is more profitable in terms of return on total assets?
(b) Which company is more profitable in terms of return on stockholders' equity?
(c) Which company has the greater net income per share of stock? Neither company issued or reacquired shares during the year.
(d) From the point of view of net income, is it advantageous to the stockholders of Jana Kingston Co. to have the long-term debt outstanding? Why?
(e) What is the book value per share for each company?

(LO 9) **E15-20** **(Trading on the Equity Analysis)** Presented below is information from the annual report of Emporia Plastics, Inc.

Operating income	$ 532,150
Bond interest expense	135,000
	397,150
Income taxes	183,432
Net income	$ 213,718
Bonds payable	$1,000,000
Common stock	875,000
Retained earnings	375,000

Instructions

    (a) Compute the return on common stock equity and the rate of interest paid on bonds. (Assume balances for debt and equity accounts approximate averages for the year.)

    (b) Is Emporia Plastics Inc. trading on the equity successfully? Explain.

(LO 10) *E15-21 (Preferred Dividends)** The outstanding capital stock of Edna Millay Corporation consists of 2,000 shares of $100 par value, 8% preferred, and 5,000 shares of $50 par value common.

Instructions

Assuming that the company has retained earnings of $90,000, all of which is to be paid out in dividends, and that preferred dividends were not paid during the 2 years preceding the current year, state how much each class of stock should receive under each of the following conditions.

    (a) The preferred stock is noncumulative and nonparticipating.

    (b) The preferred stock is cumulative and nonparticipating.

    (c) The preferred stock is cumulative and participating. (Round dividend rate percentages to four decimal places.)

(LO 10) *E15-22 (Preferred Dividends)** Matt Schmidt Company's ledger shows the following balances on December 31, 2007.

7% Preferred stock—$10 par value, outstanding 20,000 shares	$ 200,000
Common stock—$100 par value, outstanding 30,000 shares	3,000,000
Retained earnings	630,000

Instructions

Assuming that the directors decide to declare total dividends in the amount of $366,000, determine how much each class of stock should receive under each of the conditions stated below. One year's dividends are in arrears on the preferred stock.

    (a) The preferred stock is cumulative and fully participating.

    (b) The preferrred stock is noncumulative and nonparticipating.

    (c) The preferred stock is noncumulative and is participating in distributions in excess of a 10% dividend rate on the common stock.

(LO 10) *E15-23 (Preferred Stock Dividends)** Cajun Company has outstanding 2,500 shares of $100 par, 6% preferred stock and 15,000 shares of $10 par value common. The schedule on the next page shows the amount of dividends paid out over the last 4 years.

Instructions

Allocate the dividends to each type of stock under assumptions (a) and (b). Express your answers in per-share amounts using the format shown below.

		Assumptions			
		(a) Preferred, noncumulative, and nonparticipating		(b) Preferred, cumulative, and fully participating	
Year	Paid-out	Preferred	Common	Preferred	Common
2005	$13,000				
2006	$26,000				
2007	$57,000				
2008	$76,000				

(LO 10) *E15-24 (Computation of Book Value per Share)** Morgan Sondgeroth Inc. began operations in January 2005 and reported the following results for each of its 3 years of operations.

2005 $260,000 net loss   2006 $40,000 net loss   2007 $800,000 net income

At December 31, 2007, Morgan Sondgeroth Inc. capital accounts were as follows.

8% cumulative preferred stock, par value $100; authorized, issued, and outstanding 5,000 shares	$500,000
Common stock, par value $1.00; authorized 1,000,000 shares; issued and outstanding 750,000 shares	$750,000

    Morgan Sondgeroth Inc. has never paid a cash or stock dividend. There has been no change in the capital accounts since Sondgeroth began operations. The state law permits dividends only from retained earnings.

Instructions

(a) Compute the book value of the common stock at December 31, 2007.

(b) Compute the book value of the common stock at December 31, 2007, assuming that the preferred stock has a liquidating value of $106 per share.

See the book's website, www.wiley.com/college/kieso, for Additional Exercises.

PROBLEMS

(LO 3, 4, 9) **P15-1** **(Equity Transactions and Statement Preparation)** On January 5, 2007, Drabek Corporation received a charter granting the right to issue 5,000 shares of $100 par value, 8% cumulative and nonparticipating preferred stock, and 50,000 shares of $5 par value common stock. It then completed these transactions.

Jan. 11 Issued 20,000 shares of common stock at $16 per share.

Feb. 1 Issued to Robb Nen Corp. 4,000 shares of preferred stock for the following assets: machinery with a fair market value of $50,000; a factory building with a fair market value of $110,000; and land with an appraised value of $270,000.

July 29 Purchased 1,800 shares of common stock at $19 per share. (Use cost method.)

Aug. 10 Sold the 1,800 treasury shares at $14 per share.

Dec. 31 Declared a $0.25 per share cash dividend on the common stock and declared the preferred dividend.

Dec. 31 Closed the Income Summary account. There was a $175,700 net income.

Instructions

(a) Record the journal entries for the transactions listed above.

(b) Prepare the stockholders' equity section of Drabek Corporation's balance sheet as of December 31, 2007.

(LO 4, 9) **P15-2** **(Treasury Stock Transactions and Presentation)** Andruw Jones Company had the following stockholders' equity as of January 1, 2007.

Common stock, $5 par value, 20,000 shares issued	$100,000
Paid-in capital in excess of par	300,000
Retained earnings	320,000
Total stockholders' equity	$720,000

During 2007, the following transactions occurred.

Feb. 1 Jones repurchased 2,000 shares of treasury stock at a price of $18 per share.

Mar. 1 800 shares of treasury stock repurchased above were reissued at $17 per share.

Mar. 18 500 shares of treasury stock repurchased above were reissued at $14 per share.

Apr. 22 600 shares of treasury stock repurchased above were reissued at $20 per share.

Instructions

(a) Prepare the journal entries to record the treasury stock transactions in 2007, assuming Jones uses the cost method.

(b) Prepare the stockholders' equity section as of April 30, 2007. Net income for the first 4 months of 2007 was $110,000.

(LO 3, 4, 7, 8) **P15-3** **(Equity Transactions and Statement Preparation)** Amado Company has two classes of capital stock outstanding: 8%, $20 par preferred and $5 par common. At December 31, 2007, the following accounts were included in stockholders' equity.

Preferred Stock, 150,000 shares	$ 3,000,000
Common Stock, 2,000,000 shares	10,000,000
Paid-in Capital in Excess of Par—Preferred	200,000
Paid-in Capital in Excess of Par—Common	27,000,000
Retained Earnings	4,500,000

The following transactions affected stockholders' equity during 2007.

Jan. 1 25,000 shares of preferred stock issued at $22 per share.

Feb. 1 40,000 shares of common stock issued at $20 per share.

June 1 2-for-1 stock split (par value reduced to $2.50).

July 1 30,000 shares of common treasury stock purchased at $9 per share. Amado uses the cost method.

Sept. 15   10,000 shares of treasury stock reissued at $11 per share.
Dec. 31   Net income is $2,100,000.
Dec. 31   The preferred dividend is declared, and a common dividend of 50¢ per share is declared.

Instructions
Prepare the stockholders' equity section for Amado Company at December 31, 2007. Show all supporting computations.

(LO 3, 5)   **P15-4   (Stock Transactions—Lump Sum)**   Matsui Corporation's charter authorized issuance of 100,000 shares of $10 par value common stock and 50,000 shares of $50 preferred stock. The following transactions involving the issuance of shares of stock were completed. Each transaction is independent of the others.

1. Issued a $10,000, 9% bond payable at par and gave as a bonus one share of preferred stock, which at that time was selling for $106 a share.
2. Issued 500 shares of common stock for machinery. The machinery had been appraised at $7,100; the seller's book value was $6,200. The most recent market price of the common stock is $15 a share.
3. Issued 375 shares of common and 100 shares of preferred for a lump sum amounting to $11,300. The common had been selling at $14 and the preferred at $65.
4. Issued 200 shares of common and 50 shares of preferred for furniture and fixtures. The common had a fair market value of $16 per share; the furniture and fixtures have a fair value of $6,200.

Instructions
Record the transactions listed above in journal entry form.

(LO 4)   **P15-5   (Treasury Stock—Cost Method)**   Before Polska Corporation engages in the treasury stock transactions listed below, its general ledger reflects, among others, the following account balances (par value of its stock is $30 per share).

Paid-in Capital in Excess of Par	Common Stock	Retained Earnings
$99,000	$270,000	$80,000

Instructions
Record the treasury stock transactions (given below) under the cost method of handling treasury stock; use the FIFO method for purchase-sale purposes.

(a) Bought 380 shares of treasury stock at $39 per share.
(b) Bought 300 shares of treasury stock at $43 per share.
(c) Sold 350 shares of treasury stock at $42 per share.
(d) Sold 120 shares of treasury stock at $38 per share.

(LO 4, 7, 9)   **P15-6   (Treasury Stock—Cost Method—Equity Section Preparation)**   Constantine Company has the following stockholders' equity accounts at December 31, 2006.

Common Stock—$100 par value, authorized 8,000 shares	$480,000
Retained Earnings	294,000

Instructions
(a) Prepare entries in journal form to record the following transactions, which took place during 2007.
  (1) 240 shares of outstanding stock were purchased at $97 per share. (These are to be accounted for using the cost method.)
  (2) A $20 per share cash dividend was declared.
  (3) The dividend declared in No. 2 above was paid.
  (4) The treasury shares purchased in No. 1 above were resold at $102 per share.
  (5) 500 shares of outstanding stock were purchased at $103 per share.
  (6) 330 of the shares purchased in No. 5 above were resold at $96 per share.
(b) Prepare the stockholders' equity section of Constantine Company's balance sheet after giving effect to these transactions, assuming that the net income for 2007 was $94,000. State law requires restriction of retained earnings for the amount of treasury stock.

(LO 4, 7)   **P15-7   (Cash Dividend Entries)**   The books of John Dos Passos Corporation carried the following account balances as of December 31, 2006.

Cash	$ 195,000
Preferred stock, 6% cumulative, nonparticipating, $50 par	200,000
Common stock, no par value, 300,000 shares issued	1,500,000
Paid-in capital in excess of par (preferred)	150,000
Treasury stock (common 4,200 shares at cost)	33,600
Retained earnings	105,000

The company decided not to pay any dividends in 2006.

The board of directors, at their annual meeting on December 21, 2007, declared the following: "The current year dividends shall be 6% on the preferred and $.30 per share on the common. The dividends in arrears shall be paid by issuing 1,500 shares of treasury stock." At the date of declaration, the preferred is selling at $80 per share, and the common at $8 per share. Net income for 2007 is estimated at $77,000.

Instructions
    (a) Prepare the journal entries required for the dividend declaration and payment, assuming that they occur simultaneously.
    (b) Could John Dos Passos Corporation give the preferred stockholders 2 years' dividends and common stockholders a 30 cents per share dividend, all in cash?

(LO 7, 8) **P15-8 (Dividends and Splits)** Gutsy Company provides you with the following condensed balance sheet information.

Assets		Liabilities and Stockholders' Equity		
Current assets	$ 40,000	Current and long-term liabilities		$100,000
Investments in ABC stock		Stockholders' equity		
(10,000 shares at cost)	60,000	Common stock ($2 par)	$ 20,000	
Equipment (net)	250,000	Paid-in capital in excess of par	110,000	
Intangibles	60,000	Retained earnings	180,000	310,000
Total assets	$410,000	Total liabilities and		
		stockholders' equity		$410,000

Instructions
For each transaction below, indicate the dollar impact (if any) on the following five items: (1) total assets, (2) common stock, (3) paid-in capital in excess of par, (4) retained earnings, and (5) stockholders' equity. (Each situation is independent.)
    (a) Gutsy declares and pays a $0.50 per share cash dividend.
    (b) Gutsy declares and issues a 10% stock dividend when the market price of the stock is $14 per share.
    (c) Gutsy declares and issues a 40% stock dividend when the market price of the stock is $15 per share.
    (d) Gutsy declares and distributes a property dividend. Gutsy gives one share of ABC stock for every two shares of Gutsy Company stock held. ABC is selling for $10 per share on the date the property dividend is declared.
    (e) Gutsy declares a 2-for-1 stock split and issues new shares.

(LO 3, 4, 7, 9) **P15-9 (Stockholders' Equity Section of Balance Sheet)** The following is a summary of all relevant transactions of Jackson Day Corporation since it was organized in 2007.

In 2007, 15,000 shares were authorized and 7,000 shares of common stock ($50 par value) were issued at a price of $57. In 2008, 1,000 shares were issued as a stock dividend when the stock was selling for $62. Three hundred shares of common stock were bought in 2009 at a cost of $66 per share. These 300 shares are still in the company treasury.

In 2008, 10,000 preferred shares were authorized and the company issued 4,000 of them ($100 par value) at $113. Some of the preferred stock was reacquired by the company and later reissued for $4,700 more than it cost the company.

The corporation has earned a total of $610,000 in net income after income taxes and paid out a total of $312,600 in cash dividends since incorporation.

Instructions
Prepare the stockholders' equity section of the balance sheet in proper form for Jackson Day Corporation as of December 31, 2009. Account for treasury stock using the cost method.

(LO 8) **P15-10 (Stock Dividends and Stock Split)** Jenny Dill Inc. $10 par common stock is selling for $120 per share. Five million shares are currently issued and outstanding. The board of directors wishes to stimulate interest in Jenny Dill common stock before a forthcoming stock issue but does not wish to distribute capital at this time. The board also believes that too many adjustments to the stockholders' equity section, especially retained earnings, might discourage potential investors.

The board has considered three options for stimulating interest in the stock:
    1. A 20% stock dividend.
    2. A 100% stock dividend.
    3. A 2-for-1 stock split.

Instructions

Acting as financial advisor to the board, you have been asked to report briefly on each option and, considering the board's wishes, make a recommendation. Discuss the effects of each of the foregoing options.

(LO 7, 8) **P15-11 (Stock and Cash Dividends)** Gul Ducat Corporation has outstanding 2,000,000 shares of common stock of a par value of $10 each. The balance in its retained earnings account at January 1, 2007, was $24,000,000, and it then had Additional Paid-in Capital of $5,000,000. During 2007, the company's net income was $5,700,000. A cash dividend of $0.60 a share was paid June 30, 2007, and a 6% stock dividend was declared on November 30, 2007, and distributed to stockholders of record at the close of business on December 31, 2007. You have been asked to advise on the proper accounting treatment of the stock dividend.

The existing stock of the company is quoted on a national stock exchange. The market price of the stock has been as follows.

October 31, 2007	$31
November 30, 2007	$35
December 31, 2007	$38

Instructions

(a) Prepare the journal entry to record the cash dividend.
(b) Prepare the journal entry to record the stock dividend.
(c) Prepare the stockholders' equity section (including schedules of retained earnings and additional paid-in capital) of the balance sheet of Gul Ducat Corporation for the year 2007 on the basis of the foregoing information. Draft a note to the financial statements setting forth the basis of the accounting for the stock dividend, and add separately appropriate comments or explanations regarding the basis chosen.

(LO 3, 4, 7, 8, 9) **P15-12 (Analysis and Classification of Equity Transactions)** Ohio Company was formed on July 1, 2003. It was authorized to issue 300,000 shares of $10 par value common stock and 100,000 shares of 8% $25 par value, cumulative and nonparticipating preferred stock. Ohio Company has a July 1–June 30 fiscal year.

The following information relates to the stockholders' equity accounts of Ohio Company.

Common Stock

Prior to the 2005–06 fiscal year, Ohio Company had 110,000 shares of outstanding common stock issued as follows.

1. 95,000 shares were issued for cash on July 1, 2003, at $31 per share.
2. On July 24, 2003, 5,000 shares were exchanged for a plot of land which cost the seller $70,000 in 1997 and had an estimated market value of $220,000 on July 24, 2003.
3. 10,000 shares were issued on March 1, 2004, for $42 per share.

During the 2005–06 fiscal year, the following transactions regarding common stock took place.

November 30, 2005	Ohio purchased 2,000 shares of its own stock on the open market at $39 per share. Ohio uses the cost method for treasury stock.
December 15, 2005	Ohio declared a 5% stock dividend for stockholders of record on January 15, 2006, to be issued on January 31, 2006. Ohio was having a liquidity problem and could not afford a cash dividend at the time. Ohio's common stock was selling at $52 per share on December 15, 2005.
June 20, 2006	Ohio sold 500 shares of its own common stock that it had purchased on November 30, 2005, for $21,000.

Preferred Stock

Ohio issued 50,000 shares of preferred stock at $44 per share on July 1, 2004.

Cash Dividends

Ohio has followed a schedule of declaring cash dividends in December and June, with payment being made to stockholders of record in the following month. The cash dividends which have been declared since inception of the company through June 30, 2006, are shown below.

Declaration Date	Common Stock	Preferred Stock
12/15/04	$0.30 per share	$1.00 per share
6/15/05	$0.30 per share	$1.00 per share
12/15/05	—	$1.00 per share

No cash dividends were declared during June 2006 due to the company's liquidity problems.

Retained Earnings

As of June 30, 2005, Ohio's retained earnings account had a balance of $690,000. For the fiscal year ending June 30, 2006, Ohio reported net income of $40,000.

Instructions

Prepare the stockholders' equity section of the balance sheet, including appropriate notes, for Ohio Company as of June 30, 2006, as it should appear in its annual report to the shareholders.

(CMA adapted)

CONCEPTS FOR ANALYSIS

CA15-1 (Preemptive Rights and Dilution of Ownership) Alvarado Computer Company is a small, closely held corporation. Eighty percent of the stock is held by Eduardo Alvarado, president. Of the remainder, 10% is held by members of his family and 10% by Shaunda Jones, a former officer who is now retired. The balance sheet of the company at June 30, 2007, was substantially as shown below.

Assets		Liabilities and Stockholders' Equity	
Cash	$ 22,000	Current liabilities	$ 50,000
Other	450,000	Capital stock	250,000
	$472,000	Retained earnings	172,000
			$472,000

Additional authorized capital stock of $300,000 par value had never been issued. To strengthen the cash position of the company, Eduardo Alvarado issued capital stock with a par value of $100,000 to himself at par for cash. At the next stockholders' meeting, Jones objected and claimed that her interests had been injured.

Instructions

(a) Which stockholder's right was ignored in the issue of shares to Eduardo Alvarado?

(b) How may the damage to Jones' interests be repaired most simply?

(c) If Eduardo Alvarado offered Jones a personal cash settlement and they agreed to employ you as an impartial arbitrator to determine the amount, what settlement would you propose? Present your calculations with sufficient explanation to satisfy both parties.

CA15-2 (Issuance of Stock for Land) Crosby Corporation is planning to issue 3,000 shares of its own $10 par value common stock for two acres of land to be used as a building site.

Instructions

(a) What general rule should be applied to determine the amount at which the land should be recorded?

(b) Under what circumstances should this transaction be recorded at the fair market value of the land?

(c) Under what circumstances should this transaction be recorded at the fair market value of the stock issued?

(d) Assume Crosby intentionally records this transaction at an amount greater than the fair market value of the land and the stock. Discuss this situation.

CA15-3 (Conceptual Issues—Equity) Statements of Financial Accounting Concepts set forth financial accounting and reporting objectives and fundamentals that will be used by the Financial Accounting Standards Board in developing standards. *Concepts Statement No. 6* defines various elements of financial statements.

Instructions

Answer the following questions based on *SFAC No. 6*.

(a) Define and discuss the term "equity."

(b) What transactions or events change owners' equity?

(c) Define "investments by owners" and provide examples of this type of transaction. What financial statement element other than equity is typically affected by owner investments?

(d) Define "distributions to owners" and provide examples of this type of transaction. What financial statement element other than equity is typically affected by distributions?

(e) What are examples of changes within owners' equity that do not change the total amount of owners' equity?

CA15-4 (Stock Dividends and Splits) The directors of Amman Corporation are considering the issuance of a stock dividend. They have asked you to discuss the proposed action by answering the following questions.

Instructions
- (a) What is a stock dividend? How is a stock dividend distinguished from a stock split (1) from a legal standpoint, and (2) from an accounting standpoint?
- (b) For what reasons does a corporation usually declare a stock dividend? A stock split?
- (c) Discuss the amount, if any, of retained earnings to be capitalized in connection with a stock dividend.

(AICPA adapted)

CA15-5 (Stock Dividends) Kitakyushu Inc., a client, is considering the authorization of a 10% common stock dividend to common stockholders. The financial vice president of Kitakyushu wishes to discuss the accounting implications of such an authorization with you before the next meeting of the board of directors.

Instructions
- (a) The first topic the vice president wishes to discuss is the nature of the stock dividend to the recipient. Discuss the case against considering the stock dividend as income to the recipient.
- (b) The other topic for discussion is the propriety of issuing the stock dividend to all "stockholders of record" or to "stockholders of record exclusive of shares held in the name of the corporation as treasury stock." Discuss the case against issuing stock dividends on treasury shares.

(AICPA adapted)

CA15-6 (Stock Dividend, Cash Dividend, and Treasury Stock) AROD Company has 30,000 shares of $10 par value common stock authorized and 20,000 shares issued and outstanding. On August 15, 2007, AROD purchased 1,000 shares of treasury stock for $16 per share. AROD uses the cost method to account for treasury stock. On September 14, 2007, AROD sold 500 shares of the treasury stock for $20 per share.

In October 2007, AROD declared and distributed 1,950 shares as a stock dividend from unissued shares when the market value of the common stock was $21 per share.

On December 20, 2007, AROD declared a $1 per share cash dividend, payable on January 10, 2008, to shareholders of record on December 31, 2007.

Instructions
- (a) How should AROD account for the purchase and sale of the treasury stock, and how should the treasury stock be presented in the balance sheet at December 31, 2007?
- (b) How should AROD account for the stock dividend, and how would it affect the stockholders' equity at December 31, 2007? Why?
- (c) How should AROD account for the cash dividend, and how would it affect the balance sheet at December 31, 2007? Why?

(AICPA adapted)

 CA15-7 (Treasury Stock) Jean Loptien, president of Sycamore Corporation, is concerned about several large stockholders who have been very vocal lately in their criticisms of her leadership. She thinks they might mount a campaign to have her removed as the corporation's CEO. She decides that buying them out by purchasing their shares could eliminate them as opponents, and she is confident they would accept a "good" offer. Loptien knows the corporation's cash position is decent, so it has the cash to complete the transaction. She also knows the purchase of these shares will increase earnings per share, which should make other investors quite happy. (Earnings per share is calculated by dividing net income available for the common shareholders by the weighted average number of shares outstanding. Therefore, if the number of shares outstanding is decreased by purchasing treasury shares, earnings per share increases.)

Instructions
Answer the following questions.
- (a) Who are the stakeholders in this situation?
- (b) What are the ethical issues involved?
- (c) Should Loptien authorize the transaction?

USING YOUR JUDGMENT

Financial Reporting Problem

P&G The Procter & Gamble Company (P&G)

The financial statements of **P&G** are presented in Appendix 5B or can be accessed on the KWW website.

Instructions

Refer to these financial statements and the accompanying notes to answer the following questions.

(a) What is the par or stated value of P&G's preferred stock?

(b) What is the par or stated value of P&G's common stock?

(c) What percentage of P&G's authorized common stock was issued at June 30, 2004?

(d) How many shares of common stock were outstanding at June 30, 2004, and June 30, 2003?

(e) What was the dollar amount effect of the cash dividends on P&G's stockholders' equity?

(f) What is P&G's rate of return on common stock equity for 2004 and 2003?

(g) What is P&G's payout ratio for 2004 and 2003?

(h) What was the market price range (high/low) of P&G's common stock during the quarter ended June 30, 2004?

Financial Statement Analysis Case

Case 1: Kellogg Corporation

Kellogg Corporation is the world's leading producer of ready-to-eat cereal products. In recent years the company has taken numerous steps aimed at improving its profitability and earnings per share. Presented below are some basic facts for Kellogg Corporation.

(all dollars in millions)	2004	2003
Net sales	$9,614	$8,812
Net earnings	891	787
Total assets	10,790	10,143
Total liabilities	8,533	8,699
Common stock, $0.25 par value	104	104
Capital in excess of par value		25
Retained earnings	2,701	2,248
Treasury stock, at cost	108	204
Number of shares outstanding (in millions)	413	410

Instructions

(a) What are some of the reasons that management purchases its own stock?

(b) Explain how earnings per share might be affected by treasury stock transactions.

(c) Calculate the ratio of debt to total assets for 2003 and 2004, and discuss the implications of the change.

Case 2: Wiebold, Incorporated

The following note related to stockholders' equity was reported in **Wiebold, Inc.**'s annual report.

On February 1, the Board of Directors declared a 3-for-2 stock split, distributed on February 22 to shareholders of record on February 10. Accordingly, all numbers of common shares, except unissued shares and treasury shares, and all per share data have been restated to reflect this stock split.

On the basis of amounts declared and paid, the annualized quarterly dividends per share were $0.80 in the current year and $0.75 in the prior year.

Instructions

(a) What is the significance of the date of record and the date of distribution?

(b) Why might Weibold have declared a 3-for-2 for stock split?

(c) What impact does Wiebold's stock split have on (1) total stockholders' equity, (2) total par value, (3) outstanding shares, and (4) book value per share?

Comparative Analysis Case

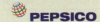

The Coca-Cola Company and PepsiCo, Inc.

Instructions
Go to the KWW website and use information found there to answer the following questions related to **The Coca-Cola Company** and **PepsiCo, Inc.**

(a) What is the par or stated value of Coca-Cola's and PepsiCo's common or capital stock?

(b) What percentage of authorized shares was issued by Coca-Cola at December 31, 2004, and by PepsiCo at December 25, 2004?

(c) How many shares are held as treasury stock by Coca-Cola at December 31, 2004, and by PepsiCo at December 25, 2004?

(d) How many Coca-Cola common shares are outstanding at December 31, 2004? How many PepsiCo shares of capital stock are outstanding at December 25, 2004?

(e) What amounts of cash dividends per share were declared by Coca-Cola and PepsiCo in 2004? What were the dollar amount effects of the cash dividends on each company's stockholders' equity?

(f) What are Coca-Cola's and PepsiCo's rate of return on common/capital stock equity for 2004 and 2003? Which company gets the higher return on the equity of its shareholders?

(g) What are Coca-Cola's and PepsiCo's payout ratios for 2004?

(h) What was the market price range (high/low) for Coca-Cola's common stock and PepsiCo's capital stock during the fourth quarter of 2004? Which company's (Coca-Cola's or PepsiCo's) stock price increased more (%) during 2004?

Research Case

The article "Leading the News: **AT&T Corp.** Resorts to Unusual Motion: Reverse Stock Split—Market Capitalization Stays Constant, but Measure Would Boost Share Price," by Deborah Solomon, was published in the *Wall Street Journal* on April 11, 2002.

Instructions
Read the article and answer the following questions.

(a) Why is AT&T doing a reverse stock split? What advantage does it expect?

(b) Why are reverse stock splits seen as a sign of weakness? How is a reverse stock split recorded, and how is it reported in the financial statements?

(c) Why are share buybacks considered "a sign of strength"? How are they recorded, and how are they reported in the financial statements?

(d) If you were an AT&T stockholder, would you agree to this reverse stock split? Why or why not?

Professional Research: Financial Accounting and Reporting

Recall from Chapter 13 that Hincapie Co. (a specialty bike-accessory manufacturer) is expecting growth in sales of some products targeted to the low-price market. Hincapie is contemplating a preferred stock issue to help finance this expansion in operations. The company is leaning toward participating preferred stock because ownership will not be diluted, but the investors will get an extra dividend if the company does well. The company management wants to be certain that its reporting of this transaction is transparent to its current shareholders and wants you to research the disclosure requirements related to its capital structure.

Instructions
Using the **Financial Accounting Research System (FARS)**, respond to the following items. (Provide text strings used in your search.)

(a) Identify the FASB standard that addresses disclosure of information about capital structure.

(b) Find definitions for the following:
  (1) Securities.
  (2) Participation rights.
  (3) Preferred stock.

(c) What information about securities must be disclosed? Discuss how the proposed Hincapie preferred stock issue will be reported.

Professional Simulation

In this simulation you are asked to address questions related to the accounting for stockholders' equity. Prepare responses to all parts.

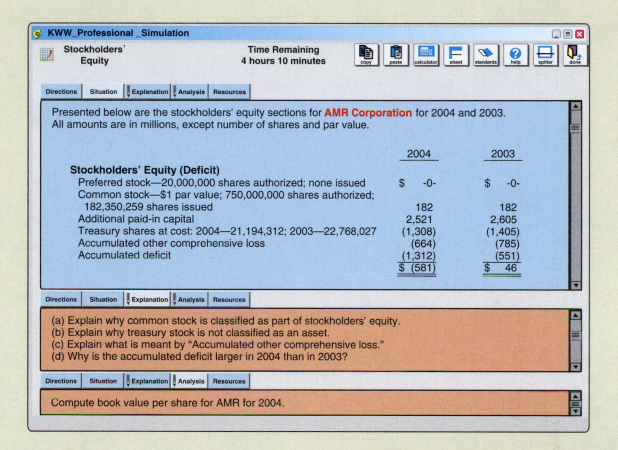

KWW_Professional _Simulation

Stockholders' Equity — Time Remaining 4 hours 10 minutes

copy | paste | calculator | sheet | standards | help | splitter | done

Directions | Situation | Explanation | Analysis | Resources

Presented below are the stockholders' equity sections for **AMR Corporation** for 2004 and 2003. All amounts are in millions, except number of shares and par value.

	2004	2003
Stockholders' Equity (Deficit)		
Preferred stock—20,000,000 shares authorized; none issued	$ -0-	$ -0-
Common stock—$1 par value; 750,000,000 shares authorized;		
182,350,259 shares issued	182	182
Additional paid-in capital	2,521	2,605
Treasury shares at cost: 2004—21,194,312; 2003—22,768,027	(1,308)	(1,405)
Accumulated other comprehensive loss	(664)	(785)
Accumulated deficit	(1,312)	(551)
	$ (581)	$ 46

Directions | Situation | Explanation | Analysis | Resources

(a) Explain why common stock is classified as part of stockholders' equity.
(b) Explain why treasury stock is not classified as an asset.
(c) Explain what is meant by "Accumulated other comprehensive loss."
(d) Why is the accumulated deficit larger in 2004 than in 2003?

Directions | Situation | Explanation | Analysis | Resources

Compute book value per share for AMR for 2004.

Remember to check the book's companion website to find additional resources for this chapter.

wiley.com/college/kieso

DILUTIVE SECURITIES AND EARNINGS PER SHARE

Kicking the Habit

Some habits die hard. Take stock options—called by some "the crack cocaine of incentives." For many years U.S. businesses were hooked. Why? The combination of a hot stock market and favorable accounting treatment made stock options the incentive of choice–they were compensation with no expense, so companies granted them with abandon. However, new accounting rules that take affect in 2006 will require expensing of stock options, which might make it easier for companies to kick this habit. Some changes are surfacing already.

For the third consecutive year, the number of new stock option grants at the 200 largest U.S. companies declined in 2003, with nearly two out of three cutting back. Compensation consultants say the trend continued through 2004 and will accelerate in 2005 and beyond. As a spokesperson at **Progress Energy** commented, "Once you begin expensing options, the attractiveness significantly drops."

By reining in options, many companies may be taking the first steps toward curbing both out-of-control executive pay and the era of corporate corruption that it spawned. In the 1990s, executives with huge option stockpiles had an almost irresistible incentive to do whatever it took to increase the stock price and cash in their options.

Some of the ways that companies are curbing option grants include replacing options with fewer shares of restricted stock. Others are simply reducing option grants, without offering a replacement. For example, in 2004 **Dell** awarded less than half the options compared to two years earlier. And some companies, like **Microsoft** and **Yahoo**, have switched to restricted stock plans.

When the new expensing rules take effect—barring any last-minute congressional intervention—option-reduction strategies likely will become more widespread as companies search for ways to reward talent without breaking the bank. The good news for companies: They have plenty of alternatives to choose from. The positive impact on corporate behavior, while hard to measure, should benefit investors in years to come.[1]

_____

[1]Adapted from: Louis Lavelle, "Kicking the Stock-Options Habit,"*BusinessWeekOnline* (February 16, 2005).

Learning Objectives

After studying this chapter, you should be able to:

1 Describe the accounting for the issuance, conversion, and retirement of convertible securities.

2 Explain the accounting for convertible preferred stock.

3 Contrast the accounting for stock warrants and for stock warrants issued with other securities.

4 Describe the accounting for stock compensation plans under generally accepted accounting principles.

5 Discuss the controversy involving stock compensation plans.

6 Compute earnings per share in a simple capital structure.

7 Compute earnings per share in a complex capital structure.

As the opening story indicates, changes are in store for stock options and their accounting. President George W. Bush, Federal Reserve Board Chair Alan Greenspan, Senators Joseph Lieberman and John McCain, and the guru of investing Warren Buffett all have strong opinions on whether stock options should be reported as an expense in corporate income statements. The purpose of this chapter is to discuss the proper accounting for stock options. In addition, the chapter examines issues related to other types of financial instruments, such as convertible securities, warrants, and contingent shares, including their effects on reporting earnings per share. The content and organization of the chapter are as follows.

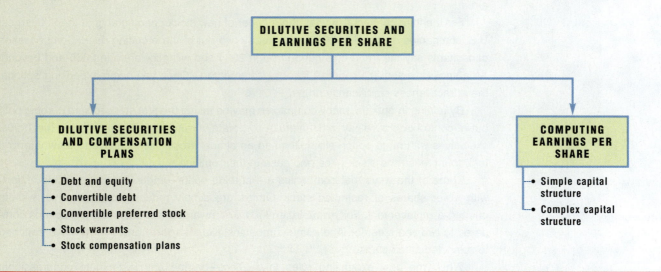

| SECTION 1 | *DILUTIVE SECURITIES AND COMPENSATION PLANS* |

DEBT AND EQUITY

Many of the controversies related to the accounting for financial instruments such as stock options, convertible securities, and preferred stock relate to whether companies should report these instruments as a liability or as equity. For example, companies should classify nonredeemable common shares as equity because the issuer has no **obligation** to pay dividends or repurchase the stock. Declaration of dividends is at the issuer's discretion, as is the decision to repurchase the stock. Similarly, preferred stock that is not redeemable does not require the issuer to pay dividends or repurchase the stock. Thus, nonredeemable common or preferred stock lacks an important characteristic of a liability—an obligation to pay the holder of the common or preferred stock at some point in the future.[2]

However the classification is not as clear-cut for other financial instruments. For example, in Chapter 15 we discussed the accounting for mandatorily redeemable preferred

---

[2] "Accounting for Certain Financial Instruments with Characteristics of Both Liabilities and Equity," *Statement of Financial Accounting Standards No. 150*, (Norwalk Conn.: FASB, 2003), par. 23.

stock. Companies originally classified this security as part of equity. The SEC then prohibited equity classification, and most companies classified these securities between debt and equity on the balance sheet in a separate section often referred to as the "mezzanine section." Recently the FASB issued a standard that requires companies to report these types of securities as a liability.[3]

In this chapter, we discuss securities that have characteristics of *both* debt and equity. For example, a convertible bond has both debt and equity characteristics. Should a company classify this security as debt, as equity, or as part debt and part equity? In addition, how should a company compute earnings per share if it has convertible bonds and other convertible securities in its capital structure? Convertible securities as well as options, warrants, and other securities are often called **dilutive securities** because upon exercise they may reduce (dilute) earnings per share.

ACCOUNTING FOR CONVERTIBLE DEBT

Convertible bonds can be converted into other corporate securities during some specified period of time after issuance. A convertible bond combines the benefits of a bond with the privilege of exchanging it for stock at the holder's option. Investors who purchase it desire the security of a bond holding (guaranteed interest and principal) plus the added option of conversion if the value of the stock appreciates significantly.

OBJECTIVE 1
Describe the accounting for the issuance, conversion, and retirement of convertible securities.

Corporations issue convertibles for two main reasons. One is to raise equity capital without giving up more ownership control than necessary. To illustrate, assume a company wants to raise $1 million; its common stock is selling at $45 a share. To raise the $1 million, the company would have to sell 22,222 shares (ignoring issue costs). By selling 1,000 bonds at $1,000 par, each convertible into 20 shares of common stock, the company could raise $1 million by committing only 20,000 shares of its common stock.

A second reason to issue convertibles is to obtain debt financing at cheaper rates. Many companies could issue debt only at high interest rates unless they attach a convertible covenant. The conversion privilege entices the investor to accept a lower interest rate than would normally be the case on a straight debt issue. For example, **Amazon.com** at one time issued convertible bonds that pay interest at an effective yield of 4.75 percent. This rate was much lower than Amazon.com would have had to pay by issuing straight debt. For this lower interest rate, the investor receives the right to buy Amazon.com's common stock at a fixed price until the bond's maturity.[4]

As indicated earlier, the accounting for convertible debt involves reporting issues at the time of (1) issuance, (2) conversion, and (3) retirement.

At Time of Issuance

The method for recording convertible bonds **at the date of issue follows the method used to record straight debt issues**. None of the proceeds are recorded as equity. Companies amortize to its maturity date any discount or premium that results from the issuance of convertible bonds. Why this treatment? Because it is difficult to predict when, if at all, conversion will occur. However, the accounting for convertible debt as a straight debt issue is controversial; we discuss it more fully later in the chapter.

---

[3]Ibid, par. 9.

[4]As with any investment, a buyer has to be careful. For example, **Wherehouse Entertainment Inc.**, which had 6¼ percent convertibles outstanding, was taken private in a leveraged buyout. As a result, the convertible was suddenly as risky as a junk bond of a highly leveraged company with a coupon of only 6¼ percent. As one holder of the convertibles noted, "What's even worse is that the company will be so loaded down with debt that it probably won't have enough cash flow to make its interest payments. And the convertible debt we hold is subordinated to the rest of Wherehouse's debt." These types of situations have made convertibles less attractive and have led to the introduction of takeover protection covenants in some convertible bond offerings. Or, sometimes convertibles are permitted to be called at par, and therefore the conversion premium may be lost.

At Time of Conversion

If converting bonds into other securities, a company uses the **book value method** to record the conversion. The book value method records the securities exchanged for the bond at the carrying amount (book value) of the bond.

To illustrate, assume that Hilton, Inc. has a $1,000 bond that is convertible into 10 shares of common stock (par value $10). At the time of conversion, the unamortized premium is $50. Hilton records the conversion of the bonds as follows.

Bonds Payable	1,000	
Premium on Bonds Payable	50	
Common Stock		100
Paid-in Capital in Excess of Par		950

Support for the book value approach is based on the argument that an agreement was established at the date of the issuance either to pay a stated amount of cash at maturity or to issue a stated number of shares of equity securities. Therefore, when the debtholder converts the debt to equity in accordance with the preexisting contract terms, the issuing company recognizes no gain or loss upon conversion.

Induced Conversions

Sometimes the issuer wishes to encourage prompt conversion of its convertible debt to equity securities in order to reduce interest costs or to improve its debt to equity ratio. Thus, the issuer may offer some form of additional consideration (such as cash or common stock), called a "sweetener," to **induce conversion**. The issuing company reports the sweetener as an expense of the current period. Its amount is the fair value of the additional securities or other consideration given.

Assume that Helloid, Inc. has outstanding $1,000,000 par value convertible debentures convertible into 100,000 shares of $1 par value common stock. Helloid wishes to reduce its annual interest cost. To do so, Helloid agrees to pay the holders of its convertible debentures an additional $80,000 if they will convert. Assuming conversion occurs, Helloid makes the following entry.

Debt Conversion Expense	80,000	
Bonds Payable	1,000,000	
Common Stock		100,000
Additional Paid-in Capital		900,000
Cash		80,000

Helloid records the additional $80,000 as **an expense of the current period** and not as a reduction of equity.

Some argue that the cost of a conversion inducement is a cost of obtaining equity capital. As a result, they contend, companies should recognize the cost of conversion as a cost of (a reduction of) the equity capital acquired, and not as an expense. However, the FASB indicated that when an issuer makes an additional payment to encourage conversion, the payment is for a service (bondholders converting at a given time) and should be reported as an expense. The issuing company does not report this expense as an extraordinary item.[5]

Retirement of Convertible Debt

As indicated earlier, the method for recording the **issuance** of convertible bonds follows that used in recording straight debt issues. Specifically this means that issuing companies should not attribute any portion of the proceeds to the conversion feature, nor should it credit Additional Paid-in Capital.

Although some raise theoretical objections to this approach, to be consistent, companies need to recognize a gain or loss on **retiring convertible debt in the same way**

---

[5]"Induced Conversions of Convertible Debt,"*Statement of Financial Accounting Standards No. 84* (Stamford, Conn.: FASB, 1985).

that they recognize a gain or loss on retiring nonconvertible debt. For this reason, companies should report differences between the cash acquisition price of debt and its carrying amount **in current income as a gain or loss.**

CONVERTIBLE PREFERRED STOCK

Convertible preferred stock includes an option for the holder to convert preferred shares into a fixed number of common shares. The major difference between accounting for a convertible bond and convertible preferred stock at the date of issue is their classification: Convertible bonds are considered liabilities, whereas convertible preferreds (unless mandatory redemption exists) are considered part of stockholders' equity.

> **OBJECTIVE 2**
> Explain the accounting for convertible preferred stock.

In addition, when stockholders exercise convertible preferred stock, there is no theoretical justification for recognizing a gain or loss. A company does not recognize a gain or loss when it deals with stockholders in their capacity as business owners. Therefore, companies do not recognize a gain or loss when stockholders exercise convertible preferred stock.

In accounting for the exercise of convertible preferred stock, a company uses the **book value method**: It debits Preferred Stock, along with any related Additional Paid-in Capital, and it credits Common Stock and Additional Paid-in Capital (if an excess exists). The treatment differs when the par value of the common stock issued **exceeds** the book value of the preferred stock. In that case, the company usually debits Retained Earnings for the difference.

To illustrate, assume Host Enterprises issued 1,000 shares of common stock (par value $2) upon conversion of 1,000 shares of preferred stock (par value $1) that was originally issued for a $200 premium. The entry would be:

Convertible Preferred Stock	1,000	
Paid-in Capital in Excess of Par (Premium on Preferred Stock)	200	
Retained Earnings	800	
Common Stock		2,000

The rationale for the debit to Retained Earnings is that Host has offered the preferred stockholders an **additional return** to facilitate their conversion to common stock. In this example, Host charges the additional return to retained earnings. Many states, however, require that this charge simply reduce additional paid-in capital from other sources.

HOW LOW CAN YOU GO?

Financial engineers are always looking for the next innovation in security design to meet the needs of both issuers and investors. Consider the convertible bonds issued by **STMicroelectronics** (STM). STM's 10-year bonds have a zero coupon and are convertible into STM common stock at an exercise price of $33.43. When issued, the bonds sold at an effective yield of −0.05 percent. That's right–a negative yield.

WHAT DO THE NUMBERS MEAN?

How could this happen? When STM issued the bonds, investors thought the options to convert were so valuable that they were willing to take zero interest payments and invest an amount *in excess of* the maturity value of the bonds. In essence, the investors are paying interest to STM, and STM records interest revenue. Why would investors do this? If the stock price rises, as many thought it would for STM and many tech companies at this time, these bond investors could convert and get a big gain in the stock.

Investors did get some additional protection in the deal: They can redeem the $1,000 bonds after three years and receive $975 (and after five and seven years, for lower amounts), if it looks like the bonds will never convert. In the end, STM has issued bonds with a significant equity component. And because the entire bond issue is classified as debt, STM records negative interest expense.

Source: STM Financial Reports. See also Floyd Norris, "Legal but Absurd: They Borrow a Billion and Report a Profit," *New York Times* (August 8, 2003), p. C1.

STOCK WARRANTS

OBJECTIVE 3
Contrast the accounting for stock warrants and for stock warrants issued with other securities.

Warrants are certificates entitling the holder to acquire shares of stock at a certain price within a stated period. This option is similar to the conversion privilege: Warrants, if exercised, become common stock and usually have a dilutive effect (reduce earnings per share) similar to that of the conversion of convertible securities. However, a substantial difference between convertible securities and stock warrants is that upon exercise of the warrants, the holder has to pay a certain amount of money to obtain the shares.

The issuance of warrants or options to buy additional shares normally arises under three situations:

1 When issuing different types of securities, such as bonds or preferred stock, companies often include warrants **to make the security more attractive**—by providing an "equity kicker."

2 Upon the issuance of additional common stock, existing stockholders have a **preemptive right to purchase common stock** first. Companies may issue warrants to evidence that right.

3 Companies give warrants, often referred to as *stock options*, **to executives and employees** as a form of **compensation**.

The problems in accounting for stock warrants are complex and present many difficulties—some of which remain unresolved.

Stock Warrants Issued with Other Securities

Warrants issued with other securities are basically long-term options to buy common stock at a fixed price. Generally the life of warrants is five years, occasionally 10 years; very occasionally, a company may offer perpetual warrants.

A warrant works like this: **Tenneco, Inc.** offered a unit comprising one share of stock and one detachable warrant. As its name implies, the **detachable stock warrant** can be "detached" from the stock and traded as a separate security. The Tenneco warrant in this example is exercisable at $24.25 per share and good for five years. The unit (share of stock plus detachable warrant) sold for 22.75 ($22.75). Since the price of the common stock the day before the sale was 19.88 ($19.88), the difference suggests a price of 2.87 ($2.87) for the warrant.

The investor pays for the warrant in order to receive the right to buy the stock, at a fixed price of $24.25, sometime in the future. It would not be profitable at present for the purchaser to exercise the warrant and buy the stock, because the price of the stock was much below the exercise price.[6] But if, for example, the price of the stock rises to $30, the investor gains $2.88 ($30 − $24.25 − $2.87) on an investment of $2.87, a 100 percent increase! If the price never rises, the investor loses the full $2.87 per warrant.[7]

A company should allocate the proceeds from the sale of debt with detachable stock warrants **between the two securities**.[8] The profession takes the position that two separable instruments are involved, that is, (1) a bond and (2) a warrant giving the holder the right to purchase common stock at a certain price. Companies can trade detachable

---

[6]Later in this discussion we will show that the value of the warrant is normally determined on the basis of a relative market-value approach because of the difficulty of imputing a warrant value in any other manner.

[7]From the illustration, it is apparent that buying warrants can be an "all or nothing" proposition.

[8]A detachable warrant means that the warrant can sell separately from the bond. *APB Opinion No. 14* makes a distinction between detachable and nondetachable warrants because companies must sell nondetachable warrants with the security as a complete package. Thus, no allocation is permitted.

warrants separately from the debt. This allows the determination of a market value. The two methods of allocation available are:

1 The proportional method.
2 The incremental method.

Proportional Method

At one time **AT&T** issued bonds with detachable five-year warrants to buy one share of common stock (par value $5) at $25. At the time, a share of AT&T stock was selling for approximately $50. These warrants enabled AT&T to price its bond offering at par with an 8¾ percent yield (quite a bit lower than prevailing rates at that time). To account for the proceeds from this offering, AT&T would place a value on the two securities: (1) the value of the bonds without the warrants, and (2) the value of the warrants. The **proportional method** then allocates the proceeds using the proportion of the two amounts, based on fair values.

For example, assume that AT&T's bonds (par $1,000) sold for 99 without the warrants soon after their issue. The market value of the warrants at that time was $30. (Prior to sale the warrants will not have a market value.) The allocation relies on an estimate of market value, generally as established by an investment banker, or on the relative market value of the bonds and the warrants soon after the company issues and trades them. The price paid for 10,000, $1,000 bonds with the warrants attached was par, or $10,000,000. Illustration 16-1 shows the proportional allocation of the bond proceeds between the bonds and warrants.

Fair market value of bonds (without warrants) ($10,000,000 × .99)	$ 9,900,000
Fair market value of warrants (10,000 × $30)	300,000
Aggregate fair market value	$10,200,000
Allocated to bonds: $\dfrac{\$9,900,000}{\$10,200,000} \times \$10,000,000 = $	$ 9,705,882
Allocated to warrants: $\dfrac{\$300,000}{\$10,200,000} \times \$10,000,000 = $	294,118
Total allocation	$10,000,000

ILLUSTRATION 16-1
Proportional Allocation of Proceeds between Bonds and Warrants

In this situation the bonds sell at a discount. AT&T records the sale as follows.

Cash	9,705,882	
Discount on Bonds Payable	294,118	
Bonds Payable		10,000,000

In addition, AT&T sells warrants that it credits to paid-in capital. It makes the following entry.

Cash	294,118	
Paid-in Capital—Stock Warrants		294,118

AT&T may combine the entries if desired. Here, we show them separately, to indicate that the purchaser of the bond is buying not only a bond, but also a possible future claim on common stock.

Assuming investors exercise all 10,000 warrants (one warrant per one share of stock), AT&T makes the following entry.

Cash (10,000 × $25)	250,000	
Paid-in Capital—Stock Warrants	294,118	
Common Stock (10,000 × $5)		50,000
Paid-in Capital in Excess of Par		494,118

What if investors fail to exercise the warrants? In that case, AT&T debits Paid-in Capital—Stock Warrants for $294,118, and credits Paid-in Capital from Expired

Warrants for a like amount. The additional paid-in capital reverts to the former stockholders.

Incremental Method

In instances where a company cannot determine the fair value of either the warrants or the bonds, it applies the **incremental method** used in lump-sum security purchases (as explained in Chapter 15, page 731). That is, the company uses the security for which it *can* determine the fair value. It allocates the remainder of the purchase price to the security for which it does not know the fair value.

For example, assume that the market price of the AT&T warrants is $300,000, but the company cannot determine the market price of the bonds without the warrants. Illustration 16-2 shows the amount allocated to the warrants and the stock in this case.

ILLUSTRATION 16-2
Incremental Allocation of Proceeds between Bonds and Warrants

Lump-sum receipt	$10,000,000
Allocated to the warrants	300,000
Balance allocated to bonds	$ 9,700,000

Conceptual Questions

The question arises whether the allocation of value to the warrants is consistent with the handling of convertible debt, in which companies allocate no value to the conversion privilege. The FASB stated that the features of a convertible security are **inseparable** in the sense that choices are mutually exclusive: The holder either converts the bonds or redeems them for cash, but cannot do both. No basis, therefore, exists for recognizing the conversion value in the accounts.

UNDERLYING CONCEPTS

Reporting a convertible bond solely as debt is not representationally faithful. However, the cost-benefit constraint is used to justify the failure to allocate between debt and equity.

The Board, however, indicated that the issuance of bonds with **detachable warrants** involves *two* securities, one a debt security, which will remain outstanding until maturity, and the other a warrant to purchase common stock. At the time of issuance, separable instruments exist. The existence of two instruments therefore justifies separate treatment. **Nondetachable warrants**, however, **do not require an allocation of the proceeds between the bonds and the warrants**. Similar to the accounting for convertible bonds, companies record the entire proceeds from nondetachable warrants as debt.

Many argue that the conversion feature of a convertible bond is not significantly different in nature from the call represented by a warrant. The question is whether, although the legal forms differ, sufficient similarities of substance exist to support the same accounting treatment. Some contend that inseparability *per se* is an insufficient basis for restricting allocation between identifiable components of a transaction. Examples of allocation between assets of value in a single transaction *do* exist, such as allocation of values in basket purchases and separation of principal and interest in capitalizing long-term leases. Critics of the current accounting for convertibles say that to deny recognition of value to the conversion feature merely looks to the form of the instrument and does not deal with the substance of the transaction.

INTERNATIONAL INSIGHT

International accounting standards require that the issuer of convertible debt record the liability and equity components separately.

In its current exposure draft on this subject, the FASB indicates that companies should separate the debt and equity components of securities such as convertible debt or bonds issued with nondetachable warrants. We agree with this position. In both situations (convertible debt and debt issued with warrants), the investor has made a payment to the company for an equity feature—the right to acquire an equity instrument in the future. The only real distinction between them is that the additional payment made when the equity instrument is formally acquired takes different forms. The warrant holder pays additional cash to the issuing company; the convertible debt holder pays for stock by forgoing the receipt of interest from conversion date until maturity date and by forgoing the receipt of the maturity value itself. Thus, the difference is one of method or form of payment only, rather than one of substance. However, until the profession officially reverses its stand in regard to accounting for convertible debt, companies will continue to report convertible debt and bonds issued with nondetachable warrants solely as debt.[9]

Rights to Subscribe to Additional Shares

If the directors of a corporation decide to issue new shares of stock, the old stockholders generally have the right (**preemptive privilege**) to purchase newly issued shares in proportion to their holdings. This privilege, referred to as a **stock right**, saves existing stockholders from suffering a dilution of voting rights without their consent. Also, it may allow them to purchase stock somewhat below its market value. Unlike the warrants issued with other securities, the warrants issued for stock rights are of short duration.

The certificate representing the stock right states the number of shares the holder of the right may purchase. Each share of stock owned ordinarily gives the owner one stock right. The certificate also states the price at which the new shares may be purchased. The price is normally less than the current market value of such shares, which gives the rights a value in themselves. From the time they are issued until they expire, holders of stock rights may purchase and sell them like any other security.

Companies make only a memorandum entry when they issue rights to existing stockholders. This entry indicates the number of rights issued to existing stockholders in order to ensure that the company has additional unissued stock registered for issuance in case the rights are exercised. Companies make no formal entry at this time because they have not yet issued stock nor received cash.

If holders exercise the stock rights, a cash payment of some type usually is involved. If the company receives cash equal to the par value, it makes an entry crediting Common Stock at par value. If the company receives cash in excess of par value, it credits Paid-in Capital in Excess of Par. If it receives cash less than par value, a debit to Paid-in Capital is appropriate.

STOCK COMPENSATION PLANS

Another form of warrant arises in stock compensation plans to pay and motivate employees. This warrant is a **stock option**, which gives key employees the option to purchase common stock at a given price over an extended period of time. As indicated in our opening story, the FASB has recently issued a new standard on stock options and other types of compensation plans that are stock-based. Illustration 16-3 (on page 786) shows how this standard is already affecting how companies are using stock options.

Illustration 16-3 indicates that option expense is considerable but that it peaked in 2002 and now is declining. The major reasons for this decline are two-fold. Critics often cited the indiscriminate use of stock options as a reason why company executives manipulated accounting numbers in an attempt to achieve higher share price. As a result, many responsible companies decided to cut back on the issuance of options, both to avoid such accounting manipulations and to head off investor doubts. In addition, the FASB's new standard will result in companies recording a higher expense when these options are granted.

---

[9]"Proposed Statement of Financial Accounting Standards Accounting for Financial Instruments with Characteristics of Liabilities, Equity, or Both; Summary (FASB, Norwalk, Conn.: October 2000). Academic research indicates that estimates of the debt and equity components of convertible bonds are subject to considerable measurement error. See Mary Barth, Wayne Landsman, and Richard Rendleman, Jr., "Option Pricing–Based Bond Value Estimates and a Fundamental Components Approach to Account for Corporate Debt," *The Accounting Review* (January 1998). This and other challenges explain in part the extended time needed to develop new standards in this area.

ILLUSTRATION 16-3
Stock Option
Compensation Expense

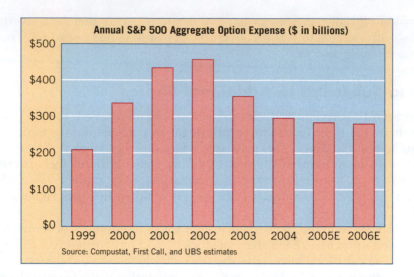

The data reported in Illustration 16-4 reinforces the point that the design of compensation plans is changing. The study documents recent compensation trends of 68 CEOs of companies in the S&P 500.

ILLUSTRATION 16-4
Compensation Elements

	2004	% Change from 2003
Total direct compensation	$7,247,903	8.8%
Salary	908,269	4.1
Bonus	975,000	32.6
Value of stock options	3,217,811	(18.7)
Restricted stock	2,679,435	34.0
Long-term incentive payouts	773,719	72.1

Sources: Compustat, First Call, UBS, Equilar, Inc.

What Illustration 16-4 shows is that cash compensation is increasing. In addition, long-term incentives are increasing, but the compensation mix is changing. For example, the use of restricted stock jumped 34 percent, but the use of options decreased approximately 19 percent. Yet, stock options remain the primary means of compensating these CEOs. As Illustrations 16-3 and 16-4 indicate, stock-based compensation is still a considerable incentive element of employee compensation.

A consensus of opinion is that effective compensation programs are ones that do the following: (1) motivate employees to high levels of performance, (2) help retain executives and allow for recruitment of new talent, (3) base compensation on employee and company performance, (4) maximize the employee's after-tax benefit and minimize the employer's after-tax cost, and (5) use performance criteria over which the employee has control. Straight cash compensation plans (salary and perhaps a bonus), though important, are oriented to the short run. Many companies recognize that they need a longer-term compensation plan in addition to the cash component.

Long-term compensation plans attempt to develop company loyalty among key employees. An effective way to do so is to give employees "a piece of the action"—that is, an equity interest. These plans, generally referred to as **stock-based compensation plans**, come in many forms. Essentially, they provide the employee with the opportunity to receive stock if the performance of the company (by whatever measure) is satisfactory. Typical performance measures focus on long-term improvements that are readily measurable and that benefit the company as a whole, such as increases in earnings per share, revenues, stock price, or market share.

The Major Reporting Issue

Suppose that as an employee for Hurdle Inc., you receive options to purchase 10,000 shares of the firm's common stock as part of your compensation. The date you receive the options is referred to as the **grant date**. The options are good for 10 years. The market price and the exercise price for the stock are both $20 at the grant date. **What is the value of the compensation you just received?**

Some believe that what you have received has no value. They reason that because the difference between the market price and the exercise price is zero, no compensation results. Others argue these options do have value: If the stock price goes above $20 any time in the next 10 years and you exercise the options, you may earn substantial compensation. For example, if at the end of the fourth year, the market price of the stock is $30 and you exercise your options, you earn $100,000 [10,000 options × ($30 − $20)], ignoring income taxes.

The question for Hurdle is how to report the granting of these options. One approach measures compensation cost by the excess of the market price of the stock over its exercise price at the grant date. This approach is referred to as the **intrinsic-value method**. It measures what the holder would receive today if the option was immediately exercised. That intrinsic value **is the difference between the market price of the stock and the exercise price of the options at the grant date.** Using the intrinsic-value method, Hurdle would not recognize any compensation expense related to your options because at the grant date the market price equaled the exercise price. (In the preceding paragraph, those who answered that the options had no value were looking at the question from the intrinsic-value approach.)

The second way to look at the question of how to report the granting of these options bases the cost of employee stock options on the **fair value** of the stock options granted. Under this **fair-value method**, companies use acceptable option-pricing models to value the options at the date of grant. These models take into account the many factors that determine an option's underlying value.[10]

Under previous accounting standards, companies could recognize stock-based compensation using *either* the intrinsic-value method *or* the fair-value method. Given a choice, most companies adopted the intrinsic-value approach because it generally resulted in lower compensation expense. However, in 2002 a number of companies began voluntarily to switch to the fair-value method. By March 2004 over 500 public companies were using the fair-value method. As indicated earlier, a major reason for the change was the desire by companies to show the investing community that they believe in fair and transparent financial reporting, particularly in the aftermath of the many financial reporting scandals.

However, the choice between two methods was not ideal. Some companies included in their income figures the cost of stock-based compensation (the fair-value approach). Others did not. Analysts raised concerns about lack of comparability, and the FASB developed a new standard for stock-based compensation.

The new FASB standard requires that companies recognize compensation cost using the fair-value method.[11] The FASB position is that companies should base the accounting for the cost of employee services on the fair value of compensation paid. This amount is presumed to be a measure of the value of the services received. We will discuss more about the politics of this new standard later (see "Debate over Stock Option Accounting," page 791). Let's first describe the procedures involved.

---

[10]These factors include the volatility of the underlying stock, the expected life of the options, the risk-free rate during the option life, and expected dividends during the option life.

[11]"Accounting for Stock-Based Compensation," *Statement of Financial Accounting Standards No. 123* (Norwalk, Conn: FASB, 1995); and "Share-Based Payment," *Statement of Financial Accounting Standard No. 123(R)* (Norwalk, Conn: FASB, 2004).

Accounting for Stock Compensation

OBJECTIVE 4
Describe the accounting for stock compensation plans under generally accepted accounting principles.

Stock option plans involve two main accounting issues:

1 How to determine compensation expense.

2 Over what periods to allocate compensation expense.

Determining Expense

Under the fair-value method, companies compute total compensation expense based on the fair value of the options expected to vest on the date they grant the options to the employee(s) (i.e., the **grant date**).[12] Public companies estimate fair value by using an option pricing model, with some adjustments for the unique factors of employee stock options. No adjustments occur after the grant date in response to subsequent changes in the stock price—either up or down.

A LITTLE HONESTY GOES A LONG WAY

WHAT DO THE NUMBERS MEAN?

Before adoption of *SFAS No. 123(R)*, companies could choose whether to expense stock-based compensation or simply disclose the estimated costs in the notes to the financial statements. You might think investors would punish companies that decided to expense stock options. After all, most of corporate America has been battling for years to avoid having to expense them, worried that accounting for those perks would destroy earnings. And indeed, **Merrill Lynch** estimated that if all S&P 500 companies were to expense options, reported profits would fall by as much as 10 percent.

Yet, as a small but growing band of big-name companies voluntarily made the switch to expensing, investors for the most part showered them with love. With a few exceptions, the stock prices of the "expensers," from **Cinergy** to **The Washington Post**, outpaced the market after they announced the change.

The few, the brave

Company	Estimated EPS Without options	Estimated EPS With options expensed	% change since announcement Company stock price
Cinergy	$ 2.80	$ 2.77	22.4%
The Washington Post	20.48	20.10	16.4
Computer Associates	−0.46	−0.62	11.1
Fannie Mae	6.15	6.02	6.7
Bank One	2.77	2.61	2.6
General Motors	5.84	5.45	2.6
Procter & Gamble	3.57	3.35	−2.3
Coca-Cola	1.79	1.70	−6.2
General Electric	1.65	1.61	−6.2
Amazon.com	0.04	−0.99	−11.4

Data sources: Merrill Lynch; company reports.

Given the market's general positive reaction to the transparent reporting of stock options, it is puzzling why some companies continued to fight implementation of *SFAS No. 123(R)*.

Source: David Stires, "A Little Honesty Goes a Long Way," *Fortune* (September 2, 2002), p. 186. Reprinted by permission. See also Troy Wolverton, "Foes of Expensing Welcome FASB Delay," *TheStreet.com* (October 15, 2004).

---

[12]"To vest" means "to earn the rights to." An employee's award becomes vested at the date that the employee's right to receive or retain shares of stock or cash under the award is no longer contingent on remaining in the service of the employer.

Allocating Compensation Expense

In general, a company recognizes compensation expense in the periods in which its employees perform the service—the **service period**. Unless otherwise specified, the service period is the vesting period—the time between the grant date and the vesting date. Thus, the company determines total compensation cost at the grant date and allocates it to the periods benefited by its employees' services.

Stock Compensation Example

An example will help show the accounting for a stock option plan.[13] Assume that on November 1, 2005, the stockholders of Chen Company approve a plan that grants the company's five executives options to purchase 2,000 shares each of the company's $1 par value common stock. The company grants the options on January 1, 2006. The executives may exercise the options at any time within the next 10 years. The option price per share is $60, and the market price of the stock at the date of grant is $70 per share.

Under the fair-value method, the company computes total compensation expense by applying an acceptable fair value option-pricing model (such as the Black-Scholes option-pricing model). To keep this illustration simple, we assume that the fair-value option-pricing model determines Chen's total compensation expense to be $220,000.

Basic Entries. Under the fair-value method, a company recognizes the value of the options as an expense in the periods in which the employee performs services. In the case of Chen Company, assume that the expected period of benefit is two years, starting with the grant date. Chen would record the transactions related to this option contract as follows.

At date of grant (January 1, 2006)

No entry.

To record compensation expense for 2006 (December 31, 2006)

Compensation Expense	110,000	
Paid-in Capital—Stock Options ($220,000 ÷ 2)		110,000

To record compensation expense for 2007 (December 31, 2007)

Compensation Expense	110,000	
Paid-in Capital—Stock Options		110,000

As indicated, Chen allocates compensation expense evenly over the two-year service period.

Exercise. If Chen's executives exercise 2,000 of the 10,000 options (20 percent of the options) on June 1, 2009 (three years and five months after date of grant), the company records the following journal entry.

June 1, 2009

Cash (2,000 × $60)	120,000	
Paid-in Capital—Stock Options (20% × $220,000)	44,000	
Common Stock (2,000 × $1.00)		2,000
Paid-in Capital in Excess of Par		162,000

Expiration. If Chen's executives fail to exercise the remaining stock options before their expiration date, the company transfers the balance in the Paid-in Capital—Stock Options account to a more properly titled paid-in capital account, such as Paid-in Capital from Expired Stock Options. Chen records this transaction at the date of expiration as follows.

January 1, 2016 (expiration date)

Paid-in Capital—Stock Options	176,000	
Paid-in Capital from Expired Stock Options		176,000
(80% × $220,000)		

---

[13]We discuss the accounting for other types of stock-based compensation in Appendix 16A.

Adjustment. An unexercised stock option does not nullify the need to record the costs of services received from executives and attributable to the stock option plan. Under GAAP, a company therefore does not adjust compensation expense upon expiration of the options.

However, if an employee forfeits a stock option because **the employee fails to satisfy a service requirement** (e.g., leaves employment), the company should adjust the estimate of compensation expense recorded in the current period (as a change in estimate). A company records this change in estimate by debiting Paid-in Capital—Stock Options and crediting Compensation Expense for the amount of cumulative compensation expense recorded to date (thus decreasing compensation expense in the period of forfeiture.)

Employee Stock Purchase Plans

Employee stock purchase plans (ESPPs) generally permit all employees to purchase stock at a discounted price for a short period of time. The company often uses such plans to secure equity capital or to induce widespread ownership of its common stock among employees. These plans are considered compensatory unless they satisfy **all three** conditions presented below.

1   Substantially all full-time employees may participate on an equitable basis.
2   The discount from market is small. That is, the discount does not exceed the per share amount of costs avoided by not having to raise cash in a public offering. If the amount of the discount is 5 percent or less, no compensation needs to be recorded.
3   The plan offers no substantive option feature.

For example, Masthead Company's stock purchase plan allowed employees who met minimal employment qualifications to purchase its stock at a 5 percent reduction from market price for a short period of time. The reduction from market price is not considered compensatory. Why? Because the per share amount of the costs avoided by not having to raise the cash in a public offering equals 5 percent.

Companies that offer their employees a compensatory ESPP should record the compensation expense over the service life of the employees. It will be difficult for some companies to claim that their ESPPs are non-compensatory (and therefore not record compensation expense) unless they change their discount policy which in the past often was 15 percent. If they change their discount policy to 5 percent, participation in these plans will undoubtedly be lower. As a result, it is likely that some companies will end up dropping these plans.

Disclosure of Compensation Plans

Companies must fully disclose the status of their compensation plans at the end of the periods presented. To meet these objectives, companies must make extensive disclosures. Specifically, a company with one or more share-based payment arrangements must disclose information that enables users of the financial statements to understand:

1   The nature and terms of such arrangements that existed during the period and the potential effects of those arrangements on shareholders.
2   The effect on the income statement of compensation cost arising from share-based payment arrangements.
3   The method of estimating the fair value of the goods or services received, or the fair value of the equity instruments granted (or offered to grant), during the period.
4   The cash flow effects resulting from share-based payment arrangements.

Illustration 16-5 presents the type of information disclosed for compensation plans.

The Company has a share-based compensation plan. The compensation cost that has been charged against income for the plan was $29.4 million, and $28.7 million for 2007 and 2006, respectively.

The Company's 2007 Employee Share Option Plan (the Plan), which is shareholder-approved, permits the grant of share options and shares to its employees for up to 8 million shares of common stock. The Company believes that such awards better align the interests of its employees with those of its shareholders. Option awards are generally granted with an exercise price equal to the market price of the Company's stock at the date of grant; those option awards generally vest based on 5 years of continuous service and have 10-year contractual terms. Share awards generally vest over five years. Certain option and share awards provide for accelerated vesting if there is a change in control (as defined by the Plan).

The fair value of each option award is estimated on the date of grant using an option valuation model based on the assumptions noted in the following table.

	2007	2006
Expected volatility	25%–40%	24%–38%
Weighted-average volatility	33%	30%
Expected dividends	1.5%	1.5%
Expected term (in years)	5.3–7.8	5.5–8.0
Risk-free rate	6.3%–11.2%	6.0%–10.0%

A summary of option activity under the Plan as of December 31, 2007, and changes during the year then ended are presented below.

Options	Shares (000)	Weighted-Average Exercise Price	Weighted-Average Remaining Contractual Term	Aggregate Intrinsic Value ($000)
Outstanding at January 1, 2007	4,660	42		
Granted	950	60		
Exercised	(800)	36		
Forfeited or expired	(80)	59		
Outstanding at December 31, 2007	4,730	47	6.5	85,140
Exercisable at December 31, 2007	3,159	41	4.0	75,816

The weighted-average grant-date fair value of options granted during the years 2007 and 2006 was $19.57 and $17.46, respectively. The total intrinsic value of options exercised during the years ended December 31, 2007 and 2006, was $25.2 million, and $20.9 million, respectively.

As of December 31, 2007, there was $25.9 million of total unrecognized compensation cost related to nonvested share-based compensation arrangements granted under the Plan. That cost is expected to be recognized over a weighted-average period of 4.9 years. The total fair value of shares vested during the years ended December 31, 2007 and 2006, was $22.8 million and $21 million, respectively.

ILLUSTRATION 16-5
Stock Option Plan Disclosure

Debate over Stock Option Accounting

The FASB faced considerable opposition when it proposed the fair-value method for accounting for stock options. This is not surprising, given that the fair-value method results in greater compensation costs relative to the intrinsic-value model. As the "What Do the Numbers Mean?" box on page 788 indicated, one study documented that, on average, companies in the Standard & Poor's 500 stock index overstated earnings in a recent year by 10 percent through the use of the intrinsic-value method. Nevertheless, some companies, such as **Coca-Cola**, **General Electric**, **Wachovia**, **Bank One**, and **The Washington Post**, decided to use the fair-value method. As the CFO of Coca-Cola stated, "There is no doubt that stock options are compensation. If they weren't, none of us would want them."

Yet many in corporate America resisted the fair-value method. Many small high-technology companies have been especially vocal in their opposition, arguing that only through offering stock options can they attract top professional management. They contend that recognizing large amounts of compensation expense under these plans places them at a competitive disadvantage against larger companies that can withstand higher compensation charges. As one high-tech executive stated, "If your goal is to attack

OBJECTIVE 5
Discuss the controversy involving stock compensation plans.

fat-cat executive compensation in multi-billion dollar firms, then please do so! But not at the expense of the people who are 'running lean and mean,' trying to build businesses and creating jobs in the process."

UNDERLYING CONCEPTS

The stock option controversy involves economic-consequence issues. The FASB believes companies should follow the neutrality concept. Others disagree, noting that factors other than accounting theory should be considered.

The stock option saga is a classic example of the difficulty the FASB faces in issuing an accounting standard. Many powerful interests aligned against the Board. Even some who initially appeared to support the Board's actions later reversed themselves. These efforts undermine the authority of the FASB at a time when it is essential that we restore faith in our financial reporting system.

Transparent financial reporting—including recognition of stock-based expense—should not be criticized because companies will report lower income. We may not like what the financial statements say, but we are always better off when the statements are representationally faithful to the underlying economic substance of transactions.

By leaving stock-based compensation expense out of income, reported income is biased. Biased reporting not only raises concerns about the credibility of companies' reports, but also of financial reporting in general. And even good companies get tainted by the biased reporting of a few "bad apples." If we write standards to achieve some social, economic, or public policy goal, financial reporting loses its credibility.

SECTION 2 | COMPUTING EARNINGS PER SHARE

Companies commonly report per share amounts for the effects of other items, such as a gain or loss on extraordinary items. The financial press also frequently reports earnings per share data. Further, stockholders and potential investors widely use this data in evaluating the profitability of a company. **Earnings per share** indicates the income earned by each share of common stock. Thus, **companies report earnings per share only for common stock**. For example, if Oscar Co. has net income of $300,000 and a weighted average of 100,000 shares of common stock outstanding for the year, earnings per share is $3 ($300,000 ÷ 100,000). Because of the importance of earnings per share information, most companies must report this information on the face of the income statement.[14] The exception, due to cost-benefit considerations, is nonpublic companies.[15] Generally, companies report earnings per share information below net income in the income statement. Illustration 16-6 shows Oscar Co.'s income statement presentation of earnings per share.

ILLUSTRATION 16-6
Income Statement Presentation of EPS

Net income	$300,000
Earnings per share	$3.00

When the income statement contains intermediate components of income, companies should disclose earnings per share for each component. The presentation in Illustration 16-7 is representative.

INTERNATIONAL INSIGHT

The FASB and the IASB are working together on a project to improve EPS accounting by simplifying the computational guidance and thereby increasing the comparability of EPS data on an international basis. A new standard is due to be effective in 2007.

---

[14]"Earnings per Share," *Statement of Financial Accounting Standards No. 128* (Norwalk, Conn: FASB, 1997). For an article on the usefulness of reported EPS data and the application of the qualitative characteristics of accounting information to EPS data, see Lola W. Dudley, "A Critical Look at EPS," *Journal of Accountancy* (August 1985), pp. 102–111.

[15]A nonpublic enterprise is an enterprise (1) whose debt or equity securities are not traded in a public market on a foreign or domestic stock exchange or in the over-the-counter market (including securities quoted locally or regionally), or (2) that is not required to file financial statements with the SEC. An enterprise is not considered a nonpublic enterprise when its financial statements are issued in preparation for the sale of any class of securities in a public market.

Earnings per share:	
Income from continuing operations	$4.00
Loss from discontinued operations, net of tax	0.60
Income before extraordinary item	3.40
Extraordinary gain, net of tax	1.00
Net income	$4.40

ILLUSTRATION 16-7
Income Statement
Presentation of EPS
Components

These disclosures enable the user of the financial statements to recognize the effects on EPS of income from continuing operations, as distinguished from income or loss from irregular items.[16]

EARNINGS PER SHARE—SIMPLE CAPITAL STRUCTURE

A corporation's capital structure is **simple** if it consists only of common stock or includes no **potential common stock** that upon conversion or exercise could dilute earnings per common share. A capital structure is **complex** if it includes securities that could have a dilutive effect on earnings per common share.

OBJECTIVE 6
Compute earnings per share in a simple capital structure.

The computation of earnings per share for a simple capital structure involves two items (other than net income)—(1) preferred stock dividends and (2) weighted-average number of shares outstanding.

Preferred Stock Dividends

As we indicated earlier, earnings per share relates to earnings per common share. When a company has both common and preferred stock outstanding, **it subtracts the current-year preferred stock dividend from net income to arrive at income available to common stockholders**. Illustration 16-8 shows the formula for computing earnings per share.

$$\text{Earnings per Share} = \frac{\text{Net Income} - \text{Preferred Dividends}}{\text{Weighted-Average Number of Shares Outstanding}}$$

ILLUSTRATION 16-8
Formula for Computing
Earnings per Share

In reporting earnings per share information, a company must calculate income available to common stockholders. To do so, the company subtracts dividends on preferred stock from each of the intermediate components of income (income from continuing operations and income before extraordinary items) and finally from net income. If a company declares dividends on preferred stock and a net loss occurs, **the company adds the preferred dividend to the loss** for purposes of computing the loss per share.

If the preferred stock is cumulative and the company declares no dividend in the current year, it subtracts (or adds) **an amount equal to the dividend that it should have declared for the current year only** from net income (or to the loss). The company should have included dividends in arrears for previous years in the previous years' computations.

Weighted-Average Number of Shares Outstanding

In all computations of earnings per share, the **weighted-average number of shares outstanding** during the period constitutes the basis for the per share amounts reported. Shares issued or purchased during the period affect the amount outstanding. Companies

---

[16]Companies should present, either on the face of the income statement or in the notes to the financial statements, per share amounts for discontinued operations and extraordinary items.

must **weight the shares by the fraction of the period they are outstanding**. The rationale for this approach is to find the equivalent number of whole shares outstanding for the year.

To illustrate, assume that Franks Inc. has changes in its common stock shares outstanding for the period as shown in Illustration 16-9.

ILLUSTRATION 16-9
Shares Outstanding, Ending Balance— Franks Inc.

Date	Share Changes	Shares Outstanding
January 1	Beginning balance	90,000
April 1	Issued 30,000 shares for cash	30,000
		120,000
July 1	Purchased 39,000 shares	39,000
		81,000
November 1	Issued 60,000 shares for cash	60,000
December 31	Ending balance	141,000

Franks computes the weighted-average number of shares outstanding as follows.

ILLUSTRATION 16-10
Weighted-Average Number of Shares Outstanding

Dates Outstanding	(A) Shares Outstanding	(B) Fraction of Year	(C) Weighted Shares (A × B)
Jan. 1–Apr. 1	90,000	3/12	22,500
Apr. 1–July 1	120,000	3/12	30,000
July 1–Nov. 1	81,000	4/12	27,000
Nov. 1–Dec. 31	141,000	2/12	23,500
Weighted-average number of shares outstanding			103,000

As Illustration 16-10 shows, 90,000 shares were outstanding for three months, which translates to 22,500 whole shares for the entire year. Because Franks issued additional shares on April 1, it must weight these shares for the time outstanding. When the company purchased 39,000 shares on July 1, it reduced the shares outstanding. Therefore from July 1 to November 1, only 81,000 shares were outstanding, which is equivalent to 27,000 shares. The issuance of 60,000 shares increases shares outstanding for the last two months of the year. Franks then makes a new computation to determine the proper weighted shares outstanding.

Stock Dividends and Stock Splits

When **stock dividends** or **stock splits** occur, companies need to restate the shares outstanding before the stock dividend or split, in order to compute the weighted-average number of shares. For example, assume that Vijay Corporation had 100,000 shares outstanding on January 1 and issued a 25 percent stock dividend on June 30. For purposes of computing a weighted-average for the current year, it assumes the additional 25,000 shares outstanding as a result of the stock dividend to be **outstanding since the beginning of the year**. Thus the weighted-average for the year for Vijay is 125,000 shares.

Companies restate the issuance of a stock dividend or stock split, but not the issuance or repurchase of stock for cash. Why? Because stock splits and stock dividends do not increase or decrease the net assets of the company. The company merely issues additional shares of stock. Because of the added shares, it must restate the weighted-average shares. Restating allows valid comparisons of earnings per share between periods before and after the stock split or stock dividend. Conversely, the issuance or purchase of stock for cash **changes the amount of net assets**. As a result, the company either earns more or less in the future as a result of this change in net assets. Stated another way, **a stock dividend or split does not change the shareholders' total investment**—it only increases (unless it is a reverse stock split) the number of common shares representing this investment.

To illustrate how a stock dividend affects the computation of the weighted-average number of shares outstanding, assume that Sabrina Company has the following changes in its common stock shares during the year.

Date	Share Changes	Shares Outstanding
January 1	Beginning balance	100,000
March 1	Issued 20,000 shares for cash	20,000
		120,000
June 1	60,000 additional shares (50% stock dividend)	60,000
		180,000
November 1	Issued 30,000 shares for cash	30,000
December 31	Ending balance	210,000

ILLUSTRATION 16-11
Shares Outstanding, Ending Balance—Sabrina Company

Sabrina computes the weighted-average number of shares outstanding as follows.

Dates Outstanding	(A) Shares Outstanding	(B) Restatement	(C) Fraction of Year	(D) Weighted Shares (A × B × C)
Jan. 1–Mar. 1	100,000	1.50	2/12	25,000
Mar. 1–June 1	120,000	1.50	3/12	45,000
June 1–Nov. 1	180,000		5/12	75,000
Nov. 1–Dec. 31	210,000		2/12	35,000
Weighted-average number of shares outstanding				180,000

ILLUSTRATION 16-12
Weighted-Average Number of Shares Outstanding—Stock Issue and Stock Dividend

Sabrina must restate the shares outstanding prior to the stock dividend. The company adjusts the shares outstanding from January 1 to June 1 for the stock dividend, so that it now states these shares on the same basis as shares issued subsequent to the stock dividend. Sabrina does not restate shares issued after the stock dividend because they are on the new basis. The stock dividend simply restates existing shares. **The same type of treatment applies to a stock split.**

If a stock dividend or stock split occurs after the end of the year, but before issuing the financial statements, a company must restate the weighted-average number of shares outstanding for the year (and any other years presented in comparative form). For example, assume that Hendricks Company computes its weighted-average number of shares as 100,000 for the year ended December 31, 2006. On January 15, 2007, before issuing the financial statements, the company splits its stock 3 for 1. In this case, the weighted-average number of shares used in computing earnings per share for 2006 is now 300,000 shares. If providing earnings per share information for 2005 as comparative information, Hendricks must also adjust it for the stock split.

Comprehensive Example

Let's study a comprehensive illustration for a simple capital structure. Darin Corporation has income before extraordinary item of $580,000 and an extraordinary gain, net of tax of $240,000. In addition, it has declared preferred dividends of $1 per share on

100,000 shares of preferred stock outstanding. Darin also has the following changes in its common stock shares outstanding during 2006.

ILLUSTRATION 16-13
Shares Outstanding, Ending Balance—Darin Corp.

Dates	Share Changes	Shares Outstanding
January 1	Beginning balance	180,000
May 1	Purchased 30,000 treasury shares	30,000
		150,000
July 1	300,000 additional shares (3-for-1 stock split)	300,000
		450,000
December 31	Issued 50,000 shares for cash	50,000
December 31	Ending balance	500,000

To compute the earnings per share information, Darin determines the weighted-average number of shares outstanding as follows.

ILLUSTRATION 16-14
Weighted-Average Number of Shares Outstanding

Dates Outstanding	(A) Shares Outstanding	(B) Restatement	(C) Fraction of Year	(D) Weighted Shares (A × B × C)
Jan. 1–May 1	180,000	3	4/12	180,000
May 1–July 1	150,000	3	2/12	75,000
July 1–Dec. 31	450,000		6/12	225,000
Weighted-average number of shares outstanding				480,000

In computing the weighted-average number of shares, the company ignores the shares sold on December 31, 2006, because they have not been outstanding during the year. Darin then divides the weighted-average number of shares into income before extraordinary item and net income to determine earnings per share. It subtracts its preferred dividends of $100,000 from income before extraordinary item ($580,000) to arrive at income before extraordinary item available to common stockholders of $480,000 ($580,000 − $100,000).

Deducting the preferred dividends from the income before extraordinary item also reduces net income without affecting the amount of the extraordinary item. The final amount is referred to as **income available to common stockholders**, as shown in Illustration 16-15.

ILLUSTRATION 16-15
Computation of Income Available to Common Stockholders

	(A) Income Information	(B) Weighted Shares	(C) Earnings per Share (A ÷ B)
Income before extraordinary item available to common stockholders	$480,000*	480,000	$1.00
Extraordinary gain (net of tax)	240,000	480,000	0.50
Income available to common stockholders	$720,000	480,000	$1.50

*$580,000 − $100,000

Darin must disclose the per share amount for the extraordinary item (net of tax) either on the face of the income statement or in the notes to the financial statements.

Illustration 16-16 shows the income and per share information reported on the face of Darin's income statement.

Income before extraordinary item	$580,000
Extraordinary gain, net of tax	240,000
Net income	$820,000
Earnings per share:	
Income before extraordinary item	$1.00
Extraordinary item, net of tax	0.50
Net income	$1.50

ILLUSTRATION 16-16
Earnings per Share, with Extraordinary Item

EARNINGS PER SHARE—COMPLEX CAPITAL STRUCTURE

The EPS discussion to this point applies to **basic EPS** for a simple capital structure. One problem with a **basic EPS** computation is that it fails to recognize the potential impact of a corporation's dilutive securities. As discussed at the beginning of the chapter, **dilutive securities** are securities that can be converted to common stock.[17] Upon conversion or exercise by the holder, the dilutive securities reduce (dilute) earnings per share. This adverse effect on EPS can be significant and, more importantly, *unexpected* unless financial statements call attention to their potential dilutive effect.

OBJECTIVE 7
Compute earnings per share in a complex capital structure.

As indicated earlier, a complex capital structure exists when a corporation has convertible securities, options, warrants, or other rights that upon conversion or exercise could dilute earnings per share. When a company has a complex capital structure, **it generally reports both basic and diluted earnings per share**.

Computing **diluted EPS** is similar to computing basic EPS. The difference is that diluted EPS includes the effect of all potential dilutive common shares that were outstanding during the period. The formula in Illustration 16-17 shows the relationship between basic EPS and diluted EPS.

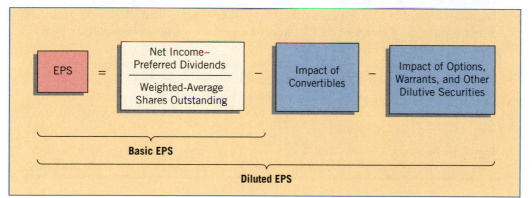

ILLUSTRATION 16-17
Relation between Basic and Diluted EPS

Some securities are antidilutive. **Antidilutive securities** are securities that upon conversion or exercise **increase** earnings per share (or reduce the loss per share). Companies with complex capital structures will not report diluted EPS if the securities in their capital structure are antidilutive. The purpose of presenting both basic and diluted EPS is to inform financial statement users of situations that will likely occur (basic EPS) and also to provide "worst case" dilutive situations (dilutive EPS) If the securities are antidilutive, the likelihood of conversion or exercise is considered remote. Thus,

---

[17]Issuance of these types of securities is typical in mergers and compensation plans.

companies that have only antidilutive securities must report only the basic EPS number. We illustrated the computation of basic EPS in the prior section. In the following sections, we address the effects of convertible and other dilutive securities on EPS calculations.

PRO FORMA EPS CONFUSION

WHAT DO THE NUMBERS MEAN?

Many companies are reporting pro forma EPS numbers along with U.S. GAAP-based EPS numbers in the financial information provided to investors. Pro forma earnings generally exceed GAAP earnings because the pro forma numbers exclude such items as restructuring charges, impairments of assets, R&D expenditures, and stock compensation expense. Here are some examples.

Company	U.S. GAAP EPS	Pro Forma EPS
Adaptec	$(0.62)	$ 0.05
Corning	(0.24)	0.09
General Motors	(0.41)	0.85
Honeywell International	(0.38)	0.44
International Paper	(0.57)	0.14
Qualcomm	(0.06)	0.20
Broadcom	(6.36)	(0.13)
Lucent Technologies	(2.16)	(0.27)

Source: Company press releases.

The SEC has expressed concern that pro forma earnings may be misleading. For example, the SEC cited **Trump Hotels & Casino Resorts (DJT)** for abuses related to a recent third-quarter pro forma EPS release. It noted that the firm misrepresented its operating results by excluding a material, one-time $81.4 million charge in its pro forma EPS statement and including an undisclosed nonrecurring gain of $17.2 million. The gain enabled DJT to post a profit in the quarter. The SEC emphasized that DJT's pro forma EPS statement deviated from conservative U.S. GAAP reporting. Therefore, it was "fraudulent" because it created a "false and misleading impression" that DJT had actually (1) recorded a profit in the third quarter and (2) exceeded consensus earnings expectations by enhancing its operating fundamentals.

As discussed in Chapter 4, SEC Regulation G now requires companies to provide a clear reconciliation between pro forma and GAAP information. And this applies to EPS measures as well. This reconciliation will be especially important, given the expected spike in pro forma reporting by companies to add back employee stock option expense after adopting *SFAS No. 123(R)*.

Sources: See M. Moran, A. J. Cohen, and K. Shaustyuk, "Stock Option Expensing: The Battle Has Been Won; Now Comes the Aftermath," *Portfolio Strategy/Accounting*. Goldman Sachs (March 17, 2005).

Diluted EPS—Convertible Securities

At conversion, companies exchange convertible securities for common stock. Companies measure the dilutive effects of potential conversion on EPS using the **if-converted method**. This method for a convertible bond assumes: (1) the conversion of the convertible securities at the beginning of the period (or at the time of issuance of the security, if issued during the period), and (2) the elimination of related interest, net of tax. Thus the additional shares assumed issued increase the **denominator**—the weighted-average number of shares outstanding. The amount of interest expense, net of tax associated with those potential common shares, increases the **numerator**—net income.

Comprehensive Example—If-Converted Method

As an example, MayField Corporation has net income of $210,000 for the year and a weighted-average number of common shares outstanding during the period of 100,000 shares. The basic earnings per share is therefore $2.10 ($210,000 ÷ 100,000). The company has two convertible debenture bond issues outstanding. One is a 6 percent issue sold at 100 (total $1,000,000) in a prior year and convertible into 20,000 common shares. The other is a 10 percent issue sold at 100 (total $1,000,000) on April 1 of the current year and convertible into 32,000 common shares. The tax rate is 40 percent.

As Illustration 16-18 shows, to determine the numerator for diluted earnings per share, Mayfield adds back the interest on the if-converted securities, less the related tax effect. Because the if-converted method assumes conversion as of the beginning of the year, MayField assumes that it pays no interest on the convertibles during the year. The interest on the 6 percent convertibles is $60,000 for the year ($1,000,000 × 6%). The increased tax expense is $24,000 ($60,000 × 0.40). The interest added back net of taxes is $36,000 [$60,000 − $24,000, or simply $60,000 × (1 − 0.40)].

Net income for the year	$210,000
Add: Adjustment for interest (net of tax)	
6% debentures ($60,000 × [1 − .40])	36,000
10% debentures ($100,000 × 9/12 × [1 − .40])	45,000
Adjusted net income	$291,000

ILLUSTRATION 16-18
Computation of Adjusted Net Income

Continuing with the information in Illustration 16-18, because Mayfield issues 10 percent convertibles subsequent to the beginning of the year, it weights the shares. In other words, it considers these shares to have been outstanding from April 1 to the end of the year. As a result, the interest adjustment to the numerator for these bonds reflects the interest for only nine months. Thus the interest added back on the 10 percent convertible is $45,000 [$1,000,000 × 10% × 9/12 year × (1 − 0.4)]. The final item in Illustration 16-18 shows the adjusted net income. This amount becomes the numerator for MayField's computation of diluted earnings per share.

MayField then calculates the weighted-average number of shares outstanding, as shown in Illustration 16-19. This number of shares becomes the denominator for May-Field's computation of diluted earnings per share.

Weighted average number of shares outstanding	100,000
Add: Shares assumed to be issued:	
6% debentures (as of beginning of year)	20,000
10% debentures (as of date of issue, April 1; 9/12 × 32,000)	24,000
Weighted-average number of shares adjusted for dilutive securities	144,000

ILLUSTRATION 16-19
Computation of Weighted-Average Number of Shares

In its income statement, MayField reports basic and diluted earnings per share.[18] Illustration 16-20 shows this dual presentation.

Net income for the year	$210,000
Earnings per Share (Note X)	
Basic earnings per share ($210,000 ÷ 100,000)	$2.10
Diluted earnings per share ($291,000 ÷ 144,000)	$2.02

ILLUSTRATION 16-20
Earnings per Share Disclosure

---

[18]Conversion of bonds is dilutive because EPS with conversion ($2.02) is less than basic EPS ($2.10).

Other Factors

The example above assumed that MayField sold its bonds at the face amount. If it instead sold the bonds at a premium or discount, the company must adjust the interest expense each period to account for this occurrence. Therefore, the interest expense reported on the income statement is the amount of interest expense, net of tax, added back to net income. (It is not the interest paid in cash during the period.)

In addition, the conversion rate on a dilutive security may change during the period in which the security is outstanding. For the diluted EPS computation in such a situation, the **company uses the most dilutive conversion rate available**. For example, assume that a company issued a convertible bond on January 1, 2005, with a conversion rate of 10 common shares for each bond starting January 1, 2007. Beginning January 1, 2010, the conversion rate is 12 common shares for each bond, and beginning January 1, 2014, it is 15 common shares for each bond. In computing diluted EPS in 2005, the company uses the conversion rate of 15 shares to one bond.

A final issue relates to preferred stock. For example, assume that MayField's 6 percent convertible debentures were instead 6 percent convertible *preferred stock.* In that case, MayField considers the convertible preferred as potential common shares. Thus, it includes them in its diluted EPS calculations as shares outstanding. The company does not subtract preferred dividends from net income in computing the numerator. Why not? Because for purposes of computing EPS, it assumes conversion of the convertible preferreds to outstanding common stock. The company uses net income as the numerator—it computes **no tax effect** because preferred dividends generally are not tax-deductible.

CUCKOO FOR CoCos

WHAT DO THE NUMBERS MEAN?

As discussed in the chapter, diluted earnings per share should reflect the potential dilution of all convertible securities, as long as the securities are not antidilutive. However, by exploiting a loophole in the GAAP for EPS, a number of companies issued contingent convertible bonds (CoCos) that bypassed EPS calculations.

CoCos have additional conditions for conversion that allow companies to avoid revealing how much earnings would be diluted if holders of the bonds exchanged them for stock. In fact, under the rules, companies were able to treat CoCos more like warrants (discussed in the next section); this resulted in the CoCos being antidilutive in EPS calculations. As indicated in the table below, CoCos avoided potential dilution of as much as 15 percent for the following companies:

Company	Potential Dilution
Cephalon	15%
FEI	14
Lattice Semi	13
General Motors	10

Source: Bear Stearns & Co.

From 2000, when the first CoCo was issued, to late 2003, over 300 companies issued CoCos, recording interest expense at lower convertible bond rates and without EPS dilution.

However, the CoCo train may be coming into the station. Due to a ruling by the Emerging Issues Task Force (EITF), companies now must include the shares underlying CoCos in diluted EPS calculations. By late 2004, over 40 companies had modified or redeemed their CoCo bonds to avoid EPS dilution.

Sources: See David Henry, "The Latest Magic in Corporate Finance,"*Business Week* (September 8, 2003), p. 88; and Pat McConnell and Janet Pegg, "Accounting for CoCo Bonds: An Update,"*Equity Research*, Bear Stearns (December 14, 2004).

Diluted EPS—Options and Warrants

A company includes in diluted earnings per share stock options and warrants outstanding (whether or not presently exercisable), unless they are antidilutive. Companies use the **treasury-stock method** to include options and warrants and their equivalents in EPS computations.

The treasury-stock method assumes that a company exercises the options or warrants at the beginning of the year (or date of issue if later), and that it uses those proceeds to purchase common stock for the treasury. If the exercise price is lower than the market price of the stock, then the proceeds from exercise are insufficient to buy back all the shares. The company then adds the incremental shares remaining to the weighted-average number of shares outstanding for purposes of computing diluted earnings per share.

For example, if the exercise price of a warrant is $5 and the fair market value of the stock is $15, the treasury-stock method increases the shares outstanding. Exercise of the warrant results in one additional share outstanding, but the $5 received for the one share issued is insufficient to purchase one share in the market at $15. The company needs to exercise three warrants (and issue three additional shares) to produce enough money ($15) to acquire one share in the market. Thus, a net increase of two shares outstanding results.

To see this computation using larger numbers, assume 1,500 options outstanding at an exercise price of $30 for a common share and a common stock market price per share of $50. Through application of the treasury-stock method, the company would have 600 incremental shares outstanding, computed as shown in Illustration 16-21.[19]

Proceeds from exercise of 1,500 options (1,500 × $30)	$45,000
Shares issued upon exercise of options	1,500
Treasury shares purchasable with proceeds ($45,000 ÷ $50)	900
Incremental shares outstanding (potential common shares)	600

ILLUSTRATION 16-21
Computation of Incremental Shares

Thus, if the exercise price of the option or warrant is **lower** than the market price of the stock, dilution occurs. An exercise price of the option or warrant **higher** than the market price of the stock reduces common shares. In this case, the options or warrants are **antidilutive** because their assumed exercise leads to an increase in earnings per share.

For both options and warrants, exercise is assumed only if the average market price of the stock exceeds the exercise price during the reported period.[20] As a practical matter, a simple average of the weekly or monthly prices is adequate, so long as the prices do not fluctuate significantly.

Comprehensive Example—Treasury-Stock Method

To illustrate application of the treasury-stock method, assume that Kubitz Industries, Inc. has net income for the period of $220,000. The average number of shares outstanding for the period was 100,000 shares. Hence, basic EPS—ignoring all dilutive securities—is $2.20. The average number of shares related to options outstanding (although not exercisable at this time), at an option price of $20 per share, is 5,000 shares.

[19]The incremental number of shares may be more simply computed:

$$\frac{\text{Market price} - \text{Option price}}{\text{Market price}} \times \text{Number of options} = \text{Number of shares}$$

$$\frac{\$50 - \$30}{\$50} \times 1{,}500 \text{ options} = 600 \text{ shares}$$

[20]Options and warrants have essentially the same assumptions and computational problems, although the warrants may allow or require the tendering of some other security, such as debt, in lieu of cash upon exercise. In such situations, the accounting becomes quite complex. *SFAS No. 128* explains the proper disposition in this situation.

The average market price of the common stock during the year was $28. Illustration 16-22 shows the computation of EPS using the treasury-stock method.

ILLUSTRATION 16-22
Computation of Earnings per Share—Treasury Stock Method

	Basic Earnings per Share	Diluted Earnings per Share
Average number of shares related to options outstanding:		5,000
Option price per share		× $20
Proceeds upon exercise of options		$100,000
Average market price of common stock		$28
Treasury shares that could be repurchased with proceeds ($100,000 ÷ $28)		3,571
Excess of shares under option over the treasury shares that could be repurchased (5,000 − 3,571)—potential common incremental shares		1,429
Average number of common shares outstanding	100,000	100,000
Total average number of common shares outstanding and potential common shares	100,000 (A)	101,429 (C)
Net income for the year	$220,000 (B)	$220,000 (D)
Earnings per share	$2.20 (B ÷ A)	$2.17 (D ÷ C)

Contingent Issue Agreement

In business combinations, the acquirer may promise to issue additional shares—referred to as **contingent shares**—under certain conditions. Sometimes the company issues these contingent shares as a result of the mere **passage of time** or upon the attainment of a **certain earnings or market price level**. If this passage of time occurs during the current year, or if the company meets the earnings or market price **by the end of the year**, the company considers the contingent shares as outstanding for the computation of diluted earnings per share.[21]

For example, assume that Watts Corporation purchased Cardoza Company and agreed to give Cardoza's stockholders 20,000 additional shares in 2010 if Cardoza's net income in 2009 is $90,000. In 2008 Cardoza's net income is $100,000. Because Cardoza has already attained the 2009 stipulated earnings of $90,000, in computing diluted earnings per share for 2008, Watts would include the 20,000 contingent shares in the shares-outstanding computation.

Antidilution Revisited

In computing diluted EPS, a company must consider the aggregate of all dilutive securities. But first it must determine which potentially dilutive securities are in fact individually dilutive and which are antidilutive. **A company should exclude any security that is antidilutive**, nor can the company use such a security to offset dilutive securities.

Recall that including antidilutive securities in earnings per share computations increases earnings per share (or reduces net loss per share). With options or warrants, whenever the exercise price exceeds the market price, the security is antidilutive. Convertible debt is antidilutive if the addition to income of the interest (net of tax) causes a greater percentage increase in income (numerator) than conversion of the bonds causes a percentage increase in common and potentially dilutive shares (denominator). In other words, convertible debt is antidilutive if conversion of the security causes common stock earnings to increase by a greater amount per additional common share than earnings per share was before the conversion.

---

[21]In addition to contingent issuances of stock, other situations that might lead to dilution are the issuance of participating securities and two-class common shares. The reporting of these types of securities in EPS computations is beyond the scope of this book.

To illustrate, assume that Martin Corporation has a 6 percent, $1,000,000 debt issue that is convertible into 10,000 common shares. Net income for the year is $210,000, the weighted-average number of common shares outstanding is 100,000 shares, and the tax rate is 40 percent. In this case, assumed conversion of the debt into common stock at the beginning of the year requires the following adjustments of net income and the weighted-average number of shares outstanding.

Net income for the year	$210,000	Average number of shares outstanding	100,000
Add: Adjustment for interest (net of tax) on 6% debentures		Add: Shares issued upon assumed conversion of debt	10,000
$60,000 × (1 − .40)	36,000	Average number of common and potential common shares	110,000
Adjusted net income	$246,000		

Basic EPS = $210,000 ÷ 100,000 = $2.10
Diluted EPS = $246,000 ÷ 110,000 = $2.24 = **Antidilutive**

ILLUSTRATION 16-23
Test for Antidilution

As a shortcut, Martin can also identify the convertible debt as antidilutive by comparing the EPS resulting from conversion, $3.60 ($36,000 additional earnings × 10,000 additional shares), with EPS before inclusion of the convertible debt, $2.10.

Companies should ignore antidilutive securities in all calculations and in computing diluted earnings per share. This approach is reasonable. The profession's intent was to inform the investor of the possible dilution that might occur in reported earnings per share and not to be concerned with securities that, if converted or exercised, would result in an increase in earnings per share. Appendix 16B to this chapter provides an extended example of how companies consider antidilution in a complex situation with multiple securities.

EPS Presentation and Disclosure

A company with a complex capital structure would present its EPS information as follows.

Earnings per common share	
Basic earnings per share	$3.30
Diluted earnings per share	$2.70

ILLUSTRATION 16-24
EPS Presentation—
Complex Capital
Structure

When the earnings of a period include irregular items, a company should show per share amounts (where applicable) for the following: income from continuing operations, income before extraordinary items, and net income. Companies that report a discontinued operation or an extraordinary item should present per share amounts **for those line items** either on the face of the income statement or in the notes to the financial statements. Illustration 16-25 shows a presentation reporting extraordinary items.

Basic earnings per share	
Income before extraordinary item	$3.80
Extraordinary item	0.80
Net income	$3.00
Diluted earnings per share	
Income before extraordinary item	$3.35
Extraordinary item	0.65
Net income	$2.70

ILLUSTRATION 16-25
EPS Presentation, with
Extraordinary Item

A company must show earnings per share amounts for all periods presented. Also, the company should restate all prior period earnings per share amounts presented for stock dividends and stock splits. If it reports diluted EPS data for at least one period, the company should report such data for all periods presented, even if it is the same as basic EPS. When a company restates results of operations of a prior period as a result of an error or a change in accounting principle, it should also restate the earnings per share data shown for the prior periods. Complex capital structures and dual presentation of earnings per share require the following additional disclosures in note form.

1   Description of pertinent rights and privileges of the various securities outstanding.

2   A reconciliation of the numerators and denominators of the basic and diluted per share computations, including individual income and share amount effects of all securities that affect EPS.

3   The effect given preferred dividends in determining income available to common stockholders in computing basic EPS.

4   Securities that could potentially dilute basic EPS in the future that were excluded in the computation because they would be antidilutive.

5   Effect of conversions subsequent to year-end, but before issuing statements.

Illustration 16-26 presents the reconciliation and the related disclosure to meet the requirements of this standard.[22]

ILLUSTRATION 16-26
Reconciliation for Basic and Diluted EPS

	For the Year Ended 2008		
	Income (Numerator)	Shares (Denominator)	Per Share Amount
Income before extraordinary item	$7,500,000		
Less: Preferred stock dividends	(45,000)		
Basic EPS			
Income available to common stockholders	7,455,000	3,991,666	$1.87
Warrants		30,768	
Convertible preferred stock	45,000	308,333	
4% convertible bonds (net of tax)	60,000	50,000	
Diluted EPS			
Income available to common stockholders + assumed conversions	$7,560,000	4,380,767	$1.73

Stock options to purchase 1,000,000 shares of common stock at $85 per share were outstanding during the second half of 2008 but were not included in the computation of diluted EPS because the options' exercise price was greater than the average market price of the common shares. The options were still outstanding at the end of year 2008 and expire on June 30, 2018.

Summary of EPS Computation

As you can see, computation of earnings per share is a complex issue. It is a controversial area because many securities, although technically not common stock, have many of its basic characteristics. Indeed, some companies have issued these other securities rather than common stock in order to avoid an adverse dilutive effect on

---

[22]"Earnings Per Share," *Statement of Financial Accounting Standards No. 128* (Norwalk, Conn.: FASB, 1997). Note that *SFAS No. 123(R)* has specific disclosure requirements regarding stock option plans and earning per share disclosures as well.

earnings per share. Illustrations 16-27 and 16-28 display the elementary points of calculating earnings per share in a simple capital structure and in a complex capital structure.

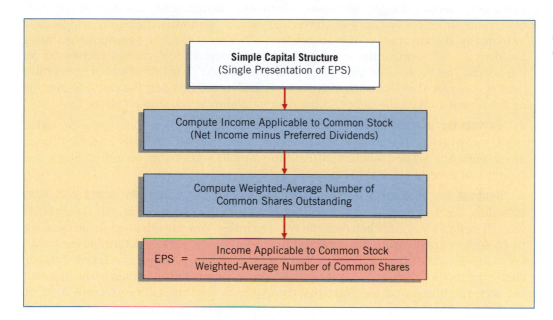

ILLUSTRATION 16-27
Calculating EPS, Simple
Capital Structure

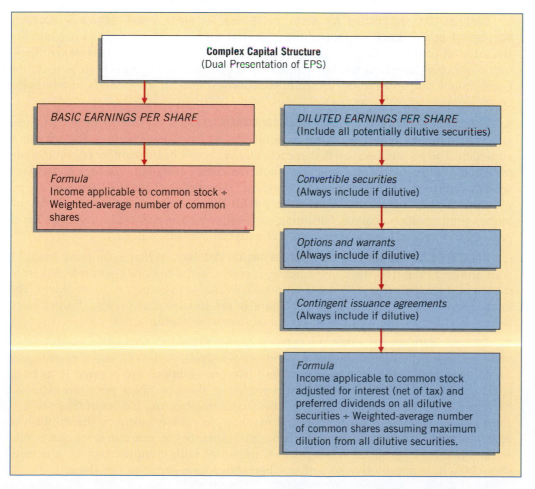

ILLUSTRATION 16-28
Calculating EPS,
Complex Capital
Structure

SUMMARY OF LEARNING OBJECTIVES

1. Describe the accounting for the issuance, conversion, and retirement of convertible securities. The method for recording convertible bonds at the date of issuance follows that used to record straight debt issues. Companies amortize any discount or premium that results from the issuance of convertible bonds, assuming the bonds will be held to maturity. If companies convert bonds into other securities, the principal accounting problem is to determine the amount at which to record the securities exchanged for the bonds. The book value method is considered GAAP. The retirement of convertible debt is considered a debt retirement, and the difference between the carrying amount of the retired convertible debt and the cash paid should result in a gain or loss.

2. Explain the accounting for convertible preferred stock. When convertible preferred stock is converted, a company uses the book value method: It debits Preferred Stock, along with any related Additional Paid-in Capital, and credits Common Stock and Additional Paid-in Capital (if an excess exists).

3. Contrast the accounting for stock warrants and for stock warrants issued with other securities. *Stock warrants*: Companies should allocate the proceeds from the sale of debt with detachable warrants between the two securities. Warrants that are detachable can be traded separately from the debt, and therefore companies can determine their market value. Two methods of allocation are available: the proportional method and the incremental method. Nondetachable warrants do not require an allocation of the proceeds between the bonds and the warrants; companies record the entire proceeds as debt. *Stock rights*: No entry is required when a company issues rights to existing stockholders. The company needs only to make a memorandum entry to indicate the number of rights issued to existing stockholders and to ensure that the company has additional unissued stock registered for issuance in case the stockholders exercise the rights.

4. Describe the accounting for stock compensation plans under generally accepted accounting principles. Companies must use the fair-value approach to account for stock-based compensation. Under this approach, a company computes total compensation expense based on the fair value of the options that it expects to vest on the grant date. Companies recognize compensation expense in the periods in which the employee performs the services.

5. Discuss the controversy involving stock compensation plans. When first proposed, there was considerable opposition to the recognition provisions contained in the fair-value approach. The reason: because that approach could result in substantial, previously unrecognized compensation expense. Corporate America, particularly the high-technology sector, vocally opposed the proposed standard. They believed that the standard would place them at a competitive disadvantage with larger companies that can withstand higher compensation charges. Offsetting such opposition is the need for greater transparency in financial reporting, on which our capital markets depend.

6. Compute earnings per share in a simple capital structure. When a company has both common and preferred stock outstanding, it subtracts the current-year preferred stock dividend from net income to arrive at income available to common stockholders. The formula for computing earnings per share is net income less preferred stock dividends, divided by the weighted-average of shares outstanding.

7. Compute earnings per share in a complex capital structure. A complex capital structure requires a dual presentation of earnings per share, each with equal prominence on the face of the income statement. These two presentations are referred to as basic earnings per share and diluted earnings per share. Basic earnings per share relies on the number of weighted-average common shares outstanding (i.e., equivalent to EPS for a simple capital structure). Diluted earnings per share indicates the dilution of earnings per share that will occur if all potential issuances of common stock that would reduce earnings per share takes place. Companies with complex capital structures should exclude antidilutive securities when computing earnings per share.

Other Stock-Based Compensation Plans

This chapter's discussion on compensation mainly addresses how to account for stock option plans. However, companies have other compensation plans that are often used to compensate employees using stock-based plans. And more companies are using these alternative plans, given that the accounting treatment for stock options is no longer as favorable as before. In other words, the playing field is now more level—the selection of the type of stock-based compensation plans a company will use will be less driven by the accounting and decided more by proper incentive design and cost considerations.

> **OBJECTIVE 8**
> **Explain the accounting for various share-based compensation plans.**

Two major plans that companies will use more extensively are: (1) restricted-stock plans and (2) stock appreciation right programs.

RESTRICTED STOCK

Restricted-stock plans transfer shares of stock to employees, subject to an agreement that the shares cannot be sold, transferred or pledged until vesting occurs. These shares are subject to forfeiture if the conditions for vesting are not met. Most companies base vesting on future service for a period of generally three to five years. Vesting may also be conditioned on some performance target such as revenue, net income, cash flows, or some combination of these three factors. The employee also collects dividends on the restricted stock, and these dividends generally must be repaid if forfeiture occurs.

Major advantages of restricted-stock plans are:

1   Restricted stock never becomes completely worthless. In contrast, if the stock price does not exceed the exercise price for a stock option, the options are worthless. The restricted stock, however, still has value.

2   Restricted stock generally results in less dilution to existing stockholders. Restricted-stock awards are usually one-half to one-third the size of stock options. For example, if a company issues stock options on 1,000 shares, an equivalent restricted-stock offering might be 333 to 500 shares. The reason for the difference is that at the end of the vesting period, the restricted stock will have value, whereas the stock options may not. As a result, fewer shares are involved in restricted-stock plans, and therefore less dilution results if the stock price rises.

3   Restricted stock better aligns the employee incentives with the companies' incentives. The holder of restricted stock is essentially a stockholder and should be more interested in the long-term objectives of the company. In contrast, the recipients of stock options often have a short-run focus which leads to taking risks to hype the stock price for short-term gain to the detriment of the long-term.

The accounting for restricted stock follows the same general principles as accounting for stock options at the date of grant. That is, the company determines the fair value of the restricted stock at the date of grant (usually the fair value of a share of stock) and then expenses that amount over the service period. Subsequent changes in the fair value of the stock are ignored for purposes of computing compensation expense.

Restricted Stock Example

Assume that on January 1, 2006, Ogden Company issues 1,000 shares of restricted stock to its CEO, Christie DeGeorge. Ogden's stock has a fair value of $20 per share on January 1, 2006. Additional information is as follows.

1 The service period related to the restricted stock is five years.
2 Vesting occurs if DeGeorge stays with the company for a five-year period.
3 The par value of the stock is $1 per share.

Ogden makes the following entry on the grant date (January 1, 2006).

Unearned Compensation	20,000	
Common Stock (1,000 × $1)		1,000
Paid-In Capital in Excess of Par (1,000 × $19)		19,000

The credits to Common Stock and Paid-In Capital in Excess of par indicate that Ogden has issued shares of stock. The debit to Unearned Compensation (often referred to as Deferred Compensation Expense) identifies the total compensation expense the company will recognize over the five-year period. **Unearned Compensation represents the cost of services yet to be performed, which is not an asset.** Consequently, the company reports Unearned Compensation in stockholders' equity in the balance sheet, as a contra-equity account (similar to the reporting of treasury stock at cost).

At December 31, 2006, Ogden records compensation expense of $4,000 (1,000 shares × $20 × 20%) as follows:

Compensation Expense	4,000	
Unearned Compensation		4,000

Ogden records compensation expense of $4,000 for each of the next four years (2007, 2008, 2009, and 2010).

What happens if DeGeorge leaves the company before the five years has elapsed? In this situation, DeGeorge forfeits her rights to the stock, and Ogden reverses the compensation expense already recorded.

For example, assume that DeGeorge leaves on February 3, 2008 (before any expense has been recorded during 2008). The entry to record this forfeiture is as follows:

Common Stock	1,000	
Paid in Capital in Excess of Par	19,000	
Compensation Expense ($4,000 × 2)		8,000
Unearned Compensation		12,000

In this situation, Ogden reverses the compensation expense of $8,000 recorded through 2007. In addition, the company debits Common Stock and Additional Paid-In Capital, reflecting DeGeorge's forfeiture. It credits the balance of Unearned Compensation since none remains when DeGeorge leaves Ogden.

This accounting is similar to accounting for stock options when employees do not fulfill vesting requirements. Recall from the chapter that once compensation expense is recorded for stock options, it is not reversed. The only exception is if the employee does not fulfill the vesting requirement, by leaving the company early.

In Ogden's restricted-stock plan, vesting never occurred because DeGeorge left the company before she met the service requirement. Because DeGeorge was never vested, she had to forfeit her shares. Therefore, the company must reverse compensation expense recorded to date.

As indicated in the chapter more companies are using restricted-stock plans. In 2004, 43.4 percent of chief executives of large companies received some form of restricted stock. This represented an increase of 5.5 percentage points from 2003. **General Electric**, for example, has reduced its stock options recently by replacing 60 percent of its options with restricted stock. **Cendant** has gone even further. An employee who received a stock option worth $1,000 now receives about $550 of stock—but only if the company meets certain financial targets.[1]

STOCK APPRECIATION RIGHTS (SARs)

A major disadvantage of many stock option plans is that an executive must pay income tax on the difference between the market price of the stock and the option price at the **date of exercise**. This feature of stock option plans (those referred to as nonqualified) can be a financial hardship for an executive who wishes to keep the stock (rather than sell it immediately) because he or she would have to pay not only income tax but the option price as well. In another type of plan (an **incentive plan**), the executive pays no taxes at exercise but may need to borrow to finance the exercise price, which leads to related interest cost.

One solution to this problem was the creation of **stock appreciation rights (SARs)**. In this type of plan, the company gives an executive the right to receive compensation equal to the share appreciation. **Share appreciation** is the excess of the market price of the stock at the date of exercise over a pre-established price. The company may pay the share appreciation in cash, shares, or a combination of both.

The major advantage of SARs is that the executive often does not have to make a cash outlay at the date of exercise, but receives a payment for the share appreciation. Unlike shares acquired under a stock option plan, the company does not issue the shares that constitute the basis for computing the appreciation in a SARs plan. Rather, the company simply awards the executive cash or stock having a market value equivalent to the appreciation. The accounting for stock appreciation rights depends on whether the company classifies the rights as equity or as a liability.

SARs—Share-Based Equity Awards

Companies classify SARs as **equity awards** if at the date of exercise, the holder receives shares of stock from the company upon exercise. In essence, SARs are essentially equivalent to a stock option. The major difference relates to the form of payment. With the stock option, the holder pays the exercise price and then receives the stock. In an equity SAR, the holder receives shares in an amount equal to the **share price appreciation** (the difference between the market price and the pre-established price). The accounting for SARs when they are equity awards follows the accounting used for stock options. At the date of grant, the company determines a fair value for the SAR and then allocates this amount to compensation expense over the service period of the employees.

SARs—Share-Based Liability Awards

Companies classify SARs as liability awards if at the date of exercise, the holder receives a cash payment. In this case the holder is not receiving additional shares of stock but a cash payment equal to the amount of share price appreciation. The company's compensation expense therefore changes as the value of the liability changes.

A company uses the following approach to record share-based liability awards:

1 Measure the fair value of the award at the grant date and accrue compensation over the service period.

2 Remeasure the fair value each reporting period, until the award is settled, and adjust the compensation cost each period for changes in fair value pro-rated for the portion of the service period completed.

---

[1]There are numerous variations on restricted stock plans, including restricted stock units (for which the shares are issued at the end of the vesting period) and restricted stock plans with performance targets, such as EPS or stock price growth.

3 Once the service period is completed, determine compensation expense each subsequent period by reporting the full change in market price as an adjustment to compensation expense.

For liability awards, the company estimates the fair value of the SARs, using an option-pricing model. The company then allocates this total estimated compensation cost over the service period, recording expense (or a decrease in expense if fair value declines) in each period. At the end of each period, total compensation expense reported to date should equal the percentage of the total service period that has elapsed, multiplied by the total estimated compensation cost.

For example, assume that the service period is 40 percent complete, and total estimated compensation is $100,000. The company reports cumulative compensation expense to date of $40,000 ($100,000 × .40).

The method of allocating compensation expense is called the **percentage approach**. In this method, in the first year of, say, a four-year plan, the company charges one-fourth of the estimated cost to date. In the second year, it charges off two-fourths, or 50 percent, of the estimated cost to date, less the amount already recognized in the first year. In the third year, it charges off three-fourths of the estimated cost to date, less the amount recognized previously. In the fourth year it charges off the remaining compensation expense.

A special problem arises when the exercise date is later than the service period. In the previous example, if the stock appreciation rights were not exercised at the end of four years, in the fifth year the company would have to account for the difference in the market price and the pre-established price. In this case, the company adjusts compensation expense whenever a change in the market price of the stock **occurs in subsequent reporting periods, until the rights expire or are exercised, whichever comes first**.

Increases or decreases in the fair value of the SAR between the date of grant and the exercise date, therefore, result in a change in the measure of compensation. Some periods will have credits to compensation expense if the fair value decreases from one period to the next. The credit to compensation expense, however, cannot exceed previously recognized compensation expense. In other words, **cumulative compensation expense cannot be negative**.

Stock Appreciation Rights Example

Assume that American Hotels, Inc. establishes a stock appreciation rights plan on January 1, 2006. The plan entitles executives to receive cash at the date of exercise for the difference between the market price of the stock and the pre-established price of $10 on 10,000 SARs. The fair value of the SARs on December 31, 2006, is $3, and the service period runs for two years (2006–2007). Illustration 16A-1 indicates the amount of

ILLUSTRATION 16A-1
Compensation Expense, Stock Appreciation Rights

STOCK APPRECIATION RIGHTS SCHEDULE OF COMPENSATION EXPENSE							
(1)	(2)	(3)	(4)	(5)			
Date	Fair Value	Cumulative Compensation Recognizable[a]	Percentage Accrued[b]	Cumulative Compensation Accrued to Date	Expense 2006	Expense 2007	Expense 2008
12/31/06	$3	$30,000	50%	$ 15,000	$15,000		
				55,000		$55,000	
12/31/07	7	70,000	100%	70,000			
				(20,000)			$(20,000)
12/31/08	5	50,000	100%	$ 50,000			

[a]Cumulative compensation for unexercised SARs to be allocated to periods of service.
[b]The percentage accrued is based upon a two-year service period (2006–2007).

compensation expense to be recorded each period, assuming that the executives hold the SARs for three years, at which time they exercise the rights.

In 2006 American Hotels records compensation expense of $15,000 because 50 percent of the $30,000 total compensation cost estimated at December 31, 2006, is allocable to 2006. In 2007 the fair value increased to $7 per right ($70,000 total). The company recorded additional compensation expense of $55,000 ($70,000 minus $15,000).

The executives held the SARs through 2008, during which time the stock decreased to $15 (and the obligation to the executives equals $50,000). American Hotels recognizes the decrease by recording a $20,000 credit to compensation expense and a debit to Liability under Stock Appreciation Plan. Note that after the service period ends, since the rights are still outstanding, the company adjusts the rights to market at December 31, 2008. Any such credit to compensation expense cannot exceed previous charges to expense attributable to that plan.

As the company records the compensation expense each period, the corresponding credit is to a liability account, because the company will pay the stock appreciation in cash. American Hotels records compensation expense in the first year as follows.

Compensation Expense	15,000	
Liability under Stock Appreciation Plan		15,000

The company would credit the liability account for $55,000 again in 2007. In 2008, when it records negative compensation expense, American would debit the account for $20,000. The entry to record the negative compensation expense is as follows.

Liability under Stock Appreciation Plan	20,000	
Compensation Expense		20,000

At December 31, 2008, the executives receive $50,000. American would remove the liability with the following entry.

Liability under Stock Appreciation Plan	50,000	
Cash		50,000

Compensation expense can increase or decrease substantially from one period to the next. The reason is that compensation expense is re-measured each year, which can lead to large swings in compensation expense.

SUMMARY OF LEARNING OBJECTIVE FOR APPENDIX 16A

KEY TERMS

percentage approach, *810*

restricted-stock plans, *807*

share appreciation, *809*

stock appreciation rights (SARs), *809*

8. Explain the accounting for various share-based compensation plans. Restricted-stock plans follow the same general accounting principles as those for stock options. Companies estimate total compensation cost at the grant date based on the fair value of the restricted stock; they expense that cost over the service period. If vesting does not occur, companies reverse the compensation expense.

The accounting for stock appreciation rights depends on whether the rights are classified as equity- or liability-based. If equity-based, the accounting is similar to that used for stock options. If liability-based, companies re-measure compensation expense each period and allocate it over the service period using the percentage approach.

APPENDIX
16B Comprehensive Earnings per Share Illustration

OBJECTIVE 9
Compute earnings per share in a complex situation.

ILLUSTRATION 16B-1
Balance Sheet for Comprehensive Illustration

This appendix illustrates the method of computing dilution when many securities are involved. We present the following section of the balance sheet of Webster Corporation for analysis. Assumptions related to the capital structure follow the balance sheet.

WEBSTER CORPORATION
BALANCE SHEET (PARTIAL)
AT DECEMBER 31, 2007

Long-term debt	
Notes payable, 14%	$ 1,000,000
8% convertible bonds payable	2,500,000
10% convertible bonds payable	2,500,000
Total long-term debt	$ 6,000,000
Stockholders' equity	
10% cumulative, convertible preferred stock, par value $100;	
100,000 shares authorized, 25,000 shares issued and outstanding	$ 2,500,000
Common stock, par value $1, 5,000,000 shares authorized,	
500,000 shares issued and outstanding	500,000
Additional paid-in capital	2,000,000
Retained earnings	9,000,000
Total stockholders' equity	$14,000,000

Notes and Assumptions
December 31, 2007

1. Options were granted in July 2005 to purchase 50,000 shares of common stock at $20 per share. The average market price of Webster's common stock during 2007 was $30 per share. All options are still outstanding at the end of 2007.
2. Both the 8 percent and 10 percent convertible bonds were issued in 2006 at face value. Each convertible bond is convertible into 40 shares of common stock. (Each bond has a face value of $1,000.)
3. The 10 percent cumulative, convertible preferred stock was issued at the beginning of 2007 at par. Each share of preferred is convertible into four shares of common stock.
4. The average income tax rate is 40 percent.
5. The 500,000 shares of common stock were outstanding during the entire year.
6. Preferred dividends were not declared in 2007.
7. Net income was $1,750,000 in 2007.
8. No bonds or preferred stock were converted during 2007.

The computation of basic earnings per share for 2007 starts with the amount based upon the weighted-average of common shares outstanding, as shown in Illustration 16B-2 (on page 813).

Note the following points concerning this calculation.

1 When preferred stock is cumulative, the company subtracts the preferred dividend to arrive at income applicable to common stock, whether the dividend is declared or not.

2 The company must compute earnings per share of $3 as a starting point, because it is the per share amount that is subject to reduction due to the existence of convertible securities and options.

Net income	$1,750,000
Less: 10% cumulative, convertible preferred stock dividend requirements	250,000
Income applicable to common stockholders	$1,500,000
Weighted-average number of common shares outstanding	500,000
Earnings per common share	$3.00

ILLUSTRATION 16B-2
Computation of Earnings per Share—Simple Capital Structure

DILUTED EARNINGS PER SHARE

The steps for computing diluted earnings per share are:

1 Determine, for each dilutive security, the per share effect assuming exercise/conversion.

2 Rank the results from step 1 from smallest to largest earnings effect per share. That is, rank the results from most dilutive to least dilutive.

3 Beginning with the earnings per share based upon the weighted-average of common shares outstanding ($3), recalculate earnings per share by adding the smallest per share effects from step 2. If the results from this recalculation are less than $3, proceed to the next smallest per share effect and recalculate earnings per share. Continue this process so long as each recalculated earnings per share is smaller than the previous amount. The process will end either because there are no more securities to test or a particular security maintains or increases earnings per share (is antidilutive).

We'll now apply the three steps to Webster Corporation. (Note that net income and income available to common stockholders are not the same if preferred dividends are declared or cumulative.) Webster Corporation has four securities that could reduce EPS: options, 8 percent convertible bonds, 10 percent convertible bonds, and the convertible preferred stock.

The first step in the computation of diluted earnings per share is to determine a per share effect for each potentially dilutive security. Illustrations 16B-3 through 16B-6 illustrate these computations.

Number of shares under option	50,000
Option price per share	× $20
Proceeds upon assumed exercise of options	$1,000,000
Average 2007 market price of common	$30
Treasury shares that could be acquired with proceeds ($1,000,000 ÷ $30)	33,333
Excess of shares under option over treasury shares that could be repurchased (50,000 − 33,333)	16,667

Per share effect:
$$\frac{\text{Incremental Numerator Effect}}{\text{Incremental Denominator Effect}} = \frac{\text{None}}{16,667 \text{ shares}} = \$0$$

ILLUSTRATION 16B-3
Per Share Effect of Options (Treasury Stock Method), Diluted Earnings per Share

Interest expense for year (8% × $2,500,000)	$200,000
Income tax reduction due to interest (40% × $200,000)	80,000
Interest expense avoided (net of tax)	$120,000
Number of common shares issued assuming conversion of bonds (2,500 bonds × 40 shares)	100,000

Per share effect:
$$\frac{\text{Incremental Numerator Effect}}{\text{Incremental Denominator Effect}} = \frac{\$120,000}{100,000 \text{ shares}} = \$1.20$$

ILLUSTRATION 16B-4
Per Share Effect of 8% Bonds (If-Converted Method), Diluted Earnings per Share

ILLUSTRATION 16B-5
Per Share Effect of 10%
Bonds (If-Converted
Method), Diluted
Earnings per Share

Interest expense for year (10% × $2,500,000)	$250,000
Income tax reduction due to interest (40% × $250,000)	100,000
Interest expense avoided (net of tax)	$150,000
Number of common shares issued assuming conversion of bonds (2,500 bonds × 40 shares)	100,000

Per share effect:
$$\frac{\text{Incremental Numerator Effect}}{\text{Incremental Denominator Effect}} = \frac{\$150,000}{100,000 \text{ shares}} = \$1.50$$

ILLUSTRATION 16B-6
Per Share Effect of 10%
Convertible Preferred
(If-Converted Method),
Diluted Earnings per
Share

Dividend requirement on cumulative preferred (25,000 shares × $10)	$250,000
Income tax effect (dividends not a tax deduction)	none
Dividend requirement avoided	$250,000
Number of common shares issued assuming conversion of preferred (4 × 25,000 shares)	100,000

Per share effect:
$$\frac{\text{Incremental Numerator Effect}}{\text{Incremental Denominator Effect}} = \frac{\$250,000}{100,000 \text{ shares}} = \$2.50$$

Illustration 16B-7 shows the ranking of all four potentially dilutive securities.

ILLUSTRATION 16B-7
Ranking of per Share
Effects (Smallest to
Largest), Diluted
Earnings per Share

	Effect per Share
1. Options	$ 0
2. 8% convertible bonds	1.20
3. 10% convertible bonds	1.50
4. 10% convertible preferred	2.50

The next step is to determine earnings per share giving effect to the ranking in Illustration 16B-7. Starting with the earnings per share of $3 computed previously, add the incremental effects of the options to the original calculation, as follows.

ILLUSTRATION 16B-8
Recomputation of EPS
Using Incremental Effect
of Options

Options	
Income applicable to common stockholders	$1,500,000
Add: Incremental numerator effect of options	none
Total	$1,500,000
Weighted-average number of common shares outstanding	500,000
Add: Incremental denominator effect of options (Illustration 16B-3)	16,667
Total	516,667
Recomputed earnings per share ($1,500,000 ÷ 516,667 shares)	$2.90

Since the recomputed earnings per share is reduced (from $3 to $2.90), the effect of the options is dilutive. Again, we could have anticipated this effect because the average market price ($30) exceeded the option price ($20).

Assuming that Webster converts the 8 percent bonds, recomputed earnings per share is as follows.

8% Convertible Bonds	
Numerator from previous calculation	$1,500,000
Add: Interest expense avoided (net of tax)	120,000
Total	$1,620,000
Denominator from previous calculation (shares)	516,667
Add: Number of common shares assumed issued upon conversion of bonds	100,000
Total	616,667
Recomputed earnings per share ($1,620,000 ÷ 616,667 shares)	$2.63

ILLUSTRATION 16B-9
Recomputation of EPS Using Incremental Effect of 8% Convertible Bonds

Since the recomputed earnings per share is reduced (from $2.90 to $2.63), the effect of the 8 percent bonds is dilutive.

Next, assuming Webster converts the 10 percent bonds, the company recomputes earnings per share as shown in Illustration 16B-10.

10% Convertible Bonds	
Numerator from previous calculation	$1,620,000
Add: Interest expense avoided (net of tax)	150,000
Total	$1,770,000
Denominator from previous calculation (shares)	616,667
Add: Number of common shares assumed issued upon conversion of bonds	100,000
Total	716,667
Recomputed earnings per share ($1,770,000 ÷ 716,667 shares)	$2.47

ILLUSTRATION 16B-10
Recomputation of EPS Using Incremental Effect of 10% Convertible Bonds

Since the recomputed earnings per share is reduced (from $2.63 to $2.47), the effect of the 10 percent convertible bonds is dilutive.

The final step is the recomputation that includes the 10 percent preferred stock. This is shown in Illustration 16B-11.

10% Convertible Preferred	
Numerator from previous calculation	$1,770,000
Add: Dividend requirement avoided	250,000
Total	$2,020,000
Denominator from previous calculation (shares)	716,667
Add: Number of common shares assumed issued upon conversion of preferred	100,000
Total	816,667
Recomputed earnings per share ($2,020,000 ÷ 816,667 shares)	$2.47

ILLUSTRATION 16B-11
Recomputation of EPS Using Incremental Effect of 10% Convertible Preferred

Since the recomputed earnings per share is not reduced, the effect of the 10 percent convertible preferred is not dilutive. Diluted earnings per share is $2.47. The per share effects of the preferred are not used in the computation.

Finally, Illustration 16B-12 shows Webster Corporation's disclosure of earnings per share on its income statement.

Net income	$1,750,000
Basic earnings per common share (Note X)	$3.00
Diluted earnings per common share	$2.47

ILLUSTRATION 16B-12
Income Statement Presentation, EPS

A company uses income from continuing operations (adjusted for preferred dividends) to determine whether potential common stock is dilutive or antidilutive. Some refer to this measure as the **control number**. To illustrate, assume that Barton Company provides the following information.

ILLUSTRATION 16B-13
Barton Company Data

Income from continuing operations	$2,400,000
Loss from discontinued operations	3,600,000
Net loss	$1,200,000
Weighted-average shares of common stock outstanding	1,000,000
Potential common stock	200,000

Barton reports basic and dilutive earnings per share as follows.

ILLUSTRATION 16B-14
Basic and Diluted EPS

Basic earnings per share	
Income from continuing operations	$2.40
Loss from discontinued operations	3.60
Net loss	$1.20
Diluted earnings per share	
Income from continuing operations	$2.00
Loss from discontinued operations	3.00
Net loss	$1.00

As Illustration 16B-14 shows, basic earnings per share from continuing operations is higher than the diluted earnings per share from continuing operations. The reason: The diluted earnings per share from continuing operations includes an additional 200,000 shares of potential common stock in its denominator.[1]

Companies use income from continuing operations as the control number because many of them show income from continuing operations (or a similar line item above net income if it appears on the income statement), but report a final net loss due to a loss on discontinued operations. If a company uses final net loss as the control number, basic and diluted earnings per share would be the same because the potential common shares are antidilutive.[2]

EPS Illustration with Multiple Dilutive Securities

wiley.com/college/kieso

KEY TERMS

control number, *816*

SUMMARY OF LEARNING OBJECTIVE FOR APPENDIX 16B

9. Compute earnings per share in a complex situation. For diluted EPS, make the following computations: (1) For each potentially dilutive security, determine the per share effect assuming exercise/conversion. (2) Rank the results from most dilutive to least dilutive. (3) Recalculate EPS starting with the most dilutive, and continue adding securities until EPS does not change.

---

[1]A company that does not report a discontinued operation but reports an extraordinary item should use that line item (for example, income before extraordinary items) as the control number.

[2]If a company reports a loss from continuing operations, basic and diluted earnings per share will be the same because potential common stock will be antidilutive, even if the company reports final net income. The FASB believes that comparability of EPS information will be improved by using income from continuing operations as the control number.

Note: All **asterisked** Questions, Brief Exercises, Exercises, and Concepts for Analysis relate to material contained in the appendixes to the chapter.

QUESTIONS

1. What is meant by a dilutive security?
2. Briefly explain why corporations issue convertible securities.
3. Discuss the similarities and the differences between convertible debt and debt issued with stock warrants.
4. Plantagenet Corp. offered holders of its 1,000 convertible bonds a premium of $160 per bond to induce conversion into shares of its common stock. Upon conversion of all the bonds, Plantagenet Corp. recorded the $160,000 premium as a reduction of paid-in capital. Comment on Plantagenet's treatment of the $160,000 "sweetener."
5. Explain how the conversion feature of convertible debt has a value (a) to the issuer and (b) to the purchaser.
6. What are the arguments for giving separate accounting recognition to the conversion feature of debentures?
7. Four years after issue, debentures with a face value of $1,000,000 and book value of $960,000 are tendered for conversion into 80,000 shares of common stock immediately after an interest payment date. At that time the market price of the debentures is 104, and the common stock is selling at $14 per share (par value $10). The company records the conversion as follows.

Bonds Payable	1,000,000	
Discount on Bonds Payable		40,000
Common Stock		800,000
Paid-in Capital in Excess of Par		160,000

Discuss the propriety of this accounting treatment.

8. On July 1, 2007, Roberts Corporation issued $3,000,000 of 9% bonds payable in 20 years. The bonds include detachable warrants giving the bondholder the right to purchase for $30 one share of $1 par value common stock at any time during the next 10 years. The bonds were sold for $3,000,000. The value of the warrants at the time of issuance was $200,000. Prepare the journal entry to record this transaction.
9. What are stock rights? How does the issuing company account for them?
10. Briefly explain the accounting requirements for stock compensation plans under *Statement of Financial Accounting Standards No. 123(R)*.
11. Weiland Corporation has an employee stock purchase plan which permits all full-time employees to purchase 10 shares of common stock on the third anniversary of their employment and an additional 15 shares on each subsequent anniversary date. The purchase price is set at the market price on the date purchased and no commission is charged. Discuss whether this plan would be considered compensatory.

12. What date or event does the profession believe should be used in determining the value of a stock option? What arguments support this position?
13. Over what period of time should compensation cost be allocated?
14. How is compensation expense computed using the fair value approach?
15. At December 31, 2007, Amad Company had 600,000 shares of common stock issued and outstanding, 400,000 of which had been issued and outstanding throughout the year and 200,000 of which were issued on October 1, 2007. Net income for 2007 was $3,000,000, and dividends declared on preferred stock were $400,000. Compute Amad's earnings per common share. (Round to the nearest penny.)
16. What effect do stock dividends or stock splits have on the computation of the weighted-average number of shares outstanding?
17. Define the following terms.
    (a) Basic earnings per share.
    (b) Potentially dilutive security.
    (c) Diluted earnings per share.
    (d) Complex capital structure.
    (e) Potential common stock.
18. What are the computational guidelines for determining whether a convertible security is to be reported as part of diluted earnings per share?
19. Discuss why options and warrants may be considered potentially dilutive common shares for the computation of diluted earnings per share.
20. Explain how convertible securities are determined to be potentially dilutive common shares and how those convertible securities that are not considered to be potentially dilutive common shares enter into the determination of earnings per share data.
21. Explain the treasury stock method as it applies to options and warrants in computing dilutive earnings per share data.
22. Earnings per share can affect market prices of common stock. Can market prices affect earnings per share? Explain.
23. What is meant by the term antidilution? Give an example.
24. What type of earnings per share presentation is required in a complex capital structure?
*25. What are the advantages of using restricted stock to compensate employees?
*26. How is antidilution determined when multiple securities are involved?

BRIEF EXERCISES

(LO 1) **BE16-1** Faital Inc. issued $5,000,000 par value, 7% convertible bonds at 99 for cash. If the bonds had not included the conversion feature, they would have sold for 95. Prepare the journal entry to record the issuance of the bonds.

(LO 1) **BE16-2** Sasha Verbitsky Corporation has outstanding 1,000 $1,000 bonds, each convertible into 50 shares of $10 par value common stock. The bonds are converted on December 31, 2008, when the unamortized discount is $30,000 and the market price of the stock is $21 per share. Record the conversion using the book value approach.

(LO 2) **BE16-3** Malik Sealy Corporation issued 2,000 shares of $10 par value common stock upon conversion of 1,000 shares of $50 par value preferred stock. The preferred stock was originally issued at $55 per share. The common stock is trading at $26 per share at the time of conversion. Record the conversion of the preferred stock.

(LO 3) **BE16-4** Divac Corporation issued 1,000 $1,000 bonds at 101. Each bond was issued with one detachable stock warrant. After issuance, the bonds were selling in the market at 98, and the warrants had a market value of $40. Use the proportional method to record the issuance of the bonds and warrants.

(LO 3) **BE16-5** Ceballos Corporation issued 1,000 $1,000 bonds at 101. Each bond was issued with one detachable stock warrant. After issuance, the bonds were selling separately at 98. The market price of the warrants without the bonds cannot be determined. Use the incremental method to record the issuance of the bonds and warrants.

(LO 4) **BE16-6** On January 1, 2008, Johnson Corporation granted 5,000 options to executives. Each option entitles the holder to purchase one share of Johnson's $5 par value common stock at $50 per share at any time during the next 5 years. The market price of the stock is $65 per share on the date of grant. The fair value of the options at the grant date is $140,000. The period of benefit is 2 years. Prepare Johnson's journal entries for January 1, 2008, and December 31, 2008 and 2009.

(LO 6) **BE16-7** Haley Corporation had 2008 net income of $1,200,000. During 2008, Haley paid a dividend of $2 per share on 100,000 shares of preferred stock. During 2008, Haley had outstanding 250,000 shares of common stock. Compute Haley's 2008 earnings per share.

(LO 6) **BE16-8** Barkley Corporation had 120,000 shares of stock outstanding on January 1, 2008. On May 1, 2008, Barkley issued 45,000 shares. On July 1, Barkley purchased 10,000 treasury shares, which were reissued on October 1. Compute Barkley's weighted-average number of shares outstanding for 2008.

(LO 6) **BE16-9** Green Corporation had 200,000 shares of common stock outstanding on January 1, 2008. On May 1, Green issued 30,000 shares. (a) Compute the weighted average number of shares outstanding if the 30,000 shares were issued for cash. (b) Compute the weighted-average number of shares outstanding if the 30,000 shares were issued in a stock dividend.

(LO 7) **BE16-10** Strickland Corporation earned net income of $300,000 in 2008 and had 100,000 shares of common stock outstanding throughout the year. Also outstanding all year was $400,000 of 10% bonds, which are convertible into 16,000 shares of common. Strickland's tax rate is 40 percent. Compute Strickland's 2008 diluted earnings per share.

(LO 7) **BE16-11** Sabonis Corporation reported net income of $400,000 in 2008 and had 50,000 shares of common stock outstanding throughout the year. Also outstanding all year were 5,000 shares of cumulative preferred stock, each convertible into 2 shares of common. The preferred stock pays an annual dividend of $5 per share. Sabonis' tax rate is 40%. Compute Sabonis' 2008 diluted earnings per share.

(LO 7) **BE16-12** Sarunas Corporation reported net income of $300,000 in 2008 and had 200,000 shares of common stock outstanding throughout the year. Also outstanding all year were 30,000 options to purchase common stock at $10 per share. The average market price of the stock during the year was $15. Compute diluted earnings per share.

(LO 6) **BE16-13** The 2008 income statement of Schrempf Corporation showed net income of $480,000 and an extraordinary loss of $120,000. Schrempf had 50,000 shares of common stock outstanding all year. Prepare Schrempf's income statement presentation of earnings per share.

(LO 8) ***BE16-14** On January 1, 2008 (the date of grant), Lee Corporation issues 2,000 shares of restricted stock to its executives. The fair value of these shares is $90,000, and their par value is $10,000. The stock is forfeited if the executives do not complete 3 years of employment with the company. Prepare the journal entry (if any) on January 1, 2008, and on December 31, 2008, assuming the service period is 3 years.

(LO 8) *BE16-15** Sam Perkins, Inc. established a stock appreciation rights (SAR) program on January 1, 2007, which entitles executives to receive cash at the date of exercise for the difference between the market price of the stock and the preestablished price of $20 on 5,000 SARs. The required service period is 2 years. The fair value of the SARs are determined to be $2 on December 31, 2007, and $9 on December 31, 2008. Compute Perkins' compensation expense for 2007 and 2008.

EXERCISES

(LO 3) **E16-1** **(Issuance and Conversion of Bonds)** For each of the unrelated transactions described below, present the entry(ies) required to record each transaction.

1. Grand Corp. issued $20,000,000 par value 10% convertible bonds at 99. If the bonds had not been convertible, the company's investment banker estimates they would have been sold at 95. Expenses of issuing the bonds were $70,000.
2. Hoosier Company issued $20,000,000 par value 10% bonds at 98. One detachable stock purchase warrant was issued with each $100 par value bond. At the time of issuance, the warrants were selling for $4.
3. **Sepracor, Inc.** called its convertible debt in 2007. Assume the following related to the transaction: The 11%, $10,000,000 par value bonds were converted into 1,000,000 shares of $1 par value common stock on July 1, 2007. On July 1, there was $55,000 of unamortized discount applicable to the bonds, and the company paid an additional $75,000 to the bondholders to induce conversion of all the bonds. The company records the conversion using the book value method.

(LO 1) **E16-2** **(Conversion of Bonds)** Aubrey Inc. issued $4,000,000 of 10%, 10-year convertible bonds on June 1, 2007, at 98 plus accrued interest. The bonds were dated April 1, 2007, with interest payable April 1 and October 1. Bond discount is amortized semiannually on a straight-line basis.

On April 1, 2008, $1,500,000 of these bonds were converted into 30,000 shares of $20 par value common stock. Accrued interest was paid in cash at the time of conversion.

Instructions
(a) Prepare the entry to record the interest expense at October 1, 2007. Assume that accrued interest payable was credited when the bonds were issued. (Round to nearest dollar.)
(b) Prepare the entry(ies) to record the conversion on April 1, 2008. (Book value method is used.) Assume that the entry to record amortization of the bond discount and interest payment has been made.

(LO 1) **E16-3** **(Conversion of Bonds)** Vargo Company has bonds payable outstanding in the amount of $500,000, and the Premium on Bonds Payable account has a balance of $7,500. Each $1,000 bond is convertible into 20 shares of preferred stock of par value of $50 per share. All bonds are converted into preferred stock.

Instructions
Assuming that the book value method was used, what entry would be made?

(LO 1) **E16-4** **(Conversion of Bonds)** On January 1, 2006, when its $30 par value common stock was selling for $80 per share, Plato Corp. issued $10,000,000 of 8% convertible debentures due in 20 years. The conversion option allowed the holder of each $1,000 bond to convert the bond into five shares of the corporation's common stock. The debentures were issued for $10,800,000. The present value of the bond payments at the time of issuance was $8,500,000, and the corporation believes the difference between the present value and the amount paid is attributable to the conversion feature. On January 1, 2007, the corporation's $30 par value common stock was split 2 for 1, and the conversion rate for the bonds was adjusted accordingly. On January 1, 2008, when the corporation's $15 par value common stock was selling for $135 per share, holders of 30% of the convertible debentures exercised their conversion options. The corporation uses the straight-line method for amortizing any bond discounts or premiums.

Instructions
(a) Prepare in general journal form the entry to record the original issuance of the convertible debentures.
(b) Prepare in general journal form the entry to record the exercise of the conversion option, using the book value method. Show supporting computations in good form.

(LO 1)   **E16-5   (Conversion of Bonds)**   The December 31, 2007, balance sheet of Kepler Corp. is as follows.

10% callable, convertible bonds payable (semiannual interest dates April 30 and October 31; convertible into 6 shares of $25 par value common stock per $1,000 of bond principal; maturity date April 30, 2013)	$500,000	
Discount on bonds payable	10,240	$489,760

On March 5, 2008, Kepler Corp. called all of the bonds as of April 30 for the principal plus interest through April 30. By April 30 all bondholders had exercised their conversion to common stock as of the interest payment date. Consequently, on April 30, Kepler Corp. paid the semiannual interest and issued shares of common stock for the bonds. The discount is amortized on a straight-line basis. Kepler uses the book value method.

Instructions
Prepare the entry(ies) to record the interest expense and conversion on April 30, 2008. Reversing entries were made on January 1, 2008. (Round to the nearest dollar.)

(LO 1)   **E16-6   (Conversion of Bonds)**   On January 1, 2007, Gottlieb Corporation issued $4,000,000 of 10-year, 8% convertible debentures at 102. Interest is to be paid semiannually on June 30 and December 31. Each $1,000 debenture can be converted into eight shares of Gottlieb Corporation $100 par value common stock after December 31, 2008.

On January 1, 2009, $400,000 of debentures are converted into common stock, which is then selling at $110. An additional $400,000 of debentures are converted on March 31, 2009. The market price of the common stock is then $115. Accrued interest at March 31 will be paid on the next interest date.

Bond premium is amortized on a straight-line basis.

Instructions
Make the necessary journal entries for:

(a)   December 31, 2008.   (c)   March 31, 2009.
(b)   January 1, 2009.   (d)   June 30, 2009.

Record the conversions using the book value method.

(LO 3)   **E16-7   (Issuance of Bonds with Warrants)**   Illiad Inc. has decided to raise additional capital by issuing $170,000 face value of bonds with a coupon rate of 10%. In discussions with investment bankers, it was determined that to help the sale of the bonds, detachable stock warrants should be issued at the rate of one warrant for each $100 bond sold. The value of the bonds without the warrants is considered to be $136,000, and the value of the warrants in the market is $24,000. The bonds sold in the market at issuance for $152,000.

Instructions
(a)   What entry should be made at the time of the issuance of the bonds and warrants?
(b)   If the warrants were nondetachable, would the entries be different? Discuss.

(LO 3)   **E16-8   (Issuance of Bonds with Detachable Warrants)**   On September 1, 2007, Sands Company sold at 104 (plus accrued interest) 4,000 of its 9%, 10-year, $1,000 face value, nonconvertible bonds with detachable stock warrants. Each bond carried two detachable warrants. Each warrant was for one share of common stock at a specified option price of $15 per share. Shortly after issuance, the warrants were quoted on the market for $3 each. No market value can be determined for the Sands Company bonds. Interest is payable on December 1 and June 1. Bond issue costs of $30,000 were incurred.

Instructions
Prepare in general journal format the entry to record the issuance of the bonds.

(AICPA adapted)

(LO 3)   **E16-9   (Issuance of Bonds with Stock Warrants)**   On May 1, 2007, Friendly Company issued 2,000 $1,000 bonds at 102. Each bond was issued with one detachable stock warrant. Shortly after issuance, the bonds were selling at 98, but the market value of the warrants cannot be determined.

Instructions
(a)   Prepare the entry to record the issuance of the bonds and warrants.
(b)   Assume the same facts as part (a), except that the warrants had a fair value of $30. Prepare the entry to record the issuance of the bonds and warrants.

(LO 4)   **E16-10   (Issuance and Exercise of Stock Options)**   On November 1, 2007, Columbo Company adopted a stock option plan that granted options to key executives to purchase 30,000 shares of the company's $10 par value common stock. The options were granted on January 2, 2008, and were exercisable 2 years after the date of grant if the grantee was still an employee of the company. The options expired 6 years from date of grant. The option price was set at $40, and the fair value option pricing model determines the total compensation expense to be $450,000.

All of the options were exercised during the year 2010: 20,000 on January 3 when the market price was $67, and 10,000 on May 1 when the market price was $77 a share.

Instructions

Prepare journal entries relating to the stock option plan for the years 2008, 2009, and 2010. Assume that the employee performs services equally in 2008 and 2009.

(LO 4) **E16-11 (Issuance, Exercise, and Termination of Stock Options)** On January 1, 2008, Titania Inc. granted stock options to officers and key employees for the purchase of 20,000 shares of the company's $10 par common stock at $25 per share. The options were exercisable within a 5-year period beginning January 1, 2010, by grantees still in the employ of the company, and expiring December 31, 2014. The service period for this award is 2 years. Assume that the fair value option pricing model determines total compensation expense to be $350,000.

On April 1, 2009, 2,000 options were terminated when the employees resigned from the company. The market value of the common stock was $35 per share on this date.

On March 31, 2010, 12,000 options were exercised when the market value of the common stock was $40 per share.

Instructions

Prepare journal entries to record issuance of the stock options, termination of the stock options, exercise of the stock options, and charges to compensation expense, for the years ended December 31, 2008, 2009, and 2010.

(LO 4) **E16-12 (Issuance, Exercise, and Termination of Stock Options)** On January 1, 2006, Nichols Corporation granted 10,000 options to key executives. Each option allows the executive to purchase one share of Nichols' $5 par value common stock at a price of $20 per share. The options were exercisable within a 2-year period beginning January 1, 2008, if the grantee is still employed by the company at the time of the exercise. On the grant date, Nichols' stock was trading at $25 per share, and a fair value option-pricing model determines total compensation to be $400,000.

On May 1, 2008, 8,000 options were exercised when the market price of Nichols' stock was $30 per share. The remaining options lapsed in 2010 because executives decided not to exercise their options.

Instructions

Prepare the necessary journal entries related to the stock option plan for the years 2006 through 2010.

(LO 6) **E16-13 (Weighted-Average Number of Shares)** Newton Inc. uses a calendar year for financial reporting. The company is authorized to issue 9,000,000 shares of $10 par common stock. At no time has Newton issued any potentially dilutive securities. Listed below is a summary of Newton's common stock activities.

1. Number of common shares issued and outstanding at December 31, 2005	2,000,000
2. Shares issued as a result of a 10% stock dividend on September 30, 2006	200,000
3. Shares issued for cash on March 31, 2007	2,000,000
Number of common shares issued and outstanding at December 31, 2007	4,200,000
4. A 2-for-1 stock split of Newton's common stock took place on March 31, 2008.	

Instructions

(a) Compute the weighted-average number of common shares used in computing earnings per common share for 2006 on the 2007 comparative income statement.

(b) Compute the weighted-average number of common shares used in computing earnings per common share for 2007 on the 2007 comparative income statement.

(c) Compute the weighted-average number of common shares to be used in computing earnings per common share for 2007 on the 2008 comparative income statement.

(d) Compute the weighted-average number of common shares to be used in computing earnings per common share for 2008 on the 2008 comparative income statement.

(CMA adapted)

(LO 6) **E16-14 (EPS: Simple Capital Structure)** On January 1, 2008, Wilke Corp. had 480,000 shares of common stock outstanding. During 2008, it had the following transactions that affected the common stock account.

February 1	Issued 120,000 shares
March 1	Issued a 10% stock dividend
May 1	Acquired 100,000 shares of treasury stock
June 1	Issued a 3-for-1 stock split
October 1	Reissued 60,000 shares of treasury stock

Instructions

(a) Determine the weighted-average number of shares outstanding as of December 31, 2008.

(b) Assume that Wilke Corp. earned net income of $3,456,000 during 2008. In addition, it had 100,000 shares of 9%, $100 par nonconvertible, noncumulative preferred stock outstanding for the entire year. Because of liquidity considerations, however, the company did not declare and pay a preferred dividend in 2008. Compute earnings per share for 2008, using the weighted-average number of shares determined in part (a).

(c) Assume the same facts as in part (b), except that the preferred stock was cumulative. Compute earnings per share for 2008.

(d) Assume the same facts as in part (b), except that net income included an extraordinary gain of $864,000 and a loss from discontinued operations of $432,000. Both items are net of applicable income taxes. Compute earnings per share for 2008.

(LO 6) **E16-15 (EPS: Simple Capital Structure)** Ace Company had 200,000 shares of common stock outstanding on December 31, 2008. During the year 2009 the company issued 8,000 shares on May 1 and retired 14,000 shares on October 31. For the year 2009 Ace Company reported net income of $249,690 after a casualty loss of $40,600 (net of tax).

Instructions

What earnings per share data should be reported at the bottom of its income statement, assuming that the casualty loss is extraordinary?

(LO 6) **E16-16 (EPS: Simple Capital Structure)** Flagstad Inc. presented the following data.

Net income	$2,500,000
Preferred stock: 50,000 shares outstanding,	
$100 par, 8% cumulative, not convertible	5,000,000
Common stock: Shares outstanding 1/1	750,000
Issued for cash, 5/1	300,000
Acquired treasury stock for cash, 8/1	150,000
2-for-1 stock split, 10/1	

Instructions

Compute earnings per share.

(LO 6) **E16-17 (EPS: Simple Capital Structure)** A portion of the combined statement of income and retained earnings of Seminole Inc. for the current year follows.

Income before extraordinary item		$15,000,000
Extraordinary loss, net of applicable		
income tax (Note 1)		1,340,000
Net income		13,660,000
Retained earnings at the beginning of the year		83,250,000
		96,910,000
Dividends declared:		
On preferred stock—$6.00 per share	$ 300,000	
On common stock—$1.75 per share	14,875,000	15,175,000
Retained earnings at the end of the year		$81,735,000

Note 1. During the year, Seminole Inc. suffered a major casualty loss of $1,340,000 after applicable income tax reduction of $1,200,000.

At the end of the current year, Seminole Inc. has outstanding 8,500,000 shares of $10 par common stock and 50,000 shares of 6% preferred.

On April 1 of the current year, Seminole Inc. issued 1,000,000 shares of common stock for $32 per share to help finance the casualty.

Instructions

Compute the earnings per share on common stock for the current year as it should be reported to stockholders.

(LO 6) **E16-18 (EPS: Simple Capital Structure)** On January 1, 2008, Lennon Industries had stock outstanding as follows.

6% Cumulative preferred stock, $100 par value,	
issued and outstanding 10,000 shares	$1,000,000
Common stock, $10 par value, issued and	
outstanding 200,000 shares	2,000,000

To acquire the net assets of three smaller companies, Lennon authorized the issuance of an additional 160,000 common shares. The acquisitions took place as shown below.

Date of Acquisition	Shares Issued
Company A April 1, 2008	50,000
Company B July 1, 2008	80,000
Company C October 1, 2008	30,000

On May 14, 2008, Lennon realized a $90,000 (before taxes) insurance gain on the expropriation of investments originally purchased in 1994.

On December 31, 2008, Lennon recorded net income of $300,000 before tax and exclusive of the gain.

Instructions

Assuming a 50% tax rate, compute the earnings per share data that should appear on the financial statements of Lennon Industries as of December 31, 2008. Assume that the expropriation is extraordinary.

(LO 6) **E16-19** **(EPS: Simple Capital Structure)** At January 1, 2008, Langley Company's outstanding shares included the following.

> 280,000 shares of $50 par value, 7% cumulative preferred stock
> 900,000 shares of $1 par value common stock

Net income for 2008 was $2,530,000. No cash dividends were declared or paid during 2008. On February 15, 2009, however, all preferred dividends in arrears were paid, together with a 5% stock dividend on common shares. There were no dividends in arrears prior to 2008.

On April 1, 2008, 450,000 shares of common stock were sold for $10 per share, and on October 1, 2008, 110,000 shares of common stock were purchased for $20 per share and held as treasury stock.

Instructions

Compute earnings per share for 2008. Assume that financial statements for 2008 were issued in March 2009.

(LO 7) **E16-20** **(EPS with Convertible Bonds, Various Situations)** In 2006 Chirac Enterprises issued, at par, 60 $1,000, 8% bonds, each convertible into 100 shares of common stock. Chirac had revenues of $17,500 and expenses other than interest and taxes of $8,400 for 2007. (Assume that the tax rate is 40%.) Throughout 2007, 2,000 shares of common stock were outstanding; none of the bonds was converted or redeemed.

Instructions

(a) Compute diluted earnings per share for 2007.

(b) Assume the same facts as those assumed for part (a), except that the 60 bonds were issued on September 1, 2007 (rather than in 2006), and none have been converted or redeemed.

(c) Assume the same facts as assumed for part (a), except that 20 of the 60 bonds were actually converted on July 1, 2007.

(LO 7) **E16-21** **(EPS with Convertible Bonds)** On June 1, 2005, Andre Company and Agassi Company merged to form Lancaster Inc. A total of 800,000 shares were issued to complete the merger. The new corporation reports on a calendar-year basis.

On April 1, 2007, the company issued an additional 400,000 shares of stock for cash. All 1,200,000 shares were outstanding on December 31, 2007.

Lancaster Inc. also issued $600,000 of 20-year, 8% convertible bonds at par on July 1, 2007. Each $1,000 bond converts to 40 shares of common at any interest date. None of the bonds have been converted to date.

Lancaster Inc. is preparing its annual report for the fiscal year ending December 31, 2007. The annual report will show earnings per share figures based upon a reported after-tax net income of $1,540,000. (The tax rate is 40%.)

Instructions

Determine the following for 2007.

(a) The number of shares to be used for calculating:
(1) Basic earnings per share.
(2) Diluted earnings per share.

(b) The earnings figures to be used for calculating:
(1) Basic earnings per share.
(2) Diluted earnings per share.

(CMA adapted)

(LO 2, 7) **E16-22** **(EPS with Convertible Bonds and Preferred Stock)** The Simon Corporation issued 10-year, $5,000,000 par, 7% callable convertible subordinated debentures on January 2, 2007. The bonds have a par value of $1,000, with interest payable annually. The current conversion ratio is 14:1, and in 2 years it will increase to 18:1. At the date of issue, the bonds were sold at 98. Bond discount is amortized on a straight-line basis. Simon's effective tax was 35%. Net income in 2007 was $9,500,000, and the company had 2,000,000 shares outstanding during the entire year.

Instructions

(a) Prepare a schedule to compute both basic and diluted earnings per share.

(b) Discuss how the schedule would differ if the security was convertible preferred stock.

(LO 2, 7) **E16-23 (EPS with Convertible Bonds and Preferred Stock)** On January 1, 2007, Crocker Company issued 10-year, $2,000,000 face value, 6% bonds, at par. Each $1,000 bond is convertible into 15 shares of Crocker common stock. Crocker's net income in 2007 was $300,000, and its tax rate was 40%. The company had 100,000 shares of common stock outstanding throughout 2007. None of the bonds were converted in 2007.

Instructions

(a) Compute diluted earnings per share for 2007.

(b) Compute diluted earnings per share for 2007, assuming the same facts as above, except that $1,000,000 of 6% convertible preferred stock was issued instead of the bonds. Each $100 preferred share is convertible into 5 shares of Crocker common stock.

(LO 7) **E16-24 (EPS with Options, Various Situations)** Venzuela Company's net income for 2007 is $50,000. The only potentially dilutive securities outstanding were 1,000 options issued during 2006, each exercisable for one share at $6. None has been exercised, and 10,000 shares of common were outstanding during 2007. The average market price of Venzuela's stock during 2007 was $20.

Instructions

(a) Compute diluted earnings per share. (Round to nearest cent.)

(b) Assume the same facts as those assumed for part (a), except that the 1,000 options were issued on October 1, 2007 (rather than in 2006). The average market price during the last 3 months of 2007 was $20.

(LO 7) **E16-25 (EPS with Contingent Issuance Agreement)** Winsor Inc. recently purchased Holiday Corp., a large midwestern home painting corporation. One of the terms of the merger was that if Holiday's income for 2007 was $110,000 or more, 10,000 additional shares would be issued to Holiday's stockholders in 2008. Holiday's income for 2006 was $120,000.

Instructions

(a) Would the contingent shares have to be considered in Winsor's 2006 earnings per share computations?

(b) Assume the same facts, except that the 10,000 shares are contingent on Holiday's achieving a net income of $130,000 in 2007. Would the contingent shares have to be considered in Winsor's earnings per share computations for 2006?

(LO 7) **E16-26 (EPS with Warrants)** Howat Corporation earned $360,000 during a period when it had an average of 100,000 shares of common stock outstanding. The common stock sold at an average market price of $15 per share during the period. Also outstanding were 15,000 warrants that could be exercised to purchase one share of common stock for $10 for each warrant exercised.

Instructions

(a) Are the warrants dilutive?

(b) Compute basic earnings per share.

(c) Compute diluted earnings per share.

(LO 8) *****E16-27 (Accounting for Restricted Stock)** Tweedie Company issues 4,000 shares of restricted stock to its CFO, Miles Hobart, on January 1, 2007. The stock has a fair value of $100,000 on this date. The service period related to this restricted stock is 4 years. Vesting occurs if Hobart stays with the company for 4 years. The par value of the stock is $5. At December 31, 2008, the fair value of the stock is $120,000.

Instructions

(a) Prepare the journal entries to record the restricted stock on January 1, 2007 (the date of grant) and December 31, 2008.

(b) On March 4, 2009, Hobart leaves the company. Prepare the journal entry (if any) to account for this forfeiture.

(LO 8) *****E16-28 (Stock Appreciation Rights)** On December 31, 2003, Beckford Company issues 150,000 stock appreciation rights to its officers entitling them to receive cash for the difference between the market price of its stock and a preestablished price of $10. The fair value of the SARs is estimated to be $4 per SAR on

December 31, 2004; $1 on December 31, 2005; $10 on December 31, 2006; and $9 on December 31, 2007. The service period is 4 years, and the exercise period is 7 years.

Instructions

(a) Prepare a schedule that shows the amount of compensation expense allocable to each year affected by the stock appreciation rights plan.

(b) Prepare the entry at December 31, 2007, to record compensation expense, if any, in 2007.

(c) Prepare the entry on December 31, 2007, assuming that all 150,000 SARs are exercised.

(LO 8) *E16-29 **(Stock Appreciation Rights)** Capulet Company establishes a stock appreciation rights program that entitles its new president Ben Davis to receive cash for the difference between the market price of the stock and a preestablished price of $30 (also market price) on December 31, 2004, on 30,000 SARs. The date of grant is December 31, 2004, and the required employment (service) period is 4 years. President Davis exercises all of the SARs in 2010. The fair value of the SARs is estimated to be $6 per SAR on December 31, 2005; $9 on December 31, 2006; $15 on December 31, 2007; $6 on December 31, 2008; and $18 on December 31, 2009.

Instructions

(a) Prepare a 5-year (2005–2009) schedule of compensation expense pertaining to the 30,000 SARs granted president Davis.

(b) Prepare the journal entry for compensation expense in 2005, 2008, and 2009 relative to the 30,000 SARs.

See the book's website, **www.wiley.com/college/kieso**, for Additional Exercises.

PROBLEMS

(LO 1, 3, 4) P16-1 **(Entries for Various Dilutive Securities)** The stockholders' equity section of McLean Inc. at the beginning of the current year appears below.

Common stock, $10 par value, authorized 1,000,000 shares, 300,000 shares issued and outstanding	$3,000,000
Paid-in capital in excess of par	600,000
Retained earnings	570,000

During the current year the following transactions occurred.

1. The company issued to the stockholders 100,000 rights. Ten rights are needed to buy one share of stock at $32. The rights were void after 30 days. The market price of the stock at this time was $34 per share.

2. The company sold to the public a $200,000, 10% bond issue at par. The company also issued with each $100 bond one detachable stock purchase warrant, which provided for the purchase of common stock at $30 per share. Shortly after issuance, similar bonds without warrants were selling at 96 and the warrants at $8.

3. All but 10,000 of the rights issued in (1) were exercised in 30 days.

4. At the end of the year, 80% of the warrants in (2) had been exercised, and the remaining were outstanding and in good standing.

5. During the current year, the company granted stock options for 5,000 shares of common stock to company executives. The company using a fair value option pricing model determines that each option is worth $10. The option price is $30. The options were to expire at year-end and were considered compensation for the current year.

6. All but 1,000 shares related to the stock option plan were exercised by year-end. The expiration resulted because one of the executives failed to fulfill an obligation related to the employment contract.

Instructions

(a) Prepare general journal entries for the current year to record the transactions listed above.

(b) Prepare the stockholders' equity section of the balance sheet at the end of the current year. Assume that retained earnings at the end of the current year is $750,000.

(LO 1) P16-2 **(Entries for Conversion, Amortization, and Interest of Bonds)** Counter Inc. issued $1,500,000 of convertible 10-year bonds on July 1, 2007. The bonds provide for 12% interest payable semiannually on January 1 and July 1. The discount in connection with the issue was $34,000, which is being amortized monthly on a straight-line basis.

The bonds are convertible after one year into 8 shares of Counter Inc.'s $100 par value common stock for each $1,000 of bonds.

On August 1, 2008, $150,000 of bonds were turned in for conversion into common. Interest has been accrued monthly and paid as due. At the time of conversion any accrued interest on bonds being converted is paid in cash.

Instructions

(Round to nearest dollar)

Prepare the journal entries to record the conversion, amortization, and interest in connection with the bonds as of the following dates.

(a) August 1, 2008. (Assume the book value method is used.)
(b) August 31, 2008.
(c) December 31, 2008, including closing entries for end-of-year.

(AICPA adapted)

(LO 4) **P16-3** **(Stock Option Plan)** ISU Company adopted a stock option plan on November 30, 2005, that provided that 70,000 shares of $5 par value stock be designated as available for the granting of options to officers of the corporation at a price of $8 a share. The market value was $12 a share on November 30, 2005.

On January 2, 2006, options to purchase 28,000 shares were granted to president Don Pedro—15,000 for services to be rendered in 2006 and 13,000 for services to be rendered in 2007. Also on that date, options to purchase 14,000 shares were granted to vice president Beatrice Leonato—7,000 for services to be rendered in 2006 and 7,000 for services to be rendered in 2007. The market value of the stock was $14 a share on January 2, 2006. The options were exercisable for a period of one year following the year in which the services were rendered. The fair value of the options on the grant date was $3 per option.

In 2007 neither the president nor the vice president exercised their options because the market price of the stock was below the exercise price. The market value of the stock was $7 a share on December 31, 2007, when the options for 2006 services lapsed.

On December 31, 2008, both president Pedro and vice president Leonato exercised their options for 13,000 and 7,000 shares, respectively, when the market price was $16 a share.

Instructions

Prepare the necessary journal entries in 2005 when the stock option plan was adopted, in 2006 when options were granted, in 2007 when options lapsed, and in 2008 when options were exercised.

(LO 7) **P16-4** **(EPS with Complex Capital Structure)** Diane Leto, controller at Dewey Yaeger Pharmaceutical Industries, a public company, is currently preparing the calculation for basic and diluted earnings per share and the related disclosure for Yaeger's external financial statements. Below is selected financial information for the fiscal year ended June 30, 2008.

DEWEY YAEGER PHARMACEUTICAL INDUSTRIES	
SELECTED STATEMENT OF	
FINANCIAL POSITION INFORMATION	
JUNE 30, 2008	
Long-term debt	
Notes payable, 10%	$ 1,000,000
7% convertible bonds payable	5,000,000
10% bonds payable	6,000,000
Total long-term debt	$12,000,000
Shareholders' equity	
Preferred stock, 8.5% cumulative, $50 par value,	
100,000 shares authorized, 25,000 shares issued	
and outstanding	$ 1,250,000
Common stock, $1 par, 10,000,000 shares authorized,	
1,000,000 shares issued and outstanding	1,000,000
Additional paid-in capital	4,000,000
Retained earnings	6,000,000
Total shareholders' equity	$12,250,000

The following transactions have also occurred at Yaeger.

1. Options were granted in 2006 to purchase 100,000 shares at $15 per share. Although no options were exercised during 2008, the average price per common share during fiscal year 2008 was $20 per share.

2. Each bond was issued at face value. The 7% convertible debenture will convert into common stock at 50 shares per $1,000 bond. It is exercisable after 5 years and was issued in 2007.
3. The 8.5% preferred stock was issued in 2006.
4. There are no preferred dividends in arrears; however, preferred dividends were not declared in fiscal year 2008.
5. The 1,000,000 shares of common stock were outstanding for the entire 2008 fiscal year.
6. Net income for fiscal year 2008 was $1,500,000, and the average income tax rate is 40%.

Instructions

For the fiscal year ended June 30, 2008, calculate the following for Dewey Yaeger Pharmaceutical Industries.

(a) Basic earnings per share.
(b) Diluted earnings per share.

(LO 6) **P16-5 (Basic EPS: Two-Year Presentation)** Hillel Corporation is preparing the comparative financial statements for the annual report to its shareholders for fiscal years ended May 31, 2006, and May 31, 2007. The income from operations for each year was $1,800,000 and $2,500,000, respectively. In both years, the company incurred a 10% interest expense on $2,400,000 of debt, an obligation that requires interest-only payments for 5 years. The company experienced a loss of $500,000 from a fire in its Scotsland facility in February 2007, which was determined to be an extraordinary loss. The company uses a 40% effective tax rate for income taxes.

The capital structure of Hillel Corporation on June 1, 2005, consisted of 2 million shares of common stock outstanding and 20,000 shares of $50 par value, 8%, cumulative preferred stock. There were no preferred dividends in arrears, and the company had not issued any convertible securities, options, or warrants.

On October 1, 2005, Hillel sold an additional 500,000 shares of the common stock at $20 per share. Hillel distributed a 20% stock dividend on the common shares outstanding on January 1, 2006. On December 1, 2006, Hillel was able to sell an additional 800,000 shares of the common stock at $22 per share. These were the only common stock transactions that occurred during the two fiscal years.

Instructions

(a) Identify whether the capital structure at Hillel Corporation is a simple or complex capital structure, and explain why.
(b) Determine the weighted-average number of shares that Hillel Corporation would use in calculating earnings per share for the fiscal year ended
(1) May 31, 2006.
(2) May 31, 2007.
(c) Prepare, in good form, a comparative income statement, beginning with income from operations, for Hillel Corporation for the fiscal years ended May 31, 2006, and May 31, 2007. This statement will be included in Hillel's annual report and should display the appropriate earnings per share presentations.

(CMA adapted)

(LO 7) **P16-6 (EPS Computation of Basic and Diluted EPS)** Edmund Halvor of the controller's office of East Aurora Corporation was given the assignment of determining the basic and diluted earnings per share values for the year ending December 31, 2007. Halvor has compiled the information listed below.

1. The company is authorized to issue 8,000,000 shares of $10 par value common stock. As of December 31, 2006, 3,000,000 shares had been issued and were outstanding.
2. The per share market prices of the common stock on selected dates were as follows.

	Price per Share
July 1, 2006	$20.00
January 1, 2007	21.00
April 1, 2007	25.00
July 1, 2007	11.00
August 1, 2007	10.50
November 1, 2007	9.00
December 31, 2007	10.00

3. A total of 700,000 shares of an authorized 1,200,000 shares of convertible preferred stock had been issued on July 1, 2006. The stock was issued at its par value of $25, and it has a cumulative dividend of $3 per share. The stock is convertible into common stock at the rate of one share of convertible preferred for one share of common. The rate of conversion is to be automatically adjusted for stock splits and stock dividends. Dividends are paid quarterly on September 30, December 31, March 31, and June 30.

4. East Aurora Corporation is subject to a 40% income tax rate.

5. The after-tax net income for the year ended December 31, 2007 was $13,550,000.

The following specific activities took place during 2007.

1. January 1—A 5% common stock dividend was issued. The dividend had been declared on December 1, 2006, to all stockholders of record on December 29, 2006.

2. April 1—A total of 200,000 shares of the $3 convertible preferred stock was converted into common stock. The company issued new common stock and retired the preferred stock. This was the only conversion of the preferred stock during 2007.

3. July 1—A 2-for-1 split of the common stock became effective on this date. The board of directors had authorized the split on June 1.

4. August 1—A total of 300,000 shares of common stock were issued to acquire a factory building.

5. November 1—A total of 24,000 shares of common stock were purchased on the open market at $9 per share. These shares were to be held as treasury stock and were still in the treasury as of December 31, 2007.

6. Common stock cash dividends—Cash dividends to common stockholders were declared and paid as follows.
April 15—$0.30 per share
October 15—$0.20 per share

7. Preferred stock cash dividends—Cash dividends to preferred stockholders were declared and paid as scheduled.

Instructions

(a) Determine the number of shares used to compute basic earnings per share for the year ended December 31, 2007.

(b) Determine the number of shares used to compute diluted earnings per share for the year ended December 31, 2007.

(c) Compute the adjusted net income to be used as the numerator in the basic earnings per share calculation for the year ended December 31, 2007.

(L0 7) **P16-7** **(Computation of Basic and Diluted EPS)** The information below pertains to Prancer Company for 2007.

Net income for the year	$1,200,000
8% convertible bonds issued at par ($1,000 per bond). Each bond is convertible into 40 shares of common stock.	2,000,000
6% convertible, cumulative preferred stock, $100 par value. Each share is convertible into 3 shares of common stock.	3,000,000
Common stock, $10 par value	6,000,000
Common stock options (granted in a prior year) to purchase 50,000 shares of common stock at $20 per share	500,000
Tax rate for 2004	40%
Average market price of common stock	$25 per share

There were no changes during 2007 in the number of common shares, preferred shares, or convertible bonds outstanding. There is no treasury stock.

Instructions

(a) Compute basic earnings per share for 2007.

(b) Compute diluted earnings per share for 2007.

(L0 6) **P16-8** **(EPS with Stock Dividend and Extraordinary Items)** Cordelia Corporation is preparing the comparative financial statements to be included in the annual report to stockholders. Cordelia employs a fiscal year ending May 31.

Income from operations before income taxes for Cordelia was $1,400,000 and $660,000, respectively, for fiscal years ended May 31, 2007 and 2006. Cordelia experienced an extraordinary loss of $500,000 because of an earthquake on March 3, 2007. A 40% combined income tax rate pertains to any and all of Cordelia Corporation's profits, gains, and losses.

Cordelia's capital structure consists of preferred stock and common stock. The company has not issued any convertible securities or warrants and there are no outstanding stock options.

Cordelia issued 50,000 shares of $100 par value, 6% cumulative preferred stock in 2003. All of this stock is outstanding, and no preferred dividends are in arrears.

There were 1,500,000 shares of $1 par common stock outstanding on June 1, 2005. On September 1, 2005, Cordelia sold an additional 400,000 shares of the common stock at $17 per share. Cordelia distributed a 20% stock dividend on the common shares outstanding on December 1, 2006. These were the only common stock transactions during the past 2 fiscal years.

Instructions

(a) Determine the weighted-average number of common shares that would be used in computing earnings per share on the current comparative income statement for:

    (1) The year ended May 31, 2006.

    (2) The year ended May 31, 2007.

(b) Starting with income from operations before income taxes, prepare a comparative income statement for the years ended May 31, 2007 and 2006. The statement will be part of Cordelia Corporation's annual report to stockholders and should include appropriate earnings per share presentation.

(c) The capital structure of a corporation is the result of its past financing decisions. Furthermore, the earnings per share data presented on a corporation's financial statements is dependent upon the capital structure.

    (1) Explain why Cordelia Corporation is considered to have a simple capital structure.

    (2) Describe how earnings per share data would be presented for a corporation that has a complex capital structure.

(CMA adapted)

CONCEPTS FOR ANALYSIS

CA16-1 (Warrants Issued with Bonds and Convertible Bonds) Incurring long-term debt with an arrangement whereby lenders receive an option to buy common stock during all or a portion of the time the debt is outstanding is a frequent corporate financing practice. In some situations the result is achieved through the issuance of convertible bonds; in others, the debt instruments and the warrants to buy stock are separate.

Instructions

(a) (1) Describe the differences that exist in current accounting for original proceeds of the issuance of convertible bonds and of debt instruments with separate warrants to purchase common stock.

    (2) Discuss the underlying rationale for the differences described in (a)1 above.

    (3) Summarize the arguments that have been presented in favor of accounting for convertible bonds in the same manner as accounting for debt with separate warrants.

(b) At the start of the year Biron Company issued $18,000,000 of 12% bonds along with warrants to buy 1,200,000 shares of its $10 par value common stock at $18 per share. The bonds mature over the next 10 years, starting one year from date of issuance, with annual maturities of $1,800,000. At the time, Biron had 9,600,000 shares of common stock outstanding, and the market price was $23 per share. The company received $20,040,000 for the bonds and the warrants. For Biron Company, 12% was a relatively low borrowing rate. If offered alone, at this time, the bonds would have been issued at a 22% discount. Prepare the journal entry (or entries) for the issuance of the bonds and warrants for the cash consideration received.

(AICPA adapted)

CA16-2 (Ethical Issues—Compensation Plan) The executive officers of Coach Corporation have a performance-based compensation plan. The performance criteria of this plan is linked to growth in earnings per share. When annual EPS growth is 12%, the Coach executives earn 100% of the shares; if growth is 16%, they earn 125%. If EPS growth is lower than 8%, the executives receive no additional compensation.

In 2006, Joanna Becker, the controller of Coach, reviews year-end estimates of bad debt expense and warranty expense. She calculates the EPS growth at 15%. Peter Reiser, a member of the executive group, remarks over lunch one day that the estimate of bad debt expense might be decreased, increasing EPS growth to 16.1%. Becker is not sure she should do this because she believes that the current estimate of bad debts is sound. On the other hand, she recognizes that a great deal of subjectivity is involved in the computation.

Instructions

Answer the following questions.

(a) What, if any, is the ethical dilemma for Becker?

(b) Should Becker's knowledge of the compensation plan be a factor that influences her estimate?

(c) How should Becker respond to Reiser's request?

 CA16-3 (Stock Warrants—Various Types) For various reasons a corporation may issue warrants to purchase shares of its common stock at specified prices that, depending on the circumstances, may be less than, equal to, or greater than the current market price. For example, warrants may be issued:

1. To existing stockholders on a pro rata basis.
2. To certain key employees under an incentive stock option plan.
3. To purchasers of the corporation's bonds.

Instructions

For each of the three examples of how stock warrants are used:

(a) Explain why they are used.

(b) Discuss the significance of the price (or prices) at which the warrants are issued (or granted) in relation to (1) the current market price of the company's stock, and (2) the length of time over which they can be exercised.

(c) Describe the information that should be disclosed in financial statements, or notes thereto, that are prepared when stock warrants are outstanding in the hands of the three groups listed above.

(AICPA adapted)

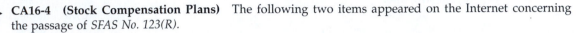

CA16-4 **(Stock Compensation Plans)** The following two items appeared on the Internet concerning the passage of *SFAS No. 123(R)*.

WASHINGTON, D.C.—*February 17, 2005*   Congressman David Dreier (R–CA), Chairman of the House Rules Committee, and Congresswoman Anna Eshoo (D–CA) reintroduced legislation today that will preserve broad-based employee stock option plans and give investors critical information they need to understand how employee stock options impact the value of their shares.

"Last year, the U.S. House of Representatives overwhelmingly voted for legislation that would have ensured the continued ability of innovative companies to offer stock options to rank-and-file employees," Dreier stated. "Both the Financial Accounting Standards Board (FASB) and the Securities and Exchange Commission (SEC) continue to ignore our calls to address legitimate concerns about the impact of FASB's new standard on workers' ability to have an ownership stake in the New Economy, and its failure to address the real need of shareholders: accurate and meaningful information about a company's use of stock options."

"In December 2004, FASB issued a stock option expensing standard that will render a huge blow to the 21st century economy," Dreier said. "Their action and the SEC's apparent lack of concern for protecting shareholders, requires us to once again take a firm stand on the side of investors and economic growth. Giving investors the ability to understand how stock options impact the value of their shares is critical. And equally important is preserving the ability of companies to use this innovative tool to attract talented employees."

"Here We Go Again!" by Jack Ciesielski (2/21/2005, http://www.accountingobserver.com/blog/2005/02/here-we-go-again)   On February 17, Congressman David Dreier (R–CA), and Congresswoman Anna Eshoo (D–CA), officially entered Silicon Valley's bid to gum up the launch of honest reporting of stock option compensation: They co-sponsored a bill to "preserve broad-based employee stock option plans and give investors critical information they need to understand how employee stock options impact the value of their shares." You know what "critical information" they mean: stuff like the stock compensation for the top five officers in a company, with a rigged value set as close to zero as possible. Investors *crave* this kind of information. Other ways the good Congresspersons want to "help" investors: The bill "also requires the SEC to study the effectiveness of those disclosures over three years, during which time, no new accounting standard related to the treatment of stock options could be recognized. Finally, the bill requires the Secretary of Commerce to conduct a study and report to Congress on the impact of broad-based employee stock option plans on expanding employee corporate ownership, skilled worker recruitment and retention, research and innovation, economic growth, and international competitiveness."

It's the old "four corners" basketball strategy: stall, stall, stall. In the meantime, hope for regime change at your opponent, the FASB.

Instructions

(a) What are the major recommendations of *SFAS No. 123(R)*, "Share-Based Payment"?

(b) How do the provisions of *SFAS No. 123(R)* differ from the bill introduced by members of Congress (Dreier and Eshoo), which would require expensing for options issued to only the top five officers in a company? Which approach do you think would result in more useful information? (Focus on comparability.)

(c) The bill in Congress urges the FASB to develop a rule that preserves "the ability of companies to use this innovative tool to attract talented employees." Write a response to these Congress-people explaining the importance of neutrality in financial accounting and reporting.

CA16-5 (EPS: Preferred Dividends, Options, and Convertible Debt) "Earnings per share" (EPS) is the most featured single financial statistic about modern corporations. Daily published quotations of stock prices have recently been expanded to include for many securities a "times earnings" figure that is based on EPS. Stock analysts often focus their discussions on the EPS of the corporations they study.

Instructions

(a) Explain how dividends or dividend requirements on any class of preferred stock that may be outstanding affect the computation of EPS.

(b) One of the technical procedures applicable in EPS computations is the "treasury stock method." Briefly describe the circumstances under which it might be appropriate to apply the treasury stock method.

(c) Convertible debentures are considered potentially dilutive common shares. Explain how convertible debentures are handled for purposes of EPS computations.

(AICPA adapted)

CA16-6 (EPS Concepts and Effect of Transactions on EPS) Fernandez Corporation, a new audit client of yours, has not reported earnings per share data in its annual reports to stockholders in the past. The treasurer, Angelo Balthazar, requested that you furnish information about the reporting of earnings per share data in the current year's annual report in accordance with generally accepted accounting principles.

Instructions

(a) Define the term "earnings per share" as it applies to a corporation with a capitalization structure composed of only one class of common stock. Explain how earnings per share should be computed and how the information should be disclosed in the corporation's financial statements.

(b) Discuss the treatment, if any, that should be given to each of the following items in computing earnings per share of common stock for financial statement reporting.

(1) Outstanding preferred stock issued at a premium with a par value liquidation right.

(2) The exercise at a price below market value but above book value of a common stock option issued during the current fiscal year to officers of the corporation.

(3) The replacement of a machine immediately prior to the close of the current fiscal year at a cost 20% above the original cost of the replaced machine. The new machine will perform the same function as the old machine that was sold for its book value.

(4) The declaration of current dividends on cumulative preferred stock.

(5) The acquisition of some of the corporation's outstanding common stock during the current fiscal year. The stock was classified as treasury stock.

(6) A 2-for-1 stock split of common stock during the current fiscal year.

(7) A provision created out of retained earnings for a contingent liability from a possible lawsuit.

CA16-7 (EPS, Antidilution) Matt Kacskos, a stockholder of Howat Corporation, has asked you, the firm's accountant, to explain why his stock warrants were not included in diluted EPS. In order to explain this situation, you must briefly explain what dilutive securities are, why they are included in the EPS calculation, and why some securities are antidilutive and thus not included in this calculation.

Instructions

Write Mr. Kacskos a 1–1.5 page letter explaining why the warrants are not included in the calculation. Use the following data to help you explain this situation.

Howat Corporation earned $228,000 during the period, when it had an average of 100,000 shares of common stock outstanding. The common stock sold at an average market price of $25 per share during the period. Also outstanding were 15,000 warrants that could be exercised to purchase one share of common stock at $30 per warrant.

*CA16-8 (Restricted Stock and Stock Appreciation Rights)** In 2005 Sanford Co. adopted a plan to give additional incentive compensation to its dealers to sell its principal product, fire extinguishers. Under the plan Sanford transferred 9,000 shares of its $1 par value stock to a trust with the provision that Sanford would have to forfeit interest in the trust and no part of the trust fund could ever revert to Sanford. The restricted shares were to be distributed to dealers on the basis of their shares of fire extinguisher purchases from Sanford (above certain minimum levels) over the 3-year period ending June 30, 2008.

In 2005 the stock was closely held. The book value of the stock was $7.90 per share as of June 30, 2005, and in 2005 additional shares were sold to existing stockholders for $8 per share. On the basis of this information, market value of the stock was determined to be $8 per share.

In 2005 when the shares were transferred to the trust, Sanford charged prepaid expenses for $72,000 ($8 per share market value) and credited common stock for $9,000 and additional paid-in capital for $63,000. The prepaid expense was charged to operations over a 3-year period ended June 30, 2008.

Sanford sold a substantial number of shares of its stock to the public in 2007 at $60 per share.

In July 2008 all shares of the stock in the trust were distributed to the dealers. The market value of the shares at date of distribution of the stock from the trust had risen to $110 per share.

Instructions

(a) How much should be reported as selling expense in each of the years noted above.

(b) Sanford is also considering other types of option plans. One such plan is a stock appreciation rights (SARs) plan. What is a stock appreciation rights plan? What is a potential disadvantage of a SAR plan from the viewpoint of the company?

USING YOUR JUDGMENT

Financial Reporting Problem

The Procter & Gamble Company (P&G)

The financial statements of (**P&G**) are presented in Appendix 5B or can be accessed on the KWW website.

Instructions

Refer to P&G's financial statements and accompanying notes to answer the following questions.

(a) Under P&G's stock-based compensation plan, stock options are granted annually to key managers and directors.

   (1) How many options were granted during 2004 under the plan?

   (2) How many options were exercisable at June 30, 2004?

   (3) How many options were exercised in 2004, and what was the average price of those exercised?

   (4) What was the range of exercise prices for options outstanding at June 30, 2004?

   (5) How many years from the grant date do the options expire?

   (6) To what accounts are the proceeds from these option exercises credited?

   (7) What was the number of outstanding options at June 30, 2004, and at what average exercise price?

(b) What number of diluted weighted average common shares outstanding was used by P&G in computing earnings per share for 2004, 2003, and 2002? What was P&G's diluted earnings per share in 2004, 2003, and 2002?

(c) What would be the amount of compensation expense reported in 2004 for P&G if it had used the fair value method? (*Hint*: See Note 1.)

Financial Statement Analysis Case

Kellogg Company

Kellogg Company in its 2004 Annual Report in Note 1—Accounting Policies made the following comment about its accounting for employee stock options and other stock-based compensation.

> **Stock compensation (in part)** The Company currently uses the intrinsic value method prescribed by *Accounting Principles Board Opinion (APB) No. 25*, "Accounting for Stock Issued to Employees," to account for its employee stock options and other stock-based compensation. Under this method, because the exercise price of the Company's employee stock options equals the market price of the underlying stock on the date of the grant, no compensation expense is recognized. The following table presents the pro forma results for the current and prior years, as if the Company had used the alternate fair value method of accounting for stock-based compensation, prescribed by *SFAS No. 123*, "Accounting for Stock-Based Compensation" (as amended by *SFAS No. 148*).

Stock-based compensation expense, net of tax:

(millions, except per share data)	2004	2003	2002
As reported	$11.4	$12.5	$10.7
Pro forma	$41.8	$42.1	$52.8
Net earnings:			
As reported	$890.6	$787.1	$720.9
Pro forma	$860.2	$757.5	$678.8
Basic net earnings per share:			
As reported	$2.16	$1.93	$1.77
Pro forma	$2.09	$1.86	$1.66
Diluted net earnings per share:			
As reported	$2.14	$1.92	$1.75
Pro forma	$2.07	$1.85	$1.65

Under this pro forma method, the fair value of each option grant (net of estimated unvested forfeitures) was estimated at the date of grant using an option-pricing model and was recognized over the vesting period, generally two years. Refer to Note 8 for further information on the Company's stock compensation programs. In December 2004, the FASB issued *SFAS No. 123(Revised)*, "Share-Based Payment," which generally requires public companies to measure the cost of employee services received in exchange for an award of equity instruments based on the grant-date fair value and to recognize this cost over the requisite service period. The Company plans to adopt *SFAS No. 123(Revised)*, as of the beginning of its 2005 fiscal third quarter and is currently considering retrospective restatement to the beginning of its 2005 fiscal year. Once this standard is adopted, management believes full-year fiscal 2005 net earnings per share will be reduced by approximately $.08.

Instructions

(a) Briefly discuss how Kellogg's financial statements will be affected by the adoption of *SFAS No. 123(R)*.

(b) Some companies argued that the recognition provisions of *SFAS No. 123(R)* are not needed, because the computation of earnings per share takes into account dilutive securities such as stock options. Do you agree? Explain, using the Kellogg disclosure provided above.

Comparative Analysis Case

The Coca-Cola Company and PepsiCo, Inc.

Instructions

Go to the KWW website and use information found there to answer the following questions related to **The Coca-Cola Company** and **PepsiCo, Inc.**

(a) What employee stock option compensation plans are offered by Coca-Cola and PepsiCo?

(b) How many options are outstanding at year-end 2004 for both Coca-Cola and PepsiCo?

(c) How many options were granted by Coca-Cola and PepsiCo to officers and employees during 2004?

(d) How many options were exercised during 2004?

(e) What was the range of option prices exercised by Coca-Cola and PepsiCo employees during 2004?

(f) What are the weighted average number of shares used by Coca-Cola and PepsiCo in 2004, 2003, and 2002 to compute diluted earnings per share?

(g) What was the diluted net income per share for Coca-Cola and PepsiCo for 2004, 2003, and 2002?

Research Case

An article by Martha Brannigan titled "Questioning the Books: **AES** Seeks to Reassure Investors Worried over Dilution of Equity" appeared in the *Wall Street Journal* on February 22, 2002.

Instructions

Read this article and answer the following questions.

(a) Where does AES get additional unregistered shares to secure its loans? How are these shares reported in its financial statements?

(b) Exactly how does a company "register shares"? How does registering shares affect the company's accounts?

(c) The article says registering the shares would dilute earnings per share. What is dilution? Why would registering the shares cause dilution?

(d) Why is measurement of dilution in earnings per share a problem for investors?

International Reporting Case

Sepracor, Inc., a U.S. drug company, reported the following information. The company prepares its financial statements in accordance with U.S. GAAP.

	2004
Current liabilities	$ 204,110
5% convertible debt	1,160,820
Total liabilities	1,370,233
Stockholders equity	(331,115)
Net income	(295,658)

Analysts attempting to compare Sepracor to international drug companies may face a challenge due to differences in accounting for convertible debt under International Financial Reporting Standards (IFRS). Under *IAS 32*, "Financial Instruments," convertible bonds, at issuance, must be classified separately into their debt and equity components based on estimated fair value.

Instructions

(a) Compute the following ratios for Sepracor, Inc. (Assume that year-end balances approximate annual averages.)
  (1) Return on assets.
  (2) Return on equity.
  (3) Debt to assets ratio.

(b) Briefly discuss the operating performance and financial position of Sepracor. Based on this analysis would you make an investment in the company's 5% convertible bonds? Explain.

(c) Assume you want to compare Sepracor to an international company, like **Bayer** (which prepares its financial statements in accordance with IFRS). Assuming that the fair value of the equity component of Sepracor's convertible bonds is $450,000, how would you adjust the analysis above to make valid comparisons between Sepracor and Bayer?

Professional Research: Financial Accounting and Reporting

Richardson Company is contemplating the establishment of a share-based compensation plan to provide long-run incentives for its top management. However, members of the compensation committee of the board of directors have voiced some concerns about adopting these plans, based on news accounts related to a recent accounting standard in this area. They would like you to conduct some research on this recent standard so they can be better informed about the accounting for these plans.

Instructions

Using the **Financial Accounting Research System (FARS)**, respond to the following items. (Provide text strings used in your search.)

(a) Identify the recent standard governing the accounting for share-based payment compensation plans.

(b) What were the principal reasons for issuing a new standard in this area?

(c) What are the key differences in the measurement of fair value between the new standard and the prior standard?

(d) The Richardson Company board is also considering an employee share-purchase plan, but the board does not want to record expense related to the plan. What criteria must be met to avoid recording expense on an employee stock-purchase plan?

Professional Simulation

In this simulation you are asked to address questions related to the accounting for stock options and earnings per share computations. Prepare responses to all parts.

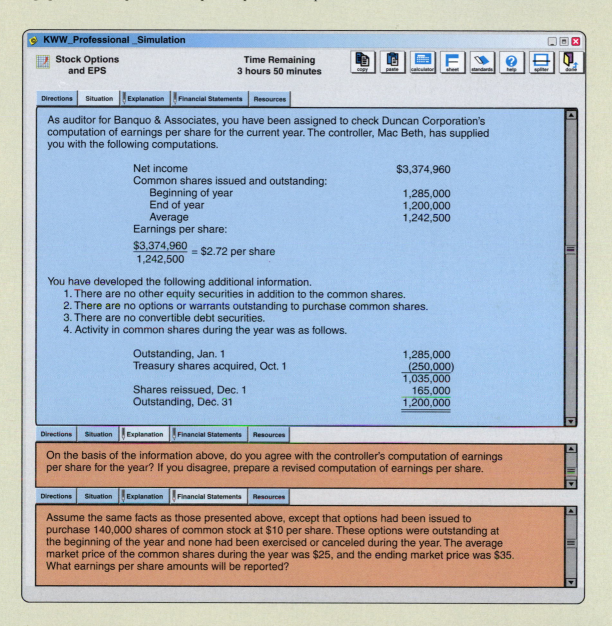

INVESTMENTS

Who's in Control Here?

The Coca-Cola Company (Coke) owns 36 percent of the shares of **Coca-Cola Enterprises** (a U.S. bottling business); **PepsiCo Inc.** owns 46 percent of **The Pepsi Bottling Group (PBG)** and 41 percent of **PepsiAmericas**. These bottling businesses are very important to Coca-Cola and PepsiCo, because they are the primary distributors of Coke and Pepsi products. In return, these companies depend on Coca-Cola and PepsiCo to provide significant marketing and distribution development support. Indeed, it can be said that Coca-Cola and PepsiCo control the bottling companies, who would not exist without their support.

However, because The Coca-Cola Company and PepsiCo own less than 50 percent of the shares in these companies, they do not prepare consolidated financial statements. Instead, Coca-Cola and PepsiCo account for these investments using the *equity method*. Under the equity method, for example, Coca-Cola reports a single income item for its profits from the bottlers, and only the net amount of its investment in the balance sheet.

Equity-method accounting gives Coca-Cola and PepsiCo pristine balance sheets and income statements, by separating the assets and liabilities and the profit margins of these bottlers from its beverage-making business. What's more, the International Accounting Standards Board (IASB) has issued *IAS No. 28* which requires that companies use the equity method. Previously, many international companies were permitted to use either the equity method or proportional consolidation for investments similar to Coke's and Pepsi's. It is good news that both U.S. and international companies are following the same rules. (On negative side, however, some of these companies should be consolidated but are not.)

A final point: In response to a recent FASB interpretation, companies are now starting to consolidate more 20 to 50 percent–owned investments. Consolidation of entities, such as the Coke and Pepsi bottlers, may be required if the risks and rewards of those investments accrue primarily to Coke and Pepsi.[1] In fact, Coke has consolidated some of its bottling companies, which should result in the reporting of more complete information on these affiliated companies.

---

[1]*Financial Accounting Standards Interpretation No. 46(R)*, "Consolidation of Variable Interest Entities (revised) —An Interpretation of *ARB No. 51*" (Norwalk, Conn.: FASB, December 2003.)

Learning Objectives

After studying this chapter, you should be able to:

1 Identify the three categories of debt securities and describe the accounting and reporting treatment for each category.

2 Understand the procedures for discount and premium amortization on bond investments.

3 Identify the categories of equity securities and describe the accounting and reporting treatment for each category.

4 Explain the equity method of accounting and compare it to the fair value method for equity securities.

5 Describe the disclosure requirements for investments in debt and equity securities.

6 Discuss the accounting for impairments of debt and equity investments.

7 Describe the accounting for transfer of investment securities between categories.

As our opening story indicates, U.S. and international standard-setters are studying the measurement, recognition, and disclosure for certain investments. In this chapter we address the accounting for debt and equity investments. Appendixes to this chapter discuss the accounting for derivative instruments and variable-interest entities. The content and organization of this chapter are as follows.

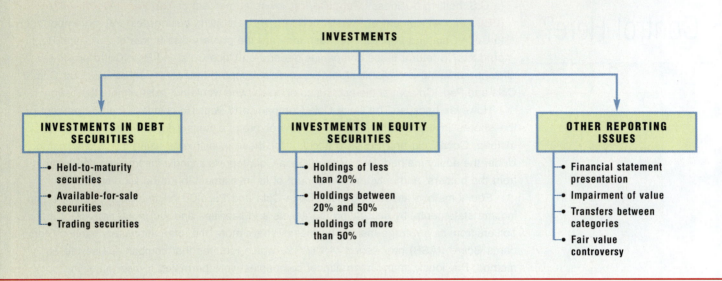

Companies have different motivations for investing in securities issued by other companies.[2] **One motivation is to earn a high rate of return.** For example, companies like **Coca-Cola** and **PepsiCo** can receive interest revenue from a debt investment or dividend revenue from an equity investment. In addition, they can realize capital gains on both types of securities. **Another motivation for investing (in equity securities) is to secure certain operating or financing arrangements with another company.** As in the opening story, **Coca-Cola** and **PepsiCo** are able to exercise some control over bottler companies based on its significant (but not controlling) equity investments.

To provide useful information, companies account for investments based on the type of security (debt or equity) and their intent with respect to the investment. As indicated in Illustration 17-1, we organize our study of investments by type of security. Within each section, we explain how the accounting for investments in debt and equity securities varies according to management intent.

---

[2]A **security** is a share, participation, or other interest in property or in an enterprise of the issuer or an obligation of the issuer that has the following three characteristics: (a) It either is represented by an instrument issued in bearer or registered form or, if not represented by an instrument, is registered in books maintained to record transfers by or on behalf of the issuer. (b) It is of a type commonly traded on securities exchanges or markets or, when represented by an instrument, is commonly recognized in any area in which it is issued or dealt in as a medium for investment. (c) It either is one of a class or series or by its terms is divisible into a class or series of shares, participations, interests, or obligations. From "Accounting for Certain Investments in Debt and Equity Securities," *Statement of Financial Accounting Standards No. 115* (Norwalk, Conn.: FASB, 1993), p. 48, par. 137.

Types of Security	Management Intent	Valuation Approach
Debt (Section 1)	No plans to sell	Amortized cost
	Plan to sell	Fair value
Equity (Section 2)	Plan to sell	Fair value
	Exercise some control	Equity method

ILLUSTRATION 17-1
Summary of Investment Accounting Approaches

INVESTMENTS IN DEBT SECURITIES | SECTION 1

Debt securities represent a creditor relationship with another entity. Debt securities include U.S. government securities, municipal securities, corporate bonds, convertible debt, and commercial paper. Trade accounts receivable and loans receivable are not debt securities because they do not meet the definition of a security.

Companies group investments in debt securities into three separate categories for accounting and reporting purposes:

- **Held-to-maturity**: Debt securities that the company has the positive intent and ability to hold to maturity.
- **Trading**: Debt securities bought and held primarily for sale in the near term to generate income on short-term price differences.
- **Available-for-sale**: Debt securities not classified as held-to-maturity or trading securities.

Illustration 17-2 identifies these categories, along with the accounting and reporting treatments required for each.

OBJECTIVE 1
Identify the three categories of debt securities and describe the accounting and reporting treatment for each category.

Category	Valuation	Unrealized Holding Gains or Losses	Other Income Effects
Held-to-maturity	Amortized cost	Not recognized	Interest when earned; gains and losses from sale.
Trading securities	Fair value	Recognized in net income	Interest when earned; gains and losses from sale.
Available-for-sale	Fair value	Recognized as other comprehensive income and as separate component of stockholders' equity	Interest when earned; gains and losses from sale.

ILLUSTRATION 17-2
Accounting for Debt Securities by Category

UNDERLYING CONCEPTS

Companies report debt securities at fair value not only because the information is relevant but also because it is reliable.

Amortized cost is the acquisition cost adjusted for the amortization of discount or premium, if appropriate. **Fair value** is the amount at which a company can exchange a financial instrument in a current transaction between willing parties, other than in a forced or liquidation sale.[3]

---

[3]Ibid., pp. 47–48. The fair value is **readily determinable** if SEC-registered exchanges provide its sale price or other quotations, or, for over-the-counter securities, recognized national publication systems publish the amounts.

HELD-TO-MATURITY SECURITIES

OBJECTIVE 2
Understand the procedures for discount and premium amortization on bond investments.

Only debt securities can be classified as held-to-maturity. By definition, equity securities have no maturity date. A company like **Starbucks** should classify a debt security as **held-to-maturity** only if it has **both (1) the positive intent** and **(2) the ability to hold those securities to maturity**. It should not classify a debt security as held-to-maturity if it intends to hold the security for an indefinite period of time. Likewise, if Starbucks anticipates that a sale may be necessary due to changes in interest rates, foreign currency risk, liquidity needs, or other asset-liability management reasons, it should not classify the security as held-to-maturity.[4]

Companies account for held-to-maturity securities **at amortized cost**, not fair value. If management intends to hold certain investment securities to maturity and has no plans to sell them, fair values (selling prices) are not relevant for measuring and evaluating the cash flows associated with these securities. Finally, because companies do not adjust held-to-maturity securities to fair value, these securities do not increase the volatility of either reported earnings or reported capital as do trading securities and available-for-sale securities.

To illustrate the accounting for held-to-maturity debt securities, assume that Robinson Company purchased $100,000 of 8 percent bonds of Evermaster Corporation on January 1, 2006, at a discount, paying $92,278. The bonds mature January 1, 2011; interest is payable each July 1 and January 1. Robinson records the investment as follows:

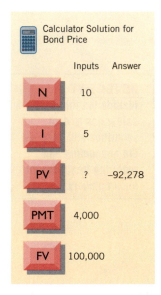

Calculator Solution for Bond Price

	Inputs	Answer
N	10	
I	5	
PV	?	–92,278
PMT	4,000	
FV	100,000	

January 1, 2006

Held-to-Maturity Securities	92,278	
Cash		92,278

Robinson uses a Held-to-Maturity Securities account to indicate the type of debt security purchased.

As indicated in Chapter 14, companies must amortize premium or discount using the **effective-interest method** unless some other method—such as the straight-line method—yields a similar result. They apply the effective-interest method to bond investments in a way similar to that for bonds payable. To compute interest revenue, companies compute the effective-interest rate or yield at the time of investment and apply that rate to the beginning carrying amount (book value) for each interest period. The investment carrying amount is increased by the amortized discount or decreased by the amortized premium in each period.

Illustration 17-3 (on page 841) shows the effect of the discount amortization on the interest revenue that Robinson records each period for its investment in Evermaster bonds. Robinson records the receipt of the first semiannual interest payment on July 1, 2006 (using the data in Illustration 17-3) as follows:

July 1, 2006

Cash	4,000	
Held-to-Maturity Securities	614	
Interest Revenue		4,614

Because Robinson is on a calendar-year basis, it accrues interest and amortizes the discount at December 31, 2006, as follows.

December 31, 2006

Interest Receivable	4,000	
Held-to-Maturity Securities	645	
Interest Revenue		4,645

Again, Illustration 17-3 shows the interest and amortization amounts.

UNDERLYING CONCEPTS

The use of some simpler method that yields results similar to the effective-interest method is an application of the materiality concept.

---

[4]The FASB defines situations where, even though a company sells a security before maturity, it has constructively held the security to maturity, and thus does not violate the held-to-maturity requirement. These include selling a security close enough to maturity (such as three months) so that interest rate risk is no longer an important pricing factor.

		8% Bonds Purchased to Yield 10%		
Date	Cash Received	Interest Revenue	Bond Discount Amortization	Carrying Amount of Bonds
1/1/06				$ 92,278
7/1/06	$ 4,000ᵃ	$ 4,614ᵇ	$ 614ᶜ	92,892ᵈ
1/1/07	4,000	4,645	645	93,537
7/1/07	4,000	4,677	677	94,214
1/1/08	4,000	4,711	711	94,925
7/1/08	4,000	4,746	746	95,671
1/1/09	4,000	4,783	783	96,454
7/1/09	4,000	4,823	823	97,277
1/1/10	4,000	4,864	864	98,141
7/1/10	4,000	4,907	907	99,048
1/1/11	4,000	4,952	952	100,000
	$40,000	$47,722	$7,722	

ᵃ$4,000 = $100,000 × .08 × $\frac{6}{12}$
ᵇ$4,614 = $92,278 × .10 × $\frac{6}{12}$
ᶜ$614 = $4,614 − $4,000
ᵈ$92,892 = $92,278 + $614

ILLUSTRATION 17-3
Schedule of Interest Revenue and Bond Discount Amortization—Effective-Interest Method

Robinson reports its investment in Evermaster bonds in its December 31, 2006, financial statements, as follows.

Balance Sheet

Current assets
    Interest receivable $ 4,000
Long-term investments
    Held-to-maturity securities, at amortized cost $93,537

Income Statement

Other revenues and gains
    Interest revenue $ 9,259

ILLUSTRATION 17-4
Reporting of Held-to-Maturity Securities

Sometimes a company sells a held-to-maturity debt security so close to its maturity date that a change in the market interest rate would not significantly affect the security's fair value. Such a sale may be considered a sale at maturity and would not call into question the company's original intent to hold the investment to maturity. Let's assume, as an example, that Robinson Company sells its investment in Evermaster bonds on November 1, 2010, at 99¾ plus accrued interest. The discount amortization from July 1, 2010, to November 1, 2010, is $635 (⁴⁄₆ × $952). Robinson records this discount amortization as follows.

November 1, 2010

Held-to-Maturity Securities   635
    Interest Revenue   635

Illustration 17-5 shows the computation of the realized gain on the sale.

Selling price of bonds (exclusive of accrued interest)		$99,750
Less: Book value of bonds on November 1, 2010:		
Amortized cost, July 1, 2010	$99,048	
Add: Discount amortized for the period July 1, 2010,		
to November 1, 2010	635	
		99,683
Gain on sale of bonds		$ 67

ILLUSTRATION 17-5
Computation of Gain on Sale of Bonds

Robinson records the sale of the bonds as:

November 1, 2010

Cash	102,417	
Interest Revenue (4/6 × $4,000)		2,667
Held-to-Maturity Securities		99,683
Gain on Sale of Securities		67

The credit to Interest Revenue represents accrued interest for four months, for which the purchaser pays cash. The debit to Cash represents the selling price of the bonds plus accrued interest ($99,750 + $2,667). The credit to Held-to-Maturity Securities represents the book value of the bonds on the date of sale. The credit to Gain on Sale of Securities represents the excess of the selling price over the book value of the bonds.

AVAILABLE-FOR-SALE SECURITIES

UNDERLYING CONCEPTS

Recognizing unrealized gains and losses is an application of the concept of comprehensive income.

Companies, like **Amazon.com**, report **available-for-sale** securities at fair value. It records the unrealized gains and losses related to changes in the fair value of available-for-sale debt securities in an unrealized holding gain or loss account. Amazon adds (subtracts) this amount to other comprehensive income for the period. Other comprehensive income is then added to (subtracted from) accumulated other comprehensive income, which is shown as a separate component of stockholders' equity until realized. Thus, **companies report available-for-sale securities at fair value on the balance sheet, but do not report changes in fair value as part of net income until after selling the security**. This approach reduces the volatility of net income.

Example: Single Security

To illustrate the accounting for available-for-sale securities, assume that Graff Corporation purchases $100,000, 10 percent, five-year bonds on January 1, 2006, with interest payable on July 1 and January 1. The bonds sell for $108,111, which results in a bond premium of $8,111 and an effective interest rate of 8 percent.

Graff records the purchase of the bonds as follows.[5]

Calculator Solution for Bond Price

Inputs	Answer
N	10
I	4
PV ?	−108,111
PMT	5,000
FV	100,000

January 1, 2006

Available-for-Sale Securities	108,111	
Cash		108,111

Illustration 17-6 (on page 843) discloses the effect of the premium amortization on the interest revenue Graff records each period using the effective-interest method.

The entry to record interest revenue on July 1, 2006, is as follows.

July 1, 2006

Cash	5,000	
Available-for-Sale Securities		676
Interest Revenue		4,324

At December 31, 2006, Graff makes the following entry to recognize interest revenue.

December 31, 2006

Interest Receivable	5,000	
Available-for-Sale Securities		703
Interest Revenue		4,297

As a result, Graff reports revenue for 2006 of $8,621 ($4,324 + $4,297).

---

[5]Companies generally record investments acquired at par, at a discount, or at a premium in the accounts at cost, including brokerage and other fees but excluding the accrued interest. They generally do not record investments at maturity value. The use of a separate discount or premium account as a valuation account is acceptable procedure for investments, but in practice companies do not widely use it.

Date	Cash Received	Interest Revenue	Bond Premium Amortization	Carrying Amount of Bonds
10% Bonds Purchased to Yield 8%				
1/1/06				$108,111
7/1/06	$ 5,000[a]	$ 4,324[b]	$ 676[c]	107,435[d]
1/1/07	5,000	4,297	703	106,732
7/1/07	5,000	4,269	731	106,001
1/1/08	5,000	4,240	760	105,241
7/1/08	5,000	4,210	790	104,451
1/1/09	5,000	4,178	822	103,629
7/1/09	5,000	4,145	855	102,774
1/1/10	5,000	4,111	889	101,885
7/1/10	5,000	4,075	925	100,960
1/1/11	5,000	4,040	960	100,000
	$50,000	$41,889	$8,111	

[a]$5,000 = $100,000 × .10 × 6/12
[b]$4,324 = $108,111 × .08 × 6/12
[c]$676 = $5,000 − $4,324
[d]$107,435 = $108,111 − $676

To apply the fair value method to these debt securities, assume that at year-end the fair value of the bonds is $105,000 and that the carrying amount of the investments is $106,732. Comparing this fair value with the carrying amount (amortized cost) of the bonds at December 31, 2006, Graff recognizes an unrealized holding loss of $1,732 ($106,732 − $105,000). It reports this loss as other comprehensive income. Graff makes the following entry.

December 31, 2006

Unrealized Holding Gain or Loss—Equity	1,732	
Securities Fair Value Adjustment (Available-for-Sale)		1,732

Graff uses a valuation account instead of crediting the Available-for-Sale Securities account. The use of the **Securities Fair Value Adjustment (Available-for-Sale) account** enables the company to maintain a record of its amortized cost. Because the adjustment account has a credit balance in this case, Graff subtracts it from the balance of the Available-for-Sale Securities account to determine fair value. Graff reports this fair value amount on the balance sheet. At each reporting date, Graff reports the bonds at fair value with an adjustment to the Unrealized Holding Gain or Loss—Equity account.

Example: Portfolio of Securities

To illustrate the accounting for a portfolio of securities, assume that Webb Corporation has two debt securities classified as available-for-sale. Illustration 17-7 identifies the amortized cost, fair value, and the amount of the unrealized gain or loss.

Available-for-Sale Debt Security Portfolio
December 31, 2007

Investments	Amortized Cost	Fair Value	Unrealized Gain (Loss)
Watson Corporation 8% bonds	$ 93,537	$103,600	$ 10,063
Anacomp Corporation 10% bonds	200,000	180,400	(19,600)
Total of portfolio	$293,537	$284,000	(9,537)
Previous securities fair value adjustment balance			–0–
Securities fair value adjustment—Cr.			$ (9,537)

The fair value of Webb's available-for-sale portfolio totals $284,000. The gross unrealized gains are $10,063, and the gross unrealized losses are $19,600, resulting in a net unrealized loss of $9,537. That is, the fair value of available-for-sale securities is $9,537 lower than its amortized cost. Webb makes an adjusting entry to a valuation allowance to record the decrease in value and to record the loss as follows.

December 31, 2007

Unrealized Holding Gain or Loss—Equity	9,537	
Securities Fair Value Adjustment (Available-for-Sale)		9,537

Webb reports the unrealized holding loss of $9,537 as other comprehensive income and a reduction of stockholders' equity. Recall that companies exclude from net income any unrealized holding gains and losses related to available-for-sale securities.

Sale of Available-for-Sale Securities

If a company sells bonds carried as investments in available-for-sale securities before the maturity date, it must make entries to remove from the Available-for-Sale Securities account the amortized cost of bonds sold. To illustrate, assume that Webb Corporation sold the Watson bonds (from Illustration 17-7) on July 1, 2008, for $90,000, at which time it had an amortized cost of $94,214. Illustration 17-8 shows the computation of the realized loss.

ILLUSTRATION 17-8
Computation of Loss on
Sale of Bonds

Amortized cost (Watson bonds)	$94,214
Less: Selling price of bonds	90,000
Loss on sale of bonds	$ 4,214

Webb records the sale of the Watson bonds as follows.

July 1, 2008

Cash	90,000	
Loss on Sale of Securities	4,214	
Available-for-Sale Securities		94,214

Webb reports this realized loss in the "Other expenses and losses" section of the income statement. Assuming no other purchases and sales of bonds in 2008, Webb on December 31, 2008, prepares the information shown in Illustration 17-9.

ILLUSTRATION 17-9
Computation of
Securities Fair Value
Adjustment—Available-
for-Sale (2008)

AVAILABLE-FOR-SALE DEBT SECURITY PORTFOLIO DECEMBER 31, 2008			
Investments	Amortized Cost	Fair Value	Unrealized Gain (Loss)
Anacomp Corporation 10% bonds (total portfolio)	$200,000	$195,000	$(5,000)
Previous securities fair value adjustment balance—Cr.			(9,537)
Securities fair value adjustment—Dr.			$ 4,537

Webb has an unrealized holding loss of $5,000. However, the Securities Fair Value Adjustment account already has a credit balance of $9,537. To reduce the adjustment account balance to $5,000, Webb debits it for $4,537, as follows.

December 31, 2008

Securities Fair Value Adjustment (Available-for-Sale)	4,537	
Unrealized Holding Gain or Loss—Equity		4,537

WHAT IS FAIR VALUE?

In the fall of 2000, Wall Street brokerage firm **Morgan Stanley** told investors that rumor of big losses in its bond portfolio were "greatly exaggerated." As it turns out, Morgan Stanley also was exaggerating.

Recently, the SEC accused Morgan Stanley of violating securities laws by overstating the value of certain bonds by $75 million. The overvaluations stemmed more from wishful thinking than reality, in violation of generally accepted accounting principles, the SEC said. "In effect, Morgan Stanley valued its positions at the price at which it thought a willing buyer and seller should enter into an exchange, rather than at a price at which a willing buyer and a willing seller would enter into a current exchange," the SEC wrote.

Especially egregious, stated one accounting expert, were the SEC's findings that Morgan Stanley in some instances used its own more optimistic assumptions as a substitute for external pricing sources. "What that is saying is: 'Fair value is what you want the value to be. Pick a number...' That's especially troublesome."

As indicated in the text, the FASB has been working on a new standard for assessing what is fair and what isn't when it comes to assigning valuations. Concerns over the issue caught fire after the collapses of **Enron Corp.** and other energy traders that abused the wide discretion given them under fair-value accounting. Investors have expressed similar worries about some financial companies, which use internal—and subjectively designed—mathematical models to come up with valuations when market quotes aren't available.

Source: Adapted from Susanne Craig and Jonathan Weil, "SEC Targets Morgan Stanley Values," *Wall Street Journal* (November 8, 2004), p. C3.

Financial Statement Presentation

Webb's December 31, 2008, balance sheet and the 2008 income statement include the following items and amounts (the Anacomp bonds are long-term investments but are not intended to be held to maturity).

ILLUSTRATION 17-10
Reporting of Available-for-Sale Securities

Balance Sheet	
Current assets	
Interest receivable	$ xxx
Investments	
Available-for-sale securities, at fair value	$195,000
Stockholders' equity	
Accumulated other comprehensive loss	$ 5,000
Income Statement	
Other revenues and gains	
Interest revenue	$ xxx
Other expenses and losses	
Loss on sale of securities	$ 4,214

Some favor including the unrealized holding gain or loss in net income rather than showing it as other comprehensive income.[6] However, some companies, particularly financial institutions, note that recognizing gains and losses on assets, but not liabilities, introduces substantial volatility in net income. They argue that hedges often exist between assets and liabilities so that gains in assets are offset by losses in liabilities, and vice versa. In short, to recognize gains and losses only on the asset side is unfair and not representative of the economic activities of the company.

This argument convinced the FASB. As a result, companies **do not include in net income** these unrealized gains and losses. However, even this approach solves only

[6]In Chapter 4, we discussed the reporting of other comprehensive income and the concept of comprehensive income. "Reporting Comprehensive Income," *Statement of Financial Accounting Standards No. 130* (Norwalk, Conn.: FASB, 1997).

some of the problems, because **volatility of capital** still results. This is of concern to financial institutions because regulators restrict financial institutions' operations based on their level of capital. In addition, companies can still manage their net income by engaging in **gains trading** (i.e., selling the winners and holding the losers).

TRADING SECURITIES

Companies hold **trading securities** with the intention of selling them in a short period of time. "Trading" in this context means frequent buying and selling. Companies thus use trading securities to generate profits from short-term differences in price. Companies generally hold these securities for less than three months, some for merely days or hours.

Companies report trading securities at fair value, with unrealized holding gains and losses reported as part of net income. Similar to held-to-maturity or available-for-sale investments, they are required to amortize any discount or premium. A **holding gain or loss** is the net change in the fair value of a security from one period to another, exclusive of dividend or interest revenue recognized but not received. In short, the FASB says to adjust the trading securities to fair value, at each reporting date. In addition, companies report the change in value as part of net income, not other comprehensive income.

To illustrate, assume that on December 31, 2007, Western Publishing Corporation determined its trading securities portfolio to be as shown in Illustration 17-11. (Assume that 2007 is the first year that Western Publishing held trading securities.) At the date of acquisition, Western Publishing recorded these trading securities at cost, including brokerage commissions and taxes, in the account entitled Trading Securities. This is the first valuation of this recently purchased portfolio.

ILLUSTRATION 17-11
Computation of Securities Fair Value Adjustment—Trading Securities Portfolio (2007)

TRADING DEBT SECURITY PORTFOLIO DECEMBER 31, 2007			
Investments	Cost	Fair Value	Unrealized Gain (Loss)
Burlington Northern 10% bonds	$ 43,860	$ 51,500	$ 7,640
GM Corporation 11% bonds	184,230	175,200	(9,030)
Time Warner 8% bonds	86,360	91,500	5,140
Total of portfolio	$314,450	$318,200	3,750
Previous securities fair value adjustment balance			–0–
Securities fair value adjustment—Dr.			$ 3,750

The total cost of Western Publishing's trading portfolio is $314,450. The gross unrealized gains are $12,780 ($7,640 + $5,140), and the gross unrealized losses are $9,030, resulting in a net unrealized gain of $3,750. The fair value of trading securities is $3,750 greater than its cost.

At December 31, Western Publishing makes an adjusting entry to a valuation allowance, referred to as Securities Fair Value Adjustment (Trading), to record the increase in value and to record the unrealized holding gain.

INTERNATIONAL INSIGHT

IFRS provides for classification as trading, available for sale, or held-to-maturity for all types of financial assets. U.S. GAAP applies these classifications only to securities.

December 31, 2007

Securities Fair Value Adjustment (Trading)	3,750	
Unrealized Holding Gain or Loss—Income		3,750

Because the Securities Fair Value Adjustment account balance is a debit, Western Publishing adds it to the cost of the Trading Securities account to arrive at a fair value for the trading securities. Western Publishing reports this fair value amount on the balance sheet.

When securities are actively traded, the FASB believes that the investments should be reported at fair value on the balance sheet. In addition, changes in fair value (unrealized gains and losses) should be reported in income. Such reporting on trading securities provides more relevant information to existing and prospective stockholders.

INVESTMENTS IN EQUITY SECURITIES | **SECTION 2**

Equity securities represent ownership interests such as common, preferred, or other capital stock. They also include rights to acquire or dispose of ownership interests at an agreed-upon or determinable price, such as in warrants, rights, and call or put options. Companies do not treat convertible debt securities as equity securities. Nor do they treat as equity securities redeemable preferred stock (which must be redeemed for common stock). The cost of equity securities includes the purchase price of the security plus broker's commissions and other fees incidental to the purchase.

> **OBJECTIVE 3**
> Identify the categories of equity securities and describe the accounting and reporting treatment for each category.

The degree to which one corporation **(investor)** acquires an interest in the common stock of another corporation **(investee)** generally determines the accounting treatment for the investment subsequent to acquisition. The classification of such investments depends on the percentage of the investee voting stock that is held by the investor:

1 Holdings of less than 20 percent (**fair value method**)—investor has passive interest.

2 Holdings between 20 percent and 50 percent (**equity method**)—investor has significant influence.

3 Holdings of more than 50 percent (**consolidated statements**)—investor has controlling interest.

Illustration 17-12 lists these levels of interest or influence and the corresponding valuation and reporting method that companies must apply to the investment.

Percentage of Ownership	0% ⟷	20% ⟷	50% ⟷	100%
Level of Influence		Little or None	Significant	Control
Valuation Method		Fair Value Method	Equity Method	Consolidation

ILLUSTRATION 17-12
Levels of Influence Determine Accounting Methods

The accounting and reporting for equity securities therefore depends upon the level of influence and the type of security involved, as shown in Illustration 17-13.

Category	Valuation	Unrealized Holding Gains or Losses	Other Income Effects
Holdings less than 20%			
1. Available-for-sale	Fair value	Recognized in "Other comprehensive income" and as separate component of stockholders' equity	Dividends declared; gains and losses from sale.
2. Trading	Fair value	Recognized in net income	Dividends declared; gains and losses from sale.
Holdings between 20% and 50%	Equity	Not recognized	Proportionate share of investee's net income.
Holdings more than 50%	Consolidation	Not recognized	Not applicable.

ILLUSTRATION 17-13
Accounting and Reporting for Equity Securities by Category

HOLDINGS OF LESS THAN 20%

When an investor has an interest of less than 20 percent, it is presumed that the investor has little or no influence over the investee. In such cases, if market prices are available subsequent to acquisition, the company values and reports the investment using the **fair value method**.[7] The fair value method requires that companies classify equity securities at acquisition as **available-for-sale securities** or **trading securities**. Because equity securities have no maturity date, companies cannot classify them as held-to-maturity.

Available-for-Sale Securities

Upon acquisition, companies record available-for-sale securities at cost.[8] To illustrate, assume that on November 3, 2007 Republic Corporation purchased common stock of three companies, each investment representing less than a 20 percent interest.

	Cost
Northwest Industries, Inc.	$259,700
Campbell Soup Co.	317,500
St. Regis Pulp Co.	141,350
Total cost	$718,550

Republic records these investments as follows.

November 3, 2007

Available-for-Sale Securities	718,550	
Cash		718,550

On December 6, 2007, Republic receives a cash dividend of $4,200 on its investment in the common stock of Campbell Soup Co. It records the cash dividend as follows.

December 6, 2007

Cash	4,200	
Dividend Revenue		4,200

All three of the investee companies reported net income for the year, but only Campbell Soup declared and paid a dividend to Republic. But, recall that when an investor owns less than 20 percent of the common stock of another corporation, it is presumed that the investor has relatively little influence on the investee. As a result, **net income earned by the investee is not a proper basis for recognizing income from the investment by the investor**. Why? Because the increased net assets resulting from profitable operations may be permanently retained for use in the investee's

---

[7]When market prices are unavailable, a company values the investment and reports it at cost in periods subsequent to acquisition. This approach is often referred to as the **cost method**. Companies recognize dividends when received. They value the portfolio and report it at acquisition cost. Companies only recognize gains or losses after selling the securities.

[8]Companies should record equity securities acquired in **exchange for noncash consideration** (property or services) at (1) the fair value of the consideration given, or (2) the fair value of the security received, whichever is more clearly determinable. Accounting for numerous purchases of securities requires the preservation of information regarding the cost of individual purchases, as well as the dates of purchases and sales. If **specific identification** is not possible, companies may use an **average cost** for multiple purchases of the same class of security. The **first-in, first-out method** (FIFO) of assigning costs to investments at the time of sale is also acceptable and normally employed.

business. Therefore, **the investor earns net income only when the investee declares cash dividends**.

At December 31, 2007, Republic's available-for-sale equity security portfolio has the cost and fair value shown in Illustration 17-14.

AVAILABLE-FOR-SALE EQUITY SECURITY PORTFOLIO DECEMBER 31, 2007			
Investments	Cost	Fair Value	Unrealized Gain (Loss)
Northwest Industries, Inc.	$259,700	$275,000	$ 15,300
Campbell Soup Co.	317,500	304,000	(13,500)
St. Regis Pulp Co.	141,350	104,000	(37,350)
Total of portfolio	$718,550	$683,000	(35,550)
Previous securities fair value adjustment balance			–0–
Securities fair value adjustment—Cr.			$(35,550)

ILLUSTRATION 17-14
Computation of Securities Fair Value Adjustment—Available-for-Sale Equity Security Portfolio (2007)

For Republic's available-for-sale equity securities portfolio, the gross unrealized gains are $15,300, and the gross unrealized losses are $50,850 ($13,500 + $37,350), resulting in a net unrealized loss of $35,550. The fair value of the available-for-sale securities portfolio is below cost by $35,550.

As with available-for-sale **debt** securities, Republic records the net unrealized gains and losses related to changes in the fair value of available-for-sale **equity** securities in an Unrealized Holding Gain or Loss—Equity account. Republic reports this amount as a **part of other comprehensive income and as a component of other accumulated comprehensive income (reported in stockholders' equity) until realized**. In this case, Republic prepares an adjusting entry debiting the Unrealized Holding Gain or Loss—Equity account and crediting the Securities Fair Value Adjustment account to record the decrease in fair value and to record the loss as follows.

December 31, 2007

Unrealized Holding Gain or Loss—Equity	35,550	
Securities Fair Value Adjustment (Available-for-Sale)		35,550

On January 23, 2008, Republic sold all of its Northwest Industries, Inc. common stock receiving net proceeds of $287,220. Illustration 17-15 shows the computation of the realized gain on the sale.

Net proceeds from sale	$287,220
Cost of Northwest shares	259,700
Gain on sale of stock	$ 27,520

ILLUSTRATION 17-15
Computation of Gain on Sale of Stock

Republic records the sale as follows.

January 23, 2008

Cash	287,220	
Available-for-Sale Securities		259,700
Gain on Sale of Stock		27,520

In addition, assume that on February 10, 2008, Republic purchased 20,000 shares of Continental Trucking at a market price of $12.75 per share plus brokerage commissions of $1,850 (total cost, $256,850).

Illustration 17-16 lists Republic's portfolio of available-for-sale securities, as of December 31, 2008.

ILLUSTRATION 17-16
Computation of
Securities Fair Value
Adjustment—Available-
for-Sale Equity Security
Portfolio (2008)

AVAILABLE-FOR-SALE EQUITY SECURITY PORTFOLIO DECEMBER 31, 2008			
Investments	Cost	Fair Value	Unrealized Gain (Loss)
Continental Trucking	$256,850	$278,350	$ 21,500
Campbell Soup Co.	317,500	362,550	45,050
St. Regis Pulp Co.	141,350	139,050	(2,300)
Total of portfolio	$715,700	$779,950	64,250
Previous securities fair value adjustment balance—Cr.			(35,550)
Securities fair value adjustment—Dr.			$ 99,800

At December 31, 2008, the fair value of Republic's available-for-sale equity securities portfolio exceeds cost by $64,250 (unrealized gain). The Securities Fair Value Adjustment account had a credit balance of $35,550 at December 31, 2008. To adjust its December 31, 2008, available-for-sale portfolio to fair value, the company debits the Securities Fair Value Adjustment account for $99,800 ($35,550 + $64,250). Republic records this adjustment as follows.

December 31, 2008

Securities Fair Value Adjustment (Available-for-Sale)	99,800	
Unrealized Holding Gain or Loss—Equity		99,800

Trading Securities

The accounting entries to record trading equity securities are the same as for available-for-sale equity securities, except for recording the unrealized holding gain or loss. For trading equity securities, companies **report the unrealized holding gain or loss as part of net income**. Thus, the account titled Unrealized Holding Gain or Loss—Income is used.

HOLDINGS BETWEEN 20% AND 50%

An investor corporation may hold an interest of less than 50 percent in an investee corporation and thus not possess legal control. However, as shown in our opening story about **Coca-Cola**, an investment in voting stock of less than 50 percent can still give Coke (the investor) the ability to exercise significant influence over the operating and financial policies of its bottlers.[9] **Significant influence** may be indicated in several ways. Examples include representation on the board of directors, participation in policy-making processes, material intercompany transactions, interchange of managerial personnel, or technological dependency.

Another important consideration is the extent of ownership by an investor in relation to the concentration of other shareholdings. To achieve a reasonable degree of uniformity in application of the "significant influence" criterion, the profession concluded that an investment (direct or indirect) of 20 percent or more of the voting stock

---

[9]"The Equity Method of Accounting for Investments in Common Stock," *Opinions of the Accounting Principles Board No. 18* (New York: AICPA, 1971), par. 17.

of an investee should lead to a presumption that in the absence of evidence to the contrary, an investor has the ability to exercise significant influence over an investee.[10]

In instances of "significant influence" (generally an investment of 20 percent or more), the investor must account for the investment using the **equity method**.

Equity Method

Under the **equity method** the investor and the investee acknowledge a substantive economic relationship. The company originally records the investment at the cost of the shares acquired but subsequently adjusts the amount each period for changes in the investee's net assets. That is, the **the investor's proportionate share of the earnings (losses) of the investee periodically increases (decreases) the investment's carrying amount. All dividends received by the investor from the investee also decrease the investment's carrying amount.** The equity method recognizes that investee's earnings increase investee's net assets, and that investee's losses and dividends decrease these net assets.

To illustrate the equity method and compare it with the fair value method, assume that Maxi Company purchases a 20 percent interest in Mini Company. To apply the fair value method in this example, assume that Maxi does not have the ability to exercise significant influence, and classifies the securities as available-for-sale. Where this example applies the equity method, assume that the 20 percent interest permits Maxi to exercise significant influence. Illustration 17-17 shows the entries.

> **OBJECTIVE 4**
> **Explain the equity method of accounting and compare it to the fair value method for equity securities.**

ILLUSTRATION 17-17
Comparison of Fair Value Method and Equity Method

ENTRIES BY MAXI COMPANY			
Fair Value Method		**Equity Method**	
On January 2, 2007, Maxi Company acquired 48,000 shares (20% of Mini Company common stock) at a cost of $10 a share.			
Available-for-Sale-Securities	480,000	Investment in Mini Stock	480,000
Cash	480,000	Cash	480,000
For the year 2007, Mini Company reported net income of $200,000; Maxi Company's share is 20%, or $40,000.			
No entry		Investment in Mini Stock	40,000
		Revenue from Investment	40,000
At December 31, 2007, the 48,000 shares of Mini Company have a fair value (market price) of $12 a share, or $576,000.			
Securities Fair Value Adjustment		No entry	
(Available-for-Sale)	96,000		
Unrealized Holding Gain			
or Loss—Equity	96,000		
On January 28, 2008, Mini Company announced and paid a cash dividend of $100,000; Maxi Company received 20%, or $20,000.			
Cash	20,000	Cash	20,000
Dividend Revenue	20,000	Investment in Mini Stock	20,000
For the year 2008, Mini reported a net loss of $50,000; Maxi Company's share is 20%, or $10,000.			
No entry		Loss on Investment	10,000
		Investment in Mini Stock	10,000
At December 31, 2008, the Mini Company 48,000 shares have a fair value (market price) of $11 a share, or $528,000.			
Unrealized Holding Gain			
or Loss—Equity	48,000	No entry	
Securities Fair Value Adjustment			
(Available-for-Sale)	48,000		

---

[10]Cases in which an investment of 20 percent or more might not enable an investor to exercise significant influence include:

(1) The investee opposes the investor's acquisition of its stock.

(2) The investor and investee sign an agreement under which the investor surrenders significant shareholder rights.

(3) The investor's ownership share does not result in "significant influence" because majority ownership of the investee is concentrated among a small group of shareholders who operate the investee without regard to the views of the investor.

(4) The investor tries and fails to obtain representation on the investee's board of directors.

"Criteria for Applying the Equity Method of Accounting for Investments in Common Stock," *Interpretations of the Financial Accounting Standards Board No. 35* (Stamford, Conn.: FASB, 1981).

Note that under the fair value method, Maxi reports as revenue only the cash dividends received from Mini. **The earning of net income by Mini (the investee) is not considered a proper basis for recognition of income from the investment by Maxi (the investor).** Why? Mini may permanently retain in the business any increased net assets resulting from its profitable operation. Therefore, Maxi only earns revenue when it receives dividends from Mini.

Under the equity method, Maxi reports as revenue its share of the net income reported by Mini. Maxi records the cash dividends received from Mini as a decrease in the investment carrying value. As a result, Maxi records its share of the net income of Mini in the year when it is earned. With significant influence, Maxi can ensure that Mini will pay dividends, if desired, on any net asset increases resulting from net income. To wait until receiving a dividend ignores the fact that Maxi is better off if the investee has earned income.

Using dividends as a basis for recognizing income poses an additional problem. For example, assume that the investee reports a net loss. However, the investor exerts influence to force a dividend payment from the investee. In this case, the investor reports income, even though the investee is experiencing a loss. **In other words, using dividends as a basis for recognizing income fails to report properly the economics of the situation.**

For some companies, equity accounting can be a real pain to the bottom line. For example, **Amazon.com**, the pioneer of Internet retailing, at one time struggled to turn a profit. Furthermore, some of Amazon's equity investments had resulted in Amazon's earnings performance going from bad to worse. In a recent year, Amazon.com disclosed equity stakes in such companies as **Altera International**, **Basis Technology**, **Drugstore.com**, and **Eziba.com**. These equity investees reported losses that made Amazon's already bad bottom line even worse, accounting for up to 22 percent of its reported loss in one year alone.

Investee Losses Exceed Carrying Amount

If an investor's share of the investee's losses exceeds the carrying amount of the investment, should the investor recognize additional losses? Ordinarily the investor should discontinue applying the equity method and not recognize additional losses.

If the investor's potential loss is not limited to the amount of its original investment (by guarantee of the investee's obligations or other commitment to provide further financial support), or if imminent return to profitable operations by the investee appears to be assured, the investor should recognize additional losses.[11]

HOLDINGS OF MORE THAN 50%

When one corporation acquires a voting interest of more than 50 percent in another corporation, it is said to have a **controlling interest**. In such a relationship, the investor corporation is referred to as the **parent** and the investee corporation as the **subsidiary**. Companies present the investment in the common stock of the subsidiary as a long-term investment on the separate financial statements of the parent.

When the parent treats the subsidiary as an investment, the parent generally prepares **consolidated financial statements**. Consolidated financial statements treat the parent and subsidiary corporations as a single economic entity. (Advanced accounting courses extensively discuss the subject of when and how to prepare consolidated financial statements.) Whether or not consolidated financial statements are prepared, the parent company generally accounts for the investment in the subsidiary **using the equity method** as explained in this chapter.

UNDERLYING CONCEPTS

Revenue to be recognized should be earned and realized or realizable. A low level of ownership indicates that a company should defer the income from an investee until cash is received.

---

[11]"The Equity Method of Accounting for Investments in Common Stock," op. cit., par. 19(i).

CONSOLIDATE THIS!

Presently the rules for consolidation seem very straightforward: If a company owns more than 50 percent of another company, it generally should be consolidated. If it owns less than 50 percent, it is generally not consolidated. However the FASB recognizes the artificiality of the present test. Determination of who really has control often relies on factors other than stock ownership.

In fact, specific guidelines force consolidation even though stock ownership is not above 50 percent in certain limited situations. For example, **Enron**'s failure to consolidate three special-purpose entities (SPEs) that it effectively controlled led to an overstatement of income of $569 million and overstatement of equity of $1.2 billion. In each of Enron's three SPEs, the GAAP guidelines would have led to consolidation. That is, the following factors indicate that consolidation should have occurred: the majority owner of the special-purpose entity (SPE) made only a modest investment; the activities of the SPE primarily benefited Enron; and the substantive risks and rewards related to the assets or debt of the SPE rested directly or indirectly with Enron.

The FASB has issued new guidelines related to SPEs, given all the reporting problems that have surfaced related to SPEs at Enron and other companies. We discuss these new rules in Appendix 17B.

WHAT DO THE NUMBERS MEAN?

OTHER REPORTING ISSUES | SECTION 3

We have identified the basic issues involved in accounting for investments in debt and equity securities. In addition, the following issues relate to both of these types of securities.

1 Financial statement presentation.
2 Impairment of value.
3 Transfers between categories.
4 Fair value controversy.

FINANCIAL STATEMENT PRESENTATION OF INVESTMENTS

OBJECTIVE 5
Describe the disclosure requirements for investments in debt and equity securities.

Companies must present individual amounts for the three categories of investments either on the balance sheet or in the related notes. Illustration 17-18 summarizes the valuation and balance sheet classification of investments.

ILLUSTRATION 17-18
Investment Valuation and Classification

Investment Category	Valuation	Classification
Trading securities (debt and equity)	Fair value	Current asset.
Held-to-maturity (debt)	Amortized cost	Current or noncurrent based on maturity date of individual security.
Available-for-sale debt	Fair value	Depends on the circumstances. Current or noncurrent based on maturities and expectations as to sales and redemptions in the following year.
Available-for-sale equity	Fair value	Depends on the circumstances. Current or noncurrent based on expectations as to sales in the following year.

Actual Company Disclosures Related to Investments and Comprehensive Income

For securities classified as available-for-sale and separately for securities classified as held-to-maturity, a company should describe:

1 Aggregate fair value, gross unrealized holding gains, gross unrealized losses, and amortized cost basis by major security type (debt and equity).

2 Information about the contractual maturities of debt securities. The company may group maturity information, for example (a) within one year, (b) after one year through five years, (c) after five years through ten years, and (d) after ten years.

In classifying investments, evidence should support management's expressed intent, such as the history of the company's investment activities, events subsequent to the balance sheet date, and the nature and purpose of the investment.

Companies must be extremely careful with debt securities held to maturity. If a company prematurely sells a debt security in this category, the sale may "taint" the entire held-to-maturity portfolio. That is, a management's statement regarding "intent" is no longer credible. Therefore the company may have to reclassify the securities. This could lead to unfortunate consequences. An interesting by-product of this situation is that companies that wish to retire their debt securities early are finding it difficult to do so. The holder will not sell because the securities are classified as held-to-maturity.

Disclosures Related to Equity Investments

Disclosures Required under the Equity Method

The significance of an investment to the investor's financial position and operating results should determine the extent of disclosures. The following disclosures in the investor's financial statements generally apply to the equity method.

WHAT DO THE NUMBERS MEAN?

MORE DISCLOSURE PLEASE

As indicated in the last two sections, the level of disclosure for investment securities is extensive. How to account for investment securities is a particularly sensitive area, given the large amounts of equity investments involved. And presently companies report investments in equity securities at cost, equity, fair value, and full consolidation, depending on the circumstances. As a recent SEC study noted, "there are so many different accounting treatments for investments that it raises the question of whether they are all needed."

Presented below is an estimate of the percentage of companies on the major exchanges that have investments in the equity of other entities.

Investments in the Equity of Other Companies

Categorized by Accounting Treatment	Percent of Companies
Presenting consolidated financial statements	91.1%
Reporting equity method investments	23.5
Reporting cost method investments*	17.4
Reporting available-for-sale investments	37.4
Reporting trading investments	6.2

*If the equity investments are not publicly traded, the company often accounts for the investment under the cost method. Changes in value are therefore not recognized unless there is impairment.

As the table indicates, many companies have equity investments of some type. These investments can be substantial. For example, based on the table above, the total amount of equity-method investments appearing on company balance sheets is approximately $403 billion and the amount shown in the income statements in any one year for all companies is approximately $38 billion.

Source: "Report and Recommendations Pursuant to Section 401(c) of the Sarbanes-Oxley Act of 2002 on Arrangements with Off-Balance Sheet Implications, Special Purpose Entities, and Transparency of Filings by Issuers," United States Securities and Exchange Commission—Office of Chief Accountant, Office of Economic Analyses, Division of Corporation Finance (June 2005), pp. 36–39.

1   The name of each investee and the percentage of ownership of common stock.
2   The accounting policies of the investor with respect to investments in common stock.
3   The difference, if any, between the amount in the investment account and the amount of underlying equity in the net assets of the investee.
4   The aggregate value of each identified investment based on quoted market price (if available).
5   When equity-method investments are, in the aggregate, material in relation to the financial position and operating results of an investor, the company may need to present summarized information concerning assets, liabilities, and results of operations of the investees, either individually or in groups, as appropriate.

In addition, the investor should disclose the reasons for not using the equity method in cases of 20 percent or more ownership interest, and for using the equity method in cases of less than 20 percent ownership interest.

UNDERLYING CONCEPTS

The consolidation of financial results of different companies follows the economic entity assumption and disregards legal entities. The key objective is to provide useful information to financial statement users.

Reclassification Adjustments

As we indicated in Chapter 4, companies report changes in unrealized holding gains and losses related to available-for-sale securities as part of other comprehensive income. Companies may display the components of other comprehensive income in one of three ways: (1) in a combined statement of income and comprehensive income, (2) in a separate statement of comprehensive income that begins with net income, or (3) in a statement of stockholders' equity.

The reporting of changes in unrealized gains or losses in comprehensive income is straightforward unless a company sells securities during the year. In that case, double counting results when the company reports realized gains or losses as part of net income but also shows the amounts as part of other comprehensive income in the current period or in previous periods.

To ensure that gains and losses are not counted twice when a sale occurs, a **reclassification adjustment** is necessary. To illustrate, assume that Open Company has the following two available-for-sale securities in its portfolio at the end of 2006 (its first year of operations).

Investments	Cost	Fair Value	Unrealized Holding Gain (Loss)
Lehman Inc. common stocks	$ 80,000	$105,000	$25,000
Woods Co. common stocks	120,000	135,000	15,000
Total of portfolio	$200,000	$240,000	40,000
Previous securities fair value adjustment balance			–0–
Securities fair value adjustment—Dr.			$40,000

ILLUSTRATION 17-19
Available-for-Sale Security Portfolio (2006)

If Open Company reports net income in 2006 of $350,000, it presents a statement of comprehensive income as follows.

OPEN COMPANY
STATEMENT OF COMPREHENSIVE INCOME
FOR THE YEAR ENDED DECEMBER 31, 2006

Net income		$350,000
Other comprehensive income		
Holding gains arising during period		40,000
Comprehensive income		$390,000

ILLUSTRATION 17-20
Statement of Comprehensive Income (2006)

During 2007, Open Company sold the Lehman Inc. common stock for $105,000 and realized a gain on the sale of $25,000 ($105,000 – $80,000). At the end of 2007, the fair value of the Woods Co. common stock increased an additional $20,000, to $155,000. Illustration 17-21 shows the computation of the change in the securities fair value adjustment account.

ILLUSTRATION 17-21
Available-for-Sale
Security Portfolio (2007)

Investments	Cost	Fair Value	Unrealized Holding Gain (Loss)
Woods Co. common stocks	$120,000	$155,000	$35,000
Previous securities fair value adjustment balance—Dr.			(40,000)
Securities fair value adjustment—Cr.			$ (5,000)

Illustration 17-21 indicates that Open should report an unrealized holding loss of $5,000 in comprehensive income in 2007. In addition, Open realized a gain of $25,000 on the sale of the Lehman common stock. **Comprehensive income includes both realized and unrealized components.** Therefore Open recognizes a total holding gain (loss) in 2007 of $20,000, computed as follows.

ILLUSTRATION 17-22
Computation of Total
Holding Gain (Loss)

Unrealized holding gain (loss)	$ (5,000)
Realized holding gain	25,000
Total holding gain recognized	$20,000

Open reports net income of $720,000 in 2007, which includes the realized gain on sale of the Lehman securities. Illustration 17-23 shows a statement of comprehensive income for 2007, indicating how Open reported the components of holding gains (losses).

ILLUSTRATION 17-23
Statement of
Comprehensive Income
(2007)

OPEN COMPANY
STATEMENT OF COMPREHENSIVE INCOME
FOR THE YEAR ENDED DECEMBER 31, 2007

Net income (includes $25,000 realized gain on Lehman shares)		$720,000
Other comprehensive income		
Total holding gains arising during period [$(5,000) + $25,000]	$20,000	
Less: Reclassification adjustment for gains included in net income	(25,000)	(5,000)
Comprehensive income		$715,000

In 2006, Open included the unrealized gain on the Lehman Co. common stock in comprehensive income. In 2007, Open sold the stock. It reported the realized gain in net income, which increased comprehensive income again. To avoid double counting this gain, Open makes a reclassification adjustment to eliminate the realized gain from the computation of comprehensive income in 2007.

A company may display reclassification adjustments on the face of the financial statement in which it reports comprehensive income. Or it may disclose these reclassification adjustments in the notes to the financial statements.

Comprehensive Example

To illustrate the reporting of investment securities and related gain or loss on available-for-sale securities, assume that on January 1, 2006, Hinges Co. had cash and common stock of $50,000.[12] At that date the company had no other asset, liability, or equity balance. On January 2, Hinges purchased for cash $50,000 of equity securities classified as available-for-sale. On June 30, Hinges sold part of the available-for-sale security portfolio, realizing a gain as shown in Illustration 17-24.

Fair value of securities sold	$22,000
Less: Cost of securities sold	20,000
Realized gain	$ 2,000

ILLUSTRATION 17-24
Computation of Realized Gain

Hinges did not purchase or sell any other securities during 2006. It received $3,000 in dividends during the year. At December 31, 2006, the remaining portfolio is as shown in Illustration 17-25.

Fair value of portfolio	$34,000
Less: Cost of portfolio	30,000
Unrealized gain	$ 4,000

ILLUSTRATION 17-25
Computation of Unrealized Gain

Illustration 17-26 shows the company's income statement for 2006.

HINGES CO.	
INCOME STATEMENT	
FOR THE YEAR ENDED DECEMBER 31, 2006	
Dividend revenue	$3,000
Realized gains on investment in securities	2,000
Net income	$5,000

ILLUSTRATION 17-26
Income Statement

The company reports its change in the unrealized holding gain in a statement of comprehensive income as follows.

HINGES CO.		
STATEMENT OF COMPREHENSIVE INCOME		
FOR THE YEAR ENDED DECEMBER 31, 2006		
Net income		$5,000
Other comprehensive income:		
Holding gains arising during the period	$6,000	
Less: Reclassification adjustment for gains included in net income	2,000	4,000
Comprehensive income		$9,000

ILLUSTRATION 17-27
Statement of Comprehensive Income

---

[12]We adapted this example from Dennis R. Beresford, L. Todd Johnson, and Cheri L. Reither, "Is a Second Income Statement Needed?" *Journal of Accountancy* (April 1996), p. 71.

Its statement of stockholders' equity appears in Illustration 17-28.

ILLUSTRATION 17-28
Statement of
Stockholders' Equity

HINGES CO.
STATEMENT OF STOCKHOLDERS' EQUITY
FOR THE YEAR ENDED DECEMBER 31, 2006

	Common Stock	Retained Earnings	Accumulated Other Comprehensive Income	Total
Beginning balance	$50,000	$–0–	$–0–	$50,000
Add: Net income		5,000		5,000
Other comprehensive Income			4,000	4,000
Ending balance	$50,000	$5,000	$4,000	$59,000

The comparative balance sheet is shown in Illustration 17-29.

ILLUSTRATION 17-29
Comparative Balance
Sheet

HINGES CO.
COMPARATIVE BALANCE SHEET

	1/1/06	12/31/06
Assets		
Cash	$50,000	$25,000
Available-for-sale securities		34,000
Total assets	$50,000	$59,000
Stockholders' equity		
Common stock	$50,000	$50,000
Retained earnings		5,000
Accumulated other comprehensive income		4,000
Total stockholders' equity	$50,000	$59,000

This example indicates how an unrealized gain or loss on available-for-sale securities affects all the financial statements. Note that a company must disclose the components that comprise accumulated other comprehensive income.

IMPAIRMENT OF VALUE

OBJECTIVE 6
Discuss the accounting for impairments of debt and equity investments.

A company should evaluate every investment, at each reporting date, to determine if it has suffered **impairment**—a loss in value that is other than temporary. For example, if an investee experiences a bankruptcy or a significant liquidity crisis, the investor may suffer a permanent loss. **If the decline is judged to be other than temporary, a company writes down the cost basis of the individual security to a new cost basis.** The company accounts for the write-down as a realized loss. Therefore, it includes the amount in net income.

For debt securities, a company uses the impairment test to determine whether "it is probable that the investor will be unable to collect all amounts due according to the contractual terms."

For equity securities, the guideline is less precise. Any time realizable value is lower than the carrying amount of the investment, a company must consider an impairment. Factors involved include the length of time and the extent to which the fair value has been less than cost; the financial condition and near-term prospects of the issuer; and the intent and ability of the investor company to retain its investment to allow for any anticipated recovery in fair value.

To illustrate an impairment, assume that Strickler Company holds available-for-sale bond securities with a par value and amortized cost of $1 million. The fair value of these securities is $800,000. Strickler has previously reported an unrealized loss on these securities of $200,000 as part of other comprehensive income. In evaluating the securities, Strickler now determines that it probably will not collect all amounts due. In this case, it reports the unrealized loss of $200,000 as a loss on impairment of $200,000. Strickler includes this amount in income, with the bonds stated at their new cost basis. It records this impairment as follows.

Loss on Impairment	200,000	
Securities Fair Value Adjustment (Available-for-Sale)	200,000	
Unrealized Holding Gain or Loss—Equity		200,000
Available-for-Sale Securities		200,000

The new cost basis of the investment in debt securities is $800,000. Strickler includes subsequent increases and decreases in the fair value of impaired available-for-sale securities as other comprehensive income.[13]

Companies base impairment for debt and equity securities on a fair value test. This test differs slightly from the impairment test for loans that we discuss in Appendix 14A. The FASB rejected the discounted cash flow alternative for securities because of the availability of market price information.

THE IRONY OF IT ALL

The **Federal National Mortgage Association** (FNMA)—known as "Fannie Mae"—is a government-sponsored company that owns or guarantees about 25 percent of all the mortgages in the United States. Recently numerous articles have detailed accounting abuses by Fannie Mae. For example, Fannie Mae has acknowledged that some of its accounting polices do not comply with GAAP. It is now preparing to restate its financial statements back to 2001 and possibly to recognize at least $9 billion in losses related to derivatives.

Interestingly, Fannie Mae has caused much hardship for many of its brethren in the financial community (such as **DNB Financial**, **Independent Bank Corporation**, and **Wilmington Trust**). The reason: Many are holding security investments in Fannie Mae. And now the institutions are taking permanent write-downs on these securities because the losses appear to be other than temporary. (In other words, the Fannie Mae securities are impaired.) The irony is that a number of the companies that are taking impairment losses are the very ones that recently fought hard to make sure the FASB did not tighten up impairment accounting rules. Even more ironic is the fact the one of their fellow lobbyers (FNMA) is the source of their impairments!

WHAT DO THE NUMBERS MEAN?

TRANSFERS BETWEEN CATEGORIES

Companies account for transfers between any of the categories at fair value. Thus, if a company transfers available-for-sale securities to held-to-maturity investments, it records the new investment (held-to-maturity) at the date of transfer at **fair value** in the new category. Similarly, if it transfers held-to-maturity investments to available-for-sale investments, it records the new investments (available-for-sale) at **fair value**. This **fair value** rule assures that a company cannot omit recognition of fair value simply by transferring securities to the held-to-maturity category. Illustration 17-30 (on page 860) summarizes the accounting treatment for transfers.

OBJECTIVE 7
Describe the accounting for transfer of investment securities between categories.

---

[13]Companies may not amortize any discount related to the debt securities after recording the impairment. The new cost basis of impaired held-to-maturity securities does not change unless additional impairment occurs.

ILLUSTRATION 17-30
Accounting for Transfers

*Examples of the Entries
for Recording Transfers
Between Categories*

Type of Transfer	Measurement Basis	Impact of Transfer on Stockholders' Equity*	Impact of Transfer on Net Income*
Transfer from trading to available-for-sale	Security transferred at fair value at the date of transfer, which is the new cost basis of the security.	The unrealized gain or loss at the date of transfer increases or decreases stockholders' equity.	The unrealized gain or loss at the date of transfer is recognized in income.
Transfer from available-for-sale to trading	Security transferred at fair value at the date of transfer, which is the new cost basis of the security.	The unrealized gain or loss at the date of transfer increases or decreases stockholders' equity.	The unrealized gain or loss at the date of transfer is recognized in income.
Transfer from held-to-maturity to available-for-sale**	Security transferred at fair value at the date of transfer.	The separate component of stockholders' equity is increased or decreased by the unrealized gain or loss at the date of transfer.	None
Transfer from available-for-sale to held-to-maturity	Security transferred at fair value at the date of transfer.	The unrealized gain or loss at the date of transfer carried as a separate component of stockholders' equity is amortized over the remaining life of the security.	None

*Assumes that adjusting entries to report changes in fair value for the current period are not yet recorded.

**Statement No. 115 states that these types of transfers should be rare.

FAIR VALUE CONTROVERSY

The reporting of investment securities is controversial. Some believe that all securities should be reported at fair value; others believe they all should be stated at amortized cost. Others favor the present approach. In this section we look at some of the major unresolved issues.

Measurement Based on Intent

Companies classify debt securities as held-to-maturity, available-for-sale, or trading. As a result, companies can report three identical debt securities in three different ways in the financial statements. Some argue such treatment is confusing. Furthermore, the held-to-maturity category relies solely on intent, a subjective evaluation. What is not subjective is the market price of the debt instrument. In other words, the three classifications are subjective, resulting in arbitrary classifications.

Gains Trading

Companies can classify certain debt securities as held-to-maturity and therefore report them at amortized cost. Companies can classify other debt and equity securities as available-for-sale and report them at fair value with the unrealized gain or loss reported as other comprehensive income. In either case, a company can become involved in "gains trading" (also referred to as "cherry picking," "snacking," or "sell the best and keep the rest"). In **gains trading**, companies sell their "winners," reporting the gains in income, and hold on to the losers.

Liabilities Not Fairly Valued

Many argue that if companies report investment securities at fair value, they also should report liabilities at fair value. Why? By recognizing changes in value on only one side of the balance sheet (the asset side), a high degree of volatility can occur in the income and stockholders' equity amounts. Further, financial institutions are involved in asset and liability management (not just asset management). Viewing only one side may lead managers to make uneconomic decisions as a result of the accounting.

Although the Board sympathized with this view, it noted that companies still reported certain debt securities at amortized cost (held-to-maturity securities) and that this standard excluded other types of securities. In addition, serious valuation issues arose in relation to some types of liabilities. As a result, liabilities were excluded from consideration.[14]

Subjectivity of Fair Values

Some question the relevance of fair value measures for investments in securities, arguing in favor of reporting based on amortized cost. They believe that amortized cost provides relevant information: it focuses on the decision to acquire the asset, the earning effects of that decision that will be realized over time, and the ultimate recoverable value of the asset. They argue that fair value ignores those concepts. Instead, fair value focuses on the effects of transactions and events that do not involve the company, reflecting opportunity gains and losses whose recognition in the financial statements is, in their view, not appropriate until realized.

SUMMARY OF REPORTING TREATMENT OF SECURITIES

Illustration 17-31 summarizes the major debt and equity securities and their reporting treatment.

Category	Balance Sheet	Income Statement
Trading (debt and equity securities)	Investments shown at fair value. Current assets.	Interest and dividends are recognized as revenue. Unrealized holding gains and losses are included in net income.
Available-for-sale (debt and equity securities)	Investments shown at fair value. Current or long-term assets. Unrealized holding gains and losses are a separate component of stockholders' equity.	Interest and dividends are recognized as revenue. Unrealized holding gains and losses are **not** included in net income but in other comprehensive income.
Held-to-maturity (debt securities)	Investments shown at amortized cost. Current or long-term assets.	Interest is recognized as revenue.
Equity method and/or consolidation (equity securities)	Investments originally are carried at cost, are periodically adjusted by the investor's share of the investee's earnings or losses, and are decreased by all dividends received from the investee. Classified as long-term.	Revenue is recognized to the extent of the investee's earnings or losses reported subsequent to the date of investment.

ILLUSTRATION 17-31
Summary of Treatment of Major Debt and Equity Securities

Discussion of Special Issues Related to Investments

---

[14]In a recent exposure draft concerning valuation of financial instruments, the FASB indicated its support for valuing liabilities at fair value. "Fair Value Measurements," Proposed Statement of Financial Accounting Standards (Norwalk, Conn.: FASB, June 23, 2004).

KEY TERMS

SUMMARY OF LEARNING OBJECTIVES

1. Identify the three categories of debt securities and describe the accounting and reporting treatment for each category. (1) Carry and report *held-to-maturity debt securities* at amortized cost. (2) Value *trading debt securities* for reporting purposes at fair value, with unrealized holding gains or losses included in net income. (3) Value *available-for-sale debt securities* for reporting purposes at fair value, with unrealized holding gains or losses reported as other comprehensive income and as a separate component of stockholders' equity.

2. Understand the procedures for discount and premium amortization on bond investments. Similar to bonds payable, companies should amortize discount or premium on bond investments using the effective-interest method. They apply the effective interest rate or yield to the beginning carrying value of the investment for each interest period in order to compute interest revenue.

3. Identify the categories of equity securities and describe the accounting and reporting treatment for each category. The degree to which one corporation (investor) acquires an interest in the common stock of another corporation (investee) generally determines the accounting treatment for the investment. Long-term investments by one corporation in the common stock of another can be classified according to the percentage of the voting stock of the investee held by the investor.

4. Explain the equity method of accounting and compare it to the fair value method for equity securities. Under the equity method the investor and the investee acknowledge a substantive economic relationship. The company originally records the investment at cost but subsequently adjusts the amount each period for changes in the net assets of the investee. That is, the investor's proportionate share of the earnings (losses) of the investee periodically increases (decreases) the investment's carrying amount. All dividends received by the investor from the investee decrease the investment's carrying amount. Under the fair value method a company reports the equity investment at fair value each reporting period irrespective of the investee's earnings or dividends paid to it. A company applies the equity method to investment holdings between 20 percent and 50 percent of ownership. It applies the fair value method to holdings below 20 percent.

5. Describe the disclosure requirements for investments in debt and equity securities. Companies should report trading securities at aggregate fair value as current assets. Companies should classify individual held-to-maturity and available-for-sale securities as current or noncurrent, depending on the circumstances. For available-for-sale and held-to-maturity securities, a company should describe: aggregate fair value, gross unrealized holding gains, gross unrealized losses, amortized cost basis by type (debt and equity), and information about the contractual maturity of debt securities. A company needs a reclassification adjustment when it reports realized gains or losses as part of net income but also shows the amounts as part of other comprehensive income in the current or in previous periods. Companies should report unrealized holding gains or losses related to available-for-sale securities in other comprehensive income and the aggregate balance as accumulated comprehensive income on the balance sheet.

6. Discuss the accounting for impairments of debt and equity investments. Impairments of debt and equity securities are losses in value that are determined to be other than temporary, are based on a fair value test, and are charged to income.

7. Describe the accounting for transfer of investment securities between categories. Transfers of securities between categories of investments should be accounted for at fair value, with unrealized holding gains or losses treated in accordance with the nature of the transfer.

Accounting for Derivative Instruments

Until the early 1970s, most financial managers worked in a cozy, if unthrilling, world. Since then, constant change caused by volatile markets, new technology, and deregulation has increased the risks to businesses. In response, the financial community developed products to manage these risks.

These products—called **derivative financial instruments** or simply, **derivatives**—are useful for managing risk. Companies use the fair values or cash flows of these instruments to offset the changes in fair values or cash flows of the at-risk assets. The development of powerful computing and communication technology has aided the growth in derivative use. This technology provides new ways to analyze information about markets as well as the power to process high volumes of payments.

UNDERSTANDING DERIVATIVES

In order to understand derivatives, consider the following examples.

Example 1—Forward Contract. Assume that a company like **Dell** believes that the price of **Google**'s stock will increase substantially in the next three months. Unfortunately, it does not have the cash resources to purchase the stock today. Dell therefore enters into a contract with a broker for delivery of 10,000 shares of Google stock in three months at the price of $110 per share.

Dell has entered into a **forward contract**, a type of derivative. As a result of the contract, Dell **has received the right** to receive 10,000 shares of Google stock in three months. Further, it **has an obligation** to pay $110 per share at that time. What is the benefit of this derivative contract? Dell can buy Google stock today and take delivery in three months. If the price goes up, as it expects, Dell profits. If the price goes down, it loses.

Example 2—Option Contract. Now suppose that Dell needs two weeks to decide whether to purchase Google stock. It therefore enters into a different type of contract, one that gives it the right to purchase Google stock at its current price any time within the next two weeks. As part of the contract, the broker charges $3,000 for holding the contract open for two weeks at a set price.

Dell has now entered into an **option contract**, another type of derivative. As a result of this contract, **it has received the right**, **but not the obligation** to purchase this stock. If the price of the Google stock increases in the next two weeks, Dell exercises its option. In this case, the cost of the stock is the price of the stock stated in the contract, plus the cost of the option contract. If the price does not increase, Dell does not exercise the contract, but still incurs the cost for the option.

The forward contract and the option contract both involve a future delivery of stock. The value of the contract relies on the underlying asset—the Google stock. Thus, these financial instruments are known as derivatives because they **derive their value from** values of other assets (e.g., stocks, bonds, or commodities). Or, their value relates to a market-determined indicator (e.g., interest rates or the Standard and Poor's 500 stock composite index).

In this appendix, we discuss the accounting for three different types of derivatives:

1 Financial forwards or financial futures.

2 Options.

3 Swaps.

Who Uses Derivatives, and Why?

Whether to protect for changes in interest rates, the weather, stock prices, oil prices, or foreign currencies, derivative contracts help to smooth the fluctuations caused by various types of risks. A company that wants to ensure against certain types of business risks often uses derivative contracts to achieve this objective.[1]

Producers and Consumers

To illustrate, assume that Heartland Ag is a large producer of potatoes for the consumer market. The present price for potatoes is excellent. Unfortunately, Heartland needs two months to harvest its potatoes and deliver them to the market. Because Heartland expects the price of potatoes to drop, it signs a forward contract. It agrees to sell its potatoes today at the current market price for delivery in two months.

Who would buy this contract? Suppose on the other side of the contract is **McDonald's Corporation**. McDonald's wants to have potatoes (for French fries) in two months and believes that prices will increase. McDonald's is therefore agreeable to delivery in two months at current prices. It knows that it will need potatoes in two months, and that it can make an acceptable profit at this price level.

In this situation, if the price of potatoes increases before delivery, Heartland loses and McDonald's wins. Conversely, if prices decrease, Heartland wins and McDonald's loses. However, the objective is not to gamble on the outcome. Regardless of which way the price moves, both Heartland and McDonald's have received a price at which they obtain an acceptable profit. In this case, although Heartland is a **producer** and McDonald's is a **consumer**, both companies are **hedgers**. They both hedge their positions to ensure an acceptable financial result.

Commodity prices are volatile. They depend on weather, crop production, and general economic conditions. For the producer and the consumer to plan effectively, it makes good sense to lock in specific future revenues or costs in order to run their businesses successfully.

Speculators and Arbitrageurs

In some cases, instead of McDonald's taking a position in the forward contract, a speculator may purchase the contract from Heartland. The **speculator** bets that the price of potatoes will rise, thereby increasing the value of the forward contract. The speculator, who may be in the market for only a few hours, will then sell the forward contract to another speculator or to a company like McDonald's.

Arbitrageurs also use derivatives. These market players attempt to exploit inefficiencies in derivative markets. They seek to lock in profits by simultaneously entering into transactions in two or more markets. For example, an arbitrageur might trade in a futures contract. At the same time, the arbitrageur will also trade in the commodity underlying the futures contract, hoping to achieve small price gains on the difference between the two. Markets rely on speculators and arbitrageurs to keep the market liquid on a daily basis.

In these illustrations, we explained why Heartland (the producer) and McDonald's (the consumer) would become involved in a derivative contract. Consider other types of situations that companies face.

---

[1]Derivatives are traded on many exchanges throughout the world. In addition, many derivative contracts (primarily interest rate swaps) are privately negotiated.

1 Airlines, like **Delta**, **Southwest**, and **United**, are affected by changes in the price of jet fuel.

2 Financial institutions, such as **Citigroup**, **Bankers Trust**, and **M&I Bank**, are involved in borrowing and lending funds that are affected by changes in interest rates.

3 Multinational corporations, like **Cisco Systems**, **Coca-Cola**, and **General Electric**, are subject to changes in foreign exchange rates.

In fact, most corporations are involved in some form of derivatives transactions. Companies give these reasons (in their annual reports) as to why they use derivatives:

1 **ExxonMobil** uses derivatives to hedge its exposure to fluctuations in interest rates, foreign currency exchange rates, and hydrocarbon prices.

2 **Caterpillar** uses derivatives to manage foreign currency exchange rates, interest rates, and commodity price exposure.

3 **Johnson & Johnson** uses derivatives to manage the impact of interest rate and foreign exchange rate changes on earnings and cash flows.

Many corporations use derivatives extensively and successfully. However, derivatives can be dangerous. All parties involved must understand the risks and rewards associated with these contracts.[2]

BASIC PRINCIPLES IN ACCOUNTING FOR DERIVATIVES

In *SFAS No. 133*, the FASB concluded that derivatives such as forwards and options are assets and liabilities. Companies should therefore report them in the balance sheet at **fair value**.[3] The Board believes that fair value will provide statement users the best information about derivatives.[4] Relying on some other basis of valuation for derivatives, such as historical cost, does not make sense. Why? Because many derivatives have a historical cost of zero. Furthermore, the markets for derivatives, and the assets upon which derivatives' values rely, are well developed. As a result, the Board believes that companies can determine reliable fair value amounts for derivatives.

On the income statement, a company should recognize any unrealized gain or loss in income, if it uses the derivative for speculation purposes. If using the derivative for hedging purposes, the accounting for any gain or loss depends on the type of hedge used. We discuss the accounting for hedged transactions later in the appendix.

In summary, companies follow these guidelines in accounting for derivatives.

1 Recognize derivatives in the financial statements as assets and liabilities.

2 Report derivatives at fair value.

> **OBJECTIVE 9**
> Understand the basic guidelines for accounting for derivatives.

---

[2]There are some well-publicized examples of companies that have suffered considerable losses using derivatives. For example, companies such as **Fannie Mae** (U.S.), **Enron** (U.S.), **Showa Shell Sekiyu** (Japan), **Metallgesellschaft** (Germany), **Procter & Gamble** (U.S.), and **Air Products & Chemicals** (U.S.) incurred significant losses from investments in derivative instruments.

[3]"Accounting for Derivative Instruments and Hedging Activities," *Statement of Financial Accounting Standards No. 133* (Stamford, Conn.: FASB, 1998). This standard covers all derivative instruments, whether financial or not. In this chapter we focus on derivative financial instruments because of their widespread use in practice.

[4]*Fair value* is the amount at which companies can willingly (i.e., not forced or in liquidation) buy (incur) or sell (settle) an asset (or liability). Quoted market prices in active markets are the best evidence of fair value. Companies should use them if available. In the absence of market prices, companies can use the prices of similar assets or liabilities or accepted present value techniques. "Disclosures About Fair Value of Financial Instruments," *Statement of Financial Accounting Standards No. 107* (Stamford, Conn.: FASB, 1991), pars. 5–6, 11. The Board's long-term objective is to require fair value measurement and recognition for all financial instruments (*SFAS No. 133*, par. 216).

3 Recognize gains and losses resulting from speculation in derivatives immediately in income.

4 Report gains and losses resulting from hedge transactions differently, depending on the type of hedge.

Example of Derivative Financial Instrument—Speculation

OBJECTIVE 10
Describe the accounting for derivative financial instruments.

To illustrate the measurement and reporting of a derivative for speculative purposes, we examine a derivative whose value depends on the market price of Laredo Inc. common stock. A company can realize a gain from the increase in the value of the Laredo shares with the use of a derivative, such as a call option.[5] A **call option** gives the holder the right, but not the obligation, to buy shares at a preset price. This price is often referred to as the **strike price** or the **exercise price**.

For example, assume a company enters into a call option contract with Baird Investment Co., which gives it the option to purchase Laredo stock at $100 per share.[6] If the price of Laredo stock increases above $100, the company can exercise this option and purchase the shares for $100 per share. If Laredo's stock never increases above $100 per share, the call option is worthless.

Accounting Entries

To illustrate the accounting for a call option, assume that the company purchases a call option contract on January 2, 2007, when Laredo shares are trading at $100 per share. The contract gives it the option to purchase 1,000 shares (referred to as the **notional amount**) of Laredo stock at an option price of $100 per share. The option expires on April 30, 2007. The company purchases the call option for $400 and makes the following entry.

January 2, 2007

Call Option	400	
Cash		400

This payment is referred to as the **option premium**. It is generally much less than the cost of purchasing the shares directly. The option premium consists of two amounts: (1) intrinsic value and (2) time value. Illustration 17A-1 shows the formula to compute the option premium.

ILLUSTRATION 17A-1
Option Premium Formula

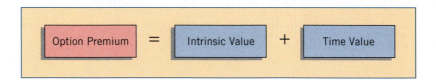

Intrinsic value is the difference between the market price and the preset strike price at any point in time. It represents the amount realized by the option holder, if exercising the option immediately. On January 2, 2007, the intrinsic value is zero because the market price equals the preset strike price.

---

[5]Investors can use a different type of option contract—a **put option**—to realize a gain if anticipating a decline in the Laredo stock value. A put option gives the holder the option to sell shares at a preset price. Thus, a put option **increases** in value when the underlying asset **decreases** in value.

[6]Baird Investment Co. is referred to as the **counterparty**. Counterparties frequently are investment bankers or other companies that hold inventories of financial instruments.

Time value refers to the option's value over and above its intrinsic value. Time value reflects the possibility that the option has a fair value greater than zero. How? Because there is some expectation that the price of Laredo shares will increase above the strike price during the option term. As indicated, the time value for the option is $400.[7]

On March 31, 2007, the price of Laredo shares increases to $120 per share. The intrinsic value of the call option contract is now $20,000. That is, the company can exercise the call option and purchase 1,000 shares from Baird Investment for $100 per share. It can then sell the shares in the market for $120 per share. This gives the company a gain of $20,000 ($120,000 − $100,000) on the option contract.[8] It records the increase in the intrinsic value of the option as follows.

March 31, 2007

Call Option	20,000	
Unrealized Holding Gain or Loss—Income		20,000

A market appraisal indicates that the time value of the option at March 31, 2007, is $100.[9] The company records this change in value of the option as follows.

March 31, 2007

Unrealized Holding Gain or Loss—Income	300	
Call Option ($400 − $100)		300

At March 31, 2007, the company reports the call option in its balance sheet at fair value of $20,100.[10] The unrealized holding gain increases net income for the period. The loss on the time value of the option decreases net income.

On April 1, 2007, the company records the settlement of the call option contract with Baird Investment as follows.

April 1, 2007

Cash	20,000	
Loss on Settlement of Call Option	100	
Call Option		20,100

Illustration 17A-2 summarizes the effects of the call option contract on net income.

Date	Transaction	Income (Loss) Effect
March 31, 2007	Net increase in value of call option ($20,000 − $300)	$19,700
April 1, 2007	Settle call option	(100)
	Total net income	$19,600

ILLUSTRATION 17A-2
Effect on Income—
Derivative Financial
Instrument

The accounting summarized in Illustration 17A-2 is in accord with *SFAS No. 133*. That is, because the call option meets the definition of an asset, the company records

---

[7]This cost is estimated using option-pricing models, such as the Black-Scholes model. The volatility of the underlying stock, the expected life of the option, the risk-free rate of interest, and expected dividends on the underlying stock during the option term affect the Black-Scholes fair value estimate.

[8]In practice, investors generally do not have to actually buy and sell the Laredo shares to settle the option and realize the gain. This is referred to as the **net settlement** feature of option contracts.

[9]The decline in value reflects both the decreased likelihood that the Laredo shares will continue to increase in value over the option period and the shorter time to maturity of the option contract.

[10]As indicated earlier, the total value of the option at any point in time equals the intrinsic value plus the time value.

it in the balance sheet on March 31, 2007. Furthermore, it reports the call option at fair value, with any gains or losses reported in income.

Differences between Traditional and Derivative Financial Instruments

How does a traditional financial instrument differ from a derivative one? A derivative financial instrument has the following three basic characteristics.[11]

1 **The instrument has (1) one or more underlyings and (2) an identified payment provision.** An **underlying** is a specified interest rate, security price, commodity price, index of prices or rates, or other market-related variable. The interaction of the underlying, with the face amount or the number of units specified in the derivative contract (the notional amounts), determines payment. For example, the value of the call option increased in value when the value of the Laredo stock increased. In this case, the underlying is the stock price. To arrive at the payment provision, multiply the change in the stock price by the number of shares (notional amount).

2 **The instrument requires little or no investment at the inception of the contract.** To illustrate, the company paid a small premium to purchase the call option—an amount much less than if purchasing the Laredo shares as a direct investment.

3 **The instrument requires or permits net settlement.** As indicated in the call option example, the company could realize a profit on the call option without taking possession of the shares. This **net settlement** feature reduces the transaction costs associated with derivatives.

Illustration 17A-3 summarizes the differences between traditional and derivative financial instruments. Here, we use a trading security for the traditional financial instrument and a call option as an example of a derivative one.

ILLUSTRATION 17A-3
Features of Traditional and Derivative Financial Instruments

Feature	Traditional Financial Instrument (Trading Security)	Derivative Financial Instrument (Call Option)
Payment provision	Stock price times the number of shares.	Change in stock price (underlying) times number of shares (notional amount).
Initial investment	Investor pays full cost.	Initial investment is much less than full cost.
Settlement	Deliver stock to receive cash.	Receive cash equivalent, based on changes in stock price times the number of shares.

DERIVATIVES USED FOR HEDGING

Flexibility in use, and the low-cost features of derivatives relative to traditional financial instruments, explain the popularity of derivatives. An additional use for derivatives is in risk management. For example, companies such as **Coca-Cola**, **ExxonMobil**, and **General Electric** borrow and lend substantial amounts in credit markets. In doing so, they are exposed to significant **interest rate risk**. That is, they face substantial risk that

[11]In *SFAS No. 133*, the FASB identifies these same features as the key characteristics of derivatives. The FASB used these broad characteristics so that companies could apply the definitions, and hence the standard, to yet-to-be-developed derivatives (par. 249).

the fair values or cash flows of interest-sensitive assets or liabilities will change if interest rates increase or decrease. These same companies also have significant international operations. As such, they are also exposed to **exchange rate risk**—the risk that changes in foreign currency exchange rates will negatively impact the profitability of their international businesses.

Companies can use derivatives to offset the negative impacts of changes in interest rates or foreign currency exchange rates. This use of derivatives is referred to as **hedging**.

SFAS No. 133 established accounting and reporting standards for derivative financial instruments used in hedging activities. The FASB allows special accounting for two types of hedges—fair value and cash flow hedges.[12]

RISKY BUSINESS

As shown in the graph below, use of derivatives has grown steadily in the past several years. In fact, close to *$200 trillion* (in notional amounts) in derivative contracts were in play at the end of 2004. The primary players in the market for derivatives are large companies and various financial institutions, which continue to find new uses for derivatives for speculation and risk management.

WHAT DO THE NUMBERS MEAN?

Total Swaps and Equity Derivatives
($ in trillions)

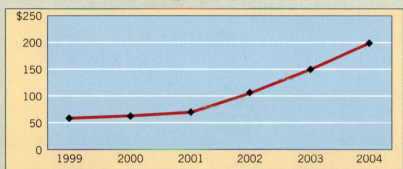

Financial engineers continue to develop new uses for derivatives, many times through the use of increasingly complex webs of transactions, spanning a number of markets. As new uses for derivatives appear, the financial system as a whole can be dramatically affected. As a result, some market-watchers are concerned about the risk that a crisis in one company or sector could bring the entire financial system to its knees.

This concern was illustrated recently when both **Fannie Mae** and **Freddie Mac** (two federally-chartered mortgage companies) indicated problems with their derivative accounting. It now appears likely that both of these companies will have to restate their financial results for prior periods. This has led Congress to study whether the concentration of mortgages in these institutions is too high. With so many home buyers dependent on Fannie and Freddie, there is concern that these companies may be too loaded down with debt, which could negatively affect the home mortgage market.

Source: Data from International Swaps and Derivatives Association Market Survey (2004).

---

[12]*SFAS No. 133* also addresses the accounting for certain foreign currency hedging transactions. In general, these transactions are special cases of the two hedges we discuss here. Understanding of foreign currency hedging transactions requires knowledge related to consolidation of multinational entities, which is beyond the scope of this textbook.

Fair Value Hedge

In a **fair value hedge**, a company uses a derivative to hedge (offset) the exposure to changes in the fair value of a recognized asset or liability or of an unrecognized commitment. In a perfectly hedged position, the gain or loss on the fair value of the derivative equals and offsets that of the hedged asset or liability.

Companies commonly use several types of fair value hedges. For example, companies use interest rate swaps to hedge the risk that changes in interest rates will impact the fair value of debt obligations. Or, they use put options to hedge the risk that an equity investment will decline in value.

To illustrate a fair value hedge, assume that on April 1, 2006, Hayward Co. purchases 100 shares of Sonoma stock at a market price of $100 per share. Hayward does not intend to actively trade this investment. It consequently classifies the Sonoma investment as available-for-sale. Hayward records this available-for-sale investment as follows.

April 1, 2006

Available-for-Sale Securities	10,000	
Cash		10,000

Hayward records available-for-sale securities at fair value on the balance sheet. It reports unrealized gains and losses in equity as part of other comprehensive income.[13] Fortunately for Hayward, the value of the Sonoma shares increases to $125 per share during 2006. Hayward records the gain on this investment as follows.

December 31, 2006

Security Fair Value Adjustment (Available-for-Sale)	2,500	
Unrealized Holding Gain or Loss—Equity		2,500

Illustration 17A-4 indicates how Hayward reports the Sonoma investment in its balance sheet.

ILLUSTRATION 17A-4
Balance Sheet Presentation of Available-for-Sale Securities

HAYWARD CO.
BALANCE SHEET (PARTIAL)
DECEMBER 31, 2006

Assets	
Available-for-sale securities (at fair value)	$12,500
Stockholders' Equity	
Accumulated other comprehensive income	
Unrealized holding gain	$2,500

While Hayward benefits from an increase in the price of Sonoma shares, it is exposed to the risk that the price of the Sonoma stock will decline. To hedge this risk, Hayward locks in its gain on the Sonoma investment by purchasing a put option on 100 shares of Sonoma stock.

Hayward enters into the put option contract on January 2, 2007, and designates the option as a fair value hedge of the Sonoma investment. This put option (which expires in two years) gives Hayward the option to sell Sonoma shares at a price of $125. Since the exercise price equals the current market price, no entry is necessary at inception of the put option.[14]

January 2, 2007

No entry required. A memorandum indicates the signing of the put option contract and its designation as a fair value hedge for the Sonoma investment.

---

[13]We discussed the distinction between trading and available-for-sale investments earlier in the chapter.

[14]To simplify the example, we assume no premium is paid for the option.

At December 31, 2007, the price of the Sonoma shares has declined to $120 per share. Hayward records the following entry for the Sonoma investment.

December 31, 2007

Unrealized Holding Gain or Loss—Income	500	
Security Fair Value Adjustment (Available-for-Sale)		500

Note that upon designation of the hedge, the accounting for the available-for-sale security changes from regular GAAP. That is, Hayward records the unrealized holding loss in income, not in equity. If Hayward had not followed this accounting, a mismatch of gains and losses in the income statement would result. Thus, special accounting for the hedged item (in this case, an available-for-sale security) is necessary in a fair value hedge.

The following journal entry records the increase in value of the put option on Sonoma shares.

December 31, 2007

Put Option	500	
Unrealized Holding Gain or Loss—Income		500

The decline in the price of Sonoma shares results in an increase in the fair value of the put option. That is, Hayward could realize a gain on the put option by purchasing 100 shares in the open market for $120 and then exercise the put option, selling the shares for $125. This results in a gain to Hayward of $500 (100 shares × [$125 − $120]).[15]

Illustration 17A-5 indicates how Hayward reports the amounts related to the Sonoma investment and the put option.

HAYWARD CO. BALANCE SHEET (PARTIAL) DECEMBER 31, 2007	
Assets	
Available-for-sale securities (at fair value)	$12,000
Put option	500

ILLUSTRATION 17A-5
Balance Sheet Presentation of Fair Value Hedge

The increase in fair value on the option offsets or hedges the decline in value on Hayward's available-for-sale security. By using fair value accounting for both financial instruments, the financial statements reflect the underlying substance of Hayward's net exposure to the risks of holding Sonoma stock. By using fair value accounting for both these financial instruments, the balance sheet reports the amount that Hayward would receive on the investment and the put option contract if Hayward sold and settled them, respectively.

Illustration 17A-6 illustrates the reporting of the effects of the hedging transaction on income for the year ended December 31, 2007.

HAYWARD CO. INCOME STATEMENT (PARTIAL) FOR THE YEAR ENDED DECEMBER 31, 2007	
Other Income	
Unrealized holding gain—put option	$ 500
Unrealized holding loss—available-for-sale securities	(500)

ILLUSTRATION 17A-6
Income Statement Presentation of Fair Value Hedge

---

[15]In practice, Hayward generally does not have to actually buy and sell the Sonoma shares to realize this gain. Rather, unless the counterparty wants to hold Hayward shares, Hayward can "close out" the contract by having the counterparty pay it $500 in cash. This is an example of the net settlement feature of derivatives.

The income statement indicates that the gain on the put option offsets the loss on the available-for-sale securities.[16] The reporting for these financial instruments, even when they reflect a hedging relationship, illustrates why the FASB argued that fair value accounting provides the most relevant information about financial instruments, including derivatives.

Cash Flow Hedge

OBJECTIVE 12
Explain how to account for a cash flow hedge.

INTERNATIONAL INSIGHT

Under IFRS, companies record unrealized holding gains or losses on cash flow hedges as adjustments to the value of the hedged item, not as "Other comprehensive income."

Companies use **cash flow hedges** to hedge exposures to **cash flow risk**, which results from the variability in cash flows. The FASB allows special accounting for cash flow hedges. Generally, companies measure and report derivatives at fair value on the balance sheet. They report gains and losses directly in net income. However, companies account for derivatives used in cash flow hedges at fair value on the balance sheet, but they **record gains or losses in equity**, **as part of other comprehensive income**.

To illustrate, assume that in September 2006 Allied Can Co. anticipates purchasing 1,000 metric tons of aluminum in January 2007. Concerned that prices for aluminum will increase in the next few months, Allied wants to hedge the risk that it might pay higher prices for inventory in January 2007. As a result, Allied enters into an aluminum futures contract.

A **futures contract** gives the holder the right and the obligation to purchase an asset at a preset price for a specified period of time.[17] In this case, the aluminum futures contract gives Allied the right and the obligation to purchase 1,000 metric tons of aluminum for $1,550 per ton. This contract price is good until the contract expires in January 2007. The underlying for this derivative is the price of aluminum. If the price of aluminum rises above $1,550, the value of the futures contract to Allied increases. Why? Because Allied will be able to purchase the aluminum at the lower price of $1,550 per ton.[18]

Allied enters into the futures contract on September 1, 2006. Assume that the price to be paid today for inventory to be delivered in January—the **spot price**—equals the contract price. With the two prices equal, the futures contract has no value. Therefore no entry is necessary.

September 2006

No entry required. A memorandum indicates the signing of the futures contract.

At December 31, 2006, the price for January delivery of aluminum increases to $1,575 per metric ton. Allied makes the following entry to record the increase in the value of the futures contract.

December 31, 2006

Futures Contract	25,000	
Unrealized Holding Gain or Loss—Equity		25,000
([$1,575 − $1,550] × 1,000 tons)		

Allied reports the futures contract in the balance sheet as a current asset. It reports the gain on the futures contract as part of other comprehensive income.

---

[16]Note that the fair value changes in the option contract will not offset **increases** in the value of the Hayward investment. Should the price of Sonoma stock increase above $125 per share, Hayward would have no incentive to exercise the put option.

[17]A **futures contract** is a firm contractual agreement between a buyer and seller for a specified asset on a fixed date in the future. The contract also has a standard specification so both parties know exactly what is being traded. A **forward** is similar but is not traded on an exchange and does not have standardized conditions.

[18]As with the earlier call option example, the actual aluminum does not have to be exchanged. Rather, the parties to the futures contract settle by paying the cash difference between the futures price and the price of aluminum on each settlement date.

Since Allied has not yet purchased and sold the inventory, this gain is an **anticipated transaction**. In this type of transaction, a company accumulates in equity gains or losses on the futures contract as part of other comprehensive income until the period in which it sells the inventory, thereby affecting earnings.

In January 2007, Allied purchases 1,000 metric tons of aluminum for $1,575 and makes the following entry.[19]

January 2007

Aluminum Inventory	1,575,000	
Cash ($1,575 × 1,000 tons)		1,575,000

At the same time, Allied makes final settlement on the futures contract. It records the following entry.

January 2007

Cash	25,000	
Futures Contract ($1,575,000 − $1,550,000)		25,000

Through use of the futures contract derivative, Allied fixes the cost of its inventory. The $25,000 futures contract settlement offsets the amount paid to purchase the inventory at the prevailing market price of $1,575,000. The result: net cash outflow of $1,550 per metric ton, as desired. As Illustration 17A-7 shows, Allied has therefore effectively hedged the cash flow for the purchase of inventory.

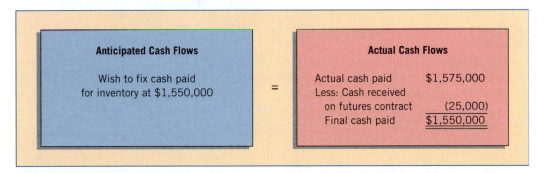

ILLUSTRATION 17A-7
Effect of Hedge on Cash Flows

There are no income effects at this point. Allied accumulates in equity the gain on the futures contract as part of other comprehensive income until the period when it sells the inventory, affecting earnings through cost of goods sold.

For example, assume that Allied processes the aluminum into finished goods (cans). The total cost of the cans (including the aluminum purchases in January 2007) is $1,700,000. Allied sells the cans in July 2007 for $2,000,000, and records this sale as follows.

July 2007

Cash	2,000,000	
Sales Revenue		2,000,000
Cost of Goods Sold	1,700,000	
Inventory (Cans)		1,700,000

Since the effect of the anticipated transaction has now affected earnings, Allied makes the following entry related to the hedging transaction.

July 2007

Unrealized Holding Gain or Loss—Equity	25,000	
Cost of Goods Sold		25,000

The gain on the futures contract, which Allied reported as part of other comprehensive income, now reduces cost of goods sold. As a result, the cost of aluminum

---

[19]In practice, futures contracts are settled on a daily basis. For our purposes we show only one settlement for the entire amount.

included in the overall cost of goods sold is $1,550,000. The futures contract has worked as planned. Allied has managed the cash paid for aluminum inventory and the amount of cost of goods sold.

OTHER REPORTING ISSUES

OBJECTIVE 13
Identify special reporting issues related to derivative financial instruments that cause unique accounting problems.

The preceding examples illustrate the basic reporting issues related to the accounting for derivatives. Next, we discuss the following additional issues:

1 The accounting for embedded derivatives.
2 Qualifying hedge criteria.
3 Disclosures about financial instruments and derivatives.

Embedded Derivatives

As we indicated at the beginning of this appendix, rapid innovation in the development of complex financial instruments drove efforts toward unifying and improving the accounting standards for derivatives. In recent years, this innovation has led to the development of **hybrid securities**. These securities have characteristics of both debt and equity. They often combine traditional and derivative financial instruments.

For example, a convertible bond (discussed in Chapter 16) is a hybrid instrument. It consists of two parts: (1) a debt security, referred to as the **host security**, combined with (2) an option to convert the bond to shares of common stock, the **embedded derivative**.

To provide consistency in accounting for similar derivatives, a company must account for embedded derivatives similarly to other derivatives. Therefore, to account for an embedded derivative, a company **should separate it from the host security** and then account for it using the accounting for derivatives. This separation process is referred to as **bifurcation**.[20] Thus, a company investing in a convertible bond must separate the stock option component of the instrument. It then accounts for the derivative (the stock option) at fair value and the host instrument (the debt) according to GAAP, as if there were no embedded derivative.[21]

Qualifying Hedge Criteria

The FASB identified certain criteria that hedging transactions must meet before requiring the special accounting for hedges. The FASB designed these criteria to ensure the use of hedge accounting in a consistent manner across different hedge transactions. The general criteria relate to the following areas.

1 **Documentation, risk management, and designation.** At inception of the hedge, there must be formal **documentation** of the hedging relationship, the company's **risk management** objective, and the strategy for undertaking the hedge. **Designation** refers to identifying the hedging instrument, the hedged item or transaction, the nature of the risk being hedged, and how the hedging instrument will offset changes in the fair value or cash flows attributable to the hedged risk.

The FASB decided that documentation and designation are critical to the implementation of the special accounting for hedges. Without these requirements, companies might try to apply the hedge accounting provisions retroactively, only

---

[20]A company can also designate such a derivative as a hedging instrument. The company would apply the hedge accounting provisions outlined earlier in the chapter.

[21]The **issuer** of the convertible bonds would not bifurcate the option component of the convertible bonds payable. *SFAS No. 133* explicitly precludes embedded derivative accounting for an embedded derivative that is indexed to a company's own common stock. If the conversion feature was tied to **another company's** stock, then the derivative would be bifurcated.

in response to negative changes in market conditions, to offset the negative impact of a transaction on the financial statements. Allowing special hedge accounting in such a setting could mask the speculative nature of the original transaction.

2 Effectiveness of the hedging relationship. At inception and on an ongoing basis, the hedging relationship should be **highly effective** in achieving offsetting changes in fair value or cash flows. Companies must assess effectiveness whenever preparing financial statements.

The general guideline for effectiveness is that the fair values or cash flows of the hedging instrument (the derivative) and the hedged item exhibit a high degree of correlation. In practice, high effectiveness is assumed when the correlation is close to one (e.g., within plus or minus .10). In our earlier hedging examples (put option and the futures contract on aluminum inventory), the fair values and cash flows are perfectly correlated. That is, when the cash payment for the inventory purchase increased, it offset, dollar for dollar, the cash received on the futures contract.

If the effectiveness criterion is not met, either at inception or because of changes following inception of the hedging relationship, the FASB no longer allows special hedge accounting. The company should then account for the derivative as a free-standing derivative.[22]

3 Effect on reported earnings of changes in fair values or cash flows. A change in the fair value of a hedged item or variation in the cash flow of a hedged forecasted transaction must have the potential to change the amount recognized in reported earnings. There is no need for special hedge accounting if a company accounts for both the hedging instrument and the hedged item at fair value under existing GAAP. In this case, earnings will properly reflect the offsetting gains and losses.

For example, special accounting is not needed for a fair value hedge of a trading security, because a company accounts for both the investment and the derivative at fair value on the balance sheet with gains or losses reported in earnings. Thus, "special" hedge accounting is necessary only when there is a mismatch of the accounting effects for the hedging instrument and the hedged item under GAAP.[23]

Disclosure Provisions

SFAS No. 133 provides comprehensive accounting guidance for derivatives. In addition, *SFAS No. 107* provides general disclosure requirements for traditional financial instruments. The primary requirements for disclosures related to financial instruments are as follows.

> **OBJECTIVE 14**
> Describe the disclosure requirements for traditional and derivative financial instruments.

1 Disclose the fair value and related carrying value of financial instruments in the body of the financial statements, in a note, or in a summary table form that makes it clear whether the amounts represent assets or liabilities.

2 Distinguish between financial instruments held or issued for purposes other than trading. For derivatives, disclose the objectives for holding or issuing those instruments (speculation or hedging), the hedging context (fair value or cash flow), and the strategies for achieving risk management objectives.

3 Do not combine, aggregate, or net the fair value of separate financial instruments, even if considering those instruments as related.

4 Display as a separate classification of other comprehensive income the net gain or loss on derivative instruments designated in cash flow hedges.

---

[22]The accounting for the part of a derivative that is not effective in a hedge is at fair value, with gains and losses recorded in income.

[23]An important criterion specific to cash flow hedges is that the forecasted transaction in a cash flow hedge "is likely to occur." A company should support this probability (defined as significantly greater than the term "more likely than not") by observable facts such as frequency of similar past transactions and its financial and operational ability to carry out the transaction.

5 Provide quantitative information about market risks of derivatives, and also of other assets and liabilities (encouraged, not required, information). Such information should be consistent with risk management procedures. Further, the information should be useful for comparing the results of the use of derivatives.

While these additional disclosures of fair value provide useful information to financial statement users, companies generally provide them as supplemental information only. The balance sheet continues to rely primarily on historical cost. Exceptions to this general rule are the fair value requirements for certain investment securities and derivatives, as we illustrated earlier. Illustration 17A-8 provides a fair value disclosure for **Caterpillar Inc.**

ILLUSTRATION 17A-8
Caterpillar Inc. Fair Value
Disclosure

Caterpillar Inc.

Notes to the Financial Statements

Fair Values of Financial Instruments

(millions of dollars)	2004 Carrying Amount	2004 Fair Value	2003 Carrying Amount	2003 Fair Value
Asset (Liability) at December 31				
Cash and short-term investments	$ 445	$ 445	$ 342	$ 342
Long-term investments	1,852	1,852	1,574	1,574
Foreign currency contracts	176	176	167	167
Finance recievables—net (excluding finance type leases)	13,457	13,445	11,439	11,489
Wholesale inventory recievables—net (excluding finance type leases)	882	857	681	666
Short-term borrowings	(4,157)	(4,157)	(2,757)	(2,757)
Long-term debt (including amounts due within one year)				
Machinery and engines	(3,669)	(4,186)	(3,635)	(4,109)
Financial products	(15,699)	(15,843)	(13,892)	(14,078)
Interest rate swaps				
Financial products—				
in a net receivable position	75	75	87	87
in a net payable position	(69)	(69)	(59)	(59)
Guarantees	(10)	(10)	(5)	(9)

UNDERLYING CONCEPTS

Providing supplemental information on the fair values of financial instruments illustrates application of the full disclosure principle.

The fair values of cash and cash equivalents, short-term investments, and short-term debt approximate cost. The reason is obvious—because of the immediate and short-term maturities of these instruments. The fair value of long-term investments (and some derivatives) relies on quoted market prices at the reporting date. The fair value of long-term debt and some derivatives relies on market prices for similar instruments or by discounting expected cash flows at rates currently available to the company for instruments with similar risks and maturities.

If a company cannot estimate fair value, it must disclose information relevant to the estimate of fair value (such as the terms of the instrument) and the reason why it is unable to arrive at an estimate of fair value.[24]

---

[24]*SFAS No. 107* lists a number of exceptions to this requirement; most of which other standards cover. The exception list includes such items as pension and postretirement benefits; employee stock options; insurance contracts; lease contracts; warranties, rights, and obligations; purchase obligations; equity method investments; minority interests; and instruments classified as stockholders' equity in the company's balance sheet.

Summary of *SFAS No. 133*

Illustration 17A-9 summarizes the accounting provisions for derivatives and hedging transactions.

Derivative Use	Accounting for Derivative	Accounting for Hedged Item	Common Example
Speculation	At fair value with unrealized holding gains and losses recorded in income.	Not applicable	Call or put option on an equity security.
Hedging Fair value	At fair value with holding gains and losses recorded in income.	At fair value with gains and losses recorded in income.	Put option to hedge an equity investment.
Cash flow	At fair value with unrealized holding gains and losses from the hedge recorded in other comprehensive income, and reclassified in income when the hedged transaction's cash flows affect earnings.	Use other generally accepted accounting principles for the hedged item.	Use of a futures contract to hedge a forecasted purchase of inventory.

ILLUSTRATION 17A-9
Summary of Derivative Accounting Under *SFAS 133*

As indicated, the general accounting for derivatives relies on fair values. *SFAS No. 133* also establishes special accounting guidance when companies use derivatives **for hedging purposes**. For example, when a company uses a put option to hedge prices changes in an available-for-sale stock investment in a fair value hedge (see the Hayward example earlier), it records unrealized gains on the investment in earnings, which is not GAAP for available-for-sale securities without such a hedge. This special accounting is justified in order to accurately report the nature of the hedging relationship in the balance sheet (recording both the put option and the investment at fair value) and in the income statement (reporting offsetting gains and losses in the same period).

Special accounting also is used for cash flow hedges. Companies account for derivatives used in qualifying cash flow hedges at fair value on the balance sheet, but record unrealized holding gains or losses in other comprehensive income until selling or settling the hedged item. In a cash flow hedge, a company continues to record the hedged item at its historical cost.

COMPREHENSIVE HEDGE ACCOUNTING EXAMPLE

To provide a comprehensive example of hedge accounting, we examine the use of an interest rate swap. First, let's consider how swaps work and why companies use them.

Options and futures trade on organized securities exchanges. Because of this, options and futures have standardized terms. Although that standardization makes the trading easier, it limits the flexibility needed to tailor contracts to specific circumstances. In addition, most types of derivatives have relatively short time horizons, thereby excluding their use for reducing long-term risk exposure.

As a result, many corporations instead turn to the swap, a very popular type of derivative. A **swap** is a transaction between two parties in which the first party promises to make a payment to the second party. Similarly, the second party promises to make a simultaneous payment to the first party.

The most common type of swap is the **interest rate swap**. In this type, one party makes payments based on a fixed or floating rate, and the second party does just the opposite. In most cases, large money-center banks bring together the two parties. These banks handle the flow of payments between the parties, as shown in Illustration 17A-10.

ILLUSTRATION 17A-10
Swap Transaction

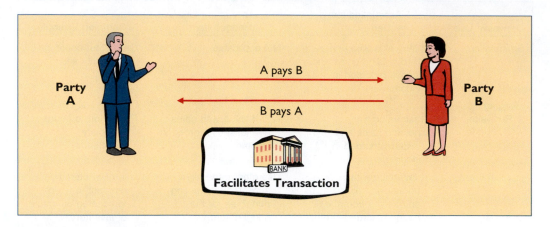

Fair Value Hedge

To illustrate the use of a swap in a fair value hedge, assume that Jones Company issues $1,000,000 of five-year, 8 percent bonds on January 2, 2007. Jones records this transaction as follows.

	January 2, 2007	
Cash	1,000,000	
Bonds Payable		1,000,000

Jones offered a fixed interest rate to appeal to investors. But Jones is concerned that if market interest rates decline, the fair value of the liability will increase. The company will then suffer an economic loss.[25] To protect against the risk of loss, Jones hedges the risk of a decline in interest rates by entering into a five-year interest rate swap contract. Jones agrees to the following terms:

1 Jones will receive fixed payments at 8 percent (based on the $1,000,000 amount).
2 Jones will pay variable rates, based on the market rate in effect for the life of the swap contract. The variable rate at the inception of the contract is 6.8 percent.

As Illustration 17A-11 shows, this swap allows Jones to change the interest on the bonds payable from a fixed rate to a variable rate.

ILLUSTRATION 17A-11
Interest Rate Swap

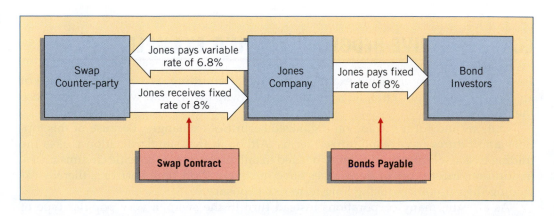

---

[25]This economic loss arises because Jones is locked into the 8 percent interest payments even if rates decline.

The settlement dates for the swap correspond to the interest payment dates on the debt (December 31). On each interest payment (settlement) date, Jones and the counterparty compute the difference between current market interest rates and the fixed rate of 8 percent, and determine the value of the swap.[26] If interest rates decline, the value of the swap contract to Jones increases (Jones has a gain), while at the same time Jones's fixed-rate debt obligation increases (Jones has an economic loss).

The swap is an effective risk-management tool in this setting. Its value relates to the same underlying (interest rates) that will affect the value of the fixed-rate bond payable. Thus, if the value of the swap goes up, it offsets the loss related to the debt obligation.

Assuming that Jones enters into the swap on January 2, 2007 (the same date as the issuance of the debt), the swap at this time has no value. Therefore no entry is necessary.

January 2, 2007

No entry required. A memorandum indicates the signing of the swap contract.

At the end of 2007, Jones makes the interest payment on the bonds. It records this transaction as follows.

December 31, 2007

Interest Expense	80,000	
Cash (8% × $1,000,000)		80,000

At the end of 2007, market interest rates have declined substantially. Therefore the value of the swap contract increases. Recall (see Illustration 17A-11) that in the swap, Jones receives a fixed rate of 8 percent, or $80,000 ($1,000,000 × 8%), and pays a variable rate (6.8%), or $68,000. Jones therefore receives $12,000 ($80,000 − $68,000) as a settlement payment on the swap contract on the first interest payment date. Jones records this transaction as follows.

December 31, 2007

Cash	12,000	
Interest Expense		12,000

In addition, a market appraisal indicates that the value of the interest rate swap has increased $40,000. Jones records this increase in value as follows.[27]

December 31, 2007

Swap Contract	40,000	
Unrealized Holding Gain or Loss—Income		40,000

Jones reports this swap contract in the balance sheet. It reports the gain on the hedging transaction in the income statement. Because interest rates have declined, the company records a loss and a related increase in its liability as follows.

December 31, 2007

Unrealized Holding Gain or Loss—Income	40,000	
Bonds Payable		40,000

Jones reports the loss on the hedging activity in net income. It adjusts bonds payable in the balance sheet to fair value.

Financial Statement Presentation of an Interest Rate Swap

Illustration 17A-12 (on page 880) indicates how Jones reports the asset and liability related to this hedging transaction on the balance sheet.

---

[26]The underlying for an interest rate swap is some index of market interest rates. The most commonly used index is the London Interbank Offer Rate, or LIBOR. In this example, we assume the LIBOR is 6.8 percent.

[27]Theoretically, this fair value change reflects the present value of expected future differences in variable and fixed interest rates.

ILLUSTRATION 17A-12
Balance Sheet
Presentation of Fair Value
Hedge

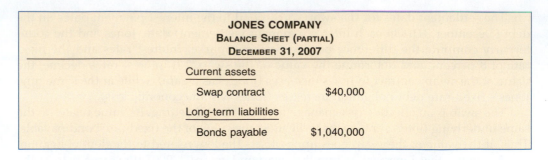

JONES COMPANY	
BALANCE SHEET (PARTIAL)	
DECEMBER 31, 2007	
Current assets	
Swap contract	$40,000
Long-term liabilities	
Bonds payable	$1,040,000

The effect on Jones's balance sheet is the addition of the swap asset and an increase in the carrying value of the bonds payable. Illustration 17A-13 indicates how Jones reports the effects of this swap transaction in the income statement.

ILLUSTRATION 17A-13
Income Statement
Presentation of Fair Value
Hedge

JONES COMPANY		
INCOME STATEMENT (PARTIAL)		
FOR THE YEAR ENDED DECEMBER 31, 2007		
Interest expense ($80,000 − $12,000)		$68,000
Other income		
Unrealized holding gain—swap contract	$40,000	
Unrealized holding loss—bonds payable	(40,000)	
Net gain (loss)		$–0–

On the income statement, Jones reports interest expense of $68,000. Jones has effectively changed the debt's interest rate from fixed to variable. That is, by receiving a fixed rate and paying a variable rate on the swap, the company converts the fixed rate on the bond payable to variable. This results in an effective interest rate of 6.8 percent in 2007.[28] Also, the gain on the swap offsets the loss related to the debt obligation. Therefore the net gain or loss on the hedging activity is zero.

Illustration 17A-14 shows the overall impact of the swap transaction on the financial statements.

ILLUSTRATION 17A-14
Impact on Financial
Statements of Fair Value
Hedge

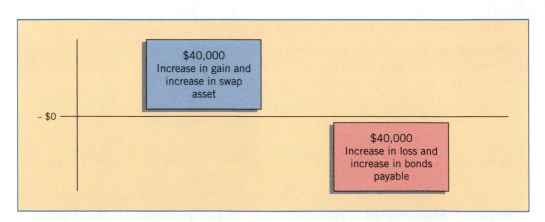

In summary, to account for fair value hedges (as illustrated in the Jones example) **record the derivative at its fair value in the balance sheet, and record any gains and losses in income**. Thus, the gain on the swap offsets or hedges the loss on the bond payable, due to the decline in interest rates.

---

[28]Jones will apply similar accounting and measurement at future interest payment dates. Thus, if interest rates increase, Jones will continue to receive 8 percent on the swap (records a loss) but will also be locked into the fixed payments to the bondholders at an 8 percent rate (records a gain).

By adjusting the hedged item (the bond payable in the Jones case) to fair value, with the gain or loss recorded in earnings, the accounting for the Jones bond payable deviates from amortized cost. This special accounting is justified in order to report accurately the nature of the hedging relationship between the swap and the bond payable in the balance sheet (both the swap and the debt obligation are recorded at fair value) and in the income statement (offsetting gains and losses are reported in the same period).[29]

INTERNATIONAL INSIGHT

International accounting for hedges (*IAS 39*) is similar to the provisions of U.S. GAAP.

CONTROVERSY AND CONCLUDING REMARKS

SFAS No. 133 represents the FASB's effort to develop accounting guidance for derivatives. Many believe that companies need these new rules to properly measure and report derivatives in financial statements. Others argue that reporting derivatives at fair value results in unrealized gains and losses that are difficult to interpret. Still others raise concerns about the complexity and cost of implementing the standard, since prior to *SFAS No. 133*, companies omitted recognizing many derivatives in financial statements.[30]

We believe that the long-term benefits of this standard will far outweigh any short-term implementation costs. As the volume and complexity of derivatives and hedging transactions continue to grow, so does the risk that investors and creditors will be exposed to unexpected losses arising from derivative transactions. Without this standard, statement readers do not have comprehensive information concerning many derivative financial instruments and the effects of hedging transactions using derivatives.

SUMMARY OF LEARNING OBJECTIVES FOR APPENDIX 17A

8. Explain who uses derivatives and why. Any company or individual that wants to ensure against different types of business risks may use derivative contracts to achieve this objective. In general, these transactions involve some type of hedge. Speculators also use derivatives, attempting to find an enhanced return. Speculators are very important to the derivatives market because they keep it liquid on a daily basis. Arbitrageurs attempt to exploit inefficiencies in various derivative contracts. A company primarily uses derivatives for purposes of hedging its exposure to fluctuations in interest rates, foreign currency exchange rates, and commodity prices.

9. Understand the basic guidelines for accounting for derivatives. Companies should recognize derivatives in the financial statements as assets and liabilities, and report them at fair value. Companies should recognize gains and losses resulting from speculation immediately in income. They report gains and losses resulting from hedge transactions in different ways, depending on the type of hedge.

10. Describe the accounting for derivative financial instruments. Companies report derivative financial instruments in the balance sheet, and record them at fair value. Except for derivatives used in hedging, companies record realized and unrealized gains and losses on derivative financial instruments in income.

KEY TERMS

anticipated transaction, *873*

arbitrageurs, *864*

bifurcation, *874*

call option, *866*

cash flow hedge, *872*

counterparty, *866(n)*

derivative financial instrument, derivative, *863*

designation, *874*

documentation, *874*

embedded derivative, *874*

fair value, *865*

fair value hedge, *870*

forward contract, *863*

futures contract, *872*

hedging, *869*

---

[29]An interest rate swap can also be used in a cash flow hedge. A common setting is the cash flow risk inherent in having variable rate debt as part of a company's debt structure. In this situation, the variable debt issuer can hedge the cash flow risk by entering into a swap contract to receive variable rate cash flows but pay fixed rate. The cash received on the swap contract will offset the variable cash flows to be paid on the debt obligation.

[30]Interestingly, some companies adopted the standard early because the rules provide better accounting for some derivatives relative to the rules in place before *SFAS No. 133*. Paula Froelich, "U.S. Companies Find New Accounting Rule Costly, Inefficient," Dow Jones News Service (March 2, 1999). In June 2000, the FASB issued guidance to ease implementation of the provisions of *SFAS No. 133*: "Accounting for Certain Derivative Hedging Instruments and Certain Hedging Activities—An Amendment to FASB Statement No. 133," *Statement of Financial Accounting Standards No. 138* (Stamford, Conn.: FASB, 2000).

11. Explain how to account for a fair value hedge. A company records the derivative used in a qualifying fair value hedge at its fair value in the balance sheet, recording any gains and losses in income. In addition, the company also accounts for the item being hedged with the derivative at fair value. By adjusting the hedged item to fair value, with the gain or loss recorded in earnings, the accounting for the hedged item may deviate from GAAP in the absence of a hedge relationship. This special accounting is justified in order to report accurately the nature of the hedging relationship between the derivative hedging instruments and the hedged item. A company reports both in the balance sheet, reporting offsetting gains and losses in income in the same period.

12. Explain how to account for a cash flow hedge. Companies account for derivatives used in qualifying cash flow hedges at fair value on the balance sheet, but record gains or losses in equity as part of other comprehensive income. Companies accumulate these gains or losses, and reclassify them in income when the hedged transaction's cash flows affect earnings. Accounting is according to GAAP for the hedged item.

13. Identify special reporting issues related to derivative financial instruments that cause unique accounting problems. A company should separate a derivative that is embedded in a hybrid security from the host security, and account for it using the accounting for derivatives. This separation process is referred to as bifurcation. Special hedge accounting is allowed only for hedging relationships that meet certain criteria. The main criteria are: (1) There is formal documentation of the hedging relationship, the company's risk management objective, and the strategy for undertaking the hedge, and the company designates the derivative as either a cash flow or fair value hedge. (2) The company expects the hedging relationship to be highly effective in achieving offsetting changes in fair value or cash flows. (3) "Special" hedge accounting is necessary only when there is a mismatch of the accounting effects for the hedging instrument and the hedged item under GAAP.

14. Describe the disclosure requirements for traditional and derivative financial instruments. Companies must disclose the fair value and related carrying value of its financial instruments. These disclosures should distinguish between amounts that represent assets or liabilities. The disclosures should also distinguish between financial instruments held or issued for purposes other than trading. For derivative financial instruments, a company should disclose whether using the instruments for speculation or hedging. In disclosing fair values of financial instruments, a company should not combine, aggregate, or net the fair value of separate financial instruments, even if it considers those instruments to be related. A company should display as a separate classification of other comprehensive income the net gain or loss on derivative instruments designated in cash flow hedges. Companies are encouraged, but not required, to provide quantitative information about market risks of derivative financial instruments.

APPENDIX
17B Variable-Interest Entities

OBJECTIVE 15
Describe the accounting for variable-interest entities.

Recently the FASB issued an interpretation to address the concern that some companies were not reporting the risks and rewards of certain investments and other financial arrangements in their consolidated financial statements.[1] As one analyst noted, **Enron** showed the world the power of the idea that "if investors can't see it, they can't ask you about it—the 'it' being assets and liabilities."

---

[1] *Financial Accounting Standards Interpretation No. 46(R)*, "Consolidation of Variable Interest Entities (revised)—An Interpretation of *ARB No. 51*," (FASB, Norwalk, Conn.: December 2003.).

What exactly did Enron do? First, it created a number of entities whose purpose was to hide debt, avoid taxes, and enrich certain management personnel to the detriment of the company and its stockholders. In effect, these entities, called **special purpose entities (SPEs)**, appeared to be separate entities for which Enron had a limited economic interest. For many of these arrangements, Enron actually had a substantial economic interest; the risks and rewards of ownership were not shifted to the entities but remained with Enron. In short, Enron was obligated to repay investors in these SPEs when they were unsuccessful. Once Enron's problems were discovered, it soon became apparent that many other companies had similar problems.

WHAT ABOUT GAAP?

A reasonable question to ask with regard to SPEs is, "Why didn't GAAP prevent companies from hiding SPE debt and other risks, by forcing companies to include these obligations in their consolidated financial statements?" To understand why, we have to look at the basic rules of consolidation.

The GAAP rules indicate that consolidated financial statements are "usually necessary for a fair presentation when one of the companies in the group directly or indirectly has a controlling financial interest in other companies." They further note that "the usual condition for a controlling financial interest is ownership of a majority voting interest."[2] In other words, if a company, like **Intel**, owns more than 50 percent of the voting stock of another company, Intel consolidates that company. GAAP also indicates that controlling financial interest may be achieved through arrangements that do not involve voting interests. However, applying these guidelines in practice is difficult.

Whenever GAAP uses a clear line, like "greater than 50 percent," companies sometimes exploit the criterion. For example, some companies set up joint ventures in which each party owns exactly 50 percent. In that case, neither party consolidates. Or like **Coca-Cola** in the opening story, a company may own less than 50 percent of the voting stock, but maintain effective control through board of director relationships, supply relationships, or through some other type of financial arrangement.

So the FASB realized that changes had to be made to GAAP for consolidations, and it issued *SFAS Interpretation No. 46 (Revised)*, "Consolidation of Variable Interest Entities." This interpretation (*FIN No. 46R*) defines when a company should use factors other than voting interest to determine controlling financial interest. In this interpretation, the FASB created a new **risk-and-reward** model to be used in situations where voting interests were unclear. The risk-and-reward model answers the basic questions of who stands to gain or lose the most from ownership in an SPE when ownership is uncertain.

In other words, we now have two models for consolidation:

1 **Voting-interest model**—If a company owns more than 50 percent of another company, then consolidate in most cases.

2 **Risk-and-reward model**—If a company is involved substantially in the economics of another company, then consolidate.

Operationally, the voting-interest model is easy to apply: It sets a "bright line" ownership standard of more than 50 percent of the voting stock. However, if companies cannot determine control based on voting interest, they may use the risk-and-reward model.

CONSOLIDATION OF VARIABLE-INTEREST ENTITIES

To answer the question of who gains or loses when voting rights do not determine consolidation, the FASB developed the risk-and-reward model. In this model, the FASB introduced the notion of a variable-interest entity. A **variable-interest entity (VIE)** is an entity that has one of the following characteristics:

---

[2]"Consolidation of Certain Special Purpose Entities," Proposed Interpretation (Norwalk, Conn.: FASB, June 28, 2002).

1 **Insufficient equity investment at risk.** Stockholders are assumed to have sufficient capital investment to support the entity's operations. If thinly capitalized, the entity is considered a VIE and is subject to the risk-and-reward model.

2 **Stockholders lack decision-making rights.** In some cases, stockholders do not have the influence to control the company's destiny.

3 **Stockholders do not absorb the losses or receive the benefits of a normal stockholder.** In some entities, stockholders are shielded from losses related to their primary risks, or their returns are capped or must be shared with other parties.

Once the company determines that an entity is a variable-interest entity, it no longer can use the voting-interest model. The question that must then be asked is, "What party is exposed to the majority of the risks and rewards associated with the VIE?" This party is called the primary beneficiary and must consolidate the VIE. Illustration 17B-1 shows the decision model for the VIE consolidation model.

ILLUSTRATION 17B-1
VIE Consolidation Model

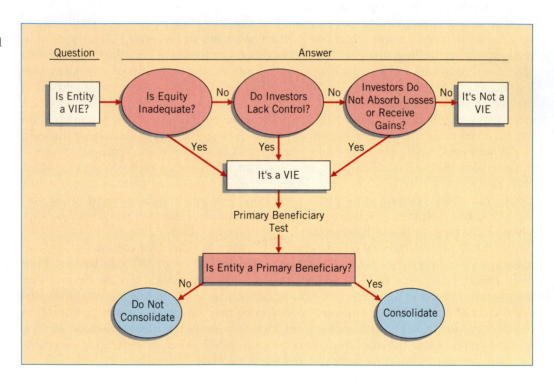

Some Examples

Let's look at a couple of examples to illustrate how this process works.

Example 1. Assume that **Citigroup** sells notes receivable to another entity called RAKO. RAKO's assets are financed in two ways: Lenders provide 90 percent, and investors provide the remaining 10 percent as an equity investment. If Citigroup does not guarantee the debt, Citigroup has low or nonexistent risk. Therefore, Citigroup would not consolidate the assets and liabilities of RAKO. On the other hand, if Citigroup guarantees RAKO's debt, then RAKO is a VIE, and Citigroup is the primary beneficiary. In that case, Citigroup must consolidate.

Example 2. **San Diego Gas and Electric (SDGE)** is required by law to buy power from small, local producers. In some cases, SDGE has contracts requiring it to purchase substantially all the power generated by these local companies over their lifetime. Because SDGE controls the outputs of the producers, they are VIEs. In this case, the risks and rewards related to ownership apply to SDGE. In other words, it is the primary beneficiary, and SDGE should include these producers in the consolidated financial statements.

Note that the primary beneficiary may have the risks and rewards of ownership through use of a variety of instruments and financial arrangements, such as equity investments, loans to the VIE, leases, derivatives, and guarantees. Potential VIEs include the following: corporations, partnerships, limited liability companies, and majority-owned subsidiaries.

What Is Happening in Practice?

For most companies, the reporting related to VIEs will not materially affect their financial statements. As shown in Illustration 17B-2, one study of 509 companies with total market values over $500 million found that just 17 percent of the companies reviewed have a material impact from *FIN No. 46R*.

Of the material VIEs disclosed in the study, the most common types (42 percent) were related to joint-venture equity investments, followed by off-balance-sheet lease arrangements (22 percent). In some cases, companies are restructuring transactions to avoid consolidation. For example, **Pep Boys**, **Choice Point, Inc.**, and **Anadarko** all appear to have restructured their lease transactions to avoid consolidation. On the other hand, companies like **eBay**, **Kimberly-Clark**, and **Williams-Sonoma Inc.** intend to or have consolidated their VIEs.

In summary, *FIN No. 46R* introduces a new model for determining if companies should include certain investments or other financial arrangements in consolidated financial statements. As a result, financial statements should be more complete in reporting the risks and rewards of these transactions.

ILLUSTRATION 17B-2
Impact of *FIN No. 46R*

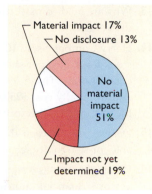

Source: Company Reports, *Glass, Lewis, & Co. Research Report* (November 6, 2003).

KEY TERMS

risk-and-reward model, *883*

special purpose entity (SPE), *883*

variable-interest entity (VIE), *883*

voting-interest model, *883*

SUMMARY OF LEARNING OBJECTIVE FOR APPENDIX 17B

15. **Describe the accounting for variable-interest entities.** Special variable-interest accounting is used in situations where control cannot be determined based on voting rights. A company is required to consolidate a variable-interest entity if it is the primary beneficiary of the variable-interest entity.

Note: All **asterisked** Questions, Exercises, and Problems relate to material contained in the appendixes to the chapter.

QUESTIONS

1. Distinguish between a debt security and an equity security.

2. What purpose does the variety in bond features (types and characteristics) serve?

3. What is the cost of a long-term investment in bonds?

4. Identify and explain the three types of classifications for investments in debt securities.

5. When should a debt security be classified as held-to-maturity?

6. Explain how trading securities are accounted for and reported.

7. At what amount should trading, available-for-sale, and held-to-maturity securities be reported on the balance sheet?

8. On July 1, 2007, Ingalls Company purchased $2,000,000 of Wilder Company's 8% bonds, due on July 1, 2014. The bonds, which pay interest semiannually on January 1 and July 1, were purchased for $1,750,000 to yield 10%. Determine the amount of interest revenue Ingalls should report on its income statement for year ended December 31, 2007.

9. If the bonds in question 8 are classified as available-for-sale and they have a fair value at December 31, 2007, of $1,802,000, prepare the journal entry (if any) at December 31, 2007, to record this transaction.

10. Indicate how unrealized holding gains and losses should be reported for investment securities classified as trading, available-for-sale, and held-to-maturity.

11. (a) Assuming no Securities Fair Value Adjustment (Available-for-Sale) account balance at the beginning of the year, prepare the adjusting entry at the end of the year if Laura Company's available-for-sale securities have a market value $70,000 below cost. (b) Assume the same information as part (a), except that Laura Company has a debit balance in its Securities Fair Value Adjustment (Available-for-Sale) account of $10,000 at the beginning of the year. Prepare the adjusting entry at year-end.

12. Identify and explain the different types of classifications for investment in equity securities.

13. Why are held-to-maturity investments applicable only to debt securities?

14. Harry Company sold 10,000 shares of Potter Co. common stock for $27.50 per share, incurring $1,770 in brokerage commissions. These securities were classified as trading and originally cost $250,000. Prepare the entry to record the sale of these securities.

15. Distinguish between the accounting treatment for available-for-sale equity securities and trading equity securities.

16. What constitutes "significant influence" when an investor's financial interest is below the 50% level?

17. Explain how the investment account is affected by investee activities under the equity method.

18. When the equity method is applied, what disclosures should be made in the investor's financial statements?

19. Hatch Co. uses the equity method to account for investments in common stock. What accounting should be made for dividends received in excess of Hatch's share of investee's earnings subsequent to the date of investment?

20. Elizabeth Corp. has an investment with a carrying value (equity method) on its books of $170,000 representing a 40% interest in Dole Company, which suffered a $620,000 loss this year. How should Elizabeth Corp. handle its proportionate share of Dole's loss?

21. Where on the asset side of the balance sheet are trading securities, available-for-sale securities, and held-to-maturity securities reported? Explain.

22. Explain why reclassification adjustments are necessary.

23. Briefly discuss how a transfer of securities from the available-for-sale category to the trading category affects stockholders' equity and income.

24. When is a debt security considered impaired? Explain how to account for the impairment of an available-for-sale debt security.

*25. What is meant by the term underlying as it relates to derivative financial instruments?

*26. What are the main distinctions between a traditional financial instrument and a derivative financial instrument?

*27. What is the purpose of a fair value hedge?

*28. In what situation will the unrealized holding gain or loss on an available-for-sale security be reported in income?

*29. Why might a company become involved in an interest rate swap contract to receive fixed interest payments and pay variable?

*30. What is the purpose of a cash flow hedge?

*31. Where are gains and losses related to cash flow hedges involving anticipated transactions reported?

*32. What are hybrid securities? Give an example of a hybrid security.

*33. Explain the difference between the voting-interest model and the risk-and-reward model used for consolidation.

*34. What is a variable interest entity?

BRIEF EXERCISES

(LO 2) **BE17-1** Moonwalker Company purchased, as a held-to-maturity investment, $50,000 of the 9%, 5-year bonds of Prime Time Corporation for $46,304, which provides an 11% return. Prepare Moonwalker's journal entries for (a) the purchase of the investment, and (b) the receipt of annual interest and discount amortization. Assume effective-interest amortization is used.

(LO 2) **BE17-2** Use the information from BE17-1, but assume the bonds are purchased as an available-for-sale security. Prepare Moonwalker's journal entries for (a) the purchase of the investment, (b) the receipt of annual interest and discount amortization, and (c) the year-end fair value adjustment. The bonds have a year-end fair value of $47,200.

(LO 2) **BE17-3** Mask Corporation purchased, as a held-to-maturity investment, $40,000 of the 8%, 5-year bonds of Phantasy Star, Inc. for $43,412, which provides a 6% return. The bonds pay interest semiannually. Prepare Mask's journal entries for (a) the purchase of the investment, and (b) the receipt of semiannual interest and premium amortization. Assume effective-interest amortization is used.

(LO 2) **BE17-4** Pete Sampras Corporation purchased trading investment bonds for $40,000 at par. At December 31, Sampras received annual interest of $2,000, and the fair value of the bonds was $38,400. Prepare Sampras' journal entries for (a) the purchase of the investment, (b) the interest received, and (c) the fair value adjustment.

$300 \times 3.25 = 975$

(LO 3) **BE17-5** Buttercup Corporation purchased 300 shares of Bubbles Inc. common stock as an available-for-sale investment for $9,900. During the year, Bubbles paid a cash dividend of $3.25 per share. At year-end, Bubbles stock was selling for $34.50 per share. Prepare Buttercup's journal entries to record (a) the purchase of the investment, (b) the dividends received, and (c) the fair value adjustment.

(LO 3) **BE17-6** Use the information from BE17-5 but assume the stock was purchased as a trading security. Prepare Buttercup's journal entries to record (a) the purchase of the investment, (b) the dividends received, and (c) the fair value adjustment.

(LO 4) **BE17-7** Penn Corporation purchased for $300,000 a 25% interest in Teller, Inc. This investment enables Penn to exert significant influence over Teller. During the year Teller earned net income of $180,000 and paid dividends of $60,000. Prepare Penn's journal entries related to this investment.

(LO 3) **BE17-8** Swartentruber Company has a stock portfolio valued at $4,000. Its cost was $3,500. If the Securities Fair Value Adjustment (Available-for-Sale) account has a debit balance of $200, prepare the journal entry at year-end.

(LO 5) **BE17-9** The following information relates to **Starbucks** for 2004: net income $391.775 million; unrealized holding loss of $4.925 million related to available-for-sale securities during the year; accumulated other comprehensive income of $14.248 million on January 1, 2004. Assuming no other changes in accumulated other comprehensive income, determine (a) other comprehensive income for 2004, (b) comprehensive income for 2004, and (c) accumulated other comprehensive income at December 31, 2004.

(LO 5) **BE17-10** Raveonette Co. has an available-for-sale investment in the bonds of No Doubt Corp. with a carrying (and fair) value of $75,000. Raveonette determined that due to poor economic prospects for No Doubt, the bonds have decreased in value to $60,000. It is determined that this loss in value is other-than-temporary. Prepare the journal entry, if any, to record the reduction in value.

EXERCISES

(LO 1, 3) **E17-1** **(Investment Classifications)** For the following investments identify whether they are:

1. Trading Securities
2. Available-for-Sale Securities
3. Held-to-Maturity Securities

Each case is independent of the other.

(a) A bond that will mature in 4 years was bought 1 month ago when the price dropped. As soon as the value increases, which is expected next month, it will be sold.
(b) 10% of the outstanding stock of Farm-Co was purchased. The company is planning on eventually getting a total of 30% of its outstanding stock.
(c) 10-year bonds were purchased this year. The bonds mature at the first of next year.
(d) Bonds that will mature in 5 years are purchased. The company would like to hold them until they mature, but money has been tight recently and they may need to be sold.
(e) Preferred stock was purchased for its constant dividend. The company is planning to hold the preferred stock for a long time.
(f) A bond that matures in 10 years was purchased. The company is investing money set aside for an expansion project planned 10 years from now.

(LO 2) **E17-2** **(Entries for Held-to-Maturity Securities)** On January 1, 2006, Dagwood Company purchased at par 12% bonds having a maturity value of $300,000. They are dated January 1, 2006, and mature January 1, 2011, with interest receivable December 31 of each year. The bonds are classified in the held-to-maturity category.

Instructions
(a) Prepare the journal entry at the date of the bond purchase.
(b) Prepare the journal entry to record the interest received for 2006.
(c) Prepare the journal entry to record the interest received for 2007.

(LO 2) **E17-3** **(Entries for Held-to-Maturity Securities)** On January 1, 2006, Hi and Lois Company purchased 12% bonds, having a maturity value of $300,000, for $322,744.44. The bonds provide the bondholders with a 10% yield. They are dated January 1, 2006, and mature January 1, 2011, with interest receivable December 31 of each year. Hi and Lois Company uses the effective-interest method to allocate unamortized discount or premium. The bonds are classified in the held-to-maturity category.

Instructions

(a) Prepare the journal entry at the date of the bond purchase.
(b) Prepare a bond amortization schedule.
(c) Prepare the journal entry to record the interest received and the amortization for 2006.
(d) Prepare the journal entry to record the interest received and the amortization for 2007.

(LO 2)   **E17-4   (Entries for Available-for-Sale Securities)**   Assume the same information as in E17-3 except that the securities are classified as available-for-sale. The fair value of the bonds at December 31 of each year-end is as follows.

2006	$320,500	2009	$310,000
2007	$309,000	2010	$300,000
2008	$308,000		

Instructions

(a) Prepare the journal entry at the date of the bond purchase.
(b) Prepare the journal entries to record the interest received and recognition of fair value for 2006.
(c) Prepare the journal entry to record the recognition of fair value for 2007.

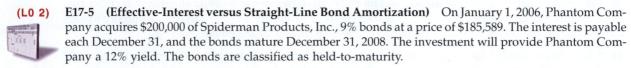

(LO 2)   **E17-5   (Effective-Interest versus Straight-Line Bond Amortization)**   On January 1, 2006, Phantom Company acquires $200,000 of Spiderman Products, Inc., 9% bonds at a price of $185,589. The interest is payable each December 31, and the bonds mature December 31, 2008. The investment will provide Phantom Company a 12% yield. The bonds are classified as held-to-maturity.

Instructions

(a) Prepare a 3-year schedule of interest revenue and bond discount amortization, applying the straight-line method.
(b) Prepare a 3-year schedule of interest revenue and bond discount amortization, applying the effective-interest method.
(c) Prepare the journal entry for the interest receipt of December 31, 2007, and the discount amortization under the straight-line method.
(d) Prepare the journal entry for the interest receipt of December 31, 2007, and the discount amortization under the effective-interest method.

(LO 3)   **E17-6   (Entries for Available-for-Sale and Trading Securities)**   The following information is available for Barkley Company at December 31, 2007, regarding its investments.

Securities	Cost	Fair Value
3,000 shares of Myers Corporation Common Stock	$40,000	$48,000
1,000 shares of Cole Incorporated Preferred Stock	25,000	22,000
	$65,000	$70,000

Instructions

(a) Prepare the adjusting entry (if any) for 2007, assuming the securities are classified as trading.
(b) Prepare the adjusting entry (if any) for 2007, assuming the securities are classified as available-for-sale.
(c) Discuss how the amounts reported in the financial statements are affected by the entries in (a) and (b).

(LO 3)   **E17-7   (Trading Securities Entries)**   On December 21, 2006, Bucky Katt Company provided you with the following information regarding its trading securities.

December 31, 2006			
Investments (Trading)	Cost	Fair Value	Unrealized Gain (Loss)
Clemson Corp. stock	$20,000	$19,000	$(1,000)
Colorado Co. stock	10,000	9,000	(1,000)
Buffaloes Co. stock	20,000	20,600	600
Total of portfolio	$50,000	$48,600	(1,400)
Previous securities fair value adjustment balance			–0–
Securities fair value adjustment—Cr.			$(1,400)

During 2007, Colorado Company stock was sold for $9,400. The fair value of the stock on December 31, 2007, was: Clemson Corp. stock—$19,100; Buffaloes Co. stock—$20,500.

Instructions

(a) Prepare the adjusting journal entry needed on December 31, 2006.

(b) Prepare the journal entry to record the sale of the Colorado Company stock during 2007.

(c) Prepare the adjusting journal entry needed on December 31, 2007.

(LO 3) **E17-8** **(Available-for-Sale Securities Entries and Reporting)** Satchel Corporation purchases equity securities costing $73,000 and classifies them as available-for-sale securities. At December 31, the fair value of the portfolio is $65,000.

Instructions

Prepare the adjusting entry to report the securities properly. Indicate the statement presentation of the accounts in your entry.

(LO 3) **E17-9** **(Available-for-Sale Securities Entries and Financial Statement Presentation)** At December 31, 2006, the available-for-sale equity portfolio for Steffi Graf, Inc. is as follows.

Security	Cost	Fair Value	Unrealized Gain (Loss)
A	$17,500	$15,000	($2,500)
B	12,500	14,000	1,500
C	23,000	25,500	2,500
Total	$53,000	$54,500	1,500
Previous securities fair value adjustment balance—Dr.			400
Securities fair value adjustment—Dr.			$1,100

On January 20, 2007, Steffi Graf, Inc. sold security A for $15,100. The sale proceeds are net of brokerage fees.

Instructions

(a) Prepare the adjusting entry at December 31, 2006, to report the portfolio at fair value.

(b) Show the balance sheet presentation of the investment related accounts at December 31, 2006. (Ignore notes presentation.)

(c) Prepare the journal entry for the 2007 sale of security A.

(LO 5) **E17-10** **(Comprehensive Income Disclosure)** Assume the same information as E17-9 and that Steffi Graf Inc. reports net income in 2006 of $120,000 and in 2007 of $140,000. Total holding gains (including any realized holding gain or loss) arising during 2007 total $40,000.

Instructions

(a) Prepare a statement of comprehensive income for 2006 starting with net income.

(b) Prepare a statement of comprehensive income for 2007 starting with net income.

(LO 3) **E17-11** **(Equity Securities Entries)** Arantxa Corporation made the following cash purchases of securities during 2007, which is the first year in which Arantxa invested in securities.

1. On January 15, purchased 10,000 shares of Sanchez Company's common stock at $33.50 per share plus commission $1,980.

2. On April 1, purchased 5,000 shares of Vicario Co.'s common stock at $52.00 per share plus commission $3,370.

3. On September 10, purchased 7,000 shares of WTA Co.'s preferred stock at $26.50 per share plus commission $4,910.

On May 20, 2007, Arantxa sold 4,000 shares of Sanchez Company's common stock at a market price of $35 per share less brokerage commissions, taxes, and fees of $3,850. The year-end fair values per share were: Sanchez $30, Vicario $55, and WTA $28. In addition, the chief accountant of Arantxa told you that Arantxa Corporation plans to hold these securities for the long term but may sell them in order to earn profits from appreciation in prices.

Instructions

(a) Prepare the journal entries to record the above three security purchases.

(b) Prepare the journal entry for the security sale on May 20.

(c) Compute the unrealized gains or losses and prepare the adjusting entries for Arantxa on December 31, 2007.

(LO 3, 4) **E17-12** **(Journal Entries for Fair Value and Equity Methods)** Presented on page 890 are two independent situations.

Situation 1
Conchita Cosmetics acquired 10% of the 200,000 shares of common stock of Martinez Fashion at a total cost of $13 per share on March 18, 2007. On June 30, Martinez declared and paid a $75,000 cash dividend. On December 31, Martinez reported net income of $122,000 for the year. At December 31, the market price of Martinez Fashion was $15 per share. The securities are classified as available-for-sale.

Situation 2
Monica, Inc. obtained significant influence over Seles Corporation by buying 30% of Seles's 30,000 outstanding shares of common stock at a total cost of $9 per share on January 1, 2007. On June 15, Seles declared and paid a cash dividend of $36,000. On December 31, Seles reported a net income of $85,000 for the year.

Instructions
Prepare all necessary journal entries in 2007 for both situations.

(LO 4) **E17-13** **(Equity Method)** Parent Co. invested $1,000,000 in Sub Co. for 25% of its outstanding stock. Sub Co. pays out 40% of net income in dividends each year.

Instructions
Use the information in the following T-account for the investment in Sub to answer the following questions.

Investment in Sub Co.

1,000,000	
110,000	
	44,000

(a) How much was Parent Co.'s share of Sub Co.'s net income for the year?
(b) How much was Parent Co.'s share of Sub Co.'s dividends for the year?
(c) What was Sub Co.'s total net income for the year?
(d) What was Sub Co.'s total dividends for the year?

(LO 3) **E17-14** **(Equity Investment—Trading)** Oregon Co. had purchased 200 shares of Washington Co. for $40 each this year and classified the investment as a trading security. Oregon Co. sold 100 shares of the stock for $45 each. At year end the price per share of the Washington Co. stock had dropped to $35.

Instructions
Prepare the journal entries for these transactions and any year-end adjustments.

(LO 3) **E17-15** **(Equity Investments—Trading)** Kenseth Company has the following securities in its trading portfolio of securities on December 31, 2006.

Investments (Trading)	Cost	Fair Value
1,500 shares of Gordon, Inc., Common	$ 73,500	$ 69,000
5,000 shares of Wallace Corp., Common	180,000	175,000
400 shares of Martin, Inc., Preferred	60,000	61,600
	$313,500	$305,600

All of the securities were purchased in 2006.
In 2007, Kenseth completed the following securities transactions.

March 1 Sold the 1,500 shares of Gordon, Inc., Common, @ $45 less fees of $1,200.
April 1 Bought 700 shares of Earnhart Corp., Common, @ $75 plus fees of $1,300.

Kenseth Company's portfolio of trading securities appeared as follows on December 31, 2007.

Investments (Trading)	Cost	Fair Value
5,000 shares of Wallace Corp., Common	$180,000	$175,000
700 shares of Earnhart Corp., Common	53,800	50,400
400 shares of Martin, Inc., Preferred	60,000	58,000
	$293,800	$283,400

Instructions
Prepare the general journal entries for Kenseth Company for:

(a) The 2006 adjusting entry.
(b) The sale of the Gordon stock.
(c) The purchase of the Earnhart stock.
(d) The 2007 adjusting entry for the trading portfolio.

(LO 3, 4) **E17-16** **(Fair Value and Equity Method Compared)** Jaycie Phelps Inc. acquired 20% of the outstanding common stock of Theresa Kulikowski Inc. on December 31, 2006. The purchase price was $1,200,000 for 50,000 shares. Kulikowski Inc. declared and paid an $0.85 per share cash dividend on June 30 and on December 31, 2007. Kulikowski reported net income of $730,000 for 2007. The fair value of Kulikowski's stock was $27 per share at December 31, 2007.

Instructions
(a) Prepare the journal entries for Jaycie Phelps Inc. for 2006 and 2007, assuming that Phelps cannot exercise significant influence over Kulikowski. The securities should be classified as available-for-sale.
(b) Prepare the journal entries for Jaycie Phelps Inc. for 2006 and 2007, assuming that Phelps can exercise significant influence over Kulikowski.
(c) At what amount is the investment in securities reported on the balance sheet under each of these methods at December 31, 2007? What is the total net income reported in 2007 under each of these methods?

(LO 4) **E17-17** **(Equity Method)** On January 1, 2007, Pennington Corporation purchased 30% of the common shares of Edwards Company for $180,000. During the year, Edwards earned net income of $80,000 and paid dividends of $20,000.

Instructions
Prepare the entries for Pennington to record the purchase and any additional entries related to this investment in Edwards Company in 2007.

(LO 6) **E17-18** **(Impairment of Debt Securities)** Hagar Corporation has municipal bonds classified as available-for-sale at December 31, 2006. These bonds have a par value of $800,000, an amortized cost of $800,000, and a fair value of $720,000. The unrealized loss of $80,000 previously recognized as other comprehensive income and as a separate component of stockholders' equity is now determined to be other than temporary. That is, the company believes that impairment accounting is now appropriate for these bonds.

Instructions
(a) Prepare the journal entry to recognize the impairment.
(b) What is the new cost basis of the municipal bonds? Given that the maturity value of the bonds is $800,000, should Hagar Corporation amortize the difference between the carrying amount and the maturity value over the life of the bonds?
(c) At December 31, 2007, the fair value of the municipal bonds is $760,000. Prepare the entry (if any) to record this information.

(LO 10) *E17-19** **(Call Option)** On January 2, 2007, Jones Company purchases a call option for $300 on Merchant common stock. The call option gives Jones the option to buy 1,000 shares of Merchant at a strike price of $50 per share. The market price of a Merchant share is $50 on January 2, 2007 (the intrinsic value is therefore $0). On March 31, 2007, the market price for Merchant stock is $53 per share, and the time value of the option is $200.

Instructions
(a) Prepare the journal entry to record the purchase of the call option on January 2, 2007.
(b) Prepare the journal entry(ies) to recognize the change in the fair value of the call option as of March 31, 2007.
(c) What was the effect on net income of entering into the derivative transaction for the period January 2 to March 31, 2007?

(LO 10) *E17-20** **(Call Option)** On August 15, 2006, Outkast Co. invested idle cash by purchasing a call option on Counting Crows Inc. common shares for $360. The notional value of the call option is 400 shares, and the option price is $40. The option expires on January 31, 2007. The following data are available with respect to the call option.

Date	Market Price of Counting Crows Shares	Time Value of Call Option
September 30, 2006	$48 per share	$180
December 31, 2006	$46 per share	65
January 15, 2007	$47 per share	30

Instructions
Prepare the journal entries for Outkast for the following dates.
(a) Investment in call option on Counting Crows shares on August 15, 2006.
(b) September 30, 2006—Outkast prepares financial statements.
(c) December 31, 2006—Outkast prepares financial statements.
(d) January 15, 2007—Outkast settles the call option on the Counting Crows shares.

(LO 10) *E17-21** **(Put and Call Options)** On February 15, 2007, Derek Co. invested idle cash by purchasing a put option on Lee Corp. common shares for $160. The notional value of the put option is 300 shares, and the option price is $50. The option expires on July 31, 2007. The following data are available with respect to the put option.

Date	Market Price of Lee Shares	Time Value of Put Option
March 31, 2007	$40 per share	$70
June 30, 2007	$42 per share	30
July 15, 2007	$39 per share	20

Instructions
Prepare the journal entries for Derek Co. for the following dates.
   (a) February 15, 2007—Investment in put option on Lee shares.
   (b) March 31, 2007—Derek prepares financial statements.
   (c) June 30, 2007—Derek prepares financial statements.
   (d) July 6, 2007—Derek settles the put option on the Lee shares.
   (e) Repeat the requirements for (a) through (d), assuming that instead of purchasing a put option, Derek purchased a call option.

(LO 11) *E17-22** **(Cash Flow Hedge)** Hart Golf Co. uses titanium in the production of its specialty drivers. Hart anticipates that it will need to purchase 200 ounces of titanium in November 2007, for clubs that will be shipped in the spring and summer of 2008. However, if the price of titanium increases, this will increase the cost to produce the clubs, which will result in lower profit margins.

To hedge the risk of increased titanium prices, on May 1, 2007, Hart enters into a titanium futures contract and designates this futures contract as a cash flow hedge of the anticipated titanium purchase. The notional amount of the contract is 200 ounces, and the terms of the contract give Hart the option to purchase titanium at a price of $500 per ounce. The price will be good until the contract expires on November 30, 2007.

Assume the following data with respect to the price of the call options and the titanium inventory purchase.

Date	Spot Price for November Delivery
May 1, 2007	$500 per ounce
June 30, 2007	520 per ounce
September 30, 2007	525 per ounce

Instructions
Present the journal entries for the following dates/transactions.
   (a) May 1, 2007—Inception of futures contract, no premium paid.
   (b) June 30, 2007—Hart prepares financial statements.
   (c) September 30, 2007—Hart prepares financial statements.
   (d) October 5, 2007—Hart purchases 200 ounces of titanium at $525 per ounce and settles the futures contract.
   (e) December 15, 2007—Hart sells clubs containing titanium purchased in October 2006 for $250,000. The cost of the finished goods inventory is $140,000.
   (f) Indicate the amount(s) reported in the income statement related to the futures contract and the inventory transactions on December 31, 2007.

(LO 11) *E17-23** **(Fair Value Hedge)** On January 2, 2007, MacCloud Co. issued a 4-year, $100,000 note at 6% fixed interest, interest payable semiannually. MacCloud now wants to change the note to a variable-rate note.

As a result, on January 2, 2007, MacCloud Co. enters into an interest rate swap where it agrees to receive 6% fixed and pay LIBOR of 5.7% for the first 6 months on $100,000. At each 6-month period, the variable rate will be reset. The variable rate is reset to 6.7% on June 30, 2007.

Instructions
   (a) Compute the net interest expense to be reported for this note and related swap transaction as of June 30, 2007.
   (b) Compute the net interest expense to be reported for this note and related swap transaction as of December 31, 2007.

(LO 11) *E17-24** **(Fair Value Hedge)** Sarazan Company issues a 4-year, 7.5% fixed-rate interest only, nonprepayable $1,000,000 note payable on December 31, 2006. It decides to change the interest rate from a fixed rate to variable rate and enters into a swap agreement with M&S Corp. The swap agreement specifies that Sarazan will receive a fixed rate at 7.5% and pay variable with settlement dates that match the interest payments on the debt. Assume that interest rates have declined during 2007 and that Sarazan received

$13,000 as an adjustment to interest expense for the settlement at December 31, 2007. The loss related to the debt (due to interest rate changes) was $48,000. The value of the swap contract increased $48,000.

Instructions
(a) Prepare the journal entry to record the payment of interest expense on December 31, 2007.
(b) Prepare the journal entry to record the receipt of the swap settlement on December 31, 2007.
(c) Prepare the journal entry to record the change in the fair value of the swap contract on December 31, 2007.
(d) Prepare the journal entry to record the change in the fair value of the debt on December 31, 2007.

See the book's website, www.wiley.com/college/kieso, for Additional Exercises.

PROBLEMS

(LO 2) **P17-1** **(Debt Securities)** Presented below is an amortization schedule related to Kathy Baker Company's 5-year, $100,000 bond with a 7% interest rate and a 5% yield, purchased on December 31, 2004, for $108,660.

Date	Cash Received	Interest Revenue	Bond Premium Amortization	Carrying Amount of Bonds
12/31/04				$108,660
12/31/05	$7,000	$5,433	$1,567	107,093
12/31/06	7,000	5,354	1,646	105,447
12/31/07	7,000	5,272	1,728	103,719
12/31/08	7,000	5,186	1,814	101,905
12/31/09	7,000	5,095	1,905	100,000

The following schedule presents a comparison of the amortized cost and fair value of the bonds at year-end.

	12/31/05	12/31/06	12/31/07	12/31/08	12/31/09
Amortized cost	$107,093	$105,447	$103,719	$101,905	$100,000
Fair value	$106,500	$107,500	$105,650	$103,000	$100,000

Instructions
(a) Prepare the journal entry to record the purchase of these bonds on December 31, 2004, assuming the bonds are classified as held-to-maturity securities.
(b) Prepare the journal entry(ies) related to the held-to-maturity bonds for 2005.
(c) Prepare the journal entry(ies) related to the held-to-maturity bonds for 2007.
(d) Prepare the journal entry(ies) to record the purchase of these bonds, assuming they are classified as available-for-sale.
(e) Prepare the journal entry(ies) related to the available-for-sale bonds for 2005.
(f) Prepare the journal entry(ies) related to the available-for-sale bonds for 2007.

(LO 2) **P17-2** **(Available-for-Sale Debt Securities)** On January 1, 2007, Rob Wilco Company purchased $200,000, 8% bonds of Mercury Co. for $184,557. The bonds were purchased to yield 10% interest. Interest is payable semiannually on July 1 and January 1. The bonds mature on January 1, 2012. Rob Wilco Company uses the effective-interest method to amortize discount or premium. On January 1, 2009, Rob Wilco Company sold the bonds for $185,363 after receiving interest to meet its liquidity needs.

Instructions
(a) Prepare the journal entry to record the purchase of bonds on January 1. Assume that the bonds are classified as available-for-sale.
(b) Prepare the amortization schedule for the bonds.
(c) Prepare the journal entries to record the semiannual interest on July 1, 2007, and December 31, 2007.
(d) If the fair value of Mercury bonds is $186,363 on December 31, 2008, prepare the necessary adjusting entry. (Assume the securities fair value adjustment balance on January 1, 2008, is a debit of $3,375.)
(e) Prepare the journal entry to record the sale of the bonds on January 1, 2009.

(LO 2, 3) **P17-3** **(Available-for-Sale Investments)** Octavio Paz Corp. carries an account in its general ledger called Investments, which contained debits for investment purchases, and no credits (see page 894).

Feb. 1, 2006	Chiang Kai-Shek Company common stock, $100 par, 200 shares	$ 37,400
April 1	U.S. government bonds, 11%, due April 1, 2016, interest payable April 1 and October 1, 100 bonds of $1,000 par each	100,000
July 1	Claude Monet Company 12% bonds, par $50,000, dated March 1, 2006 purchased at 104 plus accrued interest, interest payable annually on March 1, due March 1, 2026	54,000

Instructions

(Round all computations to the nearest dollar.)

(a) Prepare entries necessary to classify the amounts into proper accounts, assuming that all the securities are classified as available-for-sale.

(b) Prepare the entry to record the accrued interest and the amortization of premium on December 31, 2006, using the straight-line method.

(c) The fair values of the securities on December 31, 2006, were:

Chiang Kai-shek Company common stock	$ 33,800
U.S. government bonds	124,700
Claude Monet Company bonds	58,600

What entry or entries, if any, would you recommend be made?

(d) The U.S. government bonds were sold on July 1, 2007, for $119,200 plus accrued interest. Give the proper entry.

(LO 2) **P17-4 (Available-for-Sale Debt Securities)** Presented below is information taken from a bond investment amortization schedule with related fair values provided. These bonds are classified as available-for-sale.

	12/31/06	12/31/07	12/31/08
Amortized cost	$491,150	$519,442	$550,000
Fair value	$499,000	$506,000	$550,000

Instructions

(a) Indicate whether the bonds were purchased at a discount or at a premium.

(b) Prepare the adjusting entry to record the bonds at fair value at December 31, 2006. The Securities Fair Value Adjustment account has a debit balance of $1,000 prior to adjustment.

(c) Prepare the adjusting entry to record the bonds at fair value at December 31, 2007.

(LO 3) **P17-5 (Equity Securities Entries and Disclosures)** Incognito Company has the following securities in its investment portfolio on December 31, 2006 (all securities were purchased in 2006): (1) 3,000 shares of Green Day Co. common stock which cost $58,500, (2) 10,000 shares of David Sanborn Ltd. common stock which cost $580,000, and (3) 6,000 shares of Abba Company preferred stock which cost $255,000. The Securities Fair Value Adjustment account shows a credit of $10,100 at the end of 2006.

In 2007, Incognito completed the following securities transactions.

1. On January 15, sold 3,000 shares of Green Day's common stock at $23 per share less fees of $2,150.

2. On April 17, purchased 1,000 shares of Tractors' common stock at $31.50 per share plus fees of $1,980.

On December 31, 2007, the market values per share of these securities were: Green Day $20, Sanborn $62, Abba $40, and Tractors $29. In addition, the accounting supervisor of Incognito told you that, even though all these securities have readily determinable fair values, Incognito will not actively trade these securities because the top management intends to hold them for more than one year.

Instructions

(a) Prepare the entry for the security sale on January 15, 2007.

(b) Prepare the journal entry to record the security purchase on April 17, 2007.

(c) Compute the unrealized gains or losses and prepare the adjusting entry for Incognito on December 31, 2007.

(d) How should the unrealized gains or losses be reported on Incognito's balance sheet?

(LO 3) **P17-6 (Trading and Available-for-Sale Securities Entries)** Loxley Company has the following portfolio of investment securities at September 30, 2007, its last reporting date.

Trading Securities	Cost	Fair Value
Dan Fogelberg, Inc. common (5,000 shares)	$225,000	$200,000
Petra, Inc. preferred (3,500 shares)	133,000	140,000
Tim Weisberg Corp. common (1,000 shares)	180,000	179,000

On October 10, 2007, the Fogelberg shares were sold at a price of $54 per share. In addition, 3,000 shares of Los Tigres common stock were acquired at $59.50 per share on November 2, 2007. The December 31,

2007, fair values were: Petra $96,000, Los Tigres $132,000, and the Weisberg common $193,000. All the securities are classified as trading.

Instructions

(a) Prepare the journal entries to record the sale, purchase, and adjusting entries related to the trading securities in the last quarter of 2007.

(b) How would the entries in part (a) change if the securities were classified as available-for-sale?

(LO 2) **P17-7** **(Available-for-Sale and Held-to-Maturity Debt Securities Entries)** The following information relates to the debt securities investments of Yellowjackets Company.

1. On February 1, the company purchased 12% bonds of Hilton Paris Co. having a par value of $500,000 at 100 plus accrued interest. Interest is payable April 1 and October 1.
2. On April 1, semiannual interest is received.
3. On July 1, 9% bonds of Chieftains, Inc. were purchased. These bonds with a par value of $200,000 were purchased at 100 plus accrued interest. Interest dates are June 1 and December 1.
4. On September 1, bonds with a par value of $100,000, purchased on February 1, are sold at 99 plus accrued interest.
5. On October 1, semiannual interest is received.
6. On December 1, semiannual interest is received.
7. On December 31, the fair value of the bonds purchased February 1 and July 1 are 95 and 93, respectively.

Instructions

(a) Prepare any journal entries you consider necessary, including year-end entries (December 31), assuming these are available-for-sale securities.

(b) If Yellowjackets classified these as held-to-maturity securities, explain how the journal entries would differ from those in part (a).

(LO 3, 4, 5) **P17-8** **(Fair Value and Equity Methods)** Pacers Corp. is a medium-sized corporation specializing in quarrying stone for building construction. The company has long dominated the market, at one time achieving a 70% market penetration. During prosperous years, the company's profits, coupled with a conservative dividend policy, resulted in funds available for outside investment. Over the years, Pacers has had a policy of investing idle cash in equity securities. In particular, Pacers has made periodic investments in the company's principal supplier, Pierce Industries. Although the firm currently owns 12% of the outstanding common stock of Pierce Industries, Pacers does not have significant influence over the operations of Pierce Industries.

Cheryl Miller has recently joined Pacers as assistant controller, and her first assignment is to prepare the 2007 year-end adjusting entries for the accounts that are valued by the "fair value" rule for financial reporting purposes. Miller has gathered the following information about Pacers' pertinent accounts.

1. Pacers has trading securities related to Dale Davis Motors and Rik Smits Electric. During this fiscal year, Pacers purchased 100,000 shares of Davis Motors for $1,400,000; these shares currently have a market value of $1,600,000. Pacers' investment in Smits Electric has not been profitable; the company acquired 50,000 shares of Smits in April 2007 at $20 per share, a purchase that currently has a value of $620,000.
2. Prior to 2007, Pacers invested $22,500,000 in Pierce Industries and has not changed its holdings this year. This investment in Pierce Industries was valued at $21,500,000 on December 31, 2006. Pacers' 12% ownership of Pierce Industries has a current market value of $22,275,000.

Instructions

(a) Prepare the appropriate adjusting entries for Pacers as of December 31, 2007, to reflect the application of the "fair value" rule for both classes of securities described above.

(b) For both classes of securities presented above, describe how the results of the valuation adjustments made in (a) would be reflected in the body of and notes to Pacers' 2007 financial statements.

(c) Prepare the entries for the Pierce investment, assuming that Pacers owns 30% of Pierce's shares. Pierce reported income of $500,000 in 2007 and paid cash dividends of $100,000.

(LO 3, 5) **P17-9** **(Financial Statement Presentation of Available-for-Sale Investments)** Woolford Company has the following portfolio of available-for-sale securities at December 31, 2006.

Security	Quantity	Percent Interest	Per Share Cost	Per Share Market
Favre, Inc.	2,000 shares	8%	$11	$16
Brady Corp.	5,000 shares	14%	23	17
McNabb Company	4,000 shares	2%	31	24

Instructions

(a) What should be reported on Woolford's December 31, 2006, balance sheet relative to these long-term available-for-sale securities?

On December 31, 2007, Woolford's portfolio of available-for-sale securities consisted of the following common stocks.

Security	Quantity	Percent Interest	Per Share Cost	Per Share Market
Brady Corp.	5,000 shares	14%	$23	$30
McNabb Company	4,000 shares	2%	31	23
McNabb Company	2,000 shares	1%	25	23

At the end of year 2007, Woolford Company changed its intent relative to its investment in Favre, Inc. and reclassified the shares to trading securities status when the shares were selling for $9 per share.

(b) What should be reported on the face of Woolford's December 31, 2007, balance sheet relative to available-for-sale securities investments? What should be reported to reflect the transactions above in Woolford's 2007 income statement?

(c) Assuming that comparative financial statements for 2006 and 2007 are presented, draft the footnote necessary for full disclosure of Woolford's transactions and position in equity securities.

(LO 3, 5) P17-10 (Gain on Sale of Securities and Comprehensive Income) On January 1, 2006, Enid Inc. had the following balance sheet.

ENID INC.
BALANCE SHEET
AS OF JANUARY 1, 2006

Assets		Equity	
Cash	$ 50,000	Common stock	$250,000
Available-for-sale securities	240,000	Accumulated other comprehensive income	40,000
Total	$290,000	Total	$290,000

The accumulated other comprehensive income related to unrealized holding gains on available-for-sale securities. The fair value of Enid Inc.'s available-for-sale securities at December 31, 2006, was $190,000; its cost was $120,000. No securities were purchased during the year. Enid Inc.'s income statement for 2006 was as follows. (Ignore income taxes.)

ENID INC.
INCOME STATEMENT
FOR THE YEAR ENDED DECEMBER 31, 2006

Dividend revenue	$15,000
Gain on sale of available-for-sale securities	20,000
Net income	$35,000

Instructions

(Assume all transactions during the year were for cash.)

(a) Prepare the journal entry to record the sale of the available-for-sale securities in 2006.

(b) Prepare a statement of comprehensive income for 2006.

(c) Prepare a balance sheet as of December 31, 2006.

(LO 3) P17-11 (Equity Investments—Available for Sale) Big Brother Holdings, Inc. had the following available-for-sale investment portfolio at January 1, 2006.

Earl Company	1,000 shares @ $15 each	$15,000
Josie Company	900 shares @ $20 each	18,000
David Company	500 shares @ $9 each	4,500
Available-for sale securities @ cost		37,500
Securities fair value adjustment—Available-for-sale		(7,500)
Available-for-sale securities @ fair value		$30,000

During 2006, the following transactions took place.

1. On March 1, Josie Company paid a $2 per share dividend.
2. On April 30, Big Brother Holdings, Inc. sold 300 shares of David Company for $10 per share.
3. On May 15, Big Brother Holdings, Inc. purchased 50 more shares of Earl Co. stock at $16 per share.
4. At December 31, 2006, the stocks had the following price per share values: Earl $17, Josie $19, and David $8.

During 2007, the following transactions took place.

5. On February 1, Big Brother Holdings, Inc. sold the remaining David shares for $7 per share.
6. On March 1, Josie Company paid a $2 per share dividend.
7. On December 21, Earl Company declared a cash dividend of $3 per share to be paid in the next month.
8. At December 31, 2007, the stocks had the following price per shares values: Earl $19 and Josie $21.

Instructions

(a) Prepare journal entries for each of the above transactions.

(b) Prepare a partial balance sheet showing the Investments account at December 31, 2006 and 2007.

(LO 3, 5) **P17-12** **(Available-for-Sale Securities—Statement Presentation)** Alvarez Corp. invested its excess cash in available-for-sale securities during 2006. As of December 31, 2006, the portfolio of available-for-sale securities consisted of the following common stocks.

Security	Quantity	Cost	Fair Value
Keesha Jones, Inc.	1,000 shares	$ 15,000	$ 21,000
Eola Corp.	2,000 shares	50,000	42,000
Yevette Aircraft	2,000 shares	72,000	60,000
	Totals	$137,000	$123,000

Instructions

(a) What should be reported on Alvarez's December 31, 2006, balance sheet relative to these securities? What should be reported on Alvarez's 2006 income statement?

On December 31, 2007, Alvarez's portfolio of available-for-sale securities consisted of the following common stocks.

Security	Quantity	Cost	Fair Value
Keesha Jones, Inc.	1,000 shares	$ 15,000	$20,000
Keesha Jones, Inc.	2,000 shares	38,000	40,000
King Company	1,000 shares	16,000	12,000
Yevette Aircraft	2,000 shares	72,000	22,000
	Totals	$141,000	$94,000

During the year 2007, Alvarez Corp. sold 2,000 shares of Eola Corp. for $38,200 and purchased 2,000 more shares of Keesha Jones, Inc. and 1,000 shares of King Company.

(b) What should be reported on Alvarez's December 31, 2007, balance sheet? What should be reported on Alvarez's 2007 income statement?

On December 31, 2008, Alvarez's portfolio of available-for-sale securities consisted of the following common stocks.

Security	Quantity	Cost	Fair Value
Yevette Aircraft	2,000 shares	$72,000	$82,000
King Company	500 shares	8,000	6,000
	Totals	$80,000	$88,000

During the year 2008, Alvarez Corp. sold 3,000 shares of Keesha Jones, Inc. for $39,900 and 500 shares of King Company at a loss of $2,700.

(c) What should be reported on the face of Alvarez's December 31, 2008, balance sheet? What should be reported on Alvarez's 2008 income statement?

(d) What would be reported in a statement of comprehensive income at (1) December 31, 2006, and (2) December 31, 2007?

(LO 10) *****P17-13** **(Call Option)** The treasurer of Miller Co. has read on the Internet that the stock price of Ewing Inc. is about to take off. In order to profit from this potential development, Miller Co. purchased a call option on Ewing common shares on July 7, 2006, for $240. The call option is for 200 shares (notional value), and the strike price is $70. The option expires on January 31, 2007. The data shown on page 898 are available with respect to the call option.

Date	Market Price of Ewing Shares	Time Value of Call Option
September 30, 2006	$77 per share	$180
December 31, 2006	75 per share	65
January 4, 2007	76 per share	30

Instructions

Prepare the journal entries for Miller Co. for the following dates.

(a) July 7, 2006—Investment in call option on Ewing shares.
(b) September 30, 2006—Miller prepares financial statements.
(c) December 31, 2006—Miller prepares financial statements.
(d) January 4, 2007—Miller settles the call option on the Ewing shares.

(LO 10) *P17-14 **(Put Option)** Johnstone Co. purchased a put option on Ewing common shares on July 7, 2006, for $240. The put option is for 200 shares, and the strike price is $70. The option expires on January 31, 2007. The following data are available with respect to the put option.

Date	Market Price of Ewing Shares	Time Value of Put Option
September 30, 2006	$77 per share	$125
December 31, 2006	75 per share	50
January 31, 2007	78 per share	0

Instructions

Prepare the journal entries for Johnstone Co. for the following dates.

(a) January 7, 2006—Investment in put option on Ewing shares.
(b) September 30, 2006—Johnstone prepares financial statements.
(c) December 31, 2006—Johnstone prepares financial statements.
(d) January 31, 2007—Put option expires.

(LO 10) *P17-15 **(Put Option)** Warren Co. purchased a put option on Echo common shares on January 7, 2007, for $360. The put option is for 400 shares, and the strike price is $85. The option expires on July 31, 2007. The following data are available with respect to the put option.

Date	Market Price of Echo Shares	Time Value of Put Option
March 31, 2007	$80 per share	$200
June 30, 2007	82 per share	90
July 6, 2007	77 per share	25

Instructions

Prepare the journal entries for Warren Co. for the following dates.

(a) January 7, 2007—Investment in put option on Echo shares.
(b) March 31, 2007—Warren prepares financial statements.
(c) June 30, 2007—Warren prepares financial statements.
(d) July 6, 2007—Warren settles the put option on the Echo shares.

(LO 11) *P17-16 **(Fair Value Hedge Interest Rate Swap)** On December 31, 2006, Mercantile Corp. had a $10,000,000, 8% fixed-rate note outstanding, payable in 2 years. It decides to enter into a 2-year swap with Chicago First Bank to convert the fixed-rate debt to variable-rate debt. The terms of the swap indicate that Mercantile will receive interest at a fixed rate of 8.0% and will pay a variable rate equal to the 6-month LIBOR rate, based on the $10,000,000 amount. The LIBOR rate on December 31, 2006, is 7%. The LIBOR rate will be reset every 6 months and will be used to determine the variable rate to be paid for the following 6-month period.

Mercantile Corp. designates the swap as a fair value hedge. Assume that the hedging relationship meets all the conditions necessary for hedge accounting. The 6-month LIBOR rate and the swap and debt fair values are as follows.

Date	6-Month LIBOR Rate	Swap Fair Value	Debt Fair Value
December 31, 2006	7.0%	—	$10,000,000
June 30, 2007	7.5%	(200,000)	9,800,000
December 31, 2007	6.0%	60,000	10,060,000

Instructions

(a) Present the journal entries to record the following transactions.
   (1) The entry, if any, to record the swap on December 31, 2006.
   (2) The entry to record the semiannual debt interest payment on June 30, 2007.

    (3) The entry to record the settlement of the semiannual swap receivable at 8%, less amount payable at LIBOR, 7%.

    (4) The entry to record the change in the fair value of the debt on June 30, 2007.

    (5) The entry to record the change in the fair value of the swap at June 30, 2007.

(b) Indicate the amount(s) reported on the balance sheet and income statement related to the debt and swap on December 31, 2006.

(c) Indicate the amount(s) reported on the balance sheet and income statement related to the debt and swap on June 30, 2007.

(d) Indicate the amount(s) reported on the balance sheet and income statement related to the debt and swap on December 31, 2007.

(LO 12) ***P17-17** **(Cash Flow Hedge)** LEW Jewelry Co. uses gold in the manufacture of its products. LEW anticipates that it will need to purchase 500 ounces of gold in October 2006, for jewelry that will be shipped for the holiday shopping season. However, if the price of gold increases, LEW's cost to produce its jewelry will increase, which would reduce its profit margins.

    To hedge the risk of increased gold prices, on April 1, 2006, LEW enters into a gold futures contract and designates this futures contract as a cash flow hedge of the anticipated gold purchase. The notional amount of the contract is 500 ounces, and the terms of the contract give LEW the option to purchase gold at a price of $300 per ounce. The price will be good until the contract expires on October 31, 2006.

    Assume the following data with respect to the price of the call options and the gold inventory purchase.

Date	Spot Price for October Delivery
April 1, 2006	$300 per ounce
June 30, 2006	310 per ounce
September 30, 2006	315 per ounce

Instructions

Prepare the journal entries for the following transactions during 2006.

(a) April 1, Inception of the futures contract, no premium paid.

(b) June 30, LEW Co. prepares financial statements.

(c) September 30, LEW Co. prepares financial statements.

(d) October 10, LEW Co. purchases 500 ounces of gold at $315 per ounce and settles the futures contract.

(e) December 20, 2006—LEW sells jewelry containing gold purchased in October 2006 for $350,000. The cost of the finished goods inventory is $200,000.

(f) Indicate the amount(s) reported on the balance sheet and income statement related to the futures contract on June 30, 2006.

(g) Indicate the amount(s) reported in the income statement related to the futures contract and the inventory transactions on December 31, 2006.

(LO 11) ***P17-18** **(Fair Value Hedge)** On November 3, 2007, Sprinkle Co. invested $200,000 in 4,000 shares of the common stock of Johnstone Co. Sprinkle classified this investment as available-for-sale. Sprinkle Co. is considering making a more significant investment in Johnstone Co. at some point in the future but has decided to wait and see how the stock does over the next several quarters.

    To hedge against potential declines in the value of Johnstone stock during this period, Sprinkle also purchased a put option on the Johnstone stock. Sprinkle paid an option premium of $600 for the put option, which gives Sprinkle the option to sell 4,000 Johnstone shares at a strike price of $50 per share. The option expires on July 31, 2007. The following data are available with respect to the values of the Johnstone stock and the put option.

Date	Market Price of Johnstone Shares	Time Value of Put Option
December 31, 2006	$50 per share	$375
March 31, 2007	45 per share	175
June 30, 2007	43 per share	40

Instructions

(a) Prepare the journal entries for Sprinkle Co. for the following dates.

    (1) November 3, 2006—Investment in Johnstone stock and the put option on Johnstone shares.

    (2) December 31, 2006—Sprinkle Co. prepares financial statements.

    (3) March 31, 2007—Sprinkle prepares financial statements.

    (4) June 30, 2007—Sprinkle prepares financial statements.

    (5) July 1, 2007—Sprinkle settles the put option and sells the Johnstone shares for $43 per share.

(b) Indicate the amount(s) reported on the balance sheet and income statement related to the Johnstone investment and the put option on December 31, 2006.

(c) Indicate the amount(s) reported on the balance sheet and income statement related to the Johnstone investment and the put option on June 30, 2007.

CONCEPTS FOR ANALYSIS

CA17-1 **(Issues Raised about Investment Securities)** You have just started work for Andre Love Co. as part of the controller's group involved in current financial reporting problems. Jackie Franklin, controller for Love, is interested in your accounting background because the company has experienced a series of financial reporting surprises over the last few years. Recently, the controller has learned from the company's auditors that an FASB *Statement* may apply to its investment in securities. She assumes that you are familiar with this pronouncement and asks how the following situations should be reported in the financial statements.

Situation 1
Trading securities in the current assets section have a fair value that is $4,200 lower than cost.

Situation 2
A trading security whose fair value is currently less than cost is transferred to the available-for-sale category.

Situation 3
An available-for-sale security whose fair value is currently less than cost is classified as noncurrent but is to be reclassified as current.

Situation 4
A company's portfolio of available-for-sale securities consists of the common stock of one company. At the end of the prior year the fair value of the security was 50% of original cost, and this reduction in market value was reported as an other than temporary impairment. However, at the end of the current year the fair value of the security had appreciated to twice the original cost.

Situation 5
The company has purchased some convertible debentures that it plans to hold for less than a year. The fair value of the convertible debentures is $7,700 below its cost.

Instructions
What is the effect upon carrying value and earnings for each of the situations above? Assume that these situations are unrelated.

CA17-2 **(Equity Securities)** James Joyce Co. has the following available-for-sale securities outstanding on December 31, 2006 (its first year of operations).

	Cost	Fair Value
Anna Wickham Corp. Stock	$20,000	$19,000
D. H. Lawrence Company Stock	10,000	8,800
Edith Sitwell Company Stock	20,000	20,600
	$50,000	$48,400

During 2007 D. H. Lawrence Company stock was sold for $9,200, the difference between the $9,200 and the "fair value" of $8,800 being recorded as a "Gain on Sale of Securities." The market price of the stock on December 31, 2007, was: Anna Wickham Corp. stock $19,900; Edith Sitwell Company stock $20,500.

Instructions
(a) What justification is there for valuing available-for-sale securities at fair value and reporting the unrealized gain or loss as part of stockholders' equity?
(b) How should James Joyce Company apply this rule on December 31, 2006? Explain.
(c) Did James Joyce Company properly account for the sale of the D. H. Lawrence Company stock? Explain.
(d) Are there any additional entries necessary for James Joyce Company at December 31, 2007, to reflect the facts on the financial statements in accordance with generally accepted accounting principles? Explain.

(AICPA adapted)

CA17-3 **(Financial Statement Effect of Equity Securities)** Presented below are three unrelated situations involving equity securities.

Situation 1
An equity security, whose market value is currently less than cost, is classified as available-for-sale but is to be reclassified as trading.

Situation 2
A noncurrent portfolio with an aggregate market value in excess of cost includes one particular security whose market value has declined to less than one-half of the original cost. The decline in value is considered to be other than temporary.

Situation 3
The portfolio of trading securities has a cost in excess of fair value of $13,500. The available-for-sale portfolio has a fair value in excess of cost of $28,600.

Instructions
What is the effect upon carrying value and earnings for each of the situations above?

CA17-4 (Equity Securities) The Financial Accounting Standards Board issued its *Statement No. 115* to clarify accounting methods and procedures with respect to certain debt and all equity securities. An important part of the statement concerns the distinction between held-to-maturity, available-for-sale, and trading securities.

Instructions
(a) Why does a company maintain an investment portfolio of held-to-maturity, available-for-sale, and trading securities?
(b) What factors should be considered in determining whether investments in securities should be classified as held-to-maturity, available-for-sale, and trading? How do these factors affect the accounting treatment for unrealized losses?

CA17-5 (Investment Accounted for under the Equity Method) On July 1, 2007, Sylvia Warner Company purchased for cash 40% of the outstanding capital stock of Robert Graves Company. Both Sylvia Warner Company and Robert Graves Company have a December 31 year-end. Graves Company, whose common stock is actively traded in the over-the-counter market, reported its total net income for the year to Warner Company and also paid cash dividends on November 15, 2007, to Warner Company and its other stockholders.

Instructions
How should Warner Company report the above facts in its December 31, 2007, balance sheet and its income statement for the year then ended? Discuss the rationale for your answer.

(AICPA adapted)

 CA17-6 (Equity Investment) On July 1, 2007, Munns Company purchased for cash 40% of the outstanding capital stock of Huber Corporation. Both Munns and Huber have a December 31 year-end. Huber Corporation, whose common stock is actively traded on the American Stock Exchange, paid a cash dividend on November 15, 2007, to Munns Company and its other stockholders. It also reported its total net income for the year of $920,000 to Munns Company.

Instructions
Prepare a one-page memorandum of instructions on how Munns Company should report the above facts in its December 31, 2007, balance sheet and its 2007 income statement. In your memo, identify and describe the method of valuation you recommend. Provide rationale where you can. Address your memo to the chief accountant at Munns Company.

 CA17-7 (Fair Value) Addison Manufacturing holds a large portfolio of debt and equity securities as an investment. The fair value of the portfolio is greater than its original cost, even though some securities have decreased in value. Ted Abernathy, the financial vice president, and Donna Nottebart, the controller, are near year-end in the process of classifying for the first time this securities portfolio in accordance with *FASB Statement No. 115*. Abernathy wants to classify those securities that have increased in value during the period as trading securities in order to increase net income this year. He wants to classify all the securities that have decreased in value as available-for-sale (the equity securities) and as held-to-maturity (the debt securities).

Nottebart disagrees. She wants to classify those securities that have decreased in value as trading securities and those that have increased in value as available-for-sale (equity) and held-to-maturity (debt). She contends that the company is having a good earnings year and that recognizing the losses will help to smooth the income this year. As a result, the company will have built-in gains for future periods when the company may not be as profitable.

Instructions
Answer the following questions.
(a) Will classifying the portfolio as each proposes actually have the effect on earnings that each says it will?

(b) Is there anything unethical in what each of them proposes? Who are the stakeholders affected by their proposals?

(c) Assume that Abernathy and Nottebart properly classify the entire portfolio into trading, available-for-sale, and held-to-maturity categories. But then each proposes to sell just before year-end the securities with gains or with losses, as the case may be, to accomplish their effect on earnings. Is this unethical?

USING YOUR JUDGMENT

Financial Reporting Problem

The Procter & Gamble Company (P&G)

The financial statements of P&G are presented in Appendix 5B or can be accessed on the KWW website.

Instructions

Refer to P&G's financial statements and the accompanying notes to answer the following questions.

(a) What investments does P&G report in 2004, and where are these investments reported in its financial statements?

(b) How are P&G's investments valued? How does P&G determine fair value?

(c) How does P&G use derivative financial instruments?

Financial Statement Analysis Case

Union Planters

Union Planters is a Tennessee bank holding company (that is, a corporation that owns banks). (Union Planters is now part of Regions Bank.) Union Planters manages $32 billion in assets, the largest of which is its loan portfolio of $19 billion. In addition to its loan portfolio, however, like other banks it has significant debt investments. The nature of these investments varies from short-term in nature to long-term in nature. As a consequence, consistent with the requirements of accounting rules, Union Planters reports its investments in two different categories—trading and available-for-sale. The following facts were found in a recent Union Planters' annual report.

(all dollars in millions)	Amortized Cost	Gross Unrealized Gains	Gross Unrealized Losses	Fair Value
Trading account assets	$ 275	—	—	$ 275
Securities available for sale	8,209	$108	$15	8,302
Net income				224
Net securities gains (losses)				(9)

Instructions

(a) Why do you suppose Union Planters purchases investments, rather than simply making loans? Why does it purchase investments that vary in nature both in terms of their maturities and in type (debt versus stock)?

(b) How must Union Planters account for its investments in each of the two categories?

(c) In what ways does classifying investments into two different categories assist investors in evaluating the profitability of a company like Union Planters?

(d) Suppose that the management of Union Planters was not happy with its net income for the year. What step could it have taken with its investment portfolio that would have definitely increased reported profit? How much could it have increased reported profit? Why do you suppose it chose not to do this?

Comparative Analysis Case

The Coca-Cola Company

The Coca-Cola Company and PepsiCo, Inc.

PEPSICO

Instructions

Go to the KWW website and use information found there to answer the following questions related to **The Coca-Cola Company** and **PepsiCo, Inc.**

(a) Based on the information contained in these financial statements, determine each of the following for each company.

(1) Cash used in (for) investing activities during 2004 (from the statement of cash flows).

(2) Cash used for acquisitions and investments in unconsolidated affiliates (or principally bottling companies) during 2004.

(3) Total investment in unconsolidated affiliates (or investments and other assets) at the end of 2004.

(4) What conclusions concerning the management of investments can be drawn from these data?

(b) (1) Briefly identify from Coca-Cola's December 31, 2004, balance sheet the investments it reported as being accounted for under the equity method. (2) What is the amount of investments that Coca-Cola reported in its 2004 balance sheet as "cost method investments," and what is the nature of these investments?

(c) In its Note number 9 on Financial Instruments, what total amounts did Coca-Cola report at December 31, 2004, as: (1) trading securities, (2) available-for-sale securities, and (3) held-to-maturity securities?

Research Case

The March 6, 2002, edition of the *Wall Street Journal* includes an article by Susan Pulliam and Carrick Mollenkamp titled "Investors Turn Attention to **Bank One** for Its Accounting of Securitizations."

Instructions

Read the article and answer the following questions.

(a) Explain the questions that analysts are raising about Bank One's accounting for credit-card securitizations. Why does the accounting for these securities matter?

(b) Bank One treats these securities as "available-for-sale." What are the criteria for classifying securities as available-for-sale? Based on the information in the article, do you think Bank One is classifying these securities properly? Justify your answer.

(c) How should an investment in available-for-sale securities be reported in the balance sheet? How are unrealized gains and losses on these securities reported?

(d) What is materiality, and how does it affect Bank One's financial statements? Would you consider $900 million immaterial for Bank One? Why or why not?

Professional Research: Financial Accounting and Reporting

Your client, Cascade Company, is planning to invest some of its excess cash in 5-year revenue bonds issued by the county and in the stock of one of its suppliers, Teton Co. Teton's shares trade on the over-the-counter market. Cascade plans to classify these investments as available-for-sale. They would like you to conduct some research on the accounting for these investments.

Instructions

Using the **Financial Accounting Research System (FARS)**, respond to the following items. (Provide text strings used in your search.)

(a) Since the Teton shares do not trade on one of the large stock markets, Cascade argues that the fair value of this investment is not readily available. According to the authoritative literature, when is the fair value of a security "readily determinable"?

(b) How is an impairment of a security accounted for?

(c) To avoid volatility in their financial statements due to fair value adjustments, Cascade debated whether the bond investment could be classified as held-to-maturity; Cascade is pretty sure it will hold the bonds for 5 years. How close to maturity could Cascade sell an investment and still classify it as held-to-maturity?

(d) What disclosures must be made for any sale or transfer from securities classified as held-to-maturity?

Professional Simulation

In this simulation you are asked to address questions related to investments. Prepare responses to all parts.

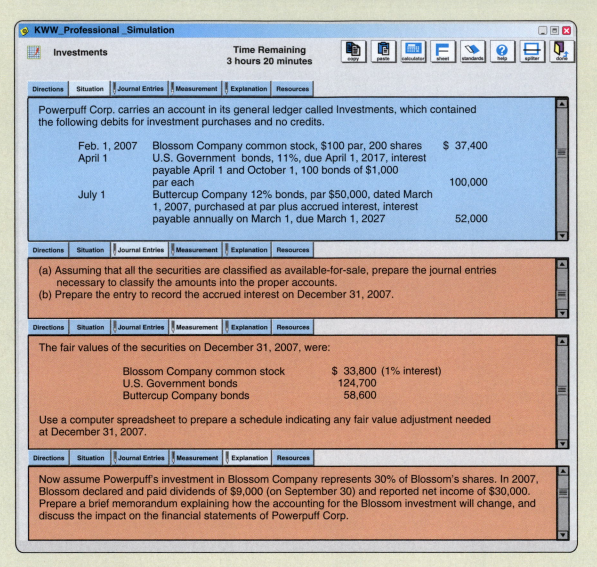

KWW_Professional_Simulation

Investments　　　　Time Remaining　　3 hours 20 minutes

copy | paste | calculator | sheet | standards | help | splitter | done

Directions | Situation | Journal Entries | Measurement | Explanation | Resources

Powerpuff Corp. carries an account in its general ledger called Investments, which contained the following debits for investment purchases and no credits.

Feb. 1, 2007	Blossom Company common stock, $100 par, 200 shares	$ 37,400
April 1	U.S. Government bonds, 11%, due April 1, 2017, interest payable April 1 and October 1, 100 bonds of $1,000 par each	100,000
July 1	Buttercup Company 12% bonds, par $50,000, dated March 1, 2007, purchased at par plus accrued interest, interest payable annually on March 1, due March 1, 2027	52,000

Directions | Situation | Journal Entries | Measurement | Explanation | Resources

(a) Assuming that all the securities are classified as available-for-sale, prepare the journal entries necessary to classify the amounts into the proper accounts.
(b) Prepare the entry to record the accrued interest on December 31, 2007.

Directions | Situation | Journal Entries | Measurement | Explanation | Resources

The fair values of the securities on December 31, 2007, were:

Blossom Company common stock	$ 33,800 (1% interest)
U.S. Government bonds	124,700
Buttercup Company bonds	58,600

Use a computer spreadsheet to prepare a schedule indicating any fair value adjustment needed at December 31, 2007.

Directions | Situation | Journal Entries | Measurement | Explanation | Resources

Now assume Powerpuff's investment in Blossom Company represents 30% of Blossom's shares. In 2007, Blossom declared and paid dividends of $9,000 (on September 30) and reported net income of $30,000. Prepare a brief memorandum explaining how the accounting for the Blossom investment will change, and discuss the impact on the financial statements of Powerpuff Corp.

Remember to check the book's companion website to find additional resources for this chapter.

It's Back

Several years after passage, the accounting world continues to be preoccupied with the Sarbanes-Oxley Act of 2002 (SOX). Unfortunately, SOX did not solve one of the classic accounting issues—how to properly account for revenue. In fact, revenue recognition practices are the most prevalent reasons why accounting restatements increased dramatically in 2004. A number of the revenue recognition issues relate to possible fraudulent behavior by company executives and employees. Consider some of the recent SEC actions:

- The SEC charged the former co-chairman and CEO of **Qwest Communications International Inc.** and eight other former Qwest officers and employees with fraud and other violations of the federal securities laws. Three of these people fraudulently characterized nonrecurring revenue from one-time sales as revenue from recurring data and Internet services. The SEC release notes that internal correspondence likened Qwest's dependence on these transactions to fill the gap between actual and projected revenue to an addiction.

- The SEC filed a complaint against three former senior officers of **iGo Corp.**, alleging that the defendants collectively caused iGo to improperly recognize revenue on consignment sales and products that were not shipped or that were shipped after the end of a fiscal quarter.

- The SEC filed a complaint against the former CEO and chairman of **Homestore Inc.** and its former executive vice president of business development, alleging that they engaged in a fraudulent scheme to overstate advertising and subscription revenues. The scheme involved a complex structure of "round-trip" transactions using various third-party companies that, in essence, allowed Homestore to recognize its own cash as revenue.

Though the cases cited involved fraud and irregularity, not all revenue recognition errors are intentional. For example, in April 2005 **American Home Mortgage Investment Corp.** announced that it would reverse revenue recognized from its fourth-quarter 2004 loan securitization, and would recognize it in the first quarter of 2005 instead. As a result, American Home restated its financial results for 2004.[1]

So, how does a company ensure that revenue transactions are recorded properly? Some answers will become apparent after you study this chapter.

---

[1]Cheryl de Mesa Graziano, "Revenue Recognition: A Perennial Problem," *Financial Executive* (July 14, 2005), *www.fei.org/mag/articles/7-2005_revenue.cfm*.

Learning Objectives

After studying this chapter, you should be able to:

1. Apply the revenue recognition principle.
2. Describe accounting issues for revenue recognition at point of sale.
3. Apply the percentage-of-completion method for long-term contracts.
4. Apply the completed-contract method for long-term contracts.
5. Identify the proper accounting for losses on long-term contracts.
6. Describe the installment-sales method of accounting.
7. Explain the cost-recovery method of accounting.

As indicated in the opening story, the issue of when revenue should be recognized is complex. The many methods of marketing products and services make it difficult to develop guidelines that will apply to all situations. This chapter provides you with general guidelines used in most business transactions. The content and organization of the chapter are as follows.

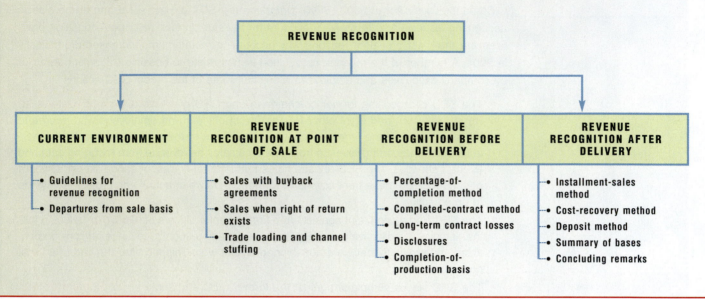

THE CURRENT ENVIRONMENT

According to one study, revenue recognition has been the largest single source of public-company restatements over the past decade. The study noted the following:

1 Restatements for improper revenue recognition result in larger drops in market capitalization than any other type of restatement.

2 Revenue problems caused eight of the top ten market value losses in a recent year.

3 Of the ten companies, the leading three lost $20 billion in market value in just three days following disclosure of revenue recognition problems.[2]

As a result of such revenue recognition problems, the SEC has increased its enforcement actions in this area (as evidenced in the opening story.) In some of these cases, companies made significant adjustments to previously issued financial statements. As Lynn Turner, former chief accountant of the SEC, indicated, "When people cross over the boundaries of legitimate reporting, the Commission will take appropriate action to ensure the fairness and integrity that investors need and depend on every day."[3]

Inappropriate recognition of revenue can occur in any industry. Products that are sold to distributors for resale pose different risks than products or services that are sold directly to customers. Sales in high-technology industries, where rapid product

---

[2]PricewaterhouseCoopers, "Current Developments for Audit Committees 2002" (Florham Park, N.J.: PricewaterhouseCoopers, 2002), p. 65.

[3]The Sarbanes-Oxley Act of 2002 also makes it clear that Congress will not tolerate abuses of the financial reporting process and that those who fail to adhere to "certain standards" will be prosecuted.

obsolescence is a significant issue, pose different risks than sale of inventory with a longer life, such as farm or construction equipment, automobiles, trucks, and appliances.[4]

As indicated in Chapter 10, telecom companies such as **Global Crossing** and **Qwest Communications** swapped fiber-optic capacity to increase revenue. The SEC has expressed concern that dot-coms also are increasing their revenue by including product sales in their revenue even though they are acting only as the distributor (intermediary) on behalf of other companies. Instead, dot-coms should be reporting only a distribution (brokerage) fee for selling another company's products.[5]

GROSSED OUT

Consider **Priceline.com**, the company made famous by William Shatner's ads about "naming your own price" for airline tickets and hotel rooms. In one of its quarterly SEC filings, Priceline reported that it earned $152 million in revenues. But that included the full amount customers paid for tickets, hotel rooms, and rental cars. Traditional travel agencies call that amount "gross bookings," not revenues. And much like regular travel agencies, Priceline keeps only a small portion of gross bookings—namely, the spread between the customers' accepted bids and the price it paid for the merchandise. The rest, which Priceline calls "product costs," it pays to the airlines and hotels that supply the tickets and rooms.

However, Priceline's product costs came to $134 million, leaving Priceline just $18 million of what it calls "gross profit" and what most other companies would call revenues. And that's before all of Priceline's other costs—like advertising and salaries—which netted out to a loss of $102 million. The difference isn't academic: Priceline stock traded at about 23 times its reported revenues but at a mind-boggling 214 times its "gross profit." This and other aggressive recognition practices led the SEC to issue stricter revenue recogniton guidance indicating that if a company performs as an agent or broker without assuming the risks and rewards of ownership of the goods, the company should report sales on a net (fee) basis.

Source: "Revenue Recognition in Financial Statements," *SEC Staff Accounting Bulletin No. 101* December 3, 1999) and "Revenue Recognition," *SEC Staff Accounting Bulletin No. 104* (December 17, 2003). See also Jeremy Kahn, "Presto Chango! Sales Are Huge," *Fortune* (March 20, 2000), p. 44.

WHAT DO THE NUMBERS MEAN?

Guidelines for Revenue Recognition

In general, the guidelines for revenue recognition are quite broad. On top of the broad guidelines, certain industries have specific additional guidelines that provide further insight into when revenue should be recognized. The **revenue recognition principle** provides that companies should recognize revenue[6] (1) when it is realized

OBJECTIVE 1
Apply the revenue recognition principle.

---

[4]Adapted from American Institute of Certified Public Accountants, Inc., *Audit Issues in Revenue Recognition* (New York: AICPA, 1999).

[5]"Revenue Recognition in Financial Statements," *SEC Staff Accounting Bulletin No. 101*, December 3, 1999).

[6]Recognition is "the process of formally recording or incorporating an item in the accounts and financial statements of an entity" (*SFAC No. 3*, par. 83). "Recognition includes depiction of an item in both words and numbers, with the amount included in the totals of the financial statements" (*SFAC No. 5*, par. 6). For an asset or liability, recognition involves recording not only acquisition or incurrence of the item but also later changes in it, including removal from the financial statements previously recognized.

Recognition is not the same as realization, although the two are sometimes used interchangeably in accounting literature and practice. *Realization* is "the process of converting noncash resources and rights into money and is most precisely used in accounting and financial reporting to refer to sales of assets for cash or claims to cash" (*SFAC No. 3*, par. 83).

or realizable and (2) when it is earned.[7] Therefore, proper revenue recognition revolves around three terms:

> Revenues are **realized** when a company exchanges goods and services for cash or claims to cash (receivables).
>
> Revenues are **realizable** when assets a company receives in exchange are readily convertible to known amounts of cash or claims to cash.
>
> Revenues are **earned** when a company has substantially accomplished what it must do to be entitled to the benefits represented by the revenues—that is, when the earnings process is complete or virtually complete.[8]

UNDERLYING CONCEPTS

Revenues are inflows of assets and/or settlements of liabilities from delivering or producing goods, providing services, or other earning activities that constitute a company's ongoing major or central operations during a period.

Four revenue transactions are recognized in accordance with this principle:

1 Companies recognize revenue from selling products at the date of sale. This date is usually interpreted to mean the date of delivery to customers.

2 Companies recognize revenue from services provided, when services have been performed and are billable.

3 Companies recognize revenue from permitting others to use enterprise assets, such as interest, rent, and royalties, as time passes or as the assets are used.

4 Companies recognize revenue from disposing of assets other than products at the date of sale.

These revenue transactions are diagrammed in Illustration 18-1.

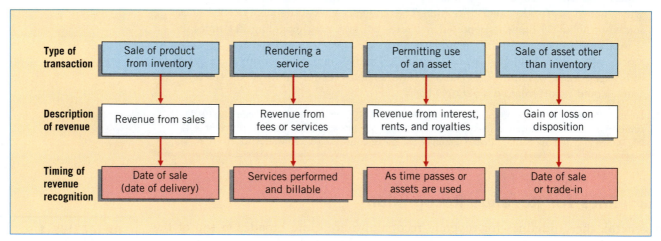

ILLUSTRATION 18-1
Revenue Recognition
Classified by Nature of
Transaction

The preceding statements are the basis of accounting for revenue transactions. Yet, in practice there are departures from the revenue recognition principle. Companies sometimes recognize revenue at other points in the earning process, owing in great measure to the considerable variety of revenue transactions.[9]

---

[7]"Recognition and Measurement in Financial Statements of Business Enterprises," *Statement of Financial Accounting Concepts No. 5* (Stamford, Conn.: FASB, 1984), par. 83.

[8]Gains (as contrasted to revenues) commonly result from transactions and other events that do not involve an "earning process." For gain recognition, being earned is generally less significant than being realized or realizable. Companies commonly recognize gains at the time of an asset's sale, disposition of a liability, or when prices of certain assets change.

[9]The FASB and IASB are now involved in a joint project on revenue recognition. The purpose of this project is to develop comprehensive conceptual guidance on when to recognize revenue. Presently, the boards are considering an approach that focuses on changes in assets and liabilities (rather than on earned and realized) as the basis for revenue recognition. It is hoped that this approach will lead to more consistent accounting in this area. (See *www.fasb.org/project/revenue_recognition.shtml*.)

Departures from the Sale Basis

An FASB study found some common **reasons for departures from the sale basis**.[10] One reason is a desire to **recognize earlier** than the time of sale the effect of earning activities. Earlier recognition is appropriate if there is a high degree of certainty about the amount of revenue earned. A second reason is a desire to **delay recognition** of revenue beyond the time of sale. Delayed recognition is appropriate if the degree of uncertainty concerning the amount of either revenue or costs is sufficiently high or if the sale does not represent substantial completion of the earnings process.

This chapter focues on two of the four general types of revenue transactions described earlier: (1) selling products and (2) providing services. Both of these are **sales transactions**. (In several other sections of the textbook, we discuss the other two types of revenue transactions—revenue from permitting others to use enterprise assets, and revenue from disposing of assets other than products.) Our discussion of product sales transactions in this chapter is organized around the following topics:

1 Revenue recognition at point of sale (delivery).
2 Revenue recognition before delivery.
3 Revenue recognition after delivery.
4 Revenue recognition for special sales transactions—franchises and consignments.

Illustration 18-2 depicts this organization of revenue recognition topics.

Examples of Revenue Recognition Policies

ILLUSTRATION 18-2
Revenue Recognition Alternatives

At date of delivery (point of sale)	Before delivery			After delivery		Special sales	
"The General Rule"	Before production	During production	At completion of production	As cash is collected	After costs are recovered	Franchises	Consignments

REVENUE RECOGNITION AT POINT OF SALE (DELIVERY)

According to the FASB's *Concepts Statement No. 5*, companies usually meet the two conditions for recognizing revenue (being realized or realizable and being earned) by the time they deliver products or render services to customers.[11] Therefore, companies commonly recognize revenues from manufacturing and selling activities at **point of sale** (usually meaning delivery).[12] Implementation problems, however, can arise. We discuss three such problematic situations on the following pages.

> **OBJECTIVE 2**
> **Describe accounting issues for revenue recognition at point of sale.**

---

[10]Henry R. Jaenicke, Survey of Present Practices in Recognizing Revenues, Expenses, Gains, and Losses, A Research Report (Stamford, Conn.: FASB, 1981), p. 11.

[11]The SEC believes that revenue is realized or realizable and earned when **all** of the following criteria are met: (1) Persuasive evidence of an arrangement exists; (2) delivery has occurred or services have been provided; (3) the seller's price to the buyer is fixed or determinable; and (4) collectibility is reasonably assured. See "Revenue Recognition in Financial Statements," *SEC Staff Accounting Bulletin No. 101* (December 3, 1999). The SEC provided more specific guidance because the general criteria were difficult to interpret.

[12]*Statement of Financial Accounting Concepts No. 5*, op. cit., par. 84.

Sales with Buyback Agreements

If a company sells a product in one period and agrees to buy it back in the next accounting period, has the company sold the product? As indicated in Chapter 8, legal title has transferred in this situation. However, the economic substance of the transaction is that the seller retains the risks of ownership. The FASB has curtailed recognition of revenue using this practice. When a repurchase agreement exists at a set price and this price covers all cost of the inventory plus related holding costs, the inventory and related liability remain on the seller's books.[13] In other words, no sale.

Sales When Right of Return Exists

Whether cash or credit sales are involved, a special problem arises with claims for returns and allowances. In Chapter 7, we presented the accounting treatment for normal returns and allowances. However, certain companies experience such a **high rate of returns**—a high ratio of returned merchandise to sales—that they find it necessary to postpone reporting sales until the return privilege has substantially expired.

For example, in the publishing industry, the rate of return approaches 25 percent for hardcover books and 65 percent for some magazines. Other types of companies that experience high return rates are perishable food dealers, distributors who sell to retail outlets, recording-industry companies, and some toy and sporting goods manufacturers. Returns in these industries are frequently made either through a right of contract or as a matter of practice involving "guaranteed sales" agreements or consignments.

Three alternative revenue recognition methods are available when the right of return exposes the seller to continued risks of ownership. These are: (1) not recording a sale until all return privileges have expired; (2) recording the sale, but reducing sales by an estimate of future returns; and (3) recording the sale and accounting for the returns as they occur. The FASB concluded that if a company sells its product but gives the buyer the right to return it, the company should recognize revenue from the sales transactions at the time of sale **only if all of the following six conditions have been met.**[14]

1 The seller's price to the buyer is substantially fixed or determinable at the date of sale.

2 The buyer has paid the seller, or the buyer is obligated to pay the seller, and the obligation is not contingent on resale of the product.

3 The buyer's obligation to the seller would not be changed in the event of theft or physical destruction or damage of the product.

4 The buyer acquiring the product for resale has economic substance apart from that provided by the seller.

5 The seller does not have significant obligations for future performance to directly bring about resale of the product by the buyer.

6 The seller can reasonably estimate the amount of future returns.

What if the six conditions are not met? In that case, the company must recognize sales revenue and cost of sales either when the return privilege has substantially expired or when those six conditions subsequently are met, **whichever occurs first**. In the income statement, the company must reduce sales revenue and cost of sales by the amount of the estimated returns.

UNDERLYING CONCEPTS

This is an example of *realized but unearned revenue*. When high rates of return exist and cannot be reasonably estimated, a question arises as to whether the earnings process has been substantially completed.

---

[13]"Accounting for Product Financing Arrangements," *Statement of Financial Accounting Standards No. 49* (Stamford, Conn.: FASB, 1981).

[14]"Revenue Recognition When Right of Return Exists," *Statement of Financial Accounting Standards No. 48* (Stamford, Conn.: FASB, 1981), par. 6.

Trade Loading and Channel Stuffing

Some companies record revenues at date of delivery with neither buyback nor unlimited return provisions. Although they appear to be following acceptable point-of-sale revenue recognition practices, they are recognizing revenues and earnings prematurely.

For example, the domestic cigarette industry at one time engaged in a distribution practice known as **trade loading**. As one commentator described this practice, "Trade loading is a crazy, uneconomic, insidious practice through which manufacturers—trying to show sales, profits, and market share they don't actually have—induce their wholesale customers, known as the trade, to buy more product than they can promptly resell."[15] In total, the cigarette industry appears to have exaggerated a couple years' operating profits by as much as $600 million by taking the profits from future years.

In the computer software industry, a similar practice is referred to as **channel stuffing**. When a software maker needed to make its financial results look good, it offered deep discounts to its distributors to overbuy, and then recorded revenue when the software left the loading dock.[16] Of course, the distributors' inventories become bloated and the marketing channel gets too filled with product, but the software maker's current-period financials are improved. However, financial results in future periods will suffer, unless the company repeats the process.

Trade loading and channel stuffing distort operating results and "window dress" financial statements. If used without an appropriate allowance for sales returns, channel stuffing is a classic example of booking tomorrow's revenue today. Business managers need to be aware of the ethical dangers of misleading the financial community by engaging in such practices to improve their financial statements.

INTERNATIONAL INSIGHT

General revenue recognition principles are provided by IFRS that are consistent with U.S. GAAP but contain limited detailed or industry-specific guidance.

NO TAKE-BACKS, REVISITED

You may recall from an earlier discussion (in Chapter 2, page 40) that investors in **Lucent Technologies** were negatively affected when Lucent violated one of the fundamental criteria for revenue recognition—the "no take-back" rule. This rule holds that revenue should not be booked on inventory that is shipped if the customer can return it at some point in the future. In this particular case, Lucent agreed to take back shipped inventory from its distributors, if the distributors were unable to sell the items to their customers.

In essence, Lucent was "stuffing the channel." By booking sales when goods were shipped, even though they most likely would get them back, Lucent was able to report continued sales growth. However, Lucent investors got a nasty surprise when distributors returned those goods and Lucent had to restate its financial results. The restatement erased $679 million in revenues, turning an operating profit into a loss. In response to this bad news, Lucent's stock price declined $1.31 per share, or 8.5 percent. Lucent is not alone in this practice. **Sunbeam** got caught stuffing the sales channel with barbeque grills and other outdoor items, which contributed to its troubles when it was forced to restate its earnings.

Investors can be tipped off to potential channel stuffing by carefully reviewing a company's revenue recognition policy for generous return policies and by watching inventory and receivable levels. When sales increase along with receivables, that's one sign that customers are not paying for goods shipped on credit. And growing inventory levels are an indicator that customers have all the goods they need. Both scenarios suggest a higher likelihood of goods being returned and revenues and income being restated. So remember, no take-backs!

Source: Adapted from S. Young, "Lucent Slashes First Quarter Outlook, Erases Revenue from Latest Quarter," *Wall Street Journal Online* (December 22, 2000); and Tracey Byrnes, "Too Many Thin Mints: Spotting the Practice of Channel Stuffing," *Wall Street Journal Online* (February 7, 2002).

WHAT DO THE NUMBERS MEAN?

---

[15]"The $600 Million Cigarette Scam," *Fortune* (December 4, 1989), p. 89.

[16]"Software's Dirty Little Secret," *Forbes* (May 15, 1989), p. 128.

REVENUE RECOGNITION BEFORE DELIVERY

For the most part, companies recognize revenue at the point of sale (delivery) because at point of sale most of the uncertainties in the earning process are removed and the exchange price is known. Under certain circumstances, however, companies recognize revenue prior to completion and delivery. The most notable example is long-term construction contract accounting, which uses the percentage-of-completion method.

Long-term contracts frequently provide that the seller (builder) may bill the purchaser at intervals, as it reaches various points in the project. Examples of long-term contracts are construction-type contracts, development of military and commercial aircraft, weapons-delivery systems, and space exploration hardware. When the project consists of separable units, such as a group of buildings or miles of roadway, contract provisions may provide for delivery in installments. In that case, the seller would bill the buyer and transfer title at stated stages of completion, such as the completion of each building unit or every 10 miles of road. The accounting records should record sales when installments are "delivered."[17]

Two distinctly different methods of accounting for long-term construction contracts are recognized.[18] They are:

- **Percentage-of-Completion Method.** Companies recognize revenues and gross profits each period based upon the progress of the construction—that is, the percentage of completion. The company accumulates construction costs **plus gross profit earned to date** in an inventory account (Construction in Process), and it accumulates progress billings in a contra inventory account (Billings on Construction in Progress).

- **Completed-Contract Method.** Companies recognize revenues and gross profit **only** when the contract is completed. The company accumulates construction costs in an inventory account (Construction in Process), and it accumulates progress billings in a contra inventory account (Billings on Construction in Progress).

The rationale for using percentage-of-completion accounting is that under most of these contracts the buyer and seller have enforceable rights. The buyer has the legal right to require specific performance on the contract. The seller has the right to require progress payments that provide evidence of the buyer's ownership interest. As a result, a continuous sale occurs as the work progresses. Companies should recognize revenue according to that progression.

Companies *must* use the percentage-of-completion method when estimates of progress toward completion, revenues, and costs are reasonably dependable and **all of the following conditions** exist.[19]

1 The contract clearly specifies the enforceable rights regarding goods or services to be provided and received by the parties, the consideration to be exchanged, and the manner and terms of settlement.
2 The buyer can be expected to satisfy all obligations under the contract.
3 The contractor can be expected to perform the contractual obligations.

Companies should use the completed-contract method when one of the following conditions applies:

---

[17]*Statement of Financial Accounting Concepts No. 5,* par. 84, item c.

[18]*Accounting Trends and Techniques—2004* reports that of the 119 of its 600 sample companies that referred to long-term construction contracts, 110 used the percentage-of-completion method and 9 used the completed-contract method.

[19]"Accounting for Performance of Construction-Type and Certain Production-Type Contracts," *Statement of Position 81-1* (New York: AICPA, 1981), par. 23.

- when a company has primarily short-term contracts, *or*
- when a company cannot meet the conditions for using the percentage-of-completion method, *or*
- when there are inherent hazards in the contract beyond the normal, recurring business risks.

The presumption is that percentage-of-completion is the better method. Therefore, companies should use the completed-contract method only when the percentage-of-completion method is inappropriate. We discuss the two methods in more detail in the following sections.

Percentage-of-Completion Method

The **percentage-of-completion method** recognizes revenues, costs, and gross profit as a company makes progress toward completion on a long-term contract. To defer recognition of these items until completion of the entire contract is to misrepresent the efforts (costs) and accomplishments (revenues) of the accounting periods during the contract. In order to apply the percentage-of-completion method, a company must have some basis or standard for measuring the progress toward completion at particular interim dates.

> **OBJECTIVE 3**
> Apply the percentage-of-completion method for long-term contracts.

Measuring the Progress toward Completion

As one practicing accountant wrote, "The big problem in applying the percentage-of-completion method . . . has to do with the ability to make reasonably accurate estimates of completion and the final gross profit."[20] Companies use various methods to determine the **extent of progress toward completion**. The most common are the *cost-to-cost* and *units-of-delivery* methods.[21]

The objective of all these methods is to measure the extent of progress in terms of costs, units, or value added. Companies identify the various measures (costs incurred, labor hours worked, tons produced, floors completed, etc.) and classify them as input or output measures. **Input measures** (costs incurred, labor hours worked) are efforts devoted to a contract. **Output measures** (with units of delivery measured as tons produced, floors of a building completed, miles of a highway completed) track results. Neither are universally applicable to all long-term projects. Their use requires the exercise of judgment and careful tailoring to the circumstances.

Both input and output measures have certain disadvantages. The input measure is based on an established relationship between a unit of input and productivity. If inefficiencies cause the productivity relationship to change, inaccurate measurements result. Another potential problem is front-end loading, in which significant up-front costs result in higher estimates of completion. To avoid this problem, companies should disregard some early-stage construction costs—for example, costs of uninstalled materials or costs of subcontracts not yet performed—if they do not relate to contract performance.

Similarly, output measures can produce inaccurate results if the units used are not comparable in time, effort, or cost to complete. For example, using floors (stories) completed can be deceiving. Completing the first floor of an eight-story building may require more than one-eighth the total cost because of the substructure and foundation construction.

The most popular input measure used to determine the progress toward completion is the **cost-to-cost basis**. Under this basis, a company like **EDS** measures the percentage of completion by comparing costs incurred to date with the most recent estimate of the total costs required to complete the contract. Illustration 18-3 (on page 914) shows the formula for the cost-to-cost basis.

---

[20]Richard S. Hickok, "New Guidance for Construction Contractors: 'A Credit Plus,'" *The Journal of Accountancy* (March 1982), p. 46.

[21]R. K. Larson and K. L. Brown, "Where Are We with Long-Term Contract Accounting?" *Accounting Horizons* (September 2004), pp. 207–219.

ILLUSTRATION 18-3
Formula for Percentage of
Completion, Cost-to-Cost
Basis

$$\frac{\text{Costs incurred to date}}{\text{Most recent estimate of total costs}} = \text{Percent complete}$$

Once EDS knows the percentage that costs incurred bear to total estimated costs, it applies that percentage to the total revenue or the estimated total gross profit on the contract. The resulting amount is the revenue or the gross profit to be recognized to date. Illustration 18-4 shows this computation.

ILLUSTRATION 18-4
Formula for Total
Revenue to Be
Recognized to Date

$$\begin{array}{c}\text{Percent}\\\text{complete}\end{array} \times \begin{array}{c}\text{Estimated}\\\text{total revenue}\\\text{(or gross profit)}\end{array} = \begin{array}{c}\text{Revenue (or gross}\\\text{profit) to be}\\\text{recognized to date}\end{array}$$

To find the amounts of revenue and gross profit recognized each period, EDS subtracts total revenue or gross profit recognized in prior periods, as shown in Illustration 18-5.

ILLUSTRATION 18-5
Formula for Amount of
Current-Period Revenue,
Cost-to-Cost Basis

$$\begin{array}{c}\text{Revenue (or gross}\\\text{profit) to be}\\\text{recognized to date}\end{array} - \begin{array}{c}\text{Revenue (or gross}\\\text{profit) recognized}\\\text{in prior periods}\end{array} = \begin{array}{c}\text{Current-period}\\\text{revenue}\\\text{(or gross profit)}\end{array}$$

Because **the cost-to-cost method is widely used** (without excluding other bases for measuring progress toward completion), we have adopted it for use in our examples.[22]

Example of Percentage-of-Completion Method—Cost-to-Cost Basis

To illustrate the percentage-of-completion method, assume that Hardhat Construction Company has a contract to construct a $4,500,000 bridge at an estimated cost of $4,000,000. The contract is to start in July 2007, and the bridge is to be completed in October 2009. The following data pertain to the construction period. (Note that by the end of 2008 Hardhat has revised the estimated total cost from $4,000,000 to $4,050,000.)

	2007	2008	2009
Costs to date	$1,000,000	$2,916,000	$4,050,000
Estimated costs to complete	3,000,000	1,134,000	—
Progress billings during the year	900,000	2,400,000	1,200,000
Cash collected during the year	750,000	1,750,000	2,000,000

Hardhat would compute the percentage complete as shown in Illustration 18-6.

ILLUSTRATION 18-6
Application of
Percentage-of-
Completion Method,
Cost-to-Cost Basis

	2007	2008	2009
Contract price	$4,500,000	$4,500,000	$4,500,000
Less estimated cost:			
Costs to date	1,000,000	2,916,000	4,050,000
Estimated costs to complete	3,000,000	1,134,000	—
Estimated total costs	4,000,000	4,050,000	4,050,000
Estimated total gross profit	$ 500,000	$ 450,000	$ 450,000
Percent complete	25%	72%	100%
	$\left(\dfrac{\$1,000,000}{\$4,000,000}\right)$	$\left(\dfrac{\$2,916,000}{\$4,050,000}\right)$	$\left(\dfrac{\$4,050,000}{\$4,050,000}\right)$

---

[22]Committee on Accounting Procedure, "Long-Term Construction-Type Contracts," *Accounting Research Bulletin No. 45* (New York: AICPA, 1955), p. 7.

On the basis of the data above, Hardhat would make the following entries to record (1) the costs of construction, (2) progress billings, and (3) collections. These entries appear as summaries of the many transactions that would be entered individually as they occur during the year.

	2007		2008		2009	
To record cost of construction:						
Construction in Process	1,000,000		1,916,000		1,134,000	
Materials, Cash,						
Payables, etc.		1,000,000		1,916,000		1,134,000
To record progress billings:						
Accounts Receivable	900,000		2,400,000		1,200,000	
Billings on Construction						
in Process		900,000		2,400,000		1,200,000
To record collections:						
Cash	750,000		1,750,000		2,000,000	
Accounts Receivable		750,000		1,750,000		2,000,000

ILLUSTRATION 18-7
Journal Entries—
Percentage-of-
Completion Method,
Cost-to-Cost Basis

In this example, the costs incurred to date are a measure of the extent of progress toward completion. To determine this, Hardhat evaluates the costs incurred to date as a proportion of the estimated total costs to be incurred on the project. The estimated revenue and gross profit that Hardhat will recognize for each year are calculated as shown in Illustration 18-8.

	2007	2008	2009
Revenue recognized in:			
2007 $4,500,000 × 25%	$1,125,000		
2008 $4,500,000 × 72%		$3,240,000	
Less: Revenue recognized in 2007		1,125,000	
Revenue in 2008		$2,115,000	
2009 $4,500,000 × 100%			$4,500,000
Less: Revenue recognized in			
2007 and 2008			3,240,000
Revenue in 2009			$1,260,000
Gross profit recognized in:			
2007 $500,000 × 25%	$ 125,000		
2008 $450,000 × 72%		$ 324,000	
Less: Gross profit recognized in 2007		125,000	
Gross profit in 2008		$ 199,000	
2009 $450,000 × 100%			$ 450,000
Less: Gross profit recognized in			
2007 and 2008			324,000
Gross profit in 2009			$ 126,000

ILLUSTRATION 18-8
Percentage-of-
Completion, Revenue
and Gross Profit, by Year

Illustration 18-9 (on page 916) shows Hardhat's entries to recognize revenue and gross profit each year and to record completion and final approval of the contract.

ILLUSTRATION 18-9
Journal Entries to
Recognize Revenue and
Gross Profit and to
Record Contract
Completion—Percentage-
of-Completion Method,
Cost-to-Cost Basis

	2007	2008	2009
To recognize revenue and gross profit:			
Construction in Process (gross profit)	125,000	199,000	126,000
Construction Expenses	1,000,000	1,916,000	1,134,000
Revenue from Long-Term Contract	1,125,000	2,115,000	1,260,000
To record completion of the contract:			
Billings on Construction in Process			4,500,000
Construction in Process			4,500,000

Note that Hardhat debits gross profit (as computed in Illustration 18-8) to Construction in Process. Similarly, it credits Revenue from Long-Term Contract for the amounts computed in Illustration 18-8. Hardhat then debits the difference between the amounts recognized each year for revenue and gross profit to a nominal account, Construction Expenses (similar to Cost of Goods Sold in a manufacturing company). It reports that amount in the income statement as the actual cost of construction incurred in that period. For example, Hardhat uses the actual costs of $1,000,000 to compute both the gross profit of $125,000 and the percent complete (25 percent).

Hardhat continues to accumulate costs in the Construction in Process account, in order to maintain a record of total costs incurred (plus recognized profit) to date. Although theoretically a series of "sales" takes place using the percentage-of-completion method, the selling company cannot remove the inventory cost until the construction is completed and transferred to the new owner. Hardhat's Construction in Process account for the bridge would include the following summarized entries over the term of the construction project.

ILLUSTRATION 18-10
Content of Construction
in Process Account—
Percentage-of-
Completion Method

Construction in Process				
2007 construction costs	$1,000,000	12/31/09	to close	
2007 recognized gross profit	125,000		completed	
2008 construction costs	1,916,000		project	$4,500,000
2008 recognized gross profit	199,000			
2009 construction costs	1,134,000			
2009 recognized gross profit	126,000			
Total	$4,500,000	Total		$4,500,000

Recall that the Hardhat Construction Company example contained a **change in estimate**: In the second year, 2008, it increased the estimated total costs from $4,000,000 to $4,050,000. The change in estimate is accounted for in a **cumulative catch-up manner**. This is done by, first, adjusting the percent completed to the new estimate of total costs. Next, Hardhat deducts the amount of revenues and gross profit recognized in prior periods from revenues and gross profit computed for progress to date. That is, it accounts for the change in estimate in the period of change. That way, the balance sheet at the end of the period of change and the accounting in subsequent periods are as they would have been if the revised estimate had been the original estimate.

Financial Statement Presentation—Percentage-of-Completion

Generally when a company records a receivable from a sale, it reduces the Inventory account. Under the percentage-of-completion method, however, the company continues to carry both the receivable and the inventory. Subtracting the balance in the **Billings account** from Construction in Process avoids double-counting the inventory. During the life of the contract, Hardhat reports in the balance sheet the difference between the

Construction in Process and the Billings on Construction in Process accounts. If that amount is a debit, Hardhat reports it **as a current asset**; if it is a credit, it reports it **as a current liability**.

At times, the costs incurred plus the gross profit recognized to date (the balance in Construction in Process) exceed the billings. In that case, Hardhat reports this excess as a current asset entitled "Cost and recognized profit in excess of billings." Hardhat can at any time calculate the unbilled portion of revenue recognized to date by subtracting the billings to date from the revenue recognized to date, as illustrated for 2007 for Hardhat Construction in Illustration 18-11.

Contract revenue recognized to date: $4,500,000 × $\frac{\$1,000,000}{\$4,000,000}$	$1,125,000
Billings to date	900,000
Unbilled revenue	$ 225,000

ILLUSTRATION 18-11
Computation of Unbilled
Contract Price at 12/31/07

At other times, the billings exceed costs incurred and gross profit to date. In that case, Hardhat reports this excess as a current liability entitled "Billings in excess of costs and recognized profit."

It probably has occurred to you that companies often have more than one project going at a time. When a company has a number of projects, costs exceed billings on some contracts and billings exceed costs on others. In such a case, the company segregates the contracts. The asset side includes only those contracts on which costs and recognized profit exceed billings. The liability side includes only those on which billings exceed costs and recognized profit. Separate disclosures of the dollar volume of billings and costs are preferable to a summary presentation of the net difference.

Using data from the bridge example, Hardhat Construction Company would report the status and results of its long-term construction activities under the perentage-of-completion method as shown in Illustration 18-12.

ILLUSTRATION 18-12
Financial Statement
Presentation—Percentage-
of-Completion Method

HARDHAT CONSTRUCTION COMPANY			
	2007	2008	2009
Income Statement			
Revenue from long-term contracts	$1,125,000	$2,115,000	$1,260,000
Costs of construction	1,000,000	1,916,000	1,134,000
Gross profit	$ 125,000	$ 199,000	$ 126,000

Balance Sheet (12/31)			
Current assets			
Accounts receivable		$ 150,000	$ 800,000
Inventories			
Construction in process	$1,125,000		
Less: Billings	900,000		
Costs and recognized profit in excess of billings		225,000	
Current liabilities			
Billings ($3,300,000) in excess of costs and recognized profit ($3,240,000)			$ 60,000

Note 1. Summary of significant accounting policies.
Long-Term Construction Contracts. The company recognizes revenues and reports profits from long-term construction contracts, its principal business, under the percentage-of-completion method of accounting. These contracts generally extend for periods in excess of one year. The amounts of revenues and profits recognized each year are based on the ratio of costs incurred to the total estimated costs. Costs included in construction in process include direct materials, direct labor, and project-related overhead. Corporate general and administrative expenses are charged to the periods as incurred and are not allocated to construction contracts.

Completed-Contract Method

Under the **completed-contract method**, companies recognize revenue and gross profit only at point of sale—that is, when the contract is completed. Under this method, companies accumulate costs of long-term contracts in process, but they make no interim charges or credits to income statement accounts for revenues, costs, or gross profit.

The principal advantage of the completed-contract method is that reported revenue reflects final results rather than *estimates* of unperformed work. Its major disadvantage is that it does not reflect current performance when the period of a contract extends into more than one accounting period. Although operations may be fairly uniform during the period of the contract, the company will not report revenue until the year of completion, creating a distortion of earnings.

Under the completed-contract method, the company would make the same **annual entries** to record costs of construction, progress billings, and collections from customers as those illustrated under the percentage-of-completion method. The significant difference is that the company **would not make entries to recognize revenue and gross profit**.

For example, under the completed-contract method for the bridge project illustrated on the preceding pages, Hardhat Construction Company would make the following entries in 2009 to recognize revenue and costs and to close out the inventory and billing accounts.

Billings on Construction in Process	4,500,000	
Revenue from Long-Term Contracts		4,500,000
Costs of Construction	4,050,000	
Construction in Process		4,050,000

Illustration 18-13 compares the amount of gross profit that Hardhat Construction Company would recognize for the bridge project under the two revenue-recognition methods.

ILLUSTRATION 18-13
Comparison of Gross Profit Recognized under Different Methods

	Percentage-of-Completion	Completed-Contract
2007	$125,000	$ 0
2008	199,000	0
2009	126,000	450,000

Under the completed-contract method, Hardhat Construction would report its long-term construction activities as follows.

ILLUSTRATION 18-14
Financial Statement Presentation—Completed-Contract Method

HARDHAT CONSTRUCTION COMPANY			
	2007	2008	2009
Income Statement			
Revenue from long-term contracts	—	—	$4,500,000
Costs of construction	—	—	4,050,000
Gross profit	—	—	$ 450,000

Balance Sheet (12/31)			
Current assets			
Accounts receivable		$150,000	$800,000
Inventories			
Construction in process	$1,000,000		
Less: Billings	900,000		
Unbilled contract costs		100,000	
Current liabilities			
Billings ($3,300,000) in excess of contract costs ($2,916,000)			$384,000

Note 1. Summary of significant accounting policies.
Long-Term Construction Contracts. The company recognizes revenues and reports profits from long-term construction contracts, its principal business, under the completed-contract method. These contracts generally extend for periods in excess of one year. Contract costs and billings are accumulated during the periods of construction, but no revenues or profits are recognized until completion of the contract. Costs included in construction in process include direct material, direct labor, and project-related overhead. Corporate general and administrative expenses are charged to the periods as incurred.

Long-Term Contract Losses

Two types of losses can become evident under long-term contracts:[23]

1 *Loss in the Current Period on a Profitable Contract.* This condition arises when, during construction, there is a significant increase in the estimated total contract costs but the increase does not eliminate all profit on the contract. Under the percentage-of-completion method only, the estimated cost increase requires a current-period adjustment of excess gross profit recognized on the project in prior periods. The company records this adjustment as a loss in the current period because it is a **change in accounting estimate** (discussed in Chapter 22).

2 *Loss on an Unprofitable Contract.* Cost estimates at the end of the current period may indicate that a loss will result on completion of the *entire* contract. Under both the percentage-of-completion and the completed-contract methods, the company must recognize in the current period the entire expected contract loss.

The treatment described for unprofitable contracts is consistent with the accounting custom of anticipating foreseeable losses to avoid overstatement of current and future income (conservatism).

Loss in Current Period

To illustrate a loss in the current period on a contract expected to be profitable upon completion, we'll continue with the Hardhat Construction Company bridge project. Assume that on December 31, 2008, Hardhat estimates the costs to complete the bridge contract at $1,468,962 instead of $1,134,000 (refer to page 914). Assuming all other data are the same as before, Hardhat would compute the percentage complete and recognize the loss as shown in Illustration 18-15. Compare these computations with those for 2008 in Illustration 18-6. The "percent complete" has dropped, from 72 percent to 66½ percent, due to the increase in estimated future costs to complete the contract.

> **OBJECTIVE 5**
> Identify the proper accounting for losses on long-term contracts.

> **UNDERLYING CONCEPTS**
> *Conservatism* justifies recognizing the losses immediately. Loss recognition does not require *realization;* it only requires evidence that an impairment of asset value has occurred.

Cost to date (12/31/08)	$2,916,000
Estimated costs to complete (revised)	1,468,962
Estimated total costs	$4,384,962
Percent complete ($2,916,000 ÷ $4,384,962)	66½%
Revenue recognized in 2008	
($4,500,000 × 66½%) − $1,125,000	$1,867,500
Costs incurred in 2008	1,916,000
Loss recognized in 2008	$ 48,500

> **ILLUSTRATION 18-15**
> Computation of Recognizable Loss, 2008—Loss in Current Period

The 2008 loss of $48,500 is a cumulative adjustment of the "excessive" gross profit recognized on the contract in 2007. Instead of restating the prior period, the company absorbs the prior period misstatement entirely in the current period. In this illustration, the adjustment was large enough to result in recognition of a loss.
Hardhat Construction would record the loss in 2008 as follows.

Construction Expenses	1,916,000	
Construction in Process (loss)		48,500
Revenue from Long-Term Contract		1,867,500

Hardhat will report the loss of $48,500 on the 2008 income statement as the difference between the reported revenues of $1,867,500 and the costs of $1,916,000.[24] **Under**

---

[23]Sak Bhamornsiri, "Losses from Construction Contracts," *The Journal of Accountancy* (April 1982), p. 26.

[24]In 2009 Hardhat Construction will recognize the remaining 33½ percent of the revenue ($1,507,500), with costs of $1,468,962 as expected, and will report a gross profit of $38,538. The total gross profit over the three years of the contract would be $115,038 [$125,000 (2007) − $48,500 (2008) + $38,538 (2009)]. This amount is the difference between the total contract revenue of $4,500,000 and the total contract costs of $4,384,962.

the completed-contract method, the company does not recognize a loss in 2008. Why not? Because the company still expects the contract to result in a profit, to be recognized in the year of completion.

Loss on an Unprofitable Contract

To illustrate the accounting for an overall loss on a long-term contract, assume that at December 31, 2008, Hardhat Construction Company estimates the costs to complete the bridge contract at $1,640,250 instead of $1,134,000. Revised estimates for the bridge contract are as follows.

	2007 Original Estimates	2008 Revised Estimates
Contract price	$4,500,000	$4,500,000
Estimated total cost	4,000,000	4,556,250*
Estimated gross profit	$ 500,000	
Estimated loss		$ (56,250)

*($2,916,000 + $1,640,250)

Under the percentage-of-completion method, Hardhat recognized $125,000 of gross profit in 2007 (see Illustration 18-8). This amount must be offset in 2008 because it is no longer expected to be realized. In addition, since losses must be recognized as soon as estimable, the company must recognize the total estimated loss of $56,250 in 2008. Therefore, Hardhat must recognize a total loss of $181,250 ($125,000 + $56,250) in 2008.

Illustration 18-16 shows Hardhat's computation of the revenue to be recognized in 2008.

ILLUSTRATION 18-16
Computation of Revenue Recognizable, 2008—Unprofitable Contract

Revenue recognized in 2008:		
Contract price		$4,500,000
Percent complete		× 64%*
Revenue recognizable to date		2,880,000
Less: Revenue recognized prior to 2008		1,125,000
Revenue recognized in 2008		**$1,755,000**
*Cost to date (12/31/08)	$2,916,000	
Estimated cost to complete	1,640,250	
Estimated total costs	$4,556,250	
Percent complete: $2,916,000 ÷ $4,556,250 = 64%		

To compute the construction costs to be expensed in 2008, Hardhat adds the total loss to be recognized in 2008 ($125,000 + $56,250) to the revenue to be recognized in 2008. Illustration 18-17 shows this computation.

ILLUSTRATION 18-17
Computation of Construction Expense, 2008—Unprofitable Contract

Revenue recognized in 2008 (computed above)		$1,755,000
Total loss recognized in 2008:		
Reversal of 2007 gross profit	$125,000	
Total estimated loss on the contract	56,250	181,250
Construction cost expensed in 2008		**$1,936,250**

Hardhat Construction would record the long-term contract revenues, expenses, and loss in 2008 as follows.

Construction Expenses	1,936,250	
Construction in Process (Loss)		181,250
Revenue from Long-Term Contracts		1,755,000

At the end of 2008, Construction in Process has a balance of $2,859,750 as shown below.[25]

Construction in Process			
2007 Construction costs	1,000,000		
2007 Recognized gross profit	125,000		
2008 Construction costs	1,916,000	2008 Recognized loss	181,250
Balance	**2,859,750**		

ILLUSTRATION 18-18
Content of Construction in Process Account at End of 2008—
Unprofitable Contract

Under the completed-contract method, Hardhat also would recognize the contract loss of $56,250, through the following entry in 2008 (the year in which the loss first became evident).

Loss from Long-Term Contracts	56,250	
Construction in Process (Loss)		56,250

Just as the Billings account balance cannot exceed the contract price, neither can the balance in Construction in Process exceed the contract price. In circumstances where the Construction in Process balance exceeds the billings the company can deduct the recognized loss from such accumulated costs on the balance sheet. That is, under both the percentage-of-completion and the completed-contract methods, the provision for the loss (the credit) may be combined with Construction in Process, thereby reducing the inventory balance. In those circumstances, however (as in the 2008 example above), where the billings exceed the accumulated costs, Hardhat must report separately on the balance sheet, as a current liability, the amount of the estimated loss. That is, under both the percentage-of-completion and the completed-contract methods, Hardhat would take the $56,250 loss, as estimated in 2008, from the Construction in Process account and report it separately as a current liability titled "Estimated liability from long-term contracts."[26]

Disclosures in Financial Statements

Construction contractors usually make some unique financial statement disclosures in addition to those required of all businesses. Generally these additional disclosures are made in the notes to the financial statements. For example, a construction contractor should disclose the following: the method of recognizing revenue,[27] the basis used to classify assets and liabilities as current (the nature and length of the operating cycle), the basis for recording inventory, the effects of any revision of estimates, the amount

---

[25]If the costs in 2009 are $1,640,250 as projected, at the end of 2009 the Construction in Process account will have a balance of $1,640,250 + $2,859,750, or $4,500,000, equal to the contract price. When the company matches the revenue remaining to be recognized in 2009 of $1,620,000 [$4,500,000 (total contract price) − $1,125,000 (2007) − $1,755,000 (2008)] with the construction expense to be recognized in 2009 of $1,620,000 [total costs of $4,556,250 less the total costs recognized in prior years of $2,936,250 (2007, $1,000,000; 2008, $1,936,250)], a zero profit results. Thus the total loss has been recognized in 2008, the year in which it first became evident.

[26]*Construction Contractors*, Audit and Accounting Guide (New York: AICPA, 1981), pp. 148–149.

[27]Ibid., p. 30.

of backlog on uncompleted contracts, and the details about receivables (billed and unbilled, maturity, interest rates, retainage provisions, and significant individual or group concentrations of credit risk).

WHAT DO THE NUMBERS MEAN?

LESS CONSERVATIVE

Halliburton provides engineering- and construction-related services, in jobs around the world. Much of the company's work is completed under contract over long periods of time. The company uses percentage-of-completion accounting. Recently the SEC started enforcement proceedings against the company related to its accounting for contract claims and disagreements with customers, including those arising from change orders and disputes about billable amounts and costs associated with a construction delay.

Prior to 1998 Halliburton took a very conservative approach to its accounting for disputed claims. As stated in the company's 1997 annual report, "Claims for additional compensation are recognized during the period such claims are resolved." That is, the company waited until all disputes were resolved before recognizing associated revenues. In contrast, in 1998 the company recognized revenue for disputed claims before their resolution, using estimates of amounts expected to be recovered. Such revenue and its related profit are more tentative and are subject to possible later adjustment than revenue and profit recognized when all claims have been resolved. As a case in point, the company noted that it incurred losses of $99 million in 1998 related to customer claims.

The accounting method put in place in 1998 is more aggressive than the company's former policy, but it is still within the boundaries of generally accepted accounting principles. However, the SEC noted that over six quarters, Halliburton failed to disclose its change in accounting practice. In the absence of any disclosure the SEC believed the investing public was misled about the precise nature of Halliburton's income in comparison to prior periods. The Halliburton situation illustrates the difficulty of using estimates in percentage-of-completion accounting and the impact of those estimates on the financial statements.

Source: "Failure to Disclose a 1998 Change in Accounting Practice," SEC (August 3, 2004), *www.sec.gov/news/press/2004-104.htm*. See also "Accounting Ace Charles Mulford Answers Accounting Questions," *Wall Street Journal Online* (June 7, 2002).

Completion-of-Production Basis

UNDERLYING CONCEPTS

This is not an exception to the revenue recognition principle. At the completion of production, realization is virtually assured and the earning process is substantially completed.

In certain cases companies recognize revenue at the completion of **production** even though no sale has been made. Examples of such situations involve precious metals or agricultural products with assured prices. Under the **completion-of-production basis**, companies recognize revenue when these metals are mined or agricultural crops harvested because the sales price is reasonably assured, the units are interchangeable, and no significant costs are involved in distributing the product.[28] (See discussion in Chapter 9, page 429, "Valuation at Net Realizable Value")

Likewise, when sale or cash receipt precedes production and delivery, as in the case of magazine subscriptions, companies recognize revenues as earned by production and delivery.[29]

---

[28]Such revenue satisfies the criteria of *Concepts Statement No. 5* since the assets are readily realizable and the earning process is virtually complete (see par. 84, item c).

[29]*Statement of Financial Accounting Concepts No. 5*, par. 84, item b.

REVENUE RECOGNITION AFTER DELIVERY

In some cases, the collection of the sales price is not reasonably assured and revenue recognition is deferred. One of two methods is generally employed to defer revenue recognition until the company receives cash: the **installment-sales method** or the **cost-recovery method**. A third method, the **deposit method**, applies in situations in which a company receives cash prior to delivery or transfer of the property; the company records that receipt as a deposit because the sale transaction is incomplete. This section examines these three methods.

Installment-Sales Accounting Method

The installment-sales method recognizes income in the periods of collection rather than in the period of sale. The logic underlying this method is that when there is no reasonable approach for estimating the degree of collectibility, companies should not recognize revenue until cash is collected.

The expression "installment sales" generally describes any type of sale for which payment is required in periodic installments over an extended period of time. All types of farm and home equipment as well as home furnishings are sold on an installment basis. The heavy equipment industry also sometimes uses the method for machine installations paid for over a long period. Another application of the method is in land-development sales.

Because payment is spread over a relatively long period, the risk of loss resulting from uncollectible accounts is greater in installment-sales transactions than in ordinary sales. Consequently, selling companies use various devices to protect themselves. Two common devices are: (1) the use of a *conditional sales contract*, which specifies that title to the item sold does not pass to the purchaser until all payments are made, and (2) use of notes secured by a *chattel* (personal property) *mortgage* on the article sold. Either of these permits the seller to "repossess" the goods sold if the purchaser defaults on one or more payments. The seller can then resell the repossessed merchandise at whatever price it will bring to compensate for the uncollected installments and the expense of repossession.

Under the installment-sales method of accounting, companies defer income recognition until the period of cash collection. They recognize both revenues and costs of sales in the period of sale, but defer the related gross profit to those periods in which they collect the cash. Thus, **instead of deferring the sale, along with related costs and expenses, to the future periods of anticipated collection, the company defers only the proportional gross profit**. This approach is equivalent to deferring both sales and cost of sales. Other expenses—that is, selling expense, administrative expense, and so on—are not deferred.

Thus, the installment-sales method matches cost and expenses against sales through the gross profit figure, but no further. Companies using the installment-sales method generally record operating expenses without regard to the fact that they will defer some portion of the year's gross profit. This practice is often justified on the basis that (1) these expenses do not follow sales as closely as does the cost of goods sold, and (2) accurate apportionment among periods would be so difficult that it could not be justified by the benefits gained.[30]

Acceptability of the Installment-Sales Method

The use of the installment-sales method for revenue recognition has fluctuated widely. At one time it was widely accepted for installment-sales transactions. Somewhat paradoxically, as installment-sales transactions increased in popularity, acceptance and

---

[30]In addition, other theoretical deficiencies of the installment-sales method could be cited. For example, see Richard A. Scott and Rita K. Scott, "Installment Accounting: Is It Inconsistent?" *The Journal of Accountancy* (November 1979).

use of the installment-sales method decreased. Finally the profession concluded that except in special circumstances, "the installment method of recognizing revenue is not acceptable."[31] The rationale for this position is simple: Because the installment method recognizes no income until cash is collected, it is not in accordance with the accrual accounting concept.

Use of the installment-sales method was often justified on the grounds that the risk of not collecting an account receivable may be so great that the sale itself is not sufficient evidence that recognition should occur. In some cases, this reasoning is valid, but not in a majority of cases. The general approach is that a company should recognize a completed sale. If the company expects bad debts, it should record this possibility as separate estimates of uncollectibles. Although collection expenses, repossession expenses, and bad debts are an unavoidable part of installment-sales activities, the incurrence of these costs and the collectibility of the receivables are reasonably predictable.

We study this topic in intermediate accounting because the method is acceptable in cases where a company believes there to be no reasonable basis of estimating the degree of collectibility. In addition, the sales method of revenue recognition has certain weaknesses when used for franchise and land-development operations. Application of the sales method to **franchise and license operations** has resulted in the abuse described earlier as "front-end loading." In some cases, franchisors recognized revenue prematurely, when they granted a franchise or issued a license, rather than when revenue was earned or the cash is received. Many **land-development** ventures were susceptible to the same abuses. As a result, the FASB prescribes application of the installment-sales method of accounting for sales of real estate under certain circumstances.[32]

Procedure for Deferring Revenue and Cost of Sales of Merchandise

One could work out a procedure that deferred both the uncollected portion of the sales price and the proportionate part of the cost of the goods sold. Instead of apportioning both sales price and cost over the period of collection, however, the installment-sales method defers **only the gross profit**. This procedure has exactly the same effect as deferring both sales and cost of sales, but it requires only one deferred account rather than two.

For the **sales in any one year**, the steps companies use to defer gross profit are as follows.

1 During the year, record both sales and cost of sales in the regular way, using the special accounts described later, and compute the rate of gross profit on installment-sales transactions.

2 At the end of the year, apply the rate of gross profit to the cash collections of the current year's installment sales, to arrive at the realized gross profit.

3 Defer to future years the gross profit not realized.

For **sales made in prior years**, companies apply the gross profit rate of each year's sales against cash collections of accounts receivable resulting from that year's sales, to arrive at the realized gross profit.

[31]"Omnibus Opinion," *Opinions of the Accounting Principles Board No. 10* (New York: AICPA, 1966), par. 12.

[32]"Accounting for Sales of Real Estate," *Statement of Financial Accounting Standards No. 66* (Norwalk, Conn.: FASB, 1982), pars. 45–47. The installment-sales method of accounting must be applied to a retail land sale that meets **all** of the following criteria: (1) the period of cancellation of the sale with refund of the down payment and any subsequent payments has expired; (2) cumulative cash payments equal or exceed 10 percent of the sales value; and (3) the seller is financially capable of providing all promised contract representations (e.g., land improvements, off-site facilities).

Special accounts must be used in the installment-sales method. These accounts provide certain special information required to determine the realized and unrealized gross profit in each year of operations. In computing net income under the installment-sales method as generally applied, the only peculiarity is the **deferral of gross profit until realized by accounts receivable collection**. We will use the following data to illustrate the installment-sales method in accounting for the sales of merchandise.

	2007	2008	2009
Installment sales	$200,000	$250,000	$240,000
Cost of installment sales	150,000	190,000	168,000
Gross profit	$ 50,000	$ 60,000	$ 72,000
Rate of gross profit on sales	25%[a]	24%[b]	30%[c]
Cash receipts			
2007 sales	$ 60,000	$100,000	$ 40,000
2008 sales		100,000	125,000
2009 sales			80,000
	[a] $\dfrac{\$50,000}{\$200,000}$	[b] $\dfrac{\$60,000}{\$250,000}$	[c] $\dfrac{\$72,000}{\$240,000}$

To simplify this example, we have excluded interest charges. Summary entries in general journal form for the year 2007 are as follows.

2007

Installment Accounts Receivable, 2007	200,000	
Installment Sales		200,000
(To record sales made on installment in 2007)		
Cash	60,000	
Installment Accounts Receivable, 2007		60,000
(To record cash collected on installment receivables)		
Cost of Installment Sales	150,000	
Inventory (or Purchases)		150,000
(To record cost of goods sold on installment in 2007 on		
either a perpetual or a periodic inventory basis)		
Installment Sales	200,000	
Cost of Installment Sales		150,000
Deferred Gross Profit, 2007		50,000
(To close installment sales and cost of installment sales		
for the year)		
Deferred Gross Profit	15,000	
Realized Gross Profit on Installment Sales		15,000
(To remove from deferred gross profit the profit realized		
through cash collections; $60,000 × 25%)		
Realized Gross Profit on Installment Sales	15,000	
Income Summary		15,000
(To close profits realized by collections)		

Illustration 18-19 shows computation of the realized and deferred gross profit for the year 2007.

2007	
Rate of gross profit current year	25%
Cash collected on current year's sales	$60,000
Realized gross profit (25% of $60,000)	15,000
Gross profit to be deferred ($50,000 − $15,000)	35,000

ILLUSTRATION 18-19
Computation of Realized and Deferred Gross Profit, 2007

Summary entries in journal form for year 2 (2008) are as follows.

2008

Installment Accounts Receivable, 2008	250,000	
Installment Sales		250,000
(To record sales made on installment in 2008)		
Cash	200,000	
Installment Accounts Receivable, 2007		100,000
Installment Accounts Receivable, 2008		100,000
(To record cash collected on installment receivables)		
Cost of Installment Sales	190,000	
Inventory (or Purchases)		190,000
(To record cost of goods sold on installment in 2008)		
Installment Sales	250,000	
Cost of Installment Sales		190,000
Deferred Gross Profit, 2008		60,000
(To close installment sales and cost of installment sales for the year)		
Deferred Gross Profit, 2007 ($100,000 × 25%)	25,000	
Deferred Gross Profit, 2008 ($100,000 × 24%)	24,000	
Realized Gross Profit on Installment Sales		49,000
(To remove from deferred gross profit the profit realized through cash collections)		
Realized Gross Profit on Installment Sales	49,000	
Income Summary		49,000
(To close profits realized by collections)		

Illustration 18-20 shows computation of the realized and deferred gross profit for the year 2008.

ILLUSTRATION 18-20
Computation of Realized and Deferred Gross Profit, 2008

2008	
Current year's sales	
Rate of gross profit	24%
Cash collected on current year's sales	$100,000
Realized gross profit (24% of $100,000)	24,000
Gross profit to be deferred ($60,000 − $24,000)	36,000
Prior year's sales	
Rate of gross profit—2007	25%
Cash collected on 2007 sales	$100,000
Gross profit realized in 2008 on 2007 sales (25% of $100,000)	25,000
Total gross profit realized in 2008	
Realized on collections of 2007 sales	$ 25,000
Realized on collections of 2008 sales	24,000
Total	$ 49,000

The entries in 2009 would be similar to those of 2008, and the total gross profit taken up or realized would be $64,000, as shown by the computations in Illustration 18-21 (on page 927).

In summary, here are the basic concepts you should understand about accounting for installment sales:

1 How to compute a proper gross profit percentage.

2 How to record installment sales, cost of installment sales, and deferred gross profit.

3 How to compute realized gross profit on installment receivables.

4 How the deferred gross profit balance at the end of the year results from applying the gross profit rate to the installment accounts receivable.

ILLUSTRATION 18-21
Computation of Realized
and Deferred Gross
Profit, 2009

2009

Current year's sales

Rate of gross profit	30%
Cash collected on current year's sales	$ 80,000
Gross profit realized on 2009 sales (30% of $80,000)	24,000
Gross profit to be deferred ($72,000 − $24,000)	48,000

Prior years' sales

2007 sales

Rate of gross profit	25%
Cash collected	$ 40,000
Gross profit realized in 2009 on 2007 sales (25% of $40,000)	10,000

2008 sales

Rate of gross profit	24%
Cash collected	$125,000
Gross profit realized in 2009 on 2008 sales (24% of $125,000)	30,000

Total gross profit realized in 2009

Realized on collections of 2007 sales	$ 10,000
Realized on collections of 2008 sales	30,000
Realized on collections of 2009 sales	24,000
Total	$ 64,000

Additional Problems of Installment-Sales Accounting

In addition to computing realized and deferred gross profit currently, other problems are involved in accounting for installment-sales transactions. These problems are related to:

1 Interest on installment contracts.

2 Uncollectible accounts.

3 Defaults and repossessions.

Interest on Installment Contracts. Because the collection of installment receivables is spread over a long period, it is customary to charge the buyer interest on the unpaid balance. The seller and buyer set up a schedule of equal payments consisting of interest and principal. Each successive payment is attributable to a smaller amount of interest and a corresondingly larger amount of principal, as shown in Illustration 18-22. This illustration assumes that a company sells for $3,000 an asset costing $2,400 (rate of gross profit = 20%), with interest of 8 percent included in the three installments of $1,164.10.

ILLUSTRATION 18-22
Installment Payment
Schedule

Date	Cash (Debit)	Interest Earned (Credit)	Installment Receivables (Credit)	Installment Unpaid Balance	Realized Gross Profit (20%)
1/2/07	—	—	—	$3,000.00	—
1/2/08	$1,164.10[a]	$240.00[b]	$ 924.10[c]	2,075.90[d]	$184.82[e]
1/2/09	1,164.10	166.07	998.03	1,077.87	199.61
1/2/10	1,164.10	86.23	1,077.87	−0−	215.57
					$600.00

[a]Periodic payment = Original unpaid balance ÷ PV of an annuity of $1.00 for three periods at 8%;
$1,164.10 = $3,000 ÷ 2.57710.
[b]$3,000.00 × .08 = $240.
[c]$1,164.10 − $240.00 = $924.10.
[d]$3,000.00 − $924.10 = $2,075.90.
[e]$924.10 × .20 = $184.82.

The company accounts for interest separate from the gross profit recognized on the installment-sales collections during the period, by recognizing interest revenue at the time of its cash receipt.

Uncollectible Accounts. The problem of bad debts or uncollectible accounts receivable is somewhat different for concerns selling on an installment basis because of a repossession feature commonly incorporated in the sales agreement. This feature gives the selling company an opportunity to recoup an uncollectible account through repossession and resale of repossessed merchandise. If the experience of the company indicates that repossessions do not, as a rule, compensate for uncollectible balances, it may be advisable to provide for such losses through charges to a special bad debt expense account, just as is done for other credit sales.

Defaults and Repossessions. Depending on the terms of the sales contract and the policy of the credit department, the seller can repossess merchandise sold under an installment arrangement if the purchaser fails to meet payment requirements. The seller may then recondition repossessed merchandise before offering it for re-sale, for cash or installment payments.

The accounting for **repossessions** recognizes that the company is not likely to collect the related installment receivable and should write it off. Along with the installment account receivable, the company must remove the applicable deferred gross profit using the following entry:

Repossessed Merchandise (an inventory account)	xxx	
Deferred Gross Profit	xxx	
Installment Accounts Receivable		xxx

This entry assumes that the company will record the repossessed merchandise at exactly the amount of the uncollected account less the deferred gross profit applicable. This assumption may or may not be proper. To determine the correct amount, the company should consider the condition of the repossessed merchandise, the cost of reconditioning, and the market for second-hand merchandise of that particular type. The objective should be to put any asset acquired on the books at its fair value, or at the best possible approximation of fair value when fair value is not determinable. A loss can occur if the fair value of the repossessed merchandise is less than the uncollected balance less the deferred gross profit. In that case, the company should record a "loss on repossession" at the date of repossession.[33]

To illustrate the required entry, assume that Klein Brothers sells a refrigerator to Marilyn Hunt for $1,500 on September 1, 2007. Terms require a down payment of $600 and $60 on the first of every month for 15 months, starting October 1, 2007. It is further assumed that the refrigerator cost $900, and that Klein Brothers priced it to provide a 40 percent rate of gross profit on selling price. At the year-end, December 31, 2007, Klein Brothers should have collected a total of $180 in addition to the original down payment.

If Hunt makes her January and February payments in 2008 and then defaults, the account balances applicable to Hunt at time of default are as shown in Illustration 18-23.

ILLUSTRATION 18-23
Computation of Installment Receivable Balances

Installment accounts receivable (September 1, 2007)		$1,500
Less: Down payment:	$600	
Payments to date ($60 × 5)	300	900
Installment accounts receivable (March 1, 2008)		$ 600
Installment accounts receivable (March 1, 2008)		$600
Gross profit rate		× 40%
Deferred gross profit		$240

[33]Some contend that a company should record repossessed merchandise at a valuation that will permit the company to make its regular rate of gross profit on resale. If the company enters the value at its approximated cost to purchase, the regular rate of gross profit could be provided for upon its ultimate sale, but that is completely a secondary consideration. It is more important that the company record the repossessed asset at fair value. This accounting would be in accordance with the general practice of carrying assets at acquisition price, as represented by the fair market value at the date of acquisition.

As indicated, Klein Brothers compute the balance of deferred gross profit applicable to Hunt's account by applying the gross profit rate for the year of sale to the balance of Hunt's account receivable: 40 percent of $600, or $240. The account balances are therefore:

Installment Account Receivable, 2007	600 (dr.)
Deferred Gross Profit, 2007	240 (cr.)

Klein repossesses the refrigerator following Hunt's default. If Klein sets the estimated fair value of the repossessed article at $150, it would make the following entry to record the repossession.

Deferred Gross Profit, 2007	240	
Repossessed Merchandise	150	
Loss on Repossession	210	
Installment Accounts Receivable, 2007		600

Klein determines the amount of the loss in two steps: (1) It subtracts the deferred gross profit from the amount of the account receivable, to determine the unrecovered cost (or book value) of the merchandise repossessed. (2) It then subtracts the estimated fair value of the merchandise repossessed from the unrecovered cost, to get the amount of the loss on repossession. Klein Brothers computes the loss on the refrigerator as shown in Illustration 18-24.

Balance of account receivable (representing uncollected selling price)	$600
Less: Deferred gross profit	240
Unrecovered cost	360
Less: Estimated fair value of merchandise repossessed	150
Loss (Gain) on repossession	$210

ILLUSTRATION 18-24
Computation of Loss on Repossession

As pointed out earlier, the loss on repossession may be charged to Allowance for Doubtful Accounts if a company carries such an account.

Financial Statement Presentation of Installment-Sales Transactions

If installment-sales transactions represent a significant part of total sales, it is desirable to make full disclosure of installment sales, the cost of installment sales, and any expenses allocable to installment sales. However, if installment-sales transactions constitute an insignificant part of total sales, it may be satisfactory to include only the realized gross profit in the income statement as a special item following the gross profit on sales. Illustration 18-25 shows this simpler presentation.

HEALTH MACHINE COMPANY
INCOME STATEMENT
FOR THE YEAR ENDED DECEMBER 31, 2008

Sales	$620,000
Cost of goods sold	490,000
Gross profit on sales	130,000
Gross profit realized on installment sales	51,000
Total gross profit on sales	$181,000

ILLUSTRATION 18-25
Disclosure of Installment-Sales Transactions—Insignificant Amount

If a company wants more complete disclosure of installment-sales transactions, it would use a presentation similar to that shown in Illustration 18-26 (on page 930).

ILLUSTRATION 18-26
Disclosure of Installment-
Sales Transactions—
Significant Amount

	Installment Sales	Other Sales	Total
HEALTH MACHINE COMPANY			
INCOME STATEMENT			
FOR THE YEAR ENDED DECEMBER 31, 2008			
Sales	$248,000	$620,000	$868,000
Cost of goods sold	182,000	490,000	672,000
Gross profit on sales	66,000	130,000	196,000
Less: Deferred gross profit on installment sales of this year	47,000		47,000
Realized gross profit on this year's sales	19,000	130,000	149,000
Add: Gross profit realized on installment sales of prior years	32,000		32,000
Gross profit realized this year	$ 51,000	$130,000	$181,000

The presentation in Illustration 18-26 is awkward. Yet the awkwardness of this method is difficult to avoid if a company wants to provide full disclosure of installment-sales transactions in the income statement. One solution, of course, is to prepare a separate schedule showing installment-sales transactions, with only the final figure carried into the income statement.

In the balance sheet it is generally considered desirable to classify installment accounts receivable by year of collectibility. There is some question as to whether companies should include in current assets installment accounts that are not collectible for two or more years. Yet if installment sales are **part of normal operations**, companies may consider them as current assets because they are collectible within the operating cycle of the business. Little confusion should result from this practice if the company fully discloses maturity dates, as illustrated in the following example.

ILLUSTRATION 18-27
Disclosure of Installment
Accounts Receivable,
by Year

Current assets		
Notes and accounts receivable		
Trade customers	$78,800	
Less: Allowance for doubtful accounts	3,700	
	75,100	
Installment accounts collectible in 2008	22,600	
Installment accounts collectible in 2009	47,200	$144,900

On the other hand, a company may have receivables from an installment contract, resulting from a transaction not related to normal operations. In that case, the company should report such receivable in the "Other assets" section if due beyond one year.

Repossessed merchandise is a part of inventory, and companies should report it as such in the "Current assets" section of the balance sheet. They should include any gain or loss on repossession in the income statement in the "Other revenues and gains" or "Other expenses and losses" section.

If a company has **deferred gross profit on installment sales**, it generally treats it as unearned revenue and classifies it as a current liability. Theoretically, deferred gross profit consists of three elements: (1) income tax liability to be paid when the sales are reported as realized revenue (current liability); (2) allowance for collection expense, bad debts, and repossession losses (deduction from installment accounts receivable); and (3) net income (retained earnings, restricted as to dividend availability). Because of the difficulty in allocating deferred gross profit among these three elements, however, companies frequently report the whole amount as unearned revenue.

In contrast, the FASB in *SFAC No. 6* states that "no matter how it is displayed in financial statements, deferred gross profit on installment sales is conceptually an asset valuation—that is, a reduction of an asset."[34] We support the FASB position, but we recognize that until an official standard on this topic is issued, financial statements will probably continue to report such deferred gross profit as a current liability.

Cost-Recovery Method

Under the **cost-recovery method**, a company recognizes no profit until cash payments by the buyer exceed the cost of the merchandise sold. After the seller has recovered all costs, it includes in income any additional cash collections. The seller's income statement for the period reports sales revenue, the cost of goods sold, and the gross profit—both the amount (if any) that is recognized during the period and the amount that is deferred. The deferred gross profit is offset against the related receivable—reduced by collections—on the balance sheet. Subsequent income statements report the gross profit as a separate item of revenue when the company recognizes it as earned.

APB Opinion No. 10 allows a seller to use the cost-recovery method to account for sales in which "there is no reasonable basis for estimating collectibility." In addition, *FASB Statements No. 45* (franchises) and *No. 66* (real estate) require use of this method where a high degree of uncertainty exists related to the collection of receivables.[35]

To illustrate the cost-recovery method, assume that early in 2007, Fesmire Manufacturing sells inventory with a cost of $25,000 to Higley Company for $36,000. Higley will make payments of $18,000 in 2007, $12,000 in 2008, and $6,000 in 2009. If the cost-recovery method applies to this transaction and Higley makes the payments as scheduled, Fesmire recognizes cash collections, revenue, cost, and gross profit as follows.[36]

	2007	2008	2009
Cash collected	$18,000	$12,000	$6,000
Revenue	$36,000	–0–	–0–
Cost of goods sold	25,000	–0–	–0–
Deferred gross profit	11,000	$11,000	$6,000
Recognized gross profit	–0–	5,000*	6,000
Deferred gross profit balance (end of period)	$11,000	$ 6,000	$ –0–

*$25,000 − $18,000 = $7,000 of unrecovered cost at the end of 2007; $12,000 − $7,000 = $5,000, the excess of cash received in 2008 over unrecovered cost.

ILLUSTRATION 18-28
Computation of Gross Profit—Cost-Recovery Method

OBJECTIVE 7
Explain the cost-recovery method of accounting.

ILLUSTRATION 18-28
Computation of Gross Profit—Cost-Recovery Method

Under the cost-recovery method, Fesmire reports total revenue and cost of goods sold in the period of sale, similar to the installment-sales method. However, unlike the installment-sales method, which recognizes income as cash is collected, Fesmire recognizes profit under the cost-recovery method **only when cash collections exceed the total cost of the goods sold**.

---

[34]*See Statement of Financial Accounting Concepts No. 6*, pars. 232–234.

[35]"Omnibus Opinion—1966," *Opinions of the Accounting Principles Board No. 10* (New York: AICPA, 1969), footnote 8, page 149; "Accounting for Franchise Fee Revenue," *Statement of Financial Accounting Standards No. 45* (Stamford, Conn.: FASB, 1981), par. 6; "Accounting for Sales of Real Estate," *Statement of Financial Accounting Standards No. 66*, pars. 62 and 63.

[36]An alternative format for computing the amount of gross profit recognized annually is shown below.

Year	Cash Received	Original Cost Recovered	Balance of Unrecovered Cost	Gross Profit Realized
Beginning balance	—	—	$25,000	—
12/31/07	$18,000	$18,000	7,000	$ –0–
12/31/08	12,000	7,000	–0–	5,000
12/31/09	6,000	–0–	–0–	6,000

Therefore, Fesmire's journal entry to record the deferred gross profit on the Higley sale transaction (after recording the sale and the cost of sale in the normal manner) at the end of 2007 is as follows.

2007

Sales	36,000	
Cost of Sales		25,000
Deferred Gross Profit		11,000
(To close sales and cost of sales and to record deferred gross profit on sales accounted for under the cost-recovery method)		

In 2008 and 2009, the deferred gross profit becomes realized gross profit as the cumulative cash collections exceed the total costs, by recording the following entries.

2008

Deferred Gross Profit	5,000	
Realized Gross Profit		5,000
(To recognize gross profit to the extent that cash collections in 2008 exceed costs)		

2009

Deferred Gross Profit	6,000	
Realized Gross Profit		6,000
(To recognize gross profit to the extent that cash collections in 2009 exceed costs)		

WHAT DO THE NUMBERS MEAN?

LIABILILTY OR REVENUE?

Suppose you purchased a gift card for spa services at Sundara Spa for $300. The gift card expires at the end of six months. When should Sundara record the revenue? Here are two choices:

1 At the time Sundara receives the cash for the gift card.

2 At the time Sundara provides the service to the gift-card holder.

If you answered number 2, you would be right. Companies should recognize revenue when the obligation is satisfied—which is when Sundara performs the service.

Now let's add a few more facts. Suppose that the gift-card holder fails to use the card in the six-month period. Statistics show that between 2 and 15 percent of gift-card holders never redeem their cards. So, do you still believe that Sundara should record the revenue at the expiration date?

If you say you are not sure, you are probably right. Here is why: Certain states (such as California) do not recognize expiration dates, and therefore the customer has the right to redeem an otherwise expired gift card at any time. Let's for the moment say we are in California. Because the card holder may never redeem, when can Sundara recognize the revenue? In that case Sundara would have to show statistically that after a certain period of time, the likelihood of redemption is remote. If it can make that case, it can recognize the revenue. Otherwise it may have to wait a long time.

Unfortunately Sundara may still have a problem. It may be required to turn over the value of the spa service to the state. The treatment for unclaimed gift cards may fall under the state abandoned-and-unclaimed-property laws. Most common unclaimed items are required to be remitted to the states after a five-year period. Failure to report and remit the property can result in additional fines and penalties. So if Sundara is in a state where unclaimed property must be sent to the state, Sundara should report a liability on its balance sheet.

Source: PricewaterhouseCoopers, "Issues Surrounding the Recognition of Gift Card Sales and Escheat Liabilities," *Quick Brief* (December 2004).

Deposit Method

In some cases, a company receives cash from the buyer before it transfers the goods or property. In such cases the seller has not performed under the contract and has no claim against the purchaser. There is not sufficient transfer of the risks and rewards of ownership for a sale to be recorded. The method of accounting for these incomplete transactions is the **deposit method**.

Under the deposit method the seller reports the cash received from the buyer as a deposit on the contract and classifies it on the balance sheet as a liability (refundable deposit or customer advance). The seller continues to report the property as an asset on its balance sheet, along with any related existing debt. Also, the seller continues to charge depreciation expense as a period cost for the property. **The seller does not recognize revenue or income until the sale is complete.**[37] At that time, it closes the deposit account and applies one of the revenue recognition methods discussed in this chapter to the sale.

The **major difference between the installment-sales and cost-recovery methods and the deposit method** relates to contract performance. In the installment-sales and cost-recovery methods it is assumed that the seller has performed on the contract, but cash collection is highly uncertain. In the deposit method, the seller has *not* performed and no legitimate claim exists. The deposit method postpones recognizing a sale until the company determines that a sale has occurred for accounting purposes. If there has not been sufficient transfer of risks and rewards of ownership, even if the selling company has received a deposit, the company postpones recognition of the sale until sufficient transfer has occurred. In that sense, the deposit method is not a revenue recognition method as are the installment-sales and cost-recovery methods.

Summary of Product Revenue Recognition Bases

Illustration 18-29 summarizes the revenue-recognition bases or methods, the criteria for their use, and the reasons for departing from the sale basis.[38]

ILLUSTRATION 18-29
Revenue Recognition Bases Other Than the Sale Basis for Products

Recognition Basis (or Method of Applying a Basis)	Criteria for Use	Reason(s) for Departing from Sale Basis
Percentage-of-completion method	Long-term construction of property; dependable estimates of extent of progress and cost to complete; reasonable assurance of collectibility of contract price; expectation that both contractor and buyer can meet obligations; and absence of inherent hazards that make estimates doubtful.	Availability of evidence of ultimate proceeds; better measure of periodic income; avoidance of fluctuations in revenues, expenses, and income; performance is a "continuous sale" and therefore not a departure from the sale basis.
Completed-contract method	Use on short-term contracts, and whenever percentage-of-completion cannot be used on long-term contracts.	Existence of inherent hazards in the contract beyond the normal, recurring business risks; conditions for using the percentage-of-completion method are absent.
Completion-of-production basis	Immediate marketability at quoted prices; unit interchangeability; and no significant distribution costs.	Known or determinable revenues; inability to determine costs and thereby defer expense recognition until sale.
Installment-sales method and cost-recovery method	Absence of reasonable basis for estimating degree of collectibility and costs of collection.	Collectibility of the receivable is so uncertain that gross profit (or income) is not recognized until cash is actually received.
Deposit method	Cash received before the sales transaction is completed.	No recognition of revenue and income because there is not sufficient transfer of the risks and rewards of ownership.

[37] *Statement of Financial Accounting Standards No. 66*, par. 65.

[38] Adapted from *Survey of Present Practices in Recognizing Revenues, Expenses, Gains, and Losses*, op. cit., pp. 12–13.

CONCLUDING REMARKS

As indicated, revenue recognition principles are sometimes difficult to apply and often vary by industry. Recently the SEC has attempted to provide more guidance in this area because of concern that the revenue recognition principle is sometimes being incorrectly applied. Many cases of intentional misstatement of revenue to achieve better financial results have recently come to light. Such practices are fraudulent, and the SEC is vigorously prosecuting these situations.

For our capital markets to be efficient, investors must have confidence that the financial information provided is both relevant and reliable. As a result, it is imperative that the accounting profession, regulators, and companies eliminate aggressive revenue recognition practices. It is our hope that recent efforts by the SEC and the accounting profession will lead to higher-quality reporting in this area.

INTERNATIONAL INSIGHT

There is no international enforcement body comparable to the U.S. SEC.

KEY TERMS

Billings account, *916*

completed-contract method, *912, 918*

completion-of-production basis, *922*

cost-recovery method, *931*

cost-to-cost basis, *913*

deposit method, *933*

earned revenues, *908*

high rate of returns, *910*

input measures, *913*

installment-sales method, *923*

output measures, *913*

percentage-of-completion method, *912, 913*

point of sale (delivery), *909*

realizable revenues, *908*

realized revenues, *908*

repossessions, *928*

revenue recognition principle, *907*

SUMMARY OF LEARNING OBJECTIVES

1. **Apply the revenue recognition principle.** The revenue recognition principle provides that a company should recognize revenue (1) when revenue is realized or realizable and (2) when it is earned. Revenues are realized when goods or services are exchanged for cash or claims to cash. Revenues are realizable when assets received in exchanges are readily convertible to known amounts of cash or claims to cash. Revenues are earned when a company has substantially accomplished what it must do to be entitled to the benefits represented by the revenues—that is, when the earnings process is complete or virtually complete.

2. **Describe accounting issues for revenue recognition at point of sale.** The two conditions for recognizing revenue are usually met by the time a company delivers products or merchandise or provides services to customers. Companies commonly recognize revenue from manufacturing and selling activities at time of sale. Problems of implementation can arise because of (1) sales with buyback agreements, (2) revenue recognition when right of return exists, and (3) trade loading and channel stuffing.

3. **Apply the percentage-of-completion method for long-term contracts.** To apply the percentage-of-completion method to long-term contracts, a company must have some basis for measuring the progress toward completion at particular interim dates. One of the most popular input measures used to determine the progress toward completion is the cost-to-cost basis. Using this basis, a company measures the percentage of completion by comparing costs incurred to date with the most recent estimate of the total costs to complete the contract. The company applies that percentage to the total revenue or the estimated total gross profit on the contract, to arrive at the amount of revenue or gross profit to be recognized to date.

4. **Apply the completed-contract method for long-term contracts.** Under this method, companies recognize revenue and gross profit only at point of sale—that is, when the company completes the contract. The company accumulates costs of long-term contracts in process and current billings. It makes no interim charges or credits to income statement accounts for revenues, costs, and gross profit. The annual entries to record costs of construction, progress billings, and collections from customers would be identical to those for the percentage-of-completion method—with the significant exclusion of the recognition of revenue and gross profit.

5. **Identify the proper accounting for losses on long-term contracts.** Two types of losses can become evident under long-term contracts: (1) *Loss in current period on a profitable contract*: Under the percentage-of-completion method only, the estimated cost increase requires a current-period adjustment of excess gross profit recognized on the project in prior periods. The company records this adjustment as a loss in the current period because it is a change in accounting estimate. (2) *Loss on an unprofitable contract*: Under

both the percentage-of-completion and the completed-contract methods, the company must recognize the entire expected contract loss in the current period.

6. Describe the installment-sales method of accounting. The installment-sales method recognizes income in the periods of collection rather than in the period of sale. The installment-sales method of accounting is justified on the basis that when there is no reasonable approach for estimating the degree of collectibility, a company should not recognize revenue until it has collected cash.

7. Explain the cost-recovery method of accounting. Under the cost-recovery method, companies do not recognize profit until cash payments by the buyer exceed the seller's cost of the merchandise sold. After the seller has recovered all costs, it includes in income any additional cash collections. The income statement for the period of sale reports sales revenue, the cost of goods sold, and the gross profit—both the amount recognized during the period and the amount deferred. The deferred gross profit is offset against the related receivable on the balance sheet. Subsequent income statements report the gross profit as a separate item of revenue when revenue is recognized as earned.

APPENDIX 18A

Revenue Recognition for Special Sales Transactions

To supplement our presentation of revenue recognition, in this appendix we cover two common yet unique types of business transactions—**franchises** and **consignments**.

FRANCHISES

OBJECTIVE 8
Explain revenue recognition for franchises and consignment sales.

As indicated throughout this chapter, companies recognize revenue on the basis of two criteria: (1) when it is realized or realizable (occurrence of an exchange for cash or claims to cash), and (2) when it is earned (completion or virtual completion of the earnings process). These criteria are appropriate for most business activities. For some sales transactions, though, they do not adequately define when a company should recognize revenue. The fast-growing franchise industry is of special concern and challenge.

In accounting for franchise sales, a company must analyze the transaction and, considering all the circumstances, use judgment in selecting one or more of the revenue recognition bases, and then possibly must monitor the situation over a long period of time.

Four types of franchising arrangements have evolved: (1) manufacturer-retailer, (2) manufacturer-wholesaler, (3) service sponsor-retailer, and (4) wholesaler-retailer. The fastest-growing category of franchising, and the one that caused a reexamination of appropriate accounting, has been the third category, **service sponsor-retailer**. Included in this category are such industries and businesses as:

Soft ice cream/frozen yogurt stores (**Tastee Freeze, TCBY, Dairy Queen**)
Food drive-ins (**McDonald's, KFC, Burger King**)
Restaurants (**TGI Friday's, Pizza Hut, Denny's**)

Motels (**Holiday Inn**, **Marriott**, **Best Western**)

Auto rentals (**Avis**, **Hertz**, **National**)

Others (**H & R Block**, **Meineke Mufflers**, **7-Eleven Stores**, **Kelly Services**)

Franchise companies derive their revenue from one or both of two sources: (1) from the sale of initial franchises and related assets or services, and (2) from continuing fees based on the operations of franchises. The **franchisor** (the party who grants business rights under the franchise) normally provides the **franchisee** (the party who operates the franchised business) with the following services.

1 Assistance in site selection: (a) analyzing location and (b) negotiating lease.

2 Evaluation of potential income.

3 Supervision of construction activity: (a) obtaining financing, (b) designing building, and (c) supervising contractor while building.

4 Assistance in the acquisition of signs, fixtures, and equipment.

5 Bookkeeping and advisory services: (a) setting up franchisee's records; (b) advising on income, real estate, and other taxes; and (c) advising on local regulations of the franchisee's business.

6 Employee and management training.

7 Quality control.

8 Advertising and promotion.[1]

In the past, it was standard practice for franchisors to recognize the entire franchise fee at the date of sale, whether the fee was received then or was collectible over a long period of time. Frequently, franchisors recorded the entire amount as revenue in the year of sale, even though many of the services were yet to be performed and uncertainty existed regarding the collection of the entire fee.[2] (In effect, the franchisors were counting their fried chickens before they were hatched.) However, a **franchise agreement** may provide for refunds to the franchisee if certain conditions are not met, and franchise fee profit can be reduced sharply by future costs of obligations and services to be rendered by the franchisor. To curb the abuses in revenue recognition that existed and to standardize the accounting and reporting practices in the franchise industry, the FASB issued *Statement No. 45*, which forms the basis for the accounting discussed below.

Initial Franchise Fees

The **initial franchise fee** is payment for establishing the franchise relationship and providing some initial services. Franchisors record initial franchise fees as revenue only when and as they make "substantial performance" of the services they are obligated to perform and when collection of the fee is reasonably assured. **Substantial performance** occurs when the franchisor has no remaining obligation to refund any cash received or excuse any nonpayment of a note and has performed all the initial services required under the contract. According to *SFAS No. 45* "commencement of operations by the franchisee shall be presumed to be the earliest point at which substantial performance has occurred, unless it can be demonstrated that substantial performance of all obligations, including services rendered voluntarily, has occurred before that time."[3]

---

[1]Archibald E. MacKay, "Accounting for Initial Franchise Fee Revenue," *The Journal of Accountancy* (January 1970), pp. 66–67.

[2]In 1987 and 1988 the SEC ordered a half-dozen fast-growing startup franchisors, including **Jiffy Lube International**, **Moto Photo, Inc.**, **Swensen's, Inc.**, and **LePeep Restaurants, Inc.**, to defer their initial franchise fee recognition until earned. See "Claiming Tomorrow's Profits Today," *Forbes* (October 17, 1988), p. 78.

[3]"Accounting for Franchise Fee Revenue," *Statement of Financial Accounting Standards No. 45* (Stamford, Conn.: FASB, 1981), par. 5.

Example of Entries for Initial Franchise Fee

To illustrate, assume that Tum's Pizza Inc. charges an initial franchise fee of $50,000 for the right to operate as a franchisee of Tum's Pizza. Of this amount, $10,000 is payable when the franchisee signs the agreement, and the balance is payable in five annual payments of $8,000 each. In return for the initial franchise fee, Tum's will help locate the site, negotiate the lease or purchase of the site, supervise the construction activity, and provide the bookkeeping services. The credit rating of the franchisee indicates that money can be borrowed at 8 percent. The present value of an ordinary annuity of five annual receipts of $8,000 each discounted at 8 percent is $31,941.68. The discount of $8,058.32 represents the interest revenue to be accrued by the franchisor over the payment period. The following examples show the entries that Tum's Pizza Inc. would make under various conditions.

1 If there is reasonable expectation that Tum's Pizza Inc. may refund the down payment and if substantial future services remain to be performed by Tum's Pizza Inc., the entry should be:

Cash	10,000.00	
Notes Receivable	40,000.00	
Discount on Notes Receivable		8,058.32
Unearned Franchise Fees		41,941.68

2 If the probability of refunding the initial franchise fee is extremely low, the amount of future services to be provided to the franchisee is minimal, collectibility of the note is reasonably assured, and substantial performance has occurred, the entry should be:

Cash	10,000.00	
Notes Receivable	40,000.00	
Discount on Notes Receivable		8,058.32
Revenue from Franchise Fees		41,941.68

3 If the initial down payment is not refundable, represents a fair measure of the services already provided, with a significant amount of services still to be performed by Tum's Pizza in future periods, and collectibility of the note is reasonably assured, the entry should be:

Cash	10,000.00	
Notes Receivable	40,000.00	
Discount on Notes Receivable		8,058.32
Revenue from Franchise Fees		10,000.00
Unearned Franchise Fees		31,941.68

4 If the initial down payment is not refundable and no future services are required by the franchisor, but collection of the note is so uncertain that recognition of the note as an asset is unwarranted, the entry should be:

Cash	10,000.00	
Revenue from Franchise Fees		10,000.00

5 Under the same conditions as those listed in case 4 above, except that the down payment is refundable or substantial services are yet to be performed, the entry should be:

Cash	10,000.00	
Unearned Franchise Fees		10,000.00

In cases 4 and 5—where collection of the note is extremely uncertain—franchisors may recognize cash collections using the installment-sales method or the cost-recovery method.[4]

[4]A study that compared four revenue recognition procedures—installment-sales basis, spreading recognition over the contract life, percentage-of-completion basis, and substantial performance—for franchise sales concluded that the percentage-of-completion method is the most acceptable revenue recognition method; the substantial-performance method was found sometimes to yield ultra-conservative results. See Charles H. Calhoun III, "Accounting for Initial Franchise Fees: Is It a Dead Issue?" *The Journal of Accountancy* (February 1975), pp. 60–67.

Continuing Franchise Fees

Continuing franchise fees are received in return for the continuing rights granted by the franchise agreement and for providing such services as management training, advertising and promotion, legal assistance, and other support. Franchisors report continuing fees as revenue when they are earned and receivable from the franchisee, unless a portion of them has been designated for a particular purpose, such as providing a specified amount for building maintenance or local advertising. In that case, the portion deferred shall be an amount sufficient to cover the estimated cost in excess of continuing franchise fees and provide a reasonable profit on the continuing services.

Bargain Purchases

In addition to paying continuing franchise fees, franchisees frequently purchase some or all of their equipment and supplies from the franchisor. The franchisor would account for these sales as it would for any other product sales.

Sometimes, however, the franchise agreement grants the franchisee the right to make **bargain purchases** of equipment or supplies after the franchisee has paid the initial franchise fee. If the bargain price is lower than the normal selling price of the same product, or if it does not provide the franchisor a reasonable profit, then the franchisor should defer a portion of the initial franchise fee. The franchisor would account for the deferred portion as an adjustment of the selling price when the franchisee subsequently purchases the equipment or supplies.

Options to Purchase

A franchise agreement may give the franchisor an **option to purchase** the franchisee's business. As a matter of management policy, the franchisor may reserve the right to purchase a profitable franchise outlet, or to purchase one that is in financial difficulty.

If it is **probable** at the time the option is given that the franchisor will ultimately purchase the outlet, then the franchisor should not recognize the initial franchise fee as revenue but should instead record it as a liability. When the franchisor exercises the option, the liability would reduce the franchisor's investment in the outlet.

Franchisor's Cost

Franchise accounting also involves proper accounting for the **franchisor's cost**. The objective is to match related costs and revenues by reporting them as components of income in the same accounting period. Franchisors should ordinarily defer **direct costs** (usually incremental costs) relating to specific franchise sales for which revenue has not yet been recognized. They should not, however, defer costs without reference to anticipated revenue and its realizability.[5] **Indirect costs** of a regular and recurring nature, such as selling and administrative expenses that are incurred irrespective of the level of franchise sales, should be expensed as incurred.

Disclosures of Franchisors

Franchisors must disclose all significant commitments and obligations resulting from franchise agreements, including a description of services that have not yet been substantially performed. They also should disclose any resolution of uncertainties regarding the collectibility of franchise fees. Franchisors segregate initial franchise fees from other franchise fee revenue if they are significant. Where possible, revenues and costs related to franchisor-owned outlets should be distinguished from those related to franchised outlets.

---

[5]"Accounting for Franchise Fee Revenue," p. 17.

CONSIGNMENTS

In some cases, manufacturers (or wholesalers) deliver goods but retain title to the goods until they are sold. This specialized method of marketing certain types of products makes use of a device known as a **consignment**. Under this arrangement, the **consignor** (manufacturer or wholesaler) ships merchandise to the **consignee** (dealer), who is to act as an agent for the consignor in selling the merchandise. Both consignor and consignee are interested in selling—the former to make a profit or develop a market, the latter to make a commission on the sale.

The consignee accepts the merchandise and agrees to exercise due diligence in caring for and selling it. The consignee remits to the consignor cash received from customers, after deducting a sales commission and any chargeable expenses.

In consignment sales, the consignor uses a modified version of the sale basis of revenue recognition. That is, the consignor recognizes revenue only after receiving notification of sale and the cash remittance from the consignee. The consignor carries the merchandise as inventory throughout the consignment, separately classified as Merchandise on Consignment. **The consignee does not record the merchandise as an asset on its books.** Upon sale of the merchandise, the consignee has **a liability for the net amount due the consignor**. The consignor periodically receives from the consignee a report called **account sales** that shows the merchandise received, merchandise sold, expenses chargeable to the consignment, and the cash remitted. Revenue is then recognized by the consignor.

To illustrate consignment accounting entries, assume that Nelba Manufacturing Co. ships merchandise costing $36,000 on consignment to Best Value Stores. Nelba pays $3,750 of freight costs, and Best Value pays $2,250 for local advertising costs that are reimbursable from Nelba. By the end of the period, Best Value has sold two-thirds of the consigned merchandise for $40,000 cash. Best Value notifies Nelba of the sales, retains a 10 percent commission, and remits the cash due Nelba. Illustration 18A-1 shows the journal entries of the consignor (Nelba) and the consignee (Best Value).

NELBA MFG. CO. (CONSIGNOR)			BEST VALUE STORES (CONSIGNEE)		
Shipment of consigned merchandise					
Inventory on Consignment	36,000		No entry (record memo of merchandise received).		
Finished Goods Inventory		36,000			
Payment of freight costs by consignor					
Inventory on Consignment	3,750		No entry.		
Cash		3,750			
Payment of advertising by consignee					
No entry until notified.			Receivable from Consignor	2,250	
			Cash		2,250
Sales of consigned merchandise					
No entry until notified.			Cash	40,000	
			Payable to Consignor		40,000
Notification of sales and expenses and remittance of amount due					
Cash	33,750		Payable to Consignor	40,000	
Advertising Expense	2,250		Receivable from		
Commission Expense	4,000		Consignor		2,250
Revenue from			Commission Revenue		4,000
Consignment Sales		40,000	Cash		33,750
Adjustment of inventory on consignment for cost of sales					
Cost of Goods Sold	26,500		No entry.		
Inventory on Consignment		26,500			
[2/3 ($36,000 + $3,750) = $26,500]					

ILLUSTRATION 18A-1
Entries for Consignment Sales

Under the consignment arrangement, the consignor accepts the risk that the merchandise might not sell and relieves the consignee of the need to commit part of its working capital to inventory. Companies use a variety of different systems and account titles to record consignments, but they all share the common goal of postponing the recognition of revenue until it is known that a sale to a third party has occurred.

KEY TERMS

account sales, *939*

consignee, *939*

consignment, *939*

consignor, *939*

continuing franchise fees, *938*

franchisee, *936*

franchisor, *936*

initial franchise fee, *936*

substantial performance, *936*

SUMMARY OF LEARNING OBJECTIVE FOR APPENDIX 18A

8. **Explain revenue recognition for franchises and consignment sales.** In a franchise arrangement, the franchisor records as revenue the initial franchise fee as it makes substantial performance of the services it is obligated to perform and collection of the fee is reasonably assured. Franchisors recognize continuing franchise fees as revenue when they are earned and receivable from the franchisee. In a consignment sale, the consignor recognizes revenue when it receives cash and notification of the sale from the consignee.

Note: All **asterisked** Questions, Brief Exercises, Exercises, and Concepts for Analysis relate to material contained in the appendix to the chapter.

QUESTIONS

1. Explain the current environment regarding revenue recognition.

2. When is revenue conventionally recognized? What conditions should exist for the recognition at date of sale of all or part of the revenue and income of any sale transaction?

3. When is revenue recognized in the following situations: (a) Revenue from selling products? (b) Revenue from services rendered? (c) Revenue from permitting others to use enterprise assets? (d) Revenue from disposing of assets other than products?

4. Identify several types of sales transactions and indicate the types of business for which that type of transaction is common.

5. What are the three alternative accounting methods available to a seller that is exposed to continued risks of ownership through return of the product?

6. Under what conditions may a seller who is exposed to continued risks of a high rate of return of the product sold recognize sales transactions as current revenue?

7. What are the two basic methods of accounting for long-term construction contracts? Indicate the circumstances that determine when one or the other of these methods should be used.

8. F. Scott Fitzgerald Construction Co. has a $60 million contract to construct a highway overpass and cloverleaf. The total estimated cost for the project is $50 million. Costs incurred in the first year of the project are $9 million. F. Scott Fitzgerald Construction Co. appropriately uses the percentage-of-completion method. How much revenue and gross profit should F. Scott Fitzgerald recognize in the first year of the project?

9. For what reasons should the percentage-of-completion method be used over the completed-contract method whenever possible?

10. What methods are used in practice to determine the extent of progress toward completion? Identify some "input measures" and some "output measures" that might be used to determine the extent of progress.

11. What are the two types of losses that can become evident in accounting for long-term contracts? What is the nature of each type of loss? How is each type accounted for?

12. Under the percentage-of-completion method, how are the Construction in Process and the Billings on Construction in Process accounts reported in the balance sheet?

13. Explain the differences between the installment-sales method and the cost-recovery method.

14. Identify and briefly describe the two methods generally employed to account for the cash received in situations where the collection of the sales price is not reasonably assured.

15. What is the deposit method and when might it be applied?

16. What is the nature of an installment sale? How do installment sales differ from ordinary credit sales?

17. Describe the installment-sales method of accounting.

18. How are operating expenses (not included in cost of goods sold) handled under the installment-sales method of accounting? What is the justification for such treatment?

19. J. K. Rowling sold her condominium for $500,000 on September 14, 2006; she had paid $310,000 for it in 1998. Rowling collected the selling price as follows: 2006, $80,000; 2007, $320,000; and 2008, $100,000. Rowling appropriately uses the installment-sales method. Prepare a schedule to determine the gross profit for 2006, 2007, and 2008 from the installment sale.

20. When interest is involved in installment-sales transactions, how should it be treated for accounting purposes?

21. How should the results of installment sales be reported on the income statement?

22. At what time is it proper to recognize income in the following cases: (a) Installment sales with no reasonable basis for estimating the degree of collectibility? (b) Sales for future delivery? (c) Merchandise shipped on consignment? (d) Profit on incomplete construction contracts? (e) Subscriptions to publications?

23. When is revenue recognized under the cost-recovery method?

24. When is revenue recognized under the deposit method? How does the deposit method differ from the installment-sales and cost-recovery methods?

*25. Why in franchise arrangements may it not be proper to recognize the entire franchise fee as revenue at the date of sale?

*26. How does the concept of "substantial performance" apply to accounting for franchise sales?

*27. How should a franchisor account for continuing franchise fees and routine sales of equipment and supplies to franchisees?

*28 What changes are made in the franchisor's recording of the initial franchise fee when the franchise agreement:

(a) Contains an option allowing the franchisor to purchase the franchised outlet, and it is likely that the option will be exercised?

(b) Allows the franchisee to purchase equipment and supplies from the franchisor at bargain prices?

*29 What is the nature of a sale on consignment? When is revenue recognized from a consignment sale?

BRIEF EXERCISES

(LO 1, 2) **BE18-1** Scooby Doo Music sold CDs to retailers and recorded sales revenue of $800,000. During 2008, retailers returned CDs to Scooby Doo and were granted credit of $78,000. Past experience indicates that the normal return rate is 15%. Prepare Scooby Doo's entries to record (a) the $78,000 of returns and (b) estimated returns at December 31, 2008.

(LO 3) **BE18-2** Shock Wave, Inc. began work on a $7,000,000 contract in 2008 to construct an office building. During 2008, Shock Wave, Inc. incurred costs of $1,715,000, billed their customers for $1,200,000, and collected $960,000. At December 31, 2008, the estimated future costs to complete the project total $3,185,000. Prepare Shock Wave's 2008 journal entries using the percentage-of-completion method.

(LO 3) **BE18-3** Shadow Blasters, Inc. began work on a $7,000,000 contract in 2008 to construct an office building. Shadow Blasters uses the percentage-of-completion method. At December 31, 2008, the balances in certain accounts were: construction in process $2,450,000; accounts receivable $240,000; and billings on construction in process $1,200,000. Indicate how these accounts would be reported in Shadow Blasters' December 31, 2008, balance sheet.

(LO 4) **BE18-4** Use the information from BE18-2, but assume Shock Wave uses the completed-contract method. Prepare the company's 2008 journal entries.

(LO 4) **BE18-5** Cordero, Inc. began work on a $7,000,000 contract in 2008 to construct an office building. Cordero uses the completed-contract method. At December 31, 2008, the balances in certain accounts were construction in process $1,715,000; accounts receivable $240,000; and billings on construction in process $1,200,000. Indicate how these accounts would be reported in Cordero's December 31, 2008, balance sheet.

(LO 5) **BE18-6** Jackie Chan Construction Company began work on a $420,000 construction contract in 2008. During 2008, Chan incurred costs of $288,000, billed its customer for $215,000, and collected $175,000. At December 31, 2008, the estimated future costs to complete the project total $162,000. Prepare Chan's journal entry to record profit or loss using (a) the percentage-of-completion method and (b) the completed-contract method, if any.

(LO 6) **BE18-7** Thunder Paradise Corporation began selling goods on the installment basis on January 1, 2008. During 2008, Thunder Paradise had installment sales of $150,000; cash collections of $54,000; cost of installment sales of $105,000. Prepare the company's entries to record installment sales, cash collected, cost of installment sales, deferral of gross profit, and gross profit recognized, using the installment-sales method.

(LO 6) **BE18-8** Buraka Inc. sells goods on the installment basis and uses the installment-sales method. Due to a customer default, Buraka repossessed merchandise that was originally sold for $800, resulting in a gross profit rate of 40%. At the time of repossession, the uncollected balance is $560, and the fair value of the repossessed merchandise is $275. Prepare Buraka's entry to record the repossession.

(LO 6) **BE18-9** At December 31, 2008, Soul Star Corporation had the following account balances.

Installment Accounts Receivable, 2007	$ 65,000
Installment Accounts Receivable, 2008	110,000
Deferred Gross Profit, 2007	23,400
Deferred Gross Profit, 2008	40,700

Most of Soul Star's sales are made on a 2-year installment basis. Indicate how these accounts would be reported in Soul Star's December 31, 2008, balance sheet. The 2007 accounts are collectible in 2009, and the 2008 accounts are collectible in 2010.

(LO 7) **BE18-10** Yogi Bear Corporation sold equipment to Magilla Company for $20,000. The equipment is on Yogi's books at a net amount of $14,000. Yogi collected $10,000 in 2007, $5,000 in 2008, and $5,000 in 2009. If Yogi uses the cost-recovery method, what amount of gross profit will be recognized in each year?

(LO 8) ***BE18-11** Speed Racer, Inc. charges an initial franchise fee of $75,000 for the right to operate as a franchisee of Speed Racer. Of this amount, $25,000 is collected immediately. The remainder is collected in 4 equal annual installments of $12,500 each. These installments have a present value of $39,623. There is reasonable expectation that the down payment may be refunded and substantial future services be performed by Speed Racer, Inc. Prepare the journal entry required by Speed Racer to record the franchise fee.

(LO 8) ***BE18-12** Tom and Jerry Corporation shipped $20,000 of merchandise on consignment to Toons Company. Tom and Jerry paid freight costs of $2,000. Toons Company paid $500 for local advertising which is reimbursable from Tom and Jerry. By year-end, 60% of the merchandise had been sold for $22,300. Toons notified Tom and Jerry, retained a 10% commission, and remitted the cash due to Tom and Jerry. Prepare Tom and Jerry's entry when the cash is received.

EXERCISES

(LO 1, 2) **E18-1** **(Revenue Recognition on Book Sales with High Returns)** Justin Huish Publishing Co. publishes college textbooks that are sold to bookstores on the following terms. Each title has a fixed wholesale price, terms f.o.b. shipping point, and payment is due 60 days after shipment. The retailer may return a maximum of 30% of an order at the retailer's expense. Sales are made only to retailers who have good credit ratings. Past experience indicates that the normal return rate is 12%, and the average collection period is 72 days.

Instructions
   (a) Identify alternative revenue recognition tests that Huish could employ concerning textbook sales.
   (b) Briefly discuss the reasoning for your answers in (a) above.
   (c) In late July, Huish shipped books invoiced at $16,000,000. Prepare the journal entry to record this event that best conforms to generally accepted accounting principles and your answer to part (b).
   (d) In October, $2 million of the invoiced July sales were returned according to the return policy, and the remaining $14 million was paid. Prepare the entries recording the return and payment.

(LO 1, 2) **E18-2** **(Sales Recorded Both Gross and Net)** On June 3, David Reid Company sold to Kim Rhode merchandise having a sale price of $5,000 with terms of 2/10, n/60, f.o.b. shipping point. An invoice totaling $120, terms n/30, was received by Rhode on June 8 from the Olympic Transport Service for the freight cost. Upon receipt of the goods, June 5, Rhode notified Reid Company that merchandise costing $400 contained flaws that rendered it worthless. The same day Reid Company issued a credit memo covering the worthless merchandise and asked that it be returned at company expense. The freight on the returned merchandise was $24, paid by Reid Company on June 7. On June 12, the company received a check for the balance due from Rhode.

Instructions
   (a) Prepare journal entries on Reid Company books to record all the events noted above under each of the following bases.
      (1) Sales and receivables are entered at gross selling price.
      (2) Sales and receivables are entered net of cash discounts.

(b) Prepare the journal entry under basis 2, assuming that Kim Rhode did not remit payment until August 5.

(LO 1, 2) **E18-3** **(Revenue Recognition on Marina Sales with Discounts)** Brooke Bennett Marina has 300 available slips that rent for $900 per season. Payments must be made in full at the start of the boating season, April 1, 2008. Slips for the next season may be reserved if paid for by December 31, 2008. Under a new policy, if payment is made by December 31, 2008, a 5% discount is allowed. The boating season ends October 31, and the marina has a December 31 year-end. To provide cash flow for major dock repairs, the marina operator is also offering a 25% discount to slip renters who pay for the 2009 season.

For the fiscal year ended December 31, 2007, all 300 slips were rented at full price. Two hundred slips were reserved and paid for for the 2008 boating season, and 60 slips were reserved and paid for for the 2009 boating season.

Instructions
(a) Prepare the appropriate journal entries for fiscal 2007.
(b) Assume the marina operator is unsophisticated in business. Explain the managerial significance of the accounting above to this person.

(LO 3, 4) **E18-4** **(Recognition of Profit on Long-Term Contracts)** During 2007 Pierson Company started a construction job with a contract price of $1,500,000. The job was completed in 2009. The following information is available.

	2007	2008	2009
Costs incurred to date	$400,000	$935,000	$1,070,000
Estimated costs to complete	600,000	165,000	–0–
Billings to date	300,000	900,000	1,500,000
Collections to date	270,000	810,000	1,425,000

Instructions
(a) Compute the amount of gross profit to be recognized each year assuming the percentage-of-completion method is used.
(b) Prepare all necessary journal entries for 2008.
(c) Compute the amount of gross profit to be recognized each year assuming the completed-contract method is used.

(LO 3) **E18-5** **(Analysis of Percentage-of-Completion Financial Statements)** In 2007, Beth Botsford Construction Corp. began construction work under a 3-year contract. The contract price was $1,000,000. Beth Botsford uses the percentage-of-completion method for financial accounting purposes. The income to be recognized each year is based on the proportion of cost incurred to total estimated costs for completing the contract. The financial statement presentations relating to this contract at December 31, 2007, follow.

Balance Sheet

Accounts receivable—construction contract billings		$21,500
Construction in progress	$65,000	
Less: Contract billings	61,500	
Cost of uncompleted contract in excess of billings		3,500

Income Statement

Income (before tax) on the contract recognized in 2007	$18,200

Instructions
(a) How much cash was collected in 2007 on this contract?
(b) What was the initial estimated total income before tax on this contract?

(AICPA adapted)

(LO 3) **E18-6** **(Gross Profit on Uncompleted Contract)** On April 1, 2007, Brad Bridgewater Inc. entered into a cost-plus-fixed-fee contract to construct an electric generator for Tom Dolan Corporation. At the contract date, Bridgewater estimated that it would take 2 years to complete the project at a cost of $2,000,000. The fixed fee stipulated in the contract is $450,000. Bridgewater appropriately accounts for this contract under the percentage-of-completion method. During 2007 Bridgewater incurred costs of $700,000 related to the project. The estimated cost at December 31, 2007, to complete the contract is $1,300,000. Dolan was billed $600,000 under the contract.

Instructions
Prepare a schedule to compute the amount of gross profit to be recognized by Bridgewater under the contract for the year ended December 31, 2007. Show supporting computations in good form.

(AICPA adapted)

(LO 3) **E18-7** **(Recognition of Profit, Percentage-of-Completion)** In 2007 Jeff Rouse Construction Company agreed to construct an apartment building at a price of $1,000,000. The information relating to the costs and billings for this contract is shown below.

	2007	2008	2009
Costs incurred to date	$280,000	$600,000	$ 785,000
Estimated costs yet to be incurred	520,000	200,000	–0–
Customer billings to date	150,000	400,000	1,000,000
Collection of billings to date	120,000	320,000	940,000

Instructions

(a) Assuming that the percentage-of-completion method is used, (1) compute the amount of gross profit to be recognized in 2007 and 2008, and (2) prepare journal entries for 2008.

(b) For 2008, show how the details related to this construction contract would be disclosed on the balance sheet and on the income statement.

(LO 3, 4) **E18-8** **(Recognition of Revenue on Long-Term Contract and Entries)** Amy Van Dyken Construction Company uses the percentage-of-completion method of accounting. In 2007, Van Dyken began work under contract #E2-D2, which provided for a contract price of $2,200,000. Other details follow:

	2007	2008
Costs incurred during the year	$ 480,000	$1,425,000
Estimated costs to complete, as of December 31	1,120,000	–0–
Billings during the year	420,000	1,680,000
Collections during the year	350,000	1,500,000

Instructions

(a) What portion of the total contract price would be recognized as revenue in 2007? In 2008?

(b) Assuming the same facts as those above except that Van Dyken uses the completed-contract method of accounting, what portion of the total contract price would be recognized as revenue in 2008?

(c) Prepare a complete set of journal entries for 2007 (using the percentage-of-completion method).

(LO 3, 4) **E18-9** **(Recognition of Profit and Balance Sheet Amounts for Long-Term Contracts)** Andre Agassi Construction Company began operations January 1, 2007. During the year, Andre Agassi Construction entered into a contract with Lindsey Davenport Corp. to construct a manufacturing facility. At that time, Agassi estimated that it would take 5 years to complete the facility at a total cost of $4,500,000. The total contract price for construction of the facility is $6,300,000. During the year, Agassi incurred $1,185,800 in construction costs related to the construction project. The estimated cost to complete the contract is $4,204,200. Lindsey Davenport Corp. was billed and paid 30% of the contract price.

Instructions

Prepare schedules to compute the amount of gross profit to be recognized for the year ended December 31, 2007, and the amount to be shown as "costs and recognized profit on uncompleted contract in excess of related billings" or "billings on uncompleted contract in excess of related costs and recognized profit" at December 31, 2007, under each of the following methods.

(a) Completed-contract method.

(b) Percentage-of-completion method.

Show supporting computations in good form.

(AICPA adapted)

(LO 4, 5) **E18-10** **(Long-Term Contract Reporting)** Derrick Adkins Construction Company began operations in 2007. Construction activity for the first year is shown below. All contracts are with different customers, and any work remaining at December 31, 2007, is expected to be completed in 2008.

Project	Total Contract Price	Billings through 12/31/07	Cash Collections through 12/31/07	Contract Costs Incurred through 12/31/07	Estimated Additional Costs to Complete
1	$ 560,000	$ 360,000	$340,000	$450,000	$140,000
2	670,000	220,000	210,000	126,000	504,000
3	500,000	500,000	440,000	330,000	–0–
	$1,730,000	$1,080,000	$990,000	$906,000	$644,000

Instructions

Prepare a partial income statement and balance sheet to indicate how the above information would be reported for financial statement purposes. Derrick Adkins Construction Company uses the completed-contract method.

(LO 6) **E18-11** **(Installment-Sales Method Calculations, Entries)** Austin Corporation appropriately uses the installment-sales method of accounting to recognize income in its financial statements. The following information is available for 2007 and 2008.

	2007	2008
Installment sales	$900,000	$1,000,000
Cost of installment sales	630,000	680,000
Cash collections on 2007 sales	370,000	350,000
Cash collections on 2008 sales	–0–	475,000

Instructions

(a) Compute the amount of realized gross profit recognized in each year.
(b) Prepare all journal entries required in 2008.

(LO 6) **E18-12** **(Analysis of Installment-Sales Accounts)** Charles Austin Co. appropriately uses the installment-sales method of accounting. On December 31, 2009, the books show balances as follows.

Installment Receivables		Deferred Gross Profit		Gross Profit on Sales	
2007	$11,000	2007	$ 7,000	2007	35%
2008	40,000	2008	26,000	2008	34%
2009	80,000	2009	95,000	2009	32%

Instructions

(a) Prepare the adjusting entry or entries required on December 31, 2009 to recognize 2009 realized gross profit. (Installment receivables have already been credited for cash receipts during 2009.)
(b) Compute the amount of cash collected in 2009 on accounts receivable each year.

(LO 6) **E18-13** **(Gross Profit Calculations and Repossessed Merchandise)** Barnes Corporation, which began business on January 1, 2007, appropriately uses the installment-sales method of accounting. The following data were obtained for the years 2007 and 2008.

	2007	2008
Installment sales	$750,000	$840,000
Cost of installment sales	525,000	604,800
General & administrative expenses	70,000	84,000
Cash collections on sales of 2007	310,000	300,000
Cash collections on sales of 2008	–0–	400,000

Instructions

(a) Compute the balance in the deferred gross profit accounts on December 31, 2007, and on December 31, 2008.
(b) A 2007 sale resulted in default in 2009. At the date of default, the balance on the installment receivable was $12,000, and the repossessed merchandise had a fair value of $8,000. Prepare the entry to record the repossession.

(AICPA adapted)

(LO 6) **E18-14** **(Interest Revenue from Installment Sale)** Gail Devers Corporation sells farm machinery on the installment plan. On July 1, 2007, Devers entered into an installment-sale contract with Gwen Torrence Inc. for a 10-year period. Equal annual payments under the installment sale are $100,000 and are due on July 1. The first payment was made on July 1, 2007.

Additional information

1. The amount that would be realized on an outright sale of similar farm machinery is $676,000.
2. The cost of the farm machinery sold to Gwen Torrence Inc. is $500,000.
3. The finance charges relating to the installment period are $324,000 based on a stated interest rate of 10%, which is appropriate.
4. Circumstances are such that the collection of the installments due under the contract is reasonably assured.

Instructions

What income or loss before income taxes should Devers record for the year ended December 31, 2007, as a result of the transaction above?

(AICPA adapted)

(LO 6, 7) **E18-15** **(Installment-Sales Method and Cost Recovery)** Kenny Corp., a capital goods manufacturing business that started on January 4, 2007, and operates on a calendar-year basis, uses the installment-sales method of profit recognition in accounting for all its sales. The following data were taken from the 2007 and 2008 records.

	2007	2008
Installment sales	$480,000	$620,000
Gross profit as a percent of costs	25%	28%
Cash collections on sales of 2007	$140,000	$240,000
Cash collections on sales of 2008	–0–	$180,000

The amounts given for cash collections exclude amounts collected for interest charges.

Instructions
(a) Compute the amount of realized gross profit to be recognized on the 2008 income statement, prepared using the installment-sales method.
(b) State where the balance of Deferred Gross Profit would be reported on the financial statements for 2008.
(c) Compute the amount of realized gross profit to be recognized on the income statement, prepared using the cost-recovery method.

(CIA adapted)

(LO 6, 7) **E18-16** **(Installment-Sales Method and Cost-Recovery Method)** On January 1, 2007, Barkly Company sold property for $200,000. The note will be collected as follows: $100,000 in 2007, $60,000 in 2008, and $40,000 in 2009. The property had cost Barkly $150,000 when it was purchased in 2005.

Instructions
(a) Compute the amount of gross profit realized each year, assuming Barkly uses the cost-recovery method.
(b) Compute the amount of gross profit realized each year, assuming Barkly uses the installment-sales method.

(LO 6) **E18-17** **(Installment Sales—Default and Repossession)** Michael Johnson Imports Inc. was involved in two default and repossession cases during the year:

1. A refrigerator was sold to Merlene Ottey for $1,800, including a 35% markup on selling price. Ottey made a down payment of 20%, four of the remaining 16 equal payments, and then defaulted on further payments. The refrigerator was repossessed, at which time the fair value was determined to be $800.

2. An oven that cost $1,200 was sold to Donovan Bailey for $1,600 on the installment basis. Bailey made a down payment of $240 and paid $80 a month for six months, after which he defaulted. The oven was repossessed and the estimated value at time of repossession was determined to be $750.

Instructions
Prepare journal entries to record each of these repossessions using a fair value approach. (Ignore interest charges.)

(LO 6) **E18-18** **(Installment Sales—Default and Repossession)** Kurt Angle Company uses the installment-sales method in accounting for its installment sales. On January 1, 2008, Angle Company had an installment account receivable from Kay Bluhm with a balance of $1,800. During 2008, $400 was collected from Bluhm. When no further collection could be made, the merchandise sold to Bluhm was repossessed. The merchandise had a fair market value of $650 after the company spent $60 for reconditioning of the merchandise. The merchandise was originally sold with a gross profit rate of 40%.

Instructions
Prepare the entries on the books of Angle Company to record all transactions related to Bluhm during 2008. (Ignore interest charges.)

(LO 8) ***E18-19** **(Franchise Entries)** Kendall Crossburgers Inc. charges an initial franchise fee of $70,000. Upon the signing of the agreement, a payment of $40,000 is due. Thereafter, three annual payments of $10,000 are required. The credit rating of the franchisee is such that it would have to pay interest at 10% to borrow money.

Instructions
Prepare the entries to record the initial franchise fee on the books of the franchisor under the following assumptions.
(a) The down payment is not refundable, no future services are required by the franchisor, and collection of the note is reasonably assured.

    (b) The franchisor has substantial services to perform, the down payment is refundable, and the collection of the note is very uncertain.

    (c) The down payment is not refundable, collection of the note is reasonably certain, the franchisor has yet to perform a substantial amount of services, and the down payment represents a fair measure of the services already performed.

(LO 8) ***E18-20** **(Franchise Fee, Initial Down Payment)** On January 1, 2007, Svetlana Masterkova signed an agreement to operate as a franchisee of Short-Track Inc. for an initial franchise fee of $50,000. The amount of $20,000 was paid when the agreement was signed, and the balance is payable in five annual payments of $6,000 each, beginning January 1, 2008. The agreement provides that the down payment is not refundable and that no future services are required of the franchisor. Svetlana Masterkova's credit rating indicates that she can borrow money at 11% for a loan of this type.

Instructions

    (a) How much should Short-Track record as revenue from franchise fees on January 1, 2007? At what amount should Svetlana record the acquisition cost of the franchise on January 1, 2007?

    (b) What entry would be made by Short-Track on January 1, 2007, if the down payment is refundable and substantial future services remain to be performed by Short-Track?

    (c) How much revenue from franchise fees would be recorded by Short-Track on January 1, 2007, if:

        (1) The initial down payment is not refundable, it represents a fair measure of the services already provided, a significant amount of services is still to be performed by Short-Track in future periods, and collectibility of the note is reasonably assured?

        (2) The initial down payment is not refundable and no future services are required by the franchisor, but collection of the note is so uncertain that recognition of the note as an asset is unwarranted?

        (3) The initial down payment has not been earned and collection of the note is so uncertain that recognition of the note as an asset is unwarranted?

(LO 8) ***E18-21** **(Consignment Computations)** On May 3, 2007, Michelle Smith Company consigned 70 freezers, costing $500 each, to Angel Martino Company. The cost of shipping the freezers amounted to $840 and was paid by Smith Company. On December 30, 2007, an account sales was received from the consignee, reporting that 40 freezers had been sold for $700 each. Remittance was made by the consignee for the amount due, after deducting a commission of 6%, advertising of $200, and total installation costs of $320 on the freezers sold.

Instructions

    (a) Compute the inventory value of the units unsold in the hands of the consignee.

    (b) Compute the profit for the consignor for the units sold.

    (c) Compute the amount of cash that will be remitted by the consignee.

> **See the book's website, www.wiley.com/college/kieso, for Additional Exercises.**

PROBLEMS

(LO 2, 3, 4, 6) **P18-1** **(Comprehensive Three-Part Revenue Recognition)** Simona Amanar Industries has three operating divisions—Gina Construction Division, Gogean Publishing Division, and Chorkina Securities Division. Each division maintains its own accounting system and method of revenue recognition.

Gina Construction Division

During the fiscal year ended November 30, 2007, Gina Construction Division had one construction project in process. A $30,000,000 contract for construction of a civic center was granted on June 19, 2007, and construction began on August 1, 2007. Estimated costs of completion at the contract date were $25,000,000 over a 2-year time period from the date of the contract. On November 30, 2007, construction costs of $7,800,000 had been incurred and progress billings of $9,500,000 had been made. The construction costs to complete the remainder of the project were reviewed on November 30, 2007, and were estimated to amount to only $16,200,000 because of an expected decline in raw materials costs. Revenue recognition is based upon a percentage-of-completion method.

Gogean Publishing Division

The Gogean Publishing Division sells large volumes of novels to a few book distributors, which in turn sell to several national chains of bookstores. Gogean allows distributors to return up to 30% of sales, and distributors give the same terms to bookstores. While returns from individual titles fluctuate greatly, the returns from distributors have averaged 20% in each of the past 5 years. A total of $8,000,000 of paperback novel sales were made to distributors during fiscal 2007. On November 30, 2007, $2,500,000 of fiscal 2007 sales were still subject to return privileges over the next 6 months. The remaining $5,500,000 of fiscal 2007 sales had actual returns of 21%. Sales from fiscal 2006 totaling $2,000,000 were collected in fiscal 2007 less 18% returns. This division records revenue according to the method referred to as revenue recognition when the right of return exists.

Chorkina Securities Division

Chorkina Securities Division works through manufacturers' agents in various cities. Orders for alarm systems and down payments are forwarded from agents, and the Division ships the goods f.o.b. factory directly to customers (usually police departments and security guard companies). Customers are billed directly for the balance due plus actual shipping costs. The company received orders for $6,000,000 of goods during the fiscal year ended November 30, 2007. Down payments of $600,000 were received, and $5,200,000 of goods were billed and shipped. Actual freight costs of $100,000 were also billed. Commissions of 10% on product price are paid to manufacturing agents after goods are shipped to customers. Such goods are warranted for 90 days after shipment, and warranty returns have been about 1% of sales. Revenue is recognized at the point of sale by this division.

Instructions

(a) There are a variety of methods of revenue recognition. Define and describe each of the following methods of revenue recognition, and indicate whether each is in accordance with generally accepted accounting principles.

    (1) Point of sale.

    (2) Completion-of-production.

    (3) Percentage-of-completion.

    (4) Installment-sales contract.

(b) Compute the revenue to be recognized in fiscal year 2007 for each of the three operating divisions of Simona Amanar Industries in accordance with generally accepted accounting principles.

(LO 3, 4)   **P18-2**   **(Recognition of Profit on Long-Term Contract)**   Jenny Thompson Construction Company has entered into a contract beginning January 1, 2007, to build a parking complex. It has been estimated that the complex will cost $600,000 and will take 3 years to construct. The complex will be billed to the purchasing company at $900,000. The following data pertain to the construction period.

	2007	2008	2009
Costs to date	$270,000	$420,000	$600,000
Estimated costs to complete	330,000	180,000	–0–
Progress billings to date	270,000	550,000	900,000
Cash collected to date	240,000	500,000	900,000

Instructions

(a) Using the percentage-of-completion method, compute the estimated gross profit that would be recognized during each year of the construction period.

(b) Using the completed-contract method, compute the estimated gross profit that would be recognized during each year of the construction period.

(LO 3, 4)   **P18-3**   **(Recognition of Profit and Entries on Long-Term Contract)**   On March 1, 2007, Winter Company entered into a contract to build an apartment building. It is estimated that the building will cost $2,000,000 and will take 3 years to complete. The contract price was $3,000,000. The following information pertains to the construction period.

	2007	2008	2009
Costs to date	$ 600,000	$1,560,000	$2,100,000
Estimated costs to complete	1,400,000	390,000	–0–
Progress billings to date	1,050,000	2,100,000	3,000,000
Cash collected to date	950,000	1,950,000	2,750,000

Instructions

(a) Compute the amount of gross profit to be recognized each year assuming the percentage-of-completion method is used.

(b) Prepare all necessary journal entries for 2009.

(c) Prepare a partial balance sheet for December 31, 2008, showing the balances in the receivables and inventory accounts.

(LO 3) **P18-4** **(Recognition of Profit and Balance Sheet Presentation, Percentage-of-Completion)** On February 1, 2007, Amanda Berg Construction Company obtained a contract to build an athletic stadium. The stadium was to be built at a total cost of $5,400,000 and was scheduled for completion by September 1, 2009. One clause of the contract stated that Berg was to deduct $15,000 from the $6,600,000 billing price for each week that completion was delayed. Completion was delayed 6 weeks, which resulted in a $90,000 penalty. Below are the data pertaining to the construction period.

	2007	2008	2009
Costs to date	$1,782,000	$3,850,000	$5,500,000
Estimated costs to complete	3,618,000	1,650,000	–0–
Progress billings to date	1,200,000	3,100,000	6,510,000
Cash collected to date	1,000,000	2,800,000	6,510,000

Instructions

(a) Using the percentage-of-completion method, compute the estimated gross profit recognized in the years 2007–2009.

(b) Prepare a partial balance sheet for December 31, 2008, showing the balances in the receivable and inventory accounts.

(LO 3, 4, 5) **P18-5** **(Completed Contract and Percentage of Completion with Interim Loss)** Gold Medal Custom Builders (GMCB) was established in 1985 by Whitney Hedgepeth and initially built high-quality customized homes under contract with specific buyers. In the 1990s, Hedgepeth's two sons joined the firm and expanded GMCB's activities into the high-rise apartment and industrial plant markets. Upon the retirement of GMCB's long-time financial manager, Hedgepeth's sons recently hired Le Jingyi as controller for GMCB. Jingyi, a former college friend of Hedgepeth's sons, has been associated with a public accounting firm for the last 6 years.

Upon reviewing GMCB's accounting practices, Jingyi observed that GMCB followed the completed-contract method of revenue recognition, a carryover from the years when individual home building was the majority of GMCB's operations. Several years ago, the predominant portion of GMCB's activities shifted to the high-rise and industrial building areas. From land acquisition to the completion of construction, most building contracts cover several years. Under the circumstances, Jingyi believes that GMCB should follow the percentage-of-completion method of accounting. From a typical building contract, Jingyi developed the following data.

DAGMAR HAZE TRACTOR PLANT

Contract price: $8,000,000

	2006	2007	2008
Estimated costs	$2,010,000	$3,015,000	$1,675,000
Progress billings	1,000,000	2,500,000	4,500,000
Cash collections	800,000	2,300,000	4,900,000

Instructions

(a) Explain the difference between completed-contract revenue recognition and percentage-of-completion revenue recognition.

(b) Using the data provided for the Dagmar Haze Tractor Plant and assuming the percentage-of-completion method of revenue recognition is used, calculate GMCB's revenue and gross profit for 2006, 2007, and 2008, under **each** of the following circumstances.

  (1) Assume that all costs are incurred, all billings to customers are made, and all collections from customers are received within 30 days of billing, as planned.

  (2) Further assume that, as a result of unforeseen local ordinances and the fact that the building site was in a wetlands area, GMCB experienced cost overruns of $800,000 in 2006 to bring the site into compliance with the ordinances and to overcome wetlands barriers to construction.

  (3) Further assume that, in addition to the cost overruns of $800,000 for this contract incurred under part (b)2, inflationary factors over and above those anticipated in the development of the original contract cost have caused an additional cost overrun of $540,000 in 2007. It is not anticipated that any cost overruns will occur in 2008.

(CMA adapted)

(LO 3, 4, 5) **P18-6** **(Long-Term Contract with Interim Loss)** On March 1, 2007, Franziska van Almsick Construction Company contracted to construct a factory building for Sandra Volker Manufacturing Inc. for a total contract price of $8,400,000. The building was completed by October 31, 2009. The annual contract costs incurred, estimated costs to complete the contract, and accumulated billings to Volker for 2007, 2008, and 2009 are given on the next page.

	2007	2008	2009
Contract costs incurred during the year	$3,200,000	$2,600,000	$1,450,000
Estimated costs to complete the contract at 12/31	3,200,000	1,450,000	–0–
Billings to Volker during the year	3,200,000	3,500,000	1,700,000

Instructions

(a) Using the percentage-of-completion method, prepare schedules to compute the profit or loss to be recognized as a result of this contract for the years ended December 31, 2007, 2008, and 2009. (Ignore income taxes.)

(b) Using the completed-contract method, prepare schedules to compute the profit or loss to be recognized as a result of this contract for the years ended December 2007, 2008, and 2009. (Ignore incomes taxes.)

(LO 3, 4, 5) **P18-7** **(Long-Term Contract with an Overall Loss)** On July 1, 2007, Kyung-wook Construction Company Inc. contracted to build an office building for Mingxia Corp. for a total contract price of $1,950,000. On July 1, Kyung-wook estimated that it would take between 2 and 3 years to complete the building. On December 31, 2009, the building was deemed substantially completed. Following are accumulated contract costs incurred, estimated costs to complete the contract, and accumulated billings to Mingxia for 2007, 2008, and 2009.

	At 12/31/07	At 12/31/08	At 12/31/09
Contract costs incurred to date	$ 150,000	$1,200,000	$2,100,000
Estimated costs to complete the contract	1,350,000	800,000	–0–
Billings to Mingxia	300,000	1,100,000	1,850,000

Instructions

(a) Using the percentage-of-completion method, prepare schedules to compute the profit or loss to be recognized as a result of this contract for the years ended December 31, 2007, 2008, and 2009. (Ignore income taxes.)

(b) Using the completed-contract method, prepare schedules to compute the profit or loss to be recognized as a result of this contract for the years ended December 2007, 2008, and 2009. (Ignore income taxes.)

(LO 6) **P18-8** **(Installment-Sales Computations and Entries)** Presented below is summarized information for Deng Yaping Co., which sells merchandise on the installment basis.

	2007	2008	2009
Sales (on installment plan)	$250,000	$260,000	$280,000
Cost of sales	150,000	163,800	182,000
Gross profit	$100,000	$ 96,200	$ 98,000
Collections from customers on:			
2007 installment sales	$ 75,000	$100,000	$ 50,000
2008 installment sales		100,000	120,000
2009 installment sales			110,000

Instructions

(a) Compute the realized gross profit for each of the years 2007, 2008, and 2009.

(b) Prepare in journal form all entries required in 2009, applying the installment-sales method of accounting. (Ignore interest charges.)

(LO 6) **P18-9** **(Installment-Sales Income Statements)** Laura Flessel Stores sells merchandise on open account as well as on installment terms.

	2007	2008	2009
Sales on account	$385,000	$426,000	$525,000
Installment sales	320,000	275,000	380,000
Collections on installment sales			
Made in 2007	110,000	90,000	40,000
Made in 2008		110,000	140,000
Made in 2009			125,000
Cost of sales			
Sold on account	270,000	277,000	341,000
Sold on installment	214,400	167,750	224,200
Selling expenses	77,000	87,000	92,000
Administrative expenses	50,000	51,000	52,000

Instructions

From the data above, which cover the 3 years since Laura Flessel Stores commenced operations, determine the net income for each year, applying the installment-sales method of accounting. (Ignore interest charges.)

(LO 6) **P18-10** **(Installment-Sales Computations and Entries)** Isabell Werth Stores sell appliances for cash and also on the installment plan. Entries to record cost of sales are made monthly.

ISABELL WERTH STORES
TRIAL BALANCE
DECEMBER 31, 2009

	Dr.	Cr.
Cash	$153,000	
Installment Accounts Receivable, 2008	48,000	
Installment Accounts Receivable, 2009	91,000	
Inventory—New Merchandise	123,200	
Inventory—Repossessed Merchandise	24,000	
Accounts Payable		$ 98,500
Deferred Gross Profit, 2008		45,600
Capital Stock		170,000
Retained Earnings		93,900
Sales		343,000
Installment Sales		200,000
Cost of Sales	255,000	
Cost of Installment Sales	128,000	
Loss on Repossessions	800	
Selling and Administrative Expenses	128,000	
	$951,000	$951,000

The accounting department has prepared the following analysis of cash receipts for the year.

Cash sales (including repossessed merchandise)	$424,000
Installment accounts receivable, 2008	104,000
Installment accounts receivable, 2009	109,000
Other	36,000
Total	$673,000

Repossessions recorded during the year are summarized as follows.

	2008
Uncollected balance	$8,000
Loss on repossession	800
Repossessed merchandise	4,800

Instructions

From the trial balance and accompanying information:
- **(a)** Compute the rate of gross profit for 2008 and 2009.
- **(b)** Prepare closing entries as of December 31, 2009, under the installment-sales method of accounting.
- **(c)** Prepare an income statement for the year ended December 31, 2009. Include only the realized gross profit in the income statement.

(LO 6) **P18-11** **(Installment-Sales Entries)** The following summarized information relates to the installment-sales activity of Lisa Jacob Stores Inc. for the year 2007.

Installment sales during 2007	$500,000
Cost of goods sold on installment basis	330,000
Collections from customers	200,000
Unpaid balances on merchandise repossessed	24,000
Estimated value of merchandise repossessed	9,200

Instructions

- **(a)** Prepare journal entries at the end of 2007 to record on the books of Lisa Jacob Stores, Inc. the summarized data above.
- **(b)** Prepare the entry to record the gross profit realized during 2007.

(LO 6) **P18-12** **(Installment-Sales Computation and Entries—Periodic Inventory)** Catherine Fox Inc. sells merchandise for cash and also on the installment plan. Entries to record cost of goods sold are made at the end of each year.

Repossessions of merchandise (sold in 2008) were made in 2009 and were recorded correctly as follows.

Deferred Gross Profit, 2008	7,200	
Repossessed Merchandise	8,000	
Loss on Repossessions	2,800	
Installment Accounts Receivable, 2008		18,000

Part of this repossessed merchandise was sold for cash during 2009, and the sale was recorded by a debit to Cash and a credit to Sales.

The inventory of repossessed merchandise on hand December 31, 2009, is $4,000; of new merchandise, $127,400. There was no repossessed merchandise on hand January 1, 2009.

Collections on accounts receivable during 2009 were:

Installment Accounts Receivable, 2008	$80,000
Installment Accounts Receivable, 2009	50,000

The cost of the merchandise sold under the installment plan during 2009 was $117,000.

The rate of gross profit on 2008 and on 2009 installment sales can be computed from the information given.

CATHERINE FOX INC.
TRIAL BALANCE
DECEMBER 31, 2009

	Dr.	Cr.
Cash	$ 98,400	
Installment Accounts Receivable, 2008	80,000	
Installment Accounts Receivable, 2009	130,000	
Inventory, Jan. 1, 2009	120,000	
Repossessed Merchandise	8,000	
Accounts Payable		$ 47,200
Deferred Gross Profit, 2008		64,000
Capital Stock, Common		200,000
Retained Earnings		40,000
Sales		400,000
Installment Sales		180,000
Purchases	380,000	
Loss on Repossessions	2,800	
Operating Expenses	112,000	
	$931,200	$931,200

Instructions

(a) From the trial balance and other information given above, prepare adjusting and closing entries as of December 31, 2009.

(b) Prepare an income statement for the year ended December 31, 2009. Include only the realized gross profit in the income statement.

(LO 6) **P18-13** **(Installment Repossession Entries)** Selected transactions of TV Lenny Company are presented below.

1. A television set costing $560 is sold to Mark Prior on November 1, 2008, for $800. Prior makes a down payment of $200 and agrees to pay $30 on the first of each month for 20 months thereafter.
2. Prior pays the $30 installment due December 1, 2008.
3. On December 31, 2008, the appropriate entries are made to record profit realized on the installment sales.
4. The first seven 2009 installments of $30 each are paid by Prior. (Make one entry.)
5. In August 2009 the set is repossessed, after Prior fails to pay the August 1 installment and indicates that he will be unable to continue the payments. The estimated fair value of the repossessed set is $100.

Instructions

Prepare journal entries to record the transactions above on the books of TV Lenny Company. Closing entries should not be made.

(LO 6) **P18-14** **(Installment-Sales Computations and Schedules)** Zambrano Company, on January 2, 2007, entered into a contract with a manufacturing company to purchase room-size air conditioners and to sell the units on an installment plan with collections over approximately 30 months with no carrying charge.

For income tax purposes Zambrano Company elected to report income from its sales of air conditioners according to the installment-sales method.

Purchases and sales of new units were as follows.

	Units Purchased		Units Sold	
Year	Quantity	Price Each	Quantity	Price Each
2007	1,400	$130	1,100	$200
2008	1,200	112	1,500	170
2009	900	136	800	182

Collections on installment sales were as follows.

	Collections Received		
	2007	2008	2009
2007 sales	$42,000	$88,000	$ 80,000
2008 sales		51,000	100,000
2009 sales			34,600

In 2009, 50 units from the 2008 sales were repossessed and sold for $80 each on the installment plan. At the time of repossession, $1,440 had been collected from the original purchasers, and the units had a fair value of $3,000.

General and administrative expenses for 2009 were $60,000. No charge has been made against current income for the applicable insurance expense from a 3-year policy expiring June 30, 2010, costing $7,200, and for an advance payment of $12,000 on a new contract to purchase air conditioners beginning January 2, 2010.

Instructions

Assuming that the weighted-average method is used for determining the inventory cost, including repossessed merchandise, prepare schedules computing for 2007, 2008, and 2009:

(a) (1) The cost of goods sold on installments.
   (2) The average unit cost of goods sold on installments for each year.
(b) The gross profit percentages for 2007, 2008, and 2009.
(c) The gain or loss on repossessions in 2009.
(d) The net income from installment sales for 2009. (Ignore income taxes.)

(AICPA adapted)

(LO 4, 5) **P18-15 (Completed-Contract Method)** Mauer Construction Company, Inc., entered into a firm fixed-price contract with Trillini Clinic on July 1, 2005, to construct a four-story office building. At that time, Mauer estimated that it would take between 2 and 3 years to complete the project. The total contract price for construction of the building is $4,500,000. Mauer appropriately accounts for this contract under the completed-contract method in its financial statements and for income tax reporting. The building was deemed substantially completed on December 31, 2007. Estimated percentage of completion, accumulated contract costs incurred, estimated costs to complete the contract, and accumulated billings to the Trillini Clinic under the contract are shown below.

	At December 31, 2005	At December 31, 2006	At December 31, 2007
Percentage of completion	30%	65%	100%
Contract costs incurred	$1,140,000	$3,055,000	$4,800,000
Estimated costs to complete the contract	$2,660,000	$1,645,000	–0–
Billings to Trillini Clinic	$1,500,000	$2,500,000	$4,300,000

Instructions

(a) Prepare schedules to compute the amount to be shown as "Cost of uncompleted contract in excess of related billings" or "Billings on uncompleted contract in excess of related costs" at December 31, 2005, 2006, and 2007. Ignore income taxes. Show supporting computations in good form.
(b) Prepare schedules to compute the profit or loss to be recognized as a result of this contract for the years ended December 31, 2005, 2006, and 2007. Ignore income taxes. Show supporting computations in good form.

(AICPA adapted)

(LO 3, 4) **P18-16 (Revenue Recognition Methods—Comparison)** Joy's Construction is in its fourth year of business. Joy performs long-term construction projects and accounts for them using the completed-contract method. Joy built an apartment building at a price of $1,000,000. The costs and billings for this contract for the first three years are as follows.

	2006	2007	2008
Costs incurred to date	$320,000	$600,000	$ 790,000
Estimated costs yet to be incurred	480,000	200,000	–0–
Customer billings to date	150,000	410,000	1,000,000
Collection of billings to date	120,000	340,000	950,000

Joy has contacted you, a certified public accountant, about the following concern. She would like to attract some investors, but she believes that in order to recognize revenue she must first "deliver" the product. Therefore, on her balance sheet, she did not recognize any gross profits from the above contract until 2008, when she recognized the entire $210,000. That looked good for 2008, but the preceding years looked grim by comparison. She wants to know about an alternative to this completed-contract revenue recognition.

Instructions

Draft a letter to Joy, telling her about the percentage-of-completion method of recognizing revenue. Compare it to the completed-contract method. Explain the idea behind the percentage-of-completion method. In addition, illustrate how much revenue she could have recognized in 2006, 2007, and 2008 if she had used this method.

(LO 3, 4) **P18-17** **(Comprehensive Problem—Long-Term Contracts)** You have been engaged by Bo Ryan Construction Company to advise it concerning the proper accounting for a series of long-term contracts. Ryan commenced doing business on January 1, 2007. Construction activities for the first year of operations are shown below. All contract costs are with different customers, and any work remaining at December 31, 2007, is expected to be completed in 2008.

Project	Total Contract Price	Billings Through 12/31/07	Cash Collections Through 12/31/07	Contract Costs Incurred Through 12/31/07	Estimated Additional Costs to Complete
A	$ 300,000	$200,000	$180,000	$248,000	$ 67,000
B	350,000	110,000	105,000	67,800	271,200
C	280,000	280,000	255,000	186,000	–0–
D	200,000	35,000	25,000	123,000	87,000
E	240,000	205,000	200,000	185,000	15,000
	$1,370,000	$830,000	$765,000	$809,800	$440,200

Instructions

(a) Prepare a schedule to compute gross profit (loss) to be reported, unbilled contract costs and recognized profit, and billings in excess of costs and recognized profit using the percentage-of-completion method.

(b) Prepare a partial income statement and balance sheet to indicate how the information would be reported for financial statement purposes.

(c) Repeat the requirements for part (a) assuming Ryan uses the completed-contract method.

(d) Using the responses above for illustrative purposes, prepare a brief report comparing the conceptual merits (both positive and negative) of the two revenue recognition approaches.

CONCEPTS FOR ANALYSIS

CA18-1 **(Revenue Recognition—Alternative Methods)** Alexsandra Isosev Industries has three operating divisions—Falilat Mining, Mourning Paperbacks, and Osygus Protection Devices. Each division maintains its own accounting system and method of revenue recognition.

Falilat Mining

Falilat Mining specializes in the extraction of precious metals such as silver, gold, and platinum. During the fiscal year ended November 30, 2007, Falilat entered into contracts worth $2,250,000 and shipped metals worth $2,000,000. A quarter of the shipments were made from inventories on hand at the beginning of the fiscal year, and the remainder were made from metals that were mined during the year. Mining totals for the year, valued at market prices, were: silver at $750,000, gold at $1,300,000, and platinum at $490,000. Falilat uses the completion-of-production method to recognize revenue, because its operations meet the specified criteria—i.e., reasonably assured sales prices, interchangeable units, and insignificant distribution costs.

Mourning Paperbacks

Mourning Paperbacks sells large quantities of novels to a few book distributors that in turn sell to several national chains of bookstores. Mourning allows distributors to return up to 30% of sales, and distributors give the same terms to bookstores. While returns from individual titles fluctuate greatly, the returns from distributors have averaged 20% in each of the past 5 years. A total of $8,000,000 of paperback novel sales were made to distributors during the fiscal year. On November 30, 2007, $3,200,000 of fiscal 2007 sales were still subject to return privileges over the next 6 months. The remaining $4,800,000 of fiscal 2007 sales had actual returns of 21%. Sales from fiscal 2006 totaling $2,500,000 were collected in fiscal 2007, with less than 18% of sales returned. Mourning records revenue according to the method referred to as revenue recognition when the right of return exits, because all applicable criteria for use of this method are met by Mourning's operations.

Osygus Protection Devices

Osygus Protection Devices works through manufacturers' agents in various cities. Orders for alarm systems and down payments are forwarded from agents, and Osygus ships the goods f.o.b. shipping point. Customers are billed for the balance due plus actual shipping costs. The firm received orders for $6,000,000 of goods during the fiscal year ended November 30, 2007. Down payments of $600,000 were received, and $5,000,000 of goods were billed and shipped. Actual freight costs of $100,000 were also billed. Commissions of 10% on product price were paid to manufacturers' agents after the goods were shipped to customers. Such goods are warranted for 90 days after shipment, and warranty returns have been about 1% of sales. Revenue is recognized at the point of sale by Osygus.

Instructions

(a) There are a variety of methods for revenue recognition. Define and describe each of the following methods of revenue recognition, and indicate whether each is in accordance with generally accepted accounting principles.
   (1) Completion-of-production method.
   (2) Percentage-of-completion method.
   (3) Installment-sales method.

(b) Compute the revenue to be recognized in the fiscal year ended November 30, 2007, for
   (1) Falilat Mining.
   (2) Mourning Paperbacks.
   (3) Osygus Protection Devices.

(CMA adapted)

CA18-2 (Recognition of Revenue—Theory) Revenue is usually recognized at the point of sale. Under special circumstances, however, bases other than the point of sale are used for the timing of revenue recognition.

Instructions

(a) Why is the point of sale usually used as the basis for the timing of revenue recognition?

(b) Disregarding the special circumstances when bases other than the point of sale are used, discuss the merits of each of the following objections to the sales basis of revenue recognition:
   (1) It is too conservative because revenue is earned throughout the entire process of production.
   (2) It is not conservative enough because accounts receivable do not represent disposable funds, sales returns and allowances may be made, and collection and bad debt expenses may be incurred in a later period.

(c) Revenue may also be recognized (1) during production and (2) when cash is received. For each of these two bases of timing revenue recognition, give an example of the circumstances in which it is properly used and discuss the accounting merits of its use in lieu of the sales basis.

(AICPA adapted)

CA18-3 (Recognition of Revenue—Theory) The earning of revenue by a business enterprise is recognized for accounting purposes when the transaction is recorded. In some situations, revenue is recognized approximately as it is earned in the economic sense. In other situations, however, accountants have developed guidelines for recognizing revenue by other criteria, such as at the point of sale.

Instructions

(Ignore income taxes.)

(a) Explain and justify why revenue is often recognized as earned at time of sale.

(b) Explain in what situations it would be appropriate to recognize revenue as the productive activity takes place.

(c)   At what times, other than those included in (a) and (b) above, may it be appropriate to recognize revenue? Explain.

CA18-4   (Recognition of Revenue—Bonus Dollars)   Alexei & Nemov Inc. was formed early this year to sell merchandise credits to merchants who distribute the credits free to their customers. For example, customers can earn additional credits based on the dollars they spend with a merchant (e.g., airlines and hotels). Accounts for accumulating the credits and catalogs illustrating the merchandise for which the credits may be exchanged are maintained online. Centers with inventories of merchandise premiums have been established for redemption of the credits. Merchants may not return unused credits to Alexei & Nemov.

The following schedule expresses Alexei & Nemov's expectations as to percentages of a normal month's activity that will be attained. For this purpose, a "normal month's activity" is defined as the level of operations expected when expansion of activities ceases or tapers off to a stable rate. The company expects that this level will be attained in the third year and that sales of credits will average $6,000,000 per month throughout the third year.

Month	Actual Credit Sales Percent	Merchandise Premium Purchases Percent	Credit Redemptions Percent
6th	30%	40%	10%
12th	60	60	45
18th	80	80	70
24th	90	90	80
30th	100	100	95

Alexei & Nemov plans to adopt an annual closing date at the end of each 12 months of operation.

Instructions
(a)   Discuss the factors to be considered in determining when revenue should be recognized in measuring the income of a business enterprise.
(b)   Discuss the accounting alternatives that should be considered by Alexei & Nemov Inc. for the recognition of its revenues and related expenses.
(c)   For each accounting alternative discussed in (b), give balance sheet accounts that should be used and indicate how each should be classified.

(AICPA adapted)

CA18-5   (Recognition of Revenue from Subscriptions)   *Cutting Edge* is a monthly magazine that has been on the market for 18 months. It currently has a circulation of 1.4 million copies. Negotiations are underway to obtain a bank loan in order to update the magazine's facilities. They are producing close to capacity and expect to grow at an average of 20% per year over the next 3 years.

After reviewing the financial statements of *Cutting Edge*, Gary Hall, the bank loan officer, had indicated that a loan could be offered to *Cutting Edge* only if it could increase its current ratio and decrease its debt to equity ratio to a specified level.

Alexander Popov, the marketing manager of *Cutting Edge*, has devised a plan to meet these requirements. Popov indicates that an advertising campaign can be initiated to immediately increase circulation. The potential customers would be contacted after the purchase of another magazine's mailing list. The campaign would include:

1.   An offer to subscribe to *Cutting Edge* at 3/4 the normal price.
2.   A special offer to all new subscribers to receive the most current world atlas whenever requested at a guaranteed price of $2.
3.   An unconditional guarantee that any subscriber will receive a full refund if dissatisfied with the magazine.

Although the offer of a full refund is risky, Popov claims that few people will ask for a refund after receiving half of their subscription issues. Popov notes that other magazine companies have tried this sales promotion technique and experienced great success. Their average cancellation rate was 25%. On average, each company increased its initial circulation threefold and in the long run increased circulation to twice that which existed before the promotion. In addition, 60% of the new subscribers are expected to take advantage of the atlas premium. Popov feels confident that the increased subscriptions from the advertising campaign will increase the current ratio and decrease the debt to equity ratio.

You are the controller of *Cutting Edge* and must give your opinion of the proposed plan.

Instructions
(a)   When should revenue from the new subscriptions be recognized?
(b)   How would you classify the estimated sales returns stemming from the unconditional guarantee?
(c)   How should the atlas premium be recorded? Is the estimated premium claims a liability? Explain.

(d) Does the proposed plan achieve the goals of increasing the current ratio and decreasing the debt to equity ratio?

 CA18-6 (Long-Term Contract—Percentage-of-Completion) Scherbo Company is accounting for a long-term construction contract using the percentage-of-completion method. It is a 4-year contract that is currently in its second year. The latest estimates of total contract costs indicate that the contract will be completed at a profit to Scherbo Company.

Instructions

(a) What theoretical justification is there for Scherbo Company's use of the percentage-of-completion method?

(b) How would progress billings be accounted for? Include in your discussion the classification of progress billings in Scherbo Company financial statements.

(c) How would the income recognized in the second year of the 4-year contract be determined using the cost-to-cost method of determining percentage of completion?

(d) What would be the effect on earnings per share in the second year of the 4-year contract of using the percentage-of-completion method instead of the completed-contract method? Discuss.

(AICPA adapted)

CA18-7 (Revenue Recognition—Real Estate Development) Pankratov Lakes is a new recreational real estate development which consists of 500 lake-front and lake-view lots. As a special incentive to the first 100 buyers of lake-view lots, the developer is offering 3 years of free financing on 10-year, 12% notes, no down payment, and one week at a nearby established resort—"a $1,200 value." The normal price per lot is $12,000. The cost per lake-view lot to the developer is an estimated average of $2,000. The development costs continue to be incurred; the actual average cost per lot is not known at this time. The resort promotion cost is $700 per lot. The notes are held by Davis Corp., a wholly owned subsidiary.

Instructions

(a) Discuss the revenue recognition and gross profit measurement issues raised by this situation.

(b) How would the developer's past financial and business experience influence your decision concerning the recording of these transactions?

(c) Assume 50 persons have accepted the offer, signed 10-year notes, and have stayed at the local resort. Prepare the journal entries that you believe are proper.

(d) What should be disclosed in the notes to the financial statements?

CA18-8 (Revenue Recognition) Nimble Health and Racquet Club (NHRC), which operates eight clubs in the Chicago metropolitan area, offers one-year memberships. The members may use any of the eight facilities but must reserve racquetball court time and pay a separate fee before using the court. As an incentive to new customers, NHRC advertised that any customers not satisfied for any reason could receive a refund of the remaining portion of unused membership fees. Membership fees are due at the beginning of the individual membership period. However, customers are given the option of financing the membership fee over the membership period at a 9% interest rate.

Some customers have expressed a desire to take only the regularly scheduled aerobic classes without paying for a full membership. During the current fiscal year, NHRC began selling coupon books for aerobic classes to accommodate these customers. Each book is dated and contains 50 coupons that may be redeemed for any regularly scheduled aerobics class over a one-year period. After the one-year period, unused coupons are no longer valid.

During 2004, NHRC expanded into the health equipment market by purchasing a local company that manufactures rowing machines and cross-country ski machines. These machines are used in NHRC's facilities and are sold through the clubs and mail order catalogs. Customers must make a 20% down payment when placing an equipment order; delivery is 60–90 days after order placement. The machines are sold with a 2-year unconditional guarantee. Based on past experience, NHRC expects the costs to repair machines under guarantee to be 4% of sales.

NHRC is in the process of preparing financial statements as of May 31, 2007, the end of its fiscal year. James Hogan, corporate controller, expressed concern over the company's performance for the year and decided to review the preliminary financial statements prepared by Barbara Hardy, NHRC's assistant controller. After reviewing the statements, Hogan proposed that the following changes be reflected in the May 31, 2007, published financial statements.

1. Membership revenue should be recognized when the membership fee is collected.
2. Revenue from the coupon books should be recognized when the books are sold.
3. Down payments on equipment purchases and expenses associated with the guarantee on the rowing and cross-country machines should be recognized when paid.

Hardy indicated to Hogan that the proposed changes are not in accordance with generally accepted accounting principles, but Hogan insisted that the changes be made. Hardy believes that Hogan wants to manage income to forestall any potential financial problems and increase his year-end bonus. At this point, Hardy is unsure what action to take.

Instructions

(a) (1) Describe when Nimble Health and Racquet Club (NHRC) should recognize revenue from membership fees, court rentals, and coupon book sales.

 (2) Describe how NHRC should account for the down payments on equipment sales, explaining when this revenue should be recognized.

 (3) Indicate when NHRC should recognize the expense associated with the guarantee of the rowing and cross-country machines.

(b) Discuss why James Hogan's proposed changes and his insistence that the financial statement changes be made is unethical. Structure your answer around or to include the following aspects of ethical conduct: competence, confidentiality, integrity, and/or objectivity.

(c) Identify some specific actions Barbara Hardy could take to resolve this situation.

(CMA adapted)

 CA18-9 (Revenue Recognition—Membership Fees) Midwest Health Club offers one-year memberships. Membership fees are due in full at the beginning of the individual membership period. As an incentive to new customers, MHC advertised that any customers not satisfied for any reason could receive a refund of the remaining portion of unused membership fees. As a result of this policy, Stanley Hack, corporate controller, recognized revenue ratably over the life of the membership.

MHC is in the process of preparing its year-end financial statements. Phyllis Cavaretta, MHC's treasurer, is concerned about the company's lackluster performance this year. She reviews the financial statements Hack prepared and tells Hack to recognize membership revenue when the fees are received.

Instructions

Answer the following questions.

(a) What are the ethical issues involved?

(b) What should Hack do?

*CA18-10 (Franchise Revenue) Badger Burrito Inc. sells franchises to independent operators throughout the northwestern part of the United States. The contract with the franchisee includes the following provisions.

1. The franchisee is charged an initial fee of $80,000. Of this amount, $30,000 is payable when the agreement is signed, and a $10,000 non-interest-bearing note is payable at the end of each of the 5 subsequent years.

2. All of the initial franchise fee collected by Badger is to be refunded and the remaining obligation canceled if, for any reason, the franchisee fails to open his or her franchise.

3. In return for the initial franchise fee, Badger agrees to (a) assist the franchisee in selecting the location for the business, (b) negotiate the lease for the land, (c) obtain financing and assist with building design, (d) supervise construction, (e) establish accounting and tax records, and (f) provide expert advice over a 5-year period relating to such matters as employee and management training, quality control, and promotion.

4. In addition to the initial franchise fee, the franchisee is required to pay to Badger a monthly fee of 2% of sales for menu planning, receipt innovations, and the privilege of purchasing ingredients from Badger at or below prevailing market prices.

Management of Badger Burrito estimates that the value of the services rendered to the franchisee at the time the contract is signed amounts to at least $30,000. All franchisees to date have opened their locations at the scheduled time, and none have defaulted on any of the notes receivable.

The credit ratings of all franchisees would entitle them to borrow at the current interest rate of 10%. The present value of an ordinary annuity of five annual receipts of $10,000 each discounted at 10% is $37,908.

Instructions

(a) Discuss the alternatives that Badger Burrito Inc. might use to account for the initial franchise fees, evaluate each by applying generally accepted accounting principles, and give illustrative entries for each alternative.

(b) Given the nature of Badger Burrito's agreement with its franchisees, when should revenue be recognized? Discuss the question of revenue recognition for both the initial franchise fee and the additional monthly fee of 2% of sales, and give illustrative entries for both types of revenue.

(c) Assume that Badger Burrito sells some franchises for $100,000, which includes a charge of $20,000 for the rental of equipment for its useful life of 10 years; that $50,000 of the fee is payable immediately and the balance on non-interest-bearing notes at $10,000 per year; that no portion of the $20,000 rental payment is refundable in case the franchisee goes out of business; and that title to the equipment remains with the franchisor. Under those assumptions, what would be the preferable method of accounting for the rental portion of the initial franchise fee? Explain.

(AICPA adapted)

USING YOUR JUDGMENT

Financial Reporting Problem

 ### The Procter & Gamble Company (P&G)

The financial statements of **P&G** are presented in Appendix 5B or can be accessed on the KWW website.

Instructions

Refer to P&G's financial statements and the accompanying notes to answer the following questions.

(a) What were P&G's sales for 2004?

(b) What was the percentage of increase or decrease in P&G's sales from 2003 to 2004? From 2002 to 2003? From 1999 to 2004?

(c) In its notes to the financial statements, what criteria does P&G use to recognize revenue?

(d) How does P&G account for trade promotions? Does the accounting conform to accrual accounting concepts? Explain.

Financial Statement Analysis Case

 ### Westinghouse Electric Corporation

The following note appears in the "Summary of Significant Accounting Policies" section of the Annual Report of **Westinghouse Electric Corporation**.

> **Note 1 (in part): Revenue Recognition.** Sales are primarily recorded as products are shipped and services are rendered. The percentage-of-completion method of accounting is used for nuclear steam supply system orders with delivery schedules generally in excess of five years and for certain construction projects where this method of accounting is consistent with industry practice.
>
> WFSI revenues are generally recognized on the accrual method. When accounts become delinquent for more than two payment periods, usually 60 days, income is recognized only as payments are received. Such delinquent accounts for which no payments are received in the current month, and other accounts on which income is not being recognized because the receipt of either principal or interest is questionable, are classified as non-earning receivables.

Instructions

(a) Identify the revenue recognition methods used by Westinghouse Electric as discussed in its note on significant accounting policies.

(b) Under what conditions are the revenue recognition methods identified in the first paragraph of Westinghouse's note above acceptable?

(c) From the information provided in the second paragraph of Westinghouse's note, identify the type of operation being described and defend the acceptability of the revenue recognition method.

Comparative Analysis Case

 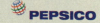

The Coca-Cola Company and PepsiCo, Inc.

Instructions

Go to KWW website and use information found there to answer the following questions related to **The Coca-Cola Company** and **PepsiCo, Inc.**

(a) What were Coca-Cola's and PepsiCo's net revenues (sales) for the year 2004? Which company increased its revenues more (dollars and percentage) from 2003 to 2004?

(b) Are the revenue recognition policies of Coca-Cola and PepsiCo similar? Explain.

(c) In which foreign countries (geographic areas) did Coca-Cola and PepsiCo experience significant revenues in 2004? Compare the amounts of foreign revenues to U.S. revenues for both Coca-Cola and PepsiCo.

Research Cases

Case 1

Companies registered with the Securities and Exchange Commission are required to file a current report on Form 8-K upon the occurrence of certain events.

Instructions

Use EDGAR or some other source to identify 8-Ks recently filed by two companies of your choice. Examine the 8-Ks and answer the following questions with regard to each.

(a) What corporate event or transaction triggered the filing of the Form 8-K?

(b) Identify any financial statements or exhibits included in the filing. How might these items help investors in evaluating the event/transaction?

Case 2

An article titled "SEC Broadens Investigation in Revenue-Boosting Tricks; Fearing Bogus Numbers Are Widespread, Agency Probes **Lucent** and Others," by Susan Pulliam and Rebecca Blumenstein, appeared in the May 16, 2002, *Wall Street Journal*.

Instructions

Read this article and answer the following questions.

(a) The article predicts that, "Probing revenue promises to be a much broader inquiry than the earlier investigations of **Enron** and other companies accused of using accounting tricks to boost their profits." What is the difference between inflating profits and inflating revenues?

(b) What are the ways in which accounting information is used (both in general and in ways specifically cited in this article)? What are the concerns about using accounting information that has been manipulated to increase revenues? To increase profits?

(c) Describe the specific techniques that may be used to inflate revenues that are enumerated in this article. Why would a practice of inflating revenues be of particular concern during the "dot-com boom"?

(d) The article says that **L90 Inc.** "lopped $8.3 million, or just over 10%, off revenue previously reported for 2000 and 2001," while booking the $250,000 net difference in the amount of wire transfers that had been used in one of these transactions as "Other income" rather than revenue. What is the difference between revenues and other income? Where might these items be found in a multi-step income statement? In a single-step income statement?

(e) What are "vendor allowances"? How might these allowances be used to inflate revenues? Consider the case of Lucent Technologies described in the article. Might Lucent's techniques also have been used to boost profits?

Professional Research: Financial Accounting and Reporting

Employees at your company disagree about the accounting for sales returns. The sales manager believes that granting more generous returns provisions can give the company a competitive edge and increase sales revenue. The controller cautions that, depending on the terms granted, loose returns provisions might lead to non-GAAP revenue recognition. The company CFO would like you to research the issue to provide an authoritative answer.

Instructions

Using the **Financial Accounting Research System (FARS)**, respond to the following items. (Provide text strings used in your search.)

(a) Which statement addresses revenue recognition when right of return exists?

(b) What is meant by "right of return"?

(c) When there is a right of return, what conditions must the company meet to recognize the revenue at the time of sale?

(d) What factors may impair the ability to make a reasonable estimate of future returns?

Professional Simulation

In this simulation you are asked to address questions related to revenue recognition issues. Prepare responses to all parts.

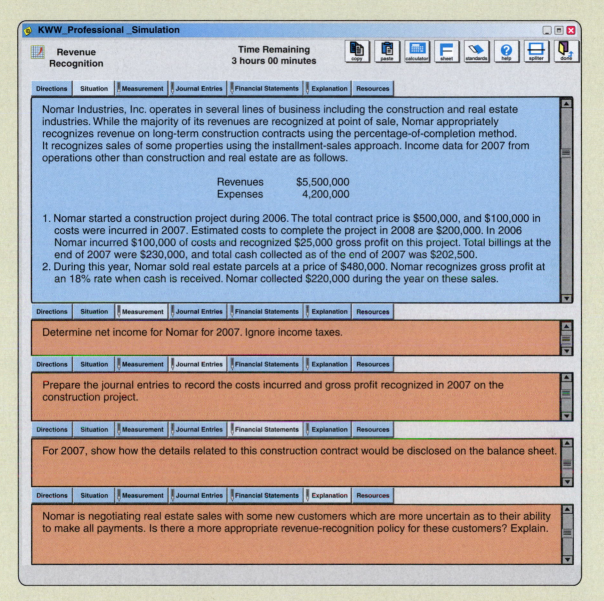

KWW_Professional _Simulation

| Revenue Recognition | Time Remaining 3 hours 00 minutes | copy paste calculator sheet standards help splitter done |

Directions | Situation | Measurement | Journal Entries | Financial Statements | Explanation | Resources

Nomar Industries, Inc. operates in several lines of business including the construction and real estate industries. While the majority of its revenues are recognized at point of sale, Nomar appropriately recognizes revenue on long-term construction contracts using the percentage-of-completion method. It recognizes sales of some properties using the installment-sales approach. Income data for 2007 from operations other than construction and real estate are as follows.

Revenues	$5,500,000
Expenses	4,200,000

1. Nomar started a construction project during 2006. The total contract price is $500,000, and $100,000 in costs were incurred in 2007. Estimated costs to complete the project in 2008 are $200,000. In 2006 Nomar incurred $100,000 of costs and recognized $25,000 gross profit on this project. Total billings at the end of 2007 were $230,000, and total cash collected as of the end of 2007 was $202,500.
2. During this year, Nomar sold real estate parcels at a price of $480,000. Nomar recognizes gross profit at an 18% rate when cash is received. Nomar collected $220,000 during the year on these sales.

Directions | Situation | Measurement | Journal Entries | Financial Statements | Explanation | Resources

Determine net income for Nomar for 2007. Ignore income taxes.

Directions | Situation | Measurement | Journal Entries | Financial Statements | Explanation | Resources

Prepare the journal entries to record the costs incurred and gross profit recognized in 2007 on the construction project.

Directions | Situation | Measurement | Journal Entries | Financial Statements | Explanation | Resources

For 2007, show how the details related to this construction contract would be disclosed on the balance sheet.

Directions | Situation | Measurement | Journal Entries | Financial Statements | Explanation | Resources

Nomar is negotiating real estate sales with some new customers which are more uncertain as to their ability to make all payments. Is there a more appropriate revenue-recognition policy for these customers? Explain.

Remember to check the book's companion website to find additional resources for this chapter.

wiley.com/college/kieso

ACCOUNTING FOR INCOME TAXES

Tax Uncertainty

One set of costs that companies manage are those related to taxes. In fact, in today's competitive markets, managers are expected to look for places in the tax code that a company can exploit to pay less tax to state and federal governments. By paying less in taxes, companies have more cash available to fund operations, finance expansion, and create new jobs. What happens, though, when companies push the tax saving envelop? Well, they may face a tax audit, the results of which could hurt their financial statements.

A notable example of corporate maneuvering to reduce taxable income involved **Limited Brands Inc.** It managed state-tax costs downward by locating part of its business in low-tax-rate states while operating retail outlets elsewhere. For example, by basing a subsidiary (which does nothing more than hold the trademarks for Bath and Body Works and Victoria's Secret) in Delaware, it is able to transfer hundreds of millions of dollars from Limited's retail outlets in high-tax states into Delaware, which has a state tax rate of zero.

However, the IRS and some states have been increasing their scrutiny of transactions that seem done only to avoid taxes and that do not serve a legitimate business purpose. In one case, an attorney for North Carolina alleged that Limited Brands Inc. ". . . engaged in hocus pocus bookkeeping and deceptive accounting," the sole purpose of which was to reduce its state-tax bill. The court agreed, and Limited Inc. had to pay millions of dollars in taxes dating back to 1994.

Limited Brands shareholders likely got an unpleasant surprise when they learned the company also had a big tax obligation from its "uncertain tax position" related to off-shore locations. The same can be said for many other companies that take tax deductions that may not hold up under the scrutiny of the tax court or an IRS audit. Current accounting rules are not very specific on when companies have to record an obligation for taxes that will be owed on uncertain tax positions. This is changing because the SEC and the FASB are concerned about non-recognition of significant tax obligations. As this text is being written, the FASB is working on a rule that would require companies to record loss contingencies for more uncertain tax provisions in their financial statements.[1]

---

[1]See Glenn Simpson, "A Tax Maneuver in Delaware Puts Squeeze on States," *Wall Street Journal* (August 9, 2002), p. A1; and FASB, "Uncertain Tax Positions: Recognition of Tax Benefits," (July 14, 2005), *www.fasb.org/project/uncertain_tax_positions.shtml*.

Learning Objectives

After studying this chapter, you should be able to:

1 Identify differences between pretax financial income and taxable income.

2 Describe a temporary difference that results in future taxable amounts.

3 Describe a temporary difference that results in future deductible amounts.

4 Explain the purpose of a deferred tax asset valuation allowance.

5 Describe the presentation of income tax expense in the income statement.

6 Describe various temporary and permanent differences.

7 Explain the effect of various tax rates and tax rate changes on deferred income taxes.

8 Apply accounting procedures for a loss carryback and a loss carryforward.

9 Describe the presentation of deferred income taxes in financial statements.

10 Indicate the basic principles of the asset-liability method.

As our opening story indicates, companies spend a considerable amount of time and effort to minimize their income tax payments. And with good reason, as income taxes are a major cost of doing business for most corporations. Yet, at the same time, companies must present financial information to the investment community that provides a clear picture of present and potential tax obligations and tax benefits. In this chapter, we discuss the basic guidelines that companies must follow in reporting income taxes. The content and organization of the chapter are as follows.

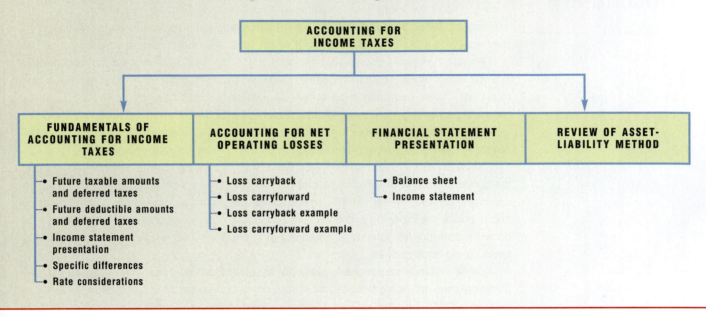

FUNDAMENTALS OF ACCOUNTING FOR INCOME TAXES

OBJECTIVE 1
Identify differences between pretax financial income and taxable income.

Up to this point, you have learned the basic guidelines that corporations use to report information to investors and creditors. Corporations also must file income tax returns following the guidelines developed by the Internal Revenue Service (IRS). Because GAAP and tax regulations differ in a number of ways, so frequently do pretax financial income and taxable income. Consequently, the amount that a company reports as tax expense will differ from the amount of taxes payable to the IRS. Illustration 19-1 highlights these differences.

Pretax financial income is a *financial reporting* term. It also is often referred to as *income before taxes*, *income for financial reporting purposes*, or *income for book purposes*. Companies determine pretax financial income according to GAAP. They measure it with the objective of providing useful information to investors and creditors.

Taxable income (income for tax purposes) is a *tax accounting* term. It indicates the amount used to compute income tax payable. Companies determine taxable income according to the Internal Revenue Code (the tax code). Income taxes provide money to support government operations.

To illustrate how differences in GAAP and IRS rules affect financial reporting and taxable income, assume that Chelsea Inc. reported revenues of $130,000 and expenses of $60,000 in each of its first three years of operations. Illustration 19-2 shows the (partial) income statement over these three years.

For tax purposes (following the tax code), Chelsea reported the same expenses to the IRS in each of the years. But, as Illustration 19-3 shows, Chelsea reported taxable revenues of $100,000 in 2007, $150,000 in 2008, and $140,000 in 2009.

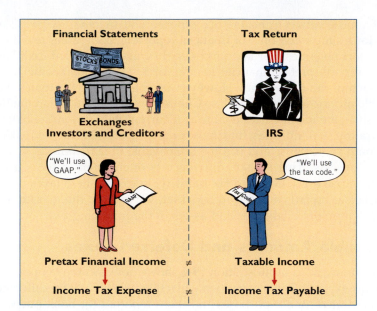

ILLUSTRATION 19-1
Fundamental Differences between Financial and Tax Reporting

ILLUSTRATION 19-2
Financial Reporting Income

CHELSEA INC.
GAAP REPORTING

	2007	2008	2009	Total
Revenues	$130,000	$130,000	$130,000	
Expenses	60,000	60,000	60,000	
Pretax financial income	$ 70,000	$ 70,000	$ 70,000	$ 210,000
Income tax expense (40%)	$ 28,000	$ 28,000	$ 28,000	$ 84,000

ILLUSTRATION 19-3
Tax Reporting Income

CHELSEA INC.
TAX REPORTING

	2007	2008	2009	Total
Revenues	$100,000	$150,000	$140,000	
Expenses	60,000	60,000	60,000	
Taxable income	$ 40,000	$ 90,000	$ 80,000	$ 210,000
Income tax payable (40%)	$ 16,000	$ 36,000	$ 32,000	$ 84,000

Income tax expense and income tax payable differed over the three years, but were equal **in total**, as Illustration 19-4 shows.

ILLUSTRATION 19-4
Comparison of Income Tax Expense to Income Tax Payable

CHELSEA INC.
INCOME TAX EXPENSE AND
INCOME TAX PAYABLE

	2007	2008	2009	Total
Income tax expense	$28,000	$28,000	$28,000	$84,000
Income tax payable	16,000	36,000	32,000	84,000
Difference	$12,000	$ (8,000)	$ (4,000)	$ 0

The differences between income tax expense and income tax payable in this example arise for a simple reason. For financial reporting, companies use the full accrual method to report revenues. For tax purposes, they use a modified cash basis. As a result, Chelsea reports pretax financial income of $70,000 and income tax expense of $28,000 for each of the three years. However, taxable income fluctuates. For example, in 2007 taxable income is only $40,000, so Chelsea owes just $16,000 to the IRS that year. Chelsea classifies the income tax payable as a current liability on the balance sheet.

As Illustration 19-4 indicates, for Chelsea the $12,000 ($28,000 − $16,000) difference between income tax expense and income tax payable in 2007 reflects taxes that it will pay in future periods. This $12,000 difference is often referred to as a **deferred tax amount**. In this case it is a **deferred tax liability**. In cases where taxes will be lower in the future, Chelsea records a **deferred tax asset**. We explain the measurement and accounting for deferred tax liabilities and assets in the following two sections.

Future Taxable Amounts and Deferred Taxes

OBJECTIVE 2
Describe a temporary difference that results in future taxable amounts.

The example summarized in Illustration 19-4 shows how income tax payable can differ from income tax expense. This can happen when there are temporary differences between the amounts reported for tax purposes and those reported for book purposes. A **temporary difference** is the difference between the tax basis of an asset or liability and its reported (carrying or book) amount in the financial statements, which will result in taxable amounts or deductible amounts in future years. **Taxable amounts** increase taxable income in future years. **Deductible amounts** decrease taxable income in future years.

In Chelsea's situation, the only difference between the book basis and tax basis of the assets and liabilities relates to accounts receivable that arose from revenue recognized for book purposes. Illustration 19-5 indicates that Chelsea reports accounts receivable at $30,000 in the December 31, 2007, GAAP-basis balance sheet. However, the receivables have a zero tax basis.

ILLUSTRATION 19-5
Temporary Difference, Sales Revenue

Per Books	12/31/07	Per Tax Return	12/31/07
Accounts receivable	$30,000	Accounts receivable	$–0–

What will happen to the $30,000 temporary difference that originated in 2007 for Chelsea? Assuming that Chelsea expects to collect $20,000 of the receivables in 2008 and $10,000 in 2009, this collection results in future taxable amounts of $20,000 in 2008 and $10,000 in 2009. These future taxable amounts will cause taxable income to exceed pretax financial income in both 2008 and 2009.

An assumption inherent in a company's GAAP balance sheet is that companies recover and settle the assets and liabilities at their reported amounts (carrying amounts). This assumption creates a requirement under accrual accounting to recognize *currently* the deferred tax consequences of temporary differences. That is, companies recognize the amount of income taxes that are payable (or refundable) when they recover and settle the reported amounts of the assets and liabilities, respectively. Illustration 19-6 shows the reversal of the temporary difference described in Illustration 19-5 and the resulting taxable amounts in future periods.

ILLUSTRATION 19-6
Reversal of Temporary Difference, Chelsea Inc.

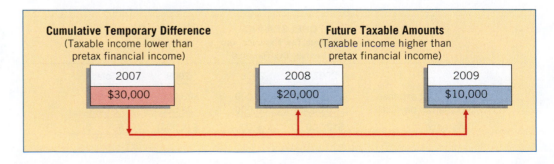

Chelsea assumes that it will collect the accounts receivable and report the $30,000 collection as taxable revenues in future tax returns. A payment of income tax in both 2008 and 2009 will occur. Chelsea should therefore record in its books in 2007 the deferred tax consequences of the revenue and related receivables reflected in the 2007 financial statements. Chelsea does this by recording a deferred tax liability.

Deferred Tax Liability

A **deferred tax liability** is the deferred tax consequences attributable to taxable temporary differences. In other words, **a deferred tax liability represents the increase in taxes payable in future years as a result of taxable temporary differences existing at the end of the current year**.

Recall from the Chelsea example that income tax payable is $16,000 ($40,000 × 40%) in 2007 (Illustration 19-4). In addition, a temporary difference exists at year-end because Chelsea reports the revenue and related accounts receivable differently for book and tax purposes. The book basis of accounts receivable is $30,000, and the tax basis is zero. Thus, the total deferred tax liability at the end of 2007 is $12,000, computed as shown in Illustration 19-7.

Book basis of accounts receivable	$30,000
Tax basis of accounts receivable	–0–
Cumulative temporary difference at the end of 2004	30,000
Tax rate	40%
Deferred tax liability at the end of 2007	$12,000

ILLUSTRATION 19-7
Computation of Deferred Tax Liability, End of 2007

Companies may also compute the deferred tax liability by preparing a schedule that indicates the future taxable amounts due to existing temporary differences. Such a schedule, as shown in Illustration 19-8, is particularly useful when the computations become more complex.

	Future Years		
	2008	2009	Total
Future taxable amounts	$20,000	$10,000	$30,000
Tax rate	40%	40%	
Deferred tax liability at the end of 2007	$ 8,000	$ 4,000	$12,000

ILLUSTRATION 19-8
Schedule of Future Taxable Amounts

Because it is the first year of operations for Chelsea, there is no deferred tax liability at the beginning of the year. Chelsea computes the income tax expense for 2007 as shown in Illustration 19-9.

Deferred tax liability at end of 2007	$12,000
Deferred tax liability at beginning of 2007	–0–
Deferred tax expense for 2007	12,000
Current tax expense for 2007 (Income tax payable)	16,000
Income tax expense (total) for 2007	$28,000

ILLUSTRATION 19-9
Computation of Income Tax Expense, 2007

This computation indicates that income tax expense has two components—**current tax expense** (the amount of income tax payable for the period) and deferred tax expense. **Deferred tax expense** is the increase in the deferred tax liability balance from the beginning to the end of the accounting period.

Companies credit taxes due and payable to Income Tax Payable, and credit the increase in deferred taxes to Deferred Tax Liability. They then debit the sum of those two items to Income Tax Expense. For Chelsea, it makes the following entry at the end of 2007.

Income Tax Expense	28,000	
Income Tax Payable		16,000
Deferred Tax Liability		12,000

At the end of 2008 (the second year), the difference between the book basis and the tax basis of the accounts receivable is $10,000. Chelsea multiplies this difference by the applicable tax rate to arrive at the deferred tax liability of $4,000 ($10,000 × 40%), which it reports at the end of 2008. Income tax payable for 2008 is $36,000 (Illustration 19-3), and the income tax expense for 2008 is as shown in Illustration 19-10.

ILLUSTRATION 19-10
Computation of Income
Tax Expense, 2008

Deferred tax liability at end of 2008	$ 4,000
Deferred tax liability at beginning of 2008	12,000
Deferred tax expense (benefit) for 2008	(8,000)
Current tax expense for 2008 (Income tax payable)	36,000
Income tax expense (total) for 2008	$28,000

Chelsea records income tax expense, the change in the deferred tax liability, and income tax payable for 2008 as follows.

Income Tax Expense	28,000	
Deferred Tax Liability	8,000	
Income Tax Payable		36,000

The entry to record income taxes at the end of 2009 reduces the Deferred Tax Liability by $4,000. The Deferred Tax Liability account appears as follows at the end of 2009.

ILLUSTRATION 19-11
Deferred Tax Liability
Account after Reversals

Deferred Tax Liability			
2008	8,000	2007	12,000
2009	4,000		

The Deferred Tax Liability account has a zero balance at the end of 2009.

"REAL LIABILITIES"

**WHAT DO THE
NUMBERS MEAN?**

Some analysts dismiss deferred tax liabilities when assessing the financial strength of a company. But the FASB indicates that the deferred tax liability meets the definition of a liability established in *Statement of Financial Accounting Concepts No. 6*, "Elements of Financial Statements" because:

1 *It results from a past transaction.* In the Chelsea example, the company performed services for customers and recognized revenue in 2007 for financial reporting purposes but deferred it for tax purposes.

2 *It is a present obligation.* Taxable income in future periods will exceed pretax financial income as a result of this temporary difference. Thus, a present obligation exists.

3 *It represents a future sacrifice.* Taxable income and taxes due in future periods will result from past events. The payment of these taxes when they come due is the future sacrifice.

A study by B. Ayers indicates that the market views deferred tax assets and liabilities similarly to other assets and liabilities. Further, the study concludes that *SFAS No. 109* increased the usefulness of deferred tax amounts in financial statements.

Source: B. Ayers, "Deferred Tax Accounting Under *SFAS No. 109*: An Empirical Investigation of Its Incremental Value-Relevance Relative to *APB No. 11*," *The Accounting Review* (April 1998).

Summary of Income Tax Accounting Objectives

One objective of accounting for income taxes is to recognize the amount of taxes payable or refundable for the current year. In Chelsea's case, income tax payable is $16,000 for 2007.

A **second objective** is to recognize deferred tax liabilities and assets for the future tax consequences of events already recognized in the financial statements or tax returns. For example, Chelsea sold services to customers that resulted in accounts receivable of $30,000 in 2007. It reported that amount on the 2007 income statement, but not on the tax return as income. That amount will appear on future tax returns as income for the period **when collected**. As a result, a $30,000 temporary difference exists at the end of 2007, which will cause future taxable amounts. Chelsea reports a deferred tax liability of $12,000 on the balance sheet at the end of 2007, which represents the increase in taxes payable in future years ($8,000 in 2008 and $4,000 in 2009) as a result of a temporary difference existing at the end of the current year. The related deferred tax liability is reduced by $8,000 at the end of 2008 and by another $4,000 at the end of 2009.

In addition to affecting the balance sheet, deferred taxes impact income tax expense in each of the three years affected. In 2007, taxable income ($40,000) is less than pretax financial income ($70,000). Income tax payable for 2007 is therefore $16,000 (based on taxable income). Deferred tax expense of $12,000 results from the increase in the Deferred Tax Liability account on the balance sheet. Income tax expense is then $28,000 for 2007.

In 2008 and 2009, however, taxable income will exceed pretax financial income, due to the reversal of the temporary difference ($20,000 in 2008 and $10,000 in 2009). Income tax payable will therefore exceed income tax expense in 2008 and 2009. Chelsea will debit the Deferred Tax Liability account for $8,000 in 2008 and $4,000 in 2009. It records credits for these amounts in Income Tax Expense. These credits are often referred to as a **deferred tax benefit** (which we discuss again later on).

Future Deductible Amounts and Deferred Taxes

Assume that during 2007, Cunningham Inc. estimated its warranty costs related to the sale of microwave ovens to be $500,000, paid evenly over the next two years. For book purposes, in 2007 Cunningham reported warranty expense and a related estimated liability for warranties of $500,000 in its financial statements. For tax purposes, **the warranty tax deduction is not allowed until paid**. Therefore, Cunningham recognizes no warranty liability on a tax-basis balance sheet. Illustration 19-12 shows the balance sheet difference at the end of 2007.

> **OBJECTIVE 3**
> Describe a temporary difference that results in future deductible amounts.

ILLUSTRATION 19-12
Temporary Difference, Warranty Liability

Per Books	12/31/07	Per Tax Return	12/31/07
Estimated liability for warranties	$500,000	Estimated liability for warranties	$–0–

When Cunningham pays the warranty liability, it reports an expense (deductible amount) for tax purposes. Because of this temporary difference, Cunningham should recognize in 2007 the tax benefits (positive tax consequences) for the tax deductions that will result from the future settlement of the liability. Cunningham reports this future tax benefit in the December 31, 2007, balance sheet as a **deferred tax asset**.

We can think about this situation another way. Deductible amounts occur in future tax returns. These **future deductible amounts** cause taxable income to be less than pretax financial income in the future as a result of an existing temporary difference. Cunningham's temporary difference originates (arises) in one period (2007) and reverses over two periods (2008 and 2009). Illustration 19-13 (page 970) diagrams this situation.

ILLUSTRATION 19-13
Reversal of Temporary
Difference, Cunningham
Inc.

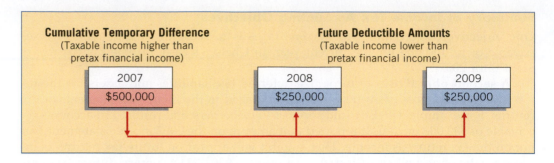

Deferred Tax Asset

A **deferred tax asset** is the deferred tax consequence attributable to deductible temporary differences. In other words, a **deferred tax asset represents the increase in taxes refundable (or saved) in future years as a result of deductible temporary differences existing at the end of the current year**.

To illustrate, assume that Hunt Co. accrues a loss and a related liability of $50,000 in 2007 for financial reporting purposes because of pending litigation. Hunt cannot deduct this amount for tax purposes until the period it pays the liability, expected in 2008. As a result, a deductible amount will occur in 2008 when Hunt settles the liability (Estimated Litigation Liability), causing taxable income to be lower than pretax financial income. Illustration 19-14 shows the computation of the deferred tax asset at the end of 2007 (assuming a 40 percent tax rate).

ILLUSTRATION 19-14
Computation of Deferred
Tax Asset, End of 2007

Book basis of litigation liability	$50,000
Tax basis of litigation liability	–0–
Cumulative temporary difference at the end of 2007	50,000
Tax rate	40%
Deferred tax asset at the end of 2007	$20,000

Hunt can also compute the deferred tax asset by preparing a schedule that indicates the future deductible amounts due to deductible temporary differences. Illustration 19-15 shows this schedule.

ILLUSTRATION 19-15
Schedule of Future
Deductible Amounts

	Future Years
Future deductible amounts	$50,000
Tax rate	40%
Deferred tax asset at the end of 2007	$20,000

Assuming that 2007 is Hunt's first year of operations, and income tax payable is $100,000, Hunt computes its income tax expense as follows.

ILLUSTRATION 19-16
Computation of Income
Tax Expense, 2007

Deferred tax asset at end of 2007	$ 20,000
Deferred tax asset at beginning of 2007	–0–
Deferred tax expense (benefit) for 2007	(20,000)
Current tax expense for 2007 (Income tax payable)	100,000
Income tax expense (total) for 2007	$ 80,000

The **deferred tax benefit** results from the increase in the deferred tax asset from the beginning to the end of the accounting period (similar to the Chelsea example earlier). The deferred tax benefit is a negative component of income tax expense. The total income tax expense of $80,000 on the income statement for 2007 thus consists of two elements—current tax expense of $100,000 and a deferred tax benefit of $20,000. For Hunt, it makes the following journal entry at the end of 2007 to record income tax expense, deferred income taxes, and income tax payable.

```
Income Tax Expense        80,000
Deferred Tax Asset        20,000
    Income Tax Payable              100,000
```

At the end of 2008 (the second year), the difference between the book value and the tax basis of the litigation liability is zero. Therefore, there is no deferred tax asset at this date. Assuming that income tax payable for 2008 is $140,000, Hunt computes income tax expense for 2008 as shown in Illustration 19-17.

Deferred tax asset at the end of 2008	$ –0–
Deferred tax asset at the beginning of 2008	20,000
Deferred tax expense (benefit) for 2008	20,000
Current tax expense for 2008 (Income tax payable)	140,000
Income tax expense (total) for 2008	$160,000

ILLUSTRATION 19-17
Computation of Income
Tax Expense, 2008

The company records income taxes for 2008 as follows.

```
Income Tax Expense       160,000
    Deferred Tax Asset             20,000
    Income Tax Payable            140,000
```

The total income tax expense of $160,000 on the income statement for 2008 thus consists of two elements—current tax expense of $140,000 and deferred tax expense of $20,000. Illustration 19-18 shows the Deferred Tax Asset account at the end of 2008.

Deferred Tax Asset

2007	20,000	2008	20,000

ILLUSTRATION 19-18
Deferred Tax Asset
Account after Reversals

"REAL ASSETS"

A key issue in accounting for income taxes is whether a company should recognize a deferred tax asset in the financial records. Based on the conceptual definition of an asset, a deferred tax asset meets the three main conditions for an item to be recognized as an asset:

WHAT DO THE NUMBERS MEAN?

1 *It results from a past transaction.* In the Hunt example, the accrual of the loss contingency is the past event that gives rise to a future deductible temporary difference.

2 *It gives rise to a probable benefit in the future.* Taxable income exceeds pretax financial income in the current year (2007). However, in the next year the exact opposite occurs. That is, taxable income is lower than pretax financial income. Because this deductible temporary difference reduces taxes payable in the future, a probable future benefit exists at the end of the current period.

3 *The entity controls access to the benefits.* Hunt can obtain the benefit of existing deductible temporary differences by reducing its taxes payable in the future. Hunt has the exclusive right to that benefit and can control others' access to it.

Market analysts' reaction to the **write-off** of deferred tax assets also supports their treatment as assets. When **Bethlehem Steel** reported a $1 billion charge in a recent year to write off a deferred tax asset, analysts believed that Bethlehem was signaling that it would not realize the future benefits of the tax deductions. Thus, Bethlehem should write down the asset like other assets.

Source: J. Weil and S. Liesman, "Stock Gurus Disregard Most Big Write-Offs But They Often Hold Vital Clues to Outlook," *Wall Street Journal Online* (December 31, 2001).

OBJECTIVE 4
Explain the purpose of
a deferred tax asset
valuation allowance.

Deferred Tax Asset—Valuation Allowance

Companies recognize a deferred tax asset for all deductible temporary differences. However, based on available evidence, a company should reduce a deferred tax asset by a **valuation allowance** if **it is more likely than not** that it **will not realize** some portion or all of the deferred tax asset. **"More likely than not"** means a level of likelihood of at least slightly more than 50 percent.

Assume that Jensen Co. has a deductible temporary difference of $1,000,000 at the end of its first year of operations. Its tax rate is 40 percent, which means it records a deferred tax asset of $400,000 ($1,000,000 × 40%). Assuming $900,000 of income taxes payable, Jensen records income tax expense, the deferred tax asset, and income tax payable as follows.

Income Tax Expense	500,000	
Deferred Tax Asset	400,000	
Income Tax Payable		900,000

After careful review of all available evidence, Jensen determines that it is more likely than not that it will not realize $100,000 of this deferred tax asset. Jensen records this reduction in asset value as follows.

Income Tax Expense	100,000	
Allowance to Reduce Deferred Tax Asset		
to Expected Realizable Value		100,000

This journal entry increases income tax expense in the current period because Jensen does not expect to realize a favorable tax benefit for a portion of the deductible temporary difference. Jensen **simultaneously establishes a valuation allowance to recognize the reduction in the carrying amount of the deferred tax asset**. This valuation account is a contra account. Jensen reports it on the financial statements in the following manner.

ILLUSTRATION 19-19
Balance Sheet
Presentation of Valuation
Allowance Account

Deferred tax asset	$400,000
Less: Allowance to reduce deferred tax asset to expected realizable value	100,000
Deferred tax asset (net)	$300,000

Jensen then evaluates this allowance account at the end of each accounting period. If, at the end of the next period, the deferred tax asset is still $400,000, but now it expects to realize $350,000 of this asset, Jensen makes the following entry to adjust the valuation account.

Allowance to Reduce Deferred Tax Asset		
to Expected Realizable Value	50,000	
Income Tax Expense		50,000

Jensen should consider all available evidence, both positive and negative, to determine whether, based on the weight of available evidence, it needs a valuation allowance. For example, if Jensen has been experiencing a series of loss years, it reasonably assumes that these losses will continue. Therefore, Jensen will lose the benefit of the future deductible amounts. We discuss the use of a valuation account under other conditions later in the chapter.

OBJECTIVE 5
Describe the
presentation of income
tax expense in the
income statement.

Income Statement Presentation

Circumstances dictate whether a company should add or subtract the change in deferred income taxes to or from income tax payable in computing income tax expense. For example, a company adds an increase in a deferred tax liability to income tax payable. On the other hand, it subtracts an increase in a deferred tax asset from income tax payable. The formula in Illustration 19-20 is used to compute income tax expense (benefit).

Income Tax Payable or Refundable	±	Change in Deferred Income Taxes	=	Total Income Tax Expense or Benefit

ILLUSTRATION 19-20
Formula to Compute Income Tax Expense

In the income statement or in the notes to the financial statements, a company should disclose the significant components of income tax expense attributable to continuing operations. Given the information related to Chelsea on page 967, Chelsea reports its income statement as follows.

CHELSEA INC.
INCOME STATEMENT
FOR THE YEAR ENDING DECEMBER 31, 2007

Revenues		$130,000
Expenses		60,000
Income before income taxes		70,000
Income tax expense		
Current	$16,000	
Deferred	12,000	28,000
Net income		$ 42,000

ILLUSTRATION 19-21
Income Statement Presentation of Income Tax Expense

As illustrated, Chelsea reports both the current portion (amount of income tax payable for the period) and the deferred portion of income tax expense. Another option is to simply report the total income tax expense on the income statement, and then indicate in the notes to the financial statements the current and deferred portions. Income tax expense is often referred to as "Provision for income taxes." Using this terminology, the current provision is $16,000, and the provision for deferred taxes is $12,000.

Specific Differences

Numerous items create differences between pretax financial income and taxable income. For purposes of accounting recognition, these differences are of two types: (1) temporary, and (2) permanent.

OBJECTIVE 6
Describe various temporary and permanent differences.

Temporary Differences

Taxable temporary differences are temporary differences that will result in taxable amounts in future years when the related assets are recovered. **Deductible temporary differences** are temporary differences that will result in deductible amounts in future years, when the related book liabilities are settled. Taxable temporary differences give rise to recording deferred tax liabilities. Deductible temporary differences give rise to recording deferred tax assets. Illustration 19-22 (page 974) provides examples of temporary differences.[2]

---

[2]*SFAS No. 109* gives more examples of temporary differences. We present the most common types in this chapter.

A. **Revenues or gains are taxable after they are recognized in financial income.**
An asset (e.g., accounts receivable or investment) may be recognized for revenues or gains that will result in **taxable amounts in future years** when the asset is recovered. Examples:
1. Sales accounted for on the accrual basis for financial reporting purposes and on the installment (cash) basis for tax purposes.
2. Contracts accounted for under the percentage-of-completion method for financial reporting purposes and a portion of related gross profit deferred for tax purposes.
3. Investments accounted for under the equity method for financial reporting purposes and under the cost method for tax purposes.
4. Gain on involuntary conversion of nonmonetary asset which is recognized for financial reporting purposes but deferred for tax purposes.

B. **Expenses or losses are deductible after they are recognized in financial income.**
A liability (or contra asset) may be recognized for expenses or losses that will result in **deductible amounts in future years** when the liability is settled. Examples:
1. Product warranty liabilities.
2. Estimated liabilities related to discontinued operations or restructurings.
3. Litigation accruals.
4. Bad debt expense recognized using the allowance method for financial reporting purposes; direct write-off method used for tax purposes.
5. Stock-based compensation expense.

C. **Revenues or gains are taxable before they are recognized in financial income.**
A liability may be recognized for an advance payment for goods or services to be provided in future years. For tax purposes, the advance payment is included in taxable income upon the receipt of cash. Future sacrifices to provide goods or services (or future refunds to those who cancel their orders) that settle the liability will result in **deductible amounts in future years**. Examples:
1. Subscriptions received in advance.
2. Advance rental receipts.
3. Sales and leasebacks for financial reporting purposes (income deferral) but reported as sales for tax purposes.
4. Prepaid contracts and royalties received in advance.

D. **Expenses or losses are deductible before they are recognized in financial income.**
The cost of an asset may have been deducted for tax purposes faster than it was expensed for financial reporting purposes. Amounts received upon future recovery of the amount of the asset for financial reporting (through use or sale) will exceed the remaining tax basis of the asset and thereby result in **taxable amounts in future years**. Examples:
1. Depreciable property, depletable resources, and intangibles.
2. Deductible pension funding exceeding expense.
3. Prepaid expenses that are deducted on the tax return in the period paid.

ILLUSTRATION 19-22
Examples of Temporary Differences

Determining a company's temporary differences may prove difficult. A company should prepare a balance sheet for tax purposes that it can compare with its GAAP balance sheet. Many of the differences between the two balance sheets are temporary differences.

Originating and Reversing Aspects of Temporary Differences. An **originating temporary difference** is the initial difference between the book basis and the tax basis of an asset or liability, regardless of whether the tax basis of the asset or liability exceeds or is exceeded by the book basis of the asset or liability. A **reversing difference**, on the other hand, occurs when eliminating a temporary difference that originated in prior periods and then removing the related tax effect from the deferred tax account.

For example, assume that Sharp Co. has tax depreciation in excess of book depreciation of $2,000 in 2003, 2004, and 2005. Further, it has an excess of book depreciation over tax depreciation of $3,000 in 2006 and 2007 for the same asset. Assuming a tax rate of 30 percent for all years involved, the Deferred Tax Liability account reflects the following.

ILLUSTRATION 19-23
Tax Effects of Originating and Reversing Differences

	Deferred Tax Liability		
Tax Effects of Reversing Differences	2006 900 2007 900	2003 600 2004 600 2005 600	Tax Effects of Originating Differences

The originating differences for Sharp in each of the first three years are $2,000. The related tax effect of each originating difference is $600. The reversing differences in 2006 and 2007 are each $3,000. The related tax effect of each is $900.

Permanent Differences

Some differences between taxable income and pretax financial income are permanent. **Permanent differences** result from items that (1) enter into pretax financial income but **never** into taxable income, or (2) enter into taxable income but **never** into pretax financial income.

Congress has enacted a variety of tax law provisions to attain certain political, economic, and social objectives. Some of these provisions exclude certain revenues from taxation, limit the deductibility of certain expenses, and permit the deduction of certain other expenses in excess of costs incurred. A corporation that has tax-free income, nondeductible expenses, or allowable deductions in excess of cost, has an effective tax rate that differs from its statutory (regular) tax rate.

Since permanent differences affect only the period in which they occur, they do not give rise to future taxable or deductible amounts. As a result, **companies recognize no deferred tax consequences**. Illustration 19-24 shows examples of permanent differences.

A. **Items are recognized for financial reporting purposes but not for tax purposes.**
   Examples:
   1. Interest received on state and municipal obligations.
   2. Expenses incurred in obtaining tax-exempt income.
   3. Proceeds from life insurance carried by the company on key officers or employees.
   4. Premiums paid for life insurance carried by the company on key officers or employees (company is beneficiary).
   5. Fines and expenses resulting from a violation of law.

B. **Items are recognized for tax purposes but not for financial reporting purposes.**
   Examples:
   1. "Percentage depletion" of natural resources in excess of their cost.
   2. The deduction for dividends received from U.S. corporations, generally 70% or 80%.

ILLUSTRATION 19-24
Examples of Permanent Differences

Examples of Temporary and Permanent Differences

To illustrate the computations used when both temporary and permanent differences exist, assume that Bio-Tech Company reports pretax financial income of $200,000 in each of the years 2005, 2006, and 2007. The company is subject to a 30 percent tax rate, and has the following differences between pretax financial income and taxable income.

1 Bio-Tech reports an installment sale of $18,000 in 2005 for tax purposes over an 18-month period at a constant amount per month beginning January 1, 2006. It recognizes the entire sale for book purposes in 2005.

2 It pays life insurance premiums for its key officers of $5,000 in 2006 and 2007. Although not tax-deductible, Bio-Tech expenses the premiums for book purposes.

The installment sale is a temporary difference, whereas the life insurance premium is a permanent difference. Illustration 19-25 shows the reconciliation of Bio-Tech's pretax financial income to taxable income and the computation of income tax payable.

	2005	2006	2007
Pretax financial income	$200,000	$200,000	$200,000
Permanent difference			
Nondeductible expense		5,000	5,000
Temporary difference			
Installment sale	(18,000)	12,000	6,000
Taxable income	182,000	217,000	211,000
Tax rate	30%	30%	30%
Income tax payable	$ 54,600	$ 65,100	$ 63,300

ILLUSTRATION 19-25
Reconciliation and Computation of Income Taxes Payable

Note that Bio-Tech **deducts** the installment sales revenue from pretax financial income to arrive at taxable income. The reason: pretax financial income includes the installment sales revenue; taxable income does not. Conversely, it **adds** the $5,000 insurance premium to pretax financial income to arrive at taxable income. The reason: pretax financial income records an expense for this premium, but for tax purposes the premium is not deductible. As a result, pretax financial income is lower than taxable income. Therefore, the life insurance premium must be added back to pretax financial income to reconcile to taxable income.

Bio-Tech records income taxes for 2005, 2006, and 2007 as follows.

December 31, 2005

Income Tax Expense ($54,600 + $5,400)	60,000	
Deferred Tax Liability ($18,000 × 30%)		5,400
Income Tax Payable ($182,000 × 30%)		54,600

December 31, 2006

Income Tax Expense ($65,100 − $3,600)	61,500	
Deferred Tax Liability ($12,000 × 30%)	3,600	
Income Tax Payable ($217,000 × 30%)		65,100

December 31, 2007

Income Tax Expense ($63,300 − $1,800)	61,500	
Deferred Tax Liability ($6,000 × 30%)	1,800	
Income Tax Payable ($211,000 × 30%)		63,300

Bio-Tech has one temporary difference, which originates in 2005 and reverses in 2006 and 2007. It recognizes a deferred tax liability at the end of 2005 because the temporary difference causes future taxable amounts. As the temporary difference reverses, Bio-Tech reduces the deferred tax liability. There is no deferred tax amount associated with the difference caused by the nondeductible insurance expense because it is a permanent difference.

Although an enacted tax rate of 30 percent applies for all three years, the effective rate differs from the enacted rate in 2006 and 2007. Bio-Tech computes the **effective tax rate** by dividing total income tax expense for the period by pretax financial income. The effective rate is 30 percent for 2005 ($60,000 ÷ $200,000 = 30%) and 30.75 percent for 2006 and 2007 ($61,500 ÷ $200,000 = 30.75%).

Tax Rate Considerations

OBJECTIVE 7
Explain the effect of various tax rates and tax rate changes on deferred income taxes.

In our previous illustrations, the enacted tax rate did not change from one year to the next. Thus, to compute the deferred income tax amount to report on the balance sheet, a company simply multiplies the cumulative temporary difference by the current tax rate. Using Bio-Tech as an example, it multiplies the cumulative temporary difference of $18,000 by the enacted tax rate, 30 percent in this case, to arrive at a deferred tax liability of $5,400 ($18,000 × 30%) at the end of 2005.

Future Tax Rates

What happens if tax rates are expected to change in the future? In this case, a company should use the **enacted tax rate** expected to apply. Therefore, a company must consider presently enacted changes in the tax rate that become effective for a particular future year(s) when determining the tax rate to apply to existing temporary differences. For example, assume that Warlen Co. at the end of 2004 has the following cumulative temporary difference of $300,000, computed as shown in Illustration 19-26.

ILLUSTRATION 19-26
Computation of Cumulative Temporary Difference

Book basis of depreciable assets	$1,000,000
Tax basis of depreciable assets	700,000
Cumulative temporary difference	$ 300,000

Furthermore, assume that the $300,000 will reverse and result in taxable amounts in the future, with the enacted tax rates shown in Illustration 19-27.

	2005	2006	2007	2008	2009	Total
Future taxable amounts	$80,000	$70,000	$60,000	$50,000	$40,000	$300,000
Tax rate	40%	40%	35%	30%	30%	
Deferred tax liability	$32,000	$28,000	$21,000	$15,000	$12,000	$108,000

ILLUSTRATION 19-27
Deferred Tax Liability
Based on Future Rates

The total deferred tax liability at the end of 2004 is $108,000. Warlen may only use tax rates other than the current rate when the future tax rates have been enacted, as is the case in this example. **If new rates are not yet enacted for future years, Warlen should use the current rate.**

In determining the appropriate enacted tax rate for a given year, companies must use the **average tax rate**. The Internal Revenue Service and other taxing jurisdictions tax income on a graduated tax basis. For a U.S. corporation, the IRS taxes the first $50,000 of taxable income at 15 percent, the next $25,000 at 25 percent, with higher incremental levels of income at rates as high as 39 percent. In computing deferred income taxes, companies for which graduated tax rates are a significant factor must therefore **determine the average tax rate and use that rate**.

Revision of Future Tax Rates

When a change in the tax rate is enacted, companies should record its effect on the existing deferred income tax accounts immediately. **A company reports the effect as an adjustment to income tax expense in the period of the change.**

Assume that on December 10, 2004, a new income tax act is signed into law that lowers the corporate tax rate from 40 percent to 35 percent, effective January 1, 2006. If Hostel Co. has one temporary difference at the beginning of 2004 related to $3 million of excess tax depreciation, then it has a Deferred Tax Liability account with a balance of $1,200,000 ($3,000,000 × 40%) at January 1, 2004. If taxable amounts related to this difference are scheduled to occur equally in 2005, 2006, and 2007, the deferred tax liability at the end of 2004 is $1,100,000, computed as follows.

	2005	2006	2007	Total
Future taxable amounts	$1,000,000	$1,000,000	$1,000,000	$3,000,000
Tax rate	40%	35%	35%	
Deferred tax liability	$ 400,000	$ 350,000	$ 350,000	$1,100,000

ILLUSTRATION 19-28
Schedule of Future
Taxable Amounts and
Related Tax Rates

Hostel, therefore, recognizes the decrease of $100,000 ($1,200,000 − $1,100,000) at the end of 2004 in the deferred tax liability as follows.

Deferred Tax Liability	100,000	
Income Tax Expense		100,000

Corporate tax rates do not change often. Therefore, companies usually employ the current rate. However, state and foreign tax rates change more frequently, and they require adjustments in deferred income taxes accordingly.[3]

---

[3]Tax rate changes nearly always will substantially impact income numbers and the reporting of deferred income taxes on the balance sheet. As a result, you can expect to hear an economic consequences argument every time that Congress decides to change the tax rates. For example, when Congress raised the corporate rate from 34 percent to 35 percent in 1993, companies took an additional "hit" to earnings if they were in a deferred tax liability position.

SHELTERED

As mentioned in our opening story, companies employ various tax strategies to reduce their tax bills and their effective tax rates. The following table reports some recent high-profile cases in which profitable companies paid little income tax and, in some cases, got tax refunds.

Company	Pre-Tax Income ($ millions)	Federal Tax Paid (Refund) ($ millions)	Tax Rate (%)
Enron	$ 1,785	$(381)	(21.34)%
El Paso Energy	1,638	(254)	(15.51)
Goodyear	442	(23)	(5.20)
Navistar	1,368	28	2.05
General Motors	12,468	740	5.94

These companies used various tools to lower their tax bills, including off-shore tax shelters, tax deferrals, and hefty use of stock options, the cost of which reduce taxable income but do not affect pretax financial income. Thus, companies can use various provisions in the tax code to reduce their effective tax rate well below the statutory rate of 35 percent.

One IRS provision designed to curb excessive tax avoidance is the **alternative minimum tax (AMT)**. Companies compute their potential tax liability under the AMT, adjusting for various preference items that reduce their tax bills under the regular tax code. (Examples of such preference items are accelerated depreciation methods and the installment method for revenue recognition.) Companies must pay the higher of the two tax obligations computed under the AMT and the regular tax code. But, as indicated by the cases above, some profitable companies avoid high tax bills, even in the presence of the AMT. Many citizens and public-interest groups cite corporate avoidance of income taxes as a reason for more tax reform.

Source: H. Gleckman, D. Foust, M. Arndt, and K. Kerwin, "Tax Dodging: Enron Isn't Alone," *Business Week* (March 4, 2002), pp. 40–41.

ACCOUNTING FOR NET OPERATING LOSSES

OBJECTIVE 8
Apply accounting procedures for a loss carryback and a loss carryforward.

Every management hopes its company will be profitable. But hopes and profits may not materialize. For a start-up company, it is common to accumulate operating losses while expanding its customer base but before realizing economies of scale. For an established company, a major event such as a labor strike, rapidly changing regulatory and competitive forces, or a disaster such as 9/11 or Hurricane Katrina can cause expenses to exceed revenues—a net operating loss.

A **net operating loss (NOL)** occurs for tax purposes in a year when tax-deductible expenses exceed taxable revenues. An inequitable tax burden would result if companies were taxed during profitable periods without receiving any tax relief during periods of net operating losses. Under certain circumstances, therefore, the federal tax laws permit taxpayers to use the losses of one year to offset the profits of other years.

Companies accomplish this income-averaging provision through the **carryback and carryforward of net operating losses**. Under this provision, a company pays no income taxes for a year in which it incurs a net operating loss. In addition, it may select one of the two options discussed below and on the following pages.

Loss Carryback

Through use of a **loss carryback**, a company may carry the net operating loss back two years and receive refunds for income taxes paid in those years. The company must apply the loss to the earlier year first and then to the second year. It may **carry**

forward any loss remaining after the two-year carryback up to 20 years to offset future taxable income. Illustration 19-29 diagrams the loss carryback procedure, assuming a loss in 2007.

ILLUSTRATION 19-29
Loss Carryback
Procedure

Loss Carryforward

A company may forgo the loss carryback and use only the **loss carryforward** option, offsetting future taxable income for up to 20 years. Illustration 19-30 shows this approach.

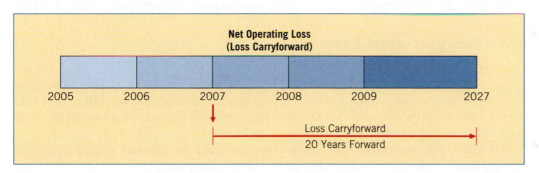

ILLUSTRATION 19-30
Loss Carryforward
Procedure

Operating losses can be substantial. For example, **Yahoo** had net operating losses of approximately $5.4 billion at year-end 2004. That amount translates into tax savings of $1.4 billion if Yahoo is able to generate taxable income before the NOLs expire.

Loss Carryback Example

To illustrate the accounting procedures for a net operating loss carryback, assume that Groh Inc. has no temporary or permanent differences. Groh experiences the following.

Year	Taxable Income or Loss	Tax Rate	Tax Paid
2003	$ 50,000	35%	$17,500
2004	100,000	30%	30,000
2005	200,000	40%	80,000
2006	(500,000)	—	–0–

In 2006, Groh incurs a net operating loss that it decides to carry back. Under the law, Groh must apply the carryback first to the **second year preceding the loss year**. Therefore, it carries the loss back first to 2004. Then, Groh carries back any unused loss to 2005. Accordingly, Groh files amended tax returns for 2004 and 2005, receiving refunds for the $110,000 ($30,000 + $80,000) of taxes paid in those years.

For accounting as well as tax purposes, the $110,000 represents the **tax effect (tax benefit)** of the loss carryback. Groh should recognize this tax effect in 2006, the loss year. Since the tax loss gives rise to a refund that is both measurable and currently realizable, Groh should recognize the associated tax benefit in this loss period.

Groh makes the following journal entry for 2006.

Income Tax Refund Receivable	110,000	
Benefit Due to Loss Carryback (Income Tax Expense)		110,000

Groh reports the account debited, **Income Tax Refund Receivable**, on the balance sheet as a current asset at December 31, 2006. It reports the account credited on the income statement for 2006 as shown in Illustration 19-31.

ILLUSTRATION 19-31
Recognition of Benefit of the Loss Carryback in the Loss Year

GROH INC.	
INCOME STATEMENT (PARTIAL) FOR **2006**	
Operating loss before income taxes	$(500,000)
Income tax benefit	
Benefit due to loss carryback	110,000
Net loss	$(390,000)

Since the $500,000 net operating loss for 2006 exceeds the $300,000 total taxable income from the 2 preceding years, Groh carries forward the remaining $200,000 loss.

Loss Carryforward Example

If a carryback fails to fully absorb a net operating loss, or if the company decides not to carry the loss back, then it can carry forward the loss for up to 20 years.[4] Because companies use carryforwards to offset future taxable income, the **tax effect of a loss carryforward** represents **future tax savings**. Realization of the future tax benefit depends on future earnings, an uncertain prospect.

The key accounting issue is whether there should be different requirements for recognition of a deferred tax asset for (a) deductible temporary differences, and (b) operating loss carryforwards. The FASB's position is that in substance these items are the same—both are tax-deductible amounts in future years. As a result, the Board concluded that there **should not be different requirements** for recognition of a deferred tax asset from deductible temporary differences and operating loss carryforwards.[5]

Carryforward Without Valuation Allowance

To illustrate the accounting for an operating loss carryforward, return to the Groh example from the preceding section. In 2006 the company records the tax effect of the $200,000 loss carryforward as a deferred tax asset of $80,000 ($200,000 × 40%), assuming that the enacted future tax rate is 40 percent. Groh records the benefits of the carryback and the carryforward in 2006 as follows.

To recognize benefit of loss carryback

Income Tax Refund Receivable	110,000	
Benefit Due to Loss Carryback (Income Tax Expense)		110,000

To recognize benefit of loss carryforward

Deferred Tax Asset	80,000	
Benefit Due to Loss Carryforward (Income Tax Expense)		80,000

---

[4]The length of the carryforward period has varied. It has increased from 7 years to 20 years over a period of time.

[5]This requirement is controversial because many believe it is inappropriate to recognize deferred tax assets except when assured beyond a reasonable doubt. Others argue that companies should never recognize deferred tax assets for loss carryforwards until realizing the income in the future.

Groh realizes the income tax refund receivable of $110,000 immediately as a refund of taxes paid in the past. It establishes a Deferred Tax Asset for the benefits of future tax savings. The two accounts credited are contra income tax expense items, which Groh presents on the 2006 income statement shown in Illustration 19-32.

GROH INC.		
INCOME STATEMENT (PARTIAL) FOR **2006**		
Operating loss before income taxes		$(500,000)
Income tax benefit		
Benefit due to loss carryback	$110,000	
Benefit due to loss carryforward	80,000	190,000
Net loss		$(310,000)

ILLUSTRATION 19-32
Recognition of the Benefit of the Loss Carryback and Carryforward in the Loss Year

The **current tax benefit** of $110,000 is the income tax refundable for the year. Groh determines this amount by applying the carryback provisions of the tax law to the taxable loss for 2006. The $80,000 is the **deferred tax benefit** for the year, which results from an increase in the deferred tax asset.

For 2007, assume that Groh returns to profitable operations and has taxable income of $250,000 (prior to adjustment for the NOL carryforward), subject to a 40 percent tax rate. Groh then realizes the benefits of the carryforward for tax purposes in 2007, which it recognized for accounting purposes in 2006. Groh computes the income tax payable for 2007 as shown in Illustration 19-33.

Taxable income prior to loss carryforward	$ 250,000
Loss carryforward deduction	(200,000)
Taxable income for 2007	50,000
Tax rate	40%
Income tax payable for 2007	$ 20,000

ILLUSTRATION 19-33
Computation of Income Tax Payable with Realized Loss Carryforward

Groh records income taxes in 2007 as follows.

Income Tax Expense	100,000	
Deferred Tax Asset		80,000
Income Tax Payable		20,000

The benefits of the NOL carryforward, realized in 2007, reduce the Deferred Tax Asset account to zero.

The 2007 income statement that appears in Illustration 19-34 does **not report** the tax effects of either the loss carryback or the loss carryforward, because Groh had reported both previously.

GROH INC.		
INCOME STATEMENT (PARTIAL) FOR **2007**		
Income before income taxes		$250,000
Income tax expense		
Current	$20,000	
Deferred	80,000	100,000
Net income		$150,000

ILLUSTRATION 19-34
Presentation of the Benefit of Loss Carryforward Realized in 2007, Recognized in 2006

Carryforward with Valuation Allowance

Let us return to the Groh example. Assume that it is more likely than not that Groh will *not* realize the entire NOL carryforward in future years. In this situation, Groh records the tax benefits of $110,000 associated with the $300,000 NOL carryback, as we previously described. In addition, it records a Deferred Tax Asset of $80,000 ($200,000 × 40%) for the potential benefits related to the loss carryforward, and an allowance to reduce the deferred tax asset by the same amount. Groh makes the following journal entries in 2006.

To recognize benefit of loss carryback

Income Tax Refund Receivable	110,000	
Benefit Due to Loss Carryback (Income Tax Expense)		110,000

To recognize benefit of loss carryforward

Deferred Tax Asset	80,000	
Benefit Due to Loss Carryforward (Income Tax Expense)		80,000

To record allowance amount

Benefit Due to Loss Carryforward (Income Tax Expense)	80,000	
Allowance to Reduce Deferred Tax Asset		
to Expected Realizable Value		80,000

The latter entry indicates that because positive evidence of sufficient quality and quantity is unavailable to counteract the negative evidence, Groh needs a valuation allowance. Illustration 19-35 shows Groh's 2006 income statement presentation.

ILLUSTRATION 19-35
Recognition of Benefit of Loss Carryback Only

GROH INC.	
INCOME STATEMENT (PARTIAL) FOR 2006	
Operating loss before income taxes	$(500,000)
Income tax benefit	
Benefit due to loss carryback	110,000
Net loss	$(390,000)

In 2007, assuming that Groh has taxable income of $250,000 (before considering the carryforward), subject to a tax rate of 40 percent, it realizes the deferred tax asset. It thus no longer needs the allowance. Groh records the following entries.

To record current and deferred income taxes

Income Tax Expense	100,000	
Deferred Tax Asset		80,000
Income Tax Payable		20,000

To eliminate allowance and recognize loss carryforward

Allowance to Reduce Deferred Tax Asset to		
Expected Realizable Value	80,000	
Benefit Due to Loss Carryforward (Income Tax Expense)		80,000

Groh reports the $80,000 Benefit Due to the Loss Carryforward on the 2007 income statement. The company did not recognize it in 2006 because it was more likely than not that it would not be realized. Assuming that Groh derives the income for 2007 from continuing operations, it prepares the income statement as shown in Illustration 19-36.

ILLUSTRATION 19-36
Recognition of Benefit of Loss Carryforward When Realized

GROH INC.		
INCOME STATEMENT (PARTIAL) FOR 2007		
Income before income taxes		$250,000
Income tax expense		
Current	$ 20,000	
Deferred	80,000	
Benefit due to loss carryforward	(80,000)	20,000
Net income		$230,000

Another method is to report only one line for total income tax expense of $20,000 on the face of the income statement and disclose the components of income tax expense in the notes to the financial statements.

Valuation Allowance Revisited

A company should consider all positive and negative information in determining whether it needs a valuation allowance. Whether the company will realize a deferred tax asset depends on whether sufficient taxable income exists or will exist within the carryforward period available under tax law. Illustration 19-37 shows possible sources of taxable income that may be available under the tax law to realize a tax benefit for deductible temporary differences and carryforwards.

ILLUSTRATION 19-37
Possible Sources of Taxable Income

Taxable Income Sources

a. Future reversals of existing taxable temporary differences

b. Future taxable income exclusive of reversing temporary differences and carryforwards

c. Taxable income in prior carryback year(s) if carryback is permitted under the tax law

d. Tax-planning strategies that would, if necessary, be implemented to:
   (1) Accelerate taxable amounts to utilize expiring carryforwards
   (2) Change the character of taxable or deductible amounts from ordinary income or loss to capital gain or loss
   (3) Switch from tax-exempt to taxable investments.[6]

If any one of these sources is sufficient to support a conclusion that a valuation allowance is unnecessary, a company need not consider other sources.

Forming a conclusion that a valuation allowance is not needed is difficult when there is negative evidence such as cumulative losses in recent years. Companies may also cite positive evidence indicating that a valuation allowance is not needed. Illustration 19-38 presents examples (not prerequisites) of evidence to consider when determining the need for a valuation allowance.

ILLUSTRATION 19-38
Evidence to Consider in Evaluating the Need for a Valuation Account

---

Negative Evidence

a. A history of operating loss or tax credit carryforwards expiring unused

b. Losses expected in early future years (by a presently profitable entity)

c. Unsettled circumstances that, if unfavorably resolved, would adversely affect future operations and profit levels on a continuing basis in future years

d. A carryback, carryforward period that is so brief that it would limit realization of tax benefits if (1) a significant deductible temporary difference is expected to reverse in a single year or (2) the enterprise operates in a traditionally cyclical business.

Positive Evidence

a. Existing contracts or firm sales backlog that will produce more than enough taxable income to realize the deferred tax asset based on existing sale prices and cost structures

b. An excess of appreciated asset value over the tax basis of the entity's net assets in an amount sufficient to realize the deferred tax asset

c. A strong earnings history exclusive of the loss that created the future deductible amount (tax loss carryforward or deductible temporary difference) coupled with evidence indicating that the loss is an aberration rather than a continuing condition (for example, the result of an unusual, infrequent, or extraordinary item).[7]

INTERNATIONAL INSIGHT

Under international accounting standards *(IAS 12)*, a company may not recognize a deferred tax asset unless realization is "probable." However, "probable" is not defined in the standard, leading to diversity in the recognition of deferred tax assets.

The use of a valuation allowance provides a company with an opportunity to manage its earnings. As one accounting expert notes, "The 'more likely than not' provision is perhaps the most judgmental clause in accounting." Some companies may set up a valuation account and then use it to increase income as needed. Others may take the income immediately to increase capital or to offset large negative charges to income.

---

[6]"Accounting for Income Taxes," *Statement of Financial Accounting Standards No. 109* (Norwalk, Conn.: FASB, 1992). Companies implement a tax-planning strategy to realize a tax benefit for an operating loss or tax credit carryforward before it expires. Companies consider tax-planning strategies when assessing the need for and amount of a valuation allowance for deferred tax assets.

[7]Ibid., pars. 23 and 24.

WHAT DO THE NUMBERS MEAN?

A recent study of companies' valuation allowances indicates that the allowances are related to the factors identified as positive and negative evidence. And though there is little evidence that companies use the valuation allowance to manage earnings, the press sometimes understates the impact of reversing the deferred tax valuation allowance.

For example, in one year **Verity, Inc.** eliminated its entire valuation allowance of $18.9 million but focused on a net deferred tax gain of $2.9 million in its press release. Why the difference? As revealed in Verity's financial statement notes, other deferred tax expense amounts totaled over $16 million. Thus, the one-time valuation reversal gave an $18.9 million bump to income, not the net $2.9 million reported in the press.

The lesson: After you read the morning paper, read the financial statement notes.

Source: G. S Miller and D. J. Skinner, "Determinants of the Valuation Allowance for Deferred Tax Assets under *SFAS No. 109*," *The Accounting Review* (April 1998).

FINANCIAL STATEMENT PRESENTATION

Balance Sheet

OBJECTIVE 9
Describe the presentation of deferred income taxes in financial statements.

Deferred tax accounts are reported on the balance sheet as assets and liabilities. Companies should classify these accounts as a net current amount and a net noncurrent amount. **An individual deferred tax liability or asset is classified as current or noncurrent based on the classification of the related asset or liability for financial reporting purposes.**

A company considers a deferred tax asset or liability to be related to an asset or liability, if reduction of the asset or liability causes the temporary difference to reverse or turn around. A company should classify a deferred tax liability or asset that is unrelated to an asset or liability for financial reporting, including a deferred tax asset related to a loss carryforward, according to the expected reversal date of the temporary difference.

To illustrate, assume that Morgan Inc. records bad debt expense using the allowance method for accounting purposes and the direct write-off method for tax purposes. It currently has Accounts Receivable and Allowance for Doubtful Accounts balances of $2 million and $100,000, respectively. In addition, given a 40 percent tax rate, Morgan has a debit balance in the Deferred Tax Asset account of $40,000 (40% × $100,000). It considers the $40,000 debit balance in the Deferred Tax Asset account to be related to the Accounts Receivable and the Allowance for Doubtful Accounts balances because collection or write-off of the receivables will cause the temporary difference to reverse. Therefore, Morgan classifies the Deferred Tax Asset account as current, the same as the Accounts Receivable and Allowance for Doubtful Accounts balances.

In practice, most companies engage in a large number of transactions that give rise to deferred taxes. Companies should classify the balances in the deferred tax accounts on the balance sheet in two categories: one for the **net current amount**, and one for the **net noncurrent amount**. We summarize this procedure as follows.

1 *Classify the amounts as current or noncurrent.* If related to a specific asset or liability, classify the amounts in the same manner as the related asset or liability. If not related, classify them on the basis of the expected reversal date of the temporary difference.

2 *Determine the net current amount* by summing the various deferred tax assets and liabilities classified as current. If the net result is an asset, report it on the balance sheet as a current asset; if a liability, report it as a current liability.

3 *Determine the net noncurrent amount* by summing the various deferred tax assets and liabilities classified as noncurrent. If the net result is an asset, report it on the balance sheet as a noncurrent asset; if a liability, report it as a long-term liability.

To illustrate, assume that K. Scott Company has four deferred tax items at December 31, 2007. Illustration 19-39 shows an analysis of these four temporary differences as current or noncurrent.

ILLUSTRATION 19-39
Classification of
Temporary Differences as
Current or Noncurrent

Temporary Difference	Resulting Deferred Tax (Asset)	Liability	Related Balance Sheet Account	Classification
1. Rent collected in advance: recognized when earned for accounting purposes and when received for tax purposes.	$(42,000)		Unearned Rent	Current
2. Use of straight-line depreciation for accounting purposes and accelerated depreciation for tax purposes.		$214,000	Equipment	Noncurrent
3. Recognition of profits on installment sales during period of sale for accounting purposes and during period of collection for tax purposes.		45,000	Installment Accounts Receivable	Current
4. Warranty liabilities: recognized for accounting purposes at time of sale; for tax purposes at time paid.	(12,000)		Estimated Liability under Warranties	Current
Totals	$(54,000)	$259,000		

K. Scott classifies as current a deferred tax asset of $9,000 ($42,000 + $12,000 − $45,000). It also reports as noncurrent a deferred tax liability of $214,000. Consequently, K. Scott's December 31, 2007, balance sheet reports deferred income taxes as shown in Illustration 19-40.

ILLUSTRATION 19-40
Balance Sheet
Presentation of Deferred
Income Taxes

Current assets	
Deferred tax asset	$ 9,000
Long-term liabilities	
Deferred tax liability	$214,000

As we indicated earlier, a deferred tax asset or liability **may not be related** to an asset or liability for financial reporting purposes. One example is an operating loss carryforward. In this case, a company records a deferred tax asset, but there is no related, identifiable asset or liability for financial reporting purposes. In these limited situations, deferred income taxes are classified according to the **expected reversal date** of the temporary difference. That is, a company should report the tax effect of any temporary difference reversing next year as current, and the remainder as noncurrent. If a deferred tax asset is noncurrent, a company should classify it in the "Other assets" section.

The total of all deferred tax liabilities, the total of all deferred tax assets, and the total valuation allowance should be disclosed. In addition, companies should disclose the following: (1) any net change during the year in the total valuation allowance, and (2) the types of temporary differences, carryforwards, or carrybacks that give rise to significant portions of deferred tax liabilities and assets.

Income tax payable is reported as a current liability on the balance sheet. Corporations make estimated tax payments to the Internal Revenue Service quarterly. They record these estimated payments by a debit to Prepaid Income Taxes. As a result, the balance of the Income Tax Payable offsets the balance of the Prepaid Income Taxes account when reporting income taxes on the balance sheet.

Income Statement

Companies should allocate income tax expense (or benefit) to continuing operations, discontinued operations, extraordinary items, and prior period adjustments. This approach is referred to as intraperiod tax allocation.

*Expanded Discussion of
Intraperiod Tax Allocation*

In addition, companies should disclose the significant components of income tax expense attributable to continuing operations:

1 Current tax expense or benefit.

2 Deferred tax expense or benefit, exclusive of other components listed below.

3 Investment tax credits.

4 Government grants (if recognized as a reduction of income tax expense).

5 The benefits of operating loss carryforwards (resulting in a reduction of income tax expense).

6 Tax expense that results from allocating tax benefits either directly to paid-in capital or to reduce goodwill or other noncurrent intangible assets of an acquired entity.

7 Adjustments of a deferred tax liability or asset for enacted changes in tax laws or rates or a change in the tax status of a company.

8 Adjustments of the beginning-of-the-year balance of a valuation allowance because of a change in circumstances that causes a change in judgment about the realizability of the related deferred tax asset in future years.

In the notes, companies must also reconcile (using percentages or dollar amounts) income tax expense attributable to continuing operations with the amount that results from applying domestic federal statutory tax rates to pretax income from continuing operations. Companies should disclose the estimated amount and the nature of each significant reconciling item. Illustration 19-41 (page 987) presents an example from the 2004 annual report of **PepsiCo, Inc.**.

These income tax disclosures are required for several reasons:

Additional Examples of Deferred Tax Disclosures

1 *Assessing Quality of Earnings.* Many investors seeking to assess the quality of a company's earnings are interested in the reconciliation of pretax financial income to taxable income. Analysts carefully examine earnings that are enhanced by a favorable tax effect, particularly if the tax effect is nonrecurring. For example, the tax disclosure in Illustration 19-41 indicates that **PepsiCo**'s effective tax rate declined from 28.5 percent in 2003 to 24.7 percent in 2004 (primarily due to settlement of a prior year's tax audit.) The decline translates into a tax savings of $38 million. These savings contributed to PepsiCo's increase in bottom-line income from 2003 to 2004.

2 *Making Better Predictions of Future Cash Flows.* Examination of the deferred portion of income tax expense provides information as to whether taxes payable are likely to be higher or lower in the future. In **PepsiCo**'s case, analysts expect significant future taxable amounts and higher tax payments, due to realization of gains on equity investments, lower depreciation in the future, and higher payments for pension expense. As a result, it may be possible to predict future reductions in deferred tax liabilities leading to a loss of liquidity. Why? Because actual tax payments will be higher than the tax expense reported on the income statement.[8]

3 *Predicting Future Cash Flows from Operating Loss Carryforwards.* Companies should disclose the amounts and expiration dates of any operating loss carryforwards for tax purposes. From this disclosure, analysts determine the amount of income that the company may recognize in the future on which it will pay no income tax. For example, the **PepsiCo** disclosure in Illustration 19-41 indicates that PepsiCo has $4.3 billion in net operating loss carryforwards that it can use to reduce future taxes up to the year 2024 and beyond. However, the valuation allowance indicates that $564 million of the deferred tax asset may not be realized in the future.

Loss carryforwards can be valuable to a potential acquirer. For example, as mentioned earlier, **Yahoo** has a substantial net operating loss carryforward. A potential acquirer would find Yahoo more valuable as a result of these carryforwards. That is, the

---

[8]An article by R. P. Weber and J. E. Wheeler, "Using Income Tax Disclosures to Explore Significant Economic Transactions," *Accounting Horizons* (September 1992), discusses how analysts use deferred tax disclosures to assess the quality of earnings and to predict future cash flows.

ILLUSTRATION 19-41
Disclosure of Income
Taxes—PepsiCo, Inc.

PepsiCo, Inc.
(in millions)

Note 13: Income Taxes	2004	2003
Income before income taxes—continuing operations		
U.S.	$2,946	$3,267
Foreign	2,600	1,725
	$5,546	$4,992
Provision for income taxes—continuing operations		
Current: U.S. Federal	$1,030	$1,326
Foreign	256	341
State	69	80
	1,355	1,747
Deferred: U.S. Federal	11	(274)
Foreign	5	(47)
State	1	(2)
	17	(323)
	$1,372	$1,424
Tax rate reconciliation—continuing operations		
U.S. Federal statutory tax rate	35.0%	35.0%
State income tax, net of U.S. Federal tax benefit	0.8	1.0
Lower taxes on foreign results	(5.4)	(5.5)
Settlement of prior years audit	(4.8)	(2.2)
Merger-related costs and impairment and restructuring charges	—	0.1
Other, net	(0.9)	0.1
Annual tax rate	24.7%	28.5%
Deferred tax liabilities		
Investments in noncontrolled affiliates	$ 850	$ 792
Property, plant and equipment	857	806
Pension benefits	669	563
Intangible assets other than nondeductible goodwill	153	146
Safe harbor leases	13	33
Zero coupon notes	46	53
Other	144	199
Gross deferred tax liabilities	2,732	2,592
Deferred tax assets		
Net carryforwards	666	535
Stock-based compensation	402	332
Retiree medical benefits	402	343
Other employee-related benefits	379	384
Various current and noncurrent liabilities	460	482
Gross deferred tax assets	2,309	2,076
Valuation allowances	(564)	(438)
Deferred tax assets, net	1,745	1,638
Net deferred tax liabilities	$ 987	$ 954
Deferred taxes included within:		
Prepaid expenses and other current assets	$ 229	$ 307
Deferred income taxes	$1,216	$1,261
Analysis of valuation allowances		
Balance, beginning of year	$ 438	$ 487
Provision/(benefit)	118	(52)
Other additions/(deductions)	8	3
Balance, end of year	$ 564	$ 438

Carryforwards, Credits and Allowances

Operating loss carryforwards totaling $4.3 billion at year-end 2004 are being carried forward in a number of foreign and state jurisdictions where we are permitted to use tax operating losses from prior periods to reduce future taxable income. These operating losses will expire as follows: $0.1 billion in 2005, $3.1 billion between 2006 and 2024 and $1.1 billion may be carried forward indefinitely. In addition, certain tax credits generated in prior periods of approximately $49.3 million are available to reduce certain foreign tax liabilities through 2011. We establish valuation allowances for our deferred tax assets when the amount of expected future taxable income is not likely to support the use of the deduction or credit.

Tax Benefit from Discontinued Operations

In the fourth quarter of 2004, we reached agreement with the taxing authorities for an open issue related to our discontinued restaurant operations which resulted in a tax benefit of $38 million or $0.02 per share.

acquirer may be able to use these carryforwards to shield future income. However the acquiring company has to be careful, because the structure of the deal may lead to a situation where the deductions will be severely limited.

Much the same issue arises in companies emerging from bankruptcy. In many cases these companies have large NOLs, but the value of the losses may be limited. This is because any gains related to the cancellation of liabilities in bankruptcy must be offset against the NOLs. For example, when **Kmart Holding Corp.** emerged from bankruptcy in early 2004, it disclosed NOL carryforwards approximating $3.8 billion. At the same time, Kmart disclosed cancellation of debt gains that reduced the value of the NOL carryforward. These reductions soured the merger between Kmart and **Sears Roebuck** because the cancellation of the indebtedness gains reduced the value of the Kmart carryforwards to the merged company by $3.74 billion.[9]

WHAT DO THE NUMBERS MEAN?

NOLs: GOOD NEWS OR BAD?

Here are some net operating loss numbers recently reported by several notable companies.

NOLs ($ in millions)

Company	2004 Income (Loss)	Operating Loss Carryforward	Tax Benefit (Deferred Tax Asset)	Comment
Delta Airlines, Inc.	($5,198.00)	$7,500.00	$2,848.00	Begins to expire in 2022. Valuation allowance recorded.
Goodyear	114.80	1,306.60*	457.30	Begins to expire in 2005. Full valuation allowance.
Kodak	556.00	509.00	234.00	Begins to expire in 2005. Valuation allowance on foreign credits only.
Krispy Kreme	57.09	26.40*	9.24	No valuation allowance.
Yahoo Inc.	42.82	5,400.00	1,443.50	State and federal carryforwards. Begins to expire in 2005. Valuation allowance recorded.

*Not reported; estimated as [(Tax benefit) ÷ 35%].

All of these companies are using the carryforward provisions of the tax code for their NOLs. For many of them, the NOL is an amount far exceeding their reported profits. Why carry forward the loss to get the tax deduction? First, the company may have already used up the carryback provision, which allows only a two-year carryback period. (Carryforwards can be claimed up to 20 years in the future.) In some cases, management expects the tax rates in the future to be higher. This difference in expected rates provides a bigger tax benefit if the losses are carried forward and matched against future income. Is there a downside? To realize the benefits of carryforwards, a company must have future taxable income in the carryforward period in order to claim the NOL deductions. As we learned, if it is more likely than not that a company will not have taxable income, it must record a valuation allowance (and increased tax expense). As the data above indicate, recording a valuation allowance to reflect the uncertainty of realizing the tax benefits has merit. But for some, the NOL benefits begin to expire in the following year, which may be not enough time to generate sufficient taxable income in order to claim the NOL deduction.

Source: Company annual reports.

---

[9]P. McConnell, J. Pegg, C. Senyak, and D. Mott, "The ABCs of NOLs," *Accounting Issues*, Bear Stearns Equity Research (June 2005). The IRS frowns on acquisitions done solely to obtain operating loss carryforwards. If it determines that the merger is solely tax motivated, the IRS disallows the deductions. But because it is very difficult to determine whether a merger is or is not tax-motivated, the "purchase of operating loss carryforwards" continues.

REVIEW OF THE ASSET-LIABILITY METHOD

The FASB believes that the **asset-liability method** (sometimes referred to as the **liability approach**) is the most consistent method for accounting for income taxes. One objective of this approach is to recognize the amount of taxes payable or refundable for the current year. A second objective is to recognize **deferred tax liabilities and assets** for the **future tax consequences** of events that have been recognized in the financial statements or tax returns.

To implement the objectives, companies apply some basic principles in accounting for income taxes at the date of the financial statements, as listed in Illustration 19-42.

Basic Principles

a. A current tax liability or asset is recognized for the estimated taxes payable or refundable on the tax return for the current year.
b. A deferred tax liability or asset is recognized for the estimated future tax effects attributable to temporary differences and carryforwards.
c. The measurement of current and deferred tax liabilities and assets is based on provisions of the enacted tax law; the effects of future changes in tax laws or rates are not anticipated.
d. The measurement of deferred tax assets is reduced, if necessary, by the amount of any tax benefits that, based on available evidence, are not expected to be realized.[10]

OBJECTIVE 10
Indicate the basic principles of the asset-liability method.

ILLUSTRATION 19-42
Basic Principles of the Asset-Liability Method

Discussion of Conceptual Approaches to Interperiod Tax Allocation

Illustration 19-43 diagrams the procedures for implementing the asset-liability method.

ILLUSTRATION 19-43
Procedures for Computing and Reporting Deferred Income Taxes

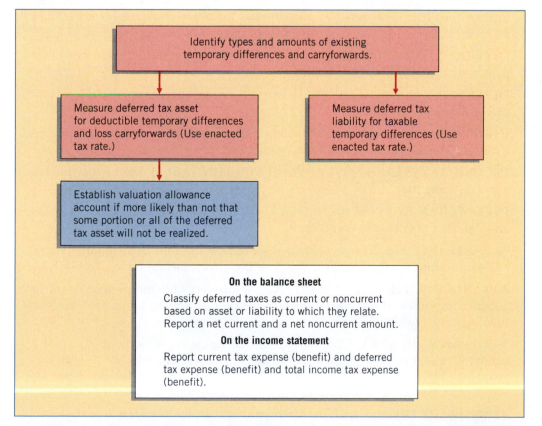

As an aid to understanding deferred income taxes, we provide the following glossary.[11]

---

[10]"Accounting for Income Taxes" (1992), pars. 6 and 8.

[11]"Accounting for Income Taxes," Appendix E.

INTERNATIONAL INSIGHT

The IFRS on income taxes is based on the same principles as the U.S. GAAP—comprehensive recognition of deferred tax assets and liabilities.

KEY DEFERRED INCOME TAX TERMS

CARRYBACKS. Deductions or credits that cannot be utilized on the tax return during a year and that may be carried back to reduce taxable income or taxes paid in a prior year. An **operating loss carryback** is an excess of tax deductions over gross income in a year. A **tax credit carryback** is the amount by which tax credits available for utilization exceed statutory limitations.

CARRYFORWARDS. Deductions or credits that cannot be utilized on the tax return during a year and that may be carried forward to reduce taxable income or taxes payable in a future year. An **operating loss carryforward** is an excess of tax deductions over gross income in a year. A **tax credit carryforward** is the amount by which tax credits available for utilization exceed statutory limitations.

CURRENT TAX EXPENSE (BENEFIT). The amount of income taxes paid or payable (or refundable) for a year as determined by applying the provisions of the enacted tax law to the taxable income or excess of deductions over revenues for that year.

DEDUCTIBLE TEMPORARY DIFFERENCE. Temporary differences that result in deductible amounts in future years when recovering or settling the related asset or liability, respectively.

DEFERRED TAX ASSET. The deferred tax consequences attributable to deductible temporary differences and carryforwards.

DEFERRED TAX CONSEQUENCES. The future effects on income taxes as measured by the enacted tax rate and provisions of the enacted tax law resulting from temporary differences and carryforwards at the end of the current year.

DEFERRED TAX EXPENSE (BENEFIT). The change during the year in a company's deferred tax liabilities and assets.

DEFERRED TAX LIABILITY. The deferred tax consequences attributable to taxable temporary differences.

INCOME TAXES. Domestic and foreign federal (national), state, and local (including franchise) taxes based on income.

INCOME TAXES CURRENTLY PAYABLE (REFUNDABLE). Refer to current tax expense (benefit).

INCOME TAX EXPENSE (BENEFIT). The sum of current tax expense (benefit) and deferred tax expense (benefit).

TAXABLE INCOME. The excess of taxable revenues over tax deductible expenses and exemptions for the year as defined by the governmental taxing authority.

TAXABLE TEMPORARY DIFFERENCE. Temporary differences that result in taxable amounts in future years when recovering or settling the related asset or liability, respectively.

TAX-PLANNING STRATEGY. An action that meets certain criteria and that a company implements to realize a tax benefit for an operating loss or tax credit carryforward before it expires. Companies consider tax-planning strategies when assessing the need for and amount of a valuation allowance for deferred tax assets.

TEMPORARY DIFFERENCE. A difference between the tax basis of an asset or liability and its reported amount in the financial statements that will result in taxable or deductible amounts in future years when recovering or settling the reported amount of the asset or liability, respectively.

VALUATION ALLOWANCE. The portion of a deferred tax asset for which it is more likely than not that a company will not realize a tax benefit.

SUMMARY OF LEARNING OBJECTIVES

1. Identify differences between pretax financial income and taxable income. Companies compute pretax financial income (or income for book purposes) in accordance with generally accepted accounting principles. They compute taxable income (or income for tax purposes) in accordance with prescribed tax regulations. Because tax regulations and GAAP differ in many ways, so frequently do pretax financial income and taxable income. Differences may exist, for example, in the timing of revenue recognition and the timing of expense recognition.

2. Describe a temporary difference that results in future taxable amounts. Revenue recognized for book purposes in the period earned but deferred and reported as revenue for tax purposes when collected results in future taxable amounts. The future taxable amounts will occur in the periods the company recovers the receivable and reports the collections as revenue for tax purposes. This results in a deferred tax liability.

3. Describe a temporary difference that results in future deductible amounts. An accrued warranty expense that a company pays for and deducts for tax purposes, in a period later than the period in which it incurs and recognizes it for book purposes, results in future deductible amounts. The future deductible amounts will occur in the periods during which the company settles the related liability for book purposes. This results in a deferred tax asset.

4. Explain the purpose of a deferred tax asset valuation allowance. A deferred tax asset should be reduced by a valuation allowance if, based on all available evidence, it is more likely than not (a level of likelihood that is at least slightly more than 50 percent) that it will not realize some portion or all of the deferred tax asset. The company should carefully consider all available evidence, both positive and negative, to determine whether, based on the weight of available evidence, it needs a valuation allowance.

5. Describe the presentation of income tax expense in the income statement. Significant components of income tax expense should be disclosed in the income statement or in the notes to the financial statements. The most commonly encountered components are the current expense (or benefit) and the deferred expense (or benefit).

6. Describe various temporary and permanent differences. Examples of temporary differences are: (1) revenue or gains that are taxable after recognition in financial income; (2) expenses or losses that are deductible after recognition in financial income; (3) revenues or gains that are taxable before recognition in financial income; (4) expenses or losses that are deductible before recognition in financial income. Examples of permanent differences are: (1) items recognized for financial reporting purposes but not for tax purposes, and (2) items recognized for tax purposes but not for financial reporting purposes.

7. Explain the effect of various tax rates and tax rate changes on deferred income taxes. Companies may use tax rates other than the current rate only after enactment of the future tax rates. When a change in the tax rate is enacted, a company should immediately recognize its effect on the deferred income tax accounts. The company reports the effects as an adjustment to income tax expense in the period of the change.

8. Apply accounting procedures for a loss carryback and a loss carryforward. A company may carry a net operating loss back two years and receive refunds for income taxes paid in those years. The loss is applied to the earlier year first and then to the second year. Any loss remaining after the two-year carryback may be carried forward up to 20 years to offset future taxable income. A company may forgo the loss carryback and use the loss carryforward, offsetting future taxable income for up to 20 years.

9. Describe the presentation of deferred income taxes in financial statements. Companies report deferred tax accounts on the balance sheet as assets and liabilities. These deferred tax accounts are classified as a net current and a net noncurrent amount.

KEY TERMS

alternative minimum tax (AMT), *978*

asset-liability method, *989*

average tax rate, *977*

current tax benefit (expense), *967, 981*

deductible amounts, *966*

deductible temporary difference, *973*

deferred tax asset, *970*

deferred tax expense (benefit), *967, 970*

deferred tax liability, *967*

effective tax rate, *976*

enacted tax rate, *976*

Income Tax Refund Receivable, *980*

loss carryback, *978*

loss carryforward, *979*

more likely than not, *972*

net current amount, *984*

net noncurrent amount, *984*

net operating loss (NOL), *978*

originating temporary difference, *974*

permanent difference, *975*

pretax financial income, *964*

reversing difference, *974*

taxable amounts, *966*

taxable income, *964*

taxable temporary difference, *973*

tax effect (tax benefit), *979*

temporary difference, *966*

valuation allowance, *972*

Companies classify an individual deferred tax liability or asset as current or noncurrent based on the classification of the related asset or liability for financial reporting. A deferred tax liability or asset that is not related to an asset or liability for financial reporting, including a deferred tax asset related to a loss carryforward, is classified according to the expected reversal date of the temporary difference.

10. Indicate the basic principles of the asset-liability method. Companies apply the following basic principles in accounting for income taxes at the date of the financial statements: (1) Recognize a current tax liability or asset for the estimated taxes payable or refundable on the tax return for the current year. (2) Recognize a deferred tax liability or asset for the estimated future tax effects attributable to temporary differences and carryforwards using the enacted tax rate. (3) Base the measurement of current and deferred tax liabilities and assets on provisions of the enacted tax law. (4) Reduce the measurement of deferred tax assets, if necessary, by the amount of any tax benefits that, based on available evidence, companies do not expect to realize.

APPENDIX
19A Comprehensive Example of Interperiod Tax Allocation

OBJECTIVE 11
Understand and apply the concepts and procedures of interperiod tax allocation.

This appendix presents a comprehensive illustration of a deferred income tax problem with several temporary and permanent differences. The example follows one company through two complete years (2006 and 2007). **Study it carefully.** It should help you understand the concepts and procedures presented in the chapter.

FIRST YEAR—2006

Allman Company, which began operations at the beginning of 2006, produces various products on a contract basis. Each contract generates a gross profit of $80,000. Some of Allman's contracts provide for the customer to pay on an installment basis. Under these contracts, Allman collects one-fifth of the contract revenue in each of the following four years. For financial reporting purposes, the company recognizes gross profit in the year of completion (accrual basis); for tax purposes, Allman recognizes gross profit in the year cash is collected (installment basis).

Presented below is information related to Allman's operations for 2006.

1 In 2006, the company completed seven contracts that allow for the customer to pay on an installment basis. Allman recognized the related gross profit of $560,000 for financial reporting purposes. It reported only $112,000 of gross profit on installment sales on the 2006 tax return. The company expects future collections on the related installment receivables to result in taxable amounts of $112,000 in each of the next four years.

2 At the beginning of 2006, Allman Company purchased depreciable assets with a cost of $540,000. For financial reporting purposes, Allman depreciates these assets using the straight-line method over a six-year service life. For tax purposes, the assets fall in the five-year recovery class, and Allman uses the MACRS system. The depreciation schedules for both financial reporting and tax purposes follow.

Year	Depreciation for Financial Reporting Purposes	Depreciation for Tax Purposes	Difference
2006	$ 90,000	$108,000	$(18,000)
2007	90,000	172,800	(82,800)
2008	90,000	103,680	(13,680)
2009	90,000	62,208	27,792
2010	90,000	62,208	27,792
2011	90,000	31,104	58,896
	$540,000	$540,000	$ –0–

3 The company warrants its product for two years from the date of completion of a contract. During 2006, the product warranty liability accrued for financial reporting purposes was $200,000, and the amount paid for the satisfaction of warranty liability was $44,000. Allman expects to settle the remaining $156,000 by expenditures of $56,000 in 2007 and $100,000 in 2008.

4 In 2006 nontaxable municipal bond interest revenue was $28,000.

5 During 2006 nondeductible fines and penalties of $26,000 were paid.

6 Pretax financial income for 2006 amounts to $412,000.

7 Tax rates enacted before the end of 2006 were:

2006	50%
2007 and later years	40%

8 The accounting period is the calendar year.

9 The company is expected to have taxable income in all future years.

Taxable Income and Income Tax Payable—2006

The first step is to determine Allman Company's income tax payable for 2006 by calculating its taxable income. Illustration 19A-1 shows this computation.

Pretax financial income for 2006	$412,000
Permanent differences:	
Nontaxable revenue—municipal bond interest	(28,000)
Nondeductible expenses—fines and penalties	26,000
Temporary differences:	
Excess gross profit per books ($560,000 – $112,000)	(448,000)
Excess depreciation per tax ($108,000 – $90,000)	(18,000)
Excess warranty expense per books ($200,000 – $44,000)	156,000
Taxable income for 2006	$100,000

ILLUSTRATION 19A-1
Computation of Taxable Income, 2006

Allman computes income tax payable on taxable income for $100,000 as follows.

Taxable income for 2006	$100,000
Tax rate	50%
Income tax payable (current tax expense) for 2006	$ 50,000

ILLUSTRATION 19A-2
Computation of Income Tax Payable, End of 2006

Computing Deferred Income Taxes—End of 2006

The schedule in Illustration 19A-3 (on page 994) summarizes the temporary differences and the resulting future taxable and deductible amounts.

ILLUSTRATION 19A-3
Schedule of Future
Taxable and Deductible
Amounts, End of 2006

	Future Years					
	2007	2008	2009	2010	2011	Total
Future taxable (deductible) amounts:						
Installment sales	$112,000	$112,000	$112,000	$112,000		$448,000
Depreciation	(82,800)	(13,680)	27,792	27,792	$58,896	18,000
Warranty costs	(56,000)	(100,000)				(156,000)

Allman computes the amounts of deferred income taxes to be reported at the end of 2006 as shown in Illustration 19A-4.

ILLUSTRATION 19A-4
Computation of Deferred
Income Taxes, End of
2006

Temporary Difference	Future Taxable (Deductible) Amounts	Tax Rate	Deferred Tax (Asset)	Liability
Installment sales	$448,000	40%		$179,200
Depreciation	18,000	40%		7,200
Warranty costs	(156,000)	40%	$(62,400)	
Totals	$310,000		$(62,400)	$186,400*

*Because only a single tax rate is involved in all relevant years, these totals can be reconciled: $310,000 × 40% = ($62,400) + $186,400.

A temporary difference is caused by the use of the accrual basis for financial reporting purposes and the installment method for tax purposes. This temporary difference will result in future taxable amounts, and hence, a deferred tax liability. Because of the installment contracts completed in 2006, a temporary difference of $448,000 originates that will reverse in equal amounts over the next four years. The company expects to have taxable income in all future years, and there is only one enacted tax rate applicable to all future years. Allman uses that rate (40 percent) to compute the entire deferred tax liability resulting from this temporary difference.

The temporary difference caused by different depreciation policies for books and for tax purposes originates over three years and then reverses over three years. This difference will cause deductible amounts in 2007 and 2008 and taxable amounts in 2009, 2010, and 2011. These amounts sum to a net future taxable amount of $18,000 (which is the cumulative temporary difference at the end of 2006). Because the company expects to have taxable income in all future years and because there is only one tax rate enacted for all of the relevant future years, Allman applies that rate to the net future taxable amount to determine the related net deferred tax liability.

The third temporary difference is caused by different methods of accounting for warranties. This difference will result in deductible amounts in each of the two future years it takes to reverse. Because the company expects to report a positive income on all future tax returns and because there is only one tax rate enacted for each of the relevant future years, Allman uses that 40 percent rate to calculate the resulting deferred tax asset.

Deferred Tax Expense (Benefit) and the Journal Entry to Record Income Taxes—2006

To determine the deferred tax expense (benefit), we need to compare the beginning and ending balances of the deferred income tax accounts. Illustration 19A-5 shows that computation.

Deferred tax asset at the end of 2006	$ 62,400
Deferred tax asset at the beginning of 2006	–0–
Deferred tax expense (benefit)	$ (62,400)
Deferred tax liability at the end of 2006	$186,400
Deferred tax liability at the beginning of 2006	–0–
Deferred tax expense (benefit)	$186,400

ILLUSTRATION 19A-5
Computation of Deferred Tax Expense (Benefit), 2006

The $62,400 increase in the deferred tax asset causes a deferred tax benefit to be reported in the income statement. The $186,400 increase in the deferred tax liability during 2006 results in a deferred tax expense. These two amounts **net** to a deferred tax expense of $124,000 for 2006.

Deferred tax expense (benefit)	$ (62,400)
Deferred tax expense (benefit)	186,400
Net deferred tax expense for 2006	$124,000

ILLUSTRATION 19A-6
Computation of Net Deferred Tax Expense, 2006

Allman then computes the total income tax expense as follows.

Current tax expense for 2006	$ 50,000
Deferred tax expense for 2006	124,000
Income tax expense (total) for 2006	$174,000

ILLUSTRATION 19A-7
Computation of Total Income Tax Expense, 2006

Allman records income tax payable, deferred income taxes, and income tax expense is as follows.

Income Tax Expense	174,000	
Deferred Tax Asset	62,400	
Income Tax Payable		50,000
Deferred Tax Liability		186,400

Financial Statement Presentation—2006

Companies should classify deferred tax assets and liabilities as current and noncurrent on the balance sheet based on the classifications of related assets and liabilities. Multiple categories of deferred taxes are classified into a net current amount and a net noncurrent amount. Illustration 19A-8 shows the classification of Allman's deferred tax accounts at the end of 2006.

Temporary Difference	Resulting Deferred Tax (Asset)	Liability	Related Balance Sheet Account	Classification
Installment sales		$179,200	Installment Receivable	Current
Depreciation		7,200	Plant Assets	Noncurrent
Warranty costs	$(62,400)		Warranty Obligation	Current
Totals	$(62,400)	$186,400		

ILLUSTRATION 19A-8
Classification of Deferred Tax Accounts, End of 2006

For the first temporary difference, there is a related asset on the balance sheet, installment accounts receivable. Allman classifies that asset as current because it has a trade practice of selling to customers on an installment basis. Allman therefore classifies the resulting deferred tax liability as a current liability.

Certain assets on the balance sheet are related to the depreciation difference—the property, plant, and equipment being depreciated. Allman would classify the plant assets as noncurrent. Therefore, it also classifies the resulting deferred tax liability as noncurrent. Since the company's operating cycle is at least four years in length, Allman classifies the entire $156,000 warranty obligation as a current liability. Thus, it also classifies the related deferred tax asset of $62,400 as current.[1]

The balance sheet at the end of 2006 reports the following amounts.

ILLUSTRATION 19A-9
Balance Sheet Presentation of Deferred Taxes, 2006

Current liabilities	
Income tax payable	$ 50,000
Deferred tax liability ($179,200 − $62,400)	116,800
Long-term liabilities	
Deferred tax liability	$ 7,200

Allman's income statement for 2006 reports the following.

ILLUSTRATION 19A-10
Income Statement Presentation of Income Tax Expense, 2006

Income before income taxes		$412,000
Income tax expense		
Current	$ 50,000	
Deferred	124,000	174,000
Net income		$238,000

SECOND YEAR—2007

1   During 2007 Allman collected $112,000 from customers for the receivables arising from contracts completed in 2006. The company expects recovery of the remaining receivables to result in taxable amounts of $112,000 in each of the following three years.

2   In 2007 the company completed four new contracts that allow for the customer to pay on an installment basis. These installment sales created new installment receivables. Future collections of these receivables will result in reporting gross profit of $64,000 for tax purposes in each of the next four years.

3   During 2007 Allman continued to depreciate the assets acquired in 2006 according to the depreciation schedules appearing on page 993. Thus, depreciation amounted to $90,000 for financial reporting purposes and $172,800 for tax purposes.

4   An analysis at the end of 2007 of the product warranty liability account showed the following details.

Balance of liability at beginning of 2007	$156,000
Expense for 2007 income statement purposes	180,000
Amount paid for contracts completed in 2006	(56,000)
Amount paid for contracts completed in 2007	(50,000)
Balance of liability at end of 2007	$230,000

---

[1]If Allman's operating cycle were less than one year in length, the company would expect to settle $56,000 of the warranty obligation within one year of the December 31, 2006, balance sheet and would use current assets to do so. Thus $56,000 of the warranty obligation would be a current liability and the remaining $100,000 warranty obligation would be a long-term (noncurrent) liability. This would mean that Allman would classify $22,000 ($56,000 × 40%) of the related deferred tax asset as a current asset, and $40,000 ($100,000 × 40%) of the deferred tax asset as a noncurrent asset. *In doing homework problems, unless it is evident otherwise, assume a company's operating cycle is not longer than a year.*

The balance of the liability is expected to require expenditures in the future as follows.

$100,000 in 2008 due to 2006 contracts
$ 50,000 in 2008 due to 2007 contracts
$ 80,000 in 2009 due to 2007 contracts

$230,000

5 During 2007 nontaxable municipal bond interest revenue was $24,000.
6 Allman accrued a loss of $172,000 for financial reporting purposes because of pending litigation. This amount is not tax-deductible until the period the loss is realized, which the company estimates to be 2015.
7 Pretax financial income for 2007 amounts to $504,800.
8 The enacted tax rates still in effect are:

| 2006 | 50% |
| 2007 and later years | 40% |

Taxable Income and Income Tax Payable—2007

Allman computes taxable income for 2007 as follows.

Pretax financial income for 2007	$504,800
Permanent difference:	
Nontaxable revenue—municipal bond interest	(24,000)
Reversing temporary differences:	
Collection on 2006 installment sales	112,000
Payments on warranties from 2006 contracts	(56,000)
Originating temporary differences:	
Excess gross profit per books—2007 contracts	(256,000)
Excess depreciation per tax	(82,800)
Excess warranty expense per books—2007 contracts	130,000
Loss accrual per books	172,000
Taxable income for 2007	$500,000

ILLUSTRATION 19A-11
Computation of Taxable
Income, 2007

Income tax payable for 2007 is as follows.

Taxable income for 2007	$500,000
Tax rate	40%
Income tax payable (current tax expense) for 2007	$200,000

ILLUSTRATION 19A-12
Computation of Income
Tax Payable, End of 2007

Computing Deferred Income Taxes—End of 2007

The schedule in Illustration 19A-13 summarizes the temporary differences existing at the end of 2007 and the resulting future taxable and deductible amounts.

ILLUSTRATION 19A-13
Schedule of Future
Taxable and Deductible
Amounts, End of 2007

	Future Years					
	2008	2009	2010	2011	2015	Total
Future taxable (deductible) amounts:						
Installment sales—2006	$112,000	$112,000	$112,000			$336,000
Installment sales—2007	64,000	64,000	64,000	$64,000		256,000
Depreciation	(13,680)	27,792	27,792	58,896		100,800
Warranty costs	(150,000)	(80,000)				(230,000)
Loss accrual					$(172,000)	(172,000)

Allman computes the amounts of deferred income taxes to be reported at the end of 2007 as follows.

ILLUSTRATION 19A-14
Computation of Deferred
Income Taxes, End of
2007

Temporary Difference	Future Taxable (Deductible) Amounts	Tax Rate	Deferred Tax (Asset)	Liability
Installment sales	$592,000*	40%		$236,800
Depreciation	100,800	40%		40,320
Warranty costs	(230,000)	40%	$ (92,000)	
Loss accrual	(172,000)	40%	(68,800)	
Totals	$290,800		$(160,800)	$277,120**

*Cumulative temporary difference = $336,000 + $256,000
**Because of a flat tax rate, these totals can be reconciled: $290,800 × 40% = $(160,800) + $277,120

Deferred Tax Expense (Benefit) and the Journal Entry to Record Income Taxes—2007

To determine the deferred tax expense (benefit), Allman must compare the beginning and ending balances of the deferred income tax accounts, as shown in Illustration 19A-15.

ILLUSTRATION 19A-15
Computation of Deferred
Tax Expense (Benefit),
2007

Deferred tax asset at the end of 2007	$160,800
Deferred tax asset at the beginning of 2007	62,400
Deferred tax expense (benefit)	$ (98,400)
Deferred tax liability at the end of 2007	$277,120
Deferred tax liability at the beginning of 2007	186,400
Deferred tax expense (benefit)	$ 90,720

The deferred tax expense (benefit) and the total income tax expense for 2007 are, therefore, as follows.

ILLUSTRATION 19A-16
Computation of Total
Income Tax Expense, 2007

Deferred tax expense (benefit)	$ (98,400)
Deferred tax expense (benefit)	90,720
Deferred tax benefit for 2007	(7,680)
Current tax expense for 2007	200,000
Income tax expense (total) for 2007	$192,320

The deferred tax expense of $90,720 and the deferred tax benefit of $98,400 net to a deferred tax benefit of $7,680 for 2007.

Allman records income taxes for 2007 with the following journal entry.

Income Tax Expense	192,320	
Deferred Tax Asset	98,400	
Income Tax Payable		200,000
Deferred Tax Liability		90,720

Financial Statement Presentation—2007

Illustration 19A-17 shows the classification of Allman's deferred tax accounts at the end of 2007.

ILLUSTRATION 19A-17
Classification of Deferred
Tax Accounts, End of 2007

Temporary Difference	Resulting Deferred Tax (Asset)	Liability	Related Balance Sheet Account	Classification
Installment sales		$236,800	Installment Receivables	Current
Depreciation		40,320	Plant Assets	Noncurrent
Warranty costs	$ (92,000)		Warranty Obligation	Current
Loss accrual	(68,800)		Litigation Obligation	Noncurrent
Totals	$(160,800)	$277,120		

The new temporary difference introduced in 2007 (due to the litigation loss accrual) results in a litigation obligation that is classified as a long-term liability. Thus, the related deferred tax asset is noncurrent.

Allman's balance sheet at the end of 2007 reports the following amounts.

ILLUSTRATION 19A-18
Balance Sheet
Presentation of Deferred
Taxes, End of 2007

Other assets (noncurrent)	
Deferred tax asset ($68,800 − $40,320)	$ 28,480
Current liabilities	
Income tax payable	$200,000
Deferred tax liability ($236,800 − $92,000)	144,800

The income statement for 2007 reports the following.

ILLUSTRATION 19A-19
Income Statement
Presentation of Income
Tax Expense, 2007

Income before income taxes		$504,800
Income tax expense		
Current	$200,000	
Deferred	(7,680)	192,320
Net income		$312,480

SUMMARY OF LEARNING OBJECTIVE FOR APPENDIX 19A

11. Understand and apply the concepts and procedures of interperiod tax allocation. Accounting for deferred taxes involves the following steps: Calculate taxable income and income tax payable for the year. Compute deferred income taxes at the end of the year. Determine deferred tax expense (benefit) and make the journal entry to record income taxes. Classify deferred tax assets and liabilities as current or noncurrent in the financial statements.

QUESTIONS

1. Explain the difference between pretax financial income and taxable income.

2. What are the two objectives of accounting for income taxes?

3. Interest on municipal bonds is referred to as a permanent difference when determining the proper amount to

report for deferred taxes. Explain the meaning of permanent differences, and give two other examples.

4. Explain the meaning of a temporary difference as it relates to deferred tax computations, and give three examples.

5. Differentiate between an originating temporary difference and a reversing difference.

6. The book basis of depreciable assets for Getty Co. is $900,000, and the tax basis is $700,000 at the end of 2007. The enacted tax rate is 34% for all periods. Determine the amount of deferred taxes to be reported on the balance sheet at the end of 2007.

7. Borg Inc. has a deferred tax liability of $68,000 at the beginning of 2007. At the end of 2007, it reports accounts receivable on the books at $80,000 and the tax basis at zero (its only temporary difference). If the enacted tax rate is 34% for all periods, and income tax payable for the period is $230,000, determine the amount of total income tax expense to report for 2007.

8. What is the difference between a future taxable amount and a future deductible amount? When is it appropriate to record a valuation account for a deferred tax asset?

9. Pretax financial income for Mott Inc. is $300,000, and its taxable income is $100,000 for 2007. Its only temporary difference at the end of the period relates to a $90,000 difference due to excess depreciation for tax purposes. If the tax rate is 40% for all periods, compute the amount of income tax expense to report in 2007. No deferred income taxes existed at the beginning of the year.

10. How are deferred tax assets and deferred tax liabilities reported on the balance sheet?

11. Describe the procedures involved in segregating various deferred tax amounts into current and noncurrent categories.

12. How is it determined whether deferred tax amounts are considered to be "related" to specific asset or liability amounts?

13. At the end of the year, North Carolina Co. has pretax financial income of $550,000. Included in the $550,000 is $70,000 interest income on municipal bonds, $30,000 fine for dumping hazardous waste, and depreciation of $60,000. Depreciation for tax purposes is $45,000. Compute income taxes payable, assuming the tax rate is 30% for all periods.

14. Raleigh Co. has one temporary difference at the beginning of 2007 of $500,000. The deferred tax liability established for this amount is $150,000, based on a tax rate of 30%. The temporary difference will provide the following taxable amounts: $100,000 in 2008; $200,000 in 2009, and $200,000 in 2010. If a new tax rate for 2010 of 25% is enacted into law at the end of 2007, what is the journal entry necessary in 2007 (if any) to adjust deferred taxes?

15. What are some of the reasons that the components of income tax expense should be disclosed and a reconciliation between the effective tax rate and the statutory tax rate be provided?

16. Differentiate between "loss carryback" and "loss carryforward." Which can be accounted for with the greater certainty when it arises? Why?

17. What are the possible treatments for tax purposes of a net operating loss? What are the circumstances that determine the option to be applied? What is the proper treatment of a net operating loss for financial reporting purposes?

18. What controversy relates to the accounting for net operating loss carryforwards?

BRIEF EXERCISES

(LO 1, 2) **BE19-1** In 2007, Speedy Gonzalez Corporation had pretax financial income of $168,000 and taxable income of $110,000. The difference is due to the use of different depreciation methods for tax and accounting purposes. The effective tax rate is 40%. Compute the amount to be reported as income taxes payable at December 31, 2007.

(LO 1, 2) **BE19-2** Murphy Corporation began operations in 2007 and reported pretax financial income of $225,000 for the year. Murphy's tax depreciation exceeded its book depreciation by $30,000. Murphy's tax rate for 2007 and years thereafter is 30%. In its December 31, 2007 balance sheet, what amount of deferred tax liability should be reported?

(LO 9) **BE19-3** Using the information from BE19-2, assume this is the only difference between Murphy's pretax financial income and taxable income. Prepare the journal entry to record the income tax expense, deferred income taxes, and income tax payable, and show how the deferred tax liability will be classified on the December 31, 2007, balance sheet.

(LO 2, 5) **BE19-4** At December 31, 2006, Yserbius Corporation had a deferred tax liability of $25,000. At December 31, 2007, the deferred tax liability is $42,000. The corporation's 2007 current tax expense is $43,000. What amount should Yserbius report as total 2007 tax expense?

(LO 1, 3) **BE19-5** At December 31, 2007, Deep Space Nine Corporation had an estimated warranty liability of $125,000 for accounting purposes and $0 for tax purposes. (The warranty costs are not deductible until paid.) The effective tax rate is 40%. Compute the amount Deep Space Nine should report as a deferred tax asset at December 31, 2007.

(LO 3, 5) **BE19-6** At December 31, 2006, Next Generation Inc. had a deferred tax asset of $35,000. At December 31, 2007, the deferred tax asset is $59,000. The corporation's 2007 current tax expense is $61,000. What amount should Next Generation report as total 2007 tax expense?

(LO 4) **BE19-7** At December 31, 2007, Stargate Corporation has a deferred tax asset of $200,000. After a careful review of all available evidence, it is determined that it is more likely than not that $80,000 of this deferred tax asset will not be realized. Prepare the necessary journal entry.

(LO 5) **BE19-8** No Doubt Corporation had income before income taxes of $175,000 in 2007. No Doubt's current income tax expense is $40,000, and deferred income tax expense is $30,000. Prepare No Doubt's 2007 income statement, beginning with income before income taxes.

(LO 2, 3) **BE19-9** Tazmania Inc. had pretax financial income of $154,000 in 2007. Included in the computation of that amount is insurance expense of $4,000 which is not deductible for tax purposes. In addition, depreciation for tax purposes exceeds accounting depreciation by $14,000. Prepare Tazmania's journal entry to record 2007 taxes, assuming a tax rate of 45%.

(LO 2) **BE19-10** Terminator Corporation has a cumulative temporary difference related to depreciation of $630,000 at December 31, 2007. This difference will reverse as follows: 2008, $42,000; 2009, $294,000; and 2010, $294,000. Enacted tax rates are 34% for 2008 and 2009, and 40% for 2010. Compute the amount Terminator should report as a deferred tax liability at December 31, 2007.

(LO 7) **BE19-11** At December 31, 2006, Tick Corporation had a deferred tax liability of $680,000, resulting from future taxable amounts of $2,000,000 and an enacted tax rate of 34%. In May 2007, a new income tax act is signed into law that raises the tax rate to 38% for 2007 and future years. Prepare the journal entry for Tick to adjust the deferred tax liability.

(LO 8) **BE19-12** Valis Corporation had the following tax information.

Year	Taxable Income	Tax Rate	Taxes Paid
2004	$300,000	35%	$105,000
2005	$325,000	30%	$ 97,500
2006	$400,000	30%	$120,000

In 2007 Valis suffered a net operating loss of $450,000, which it elected to carry back. The 2007 enacted tax rate is 29%. Prepare Valis's entry to record the effect of the loss carryback.

(LO 8) **BE19-13** Zoop Inc. incurred a net operating loss of $500,000 in 2007. Combined income for 2005 and 2006 was $400,000. The tax rate for all years is 40%. Zoop elects the carryback option. Prepare the journal entries to record the benefits of the loss carryback and the loss carryforward.

(LO 4, 8) **BE19-14** Use the information for Zoop Inc. given in BE19-13. Assume that it is more likely than not that the entire net operating loss carryforward will not be realized in future years. Prepare all the journal entries necessary at the end of 2007.

(LO 9) **BE19-15** Vectorman Corporation has temporary differences at December 31, 2007, that result in the following deferred taxes.

Deferred tax liability—current	$38,000
Deferred tax asset—current	$(52,000)
Deferred tax liability—noncurrent	$96,000
Deferred tax asset—noncurrent	$(27,000)

Indicate how these balances would be presented in Vectorman's December 31, 2007, balance sheet.

EXERCISES

(LO 2, 5) **E19-1** **(One Temporary Difference, Future Taxable Amounts, One Rate, No Beginning Deferred Taxes)** South Carolina Corporation has one temporary difference at the end of 2007 that will reverse and cause taxable amounts of $55,000 in 2008, $60,000 in 2009, and $65,000 in 2010. South Carolina's pretax financial income for 2007 is $300,000, and the tax rate is 30% for all years. There are no deferred taxes at the beginning of 2007.

Instructions

(a) Compute taxable income and income taxes payable for 2007.

(b) Prepare the journal entry to record income tax expense, deferred income taxes, and income taxes payable for 2007.

(c) Prepare the income tax expense section of the income statement for 2007, beginning with the line "Income before income taxes."

(LO 2) **E19-2** **(Two Differences, No Beginning Deferred Taxes, Tracked through 2 Years)** The following information is available for Wenger Corporation for 2006.

1. Excess of tax depreciation over book depreciation, $40,000. This $40,000 difference will reverse equally over the years 2007–2010.
2. Deferral, for book purposes, of $20,000 of rent received in advance. The rent will be earned in 2007.
3. Pretax financial income, $300,000.
4. Tax rate for all years, 40%.

Instructions
   (a) Compute taxable income for 2006.
   (b) Prepare the journal entry to record income tax expense, deferred income taxes, and income taxes payable for 2006.
   (c) Prepare the journal entry to record income tax expense, deferred income taxes, and income taxes payable for 2007, assuming taxable income of $325,000.

(LO 2, 5) **E19-3** **(One Temporary Difference, Future Taxable Amounts, One Rate, Beginning Deferred Taxes)** Bandung Corporation began 2007 with a $92,000 balance in the Deferred Tax Liability account. At the end of 2007, the related cumulative temporary difference amounts to $350,000, and it will reverse evenly over the next 2 years. Pretax accounting income for 2007 is $525,000, the tax rate for all years is 40%, and taxable income for 2007 is $405,000.

Instructions
   (a) Compute income taxes payable for 2007.
   (b) Prepare the journal entry to record income tax expense, deferred income taxes, and income taxes payable for 2007.
   (c) Prepare the income tax expense section of the income statement for 2007 beginning with the line "Income before income taxes."

(LO 2, 3, 5, 6) **E19-4** **(Three Differences, Compute Taxable Income, Entry for Taxes)** Zurich Company reports pretax financial income of $70,000 for 2007. The following items cause taxable income to be different than pretax financial income.

1. Depreciation on the tax return is greater than depreciation on the income statement by $16,000.
2. Rent collected on the tax return is greater than rent earned on the income statement by $22,000.
3. Fines for pollution appear as an expense of $11,000 on the income statement.

Zurich's tax rate is 30% for all years, and the company expects to report taxable income in all future years. There are no deferred taxes at the beginning of 2007.

Instructions
   (a) Compute taxable income and income taxes payable for 2007.
   (b) Prepare the journal entry to record income tax expense, deferred income taxes, and income taxes payable for 2007.
   (c) Prepare the income tax expense section of the income statement for 2007, beginning with the line "Income before income taxes."
   (d) Compute the effective income tax rate for 2007.

(LO 2, 3, 5) **E19-5** **(Two Temporary Differences, One Rate, Beginning Deferred Taxes)** The following facts relate to Krung Thep Corporation.

1. Deferred tax liability, January 1, 2007, $40,000.
2. Deferred tax asset, January 1, 2007, $0.
3. Taxable income for 2007, $95,000.
4. Pretax financial income for 2007, $200,000.
5. Cumulative temporary difference at December 31, 2007, giving rise to future taxable amounts, $240,000.
6. Cumulative temporary difference at December 31, 2007, giving rise to future deductible amounts, $35,000.
7. Tax rate for all years, 40%.
8. The company is expected to operate profitably in the future.

Instructions
   (a) Compute income taxes payable for 2007.
   (b) Prepare the journal entry to record income tax expense, deferred income taxes, and income taxes payable for 2007.
   (c) Prepare the income tax expense section of the income statement for 2007, beginning with the line "Income before income taxes."

(LO 6) **E19-6** **(Identify Temporary or Permanent Differences)** Listed below are items that are commonly accounted for differently for financial reporting purposes than they are for tax purposes.

Instructions

For each item below, indicate whether it involves:

    (1) A temporary difference that will result in future deductible amounts and, therefore, will usually give rise to a deferred income tax asset.

    (2) A temporary difference that will result in future taxable amounts and, therefore, will usually give rise to a deferred income tax liability.

    (3) A permanent difference.

Use the appropriate number to indicate your answer for each.

    (a) _____ The MACRS depreciation system is used for tax purposes, and the straight-line depreciation method is used for financial reporting purposes for some plant assets.

    (b) _____ A landlord collects some rents in advance. Rents received are taxable in the period when they are received.

    (c) _____ Expenses are incurred in obtaining tax-exempt income.

    (d) _____ Costs of guarantees and warranties are estimated and accrued for financial reporting purposes.

    (e) _____ Installment sales of investments are accounted for by the accrual method for financial reporting purposes and the installment method for tax purposes.

    (f) _____ For some assets, straight-line depreciation is used for both financial reporting purposes and tax purposes but the assets' lives are shorter for tax purposes.

    (g) _____ Interest is received on an investment in tax-exempt municipal obligations.

    (h) _____ Proceeds are received from a life insurance company because of the death of a key officer. (The company carries a policy on key officers.)

    (i) _____ The tax return reports a deduction for 80% of the dividends received from U.S. corporations. The cost method is used in accounting for the related investments for financial reporting purposes.

    (j) _____ Estimated losses on pending lawsuits and claims are accrued for books. These losses are tax deductible in the period(s) when the related liabilities are settled.

    (k) _____ Expenses on stock options are accrued for financial reporting purposes.

(LO 2, 3, 4, 6) **E19-7** **(Terminology, Relationships, Computations, Entries)**

Instructions

Complete the following statements by filling in the blanks.

    (a) In a period in which a taxable temporary difference reverses, the reversal will cause taxable income to be _____ (less than, greater than) pretax financial income.

    (b) If a $76,000 balance in Deferred Tax Asset was computed by use of a 40% rate, the underlying cumulative temporary difference amounts to $_____.

    (c) Deferred taxes _____ (are, are not) recorded to account for permanent differences.

    (d) If a taxable temporary difference originates in 2007, it will cause taxable income for 2007 to be _____ (less than, greater than) pretax financial income for 2007.

    (e) If total tax expense is $50,000 and deferred tax expense is $65,000, then the current portion of the expense computation is referred to as current tax _____ (expense, benefit) of $_____.

    (f) If a corporation's tax return shows taxable income of $100,000 for Year 2 and a tax rate of 40%, how much will appear on the December 31, Year 2, balance sheet for "Income tax payable" if the company has made estimated tax payments of $36,500 for Year 2? $_____.

    (g) An increase in the Deferred Tax Liability account on the balance sheet is recorded by a _____ (debit, credit) to the Income Tax Expense account.

    (h) An income statement that reports current tax expense of $82,000 and deferred tax benefit of $23,000 will report total income tax expense of $_____.

    (i) A valuation account is needed whenever it is judged to be _____ that a portion of a deferred tax asset _____ (will be, will not be) realized.

    (j) If the tax return shows total taxes due for the period of $75,000 but the income statement shows total income tax expense of $55,000, the difference of $20,000 is referred to as deferred tax _____ (expense, benefit).

(LO 2, 3, 5, 9) **E19-8** **(Two Temporary Differences, One Rate, 3 Years)** Button Company has two temporary differences between its income tax expense and income taxes payable. The information is shown on page 1004.

	2007	2008	2009
Pretax financial income	$840,000	$910,000	$945,000
Excess depreciation expense on tax return	(30,000)	(40,000)	(10,000)
Excess warranty expense in financial income	20,000	10,000	8,000
Taxable income	$830,000	$880,000	$943,000

The income tax rate for all years is 40%.

Instructions

(a) Prepare the journal entry to record income tax expense, deferred income taxes, and income tax payable for 2007, 2008, and 2009.

(b) Assuming there were no temporary differences prior to 2007, indicate how deferred taxes will be reported on the 2009 balance sheet. Button's product warranty is for 12 months.

(c) Prepare the income tax expense section of the income statement for 2009, beginning with the line "Pretax financial income."

(LO 8) **E19-9 (Carryback and Carryforward of NOL, No Valuation Account, No Temporary Differences)** The pretax financial income (or loss) figures for Jenny Spangler Company are as follows.

2002	$160,000
2003	250,000
2004	80,000
2005	(160,000)
2006	(380,000)
2007	120,000
2008	100,000

Pretax financial income (or loss) and taxable income (loss) were the same for all years involved. Assume a 45% tax rate for 2002 and 2003 and a 40% tax rate for the remaining years.

Instructions

Prepare the journal entries for the years 2004 to 2008 to record income tax expense and the effects of the net operating loss carrybacks and carryforwards assuming Jenny Spangler Company uses the carryback provision. All income and losses relate to normal operations. (In recording the benefits of a loss carryforward, assume that no valuation account is deemed necessary.)

(LO 8) **E19-10 (Two NOLs, No Temporary Differences, No Valuation Account, Entries and Income Statement)** Felicia Rashad Corporation has pretax financial income (or loss) equal to taxable income (or loss) from 1999 through 2007 as follows.

	Income (Loss)	Tax Rate
1999	$29,000	30%
2000	40,000	30%
2001	17,000	35%
2002	48,000	50%
2003	(150,000)	40%
2004	90,000	40%
2005	30,000	40%
2006	105,000	40%
2007	(60,000)	45%

Pretax financial income (loss) and taxable income (loss) were the same for all years since Rashad has been in business. Assume the carryback provision is employed for net operating losses. In recording the benefits of a loss carryforward, assume that it is more likely than not that the related benefits will be realized.

Instructions

(a) What entry(ies) for income taxes should be recorded for 2003?

(b) Indicate what the income tax expense portion of the income statement for 2003 should look like. Assume all income (loss) relates to continuing operations.

(c) What entry for income taxes should be recorded in 2004?

(d) How should the income tax expense section of the income statement for 2004 appear?

(e) What entry for income taxes should be recorded in 2007?

(f) How should the income tax expense section of the income statement for 2007 appear?

(LO 2, 3, 9) **E19-11 (Three Differences, Classify Deferred Taxes)** At December 31, 2006, Belmont Company had a net deferred tax liability of $375,000. An explanation of the items that compose this balance is as follows.

Temporary Differences	Resulting Balances in Deferred Taxes
1. Excess of tax depreciation over book depreciation	$200,000
2. Accrual, for book purposes, of estimated loss contingency from pending lawsuit that is expected to be settled in 2007. The loss will be deducted on the tax return when paid.	(50,000)
3. Accrual method used for book purposes and installment method used for tax purposes for an isolated installment sale of an investment.	225,000
	$375,000

In analyzing the temporary differences, you find that $30,000 of the depreciation temporary difference will reverse in 2007, and $120,000 of the temporary difference due to the installment sale will reverse in 2007. The tax rate for all years is 40%.

Instructions

Indicate the manner in which deferred taxes should be presented on Belmont Company's December 31, 2006, balance sheet.

(LO 2, 3, 5) **E19-12** **(Two Temporary Differences, One Rate, Beginning Deferred Taxes, Compute Pretax Financial Income)** The following facts relate to Duncan Corporation.

1. Deferred tax liability, January 1, 2007, $60,000.
2. Deferred tax asset, January 1, 2007, $20,000.
3. Taxable income for 2007, $105,000.
4. Cumulative temporary difference at December 31, 2007, giving rise to future taxable amounts, $230,000.
5. Cumulative temporary difference at December 31, 2007, giving rise to future deductible amounts, $95,000.
6. Tax rate for all years, 40%. No permanent differences exist.
7. The company is expected to operate profitably in the future.

Instructions
  (a) Compute the amount of pretax financial income for 2007.
  (b) Prepare the journal entry to record income tax expense, deferred income taxes, and income taxes payable for 2007.
  (c) Prepare the income tax expense section of the income statement for 2007, beginning with the line "Income before income taxes."
  (d) Compute the effective tax rate for 2007.

(LO 2, 7) **E19-13** **(One Difference, Multiple Rates, Effect of Beginning Balance versus No Beginning Deferred Taxes)** At the end of 2006, Lucretia McEvil Company has $180,000 of cumulative temporary differences that will result in reporting future taxable amounts as follows.

2007	$ 60,000
2008	50,000
2009	40,000
2010	30,000
	$180,000

Tax rates enacted as of the beginning of 2005 are:

2005 and 2006	40%
2007 and 2008	30%
2009 and later	25%

McEvil's taxable income for 2006 is $320,000. Taxable income is expected in all future years.

Instructions
  (a) Prepare the journal entry for McEvil to record income taxes payable, deferred income taxes, and income tax expense for 2006, assuming that there were no deferred taxes at the end of 2005.
  (b) Prepare the journal entry for McEvil to record income taxes payable, deferred income taxes, and income tax expense for 2006, assuming that there was a balance of $22,000 in a Deferred Tax Liability account at the end of 2005.

(LO 3, 4) **E19-14** **(Deferred Tax Asset with and without Valuation Account)** Jennifer Capriati Corp. has a deferred tax asset account with a balance of $150,000 at the end of 2006 due to a single cumulative temporary difference of $375,000. At the end of 2007 this same temporary difference has increased to a cumulative amount of $450,000. Taxable income for 2007 is $820,000. The tax rate is 40% for all years. No valuation account related to the deferred tax asset is in existence at the end of 2006.

Instructions

(a) Record income tax expense, deferred income taxes, and income taxes payable for 2007, assuming that it is more likely than not that the deferred tax asset will be realized.

(b) Assuming that it is more likely than not that $30,000 of the deferred tax asset will not be realized, prepare the journal entry at the end of 2007 to record the valuation account.

(LO 3, 4, 5) **E19-15** **(Deferred Tax Asset with Previous Valuation Account)** Assume the same information as E19-14, except that at the end of 2006, Jennifer Capriati Corp. had a valuation account related to its deferred tax asset of $45,000.

Instructions

(a) Record income tax expense, deferred income taxes, and income taxes payable for 2007, assuming that it is more likely than not that the deferred tax asset will be realized in full.

(b) Record income tax expense, deferred income taxes, and income taxes payable for 2007, assuming that it is more likely than not that none of the deferred tax asset will be realized.

(LO 2, 5, 7, 9) **E19-16** **(Deferred Tax Liability, Change in Tax Rate, Prepare Section of Income Statement)** Novotna Inc.'s only temporary difference at the beginning and end of 2006 is caused by a $3 million deferred gain for tax purposes for an installment sale of a plant asset, and the related receivable (only one-half of which is classified as a current asset) is due in equal installments in 2007 and 2008. The related deferred tax liability at the beginning of the year is $1,200,000. In the third quarter of 2006, a new tax rate of 34% is enacted into law and is scheduled to become effective for 2008. Taxable income for 2006 is $5,000,000, and taxable income is expected in all future years.

Instructions

(a) Determine the amount reported as a deferred tax liability at the end of 2006. Indicate proper classification(s).

(b) Prepare the journal entry (if any) necessary to adjust the deferred tax liability when the new tax rate is enacted into law.

(c) Draft the income tax expense portion of the income statement for 2006. Begin with the line "Income before income taxes." Assume no permanent differences exist.

(LO 2, 3, 7) **E19-17** **(Two Temporary Differences, Tracked through 3 Years, Multiple Rates)** Taxable income and pretax financial income would be identical for Huber Co. except for its treatments of gross profit on installment sales and estimated costs of warranties. The following income computations have been prepared.

Taxable income	2006	2007	2008
Excess of revenues over expenses (excluding two temporary differences)	$160,000	$210,000	$90,000
Installment gross profit collected	8,000	8,000	8,000
Expenditures for warranties	(5,000)	(5,000)	(5,000)
Taxable income	$163,000	$213,000	$93,000

Pretax financial income	2006	2007	2008
Excess of revenues over expenses (excluding two temporary differences)	$160,000	$210,000	$90,000
Installment gross profit earned	24,000	–0–	–0–
Estimated cost of warranties	(15,000)	–0–	–0–
Income before taxes	$169,000	$210,000	$90,000

The tax rates in effect are: 2006, 40%; 2007 and 2008, 45%. All tax rates were enacted into law on January 1, 2006. No deferred income taxes existed at the beginning of 2006. Taxable income is expected in all future years.

Instructions

Prepare the journal entry to record income tax expense, deferred income taxes, and income tax payable for 2006, 2007, and 2008.

(LO 2, 3, 7) **E19-18** **(Three Differences, Multiple Rates, Future Taxable Income)** During 2007, Kate Holmes Co.'s first year of operations, the company reports pretax financial income at $250,000. Holmes's enacted tax rate is 45% for 2007 and 40% for all later years. Holmes expects to have taxable income in each of the next 5 years. The effects on future tax returns of temporary differences existing at December 31, 2007, are summarized on the following page.

	Future Years					
	2008	2009	2010	2011	2012	Total
Future taxable (deductible) amounts:						
Installment sales	$32,000	$32,000	$32,000			$ 96,000
Depreciation	6,000	6,000	6,000	$6,000	$6,000	30,000
Unearned rent	(50,000)	(50,000)				(100,000)

Instructions

(a) Complete the schedule below to compute deferred taxes at December 31, 2007.

(b) Compute taxable income for 2007.

(c) Prepare the journal entry to record income tax payable, deferred taxes, and income tax expense for 2007.

	Future Taxable (Deductible) Amounts	Tax Rate	December 31, 2007 Deferred Tax (Asset)	Deferred Tax Liability
Installment sales	$ 96,000			
Depreciation	30,000			
Unearned rent	(100,000)			
Totals	$			

(LO 2, 3, 9) **E19-19** **(Two Differences, One Rate, Beginning Deferred Balance, Compute Pretax Financial Income)** Andy McDowell Co. establishes a $100 million liability at the end of 2007 for the estimated site-cleanup costs at two of its manufacturing facilities. All related closing costs will be paid and deducted on the tax return in 2008. Also, at the end of 2007, the company has $50 million of temporary differences due to excess depreciation for tax purposes, $7 million of which will reverse in 2008.

The enacted tax rate for all years is 40%, and the company pays taxes of $64 million on $160 million of taxable income in 2007. McDowell expects to have taxable income in 2008.

Instructions

(a) Determine the deferred taxes to be reported at the end of 2008.

(b) Indicate how the deferred taxes computed in (a) are to be reported on the balance sheet.

(c) Assuming that the only deferred tax account at the beginning of 2007 was a deferred tax liability of $10,000,000, draft the income tax expense portion of the income statement for 2007, beginning with the line "Income before income taxes." (*Hint:* You must first compute (1) the amount of temporary difference underlying the beginning $10,000,000 deferred tax liability, then (2) the amount of temporary differences originating or reversing during the year, then (3) the amount of pretax financial income.)

(LO 2, 3, 9) **E19-20** **(Two Differences, No Beginning Deferred Taxes, Multiple Rates)** Teri Hatcher Inc., in its first year of operations, has the following differences between the book basis and tax basis of its assets and liabilities at the end of 2006.

	Book Basis	Tax Basis
Equipment (net)	$400,000	$340,000
Estimated warranty liability	$200,000	$ –0–

It is estimated that the warranty liability will be settled in 2007. The difference in equipment (net) will result in taxable amounts of $20,000 in 2007, $30,000 in 2008, and $10,000 in 2009. The company has taxable income of $520,000 in 2006. As of the beginning of 2006, the enacted tax rate is 34% for 2006–2008, and 30% for 2009. Hatcher expects to report taxable income through 2009.

Instructions

(a) Prepare the journal entry to record income tax expense, deferred income taxes, and income tax payable for 2006.

(b) Indicate how deferred income taxes will be reported on the balance sheet at the end of 2006.

(LO 2, 3, 7, 9) **E19-21** **(Two Temporary Differences, Multiple Rates, Future Taxable Income)** Nadal Inc. has two temporary differences at the end of 2006. The first difference stems from installment sales, and the second one results from the accrual of a loss contingency. Nadal's accounting department has developed a schedule of future taxable and deductible amounts related to these temporary differences as follows.

	2007	2008	2009	2010
Taxable amounts	$40,000	$50,000	$60,000	$80,000
Deductible amounts		(15,000)	(19,000)	
	$40,000	$35,000	$41,000	$80,000

As of the beginning of 2006, the enacted tax rate is 34% for 2006 and 2007, and 38% for 2008–2011. At the beginning of 2006, the company had no deferred income taxes on its balance sheet. Taxable income for 2006 is $500,000. Taxable income is expected in all future years.

Instructions

(a) Prepare the journal entry to record income tax expense, deferred income taxes, and income taxes payable for 2006.

(b) Indicate how deferred income taxes would be classified on the balance sheet at the end of 2006.

(LO 2, 3, 9) **E19-22 (Two Differences, One Rate, First Year)** The differences between the book basis and tax basis of the assets and liabilities of Castle Corporation at the end of 2006 are presented below.

	Book Basis	Tax Basis
Accounts receivable	$50,000	$–0–
Litigation liability	30,000	–0–

It is estimated that the litigation liability will be settled in 2007. The difference in accounts receivable will result in taxable amounts of $30,000 in 2007 and $20,000 in 2008. The company has taxable income of $350,000 in 2006 and is expected to have taxable income in each of the following 2 years. Its enacted tax rate is 34% for all years. This is the company's first year of operations. The operating cycle of the business is 2 years.

Instructions

(a) Prepare the journal entry to record income tax expense, deferred income taxes, and income tax payable for 2006.

(b) Indicate how deferred income taxes will be reported on the balance sheet at the end of 2006.

(LO 4, 7, 8) **E19-23 (NOL Carryback and Carryforward, Valuation Account versus No Valuation Account)** Spamela Hamderson Inc. reports the following pretax income (loss) for both financial reporting purposes and tax purposes. (Assume the carryback provision is used for a net operating loss.)

Year	Pretax Income (Loss)	Tax Rate
2005	$120,000	34%
2006	90,000	34%
2007	(280,000)	38%
2008	220,000	38%

The tax rates listed were all enacted by the beginning of 2005.

Instructions

(a) Prepare the journal entries for the years 2005–2008 to record income tax expense (benefit) and income tax payable (refundable) and the tax effects of the loss carryback and carryforward, assuming that at the end of 2007 the benefits of the loss carryforward are judged more likely than not to be realized in the future.

(b) Using the assumption in (a), prepare the income tax section of the 2007 income statement beginning with the line "Operating loss before income taxes."

(c) Prepare the journal entries for 2007 and 2008, assuming that based on the weight of available evidence, it is more likely than not that one-fourth of the benefits of the loss carryforward will not be realized.

(d) Using the assumption in (c), prepare the income tax section of the 2007 income statement beginning with the line "Operating loss before income taxes."

(LO 4, 7, 8) **E19-24 (NOL Carryback and Carryforward, Valuation Account Needed)** Beilman Inc. reports the following pretax income (loss) for both book and tax purposes. (Assume the carryback provision is used where possible for a net operating loss.)

Year	Pretax Income (Loss)	Tax Rate
2005	$120,000	40%
2006	90,000	40%
2007	(280,000)	45%
2008	120,000	45%

The tax rates listed were all enacted by the beginning of 2005.

Instructions

(a) Prepare the journal entries for years 2005–2008 to record income tax expense (benefit) and income tax payable (refundable), and the tax effects of the loss carryback and loss carryforward, assuming that based on the weight of available evidence, it is more likely than not that one-half of the benefits of the loss carryforward will not be realized.

(b) Prepare the income tax section of the 2007 income statement beginning with the line "Operating loss before income taxes."

(c) Prepare the income tax section of the 2008 income statement beginning with the line "Income before income taxes."

(LO 4, 7, 8) **E19-25 (NOL Carryback and Carryforward, Valuation Account Needed)** Meyer reported the following pretax financial income (loss) for the years 2005–2009.

2005	$240,000
2006	350,000
2007	120,000
2008	(570,000)
2009	180,000

Pretax financial income (loss) and taxable income (loss) were the same for all years involved. The enacted tax rate was 34% for 2005 and 2006, and 40% for 2007–2009. Assume the carryback provision is used first for net operating losses.

Instructions

(a) Prepare the journal entries for the years 2007–2009 to record income tax expense, income tax payable (refundable), and the tax effects of the loss carryback and loss carryforward, assuming that based on the weight of available evidence, it is more likely than not that one-fifth of the benefits of the loss carryforward will not be realized.

(b) Prepare the income tax section of the 2008 income statement beginning with the line "Income (loss) before income taxes."

> **See the book's website, www.wiley.com/college/kieso, for Additional Exercises.**

PROBLEMS

(LO 2, 3, 5) **P19-1 (Three Differences, No Beginning Deferred Taxes, Multiple Rates)** The following information is available for Swanson Corporation for 2006.

1. Depreciation reported on the tax return exceeded depreciation reported on the income statement by $100,000. This difference will reverse in equal amounts of $25,000 over the years 2007–2010.
2. Interest received on municipal bonds was $10,000.
3. Rent collected in advance on January 1, 2006, totaled $60,000 for a 3-year period. Of this amount, $40,000 was reported as unearned at December 31, for book purposes.
4. The tax rates are 40% for 2006 and 35% for 2007 and subsequent years.
5. Income taxes of $360,000 are due per the tax return for 2006.
6. No deferred taxes existed at the beginning of 2006.

Instructions

(a) Compute taxable income for 2006.

(b) Compute pretax financial income for 2006.

(c) Prepare the journal entries to record income tax expense, deferred income taxes, and income taxes payable for 2006 and 2007. Assume taxable income was $980,000 in 2007.

(d) Prepare the income tax expense section of the income statement for 2006, beginning with "Income before income taxes."

(LO 3, 5, 6) **P19-2 (One Temporary Difference, Tracked for 4 Years, One Permanent Difference, Change in Rate)** The pretax financial income of Parker-Gregory Company differs from its taxable income throughout each of 4 years as follows.

Year	Pretax Financial Income	Taxable Income	Tax Rate
2007	$280,000	$180,000	35%
2008	320,000	225,000	40%
2009	350,000	270,000	40%
2010	420,000	580,000	40%

Pretax financial income for each year includes a nondeductible expense of $30,000 (never deductible for tax purposes). The remainder of the difference between pretax financial income and taxable income in each period is due to one depreciation temporary difference. No deferred income taxes existed at the beginning of 2007.

Instructions
(a) Prepare journal entries to record income taxes in all 4 years. Assume that the change in the tax rate to 40% was not enacted until the beginning of 2008.
(b) Prepare the income statement for 2008, beginning with income before income taxes.

(LO 2, 5, 6, 9) **P19-3** **(Second Year of Depreciation Difference, Two Differences, Single Rate, Extraordinary Item)** The following information has been obtained for the Kerdyk Corporation.

1. Prior to 2006, taxable income and pretax financial income were identical.
2. Pretax financial income is $1,700,000 in 2006 and $1,400,000 in 2007.
3. On January 1, 2006, equipment costing $1,000,000 is purchased. It is to be depreciated on a straight-line basis over 5 years for tax purposes and over 8 years for financial reporting purposes. (*Hint:* Use the half-year convention for tax purposes, as discussed in Appendix 11A.)
4. Interest of $60,000 was earned on tax-exempt municipal obligations in 2007.
5. Included in 2007 pretax financial income is an extraordinary gain of $200,000, which is fully taxable.
6. The tax rate is 35% for all periods.
7. Taxable income is expected in all future years.

Instructions
(a) Compute taxable income and income tax payable for 2007.
(b) Prepare the journal entry to record 2007 income tax expense, income tax payable, and deferred taxes.
(c) Prepare the bottom portion of Kerdyk's 2007 income statement, beginning with "Income before income taxes and extraordinary item."
(d) Indicate how deferred income taxes should be presented on the December 31, 2007, balance sheet.

(LO 2, 3, 5) **P19-4** **(Permanent and Temporary Differences, One Rate)** The accounting records of Anderson Inc. show the following data for 2007.

1. Life insurance expense on officers was $9,000.
2. Equipment was acquired in early January for $200,000. Straight-line depreciation over a 5-year life is used, with no salvage value. For tax purposes, Anderson used a 30% rate to calculate depreciation.
3. Interest revenue on State of New York bonds totaled $4,000.
4. Product warranties were estimated to be $60,000 in 2007. Actual repair and labor costs related to the warranties in 2007 were $10,000. The remainder is estimated to be incurred evenly in 2008 and 2009.
5. Sales on an accrual basis were $100,000. For tax purposes, $75,000 was recorded on the installment sales method.
6. Fines incurred for pollution violations were $4,200.
7. Pretax financial income was $850,000. The tax rate is 30%.

Instructions
(a) Prepare a schedule starting with pretax financial income in 2007 and ending with taxable income in 2007.
(b) Prepare the journal entry for 2007 to record income tax payable, income tax expense, and deferred income taxes.

(LO 5, 7, 8, 9) **P19-5** **(NOL without Valuation Account)** Parnevik Inc. reported the following pretax income (loss) and related tax rates during the years 2002–2008.

	Pretax Income (loss)	Tax Rate
2002	$ 40,000	30%
2003	25,000	30%
2004	60,000	30%
2005	80,000	40%
2006	(200,000)	45%
2007	70,000	40%
2008	90,000	35%

Pretax financial income (loss) and taxable income (loss) were the same for all years since Parnevik began business. The tax rates from 2005–2008 were enacted in 2005.

Instructions
(a) Prepare the journal entries for the years 2006–2008 to record income tax payable (refundable), income tax expense (benefit), and the tax effects of the loss carryback and carryforward. Assume that Parnevik elects the carryback provision where possible and expects to realize the benefits of any loss carryforward in the year that immediately follows the loss year.

    (b) Indicate the effect the 2006 entry(ies) has on the December 31, 2006, balance sheet.

    (c) Prepare the portion of the income statement, starting with "Operating loss before income taxes," for 2006.

    (d) Prepare the portion of the income statement, starting with "Income before income taxes," for 2007.

(LO 2, 3, 9) **P19-6** **(Two Differences, Two Rates, Future Income Expected)**   Presented below are two independent situations related to future taxable and deductible amounts resulting from temporary differences existing at December 31, 2006.

    1. Pirates Co. has developed the following schedule of future taxable and deductible amounts.

	2007	2008	2009	2010	2011
Taxable amounts	$300	$300	$300	$ 300	$300
Deductible amount	—	—	—	(1,400)	—

    2. Eagles Co. has the following schedule of future taxable and deductible amounts.

	2007	2008	2009	2010
Taxable amounts	$300	$300	$ 300	$300
Deductible amount	—	—	(2,000)	—

Both Pirates Co. and Eagles Co. have taxable income of $3,000 in 2006 and expect to have taxable income in all future years. The tax rates enacted as of the beginning of 2006 are 30% for 2006–2009 and 35% for years thereafter. All of the underlying temporary differences relate to noncurrent assets and liabilities.

Instructions

For each of these two situations, compute the net amount of deferred income taxes to be reported at the end of 2006, and indicate how it should be classified on the balance sheet.

(LO 2, 5, 7) **P19-7** **(One Temporary Difference, Tracked 3 Years, Change in Rates, Income Statement Presentation)** Gators Corp. sold an investment on an installment basis. The total gain of $60,000 was reported for financial reporting purposes in the period of sale. The company qualifies to use the installment sales method for tax purposes. The installment period is 3 years; one-third of the sale price is collected in the period of sale. The tax rate was 35% in 2006, and 30% in 2007 and 2008. The 30% tax rate was not enacted in law until 2007. The accounting and tax data for the 3 years is shown below.

	Financial Accounting	Tax Return
2006 (35% tax rate)		
Income before temporary difference	$ 70,000	$70,000
Temporary difference	60,000	20,000
Income	$130,000	$90,000
2007 (30% tax rate)		
Income before temporary difference	$ 70,000	$70,000
Temporary difference	–0–	20,000
Income	$ 70,000	$90,000
2008 (30% tax rate)		
Income before temporary difference	$ 70,000	$70,000
Temporary difference	–0–	20,000
Income	$ 70,000	$90,000

Instructions

    (a) Prepare the journal entries to record the income tax expense, deferred income taxes, and the income tax payable at the end of each year. No deferred income taxes existed at the beginning of 2006.

    (b) Explain how the deferred taxes will appear on the balance sheet at the end of each year. (Assume the Installment Accounts Receivable is classified as a current asset.)

    (c) Draft the income tax expense section of the income statement for each year, beginning with "Income before income taxes."

(LO 2, 3, 5, 9) **P19-8** **(Two Differences, 2 Years, Compute Taxable Income and Pretax Financial Income)** The following information was disclosed during the audit of Munter Inc.

    1.

Year	Amount Due per Tax Return
2006	$140,000
2007	112,000

2. On January 1, 2006, equipment costing $400,000 is purchased. For financial reporting purposes, the company uses straight-line depreciation over a 5-year life. For tax purposes, the company uses the elective straight-line method over a 5-year life. (*Hint:* For tax purposes, the half-year convention as discussed in Appendix 11A must be used.)

3. In January 2007, $225,000 is collected in advance rental of a building for a 3-year period. The entire $225,000 is reported as taxable income in 2007, but $150,000 of the $225,000 is reported as unearned revenue in 2007 for financial reporting purposes. The remaining amount of unearned revenue is to be earned equally in 2008 and 2009.

4. The tax rate is 40% in 2006 and all subsequent periods. (*Hint:* To find taxable income in 2006 and 2007, the related income tax payable amounts will have to be "grossed up.")

5. No temporary differences existed at the end of 2005. Munter expects to report taxable income in each of the next 5 years.

Instructions

(a) Determine the amount to report for deferred income taxes at the end of 2006, and indicate how it should be classified on the balance sheet.

(b) Prepare the journal entry to record income taxes for 2006.

(c) Draft the income tax section of the income statement for 2006 beginning with "Income before income taxes." (*Hint:* You must compute taxable income and then combine that with changes in cumulative temporary differences to arrive at pretax financial income.)

(d) Determine the deferred income taxes at the end of 2007, and indicate how they should be classified on the balance sheet.

(e) Prepare the journal entry to record income taxes for 2007.

(f) Draft the income tax section of the income statement for 2007, beginning with "Income before income taxes."

(LO 2, 3, 5, 6, 9)

P19-9 (Five Differences, Compute Taxable Income and Deferred Taxes, Draft Income Statement) King Company began operations at the beginning of 2007. The following information pertains to this company.

1. Pretax financial income for 2007 is $100,000.

2. The tax rate enacted for 2007 and future years is 40%

3. Differences between the 2007 income statement and tax return are listed below:

   (a) Warranty expense accrued for financial reporting purposes amounts to $5,000. Warranty deductions per the tax return amount to $2,000.

   (b) Gross profit on construction contracts using the percentage-of-completion method for books amounts to $92,000. Gross profit on construction contracts for tax purposes amounts to $62,000.

   (c) Depreciation of property, plant, and equipment for financial reporting purposes amounts to $60,000. Depreciation of these assets amounts to $80,000 for the tax return.

   (d) A $3,500 fine paid for violation of pollution laws was deducted in computing pretax financial income.

   (e) Interest revenue earned on an investment in tax-exempt municipal bonds amounts to $1,400. (Assume (a) is short-term in nature; assume (b) and (c) are long-term in nature.)

4. Taxable income is expected for the next few years.

Instructions

(a) Compute taxable income for 2007.

(b) Compute the deferred taxes at December 31, 2007, that relate to the temporary differences described above. Clearly label them as deferred tax asset or liability.

(c) Prepare the journal entry to record income tax expense, deferred taxes, and income taxes payable for 2007.

(d) Draft the income tax expense section of the income statement beginning with "Income before income taxes."

CONCEPTS FOR ANALYSIS

CA19-1 (Objectives and Principles for Accounting for Income Taxes) The amount of income taxes due to the government for a period of time is rarely the amount reported on the income statement for that period as income tax expense.

Instructions

(a) Explain the objectives of accounting for income taxes in general purpose financial statements.

(b) Explain the basic principles that are applied in accounting for income taxes at the date of the financial statements to meet the objectives discussed in (a).

(c) List the steps in the annual computation of deferred tax liabilities and assets.

CA19-2 **(Basic Accounting for Temporary Differences)** Majoli Company appropriately uses the asset-liability method to record deferred income taxes. Iva Majoli reports depreciation expense for certain machinery purchased this year using the modified accelerated cost recovery system (MACRS) for income tax purposes and the straight-line basis for financial reporting purposes. The tax deduction is the larger amount this year.

Majoli received rent revenues in advance this year. These revenues are included in this year's taxable income. However, for financial reporting purposes, these revenues are reported as unearned revenues, a current liability.

Instructions
- (a) What are the principles of the asset-liability approach?
- (b) How would Majoli account for the temporary differences?
- (c) How should Majoli classify the deferred tax consequences of the temporary differences on its balance sheet?

CA19-3 **(Identify Temporary Differences and Classification Criteria)** The asset-liability approach for recording deferred income taxes is an integral part of generally accepted accounting principles.

Instructions
- (a) Indicate whether each of the following independent situations should be treated as a temporary difference or as a permanent difference and explain why.
  - (1) Estimated warranty costs (covering a 3-year warranty) are expensed for financial reporting purposes at the time of sale but deducted for income tax purposes when paid.
  - (2) Depreciation for book and income tax purposes differs because of different bases of carrying the related property, which was acquired in a trade-in. The different bases are a result of different rules used for book and tax purposes to compute the basis of property acquired in a trade-in.
  - (3) A company properly uses the equity method to account for its 30% investment in another company. The investee pays dividends that are about 10% of its annual earnings.
  - (4) A company reports a gain on an involuntary conversion of a nonmonetary asset to a monetary asset. The company elects to replace the property within the statutory period using the total proceeds so the gain is not reported on the current year's tax return.
- (b) Discuss the nature of the deferred income tax accounts and possible classifications in a company's balance sheet. Indicate the manner in which these accounts are to be reported.

CA19-4 **(Accounting and Classification of Deferred Income Taxes)**
Part A
This year Sharapova Company has each of the following items in its income statement.
1. Gross profits on installment sales.
2. Revenues on long-term construction contracts.
3. Estimated costs of product warranty contracts.
4. Premiums on officers' life insurance with Sharapova as beneficiary.

Instructions
- (a) Under what conditions would deferred income taxes need to be reported in the financial statements?
- (b) Specify when deferred income taxes would need to be recognized for each of the items above, and indicate the rationale for such recognition.

Part B
Sharapova Company's president has heard that deferred income taxes can be classified in different ways in the balance sheet.

Instructions
Identify the conditions under which deferred income taxes would be classified as a noncurrent item in the balance sheet. What justification exists for such classification?

(AICPA adapted)

CA19-5 **(Explain Computation of Deferred Tax Liability for Multiple Tax Rates)** At December 31, 2007, Hingis Corporation has one temporary difference which will reverse and cause taxable amounts in 2008. In 2007 a new tax act set taxes equal to 45% for 2007, 40% for 2008, and 34% for 2009 and years thereafter.

Instructions
Explain what circumstances would call for Hingis to compute its deferred tax liability at the end of 2007 by multiplying the cumulative temporary difference by:
- (a) 45%.
- (b) 40%.
- (c) 34%.

CA19-6   (Explain Future Taxable and Deductible Amounts, How Carryback and Carryforward Affects Deferred Taxes)   Mary Joe Fernandez and Meredith McGrath are discussing accounting for income taxes. They are currently studying a schedule of taxable and deductible amounts that will arise in the future as a result of existing temporary differences. The schedule is as follows.

	Current Year	Future Years			
	2007	2008	2009	2010	2011
Taxable income	$850,000				
Taxable amounts		$375,000	$375,000	$ 375,000	$375,000
Deductible amounts				(2,400,000)	
Enacted tax rate	50%	45%	40%	35%	30%

Instructions

(a) Explain the concept of future taxable amounts and future deductible amounts as illustrated in the schedule.

(b) How do the carryback and carryforward provisions affect the reporting of deferred tax assets and deferred tax liabilities?

CA19-7   (Deferred Taxes, Income Effects)   Henrietta Aguirre, CPA, is the newly hired director of corporate taxation for Mesa Incorporated, which is a publicly traded corporation. Ms. Aguirre's first job with Mesa was the review of the company's accounting practices on deferred income taxes. In doing her review, she noted differences between tax and book depreciation methods that permitted Mesa to realize a sizable deferred tax liability on its balance sheet. As a result, Mesa paid very little in income taxes at that time.

Aguirre also discovered that Mesa has an explicit policy of selling off plant assets before they reversed in the deferred tax liability account. This policy, coupled with the rapid expansion of its plant asset base, allowed Mesa to "defer" all income taxes payable for several years, even though it always has reported positive earnings and an increasing EPS. Aguirre checked with the legal department and found the policy to be legal, but she's uncomfortable with the ethics of it.

Instructions

Answer the following questions.

(a) Why would Mesa have an explicit policy of selling plant assets before the temporary differences reversed in the deferred tax liability account?

(b) What are the ethical implications of Mesa's "deferral" of income taxes?

(c) Who could be harmed by Mesa's ability to "defer" income taxes payable for several years, despite positive earnings?

(d) In a situation such as this, what are Ms. Aguirre's professional responsibilities as a CPA?

USING YOUR JUDGMENT

Financial Reporting Problem

The Procter & Gamble Company (P&G)

The financial statements of **P&G** are presented in Appendix 5B or can be accessed on the KWW website.

Instructions

Refer to P&G's financial statements and the accompanying notes to answer the following questions.

(a) What amounts relative to income taxes does P&G report in its:

(1) 2004 income statement?

(2) June 30, 2004, balance sheet?

(3) 2004 statement of cash flows?

(b) P&G's provision for income taxes in 2002, 2003, and 2004 was computed at what effective tax rates? (See the notes to the financial statements.)

(c) How much of P&G's 2004 total provision for income taxes was current tax expense, and how much was deferred tax expense?

(d) What did P&G report as the significant components (the details) of its June 30, 2004, deferred tax assets and liabilities?

Financial Statement Analysis Case

Homestake Mining Company

Homestake Mining Company is a 120-year-old international gold mining company with substantial gold mining operations and exploration in the United States, Canada, and Australia. At year-end, Homestake reported the following items related to income taxes (thousands of dollars).

Total current taxes	$ 26,349
Total deferred taxes	(39,436)
Total income and mining taxes (the provision for taxes per its income statement)	(13,087)
Deferred tax liabilities	$303,050
Deferred tax assets, net of valuation allowance of $207,175	95,275
Net deferred tax liability	$207,775

Note 6: The classification of deferred tax assets and liabilities is based on the related asset or liability creating the deferred tax. Deferred taxes not related to a specific asset or liability are classified based on the estimated period of reversal.

Tax loss carryforwards (U.S., Canada, Australia, and Chile)	$71,151
Tax credit carryforwards	$12,007

Instructions

(a) What is the significance of Homestake's disclosure of "Current taxes" of $26,349 and "Deferred taxes" of $(39,436)?

(b) Explain the concept behind Homestake's disclosure of gross deferred tax liabilities (future taxable amounts) and gross deferred tax assets (future deductible amounts).

(c) Homestake reported tax loss carryforwards of $71,151 and tax credit carryforwards of $12,007. How do the carryback and carryforward provisions affect the reporting of deferred tax assets and deferred tax liabilities?

Comparative Analysis Case

The Coca-Cola Company and PepsiCo, Inc.

Instructions

Go to the KWW website and use information found there to answer the following questions related to **The Coca-Cola Company** and **PepsiCo, Inc.**

(a) What are the amounts of Coca-Cola's and PepsiCo's provision for income taxes for the year 2004? Of each company's 2004 provision for income taxes, what portion is current expense and what portion is deferred expense?

(b) What amount of cash was paid in 2004 for income taxes by Coca-Cola and by PepsiCo?

(c) What was the U.S. federal statutory tax rate in 2004? What was the effective tax rate in 2004 for Coca-Cola and PepsiCo? Why might their effective tax rates differ?

(d) For the year-end 2004, what amounts were reported by Coca-Cola and PepsiCo as (a) gross deferred tax assets and (b) gross deferred tax liabilities?

(e) Do either Coca-Cola or PepsiCo disclose any net operating loss carrybacks and/or carryforwards at year-end 2004? What are the amounts, and when do the carryforwards expire?

Research Cases

Case 1

As discussed in the chapter, companies must consider all positive and negative information in determining whether a deferred tax asset valuation allowance is needed.

Instructions

Examine the balance sheets and income tax footnotes for two companies that have recorded deferred tax assets, and answer the following questions with regard to each company.

(a) What is the gross amount of the deferred tax asset recorded by the company? Express this amount as a percentage of total assets.

(b) Did the company record a valuation allowance? How large was the allowance?

(c) What evidence, if any, did the company cite with regard to the need for a valuation allowance? Do you consider the company's disclosure to be adequate?

Case 2

Deferred tax liabilities require special considerations for financial statement readers.

Instructions

Obtain a recent edition of a financial statement analysis textbook, read the section related to deferred tax liabilities, and answer the following questions.

(a) What are the major analytical issues associated with deferred tax liabilities?

(b) What type of adjustments to deferred tax liabilities do analysts make when examining financial statements?

International Reporting Case

Tomkins PLC

Tomkins PLC is a British company that operates in three business sectors: industrial and automotive, air systems components, and engineering and construction products. Before 2005 Tomkins prepared its accounts in accordance with United Kingdom (U.K.) accounting standards. Like U.S. reporting, U.K. financial reporting is investor-oriented. As a result, British companies report different income amounts for tax and financial reporting purposes. British companies receive different tax treatment for such items as depreciation (capital allowances), and they receive tax credits for operating losses. In 2004 Tomkins reported income of £171.8 million and reported total shareholders' funds of £1,398.7 million at year-end. Tomkins provided the following disclosures related to taxes in its annual report.

If Tomkins had used U.S. GAAP its income would have been higher by £96.1 million in the current year. Stockholders' equity at year-end would have been £764.9 million higher if Tompkins had applied U.S. GAAP.

TOMKINS

Reconciliation to Accounting Principles Generally Accepted in the United States of America (Unaudited)—Partial

The consolidated financial statements are prepared in conformity with accounting principles generally accepted in the United Kingdom ("U.K. GAAP") which differ in certain respects from accounting principles generally accepted in the United States of America ("U.S. GAAP"). The following is a summary of the material adjustments to profit attributable to shareholders and shareholders' equity determined in accordance with U.K. GAAP, necessary to reconcile to net income and shareholders' equity determined in accordance with U.S. GAAP.

Reconciliation from U.K. GAAP to U.S. GAAP

	3 January 2004 12 months £ million
Profit attributable to shareholders	
Net income under UK GAAP	171.8
U.S. GAAP adjustments:	
Goodwill amortisation	11.9
Goodwill impairment	(30.0)
Reversal of U.K. provision for impairment	51.4
Intangibles amortisation	(1.6)
Valuation of net assets acquired in a business combination	(0.2)
Gain/(loss) on disposal of operations	22.6
Pension costs	3.4
Share options	(4.0)
Capitalised interest	2.2
Deferred income tax	(2.1)
Derivatives	29.5
Restructuring costs	13.0
Net income under U.S. GAAP	267.9

Explanation of the deferred tax difference is as follows:

In Tomkins consolidated financial statements, deferred tax is provided in full on all liabilities. Deferred tax assets are recognised to the extent it is regarded as more likely than not that there will be suitable taxable profits from which the future reversal of the underlying timing differences can be deducted, and for this purpose Tomkins considers only future periods for which forecasts are prepared. Under U.S. GAAP, deferred taxes are provided for all temporary differences on a full asset and liability basis. A valuation allowance is established in respect of those deferred tax assets where it is more likely than not that some portion will not be realised. The look forward period is not limited to the period for which forecasts are prepared.

Instructions

Use the information in the Tomkins disclosure to answer the following.

(a) Prepare the journal entry that would be required to reconcile Tomkins' income to U.S. GAAP for the differences in deferred taxes under U.S. and U.K. accounting standards.

(b) In light of the information disclosed, explain why you think Tomkins' equity under U.S. GAAP would be higher at year-end in the current year.

(c) Tomkins, like other U.K. companies, uses the intrinsic-value method to measure the expense related to stock-based compensation. Assuming similar tax treatment of stock-based compensation in the U.S. and the U.K., does the U.K. accounting cause any problems in comparing the financial statements of U.S. GAAP and U.K. GAAP companies? In your discussion, consider both compensation expense and deferred taxes.

Professional Research: Financial Accounting and Reporting

Hallscott Company started operations in 2003, and although it has grown steadily, the company reported accumulated operating losses of $450,000 in its first four years in business. In the most recent year (2007), Hallscott appears to have turned the corner and reported modest taxable income of $30,000. In addition to a deferred tax asset related to its net operating loss, Hallscott has recorded a deferred tax asset related to product warranties and a deferred tax liability related to accelerated depreciation.

Given its past operating results, Hallscott has established a full valuation allowance for its deferred tax assets. However, given its improved performance, Hallscott management wonders whether the company can now reduce or eliminate the valuation allowance. They would like you to conduct some research on the accounting for its valuation allowance.

Instructions

Using the **Financial Accounting Research System (FARS)**, respond to the following items. (Provide text strings used in your search.)

(a) Briefly explain to Hallscott management the importance of future taxable income as it relates to the valuation allowance for deferred tax assets.

(b) What are the sources of income that may be relied upon to remove the need for a valuation allowance?

(c) What are tax-planning strategies? From the information provided, does it appear that Hallscott could employ a tax-planning strategy to support reducing its valuation allowance?

Professional Simulation

In this simulation you are asked to address questions related to the accounting for taxes. Prepare responses to all parts.

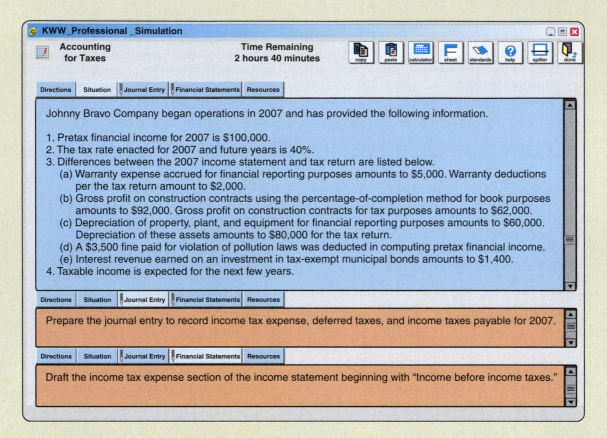

KWW_Professional _Simulation

| Accounting for Taxes | Time Remaining 2 hours 40 minutes | copy | paste | calculator | sheet | standards | help | splitter | done |

Directions | Situation | Journal Entry | Financial Statements | Resources

Johnny Bravo Company began operations in 2007 and has provided the following information.

1. Pretax financial income for 2007 is $100,000.
2. The tax rate enacted for 2007 and future years is 40%.
3. Differences between the 2007 income statement and tax return are listed below.
   (a) Warranty expense accrued for financial reporting purposes amounts to $5,000. Warranty deductions per the tax return amount to $2,000.
   (b) Gross profit on construction contracts using the percentage-of-completion method for book purposes amounts to $92,000. Gross profit on construction contracts for tax purposes amounts to $62,000.
   (c) Depreciation of property, plant, and equipment for financial reporting purposes amounts to $60,000. Depreciation of these assets amounts to $80,000 for the tax return.
   (d) A $3,500 fine paid for violation of pollution laws was deducted in computing pretax financial income.
   (e) Interest revenue earned on an investment in tax-exempt municipal bonds amounts to $1,400.
4. Taxable income is expected for the next few years.

Directions | Situation | Journal Entry | Financial Statements | Resources

Prepare the journal entry to record income tax expense, deferred taxes, and income taxes payable for 2007.

Directions | Situation | Journal Entry | Financial Statements | Resources

Draft the income tax expense section of the income statement beginning with "Income before income taxes."

Remember to check the book's companion website to find additional resources for this chapter.

wiley.com/college/kieso

ACCOUNTING FOR PENSIONS AND POSTRETIREMENT BENEFITS

Where Have All the Pensions Gone?

Many companies have benefit plans that promise income and other benefits to retired employees in exchange for services during their working years. However, a shift is on from traditional defined-benefit plans, in which employers bear the risk of meeting the benefit promises, to plans in which employees bear more of the risk. In some cases, employers are dropping retirement plans altogether. Here are some of the reasons for the shift.

Competition. Newer and foreign competitors do not have the same retiree costs that older U.S. companies do. **Southwest Airlines** does not offer a traditional pension plan, but **Northwest** and **United** both have pension deficits exceeding $100,000 per employee.

Cost. Retirees are living longer, and the costs of retirement are higher. Combined with annual retiree healthcare costs, retirement benefits are costing the S&P 500 companies over $25 billion a year and are rising at double-digit rates.

Insurance. Pensions are backed by premiums paid to the Pension Benefit Guarantee Corp (PBGC). When a company fails, the PBGC takes over the plan. But due to a number of significant company failures, the PBGC is running a deficit, and healthy companies are subsidizing the weak. For example, steel companies pay just 3 percent of PBGC premiums but account for 56 percent of the claims.

Accounting. Accounting rule makers are considering rules, to bring U.S. standards in line with international rules, that will require companies to mark their pensions to market (value them at market rates). Such a move would increase the reported volatility of the plan and company financial statements. When Britain made this shift, 25 percent of British companies closed their plans to new entrants.[1]

As a result of such factors, it is not hard to believe that experts can think of no major company that has instituted a traditional pension plan in the past decade.

---

[1]Adapted from Nanette Byrnes with David Welch, "The Benefits Trap," *BusinessWeek* (July 19, 2004), pp. 54–72.

Learning Objectives

After studying this chapter, you should be able to:

1 Distinguish between accounting for the employer's pension plan and accounting for the pension fund.

2 Identify types of pension plans and their characteristics.

3 Explain alternative measures for valuing the pension obligation.

4 List the components of pension expense.

5 Use a worksheet for employer's pension plan entries.

6 Describe the amortization of unrecognized prior service costs.

7 Explain the accounting procedure for recognizing unexpected gains and losses.

8 Explain the corridor approach to amortizing unrecognized gains and losses.

9 Explain the recognition of a minimum liability.

10 Describe the requirements for reporting pension plans in financial statements.

As our opening story indicates, the cost of retirement benefits is getting steep. For example, **General Motors'** pension and healthcare costs for retirees in a recent year totaled $6.2 billion, or approximately $1,784 per vehicle produced. General Motors and many other companies are facing substantial pension and other postretirement expenses and obligations. In this chapter we discuss the accounting issues related to these benefit plans. The content and organization of the chapter are as follows.

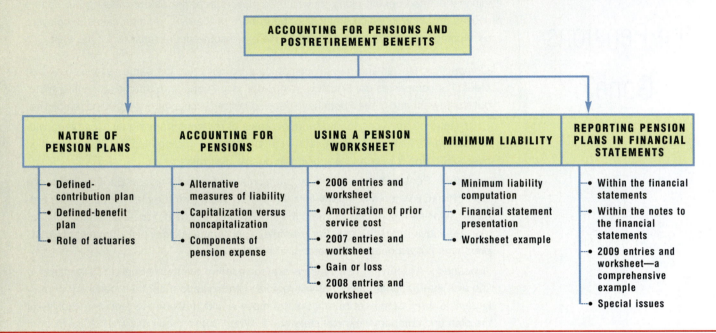

ACCOUNTING FOR PENSIONS AND POSTRETIREMENT BENEFITS				
NATURE OF PENSION PLANS	**ACCOUNTING FOR PENSIONS**	**USING A PENSION WORKSHEET**	**MINIMUM LIABILITY**	**REPORTING PENSION PLANS IN FINANCIAL STATEMENTS**
• Defined-contribution plan • Defined-benefit plan • Role of actuaries	• Alternative measures of liability • Capitalization versus noncapitalization • Components of pension expense	• 2006 entries and worksheet • Amortization of prior service cost • 2007 entries and worksheet • Gain or loss • 2008 entries and worksheet	• Minimum liability computation • Financial statement presentation • Worksheet example	• Within the financial statements • Within the notes to the financial statements • 2009 entries and worksheet—a comprehensive example • Special issues

NATURE OF PENSION PLANS

OBJECTIVE 1
Distinguish between accounting for the employer's pension plan and accounting for the pension fund.

A **pension plan** is an arrangement whereby an employer provides benefits (payments) to retired employees for services they provided in their working years. Pension accounting may be divided and separately treated as **accounting for the employer** and **accounting for the pension fund**. The *company* or *employer* is the organization sponsoring the pension plan. It incurs the cost and makes contributions to the pension fund. The *fund* or *plan* is the entity that receives the contributions from the employer, administers the pension assets, and makes the benefit payments to the retired employees (pension recipients). Illustration 20-1 shows the three entities involved in a pension plan and indicates the flow of cash among them.

ILLUSTRATION 20-1
Flow of Cash among Pension Plan Participants

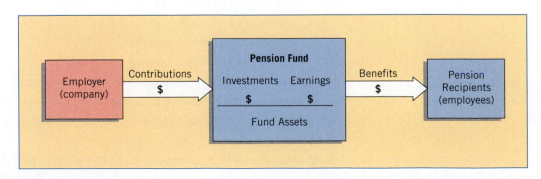

A pension plan is **funded** when the employer makes payments to a funding agency.[2] That agency accumulates the assets of the pension fund and makes payments to the recipients as the benefits come due.

Some pension plans are **contributory**. In these, the employees bear part of the cost of the stated benefits or voluntarily make payments to increase their benefits. Other plans are **noncontributory**. In these, the employer bears the entire cost. Companies generally design their pension plans so as to take advantage of federal income tax benefits. Plans that offer tax benefits are called **qualified pension plans**. They permit **deductibility of the employer's contributions to the pension fund and tax-free status of earnings from pension fund assets**.

The pension fund should be a separate legal and accounting entity. The pension fund, as a separate entity, maintains a set of books and prepares financial statements. Maintaining records and preparing financial statements for the fund, an activity known as "accounting for employee benefit plans," is not the subject of this chapter.[3] Instead, this chapter explains the pension accounting and reporting problems **of the employer** as the sponsor of a pension plan.

The need to properly administer and account for pension funds becomes apparent when you understand the size of these funds. Listed in Illustration 20-2 are the pension fund assets and pension expenses of seven major companies.

ILLUSTRATION 20-2
Pension Funds and Pension Expense

Company ($ in millions)	Size of Pension Fund	2004 Pension Expense	Pension Expense as % of Pre-Tax Income
General Motors	$ 99,909	$2,456	52.27%
Hewlett-Packard	9,168	594	14.16
Deere & Company	8,403	43	2.03
Goodyear Tire	7,720	35	10.72
Merck	5,481	397	4.98
Coca-Cola	2,800	122	1.96
Molson Coors Brewing	2,740	44	14.18%

As Illustration 2-2 indicates, pension expense is a substantial percentage of total profit for many companies.[4] The two most common types of pension plans are **defined contribution plans** and **defined benefit plans**, and we look at each of them in the following sections.

Defined-Contribution Plan

In a **defined-contribution plan**, the employer agrees to contribute to a pension trust a certain sum each period, based on a formula. This formula may consider such factors as age, length of employee service, employer's profits, and compensation level. **The plan defines only the employer's contribution.** It makes no promise regarding the ultimate benefits paid out to the employees. A common form of this plan is a "401(k)" plan.

The size of the pension benefits that the employee finally collects under the plan depends on several factors: the amounts originally contributed to the pension trust, the

OBJECTIVE 2
Identify types of pension plans and their characteristics.

[2]When used as a verb, **fund** means to pay to a funding agency (as to fund future pension benefits or to fund pension cost). Used as a noun, it refers to assets accumulated in the hands of a funding agency (trustee) for the purpose of meeting pension benefits when they become due.

[3]The FASB issued a separate standard covering the accounting and reporting for employee benefit plans. "Accounting and Reporting by Defined Benefit Pension Plans," *Statement of Financial Accounting Standards No. 35* (Stamford, Conn.: FASB, 1979).

[4]One study indicated that during the 1990s, pension funds (private and public) held or owned approximately 25 percent of the market value of corporate stock outstanding and accounted for 32 percent of the daily trading volume on the New York Stock Exchange. The enormous size (and the social significance) of these funds is staggering.

income accumulated in the trust, and the treatment of forfeitures of funds caused by early terminations of other employees. A company usually turns over to an **independent third-party trustee** the amounts originally contributed. The trustee, acting on behalf of the beneficiaries (the participating employees), assumes ownership of the pension assets and is accountable for their investment and distribution. The trust is separate and distinct from the employer.

The accounting for a defined-contribution plan is straightforward. The employee gets the benefit of gain (or the risk of loss) from the assets contributed to the pension plan. The employer simply contributes each year based on the formula established in the plan. As a result, the employer's annual cost (pension expense) is simply the amount that it is obligated to contribute to the pension trust. The employer reports a liability on its balance sheet only if it does not make the contribution in full. The employer reports an asset only if it contributes more than the required amount.

In addition to pension expense, the employer must disclose the following for a defined-contribution plan: a plan description, including employee groups covered; the basis for determining contributions; and the nature and effect of significant matters affecting comparability from period to period.[5]

Disclosures for Defined-Contribution Plans

Defined-Benefit Plan

A defined-benefit plan outlines the benefits that employees will receive when they retire. These benefits typically are a function of an employee's years of service and of the compensation level in the years approaching retirement.

To meet the defined-benefit commitments that will arise at retirement, a company must determine what the contribution should be today (a time value of money computation). Companies may use many different contribution approaches. However, the funding method should provide enough money at retirement to meet the benefits defined by the plan.

The **employees** are the beneficiaries of a defined-**contribution** trust, but the employer **is** the beneficiary of a defined-**benefit** trust. Under a defined-benefit plan, the trust's primary purpose is to safeguard and invest assets so that there will be enough to pay the employer's obligation to the employees. **In form**, the trust is a separate entity. **In substance**, the trust assets and liabilities belong to the employer. That is, **as long as the plan continues, the employer is responsible for the payment of the defined benefits (without regard to what happens in the trust).** The employer must make up any shortfall in the accumulated assets held by the trust. On the other hand, the employer can recapture any excess accumulated in the trust, either through reduced future funding or through a reversion of funds.

Because a defined-benefit plan specifies benefits in terms of uncertain future variables, a company must establish an appropriate funding pattern to ensure the availability of funds at retirement to provide the benefits promised. This funding level depends on a number of factors such as turnover, mortality, length of employee service, compensation levels, and interest earnings.

Employers are at risk with defined-benefit plans because they must contribute enough to meet the cost of benefits that the plan defines. The expense recognized each period is not necessarily equal to the cash contribution. Similarly, the liability is controversial because its measurement and recognition relate to unknown future variables. Thus, the accounting issues related to this type of plan are complex. **Our discussion in the following sections deals primarily with defined-benefit plans.**[6]

---

[5]"Employers' Accounting for Pension Plans," *Statement of Financial Accounting Standards No. 87* (Stamford, Conn.: FASB, 1985), pars. 63–66.

[6]In terms of total assets, recent Federal Reserve statistics (2004) indicate that assets in private defined-benefit and defined-contribution plans were more than $1.8 and $2.7 trillion, respectively. In many cases, companies offer a defined-contribution plan in combination with a defined-benefit plan.

WHICH PLAN IS YOR YOU?

Defined-contribution plans have become much more popular with employers than defined-benefit plans. One reason is that they are cheaper. Defined-contribution plans often cost no more than 3 percent of payroll, whereas defined-benefit plans can cost 5 to 6 percent of payroll.

In the late 1970s approximately 15 million individuals had defined-contribution plans; today over 62 million do. The following chart reflects this significant change. It shows the percentage of companies using various types of plans, based on a survey of approximately 150 CFOs and managing corporate directors.

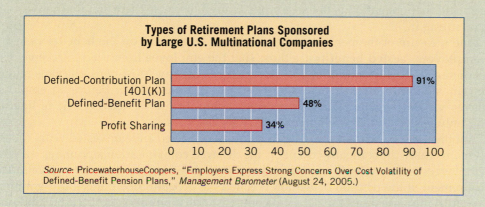

Types of Retirement Plans Sponsored by Large U.S. Multinational Companies

Defined-Contribution Plan [401(K)] 91%
Defined-Benefit Plan 48%
Profit Sharing 34%

Source: PricewaterhouseCoopers, "Employers Express Strong Concerns Over Cost Volatility of Defined-Benefit Pension Plans," *Management Barometer* (August 24, 2005.)

Although many companies are changing to defined-contribution plans, over 40 million individuals still are covered under defined-benefit plans.

The Role of Actuaries in Pension Accounting

The problems associated with pension plans involve complicated mathematical considerations. Therefore, companies engage **actuaries** to ensure that a pension plan is appropriate for the employee group covered.[7] Actuaries are individuals trained through a long and rigorous certification program to assign probabilities to future events and their financial effects. The insurance industry employs actuaries to assess risks and to advise on the setting of premiums and other aspects of insurance policies. Employers rely heavily on actuaries for assistance in developing, implementing, and funding pension funds.

Actuaries make predictions (called *actuarial assumptions*) of mortality rates, employee turnover, interest and earnings rates, early retirement frequency, future salaries, and any other factors necessary to operate a pension plan. They also compute the various pension measures that affect the financial statements, such as the pension obligation, the annual cost of servicing the plan, and the cost of amendments to the plan. In summary, accounting for defined-benefit pension plans relies heavily upon information and measurements provided by actuaries.

---

[7]An actuary's primary purpose is to ensure that the company has established an appropriate funding pattern to meet its pension obligations. This computation involves developing a set of assumptions and continued monitoring of these assumptions to ensure their realism. That the general public has little understanding of what an actuary does is illustrated by the following excerpt from the *Wall Street Journal*: "A polling organization once asked the general public what an actuary was, and received among its more coherent responses the opinion that it was a place where you put dead actors."

ACCOUNTING FOR PENSIONS

In accounting for a company's pension plan, two questions arise: (1) What is the pension obligation that a company should report in the financial statements? (2) What is the pension expense for the period? Attempting to answer the first question has produced much controversy.

Alternative Measures of the Liability

Most agree that an employer's **pension obligation** is the deferred compensation obligation it has to its employees for their service under the terms of the pension plan. Measuring that obligation is not so simple, though, because there are alternative ways of measuring it.[8]

One measure of the pension obligation is to base it only on the benefits vested to the employees. **Vested benefits** are those that the employee is entitled to receive even if he or she renders no additional services to the company. Most pension plans require a certain minimum number of years of service to the employer before an employee achieves vested benefits status. Companies compute the **vested benefit obligation** using only vested benefits, at current salary levels.

Another way to measure the obligation uses both vested and nonvested years of service. On this basis, the company computes the deferred compensation amount on all years of employees' service—**both vested and nonvested**—using current salary levels. This measurement of the pension obligation is called the **accumulated benefit obligation**.

A third measure bases the deferred compensation amount on both vested and non-vested service **using future salaries**. This measurement of the pension obligation is called the **projected benefit obligation**. Because future salaries are expected to be higher than current salaries, this approach results in the largest measurement of the pension obligation.

The choice between these measures is critical. The choice affects the amount of a company's pension liability and the annual pension expense reported. The diagram in Illustration 20-3 presents the differences in these three measurements.

ILLUSTRATION 20-3
Different Measures of the Pension Obligation

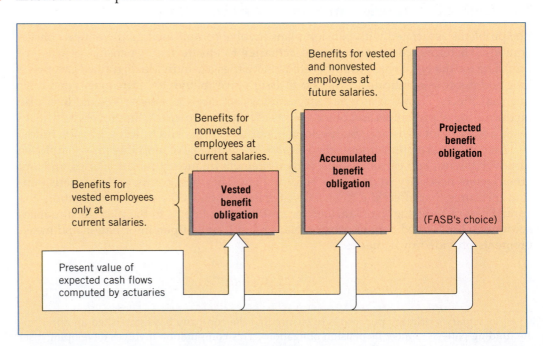

---

[8]One measure of the pension obligation is to determine the amount that the **Pension Benefit Guaranty Corporation** would require the employer to pay if it defaulted. (This amount is limited to 30 percent of the employer's net worth.) The accounting profession rejected this approach for financial reporting because it is too hypothetical and ignores the going concern concept.

Which of these alternative measures of the pension liability does the profession favor? **In general, the profession adopted the projected benefit obligation—the present value of vested and nonvested benefits accrued to date, based on employees' future salary levels.**[9] As you will learn later, however, the profession uses the accumulated benefit obligation in certain situations.

Those critical of the projected benefit obligation argue that using future salary levels is tantamount to adding future obligations to existing ones. Those in favor of the projected benefit obligation contend that a promise by an employer to pay benefits based on a percentage of the employees' future salary is far greater than a promise to pay a percentage of their current salary, and such a difference should be reflected in the pension liability and pension expense.

Regardless of the approach used, however, companies discount to present value the estimated future benefits to be paid. Minor changes in the interest rate used to discount pension benefits can dramatically affect the measurement of the employer's obligation. For example, a 1 percent decrease in the discount rate can increase pension liabilities 15 percent. Accounting rules require that, at each measurement date, a company must change the discount rate used to measure the pension liability, to reflect current interest rates.

Capitalization versus Noncapitalization

Prior to issuance of *FASB Statement No. 87*, accounting for pension plans followed a **noncapitalization approach**. Noncapitalization is also often referred to as **off-balance-sheet financing**. Under this approach, the balance sheet reported an asset or liability for the pension plan only if the amount the employer actually funded during the year was different from the amount the employer reported as pension expense for the year.

The **capitalization approach** means measuring and reporting in the financial statements the employers' pension assets and liabilities. Capitalization focuses on the **economic substance** of the pension plan arrangement over its legal form. Under this view, the employer has a liability for pension benefits that it has promised to pay for employee services already performed. As pension expense is incurred—as the employees work—the employer's liability increases. Funding the plan has no effect on the amount of the liability; only the employer's promises and the employee's services affect the liability. The employer reduces pension liability through the payment of benefits to retired employees.

In *Statement No. 87* the FASB adopted an approach that leans toward capitalization. However, the profession and the FASB strongly opposed proposals to adopt a full capitalization (total accrual) approach. *FASB Statement No. 87* **represents a compromise that combines some of the features of capitalization with some of the features of noncapitalization**. As we will learn in more detail later in this chapter, companies do not recognize (that is, do not capitalize) some elements of the pension plan in the accounts and the financial statements.

Because of this, the accounting for pensions is not perfectly logical, totally complete, or conceptually sound. Because of the financial complexity of defined-benefit pensions, many well-intentioned, competent people could not agree on the economic substance of such plans. Thus, *Statement No. 87* involves several compromises that make it less than an ideal application of the capitalization method. In its defense, however, *Statement No. 87* is a great improvement over previous accounting pronouncements; it represents a first step toward a conceptually sound approach to employers' accounting for pension plans.

---

[9]When we use the term "present value of benefits" throughout this chapter, we really mean the *actuarial* present value of benefits. **Actuarial present value** is the amount payable adjusted to reflect the time value of money *and* the probability of payment (by means of decrements for events such as death, disability, withdrawals, or retirement) between the present date and the expected date of payment. For simplicity, though, we use the term "present value" instead of "actuarial present value" in our discussion.

Components of Pension Expense

There is broad agreement that companies should account for pension cost on the **accrual basis**.[10] The profession recognizes that **accounting for pension plans requires measurement of the cost and its identification with the appropriate time periods**. The determination of pension cost, however, is extremely complicated because it is a function of the following components.

UNDERLYING CONCEPTS

The matching concept and the definition of a liability justify accounting for pension cost on the accrual basis. This requires recording an expense when employees earn the future benefits, and recognizing an existing obligation to pay pensions later based on current services received.

1 **Service Cost.** Service cost is the expense caused by the increase in pension benefits payable (the **projected benefit obligation**) to employees because of their services rendered during the current year. Actuaries compute **service cost** as the present value of the new benefits earned by employees during the year.

2 **Interest on the Liability.** Because a pension is a deferred compensation arrangement, there is a time value of money factor. As a result, companies record the pension liability on a discounted basis. **Interest expense accrues each year on the projected benefit obligation just as it does on any discounted debt.** The actuary helps to select the interest rate, referred to as the **settlement rate**.

3 **Actual Return on Plan Assets.** The return earned by the accumulated pension fund assets in a particular year is relevant in measuring the net cost to the employer of sponsoring an employee pension plan. Therefore, **a company should adjust annual pension expense for interest and dividends that accumulate within the fund, as well as increases and decreases in the market value of the fund assets.**

4 **Amortization of Unrecognized Prior Service Cost.** Pension plan amendments (including initiation of a pension plan) often include provisions to increase benefits (or in rare situations, to decrease benefits) for employee service provided in prior years. A company grants plan amendments with the expectation that it will realize economic benefits in future periods. Thus, **it allocates the cost (prior service cost) of providing these retroactive benefits to pension expense in the future, specifically to the remaining service-years of the affected employees**.

5 **Gain or Loss.** Volatility in pension expense can result from sudden and large changes in the market value of plan assets and by changes in the projected benefit obligation (which changes when actuaries modify assumptions or when actual experience differs from expected experience). Two items comprise this gain or loss: (1) the difference between the actual return and the expected return on plan assets, and (2) amortization of the unrecognized net gain or loss from previous periods. We will discuss this complex computation later in the chapter.

Illustration 20-4 (page 1027) shows the **components of pension expense** and their effect on total pension expense (increase or decrease).

Service Cost

In *FASB No. 87*, the Board states that the **service cost** component recognized in a period is the **actuarial present value** of benefits attributed by the pension benefit formula to employee service during the period. That is, the actuary predicts the additional benefits that an employer must pay under the plan's benefit formula as a result of the employees' current year's service, and then discounts the cost of those future benefits back to their present value.

---

[10]At one time, companies applied the **cash basis** of accounting to pension plans by recognizing the amount paid in a particular accounting period as the pension expense for the period. The problem was that the amount paid or funded in a fiscal period depended on financial management and was too often discretionary. For example, funding could depend on the availability of cash, the level of earnings, or other factors unrelated to the requirements of the plan. Application of the cash basis made it possible to manipulate the amount of pension expense appearing in the income statement simply by varying the cash paid to the pension fund.

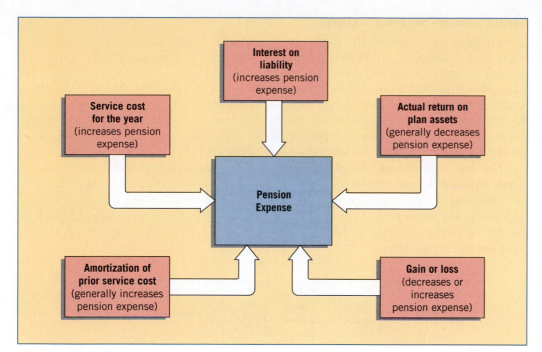

ILLUSTRATION 20-4
Components of Annual
Pension Expense

The Board concluded that **companies must consider future compensation levels in measuring the present obligation and periodic pension expense if the plan benefit formula incorporates them**. In other words, the present obligation resulting from a promise to pay a benefit of 1 percent of an employee's **final pay** differs from the promise to pay 1 percent of **current pay**. To overlook this fact is to ignore an important aspect of pension expense. Thus, FASB adopts the **benefits/years-of-service actuarial method, which determines pension expense based on future salary levels**.

Some object to this determination, arguing that a company should have more freedom to select an expense recognition pattern. Others believe that incorporating future salary increases into current pension expense is accounting for events that have not happened yet. They argue that if a company terminates the plan today, it pays only liabilities for accumulated benefits. **Nevertheless, the FASB indicates that the projected benefit obligation provides a more realistic measure of the employer's obligation under the plan on a going-concern basis and, therefore, companies should use it as the basis for determining service cost.**

Interest on the Liability

The second component of pension expense is **interest on the liability**, or **interest expense**. Because a company defers paying the liability until maturity, the company records it on a discounted basis. The liability then accrues interest over the life of the employee. **The interest component is the interest for the period on the projected benefit obligation outstanding during the period.** The FASB did not address the question of how often to compound the interest cost. To simplify our illustrations and problem materials, we use a simple interest computation, applying it to the beginning-of-the-year balance of the projected benefit liability.

How do companies determine the interest rate to apply to the pension liability? The Board states that the assumed discount rate should **reflect the rates at which companies can effectively settle pension benefits**. In determining these **settlement rates**, a company looks to available information about rates implicit in current prices of annuity contracts. (Under an annuity contract, an insurance company unconditionally guarantees to provide specific pension benefits to specific individuals in return for a fixed consideration or premium.) Companies may also employ other rates of return on high-quality fixed-income investments.

Actual Return on Plan Assets

Pension plan assets are usually investments in stocks, bonds, other securities, and real estate that a company holds to earn a reasonable return, generally at minimum risk. Employer contributions and actual returns on pension plan assets increase pension plan assets. Benefits paid to retired employees decrease them. As we indicated, the actual return earned on these assets increases the fund balance and correspondingly reduces the employer's net cost of providing employees' pension benefits. That is, the higher the actual return on the pension plan assets, the less the employer has to contribute eventually and, therefore, the less pension expense that it needs to report.

The **actual return on the plan assets** is the increase in pension funds from interest, dividends, and realized and unrealized changes in the fair-market value of the plan assets. Companies compute the actual return by adjusting the change in the plan assets for the effects of contributions during the year and benefits paid out during the year. The equation in Illustration 20-5, or a variation thereof, can be used to compute the actual return.

ILLUSTRATION 20-5
Equation for Computing Actual Return

$$\text{Actual Return} = \left(\begin{array}{c} \text{Plan Assets} \\ \text{Ending} \\ \text{Balance} \end{array} - \begin{array}{c} \text{Plan Assets} \\ \text{Beginning} \\ \text{Balance} \end{array} \right) - (\text{Contributions} - \text{Benefits Paid})$$

Stated another way, the actual return on plan assets is the difference between the **fair value of the plan assets** at the beginning of the period and at the end of the period, adjusted for contributions and benefit payments. Illustration 20-6 uses the equation above to compute the actual return, using some assumed amounts.

ILLUSTRATION 20-6
Computation of Actual Return on Plan Assets

Fair value of plan assets at end of period		$5,000,000
Deduct: Fair value of plan assets at beginning of period		4,200,000
Increase in fair value of plan assets		800,000
Deduct: Contributions to plan during period	$500,000	
Less benefits paid during period	300,000	200,000
Actual return on plan assets		$ 600,000

If the actual return on the plan assets is positive (a gain) during the period, a company subtracts it when computing pension expense. If the actual return is negative (a loss) during the period, the company adds it when computing pension expense.[11]

USING A PENSION WORKSHEET

Before covering in detail the other pension-expense components (amortization of unrecognized prior service costs and gains and losses), we will illustrate the basic accounting entries for the first three components: (1) service cost, (2) interest on the liability, and (3) actual return on plan assets.

Important to accounting for pensions is that **companies do not recognize several significant items of the pension plan in the accounts and in the financial statements**. Among the compromises the FASB made was the nonrecognition (noncapitalization) of the following pension items:

1 Projected benefit obligation.
2 Pension plan assets.

---

[11]At this point, we use the actual rate of return. Later, for purposes of computing pension expense, we use the expected rate of return.

3   Unrecognized prior service costs.
4   Unrecognized net gain or loss.

A company must **disclose in notes** to the financial statements these four noncapitalized items, but does not recognize them in the body of the financial statements. It must know the exact amount of these items at all times because it uses them in the computation of annual pension expense. **To track these off-balance-sheet pension items, a company maintains memo entries and accounts outside the formal general ledger accounting system.** To track its relevant pension plan items and components, a company uses a worksheet unique to pension accounting to determine both the formal entries and the memo entries.[12]

Illustration 20-7 shows the format of the **pension worksheet**.

OBJECTIVE 5
Use a worksheet for
employer's pension
plan entries.

ILLUSTRATION 20-7
Basic Format of Pension
Worksheet

The "General Journal Entries" columns of the worksheet (near the left side) determine the entries to record in the formal general ledger accounts. The "Memo Record" columns (on the right side) maintain balances on the unrecognized (noncapitalized) pension items.

On the first line of the worksheet, a company records the beginning balances (if any). It records subsequent transactions and events related to the pension plan using debits and credits, using both sets of records as if they were one. For each transaction or event, the debits must equal the credits. **The balance in the Prepaid/Accrued Cost column should equal the net balance in the memo record.**

2006 Entries and Worksheet

To illustrate the use of a worksheet and how it helps in accounting for a pension plan, assume that on January 1, 2006, Zarle Company accounts for its defined-benefit plan under *SFAS No. 87*. The following facts apply to the pension plan for the year 2006.

Plan assets, January 1, 2006, are $100,000.

Projected benefit obligation, January 1, 2006, is $100,000.

Annual service cost is $9,000.

Settlement rate is 10 percent.

Actual return on plan assets is $10,000.

Funding contributions are $8,000.

Benefits paid to retirees during the year are $7,000.

Using the data presented above, the worksheet in Illustration 20-8 (page 1030) presents the beginning balances and all of the pension entries recorded by Zarle in 2006. Zarle records the beginning balances for the projected benefit obligation and the pension

---

[12]The use of this pension entry worksheet is recommended and illustrated by Paul B. W. Miller, "The New Pension Accounting (Part 2)," *Journal of Accountancy* (February 1987), pp. 86–94.

plan assets on the first line of the worksheet in the memo record. It does not record them in the formal general journal and, therefore, does not report a liability and an asset in the financial statements. These two significant pension items are off-balance-sheet amounts that affect pension expense but are not recorded as assets and liabilities in the employer's books.

ILLUSTRATION 20-8
Pension Worksheet—2006

	General Journal Entries			Memo Record	
Items	Annual Pension Expense	Cash	Prepaid/ Accrued Cost	Projected Benefit Obligation	Plan Assets
Balance, Jan. 1, 2006			—	100,000 Cr.	100,000 Dr.
(a) Service cost	9,000 Dr.			9,000 Cr.	
(b) Interest cost	10,000 Dr.			10,000 Cr.	
(c) Actual return	10,000 Cr.				10,000 Dr.
(d) Contributions		8,000 Cr.			8,000 Dr.
(e) Benefits				7,000 Dr.	7,000 Cr.
Journal entry for 2006	9,000 Dr.	8,000 Cr.	1,000 Cr.*		
Balance, Dec. 31, 2006			1,000 Cr.**	112,000 Cr.	111,000 Dr.

*$9,000 − $8,000 = $1,000.
**$112,000 − $111,000 = $1,000.

Entry (a) in Illustration 20-8 records the service cost component, which increases pension expense by $9,000 and increases the liability (projected benefit obligation) by $9,000. Entry (b) accrues the interest expense component, which increases both the liability and the pension expense by $10,000 (the beginning projected benefit obligation multiplied by the settlement rate of 10 percent). Entry (c) records the actual return on the plan assets, which increases the plan assets and decreases the pension expense. Entry (d) records Zarle's contribution (funding) of assets to the pension fund, thereby decreasing cash by $8,000 and increasing plan assets by $8,000. Entry (e) records the benefit payments made to retirees, which results in equal $7,000 decreases to the plan assets and the projected benefit obligation.

Zarle makes the "formal journal entry" on December 31, which records the pension expense in 2006, as follows.

2006

Pension Expense	9,000	
Cash		8,000
Prepaid/Accrued Pension Cost		1,000

The credit to Prepaid/Accrued Pension Cost for $1,000 represents the difference between the 2006 pension expense of $9,000 and the amount funded of $8,000. Prepaid/Accrued Pension Cost (credit) is a liability because Zarle underfunds the plan by $1,000. The Prepaid/Accrued Pension Cost account balance of $1,000 also equals the net of the balances in the memo accounts. Illustration 20-9 shows the reconciliation of the off-balance-sheet items with the prepaid/accrued pension cost reported in the balance sheet.

ILLUSTRATION 20-9
Pension Reconciliation Schedule—December 31, 2006

Projected benefit obligation (Credit)	$(112,000)
Plan assets at fair value (Debit)	111,000
Prepaid/accrued pension cost (Credit)	$ (1,000)

If the net of the memo record balances is a credit, the reconciling amount in the prepaid/accrued cost column will be a credit equal in amount. If the net of the memo record balances is a debit, the prepaid/accrued cost amount will be a debit equal in amount. The worksheet is designed to produce this reconciling feature, which is useful later in the preparation of the required note disclosure related to pensions.

In this illustration, the debit to Pension Expense exceeds the credit to Cash, resulting in a credit to Prepaid/Accrued Pension Cost—the recognition of a liability. If the credit to Cash exceeded the debit to Pension Expense, Zarle would debit Prepaid/Accrued Pension Cost—the recognition of an asset.

Amortization of Unrecognized Prior Service Cost (PSC)

When either initiating (adopting) or amending a defined-benefit plan, a company often credits employees for years of service provided before the date of initiation or amendment. As a result of this prior service cost, the projected benefit obligation is increased to recognize this additional obligation. In many cases, the increase in the projected benefit obligation is substantial.

Should a company report an expense and related liability for these **prior service costs (PSC)** at the time it initiates or amends a plan? The FASB says no. The Board's rationale is that the employer would not provide credit for past years of service unless it expects to receive benefits in the future. As a result, **a company should not recognize the retroactive benefits as pension expense entirely in the year of amendment. Instead the employer recognizes the pension expense over the remaining service lives of the employees who are expected to benefit from the change in the plan**.

The cost of the retroactive benefits (including any benefits provided to existing retirees) is the increase in the projected benefit obligation at the date of the amendment. An actuary computes the amount of the prior service cost. Amortization of the unrecognized prior service cost is also an accounting function performed with the assistance of an actuary.

The Board prefers a **years-of-service** amortization method that is similar to a units-of-production computation. First, the company computes the total number of service-years to be worked by all of the participating employees. Second, it divides the unrecognized prior service cost by the total number of service-years, to obtain a cost per service-year (the unit cost). Third, the company multiplies the number of service-years consumed each year by the cost per service-year, to obtain the annual amortization charge.

To illustrate the amortization of the unrecognized service cost under the years-of-service method, assume that Zarle Company's defined-benefit pension plan covers 170 employees. In its negotiations with the employees, Zarle Company amends its pension plan on January 1, 2007, and grants $80,000 of prior service costs to its employees. The employees are grouped according to expected years of retirement, as shown below.

Group	Number of Employees	Expected Retirement on Dec. 31
A	40	2007
B	20	2008
C	40	2009
D	50	2010
E	20	2011
	170	

Illustration 20-10 (page 1032) shows computation of the service-years per year and the total service-years.

> **OBJECTIVE 6**
> Describe the amortization of unrecognized prior service costs.

ILLUSTRATION 20-10
Computation of Service-Years

	Service-Years					
Year	A	B	C	D	E	Total
2007	40	20	40	50	20	170
2008		20	40	50	20	130
2009			40	50	20	110
2010				50	20	70
2011					20	20
	40	40	120	200	100	500

Computed on the basis of a prior service cost of $80,000 and a total of 500 service-years for all years, the cost per service-year is $160 ($80,000 ÷ 500). The annual amount of amortization based on a $160 cost per service-year is computed as follows.

ILLUSTRATION 20-11
Computation of Annual
Prior Service Cost
Amortization

Year	Total Service-Years	×	Cost per Service-Year	=	Annual Amortization
2007	170		$160		$27,200
2008	130		160		20,800
2009	110		160		17,600
2010	70		160		11,200
2011	20		160		3,200
	500				$80,000

FASB Statement No. 87 allows an alternative method of computing amortization of **unrecognized prior service cost: Employers may use straight-line amortization over the average remaining service life of the employees.** In this case, with 500 service years and 170 employees, the average would be 2.94 years (500 ÷ 170). Using this method, Zarle Company would charge the $80,000 cost to expense at $27,211 ($80,000 ÷ 2.94) in 2007, $27,211 in 2008, and $25,578 ($27,211 × .94) in 2009.

2007 Entries and Worksheet

Continuing the Zarle Company illustration into 2007, we note that the company amends the pension plan on January 1, 2007, to grant employees prior service benefits with a present value of $80,000. Zarle uses the annual amortization amounts, as computed in the previous section using the years-of-service approach ($27,200 for 2007). The following additional facts apply to the pension plan for the year 2007.

Annual service cost is $9,500.

Settlement rate is 10 percent.

Actual return on plan assets is $11,100.

Annual funding contributions are $20,000.

Benefits paid to retirees during the year are $8,000.

Amortization of prior service cost (PSC) using the years-of-service method is $27,200.

Illustration 20-12 presents a worksheet of all the pension entries and information recorded by Zarle in 2007.

	General Journal Entries			Memo Record		
Items	Annual Pension Expense	Cash	Prepaid/ Accrued Cost	Projected Benefit Obligation	Plan Assets	Unrecognized Prior Service Cost
Balance, Dec. 31, 2006			1,000 Cr.	112,000 Cr.	111,000 Dr.	
(f) Prior service cost				80,000 Cr.		80,000 Dr.
Balance, Jan. 1, 2007			1,000 Cr.	192,000 Cr.	111,000 Dr.	80,000 Dr.
(g) Service cost	9,500 Dr.			9,500 Cr.		
(h) Interest cost	19,200 Dr.ᵃ			19,200 Cr.		
(i) Actual return	11,100 Cr.				11,100 Dr.	
(j) Amortization of PSC	27,200 Dr.					27,200 Cr.
(k) Contributions		20,000 Cr.			20,000 Dr.	
(l) Benefits				8,000 Dr.	8,000 Cr.	
Journal entry for 2007	44,800 Dr.	20,000 Cr.	24,800 Cr.			
Balance, Dec. 31, 2007			25,800 Cr.	212,700 Cr.	134,100 Dr.	52,800 Dr.

ᵃ$19,200 = $192,000 × 10%.

ILLUSTRATION 20-12
Pension Worksheet—2007

The first line of the worksheet shows the beginning balances of the Prepaid/Accrued Pension Cost account and the memo accounts. Entry (f) records Zarle's granting of prior service cost, by adding $80,000 to the projected benefit obligation and to the unrecognized (noncapitalized) prior service cost. Entries (g), (h), (i), (k), and (l) are similar to the corresponding entries in 2006. Entry (j) records the 2007 amortization of unrecognized prior service cost by debiting Pension Expense by $27,200 and crediting the new Unrecognized Prior Service Cost account by the same amount.

Zarle makes the following journal entry on December 31 to formally record the 2007 pension expense—the sum of the annual pension expense column.

2007

Pension Expense	44,800	
Cash		20,000
Prepaid/Accrued Pension Cost		24,800

Because the expense exceeds the funding, Zarle credits the Prepaid/Accrued Pension Cost account for the $24,800 difference. That account is a liability. In 2007, as in 2006, the balance of the Prepaid/Accrued Pension Cost account ($25,800) is equal to the net of the balances in the memo accounts, as shown in Illustration 20-13.

ILLUSTRATION 20-13
Pension Reconciliation Schedule—December 31, 2007

Projected benefit obligation (Credit)	$(212,700)
Plan assets at fair value (Debit)	134,100
Funded status	(78,600)
Unrecognized prior service cost (Debit)	52,800
Prepaid/accrued pension cost (Credit)	$ (25,800)

The reconciliation is the formula that makes the worksheet work. It relates the components of pension accounting, recorded and unrecorded, to one another.

Gain or Loss

Of great concern to companies that have pension plans are the uncontrollable and unexpected swings in pension expense that can result from (1) sudden and large changes in the market value of plan assets, and (2) changes in actuarial assumptions that affect the amount of the projected benefit obligation. If these gains or losses impact fully the financial statements in the period of realization or incurrence, substantial fluctuations in pension expense result.

OBJECTIVE 7
Explain the accounting procedure for recognizing unexpected gains and losses.

Therefore, the FASB decided to reduce the volatility associated with pension expense by using **smoothing techniques** that dampen and in some cases fully eliminate the fluctuations.

Smoothing Unexpected Gains and Losses on Plan Assets

One component of pension expense, actual return on plan assets, reduces pension expense (assuming the actual return is positive). A large change in the actual return can substantially affect pension expense for a year. Assume a company has a 40 percent return in the stock market for the year. Should this substantial, and perhaps one-time, event affect current pension expense?

Actuaries ignore current fluctuations when they develop a funding pattern to pay expected benefits in the future. They develop an **expected rate of return** and multiply it by an asset value weighted over a reasonable period of time to arrive at an **expected return on plan assets**. They then use this return to determine a company's funding pattern.

The FASB adopted the actuary's approach to dampen wide swings that might occur in the actual return. That is, a company includes the **expected return** on the plan assets as a component of pension expense, not the actual return in a given year. To achieve this goal, the company multiplies the expected rate of return by the market related value of the plan assets. The **market-related asset value** of the plan assets is either the fair value of plan assets or a calculated value that recognizes changes in fair value in a systematic and rational manner.[13]

The difference between the expected return and the actual return is referred to as the **unexpected gain or loss**; the FASB uses the term **asset gains and losses**. **Asset gains** occur when actual return exceeds expected return; **asset losses** occur when actual return is less than expected return.

What happens to unexpected gains or losses in the accounting for pensions? Companies record asset gains and asset losses in an Unrecognized Net Gain or Loss account, combining them with unrecognized gains and losses accumulated in prior years.

To illustrate the computation of an unexpected gain or loss and its related accounting, assume that in 2008, Zarle Company has an actual return on plan assets of $12,000 when the expected return in $13,410 (the expected rate of return of 10% on plan assets times the beginning of the year plan assets.) The unexpected asset loss of $1,410 ($12,000 − $13,410) is debited to the Unrecognized Gain or Loss and credited to Pension Expense.

PENSION COSTS UPS AND DOWNS

WHAT DO THE NUMBERS MEAN?

For some companies, pension plans generated real profits in the late 1990s. The plans not only paid for themselves but also increased earnings. This happens when the expected return on pension assets exceed the company's annual costs. At **Norfolk Southern**, pension income amounted to 12 percent of operating profit. It tallied 11 percent of operating profit at **Lucent Technologies**, **Coastal Corp.**, and **Unisys Corp.** The issue is important because in these cases management is not driving the operating income—pension income is. And as a result, income can change quickly.

Unfortunately, when the stock market stops booming, pension expense substantially increases for many companies. The reason: Expected return on a smaller asset base no longer offsets pension service costs and interest on the projected benefit obligation. As a result, many companies find it difficult to meet their earnings targets, and at a time when meeting such targets is crucial to maintaining the stock price.

---

[13]*FASB Statement No. 87*, par. 30. Companies may use different ways of determining the calculated market-related value for different classes of assets. For example, an employer might use fair value for bonds and a five-year-moving-average for equities. But companies should consistently apply the manner of determining market-related value from year to year for each asset class. Throughout our Zarle illustrations, we assume that market-related values based on a calculated value and the fair value of plan assets are equal. *For homework purposes*, use the fair value of plan assets as the measure for the market-related value.

Smoothing Unexpected Gains and Losses on the Pension Liability

In estimating the projected benefit obligation (the liability), actuaries make assumptions about such items as mortality rate, retirement rate, turnover rate, disability rate, and salary amounts. Any change in these actuarial assumptions affects the amount of the projected benefit obligation. Seldom does actual experience coincide exactly with actuarial predictions. These unexpected gains or losses from changes in the projected benefit obligation are called **liability gains and losses**.

Companies defer liability gains (resulting from unexpected decreases in the liability balance) and liability losses (resulting from unexpected increases). Companies combine the liability gains and losses in the same **Unrecognized Net Gain or Loss** account used for asset gains and losses. They accumulate the asset and liability gains and losses from year to year, off-balance-sheet, in a memo account.

Corridor Amortization

The asset gains and losses and the liability gains and losses can offset each other. As a result, the accumulated total unrecognized net gain or loss may not grow very large. But, it is possible that no offsetting will occur and that the balance in the Unrecognized Net Gain or Loss account will continue to grow.

To limit the growth of the Unrecognized Net Gain or Loss account, the FASB invented the **corridor approach** for amortizing the account's accumulated balance when it gets too large. How large is too large? The FASB set a limit of 10 percent of the larger of the beginning balances of the projected benefit obligation or the market-related value of the plan assets. **Above that size, the unrecognized net gain or loss balance is considered too large and must be amortized.**

To illustrate the corridor approach, data for Callaway Co.'s projected benefit obligation and plan assets over a period of six years are shown in Illustration 20-14.

> **OBJECTIVE 8**
> Explain the corridor approach to amortizing unrecognized gains and losses.

Beginning-of-the-Year Balances	Projected Benefit Obligation	Market-Related Asset Value	Corridor* +/− 10%
2005	$1,000,000	$ 900,000	$100,000
2006	1,200,000	1,100,000	120,000
2007	1,300,000	1,700,000	170,000
2008	1,500,000	2,250,000	225,000
2009	1,700,000	1,750,000	175,000
2010	1,800,000	1,700,000	180,000

*The corridor becomes 10% of the larger (in colored type) of the projected benefit obligation or the market-related plan asset value.

ILLUSTRATION 20-14
Computation of the Corridor

How the corridor works becomes apparent when we portray the data graphically, as in Illustration 20-15.

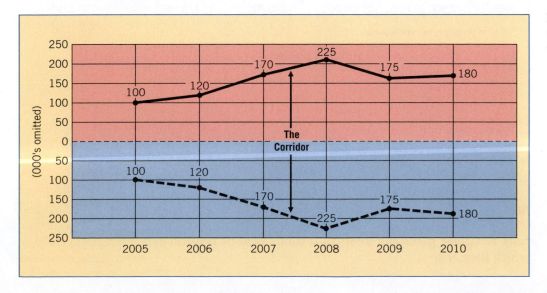

ILLUSTRATION 20-15
Graphic Illustration of the Corridor

If the balance of the Unrecognized Net Gain or Loss account stays within the upper and lower limits of the corridor, no amortization is required. In that case, Callaway carries forward the unrecognized net gain or loss balance unchanged.

If amortization is required, the minimum amortization is the excess divided by the average remaining service period of active employees who are expected to receive benefits under the plan. Callaway may use any systematic method of amortization of unrecognized gains and losses in lieu of the minimum, provided it is greater than the minimum. It must use the method consistently for both gains and losses and must disclose the amortization method used.

Example of Unrecognized Gains/Losses

In applying the corridor, companies should include amortization of the excess unrecognized net gain or loss as a component of pension expense only if, at the **beginning of the year**, the unrecognized net gain or loss exceeded the corridor. That is, if no unrecognized net gain or loss exists at the beginning of the period, the company cannot recognize pension expense gains or losses in that period.

To illustrate the amortization of unrecognized net gains and losses, assume the following information for Soft-White, Inc.

	2006	2007	2008
		(beginning of the year)	
Projected benefit obligation	$2,100,000	$2,600,000	$2,900,000
Market-related asset value	2,600,000	2,800,000	2,700,000
Unrecognized net loss	–0–	400,000	300,000

If the average remaining service life of all active employees is 5.5 years, the schedule to amortize the unrecognized net loss is as shown in Illustration 20-16.

ILLUSTRATION 20-16
Corridor Test and
Gain/Loss Amortization
Schedule

Year	Projected Benefit Obligation[a]	Plan Assets[a]	Corridor[b]	Cumulative Unrecognized Net Loss[a]	Minimum Amortization of Loss (For Current Year)
2006	$2,100,000	$2,600,000	$260,000	$ –0–	$ –0–
2007	2,600,000	2,800,000	280,000	400,000	21,818[c]
2008	2,900,000	2,700,000	290,000	678,182[d]	70,579[d]

[a]All as of the beginning of the period.
[b]10% of the greater of projected benefit obligation or plan assets market-related value.
[c]$400,000 − $280,000 = $120,000; $120,000 ÷ 5.5 = $21,818
[d]$400,000 − $21,818 + $300,000 = $678,182; $678,182 − $290,000 = $388,182; $388,182 ÷ 5.5 = $70,579.

As Illustration 20-16 indicates, the loss recognized in 2007 increased pension expense by $21,818. This amount is small in comparison with the total loss of $400,000. It indicates that the corridor approach dampens the effects (reduces volatility) of these gains and losses on pension expense.

The rationale for the corridor is that gains and losses result from refinements in estimates as well as real changes in economic value; over time, some of these gains and losses will offset one another. It therefore seems reasonable that Soft-White should not fully recognize gains and losses as a component of pension expense in the period in which they arise.

However, Soft-White should recognize certain gains and losses immediately—if they arise from a single occurrence not directly related to the operation of the pension plan and not in the ordinary course of the employer's business. For example, a gain or loss that is directly related to a plant closing, a disposal of a component, or a similar event that greatly affects the size of the employee work force, should be recognized as a part of the gain or loss associated with that event.

At one time, **Bethlehem Steel** reported a quartererly loss of $477 million. A great deal of this loss was attributable to future estimated benefits payable to workers who were permanently laid off. In this situation, the loss should be treated as an adjustment to the gain or loss on the plant closing and should not affect pension cost for the current or future periods.

Summary of Calculations for Asset Gain or Loss

The difference between the actual return on plan assets and the expected return on plan assets is the **unexpected (deferred) asset gain or loss** component. This component defers the difference between the actual return and expected return on plan assets in computing current year pension expense. Thus, after considering this component, **it is really the expected return on plan assets (not the actual return) that determines current pension expense.**

Companies determined the amortized net gain or loss by amortizing the unrecognized gain or loss at the beginning of the year subject to the corridor limitation. In other words, **if the unrecognized gain or loss is greater than the corridor, these net gains and losses are subject to amortization.** Soft-White computed this minimum amortization by dividing the net gains or losses subject to amortization by the average remaining service period. When the current-year unexpected gain or loss is combined with the amortized net gain or loss, we determine the current-year gain or loss. Illustration 20-17 summarizes these gain and loss computations.

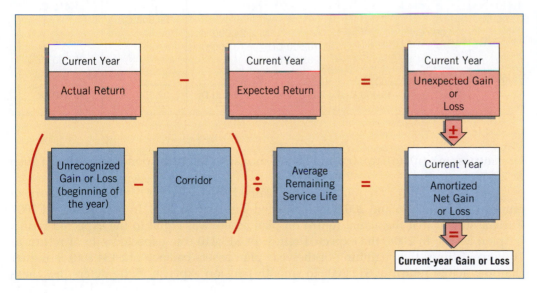

ILLUSTRATION 20-17
Graphic Summary of Gain or Loss Computation

In essence, these gains and losses are subject to *triple* smoothing. That is, companies first smooth the asset gain or loss by using the expected return. Second, they do not amortize the unrecognized gain or loss at the beginning of the year unless it is greater than the corridor. Finally, they spread the excess over the remaining service life of existing employees.

2008 Entries and Worksheet

Continuing the Zarle Company illustration, the following facts apply to the pension plan for 2008.

> Annual service cost is $13,000.
>
> Settlement rate is 10 percent; expected earnings rate is 10 percent.
>
> Actual return on plan assets is $12,000.
>
> Amortization of prior service cost (PSC) is $20,800.
>
> Annual funding contributions are $24,000.
>
> Benefits paid to retirees during the year are $10,500.
>
> Changes in actuarial assumptions establish the end-of-year projected benefit obligation at $265,000.

The worksheet in Illustration 20-18 presents all of Zarle's 2008 pension entries and related information. The first line of the worksheet records the beginning balances that relate to the pension plan. In this case, Zarle's beginning balances are the ending balances from its 2007 pension worksheet in Illustration 20-12 (page 1033).

ILLUSTRATION 20-18
Pension Worksheet—2008

	General Journal Entries			Memo Record			
Items	Annual Pension Expense	Cash	Prepaid/ Accrued Cost	Projected Benefit Obligation	Plan Assets	Unrecognized Prior Service Cost	Unrecognized Net Gain or Loss
Bal., December 31, 2007			25,800 Cr.	212,700 Cr.	134,100 Dr.	52,800 Dr.	
(m) Service cost	13,000 Dr.			13,000 Cr.			
(n) Interest cost	21,270 Dr.			21,270 Cr.			
(o) Actual return	12,000 Cr.				12,000 Dr.		
(p) Unexpected loss	1,410 Cr.						1,410 Dr.
(q) Amortization of PSC	20,800 Dr.					20,800 Cr.	
(r) Contributions		24,000 Cr.			24,000 Dr.		
(s) Benefits				10,500 Dr.	10,500 Cr.		
(t) Liability increase				28,530 Cr.			28,530 Dr.
Journal entry for 2008	41,660 Dr.	24,000 Cr.	17,660 Cr.				
Bal., December 31, 2008			43,460 Cr.	265,000 Cr.	159,600 Dr.	32,000 Dr.	29,940 Dr.

Entries (m), (n), (o), (q), (r), and (s) are similar to the corresponding entries in 2006 or 2007.

Entries (o) and (p) are related. We explained the recording of the actual return in entry (o) in both 2006 and 2007; it is recorded similarly in 2008. In both 2006 and 2007 Zarle assumed that the actual return on plan assets was equal to the expected return on plan assets. In 2008, the expected return of $13,410 (the expected rate of return of 10 percent times the beginning-of-the-year plan assets balance of $134,100) is higher than the actual return of $12,000. To smooth pension expense, Zarle defers the unexpected loss of $1,410 ($13,410 − $12,000) by debiting the Unrecognized Net Gain or Loss account and crediting Pension Expense. **As a result of this adjustment, the expected return on the plan assets is the amount actually used to compute pension expense.**

Entry (t) records the change in the projected benefit obligation resulting from a change in actuarial assumptions. As indicated, the actuary has now computed the ending balance to be $265,000. Given that the memo record balance at December 31 is $236,470 ($212,700 + $13,000 + $21,270 − $10,500), a difference of $28,530 ($265,000 − $236,470) exists. This $28,530 increase in the employer's liability is an unexpected loss.

Zarle defers that amount by debiting it to the Unrecognized Net Gain or Loss account. The journal entry on December 31 to formally record pension expense for 2008 is as follows.

2008

Pension Expense	41,660	
Cash		24,000
Prepaid/Accrued Pension Cost		17,660

As the 2008 worksheet indicates, the $43,460 balance of the Prepaid/Accrued Pension Cost account at December 31, 2008, is equal to the net of the balances in the memo accounts. Illustration 20-19 shows this computation.

Projected benefit obligation (Credit)	$(265,000)
Plan assets at fair value (Debit)	159,600
Funded status	(105,400)
Unrecognized prior service cost (Debit)	32,000
Unrecognized net loss (Debit)	29,940
Prepaid/accrued pension cost (Credit)	$ (43,460)

ILLUSTRATION 20-19
Pension Reconciliation Schedule—December 31, 2008

MINIMUM LIABILITY

If the FASB had decided to capitalize pension plan assets and liabilities, Zarle Company would have reported the following on December 31, 2008:

- a liability of $265,000
- plan assets of $159,600
- unrecognized prior service cost (goodwill) of $32,000
- and an unrecognized net loss of $29,940.

OBJECTIVE 9
Explain the recognition of a minimum liability.

Instead it reports only accrued pension cost of $43,460 as a liability.

The Board was well aware of this discrepancy. It believed that an employer with a projected benefit obligation in excess of the fair value of pension plan assets has a liability. Similarly, an employer with a fair value of plan assets in excess of projected benefit obligation has an asset. However, when the Board was faced with the final decision on this matter, it decided that to require the reporting of these amounts in the financial statements would be too great a change in practice, because up to then companies had not reported these amounts in the balance sheet.

The Board, therefore, developed a compromise approach. This approach requires immediate recognition of a liability—referred to as the minimum liability—when the accumulated benefit obligation exceeds the fair value of plan assets. The purpose of this minimum liability requirement is to ensure that if a significant plan amendment or actuarial loss occurs, a company will recognize a liability at least to the extent of the unfunded portion of the accumulated benefit obligation.

Note that the FASB requires that companies compare the plan assets to the smaller **accumulated** benefit obligation instead of the larger projected benefit obligation. The rationale for using the accumulated benefit obligation is that if the liability were settled today, it would be settled on the basis of *current* salary rates, not future salary rates. Therefore, the accumulated benefit obligation is used, not the projected benefit obligation.

Although the compromise approach frequently ignores a portion of the liability, it does help to report some balance sheet effects when a plan amendment or a large loss occurs. **The Board does not permit the recording of an additional asset if the fair value of the pension plan exceeds the accumulated benefit obligation.**

UNDERLYING CONCEPTS

Recognizing the smaller benefit obligation ignores the going concern concept. A going concern would not expect to settle the obligation today at current salaries and wages, but would expect to settle the obligation based upon future salary levels.

Minimum Liability Computation

If a company has already reported a liability for accrued pension cost, it records only an **additional liability** to equal the required minimum liability (unfunded accumulated benefit). To illustrate, assume that Largent Inc. amends its pension plan on December 31, 2006, giving retroactive benefits to its employees, as follows.

Projected benefit obligation	$8,000,000
Accumulated benefit obligation	7,000,000
Plan assets (at fair value)	5,000,000
Unrecognized prior service cost	2,500,000
Accrued pension cost	500,000

Illustration 20-20 computes the unfunded accumulated benefit obligation.

ILLUSTRATION 20-20
Computation of
Unfunded Accumulated
Benefit Obligation
(Minimum Liability)

Accumulated benefit obligation	$7,000,000
Plan assets (at fair value)	5,000,000
Unfunded accumulated benefit obligation (minimum liability)	$2,000,000

In this case, Largent must record and report on the financial statements an additional liability of $1,500,000. Illustration 20-21 shows the computation of the additional liability.[14]

ILLUSTRATION 20-21
Computation of
Additional Liability
Required—Accrued
Pension Cost Balance

Unfunded accumulated benefit obligation (minimum liability)	$2,000,000
Accrued pension cost (balance at December 31, 2006)	500,000
Additional liability required	$1,500,000

Largent Inc. would combine the **accrued pension cost** and the additional liability into one amount—$2,000,000. It would report that amount in the balance sheet as accrued pension cost or pension liability.

If Largent Inc. had a **prepaid pension cost** of $300,000, instead of an accrued pension cost of $500,000, it would record an additional liability of $2,300,000 as follows.

ILLUSTRATION 20-22
Computation of
Additional Liability
Required—Prepaid
Pension Cost Balance

Unfunded accumulated benefit obligation (minimum liability)	$2,000,000
Prepaid pension cost	300,000
Additional liability required	$2,300,000

In this case, Largent would **combine** the existing balance in the prepaid pension cost (debit) with the additional liability (credit) into one amount, and would report accrued pension cost or pension liability in the net amount of $2,000,000.

---

[14]*FASB Statement No. 87*, par. 36, requires use of the fair value of plan assets (not a calculated value) in computing the unfunded accumulated benefit obligation. Companies also must use fair value in computing the unfunded projected benefit obligation.

Financial Statement Presentation

When it is necessary to adjust the accounts to recognize a minimum liability, the company debits an intangible asset called Intangible Asset—Deferred Pension Cost. Largent records the liability and related intangible asset for the additional pension liability as follows.

Intangible Asset—Deferred Pension Cost	1,500,000	
Additional Pension Liability		1,500,000

INTERNATIONAL INSIGHT

IFRS do not account for a minimum liability.

The justification for recognizing an intangible asset up to the amount of the unrecognized prior service cost is that an amendment to an existing plan increases goodwill with employees and therefore benefits the company in the future. In other words, the cost of the additional pension benefits increases loyalty and productivity (and reduces turnover) among the affected employees.

An exception to the general rule of reporting an intangible asset occurs when the **additional liability exceeds the amount of unrecognized prior service cost**. In this case, the company debits the excess to Excess of Additional Pension Liability Over Unrecognized Prior Service Cost. The rationale: The excess must have resulted from an actuarial loss, such as an increase in the benefit obligation due to an increase in retiree longevity.

When this excess develops, companies should report it as a reduction of other comprehensive income. In addition, they report its cumulative balance as a component of "Accumulated other comprehensive income" on the balance sheet. Because the excess of additional pension liability over unrecognized prior service cost reduces stockholders' equity, it is often referred to as a contra equity account.

To illustrate, assume that Largent Inc. has common stock with a total par value of $1,000,000, additional paid-in capital of $400,000, and retained earnings of $700,000. In addition, it has an additional liability that exceeds the unrecognized prior service cost by $200,000. Illustration 20-23 shows a condensed version of Largent's stockholders' equity section.[15]

Stockholders' Equity Section	
Common stock	$1,000,000
Additional paid-in capital	400,000
Total paid-in capital	1,400,000
Retained earnings	700,000
Accumulated other comprehensive income	(200,000)
Total stockholders' equity	$1,900,000

ILLUSTRATION 20-23
Balance Sheet Presentation of Excess of Additional Pension Liability

Each reporting period, Largent should evaluate the amount of the additional liability required, along with the related intangible asset or contra equity account. At each reporting date, the company may increase, decrease, or totally eliminate these items. Neither the intangible asset nor the contra equity account is amortized from period to period; the balances are merely adjusted up or down.

[15]This treatment is similar to the reporting of the unrealized holding loss on available-for-sale securities discussed in earlier chapters. Note that companies must show the components of accumulated other comprehensive income in the stockholders' equity section of the balance sheet, in the notes, or in the statement of stockholders' equity.

The schedule in Illustration 20-24 shows the minimum liability approach for Zarle's pension plan for all three years 2006, 2007, and 2008 (values are assumed for the accumulated benefit obligation).

ILLUSTRATION 20-24
Minimum Liability
Computations

	December 31		
	2006	2007	2008
Accumulated benefit obligation	$(80,000)	$(164,000)	$(240,600)
Plan assets at fair value	111,000	134,100	159,600
Unfunded accumulated benefit obligation (minimum liability)	–0–	(29,900)	(81,000)
Accrued pension cost	1,000	25,800	43,460
Additional liability	$ –0–	(4,100)	(37,540)
Unrecognized prior service cost*		52,800	32,000
Excess of additional pension liability over unrecognized prior service cost**		$ –0–	$ (5,540)

*Maximum intangible asset recognizable.
**Reported as contra equity.

In 2006, the fair value of the plan assets exceeds the accumulated benefit obligation. Therefore, Largent reports no additional liability. **The Board does not permit the recognition of a net investment in the pension plan when the plan assets exceed the pension obligation.**

In 2007, the minimum liability amount ($29,900) exceeds the accrued pension cost liability already recorded ($25,800). Largent records an additional liability of $4,100 ($29,900 − $25,800) as follows.

December 31, 2007

Intangible Asset—Deferred Pension Cost	4,100	
Additional Pension Liability		4,100

In 2008, the minimum liability ($81,000) exceeds the accrued pension cost liability ($43,460). Largent reports an additional liability of $37,540 at the end of 2008. Since a balance of $4,100 already exists in the Additional Pension Liability account, it credits that account for $33,440 ($37,540 − $4,100). Also, since the additional liability exceeds the unrecognized prior service cost by $5,540, Largent debits the excess to the contra equity account, Excess of Additional Pension Liability over Unrecognized Prior Service Cost. It debits the remaining $27,900 ($33,440 − $5,540) to the Intangible Asset—Deferred Pension Cost. Largent makes the following entry on December 31, 2008, to adjust the minimum liability.

December 31, 2008

Intangible Asset—Deferred Pension Cost	27,900	
Excess of Additional Pension Liability over		
Unrecognized Prior Service Cost	5,540	
Additional Pension Liability		33,440

As the additional liability changes, the combined debit balance of the intangible asset and contra equity accounts fluctuates by the same amount.

Worksheet Example

To illustrate how the minimum liability computation affects the pension worksheet, we show a revised version of the 2008 worksheet of Zarle Company in Illustration 20-25. The items in blue color [entry (u)] relate to adjustments caused by recognition of the minimum liability at the end of 2007 and 2008.

	General Journal Entries					
Items	Annual Pension Expense	Cash	Prepaid/ Accrued Cost	Additional Liability	Pension Intangible	Contra Equity
Balance, Dec. 31, 2007			25,800 Cr.	4,100 Cr.	4,100 Dr.	
(m) Service cost	13,000 Dr.					
(n) Interest cost	21,270 Dr.					
(o) Actual return	12,000 Cr.					
(p) Unexpected loss	1,410 Cr.					
(q) Amortization of PSC	20,800 Dr.					
(r) Contributions		24,000 Cr.				
(s) Benefits						
(t) Liability change (Incr.)						
(u) Minimum liab. adj.				33,440 Cr.	27,900 Dr.	5,540 Dr.
Journal entry for 2008	41,660 Dr.	24,000 Cr.	17,660 Cr.			
Balance, Dec. 31, 2008			43,460 Cr.	37,540 Cr.	32,000 Dr.	5,540 Dr.

	Memo Record			
Items	Projected Benefit Obligation	Plan Assets	Unrecognized Prior Service Cost	Unrecognized Net Gain or Loss
Balance, Dec. 31, 2007	212,700 Cr.	134,100 Dr.	52,800 Dr.	
(m) Service cost	13,000 Cr.			
(n) Interest cost	21,270 Cr.			
(o) Actual return		12,000 Dr.		
(p) Unexpected loss				1,410 Dr.
(q) Amortization of PSC			20,800 Cr.	
(r) Contributions		24,000 Dr.		
(s) Benefits	10,500 Dr.	10,500 Cr.		
(t) Liability increase	28,530 Cr.			28,530 Dr.
(u) Minimum liab. adj.				
Journal entry for 2008				
Balance, Dec. 31, 2008	265,000 Cr.	159,600 Dr.	32,000 Dr.	29,940 Dr.

As prior worksheets showed, the balance in the Prepaid/Accrued Pension Cost account ($43,460) equals the net of the balances in the memo accounts ($265,000 − [$159,600 + $32,000 + $29,940]). In this case, Zarle combines the Additional Liability with the Prepaid/Accrued Pension Cost to determine the minimum pension liability in the balance sheet. This computation is shown in Illustration 20-26.

ILLUSTRATION 20-25
Revised Pension Worksheet—2008, Revised to Include Minimum Liability Computation

ILLUSTRATION 20-26
Reconciliation Schedule—2008, Revised to Show Additional Pension Liability

Projected benefit obligation (Credit)	$(265,000)
Plan assets at fair value (Debit)	159,600
Funded status	(105,400)
Unrecognized prior service cost (Debit)	32,000
Unrecognized net loss (Debit)	29,940
Prepaid/accrued pension cost (Credit)	(43,460)
Additional liability (Credit)	(37,540)
Accrued pension cost liability recognized in the balance sheet (minimum liability)	$ (81,000)

REPORTING PENSION PLANS IN FINANCIAL STATEMENTS

OBJECTIVE 10
Describe the requirements for reporting pension plans in financial statements.

As you might suspect, a phenomenon as significant and complex as pensions involves extensive reporting and disclosure requirements. We will cover these requirements in two categories: (1) those within the financial statements, and (2) those within the notes to the financial statements.

Within the Financial Statements

If the amount the employer funds (credit to Cash) to the pension trust is **less than the annual expense** (debit to Pension Expense), a liability equal to the difference results. Companies report this liability as Accrued Pension Cost, Liability for Pension Expense Not Funded, or Pension Liability. We classify a liability as current when it requires the disbursement of cash within the next year.

If the amount funded to the pension trust during the period **exceeds the amount charged to expense**, an asset equal to the difference arises. A company reports this asset as Prepaid Pension Cost, Deferred Pension Expense, or Prepaid Pension Expense. It appears in the current assets section if it is short-term in nature, and in the other assets section if it is long-term in nature.

If the **accumulated benefit obligation exceeds the fair value of pension plan assets**, companies record an additional liability. They debit either Intangible Asset—Deferred Pension Cost or a contra account to stockholders' equity entitled Excess of Additional Pension Liability Over Unrecognized Prior Service Cost. If the debit is less than unrecognized prior service cost, companies report it as an intangible asset. If the debit is greater than unrecognized prior service cost, they report the excess debit as part of other comprehensive income and the accumulated balance as a component of accumulated other comprehensive income.

WHAT DO THE NUMBERS MEAN?

PERFECT STORM

The chart below shows what has happened to the financial health of pension plans over the last few years. It is not a pretty picture.

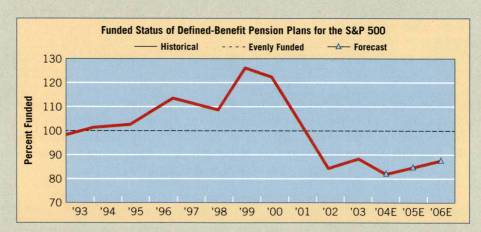

Although companies in the S&P 500 saw their pension plans bounce back from their lows in 2002, they still ended 2003 underfunded by a total of $172 billion. Estimates for 2004, 2005, and 2006 could leave funds in no better position.

A number of factors cause a fund to change from being overfunded to underfunded: First, because of low interest rates, returns on pension plan assets in the early part of this decade have been lousy. As a result, pension fund assets have not grown; in some cases, they have declined in value. Second, using low interest rates to discount the projected benefit payments leads to a higher pension liability. Finally, more individuals are retiring, which leads to a depletion of the pension plan assets. In short, we have the perfect pension storm.

Source: David Zion and Bill Carcache, "The Magical World of Pensions: An Update," *CSFB Equity Research: Accounting* (September 8, 2004).

Within the Notes to the Financial Statements

Pension plans are frequently important to understanding a company's financial position, results of operations, and cash flows. Therefore, a company discloses the following information, either in the body of the financial statements or in the notes.[16]

1 A schedule showing all the major components of pension expense.
Rationale: Information provided about the components of pension expense helps users better understand how a company determines pension expense. It also is useful in forecasting a company's net income.

2 A reconciliation showing how the projected benefit obligation and the fair value of the plan assets changed from the beginning to the end of the period.
Rationale: Disclosing the projected benefit obligation, the fair value of the plan assets, and changes in them should help users understand the economics underlying the obligations and resources of these plans. Explaining the changes in the projected benefit obligation and fair value of plan assets in the form of a reconciliation provides a more complete disclosure and makes the financial statements more understandable.

3 The funded status of the plan (difference between the projected benefit obligation and fair value of the plan assets) and the amounts recognized and not recognized in the financial statements.
Rationale: Providing a reconciliation of the plan's funded status to the amount reported in the balance sheet highlights the difference between the funded status and the balance sheet presentation.[17]

4 A disclosure of the rates used in measuring the benefit amounts (discount rate, expected return on plan assets, rate of compensation).
Rationale: Disclosure of these rates permits users to determine the reasonableness of the assumptions applied in measuring the pension liability and pension expense.

5 A table indicating the allocation of pension plan assets by category (equity securities, debt securities, real estate, and other assets), and showing the percentage of the fair value to total plan assets. In addition, a company must include a narrative description of investment policies and strategies, including the target allocation percentages (if used by the company).
Rationale: Such information helps financial statement users evaluate the pension plan's exposure to market risk and possible cash flow demands on the company. It also will help users better assess the reasonableness of the company's expected rate of return assumption.

6 The expected benefit payments to be paid to current plan participants for each of the next five fiscal years and in the aggregate for the five fiscal years thereafter. Also required is disclosure of a company's best estimate of expected contributions to be paid to the plan during the next year.

---

[16]"Employers' Disclosure about Pensions and Other Postretirement Benefits," *Statement of Financial Accounting Standards No. 132* (Stamford, Conn.: FASB, 1998; revised 2003). This statement and its revision modify the disclosure requirements of *SFAS No. 87.* The FASB issued the revised statement because of concerns about the lack of transparency in pension information. This new standard amends the existing disclosure requirements related to pensions by (1) continuing the existing disclosure requirements while (2) requiring companies to provide more details about their plan assets, benefit obligations, cash flows, and benefits costs.

[17]Companies do not need to disclose the vested benefit obligation since it is not used in the accounting for the fund. Under *SFAS 87,* they should disclose the accumulated benefit obligation (ABO) for all plans combined. Information on the ABO is relevant to assessing the minimum liability (whether the company has recognized the minimum liability or not). In addition, it provides another measure for assessing the overall funded status of the plan.

Rationale: These disclosures provide information related to the cash outflows of the company. With this information, financial statement users can better understand the potential cash outflows related to the pension plan. They can better assess the liquidity and solvency of the company, which helps in assessing the company's overall financial flexibility.

In summary, the disclosure requirements are extensive, and purposely so. One factor that has been a challenge for useful pension reporting has been the lack of consistent terminology. Furthermore, a substantial amount of offsetting is inherent in the measurement of pension expense and the pension liability. These disclosures are designed to address these concerns and take some of the mystery out of pension reporting.

Example of Pension Note Disclosure

In the following sections we provide examples and explain the key pension disclosure elements.

Components of Pension Expense. The FASB requires disclosure of the individual pension expense components (derived from the information in the pension expense worksheet column): (1) service cost, (2) interest cost, (3) expected return on assets, (4) other deferrals and amortization. The purpose of such disclosure is to clarify to more sophisticated readers how companies determine pension expense. Providing information on the components should also be useful in predicting future pension expense.

Illustration 20-27 presents an example of this part of the disclosure. It uses the information from the Zarle illustration, specifically the expense component information from the worksheets in Illustration 20-8 (page 1030), Illustration 20-12 (page 1033), and Illustration 20-18 (page 1038).

ILLUSTRATION 20-27
Summary of Expense Components—2006, 2007, 2008

ZARLE COMPANY			
	2006	2007	2008
Components of Net Periodic Pension Expense			
Service cost	$ 9,000	$ 9,500	$13,000
Interest cost	10,000	19,200	21,270
Expected return on plan assets	(10,000)	(11,100)	(13,410)*
Amortization of prior service cost	–0–	27,200	20,800
Net periodic pension expense	$ 9,000	$44,800	$41,660

*Note that the expected return must be disclosed, not the actual. In 2008, the expected return is $13,410, which is the actual gain ($12,000) adjusted by the unrecognized loss ($1,410).

Reconciliation and Funded Status of Plan. Having a reconciliation of the changes in the assets and liabilities from the beginning of the year to the end of the year, statement readers can better understand the underlying economics of the plan. In essence, this disclosure (reconciliation) contains the information in the pension worksheet for the projected benefit obligation and plan asset columns.

In addition, the FASB also requires a disclosure of the funded status of the plan. That is, a company must reconcile the off-balance-sheet assets, liabilities, and unrecognized gains and losses with the on-balance-sheet liability or asset. Many believe this is the key to understanding the accounting for pensions. Why is such a disclosure important? The delayed recognition of some pension elements may exclude the most current and the most relevant information about the pension plan from the financial statements. This disclosure, however, provides this important information.

Using the information for Zarle, the schedule in Illustration 20-28 provides an example of the reconciliation.

ILLUSTRATION 20-28
Pension Disclosure for
Zarle Company—2006,
2007, 2008

ZARLE COMPANY PENSION DISCLOSURE	2006	2007	2008
Change in benefit obligation			
Benefit obligation at beginning of year	$100,000	$112,000	$212,700
Service cost	9,000	9,500	13,000
Interest cost	10,000	19,200	21,270
Amendments (Prior service cost)	–0–	80,000	–0–
Actuarial loss	–0–	–0–	28,530
Benefits paid	(7,000)	(8,000)	(10,500)
Benefit obligation at end of year	112,000	212,700	265,000
Change in plan assets			
Fair value of plan assets at beginning of year	100,000	111,000	134,100
Actual return on plan assets	10,000	11,100	12,000
Contributions	8,000	20,000	24,000
Benefits paid	(7,000)	(8,000)	(10,500)
Fair value of plan assets at end of year	111,000	134,100	159,600
Funded status	(1,000)	(78,600)	(105,400)
Unrecognized net actuarial loss	–0–	–0–	29,940
Unrecognized prior service cost	–0–	52,800	32,000
Prepaid (accrued) benefit cost	**(1,000)**	**(25,800)**	**(43,460)**
Minimum liability adjustment included in:			
Intangible assets	–0–	(4,100)	(32,000)
Stockholders' equity	–0–	–0–	(5,540)
Accrued pension cost liability in the balance sheet	$ (1,000)	$ (29,900)	$ (81,000)

The 2006 column reveals that Zarle underfunds the projected benefit obligation by $1,000. The 2007 column reveals that Zarle reports the underfunded liability of $78,600 in the balance sheet at $29,900, due to the unrecognized prior service cost of $52,800 and the $4,100 additional liability. Finally, the 2008 column indicates that Zarle recognizes the underfunded liability of $105,400 in the balance sheet at only $81,000 because of $32,000 in unrecognized prior service costs, $29,940 of unrecognized net loss, and $37,540 additional liability (with $5,540 of the minimum liability recorded in stockholders' equity).[18]

2009 Entries and Worksheet—A Comprehensive Example

Incorporating the corridor computation, the minimum liability recognition, and the required disclosures, we continue the Zarle Company pension plan accounting based on the following facts for 2009.

Service cost is $16,000.

Settlement rate is 10 percent; expected rate of return is 10 percent.

UNDERLYING CONCEPTS

Does it make a difference to users of financial statements whether companies recognize pension information in the financial statements or disclose it only in the notes? The FASB was unsure, so in accord with the full disclosure principle, it decided to provide extensive pension plan disclosures.

Additional Postretirement Benefit Disclosures

---

[18]To see a complete postretirement benefit disclosure, including asset allocations and expected cash flow information, see **The P&G Company**'s specimen financial statements in Appendix 5B. Note that the P&G disclosure combines the disclosures for pensions and other postretirement benefits in one disclosure. This is one way that *SFAS No. 132* streamlined the reporting on benefit plans. See Appendix 20A for discussion of the accounting for other postretirement benefits.

Actual return on plan assets is $22,000.

Amortization of unrecognized prior service cost is $17,600.

Annual funding contributions are $27,000.

Benefits paid to retirees during the year are $18,000.

Accumulated benefit obligation is $263,000 at the end of 2009.

Average service life of all covered employees is 20 years.

Zarle prepares a worksheet to facilitate accumulation and recording of the components of pension expense and maintenance of the unrecognized amounts related to the pension plan. Illustration 20-29 shows that worksheet, which uses the basic data presented above. Beginning-of-the-year 2009 account balances are the December 31, 2008, balances from Zarle's revised 2008 pension worksheet in Illustration 20-25.

ILLUSTRATION 20-29
Comprehensive Pension
Worksheet—2009

	A	B	C	D	E	F	G
				General Journal Entries			
1	Items	Annual Pension Expense	Cash	Prepaid/ Accrued Cost	Additional Liability	Pension Intangible	Contra Equity
2	Balance Dec. 31, 2008			43,460 Cr.	37,540 Cr.	32,000 Dr.	5,540 Dr.
3	(aa) Service cost	16,000 Dr.					
4	(bb) Interest cost	26,500 Dr.					
5	(cc) Actual return	22,000 Cr.					
6	(dd) Unexpected gain	6,040 Dr.					
7	(ee) Amortization of PSC	17,600 Dr.					
8	(ff) Contributions		27,000 Cr.				
9	(gg) Benefits						
10	(hh) Unrecog. loss amort.	172 Dr.					
11	(ii) Minimum liab. adj.				25,912 Dr.	20,372 Dr.	5,540 Cr.
12	Journal entry for 2009	44,312 Dr.	27,000 Cr.	17,312 Cr.			
13	Balance Dec. 31, 2009			60,772 Cr.	11,628 Cr.	11,628 Dr.	—0—

	A	H	I	J	K
				Memo Record	
1	Items	Projected Benefit Obligation	Plan Assets	Unrecognized Prior Service Cost	Unrecognized Net Gain or Loss
2	Balance Dec. 31, 2008	265,000 Cr.	159,600 Dr.	32,000 Dr.	29,940 Dr.
3	(aa) Service cost	16,000 Cr.			
4	(bb) Interest cost	26,500 Cr.			
5	(cc) Actual return		22,000 Dr.		
6	(dd) Unexpected gain				6,040 Cr.
7	(ee) Amortization of PSC			17,600 Cr.	
8	(ff) Contributions		27,000 Dr.		
9	(gg) Benefits	18,000 Dr.	18,000 Cr.		
10	(hh) Unrecog. loss amort.				172 Cr.
11	(ii) Minimum liab. adj.				
12	Journal entry for 2009				
13	Balance Dec. 31, 2009	289,500 Cr.	190,600 Dr.	14,400 Dr.	23,728 Dr.

Worksheet Explanations and Entries

Entries (aa) through (gg) are similar to the corresponding entries previously explained in the prior years' worksheets, with the exception of entry (dd). In 2008 the expected return on plan assets exceeded the actual return, producing an unexpected loss. In 2009 the actual return of $22,000 exceeds the expected return of $15,960 ($159,600 × 10%), resulting in an unexpected gain of $6,040, entry (dd). By netting the gain of $6,040 against the actual return of $22,000, pension expense is affected only by the expected return of $15,960.

A new entry (hh) in Zarle's worksheet results from application of the corridor test on the accumulated balance of unrecognized net gain or loss. Zarle Company begins 2009 with a balance in the unrecognized net loss account of $29,940. The company applies the corridor criterion in 2009 to determine whether the balance is excessive and should be amortized. In 2009 the corridor is 10 percent of the larger of the beginning-of-the-year projected benefit obligation of $265,000 or the plan asset's $159,600 market-related asset value (assumed to be fair value). The corridor for 2009 is $26,500 ($265,000 × 10%). Because the balance in the Unrecognized Net Loss account is $29,940, the excess (outside the corridor) is $3,440 ($29,940 − $26,500). Zarle amortizes the $3,440 excess over the average remaining service life of all employees. Given an average remaining service life of 20 years, the amortization in 2009 is $172 ($3,440 ÷ 20). In the 2009 pension worksheet, Zarle debits Pension Expense for $172 and credits that amount to Unrecognized Net Loss. Illustration 20-30 shows the computation of the $172 amortization charge.

ILLUSTRATION 20-30
Computation of 2009
Amortization Charge
(Corridor Test)

2009 Corridor Test	
Unrecognized net (gain) or loss at beginning of year	$29,940
10% of larger of PBO or market-related asset value of plan assets	26,500
Amortizable amount	$ 3,440
Average service life of all employees	20 years
2009 amortization ($3,440 ÷ 20 years)	$172

Zarle formally records pension expense for 2009 as follows.

2009

Pension Expense	44,312	
Cash		27,000
Prepaid/Accrued Pension Cost		17,312

The company computes the minimum liability, additional liability, and the amount reported as a contra equity charge at the end of 2009 as shown in Illustration 20-31.

ILLUSTRATION 20-31
Minimum Liability
Computation—2009

	December 31, 2009
Accumulated benefit obligation (ABO)	$(263,000)
Plan assets at fair value	190,600
Unfunded accumulated benefit obligation (minimum liability)	(72,400)
Accrued pension cost	60,772
Additional liability	(11,628)
Unrecognized prior service cost	14,400
Contra equity charge	$ –0–

As indicated in the above computation, the additional liability balance on December 31, 2009, is $11,628. The balance of $37,540 of additional liability carried over from 2008 requires a downward adjustment of $25,912 ($37,540 − $11,628). The balance in the

Intangible Asset—Deferred Pension Cost account should also be $11,628. Zarle, therefore, credits that account for $20,372, to reduce the balance of $32,000 to the desired amount of $11,628. Because the unrecognized prior service cost balance exceeds the additional liability, no contra equity charge is required. Zarle makes the following entry to adjust the minimum liability (the three accounts related thereto) at December 31, 2009.

2009

Additional Pension Liability	25,912	
Intangible Asset—Deferred Pension Cost		20,372
Excess of Additional Pension Liability over Unrecognized Prior Service Cost		5,540

Financial Statement Presentation

Illustrations 20-32, 20-33, and 20-34 show Zarle's financial statements at December 31, 2009, relative to the company's pension plan.

ILLUSTRATION 20-32
Balance Sheet
Presentation of Pension
Costs—2009

ZARLE COMPANY
BALANCE SHEET
AS OF DECEMBER 31, 2009

Assets		Liabilities	
Intangible assets		Long-term liabilities	
Deferred pension cost	$11,628	Accrued pension cost	$72,400

ILLUSTRATION 20-33
Income Statement
Presentation of Pension
Expense—2009

ZARLE COMPANY
INCOME STATEMENT
FOR THE YEAR ENDED DECEMBER 31, 2009

Operating expenses

Pension expense* $44,312

*Pension expense is frequently reported as "Employee benefits."

ILLUSTRATION 20-34
Statement of Cash Flows
Presentation of Pension
Liability

ZARLE COMPANY
STATEMENT OF CASH FLOWS
FOR THE YEAR ENDED DECEMBER 31, 2009

Cash flow from operating activities
  Net income (assumed) $905,000
  Adjustments to reconcile net income to net
    cash provided by operating activities:
      Increase in accrued pension liability $17,312

Note: Significant noncash investing and financing activities
Decrease of $20,372 in intangible asset and decrease of $5,540 in contra equity due to decrease of $25,912 in minimum liability.

Note that Zarle has combined the prepaid/accrued pension cost balance of $60,772 and the additional liability balance of $11,628 from the worksheet. The balance sheet reports one amount—$72,400—for pension liability.

Note Disclosure

Illustration 20-35 shows the note disclosure of Zarle's pension plan for 2009. Note that the reconciliation schedule in that note disclosure includes the adjustment required to recognize the minimum liability of $11,628. That schedule thus reconciles the minimum liability of $11,628 to the $72,400 accrued pension cost reported in the balance sheet.

ILLUSTRATION 20-35
Minimum Note
Disclosure of Pension
Plan, Zarle Company,
2009

ZARLE COMPANY
NOTES TO THE FINANCIAL STATEMENTS

Note D. The company has a pension plan covering substantially all of its employees. The plan is noncontributory and provides pension benefits that are based on the employee's compensation during the three years immediately preceding retirement. The pension plan's assets consist of cash, stocks, and bonds. The company's funding policy is consistent with the relevant government (ERISA) and tax regulations.

Net pension expense for 2009 is comprised of the following components of pension cost.

Service cost	$16,000
Interest on projected benefit obligation	26,500
Expected return on plan assets	(15,960)
Net other components of pension expense[19]	17,772
Net pension expense	$44,312

The following schedule reports changes in the benefit obligation and plan assets during the year and reconciles the funded status of the plan with amounts reported in the company's balance sheet at December 31, 2009:

Change in benefit obligation

Benefit obligation at beginning of year	$265,000
Service cost	16,000
Interest cost	26,500
Amendments (Prior service cost)	–0–
Actuarial gain	–0–
Benefits paid	(18,000)
Benefit obligation at end of year	289,500

Change in plan assets

Fair value of plan assets at beginning of year	159,600
Actual return on plan assets	22,000
Contributions	27,000
Benefits paid	(18,000)
Fair value of plan assets at end of year	190,600
Funded status	(98,900)
Unrecognized net actuarial loss	23,728
Unrecognized prior service cost	14,400
Prepaid (accrued) benefit cost	**(60,772)**
Minimum liability adjustment included in:	
Intangible assets	(11,628)
Stockholders' equity	–0–
Accrued pension cost liability in the balance sheet	$(72,400)

The weighted-average discount rate used in determining the 2009 projected benefit obligation was 10 percent. The rate of increase in future compensation levels used in computing the 2009 projected benefit obligation was 4.5 percent. The weighted-average expected long-term rate of return on the plan's assets was 10 percent.

Illustration 20-36 (page 1052) shows the pension disclosure for **Deere & Company**.

---

[19]"Net other components of pension expense" in this example consists of amortization of prior service cost ($17,600) plus amortization of the unrecognized loss ($172).

ILLUSTRATION 20-36
Deere & Company
Pension Disclosure

Deere & Company

3. Pension and Other Postretirement Benefits (partial). The company has several defined benefit pension plans covering its U.S. employees in certain foreign countries.

The worldwide components of net periodic pension cost and the assumptions related to the cost consisted of the following in millions of dollars and in percents:

	2004	2003	2002
Pensions			
Service cost	$ 130	$ 111	$ 107
Interest cost	454	450	448
Expected return on plan assets	(619)	(558)	(619)
Amortization of actuarial loss	49	40	2
Amortization of prior service cost	41	40	30
Amortization of net transition asset			(1)
Special early-retirement benefits	3		3
Settlements/curtailments			6
Net Cost (income)	$ 58	$ 83	$ (24)
Weighted-average assumptions			
Discount rates	6.0%	6.7%	7.2%
Rate of compensation increase	3.9%	3.9%	3.9%
Expected long terms rates of return	8.5%	8.5%	9.7%

A worldwide reconciliation of the funded status of the benefit plans and the assumption related to the obligation at October 31 in millions of dollars follows:

	Pensions	
	2004	2003
Change in benefit obligations		
Beginning of year balance	$(7,790)	$(6,840)
Service cost	(130)	(111)
Interest cost	(454)	(450)
Actuarial loss	(474)	(534)
Amendments	(3)	(190)
Benefits paid	516	484
Special early-retirement benefits	(3)	
Foreign exchange and other	(65)	(149)
End of year balance	(8,403)	(7,790)
Change in plan assets (fair value)		
Beginning of year balance	5,987	5,024
Actual return on plan assets	594	958
Employer contribution	1,548	432
Benefits paid	(516)	(484)
Foreign exchange and other	22	57
End of year balance	7,635	5,987
Plan obligation more than plan assets	(768)	(1,803)
Unrecognized actuarial loss	2,551	2,094
Unrecognized prior service (credit) cost	217	254
Net amount recognized	2,000	545
Minimum pension liability adjustment	(106)	(1,964)
Net asset (liability) recognized	$1,894	$(1,419)
Amount recognized in balance sheet		
Prepaid benefit cost	$2,493	$ 63
Accrued benefit liability	(599)	(1,482)
Intangible asset	18	250
Accumulated pretax charge to other comprehensive income	88	1,714
Net amount recognized	$2,000	$545
Weighted-average assumptions		
Discount rates	5.5%	6.0%
Rate of compensation increase	3.9%	3.9%

The total accumulated benefit obligations for all pension plans at October 31, 2004 and 2003 was $7,954 million and $7,390 million respectively.

The minimum pension liability adjustment recorded by the company was $106 million and $1,964 million as of October 31, 2004 and 2003, respectively. The decrease in the adjustment, compared to last year, was a result of an increase in the fair value of plan assets due to voluntary company contributions and the return on plan assets during 2004.

Special Issues

The Pension Reform Act of 1974

The Employee Retirement Income Security Act of 1974—**ERISA**—affects virtually every private retirement plan in the United States. It attempts to safeguard employees' pension rights by mandating many pension plan requirements, including minimum funding, participation, and vesting.

These requirements can influence the employers' costs significantly. Under this legislation, annual funding is no longer discretionary. An employer now must fund the plan in accordance with an actuarial funding method that over time will be sufficient to pay for all pension obligations. If companies do not fund their plans in a reasonable manner, they may be subject to fines and/or loss of tax deductions.

The law requires plan administrators to publish a comprehensive description and summary of their plans, along with detailed annual reports that include many supplementary schedules and statements. ERISA further mandates that qualified independent public accountants audit the required reports, statements, and supplementary schedules.

Another important provision of the Act is the creation of the Pension Benefit Guaranty Corporation (PBGC). **The PBGC's purpose is to administer terminated plans** and to impose liens on an employer's assets for certain unfunded pension liabilities. If a company terminates its pension plan, the PBGC can effectively impose a lien against the employer's assets for the excess of the present value of guaranteed vested benefits over the pension fund assets. This lien generally has had the status of a tax lien; it takes priority over most other creditorship claims. This section of the Act gives the PBGC the power to force an involuntary termination of a pension plan whenever the risks related to nonpayment of the pension obligation seem too great. Because ERISA restricts to 30 percent of net worth the lien that the PBGC can impose, the PBGC must monitor all plans to ensure that net worth is sufficient to meet the pension benefit obligations.[20]

A large number of terminated plans have caused the PBGC to pay out substantial benefits. Currently the PBGC receives its funding from employers, who contribute a certain dollar amount for each employee covered under the plan.[21]

Pension Terminations

A congressman at one time noted, "employers are simply treating their employee pension plans like company piggy banks, to be raided at will." What this congressman was referring to is the practice of paying off the projected benefit obligation and pocketing any excess. ERISA prevents companies from recapturing excess assets unless they pay participants what is owed to them and then terminate the plan. As a result, companies were buying *annuities* to pay off the pension claimants and then used the excess funds for other corporate purposes.[22]

For example, at one time, pension plan terminations netted $363 million for **Occidental Petroleum Corp.**, $95 million for **Stroh's Brewery Co.**, $58 million for **Kellogg**

> ### UNDERLYING CONCEPTS
>
> Many plans are underfunded but still quite viable. For example, at one time **Loews Corp.** had a $159 million shortfall, but also had earnings of $594 million and a good net worth. Thus, the going concern assumption permits us to ignore pension underfundings in some cases because in the long run they are not significant.

---

[20]The major problems in underfunding are occurring in four labor-intensive industries—steel, autos, rubber, and airlines. For example, **General Motors**' pension plan at one time was 92 percent funded but still had a deficit of over $6 billion.

[21]**Pan American Airlines** is a good illustration of how difficult it is to assess when to terminate. When Pan Am filed for bankruptcy in 1991, it had a pension liability of $900 million. From 1983 to 1991, the IRS gave it six waivers so it did not have to make contributions. When Pan Am terminated the plan, there was little net worth left upon which to impose a lien. An additional accounting problem relates to the manner of disclosing the possible termination of a plan. For example, should Pan Am have disclosed a contingent liability for its struggling plan? At present this issue is unresolved, and considerable judgment would be needed to analyze a company with these contingent liabilities.

[22]A question exists as to whose money it is. Some argue that the excess funds belong to the employees, not the employer. In addition, given that the funds have been reverting to the employer, critics charge that cost-of-living increases and the possibility of other increased benefits are reduced, because companies will be reluctant to use those remaining funds to pay for such increases.

Co., and $29 million for **Western Airlines**. Recently, many large companies have terminated their pension plans and captured billions in surplus assets. The U.S. Treasury also benefits: Federal legislation requires companies to pay an excise tax of anywhere from 20 percent to 50 percent on the gains. All of this is quite legal.[23]

WHAT DO THE NUMBERS MEAN?

BAILING OUT

The Pension Benefit Guaranty Corp. (PBGC) recently announced that it would take over responsibility for the pilots' pension plan at **United Airlines**, to the tune of $1.4 billion. This federal agency, which acts as an insurer for corporate pension plans, has spent much of the past few years securing pension plans for "Big Steel" (U.S. steel companies), and it looks as if airlines are next.

For example, the PBGC also became the trustee of **US Airways** pilots' pensions in 2003, and it may soon announce a takeover of that struggling carrier's other three pension plans. The grand total at US Airways? It's $2.8 billion—mere pocket change next to the $6.4 billion the PBGC will owe if it has to bail out all four of United Airlines' plans. To date, the airline industry, which makes up 2 percent of participants in the program, has made 20 percent of the claims. The chart below shows how a $6.4 billion bailout would compare with the PBGC's biggest payouts to date.

Source: Kate Bonamici, "By the Numbers," *Fortune* (January 24, 2005), p. 24.

The accounting issue that arises from these terminations is whether a company should recognize a gain when pension plan assets revert back to the company (often called **asset reversion** transactions). The issue is complex because in some cases, a company starts a new defined-benefit plan after it eliminates the old one. Therefore some contend that there has been no change in substance, but merely a change in form.

---

[23]Another way that companies have reduced their pension obligations is through adoption of **cash-balance plans.** These are *hybrid* plans combining features of defined-benefit and defined-contribution plans. Although these plans permit employees to transfer their pension benefits when they change employers (like a defined contribution plan), they are controversial because the change to a cash-balance plan often reduces benefits to older workers.

The accounting for cash-balance plans is similar to that for defined-benefit plans, because employers bear the investment risk in cash-balance plans. When an employer adopts a cash-balance plan, the measurement of the future benefit obligation to employees generally is lower, compared to a traditional defined-benefit plan. See A. T. Arcady and F. Mellors, "Cash-Balance Conversions," *Journal of Accountancy* (February 2000), pp. 22–28.

As a result the FASB issued *SFAS No. 88*. It requires recognition in earnings of a gain or loss when the employer settles a pension obligation either by lump-sum cash payments to participants or by purchasing nonparticipating annuity contracts.[24]

Concluding Observation

Hardly a day goes by without the financial press analyzing in depth some issue related to pension plans in the United States. This is not surprising, since U.S. pension funds now hold over $5 trillion in assets. As you have seen, the accounting issues related to pension plans are complex. *SFAS No. 87* clarifies many of these issues and should help users understand the financial implications of a company's pension plans on its financial position, results of operations, and cash flows.

Critics still argue, however, that much remains to be done. One issue in particular relates to the delayed recognition of certain events: Currently, companies do not immediately recognize changes in pension plan obligations and changes in the value of plan assets, but systematically incorporate such changes over subsequent periods. This issue seems likely to get attention in the upcoming years. As a result, the FASB has recently decided to reexamine the accounting and reporting for pensions.

SUMMARY OF LEARNING OBJECTIVES

1. Distinguish between accounting for the employer's pension plan and accounting for the pension fund. The company or employer is the organization sponsoring the pension plan. It incurs the cost and makes contributions to the pension fund. The fund or plan is the entity that receives the contributions from the employer, administers the pension assets, and makes the benefit payments to the pension recipients (retired employees). The fund should be a separate legal and accounting entity; it maintains a set of books and prepares financial statements.

2. Identify types of pension plans and their characteristics. The two most common types of pension arrangements are: (1) *Defined-contribution plans*: The employer agrees to contribute to a pension trust a certain sum each period based on a formula. This formula may consider such factors as age, length of employee service, employer's profits, and compensation level. Only the employer's contribution is defined; no promise is made regarding the ultimate benefits paid out to the employees. (2) *Defined-benefit plans*: These plans define the benefits that the employee will receive at the time of retirement. The formula typically provides for the benefits to be a function of the employee's years of service and the compensation level when he or she nears retirement.

3. Explain alternative measures for valuing the pension obligation. One measure bases the pension obligation only on the benefits vested to the employees. Vested benefits are those that the employee is entitled to receive even if he or she renders no additional services under the plan. Companies compute the *vested benefits pension obligation* using current salary levels; this obligation includes only vested benefits. Another measure of the obligation, called the *accumulated benefit obligation*, computes the deferred compensation amount based on all years of service performed by employees under the plan—both vested and nonvested—using current salary levels. A third measure, called the

KEY TERMS

accrued pension cost, *1040*

accumulated benefit obligation, *1024*

actual return on plan assets, *1028*

actuarial present value, *1026*

actuaries, *1023*

additional liability, *1040*

asset gains and losses, *1034*

cash-balance plans, *1054(n)*

components of pension expense, *1026*

contributory pension plan, *1021*

corridor approach, *1035*

defined-benefit plan, *1022*

defined-contribution plan, *1021*

ERISA, *1053*

expected rate of return, *1034*

expected return on plan assets, *1034*

fair value of plan assets, *1028*

---

[24] "Employers' Accounting for Settlements and Curtailments of Defined Benefit Pension Plans and for Termination Benefits," *Statement of Financial Accounting Standards No. 88* (Stamford, Conn.: FASB, 1985). Some companies have established *pension poison pills* as an anti-takeover measure. These plans require asset reversions from termination of a plan to benefit employees and retirees rather than the acquiring company. For a discussion of pension poison pills, see Eugene E. Comiskey and Charles W. Mulford, "Interpreting Pension Disclosures: A Guide for Lending Officers," *Commercial Lending Review* (Winter 1993–94), Vol. 9, No. 1.

projected benefit obligation, bases the computation of the deferred compensation amount on both vested and nonvested service using future salaries.

4. List the components of pension expense. Pension expense is a function of the following components: (1) service cost, (2) interest on the liability, (3) return on plan assets, (4) amortization of unrecognized prior service cost, and (5) gain or loss.

5. Use a worksheet for employer's pension plan entries. Companies may use a worksheet unique to pension accounting. This worksheet records both the formal entries and the memo entries to keep track of all the employer's relevant pension plan items and components.

6. Describe the amortization of unrecognized prior service costs. An actuary computes the amount of the prior service cost. The FASB prefers a "years-of-service" amortization method, similar to a units-of-production computation. First, the company computes total estimated number of service-years to be worked by all of the participating employees. Second, it divides the unrecognized prior service cost by the total number of service-years, to obtain a cost per service-year (the unit cost). Third, the company multiplies the number of service-years consumed each year times the cost per service-year, to obtain the annual amortization charge.

7. Explain the accounting procedure for recognizing unexpected gains and losses. In estimating the projected benefit obligation (the liability), actuaries make assumptions about such items as mortality rate, retirement rate, turnover rate, disability rate, and salary amounts. Any change in these actuarial assumptions affects the amount of the projected benefit obligation. These unexpected gains or losses from changes in the projected benefit obligation are liability gains and losses. Liability gains result from unexpected decreases in the liability balance; liability losses result from unexpected increases. Companies defer (do not immediately recognize) liability gains and losses. They combine liability gains and losses in the same Unrecognized Net Gain or Loss account used for asset gains and losses, and then accumulate these amounts from year to year, off-balance-sheet, in a memo record account.

8. Explain the corridor approach to amortizing unrecognized gains and losses. The FASB set a limit for the size of an unrecognized net gain or loss balance. That arbitrarily selected limit (called a *corridor*) is 10 percent of the larger of the beginning balances of the projected benefit obligation or the market-related value of the plan assets. Beyond that limit, an unrecognized net gain or loss balance is considered too large and must be amortized. If the balance of the unrecognized net gain or loss account stays within the upper and lower limits of the corridor, no amortization is required.

9. Explain the recognition of a minimum liability. Companies must recognize a liability (referred to as the *minimum liability*) when the accumulated benefit obligation exceeds the fair value of plan assets. The purpose of this requirement is to ensure that if a significant plan amendment or actuarial loss occurs, a company will recognize a liability at least to the extent of the unfunded portion of the accumulated benefit obligation.

10. Describe the requirements for reporting pension plans in financial statements. Currently, companies must disclose the following pension plan information in their financial statements: (1) The components of net periodic pension expense for the period. (2) A schedule showing changes in the benefit obligation and plan assets during the year. (3) A schedule reconciling the funded status of the plan with amounts reported in the employer's statement of financial position. (4) The weighted-average assumed discount rate, the rate of compensation increase used to measure the projected benefit obligation, and the weighted-average expected long-term rate of return on plan assets. (5) A table showing the allocation of pension plan assets by category and the percentage of the fair value to total plan assets. (6) The expected benefit payments for current plan participants for each of the next five fiscal years and for the following five years in aggregate, along with an estimate of expected contributions to the plan during the next year.

Accounting for Postretirement Benefits

In March 1991 **IBM**'s adoption of a new accounting standard on postretirement benefits resulted in a $2.3 billion charge and a historical curiosity—IBM's first-ever quarterly loss. **General Electric** disclosed that its charge for adoption of the same new FASB standard would be $2.7 billion. In the fourth quarter of 1993, **AT&T** absorbed a $2.1 billion pretax hit for postretirement benefits. What is this standard, and how could its adoption have so grave an impact on companies' earnings?

ACCOUNTING GUIDANCE

After a decade of study, the FASB in December 1990 issued *Statement No. 106,* "Employers' Accounting for Postretirement Benefits Other Than Pensions." It alone was the cause for the large charges to income cited above. This standard accounts for health care and other "welfare benefits" provided to retirees, their spouses, dependents, and beneficiaries.[1] These other welfare benefits include life insurance offered outside a pension plan; medical, dental, and eye care; legal and tax services; tuition assistance; day care; and housing assistance.[2] Because healthcare benefits are the largest of the other postretirement benefits, we use this item to illustrate accounting for postretirement benefits.

For many employers (about 95 percent) this standard required a change from the predominant practice of accounting for postretirement benefits on a pay-as-you-go (cash) basis to an accrual basis. Similar to pension accounting, the accrual basis necessitates measuring the employer's obligation to provide future benefits and accrual of the cost during the years that the employee provides service.

One of the reasons companies had not prefunded these benefit plans was that payments to prefund healthcare costs, unlike excess contributions to a pension trust, are not tax-deductible. Another reason was that postretirement healthcare benefits were once perceived to be a low-cost employee benefit that could be changed or eliminated at will and therefore were not a legal liability. Now, the accounting definition of a liability goes

---

[1]*Accounting Trends and Techniques—2004* reports that of its 600 surveyed companies, 334 reported benefit plans that provide postretirement healthcare benefits. In response to rising healthcare costs and higher premiums on healthcare insurance, companies are working to get their postretirement benefit costs under control. For example, a recent study of employer health-benefit plans indicates that employers are limiting or curtailing postretirement health benefits. Of the companies surveyed, 20 percent have eliminated the plans altogether. And 17 percent indicated they have just about eliminated their liabilities for such benefits by requiring current retirees to pay healthcare premiums. In some cases, employees must work longer at a company before they are eligible for these benefits. See Kelly Greene, "Health Benefits for Retirees Continue to Shrink, Study Says," *Wall Street Journal* (September 16, 2002), p. A2.

[2]"OPEB" is the acronym frequently used to describe postretirement benefits covered by *SFAS No. 106.* This term came into being before the scope of the statement was narrowed from "other postemployment benefits" to "other postretirement benefits," thereby excluding postemployment benefits related to severance pay or wage continuation to disabled, terminated, or laid-off employees.

beyond the notion of a legally enforceable claim; the definition now encompasses equitable or constructive obligations as well, making it clear that the postretirement benefit promise is a liability.[3]

DIFFERENCES BETWEEN PENSION BENEFITS AND HEALTHCARE BENEFITS

OBJECTIVE 11
Identify the differences between pensions and postretirement healthcare benefits.

The FASB used *SFAS No. 87* on pensions as a reference for the accounting prescribed in *SFAS No. 106* on healthcare and other nonpension postretirement benefits.[4] Why didn't the FASB cover these other types of postretirement benefits in the earlier pension accounting statement? Because the apparent similarities between the two benefits mask some significant differences. Illustration 20A-1 shows these differences.[5]

ILLUSTRATION 20A-1
Differences between Pensions and Postretirement Healthcare Benefits

Item	Pensions	Healthcare Benefits
Funding	Generally funded.	Generally *NOT* funded.
Benefit	Well-defined and level dollar amount.	Generally uncapped and great variability.
Beneficiary	Retiree (maybe some benefit to surviving spouse).	Retiree, spouse, and other dependents.
Benefit payable	Monthly.	As needed and used.
Predictability	Variables are reasonably predictable.	Utilization difficult to predict. Level of cost varies geographically and fluctuates over time.

Two of the differences in Illustration 20A-1 highlight why measuring the future payments for healthcare benefit plans is so much more difficult than for pension plans.

1 Many postretirement plans do not set a limit on healthcare benefits. No matter how serious the illness or how long it lasts, the benefits continue to flow. (Even if the employer uses an insurance company plan, the premiums will escalate according to the increased benefits provided.)

2 The levels of healthcare benefit use and healthcare costs are difficult to predict. Increased longevity, unexpected illnesses (e.g., AIDS, SARS, and avian flu), along with new medical technologies and cures, cause changes in healthcare utilization.

Additionally, although the fiduciary and reporting standards for employee benefit funds under government regulations generally cover healthcare benefits, the stringent minimum vesting, participation, and funding standards that apply to pensions do not

---

[3]"Elements of Financial Statements," *Statement of Financial Accounting Concepts No. 6* (Stamford, Conn.: 1985), p. 13, footnote 21.

[4]In November 1992 the FASB issued *Statement of Financial Accounting Standards No. 112,* "Employers' Accounting for Postemployment Benefits." This standard covers postemployment benefits that are not accounted for under *SFAS No. 87* (pensions), *SFAS No. 88* (settlements, curtailments, and termination benefits), or *SFAS No. 106* (postretirement benefits other than pensions). *SFAS No. 112* requires an employer to recognize the obligation to provide postemployment benefits in accordance with *SFAS No. 43*, similar to accounting for compensated absences (see Chapter 13). These *SFAS No. 112* benefits include, but are not limited to, salary continuation, disability-related benefits, severance benefits, and continuance of healthcare benefits and life insurance for inactive or former (e.g., terminated, disabled, or deceased) employees or their beneficiaries.

[5]D. Gerald Searfoss and Naomi Erickson, "The Big Unfunded Liability: Postretirement Health-Care Benefits," *Journal of Accountancy* (November 1988), pp. 28–39.

apply to healthcare benefits. Nevertheless, as you will learn, many of the basic concepts of pensions, and much of the related accounting terminology and measurement methodology, do apply to other postretirement benefits. Therefore, in the following discussion and illustrations, we point out the similarities and differences in the accounting and reporting for these two types of postretirement benefits.

OPEBS — HOW BIG ARE THEY?

WHAT DO THE NUMBERS MEAN?

For many companies, *other postretirement benefit obligations* (OPEBs) are substantial. Generally, OPEBs are not well funded because companies are not permitted a tax deduction for contributions to the plan assets, as is the case with pensions. That is, the company may not claim a tax deduction until it makes a payment to the participant (pay-as-you-go).

Presented below are companies with the largest OPEB obligations, indicating their relationship with other financial items.

(For year ended 12/31/2003 $ in millions)	Obligation	% Underfunded	Obligation as a % of Pension Obligation (ABO)	Obligation as a % of LTD	Obligation as a % of Stockholder's Equity
General Motors	$ 67,542	85.2%	77.4%	25.1%	267.3%
Ford Motor Company	32,362	89.0%	80.0%	18.2%	277.8%
SBC Communications Inc.	27,231	74.4%	98.6%	71.2%	71.2%
Verizon Communications Inc.	24,592	81.8%	59.9%	62.4%	73.5%
General Electric	9,701	83.2%	25.6%	5.7%	12.3%
Boeing Co.	8,617	99.3%	21.6%	64.8%	105.9%
Lucent Technologies Inc.	8,511	72.7%	27.2%	152.2%	NA
Delphi Corp.	8,469	100.0%	74.2%	347.9%	539.4%
BellSouth Corp.	7,156	48.4%	61.6%	62.3%	36.3%
AT&T Corp.	6,274	67.2%	39.8%	48.0%	45.0%

So, how big are OPEB obligations? REALLY big.

Source: Jason Williams, "OPEB Plans 2003: In Worse Shape than 2002," Yellow Card Trend Alert, Glass Lewis LLP (November 1, 2004).

POSTRETIREMENT BENEFITS ACCOUNTING PROVISIONS

Healthcare and other postretirement benefits for current and future retirees and their dependents are forms of deferred compensation. They are earned through employee service and are subject to accrual during the years an employee is working.

The period of time over which the postretirement benefit cost accrues is called the **attribution period**. It is the period of service during which the employee earns the benefits under the terms of the plan. The attribution period (shown in Illustration 20A-2, on page 1060) generally begins when an employee is hired and ends on the date the employee is eligible to receive the benefits and ceases to earn additional benefits by performing service, the vesting date.[6]

---

[6]This is a benefit-years-of-service approach (the projected unit credit actuarial cost method). The FASB found no compelling reason to switch from the traditional pension accounting approach. It rejected the employee's full service period (i.e., to the estimated retirement date) because it was unable to identify any approach that would appropriately attribute benefits beyond the date when an employee attains full eligibility for those benefits. Employees attain full eligibility by meeting specified age, service, or age and service requirements of the plan.

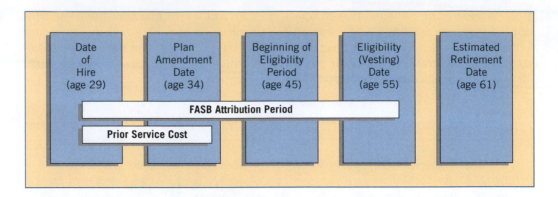

Obligations under Postretirement Benefits

In defining the obligation for postretirement benefits, the FASB maintained many concepts similar to pension accounting. It also designed some new and modified terms specifically for postretirement benefits. Two of the most important of these specialized terms are (a) expected postretirement benefit obligation and (b) accumulated postretirement benefit obligation.

The **expected postretirement benefit obligation (EPBO)** is the actuarial present value as of a particular date of **all benefits a company expects to pay after retirement to employees and their dependents**. Companies do not record the EPBO in the financial statements, but they do use it in measuring periodic expense.

The **accumulated postretirement benefit obligation (APBO)** is the actuarial present value of **future benefits attributed to employees' services rendered to a particular date**. The APBO is equal to the EPBO for retirees and active employees fully eligible for benefits. Before the date an employee achieves full eligibility, the APBO is only a portion of the EPBO. Or stated another way, the difference between the APBO and the EPBO is the future service costs of active employees who are not yet fully eligible.

Illustration 20A-3 contrasts the EPBO and the APBO.

ILLUSTRATION 20A-3
APBO and EPBO
Contrasted

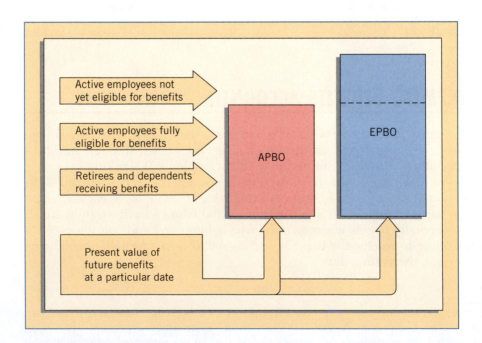

At the date an employee is fully eligible (the end of the attribution period), the APBO and the EPBO for that employee are equal.

Postretirement Expense

Postretirement expense is the employer's annual expense for postretirement benefits. Also called **net periodic postretirement benefit cost**, this expense consists of many of the familiar components used to compute annual pension expense. The components of net periodic postretirement benefit cost are as follows.[7]

1 *Service Cost:* The portion of the EPBO attributed to employee service during the period.

2 *Interest Cost:* The increase in the APBO attributable to the passage of time. Companies compute interest cost by applying the beginning-of-the-year discount rate to the beginning-of-the-year APBO, adjusted for benefit payments to be made during the period. The discount rate is based on the rates of return on high-quality, fixed-income investments that are currently available.[8]

3 *Actual Return on Plan Assets:* The change in the fair value of the plan's assets adjusted for contributions and benefit payments made during the period. Because companies charge or credit the postretirement expense for the gain or loss on plan assets (the difference between the actual and the expected return), this component is actually the expected return.

4 *Amortization of Prior Service Cost:* The amortization of the cost of retroactive benefits resulting from plan amendments after *SFAS No. 106* takes effect. The typical amortization period, beginning at the date of the plan amendment, is the remaining service periods through the full eligibility date.

5 *Gains and Losses:* In general, changes in the APBO resulting from changes in assumptions or from experience different from that assumed. For funded plans, this component also includes the difference between actual return and expected return on plan assets. (Companies compute this difference the same as for pensions—with *actual* and *expected* returns based on market-related value.) Companies can recognize gains or losses immediately or can base them on a "corridor approach" similar to that used for pension accounting.[9]

ILLUSTRATIVE ACCOUNTING ENTRIES

Like pension accounting, the accounting for postretirement plans does not recognize in the accounts and in the financial statements several significant items. These off-balance-sheet items are:

1 Expected postretirement benefit obligation (EPBO).

2 Accumulated postretirement benefit obligation (APBO).

> **OBJECTIVE 12**
> Contrast accounting for pensions to accounting for other postretirement benefits.

---

[7]"Employers' Accounting for Postretirement Benefits Other Than Pensions," *Statement of Financial Accounting Standards No. 106* (Norwalk, Conn.: FASB, 1990), pars. 46–66. Also see James R. Wilbert and Kenneth E. Dakdduk, "The New FASB 106: How to Account for Postretirement Benefits," *Journal of Accountancy* (August 1991), pp. 36–41.

[8]The FASB concluded that the discount rate for measuring the present value of the postretirement benefit obligation and the service cost component should be the same as that applied to pension measurements. It chose not to label it the *settlement rate*, in order to clarify that the objective of the discount rate is to measure the time value of money.

[9]Another component of pension expense for some companies is amortization of the transition amount. When the FASB issued its standard on OPEBs in 1991, it decided to permit companies to choose between immediate recognition (e.g., the $2.3 billion charge taken by **IBM** in the first quarter of 1991) or deferral and amortization. In general, under deferral, the company amortizes the cost over the remaining service life of existing employees. However, if the remaining service period is less than 20 years, the employer may elect a 20-year amortization period. As a consequence some companies are still amortizing this deferred cost; for most companies it is no longer an issue, and therefore we have not illustrated it here.

3 Postretirement benefit plan assets.

4 Unrecognized prior service cost.

5 Unrecognized net gain or loss.

The EPBO is not recognized in the financial statements or disclosed in the notes. Companies recompute it each year and the actuary uses it in measuring the annual service cost. Because of the numerous assumptions and actuarial complexity involved in measuring annual service cost, we have omitted these computations of the EPBO.

Companies must disclose in notes to the financial statements all five of the other off-balance-sheet items listed above. In addition, as in pension accounting, companies must know the exact amount of these items in order to compute postretirement expense. Therefore, companies use the worksheet like that for pension accounting to record both the formal general journal entries and the memo entries.

2006 Entries and Worksheet

To illustrate the use of a worksheet in accounting for a postretirement benefits plan, assume that on January 1, 2006, Quest Company adopts *Statement No. 106* to account for its healthcare benefit plan. The following facts apply to the postretirement benefits plan for the year 2006.

Plan assets at fair value on January 1, 2006, are zero.

Actual and expected returns on plan assets are zero.

APBO, January 1, 2006, is $0.

Service cost is $54,000.

No prior service cost exists.

Interest cost on the APBO is zero.

Funding contributions during the year are $38,000.

Benefit payments to employees from plan are $28,000.

Using that data, the worksheet in Illustration 20A-4 presents the postretirement benefit entries for 2006.

ILLUSTRATION 20A-4
Postretirement Benefits
Worksheet—2006

Items	General Journal Entries			Memo Record	
	Annual Postretirement Expense	Cash	Prepaid/ Accrued Cost	APBO	Plan Assets
Balance, Jan. 1, 2006					
(a) Service cost	54,000 Dr.			54,000 Cr.	
(b) Contributions		38,000 Cr.			38,000 Dr.
(c) Benefits				28,000 Dr.	28,000 Cr.
Journal entry for 2006	54,000 Dr.	38,000 Cr.	16,000 Cr.*		
Balance, Dec. 31, 2006			16,000 Cr.**	26,000 Cr.	10,000 Dr.

*$54,000 − $38,000 = $16,000.
**$26,000 − $10,000 = $16,000

Entry (a) records the service cost component, which increases postretirement expense $54,000 and increases the liability (APBO) $54,000. Entry (b) records Quest's funding of assets to the postretirement benefit fund. The funding decreases cash $38,000 and increases plan assets $38,000. Entry (c) records the benefit payments made to retirees, which results in equal $28,000 decreases to the plan assets and the liability (APBO).

Quest's December 31 adjusting entry formally records the postretirement expense in 2006, as follows.

December 31, 2006

Postretirement Expense	54,000	
Cash		38,000
Prepaid/Accrued Cost		16,000

The credit to Prepaid/Accrued Cost for $16,000 represents the difference between the 2006 postretirement expense of $54,000 and the amount funded of $38,000. The $16,000 credit balance is a liability because the plan is underfunded. The Prepaid/Accrued Cost account balance of $16,000 also equals the net of the balances in the memo accounts.

Illustration 20A-5 shows the reconciliation of the off-balance-sheet items with the prepaid/accrued cost reported in the balance sheet. (Notice its similarity to the pension reconciliation schedule.) Preparation of this reconciliation schedule is necessary as part of the required note disclosures.

Accumulated postretirement benefit obligation (Credit)	$(26,000)
Plan assets at fair value (Debit)	10,000
Prepaid/accrued cost (Credit)	$ (16,000)

ILLUSTRATION 20A-5
Postretirement Benefits Reconciliation Schedule—December 31, 2006

Recognition of Gains and Losses

Gains and losses represent changes in the APBO or the value of plan assets. These changes result either from actual experience different from that expected or from changes in actuarial assumptions. The FASB noted, "recognizing the effects of revisions in estimates in full in the period in which they occur may produce financial statements that portray more volatility than is inherent in the employer's obligation."[10] Therefore, as in pension accounting, the FASB does not require companies to recognize gains and losses immediately.[11] Instead, companies may defer such gains and losses in the period when they occur and amortize them in future years.

The Corridor Approach

Consistent with pension accounting, companies amortize deferred gains and losses as a component of net periodic expense if, at the beginning of the period, they exceed a "corridor" limit. The corridor is measured as the greater of 10 percent of the APBO or 10 percent of the market-related value of plan assets.

The intent of the **corridor approach** is to reduce volatility of postretirement expense by providing a reasonable opportunity for gains and losses to offset over time without affecting net periodic expense.

Amortization Methods

If the company must amortize gains and losses (beyond the corridor) on postretirement benefit plans, the **minimum amortization amount** is the excess gain or loss divided by the average remaining service life to expected retirement of all active employees. Companies may use any systematic method of amortization provided that: (1) the amount amortized in any period is equal to or greater than the minimum amount, (2)

---

[10]*FASB Statement No. 106,* par. 293.

[11]If a company adopts a consistent policy of immediately recognizing gains and losses, it will experience the following: (1) The amount of any **net gain** in excess of net losses previously recognized in income would first offset any unamortized **transition obligation**. (2) The amount of any **net loss** in excess of net gains previously recognized in net income would first offset any unamortized **transition asset** (existence of a transition asset, however, is unlikely).

the company applies the method consistently, and (3) the company applies the method similarly for gains and losses.

The company must recompute the amount of unrecognized gain or loss each year and amortize the gain or loss over the average remaining service life if the net amount exceeds the "corridor."

2007 Entries and Worksheet

Continuing the Quest Company illustration into 2007, the following facts apply to the postretirement benefits plan for the year 2007.

Actual return on plan assets is $600.

Expected return on plan assets is $800.

Discount rate is 8 percent.

Increase in APBO due to change in actuarial assumptions is $60,000.

Service cost is $26,000.

Funding contributions during the year are $18,000.

Benefit payments to employees during the year are $5,000.

Average remaining service to expected retirement: 25 years.

The worksheet in Illustration 20A-6 presents all of Quest's postretirement benefit entries and information for 2007. The beginning balances on the first line of worksheet are the ending balances from Quest's 2006 postretirement benefits worksheet in Illustration 20A-4.

ILLUSTRATION 20A-6
Postretirement Benefits
Worksheet—2007

	General Journal Entries			Memo Record		
Items	Annual Postretirement Expense	Cash	Prepaid/ Accrued Cost	APBO	Plan Assets	Unrecognized Net Gain or Loss
Balances, Jan. 1, 2007			16,000 Cr.	26,000 Cr.	10,000 Dr.	
(d) Service cost	26,000 Dr.			26,000 Cr.		
(e) Interest cost	2,080 Dr.			2,080 Cr.		
(f) Actual return	600 Cr.				600 Dr.	
(g) Unexpected loss	200 Cr.					200 Dr.
(h) Contributions		18,000 Cr.			18,000 Dr.	
(i) Benefits				5,000 Dr.	5,000 Cr.	
(j) Inc. in APBO—Loss				60,000 Cr.		60,000 Dr.
Journal entry for 2007	27,280 Dr.	18,000 Cr.	9,280 Cr.*			
Balance, Dec. 31, 2007			25,280 Cr.**	109,080 Cr.	23,600 Dr.	60,200 Dr.

*$27,280 − $18,000 = $9,280
**$109,080 − $23,600 − $60,200 = $25,280

Entries (d), (h), and (i) are similar to the corresponding entries previously explained for 2006. Entry (e) accrues the interest expense component, which increases both the liability and the postretirement expense by $2,080 (the beginning APBO multiplied by the discount rate of 8%). Entries (f) and (g) are related. The expected return of $800 is higher than the actual return of $600. To smooth postretirement expense, Quest defers the unexpected loss of $200 ($800 − $600) by debiting Unrecognized Net Gain or Loss and crediting Postretirement Expense. As a result of this adjustment, the expected return on the plan assets is the amount actually used to compute postretirement expense.

Entry (j) records the change in the APBO resulting from a change in actuarial assumptions. This $60,000 increase in the employer's accumulated liability is an unexpected loss. Quest defers that loss by debiting it to Unrecognized Net Gain or Loss. On December 31 Quest formally records net periodic expense for 2007 as follows.

December 31, 2007

Postretirement Expense	27,280	
Cash		18,000
Prepaid/Accrued Cost		9,280

The balance of the Prepaid/Accrued Cost account at December 31, 2007, is $25,280. This balance is equal to the net of the balances in the memo accounts as shown in the reconciliation schedule in Illustration 20A-7.

Accumulated postretirement benefit obligation (Credit)	$(109,080)
Plan assets at fair value (Debit)	23,600
Funded status (Credit)	(85,480)
Unrecognized net gain or loss (Debit)	60,200
Prepaid/accrued cost (Credit)	$ (25,280)

ILLUSTRATION 20A-7
Postretirement Benefits Reconciliation Schedule—December 31, 2007

Amortization of Unrecognized Net Gain or Loss in 2008

Quest has a beginning-of-the-year balance in unrecognized net gain or loss. Therefore, Quest must apply the corridor test for amortization of the balance at the end of 2008. Illustration 20A-8 shows the computation of the amortization charge for unrecognized net gain or loss.

2008 Corridor Test	
Unrecognized net gain or loss at beginning of year	$60,200
10% of greater of APBO or market-related value of plan assets ($109,080 × .10)	10,908
Amortizable amount	$ 49,292
Average remaining service to expected retirement	25 years
2008 amortization of loss ($49,292 ÷ 25)	$1,972

ILLUSTRATION 20A-8
Computation of Amortization Charge (Corridor Test)—2008

DISCLOSURES IN NOTES TO THE FINANCIAL STATEMENTS

The disclosures required for other postretirement benefit plans are similar to and just as detailed and extensive as those required for pensions. By recognizing these similarities, companies can combine pension and other postretirement benefit disclosures.

The FASB requires the following disclosures.

1 Postretirement expense for the period, separately identifying all components of that cost.
2 A schedule showing changes in postretirement benefit obligations and plan assets during the year.
3 A schedule reconciling the funded status of the plan with amounts reported in the employer's balance sheet, separately identifying the reconciling items.
4 The assumptions and rates used in computing the EPBO and APBO, including the following: assumed trend rates in healthcare costs; assumed discount rates; and the effect of a one-percentage-point increase in the assumed healthcare cost trend rate on the measurement of the APBO, the service cost, and the interest cost.

ACTUARIAL ASSUMPTIONS AND CONCEPTUAL ISSUES

Measurement of the EPBO, the APBO, and the net periodic postretirement benefit cost is involved and complex. Due to the uncertainties in forecasting healthcare costs, rates of use, changes in government health programs, and the differences employed in non-medical assumptions (e.g., discount rate, employee turnover, rate of pre-65 retirement, spouse-age difference), estimates of postretirement benefit costs may have a large margin of error. Is the information relevant, reliable, or verifiable? The FASB concluded that "the obligation to provide postretirement benefits meets the definition of a liability, is representationally faithful, is relevant to financial statement users, and can be measured with sufficient reliability at a justifiable cost."[12] Failure to accrue an obligation and an expense prior to payment of benefits would result in an unfaithful representation of what financial statements should represent.[13]

The FASB took a momentous step by requiring the accrual of postretirement benefits as a liability. Many opposed the requirement, warning that the standard would devastate earnings. Others argued that putting "soft" numbers on the balance sheet was inappropriate. Others noted that the requirement would force companies to curtail postretirement benefits to employees.

The authors believe that the FASB deserves special praise for this standard. Because the Board addressed this issue, companies now recognize the magnitude of these costs. This recognition has led to efforts to control escalating healthcare costs. As John Ruffle, a former president of the Financial Accounting Foundation noted, "The Board has done American industry a gigantic favor. Over the long term, industry will look back and say thanks."

KEY TERMS

accumulated postretirement benefit obligation (APBO), 1060

attribution period, 1059

corridor approach, 1063

expected postretirement benefit obligation (EPBO), 1060

SUMMARY OF LEARNING OBJECTIVES FOR APPENDIX 20A

11. Identify the differences between pensions and postretirement healthcare benefits. Pension plans are generally funded, but healthcare benefit plans are not. Pension benefits are generally well-defined and level in amount; healthcare benefits are generally uncapped and variable. Pension benefits are payable monthly; healthcare benefits are paid as needed and used. Pension plan variables are reasonably predictable, whereas healthcare plan variables are difficult to predict.

12. Contrast accounting for pensions to accounting for other postretirement benefits. Many of the basic concepts, accounting terminology, and measurement methodology that apply to pensions also apply to other postretirement benefit accounting. Because other postretirement benefit plans are unfunded, large obligations can occur. Two significant concepts peculiar to accounting for other postretirement benefits are (a) expected postretirement benefit obligation (EPBO), and (b) accumulated postretirement benefit obligation (APBO).

Note: All **asterisked** Questions, Brief Exercises, Exercises, and Problems relate to material covered in the appendix to the chapter.

---

[12]*FASB Statement No. 106,* par. 163.

[13]The FASB does not require recognition of a "minimum liability" for postretirement benefit plans. The Board concluded that the postretirement transition provisions that provide for delayed recognition should not be overridden by a requirement to recognize a liability that would accelerate recognition of that obligation in the balance sheet.

QUESTIONS

1. What is a private pension plan? How does a contributory pension plan differ from a noncontributory plan?

2. Differentiate between a defined contribution pension plan and a defined benefit pension plan. Explain how the employer's obligation differs between the two types of plans.

3. Differentiate between "accounting for the employer" and "accounting for the pension fund."

4. The meaning of the term "fund" depends on the context in which it is used. Explain its meaning when used as a noun. Explain its meaning when it is used as a verb.

5. What is the role of an actuary relative to pension plans? What are actuarial assumptions?

6. What factors must be considered by the actuary in measuring the amount of pension benefits under a defined benefit plan?

7. Name three approaches to measuring benefits from a pension plan and explain how they differ.

8. Distinguish between the noncapitalization approach and the capitalization approach with regard to accounting for pension plans. Which approach does *FASB Statement No. 87* adopt?

9. Explain how cash-basis accounting for pension plans differs from accrual-basis accounting for pension plans. Why is cash-basis accounting generally considered unacceptable for pension plan accounting?

10. Identify the five components that comprise pension expense. Briefly explain the nature of each component.

11. What is service cost, and what is the basis of its measurement?

12. In computing the interest component of pension expense, what interest rates may be used?

13. Explain the difference between service cost and prior service cost.

14. What is meant by "prior service cost"? When is prior service cost recognized as pension expense?

15. What are "liability gains and losses," and how are they accounted for?

16. If pension expense recognized in a period exceeds the current amount funded by the employer, what kind of account arises, and how should it be reported in the financial statements? If the reverse occurs—that is, current funding by the employer exceeds the amount recognized as pension expense—what kind of account arises, and how should it be reported?

17. Given the following items and amounts, compute the actual return on plan assets: fair value of plan assets at the beginning of the period $9,200,000; benefits paid during the period $1,400,000; contributions made during the period $1,000,000; and fair value of the plan assets at the end of the period $10,150,000.

18. How does an "asset gain or loss" develop in pension accounting? How does a "liability gain or loss" develop in pension accounting?

19. What is the meaning of "corridor amortization"?

20. Explain when a minimum liability is recognized and how it is reported in the financial statements.

21. Explain the nature of a debit to an intangible asset account when an additional pension liability must be recorded. How does the amount of unrecognized prior service cost influence the amount recognized as an intangible asset?

22. At the end of the current period, Jacob Inc. had an accumulated benefit obligation of $400,000, pension plan assets (at fair value) of $300,000, and a balance in prepaid pension cost of $41,000. What are the accounts and amounts that will be reported on the company's balance sheet as pension assets or pension liabilities?

23. At the end of the current year, Joshua Co. has unrecognized prior service cost of $9,150,000. In addition, it recognized a minimum liability of $10,500,000 for the year. Where should the unrecognized prior service cost be reported on the balance sheet? Where should the debit related to the establishment of the minimum liability be reported?

24. Determine the meaning of the following terms.

(a) Contributory plan.

(b) Vested benefits.

(c) Retroactive benefits.

(d) Years-of-service method.

25. Of what value to the financial statement reader is the schedule reconciling the funded status of the plan with amounts reported in the employer's balance sheet?

26. A headline in the *Wall Street Journal* stated, "Firms Increasingly Tap Their Pension Funds to Use Excess Assets." What is the accounting issue related to the use of these "excess assets" by companies?

*27. What are postretirement benefits other than pensions?

*28. Why didn't the FASB cover both types of postretirement benefits—pensions and health-care—in the earlier pension accounting statement?

*29. What are the major differences between postretirement health-care benefits and pension benefits?

*30. What is the difference between the APBO and the EPBO? What are the components of postretirement expense?

BRIEF EXERCISES

(LO 4) **BE20-1** **AMR Corporation** (parent company of **American Airlines**) reported the following for 2004 (in millions).

Service cost	$358
Interest on P.B.O.	567
Return on plan assets	569
Amortization of unrecognized prior service cost	14
Amortization of unrecognized net loss	58

Compute **AMR Corporation**'s 2004 pension expense.

(LO 4) **BE20-2** For Becker Corporation, year-end plan assets were $2,000,000. At the beginning of the year, plan assets were $1,680,000. During the year, contributions to the pension fund were $120,000, and benefits paid were $200,000. Compute Becker's actual return on plan assets.

(LO 5) **BE20-3** At January 1, 2008, Uddin Company had plan assets of $250,000 and a projected benefit obligation of the same amount. During 2008, service cost was $27,500, the settlement rate was 10%, actual and expected return on plan assets were $25,000, contributions were $20,000, and benefits paid were $17,500. Prepare a pension worksheet for Uddin Company for 2008.

(LO 4) **BE20-4** For 2004, **Campbell Soup Company** had pension expense of $43 million and contributed $65 million to the pension fund. Prepare Campbell Soup Company's journal entry to record pension income and funding.

(LO 6) **BE20-5** Duesbury Corporation amended its pension plan on January 1, 2008, and granted $120,000 of unrecognized prior service costs to its employees. The employees are expected to provide 2,000 service years in the future, with 350 service years in 2008. Compute unrecognized prior service cost amortization for 2008.

(LO 10) **BE20-6** At December 31, 2008, Conway Corporation had a projected benefit obligation of $510,000, plan assets of $322,000, unrecognized prior service cost of $127,000, and accrued pension cost of $61,000. Prepare a pension reconciliation schedule for Conway.

(LO 8) **BE20-7** Hunt Corporation had a projected benefit obligation of $3,100,000 and plan assets of $3,300,000 at January 1, 2008. Hunt's unrecognized net pension loss was $475,000 at that time. The average remaining service period of Hunt's employees is 7.5 years. Compute Hunt's minimum amortization of pension loss.

(LO 9) **BE20-8** Judy O'Neill Corporation provides the following information at December 31, 2007.

Accumulated benefit obligation	$2,800,000
Plan assets at fair value	2,000,000
Accrued pension cost	200,000
Unrecognized prior service cost	1,100,000

Compute the additional liability that O'Neill must record at December 31, 2007.

(LO 9) **BE20-9** At December 31, 2008, Judy O'Neill Corporation (see BE20-8) has the following balances.

Accumulated benefit obligation	$3,400,000
Plan assets at fair value	2,420,000
Accrued pension cost	235,000
Unrecognized prior service cost	990,000

O'Neill's Additional Pension Liability was $600,000 at December 31, 2008. Prepare O'Neill's December 31, 2008, entry to adjust Additional Pension Liability.

(LO 9) **BE20-10** At December 31, 2007, Jeremiah Corporation was not required to report any additional pension liability. At December 31, 2008, the additional liability required is $600,000, and unrecognized prior service cost was $425,000. Prepare Jeremiah's December 31, 2008, entry to adjust Additional Pension Liability.

(LO 11, 12) *****BE20-11** Caleb Corporation has the following information available concerning its postretirement benefit plan for 2008.

Service cost	$40,000
Interest cost	52,400
Actual and expected return on plan assets	26,900

Compute Caleb's 2008 postretirement expense.

(LO 11, 12) *****BE20-12** For 2008, Benjamin Inc. computed its annual postretirement expense as $240,900. Benjamin's contribution to the plan during 2008 was $160,000. Prepare Benjamin's 2008 entry to record postretirement expense.

EXERCISES

(LO 4, 6)

E20-1 **(Pension Expense, Journal Entries)** The following information is available for the pension plan of Kiley Company for the year 2007.

Actual and expected return on plan assets	$ 12,000
Benefits paid to retirees	40,000
Contributions (funding)	95,000
Interest/discount rate	10%
Prior service cost amortization	8,000
Projected benefit obligation, January 1, 2007	500,000
Service cost	60,000

Instructions

   (a) Compute pension expense for the year 2007.

   (b) Prepare the journal entry to record pension expense and the employer's contribution to the pension plan in 2007.

(LO 4, 6) **E20-2** **(Computation of Pension Expense)** Rebekah Company provides the following information about its defined benefit pension plan for the year 2008.

Service cost	$ 90,000
Contribution to the plan	105,000
Prior service cost amortization	10,000
Actual and expected return on plan assets	64,000
Benefits paid	40,000
Accrued pension cost liability at January 1, 2008	10,000
Plan assets at January 1, 2008	640,000
Projected benefit obligation at January 1, 2008	800,000
Unrecognized prior service cost balance at January 1, 2008	150,000
Interest/discount (settlement) rate	10%

Instructions

Compute the pension expense for the year 2008.

(LO 5) **E20-3** **(Preparation of Pension Worksheet with Reconciliation)** Using the information in E20-2 prepare a pension worksheet inserting January 1, 2008, balances, showing December 31, 2008, balances, the reconciliation schedule, and the journal entry recording pension expense.

(LO 5) **E20-4** **(Basic Pension Worksheet)** The following facts apply to the pension plan of Trudy Borke Inc. for the year 2008.

Plan assets, January 1, 2008	$490,000
Projected benefit obligation, January 1, 2008	490,000
Settlement rate	8.5%
Service cost	40,000
Contributions (funding)	30,000
Actual and expected return on plan assets	49,700
Benefits paid to retirees	33,400

Instructions

Using the preceding data, compute pension expense for the year 2008. As part of your solution, prepare a pension worksheet that shows the journal entry for pension expense for 2008 and the year-end balances in the related pension accounts.

(LO 6) **E20-5** **(Application of Years-of-Service Method)** Valente Company has five employees participating in its defined benefit pension plan. Expected years of future service for these employees at the beginning of 2008 are as follows.

Employee	Future Years of Service
Ed	3
Paul	4
Mary	6
Dave	6
Caroline	6

On January 1, 2008, the company amended its pension plan increasing its projected benefit obligation by $60,000.

Instructions

Compute the amount of prior service cost amortization for the years 2008 through 2013 using the years-of-service method setting up appropriate schedules.

(LO 4) **E20-6 (Computation of Actual Return)** James Paul Importers provides the following pension plan information.

Fair value of pension plan assets, January 1, 2008	$2,300,000
Fair value of pension plan assets, December 31, 2008	2,725,000
Contributions to the plan in 2008	250,000
Benefits paid retirees in 2008	350,000

Instructions

From the data above, compute the actual return on the plan assets for 2008.

(LO 5, 6) **E20-7 (Basic Pension Worksheet)** The following defined pension data of Doreen Corp. apply to the year 2008.

Projected benefit obligation, 1/1/08 (before amendment)	$560,000
Plan assets, 1/1/08	546,200
Prepaid/accrued pension cost (credit)	13,800
On January 1, 2008, Doreen Corp., through plan amendment, grants prior service benefits having a present value of	100,000
Settlement rate	9%
Service cost	58,000
Contributions (funding)	55,000
Actual (expected) return on plan assets	52,280
Benefits paid to retirees	40,000
Prior service cost amortization for 2008	17,000

Instructions

For 2008, prepare a pension worksheet for Doreen Corp. that shows the journal entry for pension expense and the year-end balances in the related pension accounts.

(LO 8) **E20-8 (Application of the Corridor Approach)** Dougherty Corp. has beginning-of-the-year present values for its projected benefit obligation and market-related values for its pension plan assets.

	Projected Benefit Obligation	Plan Assets Value
2006	$2,000,000	$1,900,000
2007	2,400,000	2,500,000
2008	2,900,000	2,600,000
2009	3,600,000	3,000,000

The average remaining service life per employee in 2006 and 2007 is 10 years and in 2008 and 2009 is 12 years. The unrecognized net gain or loss that occurred during each year is as follows: 2006, $280,000 loss; 2007, $90,000 loss; 2008, $10,000 loss; and 2009, $25,000 gain. (In working the solution the unrecognized gains and losses must be aggregated to arrive at year-end balances.)

Instructions

Using the corridor approach, compute the amount of unrecognized net gain or loss amortized and charged to pension expense in each of the four years, setting up an appropriate schedule.

(LO 10) **E20-9 (Disclosures: Pension Expense and Reconciliation Schedule)** Mildred Enterprises provides the following information relative to its defined benefit pension plan.

Balances or Values at December 31, 2008

Projected benefit obligation	$2,737,000
Accumulated benefit obligation	1,980,000
Vested benefit obligation	1,645,852
Fair value of plan assets	2,278,329
Unrecognized prior service cost	205,000
Unrecognized net loss (1/1/08 balance, –0–)	45,680
Accrued pension cost liability	207,991
Other pension plan data:	
Service cost for 2008	$ 94,000
Unrecognized prior service cost amortization for 2008	45,000
Actual return on plan assets in 2008	130,000
Expected return on plan assets in 2008	175,680
Interest on January 1, 2008, projected benefit obligation	253,000
Contributions to plan in 2008	92,329
Benefits paid	140,000

Instructions

(a) Prepare the note disclosing the components of pension expense for the year 2008.

(b) Reconcile the funded status of the plan with the amount reported in the December 31, 2008, balance sheet.

(LO 5, 10) **E20-10** **(Pension Worksheet with Reconciliation Schedule)** Buhl Corp. sponsors a defined benefit pension plan for its employees. On January 1, 2008, the following balances relate to this plan.

Plan assets	$480,000
Projected benefit obligation	625,000
Prepaid/accrued pension cost (credit)	45,000
Unrecognized prior service cost	100,000

As a result of the operation of the plan during 2008, the following additional data are provided by the actuary.

Service cost for 2008	$90,000
Settlement rate, 9%	
Actual return on plan assets in 2008	57,000
Amortization of prior service cost	19,000
Expected return on plan assets	52,000
Unexpected loss from change in projected benefit obligation,	
due to change in actuarial predictions	76,000
Contributions in 2008	99,000
Benefits paid retirees in 2008	85,000

Instructions

(a) Using the data above, compute pension expense for Buhl Corp. for the year 2008 by preparing a pension worksheet that shows the journal entry for pension expense and the year-end balances in the related pension accounts.

(b) At December 31, 2008, prepare a schedule reconciling the funded status of the plan with the pension amount reported on the balance sheet.

(LO 9) **E20-11** **(Minimum Liability Computation, Entry)** The following information is available for McGwire Corporation's defined benefit pension plan for the years 2007 and 2008.

	December 31,	
	2007	2008
Accrued pension cost balance	$ –0–	$ 45,000
Accumulated benefit obligation	260,000	370,000
Fair value of plan assets	255,000	300,000
Prepaid pension cost balance	30,000	–0–
Projected benefit obligation	350,000	455,000
Unrecognized prior service cost	125,000	110,000

Instructions

(a) Compute the amount of additional liability, if any, that McGwire must record at the end of each year.

(b) Prepare the journal entries, if any, necessary to record a minimum liability for 2007 and 2008.

(LO 4, 5, 9, 10) **E20-12** **(Pension Expense, Journal Entries, Statement Presentation, Minimum Liability)** Griseta Company sponsors a defined benefit pension plan for its employees. The following data relate to the operation of the plan for the year 2007 in which no benefits were paid.

1. The actuarial present value of future benefits earned by employees for services rendered in 2007 amounted to $56,000.

2. The company's funding policy requires a contribution to the pension trustee amounting to $145,000 for 2007.

3. As of January 1, 2007, the company had a projected benefit obligation of $1,000,000, an accumulated benefit obligation of $800,000, and an unrecognized prior service cost of $400,000. The fair value of pension plan assets amounted to $600,000 at the beginning of the year. The actual and expected return on plan assets was $54,000. The settlement rate was 9%. No gains or losses occurred in 2007 and no benefits were paid.

4. Amortization of unrecognized prior service cost was $40,000 in 2007. Amortization of unrecognized net gain or loss was not required in 2007.

Instructions

(a) Determine the amounts of the components of pension expense that should be recognized by the company in 2007.

(b) Prepare the journal entry or entries to record pension expense and the employer's contribution to the pension trustee in 2007.

(c) Indicate the amounts that would be reported on the income statement and the balance sheet for the year 2007. The accumulated benefit obligation on December 31, 2007, was $830,000.

(LO 4, 6, 7, 8, 9, 10) **E20-13 (Pension Expense, Journal Entries, Minimum Liability, Statement Presentation)** Nellie Altom Company received the following selected information from its pension plan trustee concerning the operation of the company's defined benefit pension plan for the year ended December 31, 2007.

	January 1, 2007	December 31, 2007
Projected benefit obligation	$2,000,000	$2,077,000
Market-related and fair value of plan assets	800,000	1,130,000
Accumulated benefit obligation	1,600,000	1,720,000
Actuarial (gains) losses (Unrecognized net (gain) or loss)	–0–	(200,000)

The service cost component of pension expense for employee services rendered in the current year amounted to $77,000 and the amortization of unrecognized prior service cost was $115,000. The company's actual funding (contributions) of the plan in 2007 amounted to $250,000. The expected return on plan assets and the actual rate were both 10%; the interest/discount (settlement) rate was 10%. No prepaid/accrued pension cost existed on January 1, 2007. Assume no benefits paid in 2007.

Instructions

(a) Determine the amounts of the components of pension expense that should be recognized by the company in 2007.

(b) Prepare the journal entries to record pension expense and the employer's contribution to the pension plan in 2007.

(c) Indicate the pension-related amounts that would be reported on the income statement and the balance sheet for Nellie Altom Company for the year 2007. (Compute the minimum liability.)

(LO 4, 6, 7, 8, 9, 10) **E20-14 (Computation of Actual Return, Gains and Losses, Corridor Test, Prior Service Cost, Minimum Liability, Pension Expense, and Reconciliation)** Linda Berstler Company sponsors a defined benefit pension plan. The corporation's actuary provides the following information about the plan.

	January 1, 2008	December 31, 2008
Vested benefit obligation	$1,500	$1,900
Accumulated benefit obligation	1,900	2,730
Projected benefit obligation	2,800	3,645
Plan assets (fair value)	1,700	2,620
Settlement rate and expected rate of return		10%
Prepaid/(accrued) pension cost	–0–	?
Unrecognized prior service cost	1,100	?
Service cost for the year 2008		400
Contributions (funding in 2008)		800
Benefits paid in 2008		200

The average remaining service life per employee is 20 years.

Instructions

(a) Compute the actual return on the plan assets in 2008.

(b) Compute the amount of the unrecognized net gain or loss as of December 31, 2008. (Assume the January 1, 2008, balance was zero.)

(c) Compute the amount of unrecognized net gain or loss amortization for 2008 (corridor approach).

(d) Compute the amount of prior service cost amortization for 2008.

(e) Compute pension expense for 2008.

(f) Compute the minimum liability to be reported at December 31, 2008.

(g) Prepare a schedule reconciling the plan's funded status with the amounts reported in the December 31, 2008, balance sheet.

(LO 5) **E20-15 (Worksheet for E20-14)** Using the information in E20-14 about Linda Berstler Company's defined benefit pension plan, prepare a 2008 pension worksheet with supplementary schedules of computations. Prepare the journal entries at December 31, 2008, to record pension expense and any "additional liability." Also, prepare a schedule reconciling the plan's funded status with the pension amounts reported in the balance sheet.

(LO 4, 9) **E20-16** **(Pension Expense, Minimum Liability, Journal Entries)** Walker Company provides the following information related to its defined benefit pension plan for 2007.

Accrued pension cost balance (January 1)	$ 25,000
Accumulated benefit obligation (December 31)	400,000
Actual and expected return on plan assets	15,000
Additional pension liability balance (January 1)	10,000
Contributions (funding) in 2007	150,000
Fair value of plan assets (December 31)	350,000
Settlement rate	10%
Projected benefit obligation (January 1)	700,000
Service cost	90,000

Instructions
(a) Compute pension expense and prepare the journal entry to record pension expense and the employer's contribution to the pension plan in 2007.
(b) Prepare the journal entry to record the minimum liability for 2007.

(LO 4, 6, 9, 10) **E20-17** **(Pension Expense, Minimum Liability, Statement Presentation)** Blum Foods Company obtained the following information from the insurance company that administers the company's employee-defined benefit pension plan.

	For Year Ended December 31		
	2007	2008	2009
Plan assets (at fair value)	$280,000	$398,000	$586,000
Accumulated benefit obligation	378,000	512,000	576,000
Pension expense	95,000	128,000	130,000
Employer's funding contribution	110,000	150,000	125,000
Prior service cost not yet recognized in earnings	494,230	451,365	400,438

Prior to 2007 cumulative pension expense was equal to cumulative contributions. Assume that the market-related asset value is equal to the fair value of plan assets for all three years.

Instructions
(a) Prepare the journal entries to record pension expense, employer's funding contribution, and the adjustment to a minimum pension liability for the years 2007, 2008, and 2009. (Preparation of a pension worksheet is not a requirement of this exercise; insufficient information is given to prepare one.)
(b) Indicate the pension related amounts that would be reported on the company's income statement and balance sheet for 2007, 2008, and 2009.

(LO 9, 10) **E20-18** **(Minimum Liability, Journal Entries, Balance Sheet Items)** Presented below is partial information related to the pension fund of Rose Bryhan Inc.

Funded Status (end of year)	2007	2008	2009
Assets and obligations			
Plan assets (at fair value)	1,300,000	1,670,000	1,950,000
Accumulated benefit obligation	1,150,000	1,480,000	2,060,000
Projected benefit obligation	1,600,000	1,910,000	2,500,000
Unfunded accumulated benefits			110,000
Overfunded accumulated benefits	150,000	190,000	
Amounts to be recognized			
(Accrued)/prepaid pension cost at beginning of year	$ –0–	$ 19,000	$ 16,000
Pension expense	(250,000)	(268,000)	(300,000)
Contribution	269,000	265,000	277,000
(Accrued)/prepaid pension cost at end of year	$ 19,000	$ 16,000	$ (7,000)

The company's unrecognized prior service cost is $637,000 at the end of 2009.

Instructions
(a) What pension-related amounts are reported on the balance sheet of Rose Bryhan Inc. for 2007, 2008, and 2009?
(b) What are the journal entries made to record pension expense in 2007, 2008, and 2009?
(c) What journal entries (if any) are necessary to record a minimum liability for 2007, 2008, and 2009?

(LO 6, 7, 8, 9, 10) **E20-19** **(Reconciliation Schedule, Minimum Liability, and Unrecognized Loss)** Presented below is partial information related to Jean Burr Company at December 31, 2007.

Projected benefit obligation	930,000
Accumulated benefit obligation	865,000
Plan assets (at fair value)	700,000
Vested benefits	200,000
Prior service cost not yet recognized in pension expense	120,000
Gains and losses	–0–

Instructions

(a) Present the schedule reconciling the funded status with the asset/liability reported on the balance sheet. Assume no asset or liability existed at the beginning of period for pensions on Jean Burr Company's balance sheet.

(b) Assume the same facts as in (a) except that Jean Burr Company has an unrecognized loss of $16,000 during 2007.

(c) Explain the rationale for the treatment of the unrecognized loss and the prior service cost not yet recognized in pension expense.

(LO 8) **E20-20** **(Amortization of Unrecognized Net Gain or Loss [Corridor Approach], Pension Expense Computation)** The actuary for the pension plan of Joyce Bush Inc. calculated the following net gains and losses.

	Unrecognized Net Gain or Loss

Incurred during the Year	(Gain) or Loss
2007	$300,000
2008	480,000
2009	(210,000)
2010	(290,000)

Other information about the company's pension obligation and plan assets is as follows.

As of January 1,	Projected Benefit Obligation	Plan Assets (market-related asset value)
2007	$4,000,000	$2,400,000
2008	4,520,000	2,200,000
2009	4,980,000	2,600,000
2010	4,250,000	3,040,000

Joyce Bush Inc. has a stable labor force of 400 employees who are expected to receive benefits under the plan. The total service-years for all participating employees is 5,600. The beginning balance of unrecognized net gain or loss is zero on January 1, 2007. The market-related value and the fair value of plan assets are the same for the 4-year period. Use the average remaining service life per employee as the basis for amortization.

Instructions

(Round to the nearest dollar)

Prepare a schedule which reflects the minimum amount of unrecognized net gain or loss amortized as a component of net periodic pension expense for each of the years 2007, 2008, 2009, and 2010. Apply the "corridor" approach in determining the amount to be amortized each year.

(LO 8) **E20-21** **(Amortization of Unrecognized Net Gain or Loss [Corridor Approach])** Lowell Company sponsors a defined benefit pension plan for its 600 employees. The company's actuary provided the following information about the plan.

	January 1,	December 31,	
	2007	2007	2008
Projected benefit obligation	$2,800,000	$3,650,000	$4,400,000
Accumulated benefit obligation	1,900,000	2,430,000	2,900,000
Plan assets (fair value and market related asset value)	1,700,000	2,900,000	2,100,000
Unrecognized net (gain) or loss (for purposes of the corridor calculation)	–0–	101,000	(24,000)
Discount rate (current settlement rate)	11%	8%	
Actual and expected asset return rate	10%	10%	

The average remaining service life per employee is 10.5 years. The service cost component of net periodic pension expense for employee services rendered amounted to $400,000 in 2007 and $475,000 in 2008. The unrecognized prior service cost on January 1, 2007, was $1,155,000. No benefits have been paid.

Instructions

(Round to the nearest dollar)

(a) Compute the amount of unrecognized prior service cost to be amortized as a component of net periodic pension expense for each of the years 2007 and 2008.

(b) Prepare a schedule which reflects the amount of net unrecognized gain or loss to be amortized as a component of net periodic pension expense for 2007 and 2008.

(c) Determine the total amount of net periodic pension expense to be recognized by Lowell Company in 2007 and 2008.

(LO 11, 12) *E20-22 (Postretirement Benefit Expense Computation) Chance Inc. provides the following information related to its postretirement benefits for the year 2009.

Accumulated postretirement benefit obligation at January 1, 2009	$810,000
Actual and expected return on plan assets	34,000
Unrecognized prior service cost amortization	21,000
Discount rate	10%
Service cost	88,000

Instructions

Compute postretirement benefit expense for 2009.

(LO 11, 12) *E20-23 (Postretirement Benefit Expense Computation) Marvelous Marvin Co. provides the following information about its postretirement benefit plan for the year 2008.

Service cost	$ 90,000
Prior service cost amortization	3,000
Contribution to the plan	16,000
Actual and expected return on plan assets	62,000
Benefits paid	40,000
Plan assets at January 1, 2008	710,000
Accumulated postretirement benefit obligation at January 1, 2008	810,000
Unrecognized prior service cost balance at January 1, 2008	100,000
Discount rate	9%

Instructions

Compute the postretirement benefit expense for 2008.

(LO 11, 12) *E20-24 (Postretirement Benefit Worksheet) Using the information in *E20-23 prepare a worksheet inserting January 1, 2008, balances, showing December 31, 2008, balances, and the journal entry recording postretirement benefit expense.

(LO 11, 12) *E20-25 (Postretirement Benefit Reconciliation Schedule) Presented below is partial information related to Sandra Conley Co. at December 31, 2009.

Accumulated postretirement benefit obligation	$ 950,000
Expected postretirement benefit obligation	1,000,000
Plan assets (at fair value)	650,000
Prior service cost not yet recognized in postretirement expense	60,000
Gain and losses	–0–

Instructions

(a) Present the schedule reconciling the funded status with the asset/liability reported on the balance sheet. Assume no asset or liability existed at the beginning of the period for postretirement benefits on Sandra Conley Co.'s balance sheet.

(b) Assume the same facts as in (a) except that Sandra Conley Co. has an unrecognized loss of $20,000 during 2009.

PROBLEMS

(LO 5, 6, 7, 10) **P20-1 (2-Year Worksheet and Reconciliation Schedule)** On January 1, 2008, Diana Peter Company has the following defined benefit pension plan balances.

Projected benefit obligation	$4,200,000
Fair value of plan assets	4,200,000

The interest (settlement) rate applicable to the plan is 10%. On January 1, 2009, the company amends its pension agreement so that prior service costs of $500,000 are created. Other data related to the pension plan are as follows.

	2008	2009
Service costs	$150,000	$180,000
Unrecognized prior service costs amortization	–0–	90,000
Contributions (funding) to the plan	140,000	185,000
Benefits paid	200,000	280,000
Actual return on plan assets	252,000	260,000
Expected rate of return on assets	6%	8%

Instructions

(a) Prepare a pension worksheet for the pension plan for 2008 and 2009.

(b) As of December 31, 2009, prepare a schedule reconciling the funded status with the reported liability (accrued pension cost).

(LO 5, 6, 7, 10) **P20-2 (3-Year Worksheet, Journal Entries, and Reconciliation Schedules)** Katie Day Company adopts acceptable accounting for its defined benefit pension plan on January 1, 2008, with the following beginning balances: plan assets $200,000; projected benefit obligation $200,000. Other data relating to 3 years' operation of the plan are as follows.

	2008	2009	2010
Annual service cost	$16,000	$ 19,000	$ 26,000
Settlement rate and expected rate of return	10%	10%	10%
Actual return on plan assets	17,000	21,900	24,000
Annual funding (contributions)	16,000	40,000	48,000
Benefits paid	14,000	16,400	21,000
Unrecognized prior service cost (plan amended, 1/1/09)		160,000	
Amortization of unrecognized prior service cost		54,400	41,600
Change in actuarial assumptions establishes a December 31, 2010, projected benefit obligation of:			520,000

Instructions

(a) Prepare a pension worksheet presenting all 3 years' pension balances and activities.

(b) Prepare the journal entries (from the worksheet) to reflect all pension plan transactions and events at December 31 of each year.

(c) At December 31 of each year prepare a schedule reconciling the funded status of the plan with the pension amounts reported in the financial statements.

(LO 6, 7, 8, 9, 10) **P20-3 (Pension Expense, Journal Entries, Minimum Pension Liability, Amortization of Unrecognized Loss, Reconciliation Schedule)** Paul Dobson Company sponsors a defined benefit plan for its 100 employees. On January 1, 2007, the company's actuary provided the following information.

Unrecognized prior service cost	$150,000
Pension plan assets (fair value and market-related asset value)	200,000
Accumulated benefit obligation	260,000
Projected benefit obligation	350,000

The average remaining service period for the participating employees is 10.5 years. All employees are expected to receive benefits under the plan. On December 31, 2007, the actuary calculated that the present value of future benefits earned for employee services rendered in the current year amounted to $52,000; the projected benefit obligation was $452,000; fair value of pension assets was $276,000; the accumulated benefit obligation amounted to $365,000. The expected return on plan assets and the discount rate on the projected benefit obligation were both 10%. The actual return on plan assets is $11,000. The company's current year's contribution to the pension plan amounted to $65,000. No benefits were paid during the year.

Instructions

(Round to the nearest dollar)

(a) Determine the components of pension expense that the company would recognize in 2007. (With only one year involved, you need not prepare a worksheet.)

(b) Prepare the journal entry to record the pension expense and the company's funding of the pension plan in 2007.

(c) Assume Paul Dobson Company elects to recognize the minimum pension liability in its balance sheet for the year ended December 31, 2007. Prepare the journal entry to record the minimum liability.

(d) Compute the amount of the 2007 increase/decrease in unrecognized gains or losses and the amount to be amortized in 2007 and 2008.

(e) Prepare a schedule reconciling the funded status of the plan with the pension amounts reported in the financial statement as of December 31, 2007.

(LO 5, 6, 7, 8, 9, 10)

P20-4 (Pension Expense, Minimum Liability, Journal Entries for 2 Years) Mantle Company sponsors a defined benefit pension plan. The following information related to the pension plan is available for 2007 and 2008.

	2007	2008
Plan assets (fair value), December 31	$380,000	$465,000
Projected benefit obligation, January 1	600,000	700,000
Prepaid/(accrued) pension cost balance, January 1	(40,000)	?
Unrecognized prior service cost, January 1	250,000	240,000
Service cost	60,000	90,000
Actual and expected return on plan assets	24,000	30,000
Amortization of prior service cost	10,000	12,000
Contributions (funding)	110,000	120,000
Accumulated benefit obligation, December 31	500,000	550,000
Additional pension liability balance, January 1	50,000	?
Interest/settlement rate	9%	9%

Instructions

(a) Compute pension expense for 2007 and 2008.

(b) Prepare the journal entries to record the pension expense and the company's funding of the pension plan for both years.

(c) Compute the minimum liability for 2007 and 2008.

(d) Prepare the journal entries to record the minimum liability for both years.

(LO 7, 8, 9)

P20-5 (Computation of Pension Expense, Amortization of Unrecognized Net Gain or Loss [Corridor Approach], Journal Entries for 3 Years, and Minimum Pension Liability Computation) Dubel Toothpaste Company initiates a defined benefit pension plan for its 50 employees on January 1, 2007. The insurance company which administers the pension plan provided the following information for the years 2007, 2008, and 2009.

	For Year Ended December 31,		
	2007	2008	2009
Plan assets (fair value)	$50,000	$ 85,000	$170,000
Accumulated benefit obligation	45,000	165,000	292,000
Projected benefit obligation	55,000	200,000	324,000
Unrecognized net (gain) loss (for purposes of corridor calculation)	–0–	83,950	86,121
Employer's funding contribution (made at end of year)	50,000	60,000	95,000

There were no balances as of January 1, 2007, when the plan was initiated. The actual and expected return on plan assets was 10% over the 3-year period but the settlement rate used to discount the company's pension obligation was 13% in 2007, 11% in 2008, and 8% in 2009. The service cost component of net periodic pension expense amounted to the following: 2007, $55,000; 2008, $85,000; and 2009, $119,000. The average remaining service life per employee is 12 years. No benefits were paid in 2007, $30,000 of benefits were paid in 2008, and $18,500 of benefits were paid in 2009 (all benefits paid at end of year).

Instructions

(Round to the nearest dollar)

> **(a)** Calculate the amount of net periodic pension expense that the company would recognize in 2007, 2008, and 2009.
>
> **(b)** Prepare the journal entries to record net periodic pension expense, employer's funding contribution, and the adjustment to reflect a minimum pension liability for the years 2007, 2008, and 2009.

(LO 6, 7, 8) **P20-6 (Computation of Unrecognized Prior Service Cost Amortization, Pension Expense, Journal Entries, Net Gain or Loss, and Reconciliation Schedule)** Widjaja Inc. has sponsored a noncontributory-defined benefit pension plan for its employees since 1987. Prior to 2007, cumulative net pension expense recognized equaled cumulative contributions to the plan. Other relevant information about the pension plan on January 1, 2007, is as follows.

> 1. The company has 200 employees. All these employees are expected to receive benefits under the plan. The average remaining service life per employee is 13 years.
> 2. The projected benefit obligation amounted to $5,000,000 and the fair value of pension plan assets was $3,000,000. The market-related asset value was also $3,000,000. Unrecognized prior service cost was $2,000,000.

On December 31, 2007, the projected benefit obligation and the accumulated benefit obligation were $4,750,000 and $4,025,000, respectively. The fair value of the pension plan assets amounted to $3,900,000 at the end of the year. A 10% settlement rate and a 10% expected asset return rate were used in the actuarial present value computations in the pension plan. The present value of benefits attributed by the pension benefit formula to employee service in 2007 amounted to $200,000. The employer's contribution to the plan assets amounted to $575,000 in 2007. This problem assumes no payment of pension benefits.

Instructions

(Round all amounts to the nearest dollar)

> **(a)** Prepare a schedule, based on the average remaining life per employee, showing the unrecognized prior service cost that would be amortized as a component of pension expense for 2007, 2008, and 2009.
>
> **(b)** Compute pension expense for the year 2007.
>
> **(c)** Prepare the journal entries required to report the accounting for the company's pension plan for 2007.
>
> **(d)** Compute the amount of the 2007 increase/decrease in unrecognized net gains or losses and the amount to be amortized in 2007 and 2008.
>
> **(e)** Prepare a schedule reconciling the funded status of the plan with the pension amounts reported in the financial statements as of December 31, 2007.

(LO 5, 6, 7, 8, 9) **P20-7 (Pension Worksheet, Minimum Liability)** Farber Corp. sponsors a defined benefit pension plan for its employees. On January 1, 2009, the following balances related to this plan.

Plan assets (market-related value)	$520,000
Projected benefit obligation	725,000
Prepaid/accrued pension cost (credit)	33,000
Unrecognized prior service cost	81,000
Unrecognized net gain or loss (debit)	91,000

As a result of the operation of the plan during 2009, the actuary provided the following additional data at December 31, 2009.

Service cost for 2009	$108,000
Settlement rate, 9%; expected return rate, 10%	
Actual return on plan assets in 2009	48,000
Amortization of prior service cost	25,000
Contributions in 2009	138,000
Benefits paid retirees in 2009	85,000
Average remaining service life of active employees	10 years
Accumulated benefit obligation at 12/31/09	671,000

Instructions

Using the preceding data, compute pension expense for Farber Corp. for the year 2009 by preparing a pension worksheet that shows the journal entry for pension expense and any additional pension liability. (The minimum pension liability must be computed and the corridor approach must be applied to the unrecognized gain or loss.) Use the market-related asset value to compute the expected return and for corridor amortization.

(LO 5, 6, 7, 8 9, 10)

P20-8 **(Comprehensive 2-Year Worksheet)**   Glesen Company sponsors a defined benefit pension plan for its employees. The following data relate to the operation of the plan for the years 2008 and 2009.

	2008	2009
Projected benefit obligation, January 1	$650,000	
Plan assets (fair value and market related value), January 1	410,000	
Prepaid/accrued pension cost (credit), January 1	80,000	
Additional pension liability, January 1	12,300	
Intangible asset-deferred pension cost, January 1	12,300	
Unrecognized prior service cost, January 1	160,000	
Service cost	40,000	$ 59,000
Settlement rate	10%	10%
Expected rate of return	10%	10%
Actual return on plan assets	36,000	61,000
Amortization of prior service cost	70,000	55,000
Annual contributions	72,000	81,000
Benefits paid retirees	31,500	54,000
Increase in projected benefit obligation due to changes in actuarial assumptions	87,000	–0–
Accumulated benefit obligation at December 31	721,800	789,000
Average service life of all employees		20 years
Vested benefit obligation at December 31		464,000

Instructions

(a)   Prepare a pension worksheet presenting both years 2008 and 2009 and accompanying computations including the computation of the minimum liability (2008 and 2009) and amortization of the unrecognized loss (2009) using the corridor approach.

(b)   Prepare the journal entries (from the worksheet) to reflect all pension plan transactions and events at December 31 of each year.

(c)   At December 31, 2009, prepare a schedule reconciling the funded status of the pension plan with the pension amounts reported in the financial statements.

(LO 5, 6, 7, 9)

P20-9 **(Comprehensive 2-Year Worksheet)**   Mount Co. has the following defined benefit pension plan balances on January 1, 2006.

Projected benefit obligation	$4,500,000
Fair value of plan assets	4,500,000

The interest (settlement) rate applicable to the plan is 10%. On January 1, 2007, the company amends its pension agreement so that prior service costs of $600,000 are created. Other data related to the pension plan are:

	2006	2007
Service costs	$150,000	$170,000
Unrecognized prior service costs amortization	–0–	90,000
Contributions (funding) to the plan	150,000	184,658
Benefits paid	220,000	280,000
Actual return on plan assets	252,000	250,000
Expected rate of return on assets	6%	8%

Instructions

(a)   Prepare a pension worksheet for the pension plan in 2006.

(b)   Prepare any journal entries related to the pension plan that would be needed at December 31, 2006.

(c)   Prepare a pension worksheet for 2007 and any journal entries related to the pension plan as of December 31, 2007.

(d)   As of December 31, 2007, prepare a schedule reconciling the funded status with the reported liability (accrued pension cost).

(LO 11, 12,)

*P20-10 **(Postretirement Benefit Worksheet with Reconciliation)**   Dusty Hass Foods Inc. sponsors a postretirement medical and dental benefit plan for its employees. The company adopts the provisions of *Statement No. 106* beginning January 1, 2008. The following balances relate to this plan on January 1, 2008.

Plan assets	$ 200,000
Expected postretirement benefit obligation	820,000
Accumulated postretirement benefit obligation	200,000
No prior service costs exist.	

As a result of the plan's operation during 2008, the following additional data are provided by the actuary.

> Service cost for 2008 is $70,000
> Discount rate is 9%
> Contributions to plan in 2008 are $60,000
> Expected return on plan assets is $9,000
> Actual return on plan assets is $15,000
> Benefits paid to employees from plan are $44,000
> Average remaining service to full eligibility: 20 years

Instructions

(a) Using the preceding data, compute the net periodic postretirement benefit cost for 2008 by preparing a worksheet that shows the journal entry for postretirement expense and the year-end balances in the related postretirement benefit memo accounts. (Assume that contributions and benefits are paid at the end of the year.)

(b) At December 31, 2008, prepare a schedule reconciling the funded status of the plan with the postretirement amount reported on the balance sheet.

CONCEPTS FOR ANALYSIS

CA20-1 (Pension Terminology and Theory) Many business organizations have been concerned with providing for the retirement of employees since the late 1800s. During recent decades a marked increase in this concern has resulted in the establishment of private pension plans in most large companies and in many medium- and small-sized ones.

The substantial growth of these plans, both in numbers of employees covered and in amounts of retirement benefits, has increased the significance of pension cost in relation to the financial position, results of operations, and cash flows of many companies. In examining the costs of pension plans, a CPA encounters certain terms. The components of pension costs that the terms represent must be dealt with appropriately if generally accepted accounting principles are to be reflected in the financial statements of entities with pension plans.

Instructions

(a) Define a private pension plan. How does a contributory pension plan differ from a noncontributory plan?

(b) Differentiate between "accounting for the employer" and "accounting for the pension fund."

(c) Explain the terms "funded" and "pension liability" as they relate to:
   (1) The pension fund.
   (2) The employer.

(d) (1) Discuss the theoretical justification for accrual recognition of pension costs.
   (2) Discuss the relative objectivity of the measurement process of accrual versus cash (pay-as-you-go) accounting for annual pension costs.

(e) Distinguish among the following as they relate to pension plans.
   (1) Service cost.
   (2) Prior service costs.
   (3) Vested benefits.

CA20-2 (Pension Terminology) The following items appear on Hollingsworth Company's financial statements.

1. Under the caption Assets:
   Prepaid pension cost.
   Intangible asset—Deferred pension cost.
2. Under the caption Liabilities:
   Accrued pension cost.
3. Under the caption Stockholders' Equity:
   Excess of additional pension liability over unrecognized prior service cost as a component of Accumulated Other Comprehensive Income.
4. On the income statement:
   Pension expense.

Instructions

Explain the significance of each of the items above on corporate financial statements. (*Note:* All items set forth above are not necessarily to be found on the statements of a single company.)

CA20-3 **(Basic Terminology)** In examining the costs of pension plans, Leah Hutcherson, CPA, encounters certain terms. The components of pension costs that the terms represent must be dealt with appropriately if generally accepted accounting principles are to be reflected in the financial statements of entities with pension plans.

Instructions

    (a)   **(1)**   Discuss the theoretical justification for accrual recognition of pension costs.

          (2)   Discuss the relative objectivity of the measurement process of accrual versus cash (pay-as-you-go) accounting for annual pension costs.

    (b) Explain the following terms as they apply to accounting for pension plans.

          (1)   Market-related asset value.

          (2)   Projected benefit obligation.

          (3)   Corridor approach.

    (c) What information should be disclosed about a company's pension plans in its financial statements and its notes?

(AICPA adapted)

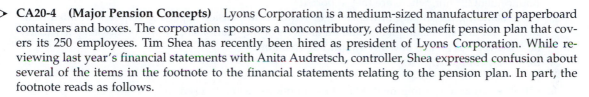 **CA20-4** **(Major Pension Concepts)** Lyons Corporation is a medium-sized manufacturer of paperboard containers and boxes. The corporation sponsors a noncontributory, defined benefit pension plan that covers its 250 employees. Tim Shea has recently been hired as president of Lyons Corporation. While reviewing last year's financial statements with Anita Audretsch, controller, Shea expressed confusion about several of the items in the footnote to the financial statements relating to the pension plan. In part, the footnote reads as follows.

> **Note J.** The company has a defined benefit pension plan covering substantially all of its employees. The benefits are based on years of service and the employee's compensation during the last four years of employment. The company's funding policy is to contribute annually the maximum amount allowed under the federal tax code. Contributions are intended to provide for benefits expected to be earned in the future as well as those earned to date.

Effective for the year ending December 31, 2007, Lyons Corporation adopted the provisions of *Statement of Financial Accounting Standard No. 87*—Employer's Accounting for Pensions. The net periodic pension expense on Lyons Corporation's comparative Income Statement was $72,000 in 2008 and $57,680 in 2007.

    The following are selected figures from the plan's funded status and amounts recognized in the Lyons Corporation's Statement of Financial Position at December 31, 2008 ($000 omitted).

Actuarial present value of benefit obligations:	
Accumulated benefit obligation	
(including vested benefits of $636)	$ (870)
Projected benefit obligation	$(1,200)
Plan assets at fair value	1,050
Projected benefit obligation in	
excess of plan assets	$ (150)

    Given that Lyons Corporation's work force has been stable for the last 6 years, Shea could not understand the increase in the net periodic pension expense. Audretsch explained that the net periodic pension expense consists of several elements, some of which may increase or decrease the net expense.

Instructions

    (a) The determination of the net periodic pension expense is a function of five elements. List and briefly describe each of the elements.

    (b) Describe the major difference and the major similarity between the accumulated benefit obligation and the projected benefit obligation.

    (c)   **(1)**   Explain why pension gains and losses are not recognized on the income statement in the period in which they arise.

          (2)   Briefly describe how pension gains and losses are recognized.

    (d) Under what conditions must Lyons recognize an additional minimum liability?

(CMA adapted)

CA20-5 **(Implications of *FASB Statement No. 87*)** Ruth Moore and Carl Nies have to do a class presentation on the pension pronouncement "Employers' Accounting for Pension Plans." In developing the class presentation, they decided to provide the class with a series of questions related to pensions and then discuss the answers in class. Given that the class has all read *FASB Statement No. 87*, they felt this approach would provide a lively discussion. Here are the situations:

1. In an article in *Business Week* prior to *FASB No. 87*, it was reported that the discount rates used by the largest 200 companies for pension reporting ranged from 5% to 11%. How can such a situation exist, and does the pension pronouncement alleviate this problem?

2. An article indicated that when *FASB Statement No. 87* was issued, it caused an increase in the liability for pensions for approximately 20% of companies. Why might this situation occur?

3. A recent article noted that while "smoothing" is not necessarily an accounting virtue, pension accounting has long been recognized as an exception—an area of accounting in which at least some dampening of market swings is appropriate. This is because pension funds are managed so that their performance is insulated from the extremes of short-term market swings. A pension expense that reflects the volatility of market swings might, for that reason, convey information of little relevance. Are these statements true?

4. Companies as diverse as **American Hospital Supply**, **Ashland Oil**, **Digital Equipment**, **GTE**, **Ralston Purina**, and **Signal Cos.** held assets twice as large as they needed to fund their pension plans at one time. Are these assets reported on the balance sheet of these companies per the pension pronouncement? If not, where are they reported?

5. Understanding the impact of the changes required in pension reporting requires detailed information about its pension plan(s) and an analysis of the relationship of many factors, particularly:
   (a) the type of plan(s) and any significant amendments.
   (b) the plan participants.
   (c) the funding status.
   (d) the actuarial funding method and assumptions currently used.
   What impact does each of these items have on financial statement presentation?

6. An article noted "You also need to decide whether to amortize gains and losses using the corridor method, or to use some other systematic method. Under the corridor approach, only gains and losses in excess of 10% of the greater of the projected benefit obligation or the plan assets would have to be amortized." What is the corridor method and what is its purpose?

7. Some companies may have to establish an intangible asset-deferred pension cost if the plan assets at fair value are less than the accumulated benefit obligation. What is the nature of this intangible asset and how is it amortized each period?

Instructions
What answers do you believe Ruth and Carl gave to each of these questions?

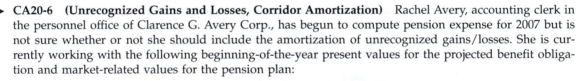 **CA20-6 (Unrecognized Gains and Losses, Corridor Amortization)**   Rachel Avery, accounting clerk in the personnel office of Clarence G. Avery Corp., has begun to compute pension expense for 2007 but is not sure whether or not she should include the amortization of unrecognized gains/losses. She is currently working with the following beginning-of-the-year present values for the projected benefit obligation and market-related values for the pension plan:

	Projected Benefit Obligation	Plan Assets Value
2004	$2,200,000	$1,900,000
2005	2,400,000	2,600,000
2006	2,900,000	2,600,000
2007	3,900,000	3,000,000

The average remaining service life per employee in 2004 and 2005 is 10 years and in 2006 and 2007 is 12 years. The unrecognized net gain or loss that occurred during each year is as follows.

2004	$280,000 loss
2005	90,000 loss
2006	12,000 loss
2007	25,000 gain

(In working the solution, you must aggregate the unrecognized gains and losses to arrive at year-end balances.)

Instructions
You are the manager in charge of accounting. Write a memo to Rachel Avery, explaining why in some years she must amortize some of the unrecognized net gains and losses and in other years she does not need to. In order to explain this situation fully, you must compute the amount of unrecognized net gain or loss that is amortized and charged to pension expense in each of the 4 years listed above. Include an appropriate amortization schedule, referring to it whenever necessary.

CA20-7 **(Nonvested Employees—An Ethical Dilemma)** Cardinal Technology recently merged with College Electronix, a computer graphics manufacturing firm. In performing a comprehensive audit of CE's accounting system, Richard Nye, internal audit manager for Cardinal Technology, discovered that the new subsidiary did not capitalize pension assets and liabilities, subject to the requirements of *FASB Statement No. 87*.

The net present value of CE's pension assets was $15.5 million, the vested benefit obligation was $12.9 million, and the projected benefit obligation was $17.4 million. Nye reported this audit finding to Renée Selma, the newly appointed controller of CE. A few days later Selma called Nye for his advice on what to do. Selma started her conversation by asking, "Can't we eliminate the negative income effect of our pension dilemma simply by terminating the employment of nonvested employees before the end of our fiscal year?"

Instructions
How should Nye respond to Selma's remark about firing nonvested employees?

USING YOUR JUDGMENT

Financial Reporting Problem

The Procter & Gamble Company (P&G)

The financial statements of **P&G** are presented in Appendix 5B or can be accessed on the KWW website.

Instructions
Refer to P&G's financial statements and the accompanying notes to answer the following questions.

(a) What kind of pension plan does P&G provide its employees in the United States?

(b) What was P&G's pension expense for 2004, 2003, and 2002 for the United States?

(c) What is the impact of P&G's pension plans for 2004 on its financial statements?

(d) What information does P&G provide on the target allocation of its pension assets? (Compare the asset allocation for "Pensions and Other Retiree Benefits.") How do the allocations relate to the expected returns on these assets?

*Financial Statement Analysis Case

General Electric

A *Wall Street Journal* article discussed a $1.8 billion charge to income made by **General Electric** for postretirement benefit costs. It was attributed to previously unrecognized health-care and life insurance cost. As financial vice president and controller for Peake, Inc., you found this article interesting because the president recently expressed interest in adopting a postemployment benefit program for Peake's employees, to complement the company's existing defined-benefit plan. The president, Martha Beyerlein, wants to know how the expense on the new plan will be determined and what impact the accounting for the plan will have on Peake's financial statements.

Instructions

(a) As financial vice president and controller of Peake, Inc., explain the calculation of postemployment benefit expense under *SFAS No. 106* and indicate how the accounting for the plan will affect Peake's financial statements.

(b) Discuss the similarities and differences in the accounting for the other postemployment benefit plan relative to the accounting for the defined-benefit plan.

Comparative Analysis Case

The Coca-Cola Company versus PepsiCo, Inc.
Instructions
Go to the KWW website and use information found there to answer the following questions related to **The Coca-Cola Company** and **PepsiCo, Inc.**

(a) What kind of pension plans do Coca-Cola and PepsiCo provide their employees?

(b) What net periodic pension expense (cost) did Coca-Cola and PepsiCo report in 2004?

(c) What is the year-end 2004 funded status of Coca-Cola's and PepsiCo's U.S. plans?

(d) What relevant rates were used by Coca-Cola and PepsiCo in computing their pension amounts?

(e) Compare the expected benefit payments and contributions for Coca-Cola and PepsiCo.

International Reporting Case

Kyowa Hakko Kogyo Co., Ltd., is an R&D–based company with special strengths in biotechnology. The company is dedicated to the creation of new value in the life sciences, especially in its two core business segments of pharmaceuticals and biochemicals, and strives to contribute to the health and well-being of people around the world. The company provided the following disclosures related to its retirement benefits in its 2005 annual report.

Kyowa Hakko Kogyo Co., Ltd.

Note 1. Basis of Presenting Consolidated Financial Statements (partial)

Kyowa Hakko Kogyo Co., Ltd. (the "Company") maintains its accounts and records in accordance with the provisions set forth in the Japanese Commercial Code and the Securities and Exchange Law and in conformity with generally accepted accounting principles and practices prevailing in Japan. . . . The Company's fiscal year is from April 1 to March 31. Therefore, "fiscal 2005" begins on April 1, 2004 and ends on March 31, 2005.

Reserve for Retirement Benefits to Employees

A reserve for retirement benefits to employees is provided at an amount equal to the present value of the projected benefit obligation less fair value of the plan assets at the year-end. Unrecognized prior service costs are amortized on a straight-line basis over five years from the year they occur. Unrecognized actuarial differences are amortized on a straight-line basis over ten years from the year after they occur.

Note 8. Reserve for Retirement Benefits to Employees

The Company and its domestic consolidated subsidiaries operate various defined benefit plans, including a corporate pension plan (the so-called cash-balanced plan), a group contributory plan, a tax-qualified pension plan and a severance payment plan.

(a) The reserve for retirement benefits as of March 31, 2005, is analyzed as follows.

	Millions of Yen 2005	Thousands of U.S. Dollars 2005
Projected benefit obligations	¥(63,854)	$(594,599)
Plan assets	31,270	291,182
Unfunded benefit obligations	(32,584)	(303,417)
Unrecognized actuarial differences	7,017	65,341
Unrecognized prior service costs (Note 2)	(5,004)	(46,597)
	¥(30,571)	$(284,673)

(b) The net periodic pension expense related to the retirement benefits for fiscal 2005 is as follows.

	Millions of Yen 2005	Thousands of U.S. Dollars 2005
Service cost	¥2,650	$24,676
Interest cost	1,583	14,741
Expected return on plan assets	(736)	(6, 854)
Amortization of unrecognized actuarial differences	1,628	15,160
Amortization of unrecognized prior service costs	(1,431)	(13,325)
	¥3,694	$34,398

(c) Assumptions used in calculation of the above information are as follows.

	2005
Discount rate	2.5%
Expected rate of return	2.8%

Instructions

Use the information on Kyowa to respond to the following requirements.

(a) What are the key differences in accounting for pensions under U.S. and Japanese standards?

(b) Briefly explain how differences in U.S. and Japanese standards for pensions would affect the amounts reported in the financial statements.

(c) In light of the differences identified above, would Kyowa's income and equity be higher or lower under U.S. GAAP compared to Japanese standards? Explain.

Research Cases

Case 1

Instructions

Examine the pension footnotes of three companies of your choice and answer the following questions.

(a) For each company, identify the following three assumptions: (1) the weighted-average discount rate, (2) the rate of compensation increase used to measure the projected benefit obligation, and (3) the weighted-average expected long-run rate of return on plan assets.

(b) Comment on any significant differences between the assumptions used by each company.

(c) Did any of the companies change their assumptions during the period covered by the footnote? If so, what was the effect on the financial statements?

Case 2

The June 15, 1999, *Wall Street Journal* included an article by Ellen E. Schultz entitled "Companies Reap a Gain off Fat Pension Plans."

Instructions

Read the article and answer the following questions.

(a) Explain how the high investment returns earned on pension plan assets in the late 1990s affected pension expense and net income. Given the down or "bear" market, what do you believe might happen to many companies' pension expense in the future?

(b) Explain what effect an overfunded pension plan can have on decisions made by management regarding various benefit costs.

(c) What is a major disadvantage of getting a pension plan too overfunded?

(d) What ethical issues are raised at the end of this article?

Professional Research: Financial Accounting and Reporting

Jack Kelly Company has grown rapidly since its founding in 2002. To instill loyalty in its employees, Kelly is contemplating establishment of a defined-benefit plan. Kelly knows that lenders and potential investors will pay close attention to the impact of the pension plan on the company's financial statements, particularly any gains or losses that develop in the plan. Kelly has asked you to conduct some research on the accounting for gains and losses in a defined-benefit plan.

Instructions

Using the **Financial Accounting Research System (FARS)**, respond to the following items. (Provide text strings used in your search.)

(a) Briefly describe how pension gains and losses are accounted for.

(b) Explain the rationale behind the accounting method described in part (a).

(c) What is the related pension asset or liability that may show up on the balance sheet? When will each of these situations occur?

(d) Kelly wants to better understand the factors that led to accounting standards for pensions. What environmental factors led to increased regulations over pension cost reporting?

Professional Simulation

In this simulation you are asked to address questions related to the accounting for pensions. Prepare responses to all parts.

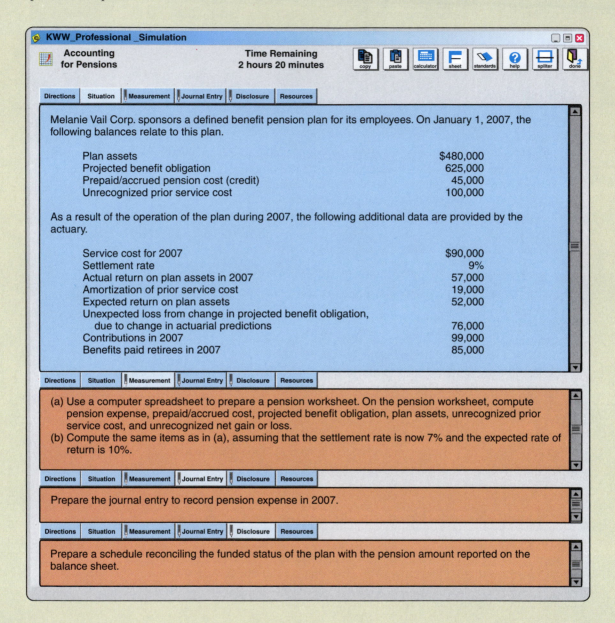

KWW_Professional _Simulation

Accounting for Pensions

Time Remaining 2 hours 20 minutes

copy   paste   calculator   sheet   standards   help   splitter   done

| Directions | Situation | Measurement | Journal Entry | Disclosure | Resources |

Melanie Vail Corp. sponsors a defined benefit pension plan for its employees. On January 1, 2007, the following balances relate to this plan.

Plan assets	$480,000
Projected benefit obligation	625,000
Prepaid/accrued pension cost (credit)	45,000
Unrecognized prior service cost	100,000

As a result of the operation of the plan during 2007, the following additional data are provided by the actuary.

Service cost for 2007	$90,000
Settlement rate	9%
Actual return on plan assets in 2007	57,000
Amortization of prior service cost	19,000
Expected return on plan assets	52,000
Unexpected loss from change in projected benefit obligation, due to change in actuarial predictions	76,000
Contributions in 2007	99,000
Benefits paid retirees in 2007	85,000

| Directions | Situation | Measurement | Journal Entry | Disclosure | Resources |

(a) Use a computer spreadsheet to prepare a pension worksheet. On the pension worksheet, compute pension expense, prepaid/accrued cost, projected benefit obligation, plan assets, unrecognized prior service cost, and unrecognized net gain or loss.
(b) Compute the same items as in (a), assuming that the settlement rate is now 7% and the expected rate of return is 10%.

| Directions | Situation | Measurement | Journal Entry | Disclosure | Resources |

Prepare the journal entry to record pension expense in 2007.

| Directions | Situation | Measurement | Journal Entry | Disclosure | Resources |

Prepare a schedule reconciling the funded status of the plan with the pension amount reported on the balance sheet.

Remember to check the book's companion website to find additional resources for this chapter.

www.wiley.com/college/kieso

ACCOUNTING FOR LEASES

More Companies Ask, "Why Buy?"

Leasing has grown tremendously in popularity. Today it is the fastest growing form of capital investment. Instead of borrowing money to buy an airplane, computer, nuclear core, or satellite, a company makes periodic payments to lease these assets. Even gambling casinos lease their slot machines. Of the 600 companies surveyed by the AICPA in 2004, 575 disclosed lease data.[1]

A classic example is the airline industry. Many travelers on airlines such as **United**, **Delta**, and **Southwest** believe these airlines own the planes on which they are flying. Often, this is not the case. Here are the lease percentages for the major U.S. airlines.

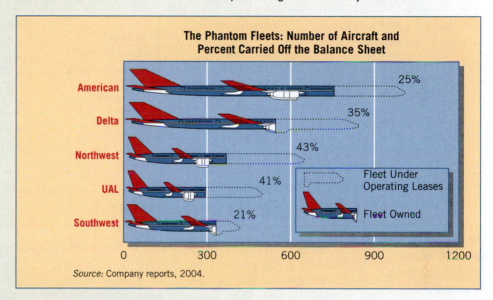

The Phantom Fleets: Number of Aircraft and Percent Carried Off the Balance Sheet

American — 25%
Delta — 35%
Northwest — 43%
UAL — 41%
Southwest — 21%

Fleet Under Operating Leases
Fleet Owned

0   300   600   900   1200

Source: Company reports, 2004.

As you will learn, airlines lease many of their airplanes due to the favorable accounting treatment they receive if they lease rather than purchase.

---

[1]AICPA, *Accounting Trends and Techniques—2004.* Eight out of 10 U.S. companies lease all or some of their equipment. Companies that lease tend to be smaller, are high growth, and are in technology-oriented industries (see *www.techlease.com*).

Learning Objectives

After studying this chapter, you should be able to:

1 Explain the nature, economic substance, and advantages of lease transactions.

2 Describe the accounting criteria and procedures for capitalizing leases by the lessee.

3 Contrast the operating and capitalization methods of recording leases.

4 Identify the classifications of leases for the lessor.

5 Describe the lessor's accounting for direct-financing leases.

6 Identify special features of lease arrangements that cause unique accounting problems.

7 Describe the effect of residual values, guaranteed and unguaranteed, on lease accounting.

8 Describe the lessor's accounting for sales-type leases.

9 List the disclosure requirements for leases.

Our opening story indicates the increased significance and prevalence of lease arrangements. As a result, the need for uniform accounting and informative reporting of these transactions has intensified. In this chapter we look at the accounting issues related to leasing. The content and organization of this chapter are as follows.

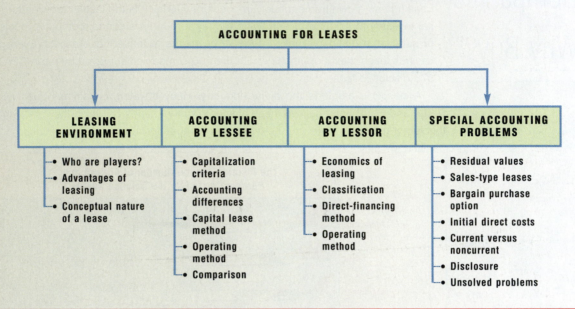

THE LEASING ENVIRONMENT

OBJECTIVE 1
Explain the nature, economic substance, and advantages of lease transactions.

Aristotle once said, "Wealth does not lie in ownership but in the use of things"! Clearly, many U.S. companies have decided that Aristotle is right, as they have become heavily involved in leasing assets rather than owning them. For example, Illustration 21-1 shows the growth in leasing transactions from 1990 to 2003.

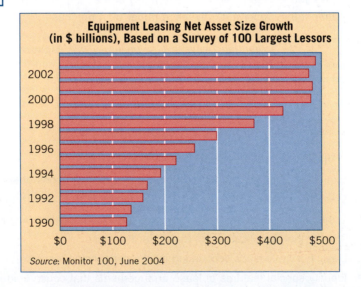

ILLUSTRATION 21-1
Equipment Leasing Growth

What types of assets are being leased? As the opening story indicated, any type of equipment can be leased, such as railcars, helicopters, bulldozers, barges, CT scanners, computers, and so on. The largest group of leased equipment involves information technology equipment, followed by assets in the transportation area (trucks, aircraft, rail), and then construction and agriculture.

Who Are the Players?

A **lease** is a contractual agreement between a lessor and a lessee. This arrangement gives the **lessee** the right to use specific property, owned by the **lessor**, for a specified period of time. In return for the use of the property, the lessee makes rental payments over the lease term to the lessor.

Who are the lessors that own this property? They generally fall into one of three categories:

1 Banks.
2 Captive leasing companies.
3 Independents.

Banks

Banks are the largest players in the leasing business. They have low-cost funds, which give them the advantage of being able to purchase assets at less cost than their competitors. Banks also have been more aggressive in the leasing markets. They have decided that there is money to be made in leasing, and as a result they have expanded their product lines in this area. Finally, leasing transactions are now more standardized, which gives banks an advantage because they do not have to be as innovative in structuring lease arrangements. Thus banks like **Wells Fargo**, **Chase**, **Citigroup**, and **PNC** have substantial leasing subsidiaries.

Captive Leasing Companies

Captive leasing companies are subsidiaries whose primary business is to perform leasing operations for the parent company. Companies like **Caterpillar Financial Services Corp.** (for Caterpillar), **Chrysler Financial** (for Daimler-Chrysler), and **IBM Global Financing** (for IBM) facilitate the sale of products to consumers. For example, suppose that **Sterling Construction Co.** wants to acquire a number of earthmovers from Caterpillar. In this case, Caterpillar Financial Services Corp. will offer to structure the transaction as a lease rather than as a purchase. Thus, Caterpillar Financial provides the financing rather than an outside financial institution.

Captive leasing companies have the point-of-sale advantage in finding leasing customers. That is, as soon as Caterpillar receives a possible order, its leasing subsidiary can quickly develop a lease-financing arrangement. Furthermore, the captive lessor has product knowledge that gives it an advantage when financing the parents' product.

The current trend is for captives to focus primarily on their company's products rather than do general lease financing. For example, **Boeing Capital** and **UPS Capital** are two captives that have left the general finance business to focus exclusively on their parent companies' products.

Independents

Independents are the final category of lessors. Independents have not done well over the last few years. Their market share has dropped fairly dramatically as banks and captive leasing companies have become more aggressive in the lease-financing area. Independents do not have point-of-sale access, nor do they have a low cost of funds advantage. What they *are* often good at is developing innovative contracts for lessees. In addition, they are starting to act as captive finance companies for some companies that do not have a leasing subsidiary.

Illustration 21-2 (page 1090) shows the new business volume by lessor type in a recent five-year period. As the chart shows, both banks and captives have increased business at the expense of the independents.

Advantages of Leasing

The growth in leasing indicates that it often has some genuine advantages over owning property, such as:

ILLUSTRATION 21-2
Lessor Types

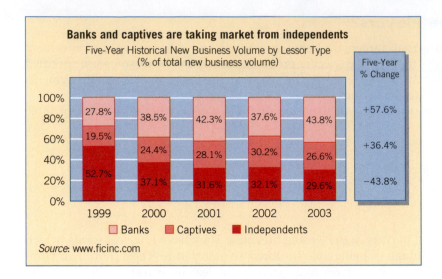

Banks and captives are taking market from independents

Five-Year Historical New Business Volume by Lessor Type
(% of total new business volume)

Year	Banks	Captives	Independents
1999	27.8%	19.5%	52.7%
2000	38.5%	24.4%	37.1%
2001	42.3%	28.1%	31.6%
2002	37.6%	30.2%	32.1%
2003	43.8%	26.6%	29.6%

Five-Year % Change

+57.6%

+36.4%

−43.8%

☐ Banks ☐ Captives ■ Independents

Source: www.ficinc.com

1 *100% Financing at Fixed Rates.* Leases are often signed without requiring any money down from the lessee. This helps the lessee conserve scarce cash—an especially desirable feature for new and developing companies. In addition, lease payments often remain fixed, which protects the lessee against inflation and increases in the cost of money. The following comment explains why companies choose a lease instead of a conventional loan: "Our local bank finally came up to 80 percent of the purchase price but wouldn't go any higher, and they wanted a floating interest rate. We just couldn't afford the down payment, and we needed to lock in a final payment rate we knew we could live with."

2 *Protection Against Obsolescence.* Leasing equipment reduces risk of obsolescence to the lessee, and in many cases passes the risk of residual value to the lessor. For example, **Merck** (a pharmaceutical maker) leases computers. Under the lease agreement, Merck may turn in an old computer for a new model at any time, canceling the old lease and writing a new one. The lessor adds the cost of the new lease to the balance due on the old lease, less the old computer's trade-in value. As one treasurer remarked, "Our instinct is to purchase." But if a new computer is likely to come along in a short time, "then leasing is just a heck of a lot more convenient than purchasing."

3 *Flexibility.* Lease agreements may contain less restrictive provisions than other debt agreements. Innovative lessors can tailor a lease agreement to the lessee's special needs. For instance, the duration of the lease—**the lease term**— may be anything from a short period of time to the entire expected economic life of the asset. The rental payments may be level from year to year, or they may increase or decrease in amount. The payment amount may be predetermined or may vary with sales, the prime interest rate, the Consumer Price Index, or some other factor. In most cases the rent is set to enable the lessor to recover the cost of the asset plus a fair return over the life of the lease.

4 *Less Costly Financing.* Some companies find leasing cheaper than other forms of financing. For example, start-up companies in depressed industries or companies in low tax brackets may lease to claim tax benefits that they might otherwise lose. Depreciation deductions offer no benefit to companies that have little if any taxable income. Through leasing, the leasing companies or financial institutions use these tax benefits. They can then pass some of these tax benefits back to the user of the asset in the form of lower rental payments.

5 *Tax Advantages.* In some cases, companies can "have their cake and eat it too" with tax advantages that leases offer. That is, for financial reporting purposes companies do not report an asset or a liability for the lease arrangement. For tax purposes, however, companies can capitalize and depreciate the leased asset. As a result, a

INTERNATIONAL INSIGHT

Some companies "double dip" on the international level too. The leasing rules of the lessor's and lessee's countries may differ, permitting both parties to own the asset. Thus, both lessor and lessee receive the tax benefits related to depreciation.

company takes deductions earlier rather than later and also reduces its taxes. A common vehicle for this type of transaction is a "synthetic lease" arrangement. (On page 1101 we discuss a synthetic lease used by **Krispy Kreme**.)

6 *Off-Balance-Sheet Financing.* Certain leases do not add debt on a balance sheet or affect financial ratios. In fact, they may add to borrowing capacity.[2] Such **off-balance-sheet financing** is critical to some companies.

OFF-BALANCE-SHEET FINANCING

As shown in our opening story, airlines use lease arrangements extensively. This results in a great deal of off-balance-sheet financing. The following chart indicates that many airlines that lease aircraft understate debt levels by a substantial amount.

WHAT DO THE NUMBERS MEAN?

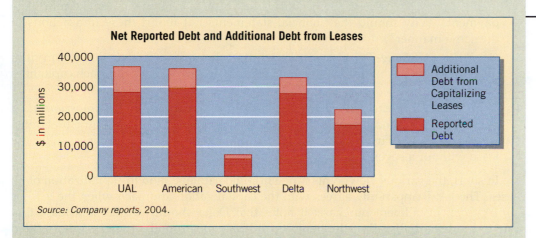

Net Reported Debt and Additional Debt from Leases

Legend: Additional Debt from Capitalizing Leases; Reported Debt

Source: Company reports, 2004.

And airlines are not the only ones playing the off-balance-sheet game. A recent SEC study estimates that for SEC registrants, off-balance-sheet lease obligations total more the $1.3 trillion, or 31 times the amount of on-balance-sheet obligations. (See SEC Off-Balance Sheet report at *www.sec.gov/news/studies/soxoffbalancerpt.pdf.*) Thus, analysts must adjust reported debt levels for the effects of non-capitalized leases. A methodology for making this adjustment is discussed in Eugene A. Imhoff, Jr., Robert C. Lipe, and David W. Wright, "Operating Leases: Impact of Constructive Capitalization," *Accounting Horizons* (March 1991).

Conceptual Nature of a Lease

If **Delta** borrows $47 million on a 10-year note from **Bank of America** to purchase a Boeing 737 jet plane, Delta should clearly report an asset and related liability at that amount on its balance sheet. Similarly, if Delta purchases the 737 for $47 million directly from Boeing through an installment purchase over 10 years, it should obviously report an asset and related liability (i.e., it should "capitalize" the installment transaction).

However, what if Delta **leases** the Boeing 737 for 10 years from **International Lease Finance Corp. (ILFC)**—the world's largest lessor of airplanes—through a noncancelable lease transaction with payments of the same amount as the installment purchase

---

[2]As demonstrated later in this chapter, certain types of lease arrangements are not capitalized on the balance sheet. The liabilities section is thereby relieved of large future lease commitments that, if recorded, would adversely affect the debt to equity ratio. The reluctance to record lease obligations as liabilities is one of the primary reasons some companies resist capitalized lease accounting.

transaction? In that case, opinion differs over how to report this transaction. The various views on **capitalization of leases** are as follows.

1 *Do Not Capitalize Any Leased Assets.* This view considers capitalization inappropriate, because Delta does not own the property. Furthermore, a lease is an **"executory" contract** requiring continuing performance by both parties. Because companies do not currently capitalize other executory contracts (such as purchase commitments and employment contracts), they should not capitalize leases either.

2 *Capitalize Leases That Are Similar to Installment Purchases.* This view holds that companies should report transactions in accordance with their economic substance. Therefore, if companies capitalize installment purchases, they should also capitalize leases that have similar characteristics. For example, Delta Airlines makes the same payments over a 10-year period for either a lease or an installment purchase. Lessees make rental payments, whereas owners make mortgage payments. Why should the financial statements not report these transactions in the same manner?

3 *Capitalize All Long-Term Leases.* This approach requires only the long-term right to use the property in order to capitalize. This property-rights approach capitalizes all long-term leases.[3]

4 *Capitalize Firm Leases Where the Penalty for Nonperformance Is Substantial.* A final approach advocates capitalizing only "firm" (noncancelable) contractual rights and obligations. "Firm" means that it is unlikely to avoid performance under the lease without a severe penalty.[4]

In short, the various viewpoints range from no capitalization to capitalization of all leases. The FASB apparently agrees with the capitalization approach when the lease is similar to an installment purchase: It notes that Delta **should capitalize a lease that transfers substantially all of the benefits and risks of property ownership**, **provided the lease is noncancelable**. **Noncancelable** means that Delta can cancel the lease contract only upon the outcome of some remote contingency, or that the cancellation provisions and penalties of the contract are so costly to Delta that cancellation probably will not occur.

This viewpoint leads to three basic conclusions: (1) Companies must identify the characteristics that indicate the transfer of substantially all of the benefits and risks of ownership. (2) The same characteristics should apply consistently to the lessee and the lessor. (3) Those leases that do **not** transfer substantially all the benefits and risks of ownership are operating leases. Companies should not capitalize operating leases. Instead, companies should account for them as rental payments and receipts.

ACCOUNTING BY THE LESSEE

OBJECTIVE 2
Describe the accounting criteria and procedures for capitalizing leases by the lessee.

If Delta Airlines (the lessee) **capitalizes** a lease, it records an asset and a liability generally equal to the present value of the rental payments. ILFC (the lessor), having transferred substantially all the benefits and risks of ownership, recognizes a sale by removing the asset from the balance sheet and replacing it with a receivable. The typical journal entries

---

[3]The property rights approach was originally recommended in a research study by the AICPA: John H. Myers, "Reporting of Leases in Financial Statements," *Accounting Research Study No. 4* (New York: AICPA, 1964), pp. 10–11. Recently, this view has received additional support. See Peter H. Knutson, "Financial Reporting in the 1990s and Beyond," Position Paper (Charlottesville, Va.: AIMR, 1993), and Warren McGregor, "Accounting for Leases: A New Approach," Special Report (Norwalk, Conn.: FASB, 1996).

[4]Yuji Ijiri, *Recognition of Contractual Rights and Obligations,* Research Report (Stamford, Conn.: FASB, 1980).

for Delta and ILFC, assuming leased and capitalized equipment, appear as shown in Illustration 21-3.

ILLUSTRATION 21-3
Journal Entries for
Capitalized Lease

Delta (Lessee)			ILFC (Lessor)		
Leased Equipment	XXX		Lease Receivable	XXX	
Lease Liability		XXX	Equipment		XXX

Having capitalized the asset, Delta records depreciation on the leased asset. Both ILFC and Delta treat the lease rental payments as consisting of interest and principal.

If Delta does not capitalize the lease, it does not record an asset, nor does ILFC remove one from its books. When Delta makes a lease payment, it records rental expense; ILFC recognizes rental revenue.

In order to record a lease as a **capital lease**, the lease must be noncancelable. Further, it must meet one or more of the four criteria listed in Illustration 21-4.

ILLUSTRATION 21-4
Capitalization Criteria
for Lessee

Capitalization Criteria (Lessee)

- The lease transfers ownership of the property to the lessee.
- The lease contains a bargain purchase option.[5]
- The lease term is equal to 75 percent or more of the estimated economic life of the leased property.
- The present value of the minimum lease payments (excluding executory costs) equals or exceeds 90 percent of the fair value of the leased property.[6]

Delta classifies and accounts for leases that **do not meet any of the four criteria** as **operating leases**. Illustration 21-5 shows that a lease meeting any one of the four criteria results in the lessee having a capital lease.

ILLUSTRATION 21-5
Diagram of Lessee's
Criteria for Lease
Classification

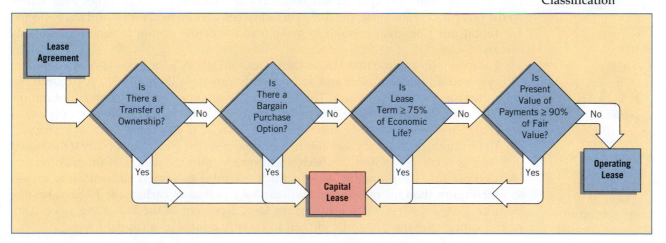

In keeping with the FASB's reasoning that a company consumes a significant portion of the value of the asset in the first 75 percent of its life, the lessee applies neither the third nor the fourth criterion when the inception of the lease occurs during the last 25 percent of the asset's life.

[5]We define a bargain purchase option in the next section.

[6]"Accounting for Leases," *FASB Statement No. 13* as amended and interpreted through May 1980 (Stamford, Conn.: FASB, 1980), par. 7.

Capitalization Criteria

Three of the four **capitalization criteria** that apply to lessees are controversial and can be difficult to apply in practice. We discuss each of the criteria in detail on the following pages.

Transfer of Ownership Test

If the lease transfers ownership of the asset to the lessee, it is a capital lease. This criterion is not controversial and easily implemented in practice.

Bargain Purchase Option Test

A **bargain purchase option** allows the lessee to purchase the leased property for a price that is **significantly lower** than the property's expected fair value at the date the option becomes exercisable. At the inception of the lease, the difference between the option price and the expected fair market value must be large enough to make exercise of the option reasonably assured.

For example, assume that Brett's Delivery Service was to lease a Honda Accord for $599 per month for 40 months, with an option to purchase for $100 at the end of the 40-month period. If the estimated fair value of the Honda Accord is $3,000 at the end of the 40 months, the $100 option to purchase is clearly a bargain. Therefore, Brett must capitalize the lease. In other cases, the criterion may not be as easy to apply, and determining *now* that a certain *future* price is a bargain can be difficult.

Economic Life Test (75% Test)

If the lease period equals or exceeds 75 percent of the asset's economic life, the lessor transfers most of the risks and rewards of ownership to the lessee. Capitalization is therefore appropriate. However, determining the lease term and the economic life of the asset can be troublesome.

The **lease term** is generally considered to be the fixed, noncancelable term of the lease. However, a bargain renewal option, if provided in the lease agreement, can extend this period. A **bargain renewal option** allows the lessee to renew the lease for a rental that is lower than the expected fair rental at the date the option becomes exercisable. At the inception of the lease, the difference between the renewal rental and the expected fair rental must be great enough to make exercise of the option to renew reasonably assured.

For example, assume that **Home Depot** leases **Dell** PCs for two years at a rental of $100 per month per computer and subsequently can lease them for $10 per month per computer for another two years. The lease clearly offers a bargain renewal option; the lease term is considered to be four years. However, with bargain renewal options, as with bargain purchase options, it is sometimes difficult to determine what is a bargain.[7]

Determining estimated economic life can also pose problems, especially if the leased item is a specialized item or has been used for a significant period of time. For example, determining the economic life of a nuclear core is extremely difficult. It is subject to much more than normal "wear and tear." As indicated earlier, the FASB takes the position that if the lease starts during the last 25 percent of the life of the asset, companies cannot use the economic life test to classify a lease as a capital lease.

INTERNATIONAL INSIGHT

In some countries (e.g., Italy, Japan), accounting principles do not specify criteria for capitalization of leases. In others (e.g., Sweden, Switzerland), such criteria exist, but capitalization of the leases is optional.

---

[7] The original lease term is also extended for leases having the following: substantial penalties for nonrenewal; periods for which the lessor has the option to renew or extend the lease; renewal periods preceding the date a bargain purchase option becomes exercisable; and renewal periods in which any lessee guarantees of the lessor's debt are expected to be in effect or in which there will be a loan outstanding from the lessee to the lessor. The lease term, however, can never extend beyond the time a bargain purchase option becomes exercisable. "Accounting for Leases: Sale-Leaseback Transactions Involving Real Estate; Sales-Type Leases of Real Estate; Definition of the Lease Term; Initial Direct Costs of Direct Financing Leases," *Statement of Financial Accounting Standards No. 98* (Stamford, Conn.: FASB, 1988).

Recovery of Investment Test (90% Test)

If the present value of the minimum lease payments equals or exceeds 90 percent of the fair market value of the asset, then a lessee like Delta should capitalize the leased asset. Why? If the present value of the minimum lease payments is reasonably close to the market price of the aircraft, Delta is effectively purchasing the asset.

Determining the present value of the minimum lease payments involves three important concepts: (1) minimum lease payments, (2) executory costs, and (3) discount rate.

Minimum Lease Payments. Delta is obligated to make, or expected to make, **minimum lease payments** in connection with the leased property. These payments include the following.

1 *Minimum Rental Payments*—Minimum rental payments are those that Delta must make to ILFC under the lease agreement. In some cases, the minimum rental payments may equal the minimum lease payments. However, the minimum lease payments may also include a guaranteed residual value (if any), penalty for failure to renew, or a bargain purchase option (if any), as we note below.

2 *Guaranteed Residual Value*—The residual value is the estimated fair (market) value of the leased property at the end of the lease term. ILFC may transfer the risk of loss to Delta or to a third party by obtaining a guarantee of the estimated residual value. The **guaranteed residual value** is either (1) the certain or determinable amount that Delta will pay ILFC at the end of the lease to purchase the aircraft at the end of the lease, or (2) the amount Delta or the third party guarantees that ILFC will realize if the aircraft is returned. (**Third-party guarantors** are, in essence, insurers who for a fee assume the risk of deficiencies in leased asset residual value.) If not guaranteed in full, the **unguaranteed residual value** is the estimated residual value exclusive of any portion guaranteed.[8]

3 *Penalty for Failure to Renew or Extend the Lease*—The amount Delta must pay if the agreement specifies that it must extend or renew the lease, and it fails to do so.

4 *Bargain Purchase Option*—As we indicated earlier (in item 1), an option given to Delta to purchase the aircraft at the end of the lease term at a price that is fixed sufficiently below the expected fair value, so that, at the inception of the lease, purchase is reasonably assured.

Delta excludes executory costs (defined below) from its computation of the present value of the minimum lease payments.

Executory Costs. Like most assets, leased tangible assets incur insurance, maintenance, and tax expenses—called **executory costs**—during their economic life. If ILFC retains responsibility for the payment of these "ownership-type costs," **it should exclude**, in computing the present value of the minimum lease payments, a portion of each lease payment that represents executory costs. Executory costs do not represent payment on or reduction of the obligation.

Many lease agreements specify that the lessee directly pays executory costs to the appropriate third parties. In these cases, the lessor can use the rental payment **without adjustment** in the present value computation.

Discount Rate. A lessee, like Delta computes the present value of the minimum lease payments using its **incremental borrowing rate**. This rate is defined as: "The rate that, at the inception of the lease, the lessee would have incurred to borrow the funds necessary to buy the leased asset on a secured loan with repayment terms similar to the payment schedule called for in the lease."[9]

---

[8]A lease provision requiring the lessee to make up a residual value deficiency that is attributable to damage, extraordinary wear and tear, or excessive usage is not included in the minimum lease payments. Lessees recognize such costs as period costs when incurred. "Lessee Guarantee of the Residual Value of Leased Property," *FASB Interpretation No. 19* (Stamford, Conn.: FASB, 1977), par. 3.

[9]*FASB Statement No. 13*, op. cit., par. 5 (l).

To determine whether the present value of these payments is less than 90 percent of the fair market value of the property, Delta discounts the payments using its incremental borrowing rate. Determining the incremental borrowing rate often requires judgment because the lessee bases it on a hypothetical purchase of the property.

However, there is one exception to this rule. If (1) Delta knows the **implicit interest rate computed by ILFC** and (2) it is less than Delta's incremental borrowing rate, then Delta **must use ILFC's implicit rate**. What is the **interest rate implicit in the lease**? It is the discount rate that, when applied to the minimum lease payments and any unguaranteed residual value accruing to the lessor, causes the aggregate present value to equal the fair value of the leased property to the lessor.[10]

The purpose of this exception is twofold. First, **the implicit rate of ILFC is generally a more realistic rate** to use in determining the amount (if any) to report as the asset and related liability for Delta. Second, the guideline ensures that Delta **does not use an artificially high incremental borrowing rate** that would cause the present value of the minimum lease payments to be less than 90 percent of the fair market value of the aircraft. Use of such a rate would thus make it possible to avoid capitalization of the asset and related liability.

Delta may argue that it cannot determine the implicit rate of the lessor and therefore should use the higher rate. However, in most cases, Delta can approximate the implicit rate used by ILFC. The determination of whether or not a reasonable estimate could be made will require judgment, particularly where the result from using the incremental borrowing rate comes close to meeting the 90 percent test. Because Delta **may not capitalize the leased property at more than its fair value** (as we discuss later), it cannot use an excessively low discount rate.

Asset and Liability Accounted for Differently

In a capital lease transaction, Delta uses the lease as a source of financing. ILFC finances the transaction (provides the investment capital) through the leased asset. Delta makes rent payments, which actually are installment payments. Therefore, over the life of the aircraft rented, **the rental payments to ILFC constitute a payment of principal plus interest**.

Asset and Liability Recorded

Under the capital lease method, Delta treats the lease transaction as if it purchases the aircraft in a financing transaction. That is, Delta acquires the aircraft and creates an obligation. Therefore, it records a capital lease as an asset and a liability at the lower of (1) the present value of the minimum lease payments (excluding executory costs) or (2) the fair-market value of the leased asset at the inception of the lease. The rationale for this approach is that companies should not record a leased asset for more than its fair market value.

Depreciation Period

One troublesome aspect of accounting for the depreciation of the capitalized leased asset relates to the period of depreciation. If the lease agreement transfers ownership of the asset to Delta (criterion 1) or contains a bargain purchase option (criterion 2), Delta depreciates the aircraft consistent with its normal depreciation policy for other aircraft, **using the economic life of the asset**.

On the other hand, if the lease does not transfer ownership or does not contain a bargain purchase option, then Delta depreciates it over the **term of the lease**. In this case, the aircraft reverts to ILFC after a certain period of time.

Effective-Interest Method

Throughout the term of the lease, Delta uses the **effective-interest method** to allocate each lease payment between principal and interest. This method produces a periodic interest expense equal to a constant percentage of the carrying value of the

---

[10]Ibid., par. 5 (k).

lease obligation. When applying the effective-interest method to capital leases, Delta must use the same discount rate that determines the present value of the minimum lease payments.

Depreciation Concept

Although Delta computes the amounts initially capitalized as an asset and recorded as an obligation at the same present value, the **depreciation of the aircraft and the discharge of the obligation are independent accounting processes** during the term of the lease. It should depreciate the leased asset by applying conventional depreciation methods: straight-line, sum-of-the-years'-digits, declining-balance, units of production, etc. The FASB uses the term "amortization" more frequently than "depreciation" to recognize intangible leased property rights. We prefer "depreciation" to describe the write-off of a tangible asset's expired services.

Capital Lease Method (Lessee)

To illustrate a capital lease, assume that **Caterpillar Financial Services Corp.** (a subsidiary of Caterpillar) and **Sterling Construction Corp**. sign a lease agreement dated January 1, 2008, that calls for Caterpillar to lease a front-end loader to Sterling beginning January 1, 2008. The terms and provisions of the lease agreement, and other pertinent data, are as follows.

- The term of the lease is five years. The lease agreement is noncancelable, requiring equal rental payments of $25,981.62 at the beginning of each year (annuity due basis).
- The loader has a fair value at the inception of the lease of $100,000, an estimated economic life of five years, and no residual value.
- Sterling pays all of the executory costs directly to third parties except for the property taxes of $2,000 per year, which it includes as part of its annual payments to Caterpillar.
- The lease contains no renewal options. The loader reverts to Caterpillar at the termination of the lease.
- Sterling's incremental borrowing rate is 11 percent per year.
- Sterling depreciates, on a straight-line basis, similar equipment that it owns.
- Caterpillar sets the annual rental to earn a rate of return on its investment of 10 percent per year; Sterling knows this fact.[11]

The lease meets the criteria for classification as a capital lease for the following reasons:

1 The lease term of five years, being equal to the equipment's estimated economic life of five years, satisfies the 75 percent test.

2 The present value of the minimum lease payments ($100,000 as computed below) exceeds 90 percent of the fair value of the loader ($100,000).

The minimum lease payments are $119,908.10 ($23,981.62 × 5). Sterling computes the amount capitalized as leased assets as the present value of the minimum lease payments (excluding executory costs—property taxes of $2,000) as shown in Illustration 21-6.

ILLUSTRATION 21-6
Computation of Capitalized Lease Payments

Capitalized amount = ($25,981.62 − $2,000) × Present value of an annuity due of 1 for 5 periods at 10% (Table 6-5)

= $23,981.62 × 4.16986

= $100,000

---

[11]If Sterling has an incremental borrowing rate of, say, 9 percent (lower than the 10 percent rate used by Caterpillar) and it did not know the rate used by Caterpillar, the present value computation would yield a capitalized amount of $101,675.35 ($23,981.62 × 4.23972). And, because this amount exceeds the $100,000 fair value of the equipment, Sterling would have to capitalize the $100,000 and use 10 percent as its effective rate for amortization of the lease obligation.

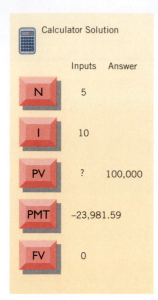

Calculator Solution

	Inputs	Answer
N	5	
I	10	
PV	?	100,000
PMT	−23,981.59	
FV	0	

Sterling uses Caterpillar's implicit interest rate of 10 percent instead of its incremental borrowing rate of 11 percent because (1) it is lower and (2) it knows about it. Sterling records the capital lease on its books on January 1, 2008, as:

Leased Equipment under Capital Leases	100,000	
Lease Liability		100,000

Note that the entry records the obligation at the net amount of $100,000 (the present value of the future rental payments) rather than at the gross amount of $119,908.10 ($23,981.62 × 5).

Sterling records the **first lease payment on January 1, 2008**, as follows:

Property Tax Expense	2,000.00	
Lease Liability	23,981.62	
Cash		25,981.62

Each lease payment of $25,981.62 consists of three elements: (1) a reduction in the lease liability, (2) a financing cost (interest expense), and (3) executory costs (property taxes). The total financing cost (interest expense) over the term of the lease is $19,908.10. This amount is the difference between the present value of the lease payments ($100,000) and the actual cash disbursed, net of executory costs ($119,908.10). Therefore, the annual interest expense, applying the effective-interest method, is a function of the outstanding liability, as Illustration 21-7 shows.

ILLUSTRATION 21-7

Lease Amortization Schedule for Lessee— Annuity-Due Basis

STERLING CONSTRUCTION
LEASE AMORTIZATION SCHEDULE
(ANNUITY-DUE BASIS)

Date	Annual Lease Payment	Executory Costs	Interest (10%) on Liability	Reduction of Lease Liability	Lease Liability
	(a)	(b)	(c)	(d)	(e)
1/1/08					$100,000.00
1/1/08	$ 25,981.62	$ 2,000	$ —0—	$ 23,981.62	76,018.38
1/1/09	25,981.62	2,000	7,601.84	16,379.78	59,638.60
1/1/10	25,981.62	2,000	5,963.86	18,017.76	41,620.84
1/1/11	25,981.62	2,000	4,162.08	19,819.54	21,801.30
1/1/12	25,981.62	2,000	2,180.32*	21,801.30	—0—
	$129,908.10	$10,000	$19,908.10	$100,000.00	

(a) Lease payment as required by lease.
(b) Executory costs included in rental payment.
(c) Ten percent of the preceding balance of (e) except for 1/1/05; since this is an annuity due, no time has elapsed at the date of the first payment and no interest has accrued.
(d) (a) minus (b) and (c).
(e) Preceding balance minus (d).
*Rounded by 19 cents.

At the end of its fiscal year, December 31, 2008, Sterling records **accrued interest** as follows.

Interest Expense	7,601.84	
Interest Payable		7,601.84

Depreciation of the leased equipment over its five-year lease term, applying Sterling's normal depreciation policy (straight-line method), results in the following entry on December 31, 2008.

Depreciation Expense—Capital Leases	20,000	
Accumulated Depreciation—Capital Leases		20,000
($100,000 ÷ 5 years)		

At December 31, 2008, Sterling separately identifies the assets recorded under capital leases on its balance sheet. Similarly, it separately identifies the related obligations. Sterling classifies the portion due within one year or the operating cycle, whichever is longer, with current liabilities, and the rest with noncurrent liabilities. For example, the current portion of the December 31, 2008, total obligation of $76,018.38 in Sterling's amortization schedule is the amount of the reduction in the obligation in 2009, or $16,379.78. Illustration 21-8 shows the liabilities section as it relates to lease transactions at December 31, 2008.

Current liabilities	
Interest payable	$ 7,601.84
Lease liability	16,379.78
Noncurrent liabilities	
Lease liability	$59,638.60

ILLUSTRATION 21-8
Reporting Current and Noncurrent Lease Liabilities

Sterling records the lease payment of January 1, 2009, as follows.

Property Tax Expense	2,000.00	
Interest Payable	7,601.84	
Lease Liability	16,379.78	
Cash		25,981.62

Entries through 2012 would follow the pattern above. Sterling records its other executory costs (insurance and maintenance) in a manner similar to how it records any other operating costs incurred on assets it owns.

Upon expiration of the lease, Sterling has fully amortized the amount capitalized as leased equipment. It also has fully discharged its lease obligation. If Sterling does not purchase the loader, it returns the equipment to Caterpillar. Sterling then removes the leased equipment and related accumulated depreciation accounts from its books.[12]

If Sterling purchases the equipment at termination of the lease, at a price of $5,000 and the estimated life of the equipment changes from five to seven years, it makes the following entry.

Equipment ($100,000 + $5,000)	105,000	
Accumulated Depreciation—Capital Leases	100,000	
Leased Equipment under Capital Leases		100,000
Accumulated Depreciation—Equipment		100,000
Cash		5,000

Operating Method (Lessee)

Under the **operating method**, rent expense (and the associated liability) accrues day by day to the lessee as it uses the property. **The lessee assigns rent to the periods benefiting from the use of the asset and ignores, in the accounting, any commitments to make future payments.** The lessee makes appropriate accruals or deferrals if the accounting period ends between cash payment dates.

For example, assume that the capital lease illustrated in the previous section did not qualify as a capital lease. Sterling therefore accounts for it as an operating lease. The first-year charge to operations is now $25,981.62, the amount of the rental payment. Sterling records this payment on January 1, 2008, as follows.

Rent Expense	25,981.62	
Cash		25,981.62

---

[12]If Sterling purchases the front-end loader **during the term of a "capital lease,"** it accounts for it like a renewal or extension of a capital lease. "Any difference between the purchase price and the carrying amount of the lease obligation shall be recorded as an adjustment of the carrying amount of the asset." See "Accounting for Purchase of a Leased Asset by the Lessee During the Term of the Lease," *FASB Interpretation No. 26* (Stamford, Conn.: FASB, 1978), par. 5.

Sterling does not report the loader, as well as any long-term liability for future rental payments, on the balance sheet. Sterling reports rent expense on the income statement. And, as discussed later in the chapter, **Sterling must disclose all operating leases that have noncancelable lease terms in excess of one year**.

RESTATEMENTS ON THE MENU

WHAT DO THE NUMBERS MEAN?

Accounting for operating leases would appear routine, so it is unusual for a bevy of companies in a single industry—restaurants—to get caught up in the accounting rules for operating leases. Getting the accounting right is particularly important for restaurant chains, because they make extensive use of leases for their restaurants and equipment.

The problem stems from the way most property (and equipment) leases cover a specific number of years (the so-called *primary lease term*) as well as renewal periods (sometimes referred to as the *option term*). In some cases, companies were calculating their lease expense for the primary term but depreciating lease-related assets over both the primary and option terms. This practice resulted in understating the total cost of the lease and thus boosted earnings.

For example, the CFO at **CKE Restaurants Inc.**, owner of the Hardee's and Carl's Jr. chains, noted that CKE ran into trouble because it was not consistent in calculating the lease and depreciation expense. Correcting the error at CKE reduced earnings by nine cents a share in fiscal 2002, nine cents a share in fiscal 2003, and 10 cents a share in fiscal 2004. The company now uses the shorter, primary lease terms for calculating both lease expense and depreciation. The change increases depreciation annually, which in turn decreases total assets.

CKE was not alone in improper operating lease accounting. Notable restaurateurs who ran afoul of the lease rules included **Brinker International Inc.**, operator of Chili's; **Darden Restaurants Inc.**, which operates Red Lobster and Olive Garden; and **Jack in the Box**. To correct their operating lease accounting, these restaurants reported restatements that resulted in lower earnings and assets.

Source: Steven D. Jones and Richard Gibson, *Wall Street Journal* (January 26, 2005). p. C3.

Comparison of Capital Lease with Operating Lease

OBJECTIVE 3
Contrast the operating and capitalization methods of recording leases.

As we indicated, if accounting for the lease as an operating lease, the first-year charge to operations is $25,981.62, the amount of the rental payment. Treating the transaction as a capital lease, however, results in a first-year charge of $29,601.84: depreciation of $20,000 (assuming straight-line), interest expense of $7,601.84 (per Illustration 21-7), and executory costs of $2,000. Illustration 21-9 shows that **while the total charges to operations are the same over the lease term whether accounting for the lease as a**

ILLUSTRATION 21-9
Comparison of Charges to Operations—Capital vs. Operating Leases

STERLING CONSTRUCTION
SCHEDULE OF CHARGES TO OPERATIONS
CAPITAL LEASE VERSUS OPERATING LEASE

| | Capital Lease | | | | Operating | |
| | | Executory | | Total | Lease | |
Year	Depreciation	Costs	Interest	Charge	Charge	Difference
2008	$ 20,000	$ 2,000	$ 7,601.84	$ 29,601.84	$ 25,981.62	$3,620.22
2009	20,000	2,000	5,963.86	27,963.86	25,981.62	1,982.24
2010	20,000	2,000	4,162.08	26,162.08	25,981.62	180.46
2011	20,000	2,000	2,180.32	24,180.32	25,981.62	(1,801.30)
2012	20,000	2,000	—	22,000.00	25,981.62	(3,981.62)
	$100,000	$10,000	$19,908.10	$129,908.10	$129,908.10	$ –0–

capital lease or as an operating lease, under the capital lease treatment the charges are higher in the earlier years and lower in the later years.[13]

If using an accelerated method of depreciation, the differences between the amounts charged to operations under the two methods would be even larger in the earlier and later years.

In addition, using the capital lease approach results in an asset and related liability of $100,000 initially reported on the balance sheet. The lessee would not report any asset or liability under the operating method. Therefore, the following differences occur if using a capital lease instead of an operating lease:

1 An increase in the amount of reported debt (both short-term and long-term).

2 An increase in the amount of total assets (specifically long-lived assets).

3 A lower income early in the life of the lease and, therefore, lower retained earnings.

Thus, many companies believe that capital leases negatively impact their financial position: Their debt to total equity ratio increases, and their rate of return on total assets decreases. As a result, the business community resists capitalizing leases.

Whether this resistance is well founded is debatable. From a cash flow point of view, the company is in the same position whether accounting for the lease as an operating or a capital lease. Managers often argue against capitalization for several reasons: First is that capitalization can more easily lead to **violation of loan covenants**. It also can affect the **amount of compensation received by owners** (for example, a stock compensation plan tied to earnings). Finally, capitalization can **lower rates of return**

DOLLARS TO DOUGHNUTS

WHAT DO THE NUMBERS MEAN?

Krispy Kreme, a chain of 217 doughnut shops, has caught the attention—some good, some bad—of Wall Street. On the good side, investors are impressed by the company's ability to grow rapidly on a relatively small bit of capital. For the first nine months of fiscal 2002, the company's capital expenditures fell to $38 million, from $59 million the year before. Yet Krispy Kreme expanded, along with its customers' waistlines, during the same period: Its earnings rose 73 percent, to $18 million, on sales that were up 27 percent to $277 million.

That's an impressive feat if you care about return on capital. But there's a hole in this doughnut. Amid much hoopla, the company announced in 2001 that it would spend $30 million on a new 187,000 square foot mixing plant and warehouse in Effingham, Illinois. Yet the financial statements failed to disclose the investments and obligations associated with that $30 million.

By financing through a synthetic lease, Krispy Kreme keeps the investment and obligation off the books. In a synthetic lease, a financial institution like **Bank of America** sets up a *special purpose entity* (SPE) that borrows money to build the plant and then leases it to Krispy Kreme. For accounting purposes, Krispy Kreme reports an operating lease, but for tax purposes the company is considered the owner of the asset and gets depreciation tax deductions.

In response to negative publicity about the use of SPEs to get favorable financial reporting and tax benefits, Krispy Kreme announced it would change its method of financing construction of its dough-making plant.

Source: Adapted from Seth Lubore and Elizabeth MacDonald, "Debt? Who, Me?" *Forbes* (February 18, 2002), p. 56.

---

[13]The higher charges in the early years is one reason lessees are reluctant to adopt the capital lease accounting method. Lessees (especially those of real estate) claim that it is really no more costly to operate the leased asset in the early years than in the later years. Thus, they advocate an even charge similar to that provided by the operating method.

and **increase debt to equity relationships,** making the company less attractive to present and potential investors.[14]

ACCOUNTING BY THE LESSOR

Earlier in this chapter we discussed leasing's advantages to the lessee. Three important benefits are available to the lessor:

1 *Interest Revenue.* Leasing is a form of financing. Banks, captives, and independent leasing companies find leasing attractive because it provides competitive interest margins.

2 *Tax Incentives.* In many cases, companies that lease cannot use the tax benefit of the asset, but leasing allows them to transfer such tax benefits to another party (the lessor) in return for a lower rental rate on the leased asset. To illustrate, **Boeing Aircraft** might sell one of its 737 jet planes to a wealthy investor who needed only the tax benefit. The investor then leased the plane to a foreign airline, for whom the tax benefit was of no use. Everyone gained. Boeing sold its airplane, the investor received the tax benefit, and the foreign airline cheaply acquired a 737.[15]

3 *High Residual Value.* Another advantage to the lessor is the return of the property at the end of the lease term. Residual values can produce very large profits. **Citigroup** at one time assumed that the commercial aircraft it was leasing to the airline industry would have a residual value of 5 percent of their purchase price. It turned out that they were worth 150 percent of their cost—a handsome profit. However, three years later these same planes slumped to 80 percent of their cost, but still far more than 5 percent.

Economics of Leasing

A lessor, such as Caterpillar Financial in our earlier example, determines the amount of the rental, basing it on the rate of return—the implicit rate—needed to justify leasing the front-end loader. In establishing the rate of return, Caterpillar considers the credit standing of Sterling Construction, the length of the lease, and the status of the residual value (guaranteed versus unguaranteed).

In the Caterpillar/Sterling example on pages 1097–1099, Caterpillar's implicit rate was 10 percent, the cost of the equipment to Caterpillar was $100,000 (also fair market value), and the estimated residual value was zero. Caterpillar determines the amount of the lease payment as follows.

ILLUSTRATION 21-10
Computation of Lease Payments

Fair market value of leased equipment	$100,000.00
Less: Present value of the residual value	–0–
Amount to be recovered by lessor through lease payments	$100,000.00
Five beginning-of-the-year lease payments to yield a 10% return ($100,000 ÷ 4.16986[a])	$ 23,981.62

[a]PV of an annuity due of 1 for 5 years at 10% (Table 6-5)

---

[14]One study indicates that management's behavior did change as a result of *FASB No. 13.* For example, many companies restructure their leases to avoid capitalization. Others increase their purchases of assets instead of leasing. Still others, faced with capitalization, postpone their debt offerings or issue stock instead. However, note that the study found no significant effect on stock or bond prices as a result of capitalization of leases. A. Rashad Abdel-khalik, "The Economic Effects on Lessees of *FASB Statement No. 13,* Accounting for Leases," Research Report (Stamford, Conn.: FASB, 1981).

[15]Some would argue that there is a loser—the U.S. government. The tax benefits enable the profitable investor to reduce or eliminate taxable income.

If a residual value is involved (whether guaranteed or not), Caterpillar would not have to recover as much from the lease payments. Therefore, the lease payments would be less. (Illustration 21-17, on page 1108, shows this situation.)

Classification of Leases by the Lessor

For accounting purposes, the **lessor** may classify leases as one of the following:

1 Operating leases.
2 Direct-financing leases.
3 Sales-type leases.

OBJECTIVE 4
Identify the classifications of leases for the lessor.

Illustration 21-11 presents two groups of capitalization criteria for the lessor. If at the date of inception, the lessor agrees to a lease that meets **one or more** of the Group I criteria (1, 2, 3, and 4) and **both** of the Group II criteria (1 and 2), the lessor shall classify and account for the arrangement as a direct-financing lease or as a sales-type lease.[16] (Note that the Group I criteria are identical to the criteria that must be met in order for a lessee to classify a lease as a capital lease, as shown in Illustration 21-4.)

Capitalization Criteria (Lessor)

Group I
1. The lease transfers ownership of the property to the lessee.
2. The lease contains a bargain purchase option.
3. The lease term is equal to 75 percent or more of the estimated economic life of the leased property.
4. The present value of the minimum lease payments (excluding executory costs) equals or exceeds 90 percent of the fair value of the leased property.

Group II
1. Collectibility of the payments required from the lessee is reasonably predictable.
2. No important uncertainties surround the amount of unreimbursable costs yet to be incurred by the lessor under the lease (lessor's performance is substantially complete or future costs are reasonably predictable).

ILLUSTRATION 21-11
Capitalization Criteria for Lessor

Why the Group II requirements? The profession wants to ensure that the lessor has really transferred the risks and benefits of ownership. If collectibility of payments is not predictable or if performance by the lessor is incomplete, then the criteria for revenue recognition have not been met. The lessor should therefore account for the lease as an operating lease.

For example, computer leasing companies at one time used to buy **IBM** equipment, lease the equipment, and remove the leased assets from their balance sheets. In leasing the assets, the computer lessors stated that they would substitute new IBM equipment if obsolescence occurred. However, when IBM introduced a new computer line, IBM refused to sell it to the computer leasing companies. As a result, a number of the lessors could not meet their contracts with their customers and had to take back the old equipment. The computer leasing companies therefore had to reinstate the assets they had taken off the books. Such a case demonstrates one reason for the Group II requirements.

The distinction for the lessor between a direct-financing lease and a sales-type lease is the presence or absence of a manufacturer's or dealer's profit (or loss): A sales-type lease involves a manufacturer's or dealer's profit, and a direct-financing lease does not. The profit (or loss) to the lessor is evidenced by the difference between the fair value of the leased property at the inception of the lease and the lessor's cost or carrying amount (book value).

Normally, sales-type leases arise when manufacturers or dealers use leasing as a means of marketing their products. For example, a computer manufacturer will lease

INTERNATIONAL INSIGHT

U.S. GAAP is consistent with *International Standard No. 17* (Accounting for Leases). However, the international standard is a relatively simple statement of basic principles, whereas the U.S. rules on leases are more prescriptive and detailed.

---

[16]*FASB Statement No. 13*, op. cit., pars. 6, 7, and 8.

its computer equipment (possibly through a captive) to businesses and institutions. Direct-financing leases generally result from arrangements with lessors that are primarily engaged in financing operations (e.g., banks). However, a lessor need not be a manufacturer or dealer to recognize a profit (or loss) at the inception of a lease that requires application of sales-type lease accounting.

ILLUSTRATION 21-12
Diagram of Lessor's
Criteria for Lease
Classification

Lessors classify and account for all leases that do not qualify as direct-financing or sales-type leases as operating leases. Illustration 21-12 shows the circumstances under which a lessor classifies a lease as operating, direct-financing, or sales-type.

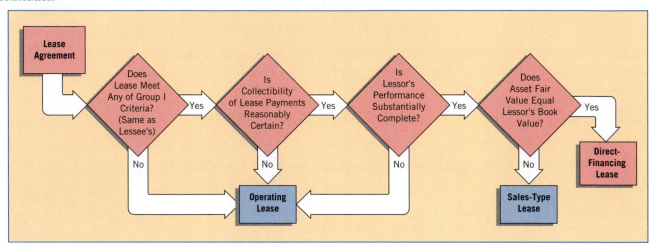

As a consequence of the additional Group II criteria for lessors, a lessor may classify a lease as an **operating** lease but the lessee may classify the same lease as a **capital** lease. In such an event, both the lessor and lessee will carry the asset on their books, and both will depreciate the capitalized asset.

For purposes of comparison with the lessee's accounting, we will illustrate only the operating and direct-financing leases in the following section. We will discuss the more complex sales-type lease later in the chapter.

Direct-Financing Method (Lessor)

OBJECTIVE 5
Describe the lessor's accounting for direct-financing leases.

Direct-financing leases are in substance the financing of an asset purchase by the lessee. In this type of lease, the lessor records a **lease receivable** instead of a leased asset. The lease receivable is the present value of the minimum lease payments. Remember that "minimum lease payments" include:

1 Rental payments (excluding executory costs).
2 Bargain purchase option (if any).
3 Guaranteed residual value (if any).
4 Penalty for failure to renew (if any).

Thus, the lessor records the residual value, whether guaranteed or not. Also, recall that if the lessor pays any executory costs, then it should reduce the rental payment by that amount in computing minimum lease payments.

The following presentation, using the data from the preceding Caterpillar/Sterling example on pages 1097–1099, illustrates the accounting treatment for a direct-financing lease. We repeat here the information relevant to Caterpillar in accounting for this lease transaction.

1 The term of the lease is five years beginning January 1, 2008, noncancelable, and requires equal rental payments of $25,981.62 at the beginning of each year. Payments include $2,000 of executory costs (property taxes).

2 The equipment (front-end loader) has a cost of $100,000 to Caterpillar, a fair value at the inception of the lease of $100,000, an estimated economic life of five years, and no residual value.

3 Caterpillar incurred no initial direct costs in negotiating and closing the lease transaction.

4 The lease contains no renewal options. The equipment reverts to Caterpillar at the termination of the lease.

5 Collectibility is reasonably assured and Caterplillar incurs no additional costs (with the exception of the property taxes being collected from Sterling).

6 Caterpillar sets the annual lease payments to ensure a rate of return of 10 percent (implicit rate) on its investment as shown in Illustration 21-13.

Fair market value of leased equipment	$100,000.00
Less: Present value of residual value	–0–
Amount to be recovered by lessor through lease payments	$100,000.00
Five beginning-of-the-year lease payments to yield a 10% return ($100,000 ÷ 4.16986ᵃ)	$ 23,981.62

ᵃPV of an annuity due of 1 for 5 years at 10% (Table 6-5).

ILLUSTRATION 21-13
Computation of Lease Payments

The lease meets the criteria for classification as a direct-financing lease for several reasons: (1) The lease term exceeds 75 percent of the equipment's estimated economic life. (2) The present value of the minimum lease payments exceeds 90 percent of the equipment's fair value. (3) Collectibility of the payments is reasonably assured. And (4) Caterpillar incurs no further costs. It is not a sales-type lease because there is no difference between the fair value ($100,000) of the loader and Caterpillar's cost ($100,000).

The Lease Receivable is the present value of the minimum lease payments (excluding executory costs which are property taxes of $2,000). Caterpillar computes it as follows.

Lease receivable = ($25,981.62 − $2,000) × Present value of an annuity due of 1 for 5 periods at 10% (Table 6-5)

= $23,981.62 × 4.16986

= $100,000

ILLUSTRATION 21-14
Computation of Lease Receivable

Caterpillar records the lease of the asset and the resulting receivable on January 1, 2008 (the inception of the lease), as follows.

Lease Receivable	100,000	
Equipment		100,000

Companies often **report** the lease receivable in the balance sheet as "Net investment in capital leases." Companies classify it either as current or noncurrent, depending on when they recover the net investment.[17]

Caterpillar replaces its investment (the leased front-end loader, a cost of $100,000), with a lease receivable. In a manner similar to Sterling's treatment of interest, Caterpillar applies the effective-interest method and recognizes interest revenue as a function of the lease receivable balance, as Illustration 21-15 (page 1106) shows.

---

[17]In the notes to the financial statements (see Illustration 21-33), the lease receivable is reported at its gross amount (minimum lease payments plus the unguaranteed residual value). In addition, the lessor also reports total unearned interest related to the lease. As a result, some lessors record lease receivable on a gross basis and record the unearned interest in a separate account. We illustrate the net approach here because it is consistent with the accounting for the lessee.

ILLUSTRATION 21-15
Lease Amortization
Schedule for Lessor—
Annuity-Due Basis

CATERPILLAR FINANCIAL
LEASE AMORTIZATION SCHEDULE
(ANNUITY-DUE BASIS)

Date	Annual Lease Payment	Executory Costs	Interest (10%) on Lease Receivable	Lease Receivable Recovery	Lease Receivable
	(a)	(b)	(c)	(d)	(e)
1/1/08					$100,000.00
1/1/08	$ 25,981.62	$ 2,000.00	$ –0–	$ 23,981.62	76,018.38
1/1/09	25,981.62	2,000.00	7,601.84	16,379.78	59,638.60
1/1/10	25,981.62	2,000.00	5,963.86	18,017.76	41,620.84
1/1/11	25,981.62	2,000.00	4,162.08	19,819.54	21,801.30
1/1/12	25,981.62	2,000.00	2,180.32*	21,801.30	–0–
	$129,908.10	$10,000.00	$19,908.10	$100,000.00	

(a) Annual rental that provides a 10% return on net investment.
(b) Executory costs included in rental payment.
(c) Ten percent of the preceding balance of (e) except for 1/1/08.
(d) (a) minus (b) and (c).
(e) Preceding balance minus (d).
*Rounded by 19 cents.

On January 1, 2008, Caterpillar records receipt of the first year's lease payment as follows.

Cash	25,981.62	
Lease Receivable		23,981.62
Property Tax Expense/Property Taxes Payable		2,000.00

On December 31, 2008, Caterpillar recognizes the interest revenue earned during the first year through the following entry.

Interest Receivable	7,601.84	
Interest Revenue—Leases		7,601.84

At December 31, 2008, Caterpillar reports the lease receivable in its balance sheet among current assets or noncurrent assets, or both. It classifies the portion due within one year or the operating cycle, whichever is longer, as a current asset, and the rest with noncurrent assets.

Illustration 21-16 shows the assets section as it relates to lease transactions at December 31, 2008.

ILLUSTRATION 21-16
Reporting Lease
Transactions by Lessor

Current assets	
Interest receivable	$ 7,601.84
Lease receivable	16,379.78
Noncurrent assets (investments)	
Lease receivable	$59,638.60

The following entries record receipt of the second year's lease payment and recognition of the interest earned.

January 1, 2009

Cash	25,981.62	
Lease Receivable		16,379.78
Interest Receivable		7,601.84
Property Tax Expense/Property Taxes Payable		2,000.00

December 31, 2009

Interest Receivable	5,963.86	
Interest Revenue—Leases		5,963.86

Journal entries through 2012 follow the same pattern except that Caterpillar records no entry in 2012 (the last year) for earned interest. Because it fully collects the receivable by January 1, 2012, no balance (investment) is outstanding during 2012. Caterpillar **recorded no depreciation**. If Sterling buys the loader for $5,000 upon expiration of the lease, Caterpillar recognizes disposition of the equipment as follows.

Cash	5,000	
Gain on Sale of Leased Equipment		5,000

Operating Method (Lessor)

Under the **operating method**, the lessor records each rental receipt as rental revenue. It **depreciates the leased asset in the normal manner**, with the depreciation expense of the period matched against the rental revenue. The amount of revenue recognized in each accounting period is a level amount (straight-line basis) regardless of the lease provisions, unless another systematic and rational basis better represents the time pattern in which the lessor derives benefit from the leased asset.

In addition to the depreciation charge, the lessor expenses maintenance costs and the cost of any other services rendered under the provisions of the lease that pertain to the current accounting period. The lessor **amortizes over the life of the lease** any costs paid to independent third parties, such as appraisal fees, finder's fees, and costs of credit checks, usually on a straight-line basis.

To illustrate the operating method, assume that the direct-financing lease illustrated in the previous section does not qualify as a capital lease. Therefore, Caterpillar accounts for it as an operating lease. It records the cash rental receipt, assuming the $2,000 was for property tax expense, as follows.

Cash	25,981.62	
Rental Revenue		25,981.62

Caterpillar records depreciation as follows (assuming a straight-line method, a cost basis of $100,000, and a five-year life).

Depreciation Expense—Leased Equipment	20,000	
Accumulated Depreciation—Leased Equipment		20,000

If Caterpillar pays property taxes, insurance, maintenance, and other operating costs during the year, it records them as expenses chargeable against the gross rental revenues.

If Caterpillar owns plant assets that it uses in addition to those leased to others, the company **separately classifies the leased equipment and accompanying accumulated depreciation** as Equipment Leased to Others or Investment in Leased Property. If significant in amount or in terms of activity, Caterpillar separates the rental revenues and accompanying expenses in the income statement from sales revenue and cost of goods sold.

SPECIAL ACCOUNTING PROBLEMS

The features of lease arrangements that cause unique accounting problems are:

1 Residual values.

2 Sales-type leases (lessor).

3 Bargain purchase options.

4 Initial direct costs.

5 Current versus noncurrent classification.

6 Disclosure.

We discuss each of these features on the following pages.

OBJECTIVE 6
Identify special features of lease arrangements that cause unique accounting problems.

1108 · *Chapter 21* **Accounting for Leases**

Residual Values

Up to this point, in order to develop the basic accounting issues related to lessee and lessor accounting, we have generally ignored residual values. Accounting for residual values is complex and will probably provide you with the greatest challenge in understanding lease accounting.

Meaning of Residual Value

The **residual value** is the estimated fair value of the leased asset at the end of the lease term. Frequently, a significant residual value exists at the end of the lease term, especially when the economic life of the leased asset exceeds the lease term. If title does not pass automatically to the lessee (criterion 1) and a bargain purchase option does not exist (criterion 2), the lessee returns physical custody of the asset to the lessor at the end of the lease term.[18]

Guaranteed versus Unguaranteed

The residual value may be unguaranteed or guaranteed by the lessee. Sometimes the lessee agrees to make up any deficiency below a stated amount that the lessor realizes in residual value at the end of the lease term. In such a case, that stated amount is the **guaranteed residual value**.

The parties to a lease use guaranteed residual value in lease arrangements for two reasons. The first is a business reason: It protects the lessor against any loss in estimated residual value, thereby ensuring the lessor of the desired rate of return on investment. The second reason is an accounting benefit that you will learn from the discussion at the end of this chapter.

Lease Payments

A guaranteed residual value—by definition—has more assurance of realization than does an unguaranteed residual value. As a result, the lessor may adjust lease payments because of the increased certainty of recovery. After the lessor establishes this rate, it makes no difference from an accounting point of view whether the residual value is guaranteed or unguaranteed. The net investment that the lessor records (once the rate is set) will be the same.

Assume the same data as in the Caterpillar/Sterling illustrations except that Caterpillar estimates a residual value of $5,000 at the end of the five-year lease term. In addition, Caterpillar assumes a 10 percent return on investment (ROI),[19] whether the residual value is guaranteed or unguaranteed. Caterpillar would compute the amount of the lease payments as follows.

ILLUSTRATION 21-17
Lessor's Computation of Lease Payments

CATERPILLAR'S COMPUTATION OF LEASE PAYMENTS (10% ROI) GUARANTEED OR UNGUARANTEED RESIDUAL VALUE (ANNUITY-DUE BASIS, INCLUDING RESIDUAL VALUE)	
Fair market value of leased asset to lessor	$100,000.00
Less: Present value of residual value ($5,000 × .62092, Table 6-2)	3,104.60
Amount to be recovered by lessor through lease payments	$ 96,895.40
Five periodic lease payments ($96,895.40 ÷ 4.16986, Table 6-5)	$ 23,237.09

[18]When the lease term and the economic life are not the same, the residual value and the salvage value of the asset will probably differ. For simplicity, we will assume that residual value and salvage value are the same, even when the economic life and lease term vary.

[19]Technically, the rate of return Caterpillar demands would differ depending upon whether the residual value was guaranteed or unguaranteed. To simplify the illustrations, we are ignoring this difference in subsequent sections.

Contrast the foregoing lease payment amount to the lease payments of $23,981.62 as computed in Illustration 21-10, where no residual value existed. In the second example, the payments are less, because the present value of the residual value reduces Caterpillar's total recoverable amount from $100,000 to $96,895.40.

Lessee Accounting for Residual Value

Whether the estimated residual value is guaranteed or unguaranteed has both economic and accounting consequence to the lessee. We saw the economic consequence—lower lease payments—in the preceding example. The accounting consequence is that the **minimum lease payments**, the basis for capitalization, include the guaranteed residual value but excludes the unguaranteed residual value.

Guaranteed Residual Value (Lessee Accounting). A guaranteed residual value affects the lessee's computation of minimum lease payments. Therefore it also affects the amounts capitalized as a leased asset and a lease obligation. In effect, the guaranteed residual value **is an additional lease payment that the lessee will pay in property or cash, or both, at the end of the lease term**.

Using the rental payments as computed by the lessor in Illustration 21-17, the minimum lease payments are $121,185.45 ([$23,237.09 × 5] + $5,000). Illustration 21-18 shows the capitalized present value of the minimum lease payments (excluding executory costs) for Sterling Construction.

OBJECTIVE 7
Describe the effect of residual values, guaranteed and unguaranteed, on lease accounting.

STERLING'S CAPITALIZED AMOUNT (10% RATE) (ANNUITY-DUE BASIS, INCLUDING **GUARANTEED** RESIDUAL VALUE)	
Present value of five annual rental payments ($23,237.09 × 4.16986, Table 6-5)	$ 96,895.40
Present value of guaranteed residual value of $5,000 due five years after date of inception: ($5,000 × .62092, Table 6-2)	3,104.60
Lessee's capitalized amount	$100,000.00

ILLUSTRATION 21-18
Computation of Lessee's Capitalized Amount—Guaranteed Residual Value

Sterling prepares a schedule of interest expense and amortization of the $100,000 lease liability. That schedule, shown in Illustration 21-19, is based on a $5,000 final guaranteed residual value payment at the end of five years.

STERLING CONSTRUCTION
LEASE AMORTIZATION SCHEDULE
(ANNUITY-DUE BASIS, **GUARANTEED** RESIDUAL VALUE—GRV)

Date	Lease Payment Plus GRV	Executory Costs	Interest (10%) on Liability	Reduction of Lease Liability	Lease Liability
	(a)	(b)	(c)	(d)	(e)
1/1/08					$100,000.00
1/1/08	$ 25,237.09	$ 2,000	–0–	$ 23,237.09	76,762.91
1/1/09	25,237.09	2,000	$ 7,676.29	15,560.80	61,202.11
1/1/10	25,237.09	2,000	6,120.21	17,116.88	44,085.23
1/1/11	25,237.09	2,000	4,408.52	18,828.57	25,256.66
1/1/12	25,237.09	2,000	2,525.67	20,711.42	4,545.24
12/31/12	5,000.00*		454.76**	4,545.24	–0–
	$131,185.45	$10,000	$21,185.45	$100,000.00	

(a) Annual lease payment as required by lease.
(b) Executory costs included in rental payment.
(c) Preceding balance of (e) × 10%, except 1/1/08.
(d) (a) minus (b) and (c).
(e) Preceding balance minus (d).

*Represents the guaranteed residual value.
**Rounded by 24 cents.

ILLUSTRATION 21-19
Lease Amortization Schedule for Lessee—Guaranteed Residual Value

Sterling records the leased asset (front-end loader) and liability, depreciation, interest, property tax, and lease payments on the basis of a guaranteed residual value. (These journal entries are shown in Illustration 21-24, on page 1112.) The format of these entries is the same as illustrated earlier, although the amounts are different because of the guaranteed residual value. Sterling records the loader at $100,000 and depreciates it over five years. To compute depreciation, it subtracts the guaranteed residual value from the cost of the loader. Assuming that Sterling uses the straight-line method, the depreciation expense each year is $19,000 ([$100,000 − $5,000] ÷ 5 years).

At the end of the lease term, before the lessee transfers the asset to Caterpillar, the lease asset and liability accounts have the following balances.

ILLUSTRATION 21-20

Account Balances on Lessee's Books at End of Lease Term—Guaranteed Residual Value

Leased equipment under capital leases	$100,000.00	Interest payable	$ 454.76
Less: Accumulated depreciation—		Lease liability	4,545.24
capital leases	95,000.00		
	$ 5,000.00		$5,000.00

If, at the end of the lease, the fair market value of the residual value is less than $5,000, Sterling will have to record a loss. Assume that Sterling depreciated the leased asset down to its residual value of $5,000 but that the fair market value of the residual value at December 31, 2012, was $3,000. In this case, Sterling would have to report a loss of $2,000. Assuming that it pays cash to make up the residual value deficiency, Sterling would make the following journal entry.

Loss on Capital Lease	2,000.00	
Interest Expense (or Interest Payable)	454.76	
Lease Liability	4,545.24	
Accumulated Depreciation—Capital Leases	95,000.00	
Leased Equipment under Capital Leases		100,000.00
Cash		2,000.00

If the fair market value *exceeds* $5,000, a gain may be recognized. Caterpillar and Sterling may apportion gains on guaranteed residual values in whatever ratio the parties initially agree.

When there is a guaranteed residual value, the lessee must be careful not to depreciate the total cost of the asset. For example, if Sterling mistakenly depreciated the total cost of the loader ($100,000), a misstatement would occur. That is, the carrying amount of the asset at the end of the lease term would be zero, but Sterling would show the liability under the capital lease at $5,000. In that case, if the asset was worth $5,000, Sterling would end up reporting a gain of $5,000 when it transferred the asset back to Caterpillar. As a result, Sterling would overstate depreciation and would understate net income in 2008–2011; in the last year (2012) net income would be overstated.

Unguaranteed Residual Value (Lessee Accounting). From the lessee's viewpoint, an **unguaranteed residual value** is the same as no residual value in terms of its effect upon the lessee's method of computing the minimum lease payments and the capitalization of the leased asset and the lease liability.

Assume the same facts as those above except that the $5,000 residual value is **unguaranteed** instead of guaranteed. The amount of the annual lease payments would be the same—$23,237.09. Whether the residual value is guaranteed or unguaranteed, Caterpillar will recover the same amount through lease rentals—that is, $96,895.40. The minimum lease payments are $116,185.45 ($23,237.09 × 5). Lessee Company would capitalize the amount shown in Illustration 21-21.

ILLUSTRATION 21-21
Computation of Lessee's Capitalized Amount—Unguaranteed Residual Value

STERLING'S CAPITALIZED AMOUNT (10% RATE)		
(ANNUITY-DUE BASIS, INCLUDING **UNGUARANTEED** RESIDUAL VALUE)		
Present value of 5 annual rental payments of $23,237.09 × 4.16986 (Table 6-5)		$96,895.40
Unguaranteed residual value of $5,000 (not capitalized by lessee)		–0–
Lessee's capitalized amount		$96,895.40

Illustration 21-22 shows Sterling's schedule of interest expense and amortization of the lease liability of $96,895.40, assuming an unguaranteed residual value of $5,000 at the end of five years.

ILLUSTRATION 21-22
Lease Amortization Schedule for Lessee—Unguaranteed Residual Value

STERLING CONSTRUCTION
LEASE AMORTIZATION SCHEDULE (10%)
(ANNUITY-DUE BASIS, **UNGUARANTEED** RESIDUAL VALUE)

Date	Annual Lease Payments	Executory Costs	Interest (10%) on Liability	Reduction of Lease Liability	Lease Liability
	(a)	(b)	(c)	(d)	(e)
1/1/08					$96,895.40
1/1/08	$ 25,237.09	$ 2,000	–0–	$23,237.09	73,658.31
1/1/09	25,237.09	2,000	$ 7,365.83	15,871.26	57,787.05
1/1/10	25,237.09	2,000	5,778.71	17,458.38	40,328.67
1/1/11	25,237.09	2,000	4,032.87	19,204.22	21,124.45
1/1/12	25,237.09	2,000	2,112.64*	21,124.45	–0–
	$126,185.45	$10,000	$19,290.05	$96,895.40	

(a) Annual lease payment as required by lease.
(b) Executory costs included in rental payment.
(c) Preceding balance of (e) × 10%.

(d) (a) minus (b) and (c).
(e) Preceding balance minus (d).
*Rounded by 19 cents.

Sterling records the leased asset and liability, depreciation, interest, property tax, and lease payments on the basis of an unguaranteed residual value. (These journal entries are shown in Illustration 21-24, on page 1112.) The format of these capital lease entries is the same as illustrated earlier. Note that Sterling records the leased asset at $96,895.40 and depreciates it over five years. Assuming that it uses the straight-line method, the depreciation expense each year is $19,379.08 ($96,895.40 ÷ 5 years). At the end of the lease term, before Sterling transfers the asset to Caterpillar, the lease asset and liability accounts have the following balances.

ILLUSTRATION 21-23
Account Balances on Lessee's Books at End of Lease Term—Unguaranteed Residual Value

Leased equipment under capital leases	$96,895	Lease liability	$–0–
Less: Accumulated depreciation—capital leases	96,895		
	$ –0–		

Assuming that Sterling has fully depreciated the leased asset and has fully amortized the lease liability, no entry is required at the end of the lease term, except to remove the asset from the books.

If Sterling depreciated the asset down to its unguaranteed residual value, a misstatement would occur. That is, the carrying amount of the leased asset would be $5,000 at the end of the lease, but the liability under the capital lease would be stated at zero before the transfer of the asset. Thus, Sterling would end up reporting a loss of $5,000 when it transferred the asset back to Caterpillar. Sterling would understate depreciation and would overstate net income in 2008–2011; in the last year (2012) net income would be understated because of the recorded loss.

Lessee Entries Involving Residual Values. Illustration 21-24 shows, in comparative form, Sterling's entries for both a guaranteed and an unguaranteed residual value.

ILLUSTRATION 21-24
Comparative Entries for Guaranteed and Unguaranteed Residual Values, Lessee Company

Guaranteed Residual Value			Unguaranteed Residual Value		
Capitalization of Lease 1/1/08:					
Leased Equipment under			Leased Equipment under		
Capital Leases	100,000.00		Capital Leases	96,895.40	
Lease Liability		100,000.00	Lease Liability		96,895.40
First Payment 1/1/08:					
Property Tax Expense	2,000.00		Property Tax Expense	2,000.00	
Lease Liability	23,237.09		Lease Liability	23,237.09	
Cash		25,237.09	Cash		25,237.09
Adjusting Entry for Accrued Interest 12/31/08:					
Interest Expense	7,676.29		Interest Expense	7,365.83	
Interest Payable		7,676.29	Interest Payable		7,365.83
Entry to Record Depreciation 12/31/08:					
Depreciation Expense—			Depreciation Expense—		
Capital Leases	19,000.00		Capital Leases	19,379.08	
Accumulated Depreciation—			Accumulated Depreciation—		
Capital Leases		19,000.00	Capital Leases		19,379.08
([$100,000 − $5,000] ÷ 5 years)			($96,895.40 ÷ 5 years)		
Second Payment 1/1/09:					
Property Tax Expense	2,000.00		Property Tax Expense	2,000.00	
Lease Liability	15,560.80		Lease Liability	15,871.26	
Interest Expense			Interest Expense		
(or Interest Payable)	7,676.29		(or Interest Payable)	7,365.83	
Cash		25,237.09	Cash		25,237.09

Lessor Accounting for Residual Value

As we indicated earlier, the lessor will recover the same net investment whether the residual value is guaranteed or unguaranteed. That is, the lessor works on the assumption that it will realize **the residual value at the end of the lease term whether guaranteed or unguaranteed**. The lease payments required in order for the company to earn a certain return on investment are the same (e.g., $23,237.09 in our example) whether the residual value is guaranteed or unguaranteed.

To illustrate, we again use the Caterpillar/Sterling data and assume classification of the lease as a direct-financing lease. With a residual value (either guaranteed or unguaranteed) of $5,000, Caterpillar determines the payments as follows.

Fair market value of leased equipment	$100,000.00
Less: Present value of residual value ($5,000 × .62092, Table 6-2)	3,104.60
Amount to be recovered by lessor through lease payments	$ 96,895.40
Five beginning-of-the-year lease payments to yield a 10% return ($96,895.40 ÷ 4.16986, Table 6-5)	$ 23,237.09

ILLUSTRATION 21-25
Computation of Direct-
Financing Lease
Payments

The amortization schedule is the same for guaranteed or unguaranteed residual value, as Illustration 21-26 shows.

CATERPILLAR FINANCIAL
LEASE AMORTIZATION SCHEDULE
(ANNUITY-DUE BASIS, **GUARANTEED** OR **UNGUARANTEED** RESIDUAL VALUE)

Date	Annual Lease Payment Plus Residual Value	Executory Costs	Interest (10%) on Lease Receivable	Lease Receivable Recovery	Lease Receivable
	(a)	(b)	(c)	(d)	(e)
1/1/08					$100,000.00
1/1/08	$ 25,237.09	$ 2,000.00	$ –0–	$ 23,237.09	76,762.91
1/1/09	25,237.09	2,000.00	7,676.29	15,560.80	61,202.11
1/1/10	25,237.09	2,000.00	6,120.21	17,116.88	44,085.23
1/1/11	25,237.09	2,000.00	4,408.52	18,828.57	25,256.66
1/1/12	25,237.09	2,000.00	2,525.67	20,711.42	4,545.24
12/31/12	5,000.00	–0–	454.76*	4,545.24	–0–
	$131,185.45	$10,000.00	$21,185.45	$100,000.00	

(a) Annual lease payment as required by lease.
(b) Executory costs included in rental payment.
(c) Preceding balance of (e) × 10%, except 1/1/08.
(d) (a) minus (b) and (c).
(e) Preceding balance minus (d).
*Rounded by 24 cents.

ILLUSTRATION 21-26
Lease Amortization
Schedule, for Lessor—
Guaranteed or
Unguaranteed Residual
Value

Using the amounts computed above, Caterpillar would make the following entries for this direct-financing lease in the first year. Note the similarity to Sterling's entries in Illustration 21-24.

Inception of Lease 1/1/08:

Lease Receivable	100,000.00	
Equipment		100,000.00

First Payment Received 1/1/08:

Cash	25,237.09	
Lease Receivable		23,237.09
Property Tax Expense/Property Taxes Payable		2,000.00

Adjusting Entry for Accrued Interest 12/31/08:

Interest Receivable	7,676.29	
Interest Revenue		7,676.29

ILLUSTRATION 21-27
Entries for Either
Guaranteed or
Unguaranteed Residual
Value, Lessor Company

Sales-Type Leases (Lessor)

As already indicated, the primary difference between a direct-financing lease and a **sales-type lease** is the manufacturer's or dealer's gross profit (or loss). The diagram in Illustration 21-28 presents the distinctions between direct-financing and sales-type leases.

OBJECTIVE 8
Describe the lessor's
accounting for sales-
type leases.

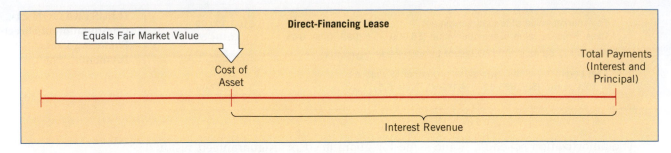

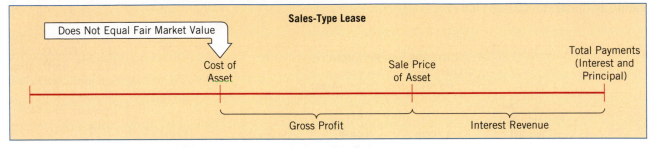

ILLUSTRATION 21-28
Direct-Financing versus
Sales-Type Leases

In a sales-type lease, the lessor records the sale price of the asset, the cost of goods sold and related inventory reduction, and the lease receivable. The information necessary to record the sales-type lease is as follows.

SALES-TYPE LEASE TERMS

LEASE RECEIVABLE (also **NET INVESTMENT**). The present value of the minimum lease payments plus the present value of any unguaranteed residual value. The lease receivable therefore includes the present value of the residual value, whether guaranteed or not.

SALES PRICE OF THE ASSET. The present value of the minimum lease payments.

COST OF GOODS SOLD. The cost of the asset to the lessor, less the present value of any unguaranteed residual value.

When recording sales revenue and cost of goods sold, there is a difference in the accounting for guaranteed and unguaranteed residual values. The guaranteed residual value can be considered part of sales revenue because the lessor knows that the entire asset has been sold. But there is less certainty that the unguaranteed residual portion of the asset has been "sold" (i.e., will be realized). Therefore, the lessor recognizes sales and cost of goods sold only for the portion of the asset for which realization is assured. However, **the gross profit amount on the sale of the asset is the same whether a guaranteed or unguaranteed residual value is involved**.

To illustrate a sales-type lease with a guaranteed residual value and with an unguaranteed residual value, assume the same facts as in the preceding direct-financing lease situation (pages 1104–1107). The estimated residual value is $5,000 (the present value of which is $3,104.60), and the leased equipment has an $85,000 cost to the dealer, Caterpillar. Assume that the fair market value of the residual value is $3,000 at the end of the lease term.

Illustration 21-29 shows computation of the amounts relevant to a sales-type lease.

	Sales-Type Lease	
	Guaranteed Residual Value	Unguaranteed Residual Value
Lease receivable	$100,000 [$23,237.09 × 4.16986 (Table 6-5) + $5,000 × .62092 (Table 6-2)]	Same
Sales price of the asset	$100,000	$96,895.40 ($100,000 − $3,104.60)
Cost of goods sold	$85,000	$81,895.40 ($85,000 − $3,104.60)
Gross profit	$15,000 ($100,000 − $85,000)	$15,000 ($96,895.40 − $81,895.40)

Caterpillar records the same profit ($15,000) at the point of sale whether the residual value is guaranteed or unguaranteed. The difference between the two is that **the sales revenue and cost of goods sold amounts are different**.

In making this computation, we deduct the present value of the unguaranteed residual value from sales revenue and cost of goods sold for two reasons: (1) The criteria for revenue recognition have not been met. (2) It is improper to match expense against revenue not yet recognized. The revenue recognition criteria have not been met **because of the uncertainty surrounding the realization of the unguaranteed residual value**.

Caterpillar makes the following entries to record this transaction on January 1, 2008, and the receipt of the residual value at the end of the lease term.

ILLUSTRATION 21-30
Entries for Guaranteed
and Unguaranteed
Residual Values, Lessor
Company—Sales-Type
Lease

Guaranteed Residual Value			Unguaranteed Residual Value		
To record sales-type lease at inception (January 1, 2008):					
Cost of Goods Sold	85,000.00		Cost of Goods Sold	81,895.40	
Lease Receivable	100,000.00		Lease Receivable	100,000.00	
Sales Revenue		100,000.00	Sales Revenue		96,895.40
Inventory		85,000.00	Inventory		85,000.00
To record receipt of the first lease payment (January 1, 2008):					
Cash	25,237.09		Cash	25,237.09	
Lease Receivable		23,237.09	Lease Receivable		23,237.09
Property Tax Exp./Pay.		2,000.00	Property Tax Exp./Pay.		2,000.00
To recognize interest revenue earned during the first year (December 31, 2008):					
Interest Receivable	7,676.29		Interest Receivable	7,676.29	
Interest Revenue		7,676.29	Interest Revenue		7,676.29
(See lease amortization schedule, Illustration 21-26 on page 1113.)					
To record receipt of the second lease payment (January 1, 2009):					
Cash	25,237.09		Cash	25,237.09	
Interest Receivable		7,676.29	Interest Receivable		7,676.29
Lease Receivable		15,560.80	Lease Receivable		15,560.80
Property Tax Exp./Pay.		2,000.00	Property Tax Exp./Pay.		2,000.00
To recognize interest revenue earned during the second year (December 31, 2009):					
Interest Receivable	6,120.21		Interest Receivable	6,120.21	
Interest Revenue		6,120.21	Interest Revenue		6,120.21
To record receipt of residual value at end of lease term (December 31, 2012):					
Inventory	3,000		Inventory	3,000	
Cash	2,000		Loss on Capital Lease	2,000	
Lease Receivable		5,000	Lease Receivable		5,000

Companies must periodically review the **estimated unguaranteed residual value in a sales-type lease**. If the estimate of the unguaranteed residual value declines, the company must revise the accounting for the transaction using the changed estimate. The decline represents a reduction in the lessor's lease receivable (net investment). The lessor recognizes the decline as a loss in the period in which it reduces the residual estimate. Companies do not recognize upward adjustments in estimated residual value.

XEROX TAKES ON THE SEC

WHAT DO THE NUMBERS MEAN?

Xerox derives much of its income from leasing equipment. Reporting such leases as sales leases, Xerox records a lease contract as a sale, therefore recognizing income immediately. One problem is that each lease receipt consists of payments for items such as supplies, services, financing, and equipment.

The SEC *accused* Xerox of inappropriately allocating lease receipts, which affects the timing of income that it reports. If Xerox applied SEC guidelines, it would report income in different time periods. Xerox contended that its methods were correct. It also noted that when the lease term is up, the bottom line is the same using either the SEC's recommended allocation method or its current method.

Although Xerox can refuse to change its method, the SEC has the right to prevent a company from selling stock or bonds to the public if the agency rejects filings of the company.

Apparently, being able to access public markets is very valuable to Xerox. The company agreed to change its accounting according to SEC wishes, and paid a fine of $10 million due to its past accounting practices.

Source: Adapted from "Xerox Takes on the SEC," *Accounting Web* (January 9, 2002) (*www.accountingweb.com*).

Bargain Purchase Option (Lessee)

As stated earlier, a bargain purchase option allows the lessee to purchase the leased property for a future price that is substantially lower than the property's expected future fair value. The price is so favorable at the lease's inception that the future exercise of the option appears to be reasonably assured. If a bargain purchase option exists, **the lessee must increase the present value of the minimum lease payments by the present value of the option price**.

For example, assume that Sterling Construction in the illustration on page 1109 had an option to buy the leased equipment for $5,000 at the end of the five-year lease term. At that point, Sterling and Caterpillar expect the fair value to be $18,000. The significant difference between the option price and the fair value creates a bargain purchase option, and the exercise of that option is reasonably assured.

A bargain purchase option affects the accounting for leases in essentially the same way as a guaranteed residual value. In other words, with a guaranteed residual value, the lessee must pay the residual value at the end of the lease. Similarly, a purchase option which is a bargain will almost certainly be paid by the lessee. Therefore, the computations, amortization schedule, and entries that would be prepared for this $5,000 bargain purchase option are identical to those shown for the $5,000 guaranteed residual value (see Illustrations 21-17, 21-18, and 21-19).

The only difference between the accounting treatment for a bargain purchase option and a guaranteed residual value of identical amounts and circumstances is in the **computation of the annual depreciation**. In the case of a guaranteed residual value, Sterling depreciates the asset over the lease term; in the case of a bargain purchase option, it uses the **economic life** of the asset.

Initial Direct Costs (Lessor)

Initial direct costs are of two types: incremental and internal.[20] **Incremental direct costs** are paid to independent third parties for originating a lease arrangement. Examples include the cost of independent appraisal of collateral used to secure a lease, the cost of an outside credit check of the lessee, or a broker's fee for finding the lessee.

Internal direct costs are directly related to specified activities performed **by the lessor** on a given lease. Examples are evaluating the prospective lessee's financial condition; evaluating and recording guarantees, collateral, and other security arrangements; negotiating lease terms and preparing and processing lease documents; and closing the transaction. The costs directly related to an employee's time spent on a specific lease transaction are also considered initial direct costs.

However, initial direct costs should **not** include **internal indirect costs**. Such costs are related to activities the lessor performs for advertising, servicing existing leases, and establishing and monitoring credit policies. Nor should the lessor include the costs for supervision and administration or for expenses such as rent and depreciation.

The accounting for initial direct costs depends on the type of lease:

* For **operating leases**, the lessor should defer initial direct costs and **allocate them over the lease term** in proportion to the recognition of rental revenue.
* For **sales-type leases**, the lessor expenses the initial direct costs **in the period** in which it recognizes the profit on the sale.
* For a **direct-financing lease**, the lessor adds initial direct costs to the net investment in the lease and **amortizes them over the life of the lease as a yield adjustment**.

In a direct-financing lease, the lessor must disclose the unamortized deferred initial direct costs that are part of its investment in the direct-financing lease. For example, if the carrying value of the asset in the lease is $4,000,000 and the lessor incurs initial direct costs of $35,000, then the lease receivable (net investment in the lease) would be $4,035,000. The yield would be lower than the initial rate of return, and the lessor would adjust the yield to ensure proper amortization of the amount over the life of the lease.

Current versus Noncurrent

Earlier in the chapter we presented the classification of the lease liability/receivable in an annuity-due situation. Illustration 21-8 indicated that Sterling's current liability is the payment of $23,981.62 (excluding $2,000 of executory costs) to be made on January 1 of the next year. Similarly, as shown in Illustration 21-16, Caterpillar's current asset is the $23,981.62 (excluding $2,000 of executory costs) it will collect on January 1 of the next year. In these annuity-due instances, the balance sheet date is December 31 and the due date of the lease payment is January 1 (less than one year), so the present value ($23,981.62) of the payment due the following January 1 is the same as the rental payment ($23,981.62).

What happens if the situation is an ordinary annuity rather than an annuity due? For example, assume that the rent is due at the **end of the year** (December 31) rather than at the beginning (January 1). *FASB Statement No. 13* does not indicate how to measure the current and noncurrent amounts. It requires that for the lessee the "obligations shall be separately identified on the balance sheet as obligations under capital leases and shall be subject to the same considerations as other obligations in classifying them with current and noncurrent liabilities in classified balance sheets."[21] **The most common**

[20]"Accounting for Nonrefundable Fees and Costs Associated with Originating or Acquiring Loans and Initial Direct Costs of Leases," *Statement of Financial Accounting Standards No. 91* (Stamford: Conn.: FASB, 1987).

[21]"Accounting for Leases," op. cit., par. 16.

method of measuring the current liability portion in ordinary annuity leases is the **change-in-the-present-value method.**[22]

To illustrate the change-in-the-present-value method, assume an ordinary-annuity situation with the same facts as the Caterpillar/Sterling case, excluding the $2,000 of executory costs. Because Sterling pays the rents at the end of the period instead of at the beginning, Caterpillar sets the five rents at $26,379.73, to have an effective interest rate of 10 percent. Illustration 21-31 shows the ordinary-annuity amortization schedule.

ILLUSTRATION 21-31
Lease Amortization Schedule—Ordinary-Annuity Basis

STERLING/CATERPILLAR
LEASE AMORTIZATION SCHEDULE
(ORDINARY-ANNUITY BASIS)

Date	Annual Lease Payment	Interest 10%	Reduction of Lease Liability/Receivable	Balance of Lease Liability/Receivable
1/1/08				$100,000.00
12/31/08	$ 26,379.73	$10,000.00	$ 16,379.73	83,620.27
12/31/09	26,379.73	8,362.03	18,017.70	65,602.57
12/31/10	26,379.73	6,560.26	19,819.47	45,783.10
12/31/11	26,379.73	4,578.31	21,801.42	23,981.68
12/31/12	26,379.73	2,398.05*	23,981.68	–0–
	$131,898.65	$31,898.65	$100,000.00	

*Rounded by 12 cents.

The current portion of the lease liability/receivable under the **change-in-the-present-value method** as of December 31, 2008, would be $18,017.70 ($83,620.27 − $65,602.57). As of December 31, 2009, the current portion would be $19,819.47 ($65,602.57 − $45,783.10). At December 31, 2008, Caterpillar classifies $65,602.57 of the receivable as noncurrent.

Thus, both the annuity-due and the ordinary-annuity situations report the reduction of principal for the next period as a current liability/current asset. In the annuity-due situation, Caterpillar accrues interest during the year but is not paid until the next period. As a result, **a current asset arises for the receivable reduction and for the interest** that was earned in the preceding period.

In the ordinary-annuity situation, the interest accrued during the period is also paid in the same period. Consequently, the lessor shows as a current asset only the principal reduction.

Disclosing Lease Data

OBJECTIVE 9
List the disclosure requirements for leases.

The FASB requires **lessees** and **lessors** to disclose certain information about leases in their financial statements or in the notes. These requirements vary based upon the type of lease (capital or operating) and whether the issuer is the lessor or lessee. These disclosure requirements provide investors with the following information:

- General description of the nature of leasing arrangements.
- The nature, timing, and amount of cash inflows and outflows associated with leases, including payments to be paid or received for each of the five succeeding years.
- The amount of lease revenues and expenses reported in the income statement each period.

[22]For additional discussion on this approach and possible alternatives, see R. J. Swieringa, "When Current Is Noncurrent and Vice Versa!" *The Accounting Review* (January 1984), pp. 123–30, and A. W. Richardson, "The Measurement of the Current Portion of the Long-Term Lease Obligations—Some Evidence from Practice," *The Accounting Review* (October 1985), pp. 744–52.

- Description and amounts of leased assets by major balance sheet classification and related liabilities.
- Amounts receivable and unearned revenues under lease agreements.[23]

Illustration 21-32 presents financial statement excerpts from the 2004 annual report of **Tasty Baking Company**. These excerpts represent the statement and note disclosures typical of a lessee having both capital leases and operating leases.

Tasty Baking Company
(dollar amounts in thousands)

	2004	2003
Current Liabilities		
Current obligations under capital leases	$ 713	$ 634
Noncurrent Liabilities		
Long-term obligations under capital leases, less current portion	4,159	4,705

Note 7: Commitments and Contingencies

The company leases certain plant and distribution facilities, machinery and automotive equipment under noncancelable lease agreements. The company expects that in the normal course of business, leases that expire will be renewed or replaced by other leases. . . .Property, plant and equipment relating to capital leases was $5,965 at December 25, 2004, and $8,310 at December 27, 2003, with accumulated amortization of $1,019 and $2,303, respectively. Depreciation and amortization of assets recorded under capital leases was $690 in 2004 and $261 in 2003.

The following is a schedule of future minimum lease payments as of December 25, 2004:

	Capital Leases	Noncancelable Operating Leases
2005	$1,142	$1,747
2006	1,142	1,440
2007	1,089	701
2008	581	487
2009	561	146
Later years	2,525	4
Total minimum lease payments	$7,040	$4,525
Less interest portion of payments	2,168	
Present value of future minimum lease payments	$4,872	

Rental expense was approximately $2,474 in 2004 and $2,194 in 2003.

ILLUSTRATION 21-32
Disclosure of Leases by Lessee

Description and amount of lease obligations

General description

Description and amounts of leased assets

Nature, timing, and amounts of cash outflows

Amount of lease rental expense

Illustration 21-33 presents the lease note disclosure from the 2004 annual report of **Hewlett-Packard Company**. The disclosure highlights required lessor disclosures.

Hewlett-Packard Company
Notes to Financial Statements
(in millions)

Note 1 (in part): Lease Financing

Lease financing consists of direct financing leases, leveraged leases and equipment on operating leases. Income on direct financing leases is recognized by a method which produces a constant periodic rate of return on the outstanding investment in the lease. . . . Initial direct costs are deferred and amortized using the interest method over the lease period. Equipment under operating leases is recorded at cost, net of accumulated depreciation. Income from operating leases is recognized ratably over the term of the leases.

continued on next page

ILLUSTRATION 21-33
Disclosure of Leases by Lessor

General description

---

[23]"Accounting for Leases," *FASB Statement No. 13*, as amended and interpreted through May 1980 (Stamford, Conn.: FASB, 1980), par. 16; par. 23.

Note 9: Financing Receivables and Operating Leases
Financing receivables represent sales-type and direct-financing leases resulting from the marketing of HP's and complementary third-party products. These receivables typically have terms from two to five years and are usually collateralized by a security interest in the underlying assets. Financing receivables also include billed receivables from operating leases. The components of net financing receivables, which are included in financing receivables and long-term financing receivables and other assets, were as follows at October 31:

	2004	2003
	(In millions)	
Minimum lease payments receivable	$ 5.328	$ 6,010
Allowance for doubtful accounts	(213)	(210)
Unguaranteed residual value	394	446
Unearned income	(396)	(475)
Financing receivables, net	5,113	5,771
Less current portion	(2,945)	(3,026)
Amounts due after one year, net	$ 2,168	$ 2,745

(left margin: Amount receivable and unearned revenues)

Scheduled maturities of HP's minimum lease payments receivable are as follows at October 31, 2004:

	2005	2006	2007	2008	2009	Thereafter	Total
			(In millions)				
Scheduled maturities of minimum lease payments receivable	$3,045	$1,381	$612	$194	$67	$29	$5,328

(left margin: Nature, timing, and amounts of cash inflows)

Equipment leased to customers under operating leases was $2.3 billion at October 31, 2004, and $2.1 billion at October 31, 2003, and is included in machinery and equipment. Accumulated depreciation on equipment under lease was $0.9 billion at October 31, 2004 and $1.2 billion at October 31, 2003. Minimum future rentals on non-cancelable operating leases related to leased equipment are as follows at October 31, 2004:

	2005	2006	2007	2008	2009	Thereafter	Total
			(In millions)				
Minimum future rentals on non-cancelable operating leases	$824	$404	$103	$18	$3	$11	$1,363

(left margin: Description of leased assets)

(left margin: Amount of future rentals)

Additional Lease Disclosures

LEASE ACCOUNTING—UNSOLVED PROBLEMS

As we indicated at the beginning of this chapter, lease accounting is subject to abuse. Companies make strenuous efforts to circumvent *Statement No. 13*. In practice, the strong desires of lessees to resist capitalization have rendered the accounting rules for capitalizing leases partially ineffective. Leasing generally involves large dollar amounts that, when capitalized, materially increase reported liabilities and adversely affect the debt-to-equity ratio. Lessees also resist lease capitalization because charges to expense made in the early years of the lease term are higher under the capital lease method than under the operating method, frequently without tax benefit. As a consequence, "let's beat *Statement No. 13*" is one of the most popular games in town.[24]

To avoid leased asset capitalization, companies design, write, and interpret lease agreements to prevent satisfying any of the four capitalized lease criteria. Companies can easily devise lease agreements in such a way, by meeting the following specifications.

1 Ensure that the lease does not specify the transfer of title of the property to the lessee.

2 Do not write in a bargain purchase option.

---

[24]Richard Dieter, "Is Lessee Accounting Working?" *CPA Journal* (August 1979), pp. 13–19. This article provides interesting examples of abuses of *Statement No. 13*, discusses the circumstances that led to the current situation, and proposes a solution.

3 Set the lease term at something less than 75 percent of the estimated economic life of the leased property.

4 Arrange for the present value of the minimum lease payments to be less than 90 percent of the fair value of the leased property.

The real challenge lies in disqualifying the lease as a capital lease to the lessee, while having the same lease qualify as a capital (sales or financing) lease to the lessor. Unlike lessees, lessors try to avoid having lease arrangements classified as operating leases.[25]

Avoiding the first three criteria is relatively simple, but it takes a little ingenuity to avoid the "90 percent recovery test" for the lessee while satisfying it for the lessor. Two of the factors involved in this effort are: (1) the use of the incremental borrowing rate by the lessee when it is higher than the implicit interest rate of the lessor, by making information about the implicit rate unavailable to the lessee; and (2) residual value guarantees.

The lessee's use of the higher interest rate is probably the more popular subterfuge. Lessees are knowledgeable about the fair value of the leased property and, of course, the rental payments. However, they generally are unaware of the estimated residual value used by the lessor. Therefore, the lessee who does not know exactly the lessor's implicit interest rate might use a different (higher) incremental borrowing rate.

The residual-value guarantee is the other unique, yet popular, device used by lessees and lessors. In fact, a whole new industry has emerged to circumvent symmetry between the lessee and the lessor in accounting for leases. The residual-value guarantee has spawned numerous companies whose principal, or even sole, function is to guarantee the residual value of leased assets.

Because the minimum lease payments include the guaranteed residual value for the lessor, this satisfies the 90 percent recovery of fair market value test. The lease is a nonoperating lease to the lessor. **But because a third-party guarantees the residual value, the minimum lease payments of the lessee exclude the guarantee.** Thus, by merely transferring some of the risk to a third party, lessees can alter substantially the accounting treatment by converting what would otherwise be capital leases to operating leases.[26]

The nature of the criteria encourages much of this circumvention, stemming from weaknesses in the basic objective of *Statement No. 13*. Accounting standards-setting bodies continue to have poor experience with arbitrary break points or other size and percentage criteria—such as rules like "90 percent of" and "75 percent of." Some believe that a more workable solution is to require capitalization of all leases that have non-cancelable payment terms in excess of one year. Under this approach, lessee acquires an asset (a property right) and a corresponding liability, rather than on the basis that the lease transfers substantially all the risks and rewards of ownership.

Three years after it issued *Statement No. 13*, a majority of the FASB expressed "the tentative view that, if *Statement 13* were to be reconsidered, they would support a property right approach in which all leases are included as 'rights to use property' and as

INTERNATIONAL INSIGHT

Recently the SEC indicated that it might be advisable for the IASB and the FASB to jointly undertake a project to reconsider lease accounting standards.

---

[25] The reason is that most lessors are banks, which are not permitted to hold these assets on their balance sheets except for relatively short periods of time. Furthermore, the capital-lease transaction from the lessor's standpoint provides higher income flows in the earlier periods of the lease life.

[26] As an aside, third-party guarantors have experienced some difficulty. **Lloyd's of London**, at one time, insured the fast-growing U.S. computer-leasing industry in the amount of $2 billion against revenue losses, and losses in residual value, for canceled leases. Because of "overnight" technological improvements and the successive introductions of more efficient and less expensive computers, lessees in abundance canceled their leases. As the market for second-hand computers became flooded, residual values plummeted, and third-party guarantor Lloyd's of London projected a loss of $400 million. The lessees' and lessors' desire to circumvent *FASB Statement No. 13* stimulated much of the third-party guarantee business.

'lease obligations' in the lessee's balance sheet."[27] The FASB and other international standard setters have issued a report on lease accounting that proposes the capitalization of more leases.[28]

WHAT DO THE NUMBERS MEAN?

Telecommunication companies have developed one of the more innovative and controversial uses of leases. In order to provide fiber-optic service to their customers in areas where they did not have networks installed, telecommunication companies such as **Global Crossing**, **Qwest Communications International**, and **Cable and Wireless** entered into agreements to swap some of their unused network capacity in exchange for the use of another company's fiber-optic cables. Here's how it works:

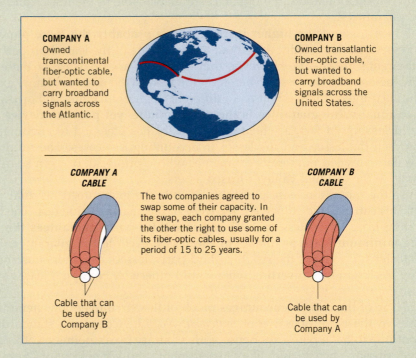

COMPANY A
Owned transcontinental fiber-optic cable, but wanted to carry broadband signals across the Atlantic.

COMPANY B
Owned transatlantic fiber-optic cable, but wanted to carry broadband signals across the United States.

COMPANY A CABLE

COMPANY B CABLE

The two companies agreed to swap some of their capacity. In the swap, each company granted the other the right to use some of its fiber-optic cables, usually for a period of 15 to 25 years.

Cable that can be used by Company B

Cable that can be used by Company A

Such trades seem like a good way to make efficient use of telecommunication assets. What got some telecommunications companies in trouble, though, was how they did the accounting for the swap.

The most conservative accounting for the capacity trades is to treat the swap as an exchange of assets, which does not affect the income statement. However, Global Crossing got into trouble with the SEC when it structured some of its capacity swaps as leases—the legal right to use capacity. Global Crossing was recognizing as revenue the payments received for the outgoing transfer of capacity, while payments for the incoming cable capacity were treated as capital expenditures, and therefore not expensed. As a result, Global Crossing was showing strong profits from its capacity swaps. However, the company's investors got an unpleasant surprise when the market for bandwidth cooled off and there was no longer demand for its broadband capacity or its long-term leasing arrangements.

Source: Simon Romero and Seth Schiesel, "The Fiber-Optic Fantasy Slips Away," *New York Times on the Web* (February 17, 2002). By permission.

[27]"Is Lessee Accounting Working?" op. cit., p. 19.

[28]H. Nailor and A. Lennard, "Capital Leases: Implementation of a New Approach," *Financial Accounting Series No. 206A* (Norwalk, Conn.: FASB, 2000).

SUMMARY OF LEARNING OBJECTIVES

1. Explain the nature, economic substance, and advantages of lease transactions. A lease is a contractual agreement between a lessor and a lessee that conveys to the lessee the right to use specific property (real or personal), owned by the lessor, for a specified period of time. In return, the lessee periodically pays cash (rent) to the lessor. The advantages of lease transactions are: (1) 100 percent financing; (2) protection against obsolescence, (3) flexibility, (4) less costly financing, (5) possible tax advantages, and (6) off-balance-sheet financing.

2. Describe the accounting criteria and procedures for capitalizing leases by the lessee. A lease is a capital lease if it meets one or more of the following (Group I) criteria: (1) The lease transfers ownership of the property to the lessee. (2) The lease contains a bargain purchase option. (3) The lease term is equal to 75 percent or more of the estimated economic life of the leased property. (4) The present value of the minimum lease payments (excluding executory costs) equals or exceeds 90 percent of the fair value of the leased property. For a capital lease, the lessee records an asset and a liability at the lower of (1) the present value of the minimum lease payments, or (2) the fair market value of the leased asset at the inception of the lease.

3. Contrast the operating and capitalization methods of recording leases. The total charges to operations are the same over the lease term whether accounting for the lease as a capital lease or as an operating lease. Under the capital lease treatment, the charges are higher in the earlier years and lower in the later years. If using an accelerated method of depreciation, the differences between the amounts charged to operations under the two methods would be even larger in the earlier and later years. If using a capital lease instead of an operating lease, the following occurs: (1) an increase in the amount of reported debt (both short-term and long-term), (2) an increase in the amount of total assets (specifically long-lived assets), and (3) lower income early in the life of the lease and, therefore, lower retained earnings.

4. Identify the classifications of leases for the lessor. A lessor may classify leases for accounting purposes as follows: (1) operating leases, (2) direct-financing leases, (3) sales-type leases. The lessor should classify and account for an arrangement as a direct-financing lease or a sales-type lease if, at the date of the lease agreement, the lease meets one or more of the Group I criteria (as shown in learning objective 2 for lessees) and *both* of the following Group II criteria. *Group II:* (1) Collectibility of the payments required from the lessee is reasonably predictable; and (2) no important uncertainties surround the amount of unreimbursable costs yet to be incurred by the lessor under the lease. The lessor classifies and accounts for all leases that fail to meet the criteria as operating leases.

5. Describe the lessor's accounting for direct-financing leases. Leases that are in substance the financing of an asset purchase by a lessee require the lessor to substitute a "lease receivable" for the leased asset. "Lease receivable" is the present value of the minimum lease payments plus the present value of the unguaranteed residual value. Therefore lessors include the residual value, whether guaranteed or unguaranteed, as part of lease receivable.

6. Identify special features of lease arrangements that cause unique accounting problems. The features of lease arrangements that cause unique accounting problems are: (1) residual values; (2) sales-type leases (lessor); (3) bargain purchase options; (4) initial direct costs; (5) current versus noncurrent; and (6) disclosures.

7. Describe the effect of residual values, guaranteed and unguaranteed, on lease accounting. Whether the estimated residual value is guaranteed or unguaranteed is of both economic and accounting consequence to the lessee. The accounting consequence

KEY TERMS

bargain purchase option, *1094*

bargain renewal option, *1094*

capital lease, *1093*

capitalization criteria, *1094*

capitalization of leases, *1092*

direct-financing lease, *1104*

effective-interest method, *1096*

executory costs, 1095

guaranteed residual value, *1095, 1108*

implicit interest rate, *1096*

incremental borrowing rate, *1095*

initial direct costs, *1117*

lease, *1089*

lease receivable, *1104*

lease term, *1090, 1094*

lessee, *1089*

lessor, *1089*

manufacturer's or dealer's profit (or loss), *1103*

minimum lease payments, *1095*

noncancelable, *1092*

off-balance-sheet financing, *1091*

operating lease, *1093*

residual value, *1108*

sales-type lease, *1113*

third-party guarantors, *1095*

unguaranteed residual value, *1110*

is that the minimum lease payments, the basis for capitalization, include the guaranteed residual value but exclude the unguaranteed residual value. A guaranteed residual value affects the lessee's computation of minimum lease payments and the amounts capitalized as a leased asset and a lease obligation. In effect, the guaranteed residual value is an additional lease payment that the lessee will pay in property or cash, or both, at the end of the lease term. An unguaranteed residual value from the lessee's viewpoint is the same as no residual value in terms of its effect upon the lessee's method of computing the minimum lease payments and the capitalization of the leased asset and the lease liability.

8. Describe the lessor's accounting for sales-type leases. A sales-type lease recognizes interest revenue like a direct-financing lease. It also recognizes a manufacturer's or dealer's profit. In a sales-type lease, the lessor records at the inception of the lease the sales price of the asset, the cost of goods sold and related inventory reduction, and the lease receivable. Sales-type leases differ from direct-financing leases in terms of the cost and fair value of the leased asset, which results in gross profit. Lease receivable and interest revenue are the same whether a guaranteed or an unguaranteed residual value is involved. The accounting for guaranteed and for unguaranteed residual values requires recording sales revenue and cost of goods sold differently. The guaranteed residual value can be considered part of sales revenue because the lessor knows that the entire asset has been sold. There is less certainty that the unguaranteed residual portion of the asset has been "sold"; therefore, lessors recognize sales and cost of goods sold only for the portion of the asset for which realization is assured. However, the gross profit amount on the sale of the asset is the same whether a guaranteed or unguaranteed residual value is involved.

*Expanded Discussion of
Real Estate Leases and
Leveraged Leases*

9. List the disclosure requirements for leases. The disclosure requirements for the lessees and lessors vary based upon the type of lease (capital or operating) and whether the issuer is the lessor or lessee. These disclosure requirements provide investors with the following information: (1) general description of the nature of leasing arrangements, (2) the nature, timing and amount of cash inflows and outflows associated with leases, including payments to be paid or received for each of the five succeeding years, (3) the amount of lease revenues and expenses reported in the income statement each period, (4) description and amounts of leased assets by major balance sheet classification and related liabilities, and (5) amounts receivable and unearned revenues under lease agreements.

APPENDIX

21A Examples of Lease Arrangements

OBJECTIVE 10
Understand and apply lease accounting concepts to various lease arrangements.

To illustrate concepts discussed in this chapter, assume that Morgan Bakeries is involved in four different lease situations. Each of these leases is noncancelable, and in no case does Morgan receive title to the properties leased during or at the end of the lease term. All leases start on January 1, 2008, with the first rental due at the beginning of the year. The additional information is shown in Illustration 21A-1.

	Harmon, Inc.	Arden's Oven Co.	Mendota Truck Co.	Appleland Computer
Type of property	Cabinets	Oven	Truck	Computer
Yearly rental	$6,000	$15,000	$5,582.62	$3,557.25
Lease term	20 years	10 years	3 years	3 years
Estimated economic life	30 years	25 years	7 years	5 years
Purchase option	None	$75,000 at end of 10 years $4,000 at end of 15 years	None	$3,000 at end of 3 years, which approximates fair market value
Renewal option	None	5-year renewal option at $15,000 per year	None	1 year at $1,500; no penalty for nonrenewal; standard renewal clause
Fair market value at inception of lease	$60,000	$120,000	$20,000	$10,000
Cost of asset to lessor	$60,000	$120,000	$15,000	$10,000
Residual value				
Guaranteed	–0–	–0–	$7,000	–0–
Unguaranteed	$5,000	–0–	–0–	$3,000
Incremental borrowing rate of lessee	12%	12%	12%	12%
Executory costs paid by	*Lessee* $300 per year	*Lessee* $1,000 per year	*Lessee* $500 per year	*Lessor* Estimated to be $500 per year
Present value of minimum lease payments				
Using incremental borrowing rate of lessee	$50,194.68	$115,153.35	$20,000	$8,224.16
Using implicit rate of lessor	Not known	Not known	Not known	Known by lessee, $8,027.48
Estimated fair market value at end of lease	$5,000	$80,000 at end of 10 years $60,000 at end of 15 years	Not available	$3,000

ILLUSTRATION 21A-1
Illustrative Lease Situations, Lessors

HARMON, INC.

The following is an analysis of the Harmon, Inc. lease.

1 **Transfer of title?** No.

2 **Bargain purchase option?** No.

3 **Economic life test (75% test).** The lease term is 20 years and the estimated economic life is 30 years. Thus it **does not** meet the 75 percent test.

4 **Recovery of investment test (90% test):**

Fair market value	$60,000		Rental payments	$ 6,000
Rate	90%		PV of annuity due for	
90% of fair market value	$54,000		20 years at 12%	× 8.36578
			PV of rental payments	$50,194.68

Because the present value of the minimum lease payments is less than 90 percent of the fair market value, the lease does not meet the 90 percent test.

Both Morgan and Harmon should account for this lease as an operating lease, as indicated by the January 1, 2008, entries shown in Illustration 21A-2 (on page 1126).

ILLUSTRATION 21A-2
Comparative Entries
for Operating Lease

Morgan Bakeries (Lessee)			Harmon, Inc. (Lessor)		
Rent Expense	6,000		Cash	6,000	
Cash		6,000	Rental Revenue		6,000

ARDEN'S OVEN CO.

The following is an analysis of the Arden's Oven Co. lease.

1 **Transfer of title?** No.

2 **Bargain purchase option?** The $75,000 option at the end of 10 years does not appear to be sufficiently lower than the expected fair value of $80,000 to make it reasonably assured that it will be exercised. However, the $4,000 at the end of 15 years when the fair value is $60,000 does appear to be a bargain. From the information given, criterion 2 is therefore met. Note that both the guaranteed and the unguaranteed residual values are assigned zero values because the lessor does not expect to repossess the leased asset.

3 **Economic life test (75% test):** Given that a bargain purchase option exists, the lease term is the initial lease period of 10 years plus the five-year renewal option since it precedes a bargain purchase option. Even though the lease term is now considered to be 15 years, this test is still not met because 75 percent of the economic life of 25 years is 18.75 years.

4 **Recovery of investment test (90% test):**

Fair market value	$120,000	Rental payments	$ 15,000.00
Rate	90%	PV of annuity due for	
90% of fair market value	$108,000	15 years at 12%	× 7.62817
		PV of rental payments	$114,422.55

PV of bargain purchase option: = $4,000 × (PVF$_{15,12\%}$) = $4,000 × .18270 = $730.80

PV of rental payments	$114,422.55
PV of bargain purchase option	730.80
PV of minimum lease payments	$115,153.35

The present value of the minimum lease payments is greater than 90 percent of the fair market value; therefore, the lease does meet the 90 percent test.

Morgan Bakeries should account for this as a capital lease because the lease meets both criteria 2 and 4. Assuming that Arden's implicit rate is less than Morgan's incremental borrowing rate, the following entries are made on January 1, 2008.

ILLUSTRATION 21A-3
Comparative Entries for
Capital Lease—Bargain
Purchase Option

Morgan Bakeries (Lessee)			Arden's Oven Co. (Lessor)		
Leased Asset—Oven 115,153.35			Lease Receivable	120,000	
Lease Liability		115,153.35	Asset—Oven		120,000

Morgan Bakeries would depreciate the leased asset over its economic life of 25 years, given the bargain purchase option. Arden's Oven Co. does not use sales-type accounting because the fair market value and the cost of the asset are the same at the inception of the lease.

MENDOTA TRUCK CO.

The following is an analysis of the Mendota Truck Co. lease.

1 **Transfer of title?** No.

2 **Bargain purchase option?** No.

3 **Economic life test (75% test):** The lease term is three years and the estimated economic life is seven years. Thus it **does not** meet the 75 percent test.

4 **Recovery of investment test (90% test):**

Fair market value	$20,000	Rental payments	$ 5,582.62
Rate	90%	PV of annuity due for	
90% of fair market value	$18,000	3 years at 12%	× 2.69005
		PV of rental payments	$15,017.54
		(Note: Adjusted for $0.01 due to rounding)	

PV of guaranteed residual value: = $7,000 × (PVF$_{3,12\%}$) = $7,000 × .71178 = $4,982.46

PV of rental payments	$15,017.54
PV of guaranteed residual value	4,982.46
PV of minimum lease payments	$20,000.00

The present value of the minimum lease payments is greater than 90 percent of the fair market value; therefore, the lease meets the 90 percent test.

Assuming that Mendota's implicit rate is the same as Morgan's incremental borrowing rate, the following entries are made on January 1, 2008.

Morgan Bakeries (Lessee)			Mendota Truck Co. (Lessor)		
Leased Asset—Truck	20,000		Lease Receivable	20,000	
Lease Liability		20,000	Cost of Goods Sold	15,000	
			Inventory—Truck		15,000
			Sales		20,000

ILLUSTRATION 21A-4
Comparative Entries for Capital Lease

Morgan depreciates the leased asset over three years to its guaranteed residual value.

APPLELAND COMPUTER

The following is an analysis of the Appleland Computer lease.

1 **Transfer of title?** No.

2 **Bargain purchase option?** No. The option to purchase at the end of three years at approximate fair market value is clearly not a bargain.

3 **Economic life test (75% test):** The lease term is three years, and no bargain renewal period exists. Therefore the 75 percent test **is not** met.

4 **Recovery of investment test (90% test):**

Fair market value	$10,000	Rental payments	$3,557.25
Rate	90%	Less executory costs	500.00
90% of fair market value	$ 9,000		3,057.25
		PV of annuity due factor for 3 years at 12%	× 2.69005
		PV of minimum lease payments using incremental borrowing rate	$8,224.16

The present value of the minimum lease payments using the incremental borrowing rate is $8,224.16; using the implicit rate, it is $8,027.48 (see Illustration 21A-1). The lessor's implicit rate is therefore higher than the incremental borrowing rate. Given this situation, the lessee uses the $8,224.16 (lower interest rate when discounting) when comparing with the 90 percent of fair market value. Because the present value of the minimum lease payments is lower than 90 percent of the fair market value, the lease does **not** meet the recovery of investment test.

The following entries are made on January 1, 2008, indicating an operating lease.

ILLUSTRATION 21A-5
Comparative Entries for
Operating Lease

Morgan Bakeries (Lessee)			Appleland Computer (Lessor)		
Rent Expense	3,557.25		Cash	3,557.25	
Cash		3,557.25	Rental Revenue		3,557.25

If the lease payments had been $3,557.25 with no executory costs involved, this lease arrangement would have qualified for capital-lease accounting treatment.

SUMMARY OF LEARNING OBJECTIVE FOR APPENDIX 21A

10. Understand and apply lease accounting concepts to various lease arrangements. The classification of leases by lessees and lessors is based on criteria that assess whether the lessor has transferred to the lessee substantially all of the risks and benefits of ownership of the asset. In addition, lessors assess two additional criteria to ensure that payment is assured and that there are not uncertainties about lessor's future costs. Lessees capitalize leases that meet any of the criteria, recording a lease asset and related lease liability. For leases that are in substance a financing of an asset purchase, lessors substitute a lease receivable for the leased asset. In a sales-type lease, the fair value of the leased asset is greater than the cost, and lessors record gross profit. Leases that do not meet capitalization criteria are classified as operating leases, on which rent expense (revenue) is recognized by lessees (lessors) for lease payments.

APPENDIX
21B Sale-Leasebacks

OBJECTIVE 11
Describe the lessee's accounting for sale-leaseback transactions.

The term **sale-leaseback** describes a transaction in which the owner of the property (seller-lessee) sells the property to another and simultaneously leases it back from the new owner. The use of the property is generally continued without interruption.

Sale-leasebacks are common. Financial institutions (e.g., **Bank of America** and **First Chicago**) have used this technique for their administrative offices, public utilities (**Ohio Edison** and **Pinnacle West Corporation**) for their generating plants, and airlines (**Continental** and **Alaska Airlines**) for their aircraft. The advantages of a sale-leaseback from the seller's viewpoint usually involve two primary considerations:

1 *Financing*—If the purchase of equipment has already been financed, a sale-leaseback can allow the seller to refinance at lower rates, assuming rates have dropped. In addition, a sale-leaseback can provide another source of working capital, particularly when liquidity is tight.

2 *Taxes*—At the time a company purchased equipment, it may not have known that it would be subject to an alternative minimum tax and that ownership might increase its minimum tax liability. By selling the property, the seller-lessee may deduct the entire lease payment, which is not subject to alternative minimum tax considerations.

DETERMINING ASSET USE

To the extent the **seller-lessee continues to use** the asset after the sale, the sale-leaseback is really a form of financing. Therefore the lessor **should not recognize a gain or loss** on the transaction. In short, the seller-lessee is simply borrowing funds.

On the other hand, if the **seller-lessee gives up the right to the use** of the asset, the transaction is in substance a sale. In that case, **gain or loss recognition** is appropriate. Trying to ascertain when the lessee has given up the use of the asset is difficult, however, and the FASB has formulated complex rules to identify this situation.[1] To understand the profession's position in this area, we discuss the basic accounting for the lessee and lessor below.

UNDERLYING CONCEPTS

A sale-leaseback is similar in substance to the parking of inventories (discussed in Chapter 8). The ultimate economic benefits remain under the control of the "seller," thus satisfying the definition of an asset.

Lessee

If the lease meets one of the four criteria for treatment as a capital lease (see Illustration 21-4), the **seller-lessee accounts for the transaction as a sale and the lease as a capital lease**. The seller-lessee should defer any profit or loss it experiences from the sale of the assets that are leased back under a capital lease; it should **amortize that profit over the lease term** (or the economic life if either criterion 1 or 2 is satisfied) in proportion to the amortization of the leased assets.

For example, assume **Scott Paper** sells equipment having a book value of $580,000 and a fair value of $623,110 to **General Electric Credit** for $623,110 and leases the equipment back for $50,000 a year for 20 years. Scott should amortize the profit of $43,110 over the 20-year period at the same rate that it depreciates the $623,110.[2] It credits the $43,110 ($623,110 − $580,000) to **Unearned Profit on Sale-Leaseback**.

If none of the capital lease criteria are satisfied, **the seller-lessee accounts for the transaction as a sale and the lease as an operating lease**. Under an operating lease, the lessee defers such profit or loss and amortizes it in proportion to the rental payments over the period when it expects to use the assets.

There are exceptions to these two general rules. They are:

1 *Losses Recognized*—When the fair value of the asset is **less than the book value** (carrying amount), the lessee must recognize a loss immediately, up to the amount of the difference between the book value and fair value. For example, if Lessee, Inc. sells equipment having a book value of $650,000 and a fair value of $623,110, it should charge the difference of $26,890 to a loss account.[3]

2 *Minor Leaseback*—Leasebacks in which the present value of the rental payments are 10 percent or less of the fair value of the asset are **minor leasebacks**. In this case, the seller-lessee gives up most of the rights to the use of the asset sold. Therefore, the transaction is a sale, and full gain or loss recognition is appropriate. It is not a financing transaction because the risks of ownership have been transferred.[4]

Lessor

If the lease meets one of the criteria in Group I and both of the criteria in Group II (see Illustration 21-11), the **purchaser-lessor** records the transaction as a purchase and a direct-financing lease. If the lease does not meet the criteria, the purchaser-lessor records the transaction as a purchase and an operating lease.

---

[1]Sales and leasebacks of real estate are often accounted for differently. A discussion of the issues related to these transactions is beyond the scope of this textbook. See *Statement of Financial Accounting Standards No. 98*, op. cit.

[2]*Statement of Financial Accounting Standards No. 28*, "Accounting for Sales with Leasebacks" (Stamford, Conn.: FASB, 1979).

[3]There can be two types of losses in sale-leaseback arrangements. One is a **real economic loss** that results when the carrying amount of the asset is higher than the fair market value of the asset. In this case, the loss should be recognized. An **artificial loss** results when the sale price is below the carrying amount of the asset but the fair market value is above the carrying amount. In this case the loss is more in the form of prepaid rent, and the lessee should defer the loss and amortize it in the future.

[4]In some cases the seller-lessee retains more than a minor part but less than substantially all. The computations to arrive at these values are complex and beyond the scope of this textbook.

SALE-LEASEBACK EXAMPLE

To illustrate the accounting treatment accorded a sale-leaseback transaction, assume that **American Airlines** on January 1, 2008, sells a used Boeing 757 having a carrying amount on its books of $75,500,000 to **Citicapital** for $80,000,000. American immediately leases the aircraft back under the following conditions:

1 The term of the lease is 15 years, noncancelable, and requires equal rental payments of $10,487,443 at the beginning of each year.

2 The aircraft has a fair value of $80,000,000 on January 1, 2008, and an estimated economic life of 15 years.

3 American pays all executory costs.

4 American depreciates similar aircraft that it owns on a straight-line basis over 15 years.

5 The annual payments assure the lessor a 12 percent return.

6 American's incremental borrowing rate is 12 percent.

This lease is a capital lease to American because the lease term exceeds 75 percent of the estimated life of the aircraft and because the present value of the lease payments exceeds 90 percent of the fair value of the aircraft to Citicapital. Assuming that collectibility of the lease payments is reasonably predictable and that no important uncertainties exist in relation to unreimbursable costs yet to be incurred by Citicapital, it should classify this lease as a direct-financing lease.

Illustration 21B-1 presents the typical journal entries to record the sale-leaseback transactions for American and Citicapital for the first year.

ILLUSTRATION 21B-1
Comparative Entries for Sale-Leaseback for Lessee and Lessor

American Airlines (Lessee)			Citicapital (Lessor)		
Sale of Aircraft by American to Citicapital, January 1, 2008:					
Cash	80,000,000		Aircraft	80,000,000	
Aircraft		75,500,000	Cash		80,000,000
Unearned Profit on					
Sale-Leaseback		4,500,000	Lease Receivable	80,000,000	
Leased Aircraft under			Aircraft		80,000,000
Capital Leases	80,000,000				
Lease Liability		80,000,000			
First Lease Payment, January 1, 2008:					
Lease Liability	10,487,443		Cash	10,487,443	
Cash		10,487,443	Lease Receivable		10,487,443
Incurrence and Payment of Executory Costs by American Corp. throughout 2008:			(No entry)		
Insurance, Maintenance,					
Taxes, etc.	XXX				
Cash or Accounts Payable		XXX			
Depreciation Expense on the Aircraft, December 31, 2008:					
Depreciation Expense	5,333,333		(No entry)		
Accumulated Depr.—					
Capital Leases		5,333,333			
($80,000,000 ÷ 15)					
Amortization of Profit on Sale-Leaseback by American, December 31, 2008:					
Unearned Profit on			(No entry)		
Sale-Leaseback	300,000				
Depreciation Expense		300,000			
($4,500,000 ÷ 15)					

Note: A case might be made for crediting Revenue instead of Depreciation Expense.

Interest for 2008, December 31, 2008:					
Interest Expense	8,341,507[a]		Interest Receivable	8,341,507	
Interest Payable		8,341,507	Interest Revenue		8,341,507[a]

[a]Partial Lease Amortization Schedule:

Date	Annual Rental Payment	Interest 12%	Reduction of Balance	Balance
1/1/08				$80,000,000
1/1/08	$10,487,443	$ –0–	$10,487,443	69,512,557
1/1/09	10,487,443	8,341,507	2,145,936	67,366,621

SUMMARY OF LEARNING OBJECTIVE FOR APPENDIX 21B

11. Describe the lessee's accounting for sale-leaseback transactions. If the lease meets one of the four criteria for treatment as a capital lease, the seller-lessee accounts for the transaction as a sale and the lease as a capital lease. The seller-lessee defers any profit it experiences from the sale of the assets that are leased back under a capital lease. The seller-lessee amortizes any profit over the lease term (or the economic life if either criterion 1 or 2 is satisfied) in proportion to the amortization of the leased assets. If the lease satisfies none of the capital lease criteria, the seller-lessee accounts for the transaction as a sale and the lease as an operating lease. Under an operating lease, the lessee defers such profit and amortizes it in proportion to the rental payments over the period of time that it expects to use the assets.

Note: All **asterisked** Questions, Brief Exercises, Exercises, and Concepts for Analysis relate to material contained in the appendixes to the chapter.

QUESTIONS

1. What are the major lessor groups in the United States? What advantage does a captive have in a leasing arrangement?

2. Jackie Remmers Co. is expanding its operations and is in the process of selecting the method of financing this program. After some investigation, the company determines that it may (1) issue bonds and with the proceeds purchase the needed assets or (2) lease the assets on a long-term basis. Without knowing the comparative costs involved, answer these questions:

   (a) What might be the advantages of leasing the assets instead of owning them?

   (b) What might be the disadvantages of leasing the assets instead of owning them?

   (c) In what way will the balance sheet be differently affected by leasing the assets as opposed to issuing bonds and purchasing the assets?

3. Identify the two recognized lease accounting methods for lessees and distinguish between them.

4. Wayne Higley Company rents a warehouse on a month-to-month basis for the storage of its excess inventory. The company periodically must rent space whenever its production greatly exceeds actual sales. For several years the company officials have discussed building their own storage facility, but this enthusiasm wavers when sales increase sufficiently to absorb the excess inventory. What is the nature of this type of lease arrangement, and what accounting treatment should be accorded it?

5. Distinguish between minimum rental payments and minimum lease payments, and indicate what is included in minimum lease payments.

6. Explain the distinction between a direct-financing lease and a sales-type lease for a lessor.

7. Outline the accounting procedures involved in applying the operating method by a lessee.

8. Outline the accounting procedures involved in applying the capital-lease method by a lessee.

9. Identify the lease classifications for lessors and the criteria that must be met for each classification.

10. Outline the accounting procedures involved in applying the direct-financing method.

11. Outline the accounting procedures involved in applying the operating method by a lessor.

12. Joan Elbert Company is a manufacturer and lessor of computer equipment. What should be the nature of its lease arrangements with lessees if the company wishes to account for its lease transactions as sales-type leases?

13. Gordon Graham Corporation's lease arrangements qualify as sales-type leases at the time of entering into the transactions. How should the corporation recognize revenues and costs in these situations?

14. Joann Skabo, M.D. (lessee) has a noncancelable 20-year lease with Countryman Realty, Inc. (lessor) for the use of a medical building. Taxes, insurance, and maintenance are paid by the lessee in addition to the fixed annual payments, of which the present value is equal to the fair market value of the leased property. At the end of the lease period, title becomes the lessee's at a nominal price. Considering the terms of the lease described above, comment on the nature of the lease transaction and the accounting treatment that should be accorded it by the lessee.

15. The residual value is the estimated fair value of the leased property at the end of the lease term.

   (a) Of what significance is (1) an unguaranteed and (2) a guaranteed residual value in the lessee's accounting for a capitalized-lease transaction?

   (b) Of what significance is (1) an unguaranteed and (2) a guaranteed residual value in the lessor's accounting for a direct-financing lease transaction?

16. How should changes in the estimated unguaranteed residual values be handled by the lessor?

17. Describe the effect of a "bargain purchase option" on accounting for a capital-lease transaction by a lessee.

18. What are "initial direct costs" and how are they accounted for?

19. What disclosures should be made by lessees and lessors related to future lease payments?

*20. What is the nature of a "sale-leaseback" transaction?

BRIEF EXERCISES

(LO 2) **BE21-1** **Callaway Golf Co.** leases telecommunication equipment. Assume the following data for equipment leased from Photon Company. The lease term is 5 years and requires equal rental payments of $30,000 at the beginning of each year. The equipment has a fair value at the inception of the lease of $138,000, an estimated useful life of 8 years, and no residual value. Callaway pays all executory costs directly to third parties. Photon set the annual rental to earn a rate of return of 10%, and this fact is known to Callaway. The lease does not transfer title or contain a bargain purchase option. How should Callaway classify this lease?

(LO 2) **BE21-2** Waterworld Company leased equipment from Costner Company. The lease term is 4 years and requires equal rental payments of $37,283 at the beginning of each year. The equipment has a fair value at the inception of the lease of $130,000, an estimated useful life of 4 years, and no salvage value. Waterworld pays all executory costs directly to third parties. The appropriate interest rate is 10%. Prepare Waterworld's January 1, 2008, journal entries at the inception of the lease.

(LO 2) **BE21-3** Rick Kleckner Corporation recorded a capital lease at $200,000 on January 1, 2008. The interest rate is 12%. Kleckner Corporation made the first lease payment of $35,947 on January 1, 2008. The lease requires eight annual payments. The equipment has a useful life of 8 years with no salvage value. Prepare Kleckner Corporation's December 31, 2008, adjusting entries.

(LO 2) **BE21-4** Use the information for Rick Kleckner Corporation from BE21-3. Assume that at December 31, 2008, Kleckner made an adjusting entry to accrue interest expense of $19,686 on the lease. Prepare Kleckner's January 1, 2009, journal entry to record the second lease payment of $35,947.

(LO 3) **BE21-5** Jana Kingston Corporation enters into a lease on January 1, 2008, that does not transfer ownership or contain a bargain purchase option. It covers 3 years of the equipment's 8-year useful life, and the present value of the minimum lease payments is less than 90% of the fair market value of the asset leased. Prepare Jana Kingston's journal entry to record its January 1, 2008, annual lease payment of $37,500.

(LO 4, 5) **BE21-6** Assume that **IBM** leased equipment that was carried at a cost of $150,000 to Sharon Swander Company. The term of the lease is 6 years beginning January 1, 2008, with equal rental payments of $30,677 at the beginning of each year. All executory costs are paid by Swander directly to third parties. The fair value of the equipment at the inception of the lease is $150,000. The equipment has a useful life of 6 years with no salvage value. The lease has an implicit interest rate of 9%, no bargain purchase option, and no transfer of title. Collectibility is reasonably assured with no additional cost to be incurred by IBM. Prepare IBM's January 1, 2008, journal entries at the inception of the lease.

(LO 4, 5) **BE21-7** Use the information for **IBM** from BE21-6. Assume the direct-financing lease was recorded at a present value of $150,000. Prepare IBM's December 31, 2008, entry to record interest.

(LO 4) **BE21-8** Jennifer Brent Corporation owns equipment that cost $72,000 and has a useful life of 8 years with no salvage value. On January 1, 2008, Jennifer Brent leases the equipment to Donna Havaci Inc. for one year with one rental payment of $15,000 on January 1. Prepare Jennifer Brent Corporation's 2008 journal entries.

(LO 6, 7) **BE21-9** Indiana Jones Corporation enters into a 6-year lease of equipment on January 1, 2008, which requires 6 annual payments of $30,000 each, beginning January 1, 2008. In addition, Indiana Jones guarantees the lessor a residual value of $20,000 at lease-end. The equipment has a useful life of 6 years. Prepare Indiana Jones' January 1, 2008, journal entries assuming an interest rate of 10%.

(LO 6, 7) **BE21-10** Use the information for Indiana Jones Corporation from BE21-9. Assume that for Lost Ark Company, the lessor, collectibility is reasonably predictable, there are no important uncertainties concerning costs, and the carrying amount of the machinery is $155,013. Prepare Lost Ark's January 1, 2008, journal entries.

(LO 8)   **BE21-11**   Starfleet Corporation manufactures replicators. On January 1, 2008, it leased to Ferengi Company a replicator that had cost $110,000 to manufacture. The lease agreement covers the 5-year useful life of the replicator and requires 5 equal annual rentals of $45,400 each. An interest rate of 12% is implicit in the lease agreement. Collectibility of the rentals is reasonably assured, and there are no important uncertainties concerning costs. Prepare Starfleet's January 1, 2008, journal entries.

(LO 10)   *****BE21-12**   On January 1, 2008, Acme Animation sold a truck to Coyote Finance for $35,000 and immediately leased it back. The truck was carried on Acme's books at $28,000. The term of the lease is 5 years, and title transfers to Acme at lease-end. The lease requires five equal rental payments of $9,233 at the end of each year. The appropriate rate of interest is 10%, and the truck has a useful life of 5 years with no salvage value. Prepare Acme's 2008 journal entries.

EXERCISES

(LO 2)   **E21-1**   **(Lessee Entries; Capital Lease with Unguaranteed Residual Value)**   On January 1, 2007, Burke Corporation signed a 5-year noncancelable lease for a machine. The terms of the lease called for Burke to make annual payments of $8,668 at the beginning of each year, starting January 1, 2007. The machine has an estimated useful life of 6 years and a $5,000 unguaranteed residual value. The machine reverts back to the lessor at the end of the lease term. Burke uses the straight-line method of depreciation for all of its plant assets. Burke's incremental borrowing rate is 10%, and the Lessor's implicit rate is unknown.

Instructions
    (a) What type of lease is this? Explain.
    (b) Compute the present value of the minimum lease payments.
    (c) Prepare all necessary journal entries for Burke for this lease through January 1, 2008.

(LO 2)   **E21-2**   **(Lessee Computations and Entries; Capital Lease with Guaranteed Residual Value)**   Pat Delaney Company leases an automobile with a fair value of $8,725 from John Simon Motors, Inc., on the following terms:

    1. Noncancelable term of 50 months.
    2. Rental of $200 per month (at end of each month). (The present value at 1% per month is $7,840.)
    3. Estimated residual value after 50 months is $1,180. (The present value at 1% per month is $715.) Delaney Company guarantees the residual value of $1,180.
    4. Estimated economic life of the automobile is 60 months.
    5. Delaney Company's incremental borrowing rate is 12% a year (1% a month). Simon's implicit rate is unknown.

Instructions
    (a) What is the nature of this lease to Delaney Company?
    (b) What is the present value of the minimum lease payments?
    (c) Record the lease on Delaney Company's books at the date of inception.
    (d) Record the first month's depreciation on Delaney Company's books (assume straight-line).
    (e) Record the first month's lease payment.

(LO 2, 7)   **E21-3**   **(Lessee Entries; Capital Lease with Executory Costs and Unguaranteed Residual Value)**   Assume that on January 1, 2008, **Kimberly-Clark Corp.** signs a 10-year noncancelable lease agreement to lease a storage building from Sheffield Storage Company. The following information pertains to this lease agreement.

    1. The agreement requires equal rental payments of $72,000 beginning on January 1, 2008.
    2. The fair value of the building on January 1, 2008 is $440,000.
    3. The building has an estimated economic life of 12 years, with an unguaranteed residual value of $10,000. Kimberly-Clark depreciates similar buildings on the straight-line method.
    4. The lease is nonrenewable. At the termination of the lease, the building reverts to the lessor.
    5. Kimberly-Clark's incremental borrowing rate is 12% per year. The lessor's implicit rate is not known by Kimberly-Clark.
    6. The yearly rental payment includes $2,470.51 of executory costs related to taxes on the property.

Instructions
Prepare the journal entries on the lessee's books to reflect the signing of the lease agreement and to record the payments and expenses related to this lease for the years 2008 and 2009. Kimberly-Clark's corporate year end is December 31.

(LO 5) **E21-4** **(Lessor Entries; Direct-Financing Lease with Option to Purchase)** Castle Leasing Company signs a lease agreement on January 1, 2008, to lease electronic equipment to Jan Way Company. The term of the noncancelable lease is 2 years, and payments are required at the end of each year. The following information relates to this agreement:

1. Jan Way has the option to purchase the equipment for $16,000 upon termination of the lease.
2. The equipment has a cost and fair value of $160,000 to Castle Leasing Company. The useful economic life is 2 years, with a salvage value of $16,000.
3. Jan Way Company is required to pay $5,000 each year to the lessor for executory costs.
4. Castle Leasing Company desires to earn a return of 10% on its investment.
5. Collectibility of the payments is reasonably predictable, and there are no important uncertainties surrounding the costs yet to be incurred by the lessor.

Instructions
(a) Prepare the journal entries on the books of Castle Leasing to reflect the payments received under the lease and to recognize income for the years 2008 and 2009.
(b) Assuming that Jan Way Company exercises its option to purchase the equipment on December 31, 2009, prepare the journal entry to reflect the sale on Castle's books.

(LO 2, 3) **E21-5** **(Type of Lease; Amortization Schedule)** Mike Macinski Leasing Company leases a new machine that has a cost and fair value of $95,000 to Sharrer Corporation on a 3-year noncancelable contract. Sharrer Corporation agrees to assume all risks of normal ownership including such costs as insurance, taxes, and maintenance. The machine has a 3-year useful life and no residual value. The lease was signed on January 1, 2008. Mike Macinski Leasing Company expects to earn a 9% return on its investment. The annual rentals are payable on each December 31.

Instructions
(a) Discuss the nature of the lease arrangement and the accounting method that each party to the lease should apply.
(b) Prepare an amortization schedule that would be suitable for both the lessor and the lessee and that covers all the years involved.

(LO 8) **E21-6** **(Lessor Entries; Sales-Type Lease)** Crosley Company, a machinery dealer, leased a machine to Dexter Corporation on January 1, 2007. The lease is for an 8-year period and requires equal annual payments of $35,013 at the beginning of each year. The first payment is received on January 1, 2007. Crosley had purchased the machine during 2006 for $160,000. Collectibility of lease payments is reasonably predictable, and no important uncertainties surround the amount of costs yet to be incurred by Crosley. Crosley set the annual rental to ensure an 11% rate of return. The machine has an economic life of 10 years with no residual value and reverts to Crosley at the termination of the lease.

Instructions
(a) Compute the amount of the lease receivable.
(b) Prepare all necessary journal entries for Crosley for 2007.

(LO 8) **E21-7** **(Lessee-Lessor Entries; Sales-Type Lease)** On January 1, 2007, Bensen Company leased equipment to Flynn Corporation. The following information pertains to this lease.

1. The term of the noncancelable lease is 6 years, with no renewal option. The equipment reverts to the lessor at the termination of the lease.
2. Equal rental payments are due on January 1 of each year, beginning in 2007.
3. The fair value of the equipment on January 1, 2007, is $150,000, and its cost is $120,000.
4. The equipment has an economic life of 8 years, with an unguaranteed residual value of $10,000. Flynn depreciates all of its equipment on a straight-line basis.
5. Bensen set the annual rental to ensure an 11% rate of return. Flynn's incremental borrowing rate is 12%, and the implicit rate of the lessor is unknown.
6. Collectibility of lease payments is reasonably predictable, and no important uncertainties surround the amount of costs yet to be incurred by the lessor.

Instructions
(Both the lessor and the lessee's accounting period ends on December 31.)
(a) Discuss the nature of this lease to Bensen and Flynn.
(b) Calculate the amount of the annual rental payment.
(c) Prepare all the necessary journal entries for Flynn for 2007.
(d) Prepare all the necessary journal entries for Bensen for 2007.

(LO 6, 7) **E21-8 (Lessee Entries with Bargain Purchase Option)** The following facts pertain to a noncancelable lease agreement between Mooney Leasing Company and Rode Company, a lessee.

Inception date:	May 1, 2007
Annual lease payment due at the beginning of	
each year, beginning with May 1, 2007	$21,227.65
Bargain purchase option price at end of lease term	$ 4,000.00
Lease term	5 years
Economic life of leased equipment	10 years
Lessor's cost	$65,000.00
Fair value of asset at May 1, 2007	$91,000.00
Lessor's implicit rate	10%
Lessee's incremental borrowing rate	10%

The collectibility of the lease payments is reasonably predictable, and there are no important uncertainties surrounding the costs yet to be incurred by the lessor. The lessee assumes responsibility for all executory costs.

Instructions
(Round all numbers to the nearest cent.)

   (a) Discuss the nature of this lease to Rode Company.
   (b) Discuss the nature of this lease to Mooney Company.
   (c) Prepare a lease amortization schedule for Rode Company for the 5-year lease term.
   (d) Prepare the journal entries on the lessee's books to reflect the signing of the lease agreement and to record the payments and expenses related to this lease for the years 2007 and 2008. Rode's annual accounting period ends on December 31. Reversing entries are used by Rode.

(LO 8) **E21-9 (Lessor Entries with Bargain Purchase Option)** A lease agreement between Mooney Leasing Company and Rode Company is described in E21-8.

Instructions
(Round all numbers to the nearest cent.)
Refer to the data in E21-8 and do the following for the lessor.

   (a) Compute the amount of the lease receivable at the inception of the lease.
   (b) Prepare a lease amortization schedule for Mooney Leasing Company for the 5-year lease term.
   (c) Prepare the journal entries to reflect the signing of the lease agreement and to record the receipts and income related to this lease for the years 2007, 2008, and 2009. The lessor's accounting period ends on December 31. Reversing entries are not used by Mooney.

(LO 5) **E21-10 (Computation of Rental; Journal Entries for Lessor)** Morgan Leasing Company signs an agreement on January 1, 2007, to lease equipment to Cole Company. The following information relates to this agreement.

   1. The term of the noncancelable lease is 6 years with no renewal option. The equipment has an estimated economic life of 6 years.
   2. The cost of the asset to the lessor is $245,000. The fair value of the asset at January 1, 2007, is $245,000.
   3. The asset will revert to the lessor at the end of the lease term at which time the asset is expected to have a residual value of $43,622, none of which is guaranteed.
   4. Cole Company assumes direct responsibility for all executory costs.
   5. The agreement requires equal annual rental payments, beginning on January 1, 2007.
   6. Collectibility of the lease payments is reasonably predictable. There are no important uncertainties surrounding the amount of costs yet to be incurred by the lessor.

Instructions
(Round all numbers to the nearest cent.)

   (a) Assuming the lessor desires a 10% rate of return on its investment, calculate the amount of the annual rental payment required. Round to the nearest dollar.
   (b) Prepare an amortization schedule that would be suitable for the lessor for the lease term.
   (c) Prepare all of the journal entries for the lessor for 2007 and 2008 to record the lease agreement, the receipt of lease payments, and the recognition of income. Assume the lessor's annual accounting period ends on December 31.

(LO 2) **E21-11 (Amortization Schedule and Journal Entries for Lessee)** Laura Leasing Company signs an agreement on January 1, 2007, to lease equipment to Plote Company. The information at the top of page 1136 relates to this agreement.

1. The term of the noncancelable lease is 5 years with no renewal option. The equipment has an estimated economic life of 5 years.
2. The fair value of the asset at January 1, 2007, is $80,000.
3. The asset will revert to the lessor at the end of the lease term, at which time the asset is expected to have a residual value of $7,000, none of which is guaranteed.
4. Plote Company assumes direct responsibility for all executory costs, which include the following annual amounts: (1) $900 to Rocky Mountain Insurance Company for insurance and (2) $1,600 to Laclede County for property taxes.
5. The agreement requires equal annual rental payments of $18,142.95 to the lessor, beginning on January 1, 2007.
6. The lessee's incremental borrowing rate is 12%. The lessor's implicit rate is 10% and is known to the lessee.
7. Plote Company uses the straight-line depreciation method for all equipment.
8. Plote uses reversing entries when appropriate.

Instructions

(Round all numbers to the nearest cent.)

(a) Prepare an amortization schedule that would be suitable for the lessee for the lease term.
(b) Prepare all of the journal entries for the lessee for 2007 and 2008 to record the lease agreement, the lease payments, and all expenses related to this lease. Assume the lessee's annual accounting period ends on December 31.

(LO 3, 4) **E21-12 (Accounting for an Operating Lease)** On January 1, 2007, Doug Nelson Co. leased a building to Patrick Wise Inc. The relevant information related to the lease is as follows.

1. The lease arrangement is for 10 years.
2. The leased building cost $4,500,000 and was purchased for cash on January 1, 2007.
3. The building is depreciated on a straight-line basis. Its estimated economic life is 50 years with no salvage value.
4. Lease payments are $275,000 per year and are made at the end of the year.
5. Property tax expense of $85,000 and insurance expense of $10,000 on the building were incurred by Nelson in the first year. Payment on these two items was made at the end of the year.
6. Both the lessor and the lessee are on a calendar-year basis.

Instructions

(a) Prepare the journal entries that Nelson Co. should make in 2007.
(b) Prepare the journal entries that Wise Inc. should make in 2007.
(c) If Nelson paid $30,000 to a real estate broker on January 1, 2007, as a fee for finding the lessee, how much should be reported as an expense for this item in 2007 by Nelson Co.?

(LO 3, 4) **E21-13 (Accounting for an Operating Lease)** On January 1, 2008, a machine was purchased for $900,000 by Young Co. The machine is expected to have an 8-year life with no salvage value. It is to be depreciated on a straight-line basis. The machine was leased to St. Leger Inc. on January 1, 2008, at an annual rental of $210,000. Other relevant information is as follows.

1. The lease term is for 3 years.
2. Young Co. incurred maintenance and other executory costs of $25,000 in 2008 related to this lease.
3. The machine could have been sold by Young Co. for $940,000 instead of leasing it.
4. St. Leger is required to pay a rent security deposit of $35,000 and to prepay the last month's rent of $17,500.

Instructions

(a) How much should Young Co. report as income before income tax on this lease for 2008?
(b) What amount should St. Leger Inc. report for rent expense for 2008 on this lease?

(LO 3, 4) **E21-14 (Operating Lease for Lessee and Lessor)** On February 20, 2007, Barbara Brent Inc., purchased a machine for $1,500,000 for the purpose of leasing it. The machine is expected to have a 10-year life, no residual value, and will be depreciated on the straight-line basis. The machine was leased to Rudy Company on March 1, 2007, for a 4-year period at a monthly rental of $19,500. There is no provision for the renewal of the lease or purchase of the machine by the lessee at the expiration of the lease term. Brent paid $30,000 of commissions associated with negotiating the lease in February 2007:

Instructions

(a) What expense should Rudy Company record as a result of the facts above for the year ended December 31, 2007? Show supporting computations in good form.

(b) What income or loss before income taxes should Brent record as a result of the facts above for the year ended December 31, 2007? (*Hint:* Amortize commissions over the life of the lease.)

(AICPA adapted)

(LO 10) ***E21-15 (Sale and Leaseback)** Assume that on January 1, 2007, **Elmer's Restaurants** sells a computer system to Liquidity Finance Co. for $680,000 and immediately leases the computer system back. The relevant information is as follows.

1. The computer was carried on Elmer's books at a value of $600,000.
2. The term of the noncancelable lease is 10 years; title will transfer to Elmer.
3. The lease agreement requires equal rental payments of $110,666.81 at the end of each year.
4. The incremental borrowing rate for Elmer is 12%. Elmer is aware that Liquidity Finance Co. set the annual rental to insure a rate of return of 10%.
5. The computer has a fair value of $680,000 on January 1, 2007, and an estimated economic life of 10 years.
6. Elmer pays executory costs of $9,000 per year.

Instructions
Prepare the journal entries for both the lessee and the lessor for 2007 to reflect the sale and leaseback agreement. No uncertainties exist, and collectibility is reasonably certain.

(LO 10) ***E21-16 (Lessee-Lessor, Sale-Leaseback)** Presented below are four independent situations.

(a) On December 31, 2008, Zarle Inc. sold computer equipment to Daniell Co. and immediately leased it back for 10 years. The sales price of the equipment was $520,000, its carrying amount is $400,000, and its estimated remaining economic life is 12 years. Determine the amount of deferred revenue to be reported from the sale of the computer equipment on December 31, 2008.

(b) On December 31, 2008, Wasicsko Co. sold a machine to Cross Co. and simultaneously leased it back for one year. The sale price of the machine was $480,000, the carrying amount is $420,000, and it had an estimated remaining useful life of 14 years. The present value of the rental payments for the one year is $35,000. At December 31, 2008, how much should Wasicsko report as deferred revenue from the sale of the machine?

(c) On January 1, 2008, McKane Corp. sold an airplane with an estimated useful life of 10 years. At the same time, McKane leased back the plane for 10 years. The sales price of the airplane was $500,000, the carrying amount $379,000, and the annual rental $73,975.22. McKane Corp. intends to depreciate the leased asset using the sum-of-the-years'-digits depreciation method. Discuss how the gain on the sale should be reported at the end of 2008 in the financial statements.

(d) On January 1, 2008, Sondgeroth Co. sold equipment with an estimated useful life of 5 years. At the same time, Sondgeroth leased back the equipment for 2 years under a lease classified as an operating lease. The sales price (fair market value) of the equipment was $212,700, the carrying amount is $300,000, the monthly rental under the lease is $6,000, and the present value of the rental payments is $115,753. For the year ended December 31, 2008, determine which items would be reported on its income statement for the sale-leaseback transaction.

See the book's website, www.wiley.com/college/kieso, for Additional Exercises.

PROBLEMS

(LO 2, 8) **P21-1 (Lessee-Lessor Entries; Sales-Type Lease)** Stine Leasing Company agrees to lease machinery to Potter Corporation on January 1, 2007. The following information relates to the lease agreement.

1. The term of the lease is 7 years with no renewal option, and the machinery has an estimated economic life of 9 years.
2. The cost of the machinery is $420,000, and the fair value of the asset on January 1, 2007, is $560,000.
3. At the end of the lease term the asset reverts to the lessor. At the end of the lease term the asset has a guaranteed residual value of $80,000. Potter depreciates all of its equipment on a straight-line basis.

4. The lease agreement requires equal annual rental payments, beginning on January 1, 2007.
5. The collectibility of the lease payments is reasonably predictable, and there are no important uncertainties surrounding the amount of costs yet to be incurred by the lessor.
6. Stine desires a 10% rate of return on its investments. Potter's incremental borrowing rate is 11%, and the lessor's implicit rate is unknown.

Instructions

(Assume the accounting period ends on December 31.)

(a) Discuss the nature of this lease for both the lessee and the lessor.
(b) Calculate the amount of the annual rental payment required.
(c) Compute the present value of the minimum lease payments.
(d) Prepare the journal entries Potter would make in 2007 and 2008 related to the lease arrangement.
(e) Prepare the journal entries Stine would make in 2007 and 2008.

(LO 3, 4)

P21-2 (Lessee-Lessor Entries; Operating Lease) Synergetics Inc. leased a new crane to M. K. Gumowski Construction under a 5-year noncancelable contract starting January 1, 2008. Terms of the lease require payments of $22,000 each January 1, starting January 1, 2008. Synergetics will pay insurance, taxes, and maintenance charges on the crane, which has an estimated life of 12 years, a fair value of $160,000, and a cost to Synergetics of $160,000. The estimated fair value of the crane is expected to be $45,000 at the end of the lease term. No bargain purchase or renewal options are included in the contract. Both Synergetics and Gumowski adjust and close books annually at December 31. Collectibility of the lease payments is reasonably certain, and no uncertainties exist relative to unreimbursable lessor costs. Gumowski's incremental borrowing rate is 10%, and Synergetics' implicit interest rate of 9% is known to Gumowski.

Instructions

(a) Identify the type of lease involved and give reasons for your classification. Discuss the accounting treatment that should be applied by both the lessee and the lessor.
(b) Prepare all the entries related to the lease contract and leased asset for the year 2008 for the lessee and lessor, assuming the following amounts.
  (1) Insurance $500.
  (2) Taxes $2,000.
  (3) Maintenance $650.
  (4) Straight-line depreciation and salvage value $10,000.
(c) Discuss what should be presented in the balance sheet, the income statement, and the related notes of both the lessee and the lessor at December 31, 2008.

(LO 2, 8, 9)

P21-3 (Lessee-Lessor Entries, Balance Sheet Presentation; Sales-Type Lease) Cascade Industries and Hardy Inc. enter into an agreement that requires Hardy Inc. to build three diesel-electric engines to Cascade's specifications. Upon completion of the engines, Cascade has agreed to lease them for a period of 10 years and to assume all costs and risks of ownership. The lease is noncancelable, becomes effective on January 1, 2008, and requires annual rental payments of $620,956 each January 1, starting January 1, 2008.

Cascade's incremental borrowing rate is 10%. The implicit interest rate used by Hardy Inc. and known to Cascade is 8%. The total cost of building the three engines is $3,900,000. The economic life of the engines is estimated to be 10 years, with residual value set at zero. Cascade depreciates similar equipment on a straight-line basis. At the end of the lease, Cascade assumes title to the engines. Collectibility of the lease payments is reasonably certain; no uncertainties exist relative to unreimbursable lessor costs.

Instructions

(Round all numbers to the nearest dollar.)

(a) Discuss the nature of this lease transaction from the viewpoints of both lessee and lessor.
(b) Prepare the journal entry or entries to record the transaction on January 1, 2008, on the books of Cascade Industries.
(c) Prepare the journal entry or entries to record the transaction on January 1, 2008, on the books of Hardy Inc.
(d) Prepare the journal entries for both the lessee and lessor to record the first rental payment on January 1, 2008.
(e) Prepare the journal entries for both the lessee and lessor to record interest expense (revenue) at December 31, 2008. (Prepare a lease amortization schedule for 2 years.)
(f) Show the items and amounts that would be reported on the balance sheet (not notes) at December 31, 2008, for both the lessee and the lessor.

(LO 2, 6, 9)

P21-4 (Balance Sheet and Income Statement Disclosure—Lessee) The following facts pertain to a noncancelable lease agreement between Alschuler Leasing Company and McKee Electronics, a lessee, for a computer system.

Inception date	October 1, 2007
Lease term	6 years
Economic life of leased equipment	6 years
Fair value of asset at October 1, 2007	$200,255
Residual value at end of lease term	–0–
Lessor's implicit rate	10%
Lessee's incremental borrowing rate	10%
Annual lease payment due at the beginning of each year, beginning with October 1, 2007	$41,800

The collectibility of the lease payments is reasonably predictable, and there are no important uncertainties surrounding the costs yet to be incurred by the lessor. The lessee assumes responsibility for all executory costs, which amount to $5,500 per year and are to be paid each October 1, beginning October 1, 2007. (This $5,500 is not included in the rental payment of $41,800.) The asset will revert to the lessor at the end of the lease term. The straight-line depreciation method is used for all equipment.

The following amortization schedule has been prepared correctly for use by both the lessor and the lessee in accounting for this lease. The lease is to be accounted for properly as a capital lease by the lessee and as a direct-financing lease by the lessor.

Date	Annual Lease Payment/ Receipt	Interest (10%) on Unpaid Liability/Receivable	Reduction of Lease Liability/Receivable	Balance of Lease Liability/Receivable
10/01/07				$200,255
10/01/07	$ 41,800		$ 41,800	158,455
10/01/08	41,800	$15,846	25,954	132,501
10/01/09	41,800	13,250	28,550	103,951
10/01/10	41,800	10,395	31,405	72,546
10/01/11	41,800	7,255	34,545	38,001
10/01/12	41,800	3,799*	38,001	–0–
	$250,800	$50,545	$200,255	

*Rounding error is $1.

Instructions

(Round all numbers to the nearest cent.)

(a) Assuming the lessee's accounting period ends on September 30, answer the following questions with respect to this lease agreement.
  (1) What items and amounts will appear on the lessee's income statement for the year ending September 30, 2008?
  (2) What items and amounts will appear on the lessee's balance sheet at September 30, 2008?
  (3) What items and amounts will appear on the lessee's income statement for the year ending September 30, 2009?
  (4) What items and amounts will appear on the lessee's balance sheet at September 30, 2009?

(b) Assuming the lessee's accounting period ends on December 31, answer the following questions with respect to this lease agreement.
  (1) What items and amounts will appear on the lessee's income statement for the year ending December 31, 2007?
  (2) What items and amounts will appear on the lessee's balance sheet at December 31, 2007?
  (3) What items and amounts will appear on the lessee's income statement for the year ending December 31, 2008?
  (4) What items and amounts will appear on the lessee's balance sheet at December 31, 2008?

(LO 5, 9) **P21-5** **(Balance Sheet and Income Statement Disclosure—Lessor)** Assume the same information as in P21-4.

Instructions

(Round all numbers to the nearest cent.)

(a) Assuming the lessor's accounting period ends on September 30, answer the following questions with respect to this lease agreement.
  (1) What items and amounts will appear on the lessor's income statement for the year ending September 30, 2008?
  (2) What items and amounts will appear on the lessor's balance sheet at September 30, 2008?

(3)   What items and amounts will appear on the lessor's income statement for the year ending September 30, 2009?

(4)   What items and amounts will appear on the lessor's balance sheet at September 30, 2009?

(b)   Assuming the lessor's accounting period ends on December 31, answer the following questions with respect to this lease agreement.

(1)   What items and amounts will appear on the lessor's income statement for the year ending December 31, 2007?

(2)   What items and amounts will appear on the lessor's balance sheet at December 31, 2007?

(3)   What items and amounts will appear on the lessor's income statement for the year ending December 31, 2008?

(4)   What items and amounts will appear on the lessor's balance sheet at December 31, 2008?

P21-6   (Lessee Entries with Residual Value)   The following facts pertain to a noncancelable lease agreement between Voris Leasing Company and Zarle Company, a lessee.

Inception date	January 1, 2007
Annual lease payment due at the beginning of each year, beginning with January 1, 2007	$81,365
Residual value of equipment at end of lease term, guaranteed by the lessee	$50,000
Lease term	6 years
Economic life of leased equipment	6 years
Fair value of asset at January 1, 2007	$400,000
Lessor's implicit rate	12%
Lessee's incremental borrowing rate	12%

The lessee assumes responsibility for all executory costs, which are expected to amount to $4,000 per year. The asset will revert to the lessor at the end of the lease term. The lessee has guaranteed the lessor a residual value of $50,000. The lessee uses the straight-line depreciation method for all equipment.

Instructions

(Round all numbers to the nearest cent.)

(a)   Prepare an amortization schedule that would be suitable for the lessee for the lease term.

(b)   Prepare all of the journal entries for the lessee for 2007 and 2008 to record the lease agreement, the lease payments, and all expenses related to this lease. Assume the lessee's annual accounting period ends on December 31 and reversing entries are used when appropriate.

(LO 2, 9)

P21-7   (Lessee Entries and Balance Sheet Presentation; Capital Lease)   Brennan Steel Company as lessee signed a lease agreement for equipment for 5 years, beginning December 31, 2007. Annual rental payments of $32,000 are to be made at the beginning of each lease year (December 31). The taxes, insurance, and the maintenance costs are the obligation of the lessee. The interest rate used by the lessor in setting the payment schedule is 10%; Brennan's incremental borrowing rate is 12%. Brennan is unaware of the rate being used by the lessor. At the end of the lease, Brennan has the option to buy the equipment for $1, considerably below its estimated fair value at that time. The equipment has an estimated useful life of 7 years, with no salvage value. Brennan uses the straight-line method of depreciation on similar owned equipment.

Instructions

(Round all numbers to the nearest dollar.)

(a)   Prepare the journal entry or entries, with explanations, that should be recorded on December 31, 2007, by Brennan. (Assume no residual value.)

(b)   Prepare the journal entry or entries, with explanations, that should be recorded on December 31, 2008, by Brennan. (Prepare the lease amortization schedule for all five payments.)

(c)   Prepare the journal entry or entries, with explanations, that should be recorded on December 31, 2009, by Brennan.

(d)   What amounts would appear on Brennan's December 31, 2009, balance sheet relative to the lease arrangement?

(LO 2, 9)

P21-8   (Lessee Entries and Balance Sheet Presentation; Capital Lease)   On January 1, 2008, Charlie Doss Company contracts to lease equipment for 5 years, agreeing to make a payment of $94,732 (including the executory costs of $6,000) at the beginning of each year, starting January 1, 2008. The taxes, the insurance, and the maintenance, estimated at $6,000 a year, are the obligations of the lessee. The leased equipment is to be capitalized at $370,000. The asset is to be depreciated on a double-declining-balance basis, and the obligation is to be reduced on an effective-interest basis. Doss's incremental borrowing rate is 12%, and the implicit rate in the lease is 10%, which is known by Doss. Title to the equipment transfers to Doss when the lease expires. The asset has an estimated useful life of 5 years and no residual value.

Instructions

(Round all numbers to the nearest dollar.)

(a) Explain the probable relationship of the $370,000 amount to the lease arrangement.

(b) Prepare the journal entry or entries that should be recorded on January 1, 2008, by Charlie Doss Company.

(c) Prepare the journal entry to record depreciation of the leased asset for the year 2008.

(d) Prepare the journal entry to record the interest expense for the year 2008.

(e) Prepare the journal entry to record the lease payment of January 1, 2009, assuming reversing entries are not made.

(f) What amounts will appear on the lessee's December 31, 2008, balance sheet relative to the lease contract?

(LO 2, 6) **P21-9 (Lessee Entries, Capital Lease with Monthly Payments)** John Roesch Inc. was incorporated in 2006 to operate as a computer software service firm with an accounting fiscal year ending August 31. Roesch's primary product is a sophisticated online inventory-control system; its customers pay a fixed fee plus a usage charge for using the system.

Roesch has leased a large, Alpha-3 computer system from the manufacturer. The lease calls for a monthly rental of $50,000 for the 144 months (12 years) of the lease term. The estimated useful life of the computer is 15 years.

Each scheduled monthly rental payment includes $4,000 for full-service maintenance on the computer to be performed by the manufacturer. All rentals are payable on the first day of the month beginning with August 1, 2007, the date the computer was installed and the lease agreement was signed. The lease is noncancelable for its 12-year term, and it is secured only by the manufacturer's chattel lien on the Alpha-3 system.

This lease is to be accounted for as a capital lease by Roesch, and it will be depreciated by the straight-line method with no expected salvage value. Borrowed funds for this type of transaction would cost Roesch 12% per year (1% per month). Following is a schedule of the present value of $1 for selected periods discounted at 1% per period when payments are made at the beginning of each period.

Periods (months)	Present Value of $1 per Period Discounted at 1% per Period
1	1.000
2	1.990
3	2.970
143	76.658
144	76.899

Instructions

Prepare, in general journal form, all entries Roesch should have made in its accounting records during August 2007 relating to this lease. Give full explanations and show supporting computations for each entry. Remember, August 31, 2007, is the end of Roesch's fiscal accounting period and it will be preparing financial statements on that date. Do not prepare closing entries.

(AICPA adapted)

(LO 4, 7, 8) **P21-10 (Lessor Computations and Entries; Sales-Type Lease with Unguaranteed RV)** Hanson Company manufactures a computer with an estimated economic life of 12 years and leases it to Flypaper Airlines for a period of 10 years. The normal selling price of the equipment is $210,482, and its unguaranteed residual value at the end of the lease term is estimated to be $20,000. Flypaper will pay annual payments of $30,000 at the beginning of each year and all maintenance, insurance, and taxes. Hanson incurred costs of $135,000 in manufacturing the equipment and $4,000 in negotiating and closing the lease. Hanson has determined that the collectibility of the lease payments is reasonably predictable, that no additional costs will be incurred, and that the implicit interest rate is 10%.

Instructions

(Round all numbers to the nearest dollar.)

(a) Discuss the nature of this lease in relation to the lessor and compute the amount of each of the following items.

　(1) Lease receivable.

　(2) Sales price.

　(3) Cost of sales.

(b) Prepare a 10-year lease amortization schedule.

(c) Prepare all of the lessor's journal entries for the first year.

(LO 2, 6, 7) **P21-11** **(Lessee Computations and Entries; Capital Lease with Unguaranteed Residual Value)** Assume the same data as in P21-10 with Flypaper Airlines Co. having an incremental borrowing rate of 10%.

Instructions

(Round all numbers to the nearest dollar.)

(a) Discuss the nature of this lease in relation to the lessee, and compute the amount of the initial obligation under capital leases.

(b) Prepare a 10-year lease amortization schedule.

(c) Prepare all of the lessee's journal entries for the first year.

P21-12 **(Basic Lessee Accounting with Difficult PV Calculation)** In 2005 Judy Yin Trucking Company negotiated and closed a long-term lease contract for newly constructed truck terminals and freight storage facilities. The buildings were erected to the company's specifications on land owned by the company. On January 1, 2006, Judy Yin Trucking Company took possession of the lease properties. On January 1, 2006 and 2007, the company made cash payments of $1,048,000 that were recorded as rental expenses.

Although the terminals have a composite useful life of 40 years, the noncancelable lease runs for 20 years from January 1, 2006, with a bargain purchase option available upon expiration of the lease.

The 20-year lease is effective for the period January 1, 2006, through December 31, 2025. Advance rental payments of $900,000 are payable to the lessor on January 1 of each of the first 10 years of the lease term. Advance rental payments of $320,000 are due on January 1 for each of the last 10 years of the lease. The company has an option to purchase all of these leased facilities for $1 on December 31, 2025. It also must make annual payments to the lessor of $125,000 for property taxes and $23,000 for insurance. The lease was negotiated to assure the lessor a 6% rate of return.

Instructions

(Round all numbers to the nearest dollar.)

(a) Prepare a schedule to compute for Judy Yin Trucking Company the discounted present value of the terminal facilities and related obligation at January 1, 2006.

(b) Assuming that the discounted present value of terminal facilities and related obligation at January 1, 2006, was $8,400,000, prepare journal entries for Judy Yin Trucking Company to record the:

(1) Cash payment to the lessor on January 1, 2008.

(2) Amortization of the cost of the leased properties for 2008 using the straight-line method and assuming a zero salvage value.

(3) Accrual of interest expense at December 31, 2008.

Selected present value factors are as follows:

Periods	For an Ordinary Annuity of $1 at 6%	For $1 at 6%
1	.943396	.943396
2	1.833393	.889996
8	6.209794	.627412
9	6.801692	.591898
10	7.360087	.558395
19	11.158117	.330513
20	11.469921	.311805

(AICPA adapted)

(LO 4, 7, 8) **P21-13** **(Lessor Computations and Entries; Sales-Type Lease with Guaranteed Residual Value)** Laura Jennings Inc. manufactures an X-ray machine with an estimated life of 12 years and leases it to Craig Gocker Medical Center for a period of 10 years. The normal selling price of the machine is $343,734, and its guaranteed residual value at the end of the noncancelable lease term is estimated to be $15,000. The hospital will pay rents of $50,000 at the beginning of each year and all maintenance, insurance, and taxes. Laura Jennings Inc. incurred costs of $210,000 in manufacturing the machine and $14,000 in negotiating and closing the lease. Laura Jennings Inc. has determined that the collectibility of the lease payments is reasonably predictable, that there will be no additional costs incurred, and that the implicit interest rate is 10%.

Instructions

(Round all numbers to the nearest dollar.)

(a) Discuss the nature of this lease in relation to the lessor and compute the amount of each of the following items.

(1) Lease receivable at inception of the lease.

(2) Sales price.

(3) Cost of sales.

(b) Prepare a 10-year lease amortization schedule.

(c) Prepare all of the lessor's journal entries for the first year.

(LO 2, 7) **P21-14** **(Lessee Computations and Entries; Capital Lease with Guaranteed Residual Value)** Assume the same data as in P21-13 and that Craig Gocker Medical Center has an incremental borrowing rate of 10%.

Instructions
(Round all numbers to the nearest dollar.)

(a) Discuss the nature of this lease in relation to the lessee, and compute the amount of the initial obligation under capital leases.
(b) Prepare a 10-year lease amortization schedule.
(c) Prepare all of the lessee's journal entries for the first year.

(LO 2, 3, 7) **P21-15** **(Operating Lease vs. Capital Lease)** You are auditing the December 31, 2006, financial statements of Sarah Shamess, Inc., manufacturer of novelties and party favors. During your inspection of the

company garage, you discovered that a 2005 Shirk automobile not listed in the equipment subsidiary ledger is parked in the company garage. You ask Sally Straub, plant manager, about the vehicle, and she tells you that the company did not list the automobile because the company was only leasing it. The lease agreement was entered into on January 1, 2006, with Jack Hayes New and Used Cars.

You decide to review the lease agreement to ensure that the lease should be afforded operating lease treatment, and you discover the following lease terms.

1. Noncancelable term of 4 years.
2. Rental of $2,160 per year (at the end of each year). (The present value at 8% per year is $7,154.)
3. Estimated residual value after 4 years is $1,100. (The present value at 8% per year is $809.) Shamess guarantees the residual value of $1,100.
4. Estimated economic life of the automobile is 5 years.
5. Shamess's incremental borrowing rate is 8% per year.

Instructions
You are a senior auditor writing a memo to your supervisor, the audit partner in charge of this audit, to discuss the above situation. Be sure to include **(a)** why you inspected the lease agreement, **(b)** what you determined about the lease, and **(c)** how you advised your client to account for this lease. Explain every journal entry that you believe is necessary to record this lease properly on the client's books. (It is also necessary to include the fact that you communicated this information to your client.)

(LO 2, 4, 7) **P21-16** **(Lessee-Lessor Accounting for Residual Values)** Lanier Dairy leases its milking equipment from Zeff Finance Company under the following lease terms.

1. The lease term is 10 years, noncancelable, and requires equal rental payments of $25,250 due at the beginning of each year starting January 1, 2007.
2. The equipment has a fair value and cost at the inception of the lease (January 1, 2007) of $185,078, an estimated economic life of 10 years, and a residual value (which is guaranteed by Lanier Dairy) of $20,000.
3. The lease contains no renewable options, and the equipment reverts to Zeff Finance Company upon termination of the lease.
4. Lanier Dairy's incremental borrowing rate is 9% per year. The implicit rate is also 9%.
5. Lanier Dairy depreciates similar equipment that it owns on a straight-line basis.
6. Collectibility of the payments is reasonably predictable, and there are no important uncertainties surrounding the costs yet to be incurred by the lessor.

Instructions
(a) Evaluate the criteria for classification of the lease, and describe the nature of the lease. In general, discuss how the lessee and lessor should account for the lease transaction.
(b) Prepare the journal entries for the lessee and lessor at January 1, 2007, and December 31, 2007 (the lessee's and lessor's year-end). Assume no reversing entries.
(c) What would have been the amount capitalized by the lessee upon the inception of the lease if:
   (1) The residual value of $20,000 had been guaranteed by a third party, not the lessee?
   (2) The residual value of $20,000 had not been guaranteed at all?
(d) On the lessor's books, what would be the amount recorded as the Net Investment (Lease Receivable) at the inception of the lease, assuming:
   (1) The residual value of $20,000 had been guaranteed by a third party?
   (2) The residual value of $20,000 had not been guaranteed at all?
(e) Suppose the useful life of the milking equipment is 20 years. How large would the residual value have to be at the end of 10 years in order for the lessee to qualify for the operating method? (Assume that the residual value would be guaranteed by a third party.) (*Hint*: The lessee's annual payments will be appropriately reduced as the residual value increases.)

CONCEPTS FOR ANALYSIS

 CA21-1 (Lessee Accounting and Reporting) On January 1, 2008, Hayes Company entered into a non-cancelable lease for a machine to be used in its manufacturing operations. The lease transfers ownership of the machine to Hayes by the end of the lease term. The term of the lease is 8 years. The minimum lease payment made by Hayes on January 1, 2008, was one of eight equal annual payments. At the inception of the lease, the criteria established for classification as a capital lease by the lessee were met.

Instructions
(a) What is the theoretical basis for the accounting standard that requires certain long-term leases to be capitalized by the lessee? Do not discuss the specific criteria for classifying a specific lease as a capital lease.
(b) How should Hayes account for this lease at its inception and determine the amount to be recorded?
(c) What expenses related to this lease will Hayes incur during the first year of the lease, and how will they be determined?
(d) How should Hayes report the lease transaction on its December 31, 2008, balance sheet?

CA21-2 (Lessor and Lessee Accounting and Disclosure) Laurie Gocker Inc. entered into a noncancelable lease arrangement with Nathan Morgan Leasing Corporation for a certain machine. Morgan's primary business is leasing; it is not a manufacturer or dealer. Gocker will lease the machine for a period of 3 years, which is 50% of the machine's economic life. Morgan will take possession of the machine at the end of the initial 3-year lease and lease it to another, smaller company that does not need the most current version of the machine. Gocker does not guarantee any residual value for the machine and will not purchase the machine at the end of the lease term.

Gocker's incremental borrowing rate is 10%, and the implicit rate in the lease is 9%. Gocker has no way of knowing the implicit rate used by Morgan. Using either rate, the present value of the minimum lease payments is between 90% and 100% of the fair value of the machine at the date of the lease agreement.

Gocker has agreed to pay all executory costs directly, and no allowance for these costs is included in the lease payments.

Morgan is reasonably certain that Gocker will pay all lease payments, and because Gocker has agreed to pay all executory costs, there are no important uncertainties regarding costs to be incurred by Morgan. Assume that no indirect costs are involved.

Instructions
(a) With respect to Gocker (the lessee), answer the following.
(1) What type of lease has been entered into? Explain the reason for your answer.
(2) How should Gocker compute the appropriate amount to be recorded for the lease or asset acquired?
(3) What accounts will be created or affected by this transaction, and how will the lease or asset and other costs related to the transaction be matched with earnings?
(4) What disclosures must Gocker make regarding this leased asset?
(b) With respect to Morgan (the lessor), answer the following:
(1) What type of leasing arrangement has been entered into? Explain the reason for your answer.
(2) How should this lease be recorded by Morgan, and how are the appropriate amounts determined?
(3) How should Morgan determine the appropriate amount of earnings to be recognized from each lease payment?
(4) What disclosures must Morgan make regarding this lease?

(AICPA adapted)

CA21-3 (Lessee Capitalization Criteria) On January 1, Shinault Company, a lessee, entered into three noncancelable leases for brand-new equipment, Lease L, Lease M, and Lease N. None of the three leases transfers ownership of the equipment to Shinault at the end of the lease term. For each of the three leases, the present value at the beginning of the lease term of the minimum lease payments, excluding that portion of the payments representing executory costs such as insurance, maintenance, and taxes to be paid by the lessor, is 75% of the fair value of the equipment.

The following information is peculiar to each lease.

1. Lease L does not contain a bargain purchase option. The lease term is equal to 80% of the estimated economic life of the equipment.
2. Lease M contains a bargain purchase option. The lease term is equal to 50% of the estimated economic life of the equipment.
3. Lease N does not contain a bargain purchase option. The lease term is equal to 50% of the estimated economic life of the equipment.

Instructions

(a) How should Shinault Company classify each of the three leases above, and why? Discuss the rationale for your answer.

(b) What amount, if any, should Shinault record as a liability at the inception of the lease for each of the three leases above?

(c) Assuming that the minimum lease payments are made on a straight-line basis, how should Shinault record each minimum lease payment for each of the three leases above?

(AICPA adapted)

CA21-4 (Comparison of Different Types of Accounting by Lessee and Lessor)

Part 1

Capital leases and operating leases are the two classifications of leases described in FASB pronouncements from the standpoint of the **lessee**.

Instructions

(a) Describe how a capital lease would be accounted for by the lessee both at the inception of the lease and during the first year of the lease, assuming the lease transfers ownership of the property to the lessee by the end of the lease.

(b) Describe how an operating lease would be accounted for by the lessee both at the inception of the lease and during the first year of the lease, assuming equal monthly payments are made by the lessee at the beginning of each month of the lease. Describe the change in accounting, if any, when rental payments are not made on a straight-line basis.

Do **not** discuss the criteria for distinguishing between capital leases and operating leases.

Part 2

Sales-type leases and direct financing leases are two of the classifications of leases described in FASB pronouncements from the standpoint of the **lessor**.

Instructions

Compare and contrast a sales-type lease with a direct financing lease as follows.

(a) Lease receivable.

(b) Recognition of interest revenue.

(c) Manufacturer's or dealer's profit.

Do **not** discuss the criteria for distinguishing between the leases described above and operating leases.

(AICPA adapted)

CA21-5 (Lessee Capitalization of Bargain Purchase Option) Brad Hayes Corporation is a diversified company with nationwide interests in commercial real estate developments, banking, copper mining, and metal fabrication. The company has offices and operating locations in major cities throughout the United States. Corporate headquarters for Brad Hayes Corporation is located in a metropolitan area of a midwestern state, and executives connected with various phases of company operations travel extensively. Corporate management is currently evaluating the feasibility of acquiring a business aircraft that can be used by company executives to expedite business travel to areas not adequately served by commercial airlines. Proposals for either leasing or purchasing a suitable aircraft have been analyzed, and the leasing proposal was considered to be more desirable.

The proposed lease agreement involves a twin-engine turboprop Viking that has a fair market value of $1,000,000. This plane would be leased for a period of 10 years beginning January 1, 2008. The lease agreement is cancelable only upon accidental destruction of the plane. An annual lease payment of $141,780 is due on January 1 of each year; the first payment is to be made on January 1, 2008. Maintenance operations are strictly scheduled by the lessor, and Brad Hayes Corporation will pay for these services as they are performed. Estimated annual maintenance costs are $6,900. The lessor will pay all insurance premiums and local property taxes, which amount to a combined total of $4,000 annually and are included in the annual lease payment of $141,780. Upon expiration of the 10-year lease, Brad Hayes Corporation can purchase the Viking for $44,440. The estimated useful life of the plane is 15 years, and its salvage value in the used plane market is estimated to be $100,000 after 10 years. The salvage value probably will never be less than $75,000 if the engines are overhauled and maintained as prescribed by the manufacturer. If the purchase option is not exercised, possession of the plane will revert to the lessor, and there is no provision for renewing the lease agreement beyond its termination on December 31, 2017.

Brad Hayes Corporation can borrow $1,000,000 under a 10-year term loan agreement at an annual interest rate of 12%. The lessor's implicit interest rate is not expressly stated in the lease agreement, but this rate appears to be approximately 8% based on ten net rental payments of $137,780 per year and the initial market value of $1,000,000 for the plane. On January 1, 2008, the present value of all net rental payments and the purchase option of $44,440 is $888,890 using the 12% interest rate. The present value of all net rental payments and the $44,440 purchase option on January 1, 2008, is $1,022,226 using the 8% interest rate implicit in the lease agreement. The financial vice-president of Brad Hayes Corporation has established that this lease agreement is a capital lease as defined in *Statement of Financial Accounting Standards No. 13,* "Accounting for Leases."

Instructions

(a) What is the appropriate amount that Brad Hayes Corporation should recognize for the leased aircraft on its balance sheet after the lease is signed?

(b) Without prejudice to your answer in part (a), assume that the annual lease payment is $141,780 as stated in the question, that the appropriate capitalized amount for the leased aircraft is $1,000,000 on January 1, 2008, and that the interest rate is 9%. How will the lease be reported in the December 31, 2008, balance sheet and related income statement? (Ignore any income tax implications.)

(CMA adapted)

 CA21-6 (Lease Capitalization, Bargain Purchase Option) Cubby Corporation entered into a lease agreement for 10 photocopy machines for its corporate headquarters. The lease agreement qualifies as an operating lease in all terms except there is a bargain purchase option. After the 5-year lease term, the corporation can purchase each copier for $1,000, when the anticipated market value is $2,500.

Glenn Beckert, the financial vice president, thinks the financial statements must recognize the lease agreement as a capital lease because of the bargain purchase agreement. The controller, Donna Kessinger, disagrees: "Although I don't know much about the copiers themselves, there is a way to avoid recording the lease liability." She argues that the corporation might claim that copier technology advances rapidly and that by the end of the lease term the machines will most likely not be worth the $1,000 bargain price.

Instructions

Answer the following questions.

(a) What ethical issue is at stake?

(b) Should the controller's argument be accepted if she does not really know much about copier technology? Would it make a difference if the controller were knowledgeable about the pace of change in copier technology?

(c) What should Beckert do?

*CA21-7 **(Sale-Leaseback)** On January 1, 2007, Laura Dwyer Company sold equipment for cash and leased it back. As seller-lessee, Laura Dwyer retained the right to substantially all of the remaining use of the equipment.

The term of the lease is 8 years. There is a gain on the sale portion of the transaction. The lease portion of the transaction is classified appropriately as a capital lease.

Instructions

(a) What is the theoretical basis for requiring lessees to capitalize certain long-term leases? **Do not discuss the specific criteria for classifying a lease as a capital lease.**

(b) (1) How should Laura Dwyer account for the sale portion of the sale-leaseback transaction at January 1, 2007?

(2) How should Laura Dwyer account for the leaseback portion of the sale-leaseback transaction at January 1, 2007?

(c) How should Laura Dwyer account for the gain on the sale portion of the sale-leaseback transaction during the first year of the lease? Why?

(AICPA adapted)

*CA21-8 **(Sale-Leaseback)** On December 31, 2007, Laura Truttman Co. sold 6-month old equipment at fair value and leased it back. There was a loss on the sale. Laura Truttman pays all insurance, maintenance, and taxes on the equipment. The lease provides for eight equal annual payments, beginning December 31, 2008, with a present value equal to 85% of the equipment's fair value and sales price. The lease's term is equal to 80% of the equipment's useful life. There is no provision for Laura Truttman to reacquire ownership of the equipment at the end of the lease term.

Instructions

(a) (1) Why is it important to compare an equipment's fair value to its lease payments' present value and its useful life to the lease term?

(2) Evaluate Laura Truttman's leaseback of the equipment in terms of each of the four criteria for determination of a capital lease.

(b) How should Laura Truttman account for the sale portion of the sale-leaseback transaction at December 31, 2007?

(c) How should Laura Truttman report the leaseback portion of the sale-leaseback transaction on its December 31, 2008, balance sheet?

USING YOUR JUDGMENT

Financial Reporting Problem

The Procter & Gamble Company (P&G)

The financial statements of **P&G** are presented in Appendix 5B or can be accessed at the KWW website.

Instructions

Refer to P&G's financial statements, accompanying notes, and management's discussion and analysis to answer the following questions.

(a) What types of leases are used by P&G?

(b) What amount of capital leases was reported by P&G in total and for less than one year?

(c) What minimum annual rental commitments under all noncancelable leases at June 30, 2004, did P&G disclose?

Financial Statement Analysis Case

Tasty Baking Company

Presented in Illustration 21-32 are the financial statement disclosures from the 2004 annual report of **Tasty Baking Company**.

Instructions

Answer the following questions related to these disclosures.

(a) What is the total obligation under capital leases at December 25, 2004, for Tasty Baking Company?

(b) What is the book value of the assets under capital lease at December 25, 2004, for Tasty Baking Company? Explain why there is a difference between the amounts reported for assets and liabilities under capital leases.

(c) What is the total rental expense reported for leasing activity for the year ended December 25, 2004, for Tasty Baking Company?

(d) Estimate the off-balance-sheet liability due to Tasty Baking's operating leases at fiscal year-end 2004.

Comparative Analysis Case

UAL, Inc. and Southwest Airlines

Instructions

Go to the KWW website or the company websites and use information found there to answer the following questions related to **UAL, Inc.** and **Southwest Airlines**.

(a) What types of leases are used by Southwest and on what assets are these leases primarily used?

(b) How long-term are some of Southwest's leases? What are some of the characteristics or provisions of Southwest's (as lessee) leases?

(c) What did Southwest report in 2004 as its future minimum annual rental commitments under non-cancelable leases?

(d) At year-end 2004, what was the present value of the minimum rental payments under Southwest's capital leases? How much imputed interest was deducted from the future minimum annual rental commitments to arrive at the present value?

(e) What were the amounts and details reported by Southwest for rental expense in 2004, 2003, and 2002?

(f) How does UAL's use of leases compare with Southwest's?

Research Cases

Case 1

The accounting for operating leases is a controversial issue. Many contend that firms employing operating leases are utilizing significantly more assets and are more highly leveraged than indicated by the balance sheet alone. As a result, analysts often use footnote disclosures to "constructively capitalize" operating lease obligations. One way to do so is to increase a firm's assets and liabilities by the present value of all future minimum rental payments.

Instructions

(a) Obtain the most recent annual report for a firm that relies heavily on operating leases. (Firms in the airline and retail industries are good candidates.) The schedule of future minimum rental payments is usually included in the "Commitments and Contingencies" footnote. Use the schedule to determine the present value of future minimum rental payments, assuming a discount rate of 10%.

(b) Calculate the company's debt-to-total-assets ratio with and without the present value of operating lease payments. Is there a significant difference?

Case 2

The January 7, 2002, edition of the *Wall Street Journal* includes an article by Judith Burns and Michael Schroeder, entitled "Accounting Firms Ask SEC for Post-**Enron** Guide."

Instructions

Read the article and answer the following questions.

(a) Why are the Big 5 firms asking the SEC to issue new guidance for disclosure?

(b) One of the areas the Big 5 suggest needs improving is reporting of lease obligations. How are off-balance-sheet lease obligations currently reported?

(c) One of the suggestions the Big 5 firms make for improving lease reporting is that firms should have to describe why these obligations aren't reported in the financial statements. Why aren't these obligations reported in the financial statements as liabilities?

International Reporting Case

As discussed in the chapter, U.S. GAAP accounting for leases allows companies to use off-balance-sheet financing for the purchase of operating assets. International accounting standards are similar to U.S. GAAP in that under these rules, companies can keep leased assets and obligations off their balance sheets. However, under *International Accounting Standard No. 17 (IAS 17)*, leases are capitalized based on the subjective evaluation of whether the risks and rewards of ownership are transferred in the lease. In Japan, virtually all leases are treated as operating leases. Furthermore, unlike U.S. and IAS standards, the Japanese rules do not require disclosure of future minimum lease payments.

Presented below are recent financial data for three major airlines that lease some part of their aircraft fleet. **American Airlines** prepares its financial statements under U.S. GAAP and leases approximately 27% of its fleet. **KLM Royal Dutch Airlines** and **Japan Airlines (JAL)** present their statements in accordance with their home country GAAP (Netherlands and Japan respectively). KLM leases about 22% of its aircraft, and JAL leases approximately 50% of its fleet.

Financial Statement Data	American Airlines (millions of dollars)	KLM Royal Dutch Airlines (millions of guilders)	Japan Airlines (millions of yen)
As-reported			
Assets	20,915	19,205	2,042,761
Liabilities	14,699	13,837	1,857,800
Income	985	606	4,619
Estimated impact of capitalizing operating leases on:[1]			
Assets	5,897	1,812	244,063
Liabilities	6,886	1,776	265,103
Income	(143)	24	(9,598)

[1]Based on *Apples to Apples: Global Airlines: Flight to Quality* (New York: N.Y.: Morgan Stanley Dean Witter, October 1998).

Instructions

(a) Using the as-reported data for each of the airlines, compute the rate of return on assets and the debt to assets ratio. Compare these companies on the basis of this analysis.

(b) Adjust the as-reported numbers of the three companies for the effects of non-capitalization of leases, and then redo the analysis in part (a).

(c) The following statement was overheard in the library: "Non-capitalization of operating leases is not that big a deal for profitability analysis based on rate of return on assets, since the operating lease payments (under operating lease accounting) are about the same as the sum of the interest and depreciation expense under capital lease treatment." Do you agree? Explain.

(d) Since the accounting for leases worldwide is similar, does your analysis above suggest there is a need for an improved accounting standard for leases? (*Hint:* Reflect on comparability of information about these companies' leasing activities, when leasing is more prevalent in one country than in others.)

Professional Research: Financial Accounting and Reporting

Henley Hardware Co. is considering alternative financing arrangements for equipment used in its warehouses. Besides purchasing the equipment outright, Henley is also considering a lease. Accounting for the outright purchase is fairly straightforward, but because Henley has not used equipment leases in the past, the accounting staff is less informed about the specific accounting rules for leases.

The staff is aware of some lease rules related to a "90 percent of fair value," "75 percent of useful life," and "residual value deficiencies," but they are unsure about the meanings of these terms in lease accounting. Henley has asked you to conduct some research on these items related to lease capitalization criteria.

Instructions

Using the **Financial Accounting Research System (FARS)**, respond to the following items. (Provide text strings used in your search.)

(a) Define "fair value of the leased property." What are some examples of the determination of fair value?

(b) Besides the noncancelable term of the lease, name at least three other considerations in determining the "lease term."

(c) A common issue in the accounting for leases concerns lease requirements that the lessee make up a residual value deficiency that is attributable to damage, extraordinary wear and tear, or excessive usage (e.g., excessive mileage on a leased vehicle). Do these features constitute a lessee guarantee of the residual value such that the estimated residual value of the leased property at the end of the lease term should be included in minimum lease payments?

Professional Simulations

Simulation 1

In this simulation you are asked to address questions related to the accounting for leases. Prepare responses to all parts.

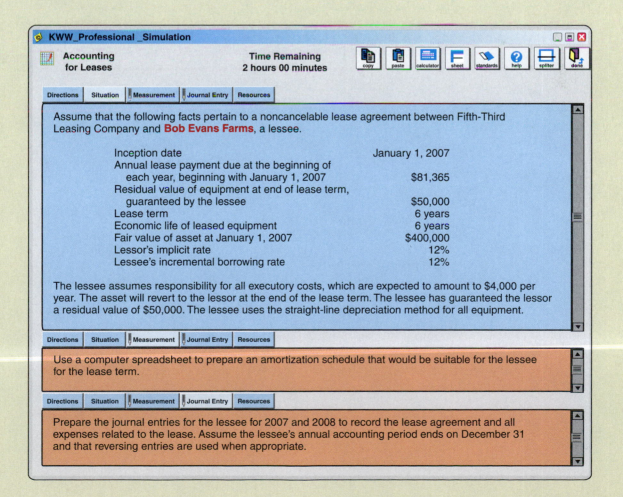

Simulation 2

In this simulation you are asked to address questions related to the accounting for leases. Prepare responses to all parts.

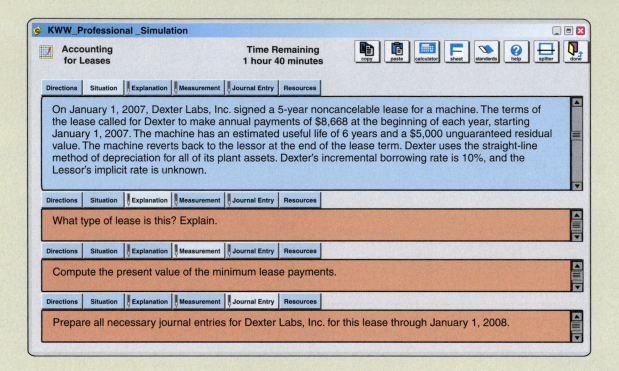

KWW_Professional _Simulation

Accounting
for Leases

Time Remaining
1 hour 40 minutes

copy | paste | calculator | sheet | standards | help | splitter | done

| Directions | Situation | Explanation | Measurement | Journal Entry | Resources |

On January 1, 2007, Dexter Labs, Inc. signed a 5-year noncancelable lease for a machine. The terms of the lease called for Dexter to make annual payments of $8,668 at the beginning of each year, starting January 1, 2007. The machine has an estimated useful life of 6 years and a $5,000 unguaranteed residual value. The machine reverts back to the lessor at the end of the lease term. Dexter uses the straight-line method of depreciation for all of its plant assets. Dexter's incremental borrowing rate is 10%, and the Lessor's implicit rate is unknown.

| Directions | Situation | Explanation | Measurement | Journal Entry | Resources |

What type of lease is this? Explain.

| Directions | Situation | Explanation | Measurement | Journal Entry | Resources |

Compute the present value of the minimum lease payments.

| Directions | Situation | Explanation | Measurement | Journal Entry | Resources |

Prepare all necessary journal entries for Dexter Labs, Inc. for this lease through January 1, 2008.

Remember to check the book's companion website to find additional resources for this chapter.

wiley.com/college/kieso

ACCOUNTING CHANGES AND ERROR ANALYSIS

So Many Changes

The FASB's conceptual framework describes comparability (including consistency) as one of the qualitative characteristics that contribute to the usefulness of accounting information. Unfortunately, companies are finding it difficult to maintain comparability and consistency due to the numerous changes in accounting principles mandated by the FASB. In addition, a number of companies have faced restatements due to errors in their financial statements. For example, the table below shows types and numbers of accounting changes.

Consolidation of variable interest entities	200	Derivatives and hedging activities	158
Liability and equity financial instruments	188	Asset retirement obligations	125
Guarantees	172	Stock compensation	122
Cost of exit or disposal activities	171	Impairments	68

The following chart indicates an increasing trend in restatements.

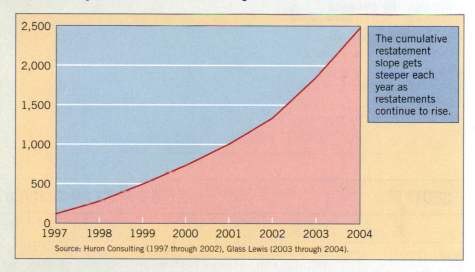

The cumulative restatement slope gets steeper each year as restatements continue to rise.

Source: Huron Consulting (1997 through 2002), Glass Lewis (2003 through 2004).

Although the percentage of companies reporting material changes or errors is small, you still must be careful. The reason: The amounts in the financial statements may have changed due to changing accounting principles and/or restatements.[1]

---

[1]Accounting change data from *Accounting Trends and Techniques—2004* (New York: AICPA, 2004). Restatement graph from T. Baldwin and D. Yoo, "Restatements—Traversing Shaky Ground," *Trend Alert* (June 2, 2005), Glass Lewis and Co., p. 7.

Learning Objectives

After studying this chapter, you should be able to:

1 Identify the types of accounting changes.

2 Describe the accounting for changes in accounting principles.

3 Understand how to account for retrospective accounting changes.

4 Understand how to account for impracticable changes.

5 Describe the accounting for changes in estimates.

6 Identify changes in a reporting entity.

7 Describe the accounting for correction of errors.

8 Identify economic motives for changing accounting methods.

9 Analyze the effect of errors.

As our opening story indicates, changes in accounting principles and errors in financial information have increased substantially in recent years. When these changes occur, companies must follow specific accounting and reporting requirements. In addition, to ensure comparability among companies, the FASB has standardized reporting of accounting changes, accounting estimates, error corrections, and related earnings per share information. In this chapter, we discuss these reporting standards, which help investors better understand a company's financial condition. The content and organization of the chapter are as follows.

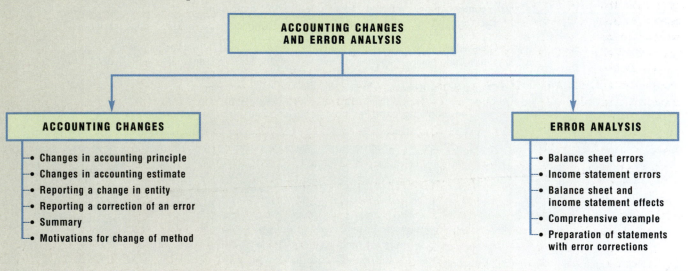

ACCOUNTING CHANGES AND ERROR ANALYSIS

ACCOUNTING CHANGES
- Changes in accounting principle
- Changes in accounting estimate
- Reporting a change in entity
- Reporting a correction of an error
- Summary
- Motivations for change of method

ERROR ANALYSIS
- Balance sheet errors
- Income statement errors
- Balance sheet and income statement effects
- Comprehensive example
- Preparation of statements with error corrections

SECTION 1	*ACCOUNTING CHANGES*

OBJECTIVE 1
Identify the types of accounting changes.

UNDERLYING CONCEPTS

While changes in accounting may enhance the qualitative characteristic of *usefulness*, these changes may adversely affect the characteristics of *comparability* and *consistency*.

Accounting alternatives diminish the comparability of financial information between periods and between companies; they also obscure useful historical trend data. For example, if **Ford** revises its estimates for equipment useful lives, depreciation expense for the current year will not be comparable to depreciation expense reported by Ford in prior years. Similarly, if **Best Buy** changes to FIFO inventory pricing while **Circuit City** uses LIFO, it will be difficult to compare these companies' reported results. A reporting framework helps preserve comparability when there is an accounting change.

The FASB has established a reporting framework, which involves three types of accounting changes.[2] The three types of accounting changes are:

1 *Change in Accounting Principle.* A change from one generally accepted accounting principle to another one. For example, a company may change its inventory valuation method from LIFO to average cost.

2 *Change in Accounting Estimate.* A change that occurs as the result of new information or additional experience. For example, a company may change its estimate of the useful lives of depreciable assets.

3 *Change in Reporting Entity.* A change from reporting as one type of entity to another type of entity. As an example, a company might change the subsidiaries for which it prepares consolidated financial statements.

A fourth category necessitates changes in accounting, though it is not classified as an accounting change.

---

[2]"Accounting Changes and Error Corrections," *Statement of Financial Accounting Standards No. 154* (Stamford, Conn.: FASB, 2005).

4 *Errors in Financial Statements.* Errors result from mathematical mistakes, mistakes in applying accounting principles, or oversight or misuse of facts that existed when preparing the financial statements. For example, a company may incorrectly apply the retail inventory method for determining its final inventory value.

The FASB classifies changes in these categories because each category involves different methods of recognizing changes in the financial statements. In this chapter we discuss these classifications. We also explain how to report each item in the accounts and how to disclose the information in comparative statements.

CHANGES IN ACCOUNTING PRINCIPLE

By definition, a **change in accounting principle** involves a change from one generally accepted accounting principle to another. For example, a company might change the basis of inventory pricing from average cost to LIFO. Or it might change its method of revenue recognition for long-term construction contracts from the completed-contract to the percentage-of-completion method.

OBJECTIVE 2
Describe the accounting for changes in accounting principles.

Companies must carefully examine each circumstance to ensure that a change in principle has actually occurred. **Adoption of a new principle** in recognition of events that have occurred for the first time or that were previously immaterial is not an accounting change. For example, a change in accounting principle has not occurred when a company adopts an inventory method (e.g., FIFO) for **newly** acquired items of inventory, even if FIFO differs from that used for **previously recorded** inventory. Another example is certain marketing expenditures that were previously immaterial and expensed in the period incurred. It would not be considered a change in accounting principle if they become material and so may be acceptably deferred and amortized.

Finally, what if a company previously followed an accounting principle that was not acceptable? Or what if the company applied a principle incorrectly? In such cases, the profession considers a change to a generally accepted accounting principle **a correction of an error**. For example, a switch from the cash (income tax) basis of accounting to the accrual basis is a correction of an error. Or, if a company deducted salvage value when computing double-declining depreciation on plant assets and later recomputed depreciation without deducting estimated salvage value, it has corrected an error.

There are three possible approaches for reporting changes in accounting principles:

Report changes currently. In this approach, companies report the cumulative effect of the change in the current year's income statement as an irregular item. The **cumulative effect** is the difference in prior years' income between the newly adopted and prior accounting method. Under this approach, the effect of the change on prior years' income appears only in the current-year income statement. The company does not change **prior-year financial statements**.

Advocates of this position argue that changing prior years' financial statements results in a loss of confidence in financial reports. How do investors react when told that the earnings computed three years ago are now entirely different? Changing prior periods, if permitted, also might upset contractual arrangements based on the old figures. For example, profit-sharing arrangements computed on the old basis might have to be recomputed and completely new distributions made, creating numerous legal problems. Many practical difficulties also exist: The cost of changing prior-period financial statements may be excessive, or determining the amount of the prior-period effect may be impossible on the basis of available data.

Report changes retrospectively. Retrospective application refers to the application of a different accounting principle to recast previously issued financial statements—**as if the new principle had always been used**. In other words, the company "goes back" and adjusts **prior years' statements** on a basis consistent with the newly adopted principle. The company shows any cumulative effect of the change as an adjustment to beginning retained earnings of the earliest year presented.

Advocates of this position argue that retrospective application ensures comparability. Think for a moment what happens if this approach is not used: The year *previous* to the change will be on the old method; the year *of the change* will report the entire cumulative adjustment; and the *following* year will present financial statements on the new basis without the cumulative effect of the change. Such lack of consistency fails to provide meaningful earnings-trend data and other financial relationships necessary to evaluate the business.

Report changes prospectively (in the future). In this approach, previously reported results remain. As a result, companies do not adjust opening balances to reflect the change in principle. Advocates of this position argue that once management presents financial statements based on acceptable accounting principles, they are final; management cannot change prior periods by adopting a new principle. According to this line of reasoning, the current-period cumulative adjustment is not appropriate, because that approach includes amounts that have little or no relationship to the current year's income or economic events.

Given these three possible approaches, which does the accounting profession prefer? The FASB **requires that companies use the retrospective approach.** Why? Because it provides financial statement users with more useful information than the cumulative-effect or prospective approaches.[3] The rationale is that changing the prior statements to be on the same basis as the newly adopted principle results in greater consistency across accounting periods. Users can then better compare results from one period to the next.[4]

INTERNATIONAL INSIGHT

IAS 8 generally requires retrospective application to prior years for accounting changes. However, *IAS 8* permits the cumulative-effect method or prospective method if a company cannot reasonably determine the amounts to which to restate prior periods.

WHAT DO THE NUMBERS MEAN?

> **QUITE A CHANGE**
>
> The cumulative-effect approach results in a loss of comparability. Also, reporting the cumulative adjustment in the period of the change can significantly affect net income, resulting in a misleading income figure. For example, at one time **Chrysler Corporation** (now **DaimlerChrysler**) changed its inventory accounting from LIFO to FIFO. If Chrysler had used the cumulative-effect approach, it would have reported a $53,500,000 adjustment to net income. That adjustment would have resulted in net income of $45,900,000, instead of a net loss of $7,600,000.
>
> A second case: In the early 1980s the railroad industry switched from the retirement-replacement method of depreciating railroad equipment to more generally used methods such as straight-line depreciation. Using cumulative treatment, railroad companies would have made substantial adjustments to income in the period of change. Many in the industry argued that including such large cumulative-effect adjustments in the current year would distort the information and make it less useful.
>
> Such situations lend support to retrospective application so that comparability is maintained.

Retrospective Accounting Change Approach

OBJECTIVE 3
Understand how to account for retrospective accounting changes.

A presumption exists that once a company adopts an accounting principle, it should not change. That presumption is understandable, given the idea that consistent use of

---

[3]"Accounting Changes and Error Corrections," *Statement of Financial Accounting Standards No. 154* (Stamford, Conn.: FASB, 2005). This recent standard carries forward many of the provisions in the previous accounting change standard (*APB Opinion No. 20*), including the accounting for errors, changes in estimates, and the disclosures related to accounting changes.

[4]Adoption of the retrospective approach contributes to international accounting convergence. The FASB and the IASB are collaborating on a project in which they have agreed to converge around high-quality solutions to resolve differences between U.S. GAAP and International Financial Reporting Standards (IFRS). By adopting the retrospective approach, which is the method used in IFRS, the FASB agreed that this approach is superior to the current approach.

an accounting principle enhances the usefulness of financial statements. However, the environment continually changes, and companies change in response. Recent standards on such subjects as stock options, exchanges of nonmonetary assets, derivatives, and so on indicate that changes in accounting principle will continue to occur.

When a company changes an accounting principle, it should report the change using retrospective application. In general terms, here is what it must do:

1 It adjusts its financial statements for each prior period presented. Thus, financial statement information about prior periods is on the same basis as the new accounting principle.

2 It adjusts the carrying amounts of assets and liabilities as of the beginning of the first year presented. By doing so, these accounts reflect the cumulative effect on periods prior to those presented of the change to the new accounting principle. The company also makes an offsetting adjustment to the opening balance of retained earnings or other appropriate component of stockholders' equity or net assets as of the beginning of the first year presented.

For example, assume that **Target** decides to change its inventory valuation method in 2007 from the retail inventory method (FIFO) to the retail inventory (average cost). It provides comparative information for 2005 and 2006 based on the new method. Target would adjust its assets, liabilities, and retained earnings for periods prior to 2005 and report these amounts in the 2005 financial statements, when it prepares comparative financial statements.

Example of Retrospective Accounting Change

To illustrate the retrospective approach, assume that Lancer Company has accounted for its inventory using the LIFO method. In 2007, the company changes to the FIFO method because management believes this approach provides a more appropriate measure of its inventory costs. Illustration 22-1 provides additional information related to Lancer Company.

ILLUSTRATION 22-1
Lancer Company Information

1. Lancer Company started its operations on January 1, 2005. At that time stockholders invested $100,000 in the business in exchange for common stock.
2. All sales, purchases, and operating expenses for the period 2005–2007 are cash transactions. Lancer's cash flows over this period are as follows.

	2005	2006	2007
Sales	$300,000	$300,000	$300,000
Purchases	90,000	110,000	125,000
Operating expenses	100,000	100,000	100,000
Cash flow from operations	$110,000	$ 90,000	$ 75,000

3. Lancer has used the LIFO method for financial reporting since its inception.
4. Inventory determined under LIFO and FIFO for the period 2005–2007 is as follows.

	LIFO Method	FIFO Method	Difference
January 1, 2005	$ 0	$ 0	$ 0
December 31, 2005	10,000	12,000	2,000
December 31, 2006	20,000	25,000	5,000
December 31, 2007	32,000	39,000	7,000

5. Cost of goods sold under LIFO and FIFO for the period 2005–2007 are as follows.

	Cost of Goods Sold LIFO	Cost of Goods Sold FIFO	Difference
January 1, 2005	$ 0	$ 0	$ 0
December 31, 2005	80,000	78,000	2,000
December 31, 2006	100,000	97,000	3,000
December 31, 2007	113,000	111,000	2,000

6. Earnings per share information is not required on the income statement.
7. All tax effects for this illustration should be ignored.

Given the information about Lancer Company, Illustration 22-2 shows its income statement, retained earnings statement, balance sheet, and statement of cash flows for 2005–2007 under LIFO.

ILLUSTRATION 22-2
Lancer Financial
Statements (LIFO)

LANCER COMPANY
INCOME STATEMENT
FOR THE YEAR ENDED DECEMBER 31

	2005	2006	2007
Sales	$300,000	$300,000	$300,000
Cost of goods sold (LIFO)	80,000	100,000	113,000
Operating expenses	100,000	100,000	100,000
Net income	$120,000	$100,000	$ 87,000

LANCER COMPANY
RETAINED EARNINGS STATEMENT
FOR THE YEAR ENDED DECEMBER 31

	2005	2006	2007
Retained earnings (beginning)	$ 0	$120,000	$220,000
Add: Net income	120,000	100,000	87,000
Retained earnings (ending)	$120,000	$220,000	$307,000

LANCER COMPANY
BALANCE SHEET
AT DECEMBER 31

	2005	2006	2007
Cash	$210,000	$300,000	$375,000
Inventory (LIFO)	10,000	20,000	32,000
Total assets	$220,000	$320,000	$407,000
Common stock	$100,000	$100,000	$100,000
Retained earnings	120,000	220,000	307,000
Total liabilities and stockholder's equity	$220,000	$320,000	$407,000

LANCER COMPANY
STATEMENT OF CASH FLOWS
FOR THE YEAR ENDED DECEMBER 31

	2005	2006	2007
Cash flows from operating activities			
Sales	$300,000	$300,000	$300,000
Purchases	90,000	110,000	125,000
Operating expenses	100,000	100,000	100,000
Net cash provided by operating activities	110,000	90,000	75,000
Cash flows from financing activities			
Issuance of common stock	100,000	—	—
Net increase in cash	210,000	90,000	75,000
Cash at beginning of year	0	210,000	300,000
Cash at end of year	$210,000	$300,000	$375,000

As Illustration 22-2 indicates, under LIFO Lancer Company reports $120,000 net income in 2005, $100,000 net income in 2006, and $87,000 net income in 2007. The amount of inventory reported on Lancer's balance sheet reflects LIFO costing.

Illustration 22-3 shows Lancer's income statement, retained earnings statement, balance sheet, and statement of cash flows for 2005–2007 under **FIFO**. You can see that **the cash flow statement under FIFO is the same as under LIFO**. Although the net incomes are different in each period, there is no cash flow effect from these differences in net income. (If we considered income taxes, a cash flow effect would result.)

ILLUSTRATION 22-3
Lancer Financial
Statements (FIFO)

LANCER COMPANY
INCOME STATEMENT
FOR THE YEAR ENDED DECEMBER 31

	2005	2006	2007
Sales	$300,000	$300,000	$300,000
Cost of goods sold (FIFO)	78,000	97,000	111,000
Operating expenses	100,000	100,000	100,000
Net income	$122,000	$103,000	$ 89,000

LANCER COMPANY
RETAINED EARNINGS STATEMENT
FOR THE YEAR ENDED DECEMBER 31

	2005	2006	2007
Retained earnings (beginning)	$ 0	$122,000	$225,000
Add: Net income	122,000	103,000	89,000
Retained earnings (ending)	$122,000	$225,000	$314,000

LANCER COMPANY
BALANCE SHEET
AT DECEMBER 31

	2005	2006	2007
Cash	$210,000	$300,000	$375,000
Inventory (FIFO)	12,000	25,000	39,000
Total assets	$222,000	$325,000	$414,000
Common stock	$100,000	$100,000	$100,000
Retained earnings	122,000	225,000	314,000
Total liabilities and stockholder's equity	$222,000	$325,000	$414,000

LANCER COMPANY
STATEMENT OF CASH FLOWS
FOR THE YEAR ENDED DECEMBER 31

	2005	2006	2007
Cash flows from operating activities			
Sales	$300,000	$300,000	$300,000
Purchases	90,000	110,000	125,000
Operating expenses	100,000	100,000	100,000
Net cash provided by operating activities	110,000	90,000	75,000
Cash flows from financing activities			
Issuance of common stock	100,000	—	—
Net increase in cash	210,000	90,000	75,000
Cast at beginning of year	0	210,000	300,000
Cash at end of year	$210,000	$300,000	$375,000

Compare the financial statements reported in Illustration 22-2 and Illustration 22-3. You can see that, under retrospective application, the change to FIFO inventory valuation affects reported inventories, cost of goods sold, net income, and retained earnings. In the following sections we discuss the accounting and reporting of Lancer's accounting change from LIFO to FIFO.

Accounting for and Reporting a Change in Principle

Given the information provided in Illustrations 22-1, 22-2, and 22-3, we now are ready to account for and report on the accounting change.

Accounting for a Change in Principle

Our first step is to adjust the financial records for the change from LIFO to FIFO. To do so, we perform the analysis in Illustration 22-4.

ILLUSTRATION 22-4
Data for Recording
Change in Accounting
Principle

| Year | Net Income | | Difference in Income |
	LIFO	FIFO	
2005	$120,000	$122,000	$2,000
2006	100,000	103,000	3,000
Total at beginning of 2007	$220,000	$225,000	$5,000
Total in 2007	$ 87,000	$ 89,000	$2,000

The entry to record the change to the FIFO method at the beginning of 2007 is as follows.

| Inventory | 5,000 | |
| Retained Earnings | | 5,000 |

The change increases the inventory account by $5,000. This amount represents the difference between the ending inventory at December 31, 2006, under LIFO ($20,000) and the ending inventory under FIFO ($25,000). The credit to Retained Earnings indicates the amount needed to change prior-year's income, assuming that Lancer had used FIFO in previous periods.

Reporting a Change in Principle

The disclosure of accounting changes is particularly important. Users of the financial statements want consistent information from one period to the next. Such consistency ensures the usefulness of financial statements. The major disclosure requirements are as follows.

1 The nature of and reason for the change in accounting principle. This must include an explanation of why the newly adopted accounting principle is preferable.

2 The method of applying the change, and:
   (a) A description of the prior-period information that has been retrospectively adjusted, if any.
   (b) The effect of the change on income from continuing operations, net income (or other appropriate captions of changes in net assets or performance indicators), any other affected line item, and any affected per-share amounts for the current period and for any prior periods retrospectively adjusted.
   (c) The cumulative effect of the change on retained earnings or other components of equity or net assets in the statement of financial position as of the beginning of the earliest period presented.[5]

Lancer Company will prepare comparative financial statements for 2006 and 2007 using FIFO (the new inventory method). Illustration 22-5 (page 1159) indicates how Lancer might present this information.

As Illustration 22-5 shows, Lancer Company reports net income under the newly adopted FIFO method for both 2006 and 2007. The company retrospectively adjusted the 2006 income statement to report the information on a FIFO basis. In addition, the note to the financial statements indicates the nature of the change, why the company made the change, and the years affected. The note also provides data on important differences between the amounts reported under LIFO versus FIFO. (When identifying

---

[5]Presentation of the effect on financial statement subtotals and totals other than income from continuing operations and net income (or other appropriate captions of changes in the applicable net assets or performance indicators) is not required *(SFAS No. 154,* par. 17.)

the significant differences, some companies show the *entire* financial statements and line-by-line differences between LIFO and FIFO.)

ILLUSTRATION 22-5
Comparative Information
Related to Accounting
Change (FIFO)

LANCER COMPANY
INCOME STATEMENT
FOR THE YEAR ENDED DECEMBER 31

	2007	2006
		As adjusted (Note A)
Sales	$300,000	$300,000
Cost of goods sold	111,000	97,000
Operating expenses	100,000	100,000
Net income	$ 89,000	$103,000

Note A

Change in Method of Accounting for Inventory Valuation On January 1, 2007, Lancer Company elected to change its method of valuing its inventory to the FIFO method; in all prior years inventory was valued using the LIFO method. The Company adopted the new method of accounting for inventory to better report cost of goods sold in the year incurred. Comparative financial statements of prior years have been adjusted to apply the new method retrospectively. The following financial statement line items for fiscal years 2007 and 2006 were affected by the change in accounting principle.

	2007			2006		
Balance Sheet	LIFO	FIFO	Difference	LIFO	FIFO	Difference
Inventory	$ 32,000	$ 39,000	$7,000	$ 20,000	$ 25,000	$5,000
Retained earnings	307,000	314,000	7,000	220,000	225,000	5,000
Income Statement						
Cost of goods sold	$113,000	$111,000	$2,000	$100,000	$ 97,000	$3,000
Net Income	87,000	89,000	2,000	100,000	103,000	3,000
Statement of Cash Flows						
(no effect)						

As a result of the accounting change, retained earnings as of January 1, 2006, increased from $120,000, as originally reported using the LIFO method, to $122,000 using the FIFO method.

Retained Earnings Adjustment

As indicated earlier, one of the disclosure requirements is to show the cumulative effect of the change on retained earnings as of the beginning of the earliest period presented. For Lancer Company, that date is January 1, 2006. Lancer disclosed that information by means of a narrative description (see Note A in Illustration 22-5). Lancer also would disclose this information in its retained earnings statement. Illustration 22-6 shows Lancer's retained earnings statement under LIFO—that is, before giving effect to the change in accounting principle. (This information comes from Illustration 22-2.)

ILLUSTRATION 22-6
Retained Earnings
Statements (LIFO)

	2007	2006	2005
Retained earnings, January 1	$220,000	$120,000	$ 0
Net income	87,000	100,000	120,000
Retained earnings, December 31	$307,000	$220,000	$120,000

If Lancer presents comparative statements for 2006 and 2007 under FIFO, then it must change the beginning balance of retained earnings at January 1, 2006. The difference between the retained earnings balances under LIFO and FIFO is computed as shown on page 1160.

Retained earnings, January 1, 2006 (FIFO)	$122,000
Retained earnings, January 1, 2006 (LIFO)	120,000
Cumulative effect difference	$ 2,000

The $2,000 difference is the cumulative effect. Illustration 22-7 shows a comparative retained earnings statement for 2006 and 2007, giving effect to the change in accounting principle to FIFO.

ILLUSTRATION 22-7
Retained Earnings
Statements after
Retrospective Application

	2007	2006
Retained earnings, January 1, as reported		$120,000
Add: Adjustment for the cumulative effect on prior years of applying retrospectively the new method of accounting for inventory		2,000
Retained earnings, January 1, as adjusted	$225,000	122,000
Net income	89,000	103,000
Retained earnings, December 31	$314,000	$225,000

Lancer adjusted the beginning balance of retained earnings on January 1, 2006, for the excess of FIFO net income over LIFO net income in 2005. This comparative presentation indicates the type of adjustment that a company needs to make. It follows that the amount of this adjustment would be much larger if a number of prior periods were involved.

Direct and Indirect Effects of Changes

Are there other effects that a company should report when it makes a change in accounting principle? For example, what happens when a company like Lancer has a bonus plan based on net income and the prior year's net income changes when FIFO is retrospectively applied? Should Lancer change the reported amount of bonus expense also? Or what happens if we had not ignored income taxes in the Lancer example? Should Lancer adjust net income, given that taxes will be different under LIFO and FIFO in prior periods? The answers depend on whether the effects are direct or indirect.

Direct Effects

The FASB takes the position that companies should retrospectively apply the **direct effects of a change in accounting principle**. An example of a **direct effect** is an adjustment to an inventory balance as a result of a change in the inventory valuation method. For example, Lancer Company should change the inventory amounts in prior periods to indicate the change to the FIFO method of inventory valuation. Another inventory-related example would be an impairment adjustment resulting from applying the lower-of-cost-or-market test to the adjusted inventory balance. Related changes, such as deferred income tax effects of the impairment adjustment, are also considered direct effects.

To illustrate the impact of a direct effect on taxes, assume that Denson Construction has accounted for its income from long-term construction contracts using the completed-contract method. In 2007 the company changed to the percentage-of-completion method. Management believes this approach provides a more appropriate measure of the income earned. For tax purposes, the company uses the completed-contract method and plans to continue doing so in the future. (We assume a 40 percent enacted tax rate.)

Illustration 22-8 shows portions of income statements for 2005–2007—for both the completed-contract and percentage-of-completion methods.

ILLUSTRATION 22-8
Comparative Income
Statements for
Completed-Contract
versus Percentage-of-
Completion Methods

COMPLETED-CONTRACT METHOD
DENSON COMPANY
INCOME STATEMENT (PARTIAL)
FOR THE YEARS ENDED DECEMBER 31

	2005	2006	2007
Income before income tax	$400,000	$160,000	$190,000
Income tax (40%)	160,000	64,000	76,000
Net income	$240,000	$ 96,000	$114,000

PERCENTAGE-OF-COMPLETION METHOD
DENSON COMPANY
INCOME STATEMENT (PARTIAL)
FOR THE YEARS ENDED DECEMBER 31

	2005	2006	2007
Income before income tax	$600,000	$180,000	$200,000
Income tax (40%)	240,000	72,000	80,000
Net income	$360,000	$108,000	$120,000

To record a change from the completed-contract to the percentage-of-completion method, we analyze the various effects, as Illustration 22-9 shows.

ILLUSTRATION 22-9
Data for Indirect Effect
Example

	Pretax Income from		Difference in Income		
Year	Percentage-of-Completion	Completed-Contract	Difference	Tax Effect 40%	Income Effect (net of tax)
Prior to 2006	$600,000	$400,000	$200,000	$80,000	$120,000
In 2006	180,000	160,000	20,000	8,000	12,000
Total at beginning of 2007	$780,000	$560,000	$220,000	$88,000	$132,000
Total in 2007	$200,000	$190,000	$ 10,000	$ 4,000	$ 6,000

The entry to record the change at the beginning of 2007 would be:

Construction in Process	220,000	
Deferred Tax Liability		88,000
Retained Earnings		132,000

The Construction in Process account increases by $220,000 (as indicated in the first column under "Difference in Income" in Illustration 22-9). The credit to Retained Earnings of $132,000 reflects the cumulative income effects prior to 2007 (third column under "Difference in Income" in Illustration 22-9). The company credits Retained Earnings because prior years' income is closed to this account each year. The credit to Deferred Tax Liability represents the adjustment to prior years' tax expense. The company now recognizes that amount, $88,000, as a tax liability for future taxable amounts. That is, in future periods, taxable income will be higher than book income as a result of current temporary differences; therefore Denson must report a deferred tax liability in the current year.

Denson reports the comparative financial statements, as shown in the lower half of Illustration 22-8. These include the new tax amounts. As indicated earlier, companies should record in the current year the direct effect of the change in taxes as a result of the change in accounting principle. They also should present information for prior periods, including changes in taxes, based on the new method.

Indirect Effects

In addition to direct effects, companies can have **indirect effects related to a change in accounting principle**. An **indirect effect** is any change to current or future cash flows of a company that result from making a change in accounting principle that is applied retrospectively. An example of an indirect effect is a change in profit-sharing or royalty payment that is based on a reported amount such as revenue or net income. **Indirect effects do not change prior-period amounts.**

For example, let's assume that Denson Construction has an employee profit-sharing plan based on net income. As Illustration 22-8 showed, Denson would report higher income in 2005 and 2006 if it used the percentage-of-completion method. In addition, let's assume that the profit-sharing plan requires that Denson pay the incremental amount due based on the percentage-of-completion income amounts. In this situation, Denson reports this additional expense **in the current period**; it would not change prior periods for this expense. If the company prepares comparative financial statements, it follows that it does not recast the prior periods for this additional expense.[6]

If the terms of the profit-sharing plan indicate that *no payment is necessary* in the current period due to this change, then the company need not recognize additional profit-sharing expense in the current period. Neither does it change amounts reported for prior periods.

When a company recognizes the indirect effects of a change in accounting principle, it includes in the financial statements a description of the indirect effects. In doing so, it discloses the amounts recognized in the current period and related per share information.

INTERNATIONAL INSIGHT

IFRS do not explicitly address the accounting and disclosure of indirect effects.

Impracticability

OBJECTIVE 4
Understand how to account for impracticable changes.

It is not always possible for companies to determine how they would have reported prior periods' financial information under retrospective application of an accounting principle change. Retrospective application is considered **impracticable** if a company cannot determine the prior-period effects using every reasonable effort to do so.

Companies should not use retrospective application if one of the following conditions exists:

1 The company cannot determine the effects of the retrospective application.

2 Retrospective application requires assumptions about management's intent in a prior period.

3 Retrospective application requires significant estimates for a prior period, and the company cannot objectively verify the necessary information to develop these estimates.

If any of the above conditions exists, it is deemed impracticable to apply the retrospective approach. In this case, the company **prospectively applies** the new accounting principle as of the earliest date it is practicable to do so.[7]

For example, assume that Williams Company changed its inventory method from FIFO to LIFO, effective January 1, 2008. Williams prepares statements on a calendar-year basis and has used the FIFO method since its inception. Williams judges it impracticable to retrospectively apply the new method. Determining prior-period effects would require subjective assumptions about the LIFO layers established in prior periods. These assumptions would ordinarily result in the computation of a number of different earnings figures.

As a result, the only adjustment necessary may be to restate the beginning inventory to a cost basis from a lower-of-cost-or-market approach. Williams must disclose only the effect of the change on the results of operations in the period of change. Also, the company should explain the reasons for omitting the computations of the cumulative

---

[6]The rationale for this approach is that companies should recognize, in the period the adoption occurs (not the prior period), the effect on the cash flows that is caused by the adoption of the new accounting principle. That is, the accounting change is a necessary "past event" in the definition of an asset or liability that gives rise to the accounting recognition of the indirect effect in the current period (*SFAS No. 154,* par. B19).

[7]*SFAS No. 154,* pars. 8–11.

effect for prior years. Finally, it should disclose the justification for the change to LIFO.[8] Illustration 22-10, from the annual report of **Quaker Oats Company**, shows the type of disclosure needed.

The Quaker Oats Company

Note 1 (In Part): Summary of Significant Accounting Policies

Inventories. Inventories are valued at the lower of cost or market, using various cost methods, and include the cost of raw materials, labor and overhead. The percentage of year-end inventories valued using each of the methods is as follows:

June 30	Current Year	Prior Year
Average quarterly cost	21%	54%
Last-in, first-out (LIFO)	65%	29%
First-in, first-out (FIFO)	14%	17%

Effective July 1, the Company adopted the LIFO cost flow assumption for valuing the majority of remaining U.S. Grocery Products inventories. The Company believes that the use of the LIFO method better matches current costs with current revenues. The cumulative effect of this change on retained earnings at the beginning of the year is not determinable, nor are the pro-forma effects of retroactive application of LIFO to prior years. The effect of this change on current-year fiscal results was to decrease net income by $16.0 million, or $.20 per share.

If the LIFO method of valuing certain inventories were not used, total inventories would have been $60.1 million higher in the current year, and $24.0 million higher in the prior year.

ILLUSTRATION 22-10
Disclosure of Change to LIFO

CHANGE MANAGEMENT

Halliburton offers a case study in the importance of good reporting of an accounting change. Recall from Chapter 18 that Halliburton uses percentage-of-completion accounting for its long-term construction-services contracts. Recently, the SEC questioned the company about its change in accounting for disputed claims.

Prior to 1998 Halliburton took a very conservative approach to its accounting for disputed claims. That is, the company waited until all disputes were resolved before recognizing associated revenues. In contrast, in 1998 the company recognized revenue for disputed claims *before* their resolution, using estimates of amounts expected to be recovered. Such revenue and its related profit are more tentative and subject to possible later adjustment. The accounting method adopted in 1998 is more aggressive than the company's former policy but is within the boundaries of GAAP.

It appears that the problem with Halliburton's accounting stems more from how the company handled its accounting change than from the new method itself. That is, Halliburton did not provide in its 1998 annual report an explicit reference to its change in accounting method. In fact, rather than stating its new policy, the company simply deleted the sentence that described how it accounted for disputed claims. Then later, in its 1999 annual report, the company stated its new accounting policy.

When companies make such changes in accounting, investors need to be informed about the change and about its effects on the financial results. With such information, investors and analysts can compare current results with those of prior periods and can make a more informed assessment about the company's future prospects.

Source: Adapted from "Accounting Ace Charles Mulford Answers Accounting Questions," *Wall Street Journal Online* (June 7, 2002).

WHAT DO THE
NUMBERS MEAN?

---

[8]*SFAS No. 154*, par. 17. In practice, many companies defer the formal adoption of LIFO until year-end. Management thus has an opportunity to assess the impact that a change to LIFO will have on the financial statements and to evaluate the desirability of a change for tax purposes. As indicated in Chapter 8, many companies use LIFO because of the advantages of this inventory valuation method in a period of inflation.

CHANGES IN ACCOUNTING ESTIMATE

<table>
<tr><td>

OBJECTIVE 5
Describe the accounting for changes in estimates.

</td></tr>
</table>

To prepare financial statements, companies must estimate the effects of future conditions and events. For example, the following items require estimates.

1   Uncollectible receivables.
2   Inventory obsolescence.
3   Useful lives and salvage values of assets.
4   Periods benefited by deferred costs.
5   Liabilities for warranty costs and income taxes.
6   Recoverable mineral reserves.
7   Change in depreciation methods.

A company cannot perceive future conditions and events and their effects with certainty. Therefore, estimating requires the exercise of judgment. Accounting estimates will change as new events occur, as a company acquires more experience, or as it obtains additional information.

Companies report prospectively changes in accounting estimates. That is, companies should not adjust previously reported results for changes in estimates. Instead, they account for the effects of all changes in estimates in (1) the period of change if the change affects that period only, or (2) the period of change and future periods if the change affects both. The FASB views changes in estimates as **normal recurring corrections and adjustments**, the natural result of the accounting process. It prohibits retrospective treatment.

The circumstances related to a change in estimate differ from those for a change in accounting principle. If companies reported changes in estimates retrospectively, continual adjustments of prior years' income would occur. It seems proper to accept the view that, because new conditions or circumstances exist, the revision fits the new situation (not the old one). Companies should therefore handle such a revision in the current and future periods.

To illustrate, Underwriters Labs Inc. purchased for $300,000 a building that it originally estimated to have a useful life of 15 years and no salvage value. It recorded depreciation for 5 years on a straight-line basis. On January 1, 2007, Underwriters Labs revises the estimate of the useful life. It now considers the asset to have a total life of 25 years. (Assume that the useful life for financial reporting and tax purposes and depreciation method are the same.) Illustration 22-11 shows the accounts at the beginning of the sixth year.

ILLUSTRATION 22-11
Book Value after Five Years' Depreciation

Building	$300,000
Less: Accumulated depreciation—building (5 × $20,000)	100,000
Book value of building	$200,000

Underwriters Labs records depreciation for the year 2007 as follows:

Depreciation Expense	10,000	
Accumulated Depreciation—Building		10,000

The company computes the $10,000 depreciation charge as shown in Illustration 22-12.

ILLUSTRATION 22-12
Depreciation after Change in Estimate

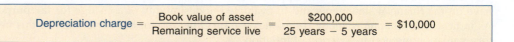

$$\text{Depreciation charge} = \frac{\text{Book value of asset}}{\text{Remaining service live}} = \frac{\$200,000}{25 \text{ years} - 5 \text{ years}} = \$10,000$$

Companies sometime find it difficult to differentiate between a change in estimate and a change in accounting principle. Is it a change in principle or a change in estimate when a company changes from deferring and amortizing marketing costs to expensing them as incurred because future benefits of these costs have become doubtful? If it is impossible to determine whether a change in principle or a change in estimate has occurred, the rule is this: **Consider the change as a change in estimate.** This is often referred to as a change in estimate effected by a change in accounting principle.

Another example of a change in estimate effected by a change in principle is a change in depreciation (as well as amortization or depletion) methods. Because companies change depreciation methods based on changes in estimates about future benefits from long-lived assets, it is not possible to separate the effect of the accounting principle change from that of the estimates. **As a result, companies account for a change in depreciation methods as a change in estimate effected by a change in accounting principle.**[9]

A similar problem occurs in differentiating between a change in estimate and a correction of an error, although here the answer is more clear-cut. How does a company determine whether it overlooked the information in earlier periods (an error), or whether it obtained new information (a change in estimate)? Proper classification is important because the accounting treatment differs for corrections of errors versus changes in estimates. The general rule is this: **Companies should consider careful estimates that later prove to be incorrect as changes in estimate.** Only when a company obviously computed the estimate incorrectly because of lack of expertise or in bad faith should it consider the adjustment an error. There is no clear demarcation line here. Companies must use good judgment in light of all the circumstances.[10]

Disclosures

Illustration 22-13 shows disclosure of a change in estimated useful lives, which appeared in the annual report of **Ampco–Pittsburgh Corporation**.

Ampco–Pittsburgh Corporation

Note 11: Change in Accounting Estimate. The Corporation revised its estimate of the useful lives of certain machinery and equipment. Previously, all machinery and equipment, whether new when placed in use or not, were in one class and depreciated over 15 years. The change principally applies to assets purchased new when placed in use. Those lives are now extended to 20 years. These changes were made to better reflect the estimated periods during which such assets will remain in service. The change had the effect of reducing depreciation expense and increasing net income by approximately $991,000 ($.10 per share).

ILLUSTRATION 22-13
Disclosure of Change in Estimated Useful Lives

For the most part, companies need not disclose changes in accounting estimate made as part of normal operations, such as bad debt allowances or inventory obsolescence, unless such changes are material. However, for a change in estimate that affects

---

[9]*SFAS No. 154*, par. 20.

[10]In evaluating reasonableness, the auditor should use one or a combination of the following approaches.

(a) Review and test the process used by management to develop the estimate.

(b) Develop an independent expectation of the estimate to corroborate the reasonableness of management's estimate.

(c) Review subsequent events or transactions occurring prior to completion of fieldwork.

"Auditing Accounting Estimates," *Statement on Auditing Standards No. 57* (New York: AICPA, 1988).

several periods (such as a change in the service lives of depreciable assets), companies should disclose the effect on income from continuing operations and related per-share amounts of the current period. When a company has a change in estimate effected by a change in accounting principle, it must indicate why the new method is preferable. In addition, companies are subject to all other disclosure guidelines established for changes in accounting principle.

REPORTING A CHANGE IN ENTITY

OBJECTIVE 6
Identify changes in a reporting entity.

Occasionally companies make changes that result in different reporting entities. In such cases, companies report the change by **changing the financial statements of all prior periods presented**. The revised statements show the financial information for the **new reporting entity** for all periods.

Examples of a change in reporting entity are:

1 Presenting consolidated statements in place of statements of individual companies.
2 Changing specific subsidiaries that constitute the group of companies for which the entity presents consolidated financial statements.
3 Changing the companies included in combined financial statements.
4 Changing the cost, equity, or consolidation method of accounting for subsidiaries and investments.[11] In this case, a change in the reporting entity does not result from creation, cessation, purchase, or disposition of a subsidiary or other business unit.

In the year in which a company changes a reporting entity, it should disclose in the financial statements the nature of the change and the reason for it. It also should report, for all periods presented, the effect of the change on income before extraordinary items, net income, and earnings per share. These disclosures need not be repeated in subsequent periods' financial statements.

Illustration 22-14 shows a note disclosing a change in reporting entity, from the annual report of **Hewlett-Packard Company**.

ILLUSTRATION 22-14
Disclosure of Change in Reporting Entity

Hewlett-Packard Company

Note: Accounting and Reporting Changes (In Part)

Consolidation of Hewlett-Packard Finance Company. The company implemented *Statement of Financial Accounting Standards No. 94 (SFAS 94)*, "Consolidation of All Majority-owned Subsidiaries." With the adoption of *SFAS 94*, the company consolidated the accounts of Hewlett-Packard Finance Company (HPFC), a wholly owned subsidiary previously accounted for under the equity method, with those of the company. The change resulted in an increase in consolidated assets and liabilities but did not have a material effect on the company's financial position. Since HPFC was previously accounted for under the equity method, the change did not affect net earnings. Prior years' consolidated financial information has been restated to reflect this change for comparative purposes.

REPORTING A CORRECTION OF AN ERROR

OBJECTIVE 7
Describe the accounting for correction of errors.

No business, large or small, is immune from errors. Unfortunately, as the opening story discussed, the number of errors in financial statements has increased dramatically. Illustration 22-15 indicates significant restatements (error adjustments) for each quarter in 2003 and 2004.

[11]An exception to retrospective application occurs when changing from the equity method. We provide an expanded illustration of the accounting for a change from or to the equity method in Appendix 22A.

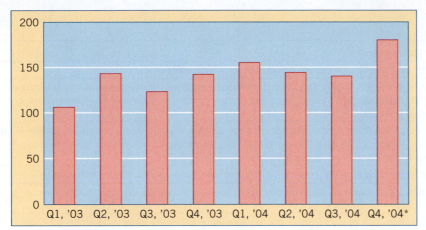

ILLUSTRATION 22-15
2003 and 2004
Restatements by Quarter

*Internal control audits mandated by Sarbanes-Oxley 404 resulted in a record number of 4th-quarter 2004 restatements.

SOURCE: T. Baldwin and D. Yoo, "Restatements—Traversing Shaky Ground," *Trend Alert*, Glass Lewis & Co. (June 2, 2005), p. 7.

Certain errors, such as misclassifications of balances within a financial statement, are not as significant to investors as other errors. Significant errors would be those resulting in overstating assets or income, for example. However, investors should know the potential impact of all errors. Even "harmless" misclassifications can affect important ratios. Also, some errors could signal important weaknesses in internal controls that could lead to more significant errors.

In general, accounting errors include the following types:

1 A change from an accounting principle that is **not** generally accepted to an accounting principle that is acceptable. The rationale is that the company incorrectly presented prior periods because of the application of an improper accounting principle. For example, a company may change from the cash (income tax) basis of accounting to the accrual basis.

2 Mathematical mistakes, such as incorrectly totaling the inventory count sheets when computing the inventory value.

3 Changes in estimates that occur because a company did not prepare the estimates in good faith. For example, a company may have adopted a clearly unrealistic depreciation rate.

4 An oversight, such as the failure to accrue or defer certain expenses and revenues at the end of the period.

5 A misuse of facts, such as the failure to use salvage value in computing the depreciation base for the straight-line approach.

6 The incorrect classification of a cost as an expense instead of an asset, and vice versa.

Accounting errors occur for a variety of reasons. Illustration 22-16 (page 1168) indicates 11 major categories of accounting errors that drive restatements.

As soon as a company discovers an error, it must correct the error. Companies record **corrections of errors** from prior periods as an adjustment to the beginning balance of retained earnings in the current period. Such corrections are called **prior period adjustments**.[12]

---

[12]"Prior Period Adjustments," *Statement of Financial Accounting Standards No. 16* (Stamford, Conn.: FASB, 1977), p. 5. See Mark L. DeFord and James Jiambalvo, "Incidence and Circumstances of Accounting Errors," *The Accounting Review* (July 1991) for examples of different types of errors and why these errors might have occurred.

ILLUSTRATION 22-16
Accounting-Error Types

Accounting Category	Type of Restatement
Expense recognition	Recording expenses in the incorrect period or for an incorrect amount
Revenue recognition	Improper revenue accounting. This category includes instances in which revenue was improperly recognized, questionable revenues were recognized, or any other number of related errors that led to misreported revenue.
Misclassification	Misclassifying significant accounting items on the balance sheet, income statement, or statement of cash flows. These include restatements due to misclassification of short- or long-term accounts or those that impact cash flows from operations
Equity—other	Improper accounting for EPS, restricted stock, warrants, and other equity instruments
Reserves/Contingencies	Errors involving accounts receivables bad debts, inventory reserves, income tax allowances, and loss contingencies
Long-lived assets	Asset impairments of property, plant, and equipment, goodwill, or other related items.
Taxes	Errors involving correction of tax provision, improper treatment of tax liabilities, and other tax-related items
Equity—other comprehensive income	Improper accounting for comprehensive income equity transactions including foreign currency items, minimum pension liability adjustments, unrealized gains and losses on certain investments in debt, equity securities, and derivatives.
Inventory	Inventory costing valuations, quantity issues, and cost of sales adjustments
Equity—stock options	Improper accounting for employee stock options
Other	Any restatement not covered by the listed categories including those related to improper accounting for acquisitions or mergers

SOURCE: T. Baldwin and D. Yoo, "Restatements—Traversing Shaky Ground," *Trend Alert*, Glass Lewis & Co. (June 2, 2005), p. 8.

If it presents comparative statements, a company should restate the prior statements affected, to correct for the error.[13] The company need not repeat the disclosures in the financial statements of subsequent periods.

Example

To illustrate, in 2008 the bookkeeper for Selectric Company discovered an error: In 2007 the company failed to record $20,000 of depreciation expense on a newly constructed building. This building is the only depreciable asset Selectric owns. The company correctly included the depreciation expense in its tax return and correctly reported its income taxes payable. Illustration 22-17 presents Selectric's income statement for 2007 (starting with income before depreciation expense) with and without the error.

ILLUSTRATION 22-17
Error Correction
Comparison

SELECTRIC COMPANY
INCOME STATEMENT
FOR THE YEAR ENDED, DECEMBER 31, 2007

	Without Error		With Error	
Income before depreciation expense		$100,000		$100,000
Depreciation expense		20,000		0
Income before income tax		80,000		100,000
Current	$32,000		$ 32,000	
Deferred	–0–	32,000	8,000	40,000
Net income		$ 48,000		$ 60,000

Illustration 22-18 shows the entries that Selectric should have made and did make for recording depreciation expense and income taxes.

---

[13]The term **"restatement"** is used for the process of revising previously issued financial statements to reflect the correction of an error. This distinguishes an error correction from a change in accounting principle (*SFAS No. 154*, par. 2, j).

ILLUSTRATION 22-18
Error Entries

Entries Company Should Have Made (Without Error)		Entries Company Did Make (With Error)	
Depreciation Expense	20,000	No entry made for depreciation	
Accumulated Depreciation			
—Buildings	20,000		
Income Tax Expense	32,000	Income Tax Expense	40,000
Income Tax Payable	32,000	Deferred Tax Liability	8,000
		Income Tax Payable	32,000

As Illustration 22-18 indicates, the $20,000 omission error in 2007 results in the following effects.

Income Statement Effects

Depreciation expense (2007) is understated $20,000.

Income tax expense (2007) is overstated $8,000 ($20,000 × 40%).

Net income (2007) is overstated $12,000 ($20,000 − $8,000).

Balance Sheet Effects

Accumulated depreciation—buildings is understated $20,000.

Deferred tax liability is overstated $8,000 ($20,000 × 40%).

To make the proper correcting entry in 2008, Selectric should recognize that net income in 2007 is overstated by $12,000, the Deferred Tax Liability is overstated by $8,000, and Accumulated Depreciation—Buildings is understated by $20,000. The entry to correct this error in 2008 is as follows:

Retained Earnings	12,000	
Deferred Tax Liability	8,000	
Accumulated Depreciation—Buildings		20,000

The debit to Retained Earnings results because net income for 2007 is overstated. The debit to the Deferred Tax Liability is made to remove this account, which was caused by the error. The credit to Accumulated Depreciation—Buildings reduces the book value of the building to its proper amount. Selectric will make the same journal entry to record the correction of the error in 2008 whether it prepares single-period (noncomparative) or comparative financial statements.

Single-Period Statements

To demonstrate how to show this information in a single-period statement, assume that Selectric Company has a beginning retained earnings balance at January 1, 2008, of $350,000. The company reports net income of $400,000 in 2008. Illustration 22-19 shows Selectric's retained earnings statement for 2008.

ILLUSTRATION 22-19
Reporting an Error—
Single-Period Financial
Statement

SELECTRIC COMPANY RETAINED EARNINGS STATEMENT FOR THE YEAR ENDED DECEMBER 31, 2008		
Retained earnings, January 1, as reported		$350,000
Correction of an error (depreciation)	$20,000	
Less: Applicable income tax reduction	8,000	(12,000)
Retained earnings, January 1, as adjusted		338,000
Add: Net income		400,000
Retained earnings, December 31		$738,000

The balance sheet in 2008 would not have any deferred tax liability related to the building, and Accumulated Depreciation—Buildings is now restated at a higher amount. The income statement would not be affected.

Comparative Statements

If preparing comparative financial statements, a company should make adjustments to correct the amounts for all affected accounts reported in the statements for **all periods** reported. The company should restate the data to the correct basis for each year presented. It should **show any catch-up adjustment as a prior period adjustment to retained earnings for the earliest period it reported**. These requirements are essentially the same as those for reporting a change in accounting principle.

For example, in the case of Selectric, the error of omitting the depreciation of $20,000 in 2007, discovered in 2008, results in the restatement of the 2007 financial statements. Illustration 22-20 shows the accounts that Selectric restates in the 2007 financial statements, presented in comparison with those of 2008.

ILLUSTRATION 22-20
Reporting an Error—
Comparative Financial
Statements

In the balance sheet:	
Accumulated depreciation—buildings	$20,000 increase
Deferred tax liability	$ 8,000 decrease
Retained earnings, ending balance	$12,000 decrease
In the income statement:	
Depreciation expense—buildings	$20,000 increase
Income tax expense	$ 8,000 decrease
Net income	$12,000 decrease
In the retained earnings statement:	
Retained earnings, ending balance (due to lower net income for the period)	$12,000 decrease

Selectric prepares the 2008 financial statements in comparative form with those of 2007 **as if the error had not occurred**. In addition, Selectric must disclose that it has restated its previously issued financial statements, and it describes the nature of the error. Selectric also must disclose the following:

1　The effect of the correction on each financial statement line item and any per-share amounts affected for each prior period presented.

2　The cumulative effect of the change on retained earnings or other appropriate components of equity or net assets in the statement of financial position, as of the beginning of the earliest period presented.[14]

SUMMARY OF ACCOUNTING CHANGES AND CORRECTIONS OF ERRORS

Having guidelines for reporting accounting changes and corrections has helped resolve several significant and long-standing accounting problems. Yet, because of diversity in situations and characteristics of the items encountered in practice, use of professional judgment is of paramount importance. In applying these guidelines, the primary objective is to serve the users of the financial statements. Achieving this objective requires accuracy, full disclosure, and an absence of misleading inferences.

Illustration 22-21 summarizes the main distinctions and treatments presented in the discussion in this chapter.

---

[14]*SFAS No. 154*, par. 26.

ILLUSTRATION 22-21
Summary of Guidelines
for Accounting Changes
and Errors

- **Changes in accounting principle**
  Employ the retrospective approach by:
  a. Changing the financial statements of all prior periods presented.
  b. Disclosing in the year of the change the effect on net income and earnings per share for all prior periods presented.
  c. Reporting an adjustment to the beginning retained earnings balance in the statement of retained earnings in the earliest year presented.
  If impracticable to determine the prior period effect (e.g., change to LIFO):
  a. Do not change prior years' income.
  b. Use opening inventory in the year the method is adopted as the base-year inventory for all subsequent LIFO computations.
  c. Disclose the effect of the change on the current year, and the reasons for omitting the computation of the cumulative effect and pro forma amounts for prior years.

- **Changes in accounting estimate.**
  Employ the current and prospective approach by:
  a. Reporting current and future financial statements on the new basis.
  b. Presenting prior period financial statements as previously reported.
  c. Making no adjustments to current-period opening balances for the effects in prior periods.

- **Changes in reporting entity.**
  Employ the retrospective approach by:
  a. Restating the financial statements of all prior periods presented.
  b. Disclosing in the year of change the effect on net income and earnings per share data for all prior periods presented.

- **Changes due to error.**
  Employ the restatement approach by:
  a. Correcting all prior period statements presented.
  b. Restating the beginning balance of retained earnings for the first period presented when the error effects occur in a period prior to that one.

Changes in accounting principle are appropriate **only** when a company demonstrates that the newly adopted generally accepted accounting principle is **preferable** to the existing one. Companies and accountants determine preferability on the basis of whether the new principle constitutes an **improvement in financial reporting**, not on the basis of the income tax effect alone.[15]

But it is not always easy to determine an improvement in financial reporting. **How does one measure preferability or improvement?** Such measurement varies from company to company. **Quaker Oats Company**, for example, argued that a change in accounting principle to LIFO inventory valuation "better matches current costs with current revenues" (see Illustration 22-10, page 1163). Conversely, another company might change from LIFO to FIFO because it wishes to report a more realistic ending inventory. How do you determine which is the better of these two arguments? Determining the preferable method requires some "standard" or "objective." Because no universal standard or objective is generally accepted, the problem of determining preferability continues to be difficult.

Initially the SEC took the position that the auditor should indicate whether a change in accounting principle was preferable. The SEC has since modified this approach, noting that greater reliance may be placed on management's judgment

UNDERLYING CONCEPTS

This is an example of two widely accepted concepts conflicting. Which is more important, matching (emphasis on the income statement) or qualitative characteristic of representational faithfulness (emphasis on the balance sheet)?

[15]A change in accounting principle, a change in the reporting entity (special type of change in accounting principle), and a correction of an error require an explanatory paragraph in the auditor's report discussing lack of consistency from one period to the next. A change in accounting estimate does not affect the auditor's opinion relative to consistency; however, if the change in estimate has a material effect on the financial statements, disclosure may still be required. Error correction not involving a change in accounting principle does not require disclosure relative to consistency.

in assessing preferability. Even though the preferability criterion is difficult to apply, the general guidelines have acted as a deterrent to capricious changes in accounting principles.[16] **If an FASB standard creates a new principle, expresses preference for, or rejects a specific accounting principle, a change is considered clearly acceptable.**

CAN I GET MY MONEY BACK?

When companies report restatements, investors usually lose money. What should investors do if a company misleads them by misstating its financial results? Join other investors in a class-action suit against the company and in some cases, the auditor.

Class-action activity has picked up in recent years, and settlements can be large. To find out about class actions, investors can go online to see if they are eligible to join any class actions. Below are some recent examples.

Company	Settlement Amount	Contact for Claim
Quaker Oats	$ 10,400,000	*www.gilardi.com*
Smart Choice Automotive	$ 2,500,000	*www.gilardi.com*
Sunbeam	$110,000,000	*www.gilardi.com*

The amounts reported are *before* attorney's fees, which can range from 15 to 30 percent of the total. Also, investors may owe taxes if the settlement results in a capital gain on the investment. Thus, investors can get back some of the money they lost due to restatements, but they should be prepared to pay an attorney and the government first.

Source: Adapted from C. Coolidge, "Lost and Found," *Forbes* (October 1, 2001), pp. 124–125.

MOTIVATIONS FOR CHANGE OF ACCOUNTING METHOD

OBJECTIVE 8
Identify economic motives for changing accounting methods.

Difficult as it is to determine which accounting standards have the strongest conceptual support, other complications make the process even more complex. These complications stem from the fact that managers have self-interest in how the financial statements make the company look. They naturally wish to show their financial performance in the best light. A **favorable profit picture** can influence investors, and a strong liquidity position can influence creditors. **Too favorable a profit picture**, however, can provide union negotiators and government regulators with ammunition during bargaining talks. Hence, managers might have varying motives for reporting income numbers.

Research has provided additional insight into why companies may prefer certain accounting methods.[17] Some of these reasons are as follows:

1 *Political Costs.* As companies become larger and more politically visible, politicians and regulators devote more attention to them. The larger the firm, the more likely it is to become subject to regulation such as antitrust, and the more likely it

---

[16]If management has not provided reasonable justification for the change in accounting principle, the auditor should express a qualified opinion. Or, if the effect of the change is sufficiently material, the auditor should express an adverse opinion on the financial statements. "Reports on Audited Financial Statements," *Statement on Auditing Standards No. 58* (New York: AICPA, 1988).

[17]See Ross L. Watts and Jerold L. Zimmerman, "Positive Accounting Theory: A Ten-Year Perspective," *The Accounting Review* (January 1990) for an excellent review of research findings related to management incentives in selecting accounting methods.

is to be required to pay higher taxes. Therefore, companies that are politically visible may seek to report low income numbers, to avoid the scrutiny of regulators. In addition, other constituents, such as labor unions, may be less willing to ask for wage increases if reported income is low. Researchers have found that the larger the company, the more likely it is to adopt income-decreasing approaches in selecting accounting methods.

2   *Capital Structure.* A number of studies have indicated that the capital structure of the company can affect the selection of accounting methods. For example, a company with a high debt-to-equity ratio is more likely to be constrained by debt covenants. The debt covenant may indicate that the company cannot pay dividends if retained earnings fall below a certain level. As a result, such a company is more likely to select accounting methods that will increase net income.

3   *Bonus Payments.* Studies have found that if compensation plans tie managers' bonus payments to income, management will select accounting methods that maximize their bonus payments.

4   *Smooth Earnings.* Substantial earnings increases attract the attention of politicians, regulators, and competitors. In addition, large increases in income are difficult to achieve in following years. Further, executive compensation plans would use these higher numbers as a baseline and make it difficult for managers to earn bonuses in subsequent years. Conversely, investors and competitors might view large decreases in earnings as a signal that the company is in financial trouble. Also, substantial decreases in income raise concerns on the part of stockholders, lenders, and other interested parties about the competency of management. For all these reasons, companies have an incentive to "manage" or "smooth" earnings. In general, management tends to believe that a steady 10 percent growth a year is much better than a 30 percent growth one year and a 10 percent decline the next.[18] In other words, managers usually prefer a gradually increasing income report and sometimes change accounting methods to ensure such a result.

Management pays careful attention to the accounting it follows and often changes accounting methods, not for conceptual reasons, but for economic reasons. As indicated throughout this textbook, such arguments have come to be known as **economic consequences** arguments. These arguments focus on the supposed impact of the accounting method on the behavior of investors, creditors, competitors, governments, or managers of the reporting companies themselves.[19]

To counter these pressures, standard setters such as the FASB have declared, as part of their conceptual framework, that they will assess the merits of proposed standards from a position of **neutrality**. That is, they evaluate the soundness of standards on the basis of conceptual soundness, not on the grounds of possible impact on behavior. It is not the FASB's place to choose standards according to the kinds of behavior it wishes to promote and the kinds it wishes to discourage. At the same time, it must be admitted that some standards often **will have** the effect of influencing behavior. Yet their justification should be conceptual, and not viewed in terms of their economic impact.

---

[18]O. Douglas Moses, "Income Smoothing and Incentives: Empirical Tests Using Accounting Changes," *The Accounting Review* (April 1987). The findings provide evidence that earnings smoothing is associated with firm size, the existence of bonus plans, and the divergence of actual earnings from expectations.

[19]Lobbyists use economic consequences arguments—and there are many of them—to put pressure on standard setters. We have seen examples of these arguments in the oil and gas industry about successful efforts versus full cost, in the technology area with the issue of mandatory expensing of research and developmental costs and stock options.

SECTION 2		*ERROR ANALYSIS*

OBJECTIVE 9
Analyze the effect of errors.

In this section, we show some additional types of accounting errors. Companies generally do not correct for errors that do not have a significant effect on the presentation of the financial statements. For example, should a company with a total annual payroll of $1,750,000 and net income of $940,000 correct its financial statements if it finds it failed to record accrued wages of $5,000? No—it would not consider this error significant.

Obviously, defining materiality is difficult, and managers and auditors must use experience and judgment to determine whether adjustment is necessary for a given error. We assume **all errors discussed in this section to be material and to require adjustment**. (Also, we ignore all tax effects in this section.)

Companies must answer three questions in error analysis:

1 What type of error is involved?
2 What entries are needed to correct for the error?
3 After discovery of the error, how are financial statements to be restated?

As indicated earlier, companies treat errors **as prior-period adjustments and report them in the current year as adjustments to the beginning balance of Retained Earnings**. If a company presents comparative statements, it restates the prior affected statements to correct for the error.

BALANCE SHEET ERRORS

Balance sheet errors affect only the presentation of an asset, liability, or stockholders' equity account. Examples are the classification of a short-term receivable as part of the investment section, the classification of a note payable as an account payable, and the classification of plant assets as inventory.

When the error is discovered, the company reclassifies the item to its proper position. If the company prepares comparative statements that include the error year, it should correctly restate the balance sheet for the error year.

INCOME STATEMENT ERRORS

Income statement errors involve the improper classification of revenues or expenses. Examples include recording interest revenue as part of sales, purchases as bad debt expense, and depreciation expense as interest expense. An income statement classification error has no effect on the balance sheet and **no effect on net income**.

A company must make a reclassification entry when it discovers the error, if it makes the discovery in the same year in which the error occurs. If the error occurred in prior periods, the company does not need to make a reclassification entry at the date of discovery because the accounts for the current year are correctly stated. (Remember that the company has closed the income statement accounts from the prior period to retained earnings.) If the company prepares comparative statements that include the error year, it restates the income statement for the error year.

BALANCE SHEET AND INCOME STATEMENT ERRORS

The third type of error involves both the balance sheet and income statement. For example, assume that the bookkeeper overlooked accrued wages payable at the end of the accounting period. The effect of this error is to understate expenses, understate liabilities, and overstate net income for that period of time. This type of error affects both the balance sheet and the income statement. We classify this type of error in one of two ways—counterbalancing or noncounterbalancing.

Counterbalancing errors are those that will be offset or corrected over two periods. For example, the failure to record accrued wages is a counterbalancing error because over a two-year period the error will no longer be present. In other words, the failure to record accrued wages in the previous period means: (1) net income for the first period is overstated; (2) accrued wages payable (a liability) is understated, and (3) wages expense is understated. In the next period, net income is understated; accrued wages payable (a liability) is correctly stated; and wages expense is overstated. For the two **years combined**: (1) net income is correct; (2) wages expense is correct; and (3) accrued wages payable at the end of the second year is correct. Most errors in accounting that affect both the balance sheet and income statement are counterbalancing errors.

Noncounterbalancing errors are those that are not offset in the next accounting period. An example would be the failure to capitalize equipment that has a useful life of five years. If we expense this asset immediately, expenses will be overstated in the first period but understated in the next four periods. At the end of the second period, the effect of the error is not fully offset. Net income is correct in the aggregate only at the end of five years, because the asset is fully depreciated at this point. Thus, **noncounterbalancing errors are those that take longer than two periods to correct themselves**.

Only in rare instances is an error never reversed. An example would be if a company initially expenses land. Because land is not depreciable, theoretically the error is never offset, unless the land is sold.

Counterbalancing Errors

We illustrate the usual types of counterbalancing errors on the following pages. In studying these illustrations, keep in mind a couple of points, discussed below.

First, determine whether the company has closed the books for the period in which the error is found:

1 **If the company has closed the books in the current year:**
   (a) If the error is already counterbalanced, no entry is necessary.
   (b) If the error is not yet counterbalanced, make an entry to adjust the present balance of retained earnings.

2 **If the company has not closed the books in the current year:**
   (a) If the error is already counterbalanced, make an entry to correct the error in the current period and to adjust the beginning balance of Retained Earnings.
   (b) If the error is not yet counterbalanced, make an entry to adjust the beginning balance of Retained Earnings.

Second, if the company presents comparative statements, it must restate the amounts for comparative purposes. **Restatement is necessary even if a correcting journal entry is not required.**

To illustrate, assume that Sanford's Cement Co. failed to accrue revenue in 2005 when earned, but recorded the revenue in 2006 when received. The company discovered the error in 2008. It does not need to make an entry to correct for this error because the effects have been counterbalanced by the time Sanford discovered the error in 2008. However, if Sanford presents comparative financial statements for 2005 through 2008, it must **restate the accounts and related amounts for the years 2005 and 2006 for financial reporting purposes**.

The sections that follow demonstrate the accounting for the usual types of counterbalancing errors.

Failure to Record Accrued Wages

On December 31, 2007, Hurley Enterprises did not accrue wages in the amount of $1,500. The entry in 2008 to correct this error, assuming Hurley has not closed the books for 2008, is:

Retained Earnings	1,500	
Wages Expense		1,500

The rationale for this entry is as follows: (1) When Hurley pays the 2007 accrued wages in 2008, it makes an additional debit of $1,500 to 2008 Wages Expense. (2) Wages Expense—2008 is overstated by $1,500. (3) Because the company did not record 2007 accrued wages as Wages Expense in 2007, the net income for 2007 was overstated by $1,500. (4) Because 2007 net income is overstated by $1,500, the Retained Earnings account is overstated by $1,500 (because net income is closed to Retained Earnings).

If Hurley has closed the books for 2008, it makes no entry, because the error is counterbalanced.

Failure to Record Prepaid Expenses

In January 2007 Hurley Enterprises purchased a two-year insurance policy costing $1,000. It debited Insurance Expense, and credited Cash. The company made no adjusting entries at the end of 2007.

The entry on December 31, 2008, to correct this error, assuming Hurley has not closed the books for 2008, is:

Insurance Expense	500	
Retained Earnings		500

If Hurley has closed the books for 2008, it makes no entry, because the error is counterbalanced.

Understatement of Unearned Revenue

On December 31, 2007, Hurley Enterprises received $50,000 as a prepayment for renting certain office space for the following year. At the time of receipt of the rent payment, the company recorded a debit to Cash and a credit to Rent Revenue. It made no adjusting entry as of December 31, 2007. The entry on December 31, 2008, to correct for this error, assuming that Hurley has not closed the books for 2008, is:

Retained Earnings	50,000	
Rent Revenue		50,000

If Hurley has closed the books for 2008, it makes no entry, because the error is counterbalanced.

Overstatement of Accrued Revenue

On December 31, 2007, Hurley Enterprises accrued as interest revenue $8,000 that applied to 2008. On that date, the company recorded a debit Interest Receivable and a credit Interest Revenue. The entry on December 31, 2008, to correct for this error, assuming that Hurley has not closed the books for 2008, is:

Retained Earnings	8,000	
Interest Revenue		8,000

If Hurley has closed the books for 2008, it makes no entry, because the error is counterbalanced.

Overstatement of Purchases

Hurley's accountant recorded a purchase of merchandise for $9,000 in 2007 that applied to 2008. The physical inventory for 2007 was correctly stated. The company uses the periodic inventory method. The entry on December 31, 2008, to correct for this error, assuming that Harley has not closed the books for 2008, is:

Purchases	9,000	
Retained Earnings		9,000

If Hurley has closed the books for 2008, it makes no entry, because the error is counterbalanced.

Noncounterbalancing Errors

The entries for noncounterbalancing errors are more complex. Companies must make correcting entries, even if they have closed the books.

Failure to Record Depreciation

Assume that on January 1, 2007, Hurley Enterprises purchased a machine for $10,000 that had an estimated useful life of five years. The accountant incorrectly expensed this machine in 2007, but discovered the error in 2008. If we assume that Hurley uses straight-line depreciation on this asset, the entry on December 31, 2008, to correct for this error, given that Hurley has not closed the books, is:

Machinery	10,000	
Depreciation Expense	2,000	
Retained Earnings		8,000[a]
Accumulated Depreciation (20% × $10,000 × 2)		4,000

[a]Computations:

Retained Earnings	
Overstatement of expense in 2007	$10,000
Proper depreciation for 2007 (20% × $10,000)	(2,000)
Retained earnings understated as of Dec. 31, 2007	$ 8,000

If Hurley has closed the books for 2008, the entry is:

Machinery	10,000	
Retained Earnings		6,000[a]
Accumulated Depreciation		4,000

[a]Computations:

Retained Earnings	
Retained earnings understated as of Dec. 31, 2007	$ 8,000
Proper depreciation for 2008 (20% × $10,000)	(2,000)
Retained earnings understated as of Dec. 31, 2008	$ 6,000

Failure to Adjust for Bad Debts

Companies sometimes use a specific charge-off method in accounting for bad debt expense when a percentage of sales is more appropriate. They then make adjustments to change from the specific write-off to some type of allowance method. For example, assume that Hurley Enterprises has recognized bad debt expense when it has the following uncollectible debts.

	2007	2008
From 2007 sales	$550	$690
From 2008 sales		700

Hurley estimates that it will charge off an additional $1,400 in 2009, of which $300 is applicable to 2007 sales and $1,100 to 2008 sales. The entry on December 31, 2008, assuming that Hurley **has not closed the books for 2008**, is:

Bad Debt Expense	410[a]	
Retained Earnings	990[a]	
Allowance for Doubtful Accounts		1,400

[a]Computations to support the amounts in this entry are on the next page.

Allowance for doubtful accounts: Additional $300 for 2007 sales and $1,100 for 2008 sales.
Bad debts and retained earnings balance:

	2007	2008
Bad debts charged for	$1,240[b]	$ 700
Additional bad debts anticipated in 2009	300	1,100
Proper bad debt expense	1,540	1,800
Charges currently made to each period	(550)	(1,390)
Bad debt adjustment	$ 990	$ 410

[b]$550 + $690 = $1,240

If Hurley **has closed the books for 2008**, the entry is:

Retained Earnings	1,400	
Allowance for Doubtful Accounts		1,400

COMPREHENSIVE EXAMPLE: NUMEROUS ERRORS

In some circumstances a combination of errors occurs. The company therefore prepares a worksheet to facilitate the analysis. The following problem demonstrates use of the worksheet. The mechanics of its preparation should be obvious from the solution format. The income statements of Hudson Company for the years ended December 31, 2006, 2007, and 2008 indicate the following net incomes.

2006	$17,400
2007	20,200
2008	11,300

An examination of the accounting records for these years indicates that Hudson Company made several errors in arriving at the net income amounts reported:

1 The company consistently omitted from the records wages earned by workers but not paid at December 31. The amounts omitted were:

December 31, 2006	$1,000
December 31, 2007	$1,400
December 31, 2008	$1,600

When paid in the year following that in which they were earned, Hudson recorded these amounts as expenses.

2 The company overstated merchandise inventory on December 31, 2006, by $1,900 as the result of errors made in the footings and extensions on the inventory sheets.

3 On December 31, 2007, Hudson expensed unexpired insurance of $1,200, applicable to 2008.

4 The company did not record on December 31, 2007, interest receivable in the amount of $240.

5 On January 2, 2007, Hudson sold for $1,800 a piece of equipment costing $3,900. At the date of sale the equipment had accumulated depreciation of $2,400. The company recorded the cash received as Miscellaneous Income in 2007. In addition, it recorded depreciation for this equipment in both 2007 and 2008 at the rate of 10 percent of cost.

The first step in preparing the worksheet is to prepare a schedule showing the corrected net income amounts for the years ended December 31, 2006, 2007, and 2008. Each correction of the amount originally reported is clearly labeled. The next step is to indicate the balance sheet accounts affected as of December 31, 2008. Illustration 22-22 shows the completed worksheet for Hudson Company.

ILLUSTRATION 22-22
Worksheet to Correct
Income and Balance
Sheet Errors

HUDSON COMPANY
Worksheet to Correct Income and Balance Sheet Errors

	A	B	C	D	E	F	G	H
1			Worksheet Analysis of Changes in Net Income				Balance Sheet Correction at December 31, 2008	
2		2006	2007	2008	Totals	Debit	Credit	Account
3	Net income as reported	$17,400	$20,200	$11,300	$48,900			
4	Wages unpaid, 12/31/06	(1,000)	1,000		–0–			
5	Wages unpaid, 12/31/07		(1,400)	1,400	–0–			
6	Wages unpaid, 12/31/08			(1,600)	(1,600)		$1,600	Wages Payable
7	Inventory overstatement, 12/31/06	(1,900)	1,900		–0–			
8	Unexpired insurance, 12/31/07		1,200	(1,200)	–0–			
9	Interest receivable, 12/31/07		240	(240)	–0–			
10	Correction for entry made upon sale of equipment, 1/2/07[a]		(1,500)		(1,500)	$2,400	3,900	Accumulated Depreciation Machinery
11	Overcharge of depreciation, 2007		390		390	390		Accumulated Depreciation
12	Overcharge of depreciation, 2008			390	390	390		Accumulated Depreciation
13	Corrected net income	$14,500	$22,030	$10,050	$46,580			
14	[a]Cost	$ 3,900						
15	Accumulated depreciation	2,400						
16	Book value	1,500						
17	Proceeds from sale	1,800						
18	Gain on sale	300						
19	Income reported	(1,800)						
20	Adjustment	$(1,500)						

Sheet1 / Sheet2 / Sheet3

Assuming that Hudson Company **has not closed the books**, correcting entries on December 31, 2008, are:

Retained Earnings	1,400	
Wages Expense		1,400
(To correct improper charge to Wages Expense for 2008)		
Wages Expense	1,600	
Wages Payable		1,600
(To record proper wages expense for 2008)		
Insurance Expense	1,200	
Retained Earnings		1,200
(To record proper insurance expense for 2008)		
Interest Revenue	240	
Retained Earnings		240
(To correct improper credit to Interest Revenue in 2008)		
Retained Earnings	1,500	
Accumulated Depreciation	2,400	
Machinery		3,900
(To record write-off of machinery in 2007 and adjustment of Retained Earnings)		
Accumulated Depreciation	780	
Depreciation Expense		390
Retained Earnings		390
(To correct improper charge for depreciation expense in 2007 and 2008)		

If Hudson Company has closed the books for 2008, the correcting entries are:

Retained Earnings	1,600	
Wages Payable		1,600
(To record proper wage expense for 2008)		
Retained Earnings	1,500	
Accumulated Depreciation	2,400	
Machinery		3,900
(To record write-off of machinery in 2007 and		
adjustment of Retained Earnings)		
Accumulated Depreciation	780	
Retained Earnings		780
(To correct improper charge for depreciation expense		
in 2007 and 2008)		

PREPARATION OF FINANCIAL STATEMENTS WITH ERROR CORRECTIONS

Up to now, our discussion of error analysis has focused on identifying the type of error involved and accounting for its correction in the records. We have noted that companies must present the correction of the error on comparative financial statements.

The following example illustrates how a company would restate a typical year's financial statements, given many different errors.

Dick & Wally's Outlet is a small retail outlet in the town of Holiday. Lacking expertise in accounting, the company does not keep adequate records, and numerous errors occurred in recording accounting information.

1 The bookkeeper inadvertently failed to record a cash receipt of $1,000 on the sale of merchandise in 2008.

2 Accrued wages expense at the end of 2007 was $2,500; at the end of 2008, $3,200. The company does not accrue for wages; all wages are charged to Administrative Expenses.

3 The company had not set up an allowance for estimated uncollectible receivables. Dick and Wally decided to set up such an allowance for the estimated probable losses, as of December 31, 2008, for 2007 accounts of $700, and for 2008 accounts of $1,500. They also decided to correct the charge against each year so that it shows the losses (actual and estimated) relating to that year's sales. The company has written off accounts to bad debt expense (selling expense) as follows.

	In 2007	In 2008
2007 accounts	$400	$2,000
2008 accounts		1,600

4 Unexpired insurance not recorded at the end of 2007 was $600, and at the end of 2008, $400. All insurance is charged to Administrative Expenses.

5 An account payable of $6,000 should have been a note payable.

6 During 2007, the company sold for $7,000 an asset that cost $10,000 and had a book value of $4,000. At the time of sale Cash was debited, and Miscellaneous Income was credited for $7,000.

7 As a result of the last transaction, the company overstated depreciation expense (an administrative expense) in 2007 by $800 and in 2008 by $1,200.

Illustration 22-23 presents a worksheet that begins with the unadjusted trial balance of Dick & Wally's Outlet. You can determine the correcting entries and their effect on the financial statements by examining the worksheet.

ILLUSTRATION 22-23
Worksheet to Analyze
Effect of Errors in
Financial Statements

DICK & WALLY'S OUTLET
Worksheet Analysis to Adjust Financial Statements for the Year 2008

	A	B Trial Balance Unadjusted		C D Adjustments	E F Adjustments	G Income Statement Adjusted	H	I Balance Sheet Adjusted	J
		Debit	Credit	Debit	Credit	Debit	Credit	Debit	Credit
3	Cash	3,100		(1) 1,000				4,100	
4	Accounts Receivable	17,600						17,600	
5	Notes Receivable	8,500						8,500	
6	Inventory	34,000						34,000	
7	Property, Plant, and Equipment	112,000			(6) 10,000^a			102,000	
8	Accumulated Depreciation		83,500	(6) 6,000^a					75,500
9				(7) 2,000					
10	Investments	24,300						24,300	
11	Accounts Payable		14,500	(5) 6,000					8,500
12	Notes Payable		10,000		(5) 6,000				16,000
13	Capital Stock		43,500						43,500
14	Retained Earnings		20,000	(3) 2,700^b					
15				(6) 4,000^a	(4) 600				
16				(2) 2,500	(7) 800				12,200
17	Sales		94,000		(1) 1,000		95,000		
18	Cost of Goods Sold	21,000				21,000			
19	Selling Expenses	22,000			(3) 500^b	21,500			
20	Administrative Expenses	23,000		(2) 700	(4) 400	22,700			
21				(4) 600	(7) 1,200				
22	Totals	265,500	265,500						
23	Wages Payable				(2) 3,200				3,200
24	Allowance for Doubtful Accounts				(3) 2,200^b				2,200
25	Unexpired Insurance			(4) 400				400	
26	Net Income					29,800			29,800
27	Totals			25,900	25,900	95,000	95,000	190,900	190,900

Sheet1 Sheet2 Sheet3

Computations:

^{a}Machinery		^{b}Bad Debts		2007	2008
Proceeds from sale	$7,000	Bad debts charged for		$2,400	$1,600
Book value of machinery	4,000	Additional bad debts anticipated		700	1,500
Gain on sale	3,000			3,100	3,100
Income credited	7,000	Charges currently made to each year		(400)	(3,600)
Retained earnings adjustment	$4,000	Bad debt adjustment		$2,700	$ (500)

SUMMARY OF LEARNING OBJECTIVES

1. **Identify the types of accounting changes.** The three different types of accounting changes are: (1) *Change in accounting principle:* a change from one generally accepted accounting principle to another generally accepted accounting principle. (2) *Change in accounting estimate:* a change that occurs as the result of new information or as additional experience is acquired. (3) *Change in reporting entity:* a change from reporting as one type of entity to another type of entity.

2. **Describe the accounting for changes in accounting principles.** A change in accounting principle involves a change from one generally accepted accounting principle to another. A change in accounting principle is not considered to result from the adoption of a new principle in recognition of events that have occurred for the first time or that were previously immaterial. If the accounting principle previously followed was not acceptable or if the principle was applied incorrectly, a change to a generally accepted accounting principle is considered a correction of an error.

KEY TERMS

change in accounting estimate, 1152, 1164

change in accounting principle, 1152, 1153

change in accounting estimate effected by a change in accounting principle, 1165

change in reporting entity, 1152

correction of an error, 1167

counterbalancing errors, 1175

3. Understand how to account for retrospective accounting changes. The general requirement for changes in accounting principle is retrospective application. Under retrospective application, companies change prior years' financial statements on a basis consistent with the newly adopted principle. They treat any part of the effect attributable to years prior to those presented as an adjustment of the earliest retained earnings presented.

4. Understand how to account for impracticable changes. Retrospective application is impracticable if the prior period effect cannot be determined using every reasonable effort to do so. For example, in changing to LIFO, the base-year inventory for all subsequent LIFO calculations is generally the opening inventory in the year the company adopts the method. There is no restatement of prior years' income because it is often too impractical to do so.

5. Describe the accounting for changes in estimates. Companies report changes in estimates prospectively. That is, companies should make no changes in previously reported results. They do not adjust opening balances nor change financial statements of prior periods.

6. Identify changes in a reporting entity. An accounting change that results in financial statements that are actually the statements of a different entity should be reported by restating the financial statements of all prior periods presented, to show the financial information for the new reporting entity for all periods.

7. Describe the accounting for correction of errors. Companies must correct errors as soon as they discover them, by proper entries in the accounts, and report them in the financial statements. The profession requires that a company treat corrections of errors as prior-period adjustments, record them in the year in which it discovered the errors, and report them in the financial statements in the proper periods. If presenting comparative statements, a company should restate the prior statements affected to correct for the errors. The company need not repeat the disclosures in the financial statements of subsequent periods.

8. Identify economic motives for changing accounting methods. Managers might have varying motives for income reporting, depending on economic times and whom they seek to impress. Some of the reasons for changing accounting methods are: (1) political costs, (2) capital structure, (3) bonus payments, and (4) smoothing of earnings.

9. Analyze the effect of errors. Three types of errors can occur: (1) *Balance sheet errors*, which affect only the presentation of an asset, liability, or stockholders' equity account. (2) *Income statement errors*, which affect only the presentation of revenue, expense, gain, or loss accounts in the income statement. (3) *Balance sheet and income statement errors*, which involve both the balance sheet and income statement. Errors are classified into two types: (1) *Counterbalancing errors* are offset or corrected over two periods. (2) *Noncounterbalancing errors* are not offset in the next accounting period and take longer than two periods to correct themselves.

As an aid to understanding accounting changes, we provide the following glossary.

KEY TERMS RELATED TO ACCOUNTING CHANGES

ACCOUNTING CHANGE. A change in (1) an accounting principle, (2) an accounting estimate, or (3) the reporting entity. The correction of an error in previously issued financial statements is not an accounting change.

CHANGE IN ACCOUNTING PRINCIPLE. A change from one generally accepted accounting principle to another generally accepted accounting principle when two or more generally accepted accounting principles apply or when the accounting principle formerly used is no longer generally accepted.

CHANGE IN ACCOUNTING ESTIMATE. A change that has the effect of adjusting the carrying amount of an existing asset or liability or altering the subsequent accounting for existing or future assets or liabilities. Changes in accounting estimates result from new information.

CHANGE IN ACCOUNTING ESTIMATE EFFECTED BY A CHANGE IN ACCOUNTING PRINCIPLE. A change in accounting estimate that is inseparable from the effect of a related change in accounting principle.

CHANGE IN THE REPORTING ENTITY. A change that results in financial statements that, in effect, are those of a different reporting entity (see page 1166).

DIRECT EFFECTS OF A CHANGE IN ACCOUNTING PRINCIPLE. Those recognized changes in assets or liabilities necessary to effect a change in accounting principle.

ERROR IN PREVIOUSLY ISSUED FINANCIAL STATEMENTS. An error in recognition, measurement, presentation, or disclosure in financial statements resulting from mathematical mistakes, mistakes in the application of GAAP, or oversight or misuse of facts that existed at the time the financial statements were prepared. A change from an accounting principle that is not generally accepted to one that is generally accepted is a correction of an error.

INDIRECT EFFECTS OF A CHANGE IN ACCOUNTING PRINCIPLE. Any changes to current or future cash flows of an entity that result from making a change in accounting principle that is applied retrospectively.

RESTATEMENT. The process of revising previously issued financial statements to reflect the correction of an error in those financial statements.

RETROSPECTIVE APPLICATION. The application of a different accounting principle to one or more previously issued financial statements, or to the statement of financial position at the beginning of the current period, as if that principle had always been used, or a change to financial statements of prior accounting periods to present the financial statements of a new reporting entity as if it had existed in those prior years.[20]

---

[20]Adapted from *SFAS No. 154*, par. 2.

Changing from or to the Equity Method

As noted in the chapter, companies generally should report an accounting change that results in financial statements for a different entity by **changing the financial statements of all prior periods presented**.

An example of a change in reporting entity is when a company's level of ownership or influence changes, such as when it changes from or to the equity method. When changing **to** the equity method, companies use retrospective application. Companies treat a change **from** the equity method prospectively. We present examples of these changes in entity in the following two sections.

CHANGE FROM THE EQUITY METHOD

OBJECTIVE 10
Make the computations and prepare the entries necessary to record a change from or to the equity method of accounting.

If the investor level of influence or ownership falls below that necessary for continued use of the equity method, a company must change from the equity method to the fair-value method. The earnings or losses that the investor previously recognized under the equity method should **remain as part of the carrying amount** of the investment, with no retrospective application to the new method.

When a company changes **from the equity method to the fair-value method, the cost basis for accounting purposes is the carrying amount of the investment at the date of the change**.[1] The investor applies the new method in its entirety once the equity method is no longer appropriate. At the next reporting date, the investor should record the unrealized holding gain or loss to recognize the difference between the carrying amount and fair value.

Dividends in Excess of Earnings

In subsequent periods, dividends received by the investor company may exceed its share of the investee's earnings for such periods (all periods following the change in method). To the extent that they do so, the investor company should account for such dividends as a **reduction of the investment carrying amount**, rather than as revenue.

To illustrate, assume that on January 1, 2006, Investor Company purchased 250,000 shares of Investee Company's 1,000,000 shares of outstanding stock for $8,500,000. Investor correctly accounted for this investment using the equity method. After accounting for dividends received and investee net income, in 2006, Investor reported its investment in Investee Company at $8,780,000 at December 31, 2006. On January 2, 2007, Investee Company sold 1,500,000 additional shares of its own common stock to the public, thereby reducing Investor Company's ownership from 25 percent to 10 percent. Illustration 22A-1 shows the net income (or loss) and dividends of Investee Company for the years 2007 through 2009.

ILLUSTRATION 22A-1
Income Earned and
Dividends Received

Year	Investor's Share of Investee Income (Loss)	Investee Dividends Received by Investor
2007	$600,000	$ 400,000
2008	350,000	400,000
2009	–0–	210,000
Totals	$950,000	$1,010,000

Assuming a change from the equity method to the fair-value method as of January 2, 2007, Investor Company's reported investment in Investee Company and its reported income would be as shown in Illustration 22A-2 (page 1185).

Investor Company would record the dividends and earnings data for the three years subsequent to the change in methods as shown by the following entries.

---

[1]In addition, when the change of methods occurs, the company stops amortizing the excess of acquisition price over the proportionate share of book value acquired attributable to undervalued depreciable assets.

Year	Dividend Revenue Recognized	Cumulative Excess of Share of Earnings Over Dividends Received	Investment at December 31
2007	$400,000	$200,000[a]	$8,780,000
2008	400,000	150,000[b]	8,780,000
2009	150,000	(60,000)[c]	$8,780,000 − $60,000 = $8,720,000

[a]$600,000 − $400,000 = $200,000
[b]($350,000 − $400,000) + $200,000 = $150,000
[c]$150,000 − $210,000 = $(60,000)

2007 and 2008

Cash	400,000	
Dividend Revenue		400,000
(To record dividend received from Investee Company)		

2009

Cash	210,000	
Available-for-Sale Securities		60,000
Dividend Revenue		150,000
(To record dividend revenue from Investee Company in 2009 and to recognize cumulative excess of dividends received over share of Investee earnings in periods subsequent to change from equity method)		

CHANGE TO THE EQUITY METHOD

When converting to the equity method, companies use retrospective application. Such a change involves adjusting the carrying amount of the investment, results of current and prior operations, and retained earnings of the investor **as if the equity method has been in effect during all of the previous periods in which this investment was held.**[2] When changing from the fair-value method to the equity method, companies also must eliminate any balances in the Unrealized Holding Gain or Loss—Equity account and the Securities Fair Value Adjustment account. In addition, they eliminate the available-for-sale classification for this investment, and they record the investment in stock under the equity method.

For example, on January 2, 2007, Amsted Corp. purchased, for $500,000 cash, 10 percent of the outstanding shares of Cable Company common stock. On that date, the net assets of Cable Company had a book value of $3,000,000. The excess of cost over the underlying equity in net assets of Cable Company is goodwill. On January 2, 2009, Amsted Corp. purchased an additional 20 percent of Cable Company's stock for $1,200,000 cash when the book value of Cable's net assets was $4,000,000. The excess of cost over book value related to this additional investment is goodwill. Now having a 30 percent interest, Amsted Corp. must use the equity method.

From January 2, 2007, to January 2, 2009, Amsted Corp. used the fair-value method and categorized these securities as available-for-sale. At January 2, 2009, Amsted has a credit balance of $92,000 in its Unrealized Holding Gain or Loss—Equity account and a debit balance in its Securities Fair Value Adjustment account of the same amount. (Income tax effects are ignored.) Illustration 22A-3 (page 1186) shows the net income reported by Cable Company and the Cable Company dividends received by Amsted during the period 2007 through 2009.

---

[2]"The Equity Method of Accounting for Investments in Common Stock," *Opinions of the Accounting Principles Board No. 18* (New York: AICPA, 1971), par. 17.

ILLUSTRATION 22A-3
Income Earned and
Dividends Received

Year	Cable Company Net Income	Cable Co. Dividends Paid to Amsted
2007	$ 500,000	$ 20,000
2008	1,000,000	30,000
2009	1,200,000	120,000

Amsted makes the following journal entries from January 2, 2007, through December 31, 2009, relative to Amsted Corp.'s investment in Cable Company, reflecting the data above and a change from the fair value method to the equity method.[3]

January 2, 2007

Available-for-Sale Securities	500,000	
Cash		500,000
(To record the purchase of a 10% interest in Cable Company)		

December 31, 2007

Cash	20,000	
Dividend Revenue		20,000
(To record the receipt of cash dividends from Cable Company)		
Securities Fair Value Adjustment (Available-for-Sale)	92,000	
Unrealized Holding Gain or Loss—Equity		92,000
(To record increase in fair value of securities)		

December 31, 2008

Cash	30,000	
Dividend Revenue		30,000
(To record the receipt of cash dividends from Cable Company)		

January 2, 2009

Investment in Cable Stock	1,300,000	
Cash		1,200,000
Retained Earnings		100,000
(To record the purchase of an additional interest in Cable Company and to reflect retrospectively a change from the fair-value method to the equity method of accounting for the investment. The $100,000 adjustment is computed as follows:		

	2007	2008	Total
Amsted Corp. equity in earnings of Cable Company (10%)	$50,000	$100,000	$150,000
Dividend received	(20,000)	(30,000)	(50,000)
Retrospective application	$30,000	$ 70,000	$100,000

January 2, 2009

Investment in Cable Stock	500,000	
Available-for-Sale Securities		500,000
(To reclassify initial 10% interest to equity method)		

January 2, 2009

Unrealized Holding Gain or Loss—Equity	92,000	
Securities Fair Value Adjustment (Available-for-Sale)		92,000
(To eliminate fair value accounts for change to equity method)		

December 31, 2009

Investment in Cable Stock	360,000	
Revenue from Investment		360,000
[To record equity in earnings of Cable Company (30% of $1,200,000)]		

[3]Adapted from Paul A. Pacter, "Applying APB Opinion No. 18—Equity Method," *Journal of Accountancy* (September 1971), pp. 59–60.

Cash	120,000	
Investment in Cable Stock		120,000
(To record the receipt of cash dividends from		
Cable Company)		

Companies change to the equity method by placing the accounts related to and affected by the investment on the same basis **as if the equity method had always been the basis of accounting for that investment**. Thus, they report the effects of this accounting change using the retrospective approach.

SUMMARY OF LEARNING OBJECTIVE FOR APPENDIX 22A

10. Make the computations and prepare the entries necessary to record a change from or to the equity method of accounting. When changing *from* the equity method to the fair-value method, the cost basis for accounting purposes is the carrying amount used for the investment at the date of change. The investor company applies the new method in its entirety once the equity method is no longer appropriate. When changing *to* the equity method, the company adjusts the accounts to be on the same basis as if the equity method had always been used for that investment.

Note: All **asterisked** Brief Exercises, Exercises, and Problems relate to material contained in the appendix to the chapter.

QUESTIONS

1. In recent years, the *Wall Street Journal* has indicated that many companies have changed their accounting principles. What are the major reasons why companies change accounting methods?

2. State how each of the following items is reflected in the financial statements.

    (a) Change from FIFO to LIFO method for inventory valuation purposes.

    (b) Charge for failure to record depreciation in a previous period.

    (c) Litigation won in current year, related to prior period.

    (d) Change in the realizability of certain receivables.

    (e) Writeoff of receivables.

    (f) Change from the percentage-of-completion to the completed-contract method for reporting net income.

3. Discuss briefly the three approaches that have been suggested for reporting changes in accounting principles.

4. Identify and describe the approach the FASB requires for reporting changes in accounting principles.

5. What is the indirect effect of a change in accounting principle? Briefly describe the reporting of the indirect effects of a change in accounting principle.

6. Define a change in estimate and provide an illustration. When is a change in accounting estimate effected by a change in accounting principle?

7. Sandwich State Bank has followed the practice of capitalizing certain marketing costs and amortizing these costs over their expected life. In the current year, the bank determined that the future benefits from these costs were doubtful. Consequently, the bank adopted the policy of expensing these costs as incurred. How should the bank report this accounting change in the comparative financial statements?

8. Indicate how the following items are recorded in the accounting records in the current year of Tami Agler Co.

    (a) Impairment of goodwill.

    (b) A change in depreciating plant assets from accelerated to the straight-line method.

    (c) Large writeoff of inventories because of obsolescence.

    (d) Change from the cash basis to accrual basis of accounting.

    (e) Change from LIFO to FIFO method for inventory valuation purposes.

    (f) Change in the estimate of service lives for plant assets.

9. R. M. Andrews Construction Co. had followed the practice of expensing all materials assigned to a construction job without recognizing any salvage inventory. On December 31, 2007, it was determined that salvage inventory should be valued at $62,000. Of this amount, $29,000 arose during the current year. How does this information affect the financial statements to be prepared at the end of 2007?

10. E. A. Basler Inc. wishes to change from the completed-contract to the percentage-of-completion method for financial reporting purposes. The auditor indicates that a change would be permitted only if it is to a preferable method. What difficulties develop in assessing preferability?

11. Discuss how a change to the LIFO method of inventory valuation is handled when it is impracticable to determine previous LIFO inventory amounts.

12. How should consolidated financial statements be reported this year when statements of individual companies were presented last year?

13. Karen Beers controlled four domestic subsidiaries and one foreign subsidiary. Prior to the current year, Beers had excluded the foreign subsidiary from consolidation. During the current year, the foreign subsidiary was included in the financial statements. How should this change in accounting principle be reflected in the financial statements?

14. Distinguish between counterbalancing and noncounterbalancing errors. Give an example of each.

15. Discuss and illustrate how a correction of an error in previously issued financial statements should be handled.

16. Prior to 2008, Mary Boudreau Inc. excluded manufacturing overhead costs from work in process and finished goods inventory. These costs have been expensed as incurred. In 2008, the company decided to change its accounting methods for manufacturing inventories to full costing by including these costs as product costs. Assuming that these costs are material, how should this change be reflected in the financial statements for 2007 and 2008?

17. Lou Brady Corp. failed to record accrued salaries for 2005, $2,000; 2006, $2,100; and 2007, $3,900. What is the amount of the overstatement or understatement of Retained Earnings at December 31, 2008?

18. In January 2007, installation costs of $8,000 on new machinery were charged to Repair Expense. Other costs of this machinery of $30,000 were correctly recorded and have been depreciated using the straight-line method with an estimated life of 10 years and no salvage value. At December 31, 2008, it is decided that the machinery has a remaining useful life of 20 years, starting with January 1, 2008. What entry(ies) should be made in 2008 to correctly record transactions related to machinery, assuming the machinery has no salvage value? The books have not been closed for 2008 and depreciation expense has not yet been recorded for 2008.

19. On January 2, 2007, $100,000 of 11%, 20-year bonds were issued for $97,000. The $3,000 discount was charged to Interest Expense. The bookkeeper, John Castle, records interest only on the interest payment dates of January 1 and July 1. What is the effect on reported net income for 2007 of this error, assuming straight-line amortization of the discount? What entry is necessary to correct for this error, assuming that the books are not closed for 2007?

20. An account payable of $13,000 for merchandise purchased on December 23, 2007, was recorded in January 2008. This merchandise was not included in inventory at December 31, 2007. What effect does this error have on reported net income for 2007? What entry should be made to correct for this error, assuming that the books are not closed for 2007?

21. Equipment was purchased on January 2, 2007, for $18,000, but no portion of the cost has been charged to depreciation. The corporation wishes to use the straight-line method for these assets, which have been estimated to have a life of 10 years and no salvage value. What effect does this error have on net income in 2007. What entry is necessary to correct for this error, assuming that the books are not closed for 2007?

BRIEF EXERCISES

(LO 3) **BE22-1** Beaty Construction Company decided at the beginning of 2008 to change from the completed-contract method to the percentage-of-completion method for financial reporting purposes. The company will continue to use the completed-contract method for tax purposes. For years prior to 2008, pre-tax income under the two methods was as follows: percentage-of-completion $128,000, and completed-contract $80,000. The tax rate is 35%. Prepare Beaty's 2008 journal entry to record the change in accounting principle.

(LO 3) **BE22-2** Refer to the accounting change by Beaty Construction Company in BE22-1. Beaty has a profit-sharing plan, which pays all employees a bonus at year-end based on 1% of pre-tax income. Compute the indirect effect of Beaty's change in accounting principle that will be reported in the 2008 income statement, assuming that the profit-sharing contract explicitly requires adjustment for changes in income numbers.

(LO 3) **BE22-3** Robert Boey, Inc., changed from the LIFO cost flow assumption to the FIFO cost flow assumption in 2008. The increase in the prior year's income before taxes is $1,000,000. The tax rate is 40%. Prepare Boey's 2008 journal entry to record the change in accounting principle.

(LO 5) **BE22-4** Bickner Company changed depreciation methods in 2008 from double-declining-balance to straight-line. Depreciation under double-declining-balance was $90,000, whereas straight-line depreciation prior to 2008 would have been $50,000. Bickner's depreciable assets had a cost of $250,000 with a $50,000 salvage value, and an 8-year remaining useful life at the beginning of 2008. Prepare the 2008 journal entries, if any, related to Bickner's depreciable assets.

(LO 5) **BE22-5** Nancy Castle Company purchased a computer system for $60,000 on January 1, 2006. It was depreciated based on a 7-year life and an $18,000 salvage value. On January 1, 2008, Castle revised these estimates to a total useful life of 4 years and a salvage value of $10,000. Prepare Castle's entry to record 2008 depreciation expense.

(LO 7) **BE22-6** In 2008, John Hiatt Corporation discovered that equipment purchased on January 1, 2006, for $75,000 was expensed at that time. The equipment should have been depreciated over 5 years, with no salvage value. The effective tax rate is 30%. Prepare Hiatt's 2008 journal entry to correct the error.

(LO 7) **BE22-7** At January 1, 2008, William R. Monat Company reported retained earnings of $2,000,000. In 2008, Monat discovered that 2007 depreciation expense was understated by $500,000. In 2008, net income was $900,000 and dividends declared were $250,000. The tax rate is 40%. Prepare a 2008 retained earnings statement for William R. Monat Company.

(LO 7) **BE22-8** Indicate the effect—**Understate**, **Overstate**, **No Effect**—that each of the following errors has on 2007 net income and 2008 net income.

	2007	2008
(a) Wages payable were not recorded at 12/31/07.	___	___
(b) Equipment purchased in 2006 was expensed.	___	___
(c) Equipment purchased in 2007 was expensed.	___	___
(d) 2007 ending inventory was overstated.	___	___
(e) Patent amortization was not recorded in 2008.	___	___

(LO 3, 5, 7) **BE22-9** Charlene Rydell Manufacturing Co. is preparing its year-end financial statements and is considering the accounting for the following items.

1. The vice president of sales had indicated that one product line has lost its customer appeal and will be phased out over the next 3 years. Therefore, a decision has been made to lower the estimated lives on related production equipment from the remaining 5 years to 3 years.
2. Estimating the lives of new products in the Leisure Products Division has become very difficult because of the highly competitive conditions in this market. Therefore, the practice of deferring and amortizing preproduction costs has been abandoned in favor of expensing such costs as they are incurred.
3. The Hightone Building was converted from a sales office to offices for the Accounting Department at the beginning of this year. Therefore, the expense related to this building will now appear as an administrative expense rather than a selling expense on the current year's income statement.

Identify and explain whether each of the above items is a change in principle, a change in estimate, or an error.

(LO 3, 5, 7) **BE22-10** Pociek Co. is evaluating the appropriate accounting for the following items.

1. When the year-end physical inventory adjustment was made for the current year, the controller discovered that the prior year's physical inventory sheets for an entire warehouse were mislaid and excluded from last year's count.
2. Management has decided to switch from the FIFO inventory valuation method to the LIFO inventory valuation method for all inventories.
3. Pociek's Custom Division manufactures large-scale, custom-designed machinery on a contract basis. Management decided to switch from the completed-contract method to the percentage-of-completion method of accounting for long-term contracts.

Identify and explain whether each of the above items is a change in accounting principle, a change in estimate, or an error.

(LO 10) *****BE22-11** Robocop Corporation owns stock of Terminator, Inc. Prior to 2008, the investment was accounted for using the equity method. In early 2008, Robocop sold part of its investment in Terminator, and began using the fair value method. In 2008, Terminator earned net income of $80,000 and paid dividends of

$95,000. Prepare Robocop's entries related to Terminator's net income and dividends, assuming Robocop now owns 8% of Terminator's stock.

(LO 10) *****BE22-12** Rocket Corporation has owned stock of Knight Corporation since 2001. At December 31, 2007, its balances related to this investment were:

Available-for-Sale Securities	$185,000
Securities Fair Value Adj (AFS)	34,000 Dr.
Unrealized Holding Gain or Loss—Equity	34,000 Cr.

On January 1, 2008, Rocket purchased additional stock of Knight Company for $445,000 and now has significant influence over Knight. If the equity method had been used in 2004–2007, income would have been $33,000 greater than dividends received. Prepare Rocket's journal entries to record the purchase of the investment and the change to the equity method.

EXERCISES

(LO 3) **E22-1** **(Change in Principle—Long-term Contracts)** Pam Erickson Construction Company changed from the completed-contract to the percentage-of-completion method of accounting for long-term construction contracts during 2008. For tax purposes, the company employs the completed-contract method and will continue this approach in the future. (*Hint:* Adjust all tax consequences through the Deferred Tax Liability account.) The appropriate information related to this change is as follows.

	Pretax Income from:		
	Percentage-of-Completion	Completed-Contract	Difference
2007	$780,000	$590,000	$190,000
2008	700,000	480,000	220,000

Instructions
(a) Assuming that the tax rate is 35%, what is the amount of net income that would be reported in 2008?
(b) What entry(ies) are necessary to adjust the accounting records for the change in accounting principle?

(LO 3, 4) **E22-2** **(Change in Principle—Inventory Methods)** Holder-Webb Company began operations on January 1, 2005, and uses the average cost method of pricing inventory. Management is contemplating a change in inventory methods for 2008. The following information is available for the years 2005–2007.

	Net Income Computed Using		
	Average Cost Method	FIFO Method	LIFO Method
2005	$15,000	$19,000	$12,000
2006	18,000	23,000	14,000
2007	20,000	25,000	17,000

Instructions
(Ignore all tax effects.)
(a) Prepare the journal entry necessary to record a change from the average cost method to the FIFO method in 2008.
(b) Determine net income to be reported for 2005, 2006, and 2007, after giving effect to the change in accounting principle.
(c) Assume Holder-Webb Company used the LIFO method instead of the average cost method during the years 2005–2007. In 2008, Holder-Webb changed to the FIFO method. Prepare the journal entry necessary to record the change in principle.

(LO 3) **E22-3** **(Accounting Change)** Taveras Co. decides at the beginning of 2007 to adopt the FIFO method of inventory valuation. Taveras had used the LIFO method for financial reporting since its inception on January 1, 2005, and had maintained records adequate to apply the FIFO method retrospectively. Taveras concluded that FIFO is the preferable inventory method because it reflects the current cost of inventory on the balance sheet. The table on page 1191 presents the effects of the change in accounting principles on inventory and cost of goods sold.

Date	Inventory Determined by		Cost of Goods Sold Determined by	
	LIFO Method	FIFO Method	LIFO Method	FIFO Method
January 1, 2005	$ 0	$ 0	$ 0	$ 0
December 31, 2005	100	80	800	820
December 31, 2006	200	240	1,000	940
December 31, 2007	320	390	1,130	1,100

Other information:
1. For each year presented, sales are $3,000 and operating expenses are $1,000.
2. Taveras provides two years of financial statements. Earnings per share information is not required.

Instructions
(a) Prepare income statements under LIFO and FIFO for 2005, 2006, and 2007.
(b) Prepare income statements reflecting the retrospective application of the accounting change from the LIFO method to the FIFO method for 2007 and 2006.
(c) Prepare the note to the financial statements describing the change in method of inventory valuation. In the note, indicate the income statement line items for 2007 and 2006 that were affected by the change in accounting principle.
(d) Prepare comparative retained earnings statements for 2006 and 2007 under FIFO. Retained earnings reported under LIFO are as follows:

	Retained Earnings Balance
December 31, 2005	$1,200
December 31, 2006	2,200
December 31, 2007	3,070

(LO 3) **E22-4** **(Accounting Change)** Gordon Company started operations on January 1, 2002, and has used the FIFO method of inventory valuation since its inception. In 2008, it decides to switch to the average cost method. You are provided with the following information.

	Net Income		Retained Earnings (Ending balance)
	Under FIFO	Under Average Cost	Under FIFO
2002	$100,000	$ 90,000	$100,000
2003	70,000	65,000	160,000
2004	90,000	80,000	235,000
2005	120,000	130,000	340,000
2006	300,000	290,000	590,000
2007	305,000	310,000	780,000

Instructions
(a) What is the beginning retained earnings balance at January 1, 2004, if Gordon prepares comparative financial statements starting in 2004?
(b) What is the beginning retained earnings balance at January 1, 2007, if Gordon prepares comparative financial statements starting in 2007?
(c) What is the beginning retained earnings balance at January 1, 2008, if Gordon prepares single-period financial statements for 2008?
(d) What is the net income reported by Gordon in the 2007 income statement if it prepares comparative financial statements starting with 2005?

(LO 3) **E22-5** **(Accounting Change)** Presented below are income statements prepared on a LIFO and FIFO basis for Kenseth Company, which started operations on January 1, 2006. The company presently uses the LIFO method of pricing its inventory and has decided to switch to the FIFO method in 2007. The FIFO income statement is computed in accordance with the requirements of *SFAS No. 154*. Kenseth's profit-sharing agreement with its employees indicates that the company will pay employees 10% of income before profit sharing. Income taxes are ignored.

	LIFO Basis		FIFO Basis	
	2007	2006	2007	2006
Sales	$3,000	$3,000	$3,000	$3,000
Cost of goods sold	1,130	1,000	1,100	940
Operating expenses	1,000	1,000	1,000	1,000
Income before profit sharing	870	1,000	900	1,060
Profit sharing expense	87	100	96	100
Net income	$ 783	$ 900	$ 804	$ 960

Instructions

Answer the following questions.

(a) If comparative income statements are prepared, what net income should Kenseth report in 2006 and 2007?

(b) Explain why, under the FIFO basis, Kenseth reports $100 in 2006 and $96 in 2007 for its profit-sharing expense.

(c) Assume that Kenseth has a beginning balance of retained earnings at January 1, 2007, of $8,000 using the LIFO method. The company declared and paid dividends of $2,000 in 2007. Prepare the retained earnings statement for 2007, assuming that Kenseth has switched to the FIFO method.

(LO 5) **E22-6 (Accounting Changes—Depreciation)** Kathleen Cole Inc. acquired the following assets in January of 2005.

Equipment, estimated service life, 5 years; salvage value, $15,000	$525,000
Building, estimated service life, 30 years; no salvage value	$693,000

The equipment has been depreciated using the sum-of-the-years'-digits method for the first 3 years for financial reporting purposes. In 2008, the company decided to change the method of computing depreciation to the straight-line method for the equipment, but no change was made in the estimated service life or salvage value. It was also decided to change the total estimated service life of the building from 30 years to 40 years, with no change in the estimated salvage value. The building is depreciated on the straight-line method.

Instructions

(a) Prepare the general journal entry to record depreciation expense for the equipment in 2008.

(b) Prepare the journal entry to record depreciation expense for the building in 2008. (Round all computations to two decimal places.)

(LO 5, 7) **E22-7 (Change in Estimate and Error; Financial Statements)** Presented below are the comparative income statements for Denise Habbe Inc. for the years 2007 and 2008.

	2008	2007
Sales	$340,000	$270,000
Cost of sales	200,000	142,000
Gross profit	140,000	128,000
Expenses	88,000	50,000
Net income	$ 52,000	$ 78,000
Retained earnings (Jan. 1)	$ 125,000	$ 72,000
Net income	52,000	78,000
Dividends	(30,000)	(25,000)
Retained earnings (Dec. 31)	$147,000	$125,000

The following additional information is provided:

1. In 2008, Denise Habbe Inc. decided to switch its depreciation method from sum-of-the-years'-digits to the straight-line method. The assets were purchased at the beginning of 2007 for $100,000 with an estimated useful life of 4 years and no salvage value. (The 2008 income statement contains depreciation expense of $30,000 on the assets purchased at the beginning of 2007.)

2. In 2008, the company discovered that the ending inventory for 2007 was overstated by $24,000; ending inventory for 2008 is correctly stated.

Instructions

Prepare the revised income and retained earnings statement for 2007 and 2008, assuming comparative statements. (Ignore income taxes.)

(LO 3, 5, 7) **E22-8 (Accounting for Accounting Changes and Errors)** Listed below are various types of accounting changes and errors.

_____ 1. Change in a plant asset's salvage value.
_____ 2. Change due to overstatement of inventory.
_____ 3. Change from sum-of-the-years'-digits to straight-line method of depreciation.
_____ 4. Change from presenting unconsolidated to consolidated financial statements.
_____ 5. Change from LIFO to FIFO inventory method.
_____ 6. Change in the rate used to compute warranty costs.
_____ 7. Change from an unacceptable accounting principle to an acceptable accounting principle.
_____ 8. Change in a patent's amortization period.
_____ 9. Change from completed-contract to percentage-of-completion method on construction contracts.
_____ 10. Change from FIFO to average-cost inventory method.

Instructions

For each change or error, indicate how it would be accounted for using the following code letters:

(a) Accounted for prospectively.
(b) Accounted for retrospectively.
(c) Neither of the above.

(LO 5, 7) **E22-9 (Error and Change in Estimate—Depreciation)** Joy Cunningham Co. purchased a machine on January 1, 2005, for $550,000. At that time it was estimated that the machine would have a 10-year life and no salvage value. On December 31, 2008, the firm's accountant found that the entry for depreciation expense had been omitted in 2006. In addition, management has informed the accountant that the company plans to switch to straight-line depreciation, starting with the year 2008. At present, the company uses the sum-of-the-years'-digits method for depreciating equipment.

Instructions

Prepare the general journal entries that should be made at December 31, 2008 to record these events. (Ignore tax effects.)

(LO 5, 7) **E22-10 (Depreciation Changes)** On January 1, 2004, Jackson Company purchased a building and equipment that have the following useful lives, salvage values, and costs.

> Building, 40-year estimated useful life, $50,000 salvage value, $800,000 cost
> Equipment, 12-year estimated useful life, $10,000 salvage value, $100,000 cost

The building has been depreciated under the double-declining balance method through 2007. In 2008, the company decided to switch to the straight-line method of depreciation. Jackson also decided to change the total useful life of the equipment to 9 years, with a salvage value of $5,000 at the end of that time. The equipment is depreciated using the straight-line method.

Instructions

(a) Prepare the journal entry(ies) necessary to record the depreciation expense on the building in 2008.
(b) Compute depreciation expense on the equipment for 2008.

(LO 5) **E22-11 (Change in Estimate—Depreciation)** Peter M. Dell Co. purchased equipment for $510,000 which was estimated to have a useful life of 10 years with a salvage value of $10,000 at the end of that time. Depreciation has been entered for 7 years on a straight-line basis. In 2008, it is determined that the total estimated life should be 15 years with a salvage value of $5,000 at the end of that time.

Instructions

(a) Prepare the entry (if any) to correct the prior years' depreciation.
(b) Prepare the entry to record depreciation for 2008.

(LO 5) **E22-12 (Change in Estimate—Depreciation)** Gerald Englehart Industries changed from the double-declining balance to the straight-line method in 2008 on all its plant assets. There was no change in the assets' salvage values or useful lives. Plant assets, acquired on January 2, 2005, had an original cost of $1,600,000, with a $100,000 salvage value and an 8-year estimated useful life. Income before depreciation expense was $270,000 in 2007 and $300,000 in 2008.

Instructions

(a) Prepare the journal entry(ies) to record the change in depreciation method in 2008.
(b) Starting with income before depreciation expense, prepare the remaining portion of the income statement for 2007 and 2008.

(LO 3) **E22-13 (Change in Principle—Long-term Contracts)** Cullen Construction Company changed from the completed-contract to the percentage-of-completion method of accounting for long-term construction contracts during 2008. For tax purposes, the company employs the completed-contract method and will continue this approach in the future. The appropriate information related to this change is as follows.

	Pretax Income from		
	Percentage-of-Completion	Completed-Contract	Difference
2007	$980,000	$590,000	$290,000
2008	900,000	480,000	420,000

Instructions

(a) Assuming that the tax rate is 40%, what is the amount of net income that would be reported in 2008?
(b) What entry(ies) are necessary to adjust the accounting records for the change in accounting principle?

(LO 3) **E22-14** **(Various Changes in Principle—Inventory Methods)** Below is the net income of Anita Ferreri Instrument Co., a private corporation, computed under the three inventory methods using a periodic system.

	FIFO	Average Cost	LIFO
2005	$26,000	$24,000	$20,000
2006	30,000	25,000	21,000
2007	28,000	27,000	24,000
2008	34,000	30,000	26,000

Instructions

(Ignore tax considerations.)

(a) Assume that in 2008 Ferreri decided to change from the FIFO method to the average cost method of pricing inventories. Prepare the journal entry necessary for the change that took place during 2008, and show net income reported for 2005, 2006, 2007, and 2008.

(b) Assume that in 2008 Ferreri, which had been using the LIFO method since incorporation in 2005, changed to the FIFO method of pricing inventories. Prepare the journal entry necessary to record the change in 2008 and show net income reported for 2005, 2006, 2007, and 2008.

(LO 7) **E22-15** **(Error Correction Entries)** The first audit of the books of Bruce Gingrich Company was made for the year ended December 31, 2008. In examining the books, the auditor found that certain items had been overlooked or incorrectly handled in the last 3 years. These items are:

1. At the beginning of 2006, the company purchased a machine for $510,000 (salvage value of $51,000) that had a useful life of 6 years. The bookkeeper used straight-line depreciation, but failed to deduct the salvage value in computing the depreciation base for the 3 years.
2. At the end of 2007, the company failed to accrue sales salaries of $45,000.
3. A tax lawsuit that involved the year 2006 was settled late in 2008. It was determined that the company owed an additional $85,000 in taxes related to 2006. The company did not record a liability in 2006 or 2007 because the possibility of loss was considered remote, and charged the $85,000 to a loss account in 2008.
4. Gingrich Company purchased a copyright from another company early in 2006 for $45,000. Gingrich had not amortized the copyright because its value had not diminished. The copyright has a useful life at purchase of 20 years.
5. In 2008, the company wrote off $87,000 of inventory considered to be obsolete; this loss was charged directly to Retained Earnings.

Instructions

Prepare the journal entries necessary in 2008 to correct the books, assuming that the books have not been closed. Disregard effects of corrections on income tax.

(LO 7) **E22-16** **(Error Analysis and Correcting Entry)** You have been engaged to review the financial statements of Gottschalk Corporation. In the course of your examination you conclude that the bookkeeper hired during the current year is not doing a good job. You notice a number of irregularities as follows.

1. Year-end wages payable of $3,400 were not recorded because the bookkeeper thought that "they were immaterial."
2. Accrued vacation pay for the year of $31,100 was not recorded because the bookkeeper "never heard that you had to do it."
3. Insurance for a 12-month period purchased on November 1 of this year was charged to insurance expense in the amount of $2,640 because "the amount of the check is about the same every year."
4. Reported sales revenue for the year is $2,120,000. This includes all sales taxes collected for the year. The sales tax rate is 6%. Because the sales tax is forwarded to the state's Department of Revenue, the Sales Tax Expense account is debited. The bookkeeper thought that "the sales tax is a selling expense." At the end of the current year, the balance in the Sales Tax Expense account is $103,400.

Instructions

Prepare the necessary correcting entries, assuming that Gottschalk uses a calendar-year basis.

(LO 7) **E22-17** **(Error Analysis and Correcting Entry)** The reported net incomes for the first 2 years of Sandra Gustafson Products, Inc., were as follows: 2007, $147,000; 2008, $185,000. Early in 2009, the following errors were discovered.

1. Depreciation of equipment for 2007 was overstated $17,000.
2. Depreciation of equipment for 2008 was understated $38,500.
3. December 31, 2007, inventory was understated $50,000.
4. December 31, 2008, inventory was overstated $16,200.

Instructions
Prepare the correcting entry necessary when these errors are discovered. Assume that the books are closed. (Ignore income tax considerations.)

(LO 7, 9) **E22-18** **(Error Analysis)** Peter Henning Tool Company's December 31 year-end financial statements contained the following errors.

	December 31, 2007	December 31, 2008
Ending inventory	$9,600 understated	$8,100 overstated
Depreciation expense	$2,300 understated	—

An insurance premium of $66,000 was prepaid in 2007 covering the years 2007, 2008, and 2009. The entire amount was charged to expense in 2007. In addition, on December 31, 2008, fully depreciated machinery was sold for $15,000 cash, but the entry was not recorded until 2009. There were no other errors during 2007 or 2008, and no corrections have been made for any of the errors. (Ignore income tax considerations.)

Instructions
  (a) Compute the total effect of the errors on 2008 net income.
  (b) Compute the total effect of the errors on the amount of Henning's working capital at December 31, 2008.
  (c) Compute the total effect of the errors on the balance of Henning's retained earnings at December 31, 2008.

(LO 7, 9) **E22-19** **(Error Analysis; Correcting Entries)** A partial trial balance of Julie Hartsack Corporation is as follows on December 31, 2008.

	Dr.	Cr.
Supplies on hand	$ 2,700	
Accrued salaries and wages		$ 1,500
Interest receivable on investments	5,100	
Prepaid insurance	90,000	
Unearned rent		–0–
Accrued interest payable		15,000

Additional adjusting data:
  1. A physical count of supplies on hand on December 31, 2008, totaled $1,100.
  2. Through oversight, the Accrued Salaries and Wages account was not changed during 2008. Accrued salaries and wages on December 31, 2008, amounted to $4,400.
  3. The Interest Receivable on Investments account was also left unchanged during 2008. Accrued interest on investments amounts to $4,350 on December 31, 2008.
  4. The unexpired portions of the insurance policies totaled $65,000 as of December 31, 2008.
  5. $28,000 was received on January 1, 2008 for the rent of a building for both 2008 and 2009. The entire amount was credited to rental income.
  6. Depreciation for the year was erroneously recorded as $5,000 rather than the correct figure of $50,000.
  7. A further review of depreciation calculations of prior years revealed that depreciation of $7,200 was not recorded. It was decided that this oversight should be corrected by a prior period adjustment.

Instructions
  (a) Assuming that the books have not been closed, what are the adjusting entries necessary at December 31, 2008? (Ignore income tax considerations.)
  (b) Assuming that the books have been closed, what are the adjusting entries necessary at December 31, 2008? (Ignore income tax considerations.)

(LO 7, 9) **E22-20** **(Error Analysis)** The before-tax income for Lonnie Holdiman Co. for 2007 was $101,000 and $77,400 for 2008. However, the accountant noted that the following errors had been made:
  1. Sales for 2007 included amounts of $38,200 which had been received in cash during 2007, but for which the related products were delivered in 2008. Title did not pass to the purchaser until 2008.
  2. The inventory on December 31, 2007, was understated by $8,640.
  3. The bookkeeper in recording interest expense for both 2007 and 2008 on bonds payable made the following entry on an annual basis.

Interest Expense	15,000	
Cash		15,000

The bonds have a face value of $250,000 and pay a stated interest rate of 6%. They were issued at a discount of $15,000 on January 1, 2007, to yield an effective interest rate of 7%. (Assume that the effective-yield method should be used.)

4. Ordinary repairs to equipment had been erroneously charged to the Equipment account during 2007 and 2008. Repairs in the amount of $8,500 in 2007 and $9,400 in 2008 were so charged. The company applies a rate of 10% to the balance in the Equipment account at the end of the year in its determination of depreciation charges.

Instructions

Prepare a schedule showing the determination of corrected income before taxes for 2007 and 2008.

(LO 7, 9) **E22-21 (Error Analysis)** When the records of Debra Hanson Corporation were reviewed at the close of 2008, the errors listed below were discovered. For each item indicate by a check mark in the appropriate column whether the error resulted in an overstatement, an understatement, or had no effect on net income for the years 2007 and 2008.

	2007			2008		
Item	Over-statement	Under-statement	No Effect	Over-statement	Under-statement	No Effect
1. Failure to record amortization of patent in 2008.						
2. Failure to record the correct amount of ending 2007 inventory. The amount was understated because of an error in calculation.						
3. Failure to record merchandise purchased in 2007. Merchandise was also omitted from ending inventory in 2007 but was not yet sold.						
4. Failure to record accrued interest on notes payable in 2007; that amount was recorded when paid in 2008.						
5. Failure to reflect supplies on hand on balance sheet at end of 2007.						

(LO 10) *****E22-22 (Change from Fair Value to Equity)** On January 1, 2007, Barbra Streisand Co. purchased 25,000 shares (a 10% interest) in Elton John Corp. for $1,400,000. At the time, the book value and the fair value of John's net assets were $13,000,000.

On July 1, 2008, Streisand paid $3,040,000 for 50,000 additional shares of John common stock, which represented a 20% investment in John. The fair value of John's identifiable assets net of liabilities was equal to their carrying amount of $14,200,000. As a result of this transaction, Streisand owns 30% of John and can exercise significant influence over John's operating and financial policies. Any excess fair value is attributed to goodwill.

John reported the following net income and declared and paid the following dividends.

	Net Income	Dividend per Share
Year ended 12/31/07	$700,000	None
Six months ended 6/30/08	500,000	None
Six months ended 12/31/08	815,000	$1.55

Instructions

Determine the ending balance that Streisand Co. should report as its investment in John Corp. at the end of 2008.

(LO 10) **E22-23* **(Change from Equity to Fair Value)** Dan Aykroyd Corp. was a 30% owner of John Belushi Company, holding 210,000 shares of Belushi's common stock on December 31, 2006. The investment account had the following entries.

Investment in Belushi			
1/1/05 Cost	$3,180,000	12/6/05 Dividend received	$150,000
12/31/05 Share of income	390,000	12/5/06 Dividend received	240,000
12/31/06 Share of income	510,000		

On January 2, 2007, Aykroyd sold 126,000 shares of Belushi for $3,440,000, thereby losing its significant influence. During the year 2007 Belushi experienced the following results of operations and paid the following dividends to Aykroyd.

	Belushi Income (Loss)	Dividends Paid to Aykroyd
2007	$300,000	$50,400

At December 31, 2007, the fair value of Belushi shares held by Aykroyd is $1,570,000. This is the first reporting date since the January 2 sale.

Instructions

(a) What effect does the January 2, 2007, transaction have upon Aykroyd's accounting treatment for its investment in Belushi?

(b) Compute the carrying amount in Belushi as of December 31, 2007.

(c) Prepare the adjusting entry on December 31, 2007, applying the fair value method to Aykroyd's long-term investment in Belushi Company securities.

See the book's website, www.wiley.com/college/kieso, for Additional Exercises.

PROBLEMS

(LO 2, 5, 7)

P22-1 (Change in Estimate and Error Correction) Brueggen Company is in the process of preparing its financial statements for 2007. Assume that no entries for depreciation have been recorded in 2007. The following information related to depreciation of fixed assets is provided to you:

1. Brueggen purchased equipment on January 2, 2004, for $65,000. At that time, the equipment had an estimated useful life of 10 years with a $5,000 salvage value. The equipment is depreciated on a straight-line basis. On January 2, 2007, as a result of additional information, the company determined that the equipment has a remaining useful life of 4 years with a $3,000 salvage value.

2. During 2007 Brueggen changed from the double-declining balance method for its building to the straight-line method. The building originally cost $300,000. It had a useful life of 10 years and a salvage value of $30,000. The following computations present depreciation on both bases for 2005 and 2006.

	2006	2005
Straight-line	$27,000	$27,000
Declining-balance	48,000	60,000

3. Brueggen purchased a machine on July 1, 2005, at a cost of $80,000. The machine has a salvage value of $8,000 and a useful life of 8 years. Brueggen's bookkeeper recorded straight-line depreciation in 2005 and 2006 but failed to consider the salvage value.

Instructions

(a) Prepare the journal entries to record depreciation expense for 2007 and correct any errors made to date related to the information provided. (Round all computations to two decimal places.)

(b) Show comparative net income for 2006 and 2007. Income before depreciation expense was $300,000 in 2007, and was $310,000 in 2006. Ignore taxes.

(LO 3, 5, 7) **P22-2 (Comprehensive Accounting Change and Error Analysis Problem)** Larry Kingston Inc. was organized in late 2005 to manufacture and sell hosiery. At the end of its fourth year of operation, the company has been fairly successful, as indicated by the following reported net incomes.

2005	$140,000[a]	2007	$205,000
2006	160,000[b]	2008	276,000

[a]Includes a $12,000 increase because of change in bad debt experience rate.
[b]Includes extraordinary gain of $40,000.

The company has decided to expand operations and has applied for a sizable bank loan. The bank officer has indicated that the records should be audited and presented in comparative statements to facilitate analysis by the bank. Larry Kingston Inc. therefore hired the auditing firm of Check & Doublecheck Co. and has provided the following additional information.

1. In early 2006, Larry Kingston Inc. changed its estimate from 2% to 1% on the amount of bad debt expense to be charged to operations. Bad debt expense for 2005, if a 1% rate had been used, would have been $12,000. The company therefore restated its net income for 2005.

2. In 2008, the auditor discovered that the company had changed its method of inventory pricing from LIFO to FIFO. The effect on the income statements for the previous years is as follows.

	2005	2006	2007	2008
Net income unadjusted—LIFO basis	$140,000	$160,000	$205,000	$276,000
Net income unadjusted—FIFO basis	155,000	165,000	215,000	260,000
	$ 15,000	$ 5,000	$ 10,000	($ 16,000)

3. In 2008 the auditor discovered that:
   a. The company incorrectly overstated the ending inventory by $11,000 in 2007.
   b. A dispute developed in 2006 with the Internal Revenue Service over the deductibility of entertainment expenses. In 2005, the company was not permitted these deductions, but a tax settlement was reached in 2008 that allowed these expenses. As a result of the court's finding, tax expenses in 2008 were reduced by $60,000.

Instructions
(a) Indicate how each of these changes or corrections should be handled in the accounting records. Ignore income tax considerations.
(b) Present comparative income statements for the years 2005 to 2008, starting with income before extraordinary items. Ignore income tax considerations.

(LO 3, 5, 7) **P22-3 (Error Corrections and Accounting Changes)** Patricia Voga Company is in the process of adjusting and correcting its books at the end of 2008. In reviewing its records, the following information is compiled.

1. Voga has failed to accrue sales commissions payable at the end of each of the last 2 years, as follows.

December 31, 2007	$4,000
December 31, 2008	$2,500

2. In reviewing the December 31, 2008, inventory, Voga discovered errors in its inventory-taking procedures that have caused inventories for the last 3 years to be incorrect, as follows.

December 31, 2006	Understated	$16,000
December 31, 2007	Understated	$21,000
December 31, 2008	Overstated	$ 6,700

Voga has already made an entry that established the incorrect December 31, 2008, inventory amount.

3. At December 31, 2008, Voga decided to change the depreciation method on its office equipment from double-declining balance to straight-line. The equipment has an original cost of $100,000 when purchased on January 1, 2006. it has a 10-year useful life and no salvage value. Depreciation expense recorded prior to 2008 under the double-declining balance method was $36,000. Voga has already recorded 2008 depreciation expense of $12,800 using the double-declining balance method.

4. Before 2008, Voga accounted for its income from long-term construction contracts on the completed-contract basis. Early in 2008, Voga changed to the percentage-of-completion basis for accounting purposes. It continues to use the completed-contract method for tax purposes. Income for 2008 has been recorded using the percentage-of-completion method. The following information (on page 1199) is available.

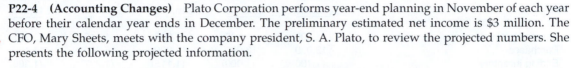

	Pretax Income	
	Percentage-of-Completion	Completed-Contract
Prior to 2008	$150,000	$95,000
2008	60,000	20,000

Instructions

Prepare the journal entries necessary at December 31, 2008, to record the above corrections and changes. The books are still open for 2008. The income tax rate is 40%. Voga has not yet recorded its 2008 income tax expense and payable amounts so current-year tax effects may be ignored. Prior-year tax effects must be considered in item 4.

(L0 5) **P22-4 (Accounting Changes)** Plato Corporation performs year-end planning in November of each year before their calendar year ends in December. The preliminary estimated net income is $3 million. The CFO, Mary Sheets, meets with the company president, S. A. Plato, to review the projected numbers. She presents the following projected information.

PLATO CORPORATION
PROJECTED INCOME STATEMENT
FOR THE YEAR ENDED DECEMBER 31, 2007

Sales		$29,000,000
Cost of goods sold	$14,000,000	
Depreciation	2,600,000	
Operating expenses	6,400,000	23,000,000
Income before income tax		6,000,000
Income tax		3,000,000
Net income		$ 3,000,000

PLATO CORPORATION
SELECTED BALANCE SHEET INFORMATION
AT DECEMBER 31, 2007

Estimated cash balance	$ 5,000,000
Available-for-sale securities (at cost)	10,000,000
Security fair value adjustment account (1/1/07)	200,000

Estimated market value at December 31, 2007:

Security	Cost	Estimated Market
A	$ 2,000,000	$ 2,200,000
B	4,000,000	3,900,000
C	3,000,000	3,000,000
D	1,000,000	2,800,000
Total	$10,000,000	$11,900,000

Other information at December 31, 2007:

Equipment	$ 3,000,000
Accumulated depreciation (5-year SL)	1,200,000
New robotic equipment (purchased 1/1/07)	5,000,000
Accumulated depreciation (5-year DDB)	2,000,000

The corporation has never used robatic equipment before, and Sheets assumed an accelerated method because of the rapidly changing technology in robotic equipment. The company normally uses straight-line depreciation for production equipment.

Plato explains to Sheets that it is important for the corporation to show an $8,000,000 net income before taxes because Plato receives a $1,000,000 bonus if the income before taxes and bonus reaches $8,000,000. Plato also does not want the company to pay more than $3,000,000 in income taxes to the government.

Instructions

(a) What can Sheets do within GAAP to accommodate the president's wishes to achieve $8,000,000 in income before taxes and bonus? Present the revised income statement based on your decision.

(b) Are the actions ethical? Who are the stakeholders in this decision, and what effect do Sheets's actions have on their interests?

(LO 3)   **P22-5   (Change in Principle—LIFO to Average Cost; Income Statements—Periodic)**   The management of Kreiter Instrument Company had concluded, with the concurrence of its independent auditors, that results of operations would be more fairly presented if Kreiter changed its method of pricing inventory from last-in, first-out (LIFO) to average cost in 2007. Given below is the 5-year summary of income under LIFO and a schedule of what the inventories would be if stated on the average cost method.

	KREITER INSTRUMENT COMPANY				
	STATEMENT OF INCOME AND RETAINED EARNINGS				
	FOR THE YEARS ENDED MAY 31				
	2003	2004	2005	2006	2007
Sales—net	$13,964	$15,506	$16,673	$18,221	$18,898
Cost of goods sold					
Beginning inventory	1,000	1,100	1,000	1,115	1,237
Purchases	13,000	13,900	15,000	15,900	17,100
Ending inventory	(1,100)	(1,000)	(1,115)	(1,237)	(1,369)
Total	12,900	14,000	14,885	15,778	16,968
Gross profit	1,064	1,506	1,788	2,443	1,930
Administrative expenses	700	763	832	907	989
Income before taxes	364	743	956	1,536	941
Income taxes (50%)	182	372	478	768	471
Net income	182	371	478	768	470
Retained earnings—beginning	1,206	1,388	1,759	2,237	3,005
Retained earnings—ending	$ 1,388	$ 1,759	$ 2,237	$ 3,005	$ 3,475
Earnings per share	$1.82	$3.71	$4.78	$7.68	$4.70

| SCHEDULE OF INVENTORY BALANCES USING AVERAGE COST METHOD | | | | | |
| | FOR THE YEARS ENDED MAY 31 | | | | |
2002	2003	2004	2005	2006	2007
$950	$1,124	$1,091	$1,270	$1,480	$1,699

Instructions

Prepare comparative statements for the 5 years, assuming that Kreiter changed its method of inventory pricing to average cost. Indicate the effects on net income and earnings per share for the years involved. Kreiter Instruments started business in 2002. (All amounts except EPS are rounded up to the nearest dollar.)

(LO 5, 7, 9)   **P22-6   (Accounting Change and Error Analysis)**   On December 31, 2008, before the books were closed, the management and accountants of Keltner Inc. made the following determinations about three depreciable assets.

1. Depreciable asset A was purchased January 2, 2005. It originally cost $495,000 and, for depreciation purposes, the straight-line method was originally chosen. The asset was originally expected to be useful for 10 years and have a zero salvage value. In 2008, the decision was made to change the depreciation method from straight-line to sum-of-the-years'-digits, and the estimates relating to useful life and salvage value remained unchanged.
2. Depreciable asset B was purchased January 3, 2004. It originally cost $120,000 and, for depreciation purposes, the straight-line method was chosen. The asset was originally expected to be useful for 15 years and have a zero salvage value. In 2008, the decision was made to shorten the total life of this asset to 9 years and to estimate the salvage value at $3,000.
3. Depreciable asset C was purchased January 5, 2004. The asset's original cost was $140,000, and this amount was entirely expensed in 2004. This particular asset has a 10-year useful life and no salvage value. The straight-line method was chosen for depreciation purposes.

Additional data:

1. Income in 2008 before depreciation expense amounted to $400,000.
2. Depreciation expense on assets other than A, B, and C totaled $55,000 in 2008.
3. Income in 2007 was reported at $370,000.
4. Ignore all income tax effects.
5. 100,000 shares of common stock were outstanding in 2007 and 2008.

Instructions

(a) Prepare all necessary entries in 2008 to record these determinations.

(b) Prepare comparative retained earnings statements for Eloise Keltner Inc. for 2007 and 2008. The company had retained earnings of $200,000 at December 31, 2006.

(LO 7, 9) **P22-7** **(Error Corrections)** You have been assigned to examine the financial statements of Vickie L. Lemke Company for the year ended December 31, 2008. You discover the following situations.

1. Depreciation of $3,200 for 2008 on delivery vehicles was not recorded.

2. The physical inventory count on December 31, 2007, improperly excluded merchandise costing $19,000 that had been temporarily stored in a public warehouse. Lemke uses a periodic inventory system.

3. The physical inventory count on December 31, 2008, improperly included merchandise with a cost of $8,500 that had been recorded as a sale on December 27, 2008, and held for the customer to pick up on January 4, 2009.

4. A collection of $5,600 on account from a customer received on December 31, 2008, was not recorded until January 2, 2009.

5. In 2008, the company sold for $3,700 fully depreciated equipment that originally cost $22,000. The company credited the proceeds from the sale to the Equipment account.

6. During November 2008, a competitor company filed a patent-infringement suit against Lemke claiming damages of $220,000. The company's legal counsel has indicated that an unfavorable verdict is probable and a reasonable estimate of the court's award to the competitor is $125,000. The company has not reflected or disclosed this situation in the financial statements.

7. Lemke has a portfolio of trading securities. No entry has been made to adjust to market. Information on cost and market value is as follows.

	Cost	Market
December 31, 2007	$95,000	$95,000
December 31, 2008	$84,000	$82,000

8. At December 31, 2008, an analysis of payroll information shows accrued salaries of $12,200. The Accrued Salaries Payable account had a balance of $16,000 at December 31, 2008, which was unchanged from its balance at December 31, 2007.

9. A large piece of equipment was purchased on January 3, 2008, for $32,000 and was charged to Repairs Expense. The equipment is estimated to have a service life of 8 years and no residual value. Lemke normally uses the straight-line depreciation method for this type of equipment.

10. A $15,000 insurance premium paid on July 1, 2007, for a policy that expires on June 30, 2010, was charged to insurance expense.

11. A trademark was acquired at the beginning of 2007 for $50,000. No amortization has been recorded since its acquisition. The maximum allowable amortization period is 10 years.

Instructions

Assume the trial balance has been prepared but the books have not been closed for 2008. Assuming all amounts are material, prepare journal entries showing the adjustments that are required. (Ignore income tax considerations.)

(LO 7, 9) **P22-8** **(Comprehensive Error Analysis)** On March 5, 2008, you were hired by Gretchen Hollenbeck Inc., a closely held company, as a staff member of its newly created internal auditing department. While reviewing the company's records for 2007 and 2008, you discover that no adjustments have yet been made for the items listed below.

Items

1. Interest income of $14,100 was not accrued at the end of 2006. It was recorded when received in February 2007.

2. A computer costing $8,000 was expensed when purchased on July 1, 2006. It is expected to have a 4-year life with no salvage value. The company typically uses straight-line depreciation for all fixed assets.

3. Research and development costs of $33,000 were incurred early in 2006. They were capitalized and were to be amortized over a 3-year period. Amortization of $11,000 was recorded for 2006 and $11,000 for 2007.

4. On January 2, 2006, Hollenbeck leased a building for 5 years at a monthly rental of $8,000. On that date, the company paid the following amounts, which were expensed when paid.

Security deposit	$25,000
First month's rent	8,000
Last month's rent	8,000
	$41,000

5. The company received $30,000 from a customer at the beginning of 2006 for services that it is to perform evenly over a 3-year period beginning in 2006. None of the amount received was reported as unearned revenue at the end of 2006.

6. Merchandise inventory costing $18,200 was in the warehouse at December 31, 2006, but was incorrectly omitted from the physical count at that date. The company uses the periodic inventory method.

Instructions

Indicate the effect of any errors on the net income figure reported on the income statement for the year ending December 31, 2006, and the retained earnings figure reported on the balance sheet at December 31, 2007. Assume all amounts are material, and ignore income tax effects. Using the following format, enter the appropriate dollar amounts in the appropriate columns. Consider each item independent of the other items. It is not necessary to total the columns on the grid.

	Net Income for 2006		Retained Earnings at 12/31/07	
Item	Understated	Overstated	Understated	Overstated

(CIA adapted)

(LO 7, 9) **P22-9** **(Error Analysis)** Mary Keeton Corporation has used the accrual basis of accounting for several years. A review of the records, however, indicates that some expenses and revenues have been handled on a cash basis because of errors made by an inexperienced bookkeeper. Income statements prepared by the bookkeeper reported $29,000 net income for 2007 and $37,000 net income for 2008. Further examination of the records reveals that the following items were handled improperly.

1. Rent was received from a tenant in December 2007. The amount, $1,300, was recorded as income at that time even though the rental pertained to 2008.

2. Wages payable on December 31 have been consistently omitted from the records of that date and have been entered as expenses when paid in the following year. The amounts of the accruals recorded in this manner were:

December 31, 2006	$1,100
December 31, 2007	1,500
December 31, 2008	940

3. Invoices for office supplies purchased have been charged to expense accounts when received. Inventories of supplies on hand at the end of each year have been ignored, and no entry has been made for them.

December 31, 2006	$1,300
December 31, 2007	740
December 31, 2008	1,420

Instructions

Prepare a schedule that will show the corrected net income for the years 2007 and 2008. All items listed should be labeled clearly. (Ignore income tax considerations.)

(LO 7, 9) **P22-10** **(Error Analysis and Correcting Entries)** You have been asked by a client to review the records of Larry Landers Company, a small manufacturer of precision tools and machines. Your client is interested in buying the business, and arrangements have been made for you to review the accounting records. Your examination reveals the following.

1. Landers Company commenced business on April 1, 2005, and has been reporting on a fiscal year ending March 31. The company has never been audited, but the annual statements prepared by the bookkeeper reflect the following income before closing and before deducting income taxes.

Year Ended March 31	Income Before Taxes
2006	$ 71,600
2007	111,400
2008	103,580

2. A relatively small number of machines have been shipped on consignment. These transactions have been recorded as ordinary sales and billed as such. On March 31 of each year, machines billed and in the hands of consignees amounted to:

2006	$6,500
2007	none
2008	5,590

Sales price was determined by adding 30% to cost. Assume that the consigned machines are sold the following year.

3. On March 30, 2007, two machines were shipped to a customer on a C.O.D. basis. The sale was not entered until April 5, 2007, when cash was received for $6,100. The machines were not included in the inventory at March 31, 2007. (Title passed on March 30, 2007.)

4. All machines are sold subject to a 5-year warranty. It is estimated that the expense ultimately to be incurred in connection with the warranty will amount to ½ of 1% of sales. The company has charged an expense account for warranty costs incurred.

Sales per books and warranty costs were as follows.

Year Ended March 31	Sales	Warranty Expense for Sales Made In			Total
		2006	2007	2008	
2006	$ 940,000	$760			$ 760
2007	1,010,000	360	$1,310		1,670
2008	1,795,000	320	1,620	$1,910	3,850

5. A review of the corporate minutes reveals the manager is entitled to a bonus of ½ of 1% of the income before deducting income taxes and the bonus. The bonuses have never been recorded or paid.

6. Bad debts have been recorded on a direct writeoff basis. Experience of similar enterprises indicates that losses will approximate ¼ of 1% of sales. Bad debts written off were:

	Bad Debts Incurred on Sales Made In			
	2006	2007	2008	Total
2006	$750			$ 750
2007	800	$ 520		1,320
2008	350	1,800	$1,700	3,850

7. The bank deducts 6% on all contracts financed. Of this amount, ½% is placed in a reserve to the credit of Landers Company that is refunded to Landers as finance contracts are paid in full. The reserve established by the bank has not been reflected in the books of Landers. The excess of credits over debits (net increase) to the reserve account with Landers on the books of the bank for each fiscal year were as follows.

2006	$ 3,000
2007	3,900
2008	5,100
	$12,000

8. Commissions on sales have been entered when paid. Commissions payable on March 31 of each year were as follows.

2006	$1,400
2007	800
2008	1,120

Instructions

(a) Present a schedule showing the revised income before income taxes for each of the years ended March 31, 2006, 2007, and 2008. Make computations to the nearest whole dollar.

(b) Prepare the journal entry or entries you would give the bookkeeper to correct the books. Assume the books have not yet been closed for the fiscal year ended March 31, 2007. Disregard correction of income taxes.

(AICPA adapted)

(LO 10) *P22-11 (Fair Value to Equity Method with Goodwill) On January 1, 2006, Latoya Inc. paid $700,000 for 10,000 shares of Jones Company's voting common stock, which was a 10% interest in Jones. At that date the net assets of Jones totaled $6,000,000. The fair values of all of Jones' identifiable assets and liabilities were equal to their book values. Latoya does not have the ability to exercise significant influence over the operating and financial policies of Jones. Latoya received dividends of $2.00 per share from Jones on October 1, 2006. Jones reported net income of $500,000 for the year ended December 31, 2006.

On July 1, 2007, Latoya paid $2,325,000 for 30,000 additional shares of Jones Company's voting common stock which represents a 30% investment in Jones. The fair values of all of Jones' identifiable assets net of liabilities were equal to their book values of $6,550,000. As a result of this transaction, Latoya has the ability to exercise significant influence over the operating and financial policies of Jones. Latoya received dividends of $2.00 per share from Jones on April 1, 2007, and $2.50 per share on October 1, 2007. Jones reported net income of $650,000 for the year ended December 31, 2007, and $400,000 for the 6 months ended December 31, 2007.

Instructions

(a) Prepare a schedule showing the income or loss before income taxes for the year ended December 31, 2006, that Latoya should report from its investment in Jones in its income statement issued in March 2007.

(b) During March 2008, Latoya issues comparative financial statements for 2006 and 2007. Prepare schedules showing the income or loss before income taxes for the years ended December 31, 2006 and 2007, that Latoya should report from its investment in Jones.

(AICPA adapted)

*P22-12 **(Change from Fair Value to Equity Method)** On January 3, 2005, Calvin Company purchased for $500,000 cash a 10% interest in Hobbes Corp. On that date the net assets of Hobbes had a book value of $3,750,000. The excess of cost over the underlying equity in net assets is attributable to undervalued depreciable assets having a remaining life of 10 years from the date of Calvin's purchase.

The fair value of Calvin's investment in Hobbes securities is as follows: December 31, 2005, $570,000, and December 31, 2006, $515,000.

On January 2, 2007, Calvin purchased an additional 30% of Hobbes's stock for $1,545,000 cash when the book value of Hobbes's net assets was $4,150,000. The excess was attributable to depreciable assets having a remaining life of 8 years.

During 2005, 2006, and 2007 the following occurred.

	Hobbes Net Income	Dividends Paid by Hobbes to Calvin
2005	$350,000	$15,000
2006	400,000	20,000
2007	550,000	70,000

Instructions

On the books of Calvin Company prepare all journal entries in 2005, 2006, and 2007 that relate to its investment in Hobbes Corp., reflecting the data above and a change from the fair value method to the equity method.

CONCEPTS FOR ANALYSIS

CA22-1 (Analysis of Various Accounting Changes and Errors) Erin Kramer Inc. has recently hired a new independent auditor, Jodie Larson, who says she wants "to get everything straightened out." Consequently, she has proposed the following accounting changes in connection with Erin Kramer Inc.'s 2008 financial statements.

1. At December 31, 2007, the client had a receivable of $820,000 from Holly Michael Inc. on its balance sheet. Holly Michael Inc. has gone bankrupt, and no recovery is expected. The client proposes to write off the receivable as a prior period item.

2. The client proposes the following changes in depreciation policies.

   (a) For office furniture and fixtures it proposes to change from a 10-year useful life to an 8-year life. If this change had been made in prior years, retained earnings at December 31, 2007, would have been $250,000 less. The effect of the change on 2008 income alone is a reduction of $60,000.

   (b) For its equipment in the leasing division the client proposes to adopt the sum-of-the-years'-digits depreciation method. The client had never used SYD before. The first year the client operated a leasing division was 2008. If straight-line depreciation were used, 2008 income would be $110,000 greater.

3. In preparing its 2007 statements, one of the client's bookkeepers overstated ending inventory by $235,000 because of a mathematical error. The client proposes to treat this item as a prior period adjustment.

4. In the past, the client has spread preproduction costs in its furniture division over 5 years. Because its latest furniture is of the "fad" type, it appears that the largest volume of sales will occur during the first 2 years after introduction. Consequently, the client proposes to amortize preproduction costs on a per-unit basis, which will result in expensing most of such costs during the first 2 years after the furniture's introduction. If the new accounting method had been used prior to 2008, retained earnings at December 31, 2007, would have been $375,000 less.

5. For the nursery division the client proposes to switch from FIFO to LIFO inventories because it believes that LIFO will provide a better matching of current costs with revenues. The effect of making this change on 2008 earnings will be an increase of $320,000. The client says that the effect of the change on December 31, 2007, retained earnings cannot be determined.

6. To achieve a better matching of revenues and expenses in its building construction division, the client proposes to switch from the completed-contract method of accounting to the percentage-of-completion method. Had the percentage-of-completion method been employed in all prior years, retained earnings at December 31, 2007, would have been $1,175,000 greater.

Instructions

(a) For each of the changes described above decide whether:
   (1) The change involves an accounting principle, accounting estimate, or correction of an error.
   (2) Restatement of opening retained earnings is required.
(b) What would be the proper adjustment to the December 31, 2007, retained earnings?

CA22-2 (Analysis of Various Accounting Changes and Errors) Various types of accounting changes can affect the financial statements of a business enterprise differently. Assume that the following list describes changes that have a material effect on the financial statements for the current year of your business enterprise.

1. A change from the completed-contract method to the percentage-of-completion method of accounting for long-term construction-type contracts.
2. A change in the estimated useful life of previously recorded fixed assets as a result of newly acquired information.
3. A change from deferring and amortizing preproduction costs to recording such costs as an expense when incurred because future benefits of the costs have become doubtful. The new accounting method was adopted in recognition of the change in estimated future benefits.
4. A change from including the employer share of FICA taxes with Payroll Tax Expenses to including it with "Retirement benefits" on the income statement.
5. Correction of a mathematical error in inventory pricing made in a prior period.
6. A change from presentation of statements of individual companies to presentation of consolidated statements.
7. A change in the method of accounting for leases for tax purposes to conform with the financial accounting method. As a result, both deferred and current taxes payable changed substantially.
8. A change from the FIFO method of inventory pricing to the LIFO method of inventory pricing.

Instructions

Identify the type of change that is described in each item above and indicate whether the prior year's financial statements should be retrospectively applied or restated when presented in comparative form with the current year's statements.

CA22-3 (Analysis of Three Accounting Changes and Errors) Listed below are three independent, unrelated sets of facts relating to accounting changes.

Situation 1
Penelope Millhouse Company is in the process of having its first audit. The company has used the cash basis of accounting for revenue recognition. Millhouse president, A. G. Shumway, is willing to change to the accrual method of revenue recognition.

Situation 2
Cheri Nestor Co. decides in January 2008 to change from FIFO to weighted-average pricing for its inventories.

Situation 3
Laura Osmund Co. determined that the depreciable lives of its fixed assets are too long at present to fairly match the cost of the fixed assets with the revenue produced. The company decided at the beginning of the current year to reduce the depreciable lives of all of its existing fixed assets by 5 years.

Instructions
For each of the situations described, provide the information indicated below.

    (a) Type of accounting change.
    (b) Manner of reporting the change under current generally accepted accounting principles including a discussion, where applicable, of how amounts are computed.
    (c) Effect of the change on the balance sheet and income statement.

CA22-4 **(Analysis of Various Accounting Changes and Errors)** Mischelle Reiners, controller of Lisa Terry Corp., is aware that a standard on accounting changes has been issued. After reading the standard, she is confused about what action should be taken on the following items related to Terry Corp. for the year 2007.

    1. In 2007, Terry decided to change its policy on accounting for certain marketing costs. Previously, the company had chosen to defer and amortize all marketing costs over at least 5 years because Terry believed that a return on these expenditures did not occur immediately. Recently, however, the time differential has considerably shortened, and Terry is now expensing the marketing costs as incurred.
    2. In 2007, the company examined its entire policy relating to the depreciation of plant equipment. Plant equipment had normally been depreciated over a 15-year period, but recent experience has indicated that the company was incorrect in its estimates and that the assets should be depreciated over a 20-year period.
    3. One division of Terry Corp., Ralph Rosentiel Co., has consistently shown an increasing net income from period to period. On closer examination of their operating statement, it is noted that bad debt expense and inventory obsolescence charges are much lower than in other divisions. In discussing this with the controller of this division, it has been learned that the controller has increased his net income each period by knowingly making low estimates related to the writeoff of receivables and inventory.
    4. In 2007, the company purchased new machinery that should increase production dramatically. The company has decided to depreciate this machinery on an accelerated basis, even though other machinery is depreciated on a straight-line basis.
    5. All equipment sold by Terry is subject to a 3-year warranty. It has been estimated that the expense ultimately to be incurred on these machines is 1% of sales. In 2007, because of a production breakthrough, it is now estimated that ½ of 1% of sales is sufficient. In 2005 and 2006, warranty expense was computed as $64,000 and $70,000, respectively. The company now believes that these warranty costs should be reduced by 50%.
    6. In 2007, the company decided to change its method of inventory pricing from average cost to the FIFO method. The effect of this change on prior years is to increase 2005 income by $65,000 and increase 2006 income by $20,000.

Instructions
Mischelle Reiners has come to you, as her CPA, for advice about the situations above. Prepare a report, indicating the appropriate accounting treatment that should be given each of these situations.

CA22-5 **(Change in Principle, Estimate)** As a certified public accountant, you have been contacted by Ben Thinken, CEO of Sports-Pro Athletics, Inc., a manufacturer of a variety of athletic equipment. He has asked you how to account for the following changes.

    1. Sports-Pro appropriately changed its depreciation method for its production machinery from the double-declining balance method to the production method effective January 1, 2007.
    2. Effective January 1, 2007, Sports-Pro appropriately changed the salvage values used in computing depreciation for its office equipment.
    3. On December 31, 2007, Sports-Pro appropriately changed the specific subsidiaries constituting the group of companies for which consolidated financial statements are presented.

Instructions
Write a 1–1.5 page letter to Ben Thinken explaining how each of the above changes should be presented in the December 31, 2007, financial statements.

CA22-6 (Change in Estimates) Andy Frain is an audit senior of a large public accounting firm who has just been assigned to the Usher Corporation's annual audit engagement. Usher has been a client of Frain's firm for many years. Usher is a fast-growing business in the commercial construction industry. In reviewing the fixed asset ledger, Frain discovered a series of unusual accounting changes, in which the useful lives of assets, depreciated using the straight-line method, were substantially lowered near the mid-point of the original estimate. For example, the useful life of one dump truck was changed from 10 to 6 years during its fifth year of service. Upon further investigation, Andy was told by Vince Lloyd, Usher's accounting manager, "I don't really see your problem. After all, it's perfectly legal to change an accounting estimate. Besides, our CEO likes to see big earnings!"

Instructions
Answer the following questions.

(a) What are the ethical issues concerning Usher's practice of changing the useful lives of fixed assets?
(b) Who could be harmed by Usher's unusual accounting changes?
(c) What should Frain do in this situation?

USING YOUR JUDGMENT

Financial Reporting Problem

 The Procter & Gamble Company (P&G)

The financial statements of **P&G** are provided in Appendix 5B or can be accessed on the KWW website.

Instructions
Refer to P&G's financial statements and the accompanying notes to answer the following questions.

(a) Were there changes in accounting principles reported by P&G during the three years covered by its income statements (2001–2004)? If so, describe the nature of the change and the year of change.
(b) What use did P&G make of estimates in 2004?

Comparative Analysis Case

The Coca-Cola Company and PepsiCo, Inc.

Instructions
Go to the KWW website and use information found there to answer the following questions related to **The Coca-Cola Company** and **PepsiCo Inc.**

(a) Identify the changes in accounting principles reported by Coca-Cola during the 3 years covered by its income statements (2002–2004). Describe the nature of the change and the year of change.
(b) Identify the changes in accounting principles reported by PepsiCo during the 3 years covered by its income statements (2002–2004). Describe the nature of the change and the year of change.
(c) For each change in accounting principle by Coca-Cola and PepsiCo, identify, if possible, the cumulative effect of each change on prior years and the effect on operating results in the year of change.

Research Cases

Case 1

Instructions
Use an appropriate source to identify two firms that recently reported a *voluntary* change in accounting principle. Answer the following questions with regard to each of the companies.

(a) What is the name of the company? What source did you use to identify the company?
(b) How did the change impact current earnings?

(c) How will the change impact future earnings?

(d) What rationale did the firm's management offer for the change? Do you agree with their stated reasons?

Case 2

The May 7, 2002 edition of the *Wall Street Journal* includes an article by James Bandler and Mark Maremont entitled "KPMG's Work With Xerox Sets Up a New Test for SEC."

Instructions

Read the article and answer the following questions.

(a) A change in estimated residual value is usually reported as a change in estimate. What distinguishes a change in estimate from an error correction?

(b) How does the reporting of a change in estimate differ from reporting of an error correction? Why would Xerox prefer to report the change in residual value as an error correction?

(c) The SEC says accounting rules ban any upward adjustments of residual value. Is the SEC correct? Justify your answer, providing citations from generally accepted accounting principles.

Professional Research: Financial Accounting and Reporting

As part of the year-end accounting process and review of operating policies, Konerko Co. is considering a change in the accounting for its equipment from the straight-line method to an accelerated method. Your supervisor wonders how the company will report this change in principle. He read in a newspaper article that the FASB has issued a standard in this area and has changed GAAP for a "change in estimate that is effected by a change in accounting principle." (Thus, the accounting may be different from that he learned in intermediate accounting.) Your supervisor wants you to research the authoritative guidance on a change in accounting principle related to depreciation methods.

Instructions

Using the **Financial Accounting Research System (FARS)**, respond to the following items. (Provide text strings used in your search.)

(a) What are the accounting and reporting guidelines for a change in accounting principle related to depreciation methods?

(b) What are the conditions that justify a change in depreciation method, as contemplated by Konerko Co?

(c) What was the FASB's reasoning for changing the accounting guidance for accounting principle changes related to depreciation?

Professional Simulation

In this simulation you are asked questions about changes in accounting principle. Prepare responses to all parts.

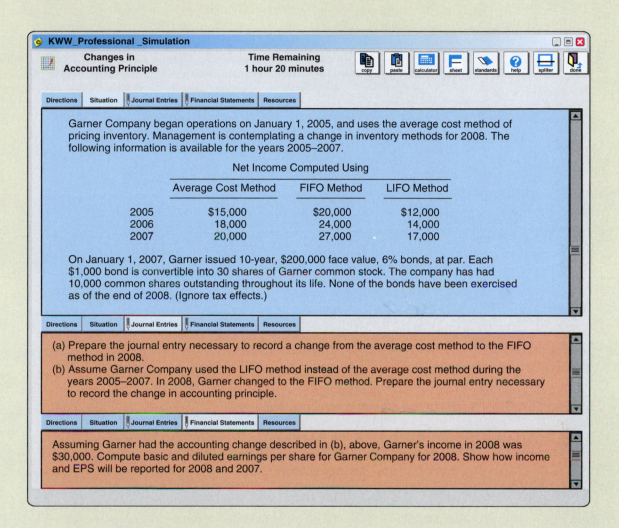

KWW_Professional _Simulation

Changes in Accounting Principle	Time Remaining 1 hour 20 minutes

copy   paste   calculator   sheet   standards   help   spliter   done

Directions | Situation | Journal Entries | Financial Statements | Resources

Garner Company began operations on January 1, 2005, and uses the average cost method of pricing inventory. Management is contemplating a change in inventory methods for 2008. The following information is available for the years 2005–2007.

Net Income Computed Using

	Average Cost Method	FIFO Method	LIFO Method
2005	$15,000	$20,000	$12,000
2006	18,000	24,000	14,000
2007	20,000	27,000	17,000

On January 1, 2007, Garner issued 10-year, $200,000 face value, 6% bonds, at par. Each $1,000 bond is convertible into 30 shares of Garner common stock. The company has had 10,000 common shares outstanding throughout its life. None of the bonds have been exercised as of the end of 2008. (Ignore tax effects.)

Directions | Situation | Journal Entries | Financial Statements | Resources

(a) Prepare the journal entry necessary to record a change from the average cost method to the FIFO method in 2008.
(b) Assume Garner Company used the LIFO method instead of the average cost method during the years 2005–2007. In 2008, Garner changed to the FIFO method. Prepare the journal entry necessary to record the change in accounting principle.

Directions | Situation | Journal Entries | Financial Statements | Resources

Assuming Garner had the accounting change described in (b), above, Garner's income in 2008 was $30,000. Compute basic and diluted earnings per share for Garner Company for 2008. Show how income and EPS will be reported for 2008 and 2007.

Remember to check the book's companion website to find additional resources for this chapter.

wiley.com/college/kieso

STATEMENT OF CASH FLOWS

Don't Take Cash Flow for Granted

Investors usually look to net income as a key indicator of a company's financial health and future prospects. The following graph shows the net income of one company over a seven-year period.

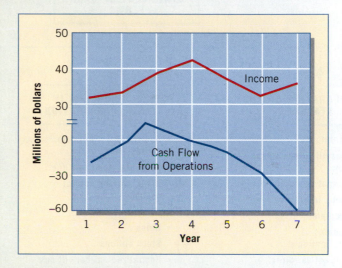

The company showed a pattern of consistent profitability and even some periods of income growth. Between years 1 and 4, net income for this company grew by 32 percent, from $31 million to $41 million. Would you expect its profitability to continue? The company had consistently paid dividends and interest. Would you expect it to continue to do so? Investors answered "yes" to these questions, by buying the company's stock. Eighteen months later, this company—**W. T. Grant**—filed for bankruptcy, in what was then the largest bankruptcy filing in the United States.

How could this happen? As indicated by the second line in the graph, the company had experienced several years of negative cash flow from its operations, even though it reported profits. How can a company have negative cash flows while reporting profits? The answer lay partly in the fact that W. T. Grant was having trouble collecting the receivables from its credit sales, causing cash flow to be less than the net income. Investors who analyzed the cash flows would have been likely to find an early warning signal of W. T. Grant's operating problems.[1]

---

[1]Adapted from James A. Largay III and Clyde P. Stickney, "Cash Flows, Ratio Analysis, and the W. T. Grant Company Bankruptcy," *Financial Analysts Journal* (July–August 1980), p. 51.

Learning Objectives

After studying this chapter, you should be able to:

1 Describe the purpose of the statement of cash flows.

2 Identify the major classifications of cash flows.

3 Differentiate between net income and net cash flows from operating activities.

4 Contrast the direct and indirect methods of calculating net cash flow from operating activities.

5 Determine net cash flows from investing and financing activities.

6 Prepare a statement of cash flows.

7 Identify sources of information for a statement of cash flows.

8 Discuss special problems in preparing a statement of cash flows.

9 Explain the use of a worksheet in preparing a statement of cash flows

As the opening story indicates, examination of **W. T. Grant**'s cash flows from operations would have shown the financial inflexibility that eventually caused the company's bankruptcy. This chapter explains the main components of a statement of cash flows and the types of information it provides. The content and organization of the chapter are as follows.

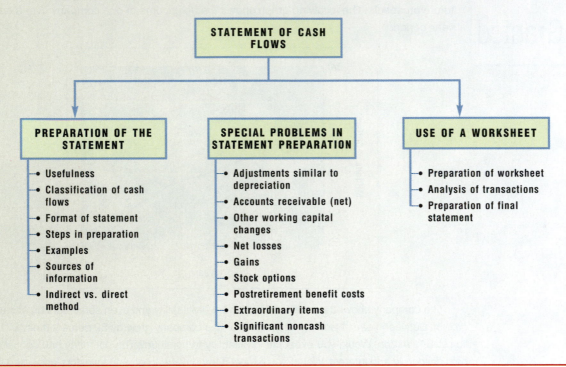

STATEMENT OF CASH FLOWS		
PREPARATION OF THE STATEMENT	**SPECIAL PROBLEMS IN STATEMENT PREPARATION**	**USE OF A WORKSHEET**
• Usefulness • Classification of cash flows • Format of statement • Steps in preparation • Examples • Sources of information • Indirect vs. direct method	• Adjustments similar to depreciation • Accounts receivable (net) • Other working capital changes • Net losses • Gains • Stock options • Postretirement benefit costs • Extraordinary items • Significant noncash transactions	• Preparation of worksheet • Analysis of transactions • Preparation of final statement

---

SECTION 1

PREPARATION OF THE STATEMENT OF CASH FLOWS

OBJECTIVE 1
Describe the purpose of the statement of cash flows.

The primary purpose of the **statement of cash flows** is to provide information about a company's cash receipts and cash payments during a period. A secondary objective is to provide cash-basis information about the company's operating, investing, and financing activities. The statement of cash flows therefore reports cash receipts, cash payments, and net change in cash resulting from a company's operating, investing, and financing activities during a period. Its format reconciles the beginning and ending cash balances for the period.

USEFULNESS OF THE STATEMENT OF CASH FLOWS

The statement of cash flows provides information to help investors, creditors, and others assess the following:[2]

1 *The entity's ability to generate future cash flows.* A primary objective of financial reporting is to provide information with which to predict the amounts, timing, and

---

[2]"The Statement of Cash Flows," *Statement of Financial Accounting Standards No. 95* (Stamford, Conn.: FASB, 1987), pars. 4 and 5.

uncertainty of future cash flows. By examining relationships between items such as sales and net cash flow from operating activities, or net cash flow from operating activities and increases or decreases in cash, it is possible to better predict the future cash flows than is possible using accrual-basis data alone.

2 *The entity's ability to pay dividends and meet obligations.* Simply put, cash is essential. Without adequate cash, a company cannot pay employees, settle debts, pay out dividends, or acquire equipment. A statement of cash flows indicates where the company's cash comes from and how the company uses its cash. Employees, creditors, stockholders, and customers should be particularly interested in this statement, because it alone shows the flows of cash in a business.

3 *The reasons for the difference between net income and net cash flow from operating activities.* The net income number is important: It provides information on the performance of a company from one period to another. But some people are critical of accrual-basis net income because companies must make estimates to arrive at it. Such is not the case with cash. Thus, as the opening story showed, financial statement readers can benefit from knowing why a company's net income and net cash flow from operating activities differ, and can assess for themselves the reliability of the income number.

4 *The cash and noncash investing and financing transactions during the period.* Besides operating activities, companies undertake investing and financing transactions. *Investing* activities include the purchase and sale of assets other than a company's products or services. *Financing* activities include borrowings and repayments of borrowings, investments by owners, and distributions to owners. By examining a company's investing and financing activities, a financial statement reader can better understand why assets and liabilities increased or decreased during the period. For example, by reading the statement of cash flows, the reader might find answers to following questions:

Why did cash decrease for **Toys R Us** when it reported net income for the period?

How much did **Southwest Airlines** spend on property, plant, and equipment last year?

Did dividends paid by **Campbell's Soup** increase?

How much money did **Coca-Cola** borrow last year?

How much cash did **Hewlett-Packard** use to repurchase its common stock?

CLASSIFICATION OF CASH FLOWS

The statement of cash flows classifies cash receipts and cash payments by operating, investing, and financing activities.[3] Transactions and other events characteristic of each kind of activity is as follows.

> **OBJECTIVE 2**
> Identify the major classifications of cash flows.

1 **Operating activities** involve the cash effects of transactions that enter into the determination of net income, such as cash receipts from sales of goods and services, and cash payments to suppliers and employees for acquisitions of inventory and expenses.

---

[3]The basis recommended by the FASB for the statement of cash flows is actually "cash and cash equivalents." **Cash equivalents** are short-term, highly liquid investments that are both: (a) readily convertible to known amounts of cash, and (b) so near their maturity that they present insignificant risk of changes in interest rates. Generally, only investments with original maturities of three months or less qualify under this definition. Examples of cash equivalents are Treasury bills, commercial paper, and money market funds purchased with cash that is in excess of immediate needs.

Although we use the term "cash" throughout our discussion and illustrations, we mean cash and cash equivalents when reporting the cash flows and the net increase or decrease in cash.

2 **Investing activities** generally involve long-term assets and include (a) making and collecting loans, and (b) acquiring and disposing of investments and productive long-lived assets.

3 **Financing activities** involve liability and stockholders' equity items and include (a) obtaining cash from creditors and repaying the amounts borrowed, and (b) obtaining capital from owners and providing them with a return on, and a return of, their investment.

Illustration 23-1 classifies the typical cash receipts and payments of a company according to operating, investing, and financing activities. The operating activities category is the most important. It shows the cash provided by company operations. This source of cash is generally considered to be the best measure of a company's ability to generate enough cash to continue as a going concern.

ILLUSTRATION 23-1
Classification of Typical Cash Inflows and Outflows

Operating 　Cash inflows 　　From sales of goods or services. 　　From returns on loans (interest) and on equity 　　　securities (dividends). 　Cash outflows 　　To suppliers for inventory. 　　To employees for services. 　　To government for taxes. 　　To lenders for interest. 　　To others for expenses.	**Income Statement Items**
Investing 　Cash inflows 　　From sale of property, plant, and equipment. 　　From sale of debt or equity securities of other entities. 　　From collection of principal on loans to other entities. 　Cash outflows 　　To purchase property, plant, and equipment. 　　To purchase debt or equity securities of other entities. 　　To make loans to other entities.	**Generally Long-Term Asset Items**
Financing 　Cash inflows 　　From sale of equity securities. 　　From issuance of debt (bonds and notes). 　Cash outflows 　　To stockholders as dividends. 　　To redeem long-term debt or reacquire capital stock.	**Generally Long-Term Liability and Equity Items**

INTERNATIONAL INSIGHT

According to International Accounting Standards, companies can define "cash and cash equivalents" as "net monetary assets"—that is, as "cash and demand deposits and highly liquid investments less short-term borrowings."

Note the following general guidelines about the classification of cash flows.

1 Operating activities involve income statement items.

2 Investing activities involve cash flows resulting from changes in investments and long-term asset items.

3 Financing activities involve cash flows resulting from changes in long-term liability and stockholders' equity items.

Companies classify some cash flows relating to investing or financing activities as operating activities.[4] For example, companies classify receipts of investment income (interest and dividends) and payments of interest to lenders as operating activities.

---

[4]For exceptions to the treatment of purchases and sales of loans and securities by banks and brokers, see *Statement of Financial Accounting Standards No. 102* (February 1989). Banks and brokers must classify cash flows from purchases and sales of loans and securities specifically for resale and carried at market value **as operating activities**. This requirement recognizes that for these firms these assets are similar to inventory in other businesses.

Why are these considered operating activities? Companies report these items in the income statement, where the results of operations are shown.

Conversely, companies classify some cash flows relating to operating activities as investing or financing activities. For example, a company classifies the cash received from the sale of property, plant, and equipment at a gain, although reported in the income statement, as an investing activity. It excludes the effects of the related gain in net cash flow from operating activities. Likewise, a gain or loss on the payment (extinguishment) of debt is generally part of the cash outflow related to the repayment of the amount borrowed. It therefore is a financing activity.

HOW'S MY CASH FLOW?

To evaluate overall cash flow, it is useful to understand where in the product life cycle a company is. Generally, companies move through several stages of development, which have implications for cash flow. As the graph below shows, the pattern of cash flows from operating, financing, and investing activities will vary depending on the stage of the product life cycle.

WHAT DO THE NUMBERS MEAN?

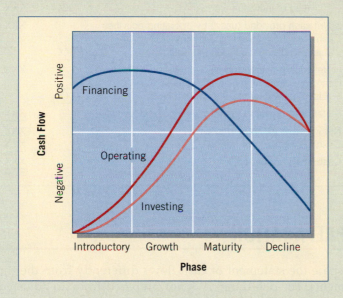

In the introductory phase, the product is likely not generating much revenue (operating cash flow is negative). Because the company is making heavy investments to get a product off the ground, cash flow from investment is negative, and financing cash flows are positive.

As the product moves to the growth and maturity phases, these cash flow relationships reverse. The product generates more cash flow from operations, which can be used to cover investments needed to support the product, and less cash is needed from financing. So is a negative operating cash flow bad? Not always. It depends on the product life cycle.

Source: Adapted from Paul D. Kimmel, Jerry J. Weygandt, and Donald E. Kieso, *Financial Accounting: Tools for Business Decision Making*, 4th ed. (New York: John Wiley & Sons, 2006), p. 591.

FORMAT OF THE STATEMENT OF CASH FLOWS

The three activities we discussed above constitute the general format of the statement of cash flows. The operating activities section always appears first. It is followed by the investing activities section and then the financing activities section.

A company reports the individual inflows and outflows from investing and financing activities separately. That is, a company reports them gross, not netted against one another. Thus, a cash outflow from the purchase of property is reported separately from the cash inflow from the sale of property. Similarly, a cash inflow from the issuance of debt is reported separately from the cash outflow from its retirement.

The net increase or decrease in cash reported during the period should reconcile the beginning and ending cash balances as reported in the comparative balance sheets. The general format of the statement of cash flows presents the results of the three activities discussed previously–operating, investing, and financing. Illustration 23-2 shows a widely used form of the statement of cash flows.

ILLUSTRATION 23-2
Format of the Statement of Cash Flows

COMPANY NAME STATEMENT OF CASH FLOWS PERIOD COVERED		
Cash flows from operating activities		
Net income		XXX
Adjustments to reconcile net income to net cash provided by operating activities:		
(List of individual items)	XX	XX
Net cash provided (used) by operating activities		XXX
Cash flows from investing activities		
(List of individual inflows and outflows)	XX	
Net cash provided (used) by investing activities		XXX
Cash flows from financing activities		
(List of individual inflows and outflows)	XX	
Net cash provided (used) by financing activities		XXX
Net increase (decrease) in cash		XXX
Cash at beginning of period		XXX
Cash at end of period		XXX

STEPS IN PREPARATION

Companies prepare the statement of cash flows differently from the three other basic financial statements. For one thing, it is not prepared from an adjusted trial balance. The cash flow statement requires detailed information concerning the changes in account balances that occurred between two points in time. An adjusted trial balance will not provide the necessary data. Second, the statement of cash flows deals with cash receipts and payments. As a result, the company must adjust the effects of the use of accrual accounting to determine cash flows. The information to prepare this statement usually comes from three sources:

1 **Comparative balance sheets** provide the amount of the changes in assets, liabilities, and equities from the beginning to the end of the period.

2 **Current income statement** data help determine the amount of cash provided by or used by operations during the period.

3 **Selected transaction data** from the general ledger provide additional detailed information needed to determine how the company provided or used cash during the period.

Preparing the statement of cash flows from the data sources above involves three major steps:

Step 1. Determine the change in cash. This procedure is straightforward. A company can easily compute the difference between the beginning and the ending cash balance from examining its comparative balance sheets.

Step 2. Determine the net cash flow from operating activities. This procedure is complex. It involves analyzing not only the current year's income statement but also comparative balance sheets as well as selected transaction data.

Step 3. Determine net cash flows from investing and financing activities. A company must analyze all other changes in the balance sheet accounts to determine their effects on cash.

On the following pages we work through these three steps in the process of preparing the statement of cash flows for Tax Consultants Inc. over several years.

FIRST EXAMPLE—2006

To illustrate a statement of cash flows, we use the **first year of operations** for Tax Consultants Inc. The company started on January 1, 2006, when it issued 60,000 shares of $1 par value common stock for $60,000 cash. The company rented its office space, furniture, and equipment, and performed tax consulting services throughout the first year. The comparative balance sheets at the beginning and end of the year 2006 appear in Illustration 23-3.

ILLUSTRATION 23-3
Comparative Balance Sheets, Tax Consultants Inc., Year 1

TAX CONSULTANTS INC.
COMPARATIVE BALANCE SHEETS

Assets	Dec. 31, 2006	Jan. 1, 2006	Change Increase/Decrease
Cash	$49,000	$–0–	$49,000 Increase
Accounts receivable	36,000	–0–	36,000 Increase
Total	$85,000	$–0–	
Liabilities and Stockholders' Equity			
Accounts payable	$ 5,000	$–0–	$ 5,000 Increase
Common stock ($1 par)	60,000	–0–	60,000 Increase
Retained earnings	20,000	–0–	20,000 Increase
Total	$85,000	$–0–	

Illustration 23-4 shows the income statement and additional information for Tax Consultants.

ILLUSTRATION 23-4
Income Statement, Tax Consultants Inc., Year 1

TAX CONSULTANTS INC.
INCOME STATEMENT
FOR THE YEAR ENDED DECEMBER 31, 2006

Revenues	$125,000
Operating expenses	85,000
Income before income taxes	40,000
Income tax expense	6,000
Net income	$ 34,000

Additional Information
Examination of selected data indicates that a dividend of $14,000 was declared and paid during the year.

Step 1: Determine the Change in Cash

To prepare a statement of cash flows, the first step is to **determine the change in cash**. This is a simple computation. Tax Consultants had no cash on hand at the beginning of the year 2006. It had $49,000 on hand at the end of 2006. Thus, cash changed (increased) in 2006 by $49,000.

Step 2: Determine Net Cash Flow from Operating Activities

OBJECTIVE 3
Differentiate between net income and net cash flows from operating activities.

To determine net cash flow from operating activities,[5] companies adjust net income in numerous ways. A useful starting point is to understand why net income must be converted to net cash provided by operating activities.

Under generally accepted accounting principles, most companies use the accrual basis of accounting. As you have learned, this basis requires that companies record revenue when earned and record expenses when incurred. Earned revenues may include credit sales for which the company has not yet collected cash. Expenses incurred may include some items that the company has not yet paid in cash. Thus, under the accrual basis of accounting, net income is not the same as net cash flow from operating activities.

To arrive at net cash flow from operating activities, a company must determine revenues and expenses on a **cash basis**. **It does this by eliminating the effects of income statement transactions that do not result in an increase or decrease in cash.** Illustration 23-5 shows the relationship between net income and net cash flow from operating activities.

ILLUSTRATION 23-5
Net Income versus Net Cash Flow from Operating Activities

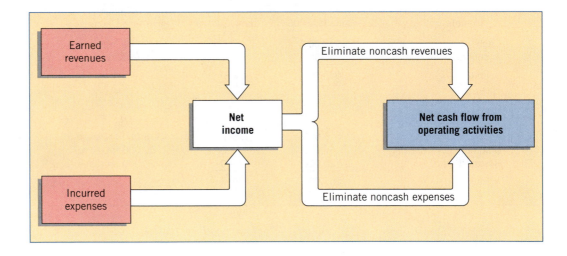

In this chapter, we use the term net income to refer to accrual-based net income. A company may convert net income to net cash flow from operating activities through either a direct method or an indirect method. We explain both methods in the following sections. The advantages and disadvantages of these two methods are discussed later in the chapter.

Direct Method

OBJECTIVE 4
Contrast the direct and indirect methods of calculating net cash flow from operating activities.

The **direct method** (also called the **income statement method**) reports cash receipts and cash disbursements from operating activities. The difference between these two amounts is the net cash flow from operating activities. In other words, the direct method deducts operating cash disbursements from operating cash receipts. The direct

---

[5]"Net cash flow from operating activities" is a generic phrase, replaced in the statement of cash flows with either "Net cash **provided by** operating activities" if operations increase cash, or "Net cash **used by** operating activities" if operations decrease cash.

method results in the presentation of a condensed cash receipts and cash disbursements statement.

As indicated from the accrual-based income statement, Tax Consultants reported revenues of $125,000. However, because the company's accounts receivable increased during 2006 by $36,000, the company collected only $89,000 ($125,000 − $36,000) in cash from these revenues. Similarly, Tax Consultants reported operating expenses of $85,000. However, accounts payable increased during the period by $5,000. Assuming that these payables relate to operating expenses, cash operating expenses were $80,000 ($85,000 − $5,000). Because no taxes payable exist at the end of the year, the company must have paid $6,000 income tax expense for 2006 in cash during the year. Tax Consultants computes net cash flow from operating activities as shown in Illustration 23-6.

Cash collected from revenues	$89,000
Cash payments for expenses	80,000
Income before income taxes	9,000
Cash payments for income taxes	6,000
Net cash provided by operating activities	$ 3,000

ILLUSTRATION 23-6
Computation of Net Cash Flow from Operating Activities, Year 1—Direct Method

"Net cash provided by operating activities" is the equivalent of cash basis net income. ("Net cash used by operating activities" is equivalent to cash basis net loss.)

Indirect Method

The **indirect method** (or **reconciliation method**) starts with net income and converts it to net cash flow from operating activities. In other words, **the indirect method adjusts net income for items that affected reported net income but did not affect cash.** To compute net cash flow from operating activities, a company adds back noncash charges in the income statement to net income and deducts noncash credits. We explain the two adjustments to net income for Tax Consultants, namely, the increases in accounts receivable and accounts payable, as follows.

Increase in Accounts Receivable—Indirect Method. Tax Consultant's accounts receivable increased by $36,000 (from $0 to $36,000) during the year. For Tax Consultants, this means that cash receipts were $36,000 lower than revenues. The Accounts Receivable account in Illustration 23-7 shows that Tax Consultants had $125,000 in revenues (as reported on the income statement), but it collected only $89,000 in cash.

	Accounts Receivable			
1/1/06	Balance	–0–	Receipts from customer	89,000
	Revenues	125,000		
12/31/06	Balance	36,000		

ILLUSTRATION 23-7
Analysis of Accounts Receivable

As shown in Illustration 23-8 (page 1220), to adjust net income to net cash provided by operating activities, Tax Consultants must deduct the increase of $36,000 in accounts receivable from net income. When the Accounts Receivable balance *decreases*, cash receipts are higher than revenue earned under the accrual basis. Therefore, the company adds to net income the amount of the decrease in accounts receivable to arrive at net cash provided by operating activities.

Increase in Accounts Payable—Indirect Method. When accounts payable increase during the year, expenses on an accrual basis exceed those on a cash basis. Why? Because Tax Consultants incurred expenses, but some of the expenses are not yet paid. To convert net income to net cash flow from operating activities, Tax Consultants must add back the increase of $5,000 in accounts payable to net income.

As a result of the accounts receivable and accounts payable adjustments, Tax Consultants determines net cash provided by operating activities is $3,000 for the year 2006. Illustration 23-8 shows this computation.

ILLUSTRATION 23-8
Computation of Net Cash
Flow from Operating
Activities, Year 1—
Indirect Method

Net income		$34,000
Adjustments to reconcile net income to net cash provided by operating activities:		
Increase in accounts receivable	$(36,000)	
Increase in accounts payable	5,000	(31,000)
Net cash provided by operating activities		$ 3,000

Note that net cash provided by operating activities is the same whether using the direct (Illustration 23-6) or the indirect method (Illustration 23-8).

PUMPING UP CASH

WHAT DO THE NUMBERS MEAN?

Due to recent concerns about a decline in quality of earnings, some investors have been focusing on cash flow. And management has an incentive to make operating cash flow look good, because Wall Street has paid a premium for companies that generate a lot of cash from operations, rather than through borrowings. However, similar to earnings, companies have ways to pump up cash flow from operations.

One way that companies boost their operating cash flow is by securitizing receivables—that is, turning their receivables into securities that can be sold. For example, at one time **Oxford Industries**, an apparel company, reported a $74 million dollar increase in cash flow from operations. This seems impressive until you read the fine print, which indicates that a big part of the increase was due to the sale of receivables. As discussed in the text, decreases in accounts receivable increase cash flow from operations. So while Oxford's core operations seemed to have improved, the company really did little more than accelerate collections of its receivables. In fact, without the cash flow boost from the securitizations, Oxford's operating cash flow would have been negative. Thus, just like earnings, cash flow can be of high or low quality.

Source: Adapted from Ann Tergesen, "Cash Flow Hocus Pocus," *Business Week* (July 16, 2002), pp. 130–131.

Step 3: Determine Net Cash Flows from Investing and Financing Activities

OBJECTIVE 5
Determine net cash flows from investing and financing activities.

After Tax Consultants has computed the net cash provided by operating activities, the next step is to determine whether any other changes in balance sheet accounts caused an increase or decrease in cash.

For example, an examination of the remaining balance sheet accounts for Tax Consultants shows increases in both common stock and retained earnings. The common stock increase of $60,000 resulted from the issuance of common stock for cash. The issuance of common stock is reported in the statement of cash flows as a receipt of cash from a financing activity.

Two items caused the retained earnings increase of $20,000:

1 Net income of $34,000 increased retained earnings.
2 Declaration of $14,000 of dividends decreased retained earnings.

Tax Consultants has converted net income into net cash flow from operating activities, as explained earlier. The additional data indicate that it paid the dividend. Thus, the company reports the dividend payment as a cash outflow, classified as a financing activity.

Statement of Cash Flows—2006

We are now ready to prepare the statement of cash flows. The statement starts with the operating activities section. Tax Consultants may use either the direct or indirect method to report net cash flow from operating activities.

The FASB **encourages** the use of the direct method over the indirect method. If a company uses the direct method of reporting net cash flow from operating activities, the FASB **requires** that the company provide in a separate schedule a reconciliation of net income to net cash flow from operating activities. If a company uses the indirect method, it can either report the reconciliation within the statement of cash flows or can provide it in a separate schedule, with the statement of cash flows reporting only the **net** cash flow from operating activities.[6] Throughout this chapter we use the indirect method, which is also used more extensively in practice.[7] *In doing homework assignments, you should follow instructions for use of either the direct or indirect method.*

Illustration 23-9 shows the statement of cash flows for Tax Consultants Inc., for year 1(2006).

> **OBJECTIVE 6**
> **Prepare a statement of cash flows.**

ILLUSTRATION 23-9
Statement of Cash Flows, Tax Consultants Inc., Year 1

TAX CONSULTANTS INC.
STATEMENT OF CASH FLOWS
FOR THE YEAR ENDED DECEMBER 31, 2006
INCREASE (DECREASE) IN CASH

Cash flows from operating activities		
Net income		$34,000
Adjustments to reconcile net income to net		
cash provided by operating activities:		
Increase in accounts receivable	$(36,000)	
Increase in accounts payable	5,000	(31,000)
Net cash provided by operating activities		3,000
Cash flows from financing activities		
Issuance of common stock	60,000	
Payment of cash dividends	(14,000)	
Net cash provided by financing activities		46,000
Net increase in cash		49,000
Cash, January 1, 2006		–0–
Cash, December 31, 2006		$49,000

As indicated, the $60,000 increase in common stock results in a financing-activity cash inflow. The payment of $14,000 in cash dividends is a financing-activity outflow of cash. The $49,000 increase in cash reported in the statement of cash flows agrees with the increase of $49,000 shown in the comparative balance sheets as the change in the cash account.

SECOND EXAMPLE—2007

Tax Consultants Inc. continued to grow and prosper in its second year of operations. The company purchased land, building, and equipment, and revenues and net income increased substantially over the first year. Illustrations 23-10 and 23-11 (page 1222) present information related to the second year of operations for Tax Consultants Inc.

---

[6]"The Statement of Cash Flows," pars. 27 and 30.

[7]*Accounting Trends and Techniques—2004* reports that out of its 600 surveyed companies, 593 (approximately 99 percent) used the indirect method, and only 7 used the direct method.

ILLUSTRATION 23-10
Comparative Balance
Sheets, Tax Consultants
Inc., Year 2

TAX CONSULTANTS INC.
COMPARATIVE BALANCE SHEETS
AS OF DECEMBER 31

Assets	2007	2006	Change Increase/Decrease
Cash	$ 37,000	$49,000	$12,000 Decrease
Accounts receivable	26,000	36,000	10,000 Decrease
Prepaid expenses	6,000	–0–	6,000 Increase
Land	70,000	–0–	70,000 Increase
Building	200,000	–0–	200,000 Increase
Accumulated depreciation—building	(11,000)	–0–	11,000 Increase
Equipment	68,000	–0–	68,000 Increase
Accumulated depreciation—equipment	(10,000)	–0–	10,000 Increase
Total	$386,000	$85,000	
Liabilities and Stockholders' Equity			
Accounts payable	$ 40,000	$ 5,000	$ 35,000 Increase
Bonds payable	150,000	–0–	150,000 Increase
Common stock ($1 par)	60,000	60,000	–0–
Retained earnings	136,000	20,000	116,000 Increase
Total	$386,000	$85,000	

ILLUSTRATION 23-11
Income Statement, Tax
Consultants Inc., Year 2

TAX CONSULTANTS INC.
INCOME STATEMENT
FOR THE YEAR ENDED DECEMBER 31, 2007

Revenues		$492,000
Operating expenses (excluding depreciation)	$269,000	
Depreciation expense	21,000	290,000
Income from operations		202,000
Income tax expense		68,000
Net income		$134,000

Additional Information
(a) The company declared and paid an $18,000 cash dividend.
(b) The company obtained $150,000 cash through the issuance of long-term bonds.
(c) Land, building, and equipment were acquired for cash.

Step 1: Determine the Change in Cash

To prepare a statement of cash flows from the available information, the first step is to determine the change in cash. As indicated from the information presented, cash decreased $12,000 ($49,000 − $37,000).

Step 2: Determine Net Cash Flow from Operating Activities—Indirect Method

Using the indirect method, we adjust net income of $134,000 on an accrual basis to arrive at net cash flow from operating activities. Explanations for the adjustments to net income follow.

Decrease in Accounts Receivable. Accounts receivable decreased during the period, because cash receipts (cash-basis revenues) are higher than revenues reported on an accrual basis. To convert net income to net cash flow from operating activities, the decrease of $10,000 in accounts receivable must be added to net income.

Increase in Prepaid Expenses. When prepaid expenses (assets) increase during a period, expenses on an accrual-basis income statement are lower than they are on a cash-basis income statement. The reason: Tax Consultants has made cash payments in the current period, but expenses (as charges to the income statement) have been deferred to future periods. To convert net income to net cash flow from operating activities, the company must deduct from net income the increase of $6,000 in prepaid expenses. An increase in prepaid expenses results in a decrease in cash during the period.

Increase in Accounts Payable. Like the increase in 2006, Tax Consultants must add the 2007 increase of $35,000 in accounts payable to net income, to convert to net cash flow from operating activities. The company incurred a greater amount of expense than the amount of cash it disbursed.

Depreciation Expense (Increase in Accumulated Depreciation). The purchase of depreciable assets is a use of cash, shown in the investing section in the year of acquisition. Tax Consultant's depreciation expense of $21,000 (also represented by the increase in accumulated depreciation) is a noncash charge; the company adds it back to net income, to arrive at net cash flow from operating activities. The $21,000 is the sum of the $11,000 depreciation on the building plus the $10,000 depreciation on the equipment.

　　Certain other periodic charges to expense do not require the use of cash. Examples are the amortization of intangible assets and depletion expense. Such charges are treated in the same manner as depreciation. Companies frequently list depreciation and similar noncash charges as the first adjustments to net income in the statement of cash flows.

　　As a result of the foregoing items, net cash provided by operating activities is $194,000 as shown in Illustration 23-12.

Net income		$134,000
Adjustments to reconcile net income to		
net cash provided by operating activities:		
Depreciation expense	$21,000	
Decrease in accounts receivable	10,000	
Increase in prepaid expenses	(6,000)	
Increase in accounts payable	35,000	60,000
Net cash provided by operating activities		$194,000

ILLUSTRATION 23-12
Computation of Net Cash Flow from Operating Activities, Year 2—Indirect Method

Step 3: Determine Net Cash Flows from Investing and Financing Activities

After you have determined the items affecting net cash provided by operating activities, the next step involves analyzing the remaining changes in balance sheet accounts. Tax Consultants Inc. analyzed the following accounts.

Increase in Land. As indicated from the change in the land account, the company purchased land of $70,000 during the period. This transaction is an investing activity, reported as a use of cash.

Increase in Building and Related Accumulated Depreciation. As indicated in the additional data, and from the change in the building account, Tax Consultants acquired an office building using $200,000 cash. This transaction is a cash outflow, reported in the investing section. The $11,000 increase in accumulated depreciation results from recording depreciation expense on the building. As indicated earlier, the reported depreciation expense has no effect on the amount of cash.

Increase in Equipment and Related Accumulated Depreciation. An increase in equipment of $68,000 resulted because the company used cash to purchase equipment. This transaction is an outflow of cash from an investing activity. The depreciation expense entry for the period explains the increase in Accumulated Depreciation—Equipment.

Increase in Bonds Payable. The bonds payable account increased $150,000. Cash received from the issuance of these bonds represents an inflow of cash from a financing activity.

Increase in Retained Earnings. Retained earnings increased $116,000 during the year. Two factors explain this increase: (1) Net income of $134,000 increased retained earnings, and (2) dividends of $18,000 decreased retained earnings. As indicated earlier, the company adjusts net income to net cash provided by operating activities in the operating activities section. Payment of the dividends is a financing activity that involves a cash outflow.

Statement of Cash Flows—2007

Combining the foregoing items, we get a statement of cash flows for 2007 for Tax Consultants Inc., using the indirect method to compute net cash flow from operating activities.

ILLUSTRATION 23-13
Statement of Cash Flows,
Tax Consultants Inc.,
Year 2

TAX CONSULTANTS INC.
STATEMENT OF CASH FLOWS
FOR THE YEAR ENDED DECEMBER 31, 2007
INCREASE (DECREASE) IN CASH

Cash flows from operating activities		
Net income		$134,000
Adjustments to reconcile net income to		
net cash provided by operating activities:		
Depreciation expense	$ 21,000	
Decrease in accounts receivable	10,000	
Increase in prepaid expenses	(6,000)	
Increase in accounts payable	35,000	60,000
Net cash provided by operating activities		194,000
Cash flows from investing activities		
Purchase of land	(70,000)	
Purchase of building	(200,000)	
Purchase of equipment	(68,000)	
Net cash used by investing activities		(338,000)
Cash flows from financing activities		
Issuance of bonds	150,000	
Payment of cash dividends	(18,000)	
Net cash provided by financing activities		132,000
Net decrease in cash		(12,000)
Cash, January 1, 2007		49,000
Cash, December 31, 2007		$ 37,000

THIRD EXAMPLE—2008

Our third example, covering the 2008 operations of Tax Consultants Inc., is more complex. It again uses the indirect method to compute and present net cash flow from operating activities.

Tax Consultants Inc. experienced continued success in 2008 and expanded its operations to include the sale of computer software used in tax-return preparation and tax planning. Thus, inventory is a new asset appearing in the company's December 31, 2008, balance sheet. Illustrations 23-14 and 23-15 show the comparative balance sheets, income statements, and selected data for 2008.

ILLUSTRATION 23-14
Comparative Balance
Sheets, Tax Consultants
Inc., Year 3

TAX CONSULTANTS INC.
COMPARATIVE BALANCE SHEETS
AS OF DECEMBER 31

Assets	2008	2007	Change Increase/Decrease
Cash	$ 54,000	$ 37,000	$ 17,000 Increase
Accounts receivable	68,000	26,000	42,000 Increase
Inventories	54,000	–0–	54,000 Increase
Prepaid expenses	4,000	6,000	2,000 Decrease
Land	45,000	70,000	25,000 Decrease
Buildings	200,000	200,000	–0–
Accumulated depreciation—buildings	(21,000)	(11,000)	10,000 Increase
Equipment	193,000	68,000	125,000 Increase
Accumulated depreciation—equipment	(28,000)	(10,000)	18,000 Increase
Totals	$569,000	$386,000	

Liabilities and Stockholders' Equity			
Accounts payable	$ 33,000	$ 40,000	$ 7,000 Decrease
Bonds payable	110,000	150,000	40,000 Decrease
Common stock ($1 par)	220,000	60,000	160,000 Increase
Retained earnings	206,000	136,000	70,000 Increase
Totals	$569,000	$386,000	

ILLUSTRATION 23-15
Income Statement, Tax
Consultants Inc., Year 3

TAX CONSULTANTS INC.
INCOME STATEMENT
FOR THE YEAR ENDED DECEMBER 31, 2008

Revenues		$890,000
Cost of goods sold	$465,000	
Operating expenses	221,000	
Interest expense	12,000	
Loss on sale of equipment	2,000	700,000
Income from operations		190,000
Income tax expense		65,000
Net income		$125,000

Additional Information
(a) Operating expenses include depreciation expense of $33,000 and amortization of prepaid expenses of $2,000.
(b) Land was sold at its book value for cash.
(c) Cash dividends of $55,000 were declared and paid.
(d) Interest expense of $12,000 was paid in cash.
(e) Equipment with a cost of $166,000 was purchased for cash. Equipment with a cost of $41,000 and a book value of $36,000 was sold for $34,000 cash.
(f) Bonds were redeemed at their book value for cash.
(g) Common stock ($1 par) was issued for cash.

Step 1: Determine the Change in Cash

The first step in the preparation of the statement of cash flows is to determine the change in cash. As the comparative balance sheets show, cash increased $17,000 in 2008.

Step 2: Determine Net Cash Flow from Operating Activities—Indirect Method

We explain the adjustments to net income of $125,000 as follows.

Increase in Accounts Receivable. The increase in accounts receivable of $42,000 represents recorded accrual-basis revenues in excess of cash collections in 2008. The company deducts this increase from net income to convert from the accrual basis to the cash basis.

Increase in Inventories. The $54,000 increase in inventories represents an operating use of cash, not an expense. Tax Consultants therefore deducts this amount from net income, to arrive at net cash flow from operations. In other words, when inventory purchased exceeds inventory sold during a period, cost of goods sold on an accrual basis is lower than on a cash basis.

Decrease in Prepaid Expenses. The $2,000 decrease in prepaid expenses represents a charge to the income statement for which Tax Consultants made no cash payment in the current period. The company adds back the decrease to net income, to arrive at net cash flow from operating activities.

Decrease in Accounts Payable. When accounts payable decrease during the year, cost of goods sold and expenses on a cash basis are higher than they are on an accrual basis. To convert net income to net cash flow from operating activities, the company must deduct the $7,000 in accounts payable from net income.

Depreciation Expense (Increase in Accumulated Depreciation). Accumulated Depreciation—Buildings increased $10,000 ($21,000 − $11,000). The Buildings account did not change during the period, which means that Tax Consultants recorded depreciation expense of $10,000 in 2008.

Accumulated Depreciation—Equipment increased by $18,000 ($28,000 − $10,000) during the year. But Accumulated Depreciation—Equipment decreased by $5,000 as a result of the sale during the year. Thus, depreciation for the year was $23,000. The company reconciled Accumulated Depreciation—Equipment as follows.

Beginning balance	$10,000
Add: Depreciation for 2008	23,000
	33,000
Deduct: Sale of equipment	5,000
Ending balance	$28,000

The company must add back to net income the total depreciation of $33,000 ($10,000 + $23,000) charged to the income statement, to determine net cash flow from operating activities.

Loss on Sale of Equipment. Tax Consultants Inc. sold for $34,000 equipment that cost $41,000 and had a book value of $36,000. As a result, the company reported a loss of $2,000 on its sale. To arrive at net cash flow from operating activities, it must add back to net income the loss on the sale of the equipment. The reason is that the loss is a noncash charge to the income statement. The loss did not reduce cash, but it did reduce net income.

From the foregoing items, the company prepares the operating activities section of the statement of cash flows, as shown in Illustration 23-16.

ILLUSTRATION 23-16
Operating Activities Section of Cash Flows Statement

Cash flows from operating activities		
Net income		$125,000
Adjustments to reconcile net income to net cash provided by operating activities:		
Depreciation expense	$33,000	
Loss on sale of equipment	2,000	
Increase in accounts receivable	(42,000)	
Increase in inventories	(54,000)	
Decrease in prepaid expenses	2,000	
Decrease in accounts payable	(7,000)	(66,000)
Net cash provided by operating activities		59,000

Step 3: Determine Net Cash Flows from Investing and Financing Activities

By analyzing the remaining changes in the balance sheet accounts, Tax Consultants identifies cash flows from investing and financing activities.

Land. Land decreased $25,000 during the period. As indicated from the information presented, the company sold land for cash at its book value. This transaction is an investing activity, reported as a $25,000 source of cash.

Equipment. An analysis of the equipment account indicates the following.

Beginning balance	$ 68,000
Purchase of equipment	166,000
	234,000
Sale of equipment	41,000
Ending balance	$193,000

The company used cash to purchase equipment with a fair value of $166,000—an investing transaction reported as a cash outflow. The sale of the equipment for $34,000 is also an investing activity, but one that generates a cash inflow.

Bonds Payable. Bonds payable decreased $40,000 during the year. As indicated from the additional information, the company redeemed the bonds at their book value. This financing transaction used $40,000 of cash.

Common Stock. The common stock account increased $160,000 during the year. As indicated from the additional information, Tax Consultants issued common stock of $160,000 at par. This financing transaction provided cash of $160,000.

Retained Earnings. Retained earnings changed $70,000 ($206,000 − $136,000) during the year. The $70,000 change in retained earnings results from net income of $125,000 from operations and the financing activity of paying cash dividends of $55,000.

Statement of Cash Flows—2008

Tax Consultants Inc. combines the foregoing items to prepare the statement of cash flows shown in Illustration 23-17.

ILLUSTRATION 23-17
Statement of Cash Flows,
Tax Consultants Inc.,
Year 3

TAX CONSULTANTS INC.
STATEMENT OF CASH FLOWS
FOR THE YEAR ENDED DECEMBER 31, 2008
INCREASE (DECREASE) IN CASH

Cash flows from operating activities		
Net income		$125,000
Adjustments to reconcile net income to		
net cash provided by operating activities:		
Depreciation expense	$ 33,000	
Loss on sale of equipment	2,000	
Increase in accounts receivable	(42,000)	
Increase in inventories	(54,000)	
Decrease in prepaid expenses	2,000	
Decrease in accounts payable	(7,000)	(66,000)
Net cash provided by operating activities		59,000
Cash flows from investing activities		
Sale of land	25,000	
Sale of equipment	34,000	
Purchase of equipment	(166,000)	
Net cash used by investing activities		(107,000)
Cash flows from financing activities		
Redemption of bonds	(40,000)	
Sale of common stock	160,000	
Payment of dividends	(55,000)	
Net cash provided by financing activities		65,000
Net increase in cash		17,000
Cash, January 1, 2008		37,000
Cash, December 31, 2008		$ 54,000

SOURCES OF INFORMATION FOR THE STATEMENT OF CASH FLOWS

OBJECTIVE 7

Identify sources of information for a statement of cash flows.

Important points to remember in the preparation of the statement of cash flows are these:

1   Comparative balance sheets provide the basic information from which to prepare the report. Additional information obtained from analyses of specific accounts is also included.

2   An analysis of the Retained Earnings account is necessary. The net increase or decrease in Retained Earnings without any explanation is a meaningless amount in the statement. Without explanation, it might represent the effect of net income, dividends declared, or prior period adjustments.

3   The statement includes all changes that have passed through cash or have resulted in an increase or decrease in cash.

4   Writedowns, amortization charges, and similar "book" entries, such as depreciation of plant assets, represent neither inflows nor outflows of cash, because they have no effect on cash. To the extent that they have entered into the determination of net income, however, the company must add them back to or subtract them from net income, to arrive at net cash provided by operating activities.

NET CASH FLOW FROM OPERATING ACTIVITIES—INDIRECT VERSUS DIRECT METHOD

As we discussed previously, the two different methods available to adjust income from operations on an accrual basis to net cash flow from operating activities are the indirect (reconciliation) method and the direct (income statement) method.

The FASB encourages use of the direct method and permits use of the indirect method. Yet, if the direct method is used, the Board requires that companies provide in a separate schedule a reconciliation of net income to net cash flow from operating activities. Therefore, under either method, companies must prepare and report information from the indirect (reconciliation) method.

Indirect Method

For consistency and comparability and because it is the most widely used method in practice, we used the indirect method in the examples just presented. We determined net cash flows from operating activities by adding back to or deducting from net income those items that had no effect on cash. Illustration 23-18 (page 1229) presents more completely the common types of adjustments that companies make to net income to arrive at net cash flow from operating activities.

The additions and deductions listed on page 1229 reconcile net income to net cash flow from operating activities, illustrating why the indirect method is also called the reconciliation method.

Direct Method—An Example

Under the direct method the statement of cash flows reports net cash flow from operating activities as major classes of *operating cash receipts* (e.g., cash collected from customers and cash received from interest and dividends) and *cash disbursements* (e.g., cash paid to suppliers for goods, to employees for services, to creditors for interest, and to government authorities for taxes).

We illustrate the direct method here in more detail to help you understand the difference between accrual-based income and net cash flow from operating activities. This

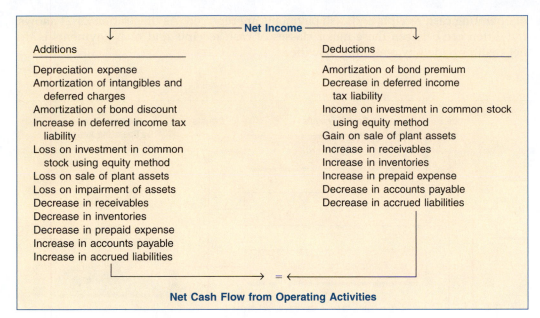

ILLUSTRATION 23-18
Adjustments Needed to
Determine Net Cash
Flow from Operating
Activities—Indirect
Method

example also illustrates the data needed to apply the direct method. Emig Company, which began business on January 1, 2008, has the following selected balance sheet information.

	December 31	
	2008	2007
Cash	$159,000	–0–
Accounts receivable	15,000	–0–
Inventory	160,000	–0–
Prepaid expenses	8,000	–0–
Property, plant, and equipment (net)	90,000	–0–
Accounts payable	60,000	–0–
Accrued expenses payable	20,000	–0–

ILLUSTRATION 23-19
Balance Sheet Accounts,
Emig Co.

Emig Company's December 31, 2008, income statement and additional information are as follows.

Revenues from sales		$780,000
Cost of goods sold		450,000
Gross profit		330,000
Operating expenses	$160,000	
Depreciation	10,000	170,000
Income before income taxes		160,000
Income tax expense		48,000
Net income		$112,000

Additional Information:
(a) Dividends of $70,000 were declared and paid in cash.
(b) The accounts payable increase resulted from the purchase of merchandise.
(c) Prepaid expenses and accrued expenses payable relate to operating expenses.

ILLUSTRATION 23-20
Income Statement,
Emig Co.

Under the **direct method**, companies compute net cash provided by operating activities by **adjusting each item in the income statement** from the accrual basis to the cash basis. To simplify and condense the operating activities section, only major classes of operating cash receipts and cash payments are reported. As Illustration 23-21 shows, the difference between these major classes of cash receipts and cash payments is the net cash provided by operating activities.

ILLUSTRATION 23-21
Major Classes of Cash Receipts and Payments

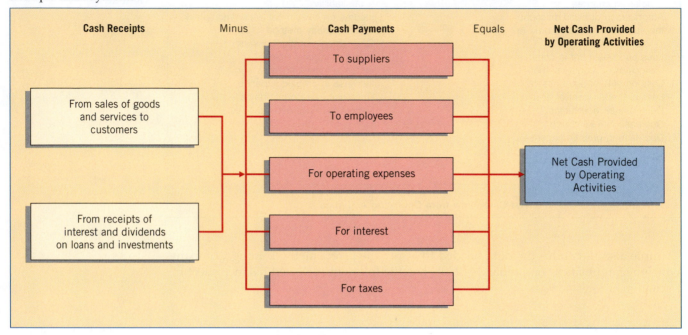

An efficient way to apply the direct method is to analyze the revenues and expenses reported in the income statement in the order in which they are listed. The company then determines cash receipts and cash payments related to these revenues and expenses. In the following sections, we present the direct method adjustments for Emig Company in 2008, to determine net cash provided by operating activities.

Cash Receipts from Customers. The income statement for Emig Company reported revenues from customers of $780,000. To determine cash receipts from customers, the company considers the change in accounts receivable during the year.

When accounts receivable increase during the year, revenues on an accrual basis are higher than cash receipts from customers. In other words, operations led to increased revenues, but not all of these revenues resulted in cash receipts. To determine the amount of increase in cash receipts, deduct the amount of the increase in accounts receivable from the total sales revenues. Conversely, a decrease in accounts receivable is added to sales revenues, because cash receipts from customers then exceed sales revenues.

For Emig Company, accounts receivable increased $15,000. Thus, cash receipts from customers were $765,000, computed as follows.

Revenues from sales	$780,000
Deduct: Increase in accounts receivable	15,000
Cash receipts from customers	$765,000

Emig could also determine cash receipts from customers by analyzing the Accounts Receivable account as shown below.

Accounts Receivable

1/1/08	Balance	–0–	Receipts from customers		765,000
	Revenue from sales	780,000			
12/31/08	Balance	15,000			

Illustration 23-22 shows the relationships between cash receipts from customers, revenues from sales, and changes in accounts receivable.

Cash receipts from customers	=	Revenues from sales	{	+ Decrease in accounts receivable or − Increase in accounts receivable

ILLUSTRATION 23-22
Formula to Compute
Cash Receipts from
Customers

Cash Payments to Suppliers. Emig Company reported cost of goods sold on its income statement of $450,000. To determine cash payments to suppliers, the company first finds purchases for the year, by adjusting cost of goods sold for the change in inventory. When inventory increases during the year, purchases this year exceed cost of goods sold. As a result, the company adds the increase in inventory to cost of goods sold, to arrive at purchases.

In 2008, Emig Company's inventory increased $160,000. The company computes purchases as follows.

Cost of goods sold	$450,000
Add: Increase in inventory	160,000
Purchases	$610,000

After computing purchases, Emig determines cash payments to suppliers by adjusting purchases for the change in accounts payable. When accounts payable increase during the year, purchases on an accrual basis are higher than they are on a cash basis. As a result, it deducts from purchases the increase in accounts payable to arrive at cash payments to suppliers. Conversely, if cash payments to suppliers exceed purchases, Emig adds to purchases the decrease in accounts payable. Cash payments to suppliers were $550,000, computed as follows.

Purchases	$610,000
Deduct: Increase in accounts payable	60,000
Cash payments to suppliers	$550,000

Emig also can determine cash payments to suppliers by analyzing Accounts Payable, as shown below.

Accounts Payable				
Payments to suppliers	550,000	1/1/08 Balance		−0−
		Purchases		610,000
		12/31/08 Balance		60,000

Illustration 23-23 shows the relationships between cash payments to suppliers, cost of goods sold, changes in inventory, and changes in accounts payable.

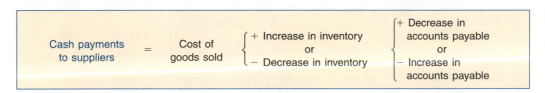

Cash payments to suppliers	=	Cost of goods sold	{	+ Increase in inventory or − Decrease in inventory	{	+ Decrease in accounts payable or − Increase in accounts payable

ILLUSTRATION 23-23
Formula to Compute
Cash Payments to
Suppliers

Cash Payments for Operating Expenses. Emig reported operating expenses of $160,000 on its income statement. To determine the cash paid for operating expenses, it must adjust this amount for any changes in prepaid expenses and accrued expenses payable.

For example, when prepaid expenses increased $8,000 during the year, cash paid for operating expenses was $8,000 higher than operating expenses reported on the income statement. To convert operating expenses to cash payments for operating expenses, the company adds to operating expenses the increase of $8,000. Conversely, if prepaid expenses decrease during the year, it deducts from operating expenses the amount of the decrease.

Emig also must adjust operating expenses for changes in accrued expenses payable. When accrued expenses payable increase during the year, operating expenses on an accrual basis are higher than they are on a cash basis. As a result, the company deducts from operating expenses an increase in accrued expenses payable, to arrive at cash payments for operating expenses. Conversely, it adds to operating expenses a decrease in accrued expenses payable, because cash payments exceed operating expenses.

Emig Company's cash payments for operating expenses were $148,000, computed as follows.

Operating expenses	$160,000
Add: Increase in prepaid expenses	8,000
Deduct: Increase in accrued expenses payable	(20,000)
Cash payments for operating expenses	$148,000

The relationships among cash payments for operating expenses, changes in prepaid expenses, and changes in accrued expenses payable are shown in Illustration 23-24.

ILLUSTRATION 23-24
Formula to Compute
Cash Payments for
Operating Expenses

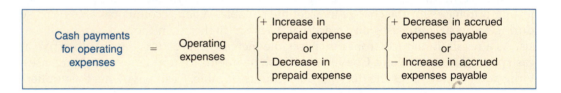

Note that the company did not consider depreciation expense, because it is a non-cash charge.

Cash Payments for Income Taxes. The income statement for Emig shows income tax expense of $48,000. This amount equals the cash paid. How do we know that? Because the comparative balance sheet indicated no income taxes payable at either the beginning or end of the year.

Summary of Net Cash Flow from Operating Activities—Direct Method

The following schedule summarizes the computations illustrated above.

ILLUSTRATION 23-25
Accrual Basis to Cash
Basis

	Accrual Basis		Adjustment	Add (Subtract)	Cash Basis
Revenues from sales	$780,000	−	Increase in accounts receivable	$(15,000)	$765,000
Cost of goods sold	450,000	+	Increase in inventory	160,000	
		−	Increase in accounts payable	(60,000)	550,000
Operating expenses	160,000	+	Increase in prepaid expenses	8,000	
		−	Increase in accrued expenses payable	(20,000)	148,000
Depreciation expense	10,000	−	Depreciation expense	(10,000)	–0–
Income tax expense	48,000				48,000
Total expense	668,000				746,000
Net income	$112,000		Net cash provided by operating activities		$ 19,000

Illustration 23-26 shows the presentation of the direct method for reporting net cash flow from operating activities for the Emig Company illustration.

ILLUSTRATION 23-26
Operating Activities
Section—Direct Method,
2008

EMIG COMPANY		
STATEMENT OF CASH FLOWS (PARTIAL)		
Cash flows from operating activities		
Cash received from customers		$765,000
Cash payments:		
To suppliers	$ 550,000	
For operating expenses	148,000	
For income taxes	48,000	746,000
Net cash provided by operating activities		$ 19,000

If Emig Company uses the direct method to present the net cash flows from operating activities, it must provide in a separate schedule the reconciliation of net income to net cash provided by operating activities. The reconciliation assumes the identical form and content of the indirect method of presentation, as shown below.

EMIG COMPANY		
RECONCILIATION		
Net income		$112,000
Adjustments to reconcile net income to net cash		
provided by operating activities:		
Depreciation expense	$ 10,000	
Increase in accounts receivable	(15,000)	
Increase in inventory	(160,000)	
Increase in prepaid expenses	(8,000)	
Increase in accounts payable	60,000	
Increase in accrued expense payable	20,000	(93,000)
Net cash provided by operating activities		$ 19,000

When the direct method is used, the company may present this reconciliation at the bottom of the statement of cash flows or in a separate schedule.

Direct Versus Indirect Controversy

The most contentious decision that the FASB faced in issuing *Statement No. 95* was choosing between the direct method and the indirect method of determining net cash flow from operating activities. Companies lobbied *against* the direct method, urging adoption of the indirect method. Commercial lending officers expressed to the FASB a strong preference in favor of the direct method. In the next two sections, we consider the arguments in favor of each of the methods.

In Favor of the Direct Method

The principal advantage of the direct method is that **it shows operating cash receipts and payments**. Thus, it is more consistent with the objective of a statement of cash flows—to provide information about cash receipts and cash payments—than the indirect method, which does not report operating cash receipts and payments.

Supporters of the direct method contend that knowledge of the specific sources of operating cash receipts and the purposes for which operating cash payments were made in past periods is useful in estimating future operating cash flows. Furthermore, information about amounts of major classes of operating cash receipts and payments is more useful than information only about their arithmetic sum (the net cash flow from operating activities). Such information is more revealing of a company's ability (1) to generate sufficient cash from operating activities to pay its debts, (2) to reinvest in its operations, and (3) to make distributions to its owners.[8]

Many companies indicate that they do not currently collect information in a manner that allows them to determine amounts such as cash received from customers or cash paid to suppliers directly from their accounting systems. But supporters of the direct method contend that the incremental cost of determining operating cash receipts and payments is not significant.

In Favor of the Indirect Method

The principal advantage of the indirect method is that **it focuses on the differences between net income and net cash flow from operating activities**. That is, it provides a useful link between the statement of cash flows and the income statement and balance sheet.

Many companies contend that it is less costly to adjust net income to net cash flow from operating activities (indirect) than it is to report gross operating cash receipts and payments (direct). Supporters of the indirect method also state that the direct method, which effectively reports income statement information on a cash rather than an accrual basis, may erroneously suggest that net cash flow from operating activities is as good as, or better than, net income as a measure of performance.

Special Rules Applying to Direct and Indirect Methods

Companies that use the direct method are required, at a minimum, to report separately the following classes of operating cash receipts and payments:

Receipts

1 Cash collected from customers (including lessees, licensees, etc.).

2 Interest and dividends received.

3 Other operating cash receipts, if any.

Payments

1 Cash paid to employees and suppliers of goods or services (including suppliers of insurance, advertising, etc.).

2 Interest paid.

3 Income taxes paid.

4 Other operating cash payments, if any.

The FASB encourages companies to provide further breakdowns of operating cash receipts and payments that they consider meaningful.

Companies using the indirect method must disclose separately changes in inventory, receivables, and payables in order to reconcile net income to net cash flow from operating activities. In addition, they must disclose, elsewhere in the financial statements or in accompanying notes, interest paid (net of amount capitalized) and income taxes paid.[9] The FASB requires these separate and additional disclosures so that users may approximate the direct method. Also, an acceptable alternative presentation of the indirect method is to report net cash flow from operating activities as a single line item in the statement of cash flows and to present the reconciliation details elsewhere in the financial statements.

---

[8]"Statement of Cash Flows," pars. 107 and 111.

[9]*Accounting Trends and Techniques—2004* reports that of the 600 companies surveyed, 310 disclosed interest paid in notes to the financial statements, 264 disclosed interest paid at the bottom of the statement of cash flows, 9 disclosed interest paid within the statement of cash flows, and 17 reported no separate amount. Income taxes paid during the year were disclosed in a manner similar to interest payments.

NOT WHAT IT SEEMS

The controversy over direct and indirect methods highlights the importance that the market attributes to operating cash flow. By showing an improving cash flow, a company can give a favorable impression of its ongoing operations. For example, **WorldCom** concealed declines in its operations by capitalizing certain operating expenses—to the tune of $3.8 billion! This practice not only "juiced up" income but also made it possible to report the cash payments in the investing section of the cash flow statement rather than as a deduction from operating cash flow.

The SEC recently addressed a similar cash flow classification issue with automakers like **Ford**, **GM**, and **Daimler-Chrysler**. For years, automakers classified lease receivables and other dealer-financing arrangements as investment cash flows. Thus, they reported an increase in lease or loan receivables from cars sold as a use of cash in the investing section of the statement of cash flows. The SEC objected and now requires automakers to report these receivables as operating cash flows, since the leases and loans are used to facilitate car sales. At GM, these reclassifications reduced its operating cash flows from $7.6 billion to $3 billion in the year before the change. So while the overall cash flow—from operations, investing, and financing—remained the same, operating cash flow at these companies looked better than it really was.

Source: Peter Elstrom, "How to Hide $3.8 Billion in Expenses," *BusinessWeek Online* (July 8, 2002); and Judith Burns, "SEC Tells US Automakers to Retool Cash-Flow Accounting," *Wall Street Journal Online* (February 28, 2005).

WHAT DO THE NUMBERS MEAN?

SPECIAL PROBLEMS IN STATEMENT PREPARATION

SECTION 2

We discussed some of the special problems related to preparing the statement of cash flows in connection with the preceding illustrations. Other problems that arise with some frequency in the preparation of this statement include the following.

OBJECTIVE 8
Discuss special problems in preparing a statement of cash flows.

1   Adjustments similar to depreciation.
2   Accounts receivable (net).
3   Other working capital changes.
4   Net losses.
5   Gains.
6   Stock options.
7   Postretirement benefit cost.
8   Extraordinary items.
9   Significant noncash transactions.

ADJUSTMENTS SIMILAR TO DEPRECIATION

Depreciation expense is the most common adjustment to net income that companies make to arrive at net cash flow from operating activities. But there are numerous other noncash expense or revenue items. Examples of expense items that companies must add back to net income are the **amortization of limited-life intangible assets** such as patents, and the **amortization of deferred costs** such as bond issue costs. These charges to expense involve expenditures made in prior periods that a company amortizes currently. These charges reduce net income without affecting cash in the current period.

Also, **amortization of bond discount or premium** on long-term bonds payable affects the amount of interest expense. However, neither changes cash. As a result, a company should add back discount amortization and subtract premium amortization from net income to arrive at net cash flow from operating activities.

In a similar manner, **changes in deferred income taxes** affect net income but have no effect on cash. For example, **Delta Airlines** reported an increase in its liability for deferred taxes of approximately $1.2 billion. This change in the liability increased tax expense and decreased net income, but did not affect cash. Therefore, Delta added back $1.2 billion to net income on its statement of cash flows.

Another common adjustment to net income is **a change related to an investment in common stock** when recording income or loss under the equity method. Recall that under the equity method, the investor (1) debits the investment account and credits revenue for its share of the investee's net income, and (2) credits dividends received to the investment account. Therefore, the net increase in the investment account does not affect cash flow. A company must deduct the net increase from net income to arrive at net cash flow from operating activities.

Assume that Victor Co. owns 40 percent of Milo Inc. During the year Milo reports net income of $100,000 and pays a cash dividend of $30,000. Victor reports this in its statement of cash flows as a deduction from net income in the following manner—Equity in earnings of Milo, net of dividends, $28,000 [($100,000 − $30,000) × 40%].

If Victor Co. does not exercise significant influence over Milo, it cannot use the equity method. Instead, it uses the fair-value method. Under the fair-value method, Victor does not recognize any of Milo's net income. Further, it records any cash dividend received as revenue. As a result, the company makes no adjustment to net income in the statement of cash flows because cash dividends received are included in income.

ACCOUNTS RECEIVABLE (NET)

Up to this point, we assumed no allowance for doubtful accounts—a contra account—to offset accounts receivable. However, if a company needs an allowance for doubtful accounts, how does that allowance affect the company's determination of net cash flow from operating activities? For example, assume that Redmark Co. reports net income of $40,000. It has the accounts receivable balances as shown in Illustration 23-28.

ILLUSTRATION 23-28
Accounts Receivable
Balances, Redmark Co.

	2008	2007	Change Increase/Decrease
Accounts receivable	$105,000	$90,000	$15,000 Increase
Allowance for doubtful accounts	(10,000)	(4,000)	6,000 Increase
Accounts receivable (net)	$ 95,000	$86,000	9,000 Increase

Indirect Method

Because an increase in the Allowance for Doubtful Accounts results from a charge to bad debts expense, a company should add back an increase in the Allowance for Doubtful Accounts to net income to arrive at net cash flow from operating activities. Illustration 23-29 shows one method for presenting this information in a statement of cash flows.

ILLUSTRATION 23-29
Presentation of
Allowance for Doubtful
Accounts—Indirect
Method

REDMARK CO. STATEMENT OF CASH FLOWS (PARTIAL) FOR THE YEAR 2008		
Cash flows from operating activities		
Net income		$40,000
Adjustments to reconcile net income to net cash provided by operating activities:		
Increase in accounts receivable	$(15,000)	
Increase in allowance for doubtful accounts	6,000	(9,000)
		$31,000

As we indicated, the increase in the Allowance for Doubtful Accounts balance results from a charge to bad debt expense for the year. Because bad debt expense is a noncash charge, a company must add it back to net income in arriving at net cash flow from operating activities.

Instead of separately analyzing the allowance account, a short-cut approach is to net the allowance balance against the receivable balance and compare the change in accounts receivable on a net basis. Illustration 23-30 shows this presentation.

ILLUSTRATION 23-30
Net Approach to Allowance for Doubtful Accounts—Indirect Method

REDMARK CO.	
STATEMENT OF CASH FLOWS (PARTIAL)	
FOR THE YEAR 2008	
Cash flows from operating activities	
Net income	$40,000
Adjustments to reconcile net income to	
net cash provided by operating activities:	
Increase in accounts receivable (net)	(9,000)
	$31,000

This short-cut procedure works also if the change in the allowance account results from a writeoff of accounts receivable. This reduces both the Accounts Receivable and the Allowance for Doubtful Accounts. No effect on cash flows occurs. Because of its simplicity, *use the net approach for your homework assignments.*

Direct Method

If using the direct method, a company **should not net** the Allowance for Doubtful Accounts against Accounts Receivable. To illustrate, assume that Redmark Co.'s net income of $40,000 consisted of the following items.

ILLUSTRATION 23-31
Income Statement, Redmark Co.

REDMARK CO.		
INCOME STATEMENT		
FOR THE YEAR 2008		
Sales		$100,000
Expenses		
Salaries	$46,000	
Utilities	8,000	
Bad debts	6,000	60,000
Net income		$ 40,000

If Redmark deducts the $9,000 increase in accounts receivable (net) from sales for the year, it would report cash sales at $91,000 ($100,000 − $9,000) and cash payments for operating expenses at $60,000. Both items would be misstated: Cash sales should be reported at $85,000 ($100,000 − $15,000), and total cash payments for operating expenses should be reported at $54,000 ($60,000 − $6,000). Illustration 23-32 shows the proper presentation.

ILLUSTRATION 23-32
Bad Debts—Direct Method

REDMARK CO.		
STATEMENT OF CASH FLOWS (PARTIAL)		
FOR THE YEAR 2008		
Cash flows from operating activities		
Cash received from customers		$85,000
Salaries paid	$46,000	
Utilities paid	8,000	54,000
Net cash provided by operating activities		$31,000

An added complication develops when a company writes off accounts receivable. Simply adjusting sales for the change in accounts receivable will not provide the proper amount of cash sales. The reason is that the writeoff of the accounts receivable is not a cash collection. Thus an additional adjustment is necessary.

OTHER WORKING CAPITAL CHANGES

Up to this point, we showed how companies handled all of the changes in working capital items (current asset and current liability items) as adjustments to net income in determining net cash flow from operating activities. You must be careful, however, because **some changes in working capital, although they affect cash, do not affect net income**. Generally, these are investing or financing activities of a current nature.

One activity is the purchase of **short-term available-for-sale securities**. For example, the purchase of short-term available-for-sale securities for $50,000 cash has no effect on net income but it does cause a $50,000 decrease in cash.[10] A company reports this transaction as a cash flow from investing activities as follows.[11]

Cash flows from investing activities
Purchase of short-term available-for-sale securities $(50,000)

What about **trading securities**? Because companies hold these investments principally for the purpose of selling them in the near term, companies should classify the cash flows from purchases and sales of trading securities as cash flows from **operating activities**.[12]

Another example is the issuance of a **short-term nontrade note payable** for cash. This change in a working capital item has no effect on income from operations but it increases cash by the amount of the note payable. For example, a company reports the issuance of a $10,000 short-term note payable for cash in the statement of cash flows as follows.

Cash flows from financing activities
Issuance of short-term note $10,000

Another change in a working capital item that has no effect on income from operations or on cash is a **cash dividend payable**. Although a company will report the cash dividends when paid as a financing activity, it does not report the declared but unpaid dividend on the statement of cash flows.

NET LOSSES

If a company reports a net loss instead of a net income, it must adjust the net loss for those items that do not result in a cash inflow or outflow. The net loss, after adjusting for the charges or credits not affecting cash, may result in a negative or a positive cash flow from operating activities.

For example, if the net loss is $50,000 and the total amount of charges to add back is $60,000, then net cash provided by operating activities is $10,000. Illustration 23-33 shows this computation.

---

[10] If the basis of the statement of cash flows is **cash and cash equivalents** and the short-term investment is considered a cash equivalent, then a company reports nothing in the statement because the transaction does not affect the balance of cash and cash equivalents. The Board notes that cash purchases of short term investments generally are part of the company's cash management activities rather than part of its operating, investing, or financing activities.

[11] "Accounting for Certain Investments in Debt and Equity Securities," *Statement of Financial Accounting Standards No. 115* (Norwalk, Conn.: 1993), par. 118.

[12] Ibid., par. 118.

Net loss		$(50,000)
Adjustments to reconcile net income to net cash provided by operating activities:		
Depreciation of plant assets	$55,000	
Amortization of patents	5,000	60,000
Net cash provided by operating activities		$ 10,000

ILLUSTRATION 23-33
Computation of Net Cash
Flow from Operating
Activities—Cash Inflow

If the company experiences a net loss of $80,000 and the total amount of the charges to add back is $25,000, the presentation appears as follows.

Net loss	$(80,000)
Adjustments to reconcile net income to net cash used by operating activities:	
Depreciation of plant assets	25,000
Net cash used by operating activities	$(55,000)

ILLUSTRATION 23-34
Computation of Net Cash
Flow from Operating
Activities—Cash Outflow

Although not illustrated in this chapter, a negative cash flow may result even if the company reports a net income.

GAINS

In the illustration for Tax Consultants, the company experienced a loss of $2,000 from the sale of equipment. The company added this loss to net income to compute net cash flow from operating activities because **the loss is a noncash charge in the income statement**.

If Tax Consultants experiences a **gain** from a sale of equipment it too requires an adjustment to net income. Because a company reports the gain in the statement of cash flows as part of the cash proceeds from the sale of equipment under investing activities, **it deducts the gain from net income to avoid double counting**—once as part of net income, and again as part of the cash proceeds from the sale.

STOCK OPTIONS

Recall for share-based compensation plans that companies are required to use the fair value method to determine total compensation cost. The compensation cost is then recognized as an expense in the periods in which the employee provides services. When Compensation Expense is debited, Paid-in Capital—Stock Options is often credited. Cash is not affected by recording the expense. **Therefore, the company must increase net income by the amount of compensation expense from stock options in computing net cash flow from operating activities.**

To illustrate how this information should be reported on a statement of cash flows, assume that First Wave Inc. grants 5,000 options to its CEO, Ann Johnson. Each option entitles Johnson to purchase one share of First Wave's $1 par value common stock at $50 per share at any time in the next two years (the service period). The fair value of the options is $200,000. First Wave records compensation expense in the first year as follows:

Compensation Expense ($200,000 ÷ 2)	100,000	
Paid-in Capital—Stock Options		100,000

In addition, if we assume that First Wave has a 35 percent tax rate, it would recognize a deferred tax asset of $35,000 ($100,000 × 35%) in the first year as follows:

Deferred Tax Asset	35,000	
Income Tax Expense		35,000

Therefore on the statement of cash flows for the first year, First Wave reports the following (assuming a net income of $600,000).

Net income	$600,000
Adjustments to reconcile net income to net cash provided by operating activities:	
Share-based compensation expense	100,000
Increase in deferred tax asset	(35,000)

As shown in First Wave's statement of cash flows, it adds the share-based compensation expense to net income because it is a non-cash expense. The increase in the deferred tax asset and the related reduction in income tax expense increase net income. Although the negative income tax expense increases net income, it does not increase cash. Therefore it should be deducted.

Subsequently, if Ann Johnson exercises her options, Third Wave reports "Cash provided by exercise of stock options" in the financing section of the statement of cash flows.[13]

POSTRETIREMENT BENEFIT COSTS

If a company has postretirement costs such as an employee pension plan, chances are that the pension expense recorded during a period will either be higher or lower than the cash funded. It will be higher when there is an unfunded liability and will be lower when there is a prepaid pension cost. When the expense is higher or lower than the cash paid, **the company must adjust net income by the difference between cash paid and the expense reported** in computing net cash flow from operating activities.

EXTRAORDINARY ITEMS

Companies should report **either as investing activities or as financing activities** cash flows from extraordinary transactions and other events whose effects are included in net income, but which are not related to operations.

For example, assume that Tax Consultants had land with a carrying value of $200,000, which was condemned by the state of Maine for a highway project. The condemnation proceeds received were $205,000, resulting in a gain of $5,000 less $2,000 of taxes. In the statement of cash flows (indirect method), the company would deduct the $5,000 gain from net income in the operating activities section. It would report the $205,000 cash inflow from the condemnation as an investing activity, as follows.

Cash flows from investing activities	
Condemnation of land	$205,000

Note that Tax Consultants handles the gain at its **gross** amount ($5,000), not net of tax. The company reports the cash received in the condemnation as an investing activity at $205,000, also exclusive of the tax effect.

The FASB requires companies to classify **all income taxes paid as operating cash outflows**. Some suggested that income taxes paid be allocated to investing and financing transactions. But the Board decided that allocation of income taxes paid to

---

[13]Companies receive a tax deduction related to share-based compensation plans at the time employees exercise their options. The amount of the deduction is equal to the difference between the market price of the stock and the exercise price at the date the employee purchases the stock, which in most cases, is much larger than the total compensation expense recorded. When the tax deduction exceeds the total compensation recorded, this provides an additional cash inflow to the company. For example, in a recent year **Cisco Systems** reported an additional cash inflow related to its stock option plans equal to $537 million. Under the provisions of *SFAS No. 123(R)*, this tax-related cash inflow is reported in the financing section of the statement of cash flows. See "Share-Based Payment," *Statement of Financial Accounting Standard No. 123(R)* (Norwalk, Conn.: FASB, 2004) par. 68.

operating, investing, and financing activities would be so complex and arbitrary that the benefits, if any, would not justify the costs involved. Under both the direct method and the indirect method, companies must disclose the total amount of income taxes paid.[14]

SIGNIFICANT NONCASH TRANSACTIONS

Because the statement of cash flows reports only the effects of operating, investing, and financing activities in terms of cash flows, it omits some **significant noncash transactions** and other events that are investing or financing activities. Among the more common of these noncash transactions that a company should report or disclose in some manner are the following.

1 Acquisition of assets by assuming liabilities (including capital lease obligations) or by issuing equity securities.

2 Exchanges of nonmonetary assets.

3 Refinancing of long-term debt.

4 Conversion of debt or preferred stock to common stock.

5 Issuance of equity securities to retire debt.

Examples of Cash Flow Statements

   A company does not incorporate these noncash items in the statement of cash flows. If material in amount, these disclosures may be either narrative or summarized in a separate schedule at the bottom of the statement, or they may appear in a separate note or supplementary schedule to the financial statements.[15] Illustration 23-35 shows the presentation of these significant noncash transactions or other events in a separate schedule at the bottom of the statement of cash flows.

Net increase in cash	$3,717,000
Cash at beginning of year	5,208,000
Cash at end of year	$8,925,000
Noncash investing and financing activities	
Purchase of land and building through issuance of 250,000 shares of common stock	$1,750,000
Exchange of Steadfast, NY, land for Bedford, PA, land	$2,000,000
Conversion of 12% bonds to 50,000 shares of common stock	$ 500,000

ILLUSTRATION 23-35
Schedule Presentation of Noncash Investing and Financing Activities

   Or, companies may present these noncash transactions in a separate note, as shown in Illustration 23-36.

Note G: Significant noncash transactions. During the year the company engaged in the following significant noncash investing and financing transactions:	
Issued 250,000 shares of common stock to purchase land and building	$1,750,000
Exchanged land in Steadfast, NY, for land in Bedford, PA	$2,000,000
Converted 12% bonds due 2007 to 50,000 shares of common stock	$ 500,000

ILLUSTRATION 23-36
Note Presentation of Noncash Investing and Financing Activities

---

[14]For an insightful article on some weaknesses and limitations in the statement of cash flows caused by implementation of *FASB Statement No. 95*, see Hugo Nurnberg, "Inconsistencies and Ambiguities in Cash Flow Statements Under *FASB Statement No. 95*," *Accounting Horizons* (June 1993), pp. 60–73. Nurnberg identifies the inconsistencies caused by the three-way classification of all cash receipts and cash payments, gross versus net of tax, the ambiguous disclosure requirements for noncash investing and financing transactions, and the ambiguous presentation of third-party financing transactions. See also Paul B. W. Miller, and Bruce P. Budge, "Nonarticulation in Cash Flow Statements and Implications for Education, Research, and Practice," *Accounting Horizons* (December 1996), pp. 1–15; and Charles Mulford and Michael Ely, "Calculating Sustainable Cash Flow: A Study of the S&P 100," *Georgia Tech Financial Analysis Lab* (October 2004).

[15]Some noncash investing and financing activities are part cash and part noncash. Companies should report only the cash portion on the statement of cash flows. The noncash component should be reported at the bottom of the statement or in a separate note.

Companies do not generally report certain other significant noncash transactions or other events in conjunction with the statement of cash flows. Examples of these types of transactions are **stock dividends**, **stock splits**, **and restrictions on retained earnings**. Companies generally report these items, neither financing nor investing activities, in conjunction with the statement of stockholders' equity or schedules and notes pertaining to changes in capital accounts.

CASH FLOW TOOL

WHAT DO THE NUMBERS MEAN?

By understanding the relationship between cash flow and income measures, analysts can gain better insights into company performance. Because earnings altered through creative accounting practices generally do not change operating cash flows, analysts can use the relationship between earnings and operating cash flow to detect suspicious accounting practices. Also, by monitoring the ratio between cash flow from operations and operating income, they can get a clearer picture of developing problems in a company.

For example, the chart below plots the ratio of operating cash flows to earnings for **Xerox Corp.** in the years leading up to the SEC singling it out in 2000 for aggressive revenue recognition practices on its leases.

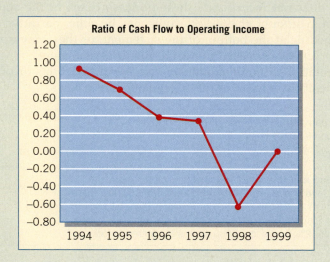

Similar to **W. T. Grant** in the chapter-opening story, Xerox was reporting earnings growth in the years leading up to its financial breakdown in 2000 but teetering near bankruptcy in 2001. However, Xerox's ratio of cash flow to earnings showed a declining trend and became negative well before its revenue recognition practices were revealed. The trend revealed in the graph should have given any analyst reason to investigate Xerox further. As one analyst noted, "Earnings growth that exceeds the growth in operating cash flow cannot continue for extended periods and should be investigated."

Source: Adapted from Charles Mulford and Eugene Comiskey, *The Financial Numbers Game: Detecting Creative Accounting Practices* (New York: John Wiley & Sons, 2002), Chapter 11, by permission.

SECTION 3 | *USE OF A WORKSHEET*

OBJECTIVE 9
Explain the use of a worksheet in preparing a statement of cash flows.

When numerous adjustments are necessary or other complicating factors are present, companies often use **a worksheet to assemble and classify the data that will appear on the statement of cash flows**. The worksheet (a **spreadsheet** when using computer software) is merely a device that aids in the preparation of the statement. Its use is optional. Illustration 23-37 shows the skeleton format of the worksheet for preparation of the statement of cash flows using the indirect method.

XYZ COMPANY
Statement of Cash Flows For the Year Ended...

	A	B	C	D	E
		End of Prior Year Balances	Reconciling Items		End of Current Year Balances
1	Balance Sheet Accounts		Debits	Credits	
2	Debit balance accounts	XX	XX	XX	XX
3		XX	XX	XX	XX
4	Totals	XXX			XXX
5	Credit balance accounts	XX	XX	XX	XX
6		XX	XX	XX	XX
7	Totals	XXX			XXX
8	Statement of Cash Flows Effects				
9	Operating activities				
10	Net income		XX		
11	Adjustments		XX	XX	
12	Investing activities				
13	Receipts and payments		XX	XX	
14	Financing activities				
15	Receipts and payments		XX	XX	
16	Totals		XXX	XXX	
17	Increase (decrease) in cash		(XX)	XX	
18	Totals		XXX	XXX	

Sheet1 / Sheet2 / Sheet3 /

ILLUSTRATION 23-37
Format of Worksheet for Preparation of Statement of Cash Flows

The following guidelines are important in using a worksheet.

1 In the balance sheet accounts section, **list accounts with debit balances separately from those with credit balances**. This means, for example, that Accumulated Depreciation is listed under credit balances and not as a contra account under debit balances. Enter the beginning and ending balances of each account in the appropriate columns. Then, enter the transactions that caused the change in the account balance during the year as reconciling items in the two middle columns.

   After all reconciling items have been entered, each line pertaining to a balance sheet account should foot across. That is, the beginning balance plus or minus the reconciling item(s) must equal the ending balance. When this agreement exists for all balance sheet accounts, all changes in account balances have been reconciled.

2 The bottom portion of the worksheet consists of the operating, investing, and financing activities sections. Accordingly, it provides the information necessary to prepare the formal statement of cash flows. **Enter inflows of cash as debits in the reconciling columns, and outflows of cash as credits in the reconciling columns.** Thus, in this section, a company would enter the sale of equipment for cash at book value as a debit under inflows of cash from investing activities. Similarly, it would enter the purchase of land for cash as a credit under outflows of cash from investing activities.

3 **Do not enter in any journal or post to any account the reconciling items shown in the worksheet.** These items do not represent either adjustments or corrections of the balance sheet accounts. They are used only to facilitate the preparation of the statement of cash flows.

PREPARATION OF THE WORKSHEET

The preparation of a worksheet involves the following steps.

Step 1. Enter the balance sheet accounts and their beginning and ending balances in the balance sheet accounts section.

Step 2. Enter the data that explain the changes in the balance sheet accounts (other than cash) and their effects on the statement of cash flows in the reconciling columns of the worksheet.

Step 3. Enter the increase or decrease in cash on the cash line and at the bottom of the worksheet. This entry should enable the totals of the reconciling columns to be in agreement.

To illustrate the preparation and use of a worksheet and to illustrate the reporting of some of the special problems discussed in the prior section, we present a comprehensive example for Satellite Corporation. Again, the indirect method serves as the basis for the computation of net cash provided by operating activities. Illustrations 23-38 and 23-39 present the balance sheet, combined statement of income and retained earnings,

ILLUSTRATION 23-38
Comparative Balance Sheet, Satellite Corporation

SATELLITE CORPORATION
Comparative Balance Sheet–December 31, 2008 and 2007

	A	B	C	D
1		2008	2007	Increase or (Decrease)
2	Assets			
3	Cash	$ 59,000	$ 66,000	$ (7,000)
4	Accounts receivable (net)	104,000	51,000	53,000
5	Inventories	493,000	341,000	152,000
6	Prepaid expenses	16,500	17,000	(500)
7	Investments in stock of Porter Co. (equity method)	18,500	15,000	3,500
8	Land	131,500	82,000	49,500
9	Equipment	187,000	142,000	45,000
10	Accumulated depreciation—equipment	(29,000)	(31,000)	(2,000)
11	Buildings	262,000	262,000	—
12	Accumulated depreciation—buildings	(74,100)	(71,000)	3,100
13	Trademark	7,600	10,000	(2,400)
14	Total assets	$1,176,000	$884,000	
15	Liabilities			
16	Accounts payable	$ 132,000	$ 131,000	1,000
17	Accrued liabilities	43,000	39,000	4,000
18	Income tax payable	3,000	16,000	(13,000)
19	Notes payable (long-term)	60,000	—	60,000
20	Bonds payable	100,000	100,000	—
21	Premium on bonds payable	7,000	8,000	(1,000)
22	Deferred tax liability (long-term)	9,000	6,000	3,000
23	Total liabilities	354,000	300,000	
24	Stockholders' Equity			
25	Common stock ($1 par)	60,000	50,000	10,000
26	Additional paid-in capital	187,000	38,000	149,000
27	Retained earnings	592,000	496,000	96,000
28	Treasury stock	(17,000)	—	17,000
29	Total stockholders' equity	822,000	584,000	
30	Total liabilities and stockholders' equity	$1,176,000	$884,000	

Sheet1 / Sheet2 / Sheet3 /

SATELLITE CORPORATION
COMBINED STATEMENT OF INCOME AND RETAINED EARNINGS
FOR THE YEAR ENDED DECEMBER 31, 2008

Net sales		$526,500
Other revenue		3,500
Total revenues		530,000
Expense		
Cost of goods sold		310,000
Selling and administrative expenses		47,000
Other expenses and losses		12,000
Total expenses		369,000
Income before income tax and extraordinary item		161,000
Income tax		
Current	$47,000	
Deferred	3,000	50,000
Income before extraordinary item		111,000
Gain on condemnation of land (net of $2,000 tax)		6,000
Net income		117,000
Retained earnings, January 1		496,000
Less:		
Cash dividends	6,000	
Stock dividend	15,000	21,000
Retained earnings, December 31		$592,000
Per share:		
Income before extraordinary item		$2.02
Extraordinary item		.11
Net income		$2.13

Additional Information

(a) Other income of $3,500 represents Satellite's equity share in the net income of Porter Co., an equity investee. Satellite owns 22% of Porter Co.

(b) An analysis of the equipment account and related accumulated depreciation indicates the following:

	Equipment Dr./(Cr.)	Accum. Dep. Dr./(Cr.)	Gain or (Loss)
Balance at end of 2007	$142,000	$(31,000)	
Purchases of equipment	53,000		
Sale of equipment	(8,000)	2,500	$(1,500)
Depreciation for the period		(11,500)	
Major repair charged to accumulated depreciation		11,000	
Balance at end of 2008	$187,000	$(29,000)	

(c) Land in the amount of $60,000 was purchased through the issuance of a long-term note; in addition, certain parcels of land costing $10,500 were condemned. The state government paid Satellite $18,500, resulting in an $8,000 gain which has a $2,000 tax effect.

(d) The change in the accumulated depreciation—buildings, trademark, and premium on bonds payable accounts resulted from depreciation and amortization entries.

(e) An analysis of the paid-in capital accounts in stockholders' equity discloses the following:

	Common Stock	Additional Paid-In Capital
Balance at end of 2007	$50,000	$ 38,000
Issuance of 2% stock dividend	1,000	14,000
Sale of stock for cash	9,000	135,000
Balance at end of 2008	$60,000	$187,000

(f) Interest paid (net of amount capitalized) is $9,000; income taxes paid is $62,000.

and additional information for Satellite Corporation. The discussion that follows these financial statements provides additional explanations related to the preparation of the worksheet.

ANALYSIS OF TRANSACTIONS

The following discussion explains the individual adjustments that appear on the worksheet in Illustration 23-40 (page 1250). Because cash is the basis for the analysis, Satellite reconciles the cash account last. Because income is the first item that appears on the statement of cash flows, it is handled first.

Change in Retained Earnings

Net income for the period is $117,000. The entry for it on the worksheet is as follows.

(1)

Operating—Net Income	117,000	
Retained Earnings		117,000

Satellite reports net income on the bottom section of the worksheet. This **is the starting point for preparation of the statement of cash flows (under the indirect method)**.

A stock dividend and a cash dividend also affected retained earnings. The retained earnings statement reports a stock dividend of $15,000. The worksheet entry for this transaction is as follows.

(2)

Retained Earnings	15,000	
Common Stock		1,000
Additional Paid-in Capital		14,000

The issuance of stock dividends is not a cash operating, investing, or financing item. Therefore, **although the company enters this transaction on the worksheet for reconciling purposes, it does not report it in the statement of cash flows**.

The $6,000 cash dividend paid represents a financing activity cash outflow. Satellite makes the following worksheet entry:

(3)

Retained Earnings	6,000	
Financing—Cash Dividends		6,000

The company reconciles the beginning and ending balances of retained earnings by entry of the three items above.

Accounts Receivable (Net)

The increase in accounts receivable (net) of $53,000 represents adjustments that did not result in cash inflows during 2008. As a result, the company would deduct from net income the increase of $53,000. Satellite makes the following worksheet entry.

(4)

Accounts Receivable (net)	53,000	
Operating—Increase in Accounts Receivable (net)		53,000

Inventories

The increase in inventories of $152,000 represents an operating use of cash. The incremental investment in inventories during the year reduces cash without increasing the cost of goods sold. Satellite makes the following worksheet entry.

(5)

Inventories	152,000	
Operating—Increase in Inventories		152,000

Prepaid Expense

The decrease in prepaid expenses of $500 represents a charge in the income statement for which there was no cash outflow in the current period. Satellite should add that amount back to net income through the following entry.

(6)

Operating—Decrease in Prepaid Expenses	500	
Prepaid Expenses		500

Investment in Stock

Satellite's investment in the stock of Porter Co. increased $3,500. This amount reflects Satellite's share of net income earned by Porter (its equity investee) during the current year. Although Satellite's revenue, and therefore its net income increased $3,500 by recording Satellite's share of Porter Co.'s net income, no cash (dividend) was provided. Satellite makes the following worksheet entry.

(7)

Investment in Stock of Porter Co.	3,500	
Operating—Equity in Earnings of Porter Co.		3,500

Land

Satellite purchased land in the amount of $60,000 through the issuance of a long-term note payable. This transaction did not affect cash. It is a significant noncash investing/financing transaction that the company would disclose either in a separate schedule below the statement of cash flows or in the accompanying notes. Satellite makes the following entry to reconcile the worksheet.

(8)

Land	60,000	
Notes Payable		60,000

In addition to the noncash transaction involving the issuance of a note to purchase land, the Land account was decreased by the condemnation proceedings. The following worksheet entry records the receipt of $18,500 for land having a book value of $10,500.

(9)

Investing—Proceeds from Condemnation of Land	18,500	
Land		10,500
Operating—Gain on Condemnation of Land		8,000

In reconciling net income to net cash flow from operating activities, Satellite deducts from net income the extraordinary gain of $8,000. The reason is that the transaction that gave rise to the gain is an item whose cash effect is already classified as an investing cash inflow. The Land account is now reconciled.

Equipment and Accumulated Depreciation

An analysis of Equipment and Accumulated Depreciation shows that a number of transactions have affected these accounts. The company purchased equipment in the amount of $53,000 during the year. Satellite records this transaction on the worksheet as follows.

(10)

Equipment	53,000	
Investing—Purchase of Equipment		53,000

In addition, Satellite sold at a loss of $1,500 equipment with a book value of $5,500. It records this transaction as follows.

(11)

Investing—Sale of Equipment	4,000	
Operating—Loss on Sale of Equipment	1,500	
Accumulated Depreciation—Equipment	2,500	
Equipment		8,000

The proceeds from the sale of the equipment provided cash of $4,000. In addition, the loss on the sale of the equipment has reduced net income, but did not affect cash. Therefore, the company adds back to net income the amount of the loss, in order to accurately report cash provided by operating activities.

Satellite reported depreciation on the equipment at $11,500 and recorded it on the worksheet as follows.

(12)

Operating—Depreciation Expense—Equipment	11,500	
Accumulated Depreciation—Equipment		11,500

The company adds depreciation expense back to net income because that expense reduced income but did not affect cash.

Finally, the company made a major repair to the equipment. It charged this expenditure, in the amount of $11,000, to Accumulated Depreciation—Equipment. This expenditure required cash, and so Satellite makes the following worksheet entry.

(13)

Accumulated Depreciation—Equipment	11,000	
Investing—Major Repairs of Equipment		11,000

After adjusting for the foregoing items, Satellite has reconciled the balances in the Equipment and related Accumulated Depreciation accounts.

Building Depreciation and Amortization of Trademark

Depreciation expense on the buildings of $3,100 and amortization of trademark of $2,400 are both expenses in the income statement that reduced net income but did not require cash outflows in the current period. Satellite makes the following worksheet entry.

(14)

Operating—Depreciation Expense—Buildings	3,100	
Operating—Amortization of Trademark	2,400	
Accumulated Depreciation—Buildings		3,100
Trademark		2,400

Other Noncash Charges or Credits

Analysis of the remaining accounts indicates that changes in the Accounts Payable, Accrued Liabilities, Income Tax Payable, Premium on Bonds Payable, and Deferred Tax Liability balances resulted from charges or credits to net income that did not affect cash. The company should individually analyze each of these items and enter them in the worksheet. The following compound entry summarizes these noncash, income-related items.

(15)

Income Tax Payable	13,000	
Premium on Bonds Payable	1,000	
Operating—Increase in Accounts Payable	1,000	
Operating—Increase in Accrued Liabilities	4,000	
Operating—Increase in Deferred Tax Liability	3,000	
Operating—Decrease in Income Tax Payable		13,000
Operating—Amortization of Bond Premium		1,000
Accounts Payable		1,000
Accrued Liabilities		4,000
Deferred Tax Liability		3,000

Common Stock and Related Accounts

Comparison of the common stock balances and the additional paid-in capital balances shows that transactions during the year affected these accounts. First, Satellite issues a stock dividend of 2 percent to stockholders. As the discussion of worksheet entry (2) indicated, no cash was provided or used by the stock dividend transaction. In addition to the shares issued via the stock dividend, Satellite sold shares of common stock at $16 per share. The company records this transaction as follows.

(16)

Financing—Sale of Common Stock	144,000	
Common Stock		9,000
Additional Paid-in Capital		135,000

Also, the company purchased shares of its common stock in the amount of $17,000. It records this transaction on the worksheet as follows.

(17)

Treasury Stock	17,000	
Financing—Purchase of Treasury Stock		17,000

Final Reconciling Entry

The final entry to reconcile the change in cash and to balance the worksheet is shown below. The $7,000 amount is the difference between the beginning and ending cash balance.

(18)

Decrease in Cash	7,000	
Cash		7,000

Once the company has determined that the differences between the beginning and ending balances per the worksheet columns have been accounted for, it can total the reconciling transactions columns, and they should balance. Satellite can prepare the statement of cash flows entirely from the items and amounts that appear at the bottom of the worksheet under "Statement of Cash Flows Effects," as shown in Illustration 23-40 on page 1250.

ILLUSTRATION 23-40
Completed Worksheet for Preparation of Statement of Cash Flows, Satellite Corporation

SATELLITE CORPORATION
Worksheet for Preparation of Statement of Cash Flows For the Year Ended December 31, 2008

	A	B	C	D	E	F	G
1		Balance 12/31/07		Reconciling Items–2008 Debits		Credits	Balance 12/31/08
2	**Debits**						
3	Cash	$ 66,000			(18)	7,000	$ 59,000
4	Accounts receivable (net)	51,000	(4)	$ 53,000			104,000
5	Inventories	341,000	(5)	152,000			493,000
6	Prepaid expenses	17,000			(6)	500	16,500
7	Investment (equity method)	15,000	(7)	3,500			18,500
8	Land	82,000	(8)	60,000	(9)	10,500	131,500
9	Equipment	142,000	(10)	53,000	(11)	8,000	187,000
10	Building	262,000					262,000
11	Trademark	10,000			(14)	2,400	7,600
12	Treasury stock		(17)	17,000			17,000
13	Total debits	$986,000					$1,296,100
14	**Credits**						
15	Accum. depr.–equipment	$ 31,000	(11)	2,500	(12)	11,500	
16			(13)	11,000			$ 29,000
17	Accum. depr.–building	71,000			(14)	3,100	74,100
18	Accounts payable	131,000			(15)	1,000	132,000
19	Accrued liabilities	39,000			(15)	4,000	43,000
20	Income tax payable	16,000	(15)	13,000			3,000
21	Notes payable	-0-			(8)	60,000	60,000
22	Bonds payable	100,000					100,000
23	Premium on bonds payable	8,000	(15)	1,000			7,000
24	Deferred tax liability	6,000			(15)	3,000	9,000
25	Common stock	50,000			(2)	1,000	
26					(16)	9,000	60,000
27	Additional paid-in capital	38,000			(2)	14,000	
28					(16)	135,000	187,000
29	Retained earnings	496,000	(2)	15,000	(1)	117,000	
30			(3)	6,000			592,000
31	Total credits	$986,000					$1,296,100
32	**Statement of Cash Flows Effects**						
33	**Operating activities**						
34	Net income		(1)	117,000			
35	Increase in accounts receivable (net)				(4)	53,000	
36	Increase in inventories				(5)	152,000	
37	Decrease in prepaid expenses		(6)	500			
38	Equity in earnings of Porter Co.				(7)	3,500	
39	Gain on condemnation of land				(9)	8,000	
40	Loss on sale of equipment		(11)	1,500			
41	Depr. expense–equipment		(12)	11,500			
42	Depr. expense–building		(14)	3,100			
43	Amortization of trademark		(14)	2,400			
44	Increase in accounts payable		(15)	1,000			
45	Increase in accrued liabilities		(15)	4,000			
46	Increase in deferred tax liability		(15)	3,000			
47	Decrease in income tax payable				(15)	13,000	
48	Amortization of bond premium				(15)	1,000	
49	**Investing activities**						
50	Proceeds from condemnation of land		(9)	18,500			
51	Purchase of equipment				(10)	53,000	
52	Sale of equipment		(11)	4,000			
53	Major repairs of equipment				(13)	11,000	
54	**Financing activities**						
55	Payment of cash dividend				(3)	6,000	
56	Issuance of common stock		(16)	144,000			
57	Purchase of treasury stock				(17)	17,000	
58	Totals			697,500		704,500	
59	Decrease in cash		(18)	7,000			
60	Totals			$704,500		$704,500	

Sheet1 / Sheet2 / Sheet3 /

PREPARATION OF FINAL STATEMENT

Illustration 23-41 presents a formal statement of cash flows prepared from the data compiled in the lower portion of the worksheet.

SATELLITE CORPORATION
STATEMENT OF CASH FLOWS
FOR THE YEAR ENDED DECEMBER 31, 2008
INCREASE (DECREASE) IN CASH

Cash flows from operating activities		
Net income		$117,000
Adjustments to reconcile net income to net cash used by operating activities:		
Depreciation expense	$ 14,600	
Amortization of trademark	2,400	
Amortization of bond premium	(1,000)	
Equity in earnings of Porter Co.	(3,500)	
Gain on condemnation of land	(8,000)	
Loss on sale of equipment	1,500	
Increase in deferred tax liability	3,000	
Increase in accounts receivable (net)	(53,000)	
Increase in inventories	(152,000)	
Decrease in prepaid expenses	500	
Increase in accounts payable	1,000	
Increase in accrued liabilities	4,000	
Decrease in income tax payable	(13,000)	(203,500)
Net cash used by operating activities		(86,500)
Cash flows from investing activities		
Proceeds from condemnation of land	18,500	
Purchase of equipment	(53,000)	
Sale of equipment	4,000	
Major repairs of equipment	(11,000)	
Net cash used by investing activities		(41,500)
Cash flows from financing activities		
Payment of cash dividend	(6,000)	
Issuance of common stock	144,000	
Purchase of treasury stock	(17,000)	
Net cash provided by financing activities		121,000
Net decrease in cash		(7,000)
Cash, January 1, 2008		66,000
Cash, December 31, 2008		$ 59,000

Supplemental Disclosures of Cash Flow Information:
Cash paid during the year for:

Interest (net of amount capitalized)	$ 9,000
Income taxes	$ 62,000

Supplemental Schedule of Noncash Investing and Financing Activities:
Purchase of land for $60,000 in exchange for a $60,000 long-term note.

ILLUSTRATION 23-41
Statement of Cash Flows,
Satellite Corporation

Discussion of the T-Account Approach to Preparation of the Statement of Cash Flows

SUMMARY OF LEARNING OBJECTIVES

1. Describe the purpose of the statement of cash flows. The primary purpose of the statement of cash flows is to provide information about cash receipts and cash payments of an entity during a period. A secondary objective is to report the entity's operating, investing, and financing activities during the period.

KEY TERMS

cash equivalents, *1213(n)*
direct method, *1218*
financing activities, *1214*
indirect method, *1219*
investing activities, *1214*

2. **Identify the major classifications of cash flows.** Companies classify cash flows as: (1) *Operating activities*—transactions that result in the revenues, expenses, gains, and losses that determine net income. (2) *Investing activities*—lending money and collecting on those loans, and acquiring and disposing of investments, plant assets, and intangible assets. (3) *Financing activities*—obtaining cash from creditors and repaying loans, issuing and reacquiring capital stock, and paying cash dividends.

3. **Differentiate between net income and net cash flows from operating activities.** Companies must adjust net income on an accrual basis to determine net cash flow from operating activities because some expenses and losses do not cause cash outflows, and some revenues and gains do not provide cash inflows.

4. **Contrast the direct and indirect methods of calculating net cash flow from operating activities.** Under the direct approach, companies calculate the major classes of operating cash receipts and cash disbursements. Companies summarize the computations in a schedule of changes from the accrual to the cash basis income statement. Presentation of the direct approach of reporting net cash flow from operating activities takes the form of a condensed cash-basis income statement. The indirect method adds back to net income the noncash expenses and losses and subtracts the noncash revenues and gains.

5. **Determine net cash flows from investing and financing activities.** Once a company has computed the net cash flow from operating activities, the next step is to determine whether any other changes in balance sheet accounts caused an increase or decrease in cash. Net cash flows from investing and financing activities can be determined by examining the changes in noncurrent balance sheet accounts.

6. **Prepare a statement of cash flows.** Preparing the statement involves three major steps: (1) *Determine the change in cash.* This is the difference between the beginning and the ending cash balance shown on the comparative balance sheets. (2) *Determine the net cash flow from operating activities.* This procedure is complex; it involves analyzing not only the current year's income statement but also the comparative balance sheets and the selected transaction data. (3) *Determine cash flows from investing and financing activities.* Analyze all other changes in the balance sheet accounts to determine the effects on cash.

7. **Identify sources of information for a statement of cash flows.** The information to prepare the statement usually comes from three sources: (1) *Comparative balance sheets.* Information in these statements indicates the amount of the changes in assets, liabilities, and equities during the period. (2) *Current income statement.* Information in this statement is used in determining the cash provided by operations during the period. (3) *Selected transaction data.* These data from the general ledger provide additional detailed information needed to determine how cash was provided or used during the period.

8. **Discuss special problems in preparing a statement of cash flows.** These special problems are: (1) adjustments similar to depreciation; (2) accounts receivable (net); (3) other working capital changes; (4) net losses; (5) gains; (6) stock options; (7) postretirement benefit costs; (8) extraordinary items; and (9) significant noncash transactions.

9. **Explain the use of a worksheet in preparing a statement of cash flows.** When numerous adjustments are necessary, or other complicating factors are present, companies often use a worksheet to assemble and classify the data that will appear on the statement of cash flows. The worksheet is merely a device that aids in the preparation of the statement. Its use is optional.

QUESTIONS

1. What is the purpose of the statement of cash flows? What information does it provide?

2. Of what use is the statement of cash flows?

3. Differentiate between investing activities, financing activities, and operating activities.

4. What are the major sources of cash (inflows) in a statement of cash flows? What are the major uses (outflows) of cash?

5. Identify and explain the major steps involved in preparing the statement of cash flows.

6. Identify the following items as (1) operating, (2) investing, or (3) financing activities: purchase of land; payment of dividends; cash sales; and purchase of treasury stock.

7. Unlike the other major financial statements, the statement of cash flows is not prepared from the adjusted trial balance. From what sources does the information to prepare this statement come, and what information does each source provide?

8. Why is it necessary to convert accrual-based net income to a cash basis when preparing a statement of cash flows?

9. Differentiate between the direct method and the indirect method by discussing each method.

10. Bonnie Raitt Company reported net income of $3.5 million in 2008. Depreciation for the year was $520,000; accounts receivable increased $500,000; and accounts payable increased $350,000. Compute net cash flow from operating activities using the indirect method.

11. Sophie B. Hawkins Co. reported sales on an accrual basis of $100,000. If accounts receivable increased $30,000, and the allowance for doubtful accounts increased $9,000 after a writeoff of $4,000, compute cash sales.

12. Your roommate is puzzled. During the last year, the company in which she is a stockholder reported a net loss of $675,000, yet its cash increased $321,000 during the same period of time. Explain to your roommate how this situation could occur.

13. The board of directors of Kenny G Corp. declared cash dividends of $260,000 during the current year. If dividends payable was $85,000 at the beginning of the year and $70,000 at the end of the year, how much cash was paid in dividends during the year?

14. Explain how the amount of cash payments to suppliers is computed under the direct method.

15. The net income for Silverchair Company for 2008 was $320,000. During 2008, depreciation on plant assets was $114,000, amortization of patent was $40,000, and the company incurred a loss on sale of plant assets of $21,000. Compute net cash flow from operating activities.

16. Each of the following items must be considered in preparing a statement of cash flows for Frogstomp Inc.

for the year ended December 31, 2008. State where each item is to be shown in the statement, if at all.

(a) Plant assets that had cost $20,000 6½ years before and were being depreciated on a straight-line basis over 10 years with no estimated scrap value were sold for $4,000.

(b) During the year, 10,000 shares of common stock with a stated value of $20 a share were issued for $41 a share.

(c) Uncollectible accounts receivable in the amount of $22,000 were written off against the Allowance for Doubtful Accounts.

(d) The company sustained a net loss for the year of $50,000. Depreciation amounted to $22,000, and a gain of $9,000 was realized on the sale of available-for-sale securities for $38,000 cash.

17. Classify the following items as (1) operating, (2) investing, (3) financing, or (4) significant noncash investing and financing activities, using the direct method.

(a) Purchase of equipment.

(b) Redemption of bonds payable.

(c) Sale of building.

(d) Cash payments to suppliers.

(e) Exchange of equipment for furniture.

(f) Issuance of preferred stock.

(g) Cash received from customers.

(h) Purchase of treasury stock.

(i) Issuance of bonds for land.

(j) Payment of dividends.

(k) Cash payments to employees.

(l) Cash payments for operating expenses.

18. Clay Walker and David Ball were discussing the presentation format of the statement of cash flows of McBride Co. At the bottom of McBride's statement of cash flows was a separate section entitled "Noncash investing and financing activities." Give three examples of significant noncash transactions that would be reported in this section.

19. During 2008, Adams Company redeemed $2,000,000 of bonds payable for $1,780,000 cash. Indicate how this transaction would be reported on a statement of cash flows, if at all.

20. What are some of the arguments in favor of using the indirect (reconciliation) method as opposed to the direct method for reporting a statement of cash flows?

21. Why is it desirable to use a worksheet when preparing a statement of cash flows? Is a worksheet required to prepare a statement of cash flows?

BRIEF EXERCISES

(LO 5) **BE23-1** American Gladhanders Corporation had the following activities in 2008.

1. Sale of land $130,000
2. Purchase of inventory $845,000
3. Purchase of treasury stock $72,000
4. Purchase of equipment $415,000
5. Issuance of common stock $320,000
6. Purchase of available-for-sale securities $59,000

Compute the amount American Gladhanders should report as net cash provided (used) by investing activities in its statement of cash flows.

(LO 5) **BE23-2** Chrono Trigger Corporation had the following activities in 2008.

1. Payment of accounts payable $770,000
2. Issuance of common stock $250,000
3. Payment of dividends $300,000
4. Collection of note receivable $100,000
5. Issuance of bonds payable $510,000
6. Purchase of treasury stock $46,000

Compute the amount Chrono Trigger should report as net cash provided (used) by financing activities in its 2008 statement of cash flows.

(LO 2) **BE23-3** Ryker Corporation is preparing its 2008 statement of cash flows, using the indirect method. Presented below is a list of items that may affect the statement. Using the code below, indicate how each item will affect Ryker's 2008 statement of cash flows.

Code Letter	Effect
A	Added to net income in the operating section
D	Deducted from net income in the operating section
R-I	Cash receipt in investing section
P-I	Cash payment in investing section
R-F	Cash receipt in financing section
P-F	Cash payment in financing section
N	Noncash investing and/or financing activity

Items

____ **(a)** Increase in accounts receivable.
____ **(b)** Decrease in accounts receivable.
____ **(c)** Issuance of stock.
____ **(d)** Depreciation expense.
____ **(e)** Sale of land at book value.
____ **(f)** Sale of land at a gain.
____ **(g)** Payment of dividends.
____ **(h)** Purchase of land and building.
____ **(i)** Purchase of available-for-sale investment.
____ **(j)** Increase in accounts payable.
____ **(k)** Decrease in accounts payable.
____ **(l)** Loan from bank by signing note.
____ **(m)** Purchase of equipment using a note.
____ **(n)** Increase in inventory.
____ **(o)** Issuance of bonds.
____ **(p)** Retirement of bonds payable.
____ **(q)** Sale of equipment at a loss.
____ **(r)** Purchase of treasury stock.

(LO 3, 4) **BE23-4** Azure Corporation had the following 2008 income statement.

Sales	$200,000
Cost of goods sold	120,000
Gross profit	80,000
Operating expenses (includes depreciation of $21,000)	50,000
Net income	$ 30,000

The following accounts increased during 2008: accounts receivable $17,000; inventory $11,000; accounts payable $13,000. Prepare the cash flows from operating activities section of Azure's 2008 statement of cash flows using the direct method.

(LO 3, 4) **BE23-5** Use the information from BE23-4 for Azure Corporation. Prepare the cash flows from operating activities section of Azure's 2008 statement of cash flows using the indirect method.

(LO 4) **BE23-6** At January 1, 2008, Cyberslider Inc. had accounts receivable of $72,000. At December 31, 2008, accounts receivable is $59,000. Sales for 2008 is $420,000. Compute Cyberslider's 2008 cash receipts from customers.

(LO 4)   **BE23-7**   Cage Corporation had January 1 and December 31 balances as follows.

	1/1/08	12/31/08
Inventory	$90,000	$113,000
Accounts payable	61,000	69,000

For 2008, cost of goods sold was $500,000. Compute Cage's 2008 cash payments to suppliers.

(LO 6)   **BE23-8**   In 2008, Fieval Corporation had net cash provided by operating activities of $531,000; net cash used by investing activities of $963,000; and net cash provided by financing activities of $585,000. At January 1, 2008, the cash balance was $333,000. Compute December 31, 2008, cash.

(LO 3, 4)   **BE23-9**   Tool Time Corporation had the following 2008 income statement.

Revenues	$100,000
Expenses	60,000
	$ 40,000

In 2008, Tool Time had the following activity in selected accounts.

Accounts Receivable					**Allowance for Doubtful Accounts**		
1/1/08	20,000					1,200	1/1/08
Revenues	100,000	1,000	Writeoffs	Writeoffs	1,000	1,540	Bad debt expense
		90,000	Collections				
12/31/08	29,000					1,740	12/31/08

Prepare Tool Time's cash flows from operating activities section of the statement of cash flows using (a) the direct method and (b) the indirect method.

(LO 3)   **BE23-10**   Red October Corporation reported net income of $50,000 in 2008. Depreciation expense was $17,000. The following working capital accounts changed.

Accounts receivable	$11,000 increase
Available-for-sale securities	16,000 increase
Inventory	7,400 increase
Nontrade note payable	15,000 decrease
Accounts payable	9,300 increase

Compute net cash provided by operating activities.

(LO 3)   **BE23-11**   In 2008, Izzy Corporation reported a net loss of $70,000. Izzy's only net income adjustments were depreciation expense $84,000, and increase in accounts receivable $8,100. Compute Izzy's net cash provided (used) by operating activities.

(LO 8)   **BE23-12**   In 2008, Mufosta Inc. issued 1,000 shares of $10 par value common stock for land worth $50,000.

  (a)   Prepare Mufosta's journal entry to record the transaction.
  (b)   Indicate the effect the transaction has on cash.
  (c)   Indicate how the transaction is reported on the statement of cash flows.

(LO 9)   **BE23-13**   Indicate in general journal form how the items below would be entered in a worksheet for the preparation of the statement of cash flows.

  (a)   Net income is $317,000.
  (b)   Cash dividends declared and paid totaled $120,000.
  (c)   Equipment was purchased for $114,000.
  (d)   Equipment that originally cost $40,000 and had accumulated depreciation of $32,000 was sold for $13,000.

EXERCISES

(LO 2)   **E23-1**   **(Classification of Transactions)**   Red Hot Chili Peppers Co. had the following activity in its most recent year of operations.

  (a)   Purchase of equipment.   **(c)**   Sale of building.
  (b)   Redemption of bonds payable.   **(d)**   Depreciation.

(e) Exchange of equipment for furniture.   (i) Issuance of bonds for land.
(f) Issuance of capital stock.   (j) Payment of dividends.
(g) Amortization of intangible assets.   (k) Increase in interest receivable on notes receivable.
(h) Purchase of treasury stock.   (l) Pension expense exceeds amount funded.

Instructions
Classify the items as (1) operating—add to net income; (2) operating—deduct from net income; (3) investing; (4) financing; or (5) significant noncash investing and financing activities. Use the indirect method.

(LO 2, 3)   **E23-2** (**Statement Presentation of Transactions—Indirect Method**)   Each of the following items must be considered in preparing a statement of cash flows (indirect method) for Turbulent Indigo Inc. for the year ended December 31, 2007.

(a) Plant assets that had cost $20,000 6 years before and were being depreciated on a straight-line basis over 10 years with no estimated scrap value were sold for $5,300.
(b) During the year, 10,000 shares of common stock with a stated value of $10 a share were issued for $43 a share.
(c) Uncollectible accounts receivable in the amount of $27,000 were written off against the Allowance for Doubtful Accounts.
(d) The company sustained a net loss for the year of $50,000. Depreciation amounted to $22,000, and a gain of $9,000 was realized on the sale of land for $39,000 cash.
(e) A 3-month U.S. Treasury bill was purchased for $100,000. The company uses a cash and cash-equivalent basis for its cash flow statement.
(f) Patent amortization for the year was $20,000.
(g) The company exchanged common stock for a 70% interest in Tabasco Co. for $900,000.
(h) During the year, treasury stock costing $47,000 was purchased.

Instructions
State where each item is to be shown in the statement of cash flows, if at all.

(LO 3, 4)   **E23-3** (**Preparation of Operating Activities Section—Indirect Method, Periodic Inventory**)   The income statement of Vince Gill Company is shown below.

VINCE GILL COMPANY
INCOME STATEMENT
FOR THE YEAR ENDED DECEMBER 31, 2008

Sales		$6,900,000
Cost of goods sold		
Beginning inventory	$1,900,000	
Purchases	4,400,000	
Goods available for sale	6,300,000	
Ending inventory	1,600,000	
Cost of goods sold		4,700,000
Gross profit		2,200,000
Operating expenses		
Selling expenses	450,000	
Administrative expenses	700,000	1,150,000
Net income		$1,050,000

Additional information:

1. Accounts receivable decreased $360,000 during the year.
2. Prepaid expenses increased $170,000 during the year.
3. Accounts payable to suppliers of merchandise decreased $275,000 during the year.
4. Accrued expenses payable decreased $100,000 during the year.
5. Administrative expenses include depreciation expense of $60,000.

Instructions
(LO 3, 4)   Prepare the operating activities section of the statement of cash flows for the year ended December 31, 2008, for Vince Gill Company, using the indirect method.

E23-4 (**Preparation of Operating Activities Section—Direct Method**)   Data for the Vince Gill Company are presented in E23-3.

Instructions
Prepare the operating activities section of the statement of cash flows using the direct method.

(LO 3, 4) **E23-5** **(Preparation of Operating Activities Section—Direct Method)** Krauss Company's income statement for the year ended December 31, 2007, contained the following condensed information.

Revenue from fees		$840,000
Operating expenses (excluding depreciation)	$624,000	
Depreciation expense	60,000	
Loss on sale of equipment	26,000	710,000
Income before income taxes		130,000
Income tax expense		40,000
Net income		$ 90,000

Krauss's balance sheet contained the following comparative data at December 31.

	2007	2006
Accounts receivable	$37,000	$54,000
Accounts payable	41,000	31,000
Income taxes payable	4,000	8,500

(Accounts payable pertains to operating expenses.)

Instructions
Prepare the operating activities section of the statement of cash flows using the direct method.

(LO 3, 4) **E23-6** **(Preparation of Operating Activities Section—Indirect Method)** Data for Krauss Company are presented in E23-5.

Instructions
Prepare the operating activities section of the statement of cash flows using the indirect method.

(LO 3, 4) **E23-7** **(Computation of Operating Activities—Direct Method)** Presented below are two independent situations.

Situation A:
Annie Lennox Co. reports revenues of $200,000 and operating expenses of $110,000 in its first year of operations, 2008. Accounts receivable and accounts payable at year-end were $71,000 and $29,000, respectively. Assume that the accounts payable related to operating expenses. Ignore income taxes.

Instructions
Using the direct method, compute net cash provided by operating activities.

Situation B:
The income statement for Blues Traveler Company shows cost of goods sold $310,000 and operating expenses (exclusive of depreciation) $230,000. The comparative balance sheet for the year shows that inventory increased $26,000, prepaid expenses decreased $8,000, accounts payable (related to merchandise) decreased $17,000, and accrued expenses payable increased $11,000.

Instructions
Compute (a) cash payments to suppliers and (b) cash payments for operating expenses.

(LO 3, 4) **E23-8** **(Schedule of Net Cash Flow from Operating Activities—Indirect Method)** Ballard Co. reported $145,000 of net income for 2008. The accountant, in preparing the statement of cash flows, noted several items occurring during 2008 that might affect cash flows from operating activities. These items are listed below and on page 1258.

1. Ballard purchased 100 shares of treasury stock at a cost of $20 per share. These shares were then resold at $25 per share.
2. Ballard sold 100 shares of IBM common at $200 per share. The acquisition cost of these shares was $145 per share. This investment was shown on Ballard's December 31, 2007, balance sheet as an available-for-sale security.
3. Ballard revised its estimate for bad debts. Before 2008, Ballard's bad debt expense was 1% of its net sales. In 2008, this percentage was increased to 2%. Net sales for 2008 were $500,000, and net accounts receivable decreased by $12,000 during 2008.
4. Ballard issued 500 shares of its $10 par common stock for a patent. The market value of the shares on the date of the transaction was $23 per share.
5. Depreciation expense is $39,000.
6. Ballard Co. holds 40% of the Nirvana Company's common stock as a long-term investment. Nirvana Company reported $27,000 of net income for 2008.

7. Nirvana Company paid a total of $2,000 of cash dividends to all investees in 2008.
8. Ballard declared a 10% stock dividend. One thousand shares of $10 par common stock were distributed. The market price at date of issuance was $20 per share.

Instructions
Prepare a schedule that shows the net cash flow from operating activities using the indirect method. Assume no items other than those listed above affected the computation of 2008 net cash flow from operating activities.

(LO 6) **E23-9** **(SCF—Direct Method)** Los Lobos Corp. uses the direct method to prepare its statement of cash flows. Los Lobos's trial balances at December 31, 2007 and 2006, are as follows.

	December 31	
	2007	2006
Debits		
Cash	$ 35,000	$ 32,000
Accounts receivable	33,000	30,000
Inventory	31,000	47,000
Property, plant, & equipment	100,000	95,000
Unamortized bond discount	4,500	5,000
Cost of goods sold	250,000	380,000
Selling expenses	141,500	172,000
General and administrative expenses	137,000	151,300
Interest expense	4,300	2,600
Income tax expense	20,400	61,200
	$756,700	$976,100
Credits		
Allowance for doubtful accounts	$ 1,300	$ 1,100
Accumulated depreciation	16,500	15,000
Trade accounts payable	25,000	15,500
Income taxes payable	21,000	29,100
Deferred income taxes	5,300	4,600
8% callable bonds payable	45,000	20,000
Common stock	50,000	40,000
Additional paid-in capital	9,100	7,500
Retained earnings	44,700	64,600
Sales	538,800	778,700
	$756,700	$976,100

Additional information:

1. Los Lobos purchased $5,000 in equipment during 2007.
2. Los Lobos allocated one-third of its depreciation expense to selling expenses and the remainder to general and administrative expenses.
3. Bad debt expense for 2007 was $5,000, and writeoffs of uncollectible accounts totaled $4,800.

Instructions
Determine what amounts Los Lobos should report in its statement of cash flows for the year ended December 31, 2007, for the following items.

1. Cash collected from customers.   4. Cash paid for income taxes.
2. Cash paid to suppliers.   5. Cash paid for selling expenses.
3. Cash paid for interest.

(LO 2, 8) **E23-10** **(Classification of Transactions)** Following are selected balance sheet accounts of Allman Bros. Corp. at December 31, 2008 and 2007, and the increases or decreases in each account from 2007 to 2008. Also presented is selected income statement information for the year ended December 31, 2008, and additional information.

Selected balance sheet accounts	2008	2007	Increase (Decrease)
Assets			
Accounts receivable	$ 34,000	$ 24,000	$ 10,000
Property, plant, and equipment	277,000	247,000	30,000
Accumulated depreciation	(178,000)	(167,000)	(11,000)

	2008	2007	Increase
Liabilities and stockholders' equity			
Bonds payable	$ 49,000	$46,000	$ 3,000
Dividends payable	8,000	5,000	3,000
Common stock, $1 par	22,000	19,000	3,000
Additional paid-in capital	9,000	3,000	6,000
Retained earnings	104,000	91,000	13,000

Selected income statement information for the year ended December 31, 2008

Sales revenue	$155,000
Depreciation	33,000
Gain on sale of equipment	14,500
Net income	31,000

Additional information:

1. During 2008, equipment costing $45,000 was sold for cash.
2. Accounts receivable relate to sales of merchandise.
3. During 2008, $20,000 of bonds payable were issued in exchange for property, plant, and equipment. There was no amortization of bond discount or premium.

Instructions

Determine the category (operating, investing, or financing) and the amount that should be reported in the statement of cash flows for the following items.

1. Payments for purchase of property, plant, and equipment.
2. Proceeds from the sale of equipment.
3. Cash dividends paid.
4. Redemption of bonds payable.

(LO 6) **E23-11** **(SCF—Indirect Method)** Condensed financial data of Pat Metheny Company for 2008 and 2007 are presented below.

PAT METHENY COMPANY
COMPARATIVE BALANCE SHEET
AS OF DECEMBER 31, 2008 AND 2007

	2008	2007
Cash	$1,800	$1,150
Receivables	1,750	1,300
Inventory	1,600	1,900
Plant assets	1,900	1,700
Accumulated depreciation	(1,200)	(1,170)
Long-term investments (Held-to-maturity)	1,300	1,420
	$7,150	$6,300
Accounts payable	$1,200	$ 900
Accrued liabilities	200	250
Bonds payable	1,400	1,550
Capital stock	1,900	1,700
Retained earnings	2,450	1,900
	$7,150	$6,300

PAT METHENY COMPANY
INCOME STATEMENT
FOR THE YEAR ENDED DECEMBER 31, 2008

Sales	$6,900
Cost of goods sold	4,700
Gross margin	2,200
Selling and administrative expense	930
Income from operations	1,270
Other revenues and gains	
Gain on sale of investments	80
Income before tax	1,350
Income tax expense	540
Net income	810
Cash dividends	260
Income retained in business	$ 550

Additional information:

During the year, $70 of common stock was issued in exchange for plant assets. No plant assets were sold in 2008.

Instructions

Prepare a statement of cash flows using the indirect method.

(LO 6) **E23-12** **(SCF—Direct Method)** Data for Pat Metheny Company are presented in E23-11.

Instructions

Prepare a statement of cash flows using the direct method. (Do not prepare a reconciliation schedule.)

(LO 6) **E23-13** **(SCF—Direct Method)** Brecker Inc., a greeting card company, had the following statements prepared as of December 31, 2008.

BRECKER INC.
COMPARATIVE BALANCE SHEET
AS OF DECEMBER 31, 2008 AND 2007

	12/31/08	12/31/07
Cash	$ 6,000	$ 7,000
Accounts receivable	62,000	51,000
Short-term investments (Available-for-sale)	35,000	18,000
Inventories	40,000	60,000
Prepaid rent	5,000	4,000
Printing equipment	154,000	130,000
Accumulated depr.—equipment	(35,000)	(25,000)
Copyrights	46,000	50,000
Total assets	$313,000	$295,000
Accounts payable	$ 46,000	$ 40,000
Income taxes payable	4,000	6,000
Wages payable	8,000	4,000
Short-term loans payable	8,000	10,000
Long-term loans payable	60,000	69,000
Common stock, $10 par	100,000	100,000
Contributed capital, common stock	30,000	30,000
Retained earnings	57,000	36,000
Total liabilities & stockholders' equity	$313,000	$295,000

BRECKER INC.
INCOME STATEMENT
FOR THE YEAR ENDING DECEMBER 31, 2008

Sales		$338,150
Cost of goods sold		175,000
Gross margin		163,150
Operating expenses		120,000
Operating income		43,150
Interest expense	$11,400	
Gain on sale of equipment	2,000	9,400
Income before tax		33,750
Income tax expense		6,750
Net income		$ 27,000

Additional information:

1. Dividends in the amount of $6,000 were declared and paid during 2008.
2. Depreciation expense and amortization expense are included in operating expenses.
3. No unrealized gains or losses have occurred on the investments during the year.
4. Equipment that had a cost of $20,000 and was 70% depreciated was sold during 2008.

Instructions

Prepare a statement of cash flows using the direct method. (Do not prepare a reconciliation schedule.)

(LO 6) **E23-14** **(SCF—Indirect Method)** Data for Brecker Inc. are presented in E23-13.

Instructions

Prepare a statement of cash flows using the indirect method.

(LO 6)   **E23-15   (SCF—Indirect Method)**   Presented below are data taken from the records of Antonio Brasileiro Company.

	December 31, 2008	December 31, 2007
Cash	$ 15,000	$ 8,000
Current assets other than cash	85,000	60,000
Long-term investments	10,000	53,000
Plant assets	335,000	215,000
	$445,000	$336,000
Accumulated depreciation	$ 20,000	$ 40,000
Current liabilities	40,000	22,000
Bonds payable	75,000	–0–
Capital stock	254,000	254,000
Retained earnings	56,000	20,000
	$445,000	$336,000

Additional information:

1. Held-to-maturity securities carried at a cost of $43,000 on December 31, 2007, were sold in 2008 for $34,000. The loss (not extraordinary) was incorrectly charged directly to Retained Earnings.
2. Plant assets that cost $50,000 and were 80% depreciated were sold during 2008 for $8,000. The loss (not extraordinary) was incorrectly charged directly to Retained Earnings.
3. Net income as reported on the income statement for the year was $57,000.
4. Dividends paid amounted to $10,000.
5. Depreciation charged for the year was $20,000.

Instructions

Prepare a statement of cash flows for the year 2008 using the indirect method.

(LO 2, 3, 5)   **E23-16   (Cash Provided by Operating, Investing, and Financing Activities)**   The balance sheet data of Brown Company at the end of 2007 and 2006 follow.

	2007	2006
Cash	$ 30,000	$ 35,000
Accounts receivable (net)	55,000	45,000
Merchandise inventory	65,000	45,000
Prepaid expenses	15,000	25,000
Equipment	90,000	75,000
Accumulated depreciation—equipment	(18,000)	(8,000)
Land	70,000	40,000
	$307,000	$257,000
Accounts payable	$ 65,000	$ 52,000
Accrued expenses	15,000	18,000
Notes payable—bank, long-term	–0–	23,000
Bonds payable	30,000	–0–
Common stock, $10 par	189,000	159,000
Retained earnings	8,000	5,000
	$307,000	$257,000

Land was acquired for $30,000 in exchange for common stock, par $30,000, during the year; all equipment purchased was for cash. Equipment costing $10,000 was sold for $3,000; book value of the equipment was $6,000. Cash dividends of $10,000 were declared and paid during the year.

Instructions

Compute net cash provided (used) by:

(a) operating activities.
(b) investing activities.
(c) financing activities.

(LO 6) **E23-17** **(SCF—Indirect Method and Balance Sheet)** Jobim Inc., had the following condensed balance sheet at the end of operations for 2007.

JOBIM INC.				
BALANCE SHEET				
DECEMBER 31, 2007				
Cash	$ 8,500	Current liabilities	$ 15,000	
Current assets other than cash	29,000	Long-term notes payable	25,500	
Investments	20,000	Bonds payable	25,000	
Plant assets (net)	67,500	Capital stock	75,000	
Land	40,000	Retained earnings	24,500	
	$165,000		$165,000	

During 2008 the following occurred.

1. A tract of land was purchased for $9,000.
2. Bonds payable in the amount of $15,000 were retired at par.
3. An additional $10,000 in capital stock was issued at par.
4. Dividends totaling $9,375 were paid to stockholders.
5. Net income was $35,250 after allowing depreciation of $13,500.
6. Land was purchased through the issuance of $22,500 in bonds.
7. Jobim Inc. sold part of its investment portfolio for $12,875. This transaction resulted in a gain of $2,000 for the company. The company classifies the investments as available-for-sale.
8. Both current assets (other than cash) and current liabilities remained at the same amount.

Instructions
(a) Prepare a statement of cash flows for 2008 using the indirect method.
(b) Prepare the condensed balance sheet for Jobim Inc. as it would appear at December 31, 2008.

(LO 6, 8) **E23-18** **(Partial SCF—Indirect Method)** The accounts below appear in the ledger of Anita Baker Company.

Retained Earnings		Dr.	Cr.	Bal.
Jan. 1, 2008	Credit Balance			$ 42,000
Aug. 15	Dividends (cash)	$15,000		27,000
Dec. 31	Net Income for 2008		$40,000	67,000

Machinery		Dr.	Cr.	Bal.
Jan. 1, 2008	Debit Balance			$140,000
Aug. 3	Purchase of Machinery	$62,000		202,000
Sept. 10	Cost of Machinery Constructed	48,000		250,000
Nov. 15	Machinery Sold		$56,000	194,000

Accumulated Depreciation—Machinery		Dr.	Cr.	Bal.
Jan. 1, 2008	Credit Balance			$ 84,000
Apr. 8	Extraordinary Repairs	$21,000		63,000
Nov. 15	Accum. Depreciation on Machinery Sold	25,200		37,800
Dec. 31	Depreciation for 2008		$16,800	54,600

Instructions
From the postings in the accounts above, indicate how the information is reported on a statement of cash flows by preparing a partial statement of cash flows using the indirect method. The loss on sale of equipment (November 15) was $5,800.

(LO 9) **E23-19** **(Worksheet Analysis of Selected Accounts)** Data for Anita Baker Company are presented in E23-18.

Instructions
Prepare entries in journal form for all adjustments that should be made on a worksheet for a statement of cash flows.

(LO 9) **E23-20** **(Worksheet Analysis of Selected Transactions)** The transactions below took place during the year 2008.

1. Convertible bonds payable with a par value of $300,000 were exchanged for unissued common stock with a par value of $300,000. The market price of both types of securities was par.
2. The net income for the year was $410,000.
3. Depreciation expense for the building was $90,000.
4. Some old office equipment was traded in on the purchase of some dissimilar office equipment and the following entry was made.

Office Equipment	50,000	
Accum. Depreciation—Office Equipment	30,000	
Office Equipment		40,000
Cash		34,000
Gain on Disposal of Plant Assets		6,000

The Gain on Disposal of Plant Assets was credited to current operations as ordinary income.
5. Dividends in the amount of $123,000 were declared. They are payable in January of next year.

Instructions
Show by journal entries the adjustments that would be made on a worksheet for a statement of cash flows.

(LO 9) **E23-21** **(Worksheet Preparation)** Below is the comparative balance sheet for Stevie Wonder Corporation.

	Dec. 31, 2008	Dec. 31, 2007
Cash	$ 16,500	$ 21,000
Short-term investments	25,000	19,000
Accounts receivable	43,000	45,000
Allowance for doubtful accounts	(1,800)	(2,000)
Prepaid expenses	4,200	2,500
Inventories	81,500	65,000
Land	50,000	50,000
Buildings	125,000	73,500
Accumulated depreciation—buildings	(30,000)	(23,000)
Equipment	53,000	46,000
Accumulated depreciation—equipment	(19,000)	(15,500)
Delivery equipment	39,000	39,000
Accumulated depreciation—delivery equipment	(22,000)	(20,500)
Patents	15,000	–0–
	$379,400	$300,000

	Dec. 31, 2008	Dec. 31, 2007
Accounts payable	$ 26,000	$ 16,000
Short-term notes payable (trade)	4,000	6,000
Accrued payables	3,000	4,600
Mortgage payable	73,000	53,400
Bonds payable	50,000	62,500
Capital stock	140,000	102,000
Additional paid-in capital	10,000	4,000
Retained earnings	73,400	51,500
	$379,400	$300,000

Dividends in the amount of $15,000 were declared and paid in 2008.

Instructions

From this information, prepare a worksheet for a statement of cash flows. Make reasonable assumptions as appropriate. The short-term investments are considered available-for-sale and no unrealized gains or losses have occurred on these securities.

See the book's website, www.wiley.com/college/kieso, for Additional Exercises.

PROBLEMS

(LO 6, 7, 8) **P23-1** **(SCF—Indirect Method)** The following is Blue Man Corp.'s comparative balance sheet accounts at December 31, 2008 and 2007, with a column showing the increase (decrease) from 2007 to 2008.

COMPARATIVE BALANCE SHEETS

	2008	2007	Increase (Decrease)
Cash	$ 807,500	$ 700,000	$107,500
Accounts receivable	1,128,000	1,168,000	(40,000)
Inventories	1,850,000	1,715,000	135,000
Property, plant and equipment	3,307,000	2,967,000	340,000
Accumulated depreciation	(1,165,000)	(1,040,000)	(125,000)
Investment in Blige Co.	305,000	275,000	30,000
Loan receivable	262,500	—	262,500
Total assets	$6,495,000	$5,785,000	$710,000
Accounts payable	$1,015,000	$ 955,000	$ 60,000
Income taxes payable	30,000	50,000	(20,000)
Dividends payable	80,000	100,000	(20,000)
Capital lease obligation	400,000	—	400,000
Capital stock, common, $1 par	500,000	500,000	—
Additional paid-in capital	1,500,000	1,500,000	—
Retained earnings	2,970,000	2,680,000	290,000
Total liabilities and stockholders' equity	$6,495,000	$5,785,000	$710,000

Additional information:

1. On December 31, 2007, Blue Man acquired 25% of Blige Co.'s common stock for $275,000. On that date, the carrying value of Blige's assets and liabilities, which approximated their fair values, was $1,100,000. Blige reported income of $120,000 for the year ended December 31, 2008. No dividend was paid on Blige's common stock during the year.
2. During 2008, Blue Man loaned $300,000 to TLC Co., an unrelated company. TLC made the first semi-annual principal repayment of $37,500, plus interest at 10%, on December 31, 2008.
3. On January 2, 2008, Blue Man sold equipment costing $60,000, with a carrying amount of $35,000, for $40,000 cash.
4. On December 31, 2008, Blue Man entered into a capital lease for an office building. The present value of the annual rental payments is $400,000, which equals the fair value of the building. Blue Man made the first rental payment of $60,000 when due on January 2, 2009.
5. Net income for 2008 was $370,000.
6. Blue Man declared and paid cash dividends for 2008 and 2007 as shown below.

	2008	2007
Declared	December 15, 2008	December 15, 2007
Paid	February 28, 2009	February 28, 2008
Amount	$80,000	$100,000

Instructions

Prepare a statement of cash flows for Blue Man Corp. for the year ended December 31, 2008, using the indirect method.

(AICPA adapted)

(LO 6, 7, 8)

P23-2 (SCF—Indirect Method) The comparative balance sheets for Shenandoah Corporation show the following information.

	December 31	
	2008	2007
Cash	$ 38,500	$13,000
Accounts receivable	12,250	10,000
Inventory	12,000	9,000
Investments	–0–	3,000
Building	–0–	29,750
Equipment	40,000	20,000
Patent	5,000	6,250
	$107,750	$91,000
Allowance for doubtful accounts	3,000	4,500
Accumulated depreciation on equipment	2,000	4,500
Accumulated depreciation on building	–0–	6,000
Accounts payable	5,000	3,000
Dividends payable	–0–	5,000
Notes payable, short-term (nontrade)	3,000	4,000
Long-term notes payable	31,000	25,000
Common stock	43,000	33,000
Retained earnings	20,750	6,000
	$107,750	$91,000

Additional data related to 2008 are as follows.

1. Equipment that had cost $11,000 and was 30% depreciated at time of disposal was sold for $2,500.
2. $10,000 of the long-term note payable was paid by issuing common stock.
3. Cash dividends paid were $5,000.
4. On January 1, 2008, the building was completely destroyed by a flood. Insurance proceeds on the building were $30,000 (net of $2,000 taxes).
5. Investments (available-for-sale) were sold at $3,700 above their cost. The company has made similar sales and investments in the past.
6. Cash of $15,000 was paid for the acquisition of equipment.
7. A long-term note for $16,000 was issued for the acquisition of equipment.
8. Interest of $2,000 and income taxes of $6,500 were paid in cash.

Instructions

Prepare a statement of cash flows using the indirect method. Flood damage is unusual and infrequent in that part of the country.

(LO 6)

P23-3 (SCF—Direct Method) Mardi Gras Company has not yet prepared a formal statement of cash flows for the 2008 fiscal year. Comparative balance sheets as of December 31, 2007 and 2008, and a statement of income and retained earnings for the year ended December 31, 2008, are presented below.

MARDI GRAS COMPANY
STATEMENT OF INCOME AND RETAINED EARNINGS
FOR THE YEAR ENDED DECEMBER 31, 2008
($000 OMITTED)

Sales		$3,800
Expenses		
Cost of goods sold	$1,200	
Salaries and benefits	725	
Heat, light, and power	75	
Depreciation	80	
Property taxes	19	
Patent amortization	25	
Miscellaneous expenses	10	
Interest	30	2,164

MARDI GRAS COMPANY
STATEMENT OF INCOME AND RETAINED EARNINGS
FOR THE YEAR ENDED DECEMBER 31, 2008
(CONTINUED)

Income before income taxes	1,636
Income taxes	818
Net income	818
Retained earnings—Jan. 1, 2008	310
	1,128
Stock dividend declared and issued	600
Retained earnings—Dec. 31, 2008	$ 528

MARDI GRAS COMPANY
COMPARATIVE BALANCE SHEETS
AS OF DECEMBER 31
($000 OMITTED)

Assets	2008	2007
Current assets		
Cash	$ 383	$ 100
U.S. Treasury notes (Available-for-sale)	–0–	50
Accounts receivable	740	500
Inventory	720	560
Total current assets	1,843	1,210
Long-term assets		
Land	150	70
Buildings and equipment	910	600
Accumulated depreciation	(200)	(120)
Patents (less amortization)	105	130
Total long-term assets	965	680
Total assets	$2,808	$1,890
Liabilities and Stockholders' Equity		
Current liabilities		
Accounts payable	$ 420	$ 340
Income taxes payable	40	20
Notes payable	320	320
Total current liabilities	780	680
Long-term notes payable—due 2010	200	200
Total liabilities	980	880
Stockholders' equity		
Common stock	1,300	700
Retained earnings	528	310
Total stockholders' equity	1,828	1,010
Total liabilities and stockholders' equity	$2,808	$1,890

Instructions

Prepare a statement of cash flows using the direct method. Changes in accounts receivable and accounts payable relate to sales and cost of goods sold. Do not prepare a reconciliation schedule.

(CMA adapted)

(LO 6, 7, 8) **P23-4 (SCF—Direct Method)** Cleveland Company had available at the end of 2007 the information on page 1267.

CLEVELAND COMPANY
COMPARATIVE BALANCE SHEETS
AS OF DECEMBER 31, 2007 AND 2006

	2007	2006
Cash	$ 15,000	$ 4,000
Accounts receivable	17,500	12,950
Short-term investments	20,000	30,000
Inventory	42,000	35,000
Prepaid rent	3,000	12,000
Prepaid insurance	2,100	900
Office supplies	1,000	750
Land	125,000	175,000
Building	350,000	350,000
Accumulated depreciation	(105,000)	(87,500)
Equipment	525,000	400,000
Accumulated depreciation	(130,000)	(112,000)
Patent	45,000	50,000
Total assets	$910,600	$871,100
Accounts payable	$ 27,000	$ 32,000
Taxes payable	5,000	4,000
Wages payable	5,000	3,000
Short-term notes payable	10,000	10,000
Long-term notes payable	60,000	70,000
Bonds payable	400,000	400,000
Premium on bonds payable	20,303	25,853
Common stock	240,000	220,000
Paid-in capital in excess of par	20,000	17,500
Retained earnings	123,297	88,747
Total liabilities and stockholders' equity	$910,600	$871,100

CLEVELAND COMPANY
INCOME STATEMENT
FOR THE YEAR ENDED DECEMBER 31, 2007

Sales revenue		$1,160,000
Cost of goods sold		(748,000)
		412,000
Gross margin		
Operating expenses		
Selling expenses	$ 79,200	
Administrative expenses	156,700	
Depreciation/Amortization expense	40,500	
Total operating expenses		(276,400)
Income from operations		135,600
Other revenues/expenses		
Gain on sale of land	8,000	
Gain on sale of short-term investment	4,000	
Dividend revenue	2,400	
Interest expense	(51,750)	(37,350)
Income before taxes		98,250
Income tax expense		(39,400)
Net income		58,850
Dividends to common stockholders		(24,300)
To retained earnings		$ 34,550

Instructions

Prepare a statement of cash flows for Cleveland Company using the direct method accompanied by a reconciliation schedule. Assume the short-term investments are available-for-sale securities.

(LO 6, 7, 8) **P23-5 (SCF—Indirect Method)** You have completed the field work in connection with your audit of Texas Hold Em Corporation for the year ended December 31, 2008. The balance sheet accounts at the beginning and end of the year are shown on the next page.

	Dec. 31, 2008	Dec. 31, 2007	Increase or (Decrease)
Cash	$ 267,900	$ 298,000	($30,100)
Accounts receivable	479,424	353,000	126,424
Inventory	741,700	610,000	131,700
Prepaid expenses	12,000	8,000	4,000
Investment in subsidiary	110,500	–0–	110,500
Cash surrender value of life insurance	2,304	1,800	504
Machinery	207,000	190,000	17,000
Buildings	535,200	407,900	127,300
Land	52,500	52,500	–0–
Patents	69,000	64,000	5,000
Copyright	40,000	50,000	(10,000)
Bond discount and expense	4,502	–0–	4,502
	$2,522,030	$2,035,200	$486,830
Accrued taxes payable	$ 90,250	$ 79,600	$ 10,650
Accounts payable	299,280	280,000	19,280
Dividends payable	70,000	–0–	70,000
Bonds payable—8%	125,000	–0–	125,000
Bonds payable—12%	–0–	100,000	(100,000)
Allowance for doubtful accounts	35,300	40,000	(4,700)
Accumulated depreciation—buildings	424,000	400,000	24,000
Accumulated depreciation—machinery	173,000	130,000	43,000
Premium on bonds payable	–0–	2,400	(2,400)
Capital stock—no par	1,176,200	1,453,200	(277,000)
Additional paid-in capital	109,000	–0–	109,000
Retained earnings—unappropriated	20,000	(450,000)	470,000
	$2,522,030	$2,035,200	$486,830

STATEMENT OF RETAINED EARNINGS
FOR THE YEAR ENDED DECEMBER 31, 2008

January 1, 2008	Balance (deficit)		$(450,000)
March 31, 2008	Net income for first quarter of 2008		25,000
April 1, 2008	Transfer from paid-in capital		425,000
	Balance		–0–
December 31, 2008	Net income for last three quarters of 2008		90,000
	Dividend declared—payable January 21, 2009		(70,000)
	Balance		$ 20,000

Your working papers contain the following information:

1. On April 1, 2008, the existing deficit was written off against paid-in capital created by reducing the stated value of the no-par stock.
2. On November 1, 2008, 29,600 shares of no-par stock were sold for $257,000. The board of directors voted to regard $5 per share as stated capital.
3. A patent was purchased for $15,000.
4. During the year, machinery that had a cost basis of $16,400 and on which there was accumulated depreciation of $5,200 was sold for $7,000. No other plant assets were sold during the year.
5. The 12%, 20-year bonds were dated and issued on January 2, 1996. Interest was payable on June 30 and December 31. They were sold originally at 106. These bonds were retired at 102 (net of $100 tax) plus accrued interest on March 31, 2008.
6. The 8%, 40-year bonds were dated January 1, 2008, and were sold on March 31 at 97 plus accrued interest. Interest is payable semiannually on June 30 and December 31. Expense of issuance was $839.
7. Texas Hold Em Corporation acquired 70% control in Amarillo Company on January 2, 2008, for $100,000. The income statement of Amarillo Company for 2008 shows a net income of $15,000.
8. Extraordinary repairs to buildings of $7,200 were charged to Accumulated Depreciation—Buildings.
9. Interest paid in 2008 was $10,500 and income taxes paid were $34,000.

Instructions

From the information given, prepare a statement of cash flows using the indirect method. A worksheet is not necessary, but the principal computations should be supported by schedules or skeleton ledger accounts.

(LO 3, 4, 6, 8) **P23-6** **(SCF—Indirect Method, and Net Cash Flow from Operating Activities, Direct Method)** Comparative balance sheet accounts of Secada Inc. are presented below.

SECADA INC.
COMPARATIVE BALANCE SHEET ACCOUNTS
AS OF DECEMBER 31, 2008 AND 2007

	December 31	
Debit Accounts	2008	2007
Cash	$ 45,000	$ 33,750
Accounts Receivable	67,500	60,000
Merchandise Inventory	30,000	24,000
Investments (available-for-sale)	22,250	38,500
Machinery	30,000	18,750
Buildings	67,500	56,250
Land	7,500	7,500
	$269,750	$238,750
Credit Accounts		
Allowance for Doubtful Accounts	$ 2,250	$ 1,500
Accumulated Depreciation—Machinery	5,625	2,250
Accumulated Depreciation—Buildings	13,500	9,000
Accounts Payable	30,000	24,750
Accrued Payables	3,375	2,625
Long-Term Note Payable	26,000	31,000
Common Stock, no par	150,000	125,000
Retained Earnings	39,000	42,625
	$269,750	$238,750

Additional data (ignoring taxes):

1. Net income for the year was $42,500.
2. Cash dividends declared during the year were $21,125.
3. A 20% stock dividend was declared during the year. $25,000 of retained earnings was capitalized.
4. Investments that cost $20,000 were sold during the year for $23,750.
5. Machinery that cost $3,750, on which $750 of depreciation had accumulated, was sold for $2,200.

Secada's 2008 income statement follows (ignoring taxes).

Sales		$540,000
Less: Cost of goods sold		380,000
Gross margin		160,000
Less: Operating expenses (includes $8,625 depreciation and $5,400 bad debts)		120,450
Income from operations		39,550
Other: Gain on sale of investments	$3,750	
Loss on sale of machinery	(800)	2,950
Net income		$ 42,500

Instructions

(a) Compute net cash flow from operating activities using the direct method.
(b) Prepare a statement of cash flows using the indirect method.

(LO 3, 4, 6, 8) **P23-7** **(SCF—Direct and Indirect Methods from Comparative Financial Statements)** George Winston Company, a major retailer of bicycles and accessories, operates several stores and is a publicly traded company. The comparative statement of financial position and income statement for Winston as of May 31, 2008, are shown on the next page. The company is preparing its statement of cash flows.

GEORGE WINSTON COMPANY
COMPARATIVE STATEMENT OF FINANCIAL POSITION
AS OF MAY 31

	2008	2007
Current assets		
Cash	$ 33,250	$ 20,000
Accounts receivable	80,000	58,000
Merchandise inventory	210,000	250,000
Prepaid expenses	9,000	7,000
Total current assets	332,250	335,000
Plant assets		
Plant assets	600,000	502,000
Less: Accumulated depreciation	150,000	125,000
Net plant assets	450,000	377,000
Total assets	$782,250	$712,000
Current liabilities		
Accounts payable	$123,000	$115,000
Salaries payable	47,250	72,000
Interest payable	27,000	25,000
Total current liabilities	197,250	212,000
Long-term debt		
Bonds payable	70,000	100,000
Total liabilities	267,250	312,000
Shareholders' equity		
Common stock, $10 par	370,000	280,000
Retained earnings	145,000	120,000
Total shareholders' equity	515,000	400,000
Total liabilities and shareholders' equity	$782,250	$712,000

GEORGE WINSTON COMPANY
INCOME STATEMENT
FOR THE YEAR ENDED MAY 31, 2008

Sales	$1,255,250
Cost of merchandise sold	722,000
Gross profit	533,250
Expenses	
Salary expense	252,100
Interest expense	75,000
Other expenses	8,150
Depreciation expense	25,000
Total expenses	360,250
Operating income	173,000
Income tax expense	43,000
Net income	$ 130,000

The following is additional information concerning Winston's transactions during the year ended May 31, 2008.

1. All sales during the year were made on account.
2. All merchandise was purchased on account, comprising the total accounts payable account.
3. Plant assets costing $98,000 were purchased by paying $48,000 in cash and issuing 5,000 shares of stock.
4. The "other expenses" are related to prepaid items.
5. All income taxes incurred during the year were paid during the year.
6. In order to supplement its cash, Winston issued 4,000 shares of common stock at par value.
7. There were no penalties assessed for the retirement of bonds.
8. Cash dividends of $105,000 were declared and paid at the end of the fiscal year.

Instructions

   (a) Compare and contrast the direct method and the indirect method for reporting cash flows from operating activities.

   (b) Prepare a statement of cash flows for Winston Company for the year ended May 31, 2008, using the direct method. Be sure to support the statement with appropriate calculations. (A reconciliation of net income to net cash provided is not required.)

   (c) Using the indirect method, calculate only the net cash flow from operating activities for Winston Company for the year ended May 31, 2008.

(LO 6, 7, 8)   **P23-8**   **(SCF—Direct and Indirect Methods)**   Comparative balance sheet accounts of Jensen Company are presented below.

JENSEN COMPANY
COMPARATIVE BALANCE SHEET ACCOUNTS
AS OF DECEMBER 31

Debit Balances	2007	2006
Cash	$ 80,000	$ 51,000
Accounts Receivable	145,000	130,000
Merchandise Inventory	75,000	61,000
Investments (Available-for-sale)	55,000	85,000
Equipment	70,000	48,000
Buildings	145,000	145,000
Land	40,000	25,000
Totals	$610,000	$545,000

Credit Balances	2007	2006
Allowance for Doubtful Accounts	$ 10,000	$ 8,000
Accumulated Depreciation—Equipment	21,000	14,000
Accumulated Depreciation—Building	37,000	28,000
Accounts Payable	70,000	60,000
Income Taxes Payable	12,000	10,000
Long-Term Notes Payable	62,000	70,000
Common Stock	310,000	260,000
Retained Earnings	88,000	95,000
Totals	$610,000	$545,000

Additional data:

  1. Equipment that cost $10,000 and was 40% depreciated was sold in 2007.
  2. Cash dividends were declared and paid during the year.
  3. Common stock was issued in exchange for land.
  4. Investments that cost $35,000 were sold during the year.
  5. There were no write-offs of uncollectible accounts during the year.

Jensen's 2007 income statement is as follows.

Sales		$950,000
Less: Cost of goods sold		600,000
Gross profit		350,000
Less: Operating expenses (includes depreciation expense and bad debt expense)		250,000
Income from operations		100,000
Other revenues and expenses		
Gain on sale of investments	$15,000	
Loss on sale of equipment	(3,000)	12,000
Income before taxes		112,000
Income taxes		45,000
Net income		$ 67,000

Instructions

   (a) Compute net cash provided by operating activities under the direct method.
   (b) Prepare a statement of cash flows using the indirect method.

(LO 6, 7, 8)

P23-9 (Indirect SCF) Seneca Corporation has contracted with you to prepare a statement of cash flows. The controller has provided the following information.

| | December 31 | |
	2007	2006
Cash	$ 43,500	$13,000
Accounts receivable	12,250	10,000
Inventory	12,000	10,000
Investments	–0–	3,000
Building	–0–	29,750
Equipment	35,000	20,000
Copyright	5,000	5,250
Totals	$107,750	$91,000
Allowance for doubtful accounts	$ 3,000	$ 4,500
Accumulated depreciation on equipment	2,000	4,500
Accumulated depreciation on building	–0–	6,000
Accounts payable	5,000	4,000
Dividends payable	–0–	5,000
Notes payable, short-term (nontrade)	3,000	4,000
Long-term notes payable	36,000	25,000
Common stock	38,000	33,000
Retained earnings	20,750	5,000
	$107,750	$91,000

Additional data related to 2007 are as follows.

1. Equipment that had cost $11,000 and was 40% depreciated at time of disposal was sold for $2,500.
2. $5,000 of the long-term note payable was paid by issuing common stock.
3. Cash dividends paid were $5,000.
4. On January 1, 2007, the building was completely destroyed by a flood. Insurance proceeds on the building were $33,000 (net of $4,000 taxes).
5. Investments (available-for-sale) were sold at $2,500 above their cost. The company has made similar sales and investments in the past.
6. Cash of $10,000 was paid for the acquisition of equipment.
7. A long-term note for $16,000 was issued for the acquisition of equipment.
8. Interest of $2,000 and income taxes of $5,000 were paid in cash.

Instructions

(a) Use the indirect method to analyze the above information and prepare a statement of cash flows for Seneca. Flood damage is unusual and infrequent in that part of the country.
(b) What would you expect to observe in the operating, investing, and financing sections of a statement of cash flows of:
    (1) a severely financially troubled firm?
    (2) a recently formed firm which is experiencing rapid growth?

CONCEPTS FOR ANALYSIS

 CA23-1 (Analysis of Improper SCF) The following statement was prepared by Abriendo Corporation's accountant.

ABRIENDO CORPORATION
STATEMENT OF SOURCES AND APPLICATION OF CASH
FOR THE YEAR ENDED SEPTEMBER 30, 2008

Sources of cash	
Net income	$ 111,000
Depreciation and depletion	70,000
Increase in long-term debt	179,000
Changes in current receivables and inventories, less current liabilities (excluding current maturities of long-term debt)	14,000
	$374,000
Application of cash	
Cash dividends	$ 60,000
Expenditure for property, plant, and equipment	214,000

Investments and other uses		20,000
Change in cash		80,000
		$374,000

The following additional information relating to Abriendo Corporation is available for the year ended September 30, 2008.

1. Wage and salary expense attributable to stock option plans was $22,000 for the year.
2. Expenditures for property, plant, and equipment — $250,000
    Proceeds from retirements of property, plant, and equipment — 36,000

    Net expenditures — $214,000

3. A stock dividend of 10,000 shares of Abriendo Corporation common stock was distributed to common stockholders on April 1, 2008, when the per-share market price was $7 and par value was $1.
4. On July 1, 2008, when its market price was $6 per share, 16,000 shares of Abriendo Corporation common stock were issued in exchange for 4,000 shares of preferred stock.
5. Depreciation expense — $ 65,000
    Depletion expense — 5,000

    — $ 70,000

6. Increase in long-term debt — $620,000
    Retirement of debt — 441,000

    Net increase — $179,000

Instructions

(a) In general, what are the objectives of a statement of the type shown above for Abriendo Corporation? Explain.
(b) Identify the weaknesses in the form and format of Abriendo Corporation's statement of cash flows without reference to the additional information. (Assume adoption of the indirect method.)
(c) For each of the six items of additional information for the statement of cash flows, indicate the preferable treatment and explain why the suggested treatment is preferable.

(AICPA adapted)

 CA23-2 (SCF Theory and Analysis of Improper SCF) Gloria Estefan and Flaco Jimenez are examining the following statement of cash flows for Tropical Clothing Store's first year of operations.

TROPICAL CLOTHING STORE
STATEMENT OF CASH FLOWS
FOR THE YEAR ENDED JANUARY 31, 2008

Sources of cash	
From sales of merchandise	$ 362,000
From sale of capital stock	400,000
From sale of investment	120,000
From depreciation	80,000
From issuance of note for truck	30,000
From interest on investments	8,000
Total sources of cash	1,000,000
Uses of cash	
For purchase of fixtures and equipment	340,000
For merchandise purchased for resale	253,000
For operating expenses (including depreciation)	170,000
For purchase of investment	85,000
For purchase of truck by issuance of note	30,000
For purchase of treasury stock	10,000
For interest on note	3,000
Total uses of cash	891,000
Net increase in cash	$ 109,000

Gloria claims that Tropical's statement of cash flows is an excellent portrayal of a superb first year, with cash increasing $109,000. Flaco replies that it was not a superb first year—that the year was an operating failure, the statement was incorrectly presented, and $109,000 is not the actual increase in cash.

Instructions

(a) With whom do you agree, Gloria or Flaco? Explain your position.

(b) Using the data provided, prepare a statement of cash flows in proper indirect method form. The only noncash items in income are depreciation and the gain from the sale of the investment (purchase and sale are related).

CA23-3 (SCF Theory and Analysis of Transactions) John Lee Hooker Company is a young and growing producer of electronic measuring instruments and technical equipment. You have been retained by Hooker to advise it in the preparation of a statement of cash flows using the indirect method. For the fiscal year ended October 31, 2008, you have obtained the following information concerning certain events and transactions of Hooker.

1. The amount of reported earnings for the fiscal year was $800,000, which included a deduction for an extraordinary loss of $110,000 (see item 5 below).
2. Depreciation expense of $315,000 was included in the income statement.
3. Uncollectible accounts receivable of $40,000 were written off against the allowance for doubtful accounts. Also, $51,000 of bad debt expense was included in determining income for the fiscal year, and the same amount was added to the allowance for doubtful accounts.
4. A gain of $9,000 was realized on the sale of a machine. It originally cost $75,000, of which $30,000 was undepreciated on the date of sale.
5. On April 1, 2008, lightning caused an uninsured building loss of $110,000 ($180,000 loss, less reduction in income taxes of $70,000). This extraordinary loss was included in determining income as indicated in 1 above.
6. On July 3, 2008, building and land were purchased for $700,000. Hooker gave in payment $75,000 cash, $200,000 market value of its unissued common stock, and signed a $425,000 mortgage note payable.
7. On August 3, 2008, $800,000 face value of Hooker's 10% convertible debentures were converted into $150,000 par value of its common stock. The bonds were originally issued at face value.

Instructions

Explain whether each of the seven numbered items above is a source or use of cash, and explain how it should be disclosed in John Lee Hooker's statement of cash flows for the fiscal year ended October 31, 2008. If any item is neither a source nor a use of cash, explain why it is not, and indicate the disclosure, if any, that should be made of the item in John Lee Hooker's statement of cash flows for the fiscal year ended October 31, 2008.

CA23-4 (Analysis of Transactions' Effect on SCF) Each of the following items must be considered in preparing a statement of cash flows for Sage Fashions Inc. for the year ended December 31, 2008.

1. Fixed assets that had cost $20,000 6½ years before and were being depreciated on a 10-year basis, with no estimated scrap value, were sold for $5,250.
2. During the year, goodwill of $15,000 was considered impaired and was completely written off to expense.
3. During the year, 500 shares of common stock with a stated value of $25 a share were issued for $34 a share.
4. The company sustained a net loss for the year of $2,100. Depreciation amounted to $2,000 and patent amortization was $400.
5. Uncollectible accounts receivable in the amount of $2,000 were written off against the Allowance for Doubtful Accounts.
6. Investments (available-for-sale) that cost $12,000 when purchased 4 years earlier were sold for $10,600. The loss was considered ordinary.
7. Bonds payable with a par value of $24,000 on which there was an unamortized bond premium of $2,000 were redeemed at 103. The gain was credited to ordinary income.

Instructions

For each item, state where it is to be shown in the statement and then how you would present the necessary information, including the amount. Consider each item to be independent of the others. Assume that correct entries were made for all transactions as they took place.

CA23-5 (Purpose and Elements of SCF) In 1987 the Financial Accounting Standards Board issued *Statement of Financial Accounting Standards (SFAS) No. 95,* "Statement of Cash Flows."

Instructions

(a) Explain the purposes of the statement of cash flows.

(b) List and describe the three categories of activities that must be reported in the statement of cash flows.

(c) Identify and describe the two methods that are allowed for reporting cash flows from operations.

(d) Describe the financial statement presentation of noncash investing and financing transactions. Include in your description an example of a noncash investing and financing transaction.

CA23-6 (Cash Flow Reporting) Durocher Guitar Company is in the business of manufacturing top-quality, steel-string folk guitars. In recent years the company has experienced working capital problems resulting from the procurement of factory equipment, the unanticipated buildup of receivables and inventories, and the payoff of a balloon mortgage on a new manufacturing facility. The founder and president of the company, Laraine Durocher, has attempted to raise cash from various financial institutions, but to no avail because of the company's poor performance in recent years. In particular, the company's lead bank, First Financial, is especially concerned about Durocher's inability to maintain a positive cash position. The commercial loan officer from First Financial told Laraine, "I can't even consider your request for capital financing unless I see that your company is able to generate positive cash flows from operations."

Thinking about the banker's comment, Laraine came up with what she believes is a good plan: With a more attractive statement of cash flows, the bank might be willing to provide long-term financing. To "window dress" cash flows, the company can sell its accounts receivables to factors and liquidate its raw materials inventories. These rather costly transactions would generate lots of cash. As the chief accountant for Durocher Guitar, it is your job to tell Laraine what you think of her plan.

Instructions

Answer the following questions.

(a) What are the ethical issues related to Laraine Durocher's idea?

(b) What would you tell Laraine Durocher?

USING YOUR JUDGMENT

Financial Reporting Problem

The Procter & Gamble Company (P&G)

The financial statements of **P&G** are presented in Appendix 5B or can be accessed on the KWW website.

Instructions

Refer to P&G's financial statements and the accompanying notes to answer the following questions.

(a) Which method of computing net cash provided by operating activities does P&G use? What were the amounts of net cash provided by operating activities for the years 2002, 2003, and 2004? Which two items were most responsible for the increase in net cash provided by operating activities in 2004?

(b) What was the most significant item in the cash flows used for investing activities section in 2004? What was the most significant item in the cash flows used for financing activities section in 2004?

(c) Where is "deferred income taxes" reported in P&G's statement of cash flows? Why does it appear in that section of the statement of cash flows?

(d) Where is depreciation reported in P&G's statement of cash flows? Why is depreciation added to net income in the statement of cash flows?

Financial Statement Analysis Case

Vermont Teddy Bear Co.

Founded in the early 1980s, the **Vermont Teddy Bear Co.** designs and manufactures American-made teddy bears and markets them primarily as gifts called Bear-Grams or Teddy Bear-Grams. Bear-Grams are personalized teddy bears delivered directly to the recipient for special occasions such as birthdays and anniversaries. The Shelburne, Vermont, company's primary markets are New York, Boston, and Chicago.

Sales have jumped dramatically in recent years. Such dramatic growth has significant implications for cash flows. Provided below are the cash flow statements for two recent years for the company.

	Current Year	Prior Year
Cash flows from operating activities:		
Net income	$ 17,523	$ 838,955
Adjustments to reconcile net income to net cash provided by operating activities		
Deferred income taxes	(69,524)	(146,590)
Depreciation and amortization	316,416	181,348
Changes in assets and liabilities:		
Accounts receivable, trade	(38,267)	(25,947)
Inventories	(1,599,014)	(1,289,293)
Prepaid and other current assets	(444,794)	(113,205)
Deposits and other assets	(24,240)	(83,044)
Accounts payable	2,017,059	(284,567)
Accrued expenses	61,321	170,755
Accrued interest payable, debentures	—	(58,219)
Other	—	(8,960)
Income taxes payable	—	117,810
Net cash provided by (used for) operating activities	236,480	(700,957)
Net cash used for investing activities	(2,102,892)	(4,422,953)
Net cash (used for) provided by financing activities	(315,353)	9,685,435
Net change in cash and cash equivalents	(2,181,765)	4,561,525

Other information:

	Current Year	Prior Year
Current liabilities	$ 4,055,465	$ 1,995,600
Total liabilities	4,620,085	2,184,386
Net sales	20,560,566	17,025,856

Instructions

(a) Note that net income in the current year was only $17,523 compared to prior-year income of $838,955, but cash flow from operations was $236,480 in the current year and a negative $700,957 in the prior year. Explain the causes of this apparent paradox.

(b) Evaluate Vermont Teddy Bear's liquidity, solvency, and profitability for the current year using cash flow-based ratios.

Comparative Analysis Case

The Coca-Cola Company and PepsiCo, Inc.

Instructions

Go to the KWW website and use information found there to answer the following questions related to **The Coca-Cola Company** and **PepsiCo, Inc.**

(a) What method of computing net cash provided by operating activities does Coca-Cola use? What method does PepsiCo use? What were the amounts of cash provided by operating activities reported by Coca-Cola and PepsiCo in 2004?

(b) What was the most significant item reported by Coca-Cola and PepsiCo in 2004 in their investing activities sections? What is the most significant item reported by Coca-Cola and PepsiCo in 2004 in their financing activities sections?

(c) What were these two companies' trends in net cash provided by operating activities over the period 2002 to 2004?

(d) Where is "depreciation and amortization" reported by Coca-Cola and PepsiCo in their statements of cash flows? What is the amount and why does it appear in that section of the statement of cash flows?

(e) Based on the information contained in Coca-Cola's and PepsiCo's financial statements, compute the following 2004 ratios for each company. These ratios require the use of statement of cash flows data. (These ratios were covered in Chapter 5.)

(1) Current cash debt coverage ratio.

(2) Cash debt coverage ratio.

(f) What conclusions concerning the management of cash can be drawn from the ratios computed in (e)?

Research Case

The March 5, 2002, edition of the *Wall Street Journal* included an article by Mark Maremont entitled "How Is Tyco Accounting for Its Cash Flow?—Its Touted Measure of Strength Leaves Room for Interpretation."

Instructions
Read the article and answer the following questions.

(a) Many analysts believe that cash flow is not as susceptible to "reporting manipulation" as income. What "complications" discussed in this article make that belief questionable?

(b) What is "free cash flow"? How was Tyco manipulating its reporting of "free cash flow"?

(c) Under U.S. GAAP, how is free cash flow determined?

(d) How is Tyco "buying earnings and operating cash flow"? Why is this practice risky for investors?

International Reporting Case

As noted in the chapter, there is international diversity in the preparation of the statement of cash flows. For example, under International Accounting Standards companies may choose how to classify dividends and interest in the cash flow statement. In some countries, like Brazil, a cash flow statement is not required. **Embraer**, a Brazilian aircraft manufacturer, prepared a statement of changes in financial position, rather than a statement of cash flows.

Instructions
Refer to Embraer's 2004 Statement of Changes in Financial Position below and on page 1278 to answer the following questions.

(a) Briefly discuss at least two similarities between Embraer's statement of changes in financial position and a statement of cash flows prepared according to U.S. GAAP.

(b) Briefly discuss at least two differences between Embraer's statement of changes in financial position and a statement of cash flows prepared according to U.S. GAAP.

Embraer
Consolidated Statement of Changes in Financial Position
for the Year Ended December 31, 2004
(in thousands of Brazilian reals)

Sources of Funds	2004
Provided from operations	
Net income	1,255,833
Items not affecting working capital	
Equity in unconsolidated subsidiary	
Translation losses on foreign investments	19,613
Minority interest	8,618
Depreciation and amortization	221,554
Net book value of permanent asset disposal	799
Interest on long-term items added to principal, net	(25,759)
Net monetary and exchange variations on long-term items	(201,030)
Provision for losses	34,268
Long-term deferred income and social contribution taxes	(47,765)
Provisions for contingencies	57,930
Funds provided from operations	1,324,061
From shareholders	
Capital increase	9,524

Sources of Funds (continued)	2004
From third parties	
Increase in long-term liabilities	
Customers' advances	257,528
Loans	1,317,535
Accounts payable and other liabilities	964,260
Tax incentives	5,672
Transfers to current asset	1,042,182
Increase in minority interest	17,997
Funds provided from third parties	3,605,174
Total sources	4,938,759
Applications of Funds	
Increase in noncurrent assets	1,390,520
Investments	41,219
Property plant and equipment	109,656
Deferred charges	415,954
Transfers to current liabilities	731,098
Interest on capital	585,173
Total applications	3,273,620
Increase in working capital	1,665,139
Working capital—end of year	
Current assets	10,329,032
Current liabilities	5,420,966
	4,908,066
Working capital—beginning of year	3,242,927
Increase in working capital	1,665,139

Professional Research: Financial Accounting and Reporting

As part of the year-end accounting process for your company, you are preparing the statement of cash flows according to GAAP. One of your team, a finance major, believes the statement should be prepared to report the change in working capital, because analysts many times use working capital in ratio analysis. Your supervisor would like research conducted to verify the basis for preparing the statement of cash flows.

Instructions

Using the **Financial Accounting Research System (FARS),** respond to the following items. (Provide text strings used in your search.)

(a) Has GAAP ever allowed the statement of cash flows to be prepared on the basis of working capital?

(b) What were the problems with using working capital as a concept of funds? Why is cash a more useful concept of funds?

(c) What information is provided in a statement of cash flows?

(d) List some of the typical cash inflows and outflows from operations.

Professional Simulation

In this simulation you are asked to address questions related to the statement of cash flows. Prepare responses to all parts.

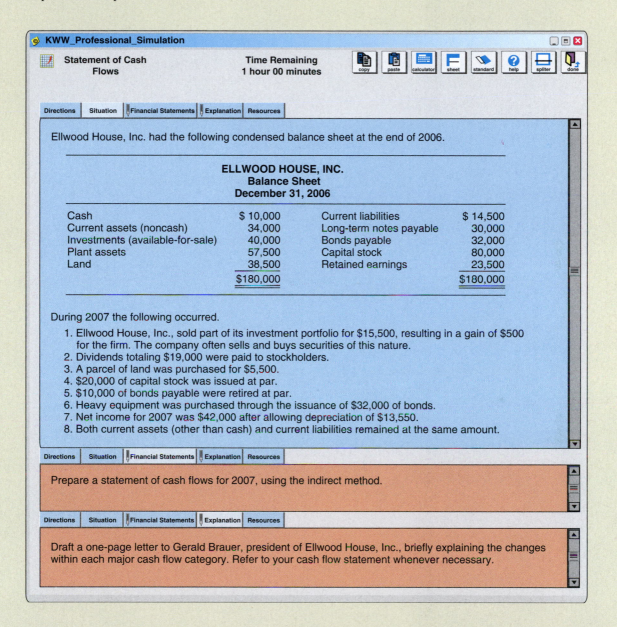

KWW_Professional_Simulation

| Statement of Cash Flows | Time Remaining 1 hour 00 minutes | copy paste calculator sheet standard help splitter done |

Directions | Situation | Financial Statements | Explanation | Resources

Ellwood House, Inc. had the following condensed balance sheet at the end of 2006.

ELLWOOD HOUSE, INC.
Balance Sheet
December 31, 2006

Cash	$ 10,000	Current liabilities	$ 14,500
Current assets (noncash)	34,000	Long-term notes payable	30,000
Investments (available-for-sale)	40,000	Bonds payable	32,000
Plant assets	57,500	Capital stock	80,000
Land	38,500	Retained earnings	23,500
	$180,000		$180,000

During 2007 the following occurred.

1. Ellwood House, Inc., sold part of its investment portfolio for $15,500, resulting in a gain of $500 for the firm. The company often sells and buys securities of this nature.
2. Dividends totaling $19,000 were paid to stockholders.
3. A parcel of land was purchased for $5,500.
4. $20,000 of capital stock was issued at par.
5. $10,000 of bonds payable were retired at par.
6. Heavy equipment was purchased through the issuance of $32,000 of bonds.
7. Net income for 2007 was $42,000 after allowing depreciation of $13,550.
8. Both current assets (other than cash) and current liabilities remained at the same amount.

Directions | Situation | Financial Statements | Explanation | Resources

Prepare a statement of cash flows for 2007, using the indirect method.

Directions | Situation | Financial Statements | Explanation | Resources

Draft a one-page letter to Gerald Brauer, president of Ellwood House, Inc., briefly explaining the changes within each major cash flow category. Refer to your cash flow statement whenever necessary.

wiley.com/college/kieso

FULL DISCLOSURE IN FINANCIAL REPORTING

High-Quality Financial Reporting— It's a Necessity

Here are excerpts from leading experts regarding the importance of high-quality financial reporting:[1]

Warren E. Buffett, Chairman and Chief Executive Officer, **Berkshire Hathaway Inc.**:

Financial reporting for Berkshire Hathaway, and for me personally, is the beginning of every decision that we make around here in terms of capital. I'm punching out 10-Ks and 10-Qs every single day. We look at the numbers and try to evaluate the quality of the financial reporting, and then we try to figure out what that means for the bonds and stocks that we're looking at, and thinking of either buying or selling.

Judy Lewent, Executive Vice President and Chief Financial Officer, Merck & Co., Inc.

. . . Higher standards, when properly implemented, drive excellence. I can make a parallel to the pharmaceutical industry. If you look around the world at where innovations come from, economists have studied and seen that where regulatory standards are the highest is where innovation is also the highest.

Floyd Norris, Chief Financial Correspondent, the **New York Times**:

We are in a situation now in our society where the temptations to provide "bad" financial reporting are probably greater than they used to be. The need to get the stock price up, or to keep it up, is intense. So, the temptation to play games, the temptation to manage earnings—some of which can be legitimate and some of which cannot be—is probably greater than it used to be.

Abby Joseph Cohen, Chair, Investment Policy Committee, **Goldman, Sachs & Co.**:

High-quality financial reporting is perhaps the most important thing we can expect from companies. For investors to make good decisions—whether those investors are buying stocks or bonds or making private investments—they need to know the truth. And we think that when information is as clear as possible and is reported as frequently as makes sense, investors can do their jobs as best they can.

In short, these comments illustrate why high-quality financial reporting is important to companies, to investors, and to the capital markets. At the heart of high-quality financial reporting is full disclosure.

---

[1]Excerpts taken from video entitled "Financially Correct with Ben Stein," Financial Accounting Standards Board (Norwalk, Conn.: FASB, 2002). By permission.

Learning Objectives

After studying this chapter, you should be able to:

1 Review the full disclosure principle and describe implementation problems.

2 Explain the use of notes in financial statement preparation.

3 Discuss the disclosure requirements for major business segments.

4 Describe the accounting problems associated with interim reporting.

5 Identify the major disclosures in the auditor's report.

6 Understand management's responsibilities for financials.

7 Identify issues related to financial forecasts and projections.

8 Describe the profession's response to fraudulent financial reporting.

As the opening story indicates, our markets will not function properly without transparent, complete, and truthful reporting of financial performance. Investors and other interested parties need to read and understand all aspects of financial reporting—the financial statements, the notes, the president's letter, and management's discussion and analysis. In this chapter, we cover the full disclosure principle in more detail and examine disclosures that must accompany financial statements so that they are not misleading. The content and organization of this chapter are as follows.

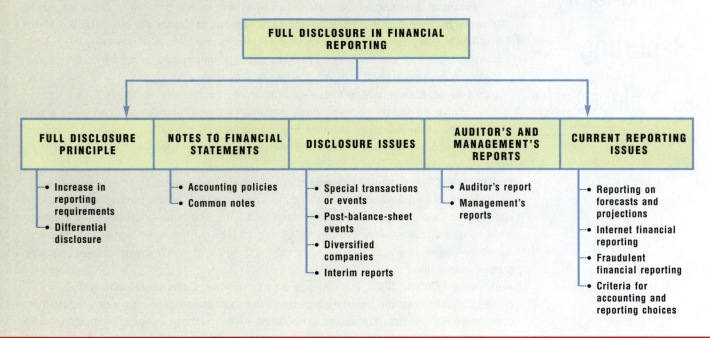

FULL DISCLOSURE PRINCIPLE

FASB Concepts Statement No. 1 notes that some useful information is best provided in the financial statements, and some is best provided by means other than in financial statements. For example, earnings and cash flows are readily available in financial statements—but investors might do better to look at comparisons to other companies in the same industry, found in news articles or brokerage house reports.

FASB standards directly affect financial statements, notes to the financial statements, and supplementary information. Other types of information found in the annual report, such as management's discussion and analysis, are not subject to FASB standards. Illustration 24-1 (page 1283) indicates the various types of financial information.

As Chapter 2 indicated, the profession has adopted a **full disclosure principle**. The full disclosure principle calls for financial reporting of **any financial facts significant enough to influence the judgment of an informed reader**. In some situations, the benefits of disclosure may be apparent but the costs uncertain. In other instances, the costs may be certain but the benefits of disclosure not as apparent.

For example, recently, the SEC required companies to provide expanded disclosures about their contractual obligations. In light of the off-balance sheet accounting frauds at companies like **Enron**, the benefits of these expanded disclosures seem fairly obvious to the investing public. While no one has documented the exact costs of disclosure in these situations, they would appear to be relatively small.

On the other hand, the cost of disclosure can be substantial in some cases and the benefits difficult to assess. For example, at one time the *Wall Street Journal* reported that

OBJECTIVE 1
Review the full disclosure principle and describe implementation problems.

UNDERLYING CONCEPTS
Here is a good example of the trade-off between cost considerations and the benefits of full disclosure.

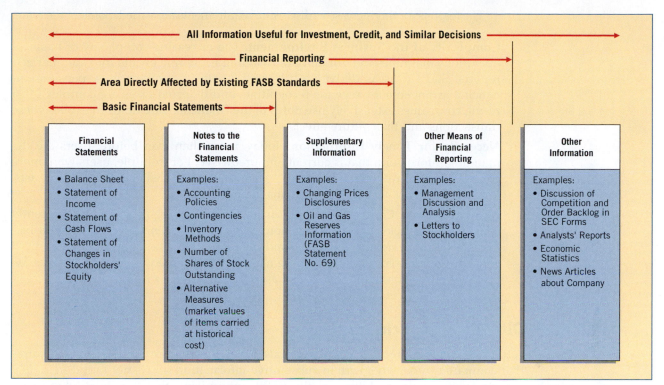

ILLUSTRATION 24-1
Types of Financial
Information

UNDERLYING CONCEPTS

The AICPA's Special Committee
on Financial Reporting notes that
business reporting is not free,
and improving it requires considering the relative costs and benefits of information. Undisciplined
expansion of mandated reporting
could result in large and need-
less costs.

if segment reporting were adopted, a company like **Fruehauf** would have had to increase its accounting staff 50 percent, from 300 to 450 individuals. In this case, the cost
of disclosure can be measured, but the benefits are less well defined.

Some even argue that the reporting requirements are so detailed and substantial
that users have a difficult time absorbing the information. These critics charge the profession with engaging in **information overload**.

Financial disasters at **Microstrategy**, **PharMor**, **WorldCom**, and **Global Crossing** highlight the difficulty of implementing the full disclosure principle. They raise the issue of
why investors were not aware of potential problems: Was the information these companies presented not comprehensible? Was it buried? Was it too technical? Was it properly
presented and fully disclosed as of the financial statement date, but the situation later de-
teriorated? Or was it simply not there? In the following sections, we describe the elements
of high-quality disclosure that will enable companies to avoid these disclosure pitfalls.

Increase in Reporting Requirements

Disclosure requirements have increased substantially. One recent survey showed that
the size of many companies' annual reports is growing in response to demands for increased transparency. For example, annual report page counts ranged from 70 pages
for **Gateway** up to a whopping 244 pages in **Eastman Kodak**'s annual report. Compared to prior years' reports, the percentage increase in pages ranged from 17 percent
at **IBM** to over 80 percent at **Siebel Systems**.[2] This result is not surprising; as illustrated throughout this textbook, the FASB has issued many standards in the last 10
years that have substantial disclosure provisions.

---

[2]Aliya Sternstein, "Heavy Lifting Required," *Forbes* (October 13, 2003) p. 58. Another earlier
study documented annual report growth for a sample of 25 large, well-known companies over
a recent 10-year period. The average number of pages of notes to the financial statements increased from 9 to 17 pages, and the average number of pages for management's discussion and
analysis grew from 7 to 12 pages. See Ray J. Groves, "Financial Disclosure: When More Is Not
Better," *Financial Executive* (May/June 1994).

The reasons for this increase in disclosure requirements are varied. Some of them are:

Complexity of the Business Environment. The increasing complexity of business operations magnifies the difficulty of distilling economic events into summarized reports. Such areas as derivatives, leasing, business combinations, pensions, financing arrangements, revenue recognition, and deferred taxes are complex. As a result, companies extensively use **notes to the financial statements** to explain these transactions and their future effects.

Necessity for Timely Information. Today, more than ever before, users are demanding information that is current and predictive. For example, users want more complete **interim data**. Also, the SEC recommends published financial forecasts, long avoided and even feared by management.

Accounting as a Control and Monitoring Device. The government has recently sought public disclosure of such phenomena as management compensation, off-balance-sheet financing arrangements, and related party transactions. An "Enronitis" concern is expressed in many of these newer disclosure requirements, and the SEC has selected accountants and auditors as the agents to assist in controlling and monitoring these concerns.

Differential Disclosure

A trend toward **differential disclosure** is also occurring. For example, the SEC requires that companies report to it certain substantive information that is not found in annual reports to stockholders. Likewise, the FASB, recognizing that certain disclosure requirements are costly and unnecessary for certain companies, has eliminated reporting requirements for nonpublic enterprises in such areas as fair value of financial instruments and segment reporting.[3]

WHAT DO THE NUMBERS MEAN?

"THE HEART OF THE MATTER"

As we discussed in the opening story, financial disclosure is one of a number of institutional features that contribute to vibrant security markets. In fact, a recent study of disclosure and other mechanisms (such as civil lawsuits and criminal sanctions) found that good disclosure is the most important contributor to a vibrant market.

The study, which compared disclosure and other legal and regulatory elements across 49 countries, found that countries with the best disclosure laws have the biggest stock markets. Countries with more successful market environments also tend to have regulations that make it relatively easy for private investors to sue corporations that provide bad information. That is, while criminal sanctions can be effective in some circumstances, disclosure and other legal and regulatory elements encouraging good disclosure are the most important determinants of highly liquid and deep securities markets.

These findings hold for nations in all stages of economic development, with particular importance for nations that are in the early stages of securities regulation. The lesson: Disclosure is good for your market.

Source: Rebecca Christie, "Study: Disclosure at Heart of Effective Securities Laws," *Wall Street Journal Online* (August 11, 2003).

---

[3]The FASB has had a disclosure-effectiveness project. The revised pension and postretirement benefit disclosures discussed in Chapter 20 [*FASB Statement No. 132* and *FASB Statement No. 132(R)*] are one example of how disclosures can be streamlined and made more useful. However, as noted by one FASB member, the usefulness of expanded required disclosure also depends on users' ability to distinguish between disclosed versus recognized items in financial statements. Research to date is inconclusive on this matter. See Katherine Schipper, "Required Disclosures in Financial Reports," Presidential Address to the American Accounting Association Annual Meeting; San Francisco, CA (August 2005).

Some still complain that the FASB has not gone far enough. They note that certain types of companies (small or nonpublic) should not have to follow complex GAAP requirements such as those for deferred income taxes, leases, or pensions. This issue, often referred to as "**big GAAP versus little GAAP**," continues to be controversial. The FASB takes the position that there should be one set of GAAP, except in unusual situations.[4]

NOTES TO THE FINANCIAL STATEMENTS

As you know from your study of this textbook, notes are an integral part of the financial statements of a business enterprise. However, readers of financial statements often overlook them because they are highly technical and often appear in small print. **Notes are the means of amplifying or explaining the items presented in the main body of the statements.** They can explain in qualitative terms information pertinent to specific financial statement items. In addition, they can provide supplementary data of a quantitative nature to expand the information in the financial statements. Notes also can explain restrictions imposed by financial arrangements or basic contractual agreements. Although notes may be technical and difficult to understand, they provide meaningful information for the user of the financial statements.

Accounting Policies

Accounting policies are the specific accounting principles and methods a company currently uses and considers most appropriate to present fairly its financial statements. *APB Opinion No. 22*, "Disclosure of Accounting Policies," states that information about the accounting policies adopted by a reporting entity is essential for financial statement users in making economic decisions. It recommended that companies should present **as an integral part of the financial statements a statement identifying the accounting policies adopted and followed by the reporting entity.** Companies should present the disclosure as the first note or in a separate Summary of Significant Accounting Policies section preceding the notes to the financial statements.

The Summary of Significant Accounting Policies answers such questions as: What method of depreciation is used on plant assets? What valuation method is employed on inventories? What amortization policy is followed in regard to intangible assets? How are marketing costs handled for financial reporting purposes?

Refer to Appendix 5B, pages 202–228, for an illustration of note disclosure of accounting policies (Note 1) and other notes accompanying the audited financial statements of **The Procter & Gamble Company**. Illustration 24-2 (pages 1286–1287) shows another example, from **Tootsie Roll Industries**.

Analysts examine carefully the summary of accounting policies to determine whether a company is using conservative or liberal accounting practices. For example, depreciating plant assets over an unusually long period of time is considered liberal. Using LIFO inventory valuation in a period of inflation is generally viewed as conservative.

Companies that fail to adopt high-quality reporting policies may be heavily penalized by the market. For example, when **Microstrategy** disclosed that it would restate prior-year results due to use of aggressive revenue recognition policies, its share

---

[4]In response to cost-benefit concerns, the SEC has exempted some small public companies from certain rules implemented in response to the Sarbanes-Oxley Act of 2002. For example, smaller companies have more time to comply with the internal control rules required by the Sarbanes-Oxley law and have more time to file annual and interim reports. Both the FASB and the AICPA are studying the big GAAP/little GAAP issue to ensure that any kind of differential reporting is conceptually sound and meets the needs of users. See Remarks of Robert H. Herz, Chairman, Financial Accounting Standards Board, 2004 AICPA National Conference on Current SEC and PCAOB Reporting Developments (December 7, 2004.)

price dropped over 60 percent in one day. Investors viewed Microstrategy's quality of earnings as low.

ILLUSTRATION 24-2
Note Disclosure of
Accounting Policies

Tootsie Roll Industries, Inc. and Subsidiaries

(Dollars in thousands, except per share amounts)

Note 1—Significant Accounting Policies (in part)

Basis of consolidation:

The consolidated financial statements include the accounts of Tootsie Roll Industries, Inc. and its wholly-owned subsidiaries (the company), which are primarily engaged in the manufacture and sale of candy products. All significant intercompany transactions have been eliminated. . . .

Revenue recognition and other accounting pronouncements:

Products are sold to customers based on accepted purchase orders which include quantity, sales price and other relevant terms of sale. Revenues are recognized when products are delivered to customers and collectibility is reasonably assured. Shipping and handling costs of $31,795, $28,217 and $28,579 in 2004, 2003 and 2002, respectively, are included in selling, marketing and administrative expenses. Accounts receivable are unsecured. Revenues from a major customer aggregated approximately 20.8%, 20.6% and 19.6% of total net sales during the years ended December 31, 2004, 2003 and 2002, respectively. . . .

Cash and cash equivalents:

The company considers temporary cash investments with an original maturity of three months or less to be cash equivalents.

Investments:

Investments consist of various marketable securities with maturities of generally up to four years. The company classifies debt and equity securities as either held to maturity, available for sale or trading. Held to maturity securities represent those securities that the company has both the positive intent and ability to hold to maturity and are carried at amortized cost. Available for sale securities represent those securities that do not meet the classification of held to maturity, are not actively traded and are carried at fair value. Unrealized gains and losses on these securities are excluded from earnings and are reported as a separate component of shareholders equity, net of applicable taxes, until realized. Trading securities relate to deferred compensation arrangements and are carried at fair value.

Hedging activities:

From time to time, the company enters into commodities futures contracts that are intended and effective as hedges of market price risks associated with the anticipated purchase of certain raw materials (primarily sugar). To qualify as a hedge, the company evaluates a variety of characteristics of these transactions, including the probability that the anticipated transaction will occur. If the anticipated transaction were not to occur, the gain or loss would then be recognized in current earnings. The company does not engage in trading or other speculative use of derivative instruments. The company does assume the risk that counterparties may not be able to meet the terms of their contracts. The company does not expect any losses as a result of counterparty defaults.

  The company's derivative instruments are being accounted for as cash flow hedges and are recorded on the balance sheet at fair value. Changes therein are recorded in other comprehensive earnings and are reclassified to earnings in the periods in which earnings are affected by the hedged item. Substantially all amounts reported in accumulated other comprehensive earnings (loss) are expected to be reclassified to cost of goods sold. During the years ended December 31, 2004, 2003 and 2002, ineffectiveness related to cash flow hedges was not material.

Inventories:

Inventories are stated at cost, not to exceed market. The cost of substantially all of the company's inventories ($54,794 and $42,735 at December 31, 2004 and 2003, respectively) has been determined by the last-in, first-out (LIFO) method. The excess of current cost over LIFO cost of inventories approximates $5,868 and $6,442 at December 31, 2004 and 2003, respectively. The cost of certain foreign inventories ($3,983 and $3,351 at December 31, 2004 and 2003, respectively) has been determined by the first-in, first-out (FIFO) method. Rebates, discounts and other cash consideration received from a vendor related to inventory purchases is reflected as a reduction in the cost of the related inventory item, and is therefore reflected in cost of sales when the related inventory item is sold.

Property, plant and equipment:

Depreciation is computed for financial reporting purposes by use of the straight-line method based on useful lives of 20 to 35 years for buildings and 5 to 20 years for machinery and equipment. Depreciation expense was $11,680, $11,379 and $12,354 in 2004, 2003 and 2002, respectively, including $744 relating to equipment disposals.

Carrying value of long-lived assets:

The company reviews long-lived assets to determine if there are events or circumstances indicating that the amount of the asset reflected in the company's balance sheet may not be recoverable. When such indicators are present, the company compares the carrying value of the long-lived asset, or asset group, to the future undiscounted cash flows of the underlying assets to determine if an impairment exists. If applicable, an impairment charge would be recorded to write down the carrying value to its fair value. The determination of fair value involves the use of estimates of future cash flows that involve considerable management judgment and are based upon assumptions about expected future operating performance. The actual cash flows could differ from management's estimates due to changes in business conditions, operating performance, and economic conditions. No impairment charges were recorded by the company during 2004, 2003 or 2002.

Postretirement health care and life insurance benefits:

The company provides certain postretirement health care and life insurance benefits. The cost of these postretirement benefits is accrued during employees' working careers. The company also provides split dollar life insurance benefits to certain executive officers. The company records an asset equal to the cumulative insurance premiums that will be recovered upon the death of a covered employee(s) or earlier under the terms of the plan. Split dollar premiums paid were $3,620, $4,237 and $6,890 in 2004, 2003 and 2002, respectively.

Intangible assets:

The company accounts for intangible assets in accordance with SFAS No. 142, "Goodwill and Other Intangible Assets," which was adopted by the company on January 1, 2002. In accordance with this statement, goodwill and intangible assets with indefinite lives are not amortized, but rather tested for impairment at least annually. All trademarks have been assessed by management to have indefinite lives because they are expected to generate cash flows indefinitely. The company has completed its annual impairment testing of its goodwill and trademarks during the fourth quarter of each of the years presented, and no impairment was found.

Income taxes:

Deferred income taxes are recorded and recognized for future tax effects of temporary differences between financial and income tax reporting. Federal income taxes are provided on the portion of income of foreign subsidiaries that is expected to be remitted to the U.S. and become taxable, but not on the portion that is considered to be permanently invested in the foreign subsidiary.

Foreign currency translation:

The company has determined the functional currency for each foreign subsidiary. The U.S. dollar is used as the functional currency where a substantial portion of the subsidiary's business is indexed to the U.S. dollar or where its manufactured products are principally sold in the U.S. All other foreign subsidiaries use the local currency as their functional currency. Where the U.S. dollar is used as the functional currency, foreign currency translation adjustments are recorded as a charge or credit to other income in the statement of earnings. Where the foreign currency is used as the functional currency, translation adjustments are recorded as a separate component of comprehensive earnings (loss).

Joint venture:

The company's 50% interest in two Spanish companies is accounted for using the equity method. The company records an increase in its investment in the joint venture to the extent of its share of the joint venture's earnings, and reduces its investment to the extent of dividends received. No dividends were received during 2004.

Comprehensive earnings:

Comprehensive earnings includes net earnings, foreign currency translation adjustments and unrealized gains/losses on commodity hedging contracts and marketable securities.

Earnings per share:

A dual presentation of basic and diluted earnings per share is not required due to the lack of potentially dilutive securities under the company's simple capital structure. Therefore, all earnings per share amounts represent basic earnings per share. . . .

Common Notes

We have discussed many of the **notes to the financial statements** throughout this textbook, and will discuss others more fully in this chapter. The more common are as shown on the next two pages.

MAJOR DISCLOSURES

Inventory. Companies should report the basis upon which inventory amounts are stated (lower of cost or market) and the method used in determining cost (LIFO, FIFO, average cost, etc.). Manufacturers should report, either in the balance sheet or in a separate schedule in the notes, the inventory composition (finished goods, work in process, raw materials). Unusual or significant financing arrangements relating to inventories that may require disclosure include transactions with related parties, product financing arrangements, firm purchase commitments, involuntary liquidation of LIFO inventories, and pledging of inventories as collateral. Chapter 9 (pages 442–443) illustrates these disclosures.

Property, Plant, and Equipment. Companies should state the basis of valuation for property, plant, and equipment. It is usually historical cost. Companies also should disclose pledges, liens, and other commitments related to these assets. In the presentation of depreciation, companies should disclose the following in the financial statements or in the notes: (1) depreciation expense for the period; (2) balances of major classes of depreciable assets, by nature and function, at the balance sheet date; (3) accumulated depreciation, either by major classes of depreciable assets or in total, at the balance sheet date; and (4) a general description of the method or methods used in computing depreciation with respect to major classes of depreciable assets. Finally, companies should explain any major impairments. Chapter 11 (pages 543–544) illustrates these disclosures.

Creditor Claims. Investors normally find it extremely useful to understand the nature and cost of creditor claims. However, the liabilities section in the balance sheet can provide the major types of liabilities only in the aggregate. Note schedules regarding such obligations provide additional information about how a company is financing its operations, the costs that it will bear in future periods, and the timing of future cash outflows. Financial statements must disclose for each of the five years following the date of the statements the aggregate amount of maturities and sinking fund requirements for all long-term borrowings. Chapter 14 (pages 694–695) illustrates these disclosures.

Equity Holders' Claims. Many companies present in the body of the balance sheet information about equity securities: the number of shares authorized, issued, and outstanding and the par value for each type of security. Or, companies may present such data in a note. Beyond that, a common equity note disclosure relates to contracts and senior securities outstanding that might affect the various claims of the residual equity holders. An example would be the existence of outstanding stock options, outstanding convertible debt, redeemable preferred stock, and convertible preferred stock. In addition, it is necessary to disclose certain types of restrictions currently in force. Generally, these types of restrictions involve the amount of earnings available for dividend distribution. Examples of these types of disclosures are illustrated in Chapter 15 (pages 749–751) and Chapter 16 (pages 803–804).

Contingencies and Commitments. A company may have gain or loss contingencies that are not disclosed in the body of the financial statements. These contingencies include litigation, debt and other guarantees, possible tax assessments, renegotiation of government contracts, and sales of receivables with recourse. In addition, companies should disclose in the notes commitments that relate to dividend restrictions, purchase agreements (through-put and take-or-pay), hedge contracts, and employment contracts. Disclosures of such items are illustrated in Chapter 7 (pages 337–338), Chapter 9 (pages 431–432), and Chapter 13 (pages 642–645).

Deferred Taxes, Pensions, and Leases. The FASB also requires extensive disclosure in the areas of deferred taxes, pensions, and leases. Chapter 19 (pages 984–988),

UNDERLYING CONCEPTS

The AICPA Special Committee on Financial Reporting notes that standard setters should address disclosures and accounting requirements for off-balance-sheet financial arrangements. The goal should be to report the risks, opportunities, resources, and obligations that result from those arrangements, consistent with users' needs for information.

Chapter 20 (pages 1043–1052), and Chapter 21 (pages 1118–1120) discuss in detail each of these disclosures. Users of financial statements should carefully read notes to the financial statements for information about off-balance-sheet commitments, future financing needs, and the quality of a company's earnings.

Changes in Accounting Principles. The profession defines various types of accounting changes and establishes guides for reporting each type. Companies discuss, either in the summary of significant accounting policies or in the other notes, changes in accounting principles (as well as material changes in estimates and corrections of errors). See Chapter 22 (pages 1158–1163 and 1165–1166).

In earlier chapters we discussed the disclosures listed above. The following sections of this chapter illustrate four additional disclosures of significance—special transactions or events, subsequent events, segment reporting, and interim reporting.

Additional Examples of Major Disclosures

MORE PAGES, BUT BETTER?

The biggest overall change in annual reports recently is that companies are now disclosing debt-rating triggers buried in their financing arrangements. These triggers can require a company to pay off a loan immediately if the debt rating collapses; they are one of the reasons **Enron** crumbled so quickly. But few Enron stockholders knew about them until the gun had gone off. Companies are also telling more about their bank credit lines, liquidity, and any special purpose entities, which were major villains in the Enron drama.

Source: Gretchen Morgenson, "Annual Reports: More Pages, But Better?" *New York Times* (March 17, 2002).

WHAT DO THE NUMBERS MEAN?

DISCLOSURE ISSUES

Disclosure of Special Transactions or Events

Related-party transactions, errors and irregularities, and illegal acts pose especially sensitive and difficult problems. The accountant/auditor who has responsibility for reporting on these types of transactions must take care to properly balance the rights of the reporting company and the needs of users of the financial statements.

Related-party transactions arise when a company engages in transactions in which one of the parties has the ability to significantly influence the policies of the other. They may also occur when a nontransacting party has the ability to influence the policies of the two transacting parties.[5] Competitive, free-market dealings may not exist in related-party transactions, and so an "arm's-length" basis cannot be assumed. Transactions such as borrowing or lending money at abnormally low or high interest rates, real estate sales at amounts that differ significantly from appraised value, exchanges of nonmonetary assets, and transactions involving enterprises that have no economic substance ("shell corporations") suggest that related parties may be involved.

---

[5]Examples of related-party transactions include transactions between (a) a parent company and its subsidiaries; (b) subsidiaries of a common parent; (c) a company and trusts for the benefit of employees (controlled or managed by the enterprise); and (d) a company and its principal owners, management, or members of immediate families, and affiliates. Two classic cases of related-party transactions were **Enron**, with its misuse of special purpose entities, and **Tyco International**, which forgave loans to its management team.

In order to make adequate disclosure, companies should report the economic substance, rather than the legal form, of these transactions. *FASB Statement No. 57* requires the following disclosures of material related-party transactions.

1 The nature of the relationship(s) involved.

2 A description of the transactions (including transactions to which no amounts or nominal amounts were ascribed) for each of the periods for which income statements are presented.

3 The dollar amounts of transactions for each of the periods for which income statements are presented.

4 Amounts due from or to related parties as of the date of each balance sheet presented.

Illustration 24-3, from the annual report of **Knight-Ridder, Inc.**, shows disclosure of related-party transactions.

ILLUSTRATION 24-3
Disclosure of Related
Party Transactions

Knight-Ridder, Inc.

Note 8 (in part): Related Party Transactions
We have ongoing purchase commitments with SP and Ponderay, our two newsprint mill partnership investments. These future commitments are for the purchase of a minimum of $42.5 million and $13.8 million of newsprint with SP and Ponderay, respectively, at current market prices. We also have a sales commitment with DN to supply them with 50% of their newsprint requirements, which will be approximately $27.4 million. We have the resources necessary to fulfill these commitments.

Many companies are involved in related-party transactions. Errors, irregularities, and illegal acts, however, are the exception rather than the rule. Accounting **errors** are *unintentional* mistakes, whereas **irregularities** are *intentional* distortions of financial statements.[6] As indicated earlier, companies should correct the financial statements when they discover errors. The same treatment should be given irregularities. The discovery of irregularities, however, gives rise to a different set of procedures and responsibilities for the accountant/auditor.[7]

Illegal acts encompass such items as illegal political contributions, bribes, kickbacks, and other violations of laws and regulations.[8] In these situations, the accountant/auditor must evaluate the adequacy of disclosure in the financial statements. For example, if a company derives revenue from an illegal act that is considered material in relation to the financial statements, this information should be disclosed. The Sarbanes-Oxley Act of 2002 is intended to deter these illegal acts. This law adds significant fines and longer jail time for those who improperly sign off on the correctness of financial statements that include willing and knowing misstatements.

Disclosure plays a very important role in these types of transactions because the events are more qualitative than quantitative and involve more subjective than objective evaluation. Users of the financial statements need some indication of the existence and nature of these transactions, through disclosures, modifications in the auditor's report, or reports of changes in auditors.

---

[6]"The Auditor's Responsibility to Detect and Report Errors and Irregularities," *Statement on Auditing Standards No. 53* (New York, AICPA, 1988). Since passage of the Sarbanes-Oxley Act of 2002, auditors of public companies are regulated by the Public Company Accounting Oversight Board (PCAOB). While the PCAOB has developed some new auditing standards, this Board has for the most part adopted the prior auditing standards issued by the Auditing Standards Board of the AICPA.

[7]The profession became so concerned with certain management frauds that affect financial statements that it established a National Commission on Fraudulent Financial Reporting. The major purpose of this organization was to determine how fraudulent reporting practices could be constrained. Fraudulent financial reporting is discussed later in this chapter.

[8]"Illegal Acts by Clients," *Statement on Auditing Standards No. 54* (New York, AICPA, 1988).

Post-Balance-Sheet Events (Subsequent Events)

Notes to the financial statements should explain any significant financial events that took place after the formal balance sheet date, but before the statement is issued. These events are referred to as **post-balance-sheet events**, or just plain **subsequent events**. Illustration 24-4 shows a time diagram of the subsequent events period.

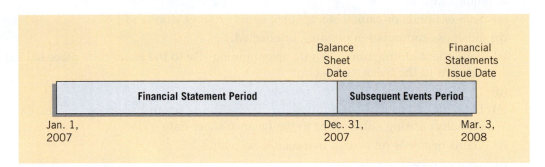

ILLUSTRATION 24-4
Time Periods for
Subsequent Events

A period of several weeks, and sometimes months, may elapse after the end of the fiscal year but before the company issues financial statements. Various activities involved in closing the books for the period and issuing the statements all take time: taking and pricing the inventory, reconciling subsidiary ledgers with controlling accounts, preparing necessary adjusting entries, ensuring that all transactions for the period have been entered, obtaining an audit of the financial statements by independent certified public accountants, and printing the annual report. During the period between the balance sheet date and its distribution to stockholders and creditors, important transactions or other events may occur that materially affect the company's financial position or operating situation.

Many who read a balance sheet believe the balance sheet condition is constant, and they project it into the future. However, readers must be told if the company has experienced a significant change—e.g., sold one of its plants, acquired a subsidiary, suffered extraordinary losses, settled significant litigation, or experienced any other important event in the post-balance-sheet period. Without an explanation in a note, the reader might be misled and draw inappropriate conclusions.

Two types of events or transactions occurring after the balance sheet date may have a material effect on the financial statements or may need disclosure so that readers interpret these statements accurately:

1 Events that provide additional evidence about conditions that existed at the balance sheet date, that affect the estimates used in preparing financial statements, and that require adjustments to the financial statement. All information available prior to the issuance of the financial statements helps investors and creditors evaluate estimates previously made. To ignore these subsequent events is to pass up an opportunity to improve the accuracy of the financial statements. This first type of event encompasses information that an accountant would have recorded in the accounts had the information been known at the balance sheet date.

For example, if a loss on an account receivable results from a customer's bankruptcy subsequent to the balance sheet date, the company adjusts the financial statements before their issuance. The bankruptcy stems from the customer's poor financial health existing at the balance sheet date.

The same criterion applies to settlements of litigation. The company must adjust the financial statements if the events that gave rise to the litigation, such as personal injury or patent infringement, took place prior to the balance sheet date.

2 Events that provide evidence about conditions that did not exist at the balance sheet date but arise subsequent to that date, and that do not require adjustment of the financial statements. To illustrate, a loss resulting from a customer's fire or flood

UNDERLYING CONCEPTS

The periodicity or time period assumption implies that economic activities of an enterprise can be divided into artificial time periods for purpose of analysis.

after the balance sheet date does not reflect conditions existing at that date. Thus, adjustment of the financial statements is not necessary. However, some of these events may have to be disclosed to keep the financial statements from being misleading. These disclosures take the form of notes, supplemental schedules, or even pro forma ("as if") financial data prepared as if the event had occurred on the balance sheet date. Examples of such events that require disclosure (but do not result in adjustment) are:

(a) Sale of bonds or capital stock; stock splits or stock dividends.

(b) Business combination pending or effected.

(c) Settlement of litigation when the event giving rise to the claim took place subsequent to the balance sheet date.

(d) Loss of plant or inventories from fire or flood.

(e) Losses on receivables resulting from conditions (such as customer's major casualty) arising subsequent to the balance sheet date.

(f) Gains or losses on certain marketable securities.[9]

Illustration 24-5 presents an example of subsequent events disclosure, excerpted from the annual report of **Goodrich Corporation**.

ILLUSTRATION 24-5
Disclosure of Subsequent Events

Goodrich Corporation

Note W. Subsequent Event
On February 16, 2004 the Company was notified by Pratt & Whitney, a United Technologies Company, that it will not meet the requirements for original equipment PW4000 engine components after the Company completes delivery of 45 shipsets (2 units per shipset) through early 2005. The Company had originally forecasted 90 shipsets to be delivered through 2009. As a result of this action, the total estimated revenue associated with this contract has been significantly reduced and anticipated cost reductions related to future deliveries under this contract will not occur.

The notice of termination is considered a Type 1 subsequent event under generally accepted accounting principles, the effects of which must be reflected in the Company's 2003 financial statements. As a result, the Company recorded a pre-tax charge of $15.1 million, as of December 31, 2003 related to this contract. The charge includes impairment of excess over average inventory of $7.0 million and $8.1 million for forward losses relating to the reduction in forecasted contract revenue and the increase in costs.

Many subsequent events or developments do not require adjustment of or disclosure in the financial statements. Typically, these are nonaccounting events or conditions that management normally communicates by other means. These events include legislation, product changes, management changes, strikes, unionization, marketing agreements, and loss of important customers.

Reporting for Diversified (Conglomerate) Companies

OBJECTIVE 3
Discuss the disclosure requirements for major business segments.

In certain business climates, companies have a tendency to diversify their operations. Take the case of conglomerate **General Electric (GE)**, whose products include locomotives and jet engines, credit card services, and water purification systems. Its

---

[9]"Subsequent Events," *Statement on Auditing Standards No. 1* (New York: AICPA, 1973), pp. 123–124. *Accounting Trends and Techniques—2004* listed the following types of subsequent events and their frequency of occurrence among the 600 companies surveyed: business combinations pending or effected, 83; debt incurred, reduced, or refinanced, 64; discontinued operations, 59; litigation, 29; and capital stock issued or repurchased, 27. The recent effects from hurricanes Katrina and Rita, which occurred after the year-end for companies with August fiscal years, require disclosure in order to keep the statements from being misleading. Some companies may have to consider whether these disasters affect their ability to continue as going concerns.

NBC Universal subsidiary owns **NBC TV**, **Vivendi Universal Entertainment**, and **Universal Pictures**. When businesses are so diversified, investors and investment analysts want more information about the details behind conglomerate financial statements. Particularly, they want income statement, balance sheet, and cash flow information on the **individual segments** that compose the total income figure.

Illustration 24-6 shows **segmented** (disaggregated) financial information of an office equipment and auto parts company.

ILLUSTRATION 24-6
Segmented Income
Statement

OFFICE EQUIPMENT AND AUTO PARTS COMPANY INCOME STATEMENT DATA (IN MILLIONS)			
	Consolidated	Office Equipment	Auto Parts
Net sales	$78.8	$18.0	$60.8
Manufacturing costs			
Inventories, beginning	12.3	4.0	8.3
Materials and services	38.9	10.8	28.1
Wages	12.9	3.8	9.1
Inventories, ending	(13.3)	(3.9)	(9.4)
	50.8	14.7	36.1
Selling and administrative expense	12.1	1.6	10.5
Total operating expenses	62.9	16.3	46.6
Income before taxes	15.9	1.7	14.2
Income taxes	(9.3)	(1.0)	(8.3)
Net income	$ 6.6	$ 0.7	$ 5.9

Much information is hidden in the aggregated totals. If the analyst has only the consolidated figures, he/she cannot tell the extent to which the differing product lines **contribute to the company's profitability**, **risk, and growth potential**. For example, in Illustration 24-6, the office equipment segment looks like a risky venture. Segmented reporting would provide useful information about the two business segments and would be useful for making an informed investment decision regarding the whole company.

A classic situation that demonstrates the need for segmented data involved **Caterpillar, Inc.** The SEC cited Caterpillar because it failed to tell investors that nearly a quarter of its income in one year came from a Brazilian unit and was nonrecurring in nature. The company knew that different economic policies in the next year would probably greatly affect earnings of the Brazilian unit. But Caterpillar presented its financial results on a consolidated basis, not disclosing the Brazilian operations. The SEC found that Caterpillar's failure to include information about Brazil left investors with an incomplete picture of the company's financial results and denied investors the opportunity to see the company "through the eyes of management."

Companies have always been somewhat hesitant to disclose segmented data for various reasons:

1 Without a thorough knowledge of the business and an understanding of such important factors as the competitive environment and capital investment requirements, the investor may find the segmented information meaningless or may even draw improper conclusions about the reported earnings of the segments.

2 Additional disclosure may be helpful to competitors, labor unions, suppliers, and certain government regulatory agencies, and thus harm the reporting company.

3 Additional disclosure may discourage management from taking intelligent business risks because segments reporting losses or unsatisfactory earnings may cause stockholder dissatisfaction with management.

4 The wide variation among companies in the choice of segments, cost allocation, and other accounting problems limits the usefulness of segmented information.

5 The investor is investing in the company as a whole and not in the particular segments, and it should not matter how any single segment is performing if the overall performance is satisfactory.

6 Certain technical problems, such as classification of segments and allocation of segment revenues and costs (especially "common costs"), are formidable.

On the other hand, the advocates of segmented disclosures offer these reasons in support of the practice:

1 Investors need segmented information to make an intelligent investment decision regarding a diversified company.

   (a) Sales and earnings of individual segments enable investors to evaluate the differences between segments in growth rate, risk, and profitability, and to forecast consolidated profits.

   (b) Segmented reports help investors evaluate the company's investment worth by disclosing the nature of a company's businesses and the relative size of the components.

2 The absence of segmented reporting by a diversified company may put its unsegmented, single product-line competitors at a competitive disadvantage because the conglomerate may obscure information that its competitors must disclose.

The advocates of segmented disclosures appear to have a much stronger case. Many users indicate that segmented data are the most useful financial information provided, aside from the basic financial statements. As a result, the FASB has issued extensive reporting guidelines in this area.

Objective of Reporting Segmented Information

The objective of reporting segmented financial data is to provide information about the **different types of business activities** in which an enterprise engages and the **different economic environments** in which it operates. Meeting this objective will help users of financial statements do the following.

(a) Better understand the enterprise's performance.

(b) Better assess its prospects for future net cash flows.

(c) Make more informed judgments about the enterprise as a whole.

Basic Principles

Financial statements can be disaggregated in several ways. For example, they can be disaggregated by products or services, by geography, by legal entity, or by type of customer. However, it is not feasible to provide all of that information in every set of financial statements. *FASB Statement No. 131* requires that general purpose financial statements include selected information on a single basis of segmentation. Thus, a company can meet the segmented reporting objective by providing financial statements segmented based on how the company's operations are managed. The method chosen is referred to as the **management approach**.[10] **The management approach reflects how management segments the company for making operating decisions.** The segments are evident from the components of the company's organization structure. These components are called **operating segments**.

Identifying Operating Segments

An **operating segment** is a component of an enterprise:

(a) That engages in business activities from which it earns revenues and incurs expenses.

---

[10]"Disclosures about Segments of an Enterprise and Related Information," *Statement of Financial Accounting Standards No. 131* (Norwalk, Conn.: FASB, 1997).

(b) Whose operating results are regularly reviewed by the company's chief operating decision maker to assess segment performance and allocate resources to the segment.

(c) For which discrete financial information is available that is generated by or based on the internal financial reporting system.

Companies may aggregate information about two or more operating segments only if the segments have the same basic characteristics in each of the following areas.

(a) The nature of the products and services provided.

(b) The nature of the production process.

(c) The type or class of customer.

(d) The methods of product or service distribution.

(e) If applicable, the nature of the regulatory environment.

After the company decides on the possible segments for disclosure, it makes a quantitative materiality test. This test determines whether the segment is significant enough to warrant actual disclosure. An operating segment is deemed significant, and therefore a reportable segment, if it satisfies **one or more** of the following quantitative thresholds.

1 Its **revenue** (including both sales to external customers and intersegment sales or transfers) is 10 percent or more of the combined revenue of all the company's operating segments.

2 The absolute amount of its **profit or loss** is 10 percent or more of the greater, in absolute amount, of **(a)** the combined operating profit of all operating segments that did not incur a loss, or **(b)** the combined loss of all operating segments that did report a loss.

3 Its **identifiable assets** are 10 percent or more of the combined assets of all operating segments.

In applying these tests, the company must consider two additional factors. First, segment data must explain a significant portion of the company's business. Specifically, the segmented results must equal or exceed 75 percent of the combined sales to unaffiliated customers for the entire company. This test prevents a company from providing limited information on only a few segments and lumping all the rest into one category.

Second, the profession recognizes that reporting too many segments may overwhelm users with detailed information. The FASB decided that 10 is a reasonable upper limit for the number of segments that a company must disclose.

To illustrate these requirements, assume a company has identified six possible reporting segments, as shown in Illustration 24-7 (000s omitted).

Segments	Total Revenue (Unaffiliated)	Operating Profit (Loss)	Identifiable Assets
A	$ 100	$10	$ 60
B	50	2	30
C	700	40	390
D	300	20	160
E	900	18	280
F	100	(5)	50
	$2,150	$85	$970

ILLUSTRATION 24-7
Data for Different Possible Reporting Segments

The company would apply the respective tests as follows:

Revenue test: 10% × $2,150 = $215; C, D, and E meet this test.

Operating profit (loss) test: 10% × $90 = $9 (note that the $5 loss is ignored, because the test is based on non-loss segments); A, C, D, and E meet this test.

Identifiable assets tests: 10% × $970 = $97; C, D, and E meet this test.

The reporting segments are therefore A, C, D, and E, assuming that these four segments have enough sales to meet the 75 percent of combined sales test. The 75 percent test is computed as follows.

75% of combined sales test: $75\% \times \$2,150 = \$1,612.50$. The sales of A, C, D, and E total $2,000 ($100 + $700 + $300 + $900); therefore, the 75 percent test is met.

Measurement Principles

The accounting principles that companies use for segment disclosure need not be the same as the principles they use to prepare the consolidated statements. This flexibility may at first appear inconsistent. But, preparing segment information in accordance with generally accepted accounting principles would be difficult because some principles are not expected to apply at a segment level. Examples are accounting for the cost of company-wide employee benefit plans, accounting for income taxes in a company that files a consolidated tax return, and accounting for inventory on a LIFO basis if the pool includes items in more than one segment.

The FASB does not require allocations of joint, common, or company-wide costs solely for external reporting purposes. **Common costs** are those incurred for the benefit of more than one segment and whose interrelated nature prevents a completely objective division of costs among segments. For example, the company president's salary is difficult to allocate to various segments. Allocations of common costs are inherently arbitrary and may not be meaningful. There is a presumption that if companies allocate common costs to segments, these allocations are either directly attributable or reasonably allocable.

Segmented Information Reported

The FASB requires that an enterprise report the following.

1 *General information about its operating segments.* This includes factors that management considers most significant in determining the company's operating segments, and the types of products and services from which each operating segment derives its revenues.

2 *Segment profit and loss and related information.* Specifically, companies must report the following information about each operating segment if the amounts are included in determining segment profit or loss.

   (a) Revenues from transactions with external customers.

   (b) Revenues from transactions with other operating segments of the same enterprise.

   (c) Interest revenue.

   (d) Interest expense.

   (e) Depreciation, depletion, and amortization expense.

   (f) Unusual items.

   (g) Equity in the net income of investees accounted for by the equity method.

   (h) Income tax expense or benefit.

   (i) Extraordinary items.

   (j) Significant noncash items other than depreciation, depletion, and amortization expense.

3 *Segment assets.* A company must report each operating segment's total assets.

4 *Reconciliations.* A company must provide a reconciliation of the total of the segments' revenues to total revenues, a reconciliation of the total of the operating segments' profits and losses to its income before income taxes, and a reconciliation of the total of the operating segments' assets to total assets.

5 *Information about products and services and geographic areas.* For each operating segment not based on geography, the company must report (unless it is impracticable): (1) revenues from external customers, (2) long-lived assets, and (3) expenditures during the period for long-lived assets. This information, if material, must be reported (a) in the enterprise's country of domicile and (b) in each other country.

6 *Major customers.* If 10 percent or more of company revenue is derived from a single customer, the company must disclose the total amount of revenue from each such customer by segment.

Illustration of Disaggregated Information

Illustration 24-8 shows the segment disclosure for **Johnson & Johnson**.

ILLUSTRATION 24-8
Segment Disclosure

Johnson&Johnson

Johnson & Johnson
(Notes excluded)
Segments of Business and Geographic Areas

			Sales to Customers		
(dollars in millions)			2004	2003	2002
Consumer—United States			$ 4,224	$ 3,968	$ 3,605
International			4,109	3,463	2,959
Total			8,333	7,431	6,564
Pharmaceutical—United States			14,960	13,271	11,919
International			7,168	6,246	5,232
Total			22,128	19,517	17,151
Medical Devices and Diagnostics—United States			8,586	8,035	6,931
International			8,301	6,879	5,652
Total			16,887	14,914	12,583
Worldwide total			$47,348	$41,862	$36,298

	Operating Profit			Identifiable Assets		
(dollars in millions)	2004	2003	2002	2004	2003	2002
Consumer	$ 1,514	$1,393	$1,229	$ 6,142	$ 5,371	$ 5,056
Pharmaceutical	7,608	5,896	5,787	16,058	15,001	11,112
Medical Devices and Diagnostics	4,091	3,370	2,489	15,805	16,082	15,052
Segments total	13,213	10,659	9,505	38,005	36,454	31,220
Expenses not allocated to segments	(375)	(351)	(214)			
General corporate				15,312	11,809	9,336
Worldwide total	$12,838	$10,308	$9,291	$53,317	$ 48,263	$40,556

	Additions to Property, Plant & Equipment			Depreciation and Amortization		
(dollars in millions)	2004	2003	2002	2004	2003	2002
Consumer	$ 227	$ 229	$ 222	$ 222	$ 246	$ 244
Pharmaceutical	1,197	1,236	1,012	1,008	765	557
Medical Devices and Diagnostics	630	639	713	769	761	776
Segments total	2,054	2,104	1,947	1,999	1,772	1,577
General corporate	121	158	152	125	97	85
Worldwide total	$2,175	$2,262	$2,099	$2,124	$1,869	$1,662

	Sales to Customers			Long-Lived Assets		
(dollars in millions)	2004	2003	2002	2004	2003	2002
United States	$27,770	$25,274	$22,455	$14,324	$14,367	$11,822
Europe	11,151	9,483	7,636	6,142	5,193	4,613
Western Hemisphere excluding U.S.	2,589	2,236	2,018	748	772	583
Asia-Pacific, Africa	5,838	4,869	4,189	620	605	555
Segments total	47,348	41,862	36,298	21,834	20,937	17,573
General corporate				444	448	383
Other non long-lived assets				31,039	26,878	22,600
Worldwide total	$47,348	$41,862	$36,298	$53,317	$48,263	$40,556

Interim Reports

Another source of information for the investor is interim reports. As noted earlier, **interim reports** cover periods of less than one year. The stock exchanges, the SEC, and the accounting profession have an active interest in the presentation of interim information.

The SEC mandates that certain companies file a **Form 10-Q**, in which a company discloses quarterly data similar to that disclosed in the annual report. It also requires those companies to disclose selected quarterly information in notes to the annual financial statements. Illustration 24-9 presents the selected quarterly disclosure of **Tootsie Roll Industries, Inc.** In addition to Form 10-Q, the APB issued *Opinion No. 28*, which attempted to narrow the reporting alternatives related to interim reports.[11]

OBJECTIVE 4
Describe the accounting problems associated with interim reporting.

ILLUSTRATION 24-9
Disclosure of Selected Quarterly Data

Tootsie Roll Industries, Inc.
For the Year Ended December 31, 2004

(Thousands of dollars except per share data)

	First	Second	Third	Fourth	Total
Net sales	$80,046	$77,157	$156,971	$105,936	$420,110
Gross margin	34,730	34,992	64,804	41,083	175,609
Net earnings	11,493	11,828	26,976	13,877	64,174
Net earnings per share	.22	.22	.52	.27	1.23

	Stock Prices 2004		Dividends 2004
	High	Low	
1st Qtr	$37.86	$35.00	$.0681
2nd Qtr	$37.60	$32.41	$.0701
3rd Qtr	$32.60	$29.08	$.0700
4th Qtr	$34.63	$29.24	$.0700

UNDERLYING CONCEPTS

For information to be relevant, it must be available to decision makers before it loses its capacity to influence their decisions (timeliness). Interim reporting is an excellent example of this concept.

Because of the short-term nature of the information in these reports, there is considerable controversy as to the general approach companies should employ. One group, which favors the **discrete approach**, believes that companies should treat each interim period as a separate accounting period. Using that treatment, companies would follow the principles for deferrals and accruals used for annual reports. In this view, companies should report accounting transactions as they occur, and expense recognition should not change with the period of time covered.

Another group, which favors the **integral approach**, believes that the interim report is an integral part of the annual report and that deferrals and accruals should take into consideration what will happen for the entire year. In this approach, companies should assign estimated expenses to parts of a year on the basis of sales volume or some other activity base.

At present, many companies follow the discrete approach for certain types of expenses and the integral approach for others, because the standards currently employed in practice are vague and lead to differing interpretations.

Interim Reporting Requirements

Generally, companies should use the same accounting principles for interim reports and for annual reports. They should recognize revenues in interim periods on the same basis as they are for annual periods. For example, if Cedars Corp. uses the installment-sales method as the basis for recognizing revenue on an annual basis, then it should

[11] "Interim Financial Reporting," *Opinions of the Accounting Principles Board No. 28* (New York: AICPA, 1973).

use the installment basis for interim reports as well. Also, Cedars should treat costs directly associated with revenues (product costs, such as materials, labor and related fringe benefits, and manufacturing overhead) in the same manner for interim reports as for annual reports.

Companies should use the same inventory pricing methods (FIFO, LIFO, etc.) for interim reports and for annual reports. However, the following exceptions are appropriate at interim reporting periods.

1 Companies may use the gross profit method for interim inventory pricing. But they must disclose the method and adjustments to reconcile with annual inventory.

2 When a company liquidates LIFO inventories at an interim date and expects to replace them by year-end, cost of goods sold should include the expected cost of replacing the liquidated LIFO base, rather than give effect to the interim liquidation.

3 Companies should not defer inventory market declines beyond the interim period unless they are temporary and no loss is expected for the fiscal year.

4 Companies ordinarily should defer planned variances under a standard cost system; such variances are expected to be absorbed by year-end.

Companies often charge to the interim period, as incurred, costs and expenses other than product costs (often referred to as **period costs**). But companies may allocate these costs among interim periods on the basis of an estimate of time expired, benefit received, or activity associated with the periods. Companies display considerable latitude in accounting for these costs in interim periods, and many believe more definitive guidelines are needed.

Regarding disclosure, companies should report the following interim data at a minimum.

1 Sales or gross revenues, provision for income taxes, extraordinary items, and net income.

2 Basic and diluted earnings per share where appropriate.

3 Seasonal revenue, cost, or expenses.

4 Significant changes in estimates or provisions for income taxes.

5 Disposal of a component of a business and extraordinary, unusual, or infrequently occurring items.

6 Contingent items.

7 Changes in accounting principles or estimates.

8 Significant changes in financial position.

The FASB encourages, but does not require, companies to publish an interim balance sheet and statement of cash flows. If a company does not present this information, it should disclose significant changes in such items as liquid assets, net working capital, long-term liabilities, and stockholders' equity.

Unique Problems of Interim Reporting

In *APB Opinion No. 28*, the Board indicated that it favored the integral approach. However, within this broad guideline, a number of unique reporting problems develop related to the following items.

Advertising and Similar Costs. The general guidelines are that companies should defer in an interim period costs such as advertising if the benefits extend beyond that period; otherwise the company should expense those costs as incurred. But such a determination is difficult, and even if the company defers the costs, how should it allocate them between quarters?

Because of the vague guidelines in this area, accounting for advertising varies widely. At one time, some companies in the food industry, such as **RJR Nabisco** and **Pillsbury**, charged advertising costs as a percentage of sales and adjusted to actual at year-end, whereas **General Foods** and **Kellogg** expensed these costs as incurred.

The same type of problem relates to such items as Social Security taxes, research and development costs, and major repairs. For example, should the company expense Social Security costs (payroll taxes) on highly paid personnel early in the year, or allocate and spread them to subsequent quarters? Should a major repair that occurs later in the year be anticipated and allocated proportionately to earlier periods?

Expenses Subject to Year-End Adjustment. Companies often do not know with a great deal of certainty amounts of bad debts, executive bonuses, pension costs, and inventory shrinkage until year-end. **They should estimate these costs and allocate them to interim periods as best they can.** Companies use a variety of allocation techniques to accomplish this objective.

Income Taxes. Not every dollar of corporate taxable income is taxed at the same rate; the tax rate is progressive. This aspect of business income taxes poses a problem in preparing interim financial statements. Should the company use the **annualized approach**, which is to annualize income to date and accrue the proportionate income tax for the period to date? Or should it follow the **marginal principle approach,** which is to apply the lower rate of tax to the first amount of income earned? At one time, companies generally followed the latter approach and accrued the tax applicable to each additional dollar of income.

The profession now, however, uses the annualized approach. This requires that "at the end of each interim period the company should make its best estimate of the effective tax rate expected to be applicable for the full fiscal year. The rate so determined should be used in providing for income taxes on income for the quarter."[12]

Because businesses did not uniformly apply this guideline in accounting for similar situations, the FASB issued *Interpretation No. 18*. This interpretation requires that to compute the year-to-date tax, companies apply the **estimated annual effective tax rate** to the year-to-date "ordinary" income at the end of each interim period. Further, the **interim period tax** related to "ordinary" income shall be the difference between the amount so computed and the amounts reported for previous interim periods of the fiscal period.[13]

Extraordinary Items. Extraordinary items consist of unusual and nonrecurring material gains and losses. In the past, companies handled them in interim reports in one of three ways: (1) absorbed them entirely in the quarter in which they occurred; (2) prorated them over four quarters; or (3) disclosed them only by note. **The required approach now is to charge or credit the loss or gain in the quarter in which it occurs**, instead of attempting some arbitrary multiple-period allocation. This approach is consistent with the way in which companies must handle extraordinary items on an annual basis. No attempt is made to prorate the extraordinary items over several years.

Some favor the omission of extraordinary items from the quarterly net income. They believe that inclusion of extraordinary items that may be large in proportion to interim results distorts the predictive value of interim reports. Many, however, consider such an omission inappropriate because it deviates from actual results.

Earnings per Share. Interim reporting of earnings per share has all the problems inherent in computing and presenting annual earnings per share, and then some. If a company issues shares in the third period, EPS for the first two periods will not reflect

---

[12]"Interim Financial Reporting," *Opinions of the Accounting Principles Board No. 28* (New York: AICPA, 1973), par. 19. The estimated annual effective tax rate should reflect anticipated tax credits, foreign tax rates, percentage depletion, capital gains rates, and other available tax planning alternatives.

[13]"Accounting for Income Taxes in Interim Periods," *FASB Interpretation No. 18* (Stamford, Conn.: FASB, March 1977), par. 9. "Ordinary" income (or loss) refers to "income (or loss) from continuing operations before income taxes (or benefits)" excluding extraordinary items, discontinued operations, and cumulative effects of changes in accounting principles.

year-end EPS. If an extraordinary item is present in one period and the company sells new equity shares in another period, the EPS figure for the extraordinary item will change for the year. On an annual basis only one EPS figure can be associated with an extraordinary item and that figure does not change; the interim figure is subject to change.

For purposes of computing earnings per share and making the required disclosure determinations, each interim period should stand alone. That is, all applicable tests should be made for that single period.

Seasonality. **Seasonality** occurs when most of a company's sales occur in one short period of the year while certain costs are fairly evenly spread throughout the year. For example, the natural gas industry has its heavy sales in the winter months. In contrast, the beverage industry has its heavy sales in the summer months.

The problem of seasonality is related to the matching concept in accounting. Expenses should be matched against the revenues they create. In a seasonal business, wide fluctuations in profits occur because off-season sales do not absorb the company's fixed costs (for example, manufacturing, selling, and administrative costs that tend to remain fairly constant regardless of sales or production).

To illustrate why seasonality is a problem, assume the following information.

Selling price per unit	$1
Annual sales for the period (projected and actual)	
100,000 units @ $1	$100,000
Manufacturing costs	
Variable	10¢ per unit
Fixed	20¢ per unit or $20,000 for the year
Nonmanufacturing costs	
Variable	10¢ per unit
Fixed	30¢ per unit or $30,000 for the year

ILLUSTRATION 24-10
Data for Seasonality Example

Sales for four quarters and the year (projected and actual) were:

		Percent of Sales
1st Quarter	$ 20,000	20%
2nd Quarter	5,000	5
3rd Quarter	10,000	10
4th Quarter	65,000	65
Total for the year	$100,000	100%

ILLUSTRATION 24-11
Sales Data for Seasonality Example

Under the present accounting framework, the income statements for the quarters might be as shown in Illustration 24-12.

	1st Qtr	2nd Qtr	3rd Qtr	4th Qtr	Year
Sales	$20,000	$ 5,000	$10,000	$65,000	$100,000
Manufacturing costs					
Variable	(2,000)	(500)	(1,000)	(6,500)	(10,000)
Fixed[a]	(4,000)	(1,000)	(2,000)	(13,000)	(20,000)
	14,000	3,500	7,000	45,500	70,000
Nonmanufacturing costs					
Variable	(2,000)	(500)	(1,000)	(6,500)	(10,000)
Fixed[b]	(7,500)	(7,500)	(7,500)	(7,500)	(30,000)
Net income	$ 4,500	$(4,500)	$ (1,500)	$31,500	$ 30,000

[a]The fixed manufacturing costs are inventoried, so that equal amounts of fixed costs do not appear during each quarter.
[b]The fixed nonmanufacturing costs are not inventoried, so equal amounts of fixed costs appear during each quarter.

ILLUSTRATION 24-12
Interim Net Income for Seasonal Business—Discrete Approach

An investor who uses the first quarter's results might be misled. If the first quarter's earnings are $4,500, should this figure be multiplied by four to predict annual earnings of $18,000? Or, if first-quarter sales of $20,000 are 20 percent of the predicted sales for the year, would the net income for the year be $22,500 ($4,500 × 5)? Both figures are obviously wrong, and after the second quarter's results occur, the investor may become even more confused.

The problem with the conventional approach is that the fixed nonmanufacturing costs are not charged in proportion to sales. Some enterprises have adopted a way of avoiding this problem by making all fixed nonmanufacturing costs follow the sales pattern, as shown in Illustration 24-13.

ILLUSTRATION 24-13
Interim Net Income for
Seasonal Business—
Integral Approach

	1st Qtr	2nd Qtr	3rd Qtr	4th Qtr	Year
Sales	$20,000	$ 5,000	$10,000	$65,000	$100,000
Manufacturing costs					
Variable	(2,000)	(500)	(1,000)	(6,500)	(10,000)
Fixed	(4,000)	(1,000)	(2,000)	(13,000)	(20,000)
	14,000	3,500	7,000	45,500	70,000
Nonmanufacturing costs					
Variable	(2,000)	(500)	(1,000)	(6,500)	(10,000)
Fixed	(6,000)	(1,500)	(3,000)	(19,500)	(30,000)
Net income	$ 6,000	$ 1,500	$ 3,000	$19,500	$ 30,000

This approach solves some of the problems of interim reporting: Sales in the first quarter are 20 percent of total sales for the year, and net income in the first quarter is 20 percent of total income. In this case, as in the previous example, the investor cannot rely on multiplying any given quarter by four, but can use comparative data or rely on some estimate of sales in relation to income for a given period.

The greater the degree of seasonality experienced by a company, the greater the possibility of distortion. Because there are no definitive guidelines for handling such items as the fixed nonmanufacturing costs, variability in income can be substantial. To alleviate this problem, the profession recommends that companies subject to material seasonal variations disclose the seasonal nature of their business and consider supplementing their interim reports with information for 12-month periods ended at the interim date for the current and preceding years.

The two illustrations above highlight the difference between the **discrete** and **integral** approaches. Illustration 24-12 represents the discrete approach, in which the fixed nonmanufacturing expenses are expensed as incurred. Illustration 24-13 shows the integral approach, in which the manufacturing expenses are charged to expense on the basis of some measure of activity.

INTERNATIONAL INSIGHT

IFRS requires that interim financial statements use the discrete method, except for the tax expenses.

UNDERLYING CONCEPTS

The AICPA Special Committee on Financial Reporting indicates that users would benefit from separate fourth-quarter reporting, including management's analysis of fourth-quarter activities and events. Also, the Committee recommended quarterly segment reporting, which companies now provide under *FASB Statement No. 131*.

Continuing Controversy. The profession has developed some standards for interim reporting, but much still has to be done. As yet, it is unclear whether the discrete or the integral method, or some combination of the two, will be settled on.

Discussion also persists about the independent auditor's involvement in interim reports. Many auditors are reluctant to express an opinion on interim financial information, arguing that the data are too tentative and subjective. On the other hand, more people are advocating some examination of interim reports. A compromise may be a limited review of interim reports. Such a review would provide some assurance that an outside party has conducted an examination and that the published information appears to be in accord with generally accepted accounting principles.[14]

---

[14]The AICPA has been involved in developing guidelines for the review of interim reports. "Limited Review of Interim Financial Statements," *Statement on Auditing Standards No. 24* (New York: AICPA, 1979) sets standards for the review of interim reports.

Analysts and investors want financial information as soon as possible, before it's old news. We may not be far from a continuous database system in which corporate financial records can be accessed via the Internet. Investors might be able to access a company's financial records whenever they wish and put the information in the format they need. Thus, they could learn about sales slippage, cost increases, or earnings changes as they happen, rather than waiting until after the quarter has ended.[15]

A steady stream of information from the company to the investor could be very positive because it might alleviate management's continual concern with short-run interim numbers. Today many contend that U.S. management is too oriented to the short-term. The truth of this statement is echoed by the words of the president of a large company who decided to retire early: "I wanted to look forward to a year made up of four seasons rather than four quarters."

I **WANT IT FASTER**

The SEC has decided that timeliness of information is of extreme importance. First, the SEC has said that large public companies will have only 60 days to complete their annual reports, down from 90 days. Quarterly reports must be done within 40 days of the close of the quarter, instead of 45. In addition, corporate executives and shareholders with more than 10 percent of a company's outstanding stock now have two days to disclose their sale or purchase of stock.

Also, in a bid to increase Internet disclosure, the SEC encourages companies to post current, quarterly, and annual reports on their websites—or explain why they don't. The Internet postings would have to be made by the day the company submits the information to the SEC, rather than within 24 hours as current rules allow.

WHAT DO THE
NUMBERS MEAN?

AUDITOR'S AND MANAGEMENT'S REPORTS

Auditor's Report

Another important source of information, which is often overlooked, is the **auditor's report**. An **auditor** is an accounting professional who conducts an independent examination of a company's accounting data.

If satisfied that the financial statements present the financial position, results of operations, and cash flows fairly in accordance with generally accepted accounting principles, the auditor expresses an **unqualified opinion**. An example is shown in Illustration 24-14 (on page 1304).[16]

In preparing the report, the auditor follows these reporting standards.

OBJECTIVE 5
Identify the major disclosures in the auditor's report.

1 The report states whether the financial statements are in accordance with generally accepted accounting principles.

2 The report identifies those circumstances in which the company has not consistently observed such principles in the current period in relation to the preceding period.

---

[15]A step in this direction is the SEC's mandate for companies to file their financial statements electronically with the SEC. The system, called EDGAR (electronic data gathering and retrieval) provides interested parties with computer access to financial information such as periodic filings, corporate prospectuses, and proxy materials.

[16]This auditor's report is in exact conformance with the specifications contained in "Reports on Audited Financial Statements," *Statement on Auditing Standards No. 58* (New York: AICPA, 1988). The last paragraph refers to the assessment of the company's internal controls, as required by the PCAOB.

3 Users are to regard the informative disclosures in the financial statements as reasonably adequate unless the report states otherwise.

4 The report contains either an expression of opinion regarding the financial statements taken as a whole or an assertion to the effect that an opinion cannot be expressed. When the auditor cannot express an overall opinion, the report should state the reasons. In all cases where an auditor's name is associated with financial statements, the report should contain a clear-cut indication of the character of the auditor's examination, if any, and the degree of responsibility being taken.

ILLUSTRATION 24-14
Auditor's Report

Best Buy Co., Inc.

Report of Independent Registered Public Accounting Firm on Consolidated Financial Statements

Shareholders and Board of Directors

We have audited the accompanying consolidated balance sheets of Best Buy Co., Inc. and subsidiaries as of February 26, 2005, and February 28, 2004, and the related consolidated statements of earnings, changes in shareholders' equity, and cash flows for each of the three years in the period ended February 26, 2005. Our audits also included the financial statement schedule listed in Item 15(a). These financial statements and schedule are the responsibility of the Company's management. Our responsibility is to express an opinion on these financial statements and schedule based on our audits.

We conducted our audits in accordance with the standards of the Public Company Accounting Oversight Board (United States). Those standards require that we plan and perform the audit to obtain reasonable assurance about whether the financial statements are free of material misstatement. An audit includes examining, on a test basis, evidence supporting the amounts and disclosures in the financial statements. An audit also includes assessing the accounting principles used and significant estimates made by management, as well as evaluating the overall financial statement presentation. We believe that our audits provide a reasonable basis for our opinion.

In our opinion, the financial statements referred to above present fairly, in all material respects, the consolidated financial position of Best Buy Co., Inc. and subsidiaries of February 26, 2005, and February 28, 2004, and the consolidated results of their operations and their cash flows for each of the three years in the period ended February 26, 2005, in conformity with U.S. generally accepted accounting principles. Also, in our opinion, the related financial statement schedule, when considered in relation to the basic financial statements taken as a whole, presents fairly, in all material respects, the information set forth therein.

As discussed in Note 5 to the financial statements, effective February 26, 2005, Best Buy Co., Inc. and subsidiaries adopted EITF Issue No. 04-08, "The Effect of Contingently Convertible Instruments on Diluted Earnings per Share," and restated earnings per share for all prior periods.

We also have audited, in accordance with the standards of the Public Company Accounting Oversight Board (United States), the effectiveness of the Best Buy Co., Inc. and subsidiaries' internal control over financial reporting as of February 26, 2005, based on the criteria established in Internal Control — Integrated Framework issued by the Committee of Sponsoring Organizations of the Treadway Commission and our report dated May 5, 2005 expressed an unqualified opinion thereon.

Ernst + Young LLP

Minneapolis, Minnesota
May 5, 2005

In most cases, the auditor issues a standard **unqualified** or **clean opinion**. That is, the auditor expresses the opinion that the financial statements present fairly, in all material respects, the financial position, results of operations, and cash flows of the entity in conformity with generally accepted accounting principles.

Certain circumstances, although they do not affect the auditor's unqualified opinion, may require the auditor to add an explanatory paragraph to the audit report. Some of the more important circumstances are as follows.

1 *Uncertainties.* A matter involving an **uncertainty** is one that is expected to be resolved at a future date, at which time sufficient evidence concerning its outcome is expected to be available. In deciding whether an explanatory paragraph is needed, the auditor should consider the likelihood of a material loss resulting from the contingency. If, for example, the possibility that a loss due to the uncertainty is remote, then an explanatory paragraph is not warranted. If the loss is probable but not estimable, or is reasonably possible and material, then an explanatory paragraph is warranted.

2 *Lack of Consistency.* If a company has changed accounting principles or the method of their application in a way that has a material effect on the comparability of its financial statements, the auditor should refer to the change in an explanatory paragraph of the report. Such an explanatory paragraph should identify the nature of the change and refer readers to the note in the financial statements that discusses the change in detail. The auditor's concurrence with a change is implicit unless the auditor takes exception to the change in expressing an opinion as to fair presentation in conformity with generally accepted accounting principles.

3 *Emphasis of a Matter.* The auditor may wish to emphasize a matter regarding the financial statements, but nevertheless intends to express an unqualified opinion. For example, the auditor may wish to emphasize that the entity is a component of a larger business enterprise or that it has had significant transactions with related parties. The auditor presents such explanatory information in a separate paragraph of the report.

In some situations, however, the auditor is required to express (1) a **qualified** opinion or (2) an **adverse** opinion, or (3) to **disclaim** an opinion.

A **qualified opinion** contains an exception to the standard opinion. Ordinarily the exception is not of sufficient magnitude to invalidate the statements as a whole; if it were, an adverse opinion would be rendered. The usual circumstances in which the auditor may deviate from the standard unqualified short-form report on financial statements are as follows.

1 The scope of the examination is limited or affected by conditions or restrictions.
2 The statements do not fairly present financial position or results of operations because of:
   (a) Lack of conformity with generally accepted accounting principles and standards.
   (b) Inadequate disclosure.

If confronted with one of the situations noted above, the auditor must offer a qualified opinion. A qualified opinion states that, except for the effects of the matter to which the qualification relates, the financial statements present fairly, in all material respects, the financial position, results of operations, and cash flows in conformity with generally accepted accounting principles.

Illustration 24-15 (page 1306) shows an example of an auditor's report with a qualified opinion. The auditor qualified the opinion because the company used an accounting principle at variance with generally accepted accounting principles.

An **adverse opinion** is required in any report in which the exceptions to fair presentation are so material that in the independent auditor's judgment, a qualified opinion is not justified. In such a case, the financial statements taken as a whole are not presented in accordance with generally accepted accounting principles. Adverse opinions are rare, because most companies change their accounting to conform with GAAP. The SEC will not permit a company listed on an exchange to have an adverse opinion.

A **disclaimer of an opinion** is appropriate when the auditor has gathered so little information on the financial statements that no opinion can be expressed.

The profession also requires the auditor to evaluate whether there is substantial doubt about the entity's **ability to continue as a going concern** for a reasonable period of time. (This period is not to exceed one year beyond the date of the financial statements.) If substantial doubt exists about the company continuing as a going

ILLUSTRATION 24-15
Qualified Auditor's
Report

Helio Company

Independent Auditor's Report

(Same first and second paragraphs as the standard report)

Helio Company has excluded, from property and debt in the accompanying balance sheets, certain lease obligations that, in our opinion, should be capitalized in order to conform with generally accepted accounting principles. If these lease obligations were capitalized, property would be increased by $1,500,000 and $1,300,000, long-term debt by $1,400,000 and $1,200,000, and retained earnings by $100,000 and $50,000 as of December 31, in the current and prior year, respectively. Additionally, net income would be decreased by $40,000 and $30,000 and earnings per share would be decreased by $.06 and $.04, respectively, for the years then ended.

In our opinion, except for the effects of not capitalizing certain lease obligations as discussed in the preceding paragraph, the financial statements referred to above present fairly, in all material respects, the financial position of Helio Company, and the results of its operations and its cash flows for the years then ended in conformity with generally accepted accounting principles.

concern, the auditor adds to the report an explanatory note describing the potential problem.[17]

The audit report should provide useful information to the investor. One investment banker noted, "Probably the first item to check is the auditor's opinion to see whether or not it is a clean one—'in conformity with generally accepted accounting principles'—or is qualified in regard to differences between the auditor and company management in the accounting treatment of some major item, or in the outcome of some major litigation."

Management's Reports

Management's Discussion and Analysis

The SEC mandates inclusion of **management's discussion and analysis (MD&A)**. This section covers three financial aspects of an enterprise's business—liquidity, capital resources, and results of operations. In it, management highlights favorable or unfavorable trends and identifies significant events and uncertainties that affect these three factors. This approach obviously involves subjective estimates, opinions, and soft data. However, the SEC believes that the relevance of this information exceeds the potential lack of reliability.

Illustration 24-16 presents an excerpt from the MD&A section (2004 "Business Risks" only) of **PepsiCo**'s annual report.

ILLUSTRATION 24-16
Management's
Discussion and Analysis

PEPSICO

PepsiCo, Inc.

Our Business Risks
We are subject to risks in the normal course of business. We manage our risks through an integrated risk management framework.

Our Reputation
We have a longstanding history of maintaining a good reputation globally which is critical to selling our branded products. If we fail to maintain high standards for product quality and integrity, our reputation could be jeopardized. In addition, we must protect our reputation by maintaining high ethical, social and environmental standards for all of our operations and activities. Damage to our reputation might result in rejection of our products by consumers and a loss of brand equity, as well as require additional resources to rebuild our reputation.

---

[17]"The Auditor's Consideration of an Entity's Ability to Continue as a Going Concern," *Statement on Auditing Standards No. 59* (New York: AICPA, 1988).

Information Technology

Information technology is becoming increasingly important as an enabler to operating efficiently and interfacing with customers, as well as maintaining financial accuracy and efficiency. If we do not allocate, and effectively manage, the resources necessary to build and sustain the proper technology infrastructure, we could be subject to transaction errors, processing inefficiencies, the loss of customers, business disruptions, or the loss of or damage to intellectual property through security breach.

Product Demand and Retail Consolidation

We are a consumer products company operating in highly competitive markets and rely on continued demand for our products. To generate revenues and profits, we must sell products that appeal to our customers and to consumers. As our chairman notes, our continued success is dependent on our product innovation, including maintaining a strong pipeline of new products, effective sales incentives, appropriate advertising campaigns and marketing programs, and the ability to secure adequate shelf space at our retailers. In addition, our success depends on our responses to consumer trends, such as low carbohydrate diets, consumer health concerns, including obesity and the consumption of certain ingredients, and changes in product category consumption and consumer demographics, including the aging of the general population. Seasonal weather conditions, particularly for sports drinks and hot cereals, can also impact demand. Our top five retail customers now represent approximately 27% of our North American net revenue reflecting the continuing consolidation of the retail trade.

Global Economic and Environmental Conditions

Unforeseen global economic and environmental changes and political unrest may result in business interruption, supply constraints, foreign currency devaluation, inflation, deflation or decreased demand. Economic conditions in North America could also adversely impact growth. For example, rising fuel costs may impact the sales of our products in convenience stores where our products are generally sold in higher margin single serve packages.

Regulatory Environment

Changes in laws, regulations and the related interpretations may alter the environment in which we do business and, therefore, impact our results or increase our liabilities. Such regulatory environment changes include changes in food and drug laws, laws related to advertising and deceptive marketing practices, accounting standards, taxation requirements, competition laws and environmental laws, including the regulation of water consumption and treatment.

Workforce Retention

Our continued growth requires us to develop our leadership bench and to implement programs, such as our long-term incentive program, designed to retain talent. We also compete to hire new employees, and then must train them and develop their skills and competencies. We have in place human resource programs, including our diversity and inclusion focus mentioned by our chairman, aimed at hiring, developing and retaining our talented and motivated workforce which provides us with competitive advantage. However, unplanned turnover could deplete our institutional knowledge base and erode our competitive advantage.

Market Risks

We are exposed to the market risks arising from adverse changes in:
- commodity prices, affecting the cost of our raw materials and energy;
- foreign exchange rates;
- interest rates;
- stock prices; and
- discount rates, affecting the measurement of our pension and retiree medical liabilities.

UNDERLYING CONCEPTS

FASB Concepts Statement No. 1 notes that management knows more about the company than users and therefore can increase the usefulness of financial information by identifying significant transactions that affect the company and by explaining their financial impact.

The MD&A section also must provide information about the effects of inflation and changing prices, if they are material to financial statement trends. The SEC has not required specific numerical computations, and companies have provided little analysis on changing prices.

An additional voluntary disclosure provided in the MD&A of many companies is discussion of the company's critical accounting policies. This disclosure identifies accounting policies that require management to make subjective judgments regarding uncertainties, resulting in potentially significant effects on the financial results.[18] For

Expanded Discussion of Accounting for Changing Prices

---

[18]See *Cautionary Advice Regarding Disclosure about Critical Accounting Policies*, Release Nos. 33-8040; 34-45149; FR-60 (Washington, D.C.: SEC); and *Proposed Rule: Disclosure in Management's Discussion and Analysis about the Application of Critical Accounting Policies*, Release Nos. 33-8098; 34-45907; International Series Release No. 1258; File No. S7-16-02 (Washington, D.C.: SEC).

example, in its critical accounting policy disclosure, **PepsiCo** showed the impact on stock-based compensation expense in response to changes in estimated interest rates and stock return volatility. Through this voluntary disclosure, companies can expand on the information contained in the notes to the financial statements to indicate the sensitivity of the financial results to accounting policy judgments.

OBJECTIVE 6
Understand manage-ment's responsibilities for financials.

Management's Responsibilities for Financial Statements

The Sarbanes-Oxley Act requires the SEC to develop guidelines for *all* publicly traded companies to report on management's responsibilities for, and assessment of, the internal control system. An example of the type of disclosure that public companies are now making is shown in Illustration 24-17.[19]

ILLUSTRATION 24-17
Report on Manage-ment's Responsibilities

Home Depot

Management's Responsibility for Financial Statements
The financial statements presented in this Annual Report have been prepared with integrity and objec-tivity and are the responsibility of the management of The Home Depot, Inc. These financial statements have been prepared in conformity with U.S. generally accepted accounting principles and properly reflect certain estimates and judgments based upon the best available information.

The financial statements of the Company have been audited by KPMG LLP, an independent regis-tered public accounting firm. Their accompanying report is based upon an audit conducted in accordance with the standards of the Public Company Accounting Oversight Board (United States).

The Audit Committee of the Board of Directors, consisting solely of outside directors, meets five times a year with the independent registered public accounting firm, the internal auditors and representatives of management to discuss auditing and financial reporting matters. In addition, a telephonic meeting is held prior to each quarterly earnings release. The Audit Committee retains the independent registered public accounting firm and regularly reviews the internal accounting controls, the activities of the inde-pendent registered public accounting firm and internal auditors and the financial condition of the Com-pany. Both the Company's independent registered public accounting firm and the internal auditors have free access to the Audit Committee.

Management's Report on Internal Control over Financial Reporting
Our management is responsible for establishing and maintaining adequate internal control over financial reporting, as such term is defined in Exchange Act Rules 13a–15(f). Under the supervision and with the participation of our management, including our principal executive officer and principal financial officer, we conducted an evaluation of the effectiveness of our internal control over financial reporting based on the framework in *Internal Control-Integrated Framework* issued by the Committee of Sponsoring Orga-nizations of the Treadway Commission (COSO). Based on our evaluation, our management concluded that our internal control over financial reporting was effective as of January 30, 2005. Our management's assessment of the effectiveness of our internal control over financial reporting as of January 30, 2005 has been audited by KPMG LLP, an independent registered public accounting firm, as stated in its re-port which is included herein.

Robert L. Nardelli
Chairman, President &
Chief Executive Officer

Carol B. Tomé
Executive Vice President &
Chief Financial Officer

Kelly H. Barrett
Vice President
Corporate Controller

[19]As indicated in this disclosure, management is responsible for preparing the financial state-ments and establishing and maintaining an effective system of internal controls. The auditor pro-vides an independent assessment of whether the financial statements are prepared in accordance with GAAP, and for public companies, whether the internal controls are effective (see the audit opinion in Illustration 24-14.)

CURRENT REPORTING ISSUES

Reporting on Financial Forecasts and Projections

In recent years, the investing public's demand for more and better information has focused on disclosure of corporate expectations for the future.[20] These disclosures take one of two forms:[21]

> *Financial forecasts.* A **financial forecast** is a set of prospective financial statements that present, to the best of the responsible party's knowledge and belief, a company's expected financial position, results of operations, and cash flows. The responsible party bases a financial forecast on conditions it expects to exist and the course of action it expects to take.

> *Financial projections.* **Financial projections** are prospective financial statements that present, to the best of the responsible party's knowledge and belief, given one or more *hypothetical assumptions*, an entity's expected financial position, results of operations, and cash flows. The responsible party bases a financial projection on conditions it expects *would* exist and the course of action it expects *would* be taken, given one or more hypothetical assumptions.

The difference between a financial forecast and a financial projection is clearcut: A forecast provides information on what is **expected** to happen, whereas a projection provides information on what **might** take place, but is not necessarily expected to happen.

Whether companies should be required to provide financial forecasts is the subject of intensive discussion with journalists, corporate executives, the SEC, financial analysts, accountants, and others. Predictably, there are strong arguments on either side. Listed below are some of the arguments.

Arguments for requiring published forecasts:

1 Investment decisions are based on future expectations. Therefore information about the future facilitates better decisions.

2 Companies already circulate forecasts informally. This situation should be regulated to ensure that the forecasts are available to all investors.

3 Circumstances now change so rapidly that historical information is no longer adequate for prediction.

Arguments against requiring published forecasts:

1 No one can foretell the future. Therefore forecasts will inevitably be wrong. Worse, they may mislead, if they convey an impression of precision about the future,.

2 Companies may strive only to meet their published forecasts, thereby failing to produce results that are in the stockholders' best interest.

3 If forecasts prove inaccurate, there will be recriminations and probably legal actions.[22]

---

[20]Some areas in which companies are using financial information about the future are equipment lease-versus-buy analysis, analysis of a company's ability to successfully enter new markets, and examination of merger and acquisition opportunities. In addition, companies also prepare forecasts and projections for use by third parties in public offering documents (requiring financial forecasts), tax-oriented investments, and financial feasibility studies. Use of forward-looking data has been enhanced by the increased capability of microcomputers to analyze, compare, and manipulate large quantities of data.

[21]"Guide for Prospective Financial Information," *Audit and Accounting Guide* (New York: AICPA, May 1999), pars. 3.04 and 3.05.

[22]The issue is serious. Over a recent three-year period, 8 percent of the companies on the NYSE were sued because of an alleged lack of financial disclosure. Companies complain that they are subject to lawsuits whenever the stock price drops. And as one executive noted, "You can even be sued if the stock price goes up—because you did not disclose the good news fast enough."

4 Disclosure of forecasts will be detrimental to organizations, because forecasts will inform competitors (foreign and domestic), as well as investors.

UNDERLYING CONCEPTS

The AICPA's Special Committee on Financial Reporting indicates that the legal environment discourages companies from disclosing forward-looking information. Companies should not have to expand reporting of forward-looking information unless there are more effective deterrents to unwarranted litigation.

The AICPA has issued a statement on standards for accountants' services on prospective financial information. This statement establishes guidelines for the preparation and presentation of financial forecasts and projections.[23] It requires accountants to provide (1) a summary of significant assumptions used in the forecast or projection and (2) guidelines for minimum presentation.

To encourage management to disclose prospective financial information, the SEC has a **safe harbor rule**. It provides protection to a company that presents an erroneous forecast, as long as the company prepared the forecast on a reasonable basis and disclosed it in good faith.[24] However, many companies note that the safe harbor rule does not work in practice, since it does not cover oral statements, nor has it kept them from investor lawsuits.

Experience in Great Britain

Great Britain has permitted financial forecasts for years, and the results have been fairly successful. Some significant differences do exist between the English and the U.S. business and legal environments.[25] But such differences probably could be overcome if influential interests in this country cooperated to produce an atmosphere conducive to quality forecasting. A typical British forecast adapted from a construction company's report to support a public offering of stock is as follows.

ILLUSTRATION 24-18
Financial Forecast of a British Company

> Profits have grown substantially over the past 10 years and directors are confident of being able to continue this expansion. . . . While the rate of expansion will be dependent on the level of economic activity in Ireland and England, the group is well structured to avail itself of opportunities as they arise, particularly in the field of property development, which is expected to play an increasingly important role in the group's future expansion.
>
> Profits before taxation for the half year ended 30th June were 402,000 pounds. On the basis of trading experiences since that date and the present level of sales and completions, the directors expect that in the absence of unforeseen circumstances, the group's profits before taxation for the year to 31st December will be not less than 960,000 pounds.
>
> No dividends will be paid in respect of the current year. In a full financial year, on the basis of above forecasts (not including full year profits) it would be the intention of the board, assuming current rates of tax, to recommend dividends totaling 40% (of after-tax profits), which will be payable in the next two years.

A general narrative-type forecast issued by a U.S. corporation might appear as follows.

ILLUSTRATION 24-19
Financial Forecast for an American Company

> On the basis of promotions planned by the company for the second half of the fiscal year, net earnings for that period are expected to be approximately the same as those for the first half of the fiscal year, with net earnings for the third quarter expected to make the predominant contribution to net earnings for the second half of the year.

---

[23]"Guide for Prospective Financial Information," op. cit., par. 1.02.

[24]"Safe-Harbor Rule for Projections," *Release No. 5993* (Washington: SEC, 1979). The Private Securities Litigation Reform Act of 1995 recognizes that some information that is useful to investors is inherently subject to less certainty or reliability than other information. By providing safe harbor for forward-looking statements, Congress has sought to facilitate access to this information by investors.

[25]The British system, for example, does not permit litigation on forecasted information, and the solicitor (lawyer) is not permitted to work on a contingent fee basis. See "A Case for Forecasting—The British Have Tried It and Find That It Works," *World* (New York: Peat, Marwick, Mitchell & Co., Autumn 1978), pp. 10–13.

Questions of Liability

What happens if a company does not meet its forecasts? Can the company and the auditor be sued? If a company, for example, projects an earnings increase of 15 percent and achieves only 5 percent, should stockholders be permitted to have some judicial recourse against the company?

One court case involving **Monsanto Chemical Corporation** has set a precedent. In this case, Monsanto predicted that sales would increase 8 to 9 percent and that earnings would rise 4 to 5 percent. In the last part of the year, the demand for Monsanto's products dropped as a result of a business turndown. Instead of increasing, the company's earnings declined. Investors sued the company because the projected earnings figure was erroneous, but a judge dismissed the suit because the forecasts were the best estimates of qualified people whose intents were honest.

As indicated earlier, the SEC's safe harbor rules are intended to protect companies that provide good-faith projections. However, much concern exists as to how the SEC and the courts will interpret such terms as "good faith" and "reasonable assumptions" when erroneous forecasts mislead users of this information.

Internet Financial Reporting

Most companies now use the power and reach of the Internet to provide more useful information to financial statement readers. All large companies have Internet sites, and a large proportion of companies' websites contain links to their financial statements and other disclosures. The popularity of such reporting is not surprising, since companies can reduce the costs of printing and disseminating paper reports with the use of Internet reporting.

Does Internet financial reporting improve the usefulness of a company's financial reports? Yes, in several ways: First, dissemination of reports via the Web allows firms **to communicate more easily and quickly with users** than do traditional paper reports. In addition, **Internet reporting allows users to take advantage of tools** such as search engines and hyperlinks to quickly find information about the firm and, sometimes, to download the information for analysis, perhaps in computer spreadsheets. Finally, **Internet reporting can help make financial reports more relevant** by allowing companies to report expanded disaggregated data and more timely data than is possible through paper-based reporting. For example, some companies voluntarily report weekly sales data and segment operating data on their websites.

While there continue to be concerns about **equality of access** to electronic financial reporting as well as the **reliability** of the information distributed via the Internet, organizations are developing new technologies and standards to further enable Internet financial reporting. An example is increasing use of extensible business reporting language (XBRL). **XBRL** is a computer language adapted from the code of the Internet. The language "tags" accounting data to correspond to financial reporting items, which are reported in the balance sheet, income statement, and the cash flow statement. Once tagged, any company's XBRL data can be easily processed using spreadsheets and other computer programs. Users can more easily search a company's reports, extract and analyze data, and perform financial comparisons within industries. As more financial statement users get on the Web, armed with tools like XBRL, we expect Internet reporting to continue to grow in popularity.[26]

---

[26]Reuters, "Lifting the Lid: Tech Seen Easing Financial Analysis," *nytimes.com* (January 22, 2005). See *www.xbrl.org/us/us/BusinessCaseForXBRL.pdf* for additional information on XBRL. The FASB has issued a report on electronic dissemination of financial reports. This report summarizes current practice and research conducted on Internet financial reporting. See Business Reporting Research Project, "Electronic Distribution of Business Reporting Information" (Norwalk, Conn.: FASB, 2000).

Fraudulent Financial Reporting

Fraudulent financial reporting is defined as "intentional or reckless conduct, whether act or omission, that results in materially misleading financial statements."[27] Fraudulent reporting can involve gross and deliberate distortion of corporate records (such as inventory count tags), or misapplication of accounting principles (failure to disclose material transactions). Although frauds are unusual, recent events involving such well-known companies as **Enron**, **WorldCom**, **Adelphia**, and **Tyco** indicate that more must be done to address this issue.

WHAT DO THE NUMBERS MEAN?

HERE'S A FRAUD

The case of **ESM Government Securities, Inc. (ESM)** exemplifies the seriousness of financial reporting frauds. ESM was a Fort Lauderdale securities dealer entrusted with monies to invest by municipalities from Toledo, Ohio to Beaumont, Texas. The cities that provided funds thought, based on the company name, that ESM was collateralized with government securities.

Examination of ESM's balance sheet indicated that the company owed about as much as it expected to collect. Unfortunately, the amount it expected to collect was from insolvent affiliates which, in effect, meant that ESM was bankrupt. In fact, ESM had been bankrupt for more than six years, and the fraud was discovered only because a customer questioned a note to the balance sheet! ESM had disguised more than $300 million of losses.

Source: For an expanded discussion of this case, see Robert J. Sack and Robert Tangreti, "ESM: Implications for the Profession," *Journal of Accountancy* (April 1987).

Causes of Fraudulent Financial Reporting

Fraudulent financial reporting usually occurs because of conditions in a company's internal or external environment.[28] Influences in the **internal environment** relate to poor internal control systems, management's poor attitude toward ethics, or perhaps a company's liquidity or profitability. Those in the **external environment** may relate to industry conditions, overall business environment, or legal and regulatory considerations.

General incentives for fraudulent financial reporting vary. Common ones are the desire to obtain a higher stock price, to avoid default on a loan covenant, or to make a personal gain of some type (additional compensation, promotion). Situational pressures on the company or an individual manager also may lead to fraudulent financial reporting. Examples of these situational pressures include the following.

- *Sudden decreases in revenue or market share* for a single company or an entire industry.
- *Unrealistic budget pressures* may occur when headquarters arbitrarily determines profit objectives (particularly for short-term results) and budgets without taking actual conditions into account.
- *Financial pressure resulting from bonus plans* that depend on short-term economic performance. This pressure is particularly acute when the bonus is a significant component of the individual's total compensation.

---

[27]"Report of the National Commission on Fraudulent Financial Reporting" (Washington, D.C., 1987), page 2. Unintentional errors as well as corporate improprieties (such as tax fraud, employee embezzlements, and so on) which do not cause the financial statements to be misleading are excluded from the definition of fraudulent financial reporting.

[28]The discussion in this section is based on the Report of the National Commission on Fraudulent Financial Reporting, pp. 23–24. See "2004 Report to the Nation on Occupational Fraud and Abuse, Association of Certified Fraud Examiners," (*www.cfenet.com/pdfs/2004RttN.pdf*) for evidence that fraudulent financial reporting causes and consequences are much the same today.

Opportunities for fraudulent financial reporting are present in circumstances when the fraud is easy to commit and when detection is difficult. Frequently these opportunities arise from:

1 *The absence of a board of directors or audit committee* that vigilantly oversees the financial reporting process.

2 *Weak or nonexistent internal accounting controls.* This situation can occur, for example, when a company's revenue system is overloaded as a result of a rapid expansion of sales, an acquisition of a new division, or the entry into a new, unfamiliar line of business.

3 *Unusual or complex transactions* such as the consolidation of two companies, the divestiture or closing of a specific operation, and the purchase and sale of derivative instruments.

4 *Accounting estimates requiring significant subjective judgment* by company management, such as the allowance for loan losses and the estimated liability for warranty expense.

5 *Ineffective internal audit staffs* resulting from inadequate staff size and severely limited audit scope.

A weak corporate ethical climate contributes to these situations. Opportunities for fraudulent financial reporting also increase dramatically when the accounting principles followed in reporting transactions are nonexistent, evolving, or subject to varying interpretations.

The AICPA has issued numerous auditing standards in response to concerns of the accounting profession, the media, and the public.[29] For example, the most recent standard on fraudulent financial reporting "raises the bar" on the performance of financial statement audits by explicitly requiring auditors to assess the risk of material financial misstatement due to fraud.[30] As indicated earlier, the Sarbanes-Oxley Act now raises the penalty substantially for executives who are involved in fraudulent financial reporting.

Criteria for Making Accounting and Reporting Choices

Throughout this textbook, we have stressed the need to provide information that is useful to predict the amounts, timing, and uncertainty of future cash flows. To achieve this objective, companies must make judicious choices between alternative accounting concepts, methods, and means of disclosure. You are probably surprised by the large number of choices that exist among acceptable alternatives.

You should recognize, however, as indicated in Chapter 1, that accounting is greatly influenced by its environment. It does not exist in a vacuum. Therefore, it is unrealistic to assume that the profession can entirely eliminate alternative presentations of certain transactions and events. Nevertheless, we are hopeful that the profession, by adhering to the conceptual framework, will be able to focus on the needs of financial statement users and eliminate diversity where appropriate. The SEC's and FASB's projects on principle-based standards are directed at these very issues. They seek to develop standards and implementation guidance that will result in accounting and financial reporting that reflects the economic substance of the transactions, not the desired financial result of management. The profession must continue its efforts to develop a sound foundation upon which to build financial standards and practice. As Aristotle said, "The correct beginning is more than half the whole."

UNDERLYING CONCEPTS

The FASB concept statements on objectives of financial reporting, elements of financial statements, qualitative characteristics of accounting information, and recognition and measurement are important steps in the right direction.

---

[29]Because the profession believes that the role of the auditor is not well understood outside the profession, much attention has been focused on the expectation gap. The **expectation gap** is the gap between (1) the expectation of financial statement users concerning the level of assurance they believe the independent auditor provides, and (2) the assurance that the independent auditor actually does provide under generally accepted auditing standards.

[30]"Consideration of Fraud in a Financial Statement Audit," *Statement on Auditing Standards No. 99* (New York: AICPA, 2002).

SUMMARY OF LEARNING OBJECTIVES

1. Review the full disclosure principle and describe implementation problems. The full disclosure principle calls for financial reporting of any financial facts significant enough to influence the judgment of an informed reader. Implementing the full disclosure principle is difficult, because the cost of disclosure can be substantial and the benefits difficult to assess. Disclosure requirements have increased because of (1) the growing complexity of the business environment, (2) the necessity for timely information, and (3) the use of accounting as a control and monitoring device.

2. Explain the use of notes in financial statement preparation. Notes are the accountant's means of amplifying or explaining the items presented in the main body of the statements. Notes can explain in qualitative terms information pertinent to specific financial statement items, and can provide supplementary data of a quantitative nature. Common note disclosures relate to such items as: accounting policies; inventories; property, plant, and equipment; creditor claims; contingencies and commitments; and subsequent events.

3. Discuss the disclosure requirements for major business segments. Aggregated figures hide much information about the composition of these consolidated figures. There is no way to tell from the consolidated data the extent to which the differing product lines contribute to the company's profitability, risk, and growth potential. As a result, the profession requires segment information in certain situations.

4. Describe the accounting problems associated with interim reporting. Interim reports cover periods of less than one year. Two viewpoints exist regarding interim reports. The discrete approach holds that each interim period should be treated as a separate accounting period. The integral approach is that the interim report is an integral part of the annual report and that deferrals and accruals should take into consideration what will happen for the entire year.

Companies should use the same accounting principles for interim reports that they use for annual reports. A number of unique reporting problems develop related to the following items: (1) advertising and similar costs, (2) expenses subject to year-end adjustment, (3) income taxes, (4) extraordinary items, (5) earnings per share, and (6) seasonality.

5. Identify the major disclosures in the auditor's report. The auditor expresses an unqualified opinion if satisfied that the financial statements present the financial position, results of operations, and cash flows fairly in accordance with generally accepted accounting principles. A qualified opinion contains an exception to the standard opinion; ordinarily the exception is not of sufficient magnitude to invalidate the statements as a whole.

An adverse opinion is required when the exceptions to fair presentation are so material that a qualified opinion is not justified. A disclaimer of an opinion is appropriate when the auditor has so little information on the financial statements that no opinion can be expressed.

6. Understand management's responsibilities for financials. Management's discussion and analysis (MD&A) section covers three financial aspects of an enterprise's business: liquidity, capital resources, and results of operations. Management's responsibility for the financial statements is often indicated in a letter to stockholders in the annual report.

7. Identify issues related to financial forecasts and projections. The SEC has indicated that companies are permitted (not required) to include profit forecasts in their reports. To encourage management to disclose such information, the SEC issued a safe harbor rule. The rule provides protection to a company that presents an erroneous forecast, as long as it prepared the projection on a reasonable basis and disclosed it in good faith. However, the safe harbor rule has not worked well in practice.

8.   **Describe the profession's response to fraudulent financial reporting.** Fraudulent financial reporting is intentional or reckless conduct, whether through act or omission, that results in materially misleading financial statements. Fraudulent financial reporting usually occurs because of poor internal control, management's poor attitude toward ethics, poor performance, and so on. The Sarbanes-Oxley Act has numerous provisions intended to help prevent fraudulent financial reporting.

APPENDIX
24A

Basic Financial Statement Analysis

What would be important to you in studying a company's financial statements? The answer depends on your particular interest—whether you are a creditor, stockholder, potential investor, manager, government agency, or labor leader. For example, **short-term creditors** such as banks are primarily interested in the ability of the firm to pay its currently maturing obligations. In that case, you would examine the current assets and their relation to short-term liabilities to evaluate the short-run solvency of the firm.

Bondholders, on the other hand, look more to long-term indicators, such as the enterprise's capital structure, past and projected earnings, and changes in financial position. **Stockholders**, present or prospective, also are interested in many of the features considered by a long-term creditor. As a stockholder, you would focus on the earnings picture, because changes in it greatly affect the market price of your investment. You also would be concerned with the financial position of the company, because it affects indirectly the stability of earnings.

The **managers** of a company are concerned about the composition of its capital structure and about the changes and trends in earnings. This financial information has a direct influence on the type, amount, and cost of external financing that the company can obtain. In addition, the company managers find financial information useful on a day-to-day operating basis in such areas as capital budgeting, breakeven analysis, variance analysis, gross margin analysis, and for internal control purposes.

PERSPECTIVE ON FINANCIAL STATEMENT ANALYSIS

Readers of financial statements can gather information by examining relationships between items on the statements and identifying trends in these relationships. The relationships are expressed numerically in ratios and percentages, and trends are identified through comparative analysis.

A problem with learning how to analyze statements is that the means may become an end in itself. Analysts could identify and calculate thousands of possible relationships and trends. If one knows only how to calculate ratios and trends without understanding how such information can be used, little is accomplished. Therefore, a logical approach to financial statement analysis is necessary, consisting of the following steps.

OBJECTIVE 9
Understand the approach to financial statement analysis.

1   *Know the questions for which you want to find answers.* As indicated earlier, various groups have different types of interest in a company.

2 *Know the questions that particular ratios and comparisons are able to help answer.* These will be discussed in this appendix.

3 *Match 1 and 2 above.* By such a matching, the statement analysis will have a logical direction and purpose.

Several caveats must be mentioned. **Financial statements report on the past.** Thus, analysis of these data is an examination of the past. When using such information in a decision-making (future-oriented) process, analysts assume that the past is a reasonable basis for predicting the future. This is usually a reasonable approach, but its limitations should be recognized.

Also, ratio and trend analyses will help identify a company's present strengths and weaknesses. They may serve as "red flags" indicating problem areas. In many cases, however, such analyses will not reveal **why** things are as they are. Finding answers about "why" usually requires an in-depth analysis and an awareness of many factors about a company that are not reported in the financial statements.

Another caveat is that a **single ratio by itself is not likely to be very useful**. For example, analysts may generally view a current ratio of 2 to 1 (current assets are twice current liabilities) as satisfactory. However, if the industry average is 3 to 1, such a conclusion may be invalid. Even given this industry average, one may conclude that the particular company is doing well if one knows the previous year's ratio was 1.5 to 1. Consequently, to derive meaning from ratios, analysts need some standard against which to compare them. Such a standard may come from industry averages, past years' amounts, a particular competitor, or planned levels.

Finally, **awareness of the limitations of accounting numbers used in an analysis** is important. We will discuss some of these limitations and their consequences later in this appendix.

RATIO ANALYSIS

In analyzing financial statement data, analysts use various devices to bring out the comparative and relative significance of the financial information presented. These devices include ratio analysis, comparative analysis, percentage analysis, and examination of related data. No one device is more useful than another. Every situation is different, and analysts often obtain the needed answers only upon close examination of the interrelationships among all the data provided. Ratio analysis is the starting point. Ratios can be classified as follows.

MAJOR TYPES OF RATIOS

Liquidity Ratios. Measures of the company's short-run ability to pay its maturing obligations.

Activity Ratios. Measures of how effectively the company is using the assets employed.

Profitability Ratios. Measures of the degree of success or failure of a given company or division for a given period of time.

Coverage Ratios. Measures of the degree of protection for long-term creditors and investors.[1]

---

[1]Some analysts use other terms to categorize these ratios. For example, liquidity ratios are sometimes referred to as *solvency* ratios; activity ratios as *turnover* or *efficiency* ratios; and coverage ratios as *leverage* or *capital structure* ratios.

We have integrated discussions and illustrations about the computation and use of these financial ratios throughout this book. Illustration 24A-1 summarizes all of the ratios presented in the book and identifies the specific chapters that presented that material.

SUMMARY OF RATIOS PRESENTED IN EARLIER CHAPTERS		
Ratio	Formula for Computation	Reference
I. Liquidity		
1. Current ratio	$\dfrac{\text{Current assets}}{\text{Current liabilities}}$	Chapter 13, p. 645
2. Quick or acid-test ratio	$\dfrac{\text{Cash, marketable securities, and net receivables}}{\text{Current liabilities}}$	Chapter 13, p. 646
3. Current cash debt coverage ratio	$\dfrac{\text{Net cash provided by operating activities}}{\text{Average current liabilities}}$	Chapter 5, p. 197
II. Activity		
4. Receivables turnover	$\dfrac{\text{Net sales}}{\text{Average trade receivables (net)}}$	Chapter 7, p. 338
5. Inventory turnover	$\dfrac{\text{Cost of goods sold}}{\text{Average inventory}}$	Chapter 9, p. 444
6. Asset turnover	$\dfrac{\text{Net sales}}{\text{Average total assets}}$	Chapter 11, p. 545
III. Profitability		
7. Profit margin on sales	$\dfrac{\text{Net income}}{\text{Net sales}}$	Chapter 11, p. 545
8. Rate of return on assets	$\dfrac{\text{Net income}}{\text{Average total assets}}$	Chapter 11, p. 545
9. Rate of return on common stock equity	$\dfrac{\text{Net income minus preferred dividends}}{\text{Average common stockholders' equity}}$	Chapter 15, p. 752
10. Earnings per share	$\dfrac{\text{Net income minus preferred dividends}}{\text{Weighted shares outstanding}}$	Chapter 16, p. 805
11. Payout ratio	$\dfrac{\text{Cash dividends}}{\text{Net income}}$	Chapter 15, p. 752
IV. Coverage		
12. Debt to total assets ratio	$\dfrac{\text{Debt}}{\text{Total assets}}$	Chapter 14, p. 695
13. Times interest earned	$\dfrac{\text{Income before interest expense and taxes}}{\text{Interest expense}}$	Chapter 14, p. 695
14. Cash debt coverage ratio	$\dfrac{\text{Net cash provided by operating activities}}{\text{Average total liabilities}}$	Chapter 5, p. 197
15. Book value per share	$\dfrac{\text{Common stockholders' equity}}{\text{Outstanding shares}}$	Chapter 15, p. 753

ILLUSTRATION 24A-1
Summary of Financial Ratios

Financial Analysis Primer

You can find additional coverage of these ratios, accompanied by assignment material, at the book's website, at **www.wiley.com/college/kieso**. This supplemental coverage takes the form of a comprehensive case adapted from the annual report of a large international chemical company that we have disguised under the name of Anetek Chemical Corporation.

Limitations of Ratio Analysis

OBJECTIVE 11
Explain the limitations of ratio analysis.

The reader of financial statements must understand the basic limitations associated with ratio analysis. As analytical tools, ratios are attractive because they are simple and convenient. But too frequently, decision makers base their decisions on only these simple computations. The ratios are only as good as the data upon which they are based and the information with which they are compared.

One important limitation of ratios is that they generally are **based on historical cost, which can lead to distortions in measuring performance**. Inaccurate assessments of the enterprise's financial condition and performance can result from failing to incorporate fair value information.

Also, investors must remember that **where estimated items (such as depreciation and amortization) are significant, income ratios lose some of their credibility**. For example, income recognized before the termination of a company's life is an approximation. In analyzing the income statement, users should be aware of the uncertainty surrounding the computation of net income. As one writer aptly noted, "The physicist has long since conceded that the location of an electron is best expressed by a probability curve. Surely an abstraction like earnings per share is even more subject to the rules of probability and risk."[2]

Probably the greatest limitation of ratio analysis is the **difficult problem of achieving comparability among firms in a given industry**. Achieving comparability requires that the analyst (1) identify basic differences in companies' accounting principles and procedures and (2) adjust the balances to achieve comparability. Basic differences in accounting usually involve one of the following areas.

UNDERLYING CONCEPTS

Consistency and comparability are important concepts for financial statement analysis. If the principles and assumptions used to prepare the financial statements are continually changing, accurate assessments of a company's progress become difficult.

1 Inventory valuation (FIFO, LIFO, average cost).
2 Depreciation methods, particularly the use of straight-line versus accelerated depreciation.
3 Capitalization versus expense of certain costs.
4 Capitalization of leases versus noncapitalization.
5 Investments in common stock carried at equity versus fair value.
6 Differing treatments of postretirement benefit costs.
7 Questionable practices of defining discontinued operations, impairments, and extraordinary items.

The use of these different alternatives can make a significant difference in the ratios computed. For example, at one time **Anheuser-Busch** noted that if it had used average cost for inventory valuation instead of LIFO, inventories would have increased approximately $33,000,000. Such an increase would have a substantive impact on the current ratio. Several studies have analyzed the impact of different accounting methods on financial statement analysis. The differences in income that can develop are staggering in some cases. Investors must be aware of the potential pitfalls if they are to be able to make the proper adjustments.[3]

Finally, analysts should recognize that a **substantial amount of important information** is not included in a company's financial statements. Events involving such things as industry changes, management changes, competitors' actions, technological developments, government actions, and union activities are often critical to a company's successful operation. These events occur continuously, and information about them must come from careful analysis of financial reports in the media and other sources. Indeed many argue, in what is known as the **efficient-market hypothesis**, that financial statements contain "no surprises" to those engaged in market activities. They contend that the effect of these events is known in the marketplace—and the price of the company's stock adjusts accordingly—well before the issuance of such reports.

---

[2]Richard E. Cheney, "How Dependable Is the Bottom Line?" *The Financial Executive* (January 1971), p. 12.

[3]See for example, Eugene A. Imhoff, Jr., Robert C. Lipe, and David W. Wright, "Operating Leases: Impact of Constructive Capitalization," *Accounting Horizons* (March 1991).

COMPARATIVE ANALYSIS

Comparative analysis presents the same information for two or more different dates or periods, so that like items may be compared. Ratio analysis provides only a single snapshot, for one given point or period in time. In a comparative analysis, an investment analyst can concentrate on a given item and determine whether it appears to be growing or diminishing year by year and the proportion of such change to related items. Generally, companies present comparative financial statements.[4] They typically include two years of balance sheet information and three years of income statement information.

In addition, many companies include in their annual reports five- or ten-year summaries of pertinent data that permit readers to examine and analyze trends. *ARB No. 43* concluded that "the presentation of comparative financial statements in annual and other reports enhances the usefulness of such reports and brings out more clearly the nature and trends of current changes affecting the enterprise." Illustration 24A-2 presents a five-year condensed statement, with additional supporting data, of Anetek Chemical Corporation.

> **OBJECTIVE 12**
> **Describe techniques of comparative analysis.**

ILLUSTRATION 24A-2
Condensed Comparative
Financial Information

ANETEK CHEMICAL CORPORATION
CONDENSED COMPARATIVE STATEMENTS
(000,000 OMITTED)

	2007	2006	2005	2004	2003	10 Years Ago 1997	20 Years Ago 1987
Sales and other revenue:							
Net sales	$1,600.0	$1,350.0	$1,309.7	$1,176.2	$1,077.5	$636.2	$170.7
Other revenue	75.0	50.0	39.4	34.1	24.6	9.0	3.7
Total	1,675.0	1,400.0	1,349.1	1,210.3	1,102.1	645.2	174.4
Costs and other charges:							
Cost of sales	1,000.0	850.0	827.4	737.6	684.2	386.8	111.0
Depreciation and amortization	150.0	150.0	122.6	115.6	98.7	82.4	14.2
Selling and administrative expenses	225.0	150.0	144.2	133.7	126.7	66.7	10.7
Interest expense	50.0	25.0	28.5	20.7	9.4	8.9	1.8
Taxes on income	100.0	75.0	79.5	73.5	68.3	42.4	12.4
Total	1,525.0	1,250.0	1,202.2	1,081.1	987.3	587.2	150.1
Net income for the year	$ 150.0	$ 150.0	$ 146.9	$ 129.2	$ 114.8	$ 58.0	$ 24.3
Other Statistics							
Earnings per share on common stock (in dollars)[a]	$ 5.00	$ 5.00	$ 4.90	$ 3.58	$ 3.11	$ 1.66	$ 1.06
Cash dividends per share on common stock (in dollars)[a]	2.25	2.15	1.95	1.79	1.71	1.11	0.25
Cash dividends declared on common stock	67.5	64.5	58.5	64.6	63.1	38.8	5.7
Stock dividend at approximate market value				46.8		27.3	
Taxes (major)	144.5	125.9	116.5	105.6	97.8	59.8	17.0
Wages paid	389.3	325.6	302.1	279.6	263.2	183.2	48.6
Cost of employee benefits	50.8	36.2	32.9	28.7	27.2	18.4	4.4
Number of employees at year end (thousands)	47.4	36.4	35.0	33.8	33.2	26.6	14.6
Additions to property	306.3	192.3	241.5	248.3	166.1	185.0	49.0

[a]Adjusted for stock splits and stock dividends.

---

[4]All 600 companies surveyed in *Accounting Trends and Techniques—2004* presented comparative 2003 amounts in their 2004 balance sheets and presented comparative 2002 and 2003 amounts in their 2004 income statements.

PERCENTAGE (COMMON-SIZE) ANALYSIS

Analysts also use percentage analysis to help them evaluate and compare companies. **Percentage analysis** consists of reducing a series of related amounts to a series of percentages of a given base. For example, analysts frequently express all items in an income statement as a percentage of sales or sometimes as a percentage of cost of goods sold. They may analyze a balance sheet on the basis of total assets. Percentage analysis facilitates comparison and is helpful in evaluating the relative size of items or the relative change in items. A conversion of absolute dollar amounts to percentages may also facilitate comparison between companies of different size.

Illustration 24A-3 shows a comparative analysis of the expense section of Anetek for the last two years.

ILLUSTRATION 24A-3
Horizontal Percentage
Analysis

ANETEK CHEMICAL CORPORATION
HORIZONTAL COMPARATIVE ANALYSIS
(000,000 OMITTED)

	2007	2006	Difference	% Change Inc. (Dec.)
Cost of sales	$1,000.0	$850.0	$150.0	17.6%
Depreciation and amortization	150.0	150.0	0	0
Selling and administrative expenses	225.0	150.0	75.0	50.0
Interest expense	50.0	25.0	25.0	100.0
Taxes	100.0	75.0	25.0	33.3

This approach, normally called **horizontal analysis**, indicates the proportionate change over a period of time. It is especially useful in evaluating trends, because absolute changes are often deceiving.

Another comparative approach, called **vertical analysis**, is the proportional expression of each financial statement item in a given period to a base figure. For example, Anetek Chemical's income statement using this approach appears in Illustration 24A-4.

ILLUSTRATION 24A-4
Vertical Percentage
Analysis

ANETEK CHEMICAL CORPORATION
INCOME STATEMENT
(000,000 OMITTED)

	Amount	Percentage of Total Revenue
Net sales	$1,600.0	96%
Other revenue	75.0	4
Total revenue	1,675.0	100
Less:		
Cost of goods sold	1,000.0	60
Depreciation and amortization	150.0	9
Selling and administrative expenses	225.0	13
Interest expense	50.0	3
Income tax	100.0	6
Total expenses	1,525.0	91
Net income	$ 150.0	9%

Vertical analysis is frequently called **common-size analysis** because it reduces all of the statement items to a "common size." That is, all of the elements within each statement are expressed in percentages of some common number and always add up to 100 percent. Common-size (percentage) analysis reveals the composition of each of the financial statements.

In the analysis of the balance sheet, common-size analysis answers such questions as: What percentage of the capital structure is stockholders' equity, current liabilities, and long-term debt? What is the mix of assets (percentage-wise) with which the company has chosen to conduct business? What percentage of current assets is in inventory, receivables, and so forth?

Common-size analysis of the income statement typically relates each item to sales. It is instructive to know what proportion of each sales dollar is absorbed by various costs and expenses incurred by the enterprise.

Analysts may use common-size statements to compare one company's statements from different years, to detect trends not evident from comparing absolute amounts. Also, common-size statements provide intercompany comparisons regardless of size because they recast financial statements into a comparable common-size format.

SUMMARY OF LEARNING OBJECTIVES FOR APPENDIX 24A

9. Understand the approach to financial statement analysis. Basic financial statement analysis involves examining relationships between items on the statements (ratio and percentage analysis) and identifying trends in these relationships (comparative analysis). Analysis is used to predict the future, but ratio analysis is limited because the data are from the past. Also, ratio analysis identifies present strengths and weaknesses of a company, but it may not reveal *why* they are as they are. Although single ratios are helpful, they are not conclusive; for maximum usefulness, analysts must compare them with industry averages, past years, planned amounts, and the like.

10. Identify major analytic ratios and describe their calculation. Ratios are classified as liquidity ratios, activity ratios, profitability ratios, and coverage ratios: (1) *Liquidity ratio analysis* measures the short-run ability of a company to pay its currently maturing obligations. (2) *Activity ratio analysis* measures how effectively a company is using its assets. (3) *Profitability ratio analysis* measures the degree of success or failure of a company to generate revenues adequate to cover its costs of operation and provide a return to the owners. (4) *Coverage ratio analysis* measures the degree of protection afforded long-term creditors and investors.

11. Explain the limitations of ratio analysis. Ratios are based on historical cost, which can lead to distortions in measuring performance. Also, where estimated items are significant, income ratios lose some of their credibility. In addition, comparability problems exist because companies use different accounting principles and procedures. Finally, analysts must recognize that a substantial amount of important information is not included in a company's financial statements.

12. Describe techniques of comparative analysis. Companies present comparative data, which generally includes two years of balance sheet information and three years of income statement information. In addition, many companies include in their annual reports five- to ten-year summaries of pertinent data that permit the reader to analyze trends.

13. Describe techniques of percentage analysis. Percentage analysis consists of reducing a series of related amounts to a series of percentages of a given base. Analysts use two approaches: *Horizontal analysis* indicates the proportionate change in financial statement items over a period of time; such analysis is most helpful in evaluating trends. *Vertical analysis* (common-size analysis) is a proportional expression of each item on the financial statements in a given period to a base amount. It analyzes the composition of each of the financial statements from different years (a) to detect trends not evident from the comparison of absolute amounts and (b) to make intercompany comparisons of different-sized enterprises.

KEY TERMS

acid-test ratio, *1317*

activity ratios, *1316*

asset turnover, *1317*

book value per share, *1317*

cash debt coverage ratio, *1317*

common-size analysis, *1320*

comparative analysis, *1319*

coverage ratios, *1316*

current cash debt coverage ratio, *1317*

current ratio, *1317*

debt to total assets ratio, *1317*

earnings per share, *1317*

horizontal analysis, *1320*

inventory turnover, *1317*

liquidity ratios, *1316*

payout ratio, *1317*

percentage analysis, *1320*

profit margin on sales, *1317*

profitability ratios, *1316*

quick ratio, *1317*

rate of return on assets, *1317*

rate of return on common stock equity, *1317*

receivables turnover, *1317*

times interest earned, *1317*

vertical analysis, *1320*

APPENDIX

24B International Accounting Standards

OBJECTIVE 14
Describe the current international accounting environment.

In Chapter 1, we noted that the former U.S. Secretary of the Treasury judged the single most important innovation shaping the capital markets to be the idea of generally accepted accounting principles. He went on to say that we need something similar internationally.

We believe the secretary is right. We also believe that environmental forces are in place to achieve a worldwide set of accounting standards in the not-too-distant future. Currently, many companies find it costly to comply with different reporting standards in different countries. Likewise, investors, attempting to diversify their holdings and manage their risks, have become very interested in investing overseas. Having one common set of accounting rules will make it easier for international investors to compare the financial results of companies from different countries.

The purpose of this appendix is to provide additional insight into the movement toward one set of accounting standards to be used by all companies.

THE PRESENT ENVIRONMENT

Most agree that, for the following reasons, there is a need for one set of globalized accounting standards.

Multinational corporations. Today companies view the entire world as their market. Some of the best-known corporations, such as **Coca-Cola**, **Intel**, and **McDonald's**, generate more than 50 percent of their sales outside the United States. These organizations no longer think of themselves as simply U.S. companies. The same situation is occurring overseas as many foreign companies find their largest market to be the United States.

Mergers and acquisitions. All you have to do is look in the *Wall Street Journal* to quickly understand the merger activity taking place between companies from different countries. The mergers of such international giants as **DaimlerChrysler** and **Vodafone/Mannesmann** suggest that we will see even more of these types of mergers in the future.

Information technology. We have witnessed an incredible transformation in the speed and scale of communications among companies and individuals across borders. As communication barriers continue to drop, companies and individuals in different countries and markets are becoming comfortable buying and selling goods and services from one another.

Financial markets. Financial markets are some of the most significant international markets today. Whether it is currency, equity securities (stocks), bonds, or derivatives, there are active markets throughout the world trading these types of instruments. With the touch of a computer key, billions of dollars are transferred from one market to another.

REASONS TO UNDERSTAND INTERNATIONAL ACCOUNTING STANDARDS

As we discuss more fully below, the FASB and international accounting standard setters are working diligently to narrow the differences between U.S. and international accounting standards. However, it is likely that a number of differences will exist for the foreseeable future. As a result, U.S. investors, regulators, and preparers who have vested interests in the reporting practices of multinational companies should be familiar with international financial accounting standards. Here is why.

Convergence. International accounting standards **converge** when differences between international and U.S. standards are eliminated. Such **convergence** is illustrated if U.S. GAAP changes to international standards. For example, a recent IASB exposure draft requires companies to record all liability contingencies at fair value, no matter the likelihood of occurrence. If this standard passes, no doubt the FASB will also consider the change. This change could affect the financial reporting practices of U.S. companies.

Reconciliation to international standards. The SEC requires foreign companies that list on the U. S. exchanges to use U.S. GAAP or provide a reconciliation between international GAAP and U.S. GAAP. Currently, U.S. companies that wish to list on the European exchanges may use U.S. GAAP. It is possible that in the future U.S. companies may have to provide a reconciliation to international GAAP if they wish to list on the European exchanges.

Investors' expectations. To attract foreign investors, U.S. companies may need to provide additional information regarding how international standards would affect their financial statements. As investors gain a better understanding of international GAAP, they may demand this additional information from U.S. companies.

Competitive factors. There is some concern that international standards may provide certain companies with a competitive advantage. For example, international standards that are more permissive for segment reporting may lead to a presentation that is more favorable but in reality is misleading. Conversely, the U.S. standards may force a U.S. company to disclose more segment information. Understanding this difference may be important in judging the competing companies.

Given these forces, it is no wonder that many are working to establish a set of accounting principles that can be used worldwide.

THE CHALLENGE OF INTERNATIONAL ACCOUNTING

The only way that international standards will work is if they are of high quality. High-quality standards must have the following characteristics.[1]

- They must permit *few alternative practices.*
- They must be *clearly stated*, to allow for easy interpretation and consistent application.
- They must be *comprehensive*, covering the major transactions facing companies, and must provide an *effective system* for responding to new transactions.
- They must provide *transparency of information* (full disclosure, understandability), to make that information relevant for making effective decisions.

Developing high-quality international standards is not easy. Accounting for transactions in the United States sometimes differs significantly from practices in other

---

[1]Adapted from Edmund L. Jenkins, "Global Financial Reporting and the Global Financial Markets," 1999 Financial Executive Summit (Vancouver, B.C., May 28, 1999).

countries. These differences in some cases are quite fundamental; they involve issues such as when companies should recognize and measure assets, liabilities, revenues, and expenses.

Here are some examples of such differences:

- The standards in the United Kingdom permit companies to value assets at fair market value using appraisals. In the United States this practice is not allowed.
- The standards in Mexico permit companies to adjust assets such as inventory and plant assets for inflation effects. Thus, Mexican companies report some financial information restated for price-level changes.
- In the United States, companies capitalize goodwill and write it off as an expense only if it is impaired. Some other countries allow different amortization periods for companies that capitalize goodwill.
- In some countries companies do not recognize as a liability certain types of benefits granted to employees (such as health benefits). Instead, companies simply record these benefits at the time they are paid. In the United States, companies recognize these benefits when incurred.
- In some countries revenue recognition follows a cash-basis approach rather than an accrual-basis approach.

The FASB and international accounting standard setters have already eliminated some differences between U.S. and international GAAP.[2] Discussions in this book have highlighted a number of the remaining differences between U.S. GAAP and international standards. The fact that there *are* differences should not be surprising, because standard setters worldwide have developed standards in response to different user needs. In some countries, the primary users of financial statements are private investors; in others, the primary users are tax authorities or central government planners. In the United States, capital market participants (investors and creditors) have driven accounting standard formulation.

WHO ARE THE KEY PLAYERS IN DEVELOPING INTERNATIONAL STANDARDS?

Throughout this book, we have discussed the FASB and its role in establishing accounting standards. We have also explained the role the SEC plays in ensuring that companies follow these standards appropriately. Both of these organizations have strongly supported the movement toward one set of international standards.

In the international arena, the primary organization involved in developing international standards is the International Accounting Standards Board (IASB).

IASB

Ed Jenkins, former chair of the FASB, noted, "We have reached a historic milestone for the future of financial reporting that will benefit investors around the world. The FASB is pleased that the **IASC**—a standard-setting organization based in London—has accepted the recommendations of its Strategy Working Party to restructure the IASC. When it is in place, the proposed restructuring would provide an independent, objective international standard setter whose standards could meet the needs of the global capital markets."[3]

[2]Notable examples are exchanges of nonmonetary assets (discussed in Chapter 10) and accounting changes (discussed in Chapter 22.)

[3]Edmund L. Jenkins, "Global Financial Reporting and the Global Financial Markets," 1999 Financial Executive Summit (Vancouver, B.C., May 28, 1999). See also SEC Concept Release, "International Accounting Standards" (Washington, D.C.: SEC, 2000).

The independent objective standard-setting body now in place is called the **International Accounting Standards Board (IASB)**. The IASB is a privately funded accounting standard setter based in London, UK. Its members currently come from nine countries and have a variety of functional backgrounds; twelve of the fourteen IASB's members have full-time positions on the Board. The Board is committed to developing, in the public interest, a single set of high-quality, understandable, and enforceable global accounting standards that require transparent and comparable information in general-purpose financial statements. In addition, the Board cooperates with national accounting standard setters to achieve convergence in accounting standards around the world.[4]

The standard-setting structure internationally is now very similar to the standard-setting structure in the United States. That is, the structure is comprised of two main bodies: The International Accounting Standards Committee Foundation (IASCF) provides oversight. The International Accounting Standards Board (IASB) develops the standards, which are referred to as **International Financial Reporting Standards (IFRS)**. In addition, the IASB has an interpretations committee (similar to the U.S. Emerging Issues Task Force) and an advisory council (similar to the FASB's Financial Accounting Standards Advisory Committee). The structure is depicted in Illustration 24B-1.

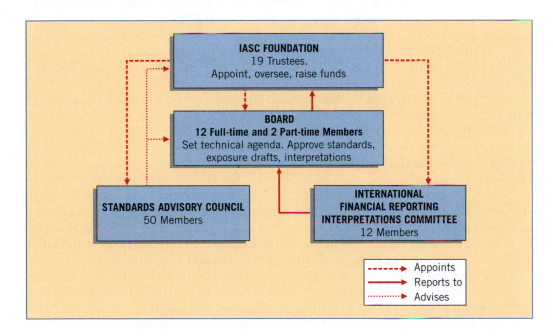

ILLUSTRATION 24B-1
International Standard-Setting Structure

Because it is a private organization, the IASB has no regulatory mandate and therefore no enforcement mechanism in place. In other words, unlike the U.S. setting, there is no SEC to enforce the use of IASB standards. Their use is completely voluntary.[5]

Other Organizations

National Standard Setters

Some countries have domestic accounting standard-setting organizations. For example, Canada and the United Kingdom have Accounting Standards Boards that develop accounting standards to be used by companies that do not list their securities on

---

[4]See *www.iasb.org/about/constitution.asp.*

[5]Effective January 1, 2005, the European Union (EU) required member country companies that list on EU securities exchanges to use IASB standards.

international exchanges. These national standard-setters often consult with the IASB in establishing accounting rules.

IOSCO

IOSCO stands for **International Organization of Securities Commissions**. IOSCO does not set accounting standards. This organization is dedicated to ensuring that the global markets can operate in an efficient and effective basis. The SEC, for example, is a member of IOSCO.

ACCOUNTING STANDARD SETTING AND INTERNATIONAL CONVERGENCE

The FASB and the IASB are working together toward the goal of a single set of high-quality accounting standards that will be used both domestically and internationally. To achieve this goal, the FASB and IASB are undertaking several joint projects. One joint project is development of a common conceptual framework for financial accounting and reporting. The goal of this project is to build a framework that both the FASB and the IASB can use when developing new and revised accounting standards.

Other joint efforts involve developing new standards on major topics. Presently, the FASB and IASB are working on such major projects as purchase method procedures, revenue recognition, and reporting on financial performance. When these issues are ultimately settled, there should be little, if any, difference between the FASB and IASB standards.

The FASB and IASB are also attempting to eliminate or narrow differences through short-term convergence projects. This approach has been quite successful so far. For example, the FASB has issued standards that mirror present IASB standards on such reporting issues as exchanges of nonmonetary assets and accounting changes. The goal of this collaboration is to select the better standard and move forward with it.

Finally, the two Boards are also coordinating interpretive activity. As often stated, "the devil is in the details." Both groups are working hard to ensure that not only are the broad conceptual approaches the same, but also the methods of applying them are the same. The Boards are not looking for mutual recognition of each other's standards. Rather, they want the **same** standards, interpretations, and language.

Regarding the FASB and convergence, Bob Herz, present chair of the FASB, has taken a position he calls "killing three birds with one stone." That is, he hopes that new standards will accomplish the following: (1) improve U.S. reporting; (2) simplify U.S. standards and standard setting; and (3) provide international convergence.

To illustrate what the FASB is trying to accomplish, consider leasing. As you learned in your study of leases in Chapter 21, there are many rules and interpretations related to the accounting for leasing transactions. Most agree that the reporting results achieved in applying the present standard often do not reflect the substance of the transaction. At some point in the future, the FASB will again address the proper accounting for these transactions. When it does, the hope is that it will (1) improve U.S. reporting, (2) simplify U.S. standards, and (3) lead to international convergence.

Challenges to Convergence

There are many challenges to convergence. Presently, domestic and international accounting parties are often starting from different places. Not only are the FASB and the IASB involved, but also numerous national standard setters are in the mix, as indicated in Illustration 24B-2.

ILLUSTRATION 24B-2
International Standard
Setters

Country(ies)	Standard Setter
Australia and New Zealand	Australian Accounting Standards Board (AASB)
	Financial Reporting Standards Board (FRSB)
Canada	Accounting Standards Board (AcSB)
France	Conseil Nationale de la Comptabilité (CNC)
Germany	German Accounting Standards Committee (DRSC)
Japan	Accounting Standards Board of Japan (ASBJ)
United Kingdom	Accounting Standards Board (ASB)
United States	Financial Accounting Standards Board (FASB)

It follows that there are significant cultural differences among countries and regions of the world. For example, Europe sometimes seems more interested in developing a *representative* IASB than an *independent* IASB. In the United States, the FASB is faced with a very litigious society, and therefore is often encouraged to write very detailed standards.

In addition, there are often institutional or legal barriers to change. For example, any time a standard is issued that affects debt versus equity classifications, loan covenants may have to be changed. In some countries, changing loan covenants is often very difficult to implement.

And there are the political issues. On both sides of the Atlantic, companies that do not want change are pleading with politicians to stop standards from being issued. In the United States, high-tech companies have fought bitterly to derail the stock option standard issued by the FASB. In Europe, the IASB issued a similar option standard and met little opposition. Conversely, bankers in Europe were up in arms regarding an IASB standard to record derivatives at fair value; U.S. GAAP requires fair value for derivatives in most situations. Although there was much opposition in the United States, the FASB passed the standard and companies now report derivatives at fair values.

RECONCILIATIONS—AN IMPORTANT ISSUE

Should the SEC accept international reporting standards, such as those issued by the IASB, for companies who wish to list on U.S. stock exchanges? The SEC's position is that foreign companies who wish to list in the United States must either follow U.S. GAAP or must file a form that **reconciles** the amounts reported under international standards (financial statements based on their home country GAAP or International Financial Reporting Standards (IFRS), as issued by the IASB) to U.S. GAAP. Illustration 24B-3 (page 1328) shows an example of a **reconciliation** form for **Nokia Corporation**.

As Illustration 24A-3 indicates, there are numerous differences between U.S. GAAP and IASB GAAP that require adjustments to make Nokia's financial statements comparable to those of a U.S. telephone maker. This is why the SEC requires reconciliation. In most cases, the U.S. GAAP reconciliation requires foreign issuers to supplement their home-country financial statements. In certain cases—when it deems a standard to be relevant and reliable—the SEC will accept the accounting standard used by the foreign company.

ILLUSTRATION 24B-3
U.S.–IFRS Reconciliation

Nokia Corporation

Note 37 (in part). The principal differences between international financial reporting standards (IFRS) and U.S. GAAP are presented below, together with explanations of certain adjustments that affect consolidated net income and total shareholders' equity as of and for the years ended December 31:

(Millions EUROs)	2004	2003
Reconciliation of net income:		
Net income reported under IFRS	3,207	3,592
U.S. GAAP adjustments		
Pension expense	—	(12)
Development costs	42	322
Provision for social security cost on stock options	(8)	(21)
Stock compensation expense	(21)	(9)
Cash flow hedges	89	9
Amortization of identifiable intangible assets acquired	(11)	(22)
Impairment of identifiable intangible assets acquired	(47)	—
Amortization of goodwill	106	162
Impairment of goodwill	—	151
Deferred tax effect of U.S. GAAP adjustments	(14)	(75)
Net income under U.S. GAAP	3,343	4,097

	2004	2003
Reconciliation of shareholders' equity:		
Total shareholders' equity reported under IFRS	14,238	15,148
U.S. GAAP adjustments		
Pension expense	(49)	(49)
Development costs	(57)	(99)
Marketable securities and unlisted investments	35	49
Provision for social security cost on stock options	6	14
Deferred compensation	(50)	(10)
Share issue premium	247	186
Stock compensation	(197)	(176)
Acquisition purchase price	2	3
Amortization of identifiable intangible assets acquired	(62)	(51)
Impairment of identifiable intangible assets acquired	(47)	—
Amortization of goodwill	502	396
Impairment of goodwill	255	255
Translation of goodwill	(319)	(293)
Deferred tax effect of U.S. GAAP adjustments	72	64
Total shareholders' equity under U.S. GAAP	14,576	15,437

Reconciliation is important because, as indicated in Illustration 24B-4, the number of foreign reporting companies in 2004 was 1,240, an increase from just 434 in 1990.

ILLUSTRATION 24B-4
Foreign Companies Registered with the SEC (1,240 Total as of December 31, 2004)

Country	Number of Companies	Country	Number of Companies
Canada	497	Bermuda	28
United Kingdom	107	Cayman Islands	26
Israel	86	Australia	24
Brazil	40	Chile	23
Mexico	39	Germany	22
Netherlands	34	British Virgin Islands	21
France	33	All other (41 Countries)	229
Japan	31		

Source: U.S. Securities and Exchange Commission

For foreign companies wishing to list in the United States, the SEC is under considerable pressure to accept the standards issued by the IASB. In the future, the SEC could follow various approaches:

- Maintain the current reconciliation requirements in all respects.
- Remove some of the current reconciliation requirements for selected IASB standards and extend the recognition to additional IASB standards as warranted, based on future review of each standard.
- Rely on the IASB standards for recognition and measurement principles, but require U.S. GAAP and SEC supplemental disclosure requirements for footnote disclosures and the level of detail for the line items in financial statements.
- Accept financial statements prepared in accordance with the IASB standards without any requirement to reconcile to U.S. GAAP.

We believe that the SEC will continue to require reconciliation for the short-run. It has indicated that the current reconciliation requirements are designed to make financial statements prepared under non-U.S. GAAP more comparable to those prepared under U.S. GAAP. Given the numerous differences contained in the Nokia disclosure presented in Illustration 24B-3, this is understandable. At the same time the SEC has stated that it expects that reconciliation to IASB standards may not be needed after 2009.

CONCLUDING REMARKS

Financial statements prepared according to U.S. GAAP have been the standard for communicating financial information to the world. Regulators from around the world have readily accepted these financial statements when a company has chosen to list on an exchange. In 2005, however, the IASB standards have become the common financial-statement language for over 7,000 listed companies in the European Union and in over 90 countries around the world. And it is conceivable that just as foreign companies may have to reconcile to U.S. GAAP when listing in the United States, U.S. companies that want to list on the European exchanges may have to provide some type of additional information in the not-too-distant future.

We believe that there still may be many bumps in the road to the establishment of one set of worldwide standards, but we view the progress to date as remarkable. We are optimistic that the goal of worldwide standards can be achieved, which will be of value to all.

SUMMARY OF LEARNING OBJECTIVE FOR APPENDIX 24B

14. Describe the current international accounting environment. Investors and creditors increasingly demand international accounting reports. The growth of multinational corporations, increased international mergers and acquisitions, and financial markets, all facilitated by technology, contribute to the demand for international accounting standards. Given these forces, many are working to establish a set of accounting principles that can be used worldwide. High-quality international standards: (1) permit *few alternative practices*, (2) are *clearly stated* to allow for easy interpretation and consistent application, (3) are *comprehensive*, covering the major transactions facing companies, (4) provide an *effective system* for responding to new transactions, and (5) provide *transparency of information* (full disclosure, understandability), to make that information relevant for making effective decisions.

The leading international accounting standard setter, the IASB, is working with the FASB to develop common, high-quality accounting standards. The U.S. SEC requires

KEY TERMS

converge, convergence, *1323*

IASC, *1324*

International Accounting Standards Board (IASB), *1325*

International Financial Reporting Standards (IFRS), *1325*

reconciles, reconciliation, *1327*

reconciliation of international accounting reports to U.S. GAAP. The current reconciliation requirements are designed to make financial statements prepared under non-U.S. GAAP more comparable to those prepared under U.S. GAAP.

Note: All **asterisked** Questions, Brief Exercises, Exercises, Problems, and Concepts for Analysis relate to materials contained in the appendixes to the chapter.

QUESTIONS

1. What are the major advantages of notes to the financial statements? What types of items are usually reported in notes?

2. What is the full disclosure principle in accounting? Why has disclosure increased substantially in the last 10 years?

3. The FASB requires a reconciliation between the effective tax rate and the federal government's statutory rate. Of what benefit is such a disclosure requirement?

4. What type of disclosure or accounting do you believe is necessary for the following items?

(a) Because of a general increase in the number of labor disputes and strikes, both within and outside the industry, there is an increased likelihood that a company will suffer a costly strike in the near future.

(b) A company reports an extraordinary item (net of tax) correctly on the income statement. No other mention is made of this item in the annual report.

(c) A company expects to recover a substantial amount in connection with a pending refund claim for a prior year's taxes. Although the claim is being contested, counsel for the company has confirmed the client's expectation of recovery.

5. The following information was described in a note of Cebar Packing Co.

"During August, A. Belew Products Corporation purchased 311,003 shares of the Company's common stock which constitutes approximately 35% of the stock outstanding. A. Belew has since obtained representation on the Board of Directors."

"An affiliate of A. Belew Products Corporation acts as a food broker for Cedar Packing in the greater New York City marketing area. The commissions for such services after August amounted to approximately $20,000."

Why is this information disclosed?

6. What are the major types of subsequent events? Indicate how each of the following "subsequent events" would be reported.

(a) Collection of a note written off in a prior period.

(b) Issuance of a large preferred stock offering.

(c) Acquisition of a company in a different industry.

(d) Destruction of a major plant in a flood.

(e) Death of the company's chief executive officer (CEO).

(f) Additional wage costs associated with settlement of a four-week strike.

(g) Settlement of a federal income tax case at considerably more tax than anticipated at year-end.

(h) Change in the product mix from consumer goods to industrial goods.

7. What are diversified companies? What accounting problems are related to diversified companies?

8. What quantitative materiality test is applied to determine whether a segment is significant enough to warrant separate disclosure?

9. Identify the segment information that is required to be disclosed by *FASB Statement No. 131*.

10. What is an operating segment, and when can information about two operating segments be aggregated?

11. The controller for Chang Lee Inc. recently commented, "If I have to disclose our segments individually, the only people who will gain are our competitors and the only people that will lose are our present stockholders." Evaluate this comment.

12. An article in the financial press entitled "Important Information in Annual Reports This Year" noted that annual reports include a management discussion and analysis section. What would this section contain?

13. "The financial statements of a company are management's, not the accountant's." Discuss the implications of this statement.

14. Olga Conrad, a financial writer, noted recently, "There are substantial arguments for including earnings projections in annual reports and the like. The most compelling is that it would give anyone interested something now available to only a relatively select few—like large stockholders, creditors, and attentive bartenders." Identify some arguments against providing earnings projections.

15. The following comment appeared in the financial press: "Inadequate financial disclosure, particularly with respect to how management views the future and its role in the marketplace, has always been a stone in the shoe.

After all, if you don't know how a company views the future, how can you judge the worth of its corporate strategy?" What are some arguments for reporting earnings forecasts?

16. What are interim reports? Why are balance sheets often not provided with interim data?

17. What are the accounting problems related to the presentation of interim data?

18. Mysteries Inc., a closely held corporation, has decided to go public. The controller, C. Keene, is concerned with presenting interim data when a LIFO inventory valuation is used. What problems are encountered with LIFO inventories when quarterly data are presented?

19. What approaches have been suggested to overcome the seasonality problem related to interim reporting?

20. What is the difference between a CPA's unqualified opinion or "clean" opinion and a qualified one?

21. Mary Beidler and Lee Pannebecker are discussing the recent fraud that occurred at LowRental Leasing, Inc. The fraud involved the improper reporting of revenue to ensure that the company would have income in excess of $1 million. What is fraudulent financial reporting, and how does it differ from an embezzlement of company funds?

*22. "The significance of financial statement data is not in the amount alone." Discuss the meaning of this statement.

*23. A close friend of yours, who is a history major and who has not had any college courses or any experience in business, is receiving the financial statements from companies in which he has minor investments (acquired for him by his now-deceased father). He asks you what he needs to know to interpret and to evaluate the financial statement data that he is receiving. What would you tell him?

*24. Distinguish between ratio analysis and percentage analysis relative to the interpretation of financial statements. What is the value of these two types of analyses?

*25. In calculating inventory turnover, why is cost of goods sold used as the numerator? As the inventory turnover increases, what increasing risk does the business assume?

*26. What is the relationship of the asset turnover ratio to the rate of return on assets?

*27. Explain the meaning of the following terms: (a) common-size analysis, (b) vertical analysis, (c) horizontal analysis, (d) percentage analysis.

*28. Presently, the profession requires that earnings per share be disclosed on the face of the income statement. What are some disadvantages of reporting ratios on the financial statements?

*29. Why is it important to understand international accounting standards?

*30. Describe some of the similarities between U.S. and international standard-setting structures.

*31. What is the reconciliation required by the SEC for international reports? Why is the reconciliation required?

BRIEF EXERCISES

(LO 2) **BE24-1** An annual report of D. Robillard Industries states, "The company and its subsidiaries have long-term leases expiring on various dates after December 31, 2007. Amounts payable under such commitments, without reduction for related rental income, are expected to average approximately $5,711,000 annually for the next 3 years. Related rental income from certain subleases to others is estimated to average $3,094,000 annually for the next 3 years." What information is provided by this note?

(LO 2) **BE24-2** An annual report of **Ford Motor Corporation** states, "Net income a share is computed based upon the average number of shares of capital stock of all classes outstanding. Additional shares of common stock may be issued or delivered in the future on conversion of outstanding convertible debentures, exercise of outstanding employee stock options, and for payment of defined supplemental compensation. Had such additional shares been outstanding, net income a share would have been reduced by 10¢ in the current year and 3¢ in the previous year. . . . As a result of capital stock transactions by the company during the current year (primarily the purchase of Class A Stock from Ford Foundation), net income a share was increased by 6¢." What information is provided by this note?

(LO 2) **BE24-3** Linden Corporation is preparing its December 31, 2006, financial statements. Two events that occurred between December 31, 2006, and March 10, 2007, when the statements were issued, are described below.

1. A liability, estimated at $150,000 at December 31, 2006, was settled on February 26, 2007, at $170,000.
2. A flood loss of $80,000 occurred on March 1, 2007.

What effect do these subsequent events have on 2006 net income?

(LO 3) **BE24-4** Bess Marvin, a student of intermediate accounting, was heard to remark after a class discussion on diversified reporting, "All this is very confusing to me. First we are told that there is merit in presenting the consolidated results, and now we are told that it is better to show segmental results. I wish they would make up their minds." Evaluate this comment.

(LO 3) **BE24-5** Roder Corporation has seven industry segments with total revenues as follows.

Genso	$600	Sergei	$225
Konami	650	Takuhi	200
RPG	250	Nippon	700
Red Moon	375		

Based only on the revenues test, which industry segments are reportable?

(LO 3) **BE24-6** Operating profits and losses for the seven industry segments of Roder Corporation are:

Genso	$ 90	Sergei	$ (20)
Konami	(40)	Takuhi	34
RPG	25	Nippon	100
Red Moon	50		

Based only on the operating profit (loss) test, which industry segments are reportable?

(LO 3) **BE24-7** Identifiable assets for the seven industry segments of Roder Corporation are:

Genso	$500	Sergei	$200
Konami	550	Takuhi	150
RPG	400	Nippon	475
Red Moon	400		

Based only on the identifiable assets test, which industry segments are reportable?

(LO 10) ***BE24-8** Answer each of the questions in the following unrelated situations.

    (a) The current ratio of a company is 5:1 and its acid-test ratio is 1:1. If the inventories and prepaid items amount to $600,000, what is the amount of current liabilities?

    (b) A company had an average inventory last year of $200,000 and its inventory turnover was 5. If sales volume and unit cost remain the same this year as last and inventory turnover is 8 this year, what will average inventory have to be during the current year?

    (c) A company has current assets of $90,000 (of which $40,000 is inventory and prepaid items) and current liabilities of $30,000. What is the current ratio? What is the acid-test ratio? If the company borrows $15,000 cash from a bank on a 120-day loan, what will its current ratio be? What will the acid-test ratio be?

    (d) A company has current assets of $600,000 and current liabilities of $240,000. The board of directors declares a cash dividend of $180,000. What is the current ratio after the declaration but before payment? What is the current ratio after the payment of the dividend?

(LO 10) ***BE24-9** Aston Martin Company's budgeted sales and budgeted cost of goods sold for the coming year are $144,000,000 and $90,000,000 respectively. Short-term interest rates are expected to average 10%. If Aston Martin can increase inventory turnover from its present level of 9 times a year to a level of 12 times per year, compute its expected cost savings for the coming year.

EXERCISES

(LO 2) **E24-1** **(Post-Balance-Sheet Events)** Madrasah Corporation issued its financial statements for the year ended December 31, 2008, on March 10, 2009. The following events took place early in 2009.

    (a) On January 10, 10,000 shares of $5 par value common stock were issued at $66 per share.

    (b) On March 1, Madrasah determined after negotiations with the Internal Revenue Service that income taxes payable for 2008 should be $1,270,000. At December 31, 2008, income taxes payable were recorded at $1,100,000.

Instructions
Discuss how the preceding post-balance sheet events should be reflected in the 2008 financial statements.

(LO 2) **E24-2** **(Post-Balance-Sheet Events)** For each of the following subsequent (post-balance-sheet) events, indicate whether a company should (a) adjust the financial statements, (b) disclose in notes to the financial statements, or (c) neither adjust nor disclose.

_____ **1.** Settlement of federal tax case at a cost considerably in excess of the amount expected at year-end.
_____ **2.** Introduction of a new product line.
_____ **3.** Loss of assembly plant due to fire.
_____ **4.** Sale of a significant portion of the company's assets.
_____ **5.** Retirement of the company president.
_____ **6.** Prolonged employee strike.
_____ **7.** Loss of a significant customer.
_____ **8.** Issuance of a significant number of shares of common stock.
_____ **9.** Material loss on a year-end receivable because of a customer's bankruptcy.
_____ **10.** Hiring of a new president.
_____ **11.** Settlement of prior year's litigation against the company.
_____ **12.** Merger with another company of comparable size.

(LO 3) **E24-3 (Segmented Reporting)** Carlton Company is involved in four separate industries. The following information is available for each of the four industries.

Operating Segment	Total Revenue	Operating Profit (Loss)	Identifiable Assets
W	$ 60,000	$15,000	$167,000
X	10,000	3,000	83,000
Y	23,000	(2,000)	21,000
Z	9,000	1,000	19,000
	$102,000	$17,000	$290,000

Instructions

Determine which of the operating segments are reportable based on the:

(a) Revenue test.
(b) Operating profit (loss) test.
(c) Identifiable assets test.

(LO 10) ***E24-4 (Ratio Computation and Analysis; Liquidity)** As loan analyst for Utrillo Bank, you have been presented the following information.

	Toulouse Co.	Lautrec Co.
Assets		
Cash	$ 120,000	$ 320,000
Receivables	220,000	302,000
Inventories	570,000	518,000
Total current assets	910,000	1,140,000
Other assets	500,000	612,000
Total assets	$1,410,000	$1,752,000
Liabilities and Stockholders' Equity		
Current liabilities	$ 305,000	$ 350,000
Long-term liabilities	400,000	500,000
Capital stock and retained earnings	705,000	902,000
Total liabilities and stockholders' equity	$1,410,000	$1,752,000
Annual sales	$ 930,000	$1,500,000
Rate of gross profit on sales	30%	40%

Each of these companies has requested a loan of $50,000 for 6 months with no collateral offered. Inasmuch as your bank has reached its quota for loans of this type, only one of these requests is to be granted.

Instructions

Which of the two companies, as judged by the information given above, would you recommend as the better risk and why? Assume that the ending account balances are representative of the entire year.

(LO 10) ***E24-5 (Analysis of Given Ratios)** Picasso Company is a wholesale distributor of professional equipment and supplies. The company's sales have averaged about $900,000 annually for the 3-year period 2006–2008. The firm's total assets at the end of 2008 amounted to $850,000.

The president of Picasso Company has asked the controller to prepare a report that summarizes the financial aspects of the company's operations for the past 3 years. This report will be presented to the board of directors at their next meeting.

In addition to comparative financial statements, the controller has decided to present a number of relevant financial ratios which can assist in the identification and interpretation of trends. At the request of the controller, the accounting staff has calculated the following ratios for the 3-year period 2006–2008.

	2006	2007	2008
Current ratio	1.80	1.89	1.96
Acid-test (quick) ratio	1.04	0.99	0.87
Accounts receivable turnover	8.75	7.71	6.42
Inventory turnover	4.91	4.32	3.42
Total debt to total assets	51.0%	46.0%	41.0%
Long-term debt to total assets	31.0%	27.0%	24.0%
Sales to fixed assets (fixed asset turnover)	1.58	1.69	1.79
Sales as a percent of 2006 sales	1.00	1.03	1.07
Gross margin percentage	36.0%	35.1%	34.6%
Net income to sales	6.9%	7.0%	7.2%
Return on total assets	7.7%	7.7%	7.8%
Return on stockholders' equity	13.6%	13.1%	12.7%

In preparation of the report, the controller has decided first to examine the financial ratios independent of any other data to determine if the ratios themselves reveal any significant trends over the 3-year period.

Instructions
(a) The current ratio is increasing while the acid-test (quick) ratio is decreasing. Using the ratios provided, identify and explain the contributing factor(s) for this apparently divergent trend.
(b) In terms of the ratios provided, what conclusion(s) can be drawn regarding the company's use of financial leverage during the 2006–2008 period?
(c) Using the ratios provided, what conclusion(s) can be drawn regarding the company's net investment in plant and equipment?

(LO 10) *E24-6 **(Ratio Analysis)** Edna Millay Inc. is a manufacturer of electronic components and accessories with total assets of $20,000,000. Selected financial ratios for Millay and the industry averages for firms of similar size are presented below.

	Edna Millay			2007 Industry Average
	2005	2006	2007	
Current ratio	2.09	2.27	2.51	2.24
Quick ratio	1.15	1.12	1.19	1.22
Inventory turnover	2.40	2.18	2.02	3.50
Net sales to stockholders' equity	2.71	2.80	2.99	2.85
Net income to stockholders' equity	0.14	0.15	0.17	0.11
Total liabilities to stockholders' equity	1.41	1.37	1.44	0.95

Millay is being reviewed by several entities whose interests vary, and the company's financial ratios are a part of the data being considered. Each of the parties listed below must recommend an action based on its evaluation of Millay's financial position.

Archibald MacLeish Bank. The bank is processing Millay's application for a new 5-year term note. Archibald MacLeish has been Millay's banker for several years but must reevaluate the company's financial position for each major transaction.

Robert Lowell Company. Lowell is a new supplier to Millay and must decide on the appropriate credit terms to extend to the company.

Robert Penn Warren. A brokerage firm specializing in the stock of electronics firms that are sold over-the-counter, Robert Penn Warren must decide if it will include Millay in a new fund being established for sale to Robert Penn Warren's clients.

Working Capital Management Committee. This is a committee of Millay's management personnel chaired by the chief operating officer. The committee is charged with the responsibility of periodically reviewing the company's working capital position, comparing actual data against budgets, and recommending changes in strategy as needed.

Instructions
(a) Describe the analytical use of each of the six ratios presented above.
(b) For each of the four entities described above, identify two financial ratios, from those ratios presented in Illustration 24A-1 (on page 1317), that would be most valuable as a basis for its decision regarding Millay.

(c) Discuss what the financial ratios presented in the question reveal about Millay. Support your answer by citing specific ratio levels and trends as well as the interrelationships between these ratios.

(CMA adapted)

See the book's website, www.wiley.com/college/kieso, for Additional Exercises.

PROBLEMS

(LO 2) **P24-1** **(Subsequent Events)** Your firm has been engaged to examine the financial statements of Sabrina Corporation for the year 2008. The bookkeeper who maintains the financial records has prepared all the unaudited financial statements for the corporation since its organization on January 2, 2002. The client provides you with the information below.

SABRINA CORPORATION
BALANCE SHEET
AS OF DECEMBER 31, 2008

Assets		Liabilities	
Current assets	$1,881,100	Current liabilities	$ 962,400
Other assets	5,171,400	Long-term liabilities	1,439,500
		Capital	4,650,600
	$7,052,500		$7,052,500

An analysis of current assets discloses the following.

Cash (restricted in the amount of $400,000 for plant expansion)	$ 571,000
Investments in land	185,000
Accounts receivable less allowance of $30,000	480,000
Inventories (LIFO flow assumption)	645,100
	$1,881,100

Other assets include:

Prepaid expenses	$ 47,400
Plant and equipment less accumulated depreciation of $1,430,000	4,130,000
Cash surrender value of life insurance policy	84,000
Unamortized bond discount	49,500
Notes receivable (short-term)	162,300
Goodwill	252,000
Land	446,200
	$5,171,400

Current liabilities include:

Accounts payable	$ 510,000
Notes payable (due 2010)	157,400
Estimated income taxes payable	145,000
Premium on common stock	150,000
	$ 962,400

Long-term liabilities include:

Unearned revenue	$ 489,500
Dividends payable (cash)	200,000
8% bonds payable (due May 1, 2013)	750,000
	$1,439,500

Capital includes:

Retained earnings	$2,810,600
Capital stock, par value $10; authorized 200,000 shares, 184,000 shares issued	1,840,000
	$4,650,600

The supplementary information below is also provided.

1. On May 1, 2008, the corporation issued at 93.4, $750,000 of bonds to finance plant expansion. The long-term bond agreement provided for the annual payment of interest every May 1. The existing plant was pledged as security for the loan. Use straight-line method for discount amortization.

2. The bookkeeper made the following mistakes.
    (a) In 2006, the ending inventory was overstated by $183,000. The ending inventories for 2007 and 2008 were correctly computed.
    (b) In 2008, accrued wages in the amount of $275,000 were omitted from the balance sheet and these expenses were not charged on the income statement.
    (c) In 2008, a gain of $175,000 (net of tax) on the sale of certain plant assets was credited directly to retained earnings.

3. A major competitor has introduced a line of products that will compete directly with Sabrina's primary line, now being produced in a specially designed new plant. Because of manufacturing innovations, the competitor's line will be of comparable quality but priced 50% below Sabrina's line. The competitor announced its new line on January 14, 2009. Sabrina indicates that the company will meet the lower prices that are high enough to cover variable manufacturing and selling expenses, but permit recovery of only a portion of fixed costs.

4. You learned on January 28, 2009, prior to completion of the audit, of heavy damage because of a recent fire to one of Sabrina's two plants; the loss will not be reimbursed by insurance. The newspapers described the event in detail.

Instructions

Analyze the above information to prepare a corrected balance sheet for Sabrina in accordance with proper accounting and reporting principles. Prepare a description of any notes that might need to be prepared. The books are closed and adjustments to income are to be made through retained earnings.

(LO 3) **P24-2 (Segmented Reporting)** Friendly Corporation is a diversified company that operates in five different industries: A, B, C, D, and E. The following information relating to each segment is available for 2007.

	A	B	C	D	E
Sales	$40,000	$ 80,000	$580,000	$35,000	$55,000
Cost of goods sold	19,000	50,000	270,000	19,000	30,000
Operating expenses	10,000	40,000	235,000	12,000	18,000
Total expenses	29,000	90,000	505,000	31,000	48,000
Operating profit (loss)	$11,000	$(10,000)	$ 75,000	$ 4,000	$ 7,000
Identifiable assets	$35,000	$ 60,000	$500,000	$65,000	$50,000

Sales of segments B and C included intersegment sales of $20,000 and $100,000, respectively.

Instructions

(a) Determine which of the segments are reportable based on the:
    (1) Revenue test.
    (2) Operating profit (loss) test.
    (3) Identifiable assets test.
(b) Prepare the necessary disclosures required by *FASB No. 131*.

(LO 10, 12) ***P24-3 (Ratio Computations and Additional Analysis)** Sandburg Corporation was formed 5 years ago through a public subscription of common stock. Robert Frost, who owns 15% of the common stock, was one of the organizers of Sandburg and is its current president. The company has been successful, but it currently is experiencing a shortage of funds. On June 10, Robert Frost approached the Spokane National Bank, asking for a 24-month extension on two $35,000 notes, which are due on June 30, 2007, and September 30, 2007. Another note of $6,000 is due on March 31, 2008, but he expects no difficulty in paying this note on its due date. Frost explained that Sandburg's cash flow problems are due primarily to the company's desire to finance a $300,000 plant expansion over the next 2 fiscal years through internally generated funds.

The Commercial Loan Officer of Spokane National Bank requested financial reports for the last 2 fiscal years. These reports are reproduced on page 1337.

SANDBURG CORPORATION
STATEMENT OF FINANCIAL POSITION
AS OF MARCH 31

Assets	2007	2006
Cash	$ 18,200	$ 12,500
Notes receivable	148,000	132,000
Accounts receivable (net)	131,800	125,500
Inventories (at cost)	95,000	50,000
Plant & equipment (net of depreciation)	1,449,000	1,420,500
Total assets	$1,842,000	$1,740,500
Liabilities and Owners' Equity		
Accounts payable	$ 69,000	$ 91,000
Notes payable	76,000	61,500
Accrued liabilities	9,000	6,000
Common stock (130,000 shares, $10 par)	1,300,000	1,300,000
Retained earnings[a]	388,000	282,000
Total liabilities and owners' equity	$1,842,000	$1,740,500

[a]Cash dividends were paid at the rate of $1 per share in fiscal year 2006 and $2 per share in fiscal year 2007.

SANDBURG CORPORATION
INCOME STATEMENT
FOR THE FISCAL YEARS ENDED MARCH 31

	2007	2006
Sales	$3,000,000	$2,700,000
Cost of goods sold[a]	1,530,000	1,425,000
Gross margin	$1,470,000	$1,275,000
Operating expenses	860,000	780,000
Income before income taxes	$ 610,000	$ 495,000
Income taxes (40%)	244,000	198,000
Net income	$ 366,000	$ 297,000

[a]Depreciation charges on the plant and equipment of $100,000 and $102,500 for fiscal years ended March 31, 2006 and 2007, respectively, are included in cost of goods sold.

Instructions

(a) Compute the following items for Sandburg Corporation.
  (1) Current ratio for fiscal years 2006 and 2007.
  (2) Acid-test (quick) ratio for fiscal years 2006 and 2007.
  (3) Inventory turnover for fiscal year 2007.
  (4) Return on assets for fiscal years 2006 and 2007. (Assume total assets were $1,688,500 at 3/31/05.)
  (5) Percentage change in sales, cost of goods sold, gross margin, and net income after taxes from fiscal year 2006 to 2007.

(b) Identify and explain what other financial reports and/or financial analyses might be helpful to the commercial loan officer of Spokane National Bank in evaluating Robert Frost's request for a time extension on Sandburg's notes.

(c) Assume that the percentage changes experienced in fiscal year 2007 as compared with fiscal year 2006 for sales and cost of goods sold will be repeated in each of the next 2 years. Is Sandburg's desire to finance the plant expansion from internally generated funds realistic? Discuss.

(d) Should Spokane National Bank grant the extension on Sandburg's notes considering Robert Frost's statement about financing the plant expansion through internally generated funds? Discuss.

(L0 13) *P24-4 **(Horizontal and Vertical Analysis)** Presented on page 1338 are comparative balance sheets for the Yevette Company.

YEVETTE COMPANY
COMPARATIVE BALANCE SHEET
AS OF DECEMBER 31, 2007 AND 2006

	December 31	
	2007	2006
Assets		
Cash	$ 180,000	$ 275,000
Accounts receivable (net)	220,000	155,000
Short-term investments	270,000	150,000
Inventories	960,000	980,000
Prepaid expense	25,000	25,000
Fixed assets	2,685,000	1,950,000
Accumulated depreciation	(1,000,000)	(750,000)
	$3,340,000	$2,785,000
Liabilities and Stockholders' Equity		
Accounts payable	$ 50,000	$ 75,000
Accrued expenses	170,000	200,000
Bonds payable	500,000	190,000
Capital stock	2,100,000	1,770,000
Retained earnings	520,000	550,000
	$3,340,000	$2,785,000

Instructions

(Round to two decimal places.)

(a) Prepare a comparative balance sheet of Yevette Company showing the percent each item is of the total assets or total liabilities and stockholders' equity.

(b) Prepare a comparative balance sheet of Yevette Company showing the dollar change and the percent change for each item.

(c) Of what value is the additional information provided in part (a)?

(d) Of what value is the additional information provided in part (b)?

(LO 10) ***P24-5 (Dividend Policy Analysis)** Remmers Inc. went public 3 years ago. The board of directors will be meeting shortly after the end of the year to decide on a dividend policy. In the past, growth has been financed primarily through the retention of earnings. A stock or a cash dividend has never been declared. Presented below is a brief financial summary of Remmers Inc. operations.

			($000 omitted)		
	2007	2006	2005	2004	2003
Sales	$20,000	$16,000	$14,000	$6,000	$4,000
Net income	2,900	1,600	800	900	250
Average total assets	22,000	19,000	11,500	4,200	3,000
Current assets	8,000	6,000	3,000	1,200	1,000
Working capital	3,600	3,200	1,200	500	400
Common shares:					
Number of shares outstanding (000)	2,000	2,000	2,000	20	20
Average market price	$9	$6	$4	—	—

Instructions

(a) Suggest factors to be considered by the board of directors in establishing a dividend policy.

(b) Compute the rate of return on assets, profit margin on sales, earnings per share, price-earnings ratio, and current ratio for each of the 5 years for Remmers Inc.

(c) Comment on the appropriateness of declaring a cash dividend at this time, using the ratios computed in part (b) as a major factor in your analysis.

CONCEPTS FOR ANALYSIS

CA24-1 (General Disclosures, Inventories, Property, Plant, and Equipment) Dan D. Lion Corporation is in the process of preparing its annual financial statements for the fiscal year ended April 30, 2007. Because all of Lion's shares are traded intrastate, the company does not have to file any reports with the

Securities and Exchange Commission. The company manufactures plastic, glass, and paper containers for sale to food and drink manufacturers and distributors.

Lion Corporation maintains separate control accounts for its raw materials, work-in-process, and finished goods inventories for each of the three types of containers. The inventories are valued at the lower of cost or market.

The company's property, plant, and equipment are classified in the following major categories: land, office buildings, furniture and fixtures, manufacturing facilities, manufacturing equipment, and leasehold improvements. All fixed assets are carried at cost. The depreciation methods employed depend upon the type of asset (its classification) and when it was acquired.

Lion Corporation plans to present the inventory and fixed asset amounts in its April 30, 2007, balance sheet as shown below.

Inventories	$4,814,200
Property, plant, and equipment (net of depreciation)	6,310,000

Instructions

What information regarding inventories and property, plant, and equipment must be disclosed by Dan D. Lion Corporation in the audited financial statements issued to stockholders, either in the body or the notes, for the 2006–2007 fiscal year?

(CMA adapted)

CA24-2 **(Disclosures Required in Various Situations)** Rem Inc. produces electronic components for sale to manufacturers of radios, television sets, and digital sound systems. In connection with her examination of Rem's financial statements for the year ended December 31, 2007, Maggie Zeen, CPA, completed field work 2 weeks ago. Ms. Zeen now is evaluating the significance of the following items prior to preparing her auditor's report. Except as noted, none of these items have been disclosed in the financial statements or notes.

Item 1

A 10-year loan agreement, which the company entered into 3 years ago, provides that dividend payments may not exceed net income earned after taxes subsequent to the date of the agreement. The balance of retained earnings at the date of the loan agreement was $420,000. From that date through December 31, 2007, net income after taxes has totaled $570,000 and cash dividends have totaled $320,000. On the basis of these data, the staff auditor assigned to this review concluded that there was no retained earnings restriction at December 31, 2007.

Item 2

Recently Rem interrupted its policy of paying cash dividends quarterly to its stockholders. Dividends were paid regularly through 2006, discontinued for all of 2007 to finance purchase of equipment for the company's new plant, and resumed in the first quarter of 2008. In the annual report dividend policy is to be discussed in the president's letter to stockholders.

Item 3

A major electronics firm has introduced a line of products that will compete directly with Rem's primary line, now being produced in the specially designed new plant. Because of manufacturing innovations, the competitor's line will be of comparable quality but priced 50% below Rem's line. The competitor announced its new line during the week following completion of field work. Ms. Zeen read the announcement in the newspaper and discussed the situation by telephone with Rem executives. Rem will meet the lower prices that are high enough to cover variable manufacturing and selling expenses but will permit recovery of only a portion of fixed costs.

Item 4

The company's new manufacturing plant building, which cost $2,400,000 and has an estimated life of 25 years, is leased from Ancient National Bank at an annual rental of $600,000. The company is obligated to pay property taxes, insurance, and maintenance. At the conclusion of its 10-year noncancellable lease, the company has the option of purchasing the property for $1. In Rem's income statement the rental payment is reported on a separate line.

Instructions

For each of the items above discuss any additional disclosures in the financial statements and notes that the auditor should recommend to her client. (The cumulative effect of the four items should not be considered.)

CA24-3 (Disclosures, Conditional and Contingent Liabilities) Presented below are three independent situations.

Situation 1

A company offers a one-year warranty for the product that it manufactures. A history of warranty claims has been compiled, and the probable amounts of claims related to sales for a given period can be determined.

Situation 2

Subsequent to the date of a set of financial statements, but prior to the issuance of the financial statements, a company enters into a contract that will probably result in a significant loss to the company. The amount of the loss can be reasonably estimated.

Situation 3

A company has adopted a policy of recording self-insurance for any possible losses resulting from injury to others by the company's vehicles. The premium for an insurance policy for the same risk from an independent insurance company would have an annual cost of $4,000. During the period covered by the financial statements, there were no accidents involving the company's vehicles that resulted in injury to others.

Instructions

Discuss the accrual or type of disclosure necessary (if any) and the reason(s) why such disclosure is appropriate for each of the three independent sets of facts above.

(AICPA adapted)

CA24-4 (Post-Balance Sheet Events) At December 31, 2007, Angie Brandt Corp. has assets of $10,000,000, liabilities of $6,000,000, common stock of $2,000,000 (representing 2,000,000 shares of $1 par common stock), and retained earnings of $2,000,000. Net sales for the year 2007 were $18,000,000, and net income was $800,000. As auditors of this company, you are making a review of subsequent events on February 13, 2008, and you find the following.

1. On February 3, 2008, one of Brandt's customers declared bankruptcy. At December 31, 2007, this company owed Brandt $300,000, of which $40,000 was paid in January, 2008.
2. On January 18, 2008, one of the three major plants of the client burned.
3. On January 23, 2008, a strike was called at one of Brandt's largest plants, which halted 30% of its production. As of today (February 13) the strike has not been settled.
4. A major electronics enterprise has introduced a line of products that would compete directly with Brandt's primary line, now being produced in a specially designed new plant. Because of manufacturing innovations, the competitor has been able to achieve quality similar to that of Brandt's products, but at a price 50% lower. Brandt officials say they will meet the lower prices, which are high enough to cover variable manufacturing and selling costs but which permit recovery of only a portion of fixed costs.
5. Merchandise traded in the open market is recorded in the company's records at $1.40 per unit on December 31, 2007. This price had prevailed for 2 weeks, after release of an official market report that predicted vastly enlarged supplies; however, no purchases were made at $1.40. The price throughout the preceding year had been about $2, which was the level experienced over several years. On January 18, 2008, the price returned to $2, after public disclosure of an error in the official calculations of the prior December, correction of which destroyed the expectations of excessive supplies. Inventory at December 31, 2007, was on a lower of cost or market basis.
6. On February 1, 2008, the board of directors adopted a resolution accepting the offer of an investment banker to guarantee the marketing of $1,200,000 of preferred stock.

Instructions

State in each case how the 2007 financial statements would be affected, if at all.

CA24-5 (Segment Reporting) You are compiling the consolidated financial statements for Vender Corporation International. The corporation's accountant, Vincent Price, has provided you with the following segment information.

Note 7: Major Segments of Business

VCI conducts funeral service and cemetery operations in the United States and Canada. Substantially all revenues of VCI's major segments of business are from unaffiliated customers. Segment information for fiscal 2007, 2006, and 2005 follows.

	Funeral	Floral	Cemetery	(thousands) Corporate	Dried Whey	Limousine	Consolidated
Revenues							
2007	$302,000	$10,000	$ 83,000	$ —	$7,000	$14,000	$416,000
2006	245,000	6,000	61,000	—	4,000	8,000	324,000
2005	208,000	3,000	42,000	—	1,000	6,000	260,000
Operating Income							
2007	79,000	1,500	18,000	(36,000)	500	2,000	65,000
2006	64,000	200	12,000	(28,000)	200	400	48,800
2005	54,000	150	6,000	(21,000)	100	350	39,600
Capital Expenditures[a]							
2007	26,000	1,000	9,000	400	300	1,000	37,700
2006	28,000	2,000	60,000	1,500	100	700	92,300
2005	14,000	25	8,000	600	25	50	22,700
Depreciation and Amortization							
2007	13,000	100	2,400	1,400	100	200	17,200
2006	10,000	50	1,400	700	50	100	12,300
2005	8,000	25	1,000	600	25	50	9,700
Identifiable Assets							
2007	334,000	1,500	162,000	114,000	500	8,000	620,000
2006	322,000	1,000	144,000	52,000	1,000	6,000	526,000
2005	223,000	500	78,000	34,000	500	3,500	339,500

[a]Includes $4,520,000, $111,480,000, and $1,294,000 for the years ended April 30, 2007, 2006, and 2005, respectively, for purchases of businesses.

Instructions

Determine which of the above segments must be reported separately and which can be combined under the category "Other." Then, write a one-page memo to the company's accountant, Vincent Price, explaining the following.

(a) What segments must be reported separately and what segments can be combined.

(b) What criteria you used to determine reportable segments.

(c) What major items for each must be disclosed.

CA24-6 (Segment Reporting—Theory) Presented below is an excerpt from the financial statements of **H. J. Heinz Company**.

Segment and Geographic Data

The company is engaged principally in one line of business—processed food products—which represents over 90% of consolidated sales. Information about the business of the company by geographic area is presented in the table below.

There were no material amounts of sales or transfers between geographic areas or between affiliates, and no material amounts of United States export sales.

(in thousands of U.S. dollars)	Domestic	United Kingdom	Canada	Foreign Western Europe	Other	Total	Worldwide
Sales	$2,381,054	$547,527	$216,726	$383,784	$209,354	$1,357,391	$3,738,445
Operating income	246,780	61,282	34,146	29,146	25,111	149,685	396,465
Identifiable assets	1,362,152	265,218	112,620	294,732	143,971	816,541	2,178,693
Capital expenditures	72,712	12,262	13,790	8,253	4,368	38,673	111,385
Depreciation expense	42,279	8,364	3,592	6,355	3,606	21,917	64,196

Instructions

(a) Why does H. J. Heinz not prepare segment information on its products or services?

(b) What are export sales, and when should they be disclosed?

(c) Why are sales by geographical area important to disclose?

CA24-7 **(Segment Reporting—Theory)** The following article appeared in the *Wall Street Journal*.

WASHINGTON—The Securities and Exchange Commission staff issued guidelines for companies grappling with the problem of dividing up their business into industry segments for their annual reports.

An industry segment is defined by the Financial Accounting Standards Board as a part of an enterprise engaged in providing a product or service or a group of related products or services primarily to unaffiliated customers for a profit.

Although conceding that the process is a "subjective task" that "to a considerable extent, depends on the judgment of management," the SEC staff said companies should consider . . . various factors . . . to determine whether products and services should be grouped together or reported as segments.

Instructions

(a) What does financial reporting for segments of a business enterprise involve?

(b) Identify the reasons for requiring financial data to be reported by segments.

(c) Identify the possible disadvantages of requiring financial data to be reported by segments.

(d) Identify the accounting difficulties inherent in segment reporting.

CA24-8 **(Interim Reporting)** J. J. Kersee Corporation, a publicly traded company, is preparing the interim financial data which it will issue to its stockholders and the Securities and Exchange Commission (SEC) at the end of the first quarter of the 2006–2007 fiscal year. Kersee's financial accounting department has compiled the following summarized revenue and expense data for the first quarter of the year.

Sales	$60,000,000
Cost of goods sold	36,000,000
Variable selling expenses	2,000,000
Fixed selling expenses	3,000,000

Included in the fixed selling expenses was the single lump sum payment of $2,000,000 for television advertisements for the entire year.

Instructions

(a) J. J. Kersee Corporation must issue its quarterly financial statements in accordance with generally accepted accounting principles regarding interim financial reporting.

(1) Explain whether Kersee should report its operating results for the quarter as if the quarter were a separate reporting period in and of itself or as if the quarter were an integral part of the annual reporting period.

(2) State how the sales, cost of goods sold, and fixed selling expenses would be reflected in Kersee Corporation's quarterly report prepared for the first quarter of the 2006–2007 fiscal year. Briefly justify your presentation.

(b) What financial information, as a minimum, must Kersee Corporation disclose to its stockholders in its quarterly reports?

(CMA adapted)

CA24-9 **(Treatment of Various Interim Reporting Situations)** The following statement is an excerpt from Paragraphs 9 and 10 of *Accounting Principles Board (APB) Opinion No. 28*, "Interim Financial Reporting."

Interim financial information is essential to provide investors and others with timely information as to the progress of the enterprise. The usefulness of such information rests on the relationship that it has to the annual results of operations. Accordingly, the Board has concluded that each interim period should be viewed primarily as an integral part of an annual period.

In general, the results for each interim period should be based on the accounting principles and practices used by an enterprise in the preparation of its latest annual financial statements unless a change in an accounting practice or policy has been adopted in the current year. The Board has concluded, however, that certain accounting principles and practices followed for annual reporting purposes may require modification at interim reporting dates so that the reported results for the interim period may better relate to the results of operations for the annual period.

Instructions

Listed below are six independent cases on how accounting facts might be reported on an individual company's interim financial reports. For each of these cases, state whether the method proposed to be used for interim reporting would be acceptable under generally accepted accounting principles applicable to interim financial data. Support each answer with a brief explanation.

(a) B. J. King Company takes a physical inventory at year-end for annual financial statement purposes. Inventory and cost of sales reported in the interim quarterly statements are based on estimated gross profit rates, because a physical inventory would result in a cessation of operations. King Company does have reliable perpetual inventory records.

(b) Florence Chadwick Company is planning to report one-fourth of its pension expense each quarter.

(c) N. Lopez Company wrote inventory down to reflect lower of cost or market in the first quarter. At year-end the market exceeds the original acquisition cost of this inventory. Consequently, management plans to write the inventory back up to its original cost as a year-end adjustment.

(d) K. Witt Company realized a large gain on the sale of investments at the beginning of the second quarter. The company wants to report one-third of the gain in each of the remaining quarters.

(e) Alice Marble Company has estimated its annual audit fee. They plan to prorate this expense equally over all four quarters.

(f) Lori McNeil Company was reasonably certain it would have an employee strike in the third quarter. As a result, it shipped heavily during the second quarter but plans to defer the recognition of the sales in excess of the normal sales volume. The deferred sales will be recognized as sales in the third quarter when the strike is in progress. McNeil Company management thinks this is more representative of normal second- and third-quarter operations.

 CA24-10 (Financial Forecasts) An article in *Barron's* noted the following.

Okay. Last fall, someone with a long memory and an even longer arm reached into that bureau drawer and came out with a moldy cheese sandwich and the equally moldy notion of corporate forecasts. We tried to find out what happened to the cheese sandwich—but, rats!, even recourse to the Freedom of Information Act didn't help. However, the forecast proposal was dusted off, polished up and found quite serviceable. The SEC, indeed, lost no time in running it up the old flagpole— but no one was very eager to salute. Even after some of the more objectionable features—compulsory corrections and detailed explanations of why the estimates went awry—were peeled off the original proposal.

Seemingly, despite the Commission's smiles and sweet talk, those craven corporations were still afraid that an honest mistake would lead them down the primrose path to consent decrees and class action suits. To lay to rest such qualms, the Commission last week approved a "Safe Harbor" rule that, providing the forecasts were made on a reasonable basis and in good faith, protected corporations from litigation should the projections prove wide of the mark (as only about 99% are apt to do).

Instructions
(a) What are the arguments for preparing profit forecasts?
(b) What is the purpose of the "safe harbor" rule?
(c) Why are corporations concerned about presenting profit forecasts?

CA24-11 (Disclosure of Estimates—Ethics) Patty Gamble, the financial vice-president, and Victoria Maher, the controller, of Castle Manufacturing Company are reviewing the financial ratios of the company for the years 2006 and 2007. The financial vice president notes that the profit margin on sales ratio has increased from 6% to 12%, a hefty gain for the 2-year period. Gamble is in the process of issuing a media release that emphasizes the efficiency of Castle Manufacturing in controlling cost. Victoria Maher knows that the difference in ratios is due primarily to an earlier company decision to reduce the estimates of warranty and bad debt expense for 2007. The controller, not sure of her supervisor's motives, hesitates to suggest to Gamble that the company's improvement is unrelated to efficiency in controlling cost. To complicate matters, the media release is scheduled in a few days.

Instructions
(a) What, if any, is the ethical dilemma in this situation?
(b) Should Maher, the controller, remain silent? Give reasons.
(c) What stakeholders might be affected by Gamble's media release?
(d) Give your opinion on the following statement and cite reasons: "Because Gamble, the vice president, is most directly responsible for the media release, Maher has no real responsibility in this matter."

 CA24-12 (Reporting of Subsequent Event—Ethics) In June 2007, the board of directors for Holtzman Enterprises Inc. authorized the sale of $10,000,000 of corporate bonds. Michelle Collins, treasurer for Holtzman Enterprises Inc., is concerned about the date when the bonds are issued. The company really needs

the cash, but she is worried that if the bonds are issued before the company's year-end (December 31, 2007) the additional liability will have an adverse effect on a number of important ratios. In July, she explains to company president Kenneth Holtzman that if they delay issuing the bonds until after December 31 the bonds will not affect the ratios until December 31, 2008. They will have to report the issuance as a subsequent event which requires only footnote disclosure. Collins expects that with expected improved financial performance in 2008 ratios should be better.

Instructions

(a) What are the ethical issues involved?

(b) Should Holtzman agree to the delay?

*CA24-13 (Effect of Transactions on Financial Statements and Ratios) The transactions listed below relate to Botticelli Inc. You are to assume that on the date on which each of the transactions occurred the corporation's accounts showed only common stock ($100 par) outstanding, a current ratio of 2.7:1, and a substantial net income for the year to date (before giving effect to the transaction concerned). On that date the book value per share of stock was $151.53.

Each numbered transaction is to be considered completely independent of the others, and its related answer should be based on the effect(s) of that transaction alone. Assume that all numbered transactions occurred during 2007 and that the amount involved in each case is sufficiently material to distort reported net income if improperly included in the determination of net income. Assume further that each transaction was recorded in accordance with generally accepted accounting principles and, where applicable, in conformity with the all-inclusive concept of the income statement.

For each of the numbered transactions you are to decide whether it:

a. Increased the corporation's 2007 net income.

b. Decreased the corporation's 2007 net income.

c. Increased the corporation's total retained earnings directly (i.e., not via net income).

d. Decreased the corporation's total retained earnings directly.

e. Increased the corporation's current ratio.

f. Decreased the corporation's current ratio.

g. Increased each stockholder's proportionate share of total owner's equity.

h. Decreased each stockholder's proportionate share of total owner's equity.

i. Increased each stockholder's equity per share of stock (book value).

j. Decreased each stockholder's equity per share of stock (book value).

k. Had none of the foregoing effects.

Instructions

List the numbers 1 through 9. Select as many letters as you deem appropriate to reflect the effect(s) of each transaction as of the date of the transaction by printing beside the transaction number the letter(s) that identifies that transaction's effect(s).

Transactions

_____ 1. Treasury stock originally repurchased and carried at $127 per share was sold for cash at $153 per share.

_____ 2. The corporation sold at a profit land and a building that had been idle for some time. Under the terms of the sale, the corporation received a portion of the sales price in cash immediately, the balance maturing at 6 month intervals.

_____ 3. In January the board directed the writeoff of certain patent rights that had suddenly and unexpectedly become worthless.

_____ 4. The corporation wrote off all of the unamortized discount and issue expense applicable to bonds that it refinanced in 2007.

_____ 5. The corporation called in all its outstanding shares of stock and exchanged them for new shares on a 2-for-1 basis, reducing the par value at the same time to $50 per share.

_____ 6. The corporation paid a cash dividend that had been recorded in the accounts at time of declaration.

_____ 7. Litigation involving Botticelli Inc. as defendant was settled in the corporation's favor, with the plaintiff paying all court costs and legal fees. In 2004 the corporation had appropriately established a special contingency for this court action. (Indicate the effect of reversing the contingency only.)

___ 8. The corporation received a check for the proceeds of an insurance policy from the company with which it is insured against theft of trucks. No entries concerning the theft had been made previously, and the proceeds reduce but do not cover completely the loss.

___ 9. Treasury stock, which had been repurchased at and carried at $127 per share, was issued as a stock dividend. In connection with this distribution, the board of directors of Botticelli Inc. had authorized a transfer from retained earnings to permanent capital of an amount equal to the aggregate market value ($153 per share) of the shares issued. No entries relating to this dividend had been made previously.

(AICPA adapted)

*ditional Financial State-
ent Analysis Problems

USING YOUR JUDGMENT

Financial Reporting Problem

P&G **The Procter & Gamble Company (P&G)**

As stated in the chapter, notes to the financial statements are the means of explaining the items presented in the main body of the statements. Common note disclosures relate to such items as accounting policies, segmented information, and interim reporting.

Instructions

Refer to **P&G**'s financial statements and the accompanying notes to answer the following questions.

(a) What specific items does P&G discuss in its Note 1—Summary of Significant Accounting Policies? (List the headings only.)

(b) For what segments did P&G report segmented information? Which segment is the largest? Who is P&G largest customer?

(c) What interim information was reported by P&G?

*Financial Statement Analysis Case

Twin Ricky Inc. (TRI) manufactures a variety of consumer products. The company's founders have run the company for 30 years and are now interested in retiring. Consequently, they are seeking a purchaser who will continue its operations, and a group of investors, Donna Inc., is looking into the acquisition of TRI. To evaluate its financial stability and operating efficiency, TRI was requested to provide the latest financial statements and selected financial ratios. Summary information provided by TRI is presented below and on the next page.

TRI
INCOME STATEMENT
FOR THE YEAR ENDED NOVEMBER 30, 2007
(IN THOUSANDS)

Sales (net)	$30,500
Interest income	500
Total revenue	31,000
Costs and expenses	
Cost of goods sold	17,600
Selling and administrative expense	3,550
Depreciation and amortization expense	1,890
Interest expense	900
Total costs and expenses	23,940
Income before taxes	7,060
Income taxes	2,900
Net income	$ 4,160

TRI
STATEMENT OF FINANCIAL POSITION
AS OF NOVEMBER 30
(IN THOUSANDS)

	2007	2006
Cash	$ 400	$ 500
Marketable securities (at cost)	500	200
Accounts receivable (net)	3,200	2,900
Inventory	5,800	5,400
Total current assets	9,900	9,000
Property, plant, & equipment (net)	7,100	7,000
Total assets	$17,000	$16,000
Accounts payable	$ 3,700	$ 3,400
Income taxes payable	900	800
Accrued expenses	1,700	1,400
Total current liabilities	6,300	5,600
Long-term debt	2,000	1,800
Total liabilities	8,300	7,400
Common stock ($1 par value)	2,700	2,700
Paid-in capital in excess of par	1,000	1,000
Retained earnings	5,000	4,900
Total shareholders' equity	8,700	8,600
Total liabilities and shareholders' equity	$17,000	$16,000

SELECTED FINANCIAL RATIOS

	TRI 2006	TRI 2005	Current Industry Average
Current ratio	1.61	1.62	1.63
Acid-test ratio	.64	.63	.68
Times interest earned	8.55	8.50	8.45
Profit margin on sales	13.2%	12.1%	13.0%
Total debt to net worth	.86	1.02	1.03
Asset turnover	1.84	1.83	1.84
Inventory turnover	3.17	3.21	3.18

Instructions

(a) Calculate a new set of ratios for the fiscal year 2007 for TRI based on the financial statements presented.

(b) Explain the analytical use of each of the seven ratios presented, describing what the investors can learn about TRI's financial stability and operating efficiency.

(c) Identify two limitations of ratio analysis.

(CMA adapted)

Comparative Analysis Case

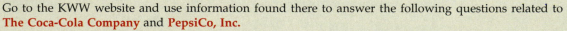

The Coca-Cola Company

PEPSICO

The Coca-Cola Company versus PepsiCo, Inc.

Instructions

Go to the KWW website and use information found there to answer the following questions related to **The Coca-Cola Company** and **PepsiCo, Inc.**

(a) (1) What specific items does Coca-Cola discuss in its **Note 1—Accounting Policies**? (Prepare a list of the headings only.)

(2) What specific items does PepsiCo discuss in its **Note 2—Our Summary of Significant Accounting Policies**? (Prepare a list of the headings only.)

(b) For what lines of business or segments do Coca-Cola and PepsiCo present segmented information?

(c) Note and comment on the similarities and differences between the auditors' reports submitted by the independent auditors of Coca-Cola and PepsiCo for the year 2004.

Research Cases

Case 1

Read the article titled "FASB Is Criticized for Inaction on Off-Balance-Sheet Debt Issue," by Steve Liesman, Jonathan Weil, and Scott Paltrow in the January 18, 2002, *Wall Street Journal*.

Instructions

Answer the following questions.

(a) Why has the FASB not set better rules for when a firm should be allowed to keep debt off its balance sheet?

(b) Who is helped (in the short term and the long term) by a firm's being able to keep debt off its balance sheet? Who is hurt (short term and long term)?

(c) According to the article, when the FASB proposes new rules that would hurt them, "corporate America and its allies invoke portents of doom as to why we shouldn't have honest accounting treatment" of what's being proposed. How does this affect the usefulness of financial reporting for investors and creditors?

(d) One of the groups criticizing the FASB for moving too slowly is the Financial Executives International (FEI), which opposed requiring firms to consolidate the results of all their entities. The FEI also opposed the FASB's proposal to require firms to expense executive stock options. Based on this, would you consider FEI "part of the solution" or "part of the problem"? Justify your answer.

Case 2

Companies registered with the Securities and Exchange Commission are required to file a quarterly report on Form 10-Q within 40 days of the end of the first three fiscal quarters.

Instructions

Use EDGAR or some other source to examine the most recent 10-Q for the company of your choice and answer the following questions.

(a) What financial information is included in Part I?

(b) Read the notes to the financial statements and identify any departures from the "integral approach."

(c) Does the 10-Q include any information under Part II? Describe the nature of the information.

Professional Research: Financial Accounting and Reporting

As part of the year-end audit, you are discussing the disclosure checklist with your client. The checklist identifies the items that must be disclosed in a set of GAAP financial statements. The client is surprised by the disclosures item related to accounting policies. Specifically, since the audit report will attest to the statements being prepared in accordance with GAAP, the client questions the accounting policy checklist item. The client has asked you to conduct some research to verify the accounting policy disclosures.

Instructions

Using the **Financial Accounting Research System (FARS)**, respond to the following items. (Provide text strings used in your search.)

(a) In general, what should disclosures of accounting policies encompass?

(b) List some examples of the most commonly required disclosures.

*Professional Simulation

In this simulation you are asked to evaluate a company's solvency and going-concern potential, by analyzing a set of ratios. You also are asked to indicate possible limitations of ratio analysis. Prepare responses to all parts.

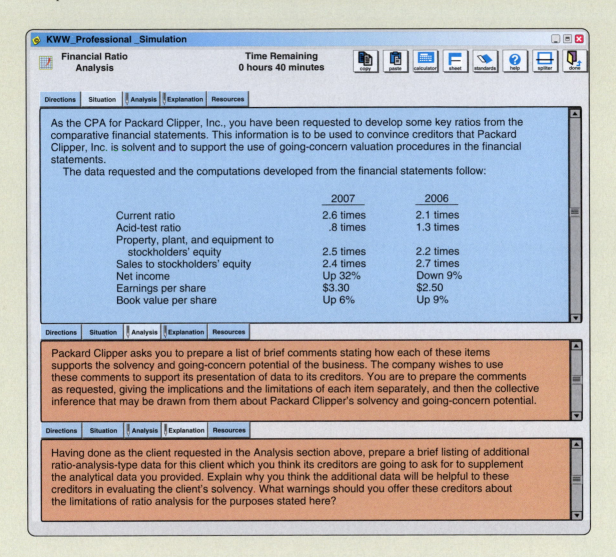

KWW_Professional _Simulation

Financial Ratio Analysis

Time Remaining
0 hours 40 minutes

copy | paste | calculator | sheet | standards | help | splitter | done

Directions | Situation | Analysis | Explanation | Resources

As the CPA for Packard Clipper, Inc., you have been requested to develop some key ratios from the comparative financial statements. This information is to be used to convince creditors that Packard Clipper, Inc. is solvent and to support the use of going-concern valuation procedures in the financial statements.

The data requested and the computations developed from the financial statements follow:

	2007	2006
Current ratio	2.6 times	2.1 times
Acid-test ratio	.8 times	1.3 times
Property, plant, and equipment to stockholders' equity	2.5 times	2.2 times
Sales to stockholders' equity	2.4 times	2.7 times
Net income	Up 32%	Down 9%
Earnings per share	$3.30	$2.50
Book value per share	Up 6%	Up 9%

Directions | Situation | Analysis | Explanation | Resources

Packard Clipper asks you to prepare a list of brief comments stating how each of these items supports the solvency and going-concern potential of the business. The company wishes to use these comments to support its presentation of data to its creditors. You are to prepare the comments as requested, giving the implications and the limitations of each item separately, and then the collective inference that may be drawn from them about Packard Clipper's solvency and going-concern potential.

Directions | Situation | Analysis | Explanation | Resources

Having done as the client requested in the Analysis section above, prepare a brief listing of additional ratio-analysis-type data for this client which you think its creditors are going to ask for to supplement the analytical data you provided. Explain why you think the additional data will be helpful to these creditors in evaluating the client's solvency. What warnings should you offer these creditors about the limitations of ratio analysis for the purposes stated here?

Remember to check the book's companion website to find additional resources for this chapter.

The following time value of money tables are also presented at the end of Chapter 6, "Accounting and the Time Value of Money" in Volume I (pages 302–311). They are presented here to facilitate your use of Volume II.

TABLE 6-1   FUTURE VALUE OF 1 (FUTURE VALUE OF A SINGLE SUM)

$$FVF_{n,i} = (1 + i)^n$$

(n) Periods	2%	2½%	3%	4%	5%	6%
1	1.02000	1.02500	1.03000	1.04000	1.05000	1.06000
2	1.04040	1.05063	1.06090	1.08160	1.10250	1.12360
3	1.06121	1.07689	1.09273	1.12486	1.15763	1.19102
4	1.08243	1.10381	1.12551	1.16986	1.21551	1.26248
5	1.10408	1.13141	1.15927	1.21665	1.27628	1.33823
6	1.12616	1.15969	1.19405	1.26532	1.34010	1.41852
7	1.14869	1.18869	1.22987	1.31593	1.40710	1.50363
8	1.17166	1.21840	1.26677	1.36857	1.47746	1.59385
9	1.19509	1.24886	1.30477	1.42331	1.55133	1.68948
10	1.21899	1.28008	1.34392	1.48024	1.62889	1.79085
11	1.24337	1.31209	1.38423	1.53945	1.71034	1.89830
12	1.26824	1.34489	1.42576	1.60103	1.79586	2.01220
13	1.29361	1.37851	1.46853	1.66507	1.88565	2.13293
14	1.31948	1.41297	1.51259	1.73168	1.97993	2.26090
15	1.34587	1.44830	1.55797	1.80094	2.07893	2.39656
16	1.37279	1.48451	1.60471	1.87298	2.18287	2.54035
17	1.40024	1.52162	1.65285	1.94790	2.29202	2.69277
18	1.42825	1.55966	1.70243	2.02582	2.40662	2.85434
19	1.45681	1.59865	1.75351	2.10685	2.52695	3.02560
20	1.48595	1.63862	1.80611	2.19112	2.65330	3.20714
21	1.51567	1.67958	1.86029	2.27877	2.78596	3.39956
22	1.54598	1.72157	1.91610	2.36992	2.92526	3.60354
23	1.57690	1.76461	1.97359	2.46472	3.07152	3.81975
24	1.60844	1.80873	2.03279	2.56330	3.22510	4.04893
25	1.64061	1.85394	2.09378	2.66584	3.38635	4.29187
26	1.67342	1.90029	2.15659	2.77247	3.55567	4.54938
27	1.70689	1.94780	2.22129	2.88337	3.73346	4.82235
28	1.74102	1.99650	2.28793	2.99870	3.92013	5.11169
29	1.77584	2.04641	2.35657	3.11865	4.11614	5.41839
30	1.81136	2.09757	2.42726	3.24340	4.32194	5.74349
31	1.84759	2.15001	2.50008	3.37313	4.53804	6.08810
32	1.88454	2.20376	2.57508	3.50806	4.76494	6.45339
33	1.92223	2.25885	2.65234	3.64838	5.00319	6.84059
34	1.96068	2.31532	2.73191	3.79432	5.25335	7.25103
35	1.99989	2.37321	2.81386	3.94609	5.51602	7.68609
36	2.03989	2.43254	2.89828	4.10393	5.79182	8.14725
37	2.08069	2.49335	2.98523	4.26809	6.08141	8.63609
38	2.12230	2.55568	3.07478	4.43881	6.38548	9.15425
39	2.16474	2.61957	3.16703	4.61637	6.70475	9.70351
40	2.20804	2.68506	3.26204	4.80102	7.03999	10.28572

TABLE 6-1   FUTURE VALUE OF 1

8%	9%	10%	11%	12%	15%	(n) Periods
1.08000	1.09000	1.10000	1.11000	1.12000	1.15000	1
1.16640	1.18810	1.21000	1.23210	1.25440	1.32250	2
1.25971	1.29503	1.33100	1.36763	1.40493	1.52088	3
1.36049	1.41158	1.46410	1.51807	1.57352	1.74901	4
1.46933	1.53862	1.61051	1.68506	1.76234	2.01136	5
1.58687	1.67710	1.77156	1.87041	1.97382	2.31306	6
1.71382	1.82804	1.94872	2.07616	2.21068	2.66002	7
1.85093	1.99256	2.14359	2.30454	2.47596	3.05902	8
1.99900	2.17189	2.35795	2.55803	2.77308	3.51788	9
2.15892	2.36736	2.59374	2.83942	3.10585	4.04556	10
2.33164	2.58043	2.85312	3.15176	3.47855	4.65239	11
2.51817	2.81267	3.13843	3.49845	3.89598	5.35025	12
2.71962	3.06581	3.45227	3.88328	4.36349	6.15279	13
2.93719	3.34173	3.79750	4.31044	4.88711	7.07571	14
3.17217	3.64248	4.17725	4.78459	5.47357	8.13706	15
3.42594	3.97031	4.59497	5.31089	6.13039	9.35762	16
3.70002	4.32763	5.05447	5.89509	6.86604	10.76126	17
3.99602	4.71712	5.55992	6.54355	7.68997	12.37545	18
4.31570	5.14166	6.11591	7.26334	8.61276	14.23177	19
4.66096	5.60441	6.72750	8.06231	9.64629	16.36654	20
5.03383	6.10881	7.40025	8.94917	10.80385	18.82152	21
5.43654	6.65860	8.14028	9.93357	12.10031	21.64475	22
5.87146	7.25787	8.95430	11.02627	13.55235	24.89146	23
6.34118	7.91108	9.84973	12.23916	15.17863	28.62518	24
6.84847	8.62308	10.83471	13.58546	17.00000	32.91895	25
7.39635	9.39916	11.91818	15.07986	19.04007	37.85680	26
7.98806	10.24508	13.10999	16.73865	21.32488	43.53532	27
8.62711	11.16714	14.42099	18.57990	23.88387	50.06561	28
9.31727	12.17218	15.86309	20.62369	26.74993	57.57545	29
10.06266	13.26768	17.44940	22.89230	29.95992	66.21177	30
10.86767	14.46177	19.19434	25.41045	33.55511	76.14354	31
11.73708	15.76333	21.11378	28.20560	37.58173	87.56507	32
12.67605	17.18203	23.22515	31.30821	42.09153	100.69983	33
13.69013	18.72841	25.54767	34.75212	47.14252	115.80480	34
14.78534	20.41397	28.10244	38.57485	52.79962	133.17552	35
15.96817	22.25123	30.91268	42.81808	59.13557	153.15185	36
17.24563	24.25384	34.00395	47.52807	66.23184	176.12463	37
18.62528	26.43668	37.40434	52.75616	74.17966	202.54332	38
20.11530	28.81598	41.14479	58.55934	83.08122	232.92482	39
21.72452	31.40942	45.25926	65.00087	93.05097	267.86355	40

TABLE 6-2   PRESENT VALUE OF 1 (PRESENT VALUE OF A SINGLE SUM)

$$PVF_{n,i} = \frac{1}{(1 + i)^n} = (1 + i)^{-n}$$

(n) Periods	2%	2½%	3%	4%	5%	6%
1	.98039	.97561	.97087	.96154	.95238	.94340
2	.96117	.95181	.94260	.92456	.90703	.89000
3	.94232	.92860	.91514	.88900	.86384	.83962
4	.92385	.90595	.88849	.85480	.82270	.79209
5	.90573	.88385	.86261	.82193	.78353	.74726
6	.88797	.86230	.83748	.79031	.74622	.70496
7	.87056	.84127	.81309	.75992	.71068	.66506
8	.85349	.82075	.78941	.73069	.67684	.62741
9	.83676	.80073	.76642	.70259	.64461	.59190
10	.82035	.78120	.74409	.67556	.61391	.55839
11	.80426	.76214	.72242	.64958	.58468	.52679
12	.78849	.74356	.70138	.62460	.55684	.49697
13	.77303	.72542	.68095	.60057	.53032	.46884
14	.75788	.70773	.66112	.57748	.50507	.44230
15	.74301	.69047	.64186	.55526	.48102	.41727
16	.72845	.67362	.62317	.53391	.45811	.39365
17	.71416	.65720	.60502	.51337	.43630	.37136
18	.70016	.64117	.58739	.49363	.41552	.35034
19	.68643	.62553	.57029	.47464	.39573	.33051
20	.67297	.61027	.55368	.45639	.37689	.31180
21	.65978	.59539	.53755	.43883	.35894	.29416
22	.64684	.58086	.52189	.42196	.34185	.22751
23	.63416	.56670	.50669	.40573	.32557	.26180
24	.62172	.55288	.49193	.39012	.31007	.24698
25	.60953	.53939	.47761	.37512	.29530	.23300
26	.59758	.52623	.46369	.36069	.28124	.21981
27	.58586	.51340	.45019	.34682	.26785	.20737
28	.57437	.50088	.43708	.33348	.25509	.19563
29	.56311	.48866	.42435	.32065	.24295	.18456
30	.55207	.47674	.41199	.30832	.23138	.17411
31	.54125	.46511	.39999	.29646	.22036	.16425
32	.53063	.45377	.38834	.28506	.20987	.15496
33	.52023	.44270	.37703	.27409	.19987	.14619
34	.51003	.43191	.36604	.26355	.19035	.13791
35	.50003	.42137	.35538	.25342	.18129	.13011
36	.49022	.41109	.34503	.24367	.17266	.12274
37	.48061	.40107	.33498	.23430	.16444	.11579
38	.47119	.39128	.32523	.22529	.15661	.10924
39	.46195	.38174	.31575	.21662	.14915	.10306
40	.45289	.37243	.30656	.20829	.14205	.09722

TABLE 6-2 PRESENT VALUE OF 1

8%	9%	10%	11%	12%	15%	(n) Periods
.92593	.91743	.90909	.90090	.89286	.86957	1
.85734	.84168	.82645	.81162	.79719	.75614	2
.79383	.77218	.75132	.73119	.71178	.65752	3
.73503	.70843	.68301	.65873	.63552	.57175	4
.68058	.64993	.62092	.59345	.56743	.49718	5
.63017	.59627	.56447	.53464	.50663	.43233	6
.58349	.54703	.51316	.48166	.45235	.37594	7
.54027	.50187	.46651	.43393	.40388	.32690	8
.50025	.46043	.42410	.39092	.36061	.28426	9
.46319	.42241	.38554	.35218	.32197	.24719	10
.42888	.38753	.35049	.31728	.28748	.21494	11
.39711	.35554	.31863	.28584	.25668	.18691	12
.36770	.32618	.28966	.25751	.22917	.16253	13
.34046	.29925	.26333	.23199	.20462	.14133	14
.31524	.27454	.23939	.20900	.18270	.12289	15
.29189	.25187	.21763	.18829	.16312	.10687	16
.27027	.23107	.19785	.16963	.14564	.09293	17
.25025	.21199	.17986	.15282	.13004	.08081	18
.23171	.19449	.16351	.13768	.11611	.07027	19
.21455	.17843	.14864	.12403	.10367	.06110	20
.19866	.16370	.13513	.11174	.09256	.05313	21
.18394	.15018	.12285	.10067	.08264	.04620	22
.17032	.13778	.11168	.09069	.07379	.04017	23
.15770	.12641	.10153	.08170	.06588	.03493	24
.14602	.11597	.09230	.07361	.05882	.03038	25
.13520	.10639	.08391	.06631	.05252	.02642	26
.12519	.09761	.07628	.05974	.04689	.02297	27
.11591	.08955	.06934	.05382	.04187	.01997	28
.10733	.08216	.06304	.04849	.03738	.01737	29
.09938	.07537	.05731	.04368	.03338	.01510	30
.09202	.06915	.05210	.03935	.02980	.01313	31
.08520	.06344	.04736	.03545	.02661	.01142	32
.07889	.05820	.04306	.03194	.02376	.00993	33
.07305	.05340	.03914	.02878	.02121	.00864	34
.06763	.04899	.03558	.02592	.01894	.00751	35
.06262	.04494	.03235	.02335	.01691	.00653	36
.05799	.04123	.02941	.02104	.01510	.00568	37
.05369	.03783	.02674	.01896	.01348	.00494	38
.04971	.03470	.02430	.01708	.01204	.00429	39
.04603	.03184	.02210	.01538	.01075	.00373	40

TABLE 6-3 FUTURE VALUE OF AN ORDINARY ANNUITY OF 1

$$\text{FVF-OA}_{n,i} = \frac{(1 + i)^n - 1}{i}$$

(n) Periods	2%	2½%	3%	4%	5%	6%
1	1.00000	1.00000	1.00000	1.00000	1.00000	1.00000
2	2.02000	2.02500	2.03000	2.04000	2.05000	2.06000
3	3.06040	3.07563	3.09090	3.12160	3.15250	3.18360
4	4.12161	4.15252	4.18363	4.24646	4.31013	4.37462
5	5.20404	5.25633	5.30914	5.41632	5.52563	5.63709
6	6.30812	6.38774	6.46841	6.63298	6.80191	6.97532
7	7.43428	7.54743	7.66246	7.89829	8.14201	8.39384
8	8.58297	8.73612	8.89234	9.21423	9.54911	9.89747
9	9.75463	9.95452	10.15911	10.58280	11.02656	11.49132
10	10.94972	11.20338	11.46338	12.00611	12.57789	13.18079
11	12.16872	12.48347	12.80780	13.48635	14.20679	14.97164
12	13.41209	13.79555	14.19203	15.02581	15.91713	16.86994
13	14.68033	15.14044	15.61779	16.62684	17.71298	18.88214
14	15.97394	16.51895	17.08632	18.29191	19.59863	21.01507
15	17.29342	17.93193	18.59891	20.02359	21.57856	23.27597
16	18.63929	19.38022	20.15688	21.82453	23.65749	25.67253
17	20.01207	20.86473	21.76159	23.69751	25.84037	28.21288
18	21.41231	22.38635	23.41444	25.64541	28.13238	30.90565
19	22.84056	23.94601	25.11687	27.67123	30.53900	33.75999
20	24.29737	25.54466	26.87037	29.77808	33.06595	36.78559
21	25.78332	27.18327	28.67649	31.96920	35.71925	39.99273
22	27.29898	28.86286	30.53678	34.24797	38.50521	43.39229
23	28.84496	30.58443	32.45288	36.61789	41.43048	46.99583
24	30.42186	32.34904	34.42647	39.08260	44.50200	50.81558
25	32.03030	34.15776	36.45926	41.64591	47.72710	54.86451
26	33.67091	36.01171	38.55304	44.31174	51.11345	59.15638
27	35.34432	37.91200	40.70963	47.08421	54.66913	63.70577
28	37.05121	39.85980	42.93092	49.96758	58.40258	68.52811
29	38.79223	41.85630	45.21885	52.96629	62.32271	73.63980
30	40.56808	43.90270	47.57542	56.08494	66.43885	79.05819
31	42.37944	46.00027	50.00268	59.32834	70.76079	84.80168
32	44.22703	48.15028	52.50276	62.70147	75.29883	90.88978
33	46.11157	50.35403	55.07784	66.20953	80.06377	97.34316
34	48.03380	52.61289	57.73018	69.85791	85.06696	104.18376
35	49.99448	54.92821	60.46208	73.65222	90.32031	111.43478
36	51.99437	57.30141	63.27594	77.59831	95.83632	119.12087
37	54.03425	59.73395	66.17422	81.70225	101.62814	127.26812
38	56.11494	62.22730	69.15945	85.97034	107.70955	135.90421
39	58.23724	64.78298	72.23423	90.40915	114.09502	145.05846
40	60.40198	67.40255	75.40126	95.02552	120.79977	154.76197

TABLE 6-3   FUTURE VALUE OF AN ORDINARY ANNUITY OF 1

8%	9%	10%	11%	12%	15%	(n) Periods
1.00000	1.00000	1.00000	1.00000	1.00000	1.00000	1
2.08000	2.09000	2.10000	2.11000	2.12000	2.15000	2
3.24640	3.27810	3.31000	3.34210	3.37440	3.47250	3
4.50611	4.57313	4.64100	4.70973	4.77933	4.99338	4
5.86660	5.98471	6.10510	6.22780	6.35285	6.74238	5
7.33592	7.52334	7.71561	7.91286	8.11519	8.75374	6
8.92280	9.20044	9.48717	9.78327	10.08901	11.06680	7
10.63663	11.02847	11.43589	11.85943	12.29969	13.72682	8
12.48756	13.02104	13.57948	14.16397	14.77566	16.78584	9
14.48656	15.19293	15.93743	16.72201	17.54874	20.30372	10
16.64549	17.56029	18.53117	19.56143	20.65458	24.34928	11
18.97713	20.14072	21.38428	22.71319	24.13313	29.00167	12
21.49530	22.95339	24.52271	26.21164	28.02911	34.35192	13
24.21492	26.01919	27.97498	30.09492	32.39260	40.50471	14
27.15211	29.36092	31.77248	34.40536	37.27972	47.58041	15
30.32428	33.00340	35.94973	39.18995	42.75328	55.71747	16
33.75023	36.97371	40.54470	44.50084	48.88367	65.07509	17
37.45024	41.30134	45.59917	50.39593	55.74972	75.83636	18
41.44626	46.01846	51.15909	56.93949	63.43968	88.21181	19
45.76196	51.16012	57.27500	64.20283	72.05244	102.44358	20
50.42292	56.76453	64.00250	72.26514	81.69874	118.81012	21
55.45676	62.87334	71.40275	81.21431	92.50258	137.63164	22
60.89330	69.53194	79.54302	91.14788	104.60289	159.27638	23
66.76476	76.78981	88.49733	102.17415	118.15524	184.16784	24
73.10594	84.70090	98.34706	114.41331	133.33387	212.79302	25
79.95442	93.32398	109.18177	127.99877	150.33393	245.71197	26
87.35077	102.72314	121.09994	143.07864	169.37401	283.56877	27
95.33883	112.96822	134.20994	159.81729	190.69889	327.10408	28
103.96594	124.13536	148.63093	178.39719	214.58275	377.16969	29
113.28321	136.30754	164.49402	199.02088	241.33268	434.74515	30
123.34587	149.57522	181.94343	221.91317	271.29261	500.95692	31
134.21354	164.03699	201.13777	247.32362	304.84772	577.10046	32
145.95062	179.80032	222.25154	275.52922	342.42945	644.66553	33
158.62667	196.98234	245.47670	306.83744	384.52098	765.36535	34
172.31680	215.71076	271.02437	341.58955	431.66350	881.17016	35
187.10215	236.12472	299.12681	380.16441	484.46312	1014.34568	36
203.07032	258.37595	330.03949	422.98249	543.59869	1167.49753	37
220.31595	282.62978	364.04343	470.51056	609.83053	1343.62216	38
238.94122	309.06646	401.44778	523.26673	684.01020	1546.16549	39
259.05652	337.88245	442.59256	581.82607	767.09142	1779.09031	40

TABLE 6-4 PRESENT VALUE OF AN ORDINARY ANNUITY OF 1

$$PVF\text{-}OA_{n,i} = \frac{1 - \dfrac{1}{(1+i)^n}}{i}$$

(n) Periods	2%	2½%	3%	4%	5%	6%
1	.98039	.97561	.97087	.96154	.95238	.94340
2	1.94156	1.92742	1.91347	1.88609	1.85941	1.83339
3	2.88388	2.85602	2.82861	2.77509	2.72325	2.67301
4	3.80773	3.76197	3.71710	3.62990	3.54595	3.46511
5	4.71346	4.64583	4.57971	4.45182	4.32948	4.21236
6	5.60143	5.50813	5.41719	5.24214	5.07569	4.91732
7	6.47199	6.34939	6.23028	6.00205	5.78637	5.58238
8	7.32548	7.17014	7.01969	6.73274	6.46321	6.20979
9	8.16224	7.97087	7.78611	7.43533	7.10782	6.80169
10	8.98259	8.75206	8.53020	8.11090	7.72173	7.36009
11	9.78685	9.51421	9.25262	8.76048	8.30641	7.88687
12	10.57534	10.25776	9.95400	9.38507	8.86325	8.38384
13	11.34837	10.98319	10.63496	9.98565	9.39357	8.85268
14	12.10625	11.69091	11.29607	10.56312	9.89864	9.29498
15	12.84926	12.38138	11.93794	11.11839	10.37966	9.71225
16	13.57771	13.05500	12.56110	11.65230	10.83777	10.10590
17	14.29187	13.71220	13.16612	12.16567	11.27407	10.47726
18	14.99203	14.35336	13.75351	12.65930	11.68959	10.82760
19	15.67846	14.97889	14.32380	13.13394	12.08532	11.15812
20	16.35143	15.58916	14.87747	13.59033	12.46221	11.46992
21	17.01121	16.18455	15.41502	14.02916	12.82115	11.76408
22	17.65805	16.76541	15.93692	14.45112	13.16300	12.04158
23	18.29220	17.33211	16.44361	14.85684	13.48857	12.30338
24	18.91393	17.88499	16.93554	15.24696	13.79864	12.55036
25	19.52346	18.42438	17.41315	15.62208	14.09394	12.78336
26	20.12104	18.95061	17.87684	15.98277	14.37519	13.00317
27	20.70690	19.46401	18.32703	16.32959	14.64303	13.21053
28	21.28127	19.96489	18.76411	16.66306	14.89813	13.40616
29	21.84438	20.45355	19.18845	16.98371	15.14107	13.59072
30	22.39646	20.93029	19.60044	17.29203	15.37245	13.76483
31	22.93770	21.39541	20.00043	17.58849	15.59281	13.92909
32	23.46833	21.84918	20.38877	17.87355	15.80268	14.08404
33	23.98856	22.29188	20.76579	18.14765	16.00255	14.23023
34	24.49859	22.72379	21.13184	18.41120	16.19290	14.36814
35	24.99862	23.14516	21.48722	18.66461	16.37419	14.49825
36	25.48884	23.55625	21.83225	18.90828	16.54685	14.62099
37	25.96945	23.95732	22.16724	19.14258	16.71129	14.73678
38	26.44064	24.34860	22.49246	19.36786	16.86789	14.84602
39	26.90259	24.73034	22.80822	19.58448	17.01704	14.94907
40	27.35548	25.10278	23.11477	19.79277	17.15909	15.04630

TABLE 6-4   PRESENT VALUE OF AN ORDINARY ANNUITY OF 1

8%	9%	10%	11%	12%	15%	(n) Periods
.92593	.91743	.90909	.90090	.89286	.86957	1
1.78326	1.75911	1.73554	1.71252	1.69005	1.62571	2
2.57710	2.53130	2.48685	2.44371	2.40183	2.28323	3
3.31213	3.23972	3.16986	3.10245	3.03735	2.85498	4
3.99271	3.88965	3.79079	3.69590	3.60478	3.35216	5
4.62288	4.48592	4.35526	4.23054	4.11141	3.78448	6
5.20637	5.03295	4.86842	4.71220	4.56376	4.16042	7
5.74664	5.53482	5.33493	5.14612	4.96764	4.48732	8
6.24689	5.99525	5.75902	5.53705	5.32825	4.77158	9
6.71008	6.41766	6.14457	5.88923	5.65022	5.01877	10
7.13896	6.80519	6.49506	6.20652	5.93770	5.23371	11
7.53608	7.16073	6.81369	6.49236	6.19437	5.42062	12
7.90378	7.48690	7.10336	6.74987	6.42355	5.58315	13
8.24424	7.78615	7.36669	6.98187	6.62817	5.72448	14
8.55948	8.06069	7.60608	7.19087	6.81086	5.84737	15
8.85137	8.31256	7.82371	7.37916	6.97399	5.95424	16
9.12164	8.54363	8.02155	7.54879	7.11963	6.04716	17
9.37189	8.75563	8.20141	7.70162	7.24967	6.12797	18
9.60360	8.95012	8.36492	7.83929	7.36578	6.19823	19
9.81815	9.12855	8.51356	7.96333	7.46944	6.25933	20
10.01680	9.29224	8.64869	8.07507	7.56200	6.31246	21
10.20074	9.44243	8.77154	8.17574	7.64465	6.35866	22
10.37106	9.58021	8.88322	8.26643	7.71843	6.39884	23
10.52876	9.70661	8.98474	8.34814	7.78432	6.43377	24
10.67478	9.82258	9.07704	8.42174	7.84314	6.46415	25
10.80998	9.92897	9.16095	8.48806	7.89566	6.49056	26
10.93516	10.02658	9.23722	8.54780	7.94255	6.51353	27
11.05108	10.11613	9.30657	8.60162	7.98442	6.53351	28
11.15841	10.19828	9.36961	8.65011	8.02181	6.55088	29
11.25778	10.27365	9.42691	8.69379	8.05518	6.56598	30
11.34980	10.34280	9.47901	8.73315	8.08499	6.57911	31
11.43500	10.40624	9.52638	8.76860	8.11159	6.59053	32
11.51389	10.46444	9.56943	8.80054	8.13535	6.60046	33
11.58693	10.51784	9.60858	8.82932	8.15656	6.60910	34
11.65457	10.56682	9.64416	8.85524	8.17550	6.61661	35
11.71719	10.61176	9.67651	8.87859	8.19241	6.62314	36
11.77518	10.65299	9.70592	8.89963	8.20751	6.62882	37
11.82887	10.69082	9.73265	8.91859	8.22099	6.63375	38
11.87858	10.72552	9.75697	8.93567	8.23303	6.63805	39
11.92461	10.75736	9.77905	8.95105	8.24378	6.64178	40

TABLE 6-5 PRESENT VALUE OF AN ANNUITY DUE OF 1

$$PVF\text{-}AD_{n,i} = 1 + \frac{1 - \dfrac{1}{(1 + i)^{n-1}}}{i}$$

(n) Periods	2%	2½%	3%	4%	5%	6%
1	1.00000	1.00000	1.00000	1.00000	1.00000	1.00000
2	1.98039	1.97561	1.97087	1.96154	1.95238	1.94340
3	2.94156	2.92742	2.91347	2.88609	2.85941	2.83339
4	3.88388	3.85602	3.82861	3.77509	3.72325	3.67301
5	4.80773	4.76197	4.71710	4.62990	4.54595	4.46511
6	5.71346	5.64583	5.57971	5.45182	5.32948	5.21236
7	6.60143	6.50813	6.41719	6.24214	6.07569	5.91732
8	7.47199	7.34939	7.23028	7.00205	6.78637	6.58238
9	8.32548	8.17014	8.01969	7.73274	7.46321	7.20979
10	9.16224	8.97087	8.78611	8.43533	8.10782	7.80169
11	9.98259	9.75206	9.53020	9.11090	8.72173	8.36009
12	10.78685	10.51421	10.25262	9.76048	9.30641	8.88687
13	11.57534	11.25776	10.95400	10.38507	9.86325	9.38384
14	12.34837	11.98319	11.63496	10.98565	10.39357	9.85268
15	13.10625	12.69091	12.29607	11.56312	10.89864	10.29498
16	13.84926	13.38138	12.93794	12.11839	11.37966	10.71225
17	14.57771	14.05500	13.56110	12.65230	11.83777	11.10590
18	15.29187	14.71220	14.16612	13.16567	12.27407	11.47726
19	15.99203	15.35336	14.75351	13.65930	12.68959	11.82760
20	16.67846	15.97889	15.32380	14.13394	13.08532	12.15812
21	17.35143	16.58916	15.87747	14.59033	13.46221	12.46992
22	18.01121	17.18455	16.41502	15.02916	13.82115	12.76408
23	18.65805	17.76541	16.93692	15.45112	14.16300	13.04158
24	19.29220	18.33211	17.44361	15.85684	14.48857	13.30338
25	19.91393	18.88499	17.93554	16.24696	14.79864	13.55036
26	20.52346	19.42438	18.41315	16.62208	15.09394	13.78336
27	21.12104	19.95061	18.87684	16.98277	15.37519	14.00317
28	21.70690	20.46401	19.32703	17.32959	15.64303	14.21053
29	22.28127	20.96489	19.76411	17.66306	15.89813	14.40616
30	22.84438	21.45355	20.18845	17.98371	16.14107	14.59072
31	23.39646	21.93029	20.60044	18.29203	16.37245	14.76483
32	23.93770	22.39541	21.00043	18.58849	16.59281	14.92909
33	24.46833	22.84918	21.38877	18.87355	16.80268	15.08404
34	24.98856	23.29188	21.76579	19.14765	17.00255	15.23023
35	25.49859	23.72379	22.13184	19.41120	17.19290	15.36814
36	25.99862	24.14516	22.48722	19.66461	17.37419	15.49825
37	26.48884	24.55625	22.83225	19.90828	17.54685	15.62099
38	26.96945	24.95732	23.16724	20.14258	17.71129	15.73678
39	27.44064	25.34860	23.49246	20.36786	17.86789	15.84602
40	27.90259	25.73034	23.80822	20.58448	18.01704	15.94907

TABLE 6-5   PRESENT VALUE OF AN ANNUITY DUE OF 1

8%	9%	10%	11%	12%	15%	(n) Periods
1.00000	1.00000	1.00000	1.00000	1.00000	1.00000	1
1.92593	1.91743	1.90909	1.90090	1.89286	1.86957	2
2.78326	2.75911	2.73554	2.71252	2.69005	2.62571	3
3.57710	3.53130	3.48685	3.44371	3.40183	3.28323	4
4.31213	4.23972	4.16986	4.10245	4.03735	3.85498	5
4.99271	4.88965	4.79079	4.69590	4.60478	4.35216	6
5.62288	5.48592	5.35526	5.23054	5.11141	4.78448	7
6.20637	6.03295	5.86842	5.71220	5.56376	5.16042	8
6.74664	6.53482	6.33493	6.14612	5.96764	5.48732	9
7.24689	6.99525	6.75902	6.53705	6.32825	5.77158	10
7.71008	7.41766	7.14457	6.88923	6.65022	6.01877	11
8.13896	7.80519	7.49506	7.20652	6.93770	6.23371	12
8.53608	8.16073	7.81369	7.49236	7.19437	6.42062	13
8.90378	8.48690	8.10336	7.74987	7.42355	6.58315	14
9.24424	8.78615	8.36669	7.98187	7.62817	6.72448	15
9.55948	9.06069	8.60608	8.19087	7.81086	6.84737	16
9.85137	9.31256	8.82371	8.37916	7.97399	6.95424	17
10.12164	9.54363	9.02155	8.54879	8.11963	7.04716	18
10.37189	9.75563	9.20141	8.70162	8.24967	7.12797	19
10.60360	9.95012	9.36492	8.83929	8.36578	7.19823	20
10.81815	10.12855	9.51356	8.96333	8.46944	7.25933	21
11.01680	10.29224	9.64869	9.07507	8.56200	7.31246	22
11.20074	10.44243	9.77154	9.17574	8.64465	7.35866	23
11.37106.	10.58021	9.88322	9.26643	8.71843	7.39884	24
11.52876	10.70661	9.98474	9.34814	8.78432	7.43377	25
11.67478	10.82258	10.07704	9.42174	8.84314	7.46415	26
11.80998	10.92897	10.16095	9.48806	8.89566	7.49056	27
11.93518	11.02658	10.23722	9.54780	8.94255	7.51353	28
12.05108	11.11613	10.30657	9.60162	8.98442	7.53351	29
12.15841	11.19828	10.36961	9.65011	9.02181	7.55088	30
12.25778	11.27365	10.42691	9.69379	9.05518	7.56598	31
12.34980	11.34280	10.47901	9.73315	9.08499	7.57911	32
12.43500	11.40624	10.52638	9.76860	9.11159	7.59053	33
12.51389	11.46444	10.56943	9.80054	9.13535	7.60046	34
12.58693	11.51784	10.60858	9.82932	9.15656	7.60910	35
12.65457	11.56682	10.64416	9.85524	9.17550	7.61661	36
12.71719	11.61176	10.67651	9.87859	9.19241	7.62314	37
12.77518	11.65299	10.70592	9.89963	9.20751	7.62882	38
12.82887	11.69082	10.73265	9.91859	9.22099	7.63375	39
12.87858	11.72552	10.75697	9.93567	9.23303	7.63805	40

LOGO CREDITS

The following companies have granted permission for their logos to be included in this text.

Avon Rubber. Reprinted by permission of Avon Rubber.

Caterpillar

The Coca-Cola Company. The world famous COCA-COLA and COCA-COLA Script Logo trademarks are registered trademarks of The Coca-Cola Company.

Eastman Kodak. Used with permission of Eastman Kodak Company.

Hewlett-Packard. Reprinted by permission of Hewlett-Packard.

Intuit Inc. Reprinted by permission of Intuit Inc.

Johnson & Johnson. Reprinted by permission of Johnson & Johnson.

Kellogg Company. © 2006 Kellogg North American Company.

Oracle. Reprinted by permission of Oracle International Corporation.

PepsiCo. All rights reserved. Used with permission.

Procter & Gamble

Southwest Airlines

Tomkins. Reprinted by permission of Tomkins PLC.

Westinghouse. Reprinted by permission of Westinghouse Electric Corporation.

OFFICIAL ACCOUNTING PRONOUNCEMENTS

The following list of official accounting pronouncements constitutes the major part of *generally accepted accounting principles* (GAAP) and represents the authoritative source documents for much of the discussion contained in this book.

Date Issued		No.	Title

Accounting Research Bulletins (ARB's), Committee on Accounting Procedures, AICPA (1953–1959)

June	1953	No. 43	Restatement and Revision of *Accounting Research Bulletins Nos. 1–42*, and *Accounting Terminology Bulletin No. 1* (originally issued 1939–1953)
Oct.	1954	No. 44	Declining-Balance Depreciation; Revised July, 1958 (amended)
Oct.	1955	No. 45	Long-term Construction-type Contracts (unchanged)
Feb.	1956	No. 46	Discontinuance of Dating Earned Surplus (unchanged)
Sept.	1956	No. 47	Accounting for Costs of Pension Plans (superseded)
Jan.	1957	No. 48	Business Combinations (superseded)
April	1958	No. 49	Earnings Per Share (superseded)
Oct.	1958	No. 50	Contingencies (superseded)
Aug.	1959	No. 51	Consolidated Financial Statements (amended and partially superseded)

Accounting Terminology Bulletins, Committee on Terminology, AICPA

Aug.	1953	No. 1	Review and Résumé (of the eight original terminology bulletins) (amended)
Mar.	1955	No. 2	Proceeds, Revenue, Income, Profit, and Earnings (amended)
Aug.	1956	No. 3	Book Value (unchanged)
July	1957	No. 4	Cost, Expense, and Loss (amended)

Accounting Principles Board (APB) Opinions, AICPA (1962–1973)

Nov.	1962	No. 1	New Depreciation Guidelines and Rules (amended)
Dec.	1962	No. 2	Accounting for the "Investment Credit" (amended)
Oct.	1963	No. 3	The Statement of Source and Application of Funds (superseded)
Mar.	1964	No. 4	Accounting for the "Investment Credit" (amending No. 2)
Sept.	1964	No. 5	Reporting of Leases in Financial Statements of Lessee (superseded)
Oct.	1965	No. 6	Status of Accounting Research Bulletins (partially superseded)
May	1966	No. 7	Accounting for Leases in Financial Statements of Lessors (superseded)
Nov.	1966	No. 8	Accounting for the Cost of Pension Plans (superseded)
Dec.	1966	No. 9	Reporting the Results of Operations (amended and partially superseded)
Dec.	1966	No. 10	Omnibus Opinion—1966 (amended and partially superseded)
Dec.	1967	No. 11	Accounting for Income Taxes (superseded)
Dec.	1967	No. 12	Omnibus Opinion—1967 (partially superseded)
Mar.	1969	No. 13	Amending Paragraph 6 of *APB Opinion No. 9*, Application to Commercial Banks (unchanged)
Mar.	1969	No. 14	Accounting for Convertible Debt and Debt Issued with Stock Purchase Warrants (unchanged)
May	1969	No. 15	Earnings per Share (superseded)
Aug.	1970	No. 16	Business Combinations (superseded)
Aug.	1970	No. 17	Intangible Assets (superseded)
Mar.	1971	No. 18	The Equity Method of Accounting for Investments in Common Stock (amended)
Mar.	1971	No. 19	Reporting Changes in Financial Position (amended)
July	1971	No. 20	Accounting Changes (superseded)
Aug.	1971	No. 21	Interest on Receivables and Payables (amended)
April	1972	No. 22	Disclosure of Accounting Policies (amended)
April	1972	No. 23	Accounting for Income Taxes—Special Areas (superseded)
April	1972	No. 24	Accounting for Income Taxes—Equity Method Investments (unchanged)
Oct.	1972	No. 25	Accounting for Stock Issued to Employees (unchanged)
Oct.	1972	No. 26	Early Extinguishment of Debt (amended)
Nov.	1972	No. 27	Accounting for Lease Transactions by Manufacturer or Dealer Lessors (superseded)
May	1973	No. 28	Interim Financial Reporting (amended and partially superseded)
May	1973	No. 29	Accounting for Nonmonetary Transactions (amended)
June	1973	No. 30	Reporting the Results of Operations (amended)
June	1973	No. 31	Disclosure of Lease Commitments by Lessees (superseded)

Financial Accounting Standards Board (FASB), Statements of Financial Accounting Standards (1973–2002)

Dec.	1973	No. 1	Disclosure of Foreign Currency Translation Information (superseded)
Oct.	1974	No. 2	Accounting for Research and Development Costs (amended)
Dec.	1974	No. 3	Reporting Accounting Changes in Interim Financial Statements (superseded)
Mar.	1975	No. 4	Reporting Gains and Losses from Extinguishment of Debt (superseded)
Mar.	1975	No. 5	Accounting for Contingencies (amended)
May	1975	No. 6	Classification of Short-term Obligations Expected to be Refinanced
June	1975	No. 7	Accounting and Reporting by Development Stage Enterprises
Oct.	1975	No. 8	Accounting for the Translation of Foreign Currency Transactions and Foreign Financial Statements (superseded)

Date Issued		No.	Title
Oct.	1975	No. 9	Accounting for Income Taxes—Oil and Gas Producing Companies (superseded)
Oct.	1975	No. 10	Extension of "Grandfather" Provisions for Business Combinations (superseded)
Dec.	1975	No. 11	Accounting for Contingencies—Transition Method
Dec.	1975	No. 12	Accounting for Certain Marketable Securities (superseded)
Nov.	1976	No. 13	Accounting for Leases (amended, interpreted, and partially superseded)
Dec.	1976	No. 14	Financial Reporting for Segments of a Business Enterprise (amended)
June	1977	No. 15	Accounting by Debtors and Creditors for Troubled Debt Restructurings (amended)
June	1977	No. 16	Prior Period Adjustments (amended)
Nov.	1977	No. 17	Accounting for Leases—Initial Direct Costs
Nov.	1977	No. 18	Financial Reporting for Segments of a Business Enterprise—Interim Financial Statements
Dec.	1977	No. 19	Financial Accounting and Reporting by Oil and Gas Producing Companies (amended)
Dec.	1977	No. 20	Accounting for Forward Exchange Contracts (superseded)
April	1978	No. 21	Suspension of the Reporting of Earnings per Share and Segment Information by Nonpublic Enterprises (amended)
June	1978	No. 22	Changes in the Provisions of Lease Agreements Resulting from Refundings of Tax-Exempt Debt (amended)
Aug.	1978	No. 23	Inception of the Lease
Dec.	1978	No. 24	Reporting Segment Information in Financial Statements That Are Presented in Another Enterprise's Financial Report
Feb.	1979	No. 25	Suspension of Certain Accounting Requirements for Oil and Gas Producing Companies
April	1979	No. 26	Profit Recognition on Sales-Type Leases of Real Estate
May	1979	No. 27	Classification of Renewals or Extensions of Existing Sales-Type or Direct Financing Leases
May	1979	No. 28	Accounting for Sales with Leasebacks
June	1979	No. 29	Determining Contingent Rentals
Aug.	1979	No. 30	Disclosure of Information about Major Customers
Sept.	1979	No. 31	Accounting for Tax Benefits Related to U.K. Tax Legislation Concerning Stock Relief
Sept.	1979	No. 32	Specialized Accounting and Reporting Principles and Practices in AICPA Statements of Position and Guides on Accounting and Auditing Matters (amended and partially superseded)
Sept.	1979	No. 33	Financial Reporting and Changing Prices (amended and partially superseded)
Oct.	1979	No. 34	Capitalization of Interest Cost (amended)
Mar.	1980	No. 35	Accounting and Reporting by Defined Benefit Pension Plans (amended)
May	1980	No. 36	Disclosure of Pension Information (superseded)
July	1980	No. 37	Balance Sheet Classification of Deferred Income Taxes (amended)
Sept.	1980	No. 38	Accounting for Preacquisition Contingencies of Purchased Enterprises (superseded)
Oct.	1980	No. 39	Financial Reporting and Changing Prices: Specialized Assets—Mining and Oil and Gas
Nov.	1980	No. 40	Financial Reporting and Changing Prices: Specialized Assets—Timberlands and Growing Timber
Nov.	1980	No. 41	Financial Reporting and Changing Prices: Specialized Assets—Income-Producing Real Estate
Nov.	1980	No. 42	Determining Materiality for Capitalization of Interest Cost
Nov.	1980	No. 43	Accounting for Compensated Absences (amended)
Dec.	1980	No. 44	Accounting for Intangible Assets of Motor Carriers (superseded)
Mar.	1981	No. 45	Accounting for Franchise Fee Revenue (amended)
Mar.	1981	No. 46	Financial Reporting and Changing Prices: Motion Picture Films
Mar.	1981	No. 47	Disclosure of Long-Term Obligations (amended)
June	1981	No. 48	Revenue Recognition When Right of Return Exists
June	1981	No. 49	Accounting for Product Financing Arrangements
Nov.	1981	No. 50	Financial Reporting in the Record and Music Industry
Nov.	1981	No. 51	Financial Reporting by Cable Television Companies (amended)
Dec.	1981	No. 52	Foreign Currency Translation (amended)
Dec.	1981	No. 53	Financial Reporting by Producers and Distributors of Motion Picture Films (superseded)
Jan.	1982	No. 54	Financial Reporting and Changing Prices: Investment Companies (superseded)
Feb.	1982	No. 55	Determining Whether a Convertible Security is a Common Stock Equivalent (superseded)
Feb.	1982	No. 56	Designation of AICPA Guide and SOP 81-1 on Contractor Accounting and SOP 81-2 on Hospital-Related Organizations as Preferable for Applying *APB Opinion 20* (superseded)
Mar.	1982	No. 57	Related Party Disclosures
April	1982	No. 58	Capitalization of Interest Cost in Financial Statements that Include Investments Accounted for by the Equity Method
April	1982	No. 59	Deferral of the Effective Date of Certain Accounting Requirements for Revision Plans of State and Local Governmental Units
June	1982	No. 60	Accounting and Reporting by Insurance Enterprises (amended)
June	1982	No. 61	Accounting for Title Plant (amended)
June	1982	No. 62	Capitalization of Interest Cost in Situations Involving Certain Tax-Exempt Borrowings and Certain Gifts and Grants
June	1982	No. 63	Financial Reporting by Broadcasters (amended)

Date Issued		No.	Title
Sept.	1982	No. 64	Extinguishment of Debt Made to Satisfy Sinking-Fund Requirements (superseded)
Sept.	1982	No. 65	Accounting for Certain Mortgage Bank Activities (amended)
Oct.	1982	No. 66	Accounting for Sales of Real Estate (amended)
Oct.	1982	No. 67	Accounting for Costs and Initial Rental Operations of Real Estate Projects (amended)
Oct.	1982	No. 68	Research and Development Arrangements (amended)
Nov.	1982	No. 69	Disclosures about Oil and Gas Producing Activities
Dec.	1982	No. 70	Financial Reporting and Changing Prices: Foreign Currency Translation
Dec.	1982	No. 71	Accounting for the Effects of Certain Types of Regulation (amended)
Feb.	1983	No. 72	Accounting for Certain Acquisitions of Banking or Thrift Institutions (amended)
Aug.	1983	No. 73	Reporting a Change in Accounting for Railroad Track Structures
Aug.	1983	No. 74	Accounting for Special Termination Benefits Paid to Employees
Nov.	1983	No. 75	Deferral of the Effective Date of Certain Accounting Requirements for Pension Plans of State and Local Governmental Units (superseded)
Nov.	1983	No. 76	Extinguishment of Debt (superseded)
Dec.	1983	No. 77	Reporting by Transferors for Transfers of Receivables with Recourse (superseded)
Dec.	1983	No. 78	Classifications of Obligations that Are Callable by the Creditor
Feb.	1984	No. 79	Elimination of Certain Disclosures for Business Combinations by Nonpublic Enterprises (superseded)
Aug.	1984	No. 80	Accounting for Futures Contracts (superseded)
Nov.	1984	No. 81	Disclosure of Postretirement Health Care and Life Insurance Benefits
Nov.	1984	No. 82	Financial Reporting and Changing Prices: Elimination of Certain Disclosures
Mar.	1985	No. 83	Designation of AICPA Guides and Statement of Position on Accounting by Brokers and Dealers in Securities, by Employee Benefit Plans, and by Banks as Preferable for Purposes of Applying *APB Opinion 20*
Mar.	1985	No. 84	Induced Conversions of Convertible Debt
Mar.	1985	No. 85	Yield Test for Determining Whether a Convertible Security Is a Common Stock Equivalent (superseded)
Aug.	1985	No. 86	Accounting for the Costs of Computer Software to be Sold, Leased, or Otherwise Marketed
Dec.	1985	No. 87	Employers' Accounting for Pensions (amended)
Dec.	1985	No. 88	Employers' Accounting for Settlements and Curtailments of Defined Benefit Pension Plans and for Termination Benefits (amended)
Dec.	1986	No. 89	Financial Reporting and Changing Prices (amended)
Dec.	1986	No. 90	Regulated Enterprises—Accounting for Abandonments and Disallowances of Plant Costs
Dec.	1986	No. 91	Accounting for Nonrefundable Fees and Costs Associated with Originating or Acquiring Loans and Initial Direct Costs of Leases
Aug.	1987	No. 92	Regulated Enterprises—Accounting for Phase-in Plans
Aug.	1987	No. 93	Recognition of Depreciation by Not-for-Profit Organizations
Oct.	1987	No. 94	Consolidation of All Majority-Owned Subsidiaries
Nov.	1987	No. 95	Statement of Cash Flows (amended)
Dec.	1987	No. 96	Accounting for Income Taxes (superseded)
Dec.	1987	No. 97	Accounting and Reporting by Insurance Enterprises for Certain Long-Duration Contracts and for Realized Gains and Losses from the Sale of Investments
June	1988	No. 98	Accounting for Leases; Sale-Leaseback Transactions Involving Real Estate; Sales-Type Leases of Real Estate; Definition of the Lease Term; Initial Direct Costs of Direct Financing Leases
Sept.	1988	No. 99	Deferral of the Effective Date of Recognition of Depreciation by Not-for-Profit Organizations
Dec.	1988	No. 100	Accounting for Income Taxes—Deferral of the Effective Date of *FASB Statement No. 96*
Dec.	1988	No. 101	Regulated Enterprises—Accounting for the Discontinuation of Application of *FASB Statement No. 71* (amended)
Feb.	1989	No. 102	Statement of Cash Flows—Exemption of Certain Enterprises and Classification of Cash Flows from Certain Securities Acquired for Resale (amended)
Dec.	1989	No. 103	Accounting for Income Taxes—Deferral of the Effective Date of *FASB Statement No. 96*
Dec.	1989	No. 104	Statement of Cash Flows—Net Reporting of Certain Cash Receipts and Cash Payments and Classification of Cash Flows from Hedging Transactions
Mar.	1990	No. 105	Disclosure of Information About Financial Instruments with Off-Balance-Sheet Risk and Financial Instruments with Concentrations of Credit Risk (superseded)
Dec.	1990	No. 106	Employers' Accounting for Postretirement Benefits Other Than Pensions (amended)
Dec.	1991	No. 107	Disclosures about Fair Value of Financial Instruments (amended)
Dec.	1991	No. 108	Accounting for Income Taxes—Deferral of the Effective Date of *FASB Statement No. 96*
Feb.	1992	No. 109	Accounting for Income Taxes (amended)
Aug.	1992	No. 110	Reporting by Defined Benefit Pension Plans of Investment Contracts
Nov.	1992	No. 111	Rescission of *FASB Statement No. 32* and Technical Corrections
Nov.	1992	No. 112	Employers' Accounting for Postemployment Benefits
Dec.	1992	No. 113	Accounting and Reporting for Reinsurance of Short-Duration and Long-Duration Contracts
May	1993	No. 114	Accounting by Creditors for Impairment of a Loan (amended)
May	1993	No. 115	Accounting for Certain Investments in Debt and Equity Securities (amended)

Date Issued		No.	Title
June	1993	No. 116	Accounting for Contributions Received and Contributions Made
June	1993	No. 117	Financial Statements of Not-for-Profit Organizations (amended)
Oct.	1994	No. 118	Accounting by Creditors for Impairments of a Loan—Income Recognition and Disclosures
Oct.	1994	No. 119	Disclosure about Derivative Financial Instruments and Fair Value of Financial Instruments (superseded)
Jan.	1995	No. 120	Accounting and Reporting by Mutual Life Insurance Enterprises
Mar.	1995	No. 121	Accounting for the Impairment of Long-Lived Assets (superseded)
May	1995	No. 122	Accounting for Mortgage Servicing Rights (superseded)
Oct.	1995	No. 123	Accounting for Stock-Based Compensation (revised)
Nov.	1995	No. 124	Accounting for Certain Investments Held by Not-for-Profit Organizations
June	1996	No. 125	Accounting for Transfers and Servicing of Financial Assets and Extinguishment of Liabilities (amended)
Dec.	1996	No. 126	Exemption from Certain Required Disclosures about Financial Instruments for Certain Nonpublic Entities
Dec.	1996	No. 127	Deferral of the Effective Date of Certain Provisions of *FASB Statement No. 125*
Feb.	1997	No. 128	Earnings per Share (amended)
Feb.	1997	No. 129	Disclosure of Information about Capital Structure
June	1997	No. 130	Reporting Comprehensive Income
June	1997	No. 131	Reporting Disaggregated Information about a Business Enterprise
Feb.	1998	No. 132	Employers' Disclosures about Pensions and Other Postretirement Benefits – an amendment of *FASB Statements No. 87, 88,* and *106* (revised)
June	1998	No. 133	Accounting for Derivative Instruments and Hedging Activities (amended)
Oct.	1998	No. 134	Accounting for Mortgage-Backed Securities Retained after the Securitization of Mortgage Loans Held for Sale by a Mortgage Banking Enterprise (an amendment of *FASB Statement No. 65*)
Feb.	1999	No. 135	Rescission of *FASB Statement No. 75* and Technical Corrections (amended)
June	1999	No. 136	Transfers of Assets to a Not-for-Profit Organization or Charitable Trust That Raises or Holds Contributions for Others (amended)
June	1999	No. 137	Accounting for Derivative Instruments and Hedging Activities—Deferral of the Effective Date for *FASB Statement No. 133* (an amendment of *Statement No. 133*)
June	2000	No. 138	Accounting for Certain Derivative Instruments and Certain Hedging Activities (an amendment of *FASB Statement No. 133*)
June	2000	No. 139	Rescission of *FASB Statement No. 53* and amendments to *FASB Statements No. 63, 89,* and *121*
Sept.	2000	No. 140	Accounting for Transfers and Servicing of Financial Assets and Extinguishments of Liabilities (a replacement of *FASB Statement 125*)
June	2001	No. 141	Business Combinations (amended)
June	2001	No. 142	Goodwill and Other Intangible Assets (amended)
June	2001	No. 143	Accounting for Asset Retirement Obligations (amended)
Aug.	2001	No. 144	Accounting for the Impairment or Disposal of Long-Lived Assets (amended)
April	2002	No. 145	Rescission of *FASB Statements No. 4, 44,* and *64,* Amendment of *FASB Statement No. 13,* and Technical Corrections
June	2002	No. 146	Accounting for Costs Associated with Exit or Disposal Activities
Oct.	2002	No. 147	Acquisitions of Certain Financial Institutions, an Amendment of *FASB Statements No. 72* and *144* and *FASB Interpretation No. 9*
Dec.	2002	No. 148	Accounting for Stock-Based Compensation—Transition and Disclosure
April	2003	No. 149	Amendment of *Statement 133* on Derivative Instruments and Hedging Activities
May	2003	No. 150	Accounting for Certain Financial Instruments with Characteristics of Both Liabilities and Equity
Nov.	2004	No. 151	Inventory Costs – an amendment of *ARB No. 43*, Chapter 4
Dec.	2004	No. 152	Accounting for Real Estate Time-Sharing Transactions
Dec.	2004	No. 153	Exchanges on Non-Monetary Assets – an amendment of *APB Opinion No. 29*
May	2005	No. 154	Accounting Changes and Error Corrections – a replacement of *APB Opinion No. 20* and *FASB Statement No. 3*

Financial Accounting Standards Board (FASB), Interpretations (1974–2002)

		No.	
June	1974	No. 1	Accounting Changes Related to the Cost of Inventory (*APB Opinion No. 20*)
June	1974	No. 2	Imputing Interest on Debt Arrangements Made Under the Federal Bankruptcy Act (*APB Opinion No. 21*) (superseded)
Dec.	1974	No. 3	Accounting for the Cost of Pension Plans Subject to the Employee Retirement Income Security Act of 1974 (*APB Opinion No. 8*)
Feb.	1975	No. 4	Applicability of *FASB Statement No. 2* to Purchase Business Combinations (amended)
Feb.	1975	No. 5	Applicability of *FASB Statement No. 2* to Development Stage Enterprises (superseded)
Feb.	1975	No. 6	Applicability of *FASB Statement No. 2* to Computer Software
Oct.	1975	No. 7	Applying *FASB Statement No. 7* in Statements of Established Enterprises
Jan.	1976	No. 8	Classification of a Short-Term Obligation Repaid Prior to Being Replaced by a Long-Term Security (*FASB Statement No. 6*)

Date Issued		No.	Title
Feb.	1976	No. 9	Applying *APB Opinion No. 16* and *17* when a Savings and Loan or Similar Institution is Acquired in a Purchase Business Combination (*APB Op. No. 16 & 17*) (amended)
Sept.	1976	No. 10	Application of *FASB Statement No. 12* to Personal Financial Statements (*FASB Statement No. 12*)
Sept.	1976	No. 11	Changes in Market Value after the Balance Sheet Date (*FASB Statement No. 12*)
Sept.	1976	No. 12	Accounting for Previously Established Allowance Accounts (*FASB Statement No. 12*)
Sept.	1976	No. 13	Consolidation of a Parent and Its Subsidiaries Having Different Balance Sheet Dates (*FASB Statement No. 12*)
Sept.	1976	No. 14	Reasonable Estimation of the Amount of a Loss (*FASB Statement No. 5*)
Sept.	1976	No. 15	Translation of Unamortized Policy Acquisition Costs by Stock Life Insurance Company (*FASB Statement No. 8*) (amended and partially superseded)
Feb.	1977	No. 16	Clarification of Definitions and Accounting for Marketable Equity Securities That Become Nonmarketable (*FASB Statement No. 12*)
Feb.	1977	No. 17	Applying the Lower of Cost or Market Rule in Translated Financial Statements (*FASB Statement No. 8*) (superseded)
Mar.	1977	No. 18	Accounting for Income Taxes in Interim Periods (*APB Op. No. 28*) (amended)
Oct.	1977	No. 19	Lessee Guarantee of the Residual Value of Leased Property (*FASB Statement No. 13*)
Nov.	1977	No. 20	Reporting Accounting Changes under AICPA Statements of Position (*APB Op. No. 20*)
April	1978	No. 21	Accounting for Leases in a Business Combination (*FASB Statement No. 13*) (amended)
April	1978	No. 22	Applicability of Indefinite Reversal Criteria to Timing Differences (*APB Op. No. 11* and *23*)
Aug.	1978	No. 23	Leases of Certain Property Owned by a Governmental Unit or Authority (*FASB Statement No. 13*)
Sept.	1978	No. 24	Leases Involving Only Part of a Building (*FASB Statement No. 13*)
Sept.	1978	No. 25	Accounting for an Unused Investment Tax Credit (*APB Op. No. 2, 4, 11,* and *16*)
Sept.	1978	No. 26	Accounting for Purchase of a Leased Asset by the Lessee During the Term of the Lease (*FASB Statement No. 13*)
Nov.	1978	No. 27	Accounting for a Loss on a Sublease (*FASB Statement No. 13* and *APB Op. No. 30*) (amended)
Dec.	1978	No. 28	Accounting for Stock Appreciation Rights and Other Variable Stock Option or Award Plans (*APB Op. No. 15* and *25*) (amended)
Feb.	1979	No. 29	Reporting Tax Benefits Realized on Disposition of Investments in Certain Subsidiaries and Other Investees (*APB Op. No. 23* and *24*)
Sept.	1979	No. 30	Accounting for Involuntary Conversions of Nonmonetary Assets to Monetary Assets (*APB Op. No. 29*)
Feb.	1980	No. 31	Treatment of Stock Compensation Plans in EPS Computations (*APB Op. No. 15* and *Interp. 28*) (superseded)
Mar.	1980	No. 32	Application of Percentage Limitations in Recognizing Investment Tax Credit (*APB Op. No. 2, 4,* and *11*)
Aug.	1980	No. 33	Applying FASB Statement No. 34 to Oil and Gas Producing Operations (*FASB Statement No. 34*)
Mar.	1981	No. 34	Disclosure of Indirect Guarantees of Indebtedness of Others (*FASB Statement No. 5*)
May	1981	No. 35	Criteria for Applying the Equity Method of Accounting for Investments in Common Stock (*APB Op. No. 18*)
Oct.	1981	No. 36	Accounting for Exploratory Wells in Progress at the End of a Period
July	1983	No. 37	Accounting for Translation Adjustments upon Sale of Part of an Investment in a Foreign Entity (Interprets *FASB Statement No. 52*)
Aug.	1984	No. 38	Determining the Measurement Date for Stock Option, Purchase, and Award Plans Involving Junior Stock (Interprets *APB Opinion No. 25*)
Mar.	1992	No. 39	Offsetting of Amounts Related to Certain Contracts (Interprets *APB Opinion No. 10* and *FASB Statement No. 105*) (amended)
Apr.	1993	No. 40	Applicability of Generally Accepted Accounting Principles to Mutual Life Insurance and Other Enterprises (Interprets *FASB Statements No. 12, 60, 97,* and *113*)
Dec.	1994	No. 41	Offsetting of Amounts Related to Certain Repurchase and Reverse Repurchase Agreements
Sept.	1996	No. 42	Accounting for Transfers of Assets in Which a Not-for-Profit Organization is Granted Variance Power
June	1999	No. 43	Real Estate Sales (Interprets FASB Statement No. 66) (amended)
		No. 44	Accounting for Certain Transactions involving Stock Compensation (an interpretation of *APB Opinion No. 25*) (amended)
Nov.	2002	No. 45	Guarantor's Accounting and Disclosure Requirements for Guarantees, Including Indirect Guarantees of Indebtedness of Others
Jan.	2003	No. 46	Consolidation of Variable Interest Entities (an interpretation of *ARB No. 51*, revised)
March	2005	No. 47	Accounting for Conditional Asset Retirement Obligations – an interpretation of *FASB Statement No. 143*

Date Issued		No.	Title

**Financial Accounting Standards Board (FASB),
Technical Bulletins (1979–2002)**

Date	Year	No.	Title
Dec.	1979	No. 79-1	Purpose and Scope of FASB Technical Bulletins and Procedures for Issuance (revised)
Dec.	1979	No. 79-2	Computer Software Costs
Dec.	1979	No. 79-3	Subjective Acceleration Clauses in Long-Term Debt Agreements
Dec.	1979	No. 79-4	Segment Reporting of Puerto Rican Operations
Dec.	1979	No. 79-5	Meaning of the Term 'Customer' as it Applies to Health Care Facilities under *FASB Statement No. 14*
Dec.	1979	No. 79-6	Valuation Allowances Following Debt Restructuring
Dec.	1979	No. 79-7	Recoveries of a Previous Writedown under a Troubled Debt Restructuring Involving a Modification of Terms
Dec.	1979	No. 79-8	Applicability of *FASB Statements 21* and *33* to Certain Brokers and Dealers in Securities
Dec.	1979	No. 79-9	Accounting in Interim Periods for Changes in Income Tax Rates
Dec.	1979	No. 79-10	Fiscal Funding Clauses in Lease Agreements
Dec.	1979	No. 79-11	Effect of a Penalty on the Term of a Lease
Dec.	1979	No. 79-12	Interest Rate Used in Calculating the Present Value of Minimum Lease Payments
Dec.	1979	No. 79-13	Applicability of *FASB Statement No. 13* to Current Value Financial Statements
Dec.	1979	No. 79-14	Upward Adjustment of Guaranteed Residual Values
Dec.	1979	No. 79-15	Accounting for Loss on a Sublease Not Involving the Disposal of a Segment
Dec.	1979	No. 79-16	Effect on a Change in Income Tax Rate on the Accounting for Leveraged Leases (revised)
Dec.	1979	No. 79-17	Reporting Cumulative Effect Adjustment from Retroactive Application of *FASB No. 13*
Dec.	1979	No. 79-18	Transition Requirements of Certain FASB Amendments and Interpretations of *FASB Statement No. 13*
Dec.	1979	No. 79-19	Investor's Accounting for Unrealized Losses on Marketable Securities Owned by an Equity Method Investee
Dec.	1980	No. 80-1	Early Extinguishment of Debt through Exchange for Common or Preferred Stock (amended)
Dec.	1980	No. 80-2	Classification of Debt Restructuring by Debtors and Creditors
Feb.	1981	No. 81-1	Disclosure of Interest Rate Futures Contracts and Forward and Standby Contracts
Feb.	1981	No. 81-2	Accounting for Unused Investment Tax Credits Acquired in a Business Combination Accounted for by the Purchase Method
Feb.	1981	No. 81-3	Multiemployer Pension Plan Amendments Act of 1980
Feb.	1981	No. 81-4	Classification as Monetary or Nonmonetary Items
Feb.	1981	No. 81-5	Offsetting Interest Cost to be Capitalized with Interest Income
Nov.	1981	No. 81-6	Applicability of Statement 15 to Debtors in Bankruptcy Situations
Jan.	1982	No. 82-1	Disclosure of the Sale or Purchase of Tax Benefits through Tax Leases (amended)
Mar.	1982	No. 82-2	Accounting for the Conversion of Stock Options into Incentive Stock Options as a Result of the Economic Recovery Tax Act of 1981
July	1983	No. 83-1	Accounting for the Reduction in the Tax Basis of an Asset Caused by the Investment Tax Credit (ITC)
Mar.	1984	No. 84-1	Accounting for Stock Issued to Acquire the Results of a Research and Development Arrangement (amended)
Sept.	1984	No. 84-2	Accounting for the Effects of the Tax Reform Act of 1984 on Deferred Income Taxes Relating to Domestic International Sales Corporations
Sept.	1984	No. 84-3	Accounting for the Effects of the Tax Reform Act of 1984 on Deferred Income Taxes of Stock Life Insurance Enterprises
Oct.	1984	No. 84-4	In-Substance Defeasance of Debt
Mar.	1985	No. 85-1	Accounting for the Receipt of Federal Home Loan Mortgage Corporation Participating Preferred Stock
Mar.	1985	No. 85-2	Accounting for Collateralized Mortgage Obligations (CMOs) (superseded)
Nov.	1985	No. 85-3	Accounting for Operating Leases with Scheduled Rent Increases
Nov.	1985	No. 85-4	Accounting for Purchases of Life Insurance (superseded)
Dec.	1985	No. 85-5	Issues Relating to Accounting for Business Combinations (amended)
Dec.	1985	No. 85-6	Accounting for a Purchase of Treasury Shares
Oct.	1986	No. 86-1	Accounting for Certain Effects of the Tax Reform Act of 1986
Dec.	1986	No. 86-2	Accounting for an Interest in the Residual Value of a Leased Asset (amended)
April	1987	No. 87-1	Accounting for a Change in Method of Accounting for Certain Postretirement Benefits
Dec.	1987	No. 87-2	Computation of a Loss on an Abandonment
Dec.	1987	No. 87-3	Accounting for Mortgage Servicing Fees and Rights (amended)
Dec.	1988	No. 88-1	Issues Relating to Accounting for Leases
Dec.	1988	No. 88-2	Definition of a Right of Setoff
Dec.	1990	No. 90-1	Accounting for Separately Priced Extended Warranty and Product Maintenance Contracts
Apr.	1994	No. 94-1	Application of *Statement 115* to Debt Securities Restructured in a Troubled Debt Restructuring
Dec.	1997	No. 97-1	Accounting under *Statement 123* for Certain Employee Stock Purchase Plans with a Look-Back Option
July	2001	No. 01-1	Effective Date for Certain Financial Institutions of Certain Provisions of *Statement No. 140* Related to the Isolation of Transferred Financial Assets

Date Issued		No.		Title

Financial Accounting Standards Board (FASB),
Statements of Financial Accounting Concepts (1978–2002)

Nov.	1978	No.	1	Objectives of Financial Reporting by Business Enterprises
May	1980	No.	2	Qualitative Characteristics of Accounting Information
Dec.	1980	No.	3	Elements of Financial Statements of Business Enterprises
Dec.	1980	No.	4	Objectives of Financial Reporting by Nonbusiness Organizations
Dec.	1984	No.	5	Recognition and Measurement in Financial Statements of Business Enterprises
Dec.	1985	No.	6	Elements of Financial Statements
Feb.	2000	No.	7	Using Cash Flow Information and Present Value in Accounting Measurements

NATIONAL ACCOUNTING BOARDS AND ORGANIZATIONS

American Accounting Association (AAA)
5717 Bessie Drive
Sarasota, FL 34233-2399
(941) 921-7747
www.aaahq.org

American Institute of Certified Public Accountants
(AICPA)
1211 Avenue of the Americas
New York, NY 10036-8775
(212) 596-6200
www.aicpa.org

Association of Government Accountants (AGA)
2208 Mount Vernon Ave.
Alexandria, VA 22301-1314
(703) 684-6931
www.agacgfm.org

Financial Accounting Standards Board (FASB)
401 Merritt 7
P.O. Box 5116
Norwalk, CT 06856-5116
(203) 847-0700
www.fasb.org

Financial Executives International (FEI)
200 Campus Drive
Florham Park, NJ 07932-0674
(973) 765-1000
www.fei.org

Governmental Accounting Standards Board (GASB)
401 Merritt 7
P.O. Box 5116
Norwalk, CT 06856-5116
(203) 847-0700
www.gasb.org

International Accounting Standards Board (IASB)
30 Cannon Street
London EC4M 6XH, United Kingdom
Telephone: +44 (0)20 7246 6410
www.iasb.org

Institute of Internal Auditors (IIA)
247 Maitland Avenue
Altamonte Springs, FL 32701-4201
(407) 937-1100
www.theiia.org

Institute of Management Accountants (IMA)
10 Paragon Drive
Montvale, NJ 07645-1718
(201) 573-9000
www.imanet.org

Securities and Exchange Commission (SEC)
100 F Street, NE
Washington, DC 20549
(202) 551-6551
www.sec.gov